CONTENTS

VOLUME 6

CRITICAL SURVEY
OF
DRAMA

CRITICAL SURVEY

OF

DRAMA

Second Revised Edition

Volume 6

Jules Romains - William Trevor

Editor, Second Revised Edition
Carl Rollyson
Baruch College, City University of New York

Editor, First Editions, English and Foreign Language Series
Frank N. Magill

SALEM PRESS, INC.
Pasadena, California   Hackensack, New Jersey

Editor in Chief: Dawn P. Dawson
Managing Editor: Christina J. Moose
Developmental Editor: R. Kent Rasmussen
Project Editor: Rowena Wildin
Research Supervisor: Jeffry Jensen
Research Assistant: Michelle Murphy

Acquisitions Editor: Mark Rehn
Photograph Editor: Philip Bader
Manuscript Editor: Sarah Hilbert
Assistant Editor: Andrea E. Miller
Production Editor: Cynthia Beres
Layout: Eddie Murillo and William Zimmerman

Library of Congress Cataloging-in-Publication Data

Critical survey of drama / edited by Carl Rollyson.-- 2nd rev. ed.

    p. cm.

Previous edition edited by Frank Northen Magill in 1994.

"Combines, updates, and expands two earlier Salem Press reference sets: Critical survey of drama, revised edition, English language series, published in 1994, and Critical survey of drama, foreign language series, published in 1986"--Pref.

Includes bibliographical references and index.

    ISBN 1-58765-102-5 (set : alk. paper) -- ISBN 1-58765-108-4 (vol. 6 : alk. paper) --

1. Drama--Dictionaries. 2. Drama--History and criticism--Dictionaries. 3. Drama--Bio-bibliography. 4. English drama--Dictionaries. 5. American drama--Dictionaries. 6. Commonwealth drama (English)--Dictionaries. 7. English drama--Bio-bibliography. 8. American drama--Bio-bibliography. 9. Commonwealth drama (English)--Bio-bibliography. I. Rollyson, Carl E. (Carl Edmund) II. Magill, Frank Northen, 1907-1997.

PN1625 .C68 2003

809.2′003—dc21   2003002190

Fourth Printing

PRINTED IN THE UNITED STATES OF AMERICA

COMPLETE LIST OF CONTENTS

VOLUME 1

VOLUME 2

VOLUME 3

VOLUME 4

VOLUME 5

VOLUME 6

VOLUME 7

AMERICAN DRAMA

VOLUME 8

CRITICAL SURVEY

OF

DRAMA

JULES ROMAINS
Louis-Henri-Jean Farigoule

Born: Saint-Julien-Chapteuil, France; August 26, 1885

Died: Paris, France; August 14, 1972

PRINCIPAL DRAMA

L'Armée dans la ville, pr., pb. 1911 (verse play)

Cromedeyre-le-Vieil, wr. 1911-1918, pr., pb. 1920 (verse play)

Le Dictateur, wr. 1911-1925, pr., pb. 1926

M. Le Trouhadec saisi par la débauche, pb. 1921, pr. 1923

Knock: Ou, Le Triomphe de la médecine, pr. 1923, pb. 1924 (*Dr. Knock*, 1925)

Amédée et les messieurs en rang, pr. 1923, pb. 1926 (*Six Gentlemen in a Row*, 1927)

La Scintillante, pr. 1924, pb. 1925 (*The Peach*, 1933)

Le Mariage de Le Trouhadec, pr., pb. 1925 (music by Georges Auric)

Démétrios, pr. 1925, pb. 1926

Jean le Maufranc, pr. 1926, pb. 1927

Volpone, pr. 1928, pb. 1929 (adaptation of Stefan Zweig's adaptation of Ben Jonson's play *Volpone*; music by Auric)

Le Déjeuner marocain, pr., pb. 1929

Donogoo, pr. 1930, pb. 1931

Musse: Ou, L'École de l'hypocrisie, pr. 1930, pb. 1931 (revision of *Jean le Maufranc*)

Boën: Ou, La Possession des biens, pr. 1930, pb. 1931

Le Roi masqué, pr. 1931, pb. 1932

Grâce encore pour la terre, pr., pb. 1941

L'An mil, pr., pb. 1947

Barbazouk, wr. 1956, pr., pb. 1963 (radio play)

OTHER LITERARY FORMS

Although Jules Romains published works in a number of genres simultaneously, his emphasis shifted. In the 1910's, he published mostly poetry, and in the 1920's, he produced primarily drama. The 1930's was his decade for writing novels, and from the 1940's to his death in 1972, his interest lay in nonfiction, especially political essays and literary criticism.

In 1904, at the age of eighteen, Romains published his first volume of poetry, *L'Âme des hommes*. Four years later came a major work, *La Vie unanime*, which illustrates his concept of unanimism, a theory of collectivity. *Europe* (1916) contrasts the peace of prewar Europe with the current chaos and expresses horror at the devastation of World War I. The contrast between peacetime and war again emerges in *Ode Génoise* (1925). In his most ambitious work, *L'Homme blanc* (1937), Romains attempted an epic poem reminiscent of Victor Hugo's five-volume *La Légende des siècles* (1859-1883).

Although Romains continued to publish poetry until the 1950's, he is better known for his fiction. He wrote several works of short fiction, including *Le Bourg régénéré* (1906) and *Nomentanus le réfugié* (1943). His first novel, *Mort de quelqu'un* (1911; *Death of a Nobody*, 1914), illustrates the formation and dynamics of groups that arise from events, in this case the death of a little-known railway engineer. *Les Copains* (1913; *The Boys in the Back Room*, 1937) is a lighthearted romp through France of seven young men, and *Psyché* (1922-1929; *The Body's Rapture*, 1933), a trilogy, explores ideal love and demonstrates the couple as a unanimist group. Romains's fame as a novelist, however, stems from *Les Hommes de bonne volonté* (1932-1946; *Men of Good Will*, 1933-1946), a vast European panorama that traces characters from before World War I to Adolf Hitler's rise to power.

Throughout his literary career, Romains also wrote a wide spectrum of nonfiction. In 1910, he published *Manuel de déification*, precepts for the development of a unanimism into a god. A scientific treatise, *La Vision extra-rétinienne et le sens paroptique* (1920; *Eyeless Sight*, 1924), claims the possibility of eyeless sight, also known as paroptic vision. Several works were concerned with war and its prevention, such as *Au-dessus de la mêlée* (1915), *Cela dépend de vous* (1938), and *Le Problème no. 1* (1947). Other later works were literary and autobiographical, such as *Confidences d'un auteur dramatique* (1953), *Souvenirs et confidences d'un écrivain* (1958), and *Ai-je fait ce que j'ai voulu?* (1964). When taken together, the variety, quantity, and quality of his literary output make Romains a major figure in twentieth century French literature.

ACHIEVEMENTS

Jules Romains is outstanding among twentieth century French authors both for his vast literary output and for unanimism, the theory of collectivity he originated and which imbues his work. Although Romains is known primarily as a novelist for his *Men of Good Will* and as a playwright for *Dr. Knock*, he made broad contributions to literature. A prolific author, over a span of nearly seventy years he produced poetry, drama, short fiction, novels, articles, and essays.

Jules Romains in 1965. (AP/Wide World Photos)

Despite having produced more than one hundred volumes of literature, Romains's fame stems primarily from his masterpiece, the twenty-seven-volume *roman-fleuve* entitled *Men of Good Will*, which he referred to as the principal work of his life. Written between 1932 and 1946, the work spans exactly one-quarter of a century, from October 6, 1908, to October 7, 1933. In the first volume, *Le 6 Octobre* (1932; *The Sixth of October*, 1933), as Parisians go about their daily activities, they read in the newspapers of the intended annexation of Bosnia-Herzegovina by the Austro-Hungarian Empire, a key event in the sequence of crises leading to the outbreak of World War I. The final volume, *Le 7 Octobre* (1946; *The Seventh of October*, 1946) is again set in Paris, where, as people head for work, they listen to news of Adolf Hitler, who has recently ascended to power. *Men of Good Will* is an uneven work, with volumes 15 and 16, *Prélude à Verdun* (1938; *The Prelude*, 1939) and *Verdun* (1938; *The Battle*, 1939) generally being the most highly touted. For contemporary readers, the value of *Men of Good Will* lies in its almost journalistic portrayal of European political, social, and economic thought and life from World War I to World War II.

Romains's depiction of collective European society in his panoramic *Men of Good Will* illustrates his theory of unanimism, a doctrine underlying most of his literary works. Romains traces his theory of unanimism to an October evening in 1903 when he was walking with his friend Georges Chennevière along the crowded rue d'Amsterdam. Suddenly he saw, among the bustling individuals, a unanimity, a unity that encompassed the entire city, shoppers and shops, passengers and taxis, into one larger collectivity. Rather than being diminished or depersonalized by being subsumed into a group, the individual, Romains believed, was heightened by his participation in a larger and greater spirit. The theory of collectivity is not unique to Romains; the relationship of the individual to the group is of prime concern to twentieth century sociologists, economists, politicians, and artists. Nevertheless, Romains's theory of unanimism is important as poetic vision rather than sociological doctrine and is central to an understanding of his work.

Romains's literature reveals several influences, mostly of the nineteenth century: He is indebted to, among others, Émile Zola, Honoré de Balzac, Charles Baudelaire, and Victor Hugo. His belief that literature should have the broad appeal that can derive only from a clear style and structure ties him to the classical tradition and explains his rejection of Surrealism and other avant-garde movements of his time. His literature remains accessible to readers because, rejecting the innovations of his era, he retained clarity of structure, plot, character, and language.

BIOGRAPHY

Jules Romains was born Louis-Henri-Jean Farigoule on August 26, 1885, in Saint-Julien-Chapteuil, a village in the Velay region of France. His parents, Henri Farigoule and Marie Richier, both came from Velay families. His father, however, had become a schoolteacher in the Montmartre district of Paris, and while Louis was still an infant, the family returned to Paris, where he spent his childhood.

A brilliant student, he studied at the Lycée Condorcet and then at the estimated École Normale Supérieure. During his school years, he read widely and began to write, producing his first volume of poetry, *L'Âme des hommes*, when he was eighteen years old, under the pseudonym Jules Romains. He associated with, but did not join, the Abbey group of young poets and artists, who published his volume of poetry *La Vie unanime* in 1908.

In 1909, already established as an author, he began his teaching career. He taught at Brest and then at Laon until the war. In 1912, he married Gabrielle Gaffé. By the outbreak of World War I, he had published several volumes of poetry, a play (*L'Armée dans la ville*), and two novels (*Death of a Nobody* and *The Boys in the Back Room*) and was a leading literary figure.

Romains had served his obligatory year of military service after leaving school in 1905 in an infantry regiment at Pithviers. He had disliked army life, and when the war broke out in 1914, he served in the auxiliary but was discharged the following year. He resumed teaching, this time in Paris at the Collège Rollin. His horror of war finds expression in the po-

etry of *Europe*, the articles in *Problèmes d'aujour-d'hui* (1931), and in *The Prelude* and *The Battle*.

By the end of the war in 1919, Romains, well established as a literary leader, had the security of a permanent publisher, Gallimard. He abandoned his teaching career, and in the years following the Armistice, he traveled extensively while also devoting himself to the theater. In December, 1923, Louis Jouvet produced and starred in *Dr. Knock*, a rollicking satire of medicine. The play was a tremendous success, adding substantially to Romains's fame and assuring his financial independence. Most of Romains's plays were written during the 1920's.

During the 1930's, Romains shifted his energies from the drama to his twenty-seven-volume novel, *Men of Good Will*. In 1936, after a two-year separation, he and Gabrielle Gaffé were divorced. In the same year, he married Lisa Dreyfus, his former secretary. In 1940, after the invasion, France was no longer safe for Romains's Jewish wife, and they fled the country, arriving eventually in New York. In 1942, they moved to Mexico City. During the 1930's and 1940's, Romains was politically active, writing and lecturing throughout Europe and in the United States. During the Occupation, he supported the Allied cause through radio broadcasts, published in *Messages aux français* (1941).

With his election to the Académie Française in 1946, Romains finally returned to his native land. Still prolific, his postwar writings included two plays (*L'An mil* and *Barbazouk*), six novels, three volumes of poetry, and two long stories. Primarily, however, he wrote nonfiction, often essays on world problems, such as *Le Problème no. 1* and *Passengers de cette planète, où allons nous?* (1955), or critical works, such as *Saints de notre calendrier* (1952), a series of critical literary evaluations, and *Confidences d'un auteur dramatique* (1953), his critique of the theater. He continued to write until 1970, two years before his death in Paris.

ANALYSIS

Although Jules Romains gained widespread popularity through the theater, his ultimate fame rests with his prose and poetry. *Cromedeyre-le-vieil* is powerful and evocative, *Dr. Knock* and *Donogoo* are delightful and cleverly plotted. Yet in all three—although they are frequently considered his best plays—plot takes precedence over character, the group dominates the individual, and the play is a didactic vehicle for a philosophy.

L'ARMÉE DANS LA VILLE

Romains began his dramatic career in 1911 with *L'Armée dans la ville*, a dramatization in verse of the conflicts between a town and the army that occupies it. Like most of his early work, *L'Armée dans la ville* was a vehicle designed to illustrate unanimism.

CROMEDEYRE-LE-VIEIL

The same year, he began writing his second and far greater drama, *Cromedeyre-le-vieil*. Said by some critics to be his masterpiece, Romains admitted that it was perhaps his favorite play. Written between 1911 and 1918, *Cromedeyre-le-vieil* was produced in 1920 at the Vieux-Colombier by Jacques Copeau. Like *L'Armée dans la ville, Cromedeyre-le-vieil* is a didactic drama in verse. The setting is Romains's native Velay region, and although many of the villages named in the play are real, Cromedeyre is, according to Romains, a synthesis of villages. Cromedeyre is also, despite realistic touches, a fantasy, with its houses linked together to form one single house and its streets interconnecting. The physical aspects of the town, such as its lack of individual homes and streets, are symbolic of the unity of its citizens, a group that, glorying in its uniqueness and solidarity, forms an ideal unanimism. The plot links two sources: One is literary, the rape of the Sabine women, and one historic, a schism within the Church caused when the village of Monedeyre decided to have and build its own church over the protest of ecclesiastic authorities. Though an unlikely combination of events, in the play both contribute to the glory of Cromedeyre.

In the first act, which is primarily exposition, Cromedeyre is described by outsiders. The village is labeled the *vieil* because of its antiquity, yet it retains a young and restless spirit. Just as the village differs physically from the others of the region, so do the inhabitants: Their relatively long legs and short torsos give them a peculiar gait that makes them recognizable at a distance. In the second act, Emmanuel, the young man who had been chosen by the village elders to go to the seminary and train to become the priest of the new church at Cromedeyre, returns to the village, dissatisfied with the teachings of the seminary. Emmanuel realizes that the god of Rome is not the god of Cromedeyre because, being a unique people, the citizens of Cromedeyre would not have sprung from the same god who created others. Despite Cromedeyre's strength and solidarity, the community is threatened, as far more males than females are born. The crisis will be solved as in the past—through the kidnapping of young women from another village. The kidnapping is described in the fourth act by the visionary Mother Agatha, an elderly woman who was carried off years before in the earlier kidnapping. The young men of the village, led by Emmanuel, return victorious. When they are followed by the young men of Lausonne, who attempt to free the captives, the Cromedeyrians set their dogs on them. In the fifth act, the couples are married in a new church with an ancient ritual recalled by Mother Agatha. She also explains to Emmanuel that, having rejected the god of others, he must now rediscover the god of Cromedeyre. In the final scenes, three emissaries from Lausonne come to persuade the women to return to their native village. Emmanuel holds sway over them, the emissaries flee, and the women remain in Cromedeyre.

As a vehicle for unanimism, the play is in many respects successful. The intertwined houses and streets of the village symbolize the unity of the group, a unity so binding that Emmanuel describes the village as being one flesh, one man, yet self-perpetuating. From this unity the villagers derive strength, pride, and a belief in their racial superiority. The play clearly demonstrates the superiority of the group to the individual. Emmanuel's name is symbolic, as is his coming to the village, and lest the comparison to Christ be overlooked, he even heals a dying child. Like Christ, Emmanuel is the young man who will lead his people to a new religion. He will be the new priest of the god of Cromedeyre, a god, like the village, both ancient and new. In its glorification of the village, *Cromedeyre-le-vieil* seems a dramatic illustration of Romains's *Manuel de déification*.

There are, however, unsettling aspects of unanimism revealed in the play. The villagers' pride in their racial superiority and their disdain for other villages can scarcely be condoned. Equally troubling is the violence. The citizens of Cromedeyre feel justified in their periodic kidnapping of women, for they are, they believe, bringing them into a superior society. Their stoning of the villagers who try to regain their women in like manner seems to them justified. They view these acts as necessary for the perpetuation of their race, and they glory in their vitality and in their triumph. The reader, however, is likely to see in the overwhelming racial pride of Cromedeyre a cause of social catastrophe, not a source of pride.

DR. KNOCK

By far Romains's most popular play is *Dr. Knock*, which was produced in December of 1923 at the Comédie des Champs-Élysées by Louis Jouvet, who also starred in the role of Dr. Knock. The play, an enormous success that added substantially to Romains's fame, has been widely performed and anthologized. This three-act play is a rollicking satire reminiscent of Molière's comedies. In the first act, Dr. Knock is traveling to the village of Saint-Maurice with Dr. and Mrs. Parpalaid in their decrepit automobile. Dr. Knock is to be Parpalaid's successor, having bought his practice from him. The practice is not promising, however, as the villagers rarely consult a doctor and traditionally pay the doctor only at the end of September. Dr. Knock, however, has a different approach from that of his predecessor. As Knock explains, healthy people are simply those unaware of their illness; lacking a clientele, he will create one. In the second act, Knock commissions the town crier to go through the town announcing free consultations on Monday mornings. He then meets with the schoolteacher and asks his collaboration in teaching health, focusing on the lurking dangers of bacteria. Knock next interviews the pharmacist, to whom he promises a much larger volume of business.

His free consultations begin: The first two patients are middle-aged women, both prosperous, and both found to be in need of daily treatments. Next come two lads from the village, intent on a practical joke. Knock shows the first illustrations of organs deteriorated by advanced alcoholism and suggests that there is no cure. The second, terrified, refuses to be examined, and the act closes as the two leave together, horrified. The third act takes place a mere three months later, but the village and its citizenry are transformed. The former hotel is now a clinic, with all rooms occupied by patients, and Dr. Knock works steadily in the clinic and on house calls. Parpalaid returns, and he and Knock compare practices. Whereas Parpalaid saw 5 patients a week, Knock sees 150. Parpalaid had no patients requiring regular treatment; Knock has 250. Dr. Knock is even better informed than the tax collector about the income of his patients. Parpalaid is first stunned, then skeptical. Unlike the villagers, Parpalaid knows of Knock's theory of health and of his intention to create a clientele; even so, he cannot resist Knock and at the end of the play is convinced that he, Parpalaid, is seriously ill. Like *Cromedeyre-le-vieil*, *Dr. Knock* illustrates unanimism—in this instance, the effect an individual can have in the creation of a group. As in *Cromedeyre-le-vieil*, the group functions almost as an individual. The newfound unity of the villagers is seen at the close, when Knock explains that at ten o'clock, 250 patients will simultaneously take their temperatures. As for Knock, he has come to exult in his role as the continual creator of the group.

Despite Knock's being a charlatan perpetrating an absurd hoax, the public is so gullible, so eager to follow, that Knock quickly rises to an unassailable dictatorship. Some critics have found in the play a warning against dictatorship, an interpretation borne out by the banning of the play in Nazi Germany. The several comic elements, however, argue against an overly serious interpretation. The situation is humorous: Dr. Parpalaid, thinking himself wily, sells a worthless practice to Knock, who quickly makes it lucrative and includes Parpalaid among his victims. The pleasure the people take in their newfound ill health and their pride in Dr. Knock are comic. The humor of the plot is enhanced by the witty repartee. The play is famous and popular not because it illustrates Romains's theory of unanimism or because it warns of the dangers of dictatorship; the play survives because it is genuinely humorous, with a clever plot and ingenious characters.

DONOGOO

In 1920, Romains wrote his only screenplay, *Donogoo-Tonka: Ou, Les Miracles de la science*. A decade later he adapted the scenario for the stage. The play, entitled *Donogoo*, was performed in October of 1930 at the Théâtre Pigalle. *Donogoo* contains characters from Romains's early comic novel *The Boys in the Back Room*, including Lamendin, the play's protagonist. *Donogoo* is one of three Le Trouhadec plays, the other two being *M. Le Trouhadec saisi par la débauche* and *Le Mariage de Le Trouhadec*. Although the last of the three to be written and staged, *Donogoo* is the first in the plot series. The play consists of a prologue, three parts, and an epilogue, further divided into tableaux and scenes.

At the beginning of the play, Lamendin, who is about to commit suicide by jumping from a bridge, meets an old cohort, Benin. Benin sends him to Professor Rufisque, a psychotherapist, who advises him to approach the first person he meets outside the Paris mosque and devote himself to this person. He meets and follows Le Trouhadec, a professor of geography at the Collège de France. Le Trouhadec had previously published a textbook describing in detail the South American city of Donogoo-Tonka, which, unfortunately for Le Trouhadec, did not exist. This error is preventing his election to the Institut de France. Lamendin, determined to devote his life to Le Trouhadec, offers to found the city. Aided by the financial backing of an unscrupulous banker, Lamendin launches a massive publicity campaign lauding the emerging, gold-rich city of Donogoo-Tonka and outlining plans for improvements and urbanization. As a result of the publicity, adventurers from around the world set off, avid to find their fortune in Donogoo-Tonka. Two such groups, exhausted from their search and growing skeptical, decide that, since they cannot find the city, they will found it. Within about ten days, a rudimentary village begins to emerge. Soon after, Lamendin and a group of "pioneers" depart for South America with the intention of creating Donogoo. On arriving at a travel agency in Rio de Janeiro, Lamendin is astonished to find not only posters and brochures advertising Donogoo but also weekly treks there. On his arrival at Donogoo, Lamendin

finds a bustling city. He immediately establishes himself as dictator. As a result of Donogoo's success, Le Trouhadec is elected to the Institut de France, the fraudulent banker Margajat's stocks are valid, and Lamendin, glorying in his position of benevolent dictator of Donogoo, creates two new gods of the country: One is scientific truth (known to the initiates as scientific error), symbolized by a perpetually pregnant woman; the other is the new national hero, Le Trouhadec. In *Donogoo*, the relativity of truth, a common twentieth century dramatic theme, finds expression in altered form: The belief in truth creates the reality; error gives rise to truth.

Donogoo has features in common with *Cromedeyre-le-vieil* and *Dr. Knock*, all three of which illustrate unanimism. In both *Cromedeyre-le-vieil* and *Donogoo*, the unanimism springs from a locality, the former an ancient village famed for its youthful vitality, the latter a vital emerging city. In both there is an animator, a person who sparks the growth and the sense of unity, and both animators bring about a deification. In *Cromedeyre-le-vieil*, Emmanuel leads the village to reject the god of others and to re-create the new yet ancient god of the village. In *Donogoo*, Lamendin, having created the city, then creates its deities. The primary distinction between the plays is that Lamendin is a hoaxer and *Donogoo* a playful satire, whereas in *Cromedeyre-le-vieil*, Emmanuel is to be viewed as a savior and the play is serious throughout.

Donogoo also bears a resemblance to *Dr. Knock*. Both are scintillating comedies. Both have similar plots and protagonists: In both, an elaborate hoax is perpetrated on a gullible public by a clever but unscrupulous charlatan who rises to become a dictator of sorts. In both plays, criticism of the characters is absent: Like Dr. Knock, Lamendin, Le Trouhadec, the banker Margajat, and the psychiatrist Rufisque are all frauds. Their actions lead to success, however, and the focus is on the pleasure of the comedy, not on the dubious morality of its characters.

OTHER MAJOR WORKS

LONG FICTION: *Mort de quelqu'un*, 1911 (*Death of a Nobody*, 1914); *Les Copains*, 1913 (*The Boys in the Back Room*, 1937); *Sur les quais de la Villette*,

1914 (reprinted as *Le Vin blanc de la Villette*, 1923); *Psyché*, 1922-1929 (*The Body's Rapture*, 1933; includes *Lucienne*, 1922 [*Lucienne's Story*]; *Le Dieu des corps*, 1928 [*The Body's Rapture*]; *Quand le navire . . .* , 1929 [*Love's Questing*]); *Les Hommes de bonne volonté*, 1932-1946 (*Men of Good Will*, 1933-1946; includes *Le 6 Octobre*, 1932 [*The Sixth of October*, 1933]; *Crime de Quinette*, 1932 [*Quinette's Crime*, 1933]; *Les Amours enfantines*, 1932 [*Children's Loves*, 1934]; *Éros de Paris*, 1932 [*Eros in Paris*, 1934]; *Les Superbes*, 1933 [*The Proud*, 1934]; *Les Humbles*, 1933 [*The Meek*, 1934]; *Recherche d'une église*, 1934 [*The Lonely*, 1935]; *Province*, 1934 [*Provincial Interlude*, 1935]; *Montée des perils*, 1935 [*Flood Warning*, 1936]; *Les Pouvoirs*, 1935 [*The Powers That Be*, 1936]; *Recours à l'abîme*, 1936 [*To the Gutter*, 1937*]; *Les Créateurs*, 1936 [*To the Stars*, 1937]; *Mission à Rome*, 1937 [*Mission to Rome*, 1938]; *Le Drapeau noir*, 1937 [*The Black Flag*, 1938]; *Prélude à Verdun*, 1938 [*The Prelude*, 1939]; *Verdun*, 1938 [*The Battle*, 1939]; *Vorge contre Quinette*, 1939 [*Vorge Against Quinette*, 1941]; *La Douceur de la vie*, 1939 [*The Sweets of Life*, 1941]; *Cette grand lueur à l'Est*, 1941 [*Promise of Dawn*, 1942]; *Le Monde est ton aventure*, 1941 [*The World Is Your Adventure*, 1942]; *Journées dans la montagne*, 1942 [*Mountain Days*, 1944]; *Les Travaux et les joies*, 1943 [*Work and Play*, 1944]; *Naissance de la bande*, 1944 [*The Gathering of the Ganges*, 1945]; *Comparutions*, 1944 [*Offered in Evidence*, 1945]; *Le Tapis magique*, 1946 [*The Magic Carpet*, 1946]; *Françoise*, 1946 [English translation, 1946]; *Le 7 Octobre*, 1946 [*The Seventh of October*, 1946]); *Le Moulin et l'hospice*, 1949; *Le Fils de Jerphanion*, 1956; *Une Femme singulière*, 1957 (*The Adventuress*, 1958); *Le Besoin de voir clair*, 1958; *Mémoires de Madame Chauverel*, 1959-1960; *Un Grand Honnête Homme*, 1961.

SHORT FICTION: *Le Bourg régénéré*, 1906; *Nomentanus le réfugié*, 1943; *Tu ne tueras point*, 1943 (*Thou Shalt Not Kill*, 1943); *Bertrand de Ganges*, 1944; *Violations de frontières*, 1951 (*Tussles with Time*, 1952); *Portraits d'inconnus*, 1962.

POETRY: *L'Âme des hommes*, 1904; *La Vie unanime*, 1908; *Un Être en marche*, 1910; *Odes et prières*, 1913; *Europe*, 1916; *Le Voyage des amants*, 1920; *Ode Génoise*, 1925; *Chants des dix années*, 1928; *L'Homme blanc*, 1937; *Choix de poèmes*, 1948; *Maisons*, 1953; *Pierres levées*, 1957.

SCREENPLAY: *Donogoo-Tonka: Ou, Les Miracles de la science*, 1920.

NONFICTION: *Manuel de déification*, 1910; *Puissances de Paris*, 1911; *Au-dessus de la mêlee*, 1915; *La Vision extra-rétinienne et le sens paroptique*, 1920 (*Eyeless Sight*, 1924); *Problèmes d'aujourd'hui*, 1931; *Problèmes européens*, 1933; *Pour l'esprit et la liberté*, 1937; *Cela dépend de vous*, 1938; *Sept Mystères du destin de l'Europe*, 1940 (*The Seven Mysteries of Europe*, 1940); *Messages aux français*, 1941; *Une Vue des choses*, 1941 (in *I Believe*, 1939); *Salsette découvre l'Amérique*, 1942 (*Salsette Discovers America*, 1942); *Le Problème no. 1*, 1947; *Saints de notre calendrier*, 1952; *Confidences d'un auteur dramatique*, 1953; *Examen de conscience des français*, 1954 (*A Frenchman Examines His Conscience*, 1955); *Passengers de cette planète, où allons nous?*, 1955; *Situation de la terre*, 1958 (*As It Is on Earth*, 1962); *Souvenirs et confidences d'un écrivain*, 1958; *Hommes, médecins, machines*, 1959; *Ai-je fait ce que j'ai voulu?*, 1964; *Lettre ouverte contre une vaste conspiration*, 1966 (*Open Letter Against a Vast Conspiracy*, 1967); *Amitiés et rencontres*, 1970.

BIBLIOGRAPHY

Boak, Denis. *Jules Romains*. Boston: Twayne, 1974. A concise yet thorough study of the life and works of Jules Romains. Bibliography.

Madden, David. "David Madden on Jules Romains's *Death of a Nobody*." In *Rediscoveries II*. New York: Carroll & Graf, 1988. Madden discusses Romains's *Death of a Nobody*, a novel in which the roots of his ideas of unanimism can be seen.

Norrish, P. J. *Drama of the Group: A Study of Unanimism in the Plays of Jules Romains*. Cambridge, England: Cambridge University Press, 1958. Norrish examines the dramatic works of Romains, placing special attention to his theories of unanimism. Index.

Edna M. Troiano

EDMOND ROSTAND

Born: Marseilles, France; April 1, 1868
Died: Paris, France; December 2, 1918

PRINCIPAL DRAMA

Le Gant rouge, pr., pb. 1888 (with Henry Lee)
Les Romanesques, pr., 1894, pb. 1917 (verse play;
  The Romantics, 1899)
La Princesse lointaine, pr. 1895, pb. 1908 (verse
  play; *The Far Princess*, 1899)
La Samaritaine, pr. 1897, pb. 1898 (verse play; *The
  Woman of Samaria*, 1921)
Cyrano de Bergerac, pr. 1897, pb. 1898 (verse
  play; English translation, 1898)
L'Aiglon, pr., pb. 1900 (verse play; *The Eaglet*,
  1898)
Chantecler, pr., pb. 1910 (verse play; *Chanticleer*,
  1910)
La Dernière nuit de Don Juan, pb. 1921, pr. 1922
  (verse play; *The Last Night of Don Juan*, 1929)
Plays of Edmond Rostand, pb. 1921

OTHER LITERARY FORMS

Although his greatest success was as a dramatist, Edmond Rostand was first of all a poet. All of his plays are written in verse, and despite his real flair for dramatic situations, it is the wit and lyricism of his verse that raise his best plays above the level of ordinary melodrama. His first published work was a volume of poetry, *Les Musardises* (1890). The title is untranslatable. Its basic meaning is "daydreams," but in a preface, Rostand explained that he also meant to evoke a kind of melancholy—*muzer*, in the Walloon dialect, meaning "to be sad"—as well as the source of poetic inspiration—the Muse. He published two later volumes of verse, *Le Cantique de l'aile* (1910; the canticle of the wing), including a paean to the first aviators, and *Le Vol de la Marseillaise* (1914; the flight of the Marseillaise), a collection of patriotic poems inspired by World War I. He wrote little prose, but a boyhood essay on Honoré d'Urfé and Émile Zola, which won for him first prize in a contest sponsored by the Academy of Moral and Political Sci-

ences of Marseilles, proved important because it introduced him to the strain in French literature known as *préciosité*, of which d'Urfé's work was a classic expression. Rostand's speech on his induction into the Académie Française is also revealing; in it, he discusses the notion of *panache*, the "spirit of bravura" central to his masterpiece, *Cyrano de Bergerac*.

ACHIEVEMENTS

Edmond Rostand is remembered, and will probably continue to be remembered, exclusively as the author of a single play, *Cyrano de Bergerac*. Its first production, in Paris in 1897, was greeted with wild enthusiasm (the ovation on opening night lasted almost an hour) and made the twenty-nine-year-old author famous overnight. His popularity did not diminish during his lifetime, and he became the youngest man ever elected to the Académie Française, but most of his plays are marred by sentimentality and have not been much revived since his death. Only one, *The Eaglet*, enjoyed a reception comparable to that of *Cyrano de Bergerac*, but this was partly because of the popularity of its theme (the fate of Napoleon II) among Rostand's contemporaries, and partly because of the acting of Sarah Bernhardt, who appeared in the title role. Rostand cannot be said to have influenced subsequent French drama, for his style was anachronistic in his own day, a reaction against what was perceived as the pessimism of the realistic theater. *Cyrano de Bergerac*, however, has proved to be a perennial favorite on the world stage and has been translated into languages as disparate as Turkish, Russian, Hebrew, and Japanese. In addition, a musical comedy, *The Fantasticks*, based on *The Romantics*, has had an incredibly long run Off-Broadway (more than twenty years) and has been produced in fifty-seven countries.

BIOGRAPHY

Edmond Eugène Alexis Rostand was born into an upper-middle-class family with deep roots in the south of France that can be traced back to the sixteenth century. His father, Eugène, and his paternal uncle Alexis were distinguished economists who also managed to cultivate their gifts for poetry and music, respectively: Eugène translated Catullus and wrote the librettos for Alexis's oratorios. The young Rostand was a shy and studious child who loved to read and play with marionettes; his favorite authors were Sir Walter Scott and Alexandre Dumas, *père*. During long summer vacations in the Pyrenees, he developed a deep attachment for the region; there he also wrote his first poems. After completing primary school and six years at the Marseilles Lycée, he was sent to the Collège Stanislas in Paris to complete his secondary education. His teachers there introduced him to the work of William Shakespeare, Johann Wolfgang von Goethe, and Alfred de Musset (some echoes of Musset's comedies may be detected in *The Romantics* and *The Far Princess*). Rostand's other literary heroes were Miguel de Cervantes and Victor Hugo.

Untouched by the naturalists and Symbolists, he was not drawn into any of the literary circles of Paris. Through his future wife, Rosemonde Gérard, he made the acquaintance of the poet Leconte de Lisle, her godfather, but received no encouragement from him. At his father's urging, he began to study law while making his first attempts at playwriting. *Le Gant rouge* (the red glove), a comedy written in collaboration with Henry Lee, his future brother-in-law, was staged in 1888 but was not well received. *Les Musardises* met with mixed reviews in 1890. In the same year Rostand married Gérard, who was herself a poet (her collection *Les Pipeaux* was published in 1889). According to Rostand's biographer Émile Ripert, Gérard was responsible in large measure for bringing her husband's work to the attention of the public. A perfectionist, Rostand revised his work repeatedly and was reluctant to publish. The couple had two sons, Maurice, a dramatist, and Jean, an eminent biologist. With *The Romantics* and *The Far Princess*,

Edmond Rostand (Hulton Archive by Getty Images)

Rostand gained some recognition. The former play won for him the Toirac Prize, and the latter, the friendship and admiration of Sarah Bernhardt, who produced the work and played the princess. The title role of *The Woman of Samaria* was created especially for Bernhardt.

The appearance of *Cyrano de Bergerac* proved a watershed in the poet's life; from that time until his death, he was a famous man, besieged by admirers and, as Ripert notes, acutely conscious of his "spiritual mission" as poet, patriot, and idealist. In spite of the nationalist tendency observable in *The Eaglet* (Rostand's father was a Bonapartist), Rostand did not support the nationalist parties of his day and, in fact, risked his popularity by maintaining the innocence of Alfred Dreyfus. In politics as in literature, he refused to align himself with a particular movement; he admired quixotic daring against all odds—the bravura of Cyrano—wherever he saw it, and wrote poems in praise of both the Greeks and the Boers in their bids for independence.

Rostand was plagued by recurrent pulmonary infections, and, after the success of *The Eaglet*, he moved with his family to Cambo in the foothills of the Pyrenees, where the weather and the relative privacy were better for his health. He returned to Paris for short periods only—for example, to deliver an acceptance speech at the Académie Française in 1903 and to supervise the staging of *Chanticleer*. Even in Cambo, where he built a villa and lived in semi-retirement for the remainder of his life, the mantle of unofficial poet laureate weighed heavily on him. He was forced to hire a secretary to answer the flood of mail he received, and he spent ten years revising *Chanticleer*, for fear of disappointing his public (the play was only a partial success). A compulsive worker who suffered from insomnia, Rostand was a rather distant father to his two sons. As Maurice Rostand put it, "Glory makes homes empty." By contrast, he corresponded with hundreds of young soldiers during World War I and visited others in the trenches. The war cast a deep gloom over his last years, during which he wrote a collection of labored patriotic verse and *The Last Night of Don Juan*, which he termed a "dramatic poem." The latter was staged in 1922, four years after his death, but without success. He died of pneumonia on December 2, 1918, shortly after the Armistice.

ANALYSIS

Despite his debt to the romantics, the strain in French literature to which Edmond Rostand really belongs is that of *préciosité*, "precious" or elaborately refined writing, usually on the subject of love. An outstanding trait of *préciosité* is the prominence it gives to form, often at the expense of content. Therefore, Rostand wrote his dramas in the regular rhymed couplets of the classical and romantic French theater, even insisting on *rime riche* in the manner of the Parnassian poet Théodore de Banville. His diction and imagery were equally studied and at times rather farfetched. When deployed with wit and grace, as in his best plays, this fastidious technique served Rostand well, but it was not equally suited to all the subjects he treated.

At heart, Rostand—like most of his protagonists—was an idealist who shunned what he saw as the negativism of modern literature. Like Edwin Arlington Robinson's Miniver Cheevy, he was in a real sense "born too late"; only instead of drinking as Miniver did, he "kept on writing" in his own vein, oblivious of his naturalist and Symbolist contemporaries. He was at his best, however, when he tempered his romantic flights with a dose of humor or with a trace of the irony that characterized his own age. Therefore, his masterpiece, *Cyrano de Bergerac*, takes as its hero a seventeenth century wit (himself a *précieux*) whose tendency to take himself too seriously is perfectly tempered by his ludicrous appearance. In Cyrano, Rostand was able to fuse his idealism and his polished wit in a character who is by turns heroic and comical—to resounding dramatic effect.

Indeed, Rostand was not only a meticulous versifier but also a man of considerable dramatic gifts. In particular, he knew how to vary the moods of successive scenes and achieve striking stage effects with surprise reversals. He was also capable of clever plot development, as his best plays, *Cyrano de Bergerac* and *The Romantics*, demonstrate. Yet because his characters are only sketchily developed, their actions can appear insufficiently motivated, and the interplay of character and action characteristic of most great drama is missing. Nor is there a structure of ideas in Rostand's plays that might compensate for this shallowness of characterization. In his dramatic effects, as in his verbal craftsmanship, he is above all a superb entertainer—albeit an idealistic one.

Indeed, *préciosité* is, in essence, a form of highly refined entertainment. It is not a school but rather a tendency that runs through much of French poetry, though its heyday was in the early seventeenth century. (Its origins may be traced to the courtly lyrics of the troubadors, and it is visible in the poetry of the sixteenth century "Pléïade" as well as in that of the nineteenth century Parnassians.) The context in which the seventeenth century *précieux* flourished was that of the salons, exclusive social circles that noble and, later, bourgeois women gathered about themselves. The members of such circles met to discuss literary topics and often to compete with one another in actual poetic contests. One of Rostand's best poems, a period piece called *La Journée d'une précieuse* (1898; a day in the life of a précieuse), describes such a contest, in which the requirement is to compose a *rondeau* with rhymes in *-al* and *-oche* "to accompany the gift of a seal of rock-crystal." Rostand's poem manages to poke gentle fun at the extravagances of his heroine and her salon while conveying some of the genuine wit and charm that such circles fostered.

In most of the salons, wit and worldly graces were prized above true erudition; writers of a "precious" cast tended to seek new, entertaining ways of saying things rather than new things to say. In general this is true of Rostand, whose imagery, diction, and versification all display the studied (*recherché*) quality proper to the *précieux*. Rostand's decision to write verse dramas in the last decade of the nineteenth and the first decade of the twentieth centuries was itself a relative anachronism (the realistic theater confined itself to prose) and as such called attention to his virtuosity. He allowed himself romantic license in his use of the Alexandrine (the twelve-syllable line that had been the medium for classical French drama): En-

jambments are frequent, and single lines are routinely divided among three, four, or even more different characters. Even in crowd scenes, however, there are no lapses into prose, and the effect is often that of a tour de force. This method works well when the theme is love or bravado, as in the famous balcony scene or in Cyrano's duel with the Vicomte de Valvert, during which he composes a *ballade*, finishing off his opponent at the end of the refrain; it is less successful when more banal topics are involved, and especially when, as in *Chanticleer*, the necessary suspension of disbelief cannot be maintained: Twentieth century farm animals cannot be made to speak heroic couplets except in farce, and Rostand exceeds the limits of his form by freighting the play with serious themes. Even in plays set in a distant or legendary past, such as *The Far Princess* and *The Woman of Samaria*, there are lapses of taste, for the finely chiseled lines and *rime riche* (rhyme involving not only the last syllable of a word but also the preceding consonant or syllable) can easily ring false outside certain contexts. The same may be said of Rostand's diction, which—largely as a result of his insistence on "rich" rhyme—includes rare and occasionally grotesque words, some of them coinages. These qualities suit the burlesque scenes to perfection but give a labored or awkward tone to some serious scenes, especially in *The Far Princess*.

Where imagery is concerned, Rostand is a true *précieux*, working best on the small scale of the individual line or speech; his recurrent or governing images are often banal (thus light is symbolic of glory, wings of daring or aspiration, lilies of chastity, and roses of fulfilled love). Even these can be effective in specific contexts—when, for example, the "Far Princess," Mélissinde, acknowledges that the strong yet overrefined scent of the lilies with which she surrounds herself may reinforce her own "solitary pride." By insisting that the stage be strewn with lilies, however—to be exchanged for roses in act 3, when Mélissinde has fallen in love with Bertrand— Rostand makes the symbolism too emphatic and obvious. Granted that hyperbole or exaggeration is also a feature of the "precious" style, this overworking is a temptation to which Rostand, like many *précieux*, succumbs all too readily. One of his loveliest images compares the Samaritan woman's gesture, as she balances a water jar on her head with one hand, to the jar itself with its graceful handle; yet instead of letting the image stand on its own, he goes on to freight it with a grandiloquence ("Immortal splendor of this rustic grace!") and a sentimentality beneath which it all but founders.

The far-fetched quality proper to "precious" imagery makes it most appropriate to, and effective in, burlesque or self-consciously witty passages. Here Rostand is in his element and can make the sparks fly. Perhaps the most famous example is the "nose tirade" in act 1 of *Cyrano de Bergerac*, in which the hero puts a man who has insulted him to scorn by improving on the insult. Instead of saying baldly, "You have a very big nose," the man might have compared the nose to a peninsula, a scissors-case, a conch, a monument—even, "when it bleeds, the Red Sea!" This kind of virtuosity is already visible in Rostand's early poem, "Charivari à la lune" (mock-serenade for the moon, in *Les Musardises*), which compares the moon to scores of different objects, including a cymbal, a mushroom, an egg, and a fingernail. More striking than the images themselves is the grace and wit with which Rostand arranges them: At first, each quatrain encompasses a single image, then two, then four, until the last frenetic strophe of the "serenade" is made to hold eight different images. Lapsing into Alexandrines, the poet admits that he is out of breath and hopes for a response from the moon—but all he hears is an ironic, "Go on!" Here as elsewhere, wit is Rostand's great redeeming grace, the pinprick deflating what otherwise might become intolerably artificial and hollow.

This is not to deny Rostand's properly dramatic talents. Even his most sentimental plays contain effective scenes, in which a sense of dramatic movement is sustained by artful development or sudden reversals. Thus, the woman of Samaria, recognizing Jesus as the Messiah, bursts into the same profane love song with which she had approached the well; thus Metternich, entering the Duke of Reichstadt's bedroom late at night, is confronted by a French grenadier standing guard and half believes for a mo-ment that Napoleon is occupying the palace as he had twenty years earlier. Indeed, the entire plot of *The Romantics* is built on a double reversal of romantic conventions, which Rostand arranges to maximum theatrical effect.

THE ROMANTICS

The Romantics might be described as an anti-*Romeo and Juliet* (pr. c. 1595-1596; deliberately so on Rostand's part—as it opens, the hero is reading Romeo's speech from the balcony scene). In the first act, two fathers foster an attachment between their children, Sylvette and Percinet, by pretending to be mortal enemies; like Ovid's Pyramus and Thisbe, the young couple meet in secret by the wall dividing the two estates. The fathers put a contrived end to their contrived hatred by hiring a knockabout named Straforel to stage an "abduction" of Sylvette, whom Percinet "rescues." As act 2 opens, the wall is down and the marriage, imminent, but a second (and this time realistic) reversal is in store: The fathers, finding each other's daily company irritating, are on the way to becoming enemies in earnest. They find it still harder to bear the condescension of their children, who believe that their own romantic ideal has won the day over the obtuse self-interest of their elders. At last unable to contain themselves, the fathers tell Sylvette the truth; she tries to hide it from Percinet but finds herself losing interest in his romantic excesses, which now strike her as pretentious and hollow. Then Percinet stumbles on Straforel's bill for the "abduction" (a masterfully comic touch, including items such as "Rumpled clothing, ten francs; Hurt pride, forty"). Though their first reaction is to reaffirm their love, which they insist is real even if their situation has been false, they soon quarrel, and Percinet runs off to seek "real" adventure. Straforel, who has yet to be paid, decides to patch it up between the two; he begins by proposing a real elopement to Sylvette, describing the hardships she will face in terms that make her long for a quiet life with Percinet. Meanwhile, her fiancé returns, disenchanted by his brushes with "adventure" in the form of barmaids and thugs, and the two lovers are reconciled.

As can be seen from this summary, the plot is clever, and Rostand unfolds it artfully, making the most of every reversal. He also maintains a consistent tone throughout the poetic dialogue—light and graceful, as in *La Journée d'une précieuse*, with exactly the right shade of gentle irony. After *Cyrano de Bergerac*, *The Romantics* is the play of Rostand that holds up best for a modern-day audience. This is largely a result of the universal appeal of its stock characters, which can be traced back as far as Menander (young lovers, burlesque fathers, jacks-of-all-trades), but it is also attributable to the essential modernity of the play's theme: the ironic unmasking of romantic ideals. The fact that Rostand arranges a happy ending—in effect, a kind of *re*-masking— makes it all the more stageworthy; it is a comedy in the classical mold. Yet it portrays middle-class disillusionment in a manner that rings true.

In this respect, *The Romantics* is unique among Rostand's plays. Most of the time, he prided himself on resisting the disillusionment of his contemporaries, choosing as heroes men whose great aim in life was to distinguish themselves. The means to this end differ considerably from play to play (poetry, fidelity in love, even, in *Chanticleer*, a rooster's crowing), yet in each case the hero justifies his endeavor by maintaining its value on an ideal plane. The distinction he seeks is not so much public recognition—though most of Rostand's heroes crave recognition as well— but rather the singularity of the romantic idealist, often purchased at the price of loneliness and self-doubt. Love is also an important theme in the plays, but it is always subordinate to the hero's struggle for distinction and is tinged with the idealism of that struggle. Hence the platonic character of the great "love affairs" in Rostand—Jaufré Rudel and Mélissinde, Cyrano and Roxane. (An extreme example can be seen in the Samaritan woman's response to Jesus, who replaces the imperfect former objects of her love.) Even Rostand's Don Juan exhibits no real sensuality; the reasons he gives for a lifetime of seduction are all intellectual, amounting to perverted or negative ideals.

It is in his idealism, which stems from the nineteenth century romantics, that Rostand least resembles the seventeenth century *précieux*; for while the latter also engaged in platonic love affairs and pro-

fessed a consuming interest in "things of the spirit," the salons in which they sought to distinguish themselves were above all social circles, little courts formed in emulation of the royal court. As such, they could be stepping-stones to worldly recognition and influence. The emphasis on form in the writings of the *précieux* thus stems from a desire to please; theirs is the art of the courtier. Rostand was far more ambivalent in his attitude toward the public for which he wrote. Though anxious lest he disappoint his audience, he believed that the poet's mission was not only to please but also to inspire. This sense of mission unfortunately had a pernicious effect on his last works, replacing the easy grace of *The Romantics* with an uneven tone that fluctuates between heavy humor and preachiness. In *Cyrano de Bergerac*, however, Rostand managed to strike the perfect compromise between his *préciosité* and his idealism.

CYRANO DE BERGERAC

Never was his sense of properly theatrical values keener than in *Cyrano de Bergerac*. The plot moves briskly, keeping the audience amused while engaging its sympathies in favor of the hero, then building to a double climax of considerable pathos. Each of the five acts has a dramatic unity of its own, yet together the acts form an almost seamless whole. A poet and soldier of uncompromising ideals, Cyrano has been cursed with an outlandish nose that he himself freely ridicules but will allow no one else to mention. His bravado dominates the first act, in which he composes a *ballade* while fighting a duel then goes alone to face one hundred men whom he learns are waiting to ambush his friend Lignière. Yet there is one person before whom he trembles: his cousin Roxane, whom he secretly loves but fears to woo because of his ugliness. He is on tenterhooks when, in the second act, she asks to meet with him in private and confesses that she is in love; but it emerges that her infatuation is for Christian de Neuvillette, a new member of Cyrano's company in the Guards, and whom she wants her cousin to befriend and protect. This Cyrano resolutely promises to do, though he warns Roxane—herself a *précieuse*— that Christian, with whom she has never spoken, may prove a fool for all of his beauty. When this prediction turns out to be true, Cyrano takes his self-sacrifice a step further and offers to coach Christian, providing him with witty and tender words that enchant Roxane. In act 3, Christian tries to speak for himself, but his awkwardness offends Roxane; in an attempt to put things right again, Cyrano has him call her to her balcony, and he himself addresses her from the shadows below. Overcome with emotion, he pours out his heart—still in Christian's name—and Roxane arranges a secret wedding for that very night, during which time Cyrano stands guard, detaining yet another of Roxane's suitors, the powerful Count de Guiche. Enraged, the count dispatches the Guards to the siege of Arras; in act 4, Roxane manages to join them there, drawn by the beauty of "Christian's" daily letters. When Roxane tells Christian that she would love him even if he were ugly, Christian urges Cyrano to tell her the truth, but a few minutes later Christian is killed, and Cyrano resolves to keep the secret. It is not until the end of act 5 (which takes place fourteen years later) that he reveals the truth, half involuntarily, on the verge of his own death.

What makes the play so compelling is the thoroughly romantic contrast between the "inner" and "outer" man: Like the dwarf Triboulet (the original of Giuseppe Verdi's Rigoletto) in Victor Hugo's play *Le Roi s'amuse* (1832; *The King Amuses Himself*, 1842), Cyrano may be tender and passionate in spite of his ridiculous face. (Similarly, in *The Eaglet*, the Duke of Reichstadt may be considered "a great prince" although he accomplishes nothing.) The weakness of Rostand's work is that the singularity of the soul that he claims for his heroes is merely assumed, never substantiated by depth or complexity of characterization. Even Cyrano, his most successful creation, is incompletely developed. One has only to ask what it is that Roxane loves in Cyrano (or, still more pointedly, what it is that Cyrano loves in Roxane) to realize that Rostand never tells. Roxane learned to love Cyrano's "soul," she says, by reading his letters, yet the only real taste that the audience gets of his eloquence is the balcony scene, in which form (witty phrasing, precious imagery) predominates and the real poignancy stems from the contrast—of which Roxane is unaware—between the beauty of Cyrano's words and the ugliness of his face.

In fact, as a survey of his other plays reveals, Rostand had only a limited repertory of characters, types to which he reverted again and again: the romantic idealist, usually his protagonist; the desirable but fickle woman, confused about what qualities are worth loving; and the hard-headed realist, who serves as foil and often friend to the hero. Because his dramas hinged on these ideal types, Rostand sought exotic settings such as twelfth century Tripoli or seventeenth century Paris; he himself admitted that he set *Chanticleer* in a barnyard because no contemporary human setting would suit his purpose.

Much of Rostand's purpose becomes clear if one compares his Cyrano with the real Cyrano, Savinien de Cyrano de Bergerac, whose life is well documented and many of whose writings survive. The greatest surprise is to discover that this Cyrano would in fact have made a very good twentieth century hero—or antihero: He gave up a military career in disgust after being wounded twice; he changed sides (possibly for pay) during the Fronde, the struggle between some nobles and the regent Cardinal Mazarin; and he almost certainly died of syphilis (like Rostand's Cyrano, he was also struck on the head by a log, but this preceded his death by some time and may have been an accident rather than an ambush). Admittedly, the real Cyrano was a man of the seventeenth century as well: An avowed "libertine" or freethinker, he is said to have returned to the faith on his deathbed, at the urging of his friend Lebret and his relative, Mother Marguérite of Jesus. Rostand, however, did not want a seventeenth century hero any more than he wanted a twentieth century one. His Cyrano is larger than life—a great lover and a great fighter, a man of immutable ideals, impossible courage, and matchless wit. He lacks psychological depth and plausibility precisely because the ideal that Rostand would have him sustain has something inhuman about it. Why, the audience may ask, does Cyrano remain silent for fourteen years? If it were out of loyalty to Christian, he betrays his friend just as surely by speaking at the end of that time as he would have by speaking at the beginning—and, in the meantime, he has deprived not only himself but also Roxane of happiness. The answer Rostand would have given, to judge by his other plays and poems, is that the essence of Cyrano's (and Roxane's) love was not denied but preserved by his silence: There could be no disillusionment, no imperfection, in such an idealized passion. This means that Roxane, too, must be something less than a real woman, because she also is expected to be something more; as Charles Pujos puts it, "The beloved has to remain unpolluted to the very end, since she represents an Idea more than she does a woman, and only the [author's] symbolic intention can justify that."

Given its wholly platonic conception of love, how does the play continue to hold the stage in the late twentieth century? In fairness to Rostand, it must be added that questions such as that of Cyrano's silence suggest themselves to a reader sooner than they do to a spectator, and perhaps to a spectator only after the play is finished. It should also be noted that Rostand has always found his most ardent admirers among the young, who see in Cyrano the courageous nonconformist and the tragic lover. Because of the play's wit, its carefully articulated plot, and the delicate balance it maintains between idealism and *préciosité*, *Cyrano de Bergerac* is a superb dramatic entertainment. As such, it will probably remain a perennial favorite with theatergoers around the world.

OTHER MAJOR WORKS

POETRY: *Les Musardises*, 1890; *La Journée d'une précieuse*, 1898; *Le Cantique de l'aile*, 1910; *Le Vol de la Marseillaise*, 1914.

BIBLIOGRAPHY

Amoia, Alba della Fazia. *Edmond Rostand*. Boston: Twayne, 1978. In this concise biography, Amoia discusses Rostand's life and works. Bibliography and index.

Chweh, Crystal R., ed. *Readings on "Cyrano de Bergerac."* Literary Companion to World Literature series. San Diego, Calif.: Greenhaven Press, 2001. This book of essays, intended for young adults, presents literary criticism of Rostand's best-known work.

Freeman, E. J. *Edmond Rostand, Cyrano de Bergerac*. Glasgow, Scotland: University of Glasgow French and German Publications, 1995. Freeman looks at Rostand and his most popular work. Bibliography.

Lillian Doherty

OLA ROTIMI

Born: Sapele, Nigeria; April 13, 1938
Died: Ile-Ife, Nigeria; August 18, 2000

PRINCIPAL DRAMA

To Stir the God of Iron, pr. 1963
Our Husband Has Gone Mad Again, pr. 1966, pb. 1974
The Gods Are Not to Blame, pr. 1968, pb. 1971 (adaptation of Sophocles' play *Oedipus Rex*)
Kurunmi, pr. 1969, pb. 1971
The Prodigal, pr. 1969
Holding Talks, pr., 1970, pb. 1979
Ovonramwen Nogbaisi, pr. 1971, pb. 1974
Akassa You Mi: A Historical Drama, pr. 1977, pb. 2001
If: A Tragedy of the Ruled, pr. 1979, pb. 1983
Hopes of the Living Dead, pr. 1985, pb. 1988
Grip 'Am, pr. 1985
Man Talk, Woman Talk, pr. 1995
When the Criminals Become Judges, pr. 1995

OTHER LITERARY FORMS

Ola Rotimi is noted only for his plays, although he also wrote critical articles on Nigerian theater.

ACHIEVEMENTS

Ola Rotimi was one of Nigeria's and Africa's foremost dramatists, both a theatrical teacher and an entertainer as well as a playwright. Two of Rotimi's plays, *Kurunmi* and *Ovonramwen Nogbaisi*, are historical tragedies that recapture pivotal moments in the history of the Yoruba people and the glorious empire of Benin. Three other plays, *Our Husband Has Gone Mad Again*, *If*, and *Hopes of the Living Dead*, constitute a dramatic sociopolitical trilogy, an extended inquiry into the themes of struggle and integrity of leadership. In these plays, as in others, Rotimi warned his people to beware political charlatans who have continued to lead postindependence Nigeria to one poor harvest after another. A dominant subject of Rotimi's plays was official and unofficial corruption on such a massive scale that the traditional African sense of community had been sacrificed to personal greed, personal power, and personal self-glorification. *The Gods Are Not to Blame*, first presented at the Ife Festival of the Arts in 1968, has as its theme that the real source of the Nigerian Civil War (1967-1970) was mutual ethnic distrust among Nigerian people and not the work of the great political gods of the freshly decolonialized world, the United States and the former Soviet Union as well as France and England.

The Gods Are Not to Blame was awarded first prize in the African Arts/Arts d'Afrique playwriting contest in 1969. The politico-domestic comedy *Our Husband Has Gone Mad Again*, written in 1965, when Rotimi was in his final year as a graduate student of playwriting and dramatic literature at Yale University, was honored as Yale Major Play of the Year. Both of these plays have seen numerous successful revivals in Europe and North America. *The Gods Are Not to Blame* has become a standard text for English literature classes in Nigeria, and *Our Husband Has Gone Mad Again* was a resounding triumph at its revival at the University of Toronto in June, 2000.

Rotimi's plays are often filled with dance, mime, music, and song. Frequently, the songs or chants are in his native Yoruba. They offer thematic commentary on the actions of individual characters and on the destiny of the community. Like the words of the Greek chorus in the plays of Sophocles, the songs articulate the views of reason and social stability; at the same time, they are often humorous, frequently with a satiric intent. Rotimi merges the serious with the humorous in nearly all of his plays, for he believed that the dramatist must entertain as well as teach. Action in the Aristotelian sense is the essence of his drama. A distinctive characteristic of Rotimi's work among that of contemporary African playwrights is the large number of characters, singers, and dancers on stage at one time. In his plays, the stage often becomes a meeting place for large crowds. Rotimi thus sought to re-create the spirit of communal participation that existed and still exists in traditional African ceremonies. However, Rotimi died before fulfilling his dream of producing a play with five hundred extras and characters.

Along with Wole Soyinka and John Pepper Clark-Bekederemo, Rotimi belonged to the vibrant first generation of modern Nigerian dramatists writing in English. Throughout Nigeria, their plays are continually produced. In the late twentieth century, new dramatists, inspired by Rotimi and his contemporaries, emerged: Zulu Sofolo, Wale Ogunyemi, Femi Osofisan, Bode Sowande, and Samson Amali. Rotimi was one of the two or three most highly regarded dramatists in Africa and as such played a major role in the development of a dramatic literature on his continent.

BIOGRAPHY

Emmanuel Gladstone Olawale Rotimi was born on April 13, 1938, the son of a Yoruba father from western Nigeria and an Ijaw mother from Rivers State in the Niger Delta of eastern Nigeria. His father, principal of the Engineering Training School of the Ports Authority in Lagos, often directed plays, and his mother had her own dance troupe. The young Rotimi took part in some amateur plays directed by his father, making his stage debut at the age of four. This tradition of family involvement in dramatic performance continued throughout his life. Rotimi met his wife, Hazel Mac Guadreau, a white woman, at Boston University when they were both undergraduates. She was always involved in his plays—on stage or backstage. A talented musician in her own right, she led the chorus in productions of *If*, while Kole Rotimi, Ola's son, has appeared in a principal role in the same play. She died a few months before her husband in May, 2000.

Ola Rotimi attended primary school in Port Harcourt in eastern Nigeria and the Methodist Boys High School in Lagos, Nigeria's capital. Capable in four languages—English, Ijaw, Yoruba, and Pidgin—the playwright Rotimi drew on his rich linguistic heritage: Although his plays are written in English, they contain a smattering of the other three languages as well, and his English is not an imitation of the language spoken in Oxford or Boston; rather, it is alive with the rhythms, the aphorisms, and the pulse of Nigerian English. His later plays increasingly included African languages and a Nigerian version of Pidgin English in their dialogue, although English remained the main language.

From 1959 until 1966, Rotimi studied in the United States. He received a Nigerian Federal Government scholarship to attend Boston University, where he majored in playwriting and directing, after which he attended Yale on a Rockefeller Foundation scholarship. Receiving his master of arts degree from Yale in 1966, he returned to Nigeria to become senior research fellow at the Institute of African Studies at the University of Ife. While living in Ife (now renamed Ile-Ife), in the heart of Yorubaland, he familiarized himself with Yoruba oral tradition, including various musical forms that he was to inculcate into his plays. During his tenure there, he directed the university theater company, the Ori-Olokun Players. This company was invited by the French government in 1971 to the World Festival of Theatre in the city of Nancy in eastern France. Rotimi left Ife and moved to the University of Port Harcourt, where he directed his plays at the University Theater, The Crab. Using both student actors and trained actors from the Arts Council of Rivers State, he brought the vibrancy of his art to the Port Harcourt area. From 1982 to 1984, Rotimi was dean of the faculty of humanities at the University of Port Harcourt. His play *Hopes of the Living Dead* was first performed at the University of Port Harcourt theater in 1985.

In April, 1992, Rotimi retired from teaching in order to found his production company, African Cradle Theatre, or ACT. Initially, the Nigerian International Bank promised to subsidize Rotimi's company, and Rotimi launched ACT with a production of his absurdist play, *Holding Talks*, in Lagos in September, 1992. Rotimi's project to take his historical play, *Hopes of the Living Dead*, on tour across Nigeria failed because of a lack of funding. The lack of economic support or independent sponsorship also led to the folding of ACT. Even though his satirical play, *Man Talk, Woman Talk*, played to a packed and enthusiastic audience in 1995, Rotimi became disillusioned with the corrupt dictatorial regime of Nigerian general Sani Abacha, who hanged Rotimi's fellow playwright, Ken Saro-Wiwa, for his a political activism in 1995.

In 1995, Rotimi, who has been described as diminutive in size but magnificent in talent, accepted a position as the Hubert H. Humphrey visiting professor of international studies and dramatic arts and dance at Macalester College in St. Paul, Minnesota. He taught at Macalester until 1997, often producing his own plays with great enthusiasm.

After the death of Abacha and the return of democratic rule to Nigeria at the end of 1998, Rotimi returned and became a professor at Cbafemi Awolowo University in lle-Ife. He died of a heart attack on August 18, 2000.

Rotimi spoke English, Yoruba, Ijaw, Igbo, Hausa, and Pidgin but wrote primarily in English. In 1989, at the Talawa Theatre's revival of *The Gods Are Not to Blame*, at London's Riverside Studios, Rotimi explained, "I believe that in Nigeria's multicultural situation writers should be less partisan. So I write in English. But I try all the time to use simple words and introduce the speech patterns and cadences of Yoruba villagers." His later plays, notably *If* and *Hopes of the Living Dead*, make use of Nigerian names and proverbs.

ANALYSIS

It would not be much of an exaggeration to claim that almost everything in most traditional African societies is a form of theater. The community itself is the central actor, and the village is the stage. Wrestling matches, funerals, initiation rites, religious ceremonies—each of these rituals involves the entire community. It is not surprising, then, that in this modern time, a time that has witnessed the effulgence of written literature, African drama has been nourished by traditional sources. Contemporary writers have returned to the marketplace to be inspired by oral storytellers, whose dramatic tales are often accompanied by musicians and dancers, all of whom are engaged with the audience-community in a statement of social value. The actor and audience are both active participants in the affirmation of the community. One cannot appreciate African drama without recognizing the essence of ritual in the nature of traditional communal activity. The theatrical stage is the village meeting ground, and the dramatist cannot function apart from the society to which he or she belongs.

The theater of Ola Rotimi, like that of fellow African Soyinka and the Greeks Aristophanes and Sophocles, is rooted in ritual. Songs, chants, dance, and mime are as elemental as dialogue and monologue. In his plays, Rotimi, the contemporary artist-historian, taught his people of their past so they can better understand the present and build a constructive future.

OUR HUSBAND HAS GONE MAD AGAIN

Rotimi's *Our Husband Has Gone Mad Again*, written in 1965, foreshadows his career as a dramatist with a sense of social responsibility. The play's protagonist, a former military major, Rahman Taslim Lejoka-Brown, takes to politics not out of feelings of patriotism but rather out of vanity. His political naïveté is matched by his marital ineptitude. When his American wife rejoins him unexpectedly to discover two other wives whom he has married without her knowledge, the major begins to suffer major symptoms of discomfort.

Our Husband Has Gone Mad Again is a drawing-room comedy of sorts. Most of the action takes place in Lejoka-Brown's living room; his political ambition is paralleled in his private life. When the play begins, the audience learns that his sophisticated American-educated wife, Lisa, is due to arrive in Lagos. Lejoka-Brown has not told her about his two other wives, Mama Rashida and Sikira, both of whom are in the

mold of market women. The play contains a very humorous scene in which Lisa, believing Sikira to be a housemaid, manages to antagonize the two other wives. They know that the newly arrived fowl needs to have her proud feathers plucked.

It is generally known in traditional Nigerian societies that if a man cannot handle his wives, he probably will not be able to handle political responsibility. Lejoka-Brown thinks that he is in control of his wives; he is not. Once the wives learn to accept one another and work together, the poor major has no chance. At the end of the play, Sikira, with the support of the market women, is to become the candidate of the National Liberation Party. Lejoka-Brown's world is turned upside down. He laments that before he became caught up in the craziness of politics, he was doing very well running his cocoa business.

The political figure in *Our Husband Has Gone Mad Again* is a former military major. His National Liberation Party mouths slogans of freedom for the people of Nigeria, for Africa. In actuality, political freedom really means unlimited license for corruption.

From the beginning, Rotimi warned Nigeria of the dangers that threaten the stability of society in the modern world. In his dramas, which examine the fate of a people in need of sociopolitical hope, he looks at Nigerian democracy and shudders. *Our Husband Has Gone Mad Again*, first staged at Yale University in 1966, was very popular in Nigeria during the hiatus from military rule that lasted from 1979 to 1983. Nigerian electioneering maneuvers seem to have changed not at all between 1966 and 1983. Party members in *Our Husband Has Gone Mad Again* are all thugs, and the politicians are nothing more than greedy charlatans interested only in instant wealth. The play has also been a critical success outside Africa.

THE GODS ARE NOT TO BLAME

Rotimi's next play, *The Gods Are Not to Blame*, was written in 1967, while the civil war was raging. The war took strength from long-standing tribal rivalries and was fostered by private political aspirations and corruption in high quarters. *The Gods Are Not to Blame* is an indictment of this Nigerian fratricide.

In *The Gods Are Not to Blame*, however, Rotimi warns Nigerians that the nation cannot excuse its own failure merely by blaming foreign powers. Written in 1967 as civil war was raging in Nigeria, *The Gods Are Not to Blame* reinterprets the Oedipus myth in the light of the Nigerian situation. Certainly the causes of the civil war are many and are rooted in the time of British colonialism. The military coup of January 15, 1966, in which the Hausa leaders of the north were killed, was followed by an orgy of slaughter of Igbo people living in the north. Those Igbo who could escaped to the safe confines of Igboland in eastern Nigeria, and on May 30, 1967, the Igbo declared that eastern Nigeria—now called Biafra—was an independent nation. Three years and millions of deaths later, Nigeria became reunited. The war inspired many works by Nigerian dramatists, poets, and novelists. Rotimi's *The Gods Are Not to Blame*, however, was one of the first literary responses to the conflict.

The play's protagonist, Odewale (Oedipus), the son of King Adetusa and Queen Oguola of Kutuji, grows up far from his native town. A man of an irascible nature, Odewale, like Oedipus, unwittingly slays his father, marries his mother, and in so doing pollutes the land. To save his people, he must be cleansed. There are, however, distinct differences between Odewale and Oedipus. Odewale's tragic flaw is not primarily pride; it is tribal animosity. When he attacks the old man (his father, the king) who has intruded on his farmland, Odewale is determined not to be violent, but when the old man refers to Odewale's tribe as a bush tribe, the protagonist loses all control and slays the intruder.

Throughout the play, the theme of tribalism reappears. When the village seer, Baba Fakunle, accuses Odewale of being the murderer of the former king, Odewale's immediate instinct is to see tribal bias. Odewale believes himself to be an Ikejun man among the people of Kutuje. Although it is not uncommon among Nigerian people for a member of one tribe to become head of another, Odewale chooses to see tribal resentment as the basis of any criticism directed toward him.

Rotimi alters the Oedipus story when necessary. For example, in the Nigerian cultural setting there

can be no justification for a young man to strike an elder in a dispute over a right-of-way, as happens in the Greek tale. A young man who resorts to violence against an elder is justified only in very specific circumstances, one of which is if the elder has stolen or intends to steal the young man's property. This is the situation that initiates the conflict between father and son in *The Gods Are Not to Blame*.

There are, however, distinct cultural similarities between the Greek society of Sophocles and traditional Yoruba society. Like the Greeks, the Yoruba have their pantheon of gods: Ogun, Shango, Obatala. These hero-gods provide the framework for traditional Yoruba religious beliefs and moral codes and also are symbolic vehicles for aiding Yoruba men in facing the ambiguities of human tragedy. There is a sense of cosmic totality among the Yoruba as there was among the Greeks. What Soyinka calls the ritual archetype is the foundation on which Rotimi's *The Gods Are Not to Blame* is built.

The title of the play refers ironically to the great political powers who became involved in the Nigerian War. The Biafrans blamed the Soviet Union and Great Britain for aiding the Nigerian Federalists in their attack on Biafra. The Federalists blamed France and the United States, through its charitable organizations, for supporting the Biafran's secession. Rotimi knew that ethnic distrust was the root of the conflict. Though Nigerian politicians play on the theme of foreign control, *The Gods Are Not to Blame* unsparingly rejects such self-serving rhetoric. In his final speech, Odewale warns the people not to blame the gods. Odewale warns those who will listen about the weakness of a man easily moved to the defense of his tribe against others. Because tribal hatred is a learned response, it can be unlearned.

The Gods Are Not to Blame was first produced by the Ori-Olokun Acting Company at the Ife Festival of the Arts in 1968; Rotimi himself played the Narrator. The rhythms of Ogun, Yoruba God of War and Iron, are never distant. The play is filled with many Yoruba proverbs and choral chants that echo principal themes. Ultimately, Rotimi is saying that when the wood insect gathers sticks, it carries them on its own head.

COLONIALISM AND DICTATORSHIP

With the military takeover in Nigeria from 1966 to 1979, Rotimi articulated the anxieties of this period of his country's history. *Ovonramwen Nogbaisi*, *Kurunmi*, *Akassa You Mi*, and *The Gods Are Not to Blame* deal with warfare, military rule, and the need for responsibility of leaders to the society. The plays also call Nigerians to a recognition of the nation's past and the need for Nigerians to be free from foreign exploitation and control. Both *Ovonramwen Nogbaisi* and *Akassa You Mi* deal with nineteenth century confrontations between England and the Nigerian people. The former tells the story of the sacking and destruction of the capital of the great empire of Benin; the latter narrates the attack by Brassmen in the Niger Delta at the British trading outpost in Akassa. These plays tell Nigerians that their ancestors did not passively accept the tyranny of colonialism; in fact, they did all they could to resist oppression and domination. The British raped Nigeria in their quest for economic expansion. Rotimi told his modern audience that unless Nigeria frees itself economically from foreign control, there can only be a continuation of a national malaise based on a feeling of unworthiness. There can be no real development if European interests come first.

OVONRAMWEN NOGBAISI

Rotimi's commitment to his people and his heritage is passionately made manifest in the three-act historical tragedy *Ovonramwen Nogbaisi*, a play that tells the story—well known to Nigerian audiences—of the brutal end of the empire of Benin.

In the fifteenth century, the empire of Benin was famous throughout West Africa. Indeed, in the mid-fifteenth century, under Oba Ewuare the Great, the fortified city of Benin, surrounded by three miles of walls, was the center of a great civilization. With organized guilds of palace artisans, the arts flourished. Most famous are the Benin bronze works, recognized today as one of the apogees of the history of art. Work in ivory and coral was also of high quality. In the sixteenth century, Oba Esigie ruled for nearly fifty years. At that time, Benin had a standing army of more than 100,000 men, and Benin City had more than thirty streets that exceeded 120 feet (37 meters)

in width. The Yoruba Wars and the incursions of Muslims from the north led to the decline, from the mid-sixteenth century, of the once powerful empire. By the end of the nineteenth century, Benin had seen its greatest days, but its bronze art was still a testament to its greatness, and its oba or chief, Ovonramwen, carried on the tradition of the god-ruler.

In 1897, the British destroyed the capital, captured Ovonramwen, and exiled him to Calabar in eastern Nigeria. The British account of the events leading up to the sacking of Benin City is as follows: An unarmed British trade delegation was massacred by the oba's men, and the British retaliated, destroying the capital, a center of human sacrifice and barbarousness. To save the bronze artwork, the British carried the statues and reliefs back to London, where they can be seen today in the British Museum. Rotimi tells a different story. He does not romanticize Ovonramwen. In the first act, the audience sees a leader trying to hold his empire together, struggling with rebellious chiefs and recalcitrant followers. Fear is his weapon in dealing with his people. The arrival of the British, who mask their desire to gain control of the rubber trees of Benin with treaties of friendship, leads to inevitable conflict. The royal bards chant hymns of hope, but their hopes are not to be fulfilled.

During the religious festival of Agwe, British traders—with arms—approach Benin. Warned that it is taboo to visit the oba at this sacred time, the white men pay no attention. They are murdered by subalterns of the oba, even though Ovonramwen had warned his subordinates to use no violence. As the second act ends, the oba is forced to flee.

In the third act, the oba confronts the British. He declares that British intentions in Benin were suspect. After all, had not the British captured King Jaja of Opobo when he fought to maintain control of his territory? Had not Jaja been traitorously captured at a putative peace conference and exiled to the West Indies? Oba Ovonramwen knows that the British interest in Benin is rubber, ivory, and palm oil. In the end, while struggling to join guerrilla forces still combating the British, the god-chief is captured. His empire, the magnificent empire of Benin, is dead. The god-king is a mere subject of the white man. A man more sinned against than sinning must suffer the humiliation of capture, a degradation emblematic of the destiny of his people.

The play is rooted in ritual. In the first act, the prophecy of the Ifa priest of the Oracle of Oghere warns that fire and blood threaten Benin, that disaster is at hand. Despite the oba's serious efforts to unify his people and maintain the integrity of the empire, collapse is inevitable. The chants of the bards chronicle the passage from fear to doubt to destruction. These songs and chants are derived in the main from the traditional folk-music repertoire of the Edo Cultural Group in Benin City, arranged by Osemwegie Ebohon.

In *Ovonramwen Nogbaisi*, Rotimi retells Nigerian history from Nigeria's point of view, not that of history books written by the English. He warns his people that continued economic exploitation of contemporary Nigeria by Western powers undermines the independence of Nigeria.

IF

With the return to democracy from 1979 to 1983, Rotimi proved to be no more tolerant of civilian political abuse than he was of military abuse. The play *If*, written and produced in 1979, focuses on a landlord-politician who threatens his tenants with eviction if they do not actively support his candidacy. The play, with seventeen characters excluding the twenty children and the twenty-four-person chorus, presents juxtaposed, variegated actions. Different scenes take place simultaneously. The rapid pace of *If* is accentuated by a series of satiric songs inspired by such different sources as African American spirituals and traditional African chants. *If* examines the problems faced by ordinary Nigerians after the country's civil war.

HOLDING TALKS

Rotimi continued to experiment in his art. He acknowledged his respect for William Shakespeare as well as for the Yoruba folk theater of Duro Lapido, and in his plays he has borrowed from diverse cultural sources. In 1979, with the publication of an absurdist drama, *Holding Talks*, a play in which characters talk and talk without achieving communication, Rotimi tried his hand at a different style, but even in this play, inspired perhaps by the techniques of Har-

old Pinter, Rotimi continued to be a writer involved with society, for its satire focuses on characters who fail when action is required. Thus, despite the evolution of his craft, Rotimi continued to devote his artistic life to further the interests of the majority of Nigerian people, who, since independence, have been victimized by self-seeking leaders.

GRIP 'AM

When the Nigerian military seized power again in 1984, Rotimi chose to stay in Nigeria until 1995, when he became completely disillusioned with the utter lack of possibilities for theatrical production under a regime that became notorious for its corruption and economic mismanagement, destroying all possible funding for the arts. While the military consolidated its power, in 1985 Rotimi moved into the field of short comedy with *Grip 'Am*. The play turns away from the charismatic leaders that had figured so predominantly in his earlier work, and focuses on common humanity. The Nigerian elite is lampooned, and the hero is granted the magic power to humiliate his greedy landlord by trapping him in a fruit tree. After the appearance of Die, the Pidgin name for death, the play closes on the message that the people need to take their fates into their own hands.

HOPES OF THE LIVING DEAD

First produced in 1985, *Hopes of the Living Dead* uses historical material and turns it into a dynamic three-act play. Here, Rotimi dramatizes the so-called Lepers' Rebellion in colonial Port Harcourt from 1928 to 1932. The British had selected forty lepers for new treatment but later lost interest in the project and proposed to send the lepers, called "the living dead" in Nigerian slang of the period, back to their individual villages. Gathering around their charismatic leader Ikoli Harcourt Whyte, the lepers finally win the right to move together into a newly built village provided by the British.

Critics have praised Rotimi for developing his presentation of leadership into a more democratic and collectivist direction. Whyte is no longer an isolated, elitist ruler, and is elected by the patients to represent their grievances. Because his resistance to the British is successful, he is spared the tragic fall of Rotimi's previous historical protagonists. The play's insistence that people need to find the right direction through which to overcome their problems, rather than to rely on charismatic saviors to rescue them from oppression, won great critical praise for the play.

In its actual production, the lepers' display of their disability can make for a powerfully moving spectacle. Rotimi's inclusion of characters who speak in their own tribal languages also highlighted again the necessity, so important for Nigeria's multitribal and multireligious society, for all members of a larger community, like the leper colony or, by analogy, a nation state, to work together toward their common goals, be it access to living space or economic prosperity.

LATER PLAYS

Rotimi's attempt to launch and maintain his African Cradle Theatre used up much of his great creative energy. Time and again, he stressed the need for economic support for the arts and drama in particular. He also spoke out against the use of untrained and unskilled actors and actresses. With economic collapse looming in Nigeria, even the critical success of his new productions for 1995, *When Criminals Become Judges* and the immensely popular social satire *Man Talk, Woman Talk* failed to provide Rotimi with much hope for the immediate future of theater in Nigeria. Audiences had become fearful for their own personal safety, and domestically produced gasoline had become unavailable, making movement expensive, unsafe, and unreliable.

His years at Macalester inspired Rotimi to begin work on what he saw as a major project of his life, a gargantuan African play with a cast of more than five hundred players. Returning to Nigeria, he died before he could realize this dream. Yet his plays, in particular *The Gods Are Not to Blame* and *Our Husband Has Gone Mad Again*, have become widely known in Nigeria and abroad and are wonderful testament to his political insight and dramatic skill.

BIBLIOGRAPHY

Banham, Martin. *Dancers in the Forest: Five West African Playwrights.* Cambridge, England: Cambridge University Press, 1998. Contains a perceptive study of Rotimi and his work. Focuses especially on his play *If* and analyzes Rotimi's use of performance space in the play.

_____. "Ola Rotimi: 'Humanity as My Tribesman.'" *Modern Drama* 33 (March, 1990): 67-81. Quotes at length from *If* and offers the first close critical look at *Hopes of the Living Dead*, which, Banham says, is more optimistic than *If.* Banham states that the strength of Rotimi's work "lies . . . in its powerful theatrical advocacy of political and social action."

Cbafemi, Clu. "Tragedy and the Recreation of History in Ola Rotimi's Plays." In *Contemporary Nigerian Theatre.* Bayreuth, Germany: Eckhard Breitinger, 1996. Excellent study of Rotimi's history plays by a Nigerian academic. Gives ample historical background, summarizes some of the controversies Rotimi's plays have created in Nigeria, and has a perceptive discussion of Rotimi's characteristic dramatic techniques.

Crow, Brian. "Melodrama and the 'Political Unconscious' in Two African Plays." *Ariel* 14 (July, 1983): 15-31. Compares Rotimi's *Ovonramwen Nogbaisi* with Ngugi wa Thiong'o's *The Trial of Dedan Kimathi* (pr. 1974, pb. 1976), written with Micere Githae-Mugo. Crow says that both playwrights "articulate and assert the immanence of good and evil in the historical conflicts that they dramatize" and invite further comparisons with traditional Western melodrama.

Dunton, Chris. "Ola Rotimi." In *Make Man Talk True: Nigerian Drama in English Since 1970.* London: Hans Zell, 1992. Thorough discussion of Rotimi's life and work up to *Hopes of the Living Dead* by an author who has witnessed actual performances of many of Rotimi's plays. His endnotes give useful details of many plays' production history.

Lindfors, Bernth, ed. *Dem-Say: Interviews with Eight Nigerian Writers.* Austin: University of Texas African and Afro-American Studies and Research Center, 1974. Recorded at the University of Ife in 1973, the interview covers Rotimi's education in the United States, his beginnings as a playwright, the influences of Wole Soyinka and John Pepper Clark-Bekederemo on his work, and his ambitions for "a full-length massiveness in music, dance and movement lasting two whole hours . . . mobilizing a five-hundred-man cast."

Okafor, Chinyere G. "Ola Rotimi: The Man, the Playwright, and the Producer on the Nigerian Theater Scene." *World Literature Today* 64 (Winter, 1990): 24-29. Okafor, an actress and assistant director in some of Rotimi's productions, offers firsthand knowledge of his work. She discusses Rotimi's canon and production practices, especially on dramatic spectacle, and his breaking of the proscenium arch.

Rotimi, Ola. "The Head Without a Cap." Interview by Adeola Solanke. *New Statesman Society* 2 (November 10, 1989): 42-43. An interview with the playwright on the occasion of the Talawa Theatre's revival of *The Gods Are Not to Blame* in 1989. Reexamines the Oedipus Rex myth as derivation of the play, quoting Rotimi's remark that "in my play the 'gods' are . . . the superpowers who control the political and economic destiny of the developing world."

Donald Burness, updated by Thomas J. Taylor and R. C. Lutz

JEAN DE ROTROU

Born: Dreux, France; August 21, 1609
Died: Dreux, France; June 28, 1650

PRINCIPAL DRAMA

L'Hypocondriaque, pr. 1628, pb. 1631
La Bague de l'oubli, pr. 1629, pb. 1635 (adaptation of Lope de Vega Carpio's play *La Sortija del olvido*)
Les Ménechmes, pr. 1630, pb. 1636 (adaptation of Plautus's play *Menaechmi*)
La Céliane, pr. 1631, pb. 1637
La Diane, pr. 1633, pb. 1635 (adaptation of Lope de Vega's play *La Villana de Getafe*)
Les Occasions perdues, pr. 1633, pb. 1635 (adaptation of Lope de Vega's play *La ocasión perdida*)
L'Heureuse Constance, pr. 1633, pb. 1636 (adaptation of Lope de Vega's play *El poder vencido*)
Célimène, pr. 1633, pb. 1636
La Pelerine amoureuse, pr. 1633, pb. 1637
Filandre, pr. 1633, pb. 1637
Amélie, pr. 1633, pb. 1637
Hercule mourant, pr. 1634, pb. 1636 (adaptation of Seneca's play *Hercules oetaeus*)
L'Innocente Infidélité, pr. 1634, pb. 1637

Cléagénor et Doristée, pr., pb. 1634 (based on Charles Sorel's novel *Histoire amoureuse de Cléagénor et de Doristée*)
L'Heureux Naufrage, pr. 1634, pb. 1637
Clorinde, pr. 1635, pb. 1637
Crisante, pr. 1635, pb. 1640
Florimonde, pr. 1635, pb. 1654
Agesilan de Colchos, pr. 1636, pb. 1637
Les Sosies, pr. 1636, pb. 1638 (adaptation of Plautus's play *Amphitryon*)
Deux Pucelles, pr. 1636, pb. 1639 (based on Miguel de Cervantes' story *Las dos doncellas*)
La Belle Alphrède, pr. 1636, pb. 1639
Laure persécutée, pr. 1637, pb. 1639 (adaptation of Lope de Vega's play *Laura perseguida*)
Antigone, pr. 1637, pb. 1639
Les Captifs, pr. 1638, pb. 1639 (adaptation of Plautus's play *Captivi*)
Iphigénie en Aulide, pr. 1640, pb. 1641 (adaptation of Euripides' play *Iphigenia e en Auludi*)
Clarice: Ou, L'Amour constant, pr. 1641, pb. 1644 (adaptation of Sforza Oddi's play *Lèro filomachia*)
Bélisaire, pr. 1643, pb. 1644 (adaptation of Antonio Mirade Amescua's play *El ejemplo mayor de la desdicha*)

Célie: Ou, Le Vice-roi de Naples, pr. 1644, pb. 1646

La Sœur, pr. 1645, pb. 1647 (adaptation of
Giambattista Della Porta's play *La sorella*)

La Véritable Saint-Genest, pr. 1646, pb. 1647
(adaptation of Lope de Vega's play *Lo fingido
verdadera*)

Dom Bernard de Cabrère, pr. 1646, pb. 1647

Venceslas, pr. 1647, pb. 1648 (adaptation of
Fernando de Rojas's play *No hay ser padre
siendo rey*; *Wenceslaus*, 1956)

Cosroès, pr. 1647, pb. 1648 (*Chosroes*, 1956)

Dom Lope de Cardone, pr. 1651, pb. 1652
(adaptation of Lope de Vega Carpio's play *Don
Lope de Cardona*)

Œuvres complètes, pb. 1820

Théâtre choisi, pb. 1928

OTHER LITERARY FORMS

Jean de Rotrou wrote exclusively for the stage.

ACHIEVEMENTS

After his death in 1650, Jean de Rotrou's plays, with a few notable exceptions, were neglected for more than two centuries. The probable reason for this is that Rotrou, the author, was forgotten while Rotrou, the man, was cloaked in the mythic mantle of the "mayor-martyr." His premature death by the plague while he was steadfastly serving a term as mayor of Dreux was taken as a beautiful example of civic duty and sacrifice. The aura of this noble death tended to distort other aspects of his life, and the distinction between fact and legend became more blurred with the passing years. By extension, erroneous notions cropped up in the literary domain. It is only in the second half of the twentieth century that a reevaluation of Rotrou's contribution to the French stage has begun; excellent studies and critical editions have appeared that deal with various aspects of his dramatic output. The immediate impression one receives from these scholarly works is that Rotrou should be ranked after Pierre Corneille, Jean Racine, and Molière as one of the foremost playwrights of his century. For a long time, he was, indeed, one of France's neglected classics. Modern scholarship has redressed historical injustice.

Rotrou excelled in the imbroglio type of play made popular by the Italian performers who came to France at the end of the sixteenth century. Unlike many of his contemporaries, Rotrou did not discard primacy of plot in favor of portrayal of manners or character. Indeed, his primary appeal lay in his plots. He liked a good story, a complex intrigue, and he knew how to develop it neatly. Moreover, it is doubtful that he could have attempted innovations in the genre of drama if he had so desired, at least not at the Hôtel de Bourgogne, the theater for which he wrote his plays. A playhouse, then as now, was in business to make money. To do so, it had to supply its audiences with the kind of entertainment that they desired, and in plays performed during this period, audiences wanted an abundance of movement, action, and surprise. Furthermore, to better accommodate the spectators' hunger for variety and exuberance, the Hôtel de Bourgogne had invested a huge sum in a system of complex and picturesque decor. It is likely, then, that when the directors of the Hôtel de Bourgogne chose Rotrou as their principal playwright, they expected him to continue producing action-filled, fast-moving plots. Rotrou did not disappoint them.

In the late 1620's when Rotrou began writing his plays, profound aesthetic changes were taking place in the French theater. There was a kind of purification taking place in author and spectator alike. Before 1630, many of the spectators were rabble-rousers, and more often than not, mediocre authors of salacious plays catered to their tastes. Around 1630, the theater ascended the social scale. The patronage of the aristocracy, headed by Cardinal Richelieu himself, led to much greater prestige for drama. Rotrou played an important role in this metamorphosis of the French theater. He and his fellow playwright, Pierre Corneille, were instrumental in helping develop a keener sense of propriety among the new theatergoers. The playwrights adapted and altered their texts according to the new exigencies of the times. (For example, they eliminated all obscene language from the stage.) They incorporated the classical unities in their plays and adopted the Alexandrine couplet as the standard meter instead of continuing to write plays in prose. This was the beginning of the famous *bienséance* in the French theater. Because Rotrou, during the decades from 1630 to 1650 wrote more plays than any other playwright, he was more instrumental than any other playwright in making the theater one of the principal *divertissements* of the so-called *honnêtes gens* (honest, or regular, people).

It is especially in his six tragedies that one sees the hand of the professional playwright who is in constant contact with the stage and who does not miss an opportunity to exploit any potential tragic situation or dramatic confrontation. In an age when it was common practice for playwrights to borrow freely from other dramatists, sometimes presenting entire scenes from another drama as their own work, Rotrou showed what could be done with the same raw material and enough originality. The tragedies show how, drawing on the same store of situations and characters as in a previous play, Rotrou availed himself of the tragic plot to blend these elements into a new dramatic whole. The manner in which he wrought changes en-

Jean de Rotrou (Courtesy of the New York Public Library)

abled him to produce heightened stage effects and to create more balanced plays. Many playwrights following in his footsteps would use his approach in the area of dramatic transposition and invention. Other dramatists borrowed freely from him without ever acknowledging their debt. It is true that, with a single exception, these tragedies fall short of being masterpieces. The sole exception—*La Véritable Saint-Genest*—is now considered by critics to be the best representation of a Baroque tragedy on the French stage. Though these plays are lacking in profound psychological insights, they reveal other qualities. They not only exhibit great technical skills on the part of the author but also show a powerful imagination at work and a fine discretion in the choice of what is shown on the stage. They were written in a verse whose equal, rhythmic movement, together with the precision and sober force of the language, answered fully to the aesthetic ideas that were then coming into vogue. It is for these reasons that Rotróu was hailed by Voltaire as the founder of French classical drama.

BIOGRAPHY

Jean de Rotrou was born into a family of magistrates on August 21, 1609, in the town of Dreux. Official records show that his ancestors had already been living there for several centuries at the time of his birth. Over the years, his forebears had provided this small Normandy town with many of its administrators and notaries. Rotrou would himself join their ranks. When he died there on June 28, 1650, it was in his official capacity as mayor. Very little is known about his early life except that he began his studies in the humanities at the college of Dreux and completed them in Paris. When he arrived in Paris, he was only thirteen. He studied philosophy under a benign tutor-priest, Father de Breda, who indulged his young student's penchant for versification. Rotrou earned his law degree in 1630.

There is no evidence to indicate what made Rotrou turn to the theater at such an early period in his life. The production of his first play, *l'Hypocondriaque*, took place before he was twenty. Tradition has it that he led a bohemian existence during the first years of his theatrical career. Like most young men engaged in belles lettres, he sought a patron and protector. He found one in the comte de Belin, who provided him with generous financial help until the count's death in 1637. Rotrou found another stable source of income as the official poet of the most prestigious theatrical playhouse in Paris, the Hôtel de Bourgogne. It was his function to furnish the playhouse's actors with plays at regular intervals. At about this time, he became associated with some of the great literary figures of his era, such as Jean Chapelain, Jean-Louis Guez de Balzac, and Pierre Corneille. His early plays were enormous successes and even found favor with the royal couple. He soon became the protégé of the king's minister, Cardinal Richelieu, who commissioned Rotrou and four other famous dramatists to write plays together. This group, known as the *Cinq Auteurs* (five authors), wrote in collaboration only two plays, both of which were failures.

By 1639, Rotrou had gained enough respectability to purchase a civil office in Dreux and, the following year, to marry a lady from good bourgeois stock, Marguerite Camus de Mantes. His responsibilities as husband, father, and civil servant forced him to stay in Dreux, but he continued writing for the theater; indeed, his best works were produced during this period. Not much is known about the remaining years of his life. He did not write about his activities, nor did his contemporaries have much to say about him. He seems to have become more withdrawn and more religious during his last years. In 1650, a plague descended on Dreux. Rotrou, who was mayor at the time, refused to abandon his official duties. In a letter to his brother dated June 22, 1650, he wrote the following memorable lines: "The bells are sounding today for the twenty-second person to die. They will sound for me when it pleases God." He died a few days later of the plague at the age of forty.

ANALYSIS

Jean de Rotrou's plays are seldom performed, yet his reputation has not suffered from this theatrical neglect. His plays are still read and appreciated by scholars and students alike. He was a prodigious composer during his short life, writing thirty-five plays that are extant; there were probably others that have been lost. His talent as a playwright was admired by the literati, and his success inspired many contemporary French authors to cultivate the imbroglio play. Indeed, his plays became a veritable gold mine for other dramatists. The appeal of his dramas lay in Rotrou's ability to construct a well-knit plot that holds together in every respect.

In the context of Rotrou's entire theater, one can say that it is, above all, eclectic. Rotrou borrowed freely not only from the classical past, but also from the courtly tradition, pastoral literature, history, and contemporary Spanish and Italian sources. The importance of his theater does not lie in profound character portrayals or in any poetic beauty of the language; it lies, instead, in the area of dramaturgy. The problem of dramaturgy doubtless occupied much of Rotrou's time, because he consistently strove to write exceptionally well-constructed scenes and acts. He gave his plays an air of verisimilitude by linking his scenes whenever possible and by arranging them in a logical pattern, by transposing or omitting scenes from the source material, and by inventing some original scenes of his own. He tried to observe a proper lapse of time between events and justified encounters of characters whenever feasible, as well as their entrances, exits, and motivations. His alterations in staging are proof that he paid particular attention to staging techniques when their effects had a significant bearing on total dramatic interest. For these reasons, Rotrou proved to be an innovative adapter who paved the way for other playwrights. At a time when the theater in France was groping toward a new direction, Rotrou showed his countrymen what good theater could be.

All of Rotrou's plays can be grouped into one of three dramatic genres: tragicomedy, comedy, or tragedy. Of the thirty-five plays that have survived, eighteen are in the genre of tragicomedy; these are typically adventure plays with characters from the upper classes or royalty, the denouements of which are almost invariably happy. The only "tragic" aspect of this type of play is the threat of death for the hero (usually in the fourth act), a threat that is quickly dispelled. Tragicomedy is, in fact, a hybrid genre, but one that was immensely popular with theatergoers of the period. The primary source for most tragicomedies was either the pastoral or the cloak-and-dagger adventure novels fashionable with the public. The nature of these plays is such as to demand a constant attention to external details, which were intended to create complicated situations. Rotrou accentuated the Romanesque elements usually associated with this genre (such as disguises, duels, mistaken identities, trickeries, and numerous intrigues). Moreover, with him, the Terentian double plot—two closely related actions involving two sets of characters—became the basic element of plot construction.

WENCESLAUS

It is the consensus of critics that *Wenceslaus* is Rotrou's finest tragicomedy. He borrowed the plot from a play by Fernando de Rojas, *No hay ser padre siendo rey* (pr. 1522). Nevertheless, Rotrou altered so extensively his source material that more than half the play is new. The plot centers on the twin themes of fraternal rivalry and paternal self-sacrifice. Wenceslas is an old monarch who is weary of ruling. He has two sons, Ladislas and Alexandre, both of whom are in love with the same woman, Cassandre. She prefers the more gentle Alexandre to the tempestuous Ladislas. A double love intrigue concerns the love of the minister, Frédéric, for the king's daughter, Théodore. In a case of mistaken identity, Ladislas enters Cassandre's palace one evening and kills her presumed lover. Unbeknownst to him, he has inadvertently killed his brother. Cassandre rushes to the king to demand justice for the death of Alexandre, slain at night by Ladislas. The king condemns the latter to death, but when he is about to be executed, Cassandre and Théodore beg for his life. Frédéric has been informed by Théodore that if he aspires to marry her, he must prevent the execution of her brother. In the meantime, the people have overrun the place of execution and revolted at the thought of their prince being put to death. The aged king solves the problem by abdicating in favor of his son, who is henceforth placed above the law of the realm. King Ladislas now gives his sister to Frédéric in marriage and asks Cassandre to marry him. She indi-

cates her intent of doing so after a suitable period of mourning.

Many critics have been drawn to this play in spite of the broader moral implications of showing vice seemingly rewarded. They praise the profound psychological portrayal of the characters, especially Wenceslas and Ladislas, and the play's excellent structural cohesiveness. The suspenseful plot is based largely on anxiety and fear and is constructed in accord with the classical unities. Certain changes in staging enabled Rotrou to achieve greater theatrical effects than were achieved in the original play. For example, the fact that the audience is kept in ignorance of the person whom Ladislas has killed makes the revelation of the fratricide in the fourth act even more dramatic than it might otherwise be. In his monumental study, *A History of French Dramatic Literature in the Seventeenth Century* (1929-1942), Henry Carrington Lancaster considers this scene to be one of the most effective in all French classical drama. Lastly, the generational conflict, the confrontation between parent and children depicted in the play, has always been a popular motif with the public. Perhaps this accounts for the fact that more than thirty editions of *Wenceslaus* appeared between 1648 and 1980, and that it was performed two hundred and fifty-seven times at the Comédie-Française between 1680 and 1980.

LES SOSIES

Rotrou affixed the label *comédie* to eleven of his plays. One of them, *La Bague de l'oubli*, shows close affinities with tragicomedy; the influence of the pastoral is evident in five others—*La Diane*, *Filandre*, *Célimène*, *Florimonde*, and *Clorinde*—all written between 1633 and 1635; three follow closely the comic tradition of antiquity found in Plautus's theater, *Les Ménechmes*, *Les Sosies*, and *Les Captifs*; and two are Italian adaptations, *Clarice* and *La Sœur*. Such is Rotrou's comic theater—eleven plays that reflect a variety of influences. Unquestionably, comedy of intrigue constitutes their principal ingredient. His two best-known comedies are *Les Sosies* and *La Sœur*.

Les Sosies proved to be immensely popular with Parisian audiences when it was first performed, rivaling Pierre Corneille's *Le Cid* (1636; *The Cid*, 1637) in setting new attendance records. The plot was taken from Plautus's *Amphitryon*, a comic play based on mistaken identity. Mercury has assumed the identity of Amphitryon's slave, Sosie, in order to aid his father, Jupiter, in the latter's scheme to seduce Amphitryon's wife, Alcmena. This disguise gives rise to a series of burlesque situations. The plot depends on random encounters among the characters. The characters cannot determine or influence the course of events: The action of the play progresses, not because of what the characters do, but because of what happens to them. Rotrou's method here is to develop his situations, not by concentration, but by pursuing as many ramifications as possible. He constantly shifts the characters on the stage, introducing a new character to give a new twist to the situation. For example, the exchange motif is frequently employed until it reaches a crescendo of confusions through a rapid shift of characters and situations in acts 4 and 5: The real husband is unable to prove his identity before the impostor, and the servant, Sosie, has to admit that somebody else is himself. In Rotrou's version, relations become more and more confused until finally every character is embroiled.

La Sœur

La Sœur was the last comedy that Rotrou wrote, and it is perhaps his finest. It was among his most successful productions: It remained in the repertory of the Hôtel de Bourgogne long after the author's death and was given several performances by Molière himself. Indeed, there are many scenes worthy of the master of French comedy, some of which the latter did incorporate into his plays. Furthermore, the play is probably the best example of the type of comedy that Rotrou wrote—comedy of intrigue. In *La Sœur*, the characters are so hopelessly mixed up by the end of the fourth act that nothing short of a *deus ex machina* can extricate them from their predicament. There is only one important comic figure in the play, but that figure, Ergaste, the hero's valet, is the best-developed model of the servant to be found in Rotrou's comic theater and embodies much of the type's comic potential. Last, *La Sœur* serves also as a good example of serious comedy—the type of com-

edy that emphasizes pathos and sentimentality. It was this kind of play that Rotrou favored late in his literary career.

He drew the plot of *La Sœur* from the Italian playwright Giambattista Della Porta, whose play bearing the title *La Sorella* was published in 1604. Long before the action of the play begins, Anselme, Lélie's father, has lost his wife and daughter to Turkish pirates, who kidnapped them. Years later, he sends Lélie with the ransom money to buy their freedom; unknown to him, the boy goes no farther than Venice. There, he falls in love with a beautiful servant girl, Sophie, uses the ransom money to buy her freedom, and secretly marries her. Because Anselme has not seen his daughter for years, he accepts Lélie's story that his wife is dead and that Sophie is Lélie's sister. The play opens then, with Lélie and his "sister" living together under the paternal roof, and will turn on the hero's efforts to hide from his father the fact that the girl he ostensibly ransomed from the Turks is not his sister. The play emphasizes those elements necessary to keep its plot complicated at all times: a dual love intrigue that is introduced early in the play, the attempts of the father to reveal the truth, the valet's multiple schemes, the recurring entanglements of the protagonist, the threat of incest introduced at the moment the outcome seems assured—the combination of all these represents the imbroglio comedy at its best. Because of the reduced set of characters, a certain economy in plot construction, and the elimination of extraneous materials and of coarse language, Rotrou's play is more polished than the original. Furthermore, *La Sœur* marks a culmination of the influence of Italian high comedy in the French theater. Comedy that displayed a dominant Italianate quality was to disappear from the French stage with the death of Rotrou, not to thrive again for more than a hundred years, until the great Italian dramatist Carlo Goldoni was invited to Paris to rejuvenate the Théâtre Italien.

Cosroès

Rotrou wrote six tragedies only. When he began to write plays, this genre did not enjoy the prestige that it would claim during the second half of the century. Nevertheless, two of his tragedies—*Cosroès* and *La*

Véritable Saint-Genest—rank among the best written in France during the first half of the seventeenth century.

Cosroès was the last tragedy that Rotrou wrote. It is a passionately violent play centering on kinship ties and the struggle for a throne. Cosroès, king of Persia, has two sons—one by a previous marriage, Syroès, and the other, Mardesane, by his current marriage to Syra. Syra is a domineering queen who wishes to secure the throne for her son; she plots her stepson's arrest and murder. The army and the people are for Syroès, however, and it is Queen Syra who ends up imprisoned. Syroès, who is in love with Narsée, Syra's supposed daughter, surrenders to her supplications to save her mother. He then finds out, however, that Narsée is not Syra's daughter; she is a girl who has been substituted in the cradle for the infant that Syra lost. Consequently, Syroès has Syra drink the poison that she had prepared for him. His stepbrother, Mardesane, then commits suicide. When the deposed Cosroès sees that his younger son is dead and that Syra has just taken poison, he drinks the rest of the fatal potion.

Cosroès is Rotrou's most classical tragedy, not only because of its complete adherence to the classical rules of dramaturgy but also because of the intense psychological portrayal of the main characters. Syroès is a victim of events that he is incapable of controlling. His stepbrother, Mardesane, is physically overwhelmed in a drama he does not fully comprehend. Their father, Cosroès, proves to be a weak and indecisive man driven to fits of insanity, while Syra is depicted as evil incarnate. The denouement is pessimistic and open-ended: Unaware of his father's suicide, will Syroès follow him to his grave as he had threatened to do if he could not prevent his father's death? The feeling of remorse and doom, which casts a pall over the play, along with the dramatic exposition and the constant clash of the protagonists, makes *Cosroès* a good example of French classical tragedy.

LA VÉRITABLE SAINT-GENEST

La Véritable Saint-Genest is generally acclaimed as Rotrou's masterpiece. It is the best representation of a Baroque tragedy on the French stage during the seventeenth century, and it is perhaps the finest example in dramatic literature of a play-within-a-play. Rotrou's drama is also permeated with major Baroque motifs such as illusion and metamorphosis. Moreover, the subject of the play—religious conversion—attests the Christian presence in the theater of that time. The play, then, successfully integrates secular and religious themes in spite of the belief by theorists of the period that the sacred and the profane should not be mixed.

The plot is relatively simple. In order to celebrate the engagement of his daughter, Valérie, to the victorious Roman general, Maximin, the emperor, Diocletian, wishes to have the court see a play depicting the martyrdom of Adrien, who was put to death by Maximin for converting to Christianity. The great actor, Genest, and his troupe have been invited onstage for this performance. During the course of the presentation, Genest is touched by divine grace and converts to the new faith in the presence of Diocletian and his court. The enraged emperor has him put to death for this blasphemous transgression. The play ends with Valérie and Maximin going off to be married. It is the structure of the plot that has elicited the most comments by critics. The play operates on three levels: The spectators are watching a play in which the characters, in turn, become spectators who are watching another play. The play-within-a-play, the martyrdom of Adrien portrayed by Genest and his troupe, begins in act 2 and ends in the fifth scene of act 4, in which Genest drops the actor's mask. The martyrdom of Genest begins at this point in the play, a martyrdom that will be similar to Adrien's.

One of the most important elements in the play is the long discussion about the theater, in general, and about acting, in particular. The difference between art and nature is emphasized, as is the problem of how to differentiate between illusion and reality in the context of the theater. For example, in the first scene of act 2, Genest is fearful that the decor is not natural enough to deceive the audience, and he makes suggestions that will enhance the illusion of reality. Genest himself is supremely confident in his ability to present lifelike illusions. He is such a good actor that, watching him, spectators do not know where illusion ends and reality begins. This is made manifest in the play when he passes from the illusionistic world of the theatrical performance to the real world of his conversion. At this moment, Diocletian and the court can no longer tell the difference between what is real and what is unreal. In playing with the problem of illusion and reality, Rotrou has engineered a metamorphosis. The change of Genest, actor, into Genest, martyr, is a change of illusion into truth. Paradoxically, this great actor is condemned to death for having abandoned his role on the stage—that is to say, for having shown himself to be a bad actor. The emperor came to the theater to see the martyrdom of Adrien, not to witness the conversion of Genest. In the end, Genest proves to be a less successful actor in his life than in his plays. It is this penetrating look into the problems of the actor and the illusion of the theater that makes Rotrou's *La Véritable Saint-Genest* such a unique and interesting play for modern viewers.

BIBLIOGRAPHY

Knutson, Harold C. *The Ironic Game: A Study of Rotrou's Comic Theater.* Berkeley: University of California Press, 1966. Knutson examines the comedic plays of Rotrou. Bibliography.

Morello, Joseph. *Jean Rotrou.* Boston: Twayne, 1980. A basic biography of Rotrou that also discusses his works. Bibliography.

Nelson, Robert. *Immanence and Transcendence: The Theater of Jean Rotrou, 1609-1650.* Columbus: Ohio State University Press, 1969. This scholarly study looks at the concepts of immanence and transcendence in the plays of Rotrou. Bibliography.

Raymond LePage

NICHOLAS ROWE

Born: Little Barford, England; June 20, 1674
Died: London, England; December 6, 1718

PRINCIPAL DRAMA

The Ambitious Step-Mother, pr. 1700, pb. 1701
Tamerlane, pr. 1701, pb. 1702
The Fair Penitent, pr., pb. 1703 (adaptation of
    Philip Massinger's play *The Fatal Dowry*)
The Biter, pr. 1704, pb. 1705
Ulysses, pr. 1705, pb. 1706
The Royal Convert, pr. 1707, pb. 1708
The Tragedy of Jane Shore, pr., pb. 1714
The Tragedy of Lady Jane Gray, pr., pb. 1715
Dramatick Works, pb. 1720 (2 volumes)

OTHER LITERARY FORMS

Nicholas Rowe adapted some odes of Horace to current affairs and published many poems on public occasions. He contributed a memoir of Nicolas Boileau-Despréaux to a translation of Boileau-Despréaux's *Le Lutrin* (1674, 1683; partial English translation, 1682) in 1708, took some part in a collective rendering of Ovid's *Metamorphoses* (c. 8 C.E. (English translation, 1567), and published translations of work by Jean de la Bruyère in the same year. In 1709, he edited William Shakespeare's works, creating the first truly modern edition, an edition still highly respected. A highly praised translation of Lucan's *Bellum civile* (60-65 C.E.; *Pharsalia,* 1614) was published posthumously.

ACHIEVEMENTS

Nicholas Rowe was an extremely cultivated man, well-acquainted with the classics and with French, Italian, and Spanish literature. He was esteemed as a conversationalist; Alexander Pope called him "the best of men" and seemed to delight in his society, both in London and in the country.

One of Rowe's chief achievements was his edition of Shakespeare's works, first published in 1709, generally regarded as the first attempt to edit Shakespeare in the modern sense. It was Rowe who first added a list of *dramatis personae* to each play. He was also the first to divide and number acts and scenes on rational principles, to mark the entrances and exits of the characters, and to modernize the spelling.

Hugh Blair and Samuel Johnson, also eighteenth century writers, found most of Rowe's drama too cold and too flowery, but two of his plays escaped such censure: *The Tragedy of Jane Shore* and *The Fair Penitent*. Johnson found Rowe's other literary efforts more enduring than his plays; he described Rowe's translation of Lucan as one of the greatest productions of English poetry.

BIOGRAPHY

Nicholas Rowe was born in the house of his mother's father at Little Barford, Bedfordshire, in 1674. His father's family settled at Lamerton, Devonshire, and one of his ancestors is said to have been distinguished as a Crusader. His father was a London barrister of the Middle Temple and a sergeant-at-law.

After attending a private school at Highgate, Rowe was in 1688 elected a king's scholar at Westminster. Not long afterward, he was removed and entered as a student at the Middle Temple. The law, however, proved to be uncongenial. From his youth, Rowe had read widely in literature, especially that of the theater, and soon he was ambitious to try his hand as a playwright. When his father died in 1692, Rowe was enabled to follow his own inclinations.

Early in 1700, Rowe saw his first play, entitled *The Ambitious Step-Mother*, produced at Lincoln's Inn Fields. Following this success, Rowe was for some years a professional playwright and soon gained the acquaintance of the leaders of literary society of eighteenth century London, including Pope and Joseph Addison. In 1702, he published his second tragedy, *Tamerlane*, the play he valued most of those he was to write. It was common knowledge that the play was really intended to portray William III, endowed with most amiable virtues, and Louis XIV, his villainous rival. The political tone of the play made it quite popular; it became tradition to perform it annually on November 5 of each year, in celebration of the anniversary of William III's landing.

In 1703, Rowe completed *The Fair Penitent*, a sentimental tragedy adapted from Philip Massinger's *The Fatal Dowry* (pr. 1616-1619). It was produced at Lincoln's Inn Fields, and the public approved its pathos; the villain Lothario acquired a proverbial reputation. Rowe's *Ulysses* was not nearly as successful, but it did enjoy a long run at the Queen's Theatre in the Haymarket in 1705. *The Royal Convert*, produced in 1707 at the Haymarket, was based on early British history. The final lines, spoken by Ethelrede, describe the blessing anticipated from the union of England and Scotland and panegyrize Queen Anne. Several years passed before Rowe wrote again, but his next play was one of his most popular ones. When first produced at Drury Lane in February, 1714, *The Tragedy of Jane Shore* ran for nineteen nights, and it long held the stage. His last tragedy, *The Tragedy of Lady Jane Gray*, was produced on April 20, 1715, at Drury Lane.

Rowe found himself involved in politics as an ardent Whig soon after he had begun writing plays. In February, 1708, he became undersecretary to the duke of Queensberry, secretary of state for Scotland, and held office until the duke's death in 1711. After some years of political service, Rowe obtained the recognition he sought. On August 1, 1715, he was made poet laureate in succession to Nahum Tate.

Later, Rowe produced official odes addressed to the king and eventually a collection entitled "State Poems." In 1717, he completed a verse translation of Lucan's *Pharsalia*, but the whole was not published until after his death.

ANALYSIS

The consensus among critics is that of all Nicholas Rowe's plays, *The Tragedy of Jane Shore* is his greatest. The tenderness and pathos of this play show how thorough and affectionate had been Rowe's study of great Elizabethan drama. The proof of Rowe's power is in the fact that such a play held the stage so long and was so popular even in an age much different from his own.

THE AMBITIOUS STEP-MOTHER

Rowe's first play, *The Ambitious Step-Mother*, produced in 1700, continues the tradition of heroic drama. It is set against the exotic Oriental background characteristic of the type. The play opens with Arsaces, the aged Persian king, on his deathbed. Real power is in the hands of the second wife, Artemisa. He had contrived to have her first husband killed and had then wedded her. She has gained control over the king, who is infatuated with her beauty. Artemisa is determined to secure the succession of the crown for her own son, Artaban. Arsaces had sent into exile his elder son, Artaxerxes, who has now returned, demanding his right of succession. In order to make her plan succeed, Artemisa finds a supporter in a scheming courtier, Mirza, who seeks revenge because the king's son Artaxerxes rejected the offer of his daughter Cleone for his bride. Instead, Artaxerxes chose to marry Amestris, the daughter of his counselor, Memnon.

The scheming Mirza then confides a plan for estranging Artaxerxes and Memnon, and Artemisa bars the way of Artaxerxes to his dying father's bedside. Their plot is complicated by the fact that Cleone, although rejected by Artaxerxes, is passionately in love with him and deaf to her father's desires. In the meantime, Mirza devises a plot to overpower his and the queen's enemies. Artaxerxes, Memnon, and Amestris are all seized by guards at the annual Festival of the Sun. It is Mirza's intent that Artaxerxes and Memnon shall be executed on the morrow, but he does not take into account Cleone. She dons masculine dress and offers the two prisoners the chance of escaping through Mirza's palace. Meanwhile, Amestris, confined in Mirza's palace, is sexually assaulted by Mirza. In the struggle, she stabs him with his own poniard. In one last revengeful attempt, he bids the captain of the guard to drag Amestris near him, and he stabs her. As she lies dying, Artaxerxes and Memnon enter to hear the tale of her wrongs and her last appeal to her lover. She dies, whereupon Artaxerxes stabs himself. So ends the tragedy, showing the innocent suffering along with the guilty.

Rowe's ending was severely criticized by many as too barbarous, even though he defended it on the basis of Aristotle's precept that terror and pity are the ends of tragedy. Others saw weakness in the characterization. Perhaps certain spectacular scenes made

up for this deficiency, however, because the play had a good run.

Tamerlane

Rowe's *Tamerlane*, produced in 1701, also employs the Oriental theme. Although Christopher Marlowe had written his *Tamburlaine the Great* (pr. 1587), on the same subject, there is little similarity between the two. Rowe intentionally perverts historical truth when he presents the Oriental conqueror as a prototype of the ideal political leader, William III. His dedicatory letter includes comments about how the two share courage, piety, moderation, justice, love of their subjects, and hatred of tyranny and oppression. It is evident that just as Tamerlane typifies William III, so Bajazet represents Louis XIV. The action of the play centers on Tamerlane's camp, where he is about to battle Bajazet. When the contest goes in Tamerlane's favor, he takes no personal pride in victory. He remarks, in fact, that all such pride is vain "pretence to greatness." Bajazet defies him as a dervish and declares his own conception of good rule, which in his view necessitates the ruler's thirst for more territory, this being the call of nature. Although in British terms, such ideas of sovereignty are villainous, Tamerlane nevertheless releases Bajazet and restores to him his captive queen, all of which will eventually be his undoing.

Tamerlane's religious tolerance is great, also—so great, in fact, that he takes into his council the Christian Italian Prince Axalla. This act alone angers Bajazet, who wants to conquer all lands and make all people followers of Mohammet. Because he is not able to win the argument, Bajazet attempts to stab Tamerlane with a concealed dagger, an act that Tamerlane forgives as he has certain others. Bajazet is not satisfied, however, and plots with a general, Omar, who supported Tamerlane in his rise to power but who now is angry with him because Tamerlane has not allowed him to take Bajazet's daughter Selima as his bride. Selima has given her love to Axalla, and Omar, in vengeance, arrests them both. Selima's father, Bajazet, attempts to kill her, but she is saved by the arrival of Tamerlane with Axalla, who has escaped in the disguise of a slave. Another pair of lovers are not so successful. Arpasia, who had been contracted to her countryman of royal lineage, Moneses, had been forced earlier to become one of Bajazet's brides. Moneses appeals to Tamerlane to undo this terrible wrong, but Tamerlane feels that he cannot interfere. Bajazet decides to have Moneses killed, and as his henchmen struggle with Moneses and strangle him, Arpasia sinks in a fatal swoon.

Tamerlane has effective dialogue, but it is less impressive theatrically than *The Ambitious Step-Mother*. Probably the greatest weakness in the play lies in the crude contrast between the high-souled Tamerlane and the villain Bajazet. It did remain a popular play, however, evidently because of its political allegory. It was acted at various London playhouses, usually on William III's birthday, until 1749, a period of forty-eight years. Dramatically, critics generally agree, the tragedy has little to recommend it. The love scenes are either insipid or unreal. Its chief merit lies in the vigorous action of the villain, who has the bragging manliness of John Dryden's heroes; also, the unhappy love of Moneses and Arpasia anticipates the "she tragedies" which were to follow. Dr. Johnson's estimate of the play is perhaps the best criticism: "This was the tragedy which Rowe valued most, and that which probably by the help of the political auxiliaries, excited most applause; but occasional poetry must often content itself with occasional praise."

THE FAIR PENITENT

Rowe's next play, *The Fair Penitent*, written in 1703 and produced in the same year, is set in Italy. The plot involves a Genoese nobleman, Sciolto, who has taken the place of Lord Altamont's father, thrust out by his ungrateful state. Sciolto, in the opening scene, is about to give his daughter Calista in marriage to Altamont. Calista, however, is cold toward Altamont because she is secretly in love with Lothario, Altamont's enemy. She has in fact allowed Lothario to seduce her and has begged him to marry her, all in vain. When she learns of her betrothal to Altamont, she writes Lothario informing him of her situation and asking for a last meeting between them, but the letter accidentally falls into the hands of Altamont's friend, Horatio. Horatio confronts Calista with the information, but she declares that the letter

was forged. She denounces Horatio as a slanderer, so he is forced then to show the letter to Altamont. Altamont, not wanting to believe the facts, strikes Horatio, and they fight until Horatio's wife, Lavinia, also Altamont's sister, runs between their swords to part the two. Shortly thereafter, Altamont surprises Lothario and Calista in a rendezvous and kills Lothario. With nothing to live for, Calista tries to kill herself by using Lothario's sword, but Altamont takes it from her. Sciolto, learning the truth, impetuously begins to slay his own daughter, but recoils. Later at night, he visits Calista where she is in mourning at Lothario's body. There, Sciolto offers his daughter a dagger, but as she lifts it, he prevents her death, because he cannot forget that she is his daughter. Altamont, too, experiences a strong passion for revenge against Calista, but like her father, controls his emotions. In the midst of this repentance, however, catastrophe erupts. Horatio comes in to announce that Sciolto has been attacked by Lothario's faction in revenge and is dying. Hearing his news, Calista stabs herself and begs for Altamont's and her father's blessings.

The Fair Penitent had an even greater success than did *Tamerlane*. The play was eventually adapted into French, and all over Europe, Lothario became proverbial as the equivalent of a rake: His name entered the English language, and even today a "lothario" is a seducer. The tragedy illustrates the working theme of most of Rowe's plays: the temptation of a more or less pure woman by a libertine. Indeed, Rowe serves as the link between Thomas Otway and George Lillo as a writer of domestic tragedy. Scholar Frank J. Kearful analyzes the play's characterization thoroughly, pointing out that Rowe was endeavoring to create something more than a melodrama of "unsuspecting virtue assailed by diabolical vice." By injecting issues of property and respectability into the drama, Rowe confronted his audience with the complexity of moral experience and the various kinds of moral problems they might encounter in their daily lives.

THE TRAGEDY OF JANE SHORE

The Tragedy of Jane Shore centers on the crowning of Prince Edward and the desire of Richard of

York to usurp the throne. The duke of Gloster, a supporter of Richard, fears that Lord Hastings, a staunch Edwardite, will stand in his way if he attempts to help put Richard into power, but he very much wants to do so. Hastings is loved by fair Alicia. Jane Shore, the mistress of the late King Edward IV, is being officially deprived of her property, and Hastings enters the scene to plead for gentle treatment of her.

To make matters worse, Dumont, Jane's husband in disguise, assures her that her husband died three years ago, leaving Jane in complete grief with no one but Alicia to reassure her. Alicia, who had persuaded Hastings to intercede for Jane, tries to comfort her friend, who ironically will become her rival, for Hastings falls in love with Jane in the process.

After Alicia has comforted Jane, she leaves to greet Hastings and berates him for his recent coldness to her. Hastings admits that he has lost his love for her and is attracted to Jane. From this point on, Alicia tries to ruin Jane in every way possible. When Hastings later confesses his love to Jane, she refuses him, only to have Hastings attempt rape. Jane is saved only by the intercession of Dumont.

Now set on revenge, Alicia tries to make Gloster hostile to Hastings. She openly accuses Hastings of blocking Gloster's plans for Richard. When Jane enters later to report that Dumont has been arrested by Hastings's men, Alicia tricks her into giving Gloster the letter she has written about Hastings's supposed treachery, rather than the letter pleading for merciful treatment toward Jane. The former not only accuses Hastings but also implicates Jane Shore in the treacherous action.

Although Gloster tries to persuade Jane to get Hastings to change his mind about supporting Edward, Jane, too, is loyal to the Edwardian line and praises the steadfastness of Hastings. In response, Gloster turns Jane into the streets and arrests Hastings for high treason. Though Alicia has found her revenge, it is not sweet, because she is sorry to see her lover Hastings in prison awaiting death.

Jane, left to beg, goes to Alicia and requests sustenance, but Alicia pushes her away. Only Dumont runs to her aid. She faints when she recognizes that Dumont is really her deserted, ill-treated husband, who

still loves her very much. All is not well, however, because Dumont is seized by guards and accused of aiding a traitor. He is taken to prison as Jane dies of starvation and suffering.

The Tragedy of Jane Shore enjoyed as much popularity as *The Fair Penitent*, perhaps because the moral taste of the audience was oriented toward justice for the wrongdoer. Though Jane repents and receives Dumont's blessing, she has erred by breaking the marriage vow. The play ran for several weeks and was even translated into French. Most critics regard it as Rowe's finest play.

THE TRAGEDY OF LADY JANE GRAY

Before Rowe ended his career as a dramatist, he penned one more play, *The Tragedy of Lady Jane Gray*. Again there is the theme of a disputed succession to the throne, but in this play, it receives the focus of attention. The issue of succession is complicated by a bitter religious feud. Edward IV is dying, and there is a rivalry for the throne between the supporters of Lady Jane and Mary, the latter being Roman Catholic. Lady Jane has been named successor by Edward, but the girl's thoughts are not on the crown but on the dying man. When Guilford Dudley promises that he will forgo a usual bridegroom's right and will join her in mourning, she consents to an immediate wedding with him. It so happens that Jane is loved also by the earl of Pembroke, hitherto Guilford's close friend. Pembroke now denounces Guilford as a betrayer to Gardiner, bishop of Winchester, who is Mary's chief supporter.

Soon, Jane's mother, who has forced her into a sudden marriage, tells her that she is to wear England's crown. She shudders at the very thought of being queen, but at last is persuaded to take the crown to save England from Rome's tyranny. Jane's fears are soon justified. The London crowd that had earlier supported her veers to Mary's side, and Jane finds herself in a precarious situation. Gardiner is appointed chancellor and orders Jane and Guilford imprisoned in the Tower. There is a touch of hope for the two, because Pembroke repays an earlier kindness from Guilford and secures from Mary a pardon for Jane and her husband. The hope is short-lived, however, for Gardiner intervenes and makes the pardon conditional on their renouncing their Protestant heresy. This they refuse to do, and they must die.

The irony of this production is that even though it did not enjoy the popularity of *The Fair Penitent* or *The Tragedy of Jane Shore*, it is in one way actually a better-written play. The interest is not dispersed; it remains focused on Lady Jane. With the writing of this play, Rowe's work for the stage came to an end.

OTHER MAJOR WORKS

POETRY: *Poems on Several Occasions*, 1714.

TRANSLATION: *Lucan's Pharsalis*, 1719.

EDITED TEXT: *The Works of Mr. William Shakespeare*, 1709 (6 volumes), 1714 (9 volumes).

MISCELLANEOUS: *The Works of Nicholas Rowe, Esq.*, 1727 (3 volumes).

BIBLIOGRAPHY

Aikins, Janet E. "To Know Jane Shore: 'Think on All Time, Backward.'" *Papers on Language and Literature* 18 (Summer, 1982): 258-277. Provides an intriguing close reading of *The Fair Penitent* and *The Tragedy of Jane Shore*, describing the nature of the two protagonists as "static." Rowe deliberately creates passive heroines to whom events happen, rather than active individuals, to suggest the role of fate in their downfall. Consequently, he creates a tragedy that arouses "generous pity" in the audience, leading them to pardon the offenders.

Burns, Landon C. *Pity and Tears: The Tragedies of Nicholas Rowe*. Salzburg, Austria: Institut für Englische Sprache und Literatur, 1974. Examines Rowe's gradual abandonment of the style of the seventeenth century heroic play for pathos and sentimentality. Rowe gives to his villains the posturing and bravado of John Dryden's heroes, while creating realistic heroes; further, Rowe redefines the drives for both love and admiration that animate heroic characters in the earlier plays.

Canfield, Douglas. *Nicholas Rowe and Christian Tragedy*. Gainesville: University Presses of Florida, 1977. Canfield's is the first book to analyze all Rowe's tragedies. He links Rowe's use of the structuring device of the "trial" of the protagonist's faith to the Christian worldview of the period. Good bibliography and a listing of Rowe's library as found in a sale catalog published after his death.

Dammers, Richard H. "The Importance of Being Female in the Tragedies of Nicholas Rowe." *McNeese Review* 26 (1979-1980): 13-20. Examines Rowe's creation of the "religious preceptress" figure and finds that the women of his plays lead their husbands to faith and virtue. Rowe's depiction of idealized married love is a shift from the "courtship" scenes of earlier dramatists. He thus critiques his society's double standards in sexual conduct and upholds humility and fidelity for both partners.

Goldstein, Malcolm. "Pathos and Personality in the Tragedies of Nicholas Rowe." In *English Writers of the Eighteenth Century*, edited by John H. Middendorf. New York: Columbia University Press, 1971. An excellent introduction to Rowe's work, with a review of the two "types" of women characters Rowe frequently used.

Hesse, Alfred W. "Who Was Bit by Rowe's *Biter*?" *Philological Quarterly* 62 (1983): 477-485. Hesse argues that Rowe's generally unsuccessful comedy possibly satirized Elihu Yale, benefactor of Yale University, then recently returned from the Orient.

Jenkins, Anibel. *Nicholas Rowe*. Boston: Twayne, 1977. Jenkins provides a brief biographical summary, then analyzes Rowe's works individually. Unlike Douglas Canfield (above), she discusses Rowe's comedy *The Biter* and his editorial and poetic work.

Kearful, Frank J. "The Nature of Tragedy in Rowe's *The Fair Penitent*." *Papers on Language and Literature* 2 (1966): 351-360. Discusses Rowe's shift from heroic drama to domestic tragedy, avoiding the sentimental treatment of character and plot common of Thomas Otway or John Banks. To essentially middle-class characters, he adds an element of moral instruction missing earlier. Kearful examines Rowe's Calista, unfaithful to her husband, yet under very real social pressures that contribute to her downfall.

John W. Crawford,
updated by Richard J. Sherry

TADEUSZ RÓŻEWICZ

Born: Radomsko, Poland; October 9, 1921

PRINCIPAL DRAMA

Kartoteka, pr., pb. 1960 (*The Card Index*, 1961)

Grupa Laokoona, pb. 1961, pr. 1962

Świadkowie albo nasza mała stabilizacja, pb.
1962, pr. in German 1963, pr. in Polish 1964
(*The Witnesses*, 1970)

Akt przerywany, pb. 1964, pr. in German 1965, pr.
in Polish 1970 (*The Interrupted Act*, 1969)

Śmieszny staruszek, pb. 1964, pr. 1965 (*The Funny Old Man*, 1970)

Spaghetti i miecz, pb. 1964, pr. 1967

Wyszedł z domu, pb. 1964, pr. 1965 (*Gone Out*, 1969)

Przyrost naturalny: Biografia sztuki teatralnej, pb.
1968, pr. 1979 (*Birth Rate: The Biography of a Play for the Theatre*, 1977)

Stara kobieta wysiaduje, pb. 1968, pr. 1969 (*The Old Woman Broods*, 1970)

The Card Index and Other Plays, pb. 1970

Teatr niekonsekwencji, pb. 1970

The Witnesses and Other Plays, pb. 1970

Na czworakach, pb. 1971, pr. 1972

Pogrzeb po polsku, pr. 1971, pb. 1972

Sztuki teatralne, pb. 1972

Białe małżeństwo, pb. 1974, pr. 1975 (*White Marriage*, 1977; also known as *Marriage Blanc*)

Odejście Głodomora, pb. 1976, pr. 1977 (*The Hunger Artist Departs*, 1987; based on Franz Kafka's story "The Hunger Artist")

Do piachu, pr., pb. 1979 (wr. 1955-1972)

Pulapka, pb. 1982, pr. 1983 (*The Trap*, 1997)

Teatr, pb. 1988

Dramaty wybrane, pb. 1994

OTHER LITERARY FORMS

When Tadeusz Różewicz's plays began appearing in the early 1960's, he was already a famous and prolific poet—one of the most influential of the postwar period in Polish literature—as well as a short-story writer. His poetry, prose, and drama are all interconnected. Różewicz himself has stated that some of his poems are minidramas, written in preparation for his plays. Thus, *The Card Index* is clearly related to the famous poem "Ocalony" (1947; "The Survivor," 1976). Similarly, *The Witnesses* seems to have developed from the poem *Zielona róża* (1961; *Green Rose*, 1982). His first two volumes of lyrics, *Niepokój* (1947; *Unease*, 1980) and *Czerwona rńkawiczka* (1948; the red glove), are funeral laments over those who perished in World War II, laments expressed through a new kind of "antipoetic" poetry. Volumes of the late 1960's, such as *Twarz trzecia* (1968; the third face) and especially *Regio* (1969), contain new elements of an existential and philosophical nature.

Like his poetry, Różewicz's prose is concerned with psychological analysis. A recurring theme is the contrast between the moral and spiritual emptiness of the present and the horror of wartime and occupation. This theme appears in the title story of a collection of five stories, *Wycieczka do muzeum* (1966; an excursion to a museum). Różewicz's most important piece of fiction is his novel *Śmierć w starych dekoracjach* (1970; death amid old stage props), which exhibits a traditional Polish theme of the hero who travels outside his native land and discovers himself in the process of his encounter with the West.

ACHIEVEMENTS

Tadeusz Różewicz is considered one of the most outstanding and influential twentieth century Polish playwrights. Together with his younger colleague, Sławomir Mrożek, Różewicz has been perhaps the postwar Polish playwright best known abroad. Most important, three of his major dramas have been acknowledged as contemporary classics: *The Card Index*, *The Witnesses*, and *The Old Woman Broods*. In postwar Polish poetry, Różewicz has been considered a renewer of poetic expression through his use of simple, colloquial, and even harsh words, as well as his emphasis on the themes of the horror of war and the corruption of human values. By the time he turned to drama in the 1960's, Różewicz had established a new kind of "antipoetic" poetry and had become the spokesperson for the wartime and postwar experiences of an entire generation.

Różewicz has regularly upset critics and audiences because of his constant exploration of dramatic form. He has refused to remain identified with any one type of drama. Różewicz himself has said that he considers all of his work to be a continuous polemic with contemporary theater. Although some of his early plays have been described as employing a "collage technique" or as having an "open form" (a phrase coined by Różewicz himself), neither of these categories applies to all of his dramas. Nevertheless, certain aesthetic and ethical constants seem to exist in Różewicz's dramaturgy. His plays often present a multileveled reality. This may be expressed through an expansion of the stage directions, through different modes of existence being present simultaneously on stage, or through discontinuity of time and juxtaposition of unconnected situations on stage. Although his plays are never moralizing, they often have profound ethical dimensions. Różewicz's hero is frequently a kind of contemporary Everyman who is, to some degree, the author, a participant, and a commentator on the events occurring around him. In his greatest plays, the ethical dimension of the content is as important as the avant-garde form of the work. An assessment of Różewicz's dramatic output is also complicated by certain factors. Many of his initially innovative techniques have become with time commonplace in avant-garde theater, so that his real contribution is difficult to evaluate. Further, Różewicz's reputation has fluctuated, depending on current official cultural policy, yet while he has been both lauded and attacked, Różewicz's significance has never been questioned. His dramaturgy has always been closely connected to the spirit of the times, shaped by Różewicz's developing concerns as a writer rather than by a need to realize a consistent theatrical program. With his revolutionizing of theatrical forms and his ultimately ethical view of reality, Różewicz's leading role in postwar Polish drama is assured.

Różewicz is the recipient of several Polish literary prizes. In 1955, he received the Art Award First Category for his *Równina* (1954; the plain) and, in 1959, a literary award from the City of Krakow. In 1962, he received the First Category Award from the Ministry of Culture and Art for his poetry. In 1966, he received the First Category Award from his government for his entire artistic output. He is also the recipient of an award from the city of Wrocław. In 1970, he received a special prize from the magazine *Odra* and in 1982 a state prize from Austria. In 1987 he received the Golden Wreath at the Struga Poetry Festival in Yugoslavia.

Biography

Tadeusz Różewicz, son of Władysław Różewicz and Stefania Golbard, came from a white-collar worker's family in Radomsko, a provincial town in the Łódź district of south-central Poland. Różewicz was born just after Poland regained independence (after 150 years of partition by Russia, Prussia, and Austria), and his childhood and early youth coincided with the euphoric first years of the new Polish Republic. This period was initially marked by a surge of national optimism, reflected in art and literature, that would gradually decline because of economic, social, and political problems. Różewicz attended secondary school in Radomsko and even then attempted to write poetry, his first verse appearing in school papers and in a religious publication for youth in 1938. Because of financial difficulties, however, he was forced to quit school in 1938.

Subsequently, Różewicz's personal fate became inextricably entwined with the larger drama of Polish and European history. The catastrophe of the German invasion in 1939 was especially tragic for him and his generation, then at the threshold of maturity. One of his brothers was shot by the Gestapo. Różewicz himself spent the Occupation in Radomsko, earning money as a tutor and also working in a factory, in a carpenter's shop, and as a messenger for the municipal authorities. After a time, Różewicz became involved with the Polish partisans. He worked with an underground press and wrote a collection of poetry and stories, which was circulated in typescript among partisan units. He also coedited an underground paper, *Czyn zbrojny* (armed action). He completed clandestine officer training in 1942 and then served in the anticommunist Home Army from 1943 to 1944.

After the war, Różewicz obtained his secondary school certificate in Częstochowa through special courses for working people. He then studied art history at the Jagiellonian University in Krakow from 1945 to 1949. His growing skepticism about the value of all the arts crystallized during these years in Krakow. Różewicz now saw the source of all artistic creation as lying elsewhere than in aesthetics. He began to reconstruct what seemed to him to be most important for both life and poetry: ethics. Life calls for some philosophy or value system, yet the war experience compromised, even utterly destroyed, the value system inherited from the past. The incalculable spiritual cost of the war and its effect on those who survived would become an obsessive theme in Róż-ewicz's early work. What he and others had lived through was most succinctly and even coldly summed up in a famous poem from this period, "The Survivor." The horror of the wartime experience with its concomitant disillusionment about humankind and civilization, and later the moral confusion experienced during the postwar years—all would become constant threads running throughout Różewicz's work. Although most starkly and dramatically appearing in his early poetry and short stories, these threads nevertheless continued to appear in later works as well.

In 1946, he published his first book, a collection of satiric works. In 1947, his first volume of poetry, *Unease*, appeared and immediately attracted the attention of critics. Perhaps to remove himself from the enforced self-criticism demanded of writers in the 1950's, Różewicz moved to the Silesian town of Gliwice in 1949. He himself has termed the move a "conscious decision." Between 1949 and 1955, he continued to publish, although some of his poetry of this period is considered the weakest of his output. On the other hand, Różewicz was also criticized at this time for continuing to write about war-related themes and for not being sufficiently ideological or optimistic.

After the Thaw of 1956, Różewicz increasingly expressed himself through drama. His early important plays of the 1960's marked new stages in the experiences of his generation, now the elders in postwar Polish society. In 1968, Różewicz again chose to remain apart from the more fashionable intellectual life centered in Warsaw or Krakow. He moved to Wrocłow, in Silesia, one of the most lively artistic centers in Poland, especially for the theater.

In 1981, in response to the renewal of Polish political, cultural, and social life inspired by the independent trade union Solidarity, Różewicz began to contribute materials to the journal *Odra*. However, the brief flowering of Polish civil society came to an abrupt end with the declaration of martial law. As a result, the following year Różewicz declined the Juliusz Słowacki Prize on political grounds.

In 1987, increasing liberalization throughout the Eastern Bloc as a result of Soviet leader Mikhail Gorbachev's program of glasnost enabled Różewicz to obtain permission to travel to the United States and attend a production of *The Hunger Artist Departs* in Buffalo. After the collapse of Poland's communist government and its replacement by a democratic one, Różewicz remained active as a literary figure in spite of advancing age, although he focused his efforts primarily on poetry.

ANALYSIS

Like many of his generation, Tadeusz Różewicz was deeply traumatized by World War II and the atrocities of the Holocaust. He seriously questioned whether it was possible to write poetry, to create art, in a world shadowed by Auschwitz and the other Nazi extermination camps. This led him to develop a new aesthetic that questioned and even outrightly rejected traditional concepts of beauty and lyricism, in favor of a deeply searching quest for the meaning of human suffering.

His daring and original plays regularly tested the boundaries of the very nature of drama. Particularly during the 1960's, Różewicz experimented with a number of plays in which seemingly random or meaningless elements break up the normal structure of managed action. In many of them he toyed with the notion of what constitutes an actor, having people appear on stage in real street clothes instead of costume as a way of challenging the systemic lies of the Soviet-inspired communist system. Several of his plays even have random collections of people improvising together on stage, rather like the happenings of the 1960's art culture in the West.

Thus it is not surprising that Różewicz drew a substantial amount of harsh and hostile criticism, and not just from the expected quarters. Almost any artist with any pretensions to originality or integrity could expect to come under fire from the stodgy communist party critics, who were in charge of making sure that all officially approved art met their ideological demands. However, Różewicz also received censure from groups who would be expected to be opposed to the effects of communist censorship, including Polish patriotic groups and even the Roman Catholic Church. He was accused of being irreverent, disrespectful of the genuine heroes of the past, and generally unacceptable in his treatment of his subject matter.

As a dramatist, Różewicz is associated with the 1960's, the period of the classic plays on which his reputation rests: *The Card Index*, *The Witnesses*, and *The Old Woman Broods*. Each of these works represents successively more daring experimentation with theatrical conventions. Thus, in the light of his entire output of the 1960's, *The Card Index*—Różewicz's most famous play—seems almost timid in form. Indeed, the protagonist, the Hero, has even been interpreted in the context of typical Polish romantic heroes. Różewicz's links to certain traditions in Polish literature (while initially noted by some critics) have become more apparent with time. For Różewicz, the 1960's was a period of extreme experimentation in form; it was the time of his unstageable essay-scenarios (*The Interrupted Act* and *Birth Rate*), deliberate attacks on the conventions of the stage (*The Funny Old Man* and *Na czworakach*), and repetition of earlier techniques (*Gone Out*). In theme, Różewicz moved from an obsession with the wartime experience to current problems, applying his ethical scalpel to the diseases of postwar Socialist Poland. He explored other topics as well, such as the role of art and the artist in society (*Grupa Laokoona* and *Na czworakach*) and the influence of clichés and stereo-

types on the popular mind (*Spaghetti i miecz* and *Pogrzeb po polsku*).

The plays of the 1970's, with their return to more traditional forms, attest Różewicz's protean ability to elude definition as a dramatist. *White Marriage* illustrates his mastery of conventional drama in the service of literary parody. Through *Do piachu*, Różewicz conveys in realistic terms the anguish of a wartime situation, a theme formerly expressed in his poetry and drama by means of avant-garde techniques.

Różewicz's works, regardless of genre, are characterized by formal experimentation and an emphasis on ethical themes. His competence as an essayist and film scriptwriter further testifies to his literary talent as well as to his sensitivity to current issues and to forms of expression. Indelibly marked by the past, Różewicz has been, at the same time, a penetrating observer of the present. In the words of the Polish critic Jan Kłossowicz:

> Różewicz wants to put into words—to express through drama—himself. And at the same time [to express] the concerns of the people and of the time in which he is fated to live. His deepest desire, though not stated directly in any program, is to tell the truth, to reach . . . what is most important in man, that which defines him and his relationship to others.

THE CARD INDEX

Różewicz's first play to be staged, *The Card Index*, startled Polish audiences with its open, fluid form. Although its initial production closed after only nine performances, the play has since become a classic of modern Polish theater. *The Card Index* is Różewicz's most frequently performed play. The play established his reputation in drama as a spokesperson for his generation—the survivors of the war and the Holocaust. The then unusual form of the play foreshadowed Różewicz's subsequent search for new and different kinds of theatrical expression with which to convey some of the most disturbing social and ethical problems of the 1960's and 1970's.

The Card Index consists of a series of incidents or images that pass before the eyes of the main character, the Hero, who is on stage throughout almost the entire play. The set is his bedroom, and he is for the most part in bed, but before him pass characters with whom he briefly interacts. The characters are primarily from his past (childhood, adolescence, wartime), but also from the present. It is as though the stage were a thoroughfare for persons and events that haunt and oppress the Hero. The logic of the play is psychological; the scenes jump from intimate but at the same time universal situations (childhood misbehavior, sexual initiation, infidelity) to particularly painful Polish experiences during the war (the shooting of a fellow Home Army soldier) and during the Stalinist period (writing "to order" for the regime in the 1950's). Thus, the structure of the play lies in an association of emotionally and morally charged events. The result is a more compelling life story of the Hero than might be produced through a conventional plot. As well as a presentation of past events, some scenes concern life in contemporary Poland, where the oppressive quality of life is contrasted with the drama of moral choices characteristic of wartime.

In addition to its open, fluid quality, the text of the play exemplifies what critics have termed Różewicz's "collage technique." The dialogue is studded with bits of other texts: fragments of classic Polish poetry recited by a ludicrous chorus of three elders, alliterative nonsense lists, grammatical exercises (such as declensions), nursery rhymes, and snatches of Socialist journalese. While such elements suggest a breakdown of communication among the characters and a fragmentation of the Hero's personality, they also carry subtle emotional significance. The poetry speaks of heroism and optimism, aspects of the Polish romantic ideal, and the alliterative list contains the name of a romantic hero.

Heroism and optimism have been completely compromised by the Hero's wartime and postwar experiences. He has looked for values in the past but has found none. All he feels now is an inner emptiness, periodically punctuated by nightmarish memories of the execution wall. The Hero has become simply a survivor; he must gather the fragments of his life—his card file—and find a place for himself in the strange new reality of postwar Poland. During the years since the premiere of *The Card Index*, the themes of the play have come to be interpreted in an increasingly universal manner. The Hero is no longer understood only as a man of the wartime generation, but as contemporary man in search of his authentic self, attempting to become a true human being. This existential level of *The Card Index* accounts in great part for the unabated popularity of the play.

GRUPA LAOKOONA

Różewicz's second play, *Grupa Laokoona* (the Laocoön group), is a comedy in four scenes satirizing aestheticism, pseudointellectualism, and institutionalized "culture." The characters are three generations of a family: Grandpa, Father, Mother, and Son, with the Mother's Girlfriend playing a minor role. Father's trip to Italy precipitates the family's loss of faith in truth and beauty. Father (named Zdzisław) recounts his disappointment at seeing only a plaster cast of the Laocoön Group in the Vatican Museum. Mother laments her lot as a woman but suddenly takes up painting to express herself. The Son cannot decide what to study at the university, loses faith in life, beauty, and work, and finally rebels. Even Grandpa's faith in aesthetics falters. In the final scene, "despite the bankruptcy of humanism," Grandpa and Zdzisław are still able to enjoy the Gorgonzola cheese brought back from Italy. Throughout the play, Różewicz uses the collage technique in language. The dialogue consists of Polish proverbs, slogans, and clichés about art and philosophy. In their pointless conversation, the characters exchange snatches from the works of Søren Kierkegaard, Gotthold Ephraim Lessing, José Ortega y Gasset, Oskar Kokoschka, and the nineteenth century Polish Romantic poets, Julius Słowacki and Cyprian Kamil Norwid. The sustained comedy and even farcical possibilities of the play contrast with the atmosphere of *The Card Index*. The hilarity of *Grupa Laokoona*, however, can be misleading. Here, as in many subsequent plays, Różewicz conducts a minute analysis of the mentality of people who have reified and trivialized spiritual values. The critic Stanisław Gębala describes the central theme of the play as the problem of the relationship between "the copy" and "the original": A commercialized pap of mass culture is dished out to the average citizen, whose real need for contact with the sustaining values of authentic art goes unfulfilled. In this interpretation, Różewicz's satire is both more subtle and more far-reaching. *Grupa Laokoona* can even be understood as describing a phenomenon that exists, albeit for different reasons, both in Eastern Europe and in the affluent West.

THE WITNESSES

In his next play, *The Witnesses*, Różewicz again formulated the problems of a generation and of a social group. This time, however, instead of war and political upheaval, Różewicz's subject is the materialism of Polish society of the early 1960's. The play portrays a society desperately clinging to the "little stabilization" of their standard of living, even at the cost of ethical values and ordinary human relations. Różewicz's play so captured the social climate of the times that "little stabilization," became a catchword for this period and this phenomenon. The Polish critic Henryk Vogler has compared the impact in Poland of Różewicz's metaphor in this play to that of Samuel Beckett's metaphor in *En attendant Godot* (pb. 1952, pr. 1953; *Waiting for Godot*, 1954) in the West. Formally, the play is composed of three parts. Part 1 presents two intertwined monologues, by a man and a woman, which introduce the play and the problem. The end of the poem foreshadows the next parts, as the themes of intimate relations and fear of losing the ordinary material achievements of life appear. Part 2 presents a man and a woman (they are not even termed husband and wife) who live in a small apartment. They speak to each other in false, saccharine endearments. They have created a pseudo-idyll of security. Now, however, their "little stabilization" is threatened by the imminent arrival of the mother-in-law. Where will she sleep and what will she do? How can they all manage in such cramped quarters? Once again they begin to exchange cloying endearments, but they are again interrupted when the man looks out the window and observes a small boy and girl playing with a kitten. He describes their activities, and although Jean-Philippe Rameau's pastoral music plays in the background, it is clear that the boy is going to kill the cat. The children's cruelty stems not from perversion but from lack of moral sensibility and human empathy. The implication is clear:

Moral principles and sensitivity make one fully human. The adults have quashed these qualities in their struggle for material things, and they are not inculcating such qualities in the next generation. A new age of barbarism may be on the horizon. The third part presents two men onstage in armchairs. Because the men are named "the Second" and "the Third," the audience is alerted to the absence of someone, presumably "the First." A siren wails, indicating some emergency situation, and one man sees a wounded figure crawling on the ground in the distance. The two men worry about whether the figure is really human or only a dog. They might help, but then they would have to leave their chairs, symbols of the positions they have attained in life. The dialogue dwindles; the men do nothing to help the figure; finally there is only silence. The title of the play clearly refers to the couple in part 2 and the men in part 3; the audience may also be witnesses, called by Różewicz to see the moral and spiritual deadness in society. *The Witnesses* is one of the most verbal of Różewicz's plays. The sets and props are simple; the stage directions even state that the lines may be declaimed. The impact of the play lies in the text itself.

While Różewicz's first three plays were not realistic or traditional in form, his next four plays exhibit even more daring in the exploration of avant-garde techniques, a testing of the basic nature of drama itself. In some of these plays Różewicz continues to treat distinctively Polish problems, but he goes beyond the concerns of his own society in the most famous play of this period, *The Old Woman Broods*.

THE INTERRUPTED ACT

The Interrupted Act is the first of two plays of this period that have been termed essay-scenarios. This play consists mainly of stage directions (two-thirds of the entire text), and thus the work becomes a theoretical essay on the inadequacies of the contemporary theater and the difficulty of creating a new realistic and poetic drama. Różewicz also criticizes the avant-garde plays of Stanisław Ignacy Witkiewicz and Witold Gombrowicz, as well as the works of the philosopher Leon Chwistek, as petrified classics. The title of the play refers both to the acts of a play and to the sexual act supposedly occurring off stage in scene 1. The main characters are an Engineer, his Daughter, the Robust Woman, the Nurse, the Stranger, the Assistant Engineer, and Workers. No plot is developed, however, and the audience is left with only fragments of action.

BIRTH RATE

In *Birth Rate*, Różewicz continues to experiment with the essay-scenario. Ten pages long, the play is in the form of a writer's diary or perhaps of a huge set of stage directions. The text describes the composition of an uncompleted play. Only an outline and several scenes are suggested. The subject of the play is the world population explosion. The problem is to be portrayed in scenes such as that of a crowded train or streetcar, so packed with people that at first the doors can hardly be closed; then the walls start to buckle; and, finally, the space overflows with people. Another scene would be of infants stacked in rows on shelves like rolls in a bakery shop. Halina Filipowicz evaluates this essay-scenario as rather negligible as a dramatic text but important as a performance score that can be realized through collaboration among the playwright, the actors, and the director. *Birth Rate* has also been compared and contrasted with Beckett's novel *Le Dépeupleur* (1971; *The Lost Ones*, 1972).

THE FUNNY OLD MAN

The Funny Old Man represents yet another kind of theatrical experimentation. The play is a monologue in which the title character testifies in court. The Old Man has been accused of indecency and sexual perversion. His female judge, her male assistants, and the defense lawyer are all life-size mannequins. In addition, the defense lawyer is headless. The stage directions also prescribe gymnastic equipment as part of the set and, during the intermission, athletic young women are to exercise on it. Children appear in the second half of the play. They are not to enact any roles but are simply to be themselves, playing noisily so that at times they nearly drown out the testimony of the Old Man. While the Old Man himself is ridiculous, his confession of his desires and weaknesses reveals the drama of his inner life. The play can be evaluated as simply a vehicle for a great actor. Critic Jan Kłossowicz suggests, however, that *The Funny*

Old Man marks a turning point in Różewicz's dramaturgy. After two attempts at writing a new kind of theater (*The Interrupted Act* and *Birth Rate*), Różewicz in *The Funny Old Man* begins to create a new theater for the stage. Three kinds of "beings" make up the cast of the play: the mannequins, the Old Man, and the children. Each of these represents a different source of theatrical conventions: the metaphor of dolls or puppets, the enacting of a role, and, finally, life itself. Różewicz plays with theatrical elements to create a multileveled drama in which different kinds of reality intersect.

THE OLD WOMAN BROODS

With his next play, *The Old Woman Broods*, Różewicz recaptured the success of earlier plays. *The Old Woman Broods* is perhaps the most visual of Różewicz's plays. More clearly than in *The Funny Old Man*, the set and props play an important role, solidifying the central idea. In contrast to *The Interrupted Act*, *Birth Rate*, or *The Funny Old Man*, the dialogue and stage directions are carefully integrated in this play. The first scene takes place in a railway café, sealed off from the outside world: Garbage is piled so high that when the windows are opened, a sea of garbage flows in. Contemporary civilization has become a great garbage heap, and all sources of water have been polluted. The Old Woman is a huge, repulsive being, dressed in layer on layer of clothing and jewelry, with varicolored hair, wrinkled skin, and false teeth. She is infertile and aggressive, obsessed by her own insatiable desire to give birth. She converses with two Waiters and with a Distinguished Gentleman, himself a relic of the past. In the second scene, garbage is everywhere on stage. The stage directions describe the set as "perhaps a battlefield. A huge garbage heap. A polygon. A necropolis. Perhaps a beach." Three young girls alternately sunbathe and wait on the Old Woman. The landscape around them seems to be pulsating debris containing people, refuse, and books. The Young Waiter appears, now returning from World War III. Despite the apocalyptic state of affairs, the stage directions relate that life seems to go on normally: "People work, entertain themselves, tell jokes, gossip. At times, agitated voices can be heard, even singing. . . . These voices arise from the pile of garbage." Guards representing the government of an authoritarian kingdom keep order and in particular forbid littering with even a scrap of paper. In the end, only the Old Woman remains on stage, frantically searching for her lost son in the garbage heap. This final scene presents a shocking visual conception of modern dehumanized life, first ruled by materialism and finally controlled by violence.

Na czworakach

Różewicz's next play, the tragicomic and even self-parodic *Na czworakach* (on all fours), was actually written between 1965 and 1971. The hero of the play, Laurenty, is a mediocre poet-dramatist, marked by complexes and erotic obsessions. In act 1, he is waited on by his cook and housekeeper, Pelasia (who is continually cooking soup for him), and he is visited by admirers, such as the student with the significant name of Margaret. Laurenty himself introduces the idea of walking, not upright, but on all fours, forcing his followers to do the same. Act 1 contains a modern variant of the Faust legend, as Laurenty is visited by Mephistopheles (in the form of a poodle). In act 2, the hero has become officially recognized and revered as a great writer, the Immortal Laurenty. He sits at his desk, a mummified exhibit, and is viewed by the public in his study, which has become a museum. In the epilogue, Laurenty performs like a circus animal under the whip of Pelasia. She gives him homemade wings; he first attempts to write, next to fly. A choir sings a song by the Polish Renaissance poet Jan Kochanowski as the play closes. *Na czworakach* ridicules the myth of the gifted artist and institutionalized cultural figures as well as public reaction to such myths and figures. The act of walking on all fours can be interpreted as Laurenty's subservience of his art to political dictates, but the device is also another of Różewicz's constant attempts to break down the illusion of realistic theater and find the most appropriate form for the content of his plays.

Gone Out

Another important play of the 1960's is *Gone Out*. The play initially seems to be a strange family drama in which the wife, Eva, and her two children, Gisela and Benjamin, search for the missing husband and father, Henry. Henry, the protagonist, is an amnesia victim as a result of a Chaplinesque situation: He went out, slipped on a banana peel, fell, and, after an hour, returned home. Because of his fall, Henry has lost his memory and forgotten who he is and what he does. Like the Hero in *The Card Index*, Henry is a kind of Everyman, whose life is constructed before the audience during the course of the play. Henry's life was ordinary and pointless, an existence from which he desired to escape. The play shows his reeducation; the other characters recall his life for him, teaching him his role in the home and family. The acts of the play are interspersed with pantomime interludes that further break up the already loose construction of the work. Because the real meaning of the drama lies in Henry's quest for freedom, the work can be considered a kind of modern morality play.

Later plays

Three of Różewicz's plays from the 1970's—*Do piachu*, *The Hunger Artist Departs*, and *White Marriage*—exhibit more conventional dramatic forms than the works so far discussed. By the 1970's, many of Różewicz's experimental techniques had become commonplace in avant-garde theater. His early plays such as *The Card Index* and *The Witnesses* were already classics of the contemporary stage. By the 1971-1972 season, Różewicz was the third most frequently produced playwright in Poland. Perhaps in a refusal to be categorized or officially accepted, Różewicz created three plays that seem quite unlike his previous works.

Do piachu (dead and buried) was written between 1955 and 1972. Because of the play's politically sensitive subject—the action involves the noncommunist wartime underground—it did not pass the censor until 1979. *Do piachu* traces a tragic course of events that leads to the death of a Home Army soldier. The play has a traditional structure, and the plot advances chronologically to the final scene of execution. *The Hunger Artist Departs* is a reworking of Franz Kafka's short story "Ein Hungerkünstler" (1924; "The Hunger Artist," 1938). The play also takes up the theme of art and the artist in contemporary life, a theme that Różewicz had treated earlier in *Grupa Laokoona* and *Na czworakach*, using more experimental techniques.

White Marriage

White Marriage, set on a Polish country estate and with Biedermeier interiors, concerns the sexual coming of age of two sisters, Bianca and Pauline. The sisters are the offspring of a wealthy but only seemingly staid family consisting of Father, Mother, Aunt, and Grandfather. The play is composed of thirteen consecutive tableaux. The tone is at first that of a comedy of manners, but the play rapidly becomes more like a farce, and the sexual theme becomes an obsession. The adolescent girls' initiation into the mysteries of sex is provoked by the impending marriage of Bianca to Benjamin. Bianca steals biology books from their father's library, and the two sisters read aloud about the sexual characteristics and habits of animals. It soon appears, however, that Pauline is the more sensuous sister. She gorges on chocolates and in fact eats with delight frequently during the play. Bianca tends to be revolted both by Pauline's eating and by her frank (but sometimes misinformed) eroticism. Bianca writes purple prose in her diary, is horrified at the onset of menstruation, and has demanded from Benjamin a "mariage blanc." Różewicz's penchant for sets and props that become part of the action (as in *The Old Woman Broods* or *The Funny Old Man*) appears in this play in the form of headdresses, masks, and especially of giant phalli appearing at inopportune moments, sexual "members" that only the apprehensive Bianca sees. The tableaux reveal that the entire household is either involved in sexual activity (Father, Grandfather, the Cook), suffering with sexual problems (Mother), or remembering past sexual situations (Aunt). Certain scenes seem like a nineteenth century French farce gone wild, as Father (wearing a bull's headdress) runs across the stage chasing the Cook or a Wench. Grandfather finds that his urges have not abated with age; he bribes the willing Pauline into voyeuristic and sadomasochistic rituals by giving her delectable chocolates. *White Marriage* is not only an erotic game, however, but also a literary one: The text contains elements of parody of nineteenth century Polish works such as Adam Mickiewicz's *Pan Tadeusz* (1834; English translation, 1917), Narcyza Żmichowska's *Poganka* (1846; the heathen woman), and perhaps the comedies of Aleksander Fredro.

A serious note enters the action when Mother and Aunt, while preparing Bianca's trousseau, discuss the dress and proprieties observed for mourning (presumably at the death of Grandfather). Perhaps Bianca is being prepared for another kind of death. Throughout the play Mother complains about her burdens: "given" in marriage but indifferent to sex, tortured by Father's relentless sexual desire, and enduring numerous pregnancies. In tableau 10, Bianca slashes her trousseau to ribbons; in tableau 11, the wedding banquet table becomes the bed for the bridal couple but one that, for Bianca, is more like a coffin. She puts off Benjamin's sexual advances, and in the final startling tableau she throws her clothes into the fireplace fire, crops her hair with big scissors, and, standing naked before Benjamin, announces that she is his brother. By the final scene, *White Marriage* is no longer simply a parodic farce. The play also raises the contemporary problem of female identity: Bianca rejects all the feminine roles proposed in the world of the play, roles embodied by the characters of Mother, Aunt, or Pauline. As usual, Różewicz provides no answers to the questions raised in his plays. In the light of its final scene, however, the earlier part of *White Marriage* may be interpreted less as farce than as ridicule of the contemporary obsession with the erotic. The work reveals the real brutality underneath the sexual conventions, however playfully portrayed, of both the nineteenth and the twentieth centuries.

Other major works

LONG FICTION: *Śmierć w starych dekoracjach*, 1970; *Echa leśne*, 1985.

SHORT FICTION: *Opadły liście z drzew*, 1955; *Przerwany egzamin*, 1960; *Wycieczka do muzeum*, 1966; *Opowiadania wybrane*, 1968; *Próba rekonstrukcji*, 1979; *Opowiadania*, 1994.

POETRY: *Niepokój*, 1947 (*Unease*, 1980); *Czerwona rńkawiczka*, 1948; *Pińc poematów*, 1950; *Czas który idzie*, 1951; *Wiersze i obrazy*, 1952; *Równina*, 1954; *Srebrny kłos*, 1955; *Uśmiechy*, 1955; *Poemat otwarty*, 1956; *Poezje zebrane*, 1957; *Formy*, 1958; *Rozmowa z ksińciem*, 1960; *Przerwany egzamin*, 1960; *Głos anonima*, 1961; *Zielona róża*, 1961

(*Green Rose*, 1982); *Nic w płaszczu Prospera*, 1962; *Niepokój: Wybór wierszy, 1945-1961*, 1963; *Twarz*, 1964; *Poezje wybrane*, 1967; *Wiersze i poematy*, 1967; *Twarz trzecia*, 1968; *Regio*, 1969; *Faces of Anxiety*, 1969; *Plaskorzezba*, 1970; *Poezje zebrane*, 1971; *Wiersze*, 1974; *Selected Poems*, 1976; *"The Survivor" and Other Poems*, 1976; *"Conversation with the Prince" and Other Poems*, 1982; *Na powierzchni poematu i w środku*, 1983; *Poezje*, 1987; *Poezja*, 1988 (2 volumes); *Tadeusz Różewicz's Bas-Relief and Other Poems*, 1991; *They Came to See a Poet*, 1991 (originally as *Conversation with the Prince*); *Opowiadania*, 1994; *Slowo po slowie*, 1994; *Niepokój: Wybór wierszy z lat, 1944-1994*, 1995; *Selected Poems*, 1995; *"Zawsze Fragment" and "Recycling,"* 1996; *Nozyk profesora*, 2001; *Recycling*, 2001.

NONFICTION: *Przygotowanie do wieczoru autorskiego*, 1971; *Nasz starszy brat*, 1992; *Forms in Relief and Other Works*, 1994; *Matka odchodzi*, 1999.

EDITED TEXT: *Kto jest ten dziwny nieznajomy*, 1964.

MISCELLANEOUS: *Poezja, dramat, proza*, 1973; *Proza*, 1973; *Reading the Apocalypse in Bed: Selected Plays and Short Pieces*, 1998; *Proza*, 1990 (2 volumes).

BIBLIOGRAPHY

Filipowicz, Halina. *A Laboratory of Impure Forms: The Plays of Tadeusz Różewicz*. New York: Greenwood Press, 1991. A discussion of the avant-garde elements in Różewicz's plays, in particular his distortion of traditional form to explore the modern world.

_____. "Theatrical Reality in the Plays of Tadeusz Różewicz." *Slavic and East European Journal* 26, no. 4 (Winter, 1982): 447-459. Discussion of how Różewicz's plays bend the appearance of reality to allow the audience to reach a higher truth about the human condition.

Gerould, Daniel, ed. *Twentieth Century Polish Avant-Garde Drama*. Ithaca, N.Y.: Cornell University Press, 1977. Różewicz's work is examined in the context of other Polish dramatists pushing the boundaries of form.

Krynski, Magnus J., and Robert A. Maguire. "Introduction." In *"The Survivor" and Other Poems*. Princeton, N.J.: Princeton University Press, 1976. A brief overview of Różewicz's work to provide context for the appreciation of his poetry; also discusses his dramatic works.

Theodosia Smith Robertson,
updated by Leigh Husband Kimmel

PAUL RUDNICK

Born: Piscataway, New Jersey; 1957

PRINCIPAL DRAMA

Poor Little Lambs, pr., 1982
I Hate Hamlet, pr., pb. 1991
Jeffrey, pr. 1993, pb. 1994
The Naked Truth, pr. 1994
Mr. Charles, Currently of Palm Beach, pr. 1998, pb. 2000
The Most Fabulous Story Ever Told, pr. 1998, pb. 2000
On the Fence, pr. 2001

OTHER LITERARY FORMS

Before Paul Rudnick turned his energies to drama, television, and film, he wrote two novels, *Social Disease* (1986) and *I'll Take It* (1989), both of which received good reviews. He has written for various journals, including *Spy* and *Vogue*. Using the pseudonym Libby Gelman-Waxner, he has written movie reviews, including the granting of satiric film awards, for Premiere. These columns were published as *If You Ask Me* (1994). In 1989 he wrote a screenplay of *Sister Act*, but when Bette Midler turned down the starring role, Disney Studios got new writers and a new star, Whoopie Goldberg. As "Joseph Howard," Rudnick did receive some screenwriting credit on the film. Although his writing was uncredited, he did substantial rewrites on *The Addams Family* (1991) and was the screenwriter for the sequel, *Addams Family Values* (1993). His other screenplays include the film adaptation of *Jeffrey* (1995), *In and Out* (1997), and *Isn't She Great* (2000) with Bette Midler as author Jacqueline Susann.

AWARDS AND ACHIEVEMENTS

Paul Rudnick is one of the dramatists who helped propel gay issues into the mainstream of American culture. Unlike earlier gay dramatists like Tennessee Williams, who worked undercover but had gay subtexts in their plays, Rudnick and Tony Kushner, whose *Angels in America*, a play about the AIDS (acquired immunodeficiency syndrome) epidemic, won the Pulitzer Prize in 1993, openly write about gay concerns, which are now regarded as being universal ones. Gay drama, fiction, and prose are now being published by major presses and being read by straight as well as gay readers. *Jeffrey*, a play about a gay man who gives up sex, was originally thought to be too controversial and sophisticated to appeal to audiences outside large cities, but it, like the film *In and Out*, has found nationwide audiences.

BIOGRAPHY

Paul Rudnick was born in 1957, the son of Selma and Norman Rudnick, second-generation Polish Jews (his father was a physicist), in largely non-Jewish Piscataway, New Jersey. His mother frequently took him and his brother to the theater and encouraged his educational and dramatic aspirations. Although he early realized that he was a homosexual, he was not stigmatized by his schoolmates and had an uneventful childhood. He attended Yale University, where he majored in drama and met playwrights Christopher Durang, Albert Innaurato, and Wendy Wasserstein. When he graduated from Yale, he followed them to New York. His Yale experience provided him with the necessary material for his first play, *Poor Little Lambs*, which was written while he was employed as a writer of book-jacket blurbs. He has lived in Green-

wich Village, which he once called "a refuge of clichéd bohemianism." One of his apartments was formerly occupied by John Barrymore and inspired Rudnick to write *I Hate Hamlet*. In the late 1980's, he wrote two satirical novels, *Social Disease* and *I'll Take It*, but gained his real reputation first as a playwright with *I Hate Hamlet*, a popular spoof that has been produced nationally, and with the controversial *Jeffrey*, which concerns homosexuality and AIDS. His plays since 1993 have all been about homosexuality. His screenplay for *In and Out*, which he says was inspired by Tom Hanks's tribute to his high-school drama teacher in his Oscar-acceptance speech for *Philadelphia* (1993), a film about a homosexual man dying of AIDS, concerns the "coming out" of a gay high-school teacher. In the 1990's he also turned to screenwriting, specializing in comedy, where he is a master of the "one-liner." In September of 2001, his *Rude Entertainment*, three one-act plays (including *On the Fence*, about the murder of homosexual Matthew Shepard in Laramie, Wyoming, and *Mr. Charles, Currently of Palm Beach*) opened in New York.

ANALYSIS

Like British playwright Joe Orton, Paul Rudnick has written primarily about homosexuality, but Rudnick parodies or satirizes what exists rather than creating original material. He targets conservatives, whether they are religious fundamentalists, Republicans, or Reaganite politicians. His comic gifts tend to consist of one-liners and outrageous skits, rather than carefully crafted plots. For the most part, his characters are a bit stereotypical, but occasionally they achieve complexity and make his audiences see that the problems he discusses are not limited to homosexuals but have much broader applications.

I HATE HAMLET

In his introduction to the published play *I Hate Hamlet*, Rudnick writes that the source of his play was an advertisement for an apartment listed in *The New York Times*. He rented the apartment, which formerly belonged to legendary actor John Barrymore. It is the setting for the play, which Rudnick claims is about his and the United States' ambivalent feelings about High Art and the classics. The play mixes comedy and tragedy, the present and the past, and High Art and television—all within the apartment, where the "ghost" of Barrymore resides and where the fate and identity of young actor Andrew Rally are determined.

Rudnick's stage directions call for the apartment to look like "a Hollywood interpretation of a King Arthur domicile; think Hollywood Jacobean." When Felicia Dantine, New York realtor, persuades Andrew Rally, a popular television actor on *LA Medical*, to take the apartment, she pairs Rally with Barrymore: "John Barrymore, the legendary star! And now you, Andrew Rally." In the course of the play, Rally discovers that he and Barrymore, who initially is visible only to Rally, have much in common and that he really is a Shakespearean actor rather than a television star. Rally has come to New York to play Hamlet, and for both Rally and Barrymore, playing Hamlet is a defining moment. In addition, both play under assumed names: Blythe (Barrymore) and Rallenberg (Rally).

Barrymore intends to save Rally from making the same mistake he did, going commercial. He tells Lillian Troy, an old flame with whom he had an affair in the apartment, that Andrew is "my cosmic lunge at redemption." Like the Ancient Mariner, Barrymore "cannot return." He "will not be accepted until my [his] task is accomplished."

In this kind of morality play (Rudnick draws freely from theatrical history), Barrymore as Good Angel is juxtaposed to Gary Peter Lefkowitz, a crass but somehow likeable Hollywood agent who equates William Shakespeare with "algebra on stage." Gary wants Rally to return to Hollywood to star as Jim Corman, a high-school teacher in *Night School*. Rudnick has acknowledged that "Gary expresses my distrust and more honest feelings about High Art."

By the time the play is staged, Rally has become like Barrymore, a change reflected in his altering the apartment to be a "truly medieval lair." Before the opening night performance, Barrymore's advice to Rally is taken verbatim from Hamlet's counsel to the players in *Hamlet, Prince of Denmark*. Barrymore also offers Rally advice about how to cope with

Deirdre, Rally's virginal girlfriend. As Rally becomes Hamlet, he becomes irresistible to Deirdre, so that sexual and acting performances are equated. Rally knows that he was "awful" opening night and would seem ready to accept Gary's television offer, but because he "got" the "to be" soliloquy, he decides to go ahead with the other "eight thousand lines." As the play ends, Rally is imitating Barrymore's legendary, theatrical bow to the audience.

JEFFREY

Jeffrey, which Rudnick describes as a play about "love, death, and wisecracks," is about how people confront disease and fear with humor and style. The first scene of the play, which involves homosexual sex and a broken condom, introduces the fear of AIDS that the gay population has to confront. To illustrate how pervasive the fear is, Rudnick has his characters all in one bed unanimously declaring, "No more sex." Jeffrey, an optimistic young gay, wants to be "politically correct" and decides to find a substitute for the sex he loves. Although he is attracted to Steve, who is HIV positive, he resolves to abstain, to no longer be "a slave to my libido, to my urges, or to my reputation as the pushover of lower Manhattan." His quest for a substitute for sex allows Rudnick to satirize a variety of contemporary institutions: the television game show *It's Just Sex*, where Jeffrey does not have the answers; an acting audition, where he wins the part of a gay; a society "hoe-down for AIDS" featuring "Dr. Sidney Greenblatt and his Mount Sinai Ramblers"; "the nation's hottest postmodern evangelist," who blends Jesus's love with obscene language; and the Lower Manhattan Gentlemen's Masturbation Society. When he is threatened by the masturbators clad in jockstraps, Jeffrey is rescued by Darius and Sterling, a gay couple whose relationship, with its "safe sex," becomes the model that Jeffrey and Steve will eventually adopt. Darius and Sterling are members of the "Pink Panthers," a gay protection group and caricature of the Black Panthers and the Gray Panthers. The need for such a group becomes evident when gay bashers later attack Jeffrey, who has as weapons only "Irony. Adjectives. Eyebrows." (Rudnick's later play *On the Fence* also concerns violence against homosexuals.)

The second act begins with another parody; this time it is Sexual Compulsives Anonymous, a group with the same kind of confessionals and greetings as Alcoholics Anonymous. This group fails to help Jeffrey, who proceeds to "cruise" a memorial for a gay who died of AIDS. After again rejecting Steve, who is on his way to spend time with the neglected AIDS babies in the hospital, Jeffrey calls his parents, whose suggestive comments prompt him to declare, "I am not going to have phone sex with you and Mom." Jeffrey's next encounter is with Religion in the form of Father Dan, a homosexual Catholic priest who describes himself as "somewhere between chorus boy and florist." Father Dan, however, defines God in a way that will make sense to Jeffrey and ultimately enable him to make the necessary commitment to Steve. For Father Dan, God is the balloon that people keep in the air as they bat it around. This definition will not please religious fundamentalists, but it does imply the kind of optimism that people need to survive. Before that commitment occurs, however, Rudnick includes an outrageous gay parade with groups such as "Dykes on Bikes" and the paradoxical "Gay Black Republicans." After learning about Darius's death, Jeffrey decides not to take refuge in Wisconsin, his home state, but instead to commit to Steve. Rudnick cannot, however, forsake some comic gay touches. Like the couples in *An Affair to Remember* (1957) and *Sleepless in Seattle* (1993), they promise to meet at the top of the Empire State Building and sing the gay favorite, Barbra Streisand's "Memories" while they bat the balloon in the air.

THE MOST FABULOUS STORY EVER TOLD

Starting with the "fabulous" of the title—"fabulous" is related to "fable," which reflects Rudnick's view of the authenticity of the Bible—Rudnick's play undercuts fundamentalist religious views that insist that the Bible is not about Adam and Steve, but about Adam and Eve. Rudnick's play is about Adam and Steve, and about lesbians Jane and Mabel. In his preface to the play, Rudnick comments, "I wanted to offend or provoke everyone equally, to allow all points of view equal mockery and equal acceptance," and he succeeds.

Like Thornton Wilder's *Our Town* (pr., pb. 1938), the play has a stage manager, but Rudnick's stage manager is Godlike in her (the first of many gender shifts) control of the scenery. After the stage manager declares, "Creation of the world, go," that creation is expressionistically shown. The first act consists of a gay view of the Old Testament, featuring Moses as "Brad" and Adam as "an idiot who ruined everything"; a Sodom destroyed by tourists; a gay pharaoh; bestiality aboard the Ark; an after-the-Flood meeting with straight, child-bearing people whose activities are presented as abnormal; Adam's admonition to "fluff and fold" rather than "grab and bunch" the laundry; and the first brunch. The first act ends with Mabel's "miraculous" pregnancy in an irreverent parody of the Nativity scene, which, according to Rudnick's stage directions, should look like a "Hallmark card."

In the second act, the gay and lesbian couples are presented in contemporary Manhattan at the Christmas season. Some changes have occurred in their situations. Steve is HIV positive, and Jane is pregnant by artificial insemination. Added to the mix are Rabbi Sharon, a lesbian who uses a wheelchair, and Cheryl Mindle, a Mormon tourist who wants to know why Mormons are being discriminated against. She is told, "This is New York. You're the Jew." Even the politically correct are targeted. When Mindle's child tells his mother he is gay, she is overjoyed and declares, "This means Yale." The one-liners, putdowns, puns, topical references, and irreverent repartee continue throughout the play. Because the play also contains full-frontal nudity, homosexual embraces, and simulated lovemaking, the play did offend many people, but for the most part, it was well received. Despite its offensive content, the tone of the play is warm, not cynical or abrasive, and the characters, who do look a bit like homosexual stereotypes (bodybuilder Steve; intuitive, spiritual Adam; flaky Jane; and "butch" Mabel) do engage audience empathy.

OTHER MAJOR WORKS

LONG FICTION: *Social Disease*, 1986; *I'll Take It*, 1989.

SCREENPLAYS: *Addams Family Values*, 1993; *Jeffrey*, 1995; *In and Out*, 1997; *Isn't She Great*, 2000.

NONFICTION: *If You Ask Me*, 1994 (as Libby Gelman-Waxner).

BIBLIOGRAPHY

Hornby, Richard. "Broadway Economics." *The Hudson Review* 44 (1991): 455-460. In the course of a review of current Broadway productions, Hornby describes *I Hate Hamlet* as the "funniest play on Broadway." Hornby provides a good discussion of the way Rudnick uses the show, which he calls a "ghost story," to contrast two kinds of acting: the bombastic, grand style of Barrymore, and the introspective style of most current actors. (Rudnick satirizes acting styles in the play.)

Pacheco, Paul. "The Success of a Subversive Wit." *Los Angeles Times*, September 19, 1993, Calendar, p. 3. Pacheco discusses *Jeffrey* and *The Addams Family*, but he also provides a great deal of biographical information unavailable elsewhere. Both Rudnick's stage and film works are covered.

Scott, Janny. "Changing the Way America Thinks About Gays." *Los Angeles Times*, April 25, 1993, p. 3. In this lengthy interview, Rudnick discusses the way that gays are portrayed in the theater and in films. According to Rudnick, audiences are more responsive to gay issues than they were, and gays are being presented as a diverse group rather than in terms of a few stereotypes.

Thomas L. Erskine

LOPE DE RUEDA

Born: Seville, Spain; 1510?
Died: Cordoba, Spain; 1565

PRINCIPAL DRAMA

Eufemia, wr. 1544?, pb. 1567 (based on Giovanni Boccaccio's *Decameron*; English translation, 1958)

Armelina, wr. 1545?, pb. 1567 (based on Anton Francesco Raineri's play *L'Altilia* and Juan María Cecchi's play *Il servigiale*)

Farsa del sordo, wr. 1549, pb. 1568?

Medora, wr. 1550?, pb. 1567 (based on Luis Arthemio Giancarli's play *La Cingana*)

Los engañados, wr. 1556?, pb. 1567 (based on an anonymous Italian play *Gl'Ingannati*)

Prendas de amor, wr. 1556?, pb. 1570

Auto de Naval y de Abigail, pr. 1559, pb. 1908

Coloquio de Tymbria, pb. 1567

El diálogo sobre la invención de las calzas, pb. 1567

El deleitoso, pb. 1567 (includes *Los criados*, *La carátula* [*The Mask*, 1964], *Cornudo y contento* [*Cuckolds Go to Heaven*, 1940], *El convidado*, *La tierra de Jauja*, and *Las aceitunas* [*The Olives*, 1846])

Registro de representantes, pb. 1570 (includes *Los lacayos ladrones*, *El rufián cobarde y barrera*, and *La generosa paliza*)

Coloquio en verso, pb. 1615

Discordia y cuestión de amor, pb. 1617 (second edition; date of first edition unknown)

Auto de los desposorios de Moisén, pb. 1908

Obras, pb. 1908 (2 volumes)

Pasos completos de Lope de Rueda, pb. 1966

The Interludes, pb. 1988 (translation of the ten *pasos* in *El deleitoso* and *Registro de representantes*)

OTHER LITERARY FORMS

Lope de Rueda is known solely for his drama.

ACHIEVEMENTS

A precursor of the Spanish Golden Age dramatists, Lope de Rueda was instrumental in the popularization of theater in the middle of the sixteenth century. Distancing himself from the liturgical works then in vogue and the pastoral *coloquios* that were occasionally performed for the Renaissance elite, he created comical plays in everyday language that appealed to uncultured, rowdy audiences. He was the first in Spain to write *pasos*, brief, dramatic interludes in prose in which ordinary characters confronted one another.

Often *pasos* were based on popular proverbs or stories. *The Olives*, for example, the seventh *paso* in *El deleitoso*, is based on the Spanish equivalent of "Don't count your chickens before they hatch." In this popular *paso*, Agueda and her husband, Toruvio, are engaged in a loud argument about the price for which their daughter Mencigüela should sell their olives in the plaza. Both parents shove and coax the girl in an effort to convince her. Finally, Mencigüela's cries and her parents' screams attract the attention of their neighbor Aloxa, who offers to buy the olives himself in the interest of peace and quiet. It is then that the bumpkins admit that Toruvio has just planted the olive trees that afternoon. It will be thirty years before they produce enough fruit to sell in the plaza.

The language of the *pasos* is that of the common people. Often, it is witty and racy and includes local jargon. After Lope de Rueda's time, this type of sketch became an integral part of Spanish drama. Miguel de Cervantes was influenced by Lope de Rueda when he wrote his *entremeses*, short theatrical interludes to be performed between the acts of a longer play. In his prologue to *Ocho comedias y ocho entremeses* (1615; eight plays and eight interludes), Cervantes describes the primitive nature of Lope de Rueda's theater and the excellence of his verses. Cervantes considered Lope de Rueda to be the initiator of theater in Spain, noting that it was he who took the *comedia* "out of swaddling clothes . . . and dressed it in elegance and ostentation." Lope de Rueda contributed more to the art of acting and to the germination of theater groups than to the development of dramatic literature. Marcelino Menéndez y Pelayo and Fernando González Ollé both argue that Lope de Rueda's importance as a writer has been exaggerated because

during his lifetime he was known as an actor rather than as a playwright.

On the other hand, the Spanish critic Francisco García Pavón writes that if it had not been for Fernando de Rojas, author of the lengthy novelesque drama *Comedia de Calisto y Melibea* (1499, rev. ed. 1502 as *Tragicomedia de Calisto y Melibea*; commonly known as *La Celestina*; *Celestina*, 1631), Lope de Rueda would be considered the father of Spanish dramatic literature. *Celestina*, too long and unwieldy to be performed in the original version, continued to be read in Lope de Rueda's time, although primarily by the intellectual elite. Lope de Rueda was undoubtedly familiar with the work and was influenced by Rojas's use of everyday language, his depiction of picaresque types, and his use of prose rather than verse for drama. Lope de Rueda wrote all of his *pasos* and dramas in prose, using verse only for his *coloquios*.

The popular bent of Lope de Rueda's *pasos* is characteristic of much of Spanish drama throughout the centuries. Lope de Vega Carpio, who was instrumental in the creation of a Spanish national theater at the end of the sixteenth century, wrote for the masses and drew much of his material from folk stories, popular ballads, proverbs, and historical events familiar to his audience. The depiction of popular types (the bumpkin, the ruffian, the thief, the cuckold) was common in Spanish Golden Age theater. The *gracioso*, a stock comic character in Golden Age plays, has roots in Lope de Rueda's *pasos*—not in his gullible simpletons, but in his cunning, conniving lackeys. Lope de Rueda's influence can be discerned in the *sainetes* (one-act farces) of the eighteenth century playwright Ramón de la Cruz, and in the quick-witted banter of the servant-class characters in the plays of Leandro Fernández de Moratín. The *zarzuelas* (musical comedies) of the late nineteenth century revitalized many of the types popularized by Lope de Rueda. The proletarian nature of much contemporary Spanish theater reflects long-standing tastes and traditions that were established during the time of Lope de Rueda. The early twentieth century author Ramón María del Valle-Inclán wrote short one-act plays called *esperpentos*, as well as longer works in which he cultivated, embellished, and transformed the savor and wit of the language of the common people. The popular theater known as *género chico* that was cultivated by such writers as Carlos Arniches at the beginning of the twentieth century depicts many of the same social types as Lope de Rueda. Finally, the social theater of contemporary writers such as Antonio Buero Vallejo, Alfonso Sastre, José Ruibal, and Antonio Martínez Ballesteros—all different from one another—reinforces the strong link between the Spanish stage and the common people that has existed since Lope de Rueda's time.

In addition to the *pasos*, Lope de Rueda wrote four full-length plays or *comedias*, two dialogues or *coloquios* in verse, and several pastoral and religious dramas. Unlike the *pasos*, the *comedias* and *coloquios* were directed at the upper strata of Spanish society, although the author made no attempt at a realistic portrayal of the aristocracy.

The chronology of Lope de Rueda's plays is not known, but the *coloquios* are thought to be his first works. They take place in a pastoral atmosphere, into which magical and mythological beings constantly intervene. The *comedias* probably represent the next step in Lope de Rueda's development. These are mostly adaptations of Italian dramas that were popularized by Italian playwrights who traveled with road companies through Spain during the first part of the sixteenth century. Lope de Rueda's lack of care in structuring and plotting his *comedias* indicates that he may have been more interested in expanding the repertoire of his own drama company than in creating truly original plays. The *comedias* contain several *pasos* that are loosely interwoven into the action. The *pasos* that make up *El deleitoso* and *Registro de representantes* are thought to be Rueda's last works. Most of Lope de Rueda's plays were published posthumously by Juan de Timoneda in 1567.

BIOGRAPHY

During the early sixteenth century, Spain was at the height of its glory. The nation was newly unified as a result of the conquest of Granada, the last Moorish stronghold, in 1492. Religious and patriotic zeal had led to the expulsion of the Jews that same year.

Christopher Columbus had discovered America, and by the time Lope de Rueda was born, probably around 1510, the exploration of the New World was under way. When Rueda was only about nine, Hernán Cortés set out for Mexico. By 1532, Francisco Pizarro had begun the conquest of Peru, thereby tapping a seemingly inexhaustible source of wealth. Charles V, king of Spain and heir to an empire on which "the sun never set," struggled against the Protestants, the French, the Papacy, and the Ottoman Turks with varying degrees of success and reached the acme of his powers by the middle of the century. It is easy to forget that, during this period of triumph and expansion, much of the Spanish population lived in poverty, ignorance, and fear, alternating between despair and wild fantasies of sudden good fortune.

The Spain that Lope de Rueda portrayed in his *pasos* is that of the *pícaro*, the street tough, the petty criminal, the student, the gypsy, the bumpkin. This was the Spain that the dramatist knew personally. He was born into a family of artisans and was by trade a gold beater (one who works gold leaf). Almost nothing is known about his early years, but it can be assumed that being of humble background, he received little formal education. Facts about Lope de Rueda's life are sparse. One of the most significant sources of information is Cervantes.

Spanish theater was in its infancy during Lope de Rueda's youth. During the Middle Ages, theatrical works—which were usually religious in nature—were normally performed in churches. During the early Renaissance, plays began to be performed in the palaces of the social and intellectual elite and, later, in the public plazas. The eclogues and farces of such early contributors to the Spanish stage as Juan del Encina, Lucas Fernández, and Gil Vicente were accessible to the general public. In the early sixteenth century, Italian theater groups were traveling across Spain, performing in towns and villages, and Spanish theater companies were forming. As a youth in Seville, Lope de Rueda probably saw some primitive productions and decided to become an actor. Emilio Cotarelo y Mori, one of the foremost authorities on early Spanish theater, conjectured that Lope de Rueda joined a traveling company, thus initiating his apprenticeship in theatrical theory and practice. Then, tired of performing the works of others, he determined to write his own plays. Lope de Rueda apparently knew Italian, since his *comedias* are adaptations of Italian works, but whether he actually traveled to Italy is not known. Documentation exists proving that in 1542 and 1543, Lope de Rueda, by then manager of his own company, performed in Seville.

During the first half of the sixteenth century, the importance of theater was increasing rapidly in Spain. Festivals and celebrations of many types included theatrical productions. For example, the festivities in honor of the wedding of Juana, daughter of Charles V, to João of Portugal included several plays. The first recorded use of the word *comediante* (actor) was in 1534, in a directive from Charles V regarding the adornment and dress of theatrical performers.

During this period, Lope de Rueda achieved great success as an actor. According to testimonials by his contemporaries, his gifts for mimicry and gesture were appreciated enthusiastically by all kinds of audiences, and he performed with equal success before boisterous, uncultured street crowds and before noblemen and kings. He often performed the role of the simpleton and was known for his ability to manipulate his voice and to reproduce the speech of the most ignorant elements of Spanish society. Whether the plays he performed were his own or those of other playwrights probably made no difference to his spectators, for whom he and not the text was the main attraction. His fame as an actor lasted for generations.

In spite of the joy and laughter he brought to others, Lope de Rueda's life was filled with adversity. In 1551 or 1552, he married a woman known only as Mariana, a famous singer and dancer at the court of the duke of Medinaceli. She died soon afterward, and, in 1560, Lope de Rueda married Ángela Rafaela Trilles. His second wife bore him a daughter, Juana Luisa, who also died.

During most of his life, Lope de Rueda experienced severe financial problems. In order to get by, he had to pawn possessions and rely heavily on loans. Like his sly, maneuvering lackeys and thieves, he was concerned primarily with survival; the descriptions of hunger and poverty in his *pasos* were undoubtedly drawn from his own struggles. His last will and testament mentions some of the debts that he incurred during his lifetime.

From 1551 until 1559, Lope de Rueda lived in Valladolid, although he continued to travel to other cities with his troupe. He was active in theater productions in Segovia, Seville, Valencia, and Toledo. He performed at court twice, in 1554 and in 1561.

Of particular importance with respect to the development of Spanish theater is the fact that, in 1552, the municipal council put Lope de Rueda in charge of public theatrical productions and agreed to pay him a fixed annual salary. In 1558, he requested authorization to build a number of houses to be used as *corrales*—primitive open-air theaters. These events reflect the growing importance of theater in Spain. Yet the support of the city of Valladolid apparently did not eradicate Lope de Rueda's financial worries. He was poor and in debt when he died in Cordoba in 1565. Actor, director, manager, playwright, Lope de Rueda was the first complete theater man in Spanish history.

Analysis

Lope de Rueda's *pasos* are short, anecdotal skits designed to entertain; they contain no philosophical or moral message. Although they depict the subculture of the poor, the *pasos* were not construed as instruments of social reform. Survival, not injustice, is Lope de Rueda's primary theme.

The pasos

Even so, the *pasos* provide a telling picture of the situation of the poor during the early part of the sixteenth century. Hunger is a constant preoccupation. In nearly all the *pasos*, characters are concerned about where they will obtain their next meal. In the first *paso* of *El deleitoso*, Luquitas and Alameda spend the afternoon enjoying themselves in a pastry shop, then worry about how to avoid punishment from their master, Salcedo. The entire first part of the play consists of comments on the excellence of the *buñuelos*, or doughnuts, that the servants have eaten. The dialogue reveals that for Alameda, especially, the visit to the pastry shop has been a special treat because he is not accustomed to eating so well.

In the second *paso*, Salcedo tries to frighten Alameda by pretending to be a ghost. One of the first questions Alameda asks his disguised master is whether ghosts eat, and if so, what. In the fourth *paso*, a hungry traveler arrives in a village, where he claims to be the friend of a certain Licenciado Xáquima, from whom he expects hospitality. Licenciado Xáquima is even poorer and hungrier than he, but feeling obligated, he invites the traveler to dinner, even though he has no money to provide a meal. In order to extricate Xáquima from this embarrassing situation, Bachiller Brazuelos hides him under the table and promises to tell the traveler that his host was called away by the archbishop on important business, but when the guest arrives, Brazuelos ruins everything by telling him the truth. In the fifth *paso*, two thieves distract their victim by describing an imaginary land full of good things to eat. All of these sketches reveal the extreme importance that getting food had for the Spanish underclass.

Because they are needy, Lope de Rueda's *paso* characters are crafty and manipulative. Among the indigent, survival demands nimble wits. An astute liar or thief is the object of admiration. In *El rufián cobarde y barrera*, the fifth paso of *Registro de representantes*, the thief Sigüenza brags about his "art," which consists of bringing home "four or five bags and purses," without buying even "the leather that they're made of." In the first *paso* of *El deleitoso*, Alameda is impressed with Luquitas's talent for filching. Hunger breeds distrust and selfishness. In *Tantico pan*, a *paso* from Rueda's *comedia*, *Medora*, Perico uses all of his resources to protect a piece of bread from Ortega, who labors to bargain it away.

Those who are dull are exploited. The *simple*, or simpleton, is a stock Lope de Rueda character, an object of hilarity rather than of compassion; just as Lope de Rueda shows no moral contempt for petty thieves, so he shows no sympathy for their victims. In the fifth *paso* of *El deleitoso*, for example, two thieves who are "dizzy with hunger" pounce on a vic-

tim and succeed with their scheme because he is too stupid to see through it.

Hunger makes many of Lope de Rueda's characters irrational or gullible. The two bumpkins in the seventh *paso*, known as *The Olives*, fantasize about a windfall precisely because they are so poor. Mendrugo, the simpleton of the fifth *paso*, falls for the thieves' story because the image of a land filled with delicacies that cry, "Eat me! Eat me!" is irresistible to a pauper. In many of Lope de Rueda's *pasos*, clever swindlers play on the dreams of their victims to cheat them out of their last coin.

To the characters who populate Lope de Rueda's underworld, the universe is a chaotic interplay of incomprehensible forces. An individual must be alert because unexpected turns of events can catch him off guard and because the strong and the clever routinely abuse the weak. Lope de Rueda's characters are plagued by superstition and fear. They feel menaced by external forces and by one another. Alameda is afraid of ghosts, which makes him easy to manipulate; he and Luquitas are both afraid of their master. In *El rufián cobarde y barrera*, the braggart-thug Sigüenza is afraid to fight Estepa, who punishes him for his cowardice by running away with Sebastiana, Sigüenza's girlfriend.

The *pasos* depict a fixed group of stock characters, the most common of which is the simpleton. Much of the humor of the *pasos* derives from the simpleton's candor, gullibility, and lack of verbal sophistication. Typically, the simpleton is manipulated by a more clever character who tells him what to do or say, but the simpleton misunderstands the instructions and says or does the wrong thing. One of the most amusing exchanges in the fourth *paso*, *Los lacayos ladrones*, of *Registro de representantes*, is a conversation between a lackey named Molina and a constable, in which the thief Madrigalejo puts words into Molina's mouth:

> CONSTABLE: Where are you from?
> MADRIGALEJO: Say from Salamanca.
> MOLINA: We're from Salamanca, si. . . .
> CONSTABLE: What did you come here for?
> MADRIGALEJO: Say to see the country.
> MOLINA: To see the country, sir.

In the end, the cunning Madrigalejo involves his companion to the point that the constable arrests Molina, even though he is innocent.

A typical example of Lope de Rueda's wordplay occurs in the first *paso* of *El deleitoso*. Luquitas wants Alameda to tell their master that they went to buy onions and cheese, when they were really amusing themselves at the doughnut baker's shop. Alameda has no qualms about lying, but in spite of Luquitas's coaching, he keeps getting confused and finds himself spilling out the truth. Luquitas assures Salcedo that instead of *buñolera* (doughnut baker), Alameda meant *vendedera* (saleswoman), but confused the words because both end in "a," a meaningless explanation, since in Spanish, most feminine nouns end in "a."

Another source of wordplay is the simpleton's inability to pronounce correctly or to choose the correct term. In the fifth *paso* of *El deleitoso*, Mendrugo pronounces the word for "bishop" *obispeso*, instead of *obispo*, as he should. In the second, Alameda mistakes *cilicio* (hair shirt used by penitents) for *silencio* (silence). Cervantes frequently uses this same type of wordplay in his *entremeses*.

Several jokes involve the simpleton's inability to follow directions. In the sixth *paso* of *El deleitoso*, a petty noble named Brezano sends his servant Cebadón to pay the rent, giving him careful instructions about how to proceed, but Cebadón gets confused and gives the money to the wrong person.

The master, the lackey, and the petty noble are other stock types that appear in Lope de Rueda's *pasos*. A shade more clever than the simpleton, these characters are nevertheless not intelligent enough to know better than to trust him. Salcedo gets his ear cuffed by Alameda; Brezano loses his money by trusting it to Cebadón.

Two other stock characters are the student and the cuckold. Typically, the student is a shrewd, manipulative type who seduces a woman with the full, if unwitting cooperation of her husband. In the third *paso* of Lope de Rueda's *El deleitoso*, Bárbara convinces Martín, her husband, that she is ill in order to stay at home with their guest, a student named Gerónimo. While Martín goes to the doctor for cures, Bárbara and Gerónimo go out together. When Martín runs into them in the street, Bárbara convinces him that the student is taking her to church, where she will be cloistered for nine days. Martín, noting how much better Bárbara seems to be feeling, gives them his blessing.

Lope de Rueda's individual *pasos*—that is, those that are not incorporated into his *comedias*—were probably the product of his mature years. Although most critics consider them to be minor works, they established many of the themes, situations, character types, and techniques that would be exploited during the Golden Age and beyond. The resources that Lope de Rueda had at his disposal were extremely limited in comparison with those that would become available to playwrights by the end of the century. Men such as Lope de Rueda laid the groundwork for the flowering of Spanish theater.

The comedias

In terms of the development of dramatic literature in Spain, Lope de Rueda's *comedias* are far less important than his *pasos*. Contrived and unoriginal, they consist of a series of tableaux, some of which are unrelated to the action. The plots typically hinge on mistaken identity and implausible turns of fortune. Standard characters include lost or stolen children who reappear as adults, separated twins, and disguised nobles. In general, the *comedias* lack the autochthonous flavor of later Spanish theater, although the servants, gypsies, and blacks who appear in Lope de Rueda's *comedias* express themselves with the same piquancy, vigor, and regional flair as his *paso* characters.

In spite of their primitive nature, Lope de Rueda's *comedias* are full of vitality. The wordplay and fast-moving dialogue of the comic characters and the inclusion of earthy types such as the slave, the lackey, the gypsy, and the simpleton—most of which would appear in the independent *pasos*—indicate that the *comedias* represented a significant step in Lope de Rueda's development.

Los engañados

Los engañados (the deceived) is an example of Lope de Rueda's early attempts. The play consists of ten scenes, preceded by an *argumento del autor*, in which the playwright establishes the time and place of the action and provides some background material. The plot involves a case of mistaken identity. Fabricio and Lelia are twins who, despite being of different sexes, are almost identical. Lost during the sacking of Rome, Fabricio has been separated from his family for many years. Verginio, the twins' father, arranges for Lelia to marry Gerardo, Clavela's father, with whom he has made a lucrative financial arrangement. When Verginio goes to Rome from Módena, where he is presently living, he leaves Lelia in a monastery, where the girl learns that her beloved, Lauro, has foresaken her for Clavela. Disguised as a page, Lelia leaves the monastery, takes the name "Fabio," and enters into Lauro's service in order to dissuade him from pursuing his relationship with Clavela. To complicate matters, Clavela becomes interested in Fabio.

In the meantime, Fabricio appears in Módena, where Gerardo and Verginio take him for Lelia and nearly everyone else takes him for Fabio. Gerardo, believing Fabricio to be a woman in disguise, leaves him in the company of his daughter, only to find the two of them kissing when he returns. Believing himself to be dishonored, Gerardo becomes enraged. Lauro, hearing that his servant Fabio was kissing Clavela, vows to kill him, but Lelia's deception is revealed to him just in time. Realizing how much Lelia cares for him, Lauro abandons Clavela and marries his first love. Fabricio's true identity is also revealed, and he marries Clavela.

For the most part, Lope de Rueda advances the action through dialogue. The important dramatic events occur off stage and are recounted by third parties. The primitive nature of the work is evident from the author's failure to exploit the dramatic possibilities of his story. For example, the audience does not witness the encounters between Lauro and Lelia or between Fabricio and Clavela. Furthermore, Fabricio and Lelia never appear on stage at the same time. Dramatic highlights are apparently inserted at random. In the fourth scene, Lauro speaks passionately to his supposed servant of his love for Clavela, which causes Lelia (disguised as Fabio) to faint. No other dramatic action occurs on stage until, in the sixth scene, Fabricio appears and is mistaken for Lelia or Fabio by the other characters.

Many of the exchanges do not advance the action at all, but serve only to elicit laughter. For example, at the beginning of the first scene, Gerardo asks Verginio for Lelia's hand in marriage but is interrupted by the simpleton Pajares, who, dressed as a woman, has soiled his clothes by falling into a latrine. The description of this mishap is highly amusing but adds little to the development of the plot. The third scene consists of a long *paso* that depicts a dispute between the saucy black slave Guiomar and Julieta, a maid. The argument contributes nothing to the dramatic action, but allows the author to display his gift for creating raunchy, substandard language. Although Guiomar's mispronunciations and misusages reflect to some degree the speech of blacks during the sixteenth century, many of her linguistic idiosyncrasies are Lope de Rueda's inventions.

Los engañados is closely modeled after *Gl' Ingannati*, an anonymous Italian play that was performed in Siena in 1531 and was itself inspired by another work, the thirty-sixth *novella* of Matteo Bandello. Lope de Rueda follows the action of the Italian play quite closely, maintaining the same title, plot, and even some of the characters' names. He did eliminate a few scenes from the original work, but his most significant innovation was the introduction of comic characters and the inclusion of several *pasos*.

BIBLIOGRAPHY

Adams, Kenneth, Ciaran Cosgrove, and James Whiston, eds. *Spanish Theatre: Studies in Honour of Victor F. Dixon*. Rochester, New York: Tamesis, 2001. A collection of studies on various aspects of the theater in Spain. Bibliography.

Hesler, R. "A New Look at the Theater of Lope de Rueda." *Educational Theatre Journal* (1964): 47-54. Hesler examines the Spanish theater during the time of Lope de Rueda, including his dramatic works.

Listerman, R. W. "Lope de Vega's Formula for Success: Practiced Previously by Lope de Rueda."

Language Quarterly (1977): 23-24. The essay examines the similarities between the structures of Lope de Vega Carpio's works and those of Lope de Rueda, demonstrating the latter's influence on the former.

Rueda, Lope de. *Las cuatro comedias*. Madrid: Cátedra, 2001. A collection of Lope de Rueda's comedies that also contains criticism and interpretation of his works. Bibliography. In Spanish.

Barbara Mujica

JUAN RUIZ DE ALARCÓN

Born: Mexico City, Mexico; 1581
Died: Madrid, Spain; August 4, 1639

PRINCIPAL DRAMA

Los favores del mundo, pr. c. 1616-1618
Las paredes oyen, pr. 1617 (*The Walls Have Ears*, 1942)
Algunas hazañas de las muchachas de don García Hurtado de Mendoza, marqués de Cañete, pb. 1622 (with Luis de Belmonte y Bermúdez, Guillén de Castro y Bellvís, Antonio Mira de Amescua, Luis Vélez de Guevara, and others)
El anticristo, pr. 1623, pb. 1634
Siempre ayuda la verdad, pr. 1623, pb. 1635
La industria y la suerte, pb. 1628
El semejante a sí mismo, pb. 1628
La cueva de Salamanca, pb. 1628
Mudarse por mejorarse, pb. 1628
Todo es ventura, pb. 1628
El desdichado en fingir, pb. 1628
Parte primera de las comedias, pb. 1628
La verdad sospechosa, pb. 1630 (as *El mentiroso* in Lope de Vega Carpio's *Parte veynte y dos de las comedias del fénix de España Lope de Vega Carpio*; *The Truth Suspected*, 1927)
Ganar amigos, pb. 1633
El examen de maridos, pb. 1633
Los empeños de un engaño, pb. 1634
El dueño de las estrellas, pb. 1634
La amistad castigada, pb. 1634
La manganilla de Melilla, pb. 1634
El tejedor de Segovia, I, pb. 1634
El tejedor de Segovia, II, pb. 1634

La prueba de las promesas, pb. 1634
Los pechos privilegiados, pb. 1634
La crueldad por el honor, pb. 1634
Parte segunda de las comedias, pb. 1634
La culpa busca la pena, y el agravio la venganza, pb. 1646
Quien mal anda en mal acaba, pb. c. 1652
No hay mal que por bien no venga: O, Don Domingo de don Blas, pb. 1653 (*Look for the Silver Lining*, 1941)
Comedias escogidas, pb. 1867 (3 volumes)
Obras completas de Juan Ruiz de Alarcón, pb. 1957-1968 (3 volumes)
Teatro, pb. 1992 (2 volumes)

OTHER LITERARY FORMS

Aside from some incidental verse of little consequence, Juan Ruiz de Alarcón is known primarily as a playwright.

ACHIEVEMENTS

There exists a curious symbiotic relationship between Juan Ruiz de Alarcón and his better-known French contemporary, Pierre Corneille. Corneille imitated a play titled *El mentiroso* that he found in a collection of works attributed to Lope de Vega Carpio, avowing that he would gladly have exchanged two of his own best pieces to be the original author of *Le Menteur* (pb. 1643; *The Liar*, 1671), as he conveniently titled his adaptation. Thus it is that Corneille is indebted to Ruiz de Alarcón for one of his best-known and most characteristic works, while the Spaniard owes a good portion of his reputation to the fact that the play now known as *The Truth Suspected* was singled out for praise, emulation, and the resulting diffusion. Carlo Goldoni's *Il bugiardo* (1750) and Samuel Foote's *The Lyar* (1762) are reworkings of Corneille's text. Consequently, *The Truth Suspected* joins Tirso de Molina's *El burlador de Sevilla* (c. 1625; *The Love-Rogue*, 1923) and Pedro Calderón de la Barca's *La vida es sueño* (1635; *Life Is a Dream*, 1830) as one of the three most widely diffused dramatic plots devised during the so-called Golden Age of Spanish drama.

There is greater subtlety in Ruiz de Alarcón's work than has sometimes been recognized. His presentation of honor-virtue, in contrast to the more mundane honor-reputation, is a case in point. *The Walls Have Ears* and *The Truth Suspected*, rather than merely condemning slander and falsehood respectively, point instead to a common cause underlying both these types of socially unacceptable behavior—namely, a lack of Stoic-Christian self-discipline. Another example is found in the treatment of poetic justice at the conclusion of *Todo es ventura*, a play based on the theme of fortune, with its implication that poetic justice is yet to be realized. Another example is Fortune itself; for Ruiz de Alarcón, Fortune is more aptly termed misguided than blind, for she operates through men of power and influence who more often than not reward or deprive for the wrong reasons. Likewise, the metaphysical question of free will is dealt with in *El dueño de las estrellas* in such a way as to insinuate that one may experience only the illusion of free choice, as opposed to its reality.

Closely related to subtlety of expression are the evident ambiguity and irony. One cannot be certain, for example, whether Ruiz de Alarcón approves or disapproves of Lycurgus's suicide in *El dueño de las estrellas*. Nor can one be certain whether Lycurgus's destiny was in the stars or in his own character. Indeed, it is not clear whether he overcomes the prophecy or ironically fulfills it in his own person. There are at the same time many direct, unambiguous statements in the plays. Particularly noteworthy are the proposed legislative reforms found in *El dueño de las estrellas* and *La crueldad por el honor*. In the category of direct statements may also be included those

relating to friendship, reason, and other values, many of which have an air of social satire about them.

Ruiz de Alarcón brings to the generic form called the *comedia* an idealism in human relations and in the evaluation of humankind, arising more from the Renaissance conception of the dignity of the individual than from theological considerations. His is essentially a naturalistic system of ethics, for which he is considerably indebted to the Stoics. His ethical system looks to the happiness of humankind on this earth for its ideal. Ruiz de Alarcón appears to favor a species of Epicureanism in morals, a system entailing the sort of pleasures that have little excitement or risk about them. He also favors a modified Stoicism, for although fate and fortune are significant themes in his work, he does not suggest that humankind is subservient to their whims. Passivity is not a part of the outlook on life that one infers from his texts.

BIOGRAPHY

Don Juan Ruiz de Alarcón y Mendoza was born in Mexico City or environs, possibly in Taxco. The year was 1581, almost certainly, but there are no records to substantiate the day or the month. His parents had emigrated from Spain, but very little is known about them beyond the fact that both bore illustrious family names; the father had some connection to the silver mines of Taxco, perhaps as an overseer, and the mother was known as Doña Leonor. The playwright's ostentatious addition of the title "Don" later in life derives from a claim to hereditary nobility through the maternal line of Mendoza.

Ruiz de Alarcón completed several courses in canon law at the Royal and Pontifical University of Mexico by 1600, but apparently he did not graduate. By October of that year, he was in Spain, enrolled at the University of Salamanca. In very short order—a matter of two weeks—he received a bachelor's degree in canon law and immediately registered to pursue the equivalent degree in civil law.

Records at the University of Salamanca suggest that he initially matriculated as simply Juan Ruiz. In time, he added "de Alarcón," and as he became more acclimatized to a new and often hostile environment, the mother's family name was appended, which served to justify the addition of Don at the other end. By the time his name assumed its full form, he was established in Madrid as a dramatist. At least one wit of the day made the comment that Ruiz de Alarcón's name had by then come to exceed the bearer's height by its inordinate length. Another commented that the somewhat questionable use of D. (the abbreviation of Don) could serve as the writer's half portrait in profile, since he was both humpbacked and pigeon-breasted. Another observed that it was impossible to tell, seen from a distance, whether he was coming or going. It was also held against him that he had reddish hair, since, according to popular superstition, hair of that shade indicated complicity with the powers of the netherworld. Nor was it in his favor that he was a Creole, by virtue of his birth in the New World, who had come to Spain against the tide of emigration.

The future playwright received a degree in civil law in 1602 and then spent three more years studying toward the equivalent of a master's, which he did not receive, likely owing to the great expense it would have entailed. He finally did receive a licentiate degree from the University of Mexico in 1609, and during the next four years he aspired to a university chair but was unsuccessful. Meanwhile, he practiced law in various capacities. By April 24, 1614, however, he had settled again in Spain, this time in Madrid, where he would spend the remainder of his life.

The legal background he possessed made Ruiz de Alarcón unique among the coterie of playwrights then active in Madrid, most of whom were or would become churchmen. His considerable training and experience in the law served to foster a predominantly secular outlook and helps to explain the proposed legal and social reforms expressed in two plays in particular, *El dueño de las estrellas* and *La crueldad por el honor*. It also helps one understand the advocacy of reason, his characteristically concise and precise style, and the pains taken everywhere in his work to offer logical explanations for behavior and to analyze actions and motivations. This intellectual formation and predisposition serve to explain many aspects that strike the casual reader as being different in his theater.

The difference, one notes, has been attributed to other factors, among them the resentment he must have felt at being treated so ill by his fellowmen of letters, by fortune, and by nature; his having been born and reared in Mexico; and his supposed classical bent. The supposed "Mexicanness" of his production has been held for naught by at least one distinguished modern Mexican critic, Antonio Alatorre, and the other two factors often adduced fare little better when submitted to scrutiny.

Finally, he was unique in that he wrote primarily to keep body and soul together while aspiring to other things, specifically to a civil service post for which his legal training had equipped him. Once he secured the post, as occurred in 1626, he began to abandon the theater, and he turned his back on it definitively when he received a promotion in 1633 that allowed for a modicum of affluence. Ignoring the good advice of an Italian acquaintance, Ruiz de Alarcón willingly exchanged "ambrosia for chocolate."

Analysis

Juan Ruiz de Alarcón was a keen observer and critic of the customs, foibles, and eccentricities of his time. He used this surrounding reality in various ways to further his dramatic art. Instances of a somewhat utopian vision occur in the series of proposed legislative and social reforms outlined in *El dueño de las estrellas* and *La crueldad por el honor*. A far more frequent posture is the more dystopian, even dyspeptic, view evident in his use of social satire. His barbs are often directed toward the injustices suffered by the poor and toward the privileges and favors commanded by the mere possession of wealth. Such are his allusions to men who seek office through bribery rather than on their merits, such as the sheriff's admission in *El tejedor de Segovia* of the corruption of his office and his remark that only the poor are guilty and of the pessimistic laments that have the ring of personal disillusionment. His use of social satire indicates a dissatisfaction with things as they are and an implicit desire to improve manners and mores; thus it can be said, in the final analysis, that his utopian and dystopian visions are complementary.

Ruiz de Alarcón's is an eminently practical outlook concerned with helping people as social animals to live more meaningfully—authentically, one might say—and to profit more fully from this temporal existence. Ruiz de Alarcón looked nostalgically to a golden age remote in the mists of time (*El dueño de las estrellas*; *Los favores del mundo*; *Los pechos privilegiados*) while also presenting negative examples from a sadly diminished present (*The Truth Suspected*), implying all the while that some semblance of utopia may yet be salvaged from the mire of dystopia. Despite the ubiquitous pessimism, otherworldliness, and religious and racial hysteria of Counter-Reformation Spain, Ruiz de Alarcón projects the image of an eternal optimist.

Several laudable efforts have been made to classify Juan Ruiz de Alarcón's modest production of some two dozen titles, but none has been entirely successful. One relatively sound approach is through the major themes that find expression in his theater. The theme of honor was one of the standard recourses of the drama of this time and place, along with love and faith. Ruiz de Alarcón made use of this hackneyed motif in virtually all of his plays, to one degree or another, but two plays in particular serve to suggest a new and vigorous reinterpretation of the topic. These are *The Truth Suspected* and *The Walls Have Ears*; his best-known works, both acknowledged masterpieces and, indeed, companion pieces.

THE TRUTH SUSPECTED

The Truth Suspected presents the misadventures of a young man who elevates falsehood to a fine art. Don García's creative imagination and verbal dexterity deceive and amaze all with whom he comes in contact. His objective, he discloses, is to become famous by whatever means, and because his forte is fabrication, that will serve his purpose. It is left for the audience to decide whether Don García is a compulsive liar who thus rationalizes his defect or whether he is in fact consciously pursuing a perverted notion of fame by attempting to excel at what he does best. It is clear, in any event, that his actions are counterproductive, as his father and his manservant frequently remind him. In the end, he is obliged to marry Lucrecia when he is in fact in love with Jacinta, partly as a result of mistaken identity earlier in the play, but mainly because he has persisted in spinning a tissue of lies. Although Don García might be said to be punished in this manner, by frustration, the resolution is patently unfair to Lucrecia, and Corneille, realizing this, changed the ending to make it more palatable to the audience of *Le Menteur*. The ending Ruiz de Alarcón provides need not be taken to illustrate poetic justice but may be seen merely as the continuation of a venerable tradition of comedy, that of the arbitrary pairing off at the end.

THE WALLS HAVE EARS

The Walls Have Ears presents a contrasting pair of suitors of a young and comely widow, Doña Ana. There is a third suitor, but he functions only as a foil. The two who concern the audience are Don Juan de Mendoza, whose name and uninviting physical appearance immediately suggest the author himself, and his more physically appealing but ignoble competitor, Don Mendo. Like Don García of *The Truth Suspected*, Don Mendo is pathological in his devotion to antisocial behavior, in this case slander. He speaks ill of one and all, and he is eventually overheard by Doña Ana as he disparages her to another, thus carrying through the motif of the title, *The Walls Have Ears*, and causing her to reject him in favor of the less prepossessing but more substantial Don Juan de Mendoza. Like Don García, Don Mendo persists in his counterproductive pattern, displaying thereby a singular lack of self-discipline—a failure to curb his tongue—which results in the negative consequences that await him. Both Don Mendo and Don García lack self-mastery, as is illustrated in their repetitive behavior, and therefore both lack honor as an intrinsic quality. The works are companion pieces in that they present analogous cases of excess, one of lying, the other of slander. A curious added dimension of the latter is the self-conscious projection of the author in the person of the noble-minded Don Juan de Mendoza and his vicarious victory, his winning the object of his affections in the face of formidable competition. Of greater significance, however, is the patterning of the two works, their commonalities and complementarity, which serve to point up the fact that the author is not condemning these two common vices so much as he is intent on demonstrating that excess in either, besides being counterproductive, has its source in a deplorable lack of Stoic-Christian self-mastery. Ruiz de Alarcón is no petty-minded moralist of the sort who would condemn an occasional prevarication or an aspersion on someone's good name. He looks beyond surface features in an attempt to get at root causes.

The theme most frequently found in his drama is that of love. It is a theme that lends itself to many variations, among which is the trite notion that love is blind. To say that love is blind is only to say that Cupid is blind or, rather, blindfolded. Love is also blinding, however, and consequently may detract from one's freedom of choice or free will and may cause one to act differently than is usual or expected. If one is not acting under one's own volition while under the spell of love, one cannot be held responsible for infractions of whatever sort. All must be forgiven. Likewise, all is fair in love and war. The spirited young men and women of Golden Age plays seem invariably to fall in love at first sight. Perhaps for personal reasons, Ruiz de Alarcón is clearly against the sort of love based on superficial outward impressions of beauty. As a result, he has his more enlightened heroines, such as Doña Ana of *The Walls Have Ears*, learn to look beyond the façade and into the soul, wherein lie true beauty and nobility. Because his theater is predominantly secular in nature, containing only two plays in which religious considerations figure prominently, there is only one passage that gives any indication of a conflict between human and divine love, and it occurs in one of these two plays, *La manganilla de Melilla*, when Alima, the leading female character, who has just converted from Muhammadanism to Christianity, turns her back on Azén, her former Moorish lover, saying that she now aspires only to the love of God and to being baptized.

GANAR AMIGOS

Although the theme of love is the one that appears and reappears with most frequency, it is noteworthy that male characters invariably subordinate love to friendship. This masculine bond is inviolate. A true friend should be like a brother. Friendship must never be feigned. According to Aristotle, friendship is a necessary virtue for humans. No normal person would want to live without friends. Friendship is the bond that holds together families and nations. People may love inanimate objects, but they cannot feel friendships for them. Friendship consists of wishing for the welfare of the person befriended, and this cannot apply to objects. Love may be directed unilaterally toward any object, animate or inanimate, but friendship centers on interpersonal relationships and must be mutual. Of the three types of friendship (for utility, for pleasure, and that of goodness), the friendship of goodness is to be preferred. *Ganar amigos* is a prime example of a play that illustrates the friendship of goodness, that type of friendship in which the good in one individual is attracted to similar goodness in another. True altruism is shown by the Marquis and by Don Fernando and Don Diego. It becomes clear, moreover, although it is perhaps paradoxical, that this ideal type of friendship is utilitarian. The friendship extended Don Diego and Don Fernando, although apparently involving no ulterior motive, turns out to be most useful to the Marquis when he is later saved from execution by their confession. One infers that all types of friendship tend to result in some sort of gain for all involved.

In *Ganar amigos*, friendship is placed even above the demands of the code of honor. The Marquis, on learning that Don Fernando has killed his brother, could be expected to take revenge. Instead, he makes the amazing statement that even though he loved his brother more than himself, he now gladly trades the brother he has lost for the friend he has gained. Similarly, Rodrigo of *Los pechos privilegiados*, out of self-respect and owing to his friendship for Count Melendo, refuses to serve as a go-between for the King, who aspires to the affections of a lady who is also being courted by Count Melendo. His refusal signifies a breach of the code of honor, which demands that a subject perform any act demanded by his king, no matter how reprehensible. Rodrigo is banished from the court for his insubordination, but he is not entirely disconsolate, for he knows that he has obeyed a higher code, that of friendship.

The rationale behind this considerable emphasis on friendship would seem to be that if humankind is alone in an indifferent, often hostile society, as this theater clearly implies, and subject, furthermore, to the vagaries of Fortune, people must stand together and lean on one another through friendship, lest the enormity of their plight overwhelm them.

LA MANGANILLA DE MELILLA

Conspicuously absent from Ruiz de Alarcón's work is any religious sentiment. This is especially noteworthy, given the fact that the historical time frame in which he wrote was the time of the Counter-Reformation, the Inquisition, and the forced conversion of the peoples indigenous to the Americas. Indeed, there is transparent sarcasm in the playwright's assessment of the religiosity of his time, as when the clown, or *gracioso*, his usual mouthpiece, observes in *El semejante a sí mismo* that the women who appear to be most fervid in their practice are only sufficiently so, so as to avoid being burned at the stake. Elsewhere, in *La manganilla de Melilla*, the words of the Jew, Salomón, exude an even deeper irony, when he asks a passerby to untie him from the tree where "Christian cruelty" has left him. It is at the end of this play that the author has Alima, a convert to Christianity, murder the unsuspecting Azén. The author could not have been unaware of the paradox involved in such an act. Christian cruelty may well have had special meaning for Ruiz de Alarcón, coming as he did from the New World, where the exploits of the conquistadores were still fresh in his memory. In this connection, Alima's advice to Azén, after she has mortally wounded him, may be significant; she counsels him to accept Christ and deny Muhammad. What is implied is that human life is a thing of small moment, that the important thing is to open the gates of Paradise for the soul and to populate the kingdom of Heaven by whatever means.

EL ANTICRISTO

Ruiz de Alarcón composed only one avowedly religious drama, *El anticristo*. It has been said that the advent of Christianity, with its plan of redemption, spelled the end of the sort of tragedy in which a character could be damned for all eternity, body and soul, without hope, like Sisyphus. Nevertheless, Satan and the Antichrist have presented two possible subjects for such a tragedy. John Milton succeeded in creating a memorable work of art with the former; Alarcón was not quite so fortunate with the latter. His material had great potential, for here was a towering figure doomed from his incestuous conception to play a certain role and to suffer a predestined fate. The possibility of writing a Christian tragedy on a larger-than-life scale, as well as an apparent fascination with the character itself, is quite likely what attracted Ruiz de Alarcón the dramatist. One can only wish that he had been more successful.

TODO ES VENTURA

In his presentation of the theme of Fortune, Ruiz de Alarcón looked to antiquity, to Seneca first and foremost, but also to Plautus and Terence. In Seneca, Fortune is almost always malignant, which means that a kind of pessimism is basic to his thought. A recurring problem is how to withstand fortuitous events, a problem made harder for man because the dice of Fortune are loaded against him. One of the basic teachings of Seneca was that a Stoic indifference must be maintained toward the accidents of daily life. This attitude is given expression in both *Los favores del mundo* and *Todo es ventura*. Several characters indicate a desire to stop the turning of Fortune's wheel, but Fortune, like Cupid, is blind; her fickle nature is proverbial, and her wheel turns inexorably. From antiquity, the blind god and goddess have been thought of together and sometimes said to accompany each other, as Beltrán reminds the audience in *The Walls Have Ears*.

Tello's good fortune in *Todo es ventura* is owing entirely to the whims of the Duke. A telling example of a reward given arbitrarily and undeservedly is the stewardship bestowed on Tello for having brought the Duke good news—a thing of small moment in comparison to the years of service rendered by the three other servants who are candidates for the post. The rejected servants' resulting frustration and envy, which leads to an attempt on Tello's life, is perhaps a foreshadowing of what the Duke himself may do in his frustration at losing Leonor—not that he will have Tello's life literally but, rather, that he will have his honor, a possession often equated with life. Tello's fortune is consistently good; there are no ups and downs. Nevertheless, from what is known of Fortune's inconstancy, added to the fact that the Duke is being used as her minister to bestow temporary good luck, there is all the more reason to conclude that Tello's gains at the end are dubious and that he will soon be disillusioned.

LOS FAVORES DEL MUNDO

Los favores del mundo, the other play devoted to the theme of Fortune, is similar in that, here also, there is a powerful figure, the Prince, who is very nearly as inconstant as Fortune herself and on whose whim García alternately experiences good and bad luck. In this play, there are the expected ups and downs, which make it a more realistic illustration of Fortune at work, yet it remains a less subtle study than *Todo es ventura*.

A major difference between García and Tello is that the former is virtuous, indeed a paragon, whereas Tello lacks not only virtue but also character. There is greater similarity between García and Enrique, Tello's first master. Although García and Enrique are both occasionally impetuous, they nevertheless exemplify, on the whole, Ruiz de Alarcón's primary virtue of self-mastery. Both are brave, and neither shows any indication of being the sycophant that Tello is. Both García and Enrique suffer and are tempered in their struggle with Fortune. It appears that Tello's suffering is yet to come. Although at the conclusion of *Los favores del mundo* García is in a difficult situation, not dissimilar to Tello's, there is every indication, based on his past performance, that he will know how to protect his honor against any attempts by the Prince and that he will, if necessary, abandon the court entirely to return to his estate in La Mancha. Tello lacks both the wherewithal to defend his honor and any alternative to remaining in the service of the Duke. His situation is therefore more vulnerable and perilous.

EL DUEÑO DE LAS ESTRELLAS

The last theme to be considered in the work of Ruiz de Alarcón is free will. In sixteenth and seventeenth century Spain, the issue was exclusively a theological one. The controversy over free will, predestination, and divine grace seems to have been continuous since the beginnings of theology. Martin Luther and Desiderius Erasmus had broached the question in the early sixteenth century—Luther in his *De servo arbitrio* (1525) and Erasmus in *De libero arbitrio* (1524). Just before the time of Ruiz de Alarcón, the matter had been warmly debated by the Dominican Domingo Báñez (1528-1604) and the Jesuit Luis de Molina (1535-1600). Báñez, like John Calvin and Martin Luther, espoused predestination, whereas Molina, in the manner of Erasmus, was a proponent of free will.

The primary theme of *El dueño de las estrellas*, as one might conjecture from the title alone, is fatalism versus free will. The astrologers have predicted that Lycurgus either will die at the hands of a king or that a king will die at his. The prediction is very nearly realized, but Lycurgus apparently asserts his free will and dominion over the stars by committing suicide. The resolution is not as skillful or as artistic as one might desire, but the point is made nevertheless that the stars may predispose behavior but cannot determine it. Ruiz de Alarcón, along with Calderón and others, rejected the self-stultifying position of the astrologers, for if their claims were true, humankind would be little more than a species of robot.

It is common knowledge that Lycurgus lived about 800 B.C.E. and that he achieved fame as a lawgiver and social reformer in the Greek state of Sparta. That he was at one time king of Sparta is not so well-known, as it is not historical. Ruiz de Alarcón made it up to serve his own purposes and further concocted the story that Lycurgus is in self-imposed exile in Crete, having abdicated the throne in favor of an unexpected heir, born several months after his father's (the former king's) demise. The suicide was likewise an invention of the playwright.

El dueño de las estrellas may be seen, figuratively, as a composite brief filed by three collaborating lawyers. Ruiz de Alarcón, the junior member, has performed the menial task of writing it; the eloquent Lycurgus pleads the case; and Seneca, who was once a distinguished advocate in Rome, provides much of the metaphysical background. It contains a tripartite statement about Stoic self-discipline, reservations over judicial astrology, and the illusional nature of free will. The thesis parallels that of Calderón's *Life Is a Dream.*

Free will is more than slightly problematic in *El dueño de las estrellas.* Lycurgus, as king-turned-regent in exile, fulfills not one but both the possibilities given in the prophecy in his own person: He kills a king and is killed by one simply by turning his sword on himself. Does he then have free will? It would appear that he does, for he makes a rational choice among six alternatives that he unemotionally enumerates in his final speech. He could have returned to Sparta, could have killed the King of Crete or have been killed by him, could have lived on with his beloved Diana, since his dishonor is more apparent than real, or could have become the central issue in a war between Sparta and Crete. He chooses the sixth alternative, however, that of putting a quick and unexpected end to his own life. The fact that he is aware of alternative courses of action and that he rejects five of these, while choosing one, suggests that he does enjoy free will—or at least the illusion that he has free will. Perhaps that is all any person can lay claim to with any certainty.

Lycurgus's decision demonstrates a moral triumph, regardless of whether it illustrates free will. Had he killed the King of Crete or let the king kill him, he not only would have made a lesser choice, morally speaking, but also would have fulfilled the prophecy. He becomes, at least during the moment of choice, the master of the stars. The fact that he had been a king and that he fulfills the prediction in every sense but the most technical is an ironic twist put in by Ruiz de Alarcón the more to emphasize moral choice.

BIBLIOGRAPHY

Claydon, Ellen. *Juan Ruiz de Alarcón: Baroque Dramatist.* Chapel Hill: University of North Carolina Press, 1970. Claydon presents a study of the life and works of Ruiz de Alarcón. Bibliography.

Halpern, Cynthia Leone. *The Political Theater of Early Seventeenth Century Spain: With Special Reference to Juan Ruiz de Alarcón.* New York: Peter Lang, 1993. Halpern examines the political theater that existed during the seventeenth century in Spain, focusing on Ruiz de Alarcón and his works. Bibliography.

Parr, James A., ed. *Critical Essays on the Life and Work of Juan Ruiz de Alarcón.* Madrid: Editorial Dos Continentes, 1972. A collection of essays discussing the life and plays of Ruiz de Alarcón. Bibliography.

Poesse, Walter. *Juan Ruiz de Alarcón.* New York: Twayne, 1972. A basic study of the life and works of the early Spanish dramatist. Bibliography.

James Allan Parr

GEORGE RYGA

Born: Deep Creek, Alberta, Canada; July 27, 1932
Died: Summerland, British Columbia, Canada; November 18, 1987

PRINCIPAL DRAMA

Indian, pr. 1962 (televised), pb. 1962, pr. 1964 (staged)
Nothing but a Man, pr., pb. 1966
The Ecstasy of Rita Joe, pr. 1967, pb. 1970
Grass and Wild Strawberries, pr. 1969, pb. 1971

The Ecstasy of Rita Joe and Other Plays, pb. 1971 (includes *Indian* and *Grass and Wild Strawberries*)
Captives of the Faceless Drummer, pr., pb. 1971 (music and lyrics by Ryga)
Sunrise on Sarah, pr. 1972, pb. 1973 (music by Ryga)
A Portrait of Angelica, pr. 1973, pb. 1976
A Feast of Thunder, pr. 1973 (music by Morris Surdin)

Paracelsus and the Hero, pb. 1974, pr. 1986

Twelve Ravens for the Sun, pr. 1975 (music by
    Mikis Theodorakis)

Ploughmen of the Glacier, pr., pb. 1976

Seven Hours to Sundown, pr., pb. 1976

Country and Western, pb. 1976 (includes *A Portrait
    of Angelica, Ploughmen of the Glacier, Seven
    Hours to Sundown*)

Laddie Boy, pb. 1978, pr. 1981

Prometheus Bound, pb. 1981 (adaptation of
    Aeschylus's play)

A Letter to My Son, pr. 1981, pb. 1982

*Two Plays: "Paracelsus" and "Prometheus
    Bound,"* pb. 1982

One More for the Road, pr. 1985

OTHER LITERARY FORMS

In addition to stage plays, plays for radio and television, poems, film scripts, and song lyrics, George Ryga wrote four novels and one fictionalized memoir of a journey through China. Ryga's first published novel, *Hungry Hills* (1963), is a story of a young man who returns to the cruel, barren prairie community that had exiled him three years earlier. Like many of Ryga's plays, *Hungry Hills* describes the suffering and isolation of the outcast whose social and spiritual alienation is further embittered by a "desperate climate which parch[es] both the soil and heart of man." Ryga's second novel, *Ballad of a Stone-Picker* (1966), tells of two brothers, one of whom stays to work on the family farm so that his younger brother can go to the university, where he becomes a Rhodes scholar; a revised edition was published in 1976. In *Night Desk* (1976), Ryga's third novel, the city (as always, in Ryga, a symbol of antilife) is given extended treatment. *In the Shadow of the Vulture* (1985), Ryga's fourth novel, is set in the desert at the Mexico-U.S. border and focuses on the hope and despair of immigrant laborers.

In a series of scenes narrated by a tough-talking Edmonton fight promoter, the city's grim and shabby underside is revealed. *Beyond the Crimson Morning: Reflections from a Journey Through Contemporary China* (1979) is based on Ryga's trip to China in 1976.

ACHIEVEMENTS

In *The Ecstasy of Rita Joe*, George Ryga wrote one of Canada's best-known and most widely produced plays. On July 9, 1969, less than two years after its premier performance in Vancouver during Canada's centennial, *The Ecstasy of Rita Joe* was performed at the festival opening of the National Arts Centre in Ottawa. The play was next produced by the Fondation Nationale de la Comédie Canadienne, Montreal, in a French version by Gratien Gélinas, Quebec's leading dramatist. Adapted as a ballet by Norbert Vesak and produced by the Royal Winnipeg Ballet, *The Ecstasy of Rita Joe* was performed on tour in 1971 throughout Canada, the United States, and Australia. Ryga received additional acclaim on accepting the Edinburgh Festival Fringe Award for his play in 1974. Widely reprinted, *The Ecstasy of Rita Joe* has established itself as a classic of the Canadian dramatic repertoire.

As one of English Canada's major dramatists, Ryga received considerable recognition in a country in which artists, even those of his stature, have had to struggle to have their work officially acknowledged. In 1972, he was awarded a Canada Council Senior Arts Grant to work on *Paracelsus and the Hero*. In 1979 he was nominated for an ACTRA Award for the *Newcomers* television series, while also in 1979 and in 1980, he received the Frankfurt Academy of Performing Arts Award for *Ploughmen of the Glacier* (Ryga had a substantial foreign audience). In 1980 he was invited to serve as writer-in-residence at the University of Ottawa.

BIOGRAPHY

George Ryga grew up in what he has referred to as "the internal third-world of Canada"—the rugged, depression-ridden prairie land of Northern Alberta. He was born in Deep Creek on July 27, 1932, the first child of George Ryga and Maria Kolodka, new immigrants from Ukraine. Though formally educated in a one-room schoolhouse, and only up to the eighth grade, Ryga read widely as a child while nurturing himself on the songs, myths, and folktales of his heritage. Ryga's Ukrainian background, the severe poverty in which he was reared, and the dominating reality of the northern landscape were all of enduring significance to his development as an artist. Of the land and language with which he grew up, Ryga commented:

> The language took the form of the land—uncompromising, hard, defiant—for three seasons of the year the long months of winter isolation made the desire for human contact a constant ache.

Having grown up beside a Cree reservation, Ryga soon discovered another kind of poverty from the one that he knew: the social and spiritual degradation of the indigenous community, alongside of whom Ryga would work as a laborer on his father's farm.

Ryga drew heavily from this experience in writing his first play, *Indian*, a play that Ryga described as a "milestone" in his development as a playwright. (The play was broadcast as part of the Canadian Broadcasting Corporation's *Quest* television series in November, 1962.) In an interview, Ryga discussed his experience:

> You know I grew up on the outskirts of a Cree reservation. The demoralization and degradation was about as total as any society can experience anywhere in the world. These people had been worked over by the Church; they had been worked over by the Hudson's Bay Co.; there was nothing left. There was no language left anymore. Even their heroes they picked up on from the dominant culture, like a chocolate-bar wrapper dropped in the street that's picked up as a piece of art and taken home and nailed on the wall.

Ryga's keen awareness of social injustice continued to develop throughout his teens and early twenties, a period of casual labor, artistic exploration, and deepening political commitment. The early to mid-1950's in particular saw Ryga performing political gestures of various kinds: In 1952, he wrote a controversial antiwar script for the Edmonton radio show *Reverie*; in 1953, he demonstrated in response to the Julius and Ethel Rosenberg trial; in 1955, he represented the Canadian peace movement at the World Peace Assembly in Helsinki, meeting the Chilean poet Pablo Neruda, the Turkish poet Nazim Hikmet, the soviet writer Ilya Ehrenberg, and other commu-

nist writers. In the same year, he traveled to Poland and Bulgaria. Though he left the Communist Party as a result of the Hungarian Revolution in 1956, Ryga claimed, in 1982, that "there has been no departure from the initial socialist commitment that I made a long time ago." In his plays, Ryga's "socialist commitment" emerges as a deep and abiding concern for the individual outcast, the person dispossessed economically, culturally, and spiritually who struggles to maintain dignity in the face of an impersonal system of domination, discrimination, and charity.

The early 1960's for Ryga marked the beginning of a great period of productivity and accomplishment. In 1960, he married Norma Lois Campbell, adopting her two daughters, Lesley and Tanya, and fathering, in 1961 and 1963, two sons, Campbell and Sergei. The early 1960's, moreover, saw Ryga coming to the theater via radio and television drama, where he had served his apprenticeship. Throughout the 1950's and into the early 1960's, Ryga had written short plays and stories for radio broadcasts in Edmonton. After the television production of *Indian* in 1962, Ryga turned to the stage, again with *Indian*, in 1964. There followed a period of major accomplishment, Ryga writing in succession *Nothing but a Man*, *The Ecstasy of Rita Joe*, *Grass and Wild Strawberries*, *Captives of the Faceless Drummer*, and *Sunrise on Sarah*. During the year that *A Portrait of Angelica* and *A Feast of Thunder* were produced, Ryga spent six months in Mexico working on *Paracelsus and the Hero*, and then, in 1976, he wrote two more plays, *Ploughmen of the Glacier* and *Seven Hours to Sundown*, both of which were produced that year. Also in 1976, Ryga traveled to China and later wrote his memoir of the journey, *Beyond the Crimson Morning*: *Reflections from a Journey Through Contemporary China* (1979).

On his own development as an artist, Ryga spoke of Edward Albee and Robert Burns, the Scottish poet, as having been major influences. Of Albee, Ryga commented:

> I credit a large part of the fact that *Indian* was written at all, to seeing *The Zoo Story* on television, and watching how that particular play was constructed. It

was the freedom that Albee was exercising in departing from the traditions as then practiced, and taking theatre into a kind of arid area, which I found fascinating and which to a great extent I have used ever since.

Ryga had gone to Dumfries in 1955 to study Burns's poetry, and while there, he discovered drafts of unpublished manuscripts, learning much from them about the interconnections of poetry and music. In Burns's rural origins and in his artistic resistance to English culture, Ryga also recognized much with which to identify:

> I began to see . . . that the English dominance of Scotland, and Burns' contribution in retaining a semblance of language, and around that language developing a rallying point for Scotland's national aspirations, were translatable indirectly to the Canadian experience.

Ryga was a guest professor at the University of British Columbia, at Banff School of Fine Arts, and at Simon Fraser University. As an active member in the Association of Canadian Television and Radio Artists, and an honorary member of the British Columbia Civil Liberties Association, he brought his liberal ideas to the political format. The travelogue, *Beyond the Crimson Morning*, published in 1979, was one of his last published works. He died in Summerland, British Columbia, November 18, 1987, of undisclosed causes, at the age of fifty-five.

ANALYSIS

George Ryga's achievements were fueled by his fierce, often embattled commitment to a national theater in Canada. From his earliest days as a dramatist, Ryga resisted the imposition of British and American styles on the Canadian theater and sought to establish a living theater fully responsive to his own country's heterogeneous culture. By his own admission, however, Ryga had equivocal success in establishing such a theater in Canada: "I have known electrifying national prominence, and I have known a decade of exclusion from the theatres of my country. . . ." Nevertheless, Ryga's plays, which transform Canadian myth and experience into a vivid dramatic language, have been of major significance in the struggle to establish a national theater. He was a major dramatist who dug into his Canadian material and reached through to some universal truths.

INDIAN

In his first play, *Indian*, the dramatist compressed into one powerful act many basic materials of Canadian language, myth, and experience that he would develop in later plays. The play examines the poverty and despair of the variously named and ultimately anonymous "Indian," who elicits the intended guilt and sympathy from the members of the audience and who then rejects them violently in an outburst of rage, anguish, and guilt of his own. In the process, the play shatters the distorted and clichéd image of the native Canadians that has often been preserved in the Canadian consciousness.

Of the play's three characters, Indian, the boss Watson, and the Agent (a "comfortable civil servant" from the Department of Indian Affairs), it is the Agent who represents the "white man's" guilt over the Indians' degradation and who symbolizes the white man's attempts, primarily through impersonal charity and social welfare, to repair a tragic, structural flaw in Canadian society. Indian, however, is not interested in charity: "I want nothing from you—jus' to talk to me—to know who I am. . . ." In particular, Indian needs to tell of his brother, whom he was forced to kill in an act of mercy. The Agent, who is unable to conceive of Indian's essential humanity and who lacks, therefore, the emotional and moral strength to receive Indian's confession, is coerced, rather more violently than Samuel Taylor Coleridge's wedding guest in *The Rime of the Ancient Mariner* (1798), into hearing a story of great sin and suffering.

Against the Agent's cries of "No . . . no! This I don't understand at all," Indian describes how he killed his own brother (his brother had been trapped and left to die at the bottom of a well he was digging for a white "bossman," only to be finally rescued more dead than alive), how he "stole" his clothes, and how he allowed a "half-breed" to take the dead man's name so that he could collect the reservation subsidy on it ("All Indians same—nobody"). As he tells his story, the stereotyped image of the drunken and worthless Indian with which the play opened must be correlated with the profound humanity and existential integrity of the man who chose, at the cost of immense anguish, to save his own brother by murdering him:

> I . . . kill . . . my . . . brother! In my arms I hold him. He was so light, like small boy. I hold him . . . rock 'im back and forward like this . . . like mother rock us when we tiny kids. I rock 'im an' I cry . . . I get my hands tight on his neck, an' I squeeze an' I squeeze. I know he dead, and I still squeeze an' cry, for everything is gone, and I am old man now . . . only hunger an' hurt left now. . . .

Although the play is fundamentally realistic, its skillful compression of language, setting, and events produces powerful symbolic effects. The setting is a "flat, grey, stark non-country," a "vast empty expanse" that is at once the Northern Albertan landscape and a spiritual wasteland, reminiscent of the elemental settings in Samuel Beckett or T. S. Eliot. This simultaneous realism and symbolism in setting is matched on the levels of language and event, where the cadences of Indian dialect or the harsh hammer blows with which the play ends resonate with poetic force. The fusion of realism and symbolism at key points of *Indian* anticipates the more ambitious, sustained, and experimental techniques of *The Ecstasy of Rita Joe*, Ryga's more wide-ranging treatment of indigenous experience.

THE ECSTASY OF RITA JOE

The vibrant combination of dance, song, mime, recorded voices, and special lighting effects in *The Ecstasy of Rita Joe* signals Ryga's departure from the basic naturalism of *Indian*. Ryga dramatizes both the inner and the outer experience of Rita Joe by making use of a variety of impressionistic, expressionistic, and symbolic techniques. Thus, on a forceful and realistic groundwork he builds a poetic structure in which Rita's subjective experience and inevitable doom emerge in flashbacks, shadow plays, and interludes of music, mime, or dance.

The groundwork of the play is the basic tragedy of Rita's life and death. Having left her father, the reserve, and her sexual innocence behind, Rita comes to the city, where she becomes trapped in a closing circle of poverty, theft, and prostitution—until she is raped and murdered by three white men. (The Three Murderers shadow Rita's presence throughout the play until they emerge, clearly illuminated, to murder Rita and her lover Jamie at the end.) The play's poetic structure, however, transforms this linear, deterministic plot into a mythical, often allegorical elaboration of Rita's fate, whereby the murder of the Indian woman becomes the ecstasy and apotheosis of the martyr. The fusion of realism and symbolism is pure and lacks sentimentality. Appropriately, the play ends with the poignant words of Rita's sister Eileen, which focus on the human being at the heart of the myth: "When Rita Joe first come to the city—she told me. . . . The cement made her feet hurt."

The main action revolves around a recurring courtroom scene in which Rita stands accused—of vagrancy, prostitution, theft, and other crimes—before a sentimental and ineffectual Magistrate, symbol of white society's superficial understanding of Indian experience. By administering lectures and jail sentences, the Magistrate rests the blame for Rita's degradation and despair on Rita herself, evading whatever responsibility he might have both as a man and as an official representative of white society. He tries unsuccessfully to harmonize the image of a tiny Indian girl he once saw in the Cariboo country with the woman Rita, whom he accuses of carrying a venereal disease, a symbol of her permanent condemnation.

The courtroom scenes are touchstones of a present reality that Rita strives to evade via memories and fantasies. In these imaginative interludes, the people of her past and the materials of her oppressed spirit emerge. In one scene of dramatic counterpoint, her old dead father, David Joe, speaks beautifully of a dragonfly emerging from its shell while her lover, Jamie Paul, rails against the white oppressors and advocates violence against them. Torn by this conflict of generations, trapped between impossible alternatives of urban despair and powerlessness and an extinct pastoral majesty, Rita stands paralyzed and doomed. When she recalls scenes of warmth and inspiration, as when she and her sister Eileen comforted each other after a storm, the Three Murderers loom menacingly in the background. Memory, then, is fraught with pain and contains the seeds of her inevitable doom.

Other significant characters who appear out of Rita's past are a Teacher, a Priest, a Policeman, and a welfare worker, Mr. Homer, all of whom, as representatives of white society, stand as accusers of Rita Joe. Throughout, Rita's essential isolation is dramatized as she is torn violently from her memories by a court policeman or as she stands alone in a shaft of light, separated by a barrier of memory from her surroundings. Often, the dialogue assumes a contrapuntal rhythm as the characters talk across one another's meanings, each alone in a fading world.

As the play progresses, it becomes more and more dominated by Rita's imagination, which strains against the tragic inevitability of events. Increasingly, as she emerges from her memories and imaginings, the present reality assumes a more hallucinatory quality, shaped as it has become by Rita's disorientation, fear, hunger, and exhaustion. At times the boundaries of time and space, of inner and outer reality, vanish completely. In a scene that approaches the nightmarish intensity of the Circe episode of James Joyce's *Ulysses* (1922), all the testimonies of white authority—of Priest, Policeman, Teacher, Magistrate—fuse into one "nightmare babble" of perpetual condemnation. Out of this babble comes the searing cry of the Magistrate, a cry that is also the voice of Rita's self-accusation, the bitter acknowledgment of her forced betrayal of sexual innocence and Indian heritage:

> MAGISTRATE: Have you any boils on your back? Any discharge? When did you bathe last?
> *The Three Murderers appear, and circle Rita.*
> MAGISTRATE: Answer me! Drunkenness! Shoplifting! Assault! Prostitution, prostitution, prostitution, prostitution!

In *Indian*, the Agent represents the audience's point of view and dramatizes its violent discovery of Indian's complex and painful reality. In *The Ecstasy of Rita Joe*, the audience almost exclusively shares Rita's point of view, which accounts for the play's nonsequential, associative order, its blending of

Rita's spirit and memory with the nightmare-present from which she struggles in vain to escape. The play inhibits a complete identification with Rita, however, by insistently recalling the members of the audience to their own identity. Before the play begins, for example, the players make their entrances in a "workmanlike and untheatrical way" with the houselights up, thus enforcing a sense of common reality and frustrating the audience's desire to escape into the suspension of disbelief that a darkened theater encourages.

Even when the lights are lowered and the play is long under way, the audience continues to be reminded of its status, sometimes rudely so. At one stunning moment, for example, Ryga calls for Jamie Paul to cross downstage and confront a member of the audience: "You know me? . . . You think I'm a dirty Indian, eh? Get outa my way!" At another equally uncomfortable moment, David Joe, Rita's father, gestures angrily toward the audience exclaiming, "And tell her what? . . . Of the animals there . . . who sleep with sore stomachs because . . . they eat too much?"

Structural among the play's alienating devices, however, is Rita's alter ego, the Singer, "a white liberal folklorist" who weaves the scenes together with wistful songs that bespeak her "limited concern and understanding of an ethnic dilemma." If the audience wishes to identify with Rita, it must simultaneously come to terms with the Singer, who sits, appropriately, off to the side and "turned away from the focus of the play." The Singer, consequently, serves as an alter ego of the audience as well. Thus, between the poles of intimacy and alienation, between the life and final ecstasy of Rita Joe and the superficial and sentimental songs of the Singer, the audience must steer in this most demanding of Ryga's plays.

PLOUGHMEN OF THE GLACIER

After *The Ecstasy of Rita Joe*, Ryga wrote several plays on subjects ranging from psychedelic culture to urban terrorism, small-town politics, and the Titan Prometheus. As might be expected, these plays use a wide variety of techniques, blending realism with myth, song, or dance while experimenting with both fluid and static settings. Among the plays Ryga wrote after 1967, however, *Ploughmen of the Glacier*, an exploration of the myth of the Canadian West, was his most profound. In *Ploughmen of the Glacier*, Ryga is a virtuoso who masters continuously the development of his materials, creating a play that is rich in character, language, and symbolism.

In the stage directions, Ryga called for a "possibly surrealistic" mountainside setting in which "all is staged and designed to highlight the elemental loneliness of the protagonists." Although the setting resembles that of *Indian* in its isolation and foreboding, the effect here is more dramatic as the Canadian Rockies loom unseen but felt in the background. The suggested mountainside functions in the play like the vast, mountainous range of the landscape painting: In both cases, the artist places human figures in the foreground of the vast scene to express human evanescence and isolation before nature's permanence and sublimity. At times, however, the lust and spirit of Ryga's characters succeed in dominating their surroundings.

The loneliness of the three protagonists is further reinforced by their distance from civilization. High on the mountain, the world below assumes a distant and obscure shape, formed only by the characters' infrequent allusion to the Gold Rush, the town, or the business "bandits" from Ontario. Thus isolated, the mountainside is free to open into abodes of myth, though its bearded, coughing men, moving about in clouds of real dust and speaking their raucous frontier language, suggest a particular history and region.

The action is structured on the periodic meeting of Volcanic and Lowery—the natural, elemental man and the bookish man of culture—who disguise their suppressed affection for each other in zealous, occasionally violent, and often bitter arguments about the best way to live. Their spirited and voluble antagonism is interrupted, however, on the entrance of Poor Boy, who wanders up and down the mountain with a pair of leaky water buckets in a futile attempt to hoard water against the coming fire. (Wandering through the scene playing his harmonica, Poor Boy pauses to speak wistfully and discontinuously about a dimly remembered Western legend.) As the play's Sisyphus, Poor Boy brings with him a whiff of the

abyss that stops Volcanic and Lowery cold. From this prospect of madness and futility, Volcanic and Lowery avert their faces, infected by a doubt that leaves them spiritually exhausted though somehow closer as men. When Poor Boy leaves, however, they resume their argument. According to this rhythm of spirited argument, despair, and brief communion, the play progresses.

The play's bleak existentialism is substantially countered throughout by its lusty language and humor. Responsible for the finest displays of both, Volcanic is also the Old West personified, a symbol of its tireless energy. As his name suggests, he is at once flowing lava and petrified rock—a living fossil from another time. Like the West itself, he combines the grandeur of the pioneering imagination with its ignorance and brutality (Volcanic once shot a man who trespassed unknowingly on his land), and like most grand personifications, he is slightly absurd: For all Volcanic's dreams of wealth and talk of founding a city in his name, he, like Anse Bundren of William Faulkner's *As I Lay Dying* (1930), is dominated by the homely and pressing need for a set of false teeth. Nevertheless, Volcanic's vigorous speech achieves the force and resonance of poetry. When he rails against Lowery, he is at his best:

> You're worn out by poverty . . . you depress me! . . . You're like a preacher in a whorehouse. I want to dress up like a monkey to show the world I'm livin'. . . . I want to bleed myself . . . show God I can do without Him . . . that I can spill my life on the ground an' still have more left in me than men like you! . . . I want to smell out a claim an' go after it . . . all alone . . . just my body with a hammer an' chisel against the whole goddamned mountain! To eat what nobody's ever cooked for me . . . to stand on a cliff, pants aroun' my ankles . . . an' shake the sperm in me over the cliff into the valley . . . an' laugh to see a gull scoop down an' swallow it before it hits the ground . . . Hah! The seeds for children I could've had . . . eaten by a seagull!

An aged and failed editorialist and languid spokesman of civilization, Lowery is impelled periodically to climb the mountain to berate Volcanic and to assail him with issues from "down below"—from the society and culture of man that Lowery has increasingly come to doubt. Though he is attracted by Volcanic's tireless optimism and arrogant independence, he is also dumbfounded and deeply annoyed by it. Unable to live like Volcanic but no longer at home in civilization, Lowery is the most isolated and pathetic of the play's characters. Lacking the robust constitution of Volcanic or the single-minded purpose of Poor Boy, Lowery is alone between the frontier and society, living primarily with a painful memory of the beautiful woman with whom he declined to make love, so ashamed was he of his own nakedness.

The argument of Volcanic and Lowery continues until they die facing each other in their tracks. When they are finally still, Poor Boy comes on to deliver the eulogy for the dead whom he is already beginning to forget. As Poor Boy wanders off playing his harmonica, he will have yet another half-remembered tale to ponder as he carries his leaky water buckets up the mountain.

OTHER MAJOR WORKS

LONG FICTION: *Hungry Hills*, 1963; *Ballad of a Stone-Picker*, 1966, revised 1976; *Night Desk*, 1976; *In the Shadow of the Vulture*, 1985.

TELEPLAYS: *The Storm*, 1962; *Bitter Grass*, 1963; *For Want of Something Better to Do*, 1963; *The Tulip Garden*, 1963; *Two Soldiers*, 1963; *The Pear Tree*, 1963; *Man Alive*, 1965; *The Kamloops Incident*, 1965; *A Carpenter by Trade*, 1967 (documentary); *Ninth Summer*, 1972; *The Mountains*, 1973 (documentary); *The Ballad of Iwan Lepa*, 1976 (documentary).

RADIO PLAYS: *Reverie*, 1952; *A Touch of Cruelty*, 1961; *Half-Caste*, 1962; *Masks and Shadows*, 1963; *Bread Route*, 1963; *Departures*, 1963; *Ballad for Bill*, 1963; *The Stone Angel*, 1965; *Seasons of a Summer Day*, 1975; *One Sad Song for Henry Doyle Matkevitch*, 1981.

NONFICTION: "Theatre in Canada: A Viewpoint on its Development," 1974; "Contemporary Theatre and Its Language," 1977; "The Need for a Mythology," 1977; *Beyond the Crimson Morning: Reflections from a Journey Through Contemporary China*, 1979; "The Artist in Resistance," 1982.

MISCELLANEOUS: *The Athabasca Ryga*, 1990 (collection); *Summerland*, 1992 (Ann Kujundzic, editor).

BIBLIOGRAPHY

Boire, Gary. "Tribunalations: George Ryga's Postcolonial Trial 'Play.'" *Ariel* 22, no. 2 (April, 1991): 5-20. A "clumsily beautiful trial play," *The Ecstasy of Rita Joe* is compared with Margaret Atwood's novel *The Handmaid's Tale* (1986) and other anticolonial literature as a paradigm for examining the "encoding of class violence under the guise of social contract . . . [a] crucial feature of anti-colonial literatures." Strong postmodern, semiotic deconstructionist look at "what postcolonial theorists call the reclamation of a world through irony."

Burgess, Patricia, ed. *Annual Obituary 1987*. Chicago: St. James Press, 1990. A good recapitulation of Ryga's themes, approaches to character, and patterns of composition during his career, along with an updated biography. "The lack of integration between land and people and between the individual and the group is the essential duality in Ryga's work," states the anonymous writer of this obituary. In his earlier life, before making a living as a writer, Ryga was concerned "with the degradation of human beings who are displaced and isolated, who lack a spiritual origin," a trait connected to Canadian life and society and one that informs Ryga's dramatic characterizations.

Carson, Neil. "George Ryga and the Lost Country." In *Dramatists in Canada: Selected Essays*, edited by William H. New. Vancouver: University of British Columbia Press, 1972. Discusses *The Ecstasy of Rita Joe*. Carson's opinion is that the play "establishes Ryga as the most exciting talent writing for the stage in Canada today." He believes that Ryga "rejects romantic and physical love, but does not preclude all meaningful human relationships."

Grace, Sherrill. "The Expressionist Legacy in the Canadian Theatre." *Canadian Literature*, no. 118 (Autumn, 1988): 47-58. This study of Ryga and Robert Gurik examines the non-naturalistic aspects of both writers. Mentions the influences of

Edward Albee, Fyodor Dostoevski, Eugene O'Neill, Franz Kafka, and Bertolt Brecht. Details *The Ecstasy of Rita Joe*, especially the characters identified by function, and the fragmented structure.

Hoffman, James. *The Ecstasy of Resistance: A Biography of George Ryga*. Toronto: ECW Press, 1995. Describes major events in Ryga's life, especially those that relate to his writing. Bibliography and index.

Saddlemyer, Ann. "Crime in Literature: Canadian Drama." In *Rough Justice: Essays on Crime in Literature*, edited by M. L. Friedland. Toronto: University of Toronto Press, 1991. Ryga's *Indian* is discussed as drama that "involves the process of judgment, assigning responsibility for action, distinguishing truth from fiction."

Michael Zeitlin,
updated by Thomas J. Taylor

S

ÁNGEL DE SAAVEDRA

Born: Córdoba, Spain; March 10, 1791
Died: Madrid, Spain; June 22, 1865

PRINCIPAL DRAMA

Aliatar, pr., pb. 1816
El duque de Aquitania, pr. 1816, pb. 1820 (based on Vittorio Alfieri's play *Oreste*)
Malek-Adhél, pr. 1818, pb. 1820 (based on Marie Cottin's novel *Mathilde*)
Lanuza, pr., pb. 1822
Arias Gonzalo, pr. 1827, pb. 1894 (verse play)
Tanto vales cuanto tienes, pr. 1834, pb. 1840 (verse play)
Don Álvaro: O, La fuerza del sino, pr., pb. 1835 (*Don Álvaro: Or, The Force of Destiny*, 1964)
Solaces de un prisionero: O, Tres noches en Madrid, pr., pb. 1841
La morisca de Alajuar, pr., pb. 1841 (verse play)
El crisol de la lealtad, pr., pb. 1842 (verse play)
El parador de Bailén, pr. 1843, pb. 1844
El desengaño en un sueño, pb. 1844, pr. 1875

OTHER LITERARY FORMS

In addition to his drama, Ángel de Saavedra produced poetry and nonfiction works.

ACHIEVEMENTS

Ángel de Saavedra was a prolific writer as well as an influential politician. Better known as the duke of Rivas to critics and the public, his literary production, especially the drama *Don Álvaro*, has been described alternatively as the best of Spanish Romanticism, by his friend and colleague Antonio Alcalá Galiano, and as a play whose main value lies in its intense theatricality, by the drama critic and historian Francisco Ruiz Ramón. In truth, Saavedra's literary career reflects the trajectory of literary tastes and fashions in Spain during the nineteenth century. He began in the waning neoclassical style, already tinted with elements of Romanticism; his early tragedies incorporate the themes of liberty, resistance to tyranny, political reform, and individual freedom that were prevalent in the literary and political milieu of mid-nineteenth century Spain.

The production of *Don Álvaro* in Madrid in 1835 was the event that signaled the dominance of Romanticism in Spain. Building on the work of his predecessors, Francisco Martínez de la Rosa and Mariano José de Larra, Saavedra added to his drama the influence of other European Romantics whose work he read while in exile in France and England. *Don Álvaro* is, then, the ultimate Romantic drama with the ultimate Romantic hero, the one who captured the imagination of the times, transcending frontiers and genre. His play was the base for numerous imitations in Europe and for the well-known opera by Giuseppe Verdi, *La forza del destino*.

Saavedra's achievements in the theater were not limited to his success with *Don Álvaro*. His work was generally popular among the public, and another major drama, *El desengaño en un sueño*, signaled the consolidation within the theater of the trend already started by Saavedra himself in two major works of narrative poetry, the *Romances históricos* (1841) and the *Leyendas* (1854), which shifted the character of Spanish Romanticism from the liberal European to the national conservative.

BIOGRAPHY

Ángel Pérez de Saavedra Ramírez de Madrid Ramírez de Baquedano was born in Córdoba, Spain, on March 10, 1791, the second son of a noble family. He received his early education from French clerks who had fled the French Revolution. From an early age, he showed an aptitude in poetry and painting. At the age of eleven, Saavedra entered the Royal Seminary for Noblemen in Madrid; at fifteen, he joined the Royal Guards and started his military career. At the same time, he began writing articles and poetry for a journal founded by friends. This was the time of the Napoleonic invasion of Spain and the beginning of the Spaniards' rebellion against Napoleon and his brother, Joseph Bonaparte, who had been made king of Spain by the French armies. This rebellion, known as the Spanish War of Independence, lasted from 1808 to 1814 and signaled the end of Napoleon's dominance in Europe.

Saavedra participated with distinction in the Spanish War of Independence. He first fought against the French as a lieutenant and was severely wounded in 1809. In 1810, he went to Cádiz, a stronghold of the Spanish armies, where he was promoted to captain, then to lieutenant colonel. In Cádiz, Saavedra became the editor of the official staff journal of the armies fighting against the Napoleonic forces. Also in Cádiz, he met the patriotic poets Juan Nicasio Gallego and Manuel José Quintana, whose influence is reflected in Saavedra's early neoclassical works. The political atmosphere in Cádiz was liberal, and the young Saavedra was a firm supporter of this political ideology and of the premises on which it was founded.

In 1814, Joseph Bonaparte was deposed and the French were expelled from Spain. That same year, Ferdinand VII returned from exile and abolished the liberal constitution of 1812 and all the reforms made by the popular regime of Cádiz. The king established literary censorship, and Saavedra's first tragedy, *Ataúlfo*, written in 1814, was banned. Saavedra joined the revolution that forced the king to reinstate the constitution, and in 1821, he became a deputy to the Cortes (Parliament) in Madrid. In 1823, however, the conservative government of France sent an army to Spain to help restore the absolute power of Ferdinand VII, and the liberals had to flee the country.

In exile, Saavedra went from Gibraltar to London, where he joined Antonio Alcalá Galiano and established friendships in the literary world, becoming familiar with the ideas of English Romanticism.

Looking for a better climate, Saavedra returned to Gibraltar, where he was married to the noblewoman Doña María de la Encarnación de Cueto y Ortega. After their marriage, they tried to settle in Italy, but the conservative government of that country and the Vatican denied entrance to Saavedra and his wife because of his liberal political stance. Following this failed attempt to enter Italy, Saavedra and Doña María settled in Malta, where they lived for five years. The stay in Malta was very important for Saavedra's literary development. There he had time to read the Spanish literary masters from the Renaissance and Baroque periods (the period called the Golden Age) and also the English Romantics.

In 1830, wanting to be closer to Spain, Saavedra and his family—he and his wife had three children by then—moved to France, where he opened a school for painters and renewed his friendships with the Spanish liberals. In 1834, after the death of Ferdinand VII, the liberal exiles returned to Spain, and Saavedra published his long poem, *El moro expósito*, a vigorous expression of Romantic precepts in literature. In that same year, he became a member of the Royal Spanish Academy and also inherited the title duke of Rivas from his brother. In the following year, 1835, he presented the play *Don Álvaro* in Madrid, and thus the Romantic movement was definitively launched in Spain. In 1841, Saavedra published the *Romances históricos*, a collection of ballads that would mark the shift of Romanticism in Spain from the European and cosmopolitan to the nationalistic and traditional.

In 1844, Saavedra was appointed ambassador to the kingdom of Naples and Sicily. There he wrote poetry, the last of his major dramas, *El desengaño en un sueño*, and continued work on another book of poetry, *Leyendas*, a collection of traditional Spanish legends. He returned to Madrid in 1850, and in 1857, he was named ambassador to France but returned once more to Madrid in 1858 because of a severe illness. In 1862, Saavedra was elected director of the Spanish Academy, and in 1863, he was elected president of the Council of State. His death in 1865 was mourned by the public, the politicians, and the writers of his time.

ANALYSIS

Ángel de Saavedra's theatrical production consists mainly of tragedies and dramas, and even those works written late in his career and called *comedias* were written in the vein of the Spanish drama of the Golden Age, mixing serious themes with some comical incidents. His only two true comedies were written, as he declared, to distract him from the preoccupations of everyday life and affairs of state. This attitude reveals the thrust of Saavedra's theater—a theater based on the intellectual concerns of the author. Thus, his early neoclassical and Romantic works focus on political freedom, the individual, and liberalism, and his later works, written when he had become more conservative, center on traditional Spanish themes and preoccupations.

ALIATAR

Among Saavedra's early plays, the tragedy *Aliatar* is noteworthy. It is neoclassical in form, divided into five acts, respecting the unities of time, place, and action. It also confines itself to one verse form, the assonant hendecasyllable, has lofty characters as protagonists, and comes to a tragic end. Despite this neoclassical format, however, *Aliatar* has definite pre-Romantic characteristics. It is the dramatization of the love of the Moorish chief Aliatar for his Christian captive, Elvira. The themes of power, passion, and impossible love are present, and the tone of the tragedy is Romantic, as it emphasizes the characters' despair in the face of the principles that rule the world. The tragedy ends with the suicide of Aliatar, who is unable to master the passion that consumes him.

EL DUQUE DE AQUITANIA

The tragedy *El duque de Aquitania* also follows the neoclassical precepts outlined above. Based on the play *Oreste* (pr. 1781, pb. 1784; *Orestes*, 1815) by the Italian Vittorio Alfieri, it tells the story of the power struggle between Reynal, the rightful duke, and Eudon, the usurper of the duchy of Acquitaine, and underlines the themes of freedom and independence. This tragedy enjoyed great popularity when it was presented because it reflected the conditions under which the Spanish people were living during the Napoleonic invasion.

MALEK-ADHÉL

Another tragedy that gained popularity was *Malek-Adhél*. This work was based on the well-known novel *Mathilde* (1805) by Madame Cottin, and it deals with the love story between Mathilde, sister of Richard the Lion-Hearted, and Malek-Adhél, brother of the Sultan Saladin. Here again is the theme of interracial, interreligious love that was presented in *Aliatar*, with the difference that in this instance the love is mutual. Again, in format, this is a neoclassical tragedy, but in spirit it is quite Romantic. The protagonist, Malek-Adhél, is overcome by desperation in his realization of the impossibility of his love for Mathilde. The tone and atmosphere of the play are somber, and the political conflict forms an appropriately turbulent background for the story of doomed love. An additional noticeably pre-Romantic characteristic of *Malek-Adhél* is the gloomy setting of the fifth act: midnight at the sepulchral chapel of the crusader Montmorency.

LANUZA

Lanuza, a neoclassical tragedy set in Renaissance Aragon, is a "liberal-oriented" tragedy. The plot delves into the story of Lanuza, the chief justice of Aragon, who revolted against the absolute power of Phillip II. Lanuza was successful at the beginning but was abandoned by his followers, captured by the royal troops, and decapitated. The tragedy ends with an impassioned speech by Lanuza before his death, calling the people to unite and fight absolutism. This thinly disguised call to arms to the Spaniards living under French power was received fervently by theatergoers.

ARIAS GONZALO

Saavedra's most important neoclassical tragedy is *Arias Gonzalo*. The setting and plot come from the siege of the city of Zamora by King Sancho of Castile in medieval Spain. This incident, recorded in the *Primera crónica general* by King Alfonso X of Castile, was also the theme for many traditional ballads and plays. The plot is as follows: King Sancho is killed in battle during the siege by the Zamoran warrior Bellido Dolfos. A Castilian knight, Diego Ordóñez de Lara, challenges the city of Zamora to a duel to decide the outcome of the siege. The city belongs to Doña Urraca, who is underage, and her tutor, Arias Gonzalo, accepts the challenge. His three sons take up the challenge, and the oldest two are killed by Ordóñez. The youngest, Gonzalo Arias, succeeds in defeating Ordóñez but is fatally wounded in combat. The subplot of the tragedy is the love between Urraca and Gonzalo Arias. This tragedy, considered by the critic Francisco Ruiz Ramón as one of the best of its time, brings to life the conflict it portrays through the use of forceful versification, colorful imagery, and well-described action. Divided into five acts and following all the neoclassical precepts, the tragedy nevertheless reflects a marked Romantic influence. The love between Urraca and Gonzalo, doomed to fail because of interference from the outside world, the melancholy displayed by the lovers, and the final lines spoken by Gonzalo's father—"Zamora is free/ But alas, how much this costs Arias Gonzalo"—all speak of the approaching new sensibility and conception of life. There is more emphasis on the individual and less on the duties that bind each person; indeed, a glimpse of the fully developed Romantic hero and heroine are already evident in *Arias Gonzalo*.

TANTO VALES CUANTO TIENES

A comedy written by Saavedra in the same period reveals the degree to which the neoclassical movement shaped his early work. Entitled *Tanto vales cuanto tienes*, it is a full-fledged comedy of manners. In the vein of Leandro Fernández de Moratín's *El sí de las niñas* (wr. 1801, pr., pb. 1806; *When a Girl Says Yes*, 1929), *Tanto vales cuanto tienes* is a didactic work that stereotypes its characters to make the moral message of the comedy evident. The story is simple. Don Blas, a rich Spaniard returning from the colonies in America, pretends that his fortune was lost in the voyage. His family, especially his sister Doña Rufina, reject and mock him as a silly man, a reception quite different from the one promised in letters before he returned from America, when they knew that he still had his fortune. The only family member to show love and understanding for Don Blas is his niece, Doña Paquita, daughter of Doña Rufina. At this point, Don Blas reveals that his fortune is intact and that the only one who will benefit from it is Paquita. The comedy ends with general re-

pentance and hilarity. The neoclassical elements of this comedy are evident. The characters are exaggerated to present extremes of behavior. Thus Doña Rufina is the villain, Doña Paquita the good daughter, and Don Blas the wise old man. Society is criticized, and greed and duplicity castigated. All of this was staged in the amiable manner preferred by neoclassical playwrights to ensure the attention of their public.

DON ÁLVARO

The year 1835 marked a definite change in the theatrical work of Saavedra. This was the year of the production and publication of his most famous work, the Romantic drama *Don Álvaro*. This play exhibits all the standard characteristics of Romanticism: freedom and unattainable love as themes; the hero as a mysterious, impassioned figure; and the heroine as a sweet, intense, passionate creature. Nature is depicted as a force that both reflects and thwarts the feelings of the individual, mostly through darkness and tempestuous panoramas. In the Romantic theater, the action typically climaxes in the destruction of the individual by the world, and this is indeed the case in *Don Álvaro*. The message of these plays seems to be that the Romantic hero—that is to say, the individual who differs from the norm in sensibility or talent, who tries to live by the concepts of love, beauty, and virtue, defying the established norms of society—is doomed to perish in the quest for happiness and self-expression.

The plot of *Don Álvaro* is a beautiful example of Romantic craftsmanship. Don Álvaro, a rich, handsome Peruvian, the son of an Inca princess and a Spanish officer, has come to Seville to clear his father's honor. He meets and falls in love with Doña Leonor, daughter of the impoverished Marquis of Calatrava. The Marquis denies permission for the marriage on the grounds that Don Álvaro is a mestizo. At this juncture, Don Álvaro asks Leonor to elope; she consents but hesitates at the moment of leaving. The Marquis of Calatrava returns home unexpectedly and finds Don Álvaro. Don Álvaro throws his pistol down to signify humility before the Marquis; the pistol fires and fatally wounds the Marquis, who dies cursing his daughter. A struggle follows, and Don Álvaro abandons Seville, thinking that Doña

Leonor is dead. He changes his name, joins the Spanish army in Italy, and tries to find death in battle. Don Carlos, oldest son of the Marquis of Calatrava, is also in Italy, and he and Don Álvaro become friends, each saving the other's life in battle. When Don Carlos discovers Don Álvaro's identity, however, he challenges him to a duel. Don Álvaro tries to avoid the confrontation, but Don Carlos's insistence makes it impossible. They fight, and Don Carlos is killed. Don Álvaro is condemned to death by a law prohibiting duels, enacted by King Charles of Naples. At this moment, an Austrian attack ensues, and Don Álvaro is able to flee. He returns to Spain and joins a monastery. Meanwhile Leonor, who has spent a year in Córdoba, has herself joined another monastery, near Don Álvaro's. Don Alfonso, the Marquis's youngest son, who has never stopped looking for Don Álvaro, finally finds him at the monastery. He accuses Don Álvaro of having disgraced Doña Leonor as well as killing both his father and brother. Don Álvaro tries to explain the circumstances and avoid further violence, but Don Alfonso, like the Marquis and Don Carlos, is intransigent. In the ensuing conflict, Leonor comes from the cave that has served as her hermitage for some years. Don Alfonso thinks that she and Don Álvaro have been living together and kills her. At this point, Don Álvaro loses all restraint and kills Don Alfonso. The last scene of the play takes place near a precipice, with Don Álvaro laughing and cursing diabolically in front of the other monks before plunging to his death.

The Romanticism of this play is undeniable. The action spans a period of some years and takes place in several countries; there is the recurring element of anagnorisis, or recognition, in which the hero is a mysterious person recognized by others as someone with a special nature. The cast of characters is large and varied, from water sellers to the nobility. Society, represented by the rigid norms of conduct set by the Marquis of Calatrava and the obsequiousness of the clerics, is viewed as retrograde and hostile. The world is in a constant state of turmoil, and any hopes of peace or happiness are constantly denied by fate.

The role of fate in *Don Álvaro* has been hotly debated by critics. On one side, critics maintain that Don Álvaro is a character doomed to failure and unable to control his own destiny. Other critics, however, see fate merely as a theatrical device used by Saavedra to develop a truculent plot. The answer may lie in the play *La vida es sueño* (pr. 1635; *Life Is a Dream*, 1830) by the great Spanish dramatist of the Golden Age, Pedro Calderón de la Barca, the basic thesis of which is that the stars influence but do not determine an individual's life. So is the role of fate in *Don Álvaro*, where unfortunate coincidences provide opportunities for mishaps, but the real catalysts for violence and doom are the actions of the characters themselves. If society had not frowned on interracial marriages, Don Álvaro would not have been rejected as a suitor for the daughter of the Marquis of Calatrava; if the nobility were not so prejudiced and prideful, none of the incidents related in the play would have occurred. Saavedra has a message to convey, even though a simple one: Eliminate prejudice and intransigence in society, and all will attain a better life. The merit of the play goes beyond the presentation of a simple moral message. The masterful portraiture of the environment, the colorful description of characters and places, and the powerful and varied versification make *Don Álvaro* one of the highlights of European Romanticism.

Saavedra's dramatic career did not end with *Don Álvaro*. He wrote one more comedy in the neoclassical style, *El parador de Bailén*, and three dramas in the style of the Golden Age *comedias*. These three dramas, *Solaces de un prisionero*, *La morisca de Alajuar*, and *El crisol de la lealtad*, marked another shift in Saavedra's work, away from the purely Romantic format and closer to the traditions of Spanish theater.

El desengaño en un sueño

El desengaño en un sueño, the last of his major works, is a good example of the new dramatic route taken by Saavedra. This play is also written in the style of the Golden Age *comedias*, and it was loosely inspired by Calderón's *Life Is a Dream*, as well as a famous story by the fourteenth century writer Juan Manuel entitled "The Magician of Toledo." It is the only play by Saavedra without a historical background; perhaps this is the reason that he called it a "fantasy drama." Divided into three acts, it has an uncomplicated plot. Marcolán the magician and his son Lisardo live on a deserted island. Lisardo is a young man who feels trapped by the isolation of their domain. He asks his father to allow him to go into the outside world. Marcolán hesitates but finally consents. Before Lisardo's departure, Marcolán puts him into a trance and makes him experience, through dreams, life in the world. Lisardo is exposed to every emotion and feels the pain of love and rejection, the struggle for power, the darkness of evil, and the horror of treachery and false friendship. When he is about to be executed by his enemies, Lisardo yearns for the house of his father; his wish breaks the incantation, and he finds himself on the island, from which in reality he never departed. Lisardo has learned his lesson in his dreams and is content to remain on the island, protected from the vagaries of society and the outside world.

The tone of *El desengaño en un sueño* is melancholic, with the exception of the imaginary "action scenes," which become almost frantic in nature to underline the difference between the serenity of the island and the folly of the outside world. This play, rich in philosophical ideas, constitutes a fit closure to the work of Saavedra, a dramatist who led and participated in the shaping of drama in Spain for more than a generation, whose works reflect not only his own growth and development as a writer but also the development of literature in Spain during his lifetime.

OTHER MAJOR WORKS

POETRY: "El faro de Malta," 1828; *El moro expósito*, 1834; *Romances históricos*, 1841; *Leyendas*, 1854.

NONFICTION: *Sublevación de Nápoles, capitaneada por Masanielo*, 1848; *Breve reseña de la historia del reino de las dos Sicilias*, 1855.

MISCELLANEOUS: *Obras completas*, 1854-1855 (5 volumes).

BIBLIOGRAPHY

Lovett, Gabriel. *The Duke of Rivas*. Boston: Twayne, 1977. A basic look at the life and works of Saavedra, the duke of Rivas. Includes bibliography.

Peers, E. Allison. *A Short History of the Romantic Movement in Spain*. 1949. Reprint. New York: AMS Press, 1976. This reprint of the 1949 edition published by the Institute of Hispanic Studies in Liverpool, England, presents a look at Romanticism in Spain, touching on Saavedra. Bibliography and index.

Schurlknight, Donald E. *Spanish Romanticism in Context: Of Subversion, Contradiction, and Politics: Espronceda, Larra, Rivas, Zorrilla*. Lanham, Md.: University Press of America, 1998. Schurlknight examines Spanish Romanticism through the works of Saavedra (the duke of Rivas), José de Espronceda, Mariano José de Larra, and José Zorrilla. Bibliography and index.

Lina L. Cofresí

HANS SACHS

Born: Nuremberg (now in Germany); November 5, 1494

Died: Nuremberg (now in Germany); January 19, 1576

PRINCIPAL DRAMA

Der Henno, pr. 1531, pb. 1880

Der schwanger Bauer, pr. 1544, pb. 1580

Der fahrende Schüler im Paradies, pr. 1550, pb. 1880 (*The Traveling Scholar*, 1910)

Der Nasentanz, pr. 1550, pb. 1880

Der böse Raunch, pr. 1551, pb. 1880

Der fahrende Schüler mit dem Teufelsbannen, pr. 1551, pb. 1880

Das haiss Eisen, pr. 1551, pb. 1880 (*The Hot Iron*, 1910)

Das Kälberbrüten, pr. 1551, pb. 1880

Der Bauer im Fegefeuer, pr. 1552, pb. 1880

Der gestohlene Bachen, pr. 1552, pb. 1880

Der Bauer mit dem Blerr, pr. 1553, pb. 1880

Das böse Weib, pr. 1553, pb. 1880

Der Fortunato mit dem Wünschhuet, pr. 1553, pb. 1880

Der Kezermaister mit wort, würz und stain, pr. 1553, pb. 1880

Der Rossdieb zu Fünsing, pr. 1553, pb. 1880 (*The Horse Thief*, 1910)

Das Weib im Brunnen, pr. 1553, pb. 1880

Herzog Wilhelm von Österreich mit seiner Agaley, pr. 1555, pb. 1880

Das Fräulein mit dem Ölkrug, pr. 1556, pb. 1880

Hugo Schapler, pr. 1556, pb. 1880

Der hörnen Siegfried, pr. 1557, pb. 1880

Ptholomeus der Thirann, pr. 1557, pb. 1880

Cleopatra die Künigin Egipti, pr. 1558, pb. 1880

Romulus und Remus, die Brüder, pr. 1558, pb. 1880

Sämtliche Fastnachtspiele von Hans Sachs, pb. 1880-1887 (7 volumes)

Seven Shrovetide Plays, pb. 1930

Nine Carnival Plays by Hans Sachs, pb. 1990

Translations of the Carnival Comedies of Hans Sachs, 1494-1576, pb. 1994

OTHER LITERARY FORMS

In addition to writing sixty-one tragedies, sixty-five comedies, and eighty-one *Fastnachtspiele* (carnival plays), Hans Sachs was a popular poet. He was undoubtedly the most notable German poet during the first half of the sixteenth century. His literary production was enormous; Adalbert Keller, his principal bibliographer, indicates the number of his pieces of verse to be more than 4,275, with more than fifty thousand lines. Hans Sachs also wrote *Erzählungen* (tales), *Schwänke* (farces or amusing stories), and *Fabeln* (fables) in addition to his *Lieder* (songs) and *Gedichte* (poems).

That Sachs was touched by the stirring events of his age is seen in the fact that he wrote several impassioned poems on the brutality and menace of the Turks. For a time, his relationship with the Lutheran Reformation was an active participation. In 1523, he published his famous *Die wittenbergisch Nachtigall* (nightingale of Wittemberg), in which he lauded Martin Luther and criticized the corruption of the Roman Catholic Church. Later, he published a group of Reformation prose dialogues (his only works written in prose), including the well-known *Disputation zwischen einem Chorherren und einem Schuchmacher* (1524; dispute between a choirmaster and a shoemaker).

ACHIEVEMENTS

Hans Sachs, the Nuremberg "shoemaker-poet," has been acclaimed and immortalized by readers—for more than four hundred years—for his literary contributions. The general consensus of most readers, critics, and scholars of German literature is that great as his achievements were in all phases of German literature, Sachs's art is at its best in the *Fastnachtspiele*, or carnival plays.

Johann Wolfgang von Goethe, perhaps Germany's best-known author and dramatist, wrote on one occasion that Sachs was the true initiator of German secular drama. Composer Richard Wagner showed his obvious admiration by immortalizing Sachs in his opera entitled *Die Meistersinger von Nürnberg* (1868; the meistersinger of Nuremberg).

It must be remembered that in Germany, as elsewhere, popular drama grew out of church plays representing biblical events. In time, humorous actions or anecdotes were gradually introduced into the performances for the amusement of the people. Eventually, these bits of humorous anecdotes or episodes were lengthened—to the delight of the spectators—and were acted out as a separate unit or "one-act," as in the case of the *Fastnachtspiele*.

The genre existed before Sachs, but whereas previous playwrights had only hinted in form and substance, Sachs created imaginative and colorful plots that moved rapidly with unity and dramatic cohesiveness. He became the master in creating and bringing to the stage a variety of characters whose humorous antics were supported by comic dialogue. For example, all classes of society, from noble to vagabond, from priest to peasant, that might be considered representative of Germany in the sixteenth century, are presented in his plays. The customs, thoughts, fears, and ideals of the time are revealed both humorously and seriously. Although he is less a humorist of details than of amusing situations, he does not always work even the situations to their highest climax but leaves something to his readers' imagination, so that they, like he, may chuckle over the fun and imagine additional dimensions. As an artist, he does not take special pains to elaborate; rather, with his broad brush of humor, he paints the circumstances that he envisions. Like a wise and subtle teacher, instead of intimidating or offending any members of his audience, he instructs them by means of his plays, which in many cases serve almost as parables.

Sachs, who lived and wrote during the Reformation, was, as noted above, a staunch supporter of Martin Luther. As such, he delighted in poking fun at and even ridiculing the representatives of the Roman Catholic Church, depicting priests as avaricious, unscrupulous, and ignorant. To Sachs's credit, his comic farces may well have played a part in the religious reforms of the period.

Hans Sachs (Hulton Archive by Getty Images)

In the dramatic art of Sachs, there was something to suit everyone's taste. No other dramatist of that era has left a clearer picture of the times. The view is not a systematic one, and in many cases it is probably unintentional, but it is significant for German literature that Sachs saw fit to look around himself and present life as he observed and experienced it. Sachs wrote and thought as a man of the people. His Pegasus rarely soared over the lofty heights of Olympus, but he achieved something better: He used his genius to help, to teach, to make easier and more cheerful the lives of his contemporaries.

BIOGRAPHY

Hans Sachs was born six years before the end of the fifteenth century and lived until 1576. Sachs, the son of a tailor, began his schooling at the age of seven at one of the four Latin schools of Nuremberg. His teacher, Herr Friedel, taught him grammar, rhetoric, singing, and, later, some Latin. For eight years he remained in this school; this was the only formal schooling he ever received. At the age of seventeen, he embarked on his *Wanderjahre*. From Regensburg, where he first stopped and remained for two months, he went to Passau, and from there down the Inn River, via Braunau, Ried, and Wells, to Salzburg. Everywhere he interested himself not only in his training as a cobbler, but also in the life of the many people with whom he came in contact. During these formative years, his interest in literature, as well as people, grew rapidly. His earliest dated and preserved literary attempt was written in 1513. This was a *Buhlscheidlied* (love poem), in which he describes the pangs of separation from a beloved.

About this same time, he obtained a copy of the Augsburg edition of Heinrich Steinhöwels's translation of some of the stories in Giovanni Boccaccio's *Decameron: O, Prencipe Galetto*, (1349-1351; *The Decameron*, 1620). In 1514, Sachs continued his travels to Munich, then to Würzburg, Frankfurt am Main, Koblenz, Cologne, and to Leipzig, when, after a total of five years' absence, he returned to his native Nuremberg in 1516. He settled down to his lifework, shoemaking and writing—or rather writing and shoemaking, for undoubtedly writing was always foremost in his mind. On September 1, 1519, he married Kunigunde Kreuzer; of this marriage, seven children, two sons and five daughters, were born.

It was during these years that Martin Luther became the center and the cause of a violent religious upheaval in Germany. Luther's principal contention was that people are justified by faith alone and not by works. On the basis of this idea of a personal faith, he favored the abolition of many church rituals and challenged the supreme authority of the pope. Luther was excommunicated in 1521 and appeared before the Diet of Worms in that year, taking a firm stand on his views, and was subsequently put under the ban of the Holy Roman Empire.

Sachs for his part must have studied Luther's new doctrine and accepted its precepts, because he became an ardent disciple of the Augustinian reformer. Sachs wrote vigorously and profusely on the subject of religious reform, and it was through his writings that many people in Nuremberg were influenced to adopt the tenets of the Reformation.

The writings that Sachs produced from his youth to his middle age breathe a spirit of kindly humor, tranquillity, and contentment that betokens a happy life. In his fifties, however, he faced heavy trials: He lost his seven children and, in 1560, his wife. It was in this year that Nuremberg was decimated by an epidemic that swept away more than ten thousand people. One year and five months after the death of Kunigunde, Sachs took a second wife, a young girl by the name of Barbara Harscherin. Despite his advanced years (he was sixty-eight) and the wide disparity in their ages (Barbara was twenty-seven), this marriage, too, seems to have been happy.

There is something to be said for the age as well as for the man who, as a cobbler, could become a humanist, a poet, a musician, acquire a good library, learn Greek literature and philosophy, write four thousand poems, and live in health and happiness until he was eighty-two.

ANALYSIS

It has been said that melodrama is the quintessence of drama, and that farce is the quintessence of theater. One cannot imagine Hans Sachs perform-

ing melodramas, yet one can readily imagine him improvising, ad-libbing lines eclectically and at will. One can readily imagine him achieving instant attention and rapport with his audience by means of a smile or gesture—all to the certain delight of the beholders.

Indeed, Sachs holds a unique position in German literature. While his predecessors and some of his contemporaries continued writing along traditional lines, he, though not abandoning his literary heritage, found ways to breathe fresh life into his dramatic creations. Others of his time, and later, obviously admired him for his innovative drama and his contribution to European letters through a wealth of humor, variety, and encouragement of the evolution of the theater. The trend toward secularization and the emergence of a more literate society during the sixteenth century created a new tenor of life in Europe. It was the genius of Sachs to have captured and portrayed humorously the life of that time in a form that is accessible to audiences even today.

Sachs's literary production was enormous. His dramatic works alone include sixty-one tragedies, sixty-five comedies, and eighty-one *Fastnachtspiele*. The comedies and tragedies have been forgotten, perhaps justifiably; they are little more than epic-didactic dialogues or sometimes chronicles in verse. Sachs's great contribution to German as well as European literature rests with his *Fastnachtspiele*, or carnival plays.

It is important to realize the overall purpose for which the *Fastnachtspiele* was composed. It was written for performance on a feast day or, more specifically, for carnival or pre-Lent season. This fact necessarily conditioned and affected the overall tone as well as the individual characteristics of these German playlets. Taking into account the chaotic circumstances and the ebullient demands of the audience, the writers of *Fastnachtspiele*, perforce, developed and popularized an entertaining medium in keeping with the occasion. It was in a sense a medium that was, at the time, *sui generis*. Whereas the ordinary drama elicited spectator identification with the hero and his ideals, the farce presented ridiculous characters who afforded the spectators a feeling of superiority over the "heroes." Hence, in accord with the rhythm of the festival spirit, the carnival play was more intent on entertaining than instructing.

Sachs strove to create a drama that would be in keeping with the spirit of carnival. A rough, physical sense of humor, blunt language, and a forthright approach to reality characterize his one-act plays. The actions were based primarily on the desire to fulfill an immediate, elemental need. The tool of trade employed by Sachs as a catalyst to initiate action was generally a mischievous trick or bantering quarrel. The ensuing dramatic excitement then hinged on the success or failure of the contrived ruse or bicker. The spectator or reader was immediately caught up in the situation, curious to see whether the characters would be able to satisfy their particular wants or protect themselves from their enemies. Situations were necessarily uncomplicated, easily understood by all in a minimum amount of time.

In his endeavor to put on a "good show," Sachs used dramatic incidents from *The Decameron*, which inspired thirteen of his pieces. In some instances, Sachs adheres closely to his source, then again he adds and omits, cuts and concentrates, or rounds out and expands his material. His purpose was to assimilate his sources and rework them dramatically via strong, actable characters. His primary source for his plays, however, was the daily life that surrounded him. He captures dramatically and portrays humorously the people and preoccupations of his era: Coarse peasants, faults of the clergy, overbearing wives, vagabonds, and so on, all were threads in the fabric of sixteenth century customs and events. Indeed, it can be said unequivocally that Sachs contributes significantly to present-day knowledge of sixteenth century Germany through his character portrayal.

Of all the characters that are presented in Sachs's dramatic works, the most prevalent are the farmer or peasant, the priest, and the evil woman. Because of the ancient hostility between the townsman and the farmer, it is only to be expected that Sachs should treat the farmer as a comic figure. The town audience, composed largely of artisans, enjoyed any spectacle that held the peasant up to ridicule. Some of the farmers' names alone illustrate this point: Fridlein Zettenscheis (Freddie Dungheap), Herman Hirnlos (Herman Brainless), and Velle Mistfinch (Vail Pigpen).

The farmer was often crude and stupid, and these qualities were readily assimilated into the carnival plays. The farmer or peasant appears in thirty-one of the total eighty-one *Fastnachtspiele*. For example, one of the earliest plays, entitled *Der Nasentanz*, presents a ridiculous peasant contest to determine who among the farmers has the largest nose. Sachs's depiction of the fierce competitiveness of the peasants to win the "longest nose award" is representative of the humor of this genre. This particular play is also interesting from the standpoint of the framing technique employed by Sachs: He depicts an actual carnival scene as the main setting for the play itself.

DAS KÄLBERBRÜTEN

One of the most amusing portrayals of the peasant occurs in *Das Kälberbrüten*. While the wife is away at the market, Hans, who is supposedly "watching the place," decides, rather than tend to the chickens and livestock, to sleep. As a result of his negligence, their calf falls in the pond and drowns. To avoid angering his wife, Hans, as the title indicates, attempts to remedy his plight by brooding or hatching a new calf. Eventually, even the village priest is called in the hope of restoring Hans to his senses and to pull him from the barrel, where he insists on sitting to do his hatching. The scene in which the priest and wife pull him from the barrel, with its hilarious dialogue, proves to be as uproarious today as it must have been when it was originally performed.

DER BAUER MIT DEM BLERR

Der Bauer mit dem Blerr is a delightfully contrived example of the incredible naïveté of the peasant. Heinz, who surprises his wife in bed with the village priest, vows revenge. His wife, aided by a neighbor girlfriend, concocts a logical explanation for the whole "affair." Seeing is believing, but seeing through the early morning haze and dew is enough to distort, dim, and blur the vision of even those with perfect eyesight.

DER SCHWANGER BAUER

Der schwanger Bauer, one of Sachs's best-written pieces, brings the peasant motif to its apogee. It features Isaac, a quack physician who capitalizes on the credulity of the peasants. His "cure-all" is a purgative, which in its effect acts more as a killer than a cure. Isaac's diagnosis of the peasant Kunz's malady is that the poor fellow is pregnant with a foal. The purge and subsequent pranks set the tone for the complete comic devaluation of the credulous Kunz.

DER KEZERMAISTER MIT WORT, WÜRZ UND STAIN

As noted above, Sachs, a staunch supporter of Martin Luther, delighted in ridiculing the priesthood. It should be noted, however, that with all his satire of priests and their foibles, Sachs wrote only one play in which a direct attack on the Catholic Church itself was made, and even in this play the primary object of the satire is a particular inquisitor and not the entire institution. The play in question, *Der Kezermaister mit wort, würz und stain*, is also significant in that it gives tangible evidence of the waning Catholic influence in Reformation Germany. This phenomenon is attested by the fact that by 1553, when Sachs wrote this play, the threat of excommunication, formerly so feared by the people, had become material for comedy. The play says clearly what many people had previously dared only to think silently—that corruption and materialism were rampant within the Church.

DER GESTOHLENE BACHEN

Der gestohlene Bachen immediately starts off in the spirit of carnival. Heinz Knol enters, complaining of a hangover. He meets Guntz Drol, who relates that their miserly neighbor has just killed a pig. Herman, the miser, refuses to share the meat. Consequently, the two neighbors plot to steal the *Bachen*. The miser is subsequently told by the village priest that he will reveal the thief—via his black magic. In fact, the priest is privy to the plot and reveals his magic to his accomplices: For them, and for himself, he prepares leaves of ginger covered with sugar; for Herman, he has a leaf covered with aloe and dog manure. The one who cannot swallow the leaf is guilty. How Herman "the guilty" not only forgives them immediately but also gives them "quiet money," in addition to the ba-

con, illustrates the adeptness of Sachsian dramatic craftsmanship.

DAS WEIB IM BRUNNEN

In addition to poking fun at the foibles of the farmer and the self-interest of the clergy, Sachs also recited over and over again in his one-act plays the ever-popular theme of *Das böse Weib*—the crude, insolent, violent, spiteful, evil woman. In order to present in realistic fashion his thematic *böses Weib*, Sachs created women who were not only unfaithful but also violent and vicious. One of the most salient examples is entitled *Das Weib im Brunnen*. In this play, Steffano becomes suspicious that his wife has been deliberately getting him drunk every night in order to be free to go out and meet her lover. One night, he feigns drunkenness and sleep, and, when his wife stealthily leaves the house, he locks her out. When he refuses to let her in on her return, she screams and threatens to kill herself. Finally, in order to gain entrance to the house, she successfully contrives a trick that assures her readmittance and, consequently, serves as title to the play.

DAS BÖSE WEIB

The *Fastnachtspiele* entitled *Das böse Weib* portrays the type most often implied by the term *Das böse Weib*—a quarrelsome, nagging, suspicious, coarse, and violent housewife. The wife in this particular farce enters abruptly, rudely interrupting her maid and her husband's journeyman, who are engaging in innocent courtship. She accuses both, with no reason whatsoever, of gross immoral conduct. Their indignant self-defense only goads her on to more extensive and violent insults. In her rage, the wife fires the girl, and the two are almost on the point of blows in a dispute over back wages when the husband enters. The husband, seeking to calm the combatants, is immediately accused by his wife of being a "strawpartner" with the maid. A neighbor enters and serves to further incite action and sparks from the wife. The ending leaves no doubt in the mind of the spectator as to why a term such as "evil woman" is apropos for this character.

The motif of the destructive woman was very definitely in keeping with the ribald spirit of the carnival play. Here, as elsewhere, Sachs knew how to derive the maximum amount of theatricality from the barest of dramatic staging and preliminaries. Sachs realized that audience attention would immediately be obtained if the farmer, priest, or evil woman appeared onstage. The selection of these characters also reflects his ability as a dramatic artist to capture and portray the fabric of human activity during his age. Although simple in conception, such recurrent and timeless motifs are still enjoyed by German audiences as they were more than four hundred years ago.

OTHER MAJOR WORKS

SHORT FICTION: *Schlauraffenland*, 1530; *Sanct Peter mit der Geiss*, 1555; *Gespräch Sanct Peter mit den Landsknechten*, 1556; *Schwank von dem frommen Adel*, 1562; *Der Schneider mit dem Pannier*, 1563.

POETRY: *Die wittenbergisch Nachtigall*, 1523.

NONFICTION: *Disputation zwischen einem Chorherren und einem Schuchmacher*, 1524.

BIBLIOGRAPHY

Aylett, Robert, and Peter Skrine, eds. *Hans Sachs and Folk Theatre in the Late Middle Ages: Studies in the History of Popular Culture.* Lewiston, N.Y.: Edwin Mellen Press, 1995. A study of Sachs and the popular theater of Germany that contains information on the staging of his works. Bibliography.

Beare, Mary, ed. *Hans Sachs: Selections.* Durham, England: University of Durham, 1983. The preface and introduction to this collection of poetic works by Sachs provide details of Sachs's life and critical analysis of his works. Bibliography.

Bernstein, Eckhard. "Hans Sachs." In *German Writers of the Renaissance and Reformation, 1280-1580*, edited by James Hardin and Max Reinhart. Vol. 179 in *Dictionary of Literary Biography.* Detroit, Mich.: The Gale Group, 1997. A concise overview of the life and works of Sachs.

Randall W. Listerman

HOWARD SACKLER

Born: New York, New York; December 19, 1929
Died: Ibiza, Spain; October 14, 1982

PRINCIPAL DRAMA

Uriel Acosta, pr. 1954

A Few Enquiries, wr. 1959, pr. 1965, pb. 1970 (4 one-acts: *Sarah, The Nine O'Clock Mail, Mr. Welk and Jersey Jim, Skippy*)

Mr. Welk and Jersey Jim, pr. 1960, pb. 1970 (one act)

The Yellow Loves, pr. 1960

The Pastime of Monsieur Robert, pr. 1966

The Great White Hope, pr. 1967, pb. 1968

Semmelweiss, pr. 1977

Goodbye Fidel, pr. 1980

OTHER LITERARY FORMS

In addition to his book of poetry, *Want My Shepherd* (1954), Howard Sackler wrote numerous screenplays, including *Desert Padre* (1950), *Fear and Desire* (1953), *A Midsummer Night's Dream* (1961), *The Great White Hope* (1970), *Bugsy* (1973), *Gray Lady Down* (1978; with James Whittaker and Frank P. Rosenberg), *Jaws II* (1978; with Carl Gottlieb and Dorothy Tristan), and *Saint Jack* (1979; with Paul Theroux and Peter Bogdanovich). *The Nine O'Clock Mail* was also televised, in 1965.

ACHIEVEMENTS

Although the triple prizes for *The Great White Hope* (the Pulitzer Prize, the New York Drama Critics Circle Award, and a Tony Award) were the highlight of Howard Sackler's career, they were by no means his first achievements. He had earlier received the Maxwell Anderson Award for his verse play *Uriel Acosta*, as well as Rockefeller Foundation and Littauer Foundation grants for work in his early twenties. A prolific director, especially of classical and verse plays, Sackler founded and became director of Caedmon Records in 1953, where he worked with the great British and American actors and authors whose work is now preserved in the Caedmon series. Sackler was busily employed in directing projects and screenwriting when, with *The Great White Hope*, he found the mature epic verse form that worked better onstage than any verse form since Maxwell Anderson's. His contribution to American drama lies in the size and scope of his vision, his meticulous research on historical subjects and personalities, and the grace and rhythms of his language. After *The Great White Hope*, Sackler succeeded in the form with *Semmelweiss*, a harrowing study of the nineteenth century physician who discovered that examining doctors were spreading infection among their patients and who was ostracized and broken for his trouble. Because of production problems outside the

script itself, *Semmelweiss* was not produced on Broadway; nevertheless, it remains one of the finest plays in modern dramatic literature. In 1980, Sackler's last Broadway play, *Goodbye Fidel*, closed after poor reviews. At his death, Sackler was working on "Klondike," a Gold Rush comedy.

BIOGRAPHY

Born on December 19, 1929, in the Bronx, Howard Sackler attended Brooklyn College, earning the bachelor of arts degree in 1950. A natural writer, Sackler wrote verse, publishing in respected poetry journals such as *The Hudson Review* and *Poetry*; his early work was gathered in *Want My Shepherd* and published by Caedmon in 1954. Combining his interest in the theater with his verse writing, Sackler wrote *Uriel Acosta*, for which he received the Maxwell Anderson Award in 1954. His tendency was always to

Howard Sackler, right, with James Earl Jones. (Courtesy of the New York Public Library)

look to historical settings for his plays; after his success with *Uriel Acosta*, about a Portuguese Jew in the generation before Baruch Spinoza, Sackler looked at the life of the French poet Tristan Corbière. The play, his first in prose, won the Sergel Award in 1959 and marked the beginning of his interest in nineteenth century health practices, which was to find its best voice in *Semmelweiss*. While building his playwriting career, Sackler founded Caedmon Records, which provided his livelihood as he built a reputation for screenwriting. Another career, in directing, took him to the New School for Social Research, where readings of several poetic plays augmented his growing number of recordings of William Shakespeare's plays at Caedmon, with such notable voices as those of Paul Scofield, Albert Finney, and Dame Edith Evans. Sackler's next venture into live theater came with *A Few Enquiries*, four one-act plays separate in setting and characters but joined in their thematic investigation of human contact and the need of the individual to find his place in a larger community. His mature work continued this investigation in more elaborate forms.

All Sackler's experiences came together in 1967, with *The Great White Hope*, the meticulously researched and carefully structured epic dramatization of the life of Jack Jefferson (based on the career of heavyweight champion Jack Johnson). The play earned for Sackler international recognition when it received the Pulitzer Prize, the New York Drama Critics Circle Award, and a Tony Award in 1969. By 1970, Sackler had turned his work into a highly successful screenplay, starring the actors who had appeared in the stage version: James Earl Jones as Jack Jefferson, and Jane Alexander, who had played Ellie Bachman, Jefferson's white mistress. Partly because of his busy screenwriting career and partly because of his insistence on very careful research into each of his historical plays, it was not until 1977 that Sackler offered his next stage work, *Semmelweiss*, which opened in Buffalo, New York, but did not reach Broadway. Sackler's last Broadway play, *Goodbye Fidel*, which opened in 1980, closed quickly after unfavorable reviews. *The New Yorker* praised it, however, saying, "So many roles and settings give the play a

welcomely old-fashioned air of amplitude, even of extravagance; we sense that the playwright has shared the novelist's luxurious privilege of inventing an abundance of characters and then letting them wander wherever they will." At his death, from pulmonary thrombosis, in Ibiza, Spain, on October 14, 1982, Sackler was near the finish of yet another major historical play, "Klondike," about the Alaskan Gold Rush. Sackler's papers are in the archives of the Humanities Research Center, University of Texas, Austin.

ANALYSIS

The quality that Howard Sackler brought to his historical subjects is not a simpleminded romanticism but rather an underlying universality of emotions that connects the past with his audience's immediate responses. These plays are more than well-researched panoramas of a time gone by; the point of Sackler's portraits is that these times are never gone, that the anguish and the joys one feels have been present in every history.

SARAH

No better example of everything Sackler tried to do in his work is available than the first play in the four-play collection, *A Few Enquiries*, entitled *Sarah*. A coroner, his assistant, some witnesses, and the mother of the victim of a tragic accident are gathered backstage in a ballet theater to reenact the circumstances of the awful event: A promising young ballerina perished when her costume caught fire from the gaslights during a performance. The businesslike voice of the coroner, the subdued retelling of the witnesses, the monosyllabic responses of the mother— all make a music of their own, to which the understudy dances, acting out the tragic events, to the very moment of the stagehand's feeble attempts to extinguish the flaming dress with his hands (now bandaged), a slow pantomime observed clinically by some and with emotion by others. The final cries of anguish by the mother of Sarah, the victim, echoing in the bare theater, bring the incident out of the mid-Victorian past (it was based on a real incident) into the dramatic present. The effect is emblematic of Sackler's writing gifts, which came to maturity in his Pulitzer Prize-winning *The Great White Hope*.

THE GREAT WHITE HOPE

The episodic treatment (nineteen scenes in three acts) of Jack Jefferson's career gives *The Great White Hope* the epic scope necessary to depict not only the character but also his era and his world. On one level, the play is a portrait of the times, when America was adolescent in its attitudes toward racial prejudice, civil rights, and the free enterprise system at work in the sports industry. The crowd scenes, effectively designed, focus the action where it belongs, not on the prizefights themselves (all occurring offstage) but on those waiting for the results of their wagers. Jefferson is the kind of gladiator who is envied to destruction, not because of his strength but because of his penetration of the folly and hypocrisy of the games he is forced to dignify with his talent. In the scenes with Ellie, his lover, one sees Jefferson preparing for his real fight, against a society that will not let him be simply a man but that demands that he live out the symbolic function it has assigned to him. His eventual and inevitable defeat in Cuba is anticlimactic in relation to his loss of Ellie, and by the time he emerges from the ring, bloody and dazed, he has already understood the fact that there is to be no refuge for him from humankind's indifference and exploitation.

SEMMELWEISS

The same pattern in a different setting is found in *Semmelweiss*. This time the fighter is the nineteenth century physician Ignaz Philipp Semmelweiss, and the indifferent and envious crowd is the closed-minded medical community, which refuses to treat seriously his hospital sanitation reforms. Without reducing the story to cheap symbolism, Sackler uses the diseases of the body, as revealed in the autopsy rooms of a government hospital for the poor, as external manifestations of the more insidious diseases of indifference, inhumanity, hypocrisy, and ambition that prevent the doctors and their student interns from experiencing and putting into practice the humanitarian principles of their profession. After risking his medical career by challenging the examination practices of his superiors in a maternity ward, Semmelweiss retreats to a safe marriage, not from cowardice but from helplessness. In the climactic scene, a lecture in which he purposely infects himself, the metaphor equating the infected patient with the corrupt medical profession is brought home in the most astounding image since the engine room scene from Eugene O'Neill's *The Hairy Ape* (pr. 1922). Driven mad by the self-inflicted infection, going blind among his plants, Semmelweiss agonizingly repeats the oath of medicine by which he tried to live but which has destroyed him. In the final, silent scene, a new group of interns begin their examination on a new anonymous cadaver, but it is the body of Semmelweiss they uncover, lying on the slab as though admonishing them from another world.

GOODBYE FIDEL

In Sackler's last Broadway play, *Goodbye Fidel*, the *mise en scène* is Cuba at the dawn of the Castro regime, and the characters are members of the privileged upper class, the jet set whose lives are disrupted by the new strength of the common people. Here the usually successful technique of embodying the ills of the world in the personal story of one man or woman falls short of Sackler's ambitions, primarily because, in an attempt to avoid oversimplification, he shows both sides of the economic and political struggle with equal strength and clarity. The central figure, Natalia, a beautiful woman forced by Fidel Castro to give up not only her lifestyle but also her clandestine affair with an attaché, is not a heroine in the easily recognizable mold. Her "tragedy" is more obscure; because it was difficult to sympathize with the idle rich being suddenly disenfranchised, first-night critics failed to see the love story and the private anguish lying inside the external political situation of the play. Natalia, too, however, has fought with considerable bravery against the danger of self-pity and nostalgia in which a lesser person would find refuge. She has lost her home, her friends, her lover, her child, her security, her sense of place. In the face of these losses, she dances a brave little dance, head held high.

OTHER MAJOR WORKS

POETRY: *Want My Shepherd*, 1954.

SCREENPLAYS: *Desert Padre*, 1950; *Fear and Desire*, 1953; *A Midsummer Night's Dream*, 1961; *The*

Great White Hope, 1970; *Bugsy*, 1973; *Gray Lady Down*, 1978 (with James Whittacker and Frank P. Rosenberg); *Jaws II*, 1978 (with Carl Gottlieb and Dorothy Tristan); *Saint Jack*, 1979 (with Paul Theroux and Peter Bogdanovich).

BIBLIOGRAPHY

Funke, Lewis. "Howard Sackler." In *Playwrights Talk About Writing: Twelve Interviews with Lewis Funke.* Chicago: Dramatic Publishing, 1975. Sackler's interview is prefaced with a summary of his professional accomplishments and a brief biography. He discusses his working habits, sources of inspiration, and the relationship between his work as a director and his work as a writer. He interprets *The Great White Hope* and *The Pastime of Monsieur Robert*, distinguishing these dramas from history, and offers opinions on drama in general.

Gill, Brendan. "Passing Losses On." Review of *Goodbye Fidel*, by Howard Sackler. *The New Yorker* 46 (May 5, 1980): 109-110. *Goodbye Fidel*, a play about upper-class Cubans who deal with changes in their lives between 1958 and 1962, suggests the richness of a novel with its large cast and historical subject. Sackler's attempt, however, to parallel the quarrels between the lovers Natalia and James Sinclair with political events is not convincing. The play closed four days after it opened.

Kroll, Jack. "The Champ." Review of *The Great White Hope*, by Howard Sackler. *Newsweek*, December 25, 1967, 73. Both strengths and weaknesses were found in the epic quality of *The Great White Hope* performed at the Arena Stage in Washington, D.C. Although the play is too long, too ambitious, and somewhat unfocused, some episodes attained real power through Edwin Sherin's direction and James Earl Jones and Jane Alexander's performances. It is the most successful use of sports in drama since Clifford Odets's *Golden Boy* (pr., pb. 1937).

Novick, Julius. "Tragic Cakewalk." Review of *The Great White Hope*, by Howard Sackler. *The Nation* 206 (January 15, 1968): 93-94. The choice of the Arena Stage to produce *The Great White Hope* fulfilled the conviction of the theater's founder, Zelda Fichandler, that drama must appeal to a broad spectrum of people through the presentation of plays that deal with current social problems. In this play, Sackler realizes the significance of his historical subject and presents it in powerful human terms.

Pressley, Nelson. "The Good Fight." *American Theatre* 17, no. 8 (October, 2000): 28-32. Pressley uses the occasion of the Arena Stage's revival of *The Great White Hope* to analyze the drama and both productions, as well as the significance of Sackler's play.

Trousdale, Marion. "Ritual Theatre: *The Great White Hope*." *Western Humanities Review* 23 (1969): 295-303. The performances of *The Great White Hope* at the Arena Stage (Washington, D.C.) and in New York were profoundly different. Those at the Arena Stage were characterized by ritualistic qualities, achieving Aristotle's definition of drama—the imitation of an action by means of an action. By contrast, the New York production reduced the play to a simple antiracist message.

Weber, Bruce. "A Washington Company Revisits a Shining Moment From a Decidedly Different Era." Review of *The Great White Hope*, by Preston Jones. *The New York Times*, September 14, 2000, p. E1. Weber presents a favorable review of the Arena Stage's revival of *The Great White Hope*.

Thomas J. Taylor,
updated by Frank Ardolino

LUIS RAFAEL SÁNCHEZ

Born: Humacao, Puerto Rico; November 17, 1936

PRINCIPAL DRAMA

La espera, pr. 1959

"Cuento de cucarachita viudita," wr. 1959

Farsa del amor compradito, pb. 1960

Los ángeles se han fatigado, pb. 1960 (*The Angels Are Exhausted*, 1964, 1973)

La hiel nuestra de cada día, pr. 1962, pb. 1976 (*Our Daily Bitterness*, 1964)

Casi el alma: Auto da fe en tres actos, pr. 1964, pb. 1966 (*A Miracle for Maggie*, 1974)

La pasión según Antígona Pérez, pr., pb. 1968 (*The Passion According to Antígona Pérez*, 1968; also known as *The Passion of Antígona Pérez*, 1971)

Teatro de Luis Rafael Sánchez, pb. 1976 (includes *Los ángeles se han fatigado*, *Farsa del amor compradito*, and *La hiel nuestra de cada día*)

Quíntuples, pr. 1984, pb. 1985 (*Quintuplets*, 1984)

OTHER LITERARY FORMS

Renowned in Puerto Rico as a dramatist, Luis Rafael Sánchez is better known on the American mainland as a novelist. His first novel, *La guaracha del Macho Camacho* (1976; *Macho Camacho's Beat*, 1980) brought him immediate recognition on the mainland. Through the novel's characters—Senator Vicente Reinosa, a sleazy politician in league with mainland business interests; his wife, Graciela, who is frigid and grossly materialistic; his mulatto mistress, China Hereje and her retarded son, the Nene; and his son Benny who cares about little but the Ferrari sports car that he uses as a sexual object in which to masturbate—Sánchez projects a jaundiced gaze at the Puerto Rico of the 1970's. His depiction is unvarnished and realistic, but his manner of telling his story, rather than its content, is what distinguishes it. Sánchez eschews conventional notions of narration and plot development, preferring instead to present fragmented glimpses of each character, darting from character to character and back again. This novel has been compared stylistically to James Joyce's *Ulysses* (1922) and Virginia Woolf's *Mrs. Dalloway* (1925). His second novel, *La importancia de llamarse Daniel Santos* (1988; the importance of being Daniel Santos), again stresses the political tensions rife in Puerto Rico.

Sánchez has produced a volume of short stories, *En cuerpo de camisa: Cuentos* (1966, rev. 1971; shirt sleeves unbuttoned), which has gone into several expanded editions. His nonfictional *Fabulación e ideología en la cuentística de Emilio S. Belavel* (1979) deals with problems unique to Puerto Rico and its relationship both to its Spanish heritage and to U.S. domination.

ACHIEVEMENTS

Luis Rafael Sánchez gained recognition while still a student at the University of Puerto Rico. His play, *La espera*, written for an undergraduate playwriting class, received an honorable mention from the Puerto Rican Ateneo in 1958 and was performed the following year. In 1959, he received a prize for his children's play, "Cuento de cucarahita viudita." The university granted him a fellowship that enabled him to attend Columbia University in New York City to study theater arts and creative writing for a year.

Following the publication of *Macho Camacho's Beat*, Sánchez's literary fortunes improved markedly. In 1979, he was awarded a Guggenheim Fellowship. In 1983, he was a guest scholar at the Woodrow Wilson Center in Washington, D.C. In 1985, he spent a year as a guest writer in Berlin thanks to a grant from the Deutscher Akademischer Austrauschdienst-Berliner Kunstler Programm. He also served as a visiting professor at the City University of New York in 1988 and at The Johns Hopkins University in 1989.

Sánchez also held a distinguished professorship at the University of Puerto Rico at Río Piedras. Upon retirement, he was granted emeritus status both by the University of Puerto Rico and the City University of New York.

BIOGRAPHY

Luis Rafael Sánchez, born on November 17, 1936, spent his first sixteen years in Humacao, at that time a city of fewer than eight thousand people on the Humacao River near the ocean in eastern Puerto Rico. Born to working-class parents, Sánchez received his early education in the local schools of Humacao. In his early teens, he wanted to reconsider and reorder his concept of reality. To do this, he realized that he would need to write, so he started to perfect his writing skills.

In 1948, with the industrialization and urbanization of Puerto Rico, Sánchez's parents moved to San Juan, where Luis attended secondary school and later the University of Puerto Rico at Río Piedras, majoring in theater studies. Here his two earliest plays were performed. The university fellowship that sent him to Columbia University made it possible for him to experience firsthand a broad spectrum of live, professional drama.

Upon graduation from the University of Puerto Rico, Sánchez acted in soap operas before he returned to the campus to teach theater studies in the university's experimental high school. He attributes some of his facility in writing and in capturing the idiom of common people to his work in soap operas.

In the early 1960's, the university offered to support Sánchez's return to the United States to study for a master's degree. He attended New York University where he majored in Spanish literature, receiving the master of arts degree in 1963. Returning to San Juan, he taught Spanish at the main campus of the University of Puerto Rico at Río Piedras. Sánchez soon returned to Columbia University to work toward a doctorate, but he did not stay long and did not complete his doctoral studies. Instead, he went to Spain where, in 1973, he earned the doctorate in literature at the University of Madrid. Returning to Puerto Rico, he was appointed professor of literature at the Río Piedras campus of the university.

The publication of *La guaracha del Macho Camacho* in Buenos Aires in 1976 and the subsequent publication of its translation, *Macho Camacho's Beat*, in the United States in 1980 clearly established Sánchez as a writer of international scope. This resulted in Sánchez's receiving support for his writing from the Guggenheim Foundation and receiving many accolades that celebrated his outstanding achievements as a writer. He has been praised especially for his ability to capture the neobaroque language and cadences of popular Puerto Rican speech and to create a rhythmic, sometimes rhyming prose that is truly unique.

ANALYSIS

The major work of Luis Rafael Sánchez represents a shift from the euphemistic writing of René Marqués, Puerto Rico's most celebrated writer of the 1950's, although his early writing was somewhat in the Marqués tradition. As he moved toward developing the style that was to distinguish most of his work and set him apart from earlier Puerto Rican writers, rather than writing with the sort of restraint that characterized much of Marqués's work, Sánchez employed overstatement, developing a grotesque, hyperbolic style that he used to satirize the political system of the island. In considering his writing, one must remember that a great deal of his writing is parody. He convincingly recreates the language that is part of the carnival tradition. He fashions his language around what he has called *la poética de lo soez* (the poetics of the low).

Sánchez creates a carnival milieu that allows him through farce to deal directly with the ills generated by political colonialism. This technique is apparent particularly in *Quintuplets*, although it exists also in *Farsa del amor compradito* (the farce of love's bargain), *The Passion According to Antígona Pérez*, and *The Angels Are Exhausted*, as well as in Sánchez's two novels, *Macho Camacho's Beat* and *La importancia de llamarse Daniel Santos*, and in many of his short stories.

Even though his writing is fraught with political commentary and criticism, both of the Spanish colonialism that early beset Puerto Rico and of the island's postcolonialism during the period of its political rule by the United States, this serious commentary is always leavened with Sánchez's unrelenting humor and with a genuine love for the light-hearted atmosphere that is present in the island and its people. In all of his writing, Sánchez's warm attachment to Puerto Rico and to Puerto Ricans is apparent.

Sánchez is fundamentally concerned with those on the fringes of mainstream society. This is clear in his collection of fifteen short stories, *En cuerpo de camisa*, which are peopled with prostitutes, the unemployed homeless, drug addicts, and gays. In these stories, as in much of Sánchez's other work, language is displaced in depicting the socially bizarre and the grotesque. The physical activities of his characters—eating, having sex, mingling socially—demonstrate their lowness, but the depiction is nonjudgmental and tempered with humor that evolves from language rather than from situation, as is the case in the best comic writing.

A Miracle for Maggie

This ironic and cynical play focuses on two sleazy people who, quite lacking in faith, became the founders of a religion called Dios Sociedad Anónima (God, Inc.). *A Miracle for Maggie* deals with the hypocrisy and irony of creating faith from an absence of faith. The objective is, obviously, to exploit whatever innocent, ignorant people these two renegades can attract. Sánchez likes to present such ironies, as he does, for example, in his story *La guagua aérea* (the flying bus), in which a Puerto Rican, asked from where in Puerto Rico she comes, responds, "New York," suggesting that the invaded has invaded the invader.

Besides making a sociopolitical statement, this play, through its inventive use of the neobaroque language of the masses, captures the essence of what the masses are like. The language is rhythmic and crude, but, at times, poetic. It generally evokes laughter, which successfully moderates the serious message of the play.

The Passion According to Antígona Pérez

Despite its obvious reference to Sophocles and to the Oedipus trilogy, none of the major figures in this play rise to the stature of Antigone, although Sánchez explores in the work questions of loyalty and blind obedience to power. *The Passion According to Antígona Pérez* had its premier at the theater festival of the Institute of Puerto Rican Culture in 1968 and had an immediate appeal to Puerto Rican audiences. It was translated into English and taken on tour by the Puerto Rican Traveling Theater. Thousands of Latin Americans saw it as well as citizens of the United States and Canada.

The play struck a responsive chord in Latin American audiences because it focused on destructive Latin American dictatorships. The play, set in a fictional banana republic in Latin America, appears to have taken particular aim at the dictatorships of Fidel Castro in Cuba and of Rafael Leonidas Trujillo Molina in the Dominican Republic, although this seeming emphasis may be coincidental.

Quintuplets

This play, like *A Miracle for Maggie*, is written for two performers, but in this case, each performer plays several roles. Critics have said that it is necessary to consult one's playbill to make sure that only two performers are involved because each one acts so convincingly in the variety of roles undertaken. Sánchez has called the play a parody of suspense comedy. It is played as a family vaudeville act that, in the course of its unfolding, comments sociopolitically and philosophically on what it means to act and what it means to produce drama.

The play is acted out before the delegates at a Conference on Family Affairs. The participants, the Morrison Quintuplets and their father, each occupy one of the play's six acts, presenting a monologue that details his or her perceptions of what it is to be a member of the Morrison family. According to Sánchez's directions, each member of the family improvises his or her part in a vaudevillian style. The play is heavy with stage directions that themselves offer commentary on the meaning of acting and of drama. The play comments stingingly on patriarchy and, indirectly, on the paternalism of the United States toward Puerto Rico, a topic that Sánchez injects into most of his writing.

Among the Morrisons, Dafne is cast as a bombshell, radiant in a provocative red dress. She rejects traditional femininity but adopts the mask of femininity. In contrast is Bianca, whose sexual identity is not clearly revealed, although it is suggested that she has lesbian tendencies. All three Morrison boys are named Ifigenio, so they adopt names that distinguish them from each other: Baby and Mandrake are particularly telling among these assumed names.

The father, Papá Morrison, referred to as El Gran Semental (the great stud), is viewed quite differently by each of the quintuplets. For Dafne, he represents perfection and is to be emulated. For Mandrake, he is the competition as a performer but also in an Oedipal sense. Bianca considers him a controlling, domineering patriarchal archetype. Baby, the least secure of the quintuplets, sees his father as someone whose example he can never live up to no matter how hard he tries.

Quintuplets is, aside from *Macho Camacho's Beat*, Sánchez's most fully realized and successful work to date. It has been performed before enthusiastic audiences in the United States, throughout Latin America, and in Spain.

OTHER MAJOR WORKS

LONG FICTION: *La guaracha del Macho Camacho*, 1976 (*Macho Camacho's Beat*, 1980); *La importancia de llamarse Daniel Santos*, 1988.

SHORT FICTION: *En cuerpo de camisa: Cuentos*, 1966, rev. 1971.

NONFICTION: *Fabulación e ideología en la cuentística de Emilio S. Belavel*, 1979; *No llores por nosotros, Puerto Rico*, 1997.

BIBLIOGRAPHY

Flores, Angel, ed. *Spanish American Writers: The Twentieth Century*. New York: H. W. Wilson, 1992. This brief overview of Sánchez's work will be helpful to the beginner. It touches on most of the author's major writing, although it does not discuss it in depth.

Gazarian Gautier, Marie-Lise. *Interviews with Latin American Writers*. Elmwood Park, Ill.: The Dalkey Archive Press, 1989. Sánchez discusses the sociopolitical orientation of his writing, emphasizing the often strained relationship between his native Puerto Rico and the United States. Contains some interesting comments on the course that his dramatic writing has followed.

Perivolaris, John Dimitri. *Puerto Rican Cultural Identity and the Work of Luis Rafael Sánchez*. Chapel Hill: University of North Carolina Press, 2000. Perivolaris is fundamentally concerned with the sociopolitical aspects of Sánchez's writing. He offers perceptive readings of some of the more important prose fiction Sánchez has produced, but he has much less to say about the plays, save for his illuminating chapter on *Quintuplets*.

Sorrentino, Gilbert. "The Frenetic Pulse of Puerto Rico." *Book World-The Washington Post*, February 8, 1981, p. 3. Although Sorrentino's discussion is largely of Sánchez's *Macho Camacho's Beat*, his grasp of the politics of what Sánchez generally writes about is impressive and useful.

R. Baird Shuman

SONIA SANCHEZ

Born: Birmingham, Alabama; September 9, 1934

PRINCIPAL DRAMA

The Bronx Is Next, pb. 1968, pr. 1970
Sister Son/ji, pb. 1969, pr. 1972
Dirty Hearts, pb. 1973
Uh Huh; But How Do It Free Us?, pb. 1974, pr. 1975
Malcolm Man/Don't Live Here No Mo', pr. 1979

I'm Black When I'm Singing, I'm Blue When I Ain't, pr. 1982
Black Cats Back and Uneasy Landings, pr. 1995

OTHER LITERARY FORMS

Sonia Sanchez's literary reputation rests primarily on her poetry. She has published more than ten volumes of poetry, beginning with *Homecoming* in 1969; had her poems included in numerous anthologies; and edited several poetry anthologies. She sees her plays as an extension of her poetic art, saying that their longer form gives her more room to express her ideas. She has written short stories, children's books, essays, literary criticism, and social commentary. She has an impressive record as a university teacher and political activist and has been a driving force behind the movement to include writings by African American authors in the college curriculum. She frequently gives public readings, performances that are noted for their dramatic power and include music, drum beats, and chanting. Some of her best-known works were inspired by the Black Arts movement of the 1960's, and her later writings have continued to focus on African American themes.

ACHIEVEMENTS

The work of Sonia Sanchez has been widely recognized by both the literary establishment and the public. Her early poetry earned a PEN Writing Award (1969), a grant from the National Institute of Arts and Letters (1970), and a National Endowment for the Arts award (1978-1979). She has received recognition for her commitment to teaching and to social activism from community organizations including the Black Students of Smith College (1982), the Mayor's Commission for Women in Philadelphia (1987), and the Young Men's Christian Association (YMCA) Women Pioneers Hall of Fame (1992). She won a PEN fellowship in the Arts (1993-1994) and was given the Legacy Award from Jomandi Productions (1995). She has been a distinguished poet-in-residence at Spelman College and was awarded an honorary doctorate by Wilberforce University.

BIOGRAPHY

Sonia Sanchez was born in Birmingham, Alabama, in 1934, as Wilsonia Benita Driver. When Sanchez was one year old, her mother died in childbirth. She and her sister were cared for by her grandmother, a woman whom Sanchez has celebrated in her poetry. This grandmother died when Sanchez was five years old, an event she says traumatized her. For several years she and her sister were passed around among relatives. She has described herself as a shy, introspective child who stuttered.

When she was nine years old, her father remarried and moved the family to New York City, where Sanchez was introduced to the African American heritage of Harlem, a culture that has had a strong influence on her work. She graduated from Hunter College in 1955 with a degree in political science. Although she had read the work of African American poets in school in the South, the encouragement of librarians and a visit to the Schomburg Library, a black culture museum, opened her eyes to the history of slavery and to the works of other African American writers. Sanchez did graduate work in poetry with Louise Bogan at New York University, who she says taught her the craft of poetry.

In the 1960's she became politically active. During the Civil Rights movement, Sanchez was an integrationist, believing that blacks and whites shared cultural values and could work together for social justice. However, after listening to Malcolm X, she rejected the white world and began writing out of her black identity. Despite criticism from her friends and family, she adopted a natural hairstyle and joined the Nation of Islam, a religious organization she later abandoned after political differences with its leaders. Her first book of poetry, *Homecoming*, was a celebration of militant blackness, written in the language of urban street culture for an audience of African Americans. She was followed and arrested by the Federal Bureau of Investigation for her work as a social activist.

Sanchez has supported herself through a series of academic appointments, beginning at San Francisco State College in 1966 and including the University of Pittsburgh, Rutgers University, City College of New York, Amherst College, University of Pennsylvania, and Temple University. She initiated the black studies movement, a drive to include African American literature in the college curriculum, in 1966 at San Francisco State College. At the University of Pittsburgh, she taught the first seminar on literature written by black women. She believes that teachers are responsible for transmitting the legacy of the past and for creating social change and is widely acclaimed as a teacher. In both her teaching and writing, Sanchez emphasizes that African Americans must refuse to see themselves as victims and must develop the self-confidence to survive in a white world that oppresses them. Her books for children promote positive self-images. She has militantly opposed drugs in the black community and sees literacy and education as the hope for the future. She believes that African Americans have a personal responsibility for self-development but must move beyond this to a larger commitment as members of the black community.

Sanchez is a prodigious worker. While raising her three children—Anita, Morani Neusi, and Mungu Neusi—and fulfilling her duties as a college professor, she continued to write in longhand from midnight to three o'clock in the morning. When asked why she writes, she responded, "I write because I must. I write because it keeps me going. I have not killed anyone in America because I write." Literary critics have said that her poetry is based on the African oral tradition, in which the poet is a source of history, instruction, and inspiration. She is gratified that white audiences have come to appreciate her work but says that she writes for herself and for an African American audience.

The reputations of many of the revolutionary poets of the Black Arts movement have faded, but Sanchez has continued to grow in her craft and attract new audiences. Although she sees writing as an instrument of political and social change, most critics agree that her artistic craft is not compromised by her beliefs.

ANALYSIS

Sonia Sanchez's strong political views have created controversy surrounding her work among both black and white audiences. Her plays are revolutionary in their content and in their blunt language describing the evils of racism. Her characters often speak in the profane language of urban black English, shocking readers and playgoers. Her exploration of the oppression of black women by black men is a constant theme in her drama, often drawing the criticism of the black community. Her views, however, are not traditionally feminist, as her central theme is the evil of racism. As in all her writing, her plays stress the responsibility of the members of the Afri-

can American community to love themselves and one another as a way of transcending racism. She has attempted to bridge the gap between the elite world of academia and the reality of the black experience in the United States.

Sanchez's plays are an outgrowth and extension of her poetic craft. She calls on her heritage from black music: blues, jazz, and gospel. Her dialogue is innovative in its typography and rhythm and rejects traditional spelling and capitalization (for example, "blk" and "u" for "black" and "you"). The language of white people, she believes, is a form of oppression. While Sanchez is skilled in playing with words and can express herself in a variety of forms, including traditional English prose and poetry and Japanese haiku, in both her poetry and drama she rejects "Eurocentric" language and traditions. She has moved away from her use of vulgarity in her earlier plays toward a more loving, spiritual expression, and her later work in poetry seems less angry, although it still has strong political content.

THE BRONX IS NEXT

Sanchez's first brief play was, she says, a condemnation of what Harlem was becoming in the 1960's. Once the site of the great outpouring of creativity called the Harlem Renaissance, the area was being destroyed by drugs and violence. The play's two major characters are Old Sister, representing the past oppression of African Americans in the Old South, and Black Bitch, a sexually promiscuous woman accused by the black male characters of sleeping with a white police officer and failing to support the revolution. When Black Bitch accuses the black male leader of abusing women, he brutally rapes her. The black male revolutionaries force both women back into the burning buildings to die. Sanchez's language is explicitly sexual and violent in this play. Although some critics believe the work contains one of the first examples of strong black women characters in drama, others find the message disturbing, with the playwright seeming to blame the women characters for not supporting the revolution.

SISTER SON/JI

The narrator in this one-act play is an African American woman in her fifties recalling important episodes of her history as a revolutionary. By changing her makeup and costumes, she recalls her early college days, her first sexual experience, her black consciousness awakening through the speeches of Malcolm X, an episode of near insanity when she loses control of her life, and the death of her teenage son in the revolution. Sanchez portrays the conflicted relationship between black men and women, with the men exploiting their power and expecting the women to take a subservient role in the movement. Sister Son/ji pleads with black men to admit women as equals and respect love and family life rather than a false idea of manhood.

By tracing Sister Son/ji's experiences, Sanchez explores themes that dominate all her work: the exploitation of black women by black men, the destructive power of drugs and violence, the urgent need for African American men and women to work together to combat racism. The play concludes with a statement of Sister Son/ji's strength and survival skills:

Death is a five o-clock door forever changing time. And wars end. Sometimes too late. i am here. still in mississippi. Near the graves of my past. We are at peace. . . . but I have my memories. . . . i have my sweet/astringent memories becuz we dared to pick up the day and shake its tail until it became evening. A time for us. blk/ness. blk/people.

UH HUH; BUT HOW DO IT FREE US?

This play, the longest of the three, is experimental in form, with three unrelated scenes connected by dance sequences. In the first scene, three characters (Malik, Waleesha, and Nefertia) represent the black male's need to dominate women to assure his manhood. Both women are pregnant and enemies of each other, rather than sisters, as they try to hold on to Malik's love.

The next scene is a surreal dramatization of male cocaine addicts, four black and one white, riding horses that represent their drug-induced fantasies. Two prostitutes, one white and one black, are whipping them and providing drugs. At the end of this scene, the white man dresses in drag, proclaiming himself the "real queen." Sanchez represents black men as superior to white men, but sees women, both black and white, as subordinate to the degenerate needs of men of both races.

The final scene portrays a black male revolutionary called Brother in relationships with both a black woman and a white woman. The white woman functions as a symbol of the white man's property. She supports him financially and makes him feel powerful. Sister, the black woman, is conflicted in her role as angry lover demeaned by Brother's betrayal with the "devil/woman" and her hopes that he will reform himself and return to his true responsibility as a man committed to his role in the black community. Sanchez stops short of supporting the sisterhood of black women, emphasizing Sister's individual strength and ability to survive both racism and her oppression by the black male.

OTHER MAJOR WORKS

POETRY: *Homecoming*, 1969; *We a BaddDDD People*, 1970; *Love Poems*, 1973; *A Blues Book for Blue Black Magical Women*, 1973; *I've Been a Woman: New and Selected Poems*, 1978; *Homegirls and Handgrenades*, 1984; *Under a Soprano Sky*, 1987; *Wounded in the House of a Friend*, 1995; *Does Your House Have Lions?*, 1997; *Like the Singing Coming off the Drums: Love Poems*, 1998; *Shake Loose My Skin: New and Selected Poems*, 1999.

NONFICTION: *Crisis in Culture: Two Speeches by Sonia Sanchez*, 1983.

CHILDREN'S LITERATURE: *It's a New Day: Poems for Young Brothas and Sistuhs*, 1971; *The Adventures of Fat Head, Small Head, and Square Head*, 1973; *A Sound Investment and Other Stories*, 1979.

EDITED TEXT: *We Be Word Sorcerers: Twenty-five Stories by Black Americans*, 1973.

BIBLIOGRAPHY

Brown-Guillory, Elizabeth, ed. Introduction to *Sister Son/ji*, by Sonia Sanchez. In *Wines in the Wilderness: Plays by African American Women from the Harlem Renaissance to the Present*. New York: Praeger, 1990. Editor Brown-Guillory provides a synopsis of the play and analysis of Sanchez's work as a whole.

Evans, Mari, ed. *Black Women Writers, 1950-1980: A*

Critical Evaluation. Garden City, N.Y.: Anchor Books, 1984. Contains an essay on Sanchez, analyzing her inventive use of urban black English in her work, and one by Sanchez, in which she explains her belief that the poet has a responsibility to change social values and discusses her personal life and working methods.

Joyce, Joyce Ann. Introduction to *Ijala: Sonia Sanchez and the African Poetic Tradition*. Chicago: Third World Press, 1996. Joyce argues that Sanchez's original contribution to African American literature is inspired by her deep knowledge and understanding of the African oral tradition in poetry.

Kelly, Susan. "Disciple and Craft: An Interview with Sonia Sanchez." *African American Review* 34, no. 4 (Winter, 2000): 679-687. Sanchez discusses the body of her work, her literary influences and personal history, and the importance of discipline and craft.

Tate, Claudia, ed. "Sonia Sanchez." In *Black Women Writers at Work*. New York: Continuum, 1983. In this interview, Sanchez discusses racism and the need for black women to refuse to see themselves as victims.

Ya Salaam, Kalamu. "Sonia Sanchez." In *Afro-American Poets Since 1955*, edited by Trudier Harris and Thadious M. Davis. Vol. 41 in *Dictionary of Literary Biography*. Detroit, Mich.: The Gale Group, 1985. A brief but comprehensive coverage of Sanchez's life and work.

Marjorie Podolsky

VICTORIEN SARDOU

Born: Paris, France; September 5, 1831
Died: Paris, France; November 8, 1908

PRINCIPAL DRAMA

La Taverne des étudiants, pr., pb. 1854
Les Premières Armes de Figaro, pr. 1859
Les Femmes fortes, pr. 1860, pb. 1861
Les Pattes de mouche, pr., pb. 1860 (*A Scrap of Paper*, 1861)
La Famille Benoîton, pr., pb. 1865
Nos Bons Villageois, pr. 1866, pb. 1867 (*Hazardous Ground*, 1868)
Patrie!, pr., pb. 1869 (*Patrie*, 1915)
Rabagas, pr., pb. 1872
L'Oncle Sam, pr. 1873, pb. 1875 (*Uncle Sam*, n.d.)
Daniel Rochat, pr., pb. 1880 (*Daniel*, 1880)
Divorçons, pr. 1880, pb. 1883 (with Émile de Naja; *Let's Get a Divorce*, 1885)
Fédora, pr. 1882, pb. 1908 (*Fedora*, 1883)
Théodora, pr. 1884, pb. 1907 (English translation, 1885)
La Tosca, pr. 1887, pb. 1909 (English translation, 1925)
Thermidor, pr. 1891, pb. 1892
Madame Sans-Gêne, pr. 1893, pb. 1907 (with Émile Moreau; *Madame Devil-May-Care*, 1901)
Théâtre complet, pb. 1934-1961 (15 volumes)

OTHER LITERARY FORMS

Victorien Sardou wrote only one novel, *La Perle noire* (1862; *The Black Pearl*, 1888), which he later adapted to the stage, and numerous pamphlets, of which the best known is *Mes Plagiats* (1881; my plagiarisms).

ACHIEVEMENTS

Victorien Sardou's range as a dramatist was exceptionally broad. He composed comedies, vaudevilles, historical dramas, political and social satires, melodramas, thesis plays, operas, and operettas—more than seventy works in all. The emphasis he gave to structure over character development has caused him to be widely regarded within the history of French theater as the successor and rival to Eugène Scribe. Although Sardou has often been criticized for overtly manipulating his characters, he is acknowledged as a master craftsman of theatrical effect. The plots of his plays follow carefully planned outlines, progressing to unusual levels of complication before reaching their elaborate solution in a final, "big" scene. During his lifetime, Sardou was one of the most popular and successful playwrights in France, and his works were frequently translated into English for performance in England and the United States. Except for the enduring fame of the operatic version of *La Tosca* and such occasional reinterpretations as a cinematic version of *Madame Devil-May-Care*, Sardou's plays are rarely seen today. Although his social satires were influential in broadening the capacity of French comedy to treat a variety of subjects it had not touched on previously, Sardou's plays are usually studied now as excellent examples of the well-made play.

Biography

Victorien Sardou's father, Antoine Léandre Sardou, was a schoolmaster; his mother, Mademoiselle Viard, the daughter of a manufacturer. The family lived in Paris, moving frequently in the course of the elder Sardou's teaching career. On completion of a secondary education at the Collège Henri IV in Paris, young Sardou began a career in medicine. This practical choice had been at his father's urging; his personal preference was literature. After eighteen months at the Necker Hospital, Sardou left to become a writer. To support himself, he contributed articles to several journals and encyclopedic works and tutored students in various subjects. Developing an interest in drama, he wrote several plays that were either rejected, or accepted but never performed. In 1854, *La Taverne des étudiants* (the students' tavern) was produced at the Théâtre National de l'Odéon. This play was canceled after only a few performances, however, because it had provoked the wrath of Parisian students. The reputation of this failure haunted the young playwright, and five years passed before he succeeded in bringing another play to the stage. During this period, Sardou pored over the works of Eugène Scribe. Beginning with the first act of a Scribe play, he would then compose his own version

Victorien Sardou (Hulton Archive by Getty Images)

in order to compare his technique to that of an acknowledged master.

Finally, Sardou managed to gain the attention of Virginie Déjazet. This popular actress produced and starred in Sardou's second play, *Les Premières Armes de Figaro* (Figaro's weapons), as well as several subsequent ones. A year later, Sardou wrote *A Scrap of Paper*, which became a great popular and critical success. From that point until the last few years of his life, very few seasons passed without the presence of at least one new Sardou play on the Parisian stage. Although he wrote most of his plays and librettos by himself, he occasionally collaborated with other dramatists such as Émile de Naja and Émile Moreau. Sardou composed a number of plays especially for theatrical talents of the period such as Sarah Bernhardt, Réjane, and Henry Irving. Some critics have said that these works represent the weakest part of Sardou's œuvre, suggesting that the playwright fell too strongly under the influence of the stars involved and conceded too readily to the popular taste of the moment.

Throughout his career, Sardou was regularly embroiled in controversy. Charges of plagiarism were brought against several of his plays. One such incident prompted him to write the self-defense *Mes Plagiats*. The political overtones of *Rabagas* nearly caused a riot. *Thermidor* was banned at the Comédie-Française after a single performance. *Uncle Sam*, a satire of American customs, was staged in New York before the French government allowed it to be produced in Paris.

Sardou was twice married, first in 1859, to a former actress, Laurentine de Brécourt, who died in 1867, and again in 1877, to Anne Soulié. He was elected to the Académie Française in 1877.

ANALYSIS

Victorien Sardou's plays blend the foreseeable and the unforeseeable. If his characters are often too entirely predictable, the same cannot be said of the situations in which they find themselves. The pleasure derived from a Sardou work, and indeed the key to the playwright's skill and talent, lies in the game of wits played out between author and audience as Sardou unravels a seemingly impossible situation into a logical but unpredictable resolution. Although most of Sardou's serious plays seem overly melodramatic and hence outmoded today, his ingenious plots can still prove absorbing, and his portraits of society as well as the humor of his comic pieces can still be appreciated. In sum, Sardou will continue to be esteemed as a skilled practitioner of the well-made play, a master of plot with a fine instinct for theatrical effect.

A SCRAP OF PAPER

A Scrap of Paper illustrates procedures, situations, character types, and themes commonly found in Sardou's comedies. The first scenes are typically expository. Many Sardou plays begin with a group of minor characters who are chatting with one another. A servants' conversation supplies the necessary background. The house has been closed for three years. The former owner died suddenly, shortly after the

marriage of her older daughter, Clarisse. This daughter has now returned, accompanied by her husband and her sister. As the servants clean the parlor, the housekeeper warns them not to touch a certain porcelain statue; only the mistresses of the house may dust it. The characters appear one by one as the first act progresses.

Sardou unites a diverse group on the common ground of marriage, a favorite theme both for him and his period. Prosper is seeking to marry in order to inherit from a rich uncle. Clarisse's sister Marthe has caught his eye, and he asks for her hand; she has also caught Paul's eye. Paul's awkward attempts at courtship are favorably received, but Madame Thirion, his tutor's wife, priggishly disapproves and tries to disrupt his advances to Marthe. Clarisse's cousin Suzanne, in her thirties and attractive, has never married. She prefers her independence, one suspects, because she has never found a man whom she could consider her equal. Clarisse and Vanhove seem to have settled into a comfortable marriage. She did not marry him for love, but she does not give any sign of disliking him after three years of wedlock. Vanhove is cold and aloof, but beneath lies a jealous, suspicious man, as he eventually reveals. The Thirions and another neighbor, Busonier, represent still other possibilities in the range of marital experience: Madame Thirion, belying her dovish name of Colomba, more resembles a harpy, while Busonier's wife, to his undisguised joy, has just run off with a lover.

When Clarisse and Prosper discuss his proposal to marry her sister Marthe, it is clear that their relationship is far from casual. The audience discovers that three years earlier, Clarisse and Prosper had been passionately in love with each other; the courtship came to an abrupt end when she was whisked off to Paris for a marriage of convenience with Vanhove. Clarisse had written a letter to Prosper imploring him to elope with her, but he had failed to respond. Now Clarisse maintains that she is quite happy, but when she mentions the letter, Prosper informs her that he never received it—indeed, that he could not have, for he was feverish in bed as the result of a duel he had fought for her honor on that fatal night when they last saw each other. Thunderstruck, Clarisse realizes that her letter must still be in its secret place—under the porcelain statue mentioned in the opening scene.

What follows is highly amusing as both Clarisse and Prosper attempt to remove the letter without anyone else becoming aware of its existence. Eventually he gains possession of it. From his first appearance, Prosper impresses the audience with his wit and spirit. It seems a foregone conclusion, therefore, that the mousy Clarisse will lose in any confrontation with him. Indeed, one wonders what attraction she had held for him. The situation becomes more interesting, then, when Suzanne appears. Prior to her entrance, she has been discussed in very complimentary terms, and when she appears, it is on the action-stopping exclamation, "I'm here!" Struck by the curious movements and remarks of both her cousin and Prosper, it does not take Suzanne long to fathom most of the truth. She joins the struggle on Clarisse's behalf, declaring war on Prosper as he amicably escorts her offstage at the end of act 1, under Vanhove's puzzled and somewhat suspicious gaze. If Clarisse was not a suitable match for Prosper, Suzanne gives all indications that she is.

In act 2, the situations outlined in act 1 begin to unfold. Paul challenges Prosper to a duel. Prosper accepts but specifies that he will elect the Japanese style of dueling, *harakiri*. The older man employs poise and address to dissuade his young rival and thereby seems to assume the lead in the contest for Marthe's hand. Paul then falls into another comical situation, as he scuttles back and forth between Marthe and Madame Thirion, attempting to carry out orders from one that countermands what the other has just asked of him. Finally, Paul leaves, and Marthe exits a few moments later, indicating in an aside her interest in following him. The balance in the Prosper-Marthe-Paul triangle has shifted; Prosper has lost favor.

Suzanne and Prosper confront each other. He refuses to relinquish the letter, promising instead to burn it only if and when he renounces his courtship of Marthe, adding that, actually, he would have burned the letter of his own accord if Suzanne's declaration of war had not piqued his gaming spirit. Suzanne accepts his challenge to discover the letter's hiding

place and promises in her turn to make Prosper burn the letter before her eyes. He retorts that if she can succeed in doing that, he will renounce his claim to Marthe and leave immediately. Such witty verbal sparring as that contained in this scene prompted some critics to compare Sardou to Pierre-Augustin Caron de Beaumarchais.

Prosper leaves, and Clarisse appears. The events that follow underline the difference between Clarisse and Suzanne: Clarisse, distraught in a stereotypically feminine fashion, loses her head; Suzanne, reasoning calmly, not only finds the letter but also manages to allay the jealous suspicions of Vanhove, who appears unexpectedly. With Suzanne's strength of character completely confirmed at this point, the action is dominated by her for the remainder of the act. Instead of destroying the letter, she rolls it up and arranges it conspicuously on the fireplace grate, where it can readily be used as tinder.

Prosper returns and discovers Suzanne in his study, apparently asleep. The scene that follows is highly entertaining. Prosper becomes visibly more and more enamored of Suzanne; it is obvious that he is preparing to propose marriage to her. Intent on getting him to burn the letter, Suzanne fends off his advances (without entirely discouraging them) as she keeps inventing excuses for him to light the lamp. Frustrated by her reticence and eager to prove his sincerity, Prosper snatches what he believes to be the letter and impulsively burns it. In fact, it is not the letter, and at the critical moment the elusive note once again escapes destruction. As Suzanne begins to explain to Prosper that he is holding the real letter in his hand without realizing what it is, Vanhove again arrives suddenly. Prosper, fearing that Suzanne will be compromised by being found alone in a darkened room with him, lights a candle with the scrap of paper in his hand. Still unaware of what it is, he tosses the burning paper out the window, but the flame is extinguished in the fall, and someone outside picks up what remains of it. The ensuing explanation places Prosper entirely at the mercy of the woman he loves. His reversal of attitude lends greatly to the humor of the situation. Suzanne commands Prosper to find what is left of the letter. His former composure now shattered by his newly discovered feelings, he hurries off to do her bidding. The shawl that she places over his shoulders to ward off the evening chill and her own shaken demeanor suggest, however, that this beautiful lady is not without mercy for her apparent victim.

Earlier, Prosper had chosen a deliberately obvious "hiding place" for the letter—he left it on his desk among other letters. Similarly, Suzanne placed the letter in plain sight on the fireplace. Sardou repeats this stratagem a third time when the letter reappears in the barrel of Thirion's hunting rifle as a container for a beetle. The paper thus remains tantalizingly in plain sight until Paul decides to write to Marthe and seizes the scrap without noticing that it already contains a message.

The finest humorous moments of act 3 stem from cases of mistaken identity. Suzanne, in order to protect Clarisse, has pretended to be Prosper's wronged and estranged mistress, and Vanhove has vowed to bring about their reconciliation and marriage. With this purpose in mind, he confronts Prosper, who thinks that when Vanhove admits that he "knows all," he means that he has discovered the former relationship between Prosper and Clarisse. Before the misconception can be clarified, Suzanne arrives and launches into a scene for Vanhove's benefit. After a few confusing moments, Prosper realizes what she is doing and cooperates because he loves her and sees his opportunity to coerce her into marrying him. The reconciliation they feign for Vanhove turns into a real one when it becomes clear to Suzanne that she is irremediably caught in her own white lie. She finds herself propelled into Prosper's open arms not entirely in spite of herself. The balance of power in the relationship now shifts a final time, in Prosper's favor.

Just when the play seems happily ended, Thirion enters, indignant that someone has sent a love letter to his wife. He demands that Vanhove identify the handwriting. Vanhove turns the letter over as he accepts it and therefore reads Paul's message and not Clarisse's. In a masterful twist of the plot, the maid to whom Paul had entrusted his note had given it to Madame Thirion. In retrospect, this outcome is not unex-pected. Earlier, the maid had commented slyly on Madame Thirion's constant whisperings to Paul, and Paul had not actually said the name of the person to whom he had wished the letter delivered. Clarisse's honor is saved, nevertheless, when Prosper, recognizing the letter, snatches it from Vanhove and claims it as his. When Suzanne is called on to witness her future husband's new breach of faith, she placidly remarks that she knows the contents of the note and that Vanhove may burn it, which he does.

A Scrap of Paper is composed around a popular formula—the couple meant for each other who resist their mutual attraction for a time before finally succumbing to it. Sardou moves this formula briskly through elaborate, surprising twists that he always meticulously prepares in advance. The first act is expository; the second act is devoted to the complication and ends on the climax of the action; and the third act contains the denouement. Thus, *A Scrap of Paper* neatly exemplifies the classic construction of the well-made play.

As sympathetic as Prosper and Suzanne are, as amusing as the development of their personal relationship is, the events in which they become involved playing hide-and-seek with Clarisse's letter are even more attractive. This is typical of Sardou's plays, in which the action commonly upstages the characters. Even in such a play as *Madame Devil-May-Care*, which was written especially to showcase the talents of Réjane, and in which the lead role offers an actress the opportunity to shine in witty dialogue, the entanglements of the plot are what ultimately hold the audience's attention. The psychology of Sardou's characters is essentially one-dimensional and, consequently, quite predictable. Dramatic tension stems from what happens rather than from why it does or to whom.

In such theater, objects and motifs assume great importance. In *A Scrap of Paper*, a letter carries the entire play forward. In *Hazardous Ground*, the key to a private garden, a young man's hat, and a woman's pearl necklace figure prominently. In *La Tosca*, the object is a carelessly forgotten fan, and in *Let's Get a Divorce*, a false telegram. Often these objects seem unimportant, but in Sardou's plots inconsequential objects regularly occasion actions of serious magnitude.

Sardou was noted for the painstaking care he devoted to the *mise en scène* of his works, often taking a personal hand in the actual realization of his specifications when a play was performed. The set for Prosper's study, with all its paraphernalia and souvenirs of a returned world traveler, provides a rich visual image. Given the role of objects in what happens during this play, many of the props are there out of practical necessity. Later in his career, especially in the historical dramas, Sardou specified elaborate settings and costumes less for any practical purpose than for that of creating a sumptuous and grandiose spectacle appropriate to the scope of his subject.

Humor in a Sardou comedy occasionally approaches slapstick. In *A Scrap of Paper*, characters who have been searching frantically on hands and knees rise suddenly and simultaneously, claiming that they had been doing nothing at all. In *Les Femmes fortes* (strong women), one character packs a large trunk, and another character, seemingly without the knowledge of the first, unpacks it. The lover of *Let's Get a Divorce* must contend with a door that the husband has booby-trapped with an alarm and automatic lock. The lover is halfway across the room as the door is shutting before he remembers this. He dashes back to the door and holds it open with an outstretched foot as he attempts to converse persuasively with the lady whom he wishes to seduce.

A Scrap of Paper represents a society that is not particularly anchored to a specific time or place. Many of Sardou's plays, however, treat questions which concerned his contemporaries. *Daniel* examines the problem of religious versus civil marriage; *Hazardous Ground* explores the tensions created when Parisians began moving to the country in search of a healthier way of life; *Les Femmes fortes* mocks American ways of educating young women; and *Let's Get a Divorce* wryly suggests what could happen if divorce were allowed.

PATRIE

Many critics regard the historical drama *Patrie* as one of Sardou's masterpieces. Written relatively early in his career, it was not influenced by the idiosyncrasies of any particular actor or actress, and while set on a grand scale, it is not lavish in the sense that many of his later historical dramas were. The play contains many elements in common with other Sardou dramas: spectacular happenings, telltale motifs, a jealous woman who brings destruction to all around her, complex stage settings, and a complicated plot that relies strongly on coincidence. It is the story of lovers' triangles, with the difference that the heroine is not a flesh-and-blood woman.

Patrie contains eight tableaux. The elaborate details of these sets and the number of episodic characters involved in them provide a colorful background for the action. The story takes place in Spanish-governed Brussels in 1568. The initial tableau evokes the disorder of military occupation: Groups of soldiers gather around fires, gaming, cooking, cleaning their weapons. Children and camp followers serve them drinks; patrols come and go. As gunfire is heard in the background, soldiers discuss the overflowing prisons and the executions that have been ordered as a consequence. That the army has set up camp in the city's meat market (whose hooks protrude from the beams) underscores the cruelty with which the Spaniards oppress the citizenry.

Two noblemen are escorted into these grim circumstances. One vociferously defies his captors; he is La Tremoïlle—Protestant, member of the French court, and, at the moment, prisoner of war. The other is Rysoor, a Flemish count. The conversation reveals both men's noble character and further details of the political and religious struggle that is taking place.

During the trial scene that follows, it becomes clear that a patriotic resistance movement exists. Rysoor trembles visibly when the Spanish tribunal discusses the failure of Karloo Van der Noot to surrender his militia's weapons. This brave young captain, Rysoor informs La Tremoïlle, is as dear to him as a brother. Karloo's case is dismissed until the next day, giving him the night in which to comply with the order. Rysoor gains release after the testimony of a Spanish captain, who swears to having seen him at home the previous evening. Rysoor is dumbfounded by this account because he had, in fact, been away. He discovers further that the Spaniard claims to have wounded the captain's hand. Rysoor reluctantly concludes that if the story is true, then his wife has been unfaithful.

Act 1 establishes the spirit of patriotism that is to be the true protagonist of the play and introduces an adulterous triangle. Act 2 immediately reveals the other two members of this triangle—Dolores, the unfaithful wife, and Karloo, the young patriot for whom Rysoor had been so concerned. Dolores is young, Spanish, and Catholic; her husband is none of these. As her sharp remarks testify, these differences have estranged her from him. Paralleling the political situation, the affair between Dolores and Karloo has now reached a crisis. Threats of rupture, however, only draw them together even more passionately.

Rysoor arrives and, setting aside his personal concerns, consults privately with Karloo about the progress of an insurrection planned for that very night. This patriotic duty accomplished, he then confronts Dolores with her infidelity. She admits her guilt but blames him for having caused the situation. He cannot imagine, she says, the terrible loneliness of a passionate heart that cries out with love only to be answered by the word "patriotism." Herein lies the primary cause of Dolores's infidelity: She had discovered a rival for her husband's affection and had reacted with uncontrollable jealousy. She cannot admit that any of Rysoor's love should be denied her, even for so worthy a cause as patriotism. A woman's country, as she informs her husband, is love. The explanation of Dolores's jealousy uncovers a second triangle behind the one that involves her with Karloo and Rysoor: herself, her husband, and their country. It points to a third one as well. Since Karloo, like Rysoor, loves his country, at some point Dolores will again be faced by patriotism as a rival.

In act 3, driven by her passions, Dolores denounces her husband to the military governor, the Duke of Alba, in exchange for the life of her lover, who remains unnamed. The duke, however, forces her to tell him the names of all the conspirators whom she had recognized when earlier she had followed her husband to their meeting. This scene is heavy with irony, for Dolores still does not know that Karloo is one of the insurgents, nor does she recognize his

sword (surrendered to the duke in an earlier scene) when she identifies the ribbon on it as the rebels' insignia. The truth is not revealed until she hears the order for Karloo's arrest. Dolores's actions in this sequence effectively undercut any sympathy that she may have gained by her initial explanation of her marital predicament: To sacrifice her husband for the lover she had taken out of jealous frustration is thoroughly reprehensible.

The political and sentimental strands of the plot fuse as the climax of the play draws near. At the moment that Rysoor is giving command of the rebel forces to Karloo, he notices Karloo's wounded hand—the sign that he is Dolores's lover. Rysoor must now choose between patriotic and personal duties. To allow himself to be dominated by personal revenge at this moment would be for him to commit a crime against the commonweal. So, consistent with his previous decisions, Rysoor once again subordinates his personal concerns to his patriotic zeal and sends Karloo forth to battle. The act ends as the Spaniards surprise and capture the conspirators.

In act 4, Dolores obtains Karloo's release by taking advantage of the fact that Karloo had recently rescued the duke's beloved daughter from an angry mob. Rysoor eventually commits suicide, but not before he has pardoned Karloo and made him promise to kill the traitor who denounced them. Act 5 is brief. Devastated by his mentor's death, Karloo confronts Dolores, determined to break with her and live only to avenge his comrades. Dolores selfishly attempts to dissuade him by visions of the freedom that now lies before them. Karloo finally agrees to leave with her. When she mentions her own safe-conduct, however, Karloo realizes that the woman he loves is the traitor he must kill. Now the necessity of choosing between patriotic and personal concerns falls to him. He hesitates a moment but then honors his patriotic vow and stabs Dolores with the same dagger that had killed her husband.

Instantly struck with remorse, Karloo heeds Dolores's dying plea to join her and leaps from the window to his death in the blazing fire that is consuming his captured comrades in the town square below. By dying, he atones for his murder of Dolores and for his betrayal of Rysoor's friendship. Furthermore, Karloo regains his patriotic honor, which had been jeopardized by Dolores's machinations. The hero's self-immolation thus reestablishes the order of things and provides an appropriate ending to a melodramatic tale of violent passions.

OTHER MAJOR WORKS

LONG FICTION: *La Perle noire*, 1862 (*The Black Pearl*, 1888).

NONFICTION: *Mes Plagiats*, 1881.

BIBLIOGRAPHY

Hart, Jerome. *Sardou and the Sardou Plays*. Philadelphia: J. P. Lippincott, 1913. In this classic work, Hart examines the French dramatist and his plays.

Nicassio, Susan Vandiver. *Tosca's Rome: The Play and the Opera in Historical Perspective*. Chicago: University of Chicago Press, 1999. Nicassio examines the play and opera *La Tosca*, examining Sardou's work, as well as that of Giacomo Puccini. Bibliography and index.

Joan M. West

FRANK SARGESON
Norris Frank Davey

Born: Hamilton, New Zealand; March 23, 1903
Died: Auckland, New Zealand; March 1, 1982

PRINCIPAL DRAMA

A Time for Sowing, pr. 1961, pb. 1964
The Cradle and the Egg, pr. 1962, pb. 1964
Wrestling with the Angel: Two Plays, pb. 1964
(comprises two previous plays)

OTHER LITERARY FORMS

Frank Sargeson, who wrote only two plays, both in the early 1960's, is much better known as a writer of short stories and novels, some of which—notably *When the Wind Blows* (1945) and *I Saw in My Dream* (1949)—are strongly autobiographical. His first book of short stories, *Conversation with My Uncle and Other Sketches* (1936), also concerns events that occurred early in his life. In his later novels he retained New Zealand life as a background but extended his themes, focusing on the individual's efforts to find freedom in a repressive, puritanical society. That effort was similar to Sargeson's own as he struggled first against his strict parents and later against a homophobic New Zealand culture. Sargeson also wrote three autobiographical volumes: *Once Is Enough* (1972), *More than Enough* (1975), and *Never Enough!*

(1977). His journalistic career, which began with his writing for *Tomorrow*, includes essays and reviews of dramatic and literary works. He also appeared extensively on radio and occasionally on television.

ACHIEVEMENTS

Frank Sargeson's achievements fall into two categories, his awards and his influence on many New Zealand writers. His short story "An Affair of the Heart" won second prize in the 1936 Christmas competition, and in 1940 he won first prize for his short story "The Making of a New Zealander" from New Zealand's Centennial Literary Competition. In 1965 he won the prestigious Katherine Mansfield Short Story Award for his "Just Trespassing, Thanks," and he won the Hubert Church Award three times, the last time for his novel *Man of England Now* (1972). Friends and colleagues were instrumental in his receiving an honorary degree in literature from the University of Auckland in 1974.

In addition to his many awards, Sargeson influenced many other New Zealand writers, who have enthusiastically acknowledged their debt to him. Among his protégés were David Ballantyne, John Reece Cole, Dan Davin, Maurice Dugan, Dennis McEldowney, C. K. Stead, and, most notably, Janet Frame. After meeting Sargeson, Frame, who had been in and out of psychiatric hospitals much of her life, moved into his army hut and lived there during 1955-1956 while she wrote her first novel, *Owls Do Cry* (1957). In her *An Angel at My Table* (1984), one of her autobiographical works, she wrote of Sargeson: "I did not realise until much later when I was writing many books, how extreme but how willing his inevitable sacrifice of part of his writing life had been." For New Zealanders, Sargeson was Katherine Mansfield's successor and occupied much the same place in New Zealand literature as Patrick White did in Australia.

BIOGRAPHY

Frank Sargeson's life may be conveniently divided into two parts, his life as Norris Frank Davey, which lasted from March 23, 1903, until 1931; and his life as the writer Frank Sargeson, the name he assumed and retained until his death in 1982. Born in Hamilton on the North Island of New Zealand, Davey was the victim of parental influences that shaped his literary themes. Edwin John Davey, his father, served as town clerk but his primary interest was in the Methodist Church, and his "puritan" beliefs and moralistic views made him unpopular with the townspeople and a source of embarrassment to his son. His mother, Rachel, was not as religious as her husband, but her concern for middle-class respectability made her his ally in promoting conformity to the status quo. As a result, young Davey experienced a conflict between the puritan conscience inculcated by his parents and what he came to regard as the life of the senses.

During the time Davey attended Hamilton High School, his mother, who was somewhat more liberal than his father regarding literature, took him to evening meetings of the local Shakespeare Club, where he was also introduced to the dramatic works of George Bernard Shaw and Euripides. She even encouraged him to learn how to act on the stage. In 1920 he began sitting for the Auckland University College extramural examinations in law and had a somewhat mediocre record. In 1921 he made his first visit to his uncle Oakley Sargeson's farm, which became a refuge for him. By 1921 he was aware of his homosexuality, but he was also still a devout Method-

ist. Chafing under the moral strictures of his parents, he left home in 1925 and moved to a "bach" (a small cabin), which his father owned in Takapuna, Auckland, where he found employment as a solicitor with a law firm. After saving some money, he left for England in 1927 and toured Europe briefly before returning to New Zealand in 1928. Within a year, one of his homosexual relationships resulted in his arrest for indecent assault, and he was convicted. Because the trial was publicized, his parents were understandably upset and then relieved when Oakley Sargeson agreed to take Davey back to his farm at Okahukura.

After writing an unpublished novel at his uncle's farm, Davey assumed the name Frank Sargeson and began his life as a writer in Auckland in 1931. For the next four years he was unemployed but did write stories and articles, most of which were not published. His writing career began in earnest when he began writing for *Tomorrow* in 1935, and in the next five years he published more than forty sketches and stories, as well as *Conversation with My Uncle and Other Sketches* (1936). As a result of surgical tuberculosis, he was considered unfit for military service in World War II and was awarded an invalidity benefit. During the next twenty years he received several literary prizes and published three novels, two collections of short stories, many other stories and sketches, and two plays, *The Cradle and the Egg* and *A Time for Sowing*, though the plays, written in the mid-1950's, were not produced until 1961 and 1962. Sargeson has described the period from 1964 to 1973 as the years in which he "became a professional writer in the most exact sense of the word," and except for *Sunset Village* (1976), his fiction writing was over by 1975. His last years were marked by the death of Harry Doyle, his lover of thirty-six years; critical acclaim; and health problems, including diabetes and prostate cancer.

ANALYSIS

Although Frank Sargeson's two plays differ in content, setting, and style, they are alike in some ways. The plays present issues that are discussed in depth (as in the plays of George Bernard Shaw) but never resolved by characters who act as spokespersons for causes. His characters seem unable to change and appear plagued with beliefs (Puritanism, idealism, progressivism) that are at odds with the real world. In the plays, Sargeson is pessimistic about human efforts to bridge cultures or to find peace; he finds people hypocritical and destructive.

A TIME FOR SOWING

A Time for Sowing takes place in the summer of 1819 and concerns Thomas Kendall, an Anglican missionary at the Bay of Islands in New Zealand and the first New Zealand anthropologist. Kendall, who wrote the first book about the Maori language, gained his experience by "going native" (sleeping with the Maori women), which led to spiritual problems and alcoholism. Sargeson's stage directions for Kendall's home include three items with symbolic import: a musket, representing Kendall's suicidal tendency; "some Maori objects," suggesting that Kendall is being "converted" instead of converting the natives; and a picture depicting the temptation of Adam by Eve, reflecting Kendall's own weakness for women. As the play opens, the Kendall boys are behaving in such a way as to suggest that they are also "going native." In the course of the first act, the audience learns that while Mrs. Kendall is aware of her husband's infidelities, she defends him to the visiting Captain Maubey but is herself attracted to Richard Stockwell, the Kendalls' manservant. Kendall's hypocrisy is matched by his wife's; she is a moral purist who objects to the Adam-and-Eve picture but commits adultery with Richard.

In act 2, Kendall puts the musket to his head but puts it down when his wife enters. He then unwittingly alludes to his wife's situation: "Have they converted you to the native way of life?" After she leaves with Richard, Kendall is torn between the Bible and the musket, and his inner conflict is reflected in his alternation of biblical texts: the Song of Solomon as opposed to Romans and 1 John. When Mrs. Kendall reminds him that there are some people "who are in need of your guidance," he fails to see that she, too, is torn between feeling and morals and decides to play cards, only to be reminded that it is Lent. In the third act when Captain Maubey returns, Kendall accuses him of selling muskets to the natives; Kendall has been doing this himself. During this act, Stockwell and both Kendalls appeal separately to Captain Maubey to be allowed to travel with him away from the Bay of Islands. Maubey rejects the requests, and at the end of the play, Kendall returns to his Maori women, and Mrs. Kendall and Richard continue their relationship. Sargeson used Kendall to suggest the problems implicit in cultural clashes and to depict the fate of people whose puritanical beliefs conflict with the life of the senses. Thus, the play uses a historical event and autobiographical material.

THE CRADLE AND THE EGG

The Cradle and the Egg differs considerably from *A Time for Sowing*. It concerns the past, present, and the future; some of the actors play multiple parts; and in the third act, set in the indefinite future, the stage props consists only of a rock and a symbolic egg. The conventional first act, set in the 1880's, presents a conflict between progress (a new railway proposed by entrepreneur George Chapel) and the status quo (coaches championed by coachmaker Hardy); and the men, who are both motivated primarily by capitalistic greed, suggest that their positions are motivated by concern for the town's economic prosperity (Chapel) and its traditional religious principles (Hardy). Sargeson adds a subplot involving Betty Hardy, who must choose between two suitors: Harry Chapel, a brash, obnoxious know-it-all who "borrows" money that he soon loses to a con man; and Arnold Townshend, an ethereal clergyman without any common sense. The first act ends on an indeterminate note: Betty has not made her choice, and there are still hard feelings about the railroad. On the other hand, Hardy's home and business is burning down, and it is implied that George Chapel may have set the fire.

The second act takes place in the early 1950's aboard an airliner, another mode of transportation that was foreshadowed by young Tim Hardy's fascination with balloons. In this act, the conflict is between Antony Treverhern, a sensitive young lover of poetry, and Ernest Trentham, the scientist and businessman who carries an egg-shaped object. Their interest in Stephanie Grantwell parallels the Betty-Arnold-Harry triangle of the first act. Another tie to the first act is provided by the entrance of an old man, the baby whose cradle Tim Hardy was rocking during the first act. Besides describing the fates of his brother, Tim; his sister, Betty; and the suicides of his parents, old man Hardy announces his intent to bring down "at least one of the big toy birds." The second act ends as the first did, with a catastrophe; Ernest explodes the bomb (the "egg-shaped object") he carries, and all perish.

The last act takes place in the future, after the burning of earth, when all have perished except for the egg, which emits a kind of light. Antony, Ernest, and Stephanie engage in a lengthy metaphysical discussion about the egg, which symbolizes not only the destruction of the second act but also the possibility of rebirth, which does not appear to be imminent. When the Voice is heard, it clearly is that of the Old Man, who assumes God-like status in the play. Rather than resolve the situation, he jokes about relocating the survivors, perhaps on a meteor. At the end of the play, Stephanie, Ernest, and Antony exit, but the ambiguous egg "appears to glow with a radiance of its own." In this play, over which the atomic bomb hovers, Sargeson seems to be pointing to the self-destructive nature of humankind, whose faith in progress is misplaced.

OTHER MAJOR WORKS

LONG FICTION: *When the Wind Blows*, 1945; *I Saw in My Dream*, 1949; *I for One*, 1956; *Memoirs of a Peon*, 1965; *The Hangover*, 1967; *Joy of the Worm*, 1969; *Man of England Now*, 1972 (pb. with *I for One* and *A Game of Hide and Seek*); *A Game of Hide and Seek*, 1972; *Sunset Village*, 1976.

SHORT FICTION: *Conversation with My Uncle and Other Sketches*, 1936; *A Man and His Wife*, 1940; *That Summer and Other Stories*, 1946; *Collected Stories, 1935-1963*, 1964; *The Stories of Frank Sargeson*, 1973.

NONFICTION: *Once Is Enough*, 1973 (memoir); *More than Enough*, 1975 (memoir); *Never Enough!*, 1977 (memoir); *Conversation in a Train and Other Critical Writing*, 1983.

EDITED TEXT: *Speaking for Ourselves: A Collection of New Zealand Stories*, 1945.

BIBLIOGRAPHY

Copland, R. A. *Frank Sargeson*. New York: Oxford University Press, 1976. Copland summarizes the plots of the two plays and finds a movement in them from realism of action to fantasy. While Copland sees *A Time for Sowing* lacking dramatically in its articulation of protagonist Thomas Kendall's personal predicament, he is more enthused about *The Cradle and the Egg*, which he regards as "Shavian" in its comic seriousness. For Copland, the second play is livelier and more challenging than its predecessor.

King, Michael. *Frank Sargeson: A Life*. New York: Viking, 1995. King's biography is divided into two parts: The first describes the life of Sargeson as Norris Davy, and the second one concerns Sargeson's life after he changed his name. For King, the turning point in Sargeson's life was his publicized conviction for indecent assault, which led to his two-year stay with his uncle and his decision to change his name. King provides the intellectual and dramatic context in which the plays were produced, rehearsal and casting information, and the story of the creation of the New Independent Theatre, which produced *The Cradle and the Egg*. King's book, which must be regarded as the definitive biography of Sargeson, also contains an extensive bibliography of Sargeson's writings and a bibliography of critical works.

McNaughton, Howard. "Drama." In *The Oxford History of New Zealand Literature in English*, edited by Terry Sturm. New York: Oxford University Press, 1991. McNaughton discusses Sargeson's plays in their intellectual context, finds the plays consistent with the dramatic theories Sargeson had stressed as a theater critic for *Tomorrow* and *Press*, and mentions the radio production of *The Cradle and the Egg* in 1968.

_____. *New Zealand Drama*. Boston: Twayne, 1981. McNaughton discusses both of Sargeson's plays, describing *A Time for Sowing* as a naturalistic drama that fails to explore visually Kendall's self-doubt and *The Cradle and the Egg* as a Shavian drama ambitious in its attempts to visualize the play's symbolic meaning. McNaughton has reservations about the coherence of the play, which contains symbolism, literary allusions, and several philosophies of time.

Rhodes, H. Winston. *Frank Sargeson*. New York: Twayne, 1969. Rhodes devotes one chapter to Sargeson's plays, which are summarized, analyzed, and discussed in terms of their critical reception and their place in the development of New Zea-

land drama. In his comments on *The Cradle and the Egg*, Rhodes points out the cosmic humor of the play and relates it to the comedy in Sargeson's fiction. According to Rhodes, the play reflects Sargeson's continuing concern with what he calls the "implications of creative endeavor."

Thomas L. Erskine

WILLIAM SAROYAN

Born: Fresno, California; August 31, 1908
Died: Fresno, California; May 18, 1981

PRINCIPAL DRAMA

The Hungerers: A Short Play, pb. 1939, pr. 1945
My Heart's in the Highlands, pr., pb. 1939
The Time of Your Life, pr., pb. 1939
Love's Old Sweet Song, pr., pb. 1940
Three Plays: My Heart's in the Highlands, The Time of Your Life, Love's Old Sweet Song, pb. 1940
Subway Circus, pb. 1940
The Ping-Pong Game, pb. 1940 (one act)
The Beautiful People, pr. 1940, pb. 1941
The Great American Goof, pr. 1940, pb. 1942
Across the Board on Tomorrow Morning, pr., pb. 1941
Three Plays: The Beautiful People, Sweeney in the Trees, Across the Board on Tomorrow Morning, pb. 1941
Hello Out There, pr. 1941, pb. 1942 (one act)
Jim Dandy, pr., pb. 1941
Razzle Dazzle, pb. 1942 (collection)
Talking to You, pr., pb. 1942
Get Away Old Man, pr. 1943, pb. 1944
Sam Ego's House, pr. 1947, pb. 1949
A Decent Birth, a Happy Funeral, pb. 1949
Don't Go Away Mad, pr., pb. 1949
The Slaughter of the Innocents, pb. 1952, pr. 1957
The Cave Dwellers, pr. 1957, pb. 1958

Once Around the Block, pb. 1959
Sam the Highest Jumper of Them All: Or, The London Comedy, pr. 1960, pb. 1961
Settled Out of Court, pr. 1960, pb. 1962
The Dogs: Or, The Paris Comedy and Two Other Plays, pb. 1969
An Armenian Trilogy, pb. 1986 (includes *Armenians*, *Bitlis*, and *Haratch*)
Warsaw Visitor, Tales from the Vienna Streets: The Last Two Plays of William Saroyan, pb. 1991

OTHER LITERARY FORMS

William Saroyan is perhaps even better known as the author of short stories, novels, and autobiographical prose than as a playwright. Early short-story collections include: *The Daring Young Man on the Flying Trapeze and Other Stories* (1934), *Inhale and Exhale* (1936), *Three Times Three* (1936), and *Love, Here Is My Hat and Other Short Romances* (1938). His best-known novel is *The Human Comedy* (1943).

ACHIEVEMENTS

William Saroyan's plays are vehicles for his vision of what one of his characters calls "the miracle of life." Like his prose, Saroyan's drama is predicated on a largely optimistic perception of life as a joyous festival whose bounty is spiritual rather than materialistic. His critical and commercial success in the theater reached a zenith with the production of *The Time of Your Life*, for which he was awarded the Pulitzer

Prize (he declined to accept). In this and many of his other plays, Saroyan drew heavily on his own and his family's experience to dramatize the rhythms, opportunities, and joy of life, particularly in the United States. In the course of his playwriting career, Saroyan experimented with dramatic styles (such as Surrealism and expressionism) and techniques (such as direct address to the audience) but never adopted a codified aesthetic theory. Although threatened by his proclivity toward sentimentality and naïveté, Saroyan's best plays still offer the sense of what he called "that quality of beauty as it is in the living, in the plainest of people."

BIOGRAPHY

William Saroyan was the fourth child of Armenian immigrants, Armenak and Takoohi Saroyan, who settled in Fresno, California. Three years after Saroyan's birth, his father died, and Saroyan, along with his brother and sisters, was sent to an orphanage in Oakland, California. His mother, while working in San Francisco, tried to maintain the family, and by 1915, they were reunited in Fresno. Saroyan's formal education ended before he completed high school, but by the age of twenty, he had committed himself to a career as a writer. In 1934, he won the O. Henry Award for his short story "The Daring Young Man on the Flying Trapeze." During the 1930's, Saroyan traveled widely, published five novels, and worked briefly as a screenwriter in Hollywood. Between 1939 and 1942, Saroyan enjoyed a meteoric career on Broadway. In the early 1940's, he produced and directed several of his own plays before entering the army in October, 1942. In 1943, he married Carol Marcus, whom he divorced in 1949, remarried in 1951, later divorced again, and by whom he had two children, Aram and Lucy. In the late 1940's, he published several plays that were not produced on Broadway. After 1943, Saroyan wrote only one important work for the theater, *The Cave Dwellers*, although he continued to write prolifically in other genres.

ANALYSIS

William Saroyan's career as a playwright covered more than forty years, but his best and most ac-

William Saroyan (Courtesy of the D.C. Public Library)

claimed work in the theater was concentrated in the period between 1939 and 1942. His dramatic reputation rests on these plays, most notably his much-acclaimed *The Time of Your Life*.

SUBWAY CIRCUS

A preliminary dramatic effort, *Subway Circus*, evocative of the *commedia dell'arte* tradition, is actually a series of sketches on the independent fantasies of ten riders of a subway car. Even this early work, however, demonstrates Saroyan's interest in the theater's potential to depict the inner, imaginary world of his characters and to create an atmosphere of carnival excitement and gaiety.

MY HEART'S IN THE HIGHLANDS

With *My Heart's in the Highlands*, which he later referred to as his first play, Saroyan displayed his ability to transform overtly autobiographical experience into drama and to work within a much more conventional (although hardly rigorous) structure. Set in Fresno in 1914 at the beginning of World War I and produced in 1939 at the beginning of World War II, *My Heart's in the Highlands* strikes a note of foreboding and anxiety, but more important is its resilient optimism. The plot revolves around the reception of an eccentric, itinerant Scots immigrant, Jasper MacGregor, who plays "My Heart's in the Highlands" on his bugle, in the home of a generous and equally eccentric California family. The play's movement is steeped in optimism: The homeless find homes; strangers recognize their common humanity; individuals are brought together, both in the pleasure of enjoying MacGregor's bugling and in the sorrow of mourning his death. In this play, Saroyan introduced what was to become a recurring structural feature of his plays, the performance of song, dance, dramatic reading, or musical composition. MacGregor has a number of qualities that reappear in Saroyan's later characters: Like Kit Carson in *The Time of Your Life*, he is a teller of tall tales, and like the king in *The Cave Dwellers*, he has played King Lear. In addition, like the majority of Saroyan's characters, he is a searcher, displaced, uprooted, and homeless.

THE TIME OF YOUR LIFE

Saroyan's most celebrated play, *The Time of Your Life*, for which he received both the Pulitzer Prize and the New York Drama Critics Circle Award, opened on Broadway only six months after *My Heart's in the Highlands*. Saroyan said that he wrote the play in only six days while staying at the Great Northern Hotel in New York City. *The Time of Your Life* effectively captures the variety and vitality of American life that is the essence of Saroyan's vision. Here, he assembles a virtual cross-section of the American people: The rich and the poor, the young and the old, the powerful and the powerless all meet at Nick's Pacific Street Saloon, Restaurant, and Entertainment Palace in San Francisco. It is, as Saroyan proclaims in his stage directions, "an American place," alive with humor, energy, and imagination. The plot of the play is diffused among its twenty-six characters whose stories provide a panoramic view of American society. Much of the action is orchestrated by Nick, the saloon's owner, and Joe, a benevolent, eccentric, philosophical man who describes himself as a student of life. When Tom, a young man in love with a prosti-

tute named Kitty, questions Joe's motive for helping strangers, Joe tells him that "when my study reveals something of beauty in a place or in a person where by all rights only ugliness or death should be revealed, then I know how full of goodness this life is." Joe is, in fact, the pivotal character in the play because he consciously tries to make every moment of his life the time of his life and seeks to ensure that others share in his enjoyment. Having worked hard to earn enough money to be comfortable, Joe now lives to be happy and to make others happy. Early in the play, he dispatches Tom to buy him some toys, simply because he knows they will bring him and others pleasure. His main accomplishment in the play is the reform of Kitty Duval, the prostitute whom Tom loves, and the uniting of Tom and Kitty. When Kitty first appears in the bar, she is abrasive, cold, and hard, but under Joe's questioning, her true nature and past are revealed. After hearing her story and seeing her response to Tom's love, Joe concludes that Kitty is "one of the few truly innocent people I have ever met." Finally, Tom and Kitty leave for San Diego to be married. Although their story serves as the focus of Joe's generosity, his amiability and robust vigor pervade the entire play.

The subplots of *The Time of Your Life* are nearly as numerous as its characters: There is the story of McCarthy, an idealistic longshoreman engaged in a strike; of Krupp, an honest cop who questions his profession after years on the force; of a wealthy couple slumming in search of adventure; of Kit Carson, a gadfly with an inexhaustible supply of outrageous stories; and of Blick, another policeman, who epitomizes the abuse of authority. Several other characters perform routines that give the play a remarkable ebullience: Harry (originally played by Gene Kelly) dances and tells jokes; Wesley plays the piano; the Newsboy sings "When Irish Eyes Are Smiling"; an Arab plays the harmonica. In an atmosphere that recalls vaudeville, each of them, like the other characters in *The Time of Your Life*, reveals a special talent or gift that can only be fully realized when shared with others. The play's bustling activity, episodic structure, and occasional mayhem enable it to range from hope to despair, from sorrow to happiness, and from loneliness to love. *The Time of Your Life* is a rich panoply of life informed by Saroyan's strongest themes: the need for compassion, understanding, and love; the search for identity and intimacy; and the importance of imagination.

While *The Time of Your Life* was still running on Broadway, two other works by Saroyan appeared in New York: a ballet-play, *The Great American Goof*, and *Love's Old Sweet Song*. As Saroyan became successful in theater, he also became increasingly involved in the direction, production, and casting of his plays; he codirected *Love's Old Sweet Song* in 1940 and later directed and produced *The Beautiful People*, *Across the Board on Tomorrow Morning*, and *Talking to You*.

LOVE'S OLD SWEET SONG

Love's Old Sweet Song tells of the courtship and marriage of Barnaby Gaul, a charming confidence man of the type familiar in American literature, and Ann Hamilton, a rather innocent, financially comfortable woman. Their story is juxtaposed with that of a family of Okies, Cabot and Lena Yearling and their fourteen children. The Yearling family camps on the front lawn of the Hamiltons' Bakersfield home, which the youngest Yearling child eventually burns to the ground. The play's conclusion, however, is a happy one: Ann and Barnaby will be married and plan to adopt the child who started the fire.

THE BEAUTIFUL PEOPLE

A large, friendly California house that welcomes both strangers and friends also serves as the setting for Saroyan's *The Beautiful People*. Jonah Webster, owner of the house and lay preacher to the beautiful people, clearly states the play's theme: "Every life in the world is a miracle." The action, characters, setting, and themes of this play are those that had by this time become typical of Saroyan's work. In *The Beautiful People*, however, the importance of the valiant human struggle against adversity has diminished because adversity amounts to little more than a pet mouse that has lost its home. In reviewing this play, Joseph Wood Krutch wrote of Saroyan's "genuine naïveté," which accounts for much of the freshness of *The Time of Your Life* but also, when coupled with Saroyan's proclivity toward sentimen-

tality, produces the simplistic vision of *The Beautiful People*.

ACROSS THE BOARD ON TOMORROW MORNING AND TALKING TO YOU

Three short plays conclude Saroyan's intensive dramatic productivity in the early 1940's. *Across the Board on Tomorrow Morning* and *Talking to You*, both directed by Saroyan, were produced as a double bill, which ran for only eight performances at the Belasco Theatre. In 1961, however, these two plays were revived and successfully produced by Arthur Storch at the East End Theatre. *Talking to You* is especially interesting for its manipulation of the fourth wall. As in his treatment of vaudevillian material in *The Time of Your Life*, Saroyan effectively integrated direct address to the audience and extradramatic material in *Talking to You*.

HELLO OUT THERE

Hello Out There, the last of Saroyan's Broadway successes in the 1940's, is an uncharacteristically grim depiction of human loneliness. Rather than chancing on the generosity and hospitality found in *My Heart's in the Highlands* or *The Beautiful People*, the itinerant protagonist of *Hello Out There* finds himself in jail, unjustly accused of rape. Trapped, injured, and desperate, he uses a spoon to telegraph a message no one receives: "Hello out there." He briefly engages the sympathies of a young cook, but finally he is murdered by the husband of the woman he is accused of raping. *Hello Out There* is decidedly more realistic and less optimistic than any of Saroyan's earlier plays. It depicts evil not as aberrations or misunderstandings but as very real threats to human happiness.

1940'S AND EARLY 1950'S

Between 1943—a year after he entered the army—and 1957, when *The Cave Dwellers* opened, Saroyan wrote few conventional full-length plays. In 1943, *Get Away Old Man* appeared at the Cort Theatre for a dismal run of thirteen performances. Subsequently, Saroyan published several plays, most of which were not initially produced in New York: *Jim Dandy* (in 1947, its first substantial edition), *Don't Go Away Mad*, *Sam Ego's House*, *A Decent Birth, a Happy Funeral*, and *The Slaughter of the Innocents*.

THE CAVE DWELLERS

In *The Cave Dwellers*, Saroyan's potential for drama crystallized once again. As its setting, *The Cave Dwellers* employs a condemned New York theater in which an ensemble of the displaced, homeless, and vulnerable take refuge from the cruelty of the world. In this setting, characters with names such as King, Queen, Boy, and Mother play out what seem to be the final days of their way of life. Characters periodically venture outside the theater in search of food and provisions, but the world outside is brutal and pitiless. Much of their time in the theater is spent recalling past glories and happiness, particularly King's former stage triumphs. The element of hope in *The Cave Dwellers* is offered by the birth of a child and by the camaraderie shared by the play's characters.

1960'S

In the early 1960's, Saroyan produced some drama that was performed in London, such as *Sam the Highest Jumper of Them All* and *Settled Out of Court*, or in American universities, and he also wrote for television.

OTHER MAJOR WORKS

LONG FICTION: *The Human Comedy*, 1943; *The Adventures of Wesley Jackson*, 1946; *Rock Wagram*, 1951; *Tracy's Tiger*, 1951; *The Laughing Matter*, 1953 (reprinted as *The Secret Story*, 1954); *Mama I Love You*, 1956; *Papa You're Crazy*, 1957; *Boys and Girls Together*, 1963; *One Day in the Afternoon of the World*, 1964.

SHORT FICTION: *The Daring Young Man on the Flying Trapeze and Other Stories*, 1934; *Inhale and Exhale*, 1936; *Three Times Three*, 1936; *The Gay and Melancholy Flux: Short Stories*, 1937; *Little Children*, 1937; *Love, Here Is My Hat and Other Short Romances*, 1938; *The Trouble with Tigers*, 1938; *Three Fragments and a Story*, 1939; *Peace, It's Wonderful*, 1939; *My Name Is Aram*, 1940; *Saroyan's Fables*, 1941; *The Insurance Salesman and Other Stories*, 1941; *Forty-eight Saroyan Stories*, 1942; *Some Day I'll Be a Millionaire: Thirty-four More Great Stories*, 1944; *Dear Baby*, 1944; *The Saroyan Special: Selected Stories*, 1948; *The Fiscal Hoboes*,

1949; *The Assyrian and Other Stories*, 1950; *The Whole Voyald and Other Stories*, 1956; *William Saroyan Reader*, 1958; *Love*, 1959; *After Thirty Years: The Daring Young Man on the Flying Trapeze*, 1964; *Best Stories of William Saroyan*, 1964; *The Tooth and My Father*, 1974; *The Man with His Heart in the Highlands and Other Early Stories*, 1989.

SCREENPLAYS: *The Good Job*, 1942; *The Human Comedy*, 1943.

NONFICTION: *Harlem as Seen by Hirschfield*, 1941; *Hilltop Russians in San Francisco*, 1941; *Why Abstract?*, 1945 (with Henry Miller and Hilaire Hiler); *The Twin Adventures: The Adventures of William Saroyan*, 1950; *The Bicycle Rider in Beverly Hills*, 1952; *Here Comes, There Goes, You Know Who*, 1961; *A Note on Hilaire Hiler*, 1962; *Not Dying*, 1963; *Short Drive, Sweet Chariot*, 1966; *Look at Us: Let's See: Here We Are*, 1967; *I Used to Believe I Had Forever: Now I'm Not So Sure*, 1968; *Letters from 74 Rue Taitbout*, 1969; *Days of Life and Death and Escape to the Moon*, 1970; *Places Where I've Done Time*, 1972; *Sons Come and Go, Mothers Hang in Forever*, 1976; *Chance Meetings*, 1978; *Obituaries*, 1979; *Births*, 1983.

CHILDREN'S LITERATURE: *Me*, 1963; *Horsey Gorsey and the Frog*, 1968; *The Circus*, 1986.

MISCELLANEOUS: *My Name Is Saroyan*, 1983 (stories, verse, play fragments, and memoirs); *The New Saroyan Reader*, 1984 (Brian Darwent, editor).

BIBLIOGRAPHY

Balakian, Nona. *The World of William Saroyan*. Lewisburg, Pa.: Bucknell University Press, 1998. A critical look at the life and works of Saroyan. Bibliography and index.

Calonne, David Stephen. *William Saroyan: My Real Work Is Being*. Chapel Hill: University of North Carolina Press, 1983. A thematic analysis of Saroyan's work. Calonne compares Saroyan's life and work to those of Walt Whitman, Sherwood Anderson, Thomas Wolfe, George Bernard Shaw, Henry Miller, and Samuel Beckett. Bibliography and index.

Foard, Elisabeth C. *William Saroyan: A Reference Guide*. Boston: G. K. Hall, 1989. An annotated bibliography of Saroyan's works and of books and articles on the author. Indexes.

Hamalian, Leo, ed. *William Saroyan: The Man and Writer Remembered*. Rutherford, N.J.: Fairleigh Dickinson University Press, 1987. A biography of Saroyan that examines both his life and his works.

Keyishian, Harry, ed. *Critical Essays on William Saroyan*. New York: G. K. Hall, 1995. A collection of essays providing critical analyses of various aspects of Saroyan's works. Bibliography and index.

Lee, Lawrence, and Barry Gifford. *Saroyan: A Biography*. 1984. Reprint. Berkeley: University of California Press, 1998. This biography of Saroyan, which contains a new preface, covers his life and works. Bibliography and index.

Saroyan, Aram. *Last Rites: The Death of William Saroyan*. New York: William Morrow, 1982. A remembrance of the death of Saroyan written by his son, Aram Saroyan.

_____. *William Saroyan*. San Diego: Harcourt Brace Jovanovich, 1983. A biography of Saroyan written by his son, Aram Saroyan. Bibliography.

Whitmore, Jon. *William Saroyan: A Research and Production Sourcebook*. Modern Dramatists Research and Production Sourcebooks. Westport, Conn.: Greenwood Press, 1994. Whitmore provides a bibliography citing resources to help determine how Saroyan's plays were staged and produced. Indexes.

Joan F. Dean,
updated by Rebecca Bell-Metereau

JEAN-PAUL SARTRE

Born: Paris, France; June 21, 1905
Died: Paris, France; April 15, 1980

PRINCIPAL DRAMA

Les Mouches, pr., pb. 1943 (*The Flies*, 1946)

Huis clos, pr. 1944, pb. 1945 (*In Camera*, 1946; better known as *No Exit*, 1947)

Morts sans sépulture, pr., pb. 1946 (*The Victors*, 1948)

La Putain respectueuse, pr., pb. 1946 (*The Respectful Prostitute*, 1947)

Les Jeux sont faits, pr., pb. 1947 (*The Chips Are Down*, 1948)

Les Mains sales, pr., pb. 1948 (*Dirty Hands*, 1949)

Le Diable et le Bon Dieu, pr. 1951, pb. 1952 (*The Devil and the Good Lord*, 1953)

Kean: Ou, Désordre et génie, pb. 1952, pr. 1953 (adaptation of Alexandre Dumas, *père*'s play; *Kean: Or, Disorder and Genius*, 1954)

Nekrassov, pr. 1955, pb. 1956 (English translation, 1956)

Les Séquestrés d'Altona, pr. 1959, pb. 1960 (*The Condemned of Altona*, 1960)

Les Troyennes, pr., pb. 1965 (adaptation of Euripides' play; *The Trojan Women*, 1967)

OTHER LITERARY FORMS

A philosopher by trade and training, Jean-Paul Sartre is best known as the principal exponent of existentialism, a philosophical attitude developed from the work of such earlier thinkers as Karl Marx, Edmund Husserl, and Sartre's older contemporary Martin Heidegger. Initially developed across such fictional texts as the early novel *La Nausée* (1938; *Nausea*, 1949) and the collected short stories of *Le Mur* (1939; *The Wall and Other Stories*, 1948), Sartre's existentialism received full academic exposition in the massive *L'Être et le néant* (1943; *Being and Nothingness*, 1956). In the meantime, Sartre had discovered in the immediacy of theater a vehicle almost ideally suited to the expression of his ideas. Further experiments with prose fiction, somewhat less successful than his playwriting, resulted in the unfinished tetralogy *The Roads to Freedom* (1947-1950), which includes *L'Âge de raison* (1945; *The Age of Reason*, 1947), *Le Sursis* (1945; *The Reprieve*, 1947), and *La Mort dans l'âme* (1949; *Troubled Sleep*, 1950). Sartre also achieved distinction with speeches and essays contained in the several volumes of the journal *Situations*, published from the 1940's through the 1960's, as well as with highly personal literary criticism devoted to such authors as Charles Baudelaire, Gustave Flaubert, and Jean Genet. In 1964, Sartre declined the Nobel Prize in Literature on grounds deemed both political and personal. His autobiographical essay *Les Mots* (*The Words*) had appeared earlier in that year to considerable critical acclaim.

ACHIEVEMENTS

With the possible exception of his younger contemporary Jean Anouilh, Jean-Paul Sartre emerged as the most accomplished and noteworthy French playwright of the 1940's and early 1950's. Interested in the stage since childhood, Sartre soon found in the

Jean-Paul Sartre in 1964. (Library of Congress)

theater an ideal vehicle for his otherwise ponderous philosophical speculations on the nature of humankind and society. Indeed, the rapid spread and acceptance of Sartre's profound and challenging ideas can be almost entirely attributed to the success of his plays, in the best of which the complex is rendered not only simple but also visible and audible. At times almost too close to such popular forms as melodrama to be considered literature, Sartre's characteristic dramatic style nevertheless provides for highly entertaining, accessible, and effective theater. Animated through rapid-fire dialogue exchanged among generally well-rounded and credible characters, Sartre's notions of truth and falsehood, of authentic and inauthentic behavior become both perceptible and memorable. In the best of his plays, most notably *The Flies* and *No Exit*, Sartre achieves the enviable goal of almost instantaneous communication with his audience. Perhaps even more remarkable, the strongest of his efforts remain valid as theater even without direct consideration of the ideas that they were written to express. In this respect, Sartre's achievement by far exceeds that of his erstwhile friend Albert Camus, an experienced actor and director whose efforts at playwriting failed, in general, to reach an audience secured in advance by the success of his essays and novels.

As a student and critic of the drama, with the best of his articles collected in *Situations* and elsewhere, Sartre advocated political commitment in the theater while stopping somewhat short of the "thesis drama," best exemplified by the work of Bertolt Brecht. In his own plays, Sartre, unlike Brecht, invites the participation and identification of his audience, even in the case of those characters who are to be weighed in the balance and found wanting. Indeed, such efforts as *The Flies, No Exit*, and *The Condemned of Altona* have managed to survive most post-Brechtian thesis dramas precisely because of Sartre's basically conventional, or Aristotelian, approach to character and plot.

BIOGRAPHY

Closely related on his mother's side to the Alsatian thinker and physician Albert Schweitzer, Jean-

Paul Sartre was born in Paris on June 21, 1905. As he would later recall in *The Words*, Sartre grew up alongside his young, widowed mother in a household dominated largely by women who spoiled him, eventually provoking a virile reaction in his mature thought and prose style. After completing his secondary studies at the highly esteemed Lycée Henri IV, Sartre went on to the even more prestigious École Normale Supérieure as a student of philosophy. Failing in his initial attempt to gain the coveted, competitive *agrégation*, or secondary teaching credential, Sartre took the examination again in 1929 and was accepted. In the meantime, he had made the acquaintance of Simone de Beauvoir, a fellow philosophy student who was to remain his friend, companion, and occasional partner for life, although they never married. During the 1930's, Sartre taught philosophy in *lycées* at Le Havre and elsewhere, and he also did some traveling before settling into the life of a professional thinker and writer. Around 1932, Sartre became acquainted with the eminent actor and director Charles Dullin, a member of the famous Cartel des Quatre that had revolutionized serious French drama during the 1920's. Although Sartre would not emerge as a dramatist for another decade or so, his abiding friendship with Dullin as early as his mid-twenties must be seen as a major influence on his life and career. During the Occupation, around the time of Sartre's first efforts at playwriting, Dullin hired Sartre as a lecturer on Greek drama in his School of Theatre Arts.

Actively involved in resistance to the Nazi Occupation after the fall of France in 1940 (and a brief period of incarceration as a prisoner of war), Sartre read widely, wrote extensively, and emerged, after the Liberation in 1944, as one of the most articulate and persuasive spokespeople of the postwar French Left, expressing his ideas in plays and novels as well as in essays. As founder and guiding spirit of the liberal periodical *Les Temps modernes*, Sartre expanded both his audience and his influence. It was this journal, for example, that served as Sartre's forum for his well-publicized break with Camus after the latter's publication of *L'Homme révolté* (1951; *The Rebel*, 1956).

Unable to find a satisfactory conclusion to his projected tetralogy of novels, Sartre, during the 1950's, continued writing essays and plays, beginning work also on the autobiographical project *The Words*. Although personally committed to Marxist theory, Sartre throughout his career shunned international communism as he did most other orthodoxies; still, he remained identified with what most foreigners considered to be the French Radical Left. After publication of *The Words*, Sartre devoted his attention almost exclusively to the life and work of Gustave Flaubert, in whom he found a most suitable context (or pretext) for his own reflections on philosophy, psychology, and art. By the time of Sartre's death in 1980, his work on Flaubert covered several thousand printed pages.

ANALYSIS

Outside philosophical circles, it is likely that Jean-Paul Sartre's reputation will ultimately be determined by the success or failure of his theater. His works of literary criticism, impressive though they may be, lie somewhat outside the critical mainstream and are perhaps more profitably read either as essays or as philosophy. With the notable exception of the early *Nausea*, his novels, although well written and occasionally rewarding, fall far short of the communication established almost without apparent effort in the plays. The best of his plays, although somewhat superseded in fashion during the 1950's by the antirationalist efforts of Samuel Beckett, Eugène Ionesco, and the early Arthur Adamov, are still considered among the strongest and most effective dramatic efforts of the twentieth century.

Unlike most of the philosophers and other thinkers who, over the centuries, have attempted to write for the stage, Sartre was endowed with a basically theatrical imagination, heavily weighted toward the visual and psychological. In the strongest of his plays, the verbal element occurs as if spontaneously and by afterthought, the inevitable and hence quite plausible result of placing particular characters in a given situation. Language, instead of forming the basis of the action, arises from it as dialectic turns to dialogue. *No Exit*, in particular, was and remains a rousing piece of theater owing mainly to almost preverbal interaction among the ironically matched characters.

Although acquainted with Charles Dullin and other personalities of the Parisian stage from the early 1930's onward, Sartre did not attempt playwriting until 1940, when, as a prisoner of war, he saw the stage as a suitable vehicle for thinly veiled propaganda directed toward his fellow prisoners. The result was *Bariona*, ostensibly a Christmas play about historical events surrounding the birth of Christ. Sartre's captors, predictably sidetracked by *Bariona*'s Roman characters and setting, allowed the play to be performed as planned.

THE FLIES

Sartre's earliest performed play, *The Flies*, brings forth in memorable, generally clear theatrical terms the distinctions between "essence" and "existence," *en-soi* and *pour-soi*, explained at great length in his contemporary treatise *Being and Nothingness*. Of all beings, Sartre maintains, only human beings are capable of creating themselves through continuous acts of choice, proceeding beyond mere essence (which humans share, at birth, with stones, plants, and animals) toward uniquely human existence. Those persons who refuse to choose or to accept responsibility for choices that they have already made are guilty of "bad faith" (*mauvaise foi*) and are indeed renouncing their truly human potential for existence in favor of subhuman, or at least nonhuman, essence or "definability" that is little more preferable than death. Indeed, as the prefigured Hell of *No Exit* makes even clearer, those who reject the anguish of choice for the comfort of convenient self-definition and labels are in fact already dead, insofar as their lives could be presumed to make a difference. Only after death, contends Sartre, should it be possible to take the measure of a human life; what it then "adds up to" is beyond progress or repair. Until that point, any effort to complete the phrase "I am . . ." with either a predicate adjective or a predicate noun is the mark of a person "in love with death" who has relinquished the privilege of existence. By contrast, those who "exist," in keeping with Sartre's apparent ideal, are too busy choosing their lives and are changing too

rapidly for labels to be applied by themselves or by anyone else.

The Flies, conceived in part as a rebuttal to Jean Giraudoux's *Électre* (pr., pb. 1937; *Electra*, 1952), presents an Orestes who arrives in Argos quite unaware of his identity, only to choose the life and deeds of Orestes after weighing the evidence of Clytemnestra's crime against his own intentions. Intended also as a political statement, its topical import, thinly veiled by Sartre's then conventional use of antique characters and setting, *The Flies* portrays an Argive people crushed beneath the weight of a collective guilt, imposed on them from without by their self-serving and murderous rulers. Even Electra, perceived as a rebel in most prior retellings of the myth, is portrayed as inauthentic in her behavior: At the moment of crisis, she remains trapped in the acceptance (or perhaps even enjoyment) of an image of herself as seen by the usurpers. Only Orestes, having opted to define himself by choice alone, is capable of meaningful action.

Trading on a current vogue for Greek myth on the French stage, Sartre in *The Flies* managed both forceful anti-Nazi polemic and a reasonably effective presentation of his developing existentialist theories. Over the years since the play was first performed, even critics friendly to Sartre and to existentialism have perceived major flaws in the play that appear to have escaped notice for at least the first decade of its performed and published life; still, *The Flies* remains deservedly among the best-known and most frequently revived French plays.

No small part of the play's effectiveness derives from Sartre's confident use of imagery and language bordering frequently on crudity. The central image of predatory insects reflected in the play's title reverberates often throughout the dialogue, supported by complementary allusions to garbage, filth, and tender, vulnerable flesh. Taking as his real object of scorn the collective guilt that had haunted the French people since the fall of France in 1940, and the subsequent establishment of a collaborationist government at Vichy, Sartre in *The Flies* effectively exploits the murder of Agamemnon and the tyrannical rule of Aegistheus to draw parallels between the Argives and the French. In Sartre's version, Aegistheus and Clytemnestra have consolidated their rule by imposing on their subjects a collective guilt symbolized in a national tradition of mourning. At the start of the play, each subject, encouraged by the rulers, believes himself or herself to be vicariously guilty of Agamemnon's murder, having willed the event in advance; annually, on the anniversary of Agamemnon's death, ruled and rulers join in an act of ritual penance, groveling and fawning in gestures made vividly real by Sartre's pungent imagery and language. Such is the scene beheld by the young and callow Orestes, who arrives in Argos as the foreign student Philebus, accompanied by his tutor. It remains therefore for the disinterested, detached Philebus voluntarily to choose his identity as Orestes, delivering the Argive people from their collective guilt with two additional assassinations for which he alone will bear the blame and guilt.

Although managed perhaps as effectively as possible within the limits of legend, Sartre's portrayal of Orestes' choice constitutes one of the play's more fundamental and abiding weaknesses. Much as Sartre would have the audience accept Orestes as the archetypal existential hero, choosing his own existence above the comforting eventuality of essence, what remains at the play's end, even in "existential" terms, is the sum of his deeds, precisely those deeds attributed to Orestes by several thousand years of legend and theatrical experience. Considerably more effective is Sartre's presentation of Electra, a truly archetypal Sartrean coward who, at the moment of crisis, disastrously lacks the courage of her frequently spoken convictions. Long identified as a rebellious child who hates her mother and stepfather, Electra prefers the comfort of collective guilt to individual responsibility for their assassination. Almost equally effective is Sartre's evocation of Jupiter, a suitably decadent Roman deity who materializes in response to Orestes' repeated appeals for help from the Greek god Zeus. Displaying all the bonhomie of a corrupt political manipulator, Jupiter shows off his superhumanity with impressive parlor tricks, only to admit after Orestes' deeds that the gods are in fact inventions of mankind, powerless against truly free men.

At the very end of *The Flies*, Sartre's mixed metaphors run somewhat out of control as Orestes leaves Argos pursued by a horde of buzzing flies, defining himself by his current behavior as a curious blend of the Paraclete and the Pied Piper of Hamelin. Claiming that he has expiated the guilt of the Argives by taking the full burden on himself, he still refuses the additional burden of government. Self-defined as "a King with neither land nor subjects," Orestes then trudges, as it were, off into the sunset, leaving each of his putative subjects free to create his or her own destiny. Perhaps impressive as polemic, the ending of *The Flies* proves a bit too weak, on reflection, to carry the full burden of Sartre's existentialist exposition. No doubt confined within the restrictions of his chosen material, Sartre in *The Flies* still fails to provide the convincing illustration of human freedom that he appears to have had in mind. Notwithstanding, *The Flies* remains a perennially rousing and thought-provoking play, even when divorced from the historical context of its conception.

No Exit

With *No Exit*, first performed within fifteen months after *The Flies*, Sartre so far transcended his earlier effort as to prove that prior success to have been no accident. Here, unbound by the constraints of established legend, Sartre exercised his own freedom to bring forth an utterly human interpersonal hell for which physical death is no prerequisite. Although supposedly dead and hence incapable of changing the sum of their lives, the womanizer, lesbian, and nymphomaniac who find themselves locked uneasily together in the eternal torture of interdependence merely replicate the suffering endured, through implied consent, by those who consistently refuse to alter or even question their daily approach to life.

Pursuing the penchant for crude if apt imagery that had transformed Orestes' Furies into a horde of biting flies, Sartre, in *No Exit*, went even further to assure himself of an audience through his use of shock tactics, including explicit if still printable speech. Although some observers continue to see in the play a reasonably successful attempt at Camus's stated goal of "modern tragedy," Sartre's most perceptible method is that of melodrama as commonly interpreted, and practiced, by the producers of broadcast serials. *No Exit*, although often read in literature courses, might well be described as subliterary; on the stage, however, it remains both audacious and compelling.

The French title of *No Exit* is drawn from legal terminology (of which the British translation, *In Camera*, is no doubt a more faithful rendering than the American) to denote a trial or hearing conducted behind closed doors. *No Exit* is in all likelihood Sartre's one true dramatic masterpiece. Its action necessarily compressed into a single act of a little more than one hour's playing time, Sartre's second professional dramatic effort goes considerably further than *The Flies* toward illustrating the author's philosophy in memorable theatrical terms. Even without consideration of the ideas involved, *No Exit* remains one of the most effective and affecting plays to emerge from France in the twentieth century.

Intended as communication rather than as literature, *No Exit* achieves its remarkable effect at what might well be considered the level of soap opera, thanks in part to the brutal frankness of expression that Sartre had all but perfected in *The Flies*. Set in an imagined Hell that, by Sartre's own admission, need not be the afterlife, *No Exit* portrays the mutual torture of three individuals defined as "dead" by their individual resistance to change or even to self-interrogation. Within the terms of the play, the three principals are portrayed as physically dead as well; yet it is soon clear that such death has merely fixed and confined a reality of long standing. Even Inès, the strongest of the three main characters and the one among them who most clearly speaks for the playwright, remains condemned by her early and unquestioning acceptance of a label applied to her from without, by perceived public opinion.

Significantly, at least two of the three main characters of *No Exit* are little surprised to find themselves in Hell. Both Garcin and Inès have died violently; moreover, the conduct of their lives has led them to expect the worst. What they have not anticipated, however, is the precise nature of the place; Garcin, first to arrive, is somewhat nonplussed to find a Second Empire drawing room instead of a medieval torture chamber. As Inès will soon observe, however, whoever is in charge has decided to save on staff by having the "clients" torture one another themselves; indeed, the three eternal inhabitants of the overdecorated room have been diabolically well matched. Garcin, formerly a journalist, is a self-styled "tough guy" who believes himself to be in Hell because of the way he treated his long-suffering wife: On at least one occasion, he recalls, he brought his mulatto mistress into their home and had his wife serve them breakfast in bed. Inès, perhaps even tougher, admitted her lesbianism early in life and has since nourished few, if any, illusions. Only the third arrival, an incipient nymphomaniac and would-be socialite named Estelle, appears surprised to find herself in Hell; she is also the only member of the trio to have died from natural causes. Although Estelle has actually committed murder, her presence in Sartre's Hell derives rather from her passive, shallow, and, above all, unexamined life: Born poor, she married for money and became an unreflective snob. Inès, although sexually attracted to Estelle, despises her because she never had to work for a living; Inès, meanwhile, remains bitterly proud of her own long service as a postal clerk.

As the action progresses, it soon becomes clear that Garcin has the most to hide. As editor of a pacifist journal in Rio de Janeiro, he left for Mexico City as soon as World War II was declared; arrested for desertion, he was subsequently executed by a firing squad. Inès, considerably more honest with herself than Garcin has ever been, loses little time in exploiting Garcin's inner fears that he has died a coward's death, thus proving that he has lived a coward's life as well. Regardless of his hopes or motivations, the line has now been drawn, and his life adds up to nothing more or less than the sum of his proven actions. In the cold light of Inès' lucidity, Garcin stands all but revealed as a coward; his only hope, as it were, is to persuade Inès that he is a hero.

Inès, although no doubt the most exemplary of the three characters portrayed in *No Exit*, proves deserving of her fate because, although lucid, she has accepted without question the condemnation of society. Trading on the French expression *femme damnée* (literally, "damned woman") to denote a lesbian, Sartre here presents a woman who has allowed society's negative judgment of her sexual preference not only to dominate her life but also to define it. Most of Inès' life has indeed been spent living up (or down) to her bad name—disrupting marriages and causing suicides. Apparently, it has never occurred to her to choose any identity or existence other than that chosen for her by perceived public opinion.

Of the three characters, Estelle is deliberately portrayed as the least interesting, the object of mildly political satire insofar as she is a mindless, useless member of the bourgeoisie. For Estelle, the greatest torture to be found in Hell is the absence of mirrors, on which she has come to depend for confirmation of her essence. In one of the play's most effective conceits, Inès is able to manipulate Estelle completely by telling her that her lipstick is off-center or that she has a pimple on her chin. Only gradually does Estelle, a woman overfond of euphemisms, come to admit that she was guilty of drowning her love child, born of a relatively poor man who later committed suicide.

Outspoken not only in her preference for women but also in her parallel antipathy toward men, Inès provides the play with most of its perceptible action. As the most lucid of the trio, she is also the most emotional and the most articulate. Garcin's inept, halfhearted efforts to make love to Estelle elicit from Inès shrill cries of envy and denunciation. Estelle, meanwhile, proves resistant to Inès's amorous advances so long as there is a man in the room. Garcin, although attracted to Estelle, insists on her reassurance that he is not a coward, but Estelle remains too flighty and shallow to care whether he is a coward, "so long as he kisses well." When the door pops open unexpectedly, however, none of the characters leaves; each has by then become too dependent on the purely negative tensions that bind them together. Garcin, for example, "needs" Inès because she alone can understand him, her judgment an immovable object against which he must continually try his supposedly irresistible force.

Although, as Sartre concedes, the principals of *No Exit* need not be physically dead, the assumption of

their demise allows for the inclusion of certain theatrical tricks that enhance the play's effectiveness. Being dead, the characters therefore cannot kill one another. As the conversation continues, moreover, it becomes increasingly evident that time in Hell has been somehow compressed (or perhaps stretched). Soon after their arrival, still somewhat attached to their lives, the characters can still see their erstwhile friends and surroundings; with time, however, their vision grows dimmer, and it soon becomes clear that each minute of their conversation is equivalent to several weeks on earth. At one point, for example, Garcin observes that his widow, alive at the start of the play, has been dead for about six months. By then, however, such details are quite without importance, as all three are well settled into the hell of mutual incomprehension that they have long since chosen through their actions.

Perennially popular with both professional and amateur theater groups, *No Exit* remains quite probably the most widely disseminated of Sartre's plays, its few flaws generally well concealed by the tightness and efficiency of its construction. Never again would Sartre the playwright express himself with such unerring aptness and economy, although at least two of his subsequent plays also give convincing dramatic form to his ideas.

Having discovered, with *No Exit*, the apparent secret of reaching and keeping an audience, Sartre continued to direct the remainder of his plays toward the same real or imagined public, with varying degrees of success. His next two plays, produced on a double bill in 1946, are deemed by most to have been failures and are seldom read or revived: *The Victors*, dealing with captured Resistance fighters during World War II, is an unconvincing blend of near-tragedy and melodrama; *The Respectful Prostitute*, incongruously set in an America that Sartre had not yet seen and based on the Scottsboro race trials of the 1930's, falls considerably short of Sartre's apparent intention of social satire with comic overtones. In both plays, however, Sartre's expressed thought remains consistent with his earlier and more successful dramatic efforts, stressing the difference between authentic and inauthentic behavior as exemplified in the individual character's perception between ends and means.

DIRTY HANDS

In 1948, Sartre undertook to combine the best of his approaches to theater with such existing conventions as the political thriller and the murder mystery. The result was *Dirty Hands* (also known as *Red Gloves*), later successfully filmed, an inversion of traditional procedure in that both victim and assassin are identified from the start. Consistent with Sartre's philosophy and general outlook, the suspense—and it can be considerable, provided that the play is competently directed—resides not in the identity but rather in the motive of the murderer, who himself participates in searching for the truth. A reluctant assassin at the very least, Hugo Barine must decide to his own satisfaction whether the shooting for which he has served time in prison was motivated by simple passion or by politics. Unsparing in its satire of expediency in leftist politics or indeed in any politics, *Dirty Hands* was interpreted by many contemporary observers, no doubt inaccurately, as Sartre's "anti-Communist" play. In fact, *Dirty Hands* is both less and more than that, a philosophical play with strong psychological overtones, which, in a sense, simply happens to be about politics. Although perhaps excessive in length, *Dirty Hands* has proved over the years to be both less topical and more durable than was at first supposed, a powerful and memorable character study evoking the thin line between the psychological and social dimensions of the individual, here exemplified by the indulged, immature, and irresolute Hugo.

Dirty Hands remains one of Sartre's more noteworthy and satisfying efforts, a vigorous melodrama with undertones of both the comic and the tragic. Psychological rather than political in substance, *Dirty Hands* offers as its central character a considerably less-than-tragic hero, one who has committed murder without quite knowing why. Based in part on the known facts surrounding the assassination of Leon Trotsky in 1940, the murder of Hoederer was planned long in advance as a political act by members of his own party; the problem, however, derives from the party's ironic choice of an assassin. Hugo

Barine, a pampered rich boy with strong radical leanings no doubt motivated by guilt, finds in the gruff, avuncular Hoederer a surrogate father figure to exceed his wildest dreams. For the longest time he cannot bring himself to kill the man, even as the party regulars grow increasingly impatient with his hesitation and plan an assault of their own. When at last Hugo does bring himself to kill Hoederer, his motives lie concealed beneath a tangled web of conflicting emotions, not the least of which is cuckoldry. In order to live with himself, however, Hugo must try to disentangle the web even after serving time in prison for the murder. By the time that Hugo regains his freedom, matters are complicated still further by the fact that Hoederer has been posthumously rehabilitated by the same political forces that engineered his death.

Exposed largely through flashbacks, the action of *Dirty Hands* involves a large cast of varied and interesting characters, ranging from the radical Olga (who probably loves Hugo but will not intervene to save his life) to the two inadvertently humorous hired thugs assigned to Hoederer as bodyguards. It is Hoederer himself, however, who emerges somewhat incongruously as the true hero of the play, one of the few truly decent and admirable characters in all of Sartre's theater. True to his character, he has done nearly all in his power to avoid romantic involvement with Hugo's wife, Jessica, who, without his knowledge, has volunteered to commit the murder herself so long as her husband refuses to do so.

With the possible exception of Hugo, Jessica is in all likelihood the most complex and fascinating character in *Dirty Hands*, although she often appears to have been cast by Sartre in the wrong play: Although her flirtatious and enigmatic behavior will provide one of the possible motivations for Hugo's act of murder, Jessica more often appears extraneous to the action, included more for her intrinsic interest than for her importance to the plot. Perhaps a borderline psychotic, Jessica is able to relate to her husband only during scenes of childish game playing that closely resemble *folies à deux*; such scenes, although they cast some doubt on Hugo's sanity, shed little light on his possible motivations.

Perhaps the major weakness of the play is that Hugo, for all his clinical interest as a psychological phenomenon, is simply not sufficiently interesting as a character to involve the spectator's interest in his possible thoughts as he pulls the trigger. His final, retrospective gesture of heroism—or suicide—thus strikes many audiences as either anticlimactic or gratuitous, robbing *Dirty Hands* of much of its apparently intended impact. Too particularized, and in a negative way, to be seen as Everyman, yet viewed too closely for Brechtian objectivity, the character of Hugo ultimately fails to bear the burden of exposition placed on his slender shoulders by an author then enamored of psychological case histories.

Heavily cut and adapted almost beyond recognition, *Dirty Hands* enjoyed a long, successful run in New York during the late 1940's as *Red Gloves*, an "anti-communist play by Jean-Paul Sartre." Sartre, believing his intentions to have been betrayed, protested vigorously, but the play went on to achieve a reputation perhaps ill-deserved. In the original French, *Dirty Hands* remains a better play than it at first may seem, but it is surely not a political play except to the extent that Sartre, like any effective satirist, casts aspersions on all sides.

The Devil and the Good Lord

Sartre's subsequent stage effort, *The Devil and the Good Lord*, is perhaps best remembered as the last play to be mounted by the eminent director Louis Jouvet, who died some two months after the play opened to somewhat mixed reviews. Perhaps overly ambitious both in theme and scope, *The Devil and the Good Lord* shares the historical setting and characters of Johann Wolfgang von Goethe's *Götz von Berlichingen mit der eisernen Hand* (pb. 1773; *Götz von Berlichingen with the Iron Hand*, 1799), which Sartre scrupulously avoided reading in order to guarantee, or prove, the authenticity of his own dramatic statement. Although considered by some critics to be among the author's finest dramatic efforts, Sartre's portrayal of Goetz and his uprising has generally failed to withstand the test of time and is seldom read or revived.

Kean

Somewhat more successful is *Kean*, adapted from Alexandre Dumas, *père*'s version of the British ac-

tor's life at the request of the French actor Pierre Brasseur, who had appeared in Jouvet's production of *The Devil and the Good Lord*. Couched, like the original, within the framework of a play-within-a-play, Sartre's adaptation successfully transforms the Romantic hero of Dumas into an anguished existentialist in search of his own authenticity. As interpreted by Brasseur, the play was not without its comic dimensions, and Sartre, thus encouraged, went on to attempt an original comedy for the first time since *The Respectful Prostitute*.

Nekrassov

The result was *Nekrassov*, a slight but generally successful satire of politics, the press, and the institution of celebrity. The protagonist, a petty criminal and confidence man named Georges de Valéra, endeavors to avoid capture by assuming the identity of one Nekrassov, a high-ranking Soviet politician who has mysteriously dropped out of sight. Abetted by the staff of a highly conservative evening newspaper, the fugitive plays his role of defector with consummate skill, only to find his authenticity compromised by right-wing political interests even after the real Nekrassov is discovered to have been sunning himself in the Crimea on a long-overdue vacation. Given the need for a Nekrassov who has defected to the West, de Valéra finds himself trapped in an unwelcome and increasingly uncomfortable role. For all its merits, *Nekrassov* nevertheless fell somewhat below the level of enlightened entertainment that audiences and critics alike had come to expect from Sartre, and in what turned out to be his last original play, Sartre appeared determined to offer something more.

The Condemned of Altona

The Condemned of Altona, first performed in 1959, ranks by any standard among Sartre's more impressive and memorable efforts, treading a thin line between realism and allegory in its evocation of contemporary history. The central character of the play is Franz von Gerlach, an erstwhile Nazi officer who has spent the postwar years in the apparent grip of madness, carefully hidden from view by his wealthy and influential family, while it is assumed by everyone else that he has died in Argentina. Determined to justify at all costs behavior that is now deemed abominable, Franz continually explains himself in taped addresses to the "tribunal of history," represented by hallucinated crabs on the ceiling that Franz sees as the future inhabitants of Earth. Like *Dirty Hands*, *The Condemned of Altona* is perhaps excessively long and somewhat confused in its plotting; yet it amply justifies the reputation that Sartre had earned with his earliest plays.

Sartre's last original play repays the spectator's attention with an ingenious, closely reasoned inquiry into the lessons of contemporary history. Although explicitly set in post-Nazi Germany, with strong topical allusions to the French presence in Algeria as well, *The Condemned of Altona*, like *Dirty Hands*, deals less with politics than with psychology. Franz von Gerlach, elder son of a wealthy shipbuilder, initially resists the Nazis with both his conscience and his deeds, until he learns to his chagrin that his inherited wealth renders true resistance impossible. Thereafter, he goes to war against the Allies with every expectation of meeting an early death in battle. Instead, he survives just long enough to inflict the torture of two captured Russian partisans and thereafter to become the Butcher of Smolensk, a full-fledged Nazi war criminal. Believed dead, he has in fact spent the better part of fifteen years in the shelter of his family home, protected from the world (in all senses of the term) by an apparent wall of madness. The only member of the family who even sees him in his attic lair is his sister Leni, with whom he has long since conceived an incestuous relationship. Leni, whose personality has by now all but fused with his own, participates willingly in his delirium and nurtures his illusion that the war is still in progress, with Germany losing all its wealth and strength to the Allies. It is the elder von Gerlach's impending death from cancer that causes a long overdue rent in the antisocial fabric of Franz's isolation. Determined that he and his elder son should die together, the old man begins hatching desperate schemes to entice Franz out of hiding. In the main, these efforts involve his daughter-in-law Johanna, with whom the crafty old fellow correctly predicts that Franz will fall in love.

As the outside world begins to invade his life in the person of Johanna, it becomes increasingly clear to characters and spectator alike that Franz's insanity is largely willful, if indeed not totally feigned. As a basically decent man formed in a tradition of Protestant faith and practice, Franz simply cannot bring himself to admit that he has been the Butcher of Smolensk. Instead, he recites the "last messages of a dying Germany" to an imagined audience of crabs on the ceiling, taking care to tape his messages for posterity. Presumably, in Franz's semilucid consciousness, the inhuman crustaceans represent the future inhabitants of earth, successors to a humankind that is about to bungle its last chance. As in *Dirty Hands*, exposition occurs largely in vivid flashbacks, evolving toward a crisis in the present as Franz learns that the war is over and Johanna, who has just succeeded in fanning Franz's last latent spark of humanity, renounces him forever on learning the guilty secret of his past. The double suicide will then take place as old von Gerlach has planned it, with only his own body to be buried with funeral honors. After all, Franz has been "buried" for years under a headstone bearing his name in Argentina.

For all the unwieldiness and implausibility of its plot, *The Condemned of Altona* is, on balance, a rather more successful and satisfying play than *Dirty Hands*, owing in part to the generally credible and not-unsympathetic character of Franz. Indeed, the conflict between memory and ideals as one contemplates the unthinkable might well lead to madness, either willful or involuntary. In any event, Franz is a more dimensional and fully realized character than is Hugo Barine of *Dirty Hands*. Together with Johanna, the spectator, even as he finds Franz ultimately repellent, cannot fail to have found him more than a little fascinating as well. Aided by some of the most compelling dialogue that Sartre had written since *No Exit*, the play tends to linger in the spectator's mind, raising questions of guilt and innocence that can never truly be resolved. Indeed, suggests Sartre, the image of humankind in the mid-twentieth century is hardly preferable to that of the crabs on Franz von Gerlach's ceiling. Whether Sartre intended this play to be his last, it nevertheless closed his playwriting career on an impressive note approximating that of triumph.

THE TROJAN WOMEN

By 1959, however, Sartre had all but lost interest in the stage as a vehicle for his thought and expression, preferring instead to practice the type of literary criticism that had occupied him earlier in his career. *The Trojan Women*, his adaptation of Euripides' *Trōiades* (415 B.C.E.; *The Trojan Women*, 1782), first performed in 1965, contains relatively few personal touches and was, in any case, his last attempt at writing for the stage.

OTHER MAJOR WORKS

LONG FICTION: *La Nausée*, 1938 (*Nausea*, 1949); *L'Âge de raison*, 1945 (*The Age of Reason*, 1947); *Le Sursis*, 1945 (*The Reprieve*, 1947); *La Mort dans l'âme*, 1949 (*Troubled Sleep*, 1950; also known as *Iron in the Soul*; previous three novels collectively known as *Les Chemins de la liberté*, in English *The Roads to Freedom*).

SHORT FICTION: *Le Mur*, 1939 (*The Wall and Other Stories*, 1948).

NONFICTION: *L'Imagination*, 1936 (*Imagination: A Psychological Critique*, 1962); *Esquisse d'une théorie des émotions*, 1939 (*The Emotions: Outline of a Theory*, 1948); *L'Imaginaire: Psychologie phénoménologique de l'imagination*, 1940 (*The Psychology of Imagination*, 1948); *L'Être et le néant*, 1943 (*Being and Nothingness*, 1956); *L'Existentialisme est un Humanisme*, 1946 (*Existentialism*, 1947; also as *Existentialism and Humanism*, 1948); *Réflexions sur la question juive*, 1946 (*Anti-Semite and Jew*, 1948); *Baudelaire*, 1947 (English translation, 1950); *Qu'est-ce que la littérature?*, 1947 (*What Is Literature?*, 1949); *Situations I-X*, 1947-1975 (10 volumes; partial translation 1965-1977); *Saint-Genet: Comédien et martyr*, 1952 (*Saint Genet: Actor and Martyr*, 1963); *Critique de la raison dialectique, précéde de question de méthode*, 1960 (*Search for a Method*, 1963); *Critique de la raison dialectique, I: Théorie des ensembles pratiques*, 1960 (*Critique of Dialectical Reason, I: Theory of Practical Ensembles*, 1976); *Les Mots*, 1964 (*The Words*, 1964); *L'Idiot de la famille: Gustave Flaubert, 1821-1857*, 1971-1972 (3 volumes; partial translation *The Family Idiot: Gustave Flaubert, 1821-1857*, 1981, 1987); *Un Théâtre de situations*, 1973 (*Sartre on Theater*, 1976); *Les Carnets de la drôle de guerre*, 1983 (*The War Diaries of Jean-Paul Sartre: November, 1939-March, 1940*, 1984); *Le scénario Freud*, 1984 (*The Freud Scenario*, 1985).

BIBLIOGRAPHY

Anderson, Thomas C. *Sartre's Two Ethics: From Authenticity to Integral Humanity.* Chicago: Open Court, 1993. This work, while focusing on Sartre's ethics, provides an explanation of the themes that pervaded his dramatic works. Bibliography and index.

Bloom, Harold, ed. *Jean-Paul Sartre.* Phildelphia: Chelsea House, 2001. A collection of critical essays on Sartre, with an introduction by Harold Bloom. Bibliography and index.

Howells, Christina, ed. *The Cambridge Companion to Sartre.* New York: Cambridge University Press, 1992. A comprehensive reference work devoted to Sartre and his life, times, and literary works. Bibliography and index.

_____. *Sartre.* Modern Literatures in Perspective. New York: Longman, 1995. Editor Howells presents critical analyses of the literary works of Sartre. Bibliography and index.

Kamber, Richard. *On Sartre.* Belmont, Calif.: Wadsworth/Thomson Learning, 2000. Although this volume focuses on Sartre as philosopher, it explicates the thought and viewpoints that permeate his literary works. Bibliography.

McBride, William L., ed. *Existentialist Literature and Aesthetics.* Vol. 7 in *Sartre and Existentialism.* New York: Garland, 1997. This volume, part of a multivolume series on Sartre and his philosophy, examines his literary works and how existentialism was expressed in them. Bibliography.

_____. *Sartre's Life, Times, and Vision du Monde.* Vol. 3 in *Sartre and Existentialism.* New York: Garland, 1997. This volume, one in a multivolume work on Sartre and existentialism, looks at his life, the times in which he lived and wrote, and his worldview. Bibliography.

Thody, Philip Malcolm Waller. *Jean-Paul Sartre.* New York: St. Martin's Press, 1992. An examination of Sartre as novelist, with some reference to his dramatic works.

Wardman, Harold W. *Jean-Paul Sartre: The Evolution of His Thought and Art*. Lewiston, N.Y.: Edwin Mellen, 1992. A critical examination of the literary works of Sartre that traces his philosophical development through his writings. Bibliography and index.

David B. Parsell

ALFONSO SASTRE

Born: Madrid, Spain; February 20, 1926

PRINCIPAL DRAMA

Ha sonado la muerte, pr. 1946, pb. 1949 (with Medardo Fraile)

Uranio 235, pr. 1946, pb. 1949

Cargamento de sueños, pr. 1948, pb. 1949

Comedia sonámbula, pb. 1949 (with Medardo Fraile)

Teatro de vanguardia, pb. 1949

Prólogo patético, wr. 1950, pb. 1964 (*Pathetic Prologue*, 1968)

El cubo de la basura, wr. 1951, pb. 1965

Escuadra hacia la muerte, pr. 1953, pb. 1960 (*The Condemned Squad*, 1961; also as *Death Squad*, 1964)

La mordaza, pr. 1954, pb. 1956

La sangre de Dios, pr. 1955

El cuervo, pr. 1957, pb. 1960

El pan de todos, pr. 1957, pb. 1963

Medea, pr. 1958, pb. 1967 (adaptation of Euripides' play)

Asalto nocturno, wr. 1959, pb. 1964

Muerte en el barrio, pr. 1959, pb. 1960

Ana Kleiber, pr., pb. 1960 (*Anna Kleiber*, 1962)

La cornada, pr., pb. 1960 (*Death Thrust*, 1964)

Guillermo Tell tiene los ojos tristes, pb. 1960, pr. 1965 (*Sad Are the Eyes of William Tell*, 1970)

Teatro, pb. 1960

Tierra roja, pb. 1960 (*Red Earth*, 1962)

En la red, pr. 1961, pb. 1966 (*In the Web*, 1964)

Oficio de tinieblas, wr. 1962, pr., pb. 1967

Los acreedores, pr. 1962, pb. 1967 (adaptation of August Strindberg's *Fordringsägare*)

El circulito de tiza: O, Historia de una muñeca abandonado, pr. 1962, pb. 1967 (*The Abandoned Doll*, 1996; adaptation of Bertolt Brecht's *The Caucasian Chalk Circle*)

Mulato, pr. 1963 (adaptation of Langston Hughes's play)

Teatro, pb. 1964

M.S.V.: O, La sangre y la ceniza; Flores rojas para Miguel Servet, wr. 1965, pr. 1976, pb. 1977

La taberna fantástica, wr. 1966, pr. 1985, pb. 1990

Marat-Sade, pb. 1966, pr. 1968 (adaptation of Peter Weiss's play)

Teatro selecto, pb. 1966

Obras completas, pb. 1967

Crónicas romanas, wr. 1968, pb. 1979, pr. 1982

Rosas rojas para mí, pr., pb. 1969 (adaptation of Sean O'Casey's *Red Roses for Me*)

Los secuestrados de Altona, pr. 1972 (adaptation of Jean-Paul Sartre's *Les Séquestrés d'Altona*)

Las cintas magnéticas, pr., pb. 1973 (radio play; *The Magnetic Tapes*, 1971)

Ejercicios de terror, pb. 1973

Ahola no es de leil, wr. 1975, pr. 1979, pb. 1980

Tragedia fantástica de la gitana Celestina, wr. 1977-1978, pr. 1979, pb. 1982

El hjjo único de Guillermo Tell, wr. 1980, pb. 1983 (*Young Billy Tell*, 1996)

Aventura en Euskadi, pr. 1982, pb. 1993

Los hombres y sus sombras, pr. 1982, pb. 1988

Jenofa Juncal, wr. 1983, pb. 1986, pr. 1988 (*The Red Gypsy*, 1990; adaptation of Velez de Guevara's *La serrana de la vera*)

El viaje infinito de Sancho Panza, wr. 1983-1984, pr. 1992

El cuento de la reforma, wr. 1984, pb. 1995

Los últimos dias de Emmanuel Kant contados por Ernesto Teodor Amadeo Hoffmann, wr. 1984-1985, pb. 1989, pr. 1990

Revelaciones inesperadas sobre Moisés, wr. 1988, pb. 1991

Asalto a una ciudad, pb. 1988 (adaptation of Lope de Vega's play *El asalto de Mastrique*)

¿Dónde estás, Ulalume, dónde estás?, pb. 1990, pr. 1994

Teatro de Alfonso Sastre, pb. 1990 (51 volumes)

¡Han matado a Prokopius!, pb. 1996

Crimen al otro lado del espejo, pb. 1997

El asesinato de la luna llena, pb. 1998

OTHER LITERARY FORMS

Alfonso Sastre has written hundreds of articles and essays. He has also published several collections of poetry, short stories, and books on dramatic theory, as well as many novels.

ACHIEVEMENTS

During the rule of General Francisco Franco, Alfonso Sastre is credited with attempting to revive the Spanish national theater during the years following the Spanish Civil War (1936-1939). After the war, economic hardship and strict censorship caused many Spanish intellectuals either to quit writing or to emigrate. Sastre was one of the few playwrights who opted to stay in Spain and to continue the effort to create meaningful, politically involved drama. Sastre's entire life has been a struggle to reform Spain's political and theatrical institutions. In 1945, before completing his university studies, he helped to found the Arte Nuevo (new art), an experimental theater group that sought to offer an alternative to the shallow, conventional plays that dominated the stage during post-civil war Spain. It also attempted to incorporate new methods of staging and acting. Although the group lasted only two years and had no immediate impact, it provided valuable training to several young men who would later be instrumental in the revitalization of Spanish theater. In 1948, Sastre became the first theater editor of a student magazine called *La hora* (the hour), thereby initiating his career as an essayist. His essays usually addressed political questions—in particular, the relationship between art and politics.

In 1950, Sastre and José María de Quinto, who had also been involved in Arte Nuevo, founded Teatro de Agitación Social (theater of social agitation, known as TAS), another new theater group. TAS attempted to introduce major foreign playwrights such as Arthur Miller, Bertolt Brecht, Jean-Paul Sartre, and Eugene O'Neill to the Spanish public. In their manifesto, Sastre and Quinto explained that their purpose was to make the spectator think about major political and social issues. The group was censored immediately by the authorities. Yet Sastre was building a reputation and, in 1956, he received a grant from UNESCO.

In 1960, Sastre and Quinto again combined forces to form the Grupo de Teatro Realista (realist theater group, known as GTR), another dissident troupe. The formation of the GTR reflected Sastre's interest in realism in the arts. Its purpose was to bring serious, politically provocative plays to the Spanish stage, as well as to explore realism in drama. Although the GTR, like its predecessors, fell victim to censorship, it met with some success. In 1961, it presented three major plays: *Vestire gli ignudi* (pr. 1922, pb. 1923; *Naked*, 1924), by Luigi Pirandello; *El tintero* (pr. 1961; the inkwell), by Carlos Muñiz; and *In the Web*, by Sastre. A relationship was established between GTR and UNESCO's International Institute of the Theatre. One of the greatest contributions that Sastre has made to theater in Spain is the introduction of European and American playwrights to Spanish audiences through TAS and GTR, as well as through his numerous essays.

In 1964, Sastre participated in a Festival of Latin American Theater, held in Cuba. He returned to Havana in 1968 to attend the Cultural Congress. Sastre's plays continue to be popular among Spanish youth and in parts of Europe and Latin America. *The Condemned Squad*, *Death Thrust*, *La mordaza* (the gag), and *Muerte en el barrio* (death in the neighborhood) have appeared in student editions in the United

Alfonso Sastre in 1974. (AP/Wide World Photos)

States. With the political liberalization of Spain following the death of General Francisco Franco, Sastre's radical stance has diminished in significance.

The death of General Franco and the ensuing full democratization of Spain enabled Sastre to have many of his previously written plays performed and published. Although other playwrights turned to entertainment fare, Sastre remained committed to intellectual and politically engaged works. Some audiences turned away from his plays, which became increasingly literary in style to the point where some are considered impossible to actually put on a stage. Yet the 1980's and 1990's saw a major international boom in the production of Sastre's plays.

In 1985, Sastre won Spain's prestigious Premio Nacional de Teatro for his stunning *La taberna fantástica* (the fantastic tavern), which had just been performed, nineteen years after being written. The same play won Sastre the prize El Espectador y la Critica (the spectator and the critic) in 1986. In 1993, Sastre received the national prize for drama again, this time for his play *Jenofa Juncal*, which had only

been performed abroad in Leeds, in Britain, when the prize was awarded. Sastre also received Spain's national prize for literature, Premio Nacional de Literatura, for his fiction in the same year.

BIOGRAPHY

Alfonso Sastre was a child of ten when the Spanish Civil War erupted and an adolescent during the harsh years following the conflict. He developed professionally during the dictatorship of Franco, when severe censorship was in effect. His work, like that of many other Spanish artists of his generation, was a response to the political absolutism that prevailed until late 1975, when Franco died.

Sastre is from an artistic family, several of whose members he characterized as Bohemian. His father did some acting and then gave it up for economic reasons. Sastre began his theater career in 1945, when he participated in the founding of the Arte Nuevo theater group. Arte Nuevo performed Sastre's first plays, *Uranio 235* (uranium 235) and *Ha sonado la muerte* (death has sounded), the latter written in collaboration with Medardo Fraile. In 1947, Sastre and Fraile wrote another play, *Comedia sonámbula* (sleepwalker's comedy), which was not performed. Arte Nuevo presented one more drama by Sastre, *Cargamento de sueños* (cargo of dreams), before it collapsed in 1948. That same year, Sastre became theater editor of a new student magazine, *La hora*. During his student years and beyond, Sastre acted in several plays.

In the late 1940's, a theater of social concern was beginning to develop in Spain. Antonio Buero Vallejo's *Historia de una escalera* (pr. 1949, pb. 1950; *Story of a Staircase*, 1955) was staged to critical acclaim. Although Buero Vallejo's works were not adamantly countercultural, Sastre's were, and they therefore provoked the animosity of the theater establishment. In 1950, when Sastre and José María de Quinto issued their manifesto for the TAS, the effort was largely futile. In 1951, when Sastre submitted his *Pathetic Prologue* to the María Guerrero National Theater, it was rejected. The next year, it was rejected a second time. Finally, in 1953, a university theater group presented *The Condemned Squad* at the María

Guerrero. Audiences responded enthusiastically, and although authorities closed the play after three performances, Sastre became known as a promising young playwright. That same year, Sastre completed his university studies but without receiving a degree, for he failed to show up for a crucial exam. He also finished writing *El pan de todos* (community bread), begun the year before.

During this period (from 1949 until 1953), Sastre wrote prolifically. His output included essays as well as plays. His articles appeared in several periodicals and consisted of commentaries on the nature of drama, criticism of Spanish theater, and reviews of books and films. During the years before 1953, Sastre underwent a religious crisis resulting from his struggle with the absolute values of Catholicism. On the one hand, he advocated a relativistic approach to life, arguing that any doctrine must be constantly questioned and reevaluated. On the other, he sought some sort of creed to replace the vacuum left by the disintegration of the faith of his childhood. Politically, Sastre was becoming more and more radical. Marxism, with its emphasis on change and, at the same time, its insistence on moral purism, was increasingly attractive to him. In addition to suggesting a means to reconcile the opposing extremes that dominated Sastre's thought, Marxism provided a basis for the theater of agitation.

In the early 1950's, Sastre was influenced by Jean-Paul Sartre's doctrine of artistic *engagement*, which claimed that the artist must put his work at the service of an ideology. In 1951, however, he opposed a proposed festival of Catholic theater on the basis that it would be nothing more than an instrument of Catholic propaganda and agitation. That is, he was drawn to the concept of an ideological theater when it promoted the goals of political reform but opposed such a theater when it promoted the ideals of Catholicism. Sastre's essays of this period reveal much vacillation. Although he adhered to the principles of *engagement*, Sastre was aware of the doctrine's weakness: If an artist seeks to advance one particular ideology exclusively, he must necessarily close his eyes to the advantages of other ideologies. The need to remain open-minded while at the same time advocating a new political system created a major dilemma for the young playwright.

During this period, Sastre continued to identify himself as a Christian, although not as a Catholic. For him, Christianity signified a truth and purity that contrasted radically with the hypocrisy and corruption of society. After 1953, Christianity ceased to be a major theme in Sastre's work; later in his life, he became an atheist. Still, the conflicts that emerged during his early years continued to appear in his mature writing. Instead of attempting to provide solutions, however, he strove to make his audiences confront the contradictions that they might face in their own lives. His mature plays do not advance a rigid ideology but rather pose questions.

The early and mid-1950's were an active time for Sastre. In 1954, the government prohibited the staging of *Pathetic Prologue* and *El pan de todos*, although Sastre's new play, *La mordaza*, was performed in Madrid under the direction of José María de Quinto. The author's first professional production, the play had a successful run. He wrote one more work that year and four the next. One of them, *La sangre de Dios* (the blood of God), was performed in Valencia, but two others, *Muerte en el barrio* and *Sad Are the Eyes of William Tell*, were banned.

In 1955, Sastre married Genoveva Forest, a psychologist and social activist. In 1956, the year of the birth of their first son, Juan, Sastre collaborated with José María Forqué on a film entitled *Amanecer en Puerta Oscura* (dawn in Puerta Oscura). That year, he was imprisoned for his political activities. At about the same time, *Drama y sociedad* (1956; *Drama and Society*, 1962) was published. A collection of essays on the nature of theater, the book contained the most important of the essays that had appeared previously in periodicals. In the years following *Drama and Society*, Sastre continued to write essays, and although he did not depart radically from the positions he adopted early in his career, he continued to grow intellectually. Many critics consider his 1957 analysis of Samuel Beckett's *En attendant Godot* (pb. 1952, pr. 1953; *Waiting for Godot*, 1954), which appeared in *Primer acto*, one of his most perceptive pieces.

In 1957, an edited version of *El pan de todos* was performed in Barcelona. Many critics interpreted the play as an antirevolutionary statement. In response, Sastre ordered the play closed. That year and the following, Sastre wrote several film scripts. One of them, *Carmen*, was banned twice before it met with official approval. In 1958, Sastre wrote his first novel, *El paralelo 38* (the thirty-eighth parallel); the same year, his son Pablo was born.

In the late 1950's, Sastre developed an intense interest in the theories of Bertolt Brecht, and in 1960 he published the first of several essays in which he analyzed Brecht's epic theater. Brecht wished to engage the audience intellectually but not emotionally, and at first Sastre objected to the distance the German playwright strove to create between spectator and spectacle. Later, he modified his views. During the 1960's, Sastre cultivated the epic drama himself, although with modifications. Sastre shared with Brecht the concept of theater as an instrument for societal transformation. The Spanish dramatist attempted to expose the spectator to experiences of change, however, rather than to convince him rationally. His techniques included shock treatment in sound, light, and scenic effects. *Asalto nocturno* (nocturnal assault), written in 1959, is Sastre's earliest epic play.

In 1960, *Death Thrust* premiered in Madrid and *Anna Kleiber* in Athens. That same year, Sastre and Quinto founded the GTR, and Sastre, along with 227 other intellectuals, signed a statement condemning censorship in Spain. In the next year, GTR performed *In the Web*, which was subsequently banned in the provinces. Sastre was once again imprisoned for his political participation, although only briefly.

In 1962, the year of the birth of his daughter Eva, Sastre wrote *Oficio de tinieblas* (office of darkness), which was prohibited by the authorities. In 1963, he joined other playwrights in protesting alleged atrocities against miners who were striking in Asturias, in the northern part of the country. As a result, Sastre's works were banned from national theaters throughout Spain.

Following his trip to Cuba in 1964, Sastre attempted to visit the United States, where he had received invitations to lecture at universities but was unable to obtain a visa. He did travel to Portugal, however, where there was considerable interest in his theater. Several of his plays have been translated into Portuguese. In 1968, Sastre, an avid supporter of Fidel Castro, made a second trip to Cuba.

In the fall of 1974, Sastre and his wife were imprisoned for crimes against the state. Genoveva was implicated in bomb explosions that took place in Madrid. She was also accused of involvement with Basque terrorists and charged with murder in the assassination of Premier Admiral Luis Carrero Blanco in 1973. Sastre was incarcerated with Genoveva because, under Spanish law, a husband was legally responsible for crimes committed by his wife. He spent six months in jail, and his wife served a term of two years for her crimes.

Many of Sastre's plays written after 1963 were not published until after General Franco's death in 1975. In 1967, *Oficio de tinieblas* premiered in Madrid but was received unenthusiastically. The increasing popularity of motion pictures, spectator sports, and television, as well as the democratization of Spain after Franco's death, contributed for a while to the dwindling interest in Sastre's theater.

Undeterred by this shift in the interests of Spanish audiences, Sastre continued to write his plays at a prolific rate in the 1980's and early 1990's. Because of his interests in fiction and theory, however, some directors felt that many of his later plays had become too literary and wordy to work as effective theater. Thus, many of his plays failed to be put onstage until the mid-1980's saw a sudden revival of Sastre's dramatic fortunes.

The widely popular production of *La taberna fantástica* in Madrid, which played to enthusiastic audiences and was a major critical and economical success, won Sastre two prestigious prizes. His adaptations of other plays, such as his award-winning *Jenofa Juncal*, which is based on a work by Velez de Guevara, were well received by his critics. As in the case of *Jenofa Juncal*, however, many of Sastre's plays saw their opening performance as foreign productions because many Spanish directors showed initial reluctance to take on his later work.

Sastre and his wife, Genoveva, reside in the northern Basque region of Spain. His influence on younger

Spanish playwrights and writers is heightened by the impact of his widely published theoretical essays and his role as a juror for theater and film festivals. Sastre enjoys great popularity in international drama. To preserve the legacy of his dramatic works, the Spanish publisher Editorial Hiru has set itself the goal of publishing all of Sastre's plays.

ANALYSIS

Alfonso Sastre sees drama as an instrument of social reform. For him, a successful play is one that works on the spectator's conscience and produces a reaction. Through his works, Sastre seeks to investigate the causes of social injustice and of individual unhappiness. He asks himself, "Why does man suffer and who is the guilty party?" In his article "El teatro de Alfonso Sastre visto por Alfonso Sastre" (Alfonso Sastre's theater seen by Alfonso Sastre), he states that he approaches theater as a form of criminal investigation. It is not surprising that some of his works, such as *Muerte en el barrio*, revolve around the investigation of a crime.

Sastre's purpose is not to provoke anarchy but to create an atmosphere of inquiry and analysis that will lead to the establishment of a new order. His plays often present no clearly defined answers but rather raise questions that produce a catharsis by leading the spectator to agonize over possible solutions. This is what Sastre calls "theater of anguish." Thus, although Sastre reflects Sartre's influence in that his plays convey existential pain and the need for reform, the Spanish playwright does believe that theater must promote a definite political ideology.

The vehicle that Sastre prefers is tragedy. According to ideas set forth in *Drama and Society*, tragedy awakens in the spectator a profound sense of guilt. This experience purifies him and makes him susceptible to change. The result may be a social revolution or, at least, a new willingness to address social problems.

Sastre's works deal with a variety of subjects, although nearly all have reformist or existential overtones. Political revolution is the theme of *Pathetic Prologue*, *El pan de todos*, *Red Earth*, *Sad Are the Eyes of William Tell*, *In the Web*, and *Crónicas romanas* (Roman chronicles). *Uranio 235* and *Asalto*

nocturno deal with atomic terror. *El cuervo* (the raven) and *Cargamento de sueños* deal with existential anguish. *Anna Kleiber* is a love story.

Structurally, Sastre's plays range from the classically Aristotelian to the highly experimental. As a rule, his plots are functional and unadorned. His language is concise, conversational, and nonrhetorical. His characters are real people with real problems, victims of an unjust society or of their own weaknesses.

Like that of Sartre, Sastre's theater is largely situational. Characters find themselves in predicaments in which they are forced to act or be overcome by circumstances. In several plays, especially among the earlier ones, characters are alienated from society and from one another. They are swept up by history; they are not makers of history. They do not act, but are acted on. These plays convey a sense of anguish and frustration.

ANNA KLEIBER

Anna Kleiber is an example of this type of drama. The play begins at a hotel in Barcelona, where The Writer, identified as Sastre, is being interviewed by two reporters who systematically misinterpret his responses. In a separate conversation, a man urges his distraught mistress to have an abortion, while she complains of feeling emotionally abandoned. This preliminary dialogue introduces the major themes of the work: lack of communication, isolation, and the individual's inability to find happiness in love. The Writer's involvement suggests a secondary theme: the creative process by which a dramatist writes a play.

Anna Kleiber, nervous and upset, asks for a room and requests that she be awakened early the next morning because she has an appointment so important that it will determine her future. During the night, she dies of a heart attack. At her funeral, The Writer encounters Anna's former lover, Alfredo Merton, who, through a series of flashbacks, tells Anna's story.

Anna and Alfredo met in Paris, when Anna was on the verge of suicide. After spending eight wonderful days with Alfredo, Anna abandons him, unable to bear the happiness and fearful of bringing him misfortune. Alfredo follows her to Germany, where she is acting in a small theater company. Cohen, Anna's former impresario, torments Alfredo with allusions to his previous relationship with her. In a rage, Alfredo kills him. Then, overcome with terror at the act he has committed, he yields to the entreaties of a young Nazi fanatic who praises him for killing the Jew and offers to recommend him to the Nazi authorities. Anna is disgusted by Alfredo's cowardliness, and once more the lovers separate. Anna, a libertine ever in search of new experiences, seeks thrills through sex and alcohol. When she once again joins Alfredo, however, they set up a household and she becomes a "model housewife."

When the war breaks out, Alfredo obeys the call to duty unquestioningly. In the meantime, Anna amuses herself with a series of lovers. Wounded in battle, Alfredo returns and hurls insults at Anna, who responds that his abuse "purifies" her. Alfredo, now bored with Anna's complexities and angry at her infidelities, attacks and almost kills her. Then he returns to the front. After the war, they write to each other and fix a date to meet at the hotel in Barcelona, where Anna dies.

Anna Kleiber explores the dark, self-destructive aspect of humanity. Throughout the play, Anna's sadomasochistic tendencies prevent her from attaining happiness. She refers to herself repeatedly as "diabolical," and indeed, she has a diabolical need to destroy what is dearest to her. She resists contentment because she fears routine and stagnation. She insists that she wants to live "intensely" and therefore rejects bourgeois domesticity in favor of a life of passion and freedom. Yet Anna is not free. She is a pawn of her persona—that of the depressive, nonconformist actress. Alfredo's disdain for her shallowness is evident in his ironic comment: "You retain a crumb of bourgeois dignity . . . which doesn't become an enigmatic, open woman like you."

Alfredo, however, is no more authentic than Anna. He runs to her when she flees him but flees from her when he senses that she really needs him. He kills a man, then fails to accept responsibility for his act, preferring, rather, to disappear into the ranks of Nazism, a cause in which he does not believe. When the war starts, Alfredo goes willingly. "It's not something you think about . . . you just hand yourself over to

it. . . . Maybe I'll get to be a hero." He is a man without convictions who allows himself to be swept by circumstances. Perhaps Anna and Alfredo are unable to be true to each other because they are not true to themselves.

Each sees in the other something pure. After Anna's death, Alfredo remarks that, in spite of everything, Anna is "clean"—although during her lifetime she repeatedly describes herself as "dirty." Who is Anna, really? Would she and Alfredo have found happiness had she lived? Sastre does not answer these questions. Rather, he shows that it is impossible for one human being ever really to know another. "Everyone must bear his own pain," The Writer tells Alfredo. "In that respect, we can help each other very little." All The Writer can do is observe and record. It is after he has heard Alfredo's story that he sits down to write *Anna Kleiber*, reproducing what he has seen and heard.

MUERTE EN EL BARRIO

While *Anna Kleiber* focuses on alienation, *Muerte en el barrio* focuses on solidarity and political action. In the prologue, a police inspector interrogates Pedro the bartender about the murder of Dr. Sanjo, and the story emerges. In a working-class neighborhood, a child is struck by a car and rushed to a clinic. Dr. Sanjo, who is supposed to be on duty, is absent, and the child dies. Anger mounts in the neighborhood, and violence erupts in the bar on the following Sunday, when a crowd attacks and kills Dr. Sanjo.

The events leading up to the outburst are depicted in flashbacks. It becomes clear that Dr. Sanjo represents a cold, impersonal system that dehumanizes the poor. He holds both his patients and his nurses in contempt. Yet he does not bear the sole responsibility for the child's death. Although he is guilty of abandoning his post, he is a cog in the wheel of social inequality and injustice.

The death of the child unifies the community and prompts people to act. Dr. Sanjo's murder constitutes a rebellion against the system. "Justice depends on us," not on the authorities, maintains the child's father. The police inspector finds it consoling that people "can kill attaching importance to what they're doing. That they can kill united by rage, dirtying their clothes with blood . . . suffering in order to kill." The experience purifies the collective psyche of the community. Yet will eliminating one element in an oppressive system really prove constructive?

Throughout their dialogue, the police inspector and the bartender complain of the asphyxiating heat. The constant mention of the weather serves to raise another question. To what extent were the neighbors impelled to act by the sheer discomfort of their physical situation? Was the doctor's murder a conscious, deliberate act or was it the result of several factors, some unrelated to Sanjo's irresponsibility? In *Muerte en el barrio*, as in other plays, Sastre raises important issues about the nature of political violence.

LA TABERNA FANTÁSTICA

Perhaps the most popular of Sastre's plays, *La taberna fantástica* is set in a Madrid bar patronized by the lowest members of its urban society. It draws some of its dramatic strengths and linguistic authenticity from Sastre's autobiographical knowledge of this scene, consisting of day laborers, petty thieves, drunks, and violent lowlifes. To most of his audience, the characters and their slang initially seemed very alien, and Sastre included introductory remarks in his program explaining some of the phrases when the play was performed first in Madrid in 1985. The people refer to themselves as *quinquilleros*, for example, which is not a word found in Spain's authoritative dictionary issued by the Royal Academy. The word refers to a group of petty peddlers, tinkerers, and small thieves, who hire themselves out to perform occasional menial work and services, and live at the very margin of Spain's modern cities.

The play's underground language has fascinated its audiences, who are confronted by a spoken Spanish few of them have heard in their own lives. The language gives much color to the characters, and serves as a Brechtian means of alienation; the audience is forced to deconstruct and decode much of the dialogue.

La taberna fantástica does not possess a clear, traditional plot. It is staged as if the audience were to invisibly observe action and talk in the bar, with characters complaining about their life situations, getting drunk, and cursing each other. To this realistic, naturalistic mix of characters, Sastre adds allegorical figures such as Terror, Sickness, Hunger and Cold, who

roam the stage. They are meant to signify the societal forces which, in Sastre's critical opinion, have made the human characters into the lowlifes they have become.

For Sastre, regular Spanish society both exploits and rejects his desperate characters. They perform the most menial of jobs for the least amount of pay, and many sell their blood. Some also work as laborers abroad, and can afford to return only rarely, while their families suffer from their absence. All of them are always threatened by the harsh eye of the law, as police and *la guardia civil*, Spain's civil guard, try to observe their every behavior.

A climax of sorts occurs when two men get drunk and start a fight over an insignificant issue. The fight escalates, and one of the combatants is lethally injured, frightening his antagonist and all bystanders who fear a massive reaction by the authorities. The precarious nature of life at the bottom of Spain's urban society, which Sastre sees as a consequence of the capitalist system exploiting the weak, is thus dramatically presented in this award-winning play.

OTHER MAJOR WORKS

LONG FICTION: *El paralelo 38*, 1965; *Necrópolis*, 1993.

SHORT FICTION: *Las noches lúgubres*, 1964; *Histórias de Califórnia*, 1994.

POETRY: *Te veo, Viet Nam*, 1973; *Balada de Carabanchel*, 1976; *El espanol al alcance de todos*, 1978; *T.B.O.*, 1978; *Vida del hombre invisible contada por él mismo*, 1994; *El evangelio de Drácula*, 1997.

NONFICTION: *Drama y sociedad*, 1956 (*Drama and Society*, 1962); *Anatomía del realismo*, 1965; *La revolucíon y la critica de la cultura*, 1970; *Critica de la imaginación*, 1978; *Lumpen, margenación, y jerigonça*, 1980; *Escrito en Euskadi*, 1982; *¿Dónde estoy yo?*, 1994; *El por venir del drama*, 1994 (*The Future of Drama*, 1994); *El drama y sus lenguajes*, 2000-2001 (2 volumes).

BIBLIOGRAPHY

Bryan, T. Avril. *Censorship and Social Conflict in the Spanish Theatre: The Case of Alfonso Sastre*. Washington, D.C.: University Press of America,

1982. Excellent, exhaustive study of the manifold problems faced by Sastre to have his plays performed and published in Spain under General Franco. Because Sastre considered himself one of the *imposibilistas*, or writers for whom accommodation with the fascist state was impossible, Bryan shows, he suffered severely from censorship and spent some time in jail. The work also relates Sastre's fate to the larger issues involved.

Hardison Londre, Felicia. "The Theatrical Gap Between Alfonso Sastre's Criticism and His Later Plays." In *The Contemporary Spanish Theater*, edited by Martha T. Halsey and Phyllis Zatlin. Lanham, Md.: University Press of America, 1988. Argues that many of the problems that have prevented the actual performance of Sastre's plays come from his theoretical approach, which favors styles and techniques more appropriate for a contemporary novel. Perceptive analysis of the problem.

Harper, Sandra N. "The Problematics of Identity in *Jenofa Juncal, La roja gitana del Monte Jaizkibel* by Alfonso Sastre." In *Entre Actos*, edited by Martha T. Halsey and Phyllis Zatlin. University Park, Pa.: Estreno, 1999. Analyzes construction and presentation of Sastre's gypsy character, who dwells in a borderline region of Spain, and relates this to problems of contemporary, post-Franco Spanish personal and political identity.

Martinez, Victoria. "Symbols of Oppression: Eliminating the Patriarch in Alfonso Sastre's *La mordaza* and Syria Poletti's 'Pisadas de Caballo'." *Hispanic Journal* 18 (1997): 67-78. Effective comparison of Sastre's 1954 play and the Argentinian short story. Argues that the two texts share an opposition to oppressive regimes and societies and even advocate violent change.

Schwartz, Kessel. "Posibilismo and Imposibilismo. The Buero Vallejo-Sastre Polemic." *Revista Hispanica Moderna* 34 (1968): 436-445. Concise presentation of the conflict between these two playwrights during the years of Franco's rule. While Buero Vallejo managed to get his plays performed by using allegory and historical analogies instead of straightforward political agitation, Sastre refused to circumvent censorship. The former position was known as "posibilismo," or the attempt to write plays which could possibly be performed in Spain, as opposed to "imposibilismo," whose writers knew it was impossible for the work to see the light of day.

Soto, Isabel. "Translation as Understanding: Alfonso Sastre's Adaptation of *Mulatto*." *Langston Hughes Review* 15 (1997): 13-23. Focus on the issues involved in Sastre's adapting a play by another author (in this case, a play by African American Langston Hughes). Analyzes to what extent Sastre's practice falls within the areas of translation, as opposed to a more freewheeling adaptation.

Vogeley, Nancy. "Alfonso Sastre on Alfonso Sastre." *Hispania* 64 (1981): 459-466. Sympathetic interview by the author, who has been Sastre's friend for more than forty years. Conducted before Sastre won his major prizes, the interview still sheds interesting light on Sastre's own assessment of his dramatic career and his intellectual goals.

Barbara Mujica,
updated by R. C. Lutz

ROBERT SCHENKKAN

Born: Chapel Hill, North Carolina; March 19, 1953

PRINCIPAL DRAMA

Final Passages, pb. 1981, pr. 1982
Intermission, pr. 1981, pb. 1983
Lunch Break, pr. 1981, pb. 1993
The Survivalist, pr. 1982, pb. 1993
Tachinoki, pr. 1987
Tall Tales, pr. 1988
Heaven on Earth, pr. 1989, pb. 1992

The Kentucky Cycle, pr. 1991, pb. 1993

Conversations with the Spanish Lady, pr. 1992, pb. 1993

Four One Act Plays, pb. 1993

The Dream Thief, pr., pb. 1999

Handler, pr. 2000

The Marriage of Miss Hollywood and King Neptune, pr. 2001

OTHER LITERARY FORMS

Besides writing plays, Robert Schenkkan has also acted in them. His stage debut came in Chicago as Captain Tim in *Tobacco Road* (1975), and his Off-Broadway debut came as Wayne Blossom, Jr., in *Last Days at the Dixie Girl Cafe* in 1979. His other New York City appearances include *The Taming of the Shrew* at the Equity Library Theatre (1977) and *G. R. Point* at the Playhouse Theatre (1979). Outside of New York City, Schenkkan appeared in *Write Me a Murder* (Buffalo, New York, 1981), *A Full Length Portrait of America* and *SWOP* (both in Louisville, Kentucky, 1981), and *A Midsummer Night's Dream* and *All the Way Home* at the Kenyon Theatre Festival in Ohio.

Schenkkan has also written for and acted in films. His cinema credits include roles in *Act of Vengeance* (1974), *Sanctuary of Fear* (1979), the Texas Voice in *Places in the Heart* (1984), *Sweet Liberty* (1986), *The Bedroom Window* (1987), *Amazing Grace and Chuck* (1987), and *Pump Up the Volume* (1990). His first television appearance was in the National Broadcasting Company's (NBC's) *Father Brown, Detective* (1979), followed by the Columbia Broadcasting System (CBS) film *Murder in Cowetta County* (1980), the CBS miniseries *George Washington* (1983), *Kane and Abel* (CBS, 1984), *Nutcracker* (CBS, 1987), and several episodes of *The Twilight Zone* (CBS). He also appeared as Lieutenant Commander Dexter Remmick in *Star Trek: The Next Generation*, Episodes 19 and 25 (1988). He edited Henrik Ibsen's *The Wild Duck* (1966), *Peer Gynt* (1966), and co-translated Ibsen's *Hedda Gabler* (1975). He wrote the teleplay for *The Long Ride Home* (TNT, 2001) and adapted *The Kentucky Cycle* for Kevin Costner for a Home Broadcasting Office (HBO) miniseries. With Christopher Hampton, he wrote the screenplay for a film adaptation of Graham Greene's *The Quiet American* (2002).

ACHIEVEMENTS

Robert Schenkkan has been widely recognized for both his long epic play, *The Kentucky Cycle*, and his one-act plays, and the profession has showered him with awards and grants. He was given the Best of the Fringe Award from the Edinburgh Festival for *The Survivalist* (1984), a Creative Artists Public Service Program (CAPS) grant from the state of New York for *Final Passages* (1985), a California Arts Council grant, grants from the Arthur and the Vogelstein Foundations, a Playwrights Forum Award for *Tall Tales* (1988), three Denver Drama Critics Awards, the Julie Harris Playwright Award from the Beverly Hills Theatre Guild for *Heaven on Earth* (1989), a Los Angeles Drama Critics Circle Award, a PEN Center Award, and the 1992 Pulitzer Prize in Drama for *The Kentucky Cycle*.

BIOGRAPHY

Robert Frederic Schenkkan, Jr., was born in Chapel Hill, North Carolina, son of Robert Fredric and Jean (McKenzie) Schenkkan. He graduated Phi Beta Kappa and magna cum laude from the University of Texas at Austin in 1975, and he received an M.F.A. in Theatre Arts from Cornell University in 1977. In 1984 he married the actress Mary Anne Dorward. He was active in theater and film as both a writer and actor, but the work that established his reputation was the sequence of nine short plays that make up *The Kentucky Cycle*, a huge box office success at its 1991 world premiere at the Intiman Theatre in Seattle and winner of five Los Angeles Drama Critics Awards. It is the only play ever to win the Pulitzer Prize in Drama without having been first produced in New York. The play germinated in Schenkkan's mind after a trip through Appalachia in the early 1980's, when he was shocked at the poverty he saw and richer people's brutal indifference to it.

ANALYSIS

In his best plays, *The Kentucky Cycle* and *Handler*, Robert Schenkkan treats southern life and history in a way that suggests the violence and sensationalism of the novelist Cormac McCarthy and earlier practitioners of the so-called southern gothic style. The broad historical sweep of the Kentucky plays is Faulknerian in its depiction of contending families, and the fascination with snake handling in *Handler* would have pleased Flannery O'Connor. *Heaven on Earth* features a cast of southern stereotypes: an alcoholic West Texas redneck, his religious grandmother and her coworker at the local beauty salon, a pompous broadcaster for the Christian Associates Television Network, and a con man who buys and sells used appliances—all familiar figures in the literature of the modern South. Schenkkan's dialogue often matches the coarse wit of such masters of the contemporary southern idiom as Barry Hannah and Harry Crews, although his one-act plays have none of these local color specifics. *Final Passages*, though not set in the South, has a solid historical incident to build on—the discovery in 1878 of the *San Christobal* floating off Nova Scotia with all crew and passengers dead. In general, these works have met with a favorable response, but some scholars have hotly disputed what they judge the hackneyed depiction of Kentucky as the benighted "Dogpatch" and brutal "Skunk Hollow" of Al Capp's famous "Li'l Abner" comic strip.

HEAVEN ON EARTH

Heaven on Earth is set in June of a recent year in the small town of Waylon, Texas, where Bobby, Jr., lives with his grandmother, Martha, in a two-bedroom, two-story bungalow resting on cinder blocks disguised by wooden latticework. On the wraparound porch are a swing, bug zapper, and a crude sign announcing "Used appliances/ bought and sold/ and REPAIRED." Cluttering the porch and the yard are numerous old televisions, radios, clocks, washing machines, and refrigerators, the centerpiece of which is an ancient freezer. A gravel strip around the house, a brown lawn, a mailbox, and some struggling rose bushes complete the décor. "The whole picture suggests a fierce if unsuccessful struggle with age, dry heat, and dwindling financial resources."

Bobby, Jr., staggers out to the porch and looks around. He is thirtyish and good-looking but dissipated and hung over. He takes a can of beer from the freezer and disappears into the house as Martha approaches with Jessie, her neighbor and coworker at the beauty parlor. Their small talk covers such banalities as praying to Ed McMahon to win the Publisher's Sweepstakes and Jessie's struggle to lose weight by filling her jellybean bowls with dietetic candies that taste like "sun-dried playdough." They worriedly discuss Bobby's frustrations, and when he emerges from the house he greets them with angry profanities and self-hating mockery of his prospects in life. This first scene ends with Jessie's bitter statement of her lack of religious faith and the religious but despairing Martha's query of "What's faith without hope?"

In scene 2, Bobby and his friend Miguel are smoking dope and drinking beer at two o'clock in the morning. Their drunken raucous behavior produces some crude but funny dialogue. When Miguel leaves after a disagreement, Bobby turns in a rage to a standing lamp, which he swings in fury, singing "Plastic Jesus" and hitting the porch light in an explosion of sparks that shocks him onto his back. Martha appears on the darkened porch, engaging the cruelly insulting Bobby in a plea for religious faith and hopes for a miracle. Jessie comes over to join in the hubbub, and in the uncertain light, she perceives the face of Jesus on the freezer door. The excited women think their miracle has occurred (the image in truth is a stain from Bobby's many gushers of hot beer opened at the freezer), and act 1 ends with Martha shouting, "BOBBY GET YOUR ASS OUT HERE, BOY, WE GOT US A *MIRACLE!*"

Act 2 opens on the miraculous freezer surrounded by walkers, canes, crutches, slings, and all the other devices used by the disabled. A large banner proclaims "The home of the WAYLON WONDER." The con man John Morrow of the Christian Associates Television Network is interviewing Jessie, while Miguel parades a sign announcing "MIRACLE HOURS: SUNSET TO 10:00 P.M. PLEASE STAY BEHIND THE BARRICADES. NO SHIRT, NO SHOES, NO SERVICE." When John inquires, "¿Cuanto tiempo duraron para llegar aqui?" (How long did you have to travel, pilgrim, to get here?), Miguel replies, "I live around the corner. Where'd you learn to speak Spanish, Taco Bell?" This exchange typifies the vulgar but hilarious tone of the whole scene, concluding with the exasperated John's outburst of "You're gonna have to edit the shit out of this thing, Darleen." In scene 2, Jessie explains to Bobby that Martha has lost her job because of the freezer circus, and Jessie then turns off her porch light, revealing that the miraculous face of Jesus on the freezer was a mere illusion created by artificial light shining on a beer stain. Jessie's consolation is inspired: "I guess you and Miguel could always take turns makin' hand shadows. Look at the nice elephant and the dog and the chicken and the two dead ducks."

The long finale, act 2, scene 3, begins around midnight, and the dialogue turns serious with Bobby raging to Martha about God's cruelty in letting his parents die in a car crash when he was ten. Martha's own faith seems to be wavering, when a mysterious savior appears in the yard—Tom Dooley, buyer of used appliances, amateur magician, and a purveyor of Whitmanian cosmic optimism ("Now why would you want Christ on a freezer when you got the Milky Way?"). After Bobby goes off to sleep, Dooley strokes Martha's temples, and when she falls asleep, Dooley remarks, "Heaven on earth," and the lights fade. When they both awake, Dooley has vanished, Bobby's anger at the world has apparently been drained off in an unusual dream, and he and Martha settle into an easy companionability over breakfast. This conclusion comes unexpectedly, evidently the result of some theodicy Martha and Bobby have been converted to by the mysterious stranger.

THE KENTUCKY CYCLE

This Pulitzer Prize-winning success, structured around nine short plays that take six hours to perform, follows the interrelated fortunes of three Kentucky families—the Biggses, the Rowens, and the Talberts—over two hundred years. In play 1, somewhere in the forest of eastern Kentucky, the Irish indentured servant Michael Rowen, age thirty-four, murders both Earl Tod, who has been selling rifles to the Cherokees, and an innocent Virginia farmer before selling smallpox-infected blankets to a band of Cherokees. In play 2, a year later, Michael is seen

dragging a young Cherokee woman, Morning Star, into his rude Kentucky cabin. Play 3, "The Homecoming," set in 1792, introduces the romance of Michel's son, Patrick, and a neighbor girl, Rebecca Talbert, and witnesses the murder of Michael by Morning Star and Patrick after Michael comes home with a slave girl, Sallie. When Rebecca's father, Joe Talbert, arrives on the scene, it becomes clear that he and Morning Star are romantically paired, but when Joe threatens Patrick with a murder charge Patrick kills him too.

When play 4 opens in 1819, Rebecca is dead, but Patrick lives with his two sons, Zeke and Zach, Morning Star, and Sallie Biggs, the slave, and her twenty-six-year-old son, Jessie, also a slave. A circuit court judge rides up to the farmhouse and announces that Patrick's mortgage is being foreclosed. With the judge is the dead Joe Talbert's son, Jeremiah, who has bought the mortgage from the defunct bank. After hard negotiations, Jeremiah assumes ownership of the large Rowen property, taking Sallie and Jessie with him and allowing the Rowens to live on their former land as sharecroppers. Part 1 ends with play 5, "God's Great Supper," set in 1861 and featuring the largest cast of any play in the cycle. Jed Rowen, Zeke's twenty-eight-year-old son, dominates the action as he agrees to accompany Jeremiah Talbert's son Richard on his military expedition to fight the Union army. His real purpose, it turns out, is to wait for an opportunity to kill Richard so that the Rowens can claim their former land back. His occasion comes when Richard and his men are crossing the river from Kentucky into Missouri and Jed pushes Richard into the water. After a tour with Quantrill's Raiders, Jed returns to Kentucky and the Rowens reclaim their farmland in a bloody takeover.

In play 6, set in 1890, J. T. ("Just Terrific") Wells shows up at the Rowens, sweet talking Jed's young daughter, Mary Anne, and striking a deal with Jed for the mineral rights—that is, the right to brutalize the land in digging for coal—and the twelve scenes of play 7 are set around the Blue Star Mining Company's camp. Andrew Talbert Winston, old Richard's grandson, is the mine boss, Abe Steinman is a union organizer, and Cassius Biggs, descended from Jessie

Biggs, is a miner and bootlegger. The strike incited by Steinman is cruelly suppressed, but play 7 concludes dramatically with a celebration of faith in what miners unions will be able to achieve.

In play 8, Joshua Rowen is president of United Mine Workers, District 16; James Talbert Winston is the owner of Blue Star Mining Company, and Franklin Biggs is the prosperous owner of Biggs & Son Liquor. It ends with James reading the names of those lost in a mine collapse. The final play, "The War on Poverty," jumps to 1975 and the abandoned Rowen homestead, now a trash heap. James, Joshua, and Franklin gather just in time to drive off two men who have just dug up a buckskin-wrapped bundle adorned with beadwork. As these three old men, their ancestries intertwined in history, muse around the stump of the huge oak tree that once dominated the land, they discover in the buckskin a perfectly preserved baby that we learn was born to Morning Star. As Joshua kneels down to bury the baby once again, he tucks the Rowen family's gold watch in the buckskin shroud and begins to weep as he prays. In the fantastic, triumphant finale, the ground erupts with the ghosts of the many Rowens, Talberts, and Biggses who struggled with each other and the recalcitrant land.

OTHER MAJOR WORKS

SCREENPLAY: *The Quiet American*, 2002 (with Christopher Hampton; adaptation of Graham Greene's novel).

TELEPLAYS: *Crazy Horse*, 1996; *The Long Ride Home*, 2001.

BIBLIOGRAPHY

American Theatre. Review of *Handler*, by Robert Schenkkan. 17, no. 4 (April, 2000): 34. A review of one of Schenkkan's early plays.

Billings, Dwight B., Gurney Norman, and Katherine Ledford. *Confronting Appalachian Stereotypes: Back Talk from an American Region*. Lexington: University Press of Kentucky, 1999. The twenty-one essays in this collection aim at a truer picture of Appalachia than the editors feel is given in Schenkkan's *The Kentucky Cycle*. The contributors are from various disciplines, including anthropology, history, health care, sociology, and political science.

Caudill, Harry. *Night Comes to the Cumberlands: A Biography of a Depressed Area*. 1976. Reprint. Ashland, Ky.: Jesse Stuart Foundation, 2001. Caudill was a journalist who wrote extensively about Kentucky history and was a source for Schenkkan's work.

Reeves, Rhonda. "Fightin' Words: Chris Offutt's Latest Work Stirs the Home Fires." *Ace Weekly*, April 2, 2002. Sharp criticism of Schenkkan mixed with other commentary on Southern writers.

Regan, Margaret. "Ravaged Landscape." Review of *The Kentucky Cycle*, by Robert Schenkkan. *Tucson Weekly* (November 10, 1997). An examination of a performance of *The Kentucky Cycle*.

U.S. News and World Report. Review of *The Kentucky Cycle*, by Robert Schenkkan. 115 (September 20, 1993): 72-73. One of the most appreciative pieces on *The Kentucky Cycle*.

Frank Day

FRIEDRICH SCHILLER

Born: Marbach, Württemberg (now in Germany); November 10, 1759

Died: Weimar, Sace-Weimar (now in Germany); May 9, 1805

PRINCIPAL DRAMA

Die Räuber, pb. 1781, pr. 1782 (*The Robbers*, 1792)

Die Verschwörung des Fiesko zu Genua, pr., pb. 1783 (*Fiesco: Or, The Genoese Conspiracy*, 1796)

Kabale und Liebe, pr., pb. 1784 (*Cabal and Love*, 1795)

Don Carlos, Infant von Spanien, pr., pb. 1787 (*Don Carlos, Infante of Spain*, 1798)

Wallensteins Lager, pr. 1798, pb. 1800 (*The Camp of Wallenstein*, 1846)

Die Piccolomini, pr. 1799, pb. 1800 (*The Piccolominis*, 1800)

Wallensteins Tod, pr. 1799, pb. 1800 (*The Death of Wallenstein*, 1800)

Wallenstein, pr. 1799, pb. 1800 (trilogy includes *The Camp of Wallenstein*, *The Piccolominis*, and *The Death of Wallenstein*)

Maria Stuart, pr. 1800, pb. 1801 (*Mary Stuart*, 1801)

Die Jungfrau von Orleans, pr. 1801, pb. 1802 (*The Maid of Orleans*, 1835)

Die Braut von Messina: Oder, Die feindlichen Brüder, pr., pb. 1803 (*The Bride of Messina*, 1837)

Wilhelm Tell, pr., pb. 1804 (*William Tell*, 1841)

Historical Dramas, pb. 1847

Early Dramas and Romances, pb. 1849

Dramatic Works, pb. 1851

OTHER LITERARY FORMS

George Joachim Göschen in Leipzig published most of Friedrich Schiller's early work, including the early plays and the *Historischer Kalender für Damen* (1790, 1791), which included many of Schiller's essays and was his only best-seller during his lifetime. After *Don Carlos, Infante of Spain*, Schiller's plays were published by Johann Friedrich Cotta in Tübingen. Schiller's poems, reviews, and short stories appeared in literary journals such as the *Musenalmanach* (edited by Schiller), *Die Horen* (edited by Johann Wolfgang von Goethe and Schiller in Weimar), *Die Thalia*, and *Merkur*. Schiller's letters, published posthumously, not only are an indispensable key to the philosophical and historical background of his works, but also are autobiographical documents evocative of the man Schiller, his daily life, and his great gift for friendship. Schiller's collected works are available in several editions.

ACHIEVEMENTS

Friedrich Schiller's audience might not have been ready to make the transition from the wildly emotional Sturm und Drang (storm and stress) of his first play, *The Robbers*, to the more philosophical and idealistic fervor of subsequent plays, but Schiller won them over with his ever more complex dramas. Schiller's work spans two literary periods, Sturm und Drang and classicism, and it paves the way for a third, Romanticism. At the same time, his work clearly has ties to the Enlightenment, with its emphasis on the perfectibility of humankind. In Schiller's work, German idealism attained its highest form. The lonely poet who wrote from his sickbed, however, never lost sight of the wishes of his audience. After his plays had accustomed later generations to his system of thought, Schiller became for them a poet of the people. He was acclaimed particularly by the middle class of the nineteenth century, which did not appear to notice the radical quality of freedom demanded by Schiller.

Schiller threw himself into his sources and settings, mostly historical, in order to demonstrate their

Friedrich Schiller (Library of Congress)

true range and potential—what they might have been. His plays, showing his dialectical consciousness, express the struggle between reality and the ideal. His heroes are larger than life, their struggles overshadowing their time. The fiery younger generation was his first audience, but his idealism determined the intellectual horizon of the era. The romanticists turned away from Schiller's political idealism to pursue mysticism and the indefinable, but even among them, Friedrich Hölderlin and Novalis were profoundly influenced by Schiller. The German drama was dominated by Schiller's plays for almost a century, until the advent of naturalism. Then the theater of expressionism rediscovered the revolutionary passion and the power of Schiller's tragic pathos. Georg Kaiser and Bertolt Brecht, among others, brought Schiller's influence to bear on twentieth century drama.

Schiller equated the concept of patriotism with such ideals as truth, beauty, nobility, love, freedom, and immortality. He bound all these ideals with a religious sense of duty, as in his latter dramas, in which history appears as the fulfillment of a divine plan. Schiller was a subject of several absolute monarchs in a time of democratic and republican revolutions and reactionary wars and upheavals. He created, for the Germany that did not yet exist, a model of the political tragedy. In it the hero is seen not only as an energetic but also as a suffering human being, living out a metaphysical tragedy, a conflict between ideals and fate.

Schiller gave German literature basic concepts of structure, both of the art of tragedy and of aesthetics. The history of tragedy to the present day has been, to a great extent, a confrontation with Schiller.

BIOGRAPHY

The early years of Johann Christoph Friedrich von Schiller were deeply imprinted with the tyranny of two fathers. Johann Kaspar Schiller, barber-surgeon, military officer, and later, Royal Head Forester, ruled his family with an iron hand. Duke Karl Eugen, founder of a military academy for promising young men, considered himself the father of the talented boys he chose to attend the school. After two invitations, Johann Schiller no longer had any choice about sending his son, who had wanted to become a pastor, to the duke's academy.

The academy was strict in a sense of the word no longer meaningful today. Every moment of the day was organized. No boy had any time to himself, not even on the compulsory "pleasure" strolls. Army officers maintained discipline. Duke Karl had a discriminating eye for talented men; many of the teachers he brought to his new school were gifted. Professor Abel, for example, who taught Latin and Greek, expounded principles of the Enlightenment, particularly a quest for the ideal not dependent on religious conviction.

The duke's academy was unusual for its time because it admitted both Protestant and Catholic boys. The atmosphere of religious tolerance, when combined with the secular idealism of the Enlightenment, tended to dilute the students' religious convictions, including Schiller's. Young Schiller was Professor Abel's finest student of Latin and Greek. He learned French partly to communicate with some of his fellow students from the French-speaking section of the Duchy of Württemberg. Soon, as the reputation of the school grew, boys began to appear from northern German areas, Switzerland, Scandinavia, and even from England.

Young Schiller studied law, but it was the duke's choice, not his, and after a few years, illness began making serious inroads into his accomplishments. As a result he was allowed to study medicine, including surgery. Anatomy classes never bothered Schiller, and it is possible that he escaped rigorous supervision because the military watchdogs were less vigilant in the dissection room. He was not permitted to visit his family more than one or two days a year. These ties were cut early; by age twelve, he was already at the academy.

By age twenty, Schiller had written one dissertation, which had been turned down as too speculative and theoretical, had seen himself relegated to another year at the academy to write another research paper, and had finished a manuscript of his first play, *The Robbers*, which was well in hand. The battle of sons against fathers, both in a political sense and in a familial sense, finds expression in this wildly emotional play. Above everything else, however, the protagonist is ruled by a morality that is not less strict for being his own, rather than society's. The play was written clandestinely, probably by candlelight late at night. Schiller kept it concealed, except from a few friends.

After presentation of a more technical dissertation, Schiller was graduated. Although he had every reason to expect favorable treatment from the duke, he was assigned a position as military surgeon, no higher than his unstudied father. Schiller was not well paid, was extremely restricted, and was bored. He borrowed money to publish *The Robbers* privately, the beginning of a lifetime of worry with creditors. He made several trips out of the country to Mannheim, to present his play for performance. Sometimes he traveled with official permission, sometimes not. The subject of his play was considered dangerously controversial in its contemporary context. Because Mannheim's censor might not have permitted it to be performed, Schiller had to rewrite the play as if it were happening in the 1400's, the end of the age of knighthood. Although Schiller had based his story on a contemporary robber chieftain, the theater director insisted that bands of marauders were simply not believable in eighteenth century Europe.

After the performance of *The Robbers* in Mannheim, Duke Karl Eugen forbade Schiller to publish anything further except medical research. Schiller fled the country, became a nearly penniless refugee in Mannheim until he was given a position of playwright for the theater, then contracted malaria and nearly died. His health, never robust, was permanently undermined. He was not able to fulfill some of the conditions of his contract, and the play he did complete, *Fiesco: Or, The Genoese Conspiracy*, puzzled the Mannheim audience with its political subtlety. They had been expecting more bombast. Schiller's contract was not renewed.

Schiller spent the next years, during the writing of *Cabal and Love* and *Don Carlos, Infante of Spain*, moving from the refuge of one set of friends to another, ever more deeply in debt, often despairing of finding a home. During this time he met Christian

Gottfried Körner. Their letters offer insight into Schiller's life and thought. The friendship lasted for the rest of his life.

In 1787, Duke Karl August of Saxony-Weimar, impressed by Schiller's historical essays, called him to the new university at Jena and later knighted him for his accomplishments. Johann Wolfgang von Goethe, a high official in the duchy, had suggested that Schiller be named professor of history. He did not know Schiller, but as time passed Goethe and Schiller were to become working partners, inspiration for each other, and close friends. Schiller's and Goethe's works from this point bear the mark of each other's genius, as well as their own. Schiller's work also influenced Wilhelm von Humboldt, Heinrich von Kleist, Hölderlin, and Novalis. He was kindness itself to the visiting Madame de Staël, who "discovered" for the French, and ultimately for the rest of the world, the giants of German classicism, Schiller and Goethe.

During the Weimar years, Schiller was ill so often that he seemed to live in bed. The Wallenstein trilogy, *Mary Stuart*, *The Maid of Orleans*, *William Tell*, and the others were composed in the rare moments Schiller felt well enough to work. He had to stop lecturing at the university because his small store of energy would not permit it. At the age of forty-six he died, presumably of a combination of pneumonia and tuberculosis.

ANALYSIS

It is not necessary to have studied Friedrich Schiller's theoretical writings or Immanuel Kant's *Kritik der reinen Vernunft* (1781; *Critique of Pure Reason*, 1838), which influenced him profoundly, to understand Schiller's works, but it is helpful to understand two concepts that are the source of tragic conflict in most of his plays: the concept of the "naïve" and of the "sentimental." For each word, a special sense is intended: "Sentimental" means reflective, analytical, conscious of oneself, intellectual; "naïve" means unselfconscious, natural, original, pure, unreflective. There can be sentimental modes of existence as well as sentimental art. In referring to people, Schiller used the terms "dignity" (roughly corresponding to sentimentality) and "grace" (naïveté). Homer's is an example of naïve art—that is, an outpouring of natural gifts. Eighteenth century art, with its conventions and rules, could only be sentimental. In terms of the artistic process, although the original act of creation is always naïve, it acquires a sentimental aspect as it is analyzed, structured, and contemplated by the artist. A naïve work of art is the outpouring of genius. A sentimental work of art has goals. Where a sentimental work of art has a moral, a naïve work of art is itself moral. Art is to be valued for its own sake and by its own rules. Schiller's essays *Briefe über die ästhetische Erziehung des Menschen*, 1795 (*On the Aesthetic Education of Man*, 1845), *Über Anmut und Würde* (1793; *On Grace and Dignity*, 1875), and *Über naïve und sentimentalische Dichtung* (1795; *On Naïve and Sentimental Poetry*, 1845), delineate this system of thought exemplified in the plays.

The Robbers

In Schiller's first play, *The Robbers*, critic Ilse Graham sees a version of the biblical Jacob and Esau conflict. The younger brother, who by virtue of his talent and charm has unintentionally stolen the father's affection, is tricked by the cunning, analytical older brother, and is eventually disinherited and disowned. Stunned, the younger brother takes charge of a group of marauders, looking to avenge social and political injustice in a very concrete manner. Meanwhile, the older brother uses the political power of feudalism to ruin the already weak father, while keeping the feared younger brother at bay. Although the robber chieftain makes a considerable effort to disclaim responsibility for his men's atrocities by holding himself aloof from scenes of carnage, his realization that he has become incurably tainted with moral degeneracy—that there is no way back—forms the central crisis of the play. In this moment of reflection on his actions, the robber chieftain crosses the boundary from naïve to sentimental. Like Hamlet, he contemplates suicide, but decides from pride in his own greatness to live out his bitter choice to the end: "I am my Heaven and my Hell." "Revenge is my trade." "Two such as I would bring down the whole structure of the civilized world."

Fiesco

The masks in Schiller's next play, *Fiesco*, are not confined to the operalike costume ball of the first scene. Andreas Doria, illegal dictator of Genua, is about to be toppled by another member of the hereditary oligarchy, a Machiavellian republican leader named Fiesco. Fiesco must be seen as an artist, rather than a politician, for he manipulates people much as a stage director moves actors. As the aesthetic mode of existence in which human genius can reach its full potential is possible only in the perfect freedom of play, Fiesco plays with his opponents, just as Schiller plays with the plot, drawing out the denouement with one complication after another. Fiesco, a sentimental artist in the sense of combining natural genius and reflection, is a charismatic villain with more than a hint of the subsequent century's Napoleon Bonaparte. If the robber chieftain's downfall was his naïve reaction—choosing outlawry—to a blow of fate, then Fiesco's downfall is his excessive commitment to sentimental artistry, playing with his own coup until at last he is murdered by a republican fellow-conspirator. Incredibly, the assassin rushes away from the scene to the side of the previous dictator. This is the last stroke of Schiller's "republican tragedy."

Cabal and Love

Cabal and Love includes many features of the comedy. Before Gotthold Ephraim Lessing's bourgeois tragedy *Miss Sara Sampson* (1755; English translation, 1933) and the subsequent *Emilia Galotti* (1772; English translation, 1786), only members of the nobility served as protagonists in tragedy. The middle classes were considered more suitable for comedy. Schiller, a lifelong believer in the aristocracy of art and intellect, rather than birth, brought a Shakespearean mixture of comic doings and tragic conflict to the stage in *Cabal and Love*. In this play, the potential of ideal love cannot be realized. Those who would pursue it are destroyed, on one level by their membership in diverse social classes, on another by their membership in the corrupt human race.

The play, retitled by the actor August Wilhelm Iffland, had been named after the main character, Luise Millerin, the first figure in Schiller's dramas to exemplify the *schöne Seele* (beautiful soul). Just as a naïve work of art is beautiful in and of itself, so the beautiful soul is the epitome of the naïve in a human life, a naturally pure and unspoiled being.

Cabal and Love contains some of Schiller's harshest social criticism. A despotic court conspires to deprive the lovers of any vestige of hope, seeking to destroy their vision of love and each other as well as to deprive them of the opportunity to marry. In another abuse of courtly power, the prince manages to pay for his latest gift of jewels to his mistress by selling many hundreds of young recruits to the English to be sent to fight in America. After the first few who protest are shot, their brains splashing on the pavement, the rest cheer, "Off to America! Hurrah!"

DON CARLOS, INFANTE OF SPAIN

The transitional play *Don Carlos, Infante of Spain* has an uneven plot, but is one of Schiller's most popular plays. "Geben Sie Gedankenfreiheit!" (give freedom of thought) a character demands of the startled King Philip of Spain in perhaps the most famous single line in all of German literature. As the scene develops, however, it becomes obvious that such a change would bring about the inevitable end of absolutism, and that on the other hand, anyone who became king would of necessity become a Philip.

It was not until the Wallenstein trilogy that Schiller showed that the unwillingness to act is a fateful action in itself. Thought by many to be Schiller's greatest work, the trilogy covers four days in the life of Wallenstein, duke of Friedland and supreme commander of the Imperial armies, during the Thirty Years' War (1618-1648). Having started his career as a naïve, naturally gifted military genius, Wallenstein was deposed as general for a period of time as a result of political conniving by the emperor and others. As things began to go badly for the Imperial armies in the so-called religious wars between Protestants and Catholics, Wallenstein was recalled. At the time of his fall from power, however, the general became aware of the treachery and ungratefulness of the emperor in contrast to his own loyalty and incomparable achievements for the Catholic side. All of this has taken place before the action of the trilogy: Wallenstein has already made the transition from naïve to sentimental. As Schiller depicts him in the drama, he relies on the counsel of the stars, broods on destiny, and negotiates with the Swedes (Protestants) to change his and his armies' allegiance, thus forcing the emperor to accept a compromised peace.

THE CAMP OF WALLENSTEIN

The calculating realist Wallenstein never appears in the first play, *The Camp of Wallenstein*, which shows the bright color and comedy of the military universe solely subject to, and dependent on, Wallenstein. In legends and anecdotes, the troops pay homage to their general, the charismatic god of the camp. Neither language, patriotism, nor religion can serve as a common point of allegiance for the camp, only Wallenstein.

Although Wallenstein's greatness is obvious, he is not a virtuous man. The intellectual, sentimental characteristics of the general come into sharp contrast with the naïve qualities of Max Piccolomini, a young officer who idolizes Wallenstein. For Max, the final judge of any matter is the heart, which in Schiller's works is the organ of religion as well as love, a direct connection with a divine realm.

THE PICCOLOMINIS

In the second play, *The Piccolominis*, Wallenstein's downfall has been planned and ordered by the emperor. All that remains is to determine the manner of execution. At the same time Wallenstein, ignorant of approaching doom, is fully prepared to sacrifice the ideal love between two young people very dear to him, his daughter Thekla and Max Piccolomini, in order to arrange a politically propitious marriage for her. Max and Thekla, two beautiful souls, speak with the voice of the playwright in sadly prophesying the general's downfall at the end of the play. If *The Camp of Wallenstein* is a comedy, then *The Piccolominis*, with its plot exposition lacking fulfillment, is reminiscent of William Shakespeare's historical plays.

THE DEATH OF WALLENSTEIN

The Death of Wallenstein is a tragedy. At the time he was working on the Wallenstein trilogy, Schiller translated a play by Jean Racine. He seems to have taken seriously literary journal editor Christoph Martin Wieland's call for German drama to adhere more closely to Aristotelian unities of time and place. Also, by this time Schiller and Goethe, with *Egmont* (1788;

English translation, 1841) and *Don Carlos, Infante of Spain*, had established iambic pentameter as the meter of classical German tragedy.

MARY STUART

Mary Stuart, containing a face-to-face confrontation never recorded in history between Elizabeth I and the Scottish queen, is also restricted in time and place, as in classical French tragedy. Schiller portrays the two queens as young women, Mary basically naïve—guilty of sexual transgressions and sins of impulsiveness—Elizabeth conniving and sentimental. Both love and are wooed by the same man, Leicester. Where enough humility and docility from Mary toward Elizabeth might have saved Mary from her death sentence, the Scottish queen seizes the freedom to assert her integrity and pride. Some critics, including Ilse Graham, see the two queens as two halves of the same being or personality, neither able to function without the other.

THE MAID OF ORLEANS

"This play flowed from my heart," Schiller wrote in 1802 about *The Maid of Orleans*, "and it ought to speak to the hearts of the audience. It is not always true, unfortunately, that others have a heart." Where *The Death of Wallenstein* and *Mary Stuart* had demanded intellectual discipline from the playwright, the material concerning Joan of Arc also enjoyed his affection and sympathy. Goethe considered it Schiller's best play.

Although Schiller wrote *The Maid of Orleans* in Weimar, it opened in Leipzig, Berlin, and Hamburg. Duke Karl August of Saxony-Weimar thought the play ridiculous in comparison to Voltaire's satiric mock-epic poem *La Pucelle d'Orleans* (1755; *La Pucelle: Or, the Maid of Orleans*, 1785-1786). In addition, the only actress in Weimar suitable for playing the lead was the duke's mistress. The duke did not want her lack of qualifications for the role of a holy maiden to become the subject of gossip.

Schiller did not strive for an episodic style and frequent changes of scene, as did the romantic Ludwig Tieck in his *Leben und Tod der heiligen Genoveva* (pb. 1800, pr. 1807). Actually, Schiller missed the simplicity and structural unity of the *Mary Stuart* material. To convey the Joan of Arc material, Schiller

had to let the demands of the plot determine the structure of the play, a procedure bringing him closer again to Shakespearean than to French models. Even so, Schiller felt free to let the Joan of his play differ from the historical Joan, probably most markedly in the manner of her death.

Instead of a witchcraft trial and a heretic's death at the stake, Schiller's Joan dies a victorious, glorious death from the wounds of battle. Schiller's Joan speaks more words of prophecy than the historical Joan, taking on some of the qualities of a heathen seeress. Saints Catharine and Margaret, who appeared to the historical Joan, are replaced by the repeated dream of the Virgin as Queen of Heaven. Where the historical Joan, although garbed in battle dress, limited herself to carrying a banner at the head of her troops, Schiller's Joan is commanded by God to kill the enemy mercilessly, and she does so with supernatural efficiency and cold-bloodedness. The English, typified by Montgomery, call her "terrible, dreadful."

Some critics saw in the play Schiller's intention to let the ideal qualities of form triumph over the violence of the plot in order to propel the audience into a sudden insight about the nature of beauty. Schiller used some techniques of the romantics in orchestrating the spoken voice, moving from dramatic speeches to lyric arias with their additional musical element, rhyme. There are iambic and folk-song stanzas, but also lines reminiscent of the classical hexameter and trimeter. Schiller must have called his tragedy "romantic" because of the presence of miracles and the story's proximity to medieval Christian mythology. The play also contains the motif of national liberation dear to the romantics.

Although Schiller's Joan is a heroic figure, she is not a sympathetic protagonist. She is characterized by a kind of inhuman heartlessness, required of her by God, but also proclaimed by her repeatedly. The pure and obedient shepherdess soon becomes an amazon, who even calls herself a pitiless spirit of terror. In the heat of battle she says, "My armor does not cover a heart. . . . Defend yourself; death is calling you. . . . Don't appeal to my sex; don't call me woman." She is in the human world, but not of it, her allegiance and activities forming a direct conduit from a supernatural realm. Indeed, *The Maid of Orleans*, according to some critics, shows the fate of the transcendent in the midst of a vain, impure, degrading world; its reconciliation with and return to its origin forms the culmination.

Schiller himself stated explicitly that the Joan of the last act and the shepherdess Joan of the prologue reflect each other. In 1801, he wrote in a letter to Goethe:

> I predict a good and proper effect for my last act; it explains the first act, and so the snake bites itself on the tail. Because my hero stands alone, quite deserted by the gods in her misfortune, quite free and independent, her worthiness for the role of prophet is demonstrated. The end of the fourth act is very theatrical, and the thundering *deus ex machina* will bring about the desired result.

The end of the fourth act, when the unprotesting Joan is cast out from the French army, is indeed theatrical, but also provides the point of departure for the process of tragedy: previous worldly adoration and internally, a steep fall. On the one side is the sumptuous coronation parade led by Joan with her banner of the Holy Virgin, on the other, the subsequent bitter accusations. Joan's speechlessness gives rise to the belief by all that the accusations are true, but Joan cannot deny that the enemy is in her heart—not the Devil, of course, but the Englishman Lionel. She is deeply conscious of her transgression against God, not in the form of witchcraft but in the form of love.

Seldom are Schiller's characters completely silent. Luise Miller in *Cabal and Love* is an example. Her silence might be seen as powerlessness at the beginning of the play, later the result of a forced oath to deny her love, and finally as an expression of helplessness. Joan is intransigent in her silence, which is emphasized by the clap of thunder from on high. Unfortunately, this sign from Heaven is just as subject to misinterpretation as Joan's speechlessness. Joan is mute as a sign of the fissure in her soul: She belongs neither in this world nor in the next. That is the tragic moment in this play, Joan's total isolation; not even those who love her and believe in her are able to

break through it. Everyone believes that she is guilty of witchcraft, including her infatuated companion-in-exile. Thus, Joan remains uncanny—whether in love or hate—and inaccessible to other people, a figure from an alien world, yet human enough to awaken passion in others and succumb to it herself.

Joan's silence is also an indication that she accepts her downfall and humiliation as a just punishment for her transgression, although the nature of her sin is completely misunderstood by her human judges. The process of reflection by which she arrives at this point shows that the faculty of sentimentality is added to her previous naïveté, much the same as the sentimentality of Mary Stuart. Although not guilty of the crime with which she is charged, like Mary, Joan accepts the punishment to expiate another sin. Just as Mary Stuart receives absolution in the religious rites of the execution scene, so Joan, the outcast, finds her way back to God. By honoring and accepting her just punishment Joan again becomes God's prophet and messenger. Her love for Lionel cannot distract her from the immediacy of France's peril and her mission.

The final scene of the play is not one of martyrdom but of resplendence. Joan is not seen as a figure of Christian charity, but rather as a warrior as fierce and deadly as was Achilles. Schiller created her from many sources, not only from the historical Joan but also from Shakespeare, Greek antiquity, German classicism and romanticism, the Christian Middle Ages, and the Old Testament. Through Joan of Arc's glorious death, Schiller exalted the tragedy to a religious rite. Joan is immortal because art triumphs with her over earthly restrictions and imperfections, because humanity sees in her its own potential for transcendence.

Schiller's morality, like his characteristic victories over illness in order to create, had a Promethean cast. He was consistently moral to the point of impetuosity, trying to transform his bourgeois era into an age receptive to the demanding aesthetic values and radical idealism of his work. It seemed to him the duty of human beings surrounded by a materialist and rationalist environment, on an earth haunted by evil and lacking in religion, to rediscover divine values and concepts that had lain hidden, and to bring them out and to make them visible in a new way. The tragedy as religious celebration would serve this purpose. In tragedy, Schiller believed, ideals celebrate their purest triumph over the material world.

WILLIAM TELL

If *William Tell* seems like a collection of clichés to people in the German-speaking world, it is because this greatly beloved last play of Schiller's is perhaps the most quoted work of German literature. Schiller's lines have been repeated so often for so many decades and generations that they have become part of the German language, just as many lines of Shakespeare's *Hamlet, Prince of Denmark* (pr. c. 1600-1601) might hardly seem original to a speaker of English. Schiller's *William Tell* was originally performed March 17, 1804, under the personal direction of Schiller's great collaborator and friend, Goethe. So beloved did the play become that in a performance at the court of William II, emperor of Germany, the emperor and the entire audience stood during the oath-taking scene, repeating from memory with the actors the words of the pledge of allegiance of republican Switzerland. In this, Schiller's own favorite play, one sees that his realization of ideal humanity is the unity of nature and the psyche. Where the conflict of a natural drive (love) with heroic ideals nearly destroyed Joan of Arc in *The Maid of Orleans*, the unity of naïve and sentimental forces in the hero moves *William Tell* away from tragedy and into the realm of pageantry or ritual.

OTHER MAJOR WORKS

LONG FICTION: *Der Verbrecher aus verlorener Ehre*, 1786 (*The Criminal, in Consequence of Lost Reputation*, 1841); *Der Geisterseher*, 1789 (*The Ghost-Seer: Or, The Apparitionist*, 1795).

POETRY: *Anthologie auf das Jahr 1782*, 1782; *Xenien*, 1796 (with Johann Wolfgang von Goethe); *Gedichte*, 1800, 1803; *The Poems of Schiller*, 1851; *The Ballads and Shorter Poems of Fredrick v. Schiller*, 1901.

NONFICTION: *Die Schaubühne als eine moralische Anstalt betrachtet*, 1784 (*The Theater as a Moral Institution*, 1845); *Historischer Kalender für Damen*,

1790, 1791; *Geschichte des dreissigjährigen Krieges*, 1791-1793 (3 volumes; *History of the Thirty Years' War*, 1799); *Über den Grund des Vergnügens an tragischen Gegenständen*, 1792 (*On the Pleasure in Tragic Subjects*, 1845); *Über das Pathetische*, 1793 (*On the Pathetic*, 1845); *Über Anmut und Würde*, 1793 (*On Grace and Dignity*, 1845); *Briefe über die ästhetische Erziehung des Menschen*, 1795 (*On the Aesthetic Education of Man*, 1845); *Über naïve und sentimentalische Dichtung*, 1795-1796 (*On Naïve and Sentimental Poetry*, 1845); *Über das Erhabene*, 1801 (*On the Sublime*, 1845); *Briefwechsel Zwischen Schiller und Goethe*, 1829 (*The Correspondence Between Schiller and Goethe*, 1845); *Aesthetical and Philosophical Essays*, 1845; *Schillers Briefwechsel mit Körner von 1784 bis zum Tode Schillers*, 1847 (*Schiller's Correspondence with Körner*, 1849).

MISCELLANEOUS: *Sämmtliche Werke*, 1812-1815 (12 volumes; *Complete Works in English*, 1870).

BIBLIOGRAPHY

Graham, Ilse. *Schiller's Drama: Talent and Integrity.* London: Methuen, 1974. Graham provides an analysis of Schiller's plays, including *The Robbers* and *Mary Stuart.* He looks at both content and technique. Bibliography.

Hammer, Stephanie Barbé. *Schiller's Wound: The Theater of Trauma from Crisis to Commodity.* Detroit, Mich.: Wayne State University Press, 2001. Hammer examines Schiller's plays from a psychological standpoint, analyzing the thought behind them. Bibliography and index.

Miller, R. D. *A Study of Schiller's "Jungfrau von Orleans."* Harrogate, England: Duchy Press, 1995. Miller provides a close examination of Schiller's play about Joan of Arc, *The Maid of Orleans.* Bibliography and index.

Pugh, David. *Schiller's Early Dramas: A Critical History.* Rochester, N.Y.: Camden House, 2000. One volume in the series Studies in German Literature, Linguistics, and Culture: Literary Criticism in Perspective. Focuses on the early works of Schiller, their impact and controversies.

Reed, T. J. *Schiller.* New York: Oxford University Press, 1991. A biography of the German writer, which sheds light on his writing of dramas. Bibliography and index.

Sharpe, Lesley. *Friedrich Schiller: Drama, Thought, and Politics*. New York: Cambridge University Press, 1991. Part of the Cambridge Studies in Ger-

man series, this scholarly study looks at Schiller's views and how they infused his drama and other works. Bibliography and index.

Fredericka A. Schmadel

MURRAY SCHISGAL

Born: Brooklyn, New York; November 25, 1926

PRINCIPAL DRAMA

A Simple Kind of Love Story, pr. 1960, pb. 1980
The Postman, pr. 1960 (one act)
The Typists, pr. 1960, pb. 1963 (one act)
Ducks and Lovers, pr. 1961, pb. 1972
The Tiger, pr., pb. 1963 (one act; originally as *The Postman*)
Knit One, Purl Two, pr. 1963
Luv, pr. 1963, pb. 1965
Windows, pr., pb. 1965
Reverberations, pb. 1965, pr. 1967 (as *The Basement*)
The Old Jew, pb. 1965, pr. 1967
Fragments, pb. 1965, pr. 1967
Memorial Day, pb. 1965, pr. 1968
Fragments, Windows and Other Plays, pb. 1965 (includes *Reverberations*, *The Old Jew*, *Memorial Day*)
Jimmy Shine, pr. 1968, pb. 1969 (music by John Sebastian)
The Chinese, pr. 1968, pb. 1970
A Way of Life, pr. 1969
Dr. Fish, pr., pb. 1970
An American Millionaire, pr., pb. 1974
All over Town, pr. 1974, pb. 1975
Roseland, pr. 1975
Popkins, pr. 1978, pb. 1984
The Pushcart Peddlers, pr. 1979, pb. 1980
The Downstairs Boys, pr. 1980 (revision of *Roseland*)
Walter, and The Flautist, pr., pb. 1980 (2 plays)

Little Johnny, pb. 1980
The Pushcart Peddlers, The Flautist, and Other Plays, pb. 1980 (includes *A Simple Kind of Love Story*, *Little Johnny*, *Walter*)
Twice Around the Park, pr. 1982, pb. 1983 (2 one-act comedies: *A Need for Brussels Sprouts* and *A Need for Less Expertise*)
Luv and Other Plays, pb. 1983
Closet Madness and Other Plays, pb. 1984
The Rabbi and the Toyota Dealer, pb. 1984, pr. 1985
Road Show, pr., pb. 1987
Songs of War, pr. 1989
Extensions, pr., pb. 1991 (one act)
Theatrical Release, pr. 1991
The Cowboy, the Indian, and the Fervent Feminist, pr., pb. 1993
Angel Wings, pr. 1994
Sexaholics and Other Plays, pb. 1995
Slouching Towards the Millennium, pr. 1997
Play Time, pr. 1991, pb. 1997
Fifty Years Ago, pb. 1998
The Man Who Couldn't Stop Crying, pb. 2000
First Love, pb. 2001
We Are Family, pr. 2001

OTHER LITERARY FORMS

Murray Schisgal has published the novel *Days and Nights of a French Horn Player* (1980) and has written television plays, *The Love Song of Barney Kempenski* (1966) and *Natasha Kovolina Pipishinsky* (1976), and an expanded version of his one-act play *The Tiger*, which was produced as a screenplay, *The*

Tiger Makes Out (1967), starring Eli Wallach. Schisgal's play *Luv* was also produced as a screenplay (1965). Schisgal and Larry Gelbart collaborated to produce the screenplay for the hit 1982 film *Tootsie*.

ACHIEVEMENTS

Murray Schisgal is known for his experimental plays (*The Typists*) and, even more so, for his farces, including *Luv* and *The Tiger*. He is prominent in the theater world and a friend of many on the New York theater scene, such as Eli Wallach, Anne Jackson, and Dustin Hoffman (to whom he dedicated a number of his scripts, including *Popkins*). His plays reflect some of the mainstream comic situations and themes of New York theater from the mid-twentieth century to the present day. His forte, light comedy and satire, manifests itself in witty, often topical plays that are written primarily to evoke quick laughter and that have been produced by some of the best professional theater troupes of modern times.

BIOGRAPHY

Murray Joseph Schisgal was born on November 25, 1926, to Abraham and Irene (née Sperling) Schisgal, in Brooklyn, New York. His father was a tailor in the East New York section of Brooklyn. Schisgal was in high school during World War II, but he quit to join the United States Navy in 1943, in which he served until 1946, earning the rank of radioman, third class. He returned to his high school diploma at night and attended Long Island University. He gained a bachelor of laws degree in 1953 from Brooklyn Law School and a bachelor of arts from New York's New School for Social Research in 1959.

From the age of twenty-one, Schisgal knew that his main professional interest was in writing. His initial efforts in the world of letters were in prose fiction: more than sixty stories and three novels, none of which was immediately published. He supported himself through a variety of odd jobs, including setting pins in a bowling alley, pushing clothing racks in the garment district, and playing saxophone and clarinet in a small band. After receiving his law degree, Schisgal practiced law for two years on Delancey

Murray Schisgal in 1970. (AP/Wide World Photos)

Street, near Greenwich Village, but he gave this up to devote more time to his writing. He then turned to teaching English while he continued to write on the side. From 1955 through 1960, he taught English at James Fenimore Cooper Junior High School in East Harlem, New York City. While teaching, he turned to writing plays.

Like his contemporary Edward Albee, Schisgal saw his first commercial production mounted in another country. While traveling to Europe to spend time writing, he succeeded in arranging for his first works, *The Typists* and *The Tiger*, to be produced by the British Drama League. After this breakthrough, Schisgal became a full-time playwright; since 1960, he has been able to practice his craft on a full-time basis.

Schisgal's best-known work is the comedy *Luv*, which premiered in London in 1963 and opened in the United States in November, 1964, at the Booth Theatre in New York. Directed by Mike Nichols—a television actor and comic who was to become famous as a film director with his work in *The Graduate*—*Luv*'s three-person cast consisted of Alan Arkin, recently moved over from Second City in Chicago, and Eli Wallach and Anne Jackson, two well-known personalities of the New York stage and the world of cinema. The recognition that Schisgal first gained with *The Typists* and *The Tiger* turned into financial and commercial success with the long-running *Luv*, and he became a fixture of the Broadway scene.

In 1975, however, disillusioned by the failure of the ambitious *All over Town*, Schisgal stopped writing for Broadway. He turned his attention to film and television work and received an Academy Award nomination for his work on *Tootsie*; he also wrote his first novel. He continued to write plays for Off-Broadway production before returning to Broadway with *Twice Around the Park* in 1982. He has continued to write plays, largely for European production; *Popkins* was produced in Paris in 1990, and *Theatrical Release* was performed there in 1991.

ANALYSIS

Murray Schisgal's forte is the light comedy, with genial satire and topical references often worked into the content of the play. Schisgal's plays have often enjoyed commercial success. *Luv* had a long run on Broadway in the mid-1960's, and *The Tiger* (which Schisgal revised as the screenplay *The Tiger Makes Out*) was a moderately successful movie in 1967. For several decades, Schisgal has been a commercially successful, full-time playwright and theater person—no mean accomplishment in the financially difficult medium of playwriting. He has earned the friendship of influential theater persons in New York and elsewhere.

In their zany, topical, and often absurd touches, Schisgal's light comedies are similar to those of his contemporaries Neil Simon and Saul Bellow and of the younger but similarly satiric filmmaker Woody Allen. His people are usually wealthy New Yorkers who remember a younger, poorer time in their lives

and who are often comically bored with their marriages—sexual or psychological problems provide the motivation for the plots of most of Schisgal's works. Schisgal often writes to evoke laughter and spectacle. His dramas are characterized by humorous sexual references and by satiric references to current fads in contemporary culture in general (especially New York City culture) and to the theater world in particular. Schisgal's plays tend to refer to current trends in mainstream commercial New York or related milieus during the time of the particular play's production. Although he made his initial breakthrough Off-Off-Broadway, Schisgal has become a central figure of commercial Broadway. His dramatic voice is conservative, urbane, witty, slightly cynical, and lightly comic.

Schisgal's best plays are distinguished by a flair for light comedy. There is in much of his work a nostalgia for a youthful, less financially comfortable past, a winking understanding of adultery (especially male adultery), a tendency to satirize fads, and a general assumption of familiarity with New York locations; a belief in the old verities is just below the surface of his satire. Things are not so bad, Schisgal seems to be saying: People are basically good if limited, sexual creatures given to little adventures that tend to right themselves.

LUV

Typical of Schisgal's drama is the 1960's comedy *Luv*, which has two major comic targets: the nihilistic tradition of theater, often called Theater of the Absurd, and some of the insincere posturings that are often substituted for a deeper definition of "love." Like the Theater of the Absurd that Schisgal's play satirizes, *Luv* is not literally realistic or even psychologically plausible in its presentation of characters; rather, it is an idea play, a series of gags and satiric jabs at its targets. Two men, Harry Berlin and Milt Manville, in effect pass a somewhat overbearing, bluestocking woman back and forth between them in the twists and turns of the plot. The action is rapid, basically lighthearted, played with gusto, and aimed at provoking laughter. Foibles and fads, not major cultural undercurrents, are the butt of Schisgal's comic critique.

Luv is set at the edge of a bridge on a dark, isolated night. Harry Berlin, an out-at-the-elbows Bohemian character (his nickname in high school, we learn, was "Dostoyevsky"), is about to leap off the bridge when his suicide is halted by an old friend, Milt Manville. Manville is as crass and philistine as Berlin is neurotic and typical of the counterculture. Manville has come to the bridge to pick valuables out of the garbage, thereby to add further wealth to his already considerable income. Berlin tells Manville that his (Berlin's) life is meaningless, that he has abandoned all of his projects and education. Milt attempts to cheer Harry and restore in him a sense of life's significance by reiterating the key word of the play, "love." Harry responds, saying that he feels suddenly, absurdly alive again simply when the word is mentioned. The audience soon learns that love has its meaning for Manville as well—sending him to walk by the bridge, for he is in love with a woman, Linda, who is not his wife. In short order, Milt arranges for Harry to meet his wife, Ellen. In comically fast fashion, Harry falls for Ellen. With the second act, Milt has returned to the bridge, now bored with his new marriage with Linda, and Ellen returns there, discontented with her marriage with the neurotic Harry. Milt and Ellen rapidly come back together, and the play ends with Harry being pursued by a zealous dog snapping at his pants leg as he vainly pursues the once-again-happy pair, Milt and Ellen.

The stock dramatic techniques and situations of a typical Schisgal comedy are apparent in the plot of *Luv*. There is the contrast between the commercially successful Milt Manville and the artistic, neurotic Bohemian Harry Berlin. There is a comic love triangle, some version of which is in each of Schisgal's plays. A current fashion is satirized—here, the nihilistic despair largely mouthed by Harry Berlin, especially in act 1. There are also many one-liners about adultery; the comical treatment of a potentially serious subject is typical of Schisgal's drama.

Luv can be seen as a kind of a farce-parody of a slightly older, also very successful play that eventually ran well in New York—Edward Albee's *The Zoo Story* (pr., pb. 1959). In Albee's play, a tragic, neurotic isolate meets a relatively conservative philistine

and has the philistine assist him in his own suicide. *The Zoo Story*, however, is serious, downbeat, somber, whereas *Luv* is a lighthearted and satiric reversal of a similar situation. Even the attempted suicides off the bridge, complete with water splashing up on the stage, prove humorously unsuccessful. Each time, the character comes back wet but very much alive. The human condition is not nearly as bad as the nihilistic absurdists would have us believe, Schisgal implies in *Luv*. Schisgal's is a conservative, mainstream comedy.

THE TIGER

The Tiger illustrates another version of Schisgal's satiric comedy. The play's premise provoked some adverse commentary (a man carries a woman off to his apartment by force, and she proceeds to fall for him), yet the action of the play proves far less upsetting or radical than a bare summary of the plot would indicate. A one-act play, *The Tiger* is set in a secluded New York apartment owned by Ben, a pseudo-Nietzschean isolate. Ben carries Gloria into the apartment as the play opens; she is over his shoulder, kicking and fighting. He ties her up and they talk—which constitutes the main action of the play until its climax, their love scene. Ben calls himself a "tiger," and his posturing language is full of animal imagery. He threatens Gloria with references to how he will "finish her off" and "claw" her. One learns that Ben is forty-two, insecure about his middle-aged bachelordom, a college dropout who works as a postman. Gloria is a former social worker, now a bored Long Island suburban housewife. Soon, Ben and Gloria find common ground, agreeing that conformity and boredom permeate American culture of the day (around 1963), and, speaking French to each other, they grow romantic, the lights are cut, and a love scene takes place. When the lights come back up, Gloria is dressed again and they fix a date for another adulterous tryst.

Both the play and the subsequent screenplay, *The Tiger Makes Out*, can be seen as presenting the fantasies of the middle-aged American male: Gloria is submissive and sexually accessible in an almost dreamlike way. What is being satirized in this fantasy-comedy is conformity, but the play's patent wish fulfillment almost overwhelms its satire.

JIMMY SHINE

Jimmy Shine is one of Schisgal's most elaborate plays. Its two acts embrace large sweeps of space and time, and it is designed for a three-level stage somewhat reminiscent of the set of Arthur Miller's *Death of a Salesman* (pr., pb. 1949). One follows the title character through some significant steps in his life. Schisgal's triangle theme becomes evident when Jimmy's youthful romantic interest marries his best friend. The best friend talks Jimmy into dropping out of business society and living in Greenwich Village to pursue a life of painting and the arts. Then Jimmy's friend ironically reneges and becomes a wealthy businessman, while Jimmy stays artistically pure and first flees to San Francisco, then returns to New York, where he takes up with a prostitute and continues to work as a painter. The flashback technique is similar to that of Schisgal's novel, *Days and Nights of a French Horn Player:* Like the novel, *Jimmy Shine* charts the development of a wisecracking protagonist who happens to be an artist, someone who pursues his vision and who learns through experience, particularly through his love affairs.

TWICE AROUND THE PARK

Twice Around the Park, consisting of the one-act plays *A Need for Brussels Sprouts* and *A Need for Less Expertise*, marked Schisgal's return to Broadway after a prolonged absence. *A Need for Brussels Sprouts* portrays the unorthodox courtship of Margaret, a policewoman, and Leon, an aging, unemployed actor. The play was Schisgal's first written for specific performers, and his characterizations of Margaret and Leon were strongly influenced by the performers (Anne Jackson and Eli Wallach) who inaugurated the roles. *A Need for Less Expertise* depicts the disastrous yet comic results of a marriage counselor's bizarre advice to a middle-aged couple. The playwright later observed, "I don't have more than a few themes that interest me: the 'accredited' expert telling others how to live is one of them."

OTHER MAJOR WORKS

LONG FICTION: *Days and Nights of a French Horn Player*, 1980.

SCREENPLAYS: *Ducks and Lovers*, 1962 (co-adaptor; adaptation of his play); *Luv*, 1965 (adapted from his play); *The Tiger Makes Out*, 1967 (adaptation of his *The Tiger*); *Tootsie*, 1982 (with Larry Gelbart); *Snowball*, 1994 (with David Ives); *A Hero of Our Times*, 1994; *Pen Pals*, 1995; *Medusa*, 1995-1996; *Night Cries*, 1996; *Call Me Lucky*, 1997.

TELEPLAYS: *The Love Song of Barney Kempenski*, 1966; *Natasha Kovolina Pipishinsky*, 1976.

BIBLIOGRAPHY

Herman, Jan. "Murray Schisgal Puts on a Show—So What Else Is New?" *Los Angeles Times*, July 11, 1989, p. F2. This preview of *Songs of War*, which includes a biographical profile, chronicles Schisgal's American and European reputation and recalls the fresh voice of *Luv* in 1965. *Songs of War*, with "refrains of family skirmishes," is reviewed by Don Shirley three days later.

Klein, Alvin. "*Luv* Offers Vaudeville of Neuroses." Review of *Luv*, by Murray Schisgal. *The New York Times*, February 9, 1992, p. 15. This review of the New Jersey Forum Theater Group's revival of *Luv* appeared in the New Jersey section of the newspaper. Klein includes a brief biography and a fairly long appreciation of Schisgal's sense of theater and his contribution to light comedy over several decades.

Lambert, Mike. "Awards Close Out Menu of Delicious One-Act Plays." *The Washington Post*, July 25, 1991, p. 5. The occasion, a one-act play festival at the Northern Virginia Theatre Alliance, included Schisgal's play *A Need for Brussels Sprouts*. The play went on in September to another production, directed by Stephen Rothman, at the West Hollywood Tiffany Theater.

Miller, Daryl H. "Missteps Undo *We Are Family:* Murray Schisgal's Comedy, at the Odyssey, Steps over the Line in Its Tale of Two Men Who 'Turn Gay.'" Review of *We Are Family*, by Murray Schisgal. *Los Angeles Times*, February 28, 2002, p. F47. Miller is critical of Schisgal's *We Are Family*, the story of two men who become gay in response to increased aggressiveness in women, playing at the Odyssey Theatre in Los Angeles.

Pressley, Nelson. "In Arlington, It's *Luv* in a New York Minute: A High-Speed Take on the Biting Comedy." Review of *Luv*, by Murray Schisgal. *The Washington Post*, June 19, 2000, p. C2. This review of a revival of *Luv* by the American Century Theater at the Gunston Arts Center in Arlington, Virginia, is critical of the production but not of Schisgal's comedy.

Stein, Howard, and Glenn Young, eds. *The Best American Short Plays, 1991-1992*. New York: Applause, 1992. As a preface to *Extensions*, the editors sum up Schisgal's career and his success with *Luv*, discuss his promising future, and bring into focus his later work.

Raymond Miller, Jr., updated by Thomas J. Taylor and Robert McClenaghan

ARTHUR SCHNITZLER

Born: Vienna, Austria; May 15, 1862
Died: Vienna, Austria; October 21, 1931

PRINCIPAL DRAMA

Alkandis Lied, pb. 1890

Das Märchen, pb. 1891, pr. 1893

Anatol, pr., pb. in Czech 1893, pr. in German 1910 (English translation, 1911)

Liebelei, pr. 1895, pb. 1896 (*Light-O'-Love*, 1912)

Die überspannte Person, pb. 1896, pr. 1932

Freiwild, pr. 1896, pb. 1898 (*Free Game*, 1913)

Halbzwei, pb. 1897, pr. 1932

Das Vermächtnis, pr. 1898, pb. 1899 (*The Legacy*, 1911)

Paracelsus, pb. 1898, pr. 1899 (English translation, 1913)

Die Gefährtin, pr., pb. 1899 (*The Mate*, 1913)

Der grüne Kakadu, pr., pb. 1899 (*The Green Cockatoo*, 1913)

Reigen, pb. 1900, pr. 1920 (*Hands Around*, 1920; also as *La Ronde*, 1959)

Der Schleier der Beatrice, pr. 1900, pb. 1901

Lebendige Stunden, pr. 1901, pb. 1902 (includes *Lebendige Stunden* [*Living Hours*, 1906]; *Die Frau mit dem Dolche* [*The Lady with the Dagger*, 1904]; *Die letzen Masken* [*Last Masks*, 1913]; *Literatur* [*Literature*, 1917])

Sylvesternacht, pb. 1901, pr. 1926

Der Puppenspieler, pr., pb. 1903 (*The Puppeteer*, 1995)

Der einsame Weg, pr., pb. 1904 (*The Lonely Way*, 1915)

Der tapfere Kassian, pr. 1904, pb. 1909 (*Gallant Cassian*, 1914)

Zum grossen Wurstel, pb. 1905, pr. 1906

Zwischenspiel, pr. 1905, pb. 1906 (*Intermezzo*, 1915)

Der Ruf des Lebens, pr., pb. 1906

Komtesse Mizzi: Oder, Der Familientag, pb. 1907, pr. 1909 (*Countess Mizzie*, 1907)

Die Verwandlungen des Pierrot, pb. 1908 (*The Transformation of Pierrot*, 1995)

Der junge Medardus, pr., pb. 1910

Der Schleier der Pierrette, pr., pb. 1910 (*The Veil of Pierette*, 1995)

Das weite Land, pr., pb. 1911 (*The Vast Land*, 1921)

Professor Bernhardi, pr., pb. 1912 (English translation, 1913)

The Green Cockatoo and Other Plays, pb. 1913

The Lonely Way, Intermezzo, Countess Mizzie, pb. 1915

Komödie der Worte, pr., pb. 1915 (*Comedy of Words*, 1917; includes *Stunde des Erkennens* [*The Hour of Recognition*], *Grosse Szene* [*The Big Scene*], and *Das Bacchusfest* [*The Festival of Bacchus*])

Fink und Fliederbusch, pr., pb. 1917

Die Schwestern: Oder, Casanova in Spa, pb. 1919,

pr. 1920 (*The Sisters: Or, Casanova in Spa*, 1992)

Komödie der Verführung, pr., pb. 1924 (*Seduction Comedy*, 1992)

Der Gang zum Weiher, pb. 1926, pr. 1931 (*The Way to the Pond*, 1992)

Im Spiel der Sommerlüfte, pr. 1929, pb. 1930 (*In the Play of the Summer Breezes*, 1996)

Reigen, The Affairs of Anatol, and Other Plays, pb. 1933

Die Dramatischen Werke, pb. 1962 (2 volumes)

Meisterdramen, pb. 1971

Three Late Plays, pb. 1992 (includes *The Sisters: Or, Casanova in Spa, Seduction Comedy*, and *The Way to the Pond*)

OTHER LITERARY FORMS

In addition to his dramas, Arthur Schnitzler wrote a large number of novellas, several novels, a collection of poems, and an autobiography entitled *Jugend in Wien* (1968; *My Youth in Vienna*, 1970).

ACHIEVEMENTS

The wealth and the variety of Arthur Schnitzler's creations tend to provoke different appraisals of the various aspects of his works. For some people, the name Schnitzler evokes only sweet Viennese girls being seduced by callous young men; others think primarily of the scandal that erupted at the premiere of *La Ronde*, a sequence of ten erotic scenes. Yet others think of Schnitzler's trenchant treatment of such social problems as dueling and anti-Semitism. The truth is that Schnitzler's œuvre is greater than the sum of these components. At his best, he represented Viennese society of the late nineteenth and early twentieth centuries in such a manner as to bring out its universal qualities. In Schnitzler's plays, universal topics of love, hate, cruelty, tenderness, faithfulness, infidelity, callousness, gentleness, and death are presented in the contemporary settings that were congenial to him. Whenever his characters speak with a Viennese inflection and whenever the setting is contemporary Vienna, his plays range from good to first-rate. He is much less successful with historical plays and with settings in foreign countries.

BIOGRAPHY

Arthur Schnitzler was born in Vienna on May 15, 1862. His father was a physician and the director of the Vienna General Hospital. Schnitzler grew up in the enlightened liberal atmosphere that was typical of emancipated Viennese Jews. He was at first taught by a governess (who introduced him to the dramatic works of Gotthold Ephraim Lessing, Friedrich Schiller, and William Shakespeare, and to the Viennese folk theater) and by private tutors. He then attended the Akademisches Gymnasium (high school), from which he was graduated in 1879. In the fall of that year, he began studying medicine at the University of Vienna, mostly to please his father. Except for nervous and mental diseases, Schnitzler was not really interested in medicine, and his early efforts at writing were not very promising either. Starting in 1882, he had to fulfill his military obligation by serving as a medical assistant. He hated life in the army and all forms of militarism and indulged in a "melancholy-cynical feeling of the world." This feeling and a series of fleeting love affairs seem to have coalesced into the psychological substratum from which he eventually created the cycle of one-act plays that make up the drama *Anatol*. In 1885, Schnitzler completed his master's degree and began working as a physician at the Vienna General Hospital.

The period of Schnitzler's university studies coincided with a marked change in the political climate in the Austro-Hungarian monarchy: The political power of the enlightened liberal parties declined considerably. At the same time, the clerical and nationalist parties gained majorities, both in the parliament and in the Vienna city council. Simultaneously with this shift in political power there occurred a marked increase in the hostility exhibited toward Jews. This latent and overt anti-Semitism was to become an important aspect of Schnitzler's social criticism, both in his dramas and in his fiction.

While working at the general hospital, Schnitzler developed an interest in the work of the psychiatrist Theodor Meynert. Schnitzler's involvement with psychiatry soon led him to a recognition of the social causes of many psychic diseases. A problem that preoccupied him particularly was the conflict between the sexual needs of young people and the demands of conventional morality. All these concerns were eventually reflected in his literary works.

When his father died in 1893, Schnitzler left the hospital and went into private practice. By that time he had already written several novellas, parts of *Anatol*, and the play *Alkandis Lied*. As early as in 1890, he had become part of the literary circle called "Young Vienna," which included Hugo von Hofmannsthal, Felix Salten, Richard Beer-Hofmann, and the famous critic Hermann Bahr. Roughly from 1893 on, Schnitzler turned his attention more and more toward literature and away from medicine. In 1895 he had his first major breakthrough with the premiere of *Liebelei* at the Burgtheater in Vienna. During the same year, he signed a contract with the important German publishing company S. Fischer for all of his future literary productions. During approximately the next twenty-five years, publication followed on publication and premiere on premiere. During that period, Schnitzler was considered to be *the* Austrian playwright. In 1903 he married the actress and singer Olga Gussmann, and in 1910 he was able to move into his own villa in the fashionable Viennese district of Währing.

In 1900, Schnitzler published the stream-of-consciousness novella *Leutnant Gustl* (1900; *None But the Brave*, 1925), which, besides being a literary masterpiece, contained strong criticisms of anti-Semitism and the practice of dueling. As a result of the publication of *None But the Brave*, Schnitzler was stripped of his rank as an officer in the Imperial Army. During World War I, he expressed, but did not dare to publish, strong antiwar sentiments and attacked the mindless glorification of war that was so prevalent then. He welcomed the demise of the monarchy and the advent of the first Austrian Republic with its promise of more democracy.

The postwar years, however, were difficult for Schnitzler. He took little interest in the political and economic questions of the day, and the public was no longer interested in the problems of the *fin de siècle*. His income decreased, and he was able to maintain his lifestyle only through royalties from films that had been made of several of his plays. In 1928, his

daughter Lili committed suicide. This event considerably accelerated the aging process in the dramatist. Schnitzler died of a brain hemorrhage on October 21, 1931.

ANALYSIS

The assonance between Arthur Schnitzler's first name and the name of his first major dramatic character, Anatol, points to a certain affinity between author and character, to certain autobiographical traits. The *Anatol* cycle consists of seven short one-act plays or sketches. The protagonist of each of them is Anatol, a wealthy, well-educated young man of the upper classes. He is usually melancholy, slightly cynical, but capable of recognizing and experiencing subtly differentiated feelings, moods, and pleasures. In each of the seven sketches, he interacts with one woman, and in some of them, also with his friend Max. The latter is a commonsense and practical foil to the high-strung and nervous protagonist. These simple dramatic constructs are full of psychological insights: They are witty and yet imbued with a certain sadness.

LIEBELEI

After the *Anatol* sketches, Schnitzler began writing plays whose plots are more complex and whose characters are more variegated. Even in these full-fledged dramas, however, certain stock characters and certain typical dramatic conflicts continually recur. For this reason, *Liebelei* is representative, at least in part, of several of Schnitzler's plays of that period.

The main characters in *Liebelei* are Fritz Lobheimer, the typical young man of the upper classes (very much like Anatol); Christine Weiring, the typical sweet Viennese girl of the lower classes; Theodor's current girlfriend; and Hans Weiring, Christine's father. In an expository scene in Fritz's living room, Fritz tells his friend Theodor about his affair with a married woman of the upper classes. The latter advises him to concentrate his attentions on Christine, who is similar to Theodor's girlfriend Mizi and who meets Theodor's primary requirement when it comes to women: "Women are not to be interesting, but pleasant."

Fritz and Theodor's conversation is terminated by the arrival of Christine and Mizi, whom Theodor has invited for the purpose of a surprise party. After some time, the party is interrupted by repeated rings of the doorbell. Having answered the bell, Fritz asks his guests to step into the adjoining room, and then admits "a gentleman." The latter turns out to be the husband of the woman with whom Fritz is having an affair. He returns a packet of letters written by Fritz to her. After reaching an understanding regarding the inevitable duel, the gentleman departs. Shortly afterward, Fritz's guests leave. Act 2 takes place during the following evening in Christine's room in a modest house in the suburbs. During a series of brief discussions between Christine, Katharina Binder (a well-meaning neighbor), Christine's father, and Mizi, Christine finds her situation becoming clearer: Her relationship with Fritz is becoming known in the neighborhood, and she is being pressured by Katharina to remain "decent" and to marry a decent young man of her own class who happens to have a regular job. Mr. Weiring, one of the most remarkable characters in the play, defends his daughter's right to happiness, or at least to a few happy memories before she settles down to a humdrum life. As a further aspect of Christine's characterization, her pure love for Fritz is contrasted to the more casual approach taken by Mizi in her relationships with men. The culminating scene of the second act is the encounter between Christine and Fritz, who comes to visit her and who sees her room for the first time. He is genuinely touched by her love and sincerity and by her petit bourgeois furnishings, including the obligatory bust of Franz Schubert and the encyclopedia that, alas, is only complete to the letter "G." Fritz experiences a few moments of true emotion; he feels sheltered while he is with Christine and in her world. The idyll, however, is soon shattered by Theodor's arrival. Theodor wants Fritz to get some rest before the duel, which is set for the next morning.

Act 3 takes place in Christine's room, two days later. Neither Christine nor Mizi has any news from Fritz and Theodor, who have pretended to go to the country for a day or two. Eventually, Theodor arrives and informs them that Fritz has been killed in the duel and that he has already been buried. After a powerful emotional outcry, Christine rushes out of the room, ostensibly to look for Fritz's grave, but the audience is led to agree with her father's assessment that she will never return.

Schnitzler himself, as well as contemporary critics, considered *Liebelei* to be a first-rate play. A century after its premiere, the universal elements of its subject matter remain relevant: unrequited love, a likable but unstable young man between two women, the conflict between private happiness and public morality. The topic of dueling, which assumes such an inordinate importance in some of Schnitzler's other dramas, is downplayed in *Liebelei*. In this drama, Schnitzler does not attack the social code that demands that Fritz and the cuckolded husband engage in a duel. Rather, the duel is subsumed in the topic of the unhappy relationship between Christine and Fritz. While she loves him and thinks of him day and night, he gets himself killed for the sake of another woman.

The plot of *Liebelei* is tautly constructed. Every scene has a strictly defined purpose, either for the characterization of the protagonists, or for the propulsion of the dramatic action. Similarly, Schnitzler's use of the German language (with the proper Viennese inflection) for purposes of characterization is superb.

THE VAST LAND

In *Liebelei*, part of the dramatic conflict arises from the difference in Fritz's and Christine's social standing. There is no such class conflict in *The Vast Land*, whose long list of characters includes more than a dozen protagonists, all of whom belong to the upper bourgeoisie. The main topic of the play is again the relationship between man and woman, but only between members of the upper classes. At the same time, the scope is broadened to a portrayal of the moral disintegration and emotional impoverishment of this social class. The settings of this tragicomedy are a villa in a resort near Vienna and a fashionable hotel in a resort in the Alps. The time of the play is the early twentieth century—the advent of modernity. The exterior dramatic action consists of four adulterous relationships, which are begun with varying degrees of attraction or passion, and which are terminated with varying degrees of nostalgia or resignation. The real dramatic conflict, however, takes place within "the vast land" of the protagonists' souls, and there the beginning, the middle, and the end remain one big riddle.

The main character of the play is Friedrich Hofreiter, the owner of a large lightbulb factory. During a few expository scenes, the audience learns that Friedrich has recently terminated an affair with Adele Natter, the wife of his banker, and that Alexei Korsakow, a young pianist who had been Friedrich's friend, has recently committed suicide. During several scenes in act 1, Friedrich discusses Korsakow's suicide with his wife, Genia. At first he believes that Genia had an affair with Korsakow, but then she shows him a love letter that Korsakow had written to her shortly before his death. From this letter it becomes manifest that Genia had remained faithful to her husband and that, moreover, she still loves him, in spite of his own infidelity. In a series of syllogistic arguments, Friedrich explains to Genia his shock at losing his friend Korsakow, whom she, by her "so-called fidelity," has driven to suicide. For this reason, she has become so strange and uncanny to him that he wishes to leave her for a few days. He decides, on the spur of a moment, to accompany his friend Dr. Mauer on a hiking holiday in the Alps.

The conversation between Friedrich and Genia is the starting point of a series of entanglements that eventually leads to disastrous results. Friedrich, Dr. Mauer, and Erna Wahl (a young woman in her twenties who loves Friedrich, but who is being wooed by Dr. Mauer) together brave death as they scale a dangerous mountain peak. During this expedition and back at their hotel, Friedrich starts an affair with Erna. Meanwhile, at home in the villa, Genia, who during her conversation with her husband had prided herself on being faithful to him "for her own sake," now begins an affair with a young ensign of the Austrian navy. Adele Natter starts another affair, this time with an army officer. Friedrich returns to the villa earlier than expected and observes the ensign as he climbs out of Genia's bedroom window in the middle of the night. He challenges the ensign to a duel and kills him.

The starkness of the dramatic action is relieved by several humorous episodes, but in essence *The Vast Land* is a very serious drama. Throughout the play, there occur exchanges of views that merit close attention because they illuminate Schnitzler's concern with contemporary society. One example is the conversation between Friedrich and Dr. von Aigner, the manager of the hotel in the Alps. About twenty years before the action of the play, von Aigner had been happily married and yet had had an affair with another woman. He had felt compelled to confess the affair to his wife, and they had both sensed that their marriage had come to an irrevocable end. Musing on this, Dr. von Aigner undoubtedly speaks with the voice of the compassionate psychologist Arthur Schnitzler:

> Has it not occurred to you what kind of complicated beings we humans are? There is room for so much at the same time within us! Love and deception . . . faithfulness and infidelity . . . adoration for one and desire for another one, or for several others. We do try to create some order within us, as well as it can be done, but this order is only something artificial. . . . That which is natural is chaos. Yes . . . the soul . . . is a vast land. . . .

Dr. von Aigner has reached this insight and this serenity twenty years after the breakup of his marriage. He maintains the clean break and his clear and honest position and will presumably continue to do so for the rest of his life. This attitude stands in marked contrast to the new generation, with its practice of "sliding" in and out of affairs, which is so roundly condemned by Dr. Mauer:

> I would have no objections at all against a world in which love would be nothing but a precious game. . . . But then . . . honesty, if you please! Honesty to the point of an orgy . . . that I would accept. But this mixture of caution and impudence, of cowardly jealousy and mendacious equanimity, of raging passion and empty pleasure that I see here—that I find wretched and horrible.

Dr. Mauer's condemnation of the mendacity of the "love" relationships of the upper classes occurs toward the end of act 4; the entire previous action has prepared the audience for it. Thus, this scene might provide an effective end for a tragicomedy, but the playwright had not yet finished with his main character: Friedrich, who has been quite indifferent to his wife's affair with the ensign, suddenly provokes a duel with him. Friedrich admits to Genia that he feels neither hatred, nor rage, nor jealousy, nor love. Yet this "enlightened" modern man must save his honor by killing his wife's lover. During act 5, Friedrich is revealed as being capable of emotions, after all: first when he admits to having experienced hatred when he confronted the ensign during the duel and again in the very last lines of the play when he "whines softly" at the approach of his son. Act 5 illustrates the cruelty and immorality inherent in the practice of dueling. It therefore does have a function in arousing audience response in an Aristotelian sense. In terms of plot structure, however, the final act is an anticlimactic appendage.

PROFESSOR BERNHARDI

In *Professor Bernhardi*, Schnitzler dealt with a topic that was so sensitive that the censorship office prevented its premiere in Austria in 1912. The play finally had its premiere in Vienna on December 21, 1918, after the abolition of censorship and the demise of the monarchy. The dramatic conflict revolves around the person of Professor Bernhardi, a professor of internal medicine and the director and cofounder of a prestigious private clinic in Vienna. The action takes place around 1900. Bernhardi is a Jew, as are several of his colleagues in the clinic. During act 1 two main strands of action emerge: A young woman is dying of the aftereffects of an abortion. As the result of an injection, she is filled with euphoria and happiness during her last hour; she even expects her lover to appear and to take her with him. When the Catholic priest arrives to hear her confession and to give her extreme unction, Bernhardi refuses him access to the patient so as not to destroy her euphoric happiness. She dies without having received the sacraments of the church. The secondary action concerns the headship of the department of dermatology, which has recently become vacant.

During the remainder of the play, these two strands of action become intertwined. Bernhardi's re-fusal to allow the priest access to the dying girl has outraged members of the clerical-nationalist and anti-Semitic parties. The clinic's board of trustees resigns, which entails the risk of severe financial setbacks for the institution. A member of the clerical-nationalist party is about to launch a parliamentary inquiry. Through an intermediary, Bernhardi is offered a deal: If he agrees to the appointment of a less qualified (but non-Jewish) candidate to the headship of the dermatology department, the parliamentary inquiry will not be held. Bernhardi refuses. The selection committee chooses the most competent candidate (who happens to be Jewish), with Bernhardi, as director, breaking a tie vote. A few days later the parliamentary inquiry is launched. In his reply, the Minister of Culture and Instruction, who is also a physician and supposedly Bernhardi's friend, at first defends Bernhardi but toward the end of his speech suggests that the Minister of Justice should conduct an investigation to clear the air. Consequently, Bernhardi is charged with having interfered with religious practices. During the trial, a nurse and one doctor testify that Bernhardi had shoved the priest. Even though the priest himself contradicts this false testimony, Bernhardi is sentenced to two months in jail. He refuses to appeal or to ask for clemency, and he serves his full sentence. Meanwhile, both the liberal and the social-democratic presses portray him as a hero. On his release he is greeted with ovations and conducted to his home in triumph. On the afternoon of his release, Bernhardi confronts his "friend," the Minister of Culture, ostensibly to get back his license to practice medicine, which he has lost as a consequence of his term in jail and which he needs in order to treat a prince who has summoned him. The ensuing conversation is interrupted by a telephone call from the Ministry of Justice: The nurse who had testified against Bernhardi has retracted her false testimony; a new trial will have to be held during which Bernhardi will presumably be completely rehabilitated. Bernhardi flatly refuses to cooperate with the "fraud" of a new trial; all he wants is his peace and quiet.

Throughout the play, Bernhardi's "medical-humane inspiration" in respecting the dying girl's final hour of happiness is mentioned again and again.

In this way, considerable empathy for the humane, freethinking Professor Bernhardi is created, particularly in view of the fact that his adversaries condemn his ethical and philosophical stance in the same breath as they condemn his Jewishness. This is especially true of the speech by the member of parliament who launches the inquiry and who speaks of "personalities who, through origin, education, and qualities of character, are not in a position to understand the religious feelings of the ancestral Christian population." During the last scene, the audience's feeling of complete empathy for Bernhardi is attenuated by the fact that his rehabilitation will be achieved (even without his participation) through the confession and repentance of the simpleminded Catholic nurse Ludmilla and through the urgings of her father confessor. Thus, at the end of the play, a measure of justice is reestablished in the world around Bernhardi. It is characteristic of Schnitzler's acute sense of justice that, writing in 1912, he was able to end his play on such a humane note.

OTHER MAJOR WORKS

LONG FICTION: *Der Weg ins Freie*, 1908 (*The Road to Open*, 1923); *Casanovas heimfahrt*, 1918 (*Casanova's Homecoming*, 1921); *Spiel im Morgengrauen*, 1927 (*Daybreak*, 1927); *Therese*, 1928 (*Theresa: The Chronicle of a Woman's Life*, 1928); *Flucht in die Finsternis*, 1931 (*Flight into Darkness*, 1931).

SHORT FICTION: *Sterben*, 1895; *Leutnant Gustl*, 1900 (*None but the Brave*, 1925); *Der blinde Geronimo und sein Bruder*, 1900 (*The Blind Geronimo and His Brother*, 1913); *Frau Bertha Garlan*, 1901 (*Bertha Garlen*, 1913); *Die Hirtenflöte*, 1911 (*The Shepherd's Pipe*, 1922); *Der Mörder*, 1911 (*The Murderer*, 1922); *Frau Beate und ihr Sohn*, 1913 (*Beatrice*, 1926); *Viennese Idylls*, 1913; *The Shepherd's Pipe and Other Stories*, 1922; *Fräulein Else*, 1924 (English translation, 1925); *Traumnovelle*, 1926 (*Rhapsody*, 1927); *Little Novels*, 1929; *Viennese Novelettes*, 1931.

NONFICTION: *Buch der Sprüche und Bedenken*, 1927 (*Aphorisms: From an Unpublished Book "Prov-* erbs and Reflections,"* 1928); *Der Geist im Wort und der Geist in der Tat*, 1927 (*The Mind in Words and Actions*, 1971); *Jugend in Wien*, 1968 (autobiography; *My Youth in Vienna*, 1970).

BIBLIOGRAPHY

Gay, Peter. *Schnitzler's Century: The Making of Middle-Class Culture, 1815-1914*. New York: W. W. Norton, 2002. A look at Schnitzler and the times in which he lived. Schnitzler portrayed the middle class of Vienna in his dramatic works. Bibliography and index.

Keiser, Brenda. *Deadly Dishonor: The Duel and the Honor Code in the Works of Arthur Schnitzler*. New York: Peter Lang, 1990. An examination of the works of Schnitzler in relation to his portrayal of the honor code and the practice of dueling. Bibliography and index.

Schneider-Halvorson, Brigitte L. *The Late Dramatic Works of Arthur Schnitzler*. New York: Peter Lang, 1983. A critical examination of Schnitzler's later plays. Bibliography and index.

Skrine, Peter N. *Hauptmann, Wedekind, and Schnitzler*. New York: St. Martin's Press, 1989. Skrine compares and contrasts the dramatic works of Schnitzler, Frank Wedekind, and Gerhart Hauptmann. Bibliography and index.

Weinberger, G. J. *Arthur Schnitzler's Late Plays: A Critical Study*. New York: Peter Lang, 1997. A study that looks at Schnitzler's dramatic works, particularly the later period works. Bibliography and index.

Wisely, Andrew C. *Arthur Schnitzler and the Discourse of Honor and Dueling*. New York: Peter Lang, 1996. An examination of the topics of honor and dueling as they are presented in the works of Schnitzler. Bibliography and index.

Yates, W. E. *Schnitzler, Hofmannsthal, and the Austrian Theatre*. New Haven, Conn.: Yale University Press, 1992. Yates compares and contrasts the lives and works of Schnitzler and Hugo von Hofmannsthal in his discussion of the Austrian theater. Bibliography and index.

Franz P. Haberl

EUGÈNE SCRIBE

Born: Paris, France; December 24, 1791
Died: Paris, France; February 20, 1861

PRINCIPAL DRAMA

Une Nuite de la garde nationale, pr., pb. 1815
Le Solliciteur, pr., pb. 1817
Le Charlatanisme, pr. 1825
La Dame blanche, pr., pb. 1825 (libretto, music by
    Adrien Boïeldieu; *The White Lady: Or, The
    Spirit of Abenel*, 1863)
La Demoiselle à marier, pr., pb. 1826
Le Mariage d'argent, pr., pb. 1827
Avant, pendant et après, pr., pb. 1828
La Muette de Portici, pr., pb. 1828 (libretto, music
    by Daniel Auber; *Masaniello: Or, The Dumb
    Girl of Portici*, 1871)
Le Comte Ory, pr., pb. 1828 (libretto, music by
    Gioacchino Rossini)
Fra Diavolo, pr., pb. 1830 (libretto, music by
    Auber; English translation, 1944)
Robert le Diable, pr., pb. 1831 (libretto, music by
    Giacomo Meyerbeer)
*La Famille Riquebourg: Ou, Le Mariage mal
    assorti*, pr., pb. 1831
Bertrand et Raton: Ou, L'Art de conspirer, pr., pb.
    1833 (*The School for Politicians: Or, Non-
    committal*, 1840)
L'Ambitieux, pr., pb. 1834 (*Ambition*, 1835)
La Juive, pr., pb. 1835 (libretto, music by Jacques
    Halévy; *The Jewess*, 1880)
Les Huguenots, pr., pb. 1836 (libretto, music by
    Meyerbeer; *The Huguenots*, 1870)
Le Domino noir, pr., pb. 1837 (libretto, music by
    Auber)
La Camaraderie: Ou, La Courte Échelle, pr., pb.
    1837
La Calomnie, pr., pb. 1840
La Verre d'eau: Ou, Les effets et les causes, pr., pb.
    1840 (*The Glass of Water*, 1850)
Une chaîne, pr., pb. 1841
Le Puff, pr., pb. 1848
Le Prophète, pr., pb. 1849 (libretto, music by

Meyerbeer; *The Prophet*, 1850)
Adrienne Lecouvreur, pr., pb. 1849 (with Ernest
    Legouvé; English translation, 1855)
Bataille de dames, pr., pb. 1851 (with Legouvé;
    The Ladies' Battle, 1851)
Les Vêpres siciliennes, pr., pb. 1855 (libretto,
    music by Giuseppe Verdi; *Sicilian Vespers*,
    1860)
Doigts de fée, pr., pb. 1858
L'Africaine, pr., pb. 1865 (libretto, music by
    Meyerbeer; English translation, 1866)

OTHER LITERARY FORMS

Eugène Scribe is remembered primarily for his
dramas.

ACHIEVEMENTS

One of the most prolific playwrights of all time,
the author of more than three hundred dramatic
works, Eugène Scribe is best remembered as the orig-
inator of the well-made play. His insistence on expert
dramatic craftsmanship and his remarkable success
in pleasing the public brought him power, prestige,
and wealth. While he was always sensitive to popular taste and could give his audience what it wanted,
he elevated the middlebrow comedy-vaudeville both
in form and in content, and he renovated serious comedy. He is also considered to be the principal inventor of grand opera. In his day, Scribe virtually controlled all the theaters in Paris and exerted a powerful
influence on the next several generations of dramatists.

Perhaps his most enduring legacy to his colleagues was the Société des Auteurs et Compositeurs
Dramatiques, which he helped to establish in 1827 to
protect authors' rights and grant them a fair share of
the profits. As for his dramatic technique, it has been
said that for the remainder of the nineteenth century,
all French drama was either a continuation of Scribe
or a reaction against him. The influence took many
forms, from the madcap farces of Eugène Labiche
and Georges Feydeau to the problem plays of

Alexandre Dumas, *fils*, and Émile Augier to the thrillers of Victorien Sardou, and that influence was by no means limited to France. Scribe's drama was translated and performed with great success throughout Europe and the New World. Henrik Ibsen, who in the 1850's directed more than twenty plays of Scribe, was the most brilliant of the many playwrights who learned their technique from the French master.

Critical reception of Scribe's work was mixed even in his lifetime. Although elected to the Académie Français in 1836, he provoked the wrath of the Romantics, of whose moral and aesthetic ideas he disapproved, and of elitist critics who objected both to Scribe's willingness to cater to the masses and to the financial rewards he reaped in the process. His supporters noted with approbation the lively situations and interesting characters, the logical and carefully constructed plots, the attempt to address serious issues and vices of the age, and the uncanny ability to select and represent the manners of middle-class Parisian society. In fact, Scribe's vivid rendering of that society, while not as thorough and ambitious as that of his younger contemporary Honoré de Balzac, remains one of his claims to the attention of modern readers.

At the end of the nineteenth century, Scribe fell into critical disrepute, a result both of increasing opposition to the well-made play and of the harsh judgment of eminent historians of literature, such as Gustave Lanson, who objected to Scribe's mediocre style, superficiality, and lack of idealism. None of these accusations can be denied. In particular, Scribe's undistinguished style has never had any defenders, and it continues to deter some readers. It is also true, however, that he composed his plays to be performed rather than read and did not hesitate to sacrifice purity of style for the dramatic situation. A number of studies have helped to rehabilitate Scribe by shedding new light on his extraordinary variety and originality, his technical wizardry, and even his role as moralist and social critic. The real proof of Scribe's continued vitality lies in live performance, and continuing revivals of some of his best plays demonstrate that audiences can still derive pleasure from his work.

BIOGRAPHY

Augustin-Eugène Scribe, son of a Parisian silk merchant, was born during the early years of the French Revolution. His father having died while he was an infant, he was brought up by his industrious and loving mother. He distinguished himself in his studies at the Collège de Sainte-Barbe and proceeded to begin the study of law, in deference to his mother's wishes, but he could muster no enthusiasm for it. The death of his mother in 1807 gave him enough financial independence to pursue his first love, the theater, and by 1810 he had had his first one-act comedy-vaudeville accepted at the Variétés theater. Following a string of dismal failures punctuated with a few moderate successes, Scribe achieved an overwhelming triumph in 1815 with *Une Nuite de la garde nationale*. Here for the first time he employed the two elements that were to guarantee his fame in the theater: realistic (in this case, topical) situations and ingeniously complicated plots.

In 1820, Scribe, together with two friends and former collaborators, opened a new theater called the Gymnase. As principal playwright, Scribe had to sign a contract pledging not to write for any theater in direct competition. In the 1820's alone, he furnished more than one hundred plays, many of them highly successful, to the Gymnase and made occasional forays into the Comédie-Française, the Opéra-Comique, the Opéra, and various lesser theaters. For the vast majority of his plays, he used collaborators, but with few exceptions he wrote the full text himself. Scribe generously gave credit (and a share of the royalties) to anyone who provided him with a subject or even the idea for a single scene. In certain cases he took a play that another author had submitted to him and revised it so radically that the collaborator did not even recognize the work in its performed version. By the end of the 1820's, Scribe was a millionaire, had acquired an elegant mansion in Paris and a country house, and was respected as the arbiter of Parisian theatrical taste. His success, far from turning his head, brought out his generous instincts, for he gave assistance to numerous needy individuals and charities, as well as fighting to protect the rights of fellow authors.

With the July Revolution of 1830, Scribe temporarily lost public favor. As a result, he produced a smaller percentage of his plays at the Gymnase while increasing his contributions to the Comédie-Française, including some of his most ambitious historical and social dramas, and to the lyric theaters. During the next few decades, Scribe collaborated with practically every major opera composer working in or passing through Paris. The list includes Daniel Auber, Adrien Boïeldieu, Jacques Halévy, Giacomo Meyerbeer, Jacques Offenbach, Ambroise Thomas, Luigi Cherubini, Gaetano Donizetti, Gioacchino Rossini, and Giusseppi Verdi.

In his later years, Scribe devoted more of his energies to his family (he had married in 1839) and reduced the volume of his dramatic output. In collaboration with Ernest Legouvé, he wrote several of his most celebrated plays, including his closest attempt at a tragedy, *Adrienne Lecouvreur*, designed as a vehicle for the brilliant actress Rachel. Active and loved by the public until the end, Scribe died suddenly at the age of sixty-nine, on the way home from a meeting at a colleague's house. In all, he left 374 dramatic works, a handful of novels and short stories, and a voluminous correspondence.

ANALYSIS

Eugène Scribe left two brief theoretical documents summing up his ideas about his art. In his inaugural speech at the Académie Français in 1836, he combines respect for France's classical tradition with an appreciation of popular culture, especially the satiric songs (ancestors of his own vaudevilles) that reflected their time more accurately than did the theater. The preface composed for an edition of the plays of his friend Jean-François-Alfred Bayard in 1855 goes further in proclaiming Scribe's affiliation with classicism, declaring that the artist cannot dispense with order, rules, and hard work, and that comedy, based on mirth and truth, is harder to write than serious drama. It also provides an early definition of the well-made play: the skillful presentation of a subject, rapid action, sudden reversals, obstacles created and overcome, and unexpected but carefully prepared denouement.

Love and marriage have always been a principal theme of comedy, but Scribe placed more emphasis on the pragmatic than on the romantic side. In contrast to Romantic drama, Scribe never condones the excesses of violent passion, and in particular, he condemns marital infidelity on the part of husband and wife alike. As a champion of middle-class values, he chooses for the sympathetic characters of his comedies honest, caring, simple, hardworking people. In such a milieu, love, although sincere and abiding, is not an explosive or antisocial force. Instead, it is a gentle and respectful emotion that needs to be grounded in mutual esteem, together with compatibility of personality, education and, usually, social rank. Despite the charges of Scribe's detractors, it is simply not true that he viewed money as the main consideration in marriage: *Le Mariage d'argent*, his first experiment in the five-act form, is a clear condemnation of those who betray love and principles for the sake of ambition and greed. Even in *Malvina: Ou, Un Mariage d'inclination* (1828), in which he takes the side of the parents over the young lovers, he gives his blessing to love, provided that the young people are mature enough to know what they are doing and that they act in accord with their parents. It is also true that bourgeois parents in Scribe's plays are normally idealized figures, extremely caring and indulgent and situated at the furthest extreme from the tyrannical fathers that one associates with the comedies of Molière.

LA DEMOISELLE À MARIER

La Demoiselle à marier is a one-act vaudeville. This genre, in which Scribe honed his dramatic skills and acquired his early successes, may be defined as a little operetta, usually in one act but sometimes expanded to two or three, in which new words are set to well-known tunes, ranging from popular songs to operatic selections. The use of unoriginal music provides a kind of complicity between the spectators and the characters. The mood may range from farce to sentimentality, but the appeal is always to a respectable, middle-class, family audience. Scribe elevated this form of frivolous entertainment to real drama by introducing exciting, complicated plots and more realistic characters and situations. His favorite device was to spend the first half of the play presenting the characters and involving them in an awkward predicament, and the second half in extricating them in a plausible, yet unexpected manner.

La Demoiselle à marier is a charming story of ordinary, middle-class people, temporarily harmed by a moment of vanity and pretension but saved by their basic simplicity and honesty. When the wealthy young Alphonse buys an estate in the country and finds that his new neighbors have a daughter of suitable age, he arranges to pay them a visit with the possible intention of matrimony, but he specifically requests that they abstain from formality and not inform the girl in advance of his visit. Camille, however, learns the truth, the parents yield to an impulse of vanity and put on great airs for Alphonse, and the arrival of an old family friend (who is in the process of arranging another match for the girl and is irked to find that he has not been consulted about this one) completes the complications. At first meeting, Alphonse and the family make a dreadful impression on one another, and the match is broken off at once. Now that they need treat him only as a neighbor and friend, the Dumesnils quickly revert to their normal selves, relations immediately become cordial, Alphonse discovers that his late uncle was the family friend's old schoolmate and chum, and the young people, alone for the second time but now chatting informally, find much in common and finally fall in love. Unfortunately, the change seems to have come too late, for the father has already sent a letter to the other suitor making the engagement official. The day is saved by a seemingly trivial remark made near the start of the play by the good-hearted servant Baptiste: A man of sober habits, he has vowed to get drunk on the day of his young mistress' wedding. In the process, he has fallen asleep and failed to deliver the letter, which is retrieved and torn up. Alphonse can marry Camille after all, and they join in the obligatory final chorus in which the characters sing of their happiness.

The play is in part an ingenious reversal of the timeworn convention of love at first sight and in part a satire of petty human vanity. Most of all, however, it is a celebration of ordinary life and bourgeois values. The dying words of Alphonse's uncle may be seen as a summation of Scribe's own code of conduct and

one that he assumed his audience to share: Wealth is honorable when acquired honestly, and money is not to be worshiped for its own sake but is to be valued as a means to procure independence. In addition, one must not sell one's liberty by seeking positions of influence or contracting an opulent marriage, but should live within one's means, choose a good wife, and rear one's own children.

The Glass of Water

Scribe's masterpiece in the field of full-length comedy is usually considered to be *The Glass of Water*. Never overly concerned with factual accuracy, Scribe concentrated in his historical plays on intricate plots mixing real and fictional characters. As critics have noted, Scribe had no passion for history and, unlike the Romantics, felt no urge to reconstruct the manners and attitudes of past eras. Yet Scribe's motivation in writing historical drama was not limited to catering to popular taste. Political upheavals provided a suitable backdrop for a five-act drama of constant reversals and intrigues and allowed Scribe to depict the past as a metaphor for the present.

Set in England in 1712, during the final months of the War of the Spanish Succession, *The Glass of Water* exemplifies Scribe's theory that history consists of great effects arising from small causes. Rather than presenting likenesses of heroes of epic or tragedy, Scribe depicts political leaders as basically ordinary people, ambitious and selfish, sometimes petty or inept. The major antagonists of *The Glass of Water*, the Duchess of Marlborough and Henri de Saint-Jean, later Lord Bolingbroke, are of a higher caliber—geniuses at calculation and manipulation, who fascinate with their quick wits and vitality while failing to demonstrate genuine loyalty to any moral or political ideas beyond their own self-interest.

What makes *The Glass of Water* a marvelous theatrical experience is the complexity and dizzying pace of the action. The opening act sets forth the obstacles confronting the hero: Saint-Jean is penniless and heavily in debt, and the family fortune is in the hands of an obnoxious and stupid cousin with whom he is on bad terms. His enemy, the duchess, has bought up his debts and threatens to send him to prison. There is no immediate prospect of his party's regaining power and his returning to the post of prime minister, and the duchess will not let any of his letters reach the queen. Although England's finances have been seriously depleted by the protracted war, and the French are anxious to negotiate peace, the duchess, whose husband commands the English forces and who stands to gain handsomely from continued hostilities, will not let the French envoy approach the queen. As if this were not enough, the hero's friends also face serious hurdles. The shopgirl Abigail, whom Saint-Jean has befriended, finds the duchess opposed to her taking a position in the palace that the queen (who owes the girl a sum of money) has promised. The young and handsome officer Masham, another protégé of Saint-Jean, is penniless and loves Abigail but cannot marry her until he has made his fortune. In addition, he has been warned by a secret protector never to marry and has been repeatedly insulted by an arrogant but unknown nobleman. The denouement is easy enough to predict: Masham marries Abigail, who becomes the queen's new favorite; the duchess and her faction are disgraced; and Saint-Jean, having inherited his cousin's title and fortune, regains the post of prime minister and persuades the queen to sign a peace treaty with France. As in a mystery novel, it is not the ending but the means of achieving it that create interest and suspense.

To effect the proper resolution as speedily and efficiently as possible, for the action takes only a few days, Scribe employs several basic techniques: decisive confrontations of adversaries, revelation of secrets at unexpected moments, and the main characters' talent (or lack thereof) for improvisation and for a quick response to new developments. The "duels" of Saint-Jean and the duchess, who confront each other once each act, are the most exciting, but there are others with equally important results, such as the offstage duel of Masham and his mysterious foe (who turns out to be Saint-Jean's cousin) and the spectacular climax in act 4 when the queen and the duchess discover that they are rivals for the love of Masham. Their jealousy erupts into a serious rift when the angry duchess accidentally spills a glass of water over the queen. In the heated exchange that follows, she offers her resignation, and the queen accepts it.

It is hard to derive much of a moral or philosophical lesson from this play. Voltaire, referring to this very episode in his *Le Siècle de Louis XIV* (1751), cited it as an example of trivial causes giving rise to great historical events, though he was careful not to attribute the downfall of Marlborough and the peace of Utrecht solely to this one incident. One has the impression at the end of the play that England will be better off with Lord Bolingbroke's return to power, but this is merely a result of the hero's jovial personality, his gift for bouncing back after each reversal, and his enthusiastic acceptance of the comic view of history and politics. Hardly a visionary, he at least favors peace and shows genuine concern for other people. The duchess, who represents repression and tyranny, must be disgraced primarily because she demonstrates rigidity and joylessness—the characteristics of the blocking figure in comedy. The denouement is essentially the triumph of youth and the affirmation of life, as in all comedy. One might say that the political and historical dimensions of Scribe's play furnish an unusually elaborate network of complications that delay the happy ending and temporarily distract the audience from noticing the author's optimistic view of life.

LA CAMARADERIE

Scribe was also preoccupied with social issues in his full-length comedies, and he did not hesitate to attack such vices as hypocrisy, imposture, calumny, ambition, and social climbing. Among the finest of these plays is *La Camaraderie*. A group of mediocre men in a variety of professions have formed an alliance to promote the career of each member. Dominating the group and heading its major publicity weapon, a newspaper, is a leading senator's crafty and domineering young wife, appropriately named Césarine. The supposed friendship of the men is soon revealed as hypocritical, for they know that their allies are far from being the geniuses that they have all proclaimed themselves. When Edmond, a talented, idealistic, and unswervingly honest young lawyer, is introduced to the group, he is appalled by their methods and refuses to join, despite his great need for assistance. Fortunately, his shrewd friend Zoé, working without his knowledge, succeeds in manipulating

Césarine, and through her the whole alliance, into supporting Edmond in a parliamentary election. For the first time, the alliance achieves recognition for a truly deserving individual, but by unleashing the selfishness and mutual scorn of its members it destroys itself in the process.

Although Théophile Gautier, one of the play's most vehement critics, perceived it as a direct attack on the Romantic movement, Scribe's satire is more far-reaching. To be sure, certain gibes at the poets of the "camaraderie," who are shown as hack writers who cultivate exotic themes and genres to avoid competing with poets of real talent, seem aimed at the Romantics, though other associations, literary or otherwise, operating their own journals and lauding their members in hyperbolic terms, existed in Scribe's day. The most devastating ridicule is reserved for the political establishment, portrayed as bungling, corrupt, and easily influenced by anyone with a gift for manipulation. The Count de Miremont, the revered elder statesman, is incapable of serious thought, lets his wife make his decisions for him, and conveniently becomes bedridden before each major crisis or vote. Elections to academies and parliamentary seats are rigged with extraordinary facility, and Edmond finds himself the elected deputy only a few hours after Césarine decides to announce his candidacy.

Although Scribe lived through a number of major political upheavals, he never used the stage to discuss politics except, in his role as moralist, to castigate dishonesty and mediocrity, as in this comedy. His own political sympathies apparently lay with the republicans rather than the monarchists, but he was never doctrinaire and sometimes preferred to side with whichever party was out of power.

Critics have sometimes compared *La Camaraderie* unfavorably to Scribe's delightful one-act comedy-vaudeville *Le Charlatanisme*, ignoring the fundamental differences between them. Although the plots are quite similar, the conspirators in *Le Charlatanisme* are exuberant and gifted young people, overjoyed at the prospect of helping a man with real ability. The allies of the later play are models of stodgy respectability and are conceited, untalented, and somewhat sinister. Furthermore, Scribe used the five-act format of *La Camaraderie* to expand the moral framework of his subject. Thus, the denouement is most explicit in allotting rewards and punishments and in suggesting that both are inevitable, at least in the long run. The "good" characters are well developed, and they frequently argue with members of the "camaraderie" on such basic issues as the nature of genius and true friendship. Although most of the comrades are little more than idiots, Scribe does try to provide motivation for the villainess, Césarine. Unrequited affection for Edmond and the frustration of a loveless marriage help to explain the ruthlessness of her character, but any sympathy she might inspire is far outweighed by her constant exploitation or persecution of others and by the overconfidence and lack of self-knowledge that cause her to fall into Zoé's trap. Césarine, like the vast majority of Scribe's characters, is not shown as having internal conflicts. Even in soliloquies there is hardly time for introspection; moving from one crisis to the next usually suffices to absorb all the character's attention.

THE WHITE LADY

As Scribe's earliest contact with the theater was the comedy-vaudeville, it is hardly surprising that he was drawn almost at once to the related genre of comic opera (alternating spoken dialogue with original and more complex music, performed by professional singers and full orchestra). In 1825, he produced a work which virtually revolutionized the genre, *The White Lady*. Scribe provided an engrossing, well-constructed plot, combining the mystery of a ghost story with a perfectly logical explanation; he also showed great skill in arranging the musical numbers to coincide with the high points of the action, rather than interrupting its progress.

MASANIELLO

Scribe was no less innovative in the field of opera (sung throughout and including a mandatory full-length ballet). His verse, while quite singable, is uninspired and at times inferior, but as usual his main contribution is excellence of plot selection and construction. Beginning with the epoch-making *Masaniello*, in which the title role was performed by a dancer, Scribe broke definitively with the static and slow-paced settings of mythological stories that characterized most of earlier French opera to compose sweeping historical epics that he often set in the Middle Ages or in the Renaissance. As in the historical plays, the adventures of invented characters are intertwined with those of historical figures, allowing for constant excitement and suspense. In comparison to the plays, however, the librettos generally feature less-complicated plots, for Scribe knew that singing is harder to understand than speech; instead, there is far more pageantry and local color, which is splendidly integrated with the new prominence of the chorus (especially in mob scenes) and with the required ballet. In many cases, Scribe provides an unhappy ending in which innocent characters become the victims of a larger tragedy, such as civil war or religious persecution. In contrast to Italian librettos of the same period, those of Scribe contain few arias, concentrating far more on duets, trios, choruses, and large ensembles. The arias, however, are dramatically effective, for here characters often undergo agonizing internal conflicts and are torn between incompatible emotions and obligations.

THE HUGUENOTS

The Huguenots, one of Scribe's most powerful grand operas, has seen occasional revivals in the twentieth century, but because of the extreme difficulty of Meyerbeer's score, as well as the huge expense required for the elaborate costumes, scenery, and special effects, the work has little chance of becoming part of the standard repertory. Set in Paris in 1572, *The Huguenots* dramatizes one of the blackest chapters in French history, the Saint Bartholomew's Day massacre in which Catholics murdered nearly all the Protestants in Paris during a truce declared in honor of a royal wedding celebration. As in the story of Romeo and Juliet, a Protestant knight and a Catholic noblewoman fall in love and are destroyed by the religious strife. To emphasize his own abhorrence of religious persecution, Scribe made four of the main characters advocates of toleration, flanked by fanatics of both camps. Marguerite of Valois, sister of King Charles IX, is to be married to the Protestant Henri of Navarre (later Henri IV). Learning that her favorite lady-in-waiting, Valentine, loves the Huguenot Raoul, Marguerite decides to unite them, in con-

junction with her own wedding, as a gesture designed to discourage further bloodshed. Because of a misunderstanding, Raoul publicly refuses the match, and Valentine is forced to wed another man. Although the plan of the Catholic fanatics, headed by the heroine's father, to assassinate Raoul in retaliation for this insult is foiled, their general massacre of the Huguenot community shortly thereafter succeeds all too well.

The pageantry and special effects that distinguish grand opera are lavishly displayed in *The Huguenots*. There are three indoor settings and three outdoor settings (not counting the brief final scenes) of great complexity. Act 1 shows a dinner party in the home of Count de Nevers, with a full view of the gardens. Although largely concerned with exposition, the act does surround Raoul with an aura of mystery, for he tells how he has fallen in love with a beautiful woman whom he has rescued from a mob but whose identity he does not know, and soon thereafter he receives an invitation to be taken blindfolded to a meeting with another unknown lady (Marguerite). Act 2, set in gardens of the Château de Chenonceaux, includes a dance for female bathers and ends with the ceremony in which Marguerite's attempt to reconcile the factions ends in failure. Act 3 is the most spectacular of all, requiring a complex set portraying the banks of the Seine with two cabarets, a chapel, and a view of Paris in the rear, as well as an illuminated barge that sails into view at the end of the act, carrying musicians, servants, and wedding guests. Choruses of Huguenot soldiers, Parisian students, workers, townsmen, and police are active, engaging at one point in a street brawl that manages to save Raoul's life. For good measure, Scribe adds a ballet for a troupe of gypsies. Act 4, set in the home of de Nevers, now the husband of Valentine, features the chilling scene in which the Catholic leaders, soon joined by an armed crowd, give the orders for the massacre of the Huguenots and have the swords blessed by a trio of monks. Raoul, having sneaked into the house and overheard the plot, jumps off a balcony to warn his friends. Act 5 opens in the ballroom of the Hôtel de Sens, where a bloodstained Raoul interrupts the royal festivities to announce that the massacre has already begun. The scene then shifts to a cloister where women and children have come to take refuge. As Valentine, now a widow, is married to Raoul, Catholics break into the church and murder those within. This grisly scene is followed by another in which the lovers, having managed to escape, are slain in a dark street by Valentine's father, as the horrified Marguerite tries to restore order. The opera unquestionably captures much of the grandeur, the brutality, and the unbridled energy of sixteenth century France.

Scribe certainly did not invent grand opera by himself. Meyerbeer and Doctor Louis-Desire Véron, the director of the Paris Opera who was not afraid to take risks to make that institution profitable, deserve much of the credit, as does the Romantic movement that Scribe disdained in his spoken drama. He was among the first, however, to appreciate the suitability to musical drama of the Romantic fascination with history, the supernatural, the horrifying, and the cosmic, along with chiaroscuro effects and impetuous, antisocial heroes. Ultimately, the popularity of Scribe's grand operas would outshine the Romantic theater of Victor Hugo and Alexandre Dumas, *père*. Scribe understood better than most how much of a framework the text must provide and how much could and should be left for the composer. At the same time, he always insisted on keeping opera firmly within the bounds of theater, integrating the music with well-crafted, exciting plots and an abundance of visual splendor.

BIBLIOGRAPHY

Canby, Vincent. "Getting to Know Scribe as More Than a Street." Review of *The Ladies' Battle*, by Eugène Scribe. *The New York Times*, December 25, 1995, p. A31. A review of the Pearl Theater Company's performance of Scribe and Ernest Legouvé's *The Ladies' Battle* (entitled *When Ladies Battle* for the New York performance).

Cardwell, Douglas. "The Role of Stage Properties in the Plays of Eugène Scribe." *Nineteenth-Century French Studies* 16 (Spring-Summer, 1988): 290-309. An examination of the staging of the plays of Scribe.

Koon, Helene, and Richard Switzer. *Eugène Scribe.* Boston: Twayne, 1980. A basic biography of Scribe that covers his life and works. Bibliography and index.

Pendle, Karin. *Eugène Scribe and French Opera of the Nineteenth Century.* Ann Arbor, Mich.: UMI Research, 1979. A looks at Scribe's role in developing the opera of nineteenth century France. Bibliography and index.

Perry Gethner

SENECA

Born: Corduba (now Córdoba, Spain); 4 B.C.E.
Died: Rome; 65 C.E.

PRINCIPAL DRAMA

The dating of Seneca's plays is approximate; the following were written c. 40-55 C.E.:

Agamemnon (English translation, 1581)
Hercules furens (*Mad Hercules*, 1581)
Hercules Oetaeus (*Hercules on Oeta*, 1581)
Medea (English translation, 1581)
Oedipus (English translation, 1581)
Phaedra (English translation, 1581)
Phoenissae (*The Phoenician Women*, 1581)
Thyestes (English translation, 1581)
Troades (*The Trojan Women*, 1581)

OTHER LITERARY FORMS

In addition to tragedies, Seneca wrote a number of moral essays, or "dialogues," each dealing with a particular philosophical concept, such as providence, anger, and the happy life, and several consolatory essays (one addressed to Marcia on the loss of her son, another to Polybius on the loss of his brother, a third to his mother, Helvia, to console her for his absence when he was exiled to Corsica). He also wrote a treatise, *De clementia* (c. 55-56 C.E.; *On Clemency*, 1614), addressed to the young Emperor Nero, a lengthy discourse, *De beneficiis* (c. 58-63 C.E.; *On Benefits*, 1614), a scientific work entitled *Quaestiones naturales* (c. 62-64 C.E.; *Natural Questions*, 1614), and more than one hundred moral epistles covering innumerable ethical and philosophical topics pertinent to humankind's daily existence: the quest for virtue, the exposure of vice, the extolling of friendship, the condemnation of war, beneficence to slaves, and the distempers of modern humanity—people's boredom, despair, restlessness, and insecurity. Finally Seneca wrote a satire concerning the dead Emperor Claudius entitled *Apocolocyntosis divi Claudii* (c. 54 C.E.; *The Deification of Claudius*, 1614).

ACHIEVEMENTS

Seneca—philosopher, statesman, tutor, minister, and victim of Nero—was one of the most renowned political and literary figures of Imperial Rome. A writer accomplished in many genres, Seneca was the author of intense tragedies, brilliant moral epistles, persuasive philosophical essays, learned scientific treatises, and a witty, entertaining satire. This polymath, this Renaissance man, was an innovative, creative artist, one who originated a new type of drama, as well as a new literary prose style. He not only transmitted Stoic philosophy to his contemporaries but also altered and improved it, making its doctrines less rigid, more personal, more humane.

Although Seneca allied himself to the Stoics more closely than to any other philosophical sect, it was his practice to cull his precepts from many varied sources, binding himself to the dogmas of no particular school, philosopher, or author. His writings reveal him as an eclectic and a seeker after truth: "I can dispute with Socrates, doubt with Carneades, achieve tranquility with Epicurus, conquer human nature with the Stoics, exceed it with the Cynics."

Seneca's wide-ranging eclecticism stems from the varied nature of his life, his studies, and his interests. As a youth, he came under the influence of philoso-

Seneca (Library of Congress)

phers of the various schools. At the outset of his career, he pursued a legal practice. He traveled to Egypt, took an interest in farming and in vine-growing, and achieved prominence in politics. From his father, he learned the art of rhetoric, and from his mother, he gained that philosophical and psychological strain that is so concerned with the interior life.

Seneca distinguished himself not only as a learned eclectic philosopher but also as a brilliant stylist, a master of word and phrase. He brought to the height of its perfection in Latin the *style coupé*—a style characterized by epigrammatic brevity, point, antithesis, balance, a style diametrically opposed to the long, periodic sentences of Ciceronian prose.

Finally, Seneca's legacy includes the only extant Latin tragedies. His dramatic verse is taut, vigorous as well as various, his content frequently tense, terse, and stichomythic. He was not, as has at times been asserted, merely the translator and dull copyist of the great Greek dramas of Aeschylus, Sophocles, and Euripides of five centuries earlier. In plays that tend to dramatize hateful, evil characters running amok, Seneca shaped a new poetic species of tone-poem. He dramatized the psychological states of agitation that beset ordinary people, reducing the heroic prototypes of his characters to human dimensions, and his tragedies were the vital spark that initiated and motivated the growth of Elizabethan and Jacobean drama in England many centuries later. As a creative dramatist, as a brilliant stylist, and as a profound moralist, Seneca has influenced the great writers and thinkers of all subsequent ages, but especially those of the Renaissance.

BIOGRAPHY

Lucius Annaeus Seneca was born in Corduba, Spain, about 4 B.C.E. He came from a learned and wealthy family: His father, Seneca the Elder, was a well-known rhetorician, and his mother, Helvia, was an attractive, erudite woman with a deep interest in philosophy and the liberal arts. They had three sons: Annaeus Novatus, the oldest, an accomplished orator, writer, and politician; Annaeus Mela, the youngest, remembered as the father of the Roman poet Lucan; and Lucius Annaeus, renowned philosopher, statesman, orator, and playwright.

During infancy, Seneca left Spain for Rome, where his family established permanent residence. When he came of age, he received instruction in grammar, rhetoric, and philosophy. He was bored by the teachings of dull grammarians, spurred on by the training of outstanding rhetors, and fascinated by the discussion of leading philosophers. By combining philosophy with rhetoric, the young Seneca aimed to pursue a philosophical, contemplative life along with an oratorical, political career.

Seneca's active political career was interrupted by the poor health that he had endured since childhood. Because of his illness and in order to have a change of scene, he went to Egypt, where his maternal aunt, the wife of the governor, aided him, through her devotion and care, in regaining his strength. On his return to Rome, through the influence of this devoted aunt, he obtained the quaestorship about 33 C.E., perhaps becoming *aedile* or tribune of the plebeians about 36 or 37.

While advancing politically, Seneca also distinguished himself as a lawyer, a philosopher, and an author, winning not only glory and riches but also the jealousy of the mad Emperor Caligula, who threatened to put the philosopher to death. Only Seneca's chronic ill-health and rumors that he would soon die of natural causes dissuaded the emperor from ordering his execution.

Having almost lost his life, Seneca decided to relinquish his dangerous oratorical career to devote himself more and more to philosophy and literature. After Caligula's assassination (41 C.E.) and the ascension of his uncle Claudius, Seneca was accused by Messalina, Claudius's third wife, of an illicit intrigue with Julia, sister of Caligula and niece of Claudius. On this unfounded charge, Seneca was banished to Corsica for eight years from 41 to 49 C.E. He was recalled by Agrippina, Claudius's fourth wife, with the stipulation that he become the tutor of her twelve-year-old son, Nero. To assist the philosopher in educating Nero, she appointed Burrus, later elevated by her to the post of prefect of the Praetorian Guard. Both men attempted to restrain Nero's excesses and Agrippina's lust for power. When Claudius was murdered by Agrippina in 54, Nero became emperor at the age of seventeen. Under the tutelage and guidance of Seneca and Burrus, the early principate of Nero, known as the Quinquennium Neronis, was marked by clemency and equity in government.

This era of good government, however, was soon to end. Agrippina, coveting for herself supreme control of the state and becoming annoyed by the humane administration of Seneca and Burrus, threatened to give the throne to Britannicus, son of Claudius by Messalina. Nero, filled with dread, ordered Britannicus's murder. Hostility between mother and son continued to mount until Nero finally succeeded in having his mother bludgeoned to death. The emperor's increasing waywardness, Burrus's sudden and unexplained death in 62 C.E., and the debauched Tigellinus's elevation as court favorite led Seneca to request permission to retire. When Nero refused to grant this request, the philosopher bravely withdrew of his own accord from the court and the city and commenced a life of self-exile, seclusion and study, composing during these three years of retirement some of his most famous literary works.

Retirement, however, could not rescue Seneca from Nero's malevolence. Accused of complicity in the Pisonian Conspiracy—a conspiracy that had as its aim the murder of Nero and the transfer of power to Piso—Seneca was ordered by Nero's military officers to commit suicide. Seneca, like Socrates, faced death with fortitude, courage, and dignity, relying on the precepts of the Stoic philosophy that had so strongly and for so long molded his own character. Forbidden to make his last will, Seneca turned to his friends and observed that he could only leave them his richest possession—"the image of his life."

ANALYSIS

In spite of the high esteem in which Seneca's tragedies have been held throughout the centuries, particularly in the Renaissance, a number of critics have regarded his plays as second-rate imitations of Greek originals. They have complained about his extensive use of rhetoric and mythology, his employment of melodrama, of the bloody, the horrible, the sensational on the stage, and have accused him of lacking dramatic force. Such critics have failed to observe that Seneca did not aim to write or to reproduce Greek tragedy but to create an original genre of his own.

To demonstrate Seneca's dramatic talent, it is necessary to analyze the ways in which his plays are distinct from Greek tragedy. Greek tragedy is expansive, richly embroidered; Senecan tragedy is lean, often disjunct, without transitions from one scene to another. Greek tragedy is filled with action; Senecan tragedy abounds in declamation, monologues replacing dialogues, and scenes drastically reduced. In Senecan drama, characters do not develop; they remain the same throughout. There is no catharsis—no sense, at the play's close, of the working out of justice. The Senecan protagonist is evil and unheroic. His violent deeds are enacted on the stage rather than decorously recounted to the audience by messengers. As a result of such violence, Seneca's plays are referred to as "tragedies of blood." In fact, it was his emphasis on the macabre, the grotesque, and the pathological that

especially appealed to later playwrights: the frequent appearance of spirits and ghosts; the employment of religious signs and omens foretelling disaster; the use of lengthy, nervous, and psychologically revealing monologues and soliloquies; the emphasis on the theme of revenge; and the presentation of a protagonist who is utterly evil, furious, and demented. The above traits are especially evident in his most popular plays—*Thyestes*, *Medea*, and *Phaedra*.

THYESTES

Thyestes, perhaps Seneca's most powerful play, concerns Atreus's revenge on his brother Thyestes. Thyestes returns to Argos after having been exiled by Atreus, who had seized the throne from him. The deceitful Atreus feigns a loving reception of his exiled brother but in reality seeks to destroy him, believing that he had seduced his wife. In his quest for inordinate revenge, Atreus devises the scheme of butchering Thyestes' children and serving their flesh to their father at the dinner table. In an unsurpassed final scene, one beholds the sated, drunken Thyestes at the banquet table, unwittingly having feasted on the meat of his three murdered sons, trying meekly to sing, though beset by premonitions of disaster. Such disaster is underscored by the dominant imagery of the play—storms, tides, winds that foreshadow the anarchic whirlpool of vengeance and the drama of blood. The characters are not only impelled to their doom by Fate but also by their own excessive passions. The prologue between the Fury and the ghost of Tantalus (grandfather of Atreus and Thyestes) unfolds for the audience the bloody events that are to follow. The Fury insists that Tantalus's shade must infect his grandchildren with madness, leading to the slaughter and the cannibal feast. After Tantalus's base spirit corrupts the house of his grandchildren, it returns to its infernal abode. Melodrama is the dominant feature of *Thyestes*. Characters speak at fever pitch, ranting, raving, and shouting. Atreus employs jokes, puns, and double entendres similar to the gruesome humor and sick jokes of Hamlet; he epitomizes the vice and the insanity of a tyrant, the deadly guile of a Iago. For all of Atreus's bile and his sacrilegious boasts and celebrations, Seneca makes it perfectly clear, in the play's most telling irony, that Atreus can never be content. "Bene est, abunde est," Atreus pronounces at the high point of his revenge, but he can never find good or be satisfied. Such savage fury and ire can never be forsaken; such restlessness can never find quietus. Hence, even at the play's end, the tormenting ruler is still savagely tormented: He finds that no revenge on Thyestes can ever be adequate; he still rankles with the agonizing thought that his wife might have been unfaithful, that his sons might not be his own. Such a madman, like Satan, can never find peace or regulation, for his desires exceed the boundaries of possibility. Because Atreus has surrendered reason itself, Seneca seems to imply, the final tragedy is not Thyestes', but sadly, senselessly, his own.

MEDEA

Medea, too, is a play of bloody revenge. Medea, angry at her husband, Jason, who has cast her aside for a new bride, Creusa, daughter of Creon, king of Corinth, decides to exact vengeance on Jason by slaying their own children. She never falters or changes her decision. Her opening speech is a soliloquy of violence, of towering rage, in which she appeals to the gods to assist her in obtaining vengeance. She continues throughout the drama in the same irrational state, calling on the deities for help and speaking of torches and fire. She is a barbarian witch, filled with venom and madness. The Nurse, too, shows no character development. She continually recommends patience and flight to her mistress and has nothing more to say. Jason, unlike his Euripidean counterpart, is neither tricky nor cunning. He is a constant: self-seeking, pursuing an advantageous new marital connection, unconcerned for his own and Medea's sons, although he recites the traditional commonplaces about paternal love.

Where the Euripidean messenger describes at length the horrible deaths of Creusa and Creon, Seneca limits the description to a few lines regarding the general conflagration in the palace. Where in Euripides the audience does not behold the butchery of the children onstage, Seneca's Medea murders one child offstage but brings the other out on the roof and destroys him before Jason's very eyes. Such horror onstage justifies the reputation of Senecan tragedy as a "tragedy of blood."

By her vengeance, Medea pathetically claims that she is regaining the chastity, the youth that she had enjoyed before her marriage to Jason while at the same time atoning for her former crimes—the murder of her own brother and of King Pelias of Iolchos, both of whom she destroyed in order to aid Jason. Yet like Atreus's triumph in *Thyestes*, Medea's, too, is a Pyrrhic victory. Her savagery and lunatic extremes of vengeance have left her bereft of the children she loved, and she is sorely dissatisfied. The bitter irony is that, ultimately, the revenge has really been taken on herself.

PHAEDRA

The emphasis in Senecan tragedy on human wickedness, self-willed and unnatural excess, is readily apparent in *Phaedra*. Phaedra, daughter of King Minos of Crete, is given in marriage as a prize to the hero Theseus, the slayer of the Minotaur. Phaedra, much younger than her husband, falls desperately in love with her stepson Hippolytus. Unlike Euripides *Hippolytos* (428 B.C.E.; *Hippolytus*, 1781), which blames the gods for Phaedra's passion, *Phaedra* treats human passions without extenuation. In Euripides, Venus, jealous of Hippolytus's devotion to Diana and angered by his scorn of Love, causes Phaedra to fall in love with her stepson in order to dishonor him. In Seneca's play, Phaedra herself, like Medea, generates her own villainy. Her irrational love for Hippolytus turns to frenzy and madness when she is rebuffed. In fact, all three characters of the triangle—the wife, Phaedra, the husband, Theseus, and the stepson, Hippolytus—are basically evil. Theseus has been absent from his wife for four years, seeking adultery with Persephone, the Queen of Hades. Hippolytus's intemperance, misogyny, and insensitivity stem from his own nature rather than from any external causes. All three, in fact, are self-willed and given over to unnatural excess.

Moreover, Seneca stresses the fact that the unnatural vices of these characters stem from family diseases: "Offspring returns to its source and degenerate blood recreates its primal stock." Hippolytus's mother, Antiope, was a well-known Amazon, a member of the fierce tribe of warlike women. It is not surprising that the son of such a mother rejects womankind and pursues a career of warlike hunting. Theseus had cruelly abandoned Phaedra's sister Ariadne before his marriage with Phaedra, had subsequently put to death his Amazonian wife, and had sought illicit love with Persephone. Phaedra's mother, Pasiphae, was renowned for her unnatural passion for Poseidon's bull, a passion that issued in the birth of the Minotaur, which Theseus later killed. Although this mythological background was commonplace to his audience, Seneca repeated and exaggerated familiar myths to lend impetus to his dramatic motifs, motifs that stress the excessive, the unnatural, and the bestial. The final scenes ironically underscore these inhuman traits. The perverse and rebuffed Phaedra, before committing suicide, condemns the man she supposedly loves; Hippolytus, accursed by his father, is destroyed by a monstrous sea bull that emerges from the depths of the sea; and Theseus is irrationally led to curse his own son and to bring about his death; hence, the bull-slayer is defeated by another bull. Theseus's comeuppance is the more lurid and absurd in that he has just returned from the Underworld, for the darkness and hellish torment of the land of the living exceed the horror of Hades. Thus does Seneca's heated drama of incestuous and violent passions come to a close.

OEDIPUS

A second group of Senecan tragedies varies considerably from the attention-getting pattern that has been described thus far. This second class of dramas does not feature spurts of evil, stentorian shouts of villainy, nor the presence of an overpoweringly vile protagonist galvanizing others on the stage. Instead, in this second group of plays, one encounters a mood of quiet, gloom, loss, and despair. The focus is not so much on the triumph of vice as on the inevitable destruction of the weak and the vulnerable. In the absence of an all-powerful protagonist, such plays seem headless, leaderless, without direction and control. The action is muted and appears fatalistic, for lesser characters are being manipulated, violated, and defeated. The most obvious example of such an action is the Senecan *Oedipus*. Unlike the great Sophoclean prototype, this Oedipus is a wavering, weakened, bemused, depressed character, utterly lacking in quali-

ties of leadership and virtually paralyzed by the sense of his impending doom. The play stands out as a gloomy set piece. Ghosts, omens, divination, and other supernatural machinery suggest that a weakened man is being hastened to his doom. There is none of that Sophoclean suggestion that Oedipus and Jocasta are mighty wills or powerful egos shaping their destinies, nor is there the implication that Oedipus's relentless driving quest is powerfully and ironically responsible for his own undoing. Instead, the rather effete Senecan Oedipus stands bewildered and stunned as events implacably reveal that he is himself the cause of the plague at Thebes, is himself the sacrilegious assassin of his own father and the incestuous marriage partner of his own mother. In short, the Senecan Oedipus is noteworthy for his lack of vim and virility; he is the exact opposite of the Stoic *vir bonus* who faces his destiny with courage and candor. He is an ignoble, wavering, suspicious, and timorous man, hounded and shuffled along toward his ignominious catastrophe. Indeed, imagery throughout the play stresses the sense of fatality and the broader theme of many generations—that a general curse lies on the land and the family of Antiope, Amphion, Pentheus, and Cadmus. The Senecan *Oedipus* consistently explores the workings of fatality, revealing a man who, without self-assertion, self-regulation, and self-mastery, becomes a helpless victim and scapegoat.

AGAMEMNON

Like his *Oedipus*, Seneca's *Agamemnon* concerns a major figure in the Greek dramatic tradition. Agamemnon, in particular, is a figure of imposing public significance: the victorious Greek general in the Trojan War, leader of a major dynasty at Mycenae, and hero of myth and legend. In Seneca's play, however, he is rigorously diminished in stature and import. His return home from Troy is without pomp and celebration; his speech is confined to talk with the enslaved captive Cassandra; and his assassination by his wife Clytaemestra is demeaning—he is caught in a net and slaughtered like a bull. Also reductive in *Agamemnon* is the treatment of other characters traditionally given heroic stature. Clytaemestra is presented as vacillating and insecure. She is seen chiefly as engaged in a sordid love affair with Aegisthus. Aegisthus, too, is hardly heroic. Rather than stressing his role as the just avenger of Thyestes' mistreatment at the hands of Atreus, Seneca portrays Aegisthus as bumbling, indecisive, and even effeminate. At the assassination of Agamemnon, surely the play's key moment, he hangs back ineptly and is described as a "halfman." Even the ghost of Thyestes, which appears at the play's outset to goad Aegisthus on to just revenge, is dramatized as wavering and insecure. All the main characters are tremulous and ill at ease, hardly figures of force and presence. Indeed, in the absence of significant heroes in this drama, the defeated Trojan slaves emerge—ironically enough—to fill up the vacuum; it is clearly the conquered who, by comparison with the uncertain Greeks, appear stately and victorious. Cassandra herself, despite all the pathos of her suffering and madness at the hands of the seer-god Apollo, ironically looms over the play at last as a heroine by default. Ironically, too, no one else is on hand to fulfill that role. Thus, Seneca's version of the classic play tilts and overturns heroic tradition and renders the actions subsequent to Troy's downfall as trifling, unmanly, and incomplete. Seneca's ancient Greeks to some extent mirror the nature of Nero's decadent Rome: jaded and a bit debased.

MAD HERCULES

In a class by itself is Seneca's last major play, *Mad Hercules*. In theme, *Hercules on Oeta* is quite similar (some critics believe it not to be by Seneca but by a careful imitator). *The Phoenician Women*, in the form in which it has survived, is doubtless by Seneca but is no more than a fragment. In *Mad Hercules*, the greatest mythic hero, the exemplar of heroism for Cynics and Stoics alike, is, like a Thyestes or a Cassandra, confronted by the malice of the universe and all but defeated and destroyed. Hercules has just completed his twelve great labors and returned from his most challenging test—a triumphant harrowing of the Underworld, the land of death, from which he emerges alive and victorious, leading captive the formidable triple-headed dog of Hades, Cerberus. His troubles have not concluded, however, and he must slay the tyrant Lycus, who has threatened the life of

Hercules' wife, Megara, and their children. At this highest point in his career, fate engineers its cruelest reversal. The jealous goddess Juno infects Hercules with a temporary madness, and he slays his own wife and offspring. When he awakens from this madness and learns from his father, Amphitryon, of the magnitude and heinousness of his deed, Hercules confronts his severest trial. His immediate inclination—with a fit of heroic revulsion—is to commit suicide. The saddened and aged Amphitryon attempts to dissuade him, urging on him his innocence, his filial obligations, and his duties to humankind and to the world. Hercules endures momentous inner strife and torment and does at last overcome his self-destructive urge, electing more calmly, though chafed by misery and despair, to live and to confront the void. Here, for the first time, the heroic theme is permitted to shine forth in Senecan drama: Hercules, a rare and certainly great hero, will suffer like the rest of humankind, harried by the senseless, malevolent universe; but such a hero (in this case, son of Zeus) bravely endures and, in so doing, wins a victory.

In Seneca's dramatic world, heroism is all but dead. The forces of frenzy and vice appear stronger than ever before. Most men in such a contest with the universe waver, tremble, and subside. Only the rare individual will marshall enough self-mastery to permit him to tolerate, withstand, and endure. Hercules is such an individual. For once, the human lot is vindicated, and the heavy irony of Senecan drama falls on a goddess—for it is Juno who surrenders to irrational envy, furor, and spite in her attempt to overthrow Hercules. The hero, in contrast, after a monumental struggle, achieves self-mastery. It is his greatest contest, and his victory, which the Stoics often paradoxically extolled, is a victory over the world and over the gods themselves. Such heroism is possible, Seneca seems to acknowledge, but in the fallen world it is more and more an unlikely eventuality. Such a struggle, and against such odds, only serves to accentuate the tension and the drama in Seneca's plays. Victory is possible in his pages, but defeat is by far the more common result when humans grapple with deities and Fate herself on Earth's great moving stage.

OTHER MAJOR WORKS

NONFICTION: *Ad Marciam de consolatione*, c. 40-41 C.E. (*To Marcia, on Consolation*, 1614); *Ad Helviam matrem de consolatione*, c. 41-42 C.E. (*To My Mother Helvia, on Consolation*, 1614); *De ira libri tres*, c. 41-49 C.E. (*Three Essays on Anger*, 1614); *Epigrammata super exilio*, c. 41-49 C.E.; *Ad Polybium de consolatione*, c. 43-44 C.E. (*To Polybius, on Consolation*, 1614); *De brevitate vitae*, c. 49 C.E. (*On the Shortness of Life*, 1614); *Apocolocyntosis divi Claudii*, c. 54 C.E. (*The Deification of Claudius*, 1614); *De constantia sapientis*, c. 55-56 C.E. (*On the Constancy of the Wise Man*, 1614); *De clementia*, c. 55-56 C.E. (*On Clemency*, 1614); *De beneficiis*, c. 58-63 C.E. (*On Benefits*, 1614); *De tranquillitate animi*, c. 59-61 C.E. (*On the Tranquility of the Soul*, 1614); *De otio*, c. 62 C.E. (*On Leisure*, 1614); *Quaestiones naturales*, c. 62-64 C.E. (*Natural Questions*, 1614); *Epistulae morales ad Lucilium*, c. 62-65 C.E. (*Letters to Lucilius*, 1917-1925); *De providentia*, c. 63-64 C.E. (*On Providence*, 1614); *Workes: Both Morall and Naturall*, 1614; *Ad Lucilium epistulae morales*, 1917-1925 (3 volumes); *Seneca, Moral Essays*, 1928-1935 (3 volumes).

BIBLIOGRAPHY

Boyle, A. J. *Tragic Seneca: An Essay in the Theatrical Tradition*. New York: Routledge, 1997. A study of Seneca's tragedies and his influence on Renaissance dramatists. Bibliography and index.

Davis, Peter J. *Shifting Song: The Chorus in Seneca's Tragedies*. New York: Olms-Weidmann, 1993. An examination of Seneca's tragedies and Latin drama, with emphasis on the use of the chorus. Bibliography.

Griffin, Miriam T. *Seneca: A Philosopher in Politics*. 1976. Reprint. Oxford, England: Clarendon, 1992. A biography of Seneca that examines his political viewpoints and his participation in government. Bibliography and index.

Harrison, George W. M., ed. *Seneca in Performance*. London: Duckworth with the Classical Press of Wales, 2000. An analysis of Seneca's dramas that looks at production and staging issues. Bibliography and index.

Motto, Anna Lydia. *Further Essays on Seneca*. New York: Peter Lang, 2001. A collection of essays presenting interpretation and critical analysis of the works of Seneca. Bibliography and index.

Motto, Anna Lydia, and John R. Clark. *Essays on Seneca*. New York: Peter Lang, 1993. A collection of articles on the Roman dramatist and his literary works. Bibliography and index.

Tietze Larson, Victoria. *The Role of Description in Senecan Tragedy*. New York: Peter Lang, 1994. A study of the tragedies of Seneca with emphasis on the role of description in these plays. Bibliography.

Anna Lydia Motto and John R. Clark

THOMAS SHADWELL

Born: Norfolk, England; 1640(?)
Died: Chelsea, England; November 19, 1692

PRINCIPAL DRAMA

The Sullen Lovers: Or, The Impertinents, pr., pb. 1668
The Royal Shepherdess, pr., pb. 1669
The Humorists, pr. 1670, pb. 1671
The Miser, pr. c. 1671-1672, pb. 1672 (adaptation of Molière's play *L'Avare*)

Epsom-Wells, pr. 1672, pb. 1673
The Tempest: Or, The Enchanted Island, pr., pb. 1674 (libretto)
Psyche, pr., pb. 1675 (libretto)
The Libertine: A Tragedy, pr. 1675, pb. 1676
The Virtuoso, pr., pb. 1676
The History of Timon of Athens, the Man-Hater, pr., pb. 1678
A True Widow, pr. 1678, pb. 1679

The Woman-Captain, pr. 1679. pb. 1680

The Lancashire Witches, and Tegue o Divelly the
Irish Priest, pr. 1681, pb. 1682

The Squire of Alsatia, pr., pb. 1688

The Amorous Bigot, with the Second Part of Tegue
o Divelly, pr. c. 1689, pb. 1690

Bury Fair, pr., pb. 1689

The Scowrers, pr. 1690, pb. 1691

The Volunteers: Or, The Stock Jobbers, pr. 1692,
pb. 1693

OTHER LITERARY FORMS

Thomas Shadwell, a prolific writer of comic drama, was also an energetic theatrical critic and polemicist, and a writer of pastorals, operas, and adaptations. His poetic output is divided into four categories: prologues and largely satiric epilogues that are found included in the printed texts of his own or others' drama; songs from his plays; satires and lampoons; and a translation of *The Tenth Satyr of Juvenal* (1687), to which is prefixed the translation of a short poem by Lucan. Shadwell was an active and fierce participant in the literary wars of his time and produced many pamphlets flaying the enemies of the Whig cause. *The Horrid Sin of Man-Catching, the Second Part* (1681) is dedicated to the Whig leader, the earl of Shaftesbury. *Some Reflections upon the Pretended Parallel in the Play Called "The Duke of Guise"* (1683) provoked a savage attack from Thomas Otway in his play *The Atheist: Or, The Second Part of the Soldier's Fortune* (pr. 1683). A few of Shadwell's letters have survived, but the chief interest of his nondramatic work lies in the theatrical polemics found in the prose dedications to his plays. The ideas Shadwell presented in these dedications constitute a theory of dramatic method. His prologues are used as pleas for a reintroduction of Jonsonian classical values into dramatic structure as an alternative to prevailing Restoration comic misrule.

ACHIEVEMENTS

Thomas Shadwell owes his immortality in large part to ridicule. John Dryden, his former friend, reserved some of his fiercest satiric lines for Shadwell. Dryden wrote in his mock paean of praise to fools,

MacFlecknoe (1682): "Sh— alone, of all my sons, is he/ Who stands confirm'd in full stupidity./ The rest to some faint meaning make pretense,/ But Sh— never deviates into sense." It is a tribute of sorts to Shadwell that he generated such brilliant and lasting malice. In far less memorable lines, another contemporary poet and dramatist, John Wilmot, earl of Rochester, in his "Allusion to the Tenth Satyr . . . of Horace" (1675), indicates some other elements in Shadwell's achievements: "Of all our Modern Wits, none seems to me/ Once to have toucht upon true Comedy,/ But hasty *Shadwell*, and slow *Wycherley*./ *Shadwell's* unfinish'd works do yet impart/ Great proofs of Nature, none of Art."

Shadwell's plays were performed on the London stage well into the eighteenth century. He has not been regarded as a great dramatist but as one of interest in theatrical history. Contemporaries saw him as a force to be reckoned with, as an advocate of once fashionable Jonsonian classicism. Sir Walter Scott, writing on Restoration drama long after Dryden and Shadwell and their quarrels had turned to dust, felt compelled to defend Shadwell. Scott pointed out that Shadwell's strengths lie in his comedies, which, although lacking "any brilliancy of wit, or ingenuity of intrigue," have "characters that are truly dramatic, original and well drawn, and the picture of manners which they exhibit gives us a lively idea of those of the author's age."

Between 1887 and 1907, at least eight doctoral dissertations, largely concentrating on Shadwell's use of his source materials in his comedies, appeared in Germany and Switzerland. Praise for Shadwell's "uncompromising and at the same time felicitous realism" in George Saintsbury's introduction to the Mermaid edition of four of Shadwell's plays, which appeared in the early twentieth century, contributed to creating the climate for Montague Summers's sumptuous five-volume *The Complete Works of Thomas Shadwell*, which was published in 1927. Limited to 1,290 sets, privately printed in magnificent typography by the Fortune Press (which produced ninety five-volume sets on Kelmscott unbleached handmade paper, and the remainder on machine-made paper, with lavish illustrative portraits), the volumes are collectors' items. The bibliophilic elements in Summers's edition reflect the fact that Shadwell's reputation is largely confined to scholarly circles and to students of dramatic history. Summers concludes his introduction of more than two hundred pages by asserting that Shadwell's work is "incalculably important as a picture of his times." In his comedies, "we have the whole tribe of fops, virtuosos, debauches, cuckolds, coarse country clowns, crooked politicians, business men, minor poets, sportsmen, loose wives, whores, puritans, cavaliers, the whole kaleidoscope of Restoration life."

Among twentieth century scholars, there is a consensus that Shadwell's plays, whatever their artistic deficiencies, are of great value as a reservoir of information about their times. Shadwell's canvas is a wide one, and, in this respect, he differs from other late seventeenth century dramatists of comparable stature, who generally limited their attentions to narrow court circles. Shadwell has survived Dryden's mockery to become recognized as an adherent of Jonsonian traditions on the Restoration stage, as a superb recorder of contemporary life and manners, and, at his best, as a master of vibrant comedy.

BIOGRAPHY

The facts of Thomas Shadwell's life are unclear, and even the date of his birth is shrouded in uncertainty. He was born between 1640 and 1642, probably at Santon Hall in Norfolk, to John and Sarah Shadwell; his father was a Royalist lawyer. After receiving a liberal education, being tutored from an early age in music and the general arts, he attended the King Edward VI Grammar School at Bury St. Edmunds. The theme of the apposite education for a young man entering the world is especially prominent in Shadwell's later drama. His early years on the family estate provided the foundation for the pastoral and Horatian ideals that pervade his writings, in which they are more than a mere literary convention.

Shadwell was admitted to Gonville and Caius College, Cambridge, which he left without taking a degree on July 7, 1658. He enrolled in the Middle Temple, London, no doubt hoping to follow his father in a legal career. There is evidence that between 1664 and 1665, Shadwell was with his father, recorder of Galway and Attorney General of Connacht, in Ireland. In the years immediately preceding the 1668 production of his first comedy, *The Sullen Lovers*, Shadwell met the man who was to become his patron, the influential and well-connected William Cavendish, duke of Newcastle. Dedications in printed texts of Shadwell's plays to Cavendish and members of his family attest Shadwell's indebtedness to a man who had known Ben Jonson and had patronized the arts for a long period. Sometime between 1663 and 1667, Shadwell married a leading lady in the Duke's Company, Anne Gibbs, who appeared in the prominent role of Emilia in his first produced drama. Subsequently, Shadwell's life followed the routine of the professional writer and dramatist heavily engaged in literary activity in post-Restoration London. In defense of his artistic beliefs and as a paid propagandist for the Whig cause, Shadwell was constantly involved in literary feuds with rivals. In 1681, a year of particularly intense political activity, Shadwell was forced to leave the theater and to write under assumed names. In 1688, the year of the Glorious Revolution, and the start of the reign of William and Queen Mary, Shadwell's personal and theatrical fortunes were restored. He returned to the London stage with *The Squire of Alsatia*, became the poet laureate, and enjoyed prestige and success until his death.

Evidence suggests that physically, Shadwell was big and by character blustering, hardly noted for tact, but rather for crudity of expression. He died in 1692 from an overdose of opium, to which he was addicted (in common with many of his contemporaries, he suffered from severe gout), and is buried at St. Luke's Church, Chelsea, London. Shadwell had five children, one of whom, John, achieved eminence as Queen Anne's royal physician and was knighted by her.

ANALYSIS

The 1680's were times of personal danger for Thomas Shadwell. He was lampooned, personally assaulted by Tory bullyboys, and his plays were hissed off the stage. Attacks on Catholicism in his *The*

Lancashire Witches, and Tegue o Divelly the Irish Priest, and his known association with the earl of Shaftesbury and his circle, made Shadwell particularly vulnerable after the failure of the 1678 Popish Plot. Shadwell's creative works are indissolubly intertwined with the attitudes of his age. He spiritedly defended himself against his enemies. Of particular relevance to analysis of his work is his philosophical, rather than political, battle with the earl of Rochester. Conducted in poems, pamphlets, and plays, it was a conflict between two basically opposed attitudes toward life and ways of living: Rochester's hedonism and love of extremes had their foundations in the writings of Thomas Hobbes; Shadwell's love of the middle way and his adherence to altruism were rooted in the classics. These contrasting ideologies found their way in one form or another into Shadwell's eighteen known dramas, which move from adherence to Jonsonian principles, through the fierce satires of the late 1670's and early 1680's, to the mellow, less intemperate, late plays extolling the middle way of conduct.

George Saintsbury, in his introduction to *Thomas Shadwell* (1903), draws attention to Shadwell's accuracy of observation, his keen eye for contemporary manners, and his dramatic energy and gusto. Attacked by some critics for a seeming lack of selectivity, Shadwell was in fact a dramatist whose techniques reveal careful selective principles at work: the pairing of characters into types and humors in order to present antithetical viewpoints; the reworking of source materials; the interesting use of metaphor and place to convey meaning. Shadwell is, in the words of John Loftis in *The Revels History of Drama in English, Volume V: 1660-1750* (1976), "Among the major dramatists" of the Restoration, the only one who "broadens the social range, providing engaging portraits of men outside fashionable society and venturing to criticize gentlemen not only for social affectation." Shadwell's dramatic rendering of the conflict between hedonism and altruism is universal. As the shrewd Sir Walter Scott observed, in his notes to *Peveril of the Peak* (1823), acknowledging his debt to Shadwell's *The Volunteers*, Shadwell was indeed "no mean observer of human nature."

THE SULLEN LOVERS

The Sullen Lovers, Shadwell's first London comedy, created a stage sensation with its caricaturing of contemporary court personalities. Samuel Pepys went to see the play three times in three days, noting in his diary that "Sir Positive At-all . . . is . . . Sir Robert Howard." Both men were singularly competent in pronouncing opinions on everything from warfare and domestic architecture to ball games and how they should be played. Pepys's enthusiasm also owed something to his fascination with the reaction of court figures to the play as they watched it being performed early in May, 1668. Pepys saw it again in April, 1669; Charles II chose *The Sullen Lovers* as one of the plays to be acted at Dover when his court, in May, 1670, went to meet his sister the duchess of Orleans on her return from overseas. There was a revival at Lincoln's Inn Fields on October 5, 1703, when it was announced that the play had not been acted for twenty-eight years. Shadwell's main source was Molière's *Les Fâcheux* (pr., pb. 1661; *The Impertinents*, 1732; also known as *The Bores*, 1891). Shadwell utilizes Molière's method of exhibiting various fools, individually and in pairs or various combinations, before the audience. In Shadwell's play, the fools represent the humors of classical Jonsonian drama. *The Sullen Lovers* is interesting as a Jonsonian play of humors using neoclassic structural and characterization devices, as an attempt to produce a psychological drama, and as a satire on contemporary court figures. Each character represents an idea or controlling thesis, the idea being made concrete by the dramatist's skillful play of contemporary allusions juxtaposed to the specific gestures, mannerisms, and speech peculiarities of living persons.

In *The Sullen Lovers*, Shadwell considers various modes of living in a world of utter folly. Contrast is provided by the device of marrying three pairs of humors: a pair of social misfits, Emilia and Stanford; a couple, appositely named Sir Positive At-All and Lady Vaine, totally devoted to the pursuit of folly; and Lovel and Carolina, wry and detached. Lovel and Carolina best represent the Shadwellian middle course, in contrast to the total isolation of the first pair, Emilia and Stanford, and the uncritical participation of the second pair, Sir Positive At-All and Lady Vaine, in the vanities and follies of the world in which they live. The plot dynamics revolve around the two self-confessed misanthropes, Emilia and Stanford, who are given much of Shadwell's powerful satiric invective and who are persistently pursued by a gang of idiots. The misanthropes escape from London, which is identified, as in so many of Shadwell's dramas, with corruption and vice. Emilia, influenced by Robert Burton's *The Anatomy of Melancholy* (1621), cultivates privacy and thinks of taking vows and entering a nunnery. Stanford dreams of an escape to a deserted Caribbean island. Deliberately refusing the company of others, they attract some idiosyncratic characters. The attack on Stanford's citadel is led by the self-obsessed dramatist, Sir Positive At-all, while Lady Vaine, a prostitute disguised as an aristocrat and the first of Shadwell's long line of theatrical hedonists, leads the attack on Emilia. In the second act, the "sullen lovers" of the title, Stanford and Emilia, meet. Acts 3 and 4 trace the development of their relationship and their realization that dissembling is the sole way to deal with idiocy. In the final act, they marry. Shadwell's *The Sullen Lovers* is an interesting synthesis of Jonsonian and Restoration modes of drama. Its use of humors is decidedly Jonsonian, while its emphasis on wit, sexual intrigue, and satire are typical of Restoration comedy.

EPSOM-WELLS

In *Epsom-Wells*, in many ways his most representative Restoration drama, Shadwell brilliantly utilizes the indecent characters and libertines about whom he complained in the preface to *The Sullen Lovers*. *Epsom-Wells* has as its setting a fashionable spa not too far from London where a rich galaxy of bawds, pimps, courtesans, gamblers, fops, and other contemporary types gather. The plot structure is multidimensional. Lucia and Carolina, two honorable young girls on holiday, are pursued by two rakes, Rains and Bevil, who have deliberately gone to Epsom to seduce women and to drink. They are debauchees whom Shadwell uses as commentators on the folly of their world. Lucia and Carolina are representatives of freedom. They prefer Rains's and Bevil's antics,

without succumbing to them, to the hypocrisy of London. According to Shadwell's *dramatis personae*, usually a rich source of information about the humors of his characters or their dominating ideas, Lucia and Carolina are "Two young ladies, of Wit, Beauty and Fortune," not pressured, as are so many of their contemporaries, into finding a rich husband or forced into marriage by their father. They have the privilege of bestowing their virginity on men of their own choosing. After having tantalized Rains and Bevil throughout the play, they marry them in the final act.

Other plot strands focus on the Woodlys, a young married couple. Mr. Woodly romps with Rains and Bevil: Mrs. Woodly, driven by licentious passion, sleeps with them. The last act sees them divorcing and celebrating their freedom. In addition to the Woodlys, Shadwell's *Epsom-Wells* is inhabited by the Biskets, Fribbles, and Justice Clodpates of the world. Bisket and Fribble, both London merchants, are cuckolded in the liberating Epsom atmosphere. Bisket is a "Comfit-maker, a quiet, humble, civil Cuckold, governed by his Wife, whom he very much fears and loves at the same time, and is very proud of." Fribble, on the other hand, is "A Haberdasher, a surly Cuckold, very conceited and proud of his Wife, but pretends to govern and keep her under." Mrs. Bisket is "An impertinent, imperious Strumpet, Wife to Bisket." Dorothy Fribble is "an humble, submitting Wife, who Jilts her Husband that way, a very Whore." Bisket and Fribble transform everything, including their own wives, into objects for materialistic exploitation, and value their wives' sexual indiscretions for the business opportunities thereby created. Clodpate is "A Country Justice, a publick spirited, politick, discontented Fop, an immoderate Hater of London, and a Lover of the Country above measure, a hearty true English coxcomb." Clodpate is given some magnificent lines of raillery against London, a "Sodom" full of "Pride, Popery, Folly, Lust, Prodigality, Cheating Knaves, and Jilting Whores; Wine of half a crown a quart, and Ale of twelve pence." Clodpate pursues Lucia and Carolina; jilted by them, he turns to Mrs. Jilt, a London prostitute in search of a wealthy husband and pretending at Epsom to be a lady of virtue. Luckily for Clodpate, the marriage between them turns out to be invalid. He returns to the country having enjoyed Epsom. Mrs. Jilt returns considerably richer to London. She is more in accord with Kick and Cuff, "cheating, sharking, cowardly Bullies," gigolos who fill out Shadwell's rich galaxy of the various humors congealing in a world such as Epsom-Wells.

Underpinning the play are differing attitudes to life and how it should be lived. The play opens with its characters taking the waters of the wells, waters that liberate the self from the inhibitions and artificial disguises of London and its social world. In Epsom, the true, animalistic Hobbesian nature of people is allowed to run rife. Cuff and Kick are unabashed animals, visualizing the vacationing women as wild beasts. Cuff has "a great mind to run roaring in amongst 'em," although there is a danger that he will be torn "in pieces." Bevil and Rains are intellectual hedonists. The chief target of their invective is Clodpate, the failed hedonist forced to spend his existence in far away Sussex, railing at folly. In his epilogue, Shadwell urges "Gallants, leave your lewd whoring and take wives,/ Repent for shame your Covent-Garden lives," although this message ill accords a play in which marriage encourages whoring. *Epsom-Wells* is a fascinating mixture of sexual intrigue, philosophical debate, satire, allusion, and sheer entertainment. It is hardly a wonder that it was a contemporary hit, first performed December 2, 1672, and seen three times in a single month by Charles II, who included it among his Christmas revels. *Epsom-Wells* remained in the London repertory for many years; Henry Purcell wrote music for a 1693 revival, and there is a record of a 1724 performance.

THE LIBERTINE

Shadwell's comedies have obscured his efforts in other dramatic modes. Like many other Restoration dramatists, he turned his talents to adaptation. *The Libertine*, based largely on Molière's *Dom Juan: Ou, Le Festin de Pierre* (pr. 1665, pb. 1682; *Don Juan*, 1755), is a variation on the Don Juan theme. Written in prose, the play exhibits fantastic extremes, coincidences, masques, brutality, and farce. Shadwell revels in the Hobbesian hedonism epitomized in his presentation of the flouting of all religious and civil authority by Don Juan (named "Don John" by Shadwell).

THE HISTORY OF TIMON OF ATHENS, THE MAN-HATER

It is not surprising that Shadwell's next adaptation should be a rewriting of William Shakespeare's *Timon of Athens* (pr. c. 1607-1608). In *The History of Timon of Athens, the Man-Hater*, his major deviation from Shakespeare's text is to give Timon a faithful mistress named Evandra and an unfaithful one named Melissa; further, he allows Timon to die onstage with Evandra, who stays with him when all his seemingly faithful but false friends have deserted him. Shadwell makes his spectacle serve a purpose, uses cosmopolitan scenes and stage devices such as machines, and deals with Restoration social problems. The play is of interest both in the history of Shakespearean adaptations and as an illustration of Shadwell's recurring devices, particularly the use of paired characters.

THE ROYAL SHEPHERDESS

Shadwell's experiments with pastoral and opera are not without interest. *The Royal Shepherdess* exhibits his use of dance, song, and exaggerated farce not in a comic mode but in a pastoral form, drawing on his master Ben Jonson and using his masque forms. Didacticism creeps in with a contrast between Horatian genteel life and the squalor of low life presented against a backdrop of pastoral illusion.

THE TEMPEST AND PSYCHE

Shadwell's two operas, the first, *The Tempest*, based on Dryden and Sir William Davenant's *The Tempest* (1667), the second, *Psyche*, on the Molière-Corneille-Quinault tragedy ballet, were considered "significant milestones in the evolution of English opera" by Michael W. Alssid. Both illustrate Shadwell's dexterity at stagecraft. In *The Tempest*, he shortens and rearranges between forty and fifty speeches, creating space and time for dancing, singing, and dramatic spectacle. In *Psyche*, he produces a moral allegory of the struggle within the heroine, Psyche, between the forces of ambition, power, plenty, and peace. Both operas and the pastoral are professional theatrical pieces written to make money. They reveal Shadwell's mastery of stagecraft, his didactic strain, and his sense of spectacle, providing as well an insight into the multiple forms of drama found on the Restoration stage.

THE LANCASHIRE WITCHES, AND TEGUE O DIVELLY THE IRISH PRIEST

For a number of reasons, *The Lancashire Witches, and Tegue o Divelly the Irish Priest* is among Shadwell's most interesting works. The genesis of this play was deeply political, reflecting Shadwell's role as a Whig propagandist. Shadwell's address to his readers gives an account of the delays and excisions in the text of the play demanded by his Tory political opponents before it could be performed in the autumn of 1681. Shadwell was forced to omit most of his political materials, and censorship transformed the play into an absurd but highly popular farce. Explicit political ideology was replaced by supernatural motifs that implicitly represent forces of disruption at work in society.

The play is set far away from the intrigues of London, on a country estate, an emblem for tranquillity and positive values. The action focuses on the master of the estate, Sir Edward Hartford, "a worthy Hospitable true English Gentleman, of good understanding, and honest Principles." Sir Edward detests "Foppery, slavish Principles, and Popish Religion." He is an empiricist who argues that witchcraft has natural causes. Often misled in personal matters and motivated by materialistic considerations, he tries to marry his daughter Isabella to Sir Timothy Shacklehead, "a very pert, confident, simple Fellow." Sir Edward's son Hartfort—"A Clownish, sordid Country Fool, that loves nothing but drinking Ale, and Country Sports"—is intended for the highly intelligent Theodosia Shacklehead. Witchcraft conspires to bring two reformed rakes, Bellfort and Doubty, to Sir Edward's estate. Much of the action of the play is concerned with the ways in which Isabella and Theodosia disrupt the estate, play elaborate games with Bellfort and Doubty, and disguise themselves as witches. Mistaken identity and disguise give Shadwell the opportunity to present highly amusing dramatic moments. In act 4, Lady Shacklehead, on the way to a nighttime assignation with Doubty, finds herself attacked by a lecherous priest named Tegue, who mistakenly has intercourse with a witch, Mother Dickenson, thinking that she is Lady Shacklehead. In act 5, Sir Edward's friend Sir Jeffery Shacklehead discovers his scarcely clothed wife wandering around in the dark. He is duped by her sleepwalking performance and quickly improvised nightmare, in which she exclaims "Oh! the Witch, the Witch, oh she pulls the cloaths off me. Hold me, Sir Jeffery, hold me."

Although there are many farcical elements in the play, ranging from rock throwing, chair pulling, disrobing on a darkened stage, and chases, the chaos has a serious side. The buffoons, witches, Smerk, Sir Edward's chaplain, and Tegue are representatives of the forces of disorder threatening the ordered Hartford estate and, by implication, Charles II and England itself. Shadwell, playing on audience prejudice, depicts his arch-villain Tegue as both Irish and Catholic, a dissembling troublemaker plotting insurrection. Lively theater is created by Tegue's lecherous drunken antics and by the highly energetic activities of the witches.

Shadwell even includes a witchhunt that degenerates "into a mad farce controlled by secular and religious professionals seeking to enhance their own reputations by finding and condemning great numbers," according to Kunz. Passages in the play expunged by the censor are printed in italics in the printed text, revealing that Sir Edward's estate is but a microcosm for the garden of England, which—if it is to survive—must be cultivated according to solid Whig principles. This political statement forced Shadwell as a dramatist and verse satirist into seven years of submerged existence while the country changed religions and rulers and then did an about-face.

OTHER MAJOR WORKS

POETRY: *The Medal of John Bayes: A Satyr Against Folly and Knavery*, 1682; *A Congratulatory Poem on His Highness the Prince of Orange His Coming into England*, 1689; *Ode on the Anniversary of the King's Birth*, 1690; *Votum Perenne*, 1692.

NONFICTION: *Notes and Observations on the Empress of Morocco*, 1674; *The Horrid Sin of Man-Catching, the Second Part*, 1681; *Some Reflections upon the Pretended Parallel in the Play Called "The Duke of Guise,"* 1683.

TRANSLATION: *The Tenth Satyr of Juvenal*, 1687.

MISCELLANEOUS: *The Complete Works of Thomas Shadwell*, 1927 (5 volumes; Montague Summers, editor).

BIBLIOGRAPHY

Alssid, Michael W. *Thomas Shadwell*. New York: Twayne, 1967. This volume, part of Twayne's English Authors series, gives a straightforward account of Shadwell's life and drama, attempting some critical evaluation. A useful introduction. Supplemented by a bibliography and an index.

Armistead, J. M., and Werner Bies. *Four Restoration Playwrights: A Reference Guide to Thomas Shadwell, Aphra Behn, Nathaniel Lee, and Thomas Otway*. Boston: G. K. Hall, 1984. Part of the Reference Guides to Literature series, this volume carries basic information on dates, plays, and editions, and includes a bibliography. It is invaluable for research papers.

Bruce, Donald. *Topics of Restoration Comedy*. New York: St. Martin's Press, 1974. This survey of Restoration comedy concentrates on it as a "debating" comedy, with a moral pupose in this debate. Bruce refers to Shadwell's plays extensively and examines seven of his plays within the context of the moral topics enumerated. Notes, bibliography, chronology, and index.

Burns, Edward. *Restoration Comedy: Crises of Desire and Identity*. New York: St. Martin's Press, 1987. Chapter 4 deals with Shadwell as a professional dramatist, as one of a group of dramatists whose plays are still underrated. Burns praises these writers for their energy and ferocity, opposing them to the suavity of the gentlemen playwrights. Chronology, notes, short bibliography, and index.

Hume, Robert D. *The Development of English Drama in the Late Seventeenth Century*. 1976. Reprint. Oxford, England: Clarendon Press, 1990. Hume tries to correct earlier stereotypes of Restoration drama by examining a large number of plays and paying special attention to their chronological sequencing. Contains many references to Shadwell and a full analysis of his *The Squire of Alsatia*. Two indexes.

Kunz, Don Richard. *The Drama of Thomas Shadwell*. Salzburg, Austria: University of Salzburg Press, 1972. This volume looks at the life and works of Thomas Shadwell, particularly his plays and the techniques used therein.

Loftis, John, Richard Southern, Marion Jones, and A. H. Scouten. *The Revels History of Drama in English, Volume V: 1660-1750*. London: Methuen, 1976. Contains a section on Shadwell in connection with the comedy of humors and includes other useful references to his plays throughout the volume. Complemented by a bibliography and an index.

Wheatley, Christopher J. *Without God or Reason: The Plays of Thomas Shadwell and Secular Ethics in the Restoration*. Cranbury, N.J.: Associated University Presses, 1993. Wheatley examines ethics during the Restoration, focusing on Shadwell's plays. Bibliography and index.

William Baker,
updated by David Barratt

PETER SHAFFER

Born: Liverpool, England; May 15, 1926

PRINCIPAL DRAMA

Five Finger Exercise, pr., pb. 1958
The Private Ear, pr., pb. 1962 (one act)
The Public Eye, pr., pb. 1962 (one act)
The Merry Roosters Panto, pr. 1963 (music by Stanley Myers, lyrics by Lionel Bart)
The Royal Hunt of the Sun, pr., pb. 1964
Black Comedy, pr. 1965, pb. 1967 (one act)
The White Liars, pb. 1967, 1968 (one act; originally as *White Lies*, pr., pb. 1967)

Shrivings, pb. 1973 (with *Equus*; originally as *The Battle of Shrivings*, pr. 1970)

Equus, pr., pb. 1973

Amadeus, pr. 1979, pb. 1980

The Collected Plays of Peter Shaffer, pb. 1982

Yonadab: The Watcher, pr. 1985, pb. 1988

Lettice and Lovage, pr., pb. 1987

The Gift of the Gorgon, pr. 1992, pb. 1993

OTHER LITERARY FORMS

Peter Shaffer began his writing career with a teleplay, *The Salt Land* (1955), and a radio play, *The Prodigal Father* (1955). Shaffer has also written several novels. With his twin brother, Anthony Shaffer, he wrote *The Woman in the Wardrobe* (1951), published in England under the collective pen name Peter Antony. The two brothers also collaborated on two more novels: *How Doth the Little Crocodile?* (1952), likewise issued under the pen name Peter Antony, and *Withered Murder* (1955), published under both authors' real names. Macmillan published *Withered Murder* (1956) and *How Doth the Little Crocodile?* (1957) in the United States, using the authors' real names. Shaffer also wrote the screenplays for *The Public Eye* (1972), *Equus* (1977), and *Amadeus* (1984), the last of which won the 1985 Academy Award for Best Screenplay Adaptation.

ACHIEVEMENTS

Once Peter Shaffer settled on playwriting as a career, most of his plays succeeded on both sides of the Atlantic. *Five Finger Exercise*, his first work for the stage, earned the London *Evening Standard* Drama Award for 1958 and the New York Drama Critics Circle Award for Best Foreign Play of the season in 1960. The one-act comedies *The Private Ear* and *The Public Eye* sustained Shaffer's reputation as a skilled playwright, as did the exceptional pageantry of *The Royal Hunt of the Sun*. *Equus* won the Tony Award for Best Play of the 1974-1975 season, the New York Drama Critics Circle Award, the Outer Critics Circle Award, and the Los Angeles Drama Critics Award. With 1,207 performances on Broadway, *Equus* ranks among the top twenty-five longest-running plays in the history of New York theater. *Amadeus* again took the *Evening Standard* Drama Award, the Plays and Players Award, and the London Theatre Critics Award for Best Play. The New York production won the New York Drama Critics Circle Award and the Outer Critics Circle Award for 1981. The film version of *Amadeus* won eight Oscars in 1984, including Best Film and Best Adapted Screenplay. In 1987, Shaffer was honored with the title of Commander of the British Empire.

BIOGRAPHY

Peter Levin Shaffer was born to Orthodox Jewish parents, Jack and Reka Shaffer, in Liverpool, England, on May 15, 1926, with a twin brother, Anthony. Another brother, Brian, was born in 1929. Anthony is also a writer, author of the prizewinning play *Sleuth* (pr. 1970). Brian is a biophysicist.

A middle-class British family, the Shaffers moved to London in 1936. World War II brought several relocations, in part because of safety concerns and in part because of the demands of Jack Shaffer's real estate business. In 1942, Shaffer was enrolled in St. Paul's School in London. In 1944, the twin brothers were conscripted for duty in the coal mines, working

Peter Shaffer in 1979. (Hulton Archive by Getty Images)

first in Kent, then in Yorkshire. Shaffer entered Trinity College, Cambridge University, on a scholarship in 1947.

At Cambridge, Shaffer discovered his talent and taste for writing while editing a college magazine. Taking his degree in history in 1950, he sought employment with various publishers in England, to no avail. He moved to New York in 1951. From a brief stint as a salesperson in a Doubleday bookstore, he moved to a job in the acquisitions section of a branch of the New York Public Library. Shaffer returned to London in 1954 and worked for the music publisher Boosey and Hawkes for about a year. With the broadcast of his teleplay *The Salt Land* and his radio play *The Prodigal Father* in 1955, he decided to turn to writing as a full-time career.

The 1958 success of *Five Finger Exercise* at London's Comedy Theater in the West End brought Shaffer renown as a serious playwright. The play opened in New York in December, 1959, setting a pattern followed by most of his subsequent stage plays. His pair of one-act plays, *The Private Ear* and *The Public Eye*, opened in London in 1962 and in New York in 1963. The Christmas season of 1963 saw the production of *The Merry Roosters Panto* in London.

During 1964, Shaffer and Peter Brook worked on a film script of William Golding's *Lord of the Flies* (1954), but it was not used for the eventual film version of the novel. Shaffer's *The Royal Hunt of the Sun* opened at the National Theatre in Chichester, England, in July, 1964; in London in December of that year; and in New York in October of 1965. At the behest of Sir Laurence Olivier, the director of the National Theatre, Shaffer wrote *Black Comedy*. It played at Chichester in July, 1965, then in London, and was presented in tandem with *White Lies* in 1967. This second pair of one-act plays was staged again in London in 1968, by which time Shaffer had rewritten *White Lies* and retitled it *The White Liars*.

For Shaffer, the 1970's began with a lull: *The Battle of Shrivings* opened in London in February, 1970, but did not run for long. July, 1973, however, saw the London premiere of *Equus*, which in October, 1974, opened in New York for its remarkably long run.

When Atheneum issued its edition of *Equus* in 1973, Shaffer included in it the book *Shrivings*, his revised version of *The Battle of Shrivings*, which had not survived onstage. In this general time period, Shaffer also developed the screenplay for the film version of *Equus*, which was released in 1977.

Finishing the 1970's with the highly successful *Equus*, Shaffer moved into the 1980's with the equally noteworthy *Amadeus*, which opened at the National Theatre, Chichester, in November, 1979, and subsequently opened in London. Shaffer revised his already very successful script during a run of the production in Washington, D.C., prior to its December, 1980, opening at New York's Broadhurst Theater. A film version was released in 1984 under the direction of Miloš Forman.

After the unsuccessful *Yonadab*, based on biblical themes, Shaffer returned to comedy with a star vehicle written for Maggie Smith, *Lettice and Lovage*, which received favorable reviews. Shaffer calls New York City home, despite his British citizenship and frequent returns to England.

ANALYSIS

Writing for *Theatre Arts* in February, 1960, Peter Shaffer made a declaration of independence: "Labels aren't for playwrights." His independence shows in both his life and his art. Shaffer admits in a 1963 article in *Transatlantic Review*, "All art is autobiographical inasmuch as it refers to personal experience," but the adolescent torment in *Five Finger Exercise* and the passions he stages in other works stem from his personal experience only in a general sense. Shaffer does tell of seeing, hearing, or reading of events that trigger ideas for his plays. Seeing, in 1968 and 1969, pro- and anti-Vietnam War demonstrations in New York and watching the American people agonize over the war led him to write *Shrivings*. Still, he maintains a degree of distance between his personal life and his plays. John Russell Taylor sees in *Five Finger Exercise* the sort of detachment other critics agree is characteristic of Shaffer's work: "The playwright does not seem to be personally involved in his play. . . . This balance of sympathy in a dramatist . . . makes for effective drama."

Within the mainstream of theatrical tradition, Shaffer maintains his artistic independence, varying conventional form or shifting his approach to a theme in almost every play. *Five Finger Exercise* is a middle-class domestic drama written at a time when numerous domestic dramas were in vogue, but Shaffer did not repeat himself. He moved on to romantic triangles in his one-act plays, then to epic drama with *The Royal Hunt of the Sun*, to psychological drama in *Equus*, and to a historical play, *Amadeus*.

Sets of the earlier plays are realistic. *The Royal Hunt of the Sun*, *Equus*, and *Amadeus*, however, use impressionistic sets, rely on varying amounts of flashback technique, and employ varying amounts of coordinate action. Besides varying set types and play genres, Shaffer varies emphasis in theatrical appeal. Sounds or music are important secondary factors in *Five Finger Exercise*, *The Royal Hunt of the Sun*, and *Equus* and are central to the plots of *The Private Ear* and *Amadeus*. Seeing in silence is the proposed cure for a troubled marriage in *The Public Eye*, visual display is lavish in *The Royal Hunt of the Sun*, and the sight of characters groping and stumbling through the action as though in pitch dark makes *Black Comedy* a vivid farce.

COMMON TRENDS

Given Shaffer's drive for fresh rendering of theatrical matter, various trends do appear in his plays. One such trait is cultural or ethnic variety. Possibly, being reared by Orthodox Jewish parents in nominally Protestant England sensitized him to the assets of ethnic identities and the liabilities of stereotypes. Whatever the reason, Shaffer commonly includes multicultural groupings of characters. *Five Finger Exercise* includes Louise, overly proud of her French ancestry, and Walter, the young German tutor who wants desperately to become a British subject. The protagonist of *The Public Eye*, Julian Christoforou, is Greek. To emphasize his foreignness, Christoforou was played in the film version by Topol, an Israeli actor. *Black Comedy* includes both an electrician and a prospective buyer of a young sculptor's art who are German. *Shrivings* includes an American secretary and an English poet who spends most of his time on the island of Corfu. *Amadeus* features an Italian com-

poser in the Austrian court at Vienna, and the dialogue occasionally includes Italian and French exchanges.

Generally, Shaffer's Northern European characters are identified with more rational or more placid behavior, while the Mediterranean characters are posed as more vivacious or romantic. Whatever the specific mix in a given play, each cultural alternative usually exposes a deficit in the *status quo* or brings a valuable influence to compensate for some perceived lack. The Greek private detective, Christoforou, is able to explain to the older, middle-class accountant that the young wife he suspects of infidelity really only needs some excitement in her life with her mate. Martin Dysart, the controlled, rational psychiatrist, tells of traveling each summer through Greece, yearning for the wild passion of the ancient festivals of Dionysus. Mozart, bored with writing opera according to the dominant Italian conventions, is glad for a commission from the Austrian King Joseph to write opera in German.

Despite the cosmopolitan flavor of Shaffer's work, his plays are consistently male-dominated. Significant conflicts tend to be between males. In *The Private Ear*, Tchaik loses Doreen to Ted. In *The Public Eye*, while following the wife is a major factor in the action, it is reported in dialogue between the two men. The wife does appear and interact with her husband and the detective, but she does not have equivalent exposure onstage. *The Royal Hunt of the Sun*, *Equus*, and *Amadeus* all feature conflicts between males. Only in *White Lies*, one of Shaffer's less notable efforts, is there a female protagonist. While she achieves a moral victory in that she sees and tells the truth in the end, she is forced to return her fortune-telling fee to the belligerent male antagonist and thereby faces an ethical defeat. In rewriting *Shrivings*, Shaffer strengthened the conflict by removing Sir Gideon Petrie's wife altogether, leaving the American secretary, Lois Neal, as the sole female party in a struggle primarily among men.

Significantly, Shaffer's strongest plays have usually included either more female characters or more active female characters than have the less successful plays. Even in their activity, however, the women may not be wholly ideal types. Louise in *Five Finger Exercise* is a domineering mother. Her daughter Pamela is aware of the family politics but is never permitted significant access to the actual struggles played out among the older members of the family, since she is only fourteen. *Black Comedy* features young Brindsley contending with Carol, his current and very superficial fiancée, on the night his former lover, Clea, returns. His upstairs neighbor, Miss Furnival, helps build the farce as a typical middle-aged spinster getting tipsy during the action, but she remains a convenient comic stereotype. All three women are actively involved in the plot, and all three have considerable dialogue. The protagonist, though, is a male.

Equus and *Amadeus*, Shaffer's strongest works, include women as supporting characters. Dysart turns several times to Hester Salomon for emotional support during the course of *Equus*. Wise and compassionate, she is the most wholesome of Shaffer's female characters. Constanze Mozart, too, is a support for her husband in *Amadeus* and is the only woman in the play who has a speaking role. The few others onstage are seen but not heard.

Because Shaffer is a twin, Jules Glenn suggests that his various pairs of male characters embody the conflicts and complementary satisfactions typical of twins. Although none of the character-pairs is portrayed as biological twins in the plays, their roles often have parallel aspects. Two men are involved with a single woman in *The Private Ear*, *The Public Eye*, and *White Lies*; two men in *Equus*, Martin Dysart and his patient Alan Strang, are inadequate in their sexual relationships with women. In *Amadeus*, both Mozart and Salieri have affairs with Katherina Cavalieri. *The Royal Hunt of the Sun* features two men who claim the role of a god.

ROLE OF SELF-DISCLOSURE

The key to an overview of Shaffer's work is his talent for revelation of character through self-disclosure. *Five Finger Exercise*, conventional in many respects, is outstanding for its characters' multiple levels of self-disclosure, from Stanley, who rants without understanding, to Walter, who understands both the Harringtons' needs and his own and attempts

suicide when fulfillment of his needs seems impossible. Shaffer's other plays take their depth and texture from this technique, if not their basic purpose. Self-disclosure is the major structural pattern for *The Royal Hunt of the Sun*, *Equus*, and *Amadeus*, each of which is presented by a narrator recalling past events. Similarly, Shaffer's choice of themes as his craft matures leads to a progressive revelation of the human condition. Clive, Shaffer's first stage protagonist, searches for individual identity and independence. Protagonists in the one-act plays, both the serious and the comic, are generally reaching for satisfactory relationships with other individuals. Leading characters in the major serious plays probe the ambitions, ideals, and institutions of humankind in the world at large.

Shaffer's comments on *The Royal Hunt of the Sun* reveal a salient concern obvious in that play and others overtly dealing with worship: He is disturbed that "man constantly trivializes the immensity of his experience" and "settles for a Church or Shrine or Synagogue . . . and over and over again puts into the hands of other men the reins of oppression. . . ." Even his earliest play, though portraying domestic rather than political or religious struggles, shows that revelation of character, the self-disclosure essential to informed, mature relationships, makes the individual human being vulnerable to another's control.

FIVE FINGER EXERCISE

Dennis A. Klein observes that "there is not one happy marriage in all of Shaffer's plays . . . and the prototype is the marriage between Louise and Stanley Harrington." Clive Harrington, the protagonist of *Five Finger Exercise*, is his mother's pet; he is also the target of his father's criticism because he lacks "practical" or "useful" interests. Struggling for identity and independence, Clive is never safe in the family bickering. Agreeing with Stanley that the new tutor is a needless expense draws reproach from Louise. Admitting that he is writing a review of a performance of the Greek play *Electra* triggers one more paternal lecture on the really useful pursuits in life. Clive shows contradictory responses to Walter Langer, the young German whom his mother has hired as the family tutor. Clive needs and wants the contact with an understanding, mature role model. At the same time, he is jealous of his mother's attraction to Walter, and therefore opposes Walter's efforts to become part of the Harrington family.

Home from Cambridge, Clive drinks to avoid parental control. Walter advises him to get out on his own but declines to travel with him during the coming holidays. Seeing Louise cradle Walter's head in her arms during a tender moment, Clive reports to Stanley that the two were engaged in lovemaking. Warmed by Walter's Continental graces—he is fluent in French, plays classical music on the piano and on his phonograph, and brings her wildflowers—Louise enjoys toying with the young man in somewhat the same fashion as she toys with Clive. When Walter makes it clear that he esteems her as a mother, though, Louise urges Stanley to fire Walter for being "a bad influence on Pamela."

Stanley, although he doubts that Clive's accusation is true, resents Walter's advice to Clive and uses the claim of an illicit relationship as a reason for dismissal. The lie is a very versatile weapon. It can help rid Stanley of the unwanted cost of the tutor and simultaneously serve vengeance on the young German for counseling Clive to leave home. It will punish Louise for her affectations. It will embarrass Clive—due vengeance for the boy's lack of filial piety—and weaken Clive's relationship with his mother, a bond Stanley could never match in his attempts at fathering and could never before attack so severely. Though he still understands his family no better than before, Stanley can dominate them all in one stroke.

Clive is shocked that the lie he told in private becomes his father's bludgeon in public. He realizes that his capacity to injure others is as great as that of his parents. Walter, who has opened himself to Clive and Louise in his bid for acceptance as a family member, cannot tolerate the betrayal, the victimization, resulting from his vulnerability. Walter's suicide attempt shows Clive the need for all the Harringtons to change: "The courage. For all of us. Oh God—give it."

THE ROYAL HUNT OF THE SUN

Pairs of one-act plays bracket Shaffer's epic drama *The Royal Hunt of the Sun*, which turns squarely to the issue of worship in both institutional and individual dimensions. Old Martin, the narrator, tells of his youthful adventure as page boy to Pizarro, conqueror of Peru. To Young Martin, Pizarro is a hero to worship. To the priests Valverde and De Nizza, military conquest is a necessary evil that will bring the Incas the good of institutional Christianity. To Estete, the Royal Overseer, Pizarro's personal ambition and the blessings of the Church are the necessary tools for advancing the dominion of King Carlos and thus for increasing his personal status within the king's domain. Pizarro takes the noble justifications of Church and State and the outright greed of his soldiers as the means for attaining personal glory. A hard man, he warns Young Martin never to trust him: He will surely betray anyone and anything in his drive for fame.

Atahuallpa, god-king of the Incas, believes the approaching Pizarro must be the White God of ancient legend returning as foretold. Estete declares to the Inca general, Challcuchima, that the Spanish come in the names of King Carlos of Spain and of Jesus Christ, the Son of God. Challcuchima insists that it is he who comes to them in the name of the Son of God—Atahuallpa, Son of the Sun. The two leaders are fascinated with each other. When cautioned against blasphemy in this duel of rank, Pizarro exclaims, "He is a God: I am a God."

Young Martin's faith in his hero and their cause is challenged when the Spanish massacre three thousand unarmed Inca warriors and capture Atahuallpa. Hernando de Soto gives the boy the stock rationale for the "huntsmen of God": "There must always be dying to make new life." Young Martin replaces a treacherous native translator for Pizarro and Atahuallpa and witnesses their growing kinship. The thirty-three-year-old Inca ruler learns Spanish and swordsmanship from his sixty-year-old captor. In return, Atahuallpa teaches Pizarro Inca songs and dances as the subdued empire collects gold to ransom its god-king.

Once the ransom is paid, Pizarro demands that Atahuallpa pledge that the Spanish will have safe passage out of Peru. He refuses, and Pizarro's officers insist that Atahuallpa must die. Though he himself has found no special meaning in his mother Church,

Pizarro persuades the Inca to accept Christian baptism. Without it, he would be burned to ashes. The god-king does not fear death; he believes his Father Sun will resurrect him. By accepting the rites of the Spanish Church, he earns death by strangulation and will leave a body to be restored.

There is no resurrection. Pizarro, however, weeps for his personal loss for the first time in his life and takes solace in the humanistic observation that at least Atahuallpa and he will be buried in the same earth under the same sun.

For Young Martin, Pizarro's betrayal of Atahuallpa is the end of faith: "Devotion never came again." Thus, Shaffer poses the high personal cost of trusting individuals and institutions further than they merit. The conquest was possible because Church and State accepted each other as justifications for destroying competing systems—and both fed on human greed and ambition. The Inca empire fell because its supreme ruler was convinced of his own divinity and was fascinated by the invader's claim of equal status. He never ordered a significant counterattack.

EQUUS

Shaffer gives a macrocosmic study of worship through the conflict of whole systems in *The Royal Hunt of the Sun*, with glimpses of the personal cost of faith in such systems in the lives of Atahuallpa, Pizarro, and Young Martin. *Equus*, by contrast, provides a detailed microcosmic study of the elements of worship. Seventeen-year-old Alan Strang has blinded six horses in the stable where he works. Hester Salomon, a magistrate and friend of psychiatrist Martin Dysart, brings the boy to Dysart for treatment. The psychoanalyst uncovers, little by little, the attitudes and symbols Alan has fashioned into a mysterious personal religion—worship of Equus, the horse-god.

Alan Strang is more than the average troubled adolescent of the usual domestic drama. He is the most isolated, most disturbed of all Shaffer's characters. The son of a printer and former schoolteacher, Alan is practically illiterate. His father forbids television in the home, so Alan sneaks off to watch Westerns at the neighbors' house. An avowed atheist, Frank Strang considers the religious instruction Dora gives to Alan just so much "bad sex." Dora, for her part, assures Alan that God sees him everywhere; she has read the Bible to him often. Alan especially enjoyed passages from Job and Revelation that refer to the strength and power of horses. Not wanting to interfere with her son, Dora allowed him to have a graphic poster of Christ being flogged by Roman centurions even though she believed it was a little "extreme." After an argument over religion, Frank once stormed into Alan's room and ripped the poster off the wall. Alan was devastated. A few weeks later, Frank gave Alan a picture of a horse, which Alan hung in the same spot at the foot of his bed. Frank once observed Alan chanting a genealogy, haltering himself with string, and beating himself with a coathanger before the horse picture. Frank never discussed sex with his son; Dora did so only in generalities that linked it with the love of God.

Shaffer opens both the first and second acts of *Equus* with Dysart pondering what the horse might want of Alan, and why, of all the things in the world "equal in their power to enslave . . . one suddenly strikes." When Dysart questions the propriety of "curing" Alan, whose exotic worship is "the core of his life," Hester Salomon assures the doctor that the boy must be relieved of his pain and helped to normal living. Expert in his profession, Dysart knows what he must do in order to lead the minds of troubled children into normal patterns, but he is himself led back to the borders of the rational, sensing something vital beyond: "that boy has known a passion more ferocious than I have felt in any second of my life. . . . I envy it."

The self-disclosure integral to Shaffer's drama, which built the dialogue and plot of *Five Finger Exercise* and which became a structural device as well via the narrator in *The Royal Hunt of the Sun*, rises to full force in *Equus*. Dysart is both narrator and protagonist. He relates the numerous episodes that present and then unravel the mystery of Alan's attack on the horses. Through his speeches to the audience about the plot and through his confidences shared with Hester Salomon as the protagonist within the action, Dysart exposes his own character, just as he exposes Alan's. Shaffer's use of games—which appears in the follow-the-leader ploy of *The Public Eye*, the pretended shock-treatment scene of *Shrivings*, and so on—is important in *Equus* as well. As Dysart elicits one disclosure after another from Alan, the boy extracts significant answers from Dysart in return. The methods of revelation become more intimate as the plot advances. Alan at first sings commercials when Dysart asks questions. He later divulges information via tape recordings. He finally responds in direct encounters, first with resistance, then relying on supposed hypnosis, and finally under the pretended use of a truth drug that allows him to reenact the events of the night he attacked the horses.

Alan had been out with Jill Mason, who suggested a tryst in the stable—the Holy of Holies for Equus. Alan's worship was so exclusive that his god blocked intimacy with any other. Caught between passion for another human being and passion for his horse-god—which, like his mother's God, could see him everywhere—Alan struck out to blind the god who thwarted his relationship with Jill Mason.

Martin Dysart concludes that he can lead Alan into a normal existence, but it will probably be a drab, routine life. He himself remains drawn to the nonrational source of human passion: "I need—more desperately than my children need me—a way of seeing in the dark." His need is marked with a remnant of the worship he is taking away from Alan; "There is now, in my mouth, this sharp chain. And it never comes out."

For Pizarro, the late attraction of a meaningful, dominating force appeared and died with Atahuallpa, a confident believer in an alien faith, but a faith with numerous parallels to the Christian tradition familiar to the conquistador. Pizarro had used his own religious heritage as a weapon for so long that he could only hope for meaning among a new set of symbols enlivened by a personal contact with the god-king the symbols supported. Martin Dysart's relationship with his patient also draws him into confrontation with passionate worship. The motion from Pizarro to Dysart, however, is an ideological step from a protagonist who concludes that human beings make their own gods to one who can destroy a god and still sense some force beyond human reason that endures regardless of whether the belief-system of a given worshiper is destroyed. Shaffer's next protagonist steps further into premises consistent with those of the Judeo-Christian tradition.

AMADEUS

Antonio Salieri continues Shaffer's trend of self-disclosing characters by serving as both narrator and protagonist of *Amadeus*. Old Martin and Young Martin in *The Royal Hunt of the Sun* give the narrator's view and the more passionate view of Pizarro's page, respectively, and are cast as separate characters who both may be onstage at once. Dysart serves as narrator and protagonist in turn for *Equus*, not needing a distinction in age for the separate facets of the character, because the story Dysart tells took place in the recent past. His explanations and deliberations unify the flow of cinematic scenes, which include recent events retold from Dysart's viewpoint and flashbacks to some more distant events in Alan's past. Salieri, too, serves as both narrator and protagonist, but he must bridge a temporal gap of decades, as must Old Martin. Shaffer keeps Salieri a single character, similar to Dysart, but has Salieri change costume onstage and specify the shifts in time—covering two different eras in his life through changes in the character before the eyes of the audience. The transitions are yet one more method for effecting character revelation without simply repeating a narrative technique.

Salieri is Shaffer's first protagonist to operate so nearly within traditional premises of religious devotion. Salieri interacts with a God anthropomorphic enough to respond to his prayers—but a deity shaped by the Salieri family's mercantile values. In his youth, Salieri knelt "before the God of Bargains" and prayed to be a composer. In return, he would live virtuously, help other musicians, and "honor God with much music." Mozart's appearance in Vienna threatens the established Salieri's self-esteem. Mozart the man is rash, vulgar, and obnoxious. For all the faults of the man, however, Salieri hears the voice of God in some of Mozart's music. He prays for such inspiration in his own work, since "music is God's art," but to no avail.

Salieri's star voice pupil, Katherina Cavalieri, sings the lead in Mozart's opera *The Abduction from the Seraglio* and has an affair with him as well. A jealous Salieri considers seducing Mozart's fiancée, Constanze, in revenge. Mozart marries Constanze, despite his father's objections, and struggles to support himself and his wife. Constanze Mozart approaches Salieri for help in securing an appointment for her husband. Salieri nearly exacts her virtue as the price for any assistance, but in the musical scores she has brought to further her husband's cause, Salieri has seen Absolute Beauty. He recognizes his own mediocrity and rages at his God, "To my last breath, I shall block You on earth as far as I am able!"

Narrator Salieri introduces act 2 as his "battle with God" in which "Mozart was the battleground." Salieri soon breaks his vow of virtue. Although he turns away a resentful offer of an interlude with Constanze, he takes Katherina Cavalieri as his mistress. Breaking his vow to help fellow musicians, he hinders Mozart's career whenever possible. He recommends that Mozart not be appointed to tutor the Princess Elizabeth. He does suggest that Mozart be appointed chamber composer after the death of Christoph Gluck—but at one tenth the former salary. Salieri is determined to "starve out the God." As Mozart thinks through the plot of *The Magic Flute*, Salieri raises the notion of using the rites and ideals of the Masonic order in the opera. The two composers were among many notables in Vienna who belonged to the lodge. As all the rituals and doctrines are to be kept secret, Mozart's stage parallels of Masonic practices alienate the very lodge brothers who have helped him to find what work he can get.

Alone and ailing, Mozart begs God for time to complete his *Requiem Mass*. He asks Salieri to speak for God and to explain the continual suffering of his adult years. Salieri declares, "God does not love! He can only use!"

Salieri lives to see Mozart's music come into vogue after the composer's death. His own music dies before he does. He takes this as his punishment; "I must survive to see myself become extinct." His claim to be Mozart's murderer is his last attack on God. If his fame cannot last, perhaps his infamy can. Even so negative a grasping for glory proves vain: No one really believes him.

Salieri's actions are reminiscent of those of the ancient Hebrew heroes who were held to covenants with their God. Salieri's assertion that his virtue merits blessing while Mozart's vices deserve punishment echoes a plaint recurrent in the Psalms. The pattern of Israel's God favoring the unworthy or the unlikely candidate for leadership—the naïve Gideon, the young shepherd David, and so on—also has its reflex in *Amadeus* as the esteemed court composer finds the voice of God in the music of an immature, foul-mouthed upstart. In a sense, Salieri also is a failed Cain. Jealous of God's favor to Mozart regardless of all of Salieri's musical and moral efforts, the aging narrator cannot even secure for himself the name of murderer. The biblical Cain bore a mark to signify his archetypal fratricide. Salieri cannot even invent the curse for himself. His God of Bargains wins the battle. Salieri gets no more and no less than he asked for when the bargain was struck, and he is punished for failing to keep his part of the covenant.

Thus, the trend of character revelation begun in the Harrington household persists. The issues of self-control versus domination by authority are broached from varying perspectives, institutional and individual, as Shaffer moves from a protagonist searching for self, through others searching for meaningful relationships with individuals, to characters exploring the human being's relationship to the structures and forces of the world at large. From *The Royal Hunt of the Sun* to *Shrivings* (which probes the limits of secular humanism as thoroughly as other plays challenge aspects of traditional religion) and on through *Equus* and *Amadeus*, Shaffer's protagonists become more overtly self-revealing and steadily more concerned with a focused search for meaning. Shaffer's mature use of a character's personal disclosures culminates in the award-winning cinematic narratives of *Equus* and *Amadeus*, in which there is a great passion to pursue, and in which the revelation of character shapes form, theme, and technique all at once.

THE GIFT OF THE GORGON

The Gift of the Gorgon combines naturalism of plot and dialogue with highly imaginative staging. Through the use of lighting, screens, and a wall that can part centrally into halves, one set becomes half a dozen or so locales. The action takes place during the years 1975 to 1993. The role of the playwright and the plays he or she writes is combined with elements of Greek mythology and the contemporary phenomenon of terrorism. *The Gift of the Gorgon* opened to mixed reviews in December 1992. Peter Hall, who directed the play, praised Shaffer for undertaking such a bold, ambitious task at his age (Shaffer was sixty-six years of age at the time). Hall asserts that most dramatists in their sixties are content to sit and collect their royalties.

The setting is a villa on the Greek island of Thera but often becomes England during scenes of recollection. The protagonist is Edward Damson, a once successful but now reclusive English playwright. He has Anglicized his name from Damsinski, that of his father, a whining, bigoted Russian émigré. Edward's wife is the former Helen Jarvis, whose father is a liberal Cambridge professor, a prominent member of the Peace League. Helen was a promising classical scholar until she gave up her own pursuits to devote herself totally to her husband and his career. Edward despises academic critics. Ironically, that is what his illegitimate son, Philip—never acknowledged by him—has become. As the play opens, Edward has recently died, and Philip has traveled to Thera to learn more about the father he never met. Helen is at first unwilling but does eventually review the Damson's eighteen-year relationship in a series of flashbacks. One of Edward's curious practices over those years was communicating with his wife through unpublished dramatic scenes he would leave on her pillow or in his desk where she would find them. In these scenes, Perseus, the Greek hero, represents Edward, and Athena, the goddess of wisdom, represents Helen. Early in their relationship, Athena-Helen empowers Perseus-Edward to slay the Gorgon, a monster so horrible that the beholder is turned to stone. The Gorgon represents Edward's initial inability to complete a play without his wife's inspiration.

Edward is a man of extremes, violent in language if not in behavior. The rational Helen persuades him to tone down violent scenes in his plays *Icons* and *Prerogative*, which become great successes. Later, after Edward has come to believe that Helen is more stultifying than inspiring, he writes a play, *I.R.E.*, about an Irish terrorist and a mother whose child he has killed. In the climactic scene (against which Helen has strongly recommended), the mother ritually murders the terrorist, then dances around his bloody corpse. The audience is repulsed, the play fails, and Edward exiles himself to Thera for the last five years of his life. There, he drinks, hangs about bars with pretty young tourists, and abuses Helen through total neglect. Eventually, the couple experiences something of a role reversal. The once pacific Helen writes a scene and leaves it in her husband's desk. In the scene, Athena tongue-lashes a cowering Perseus, concluding with the accusation that Perseus himself has become the Gorgon. Edward appears contrite but plots to have his wife deal him a mortal blow. The scene mimics Clytemnestra's murder of her husband, Agamemnon, in his bath in the classical tragedy, an act that Edward has earlier characterized as totally justified. He persuades Helen to give him a ritually cleansing shower, but he secretes a razor blade in the soap with which she will scrub his body. Philip, who has worshiped his father from afar, is forced to face the reality of his life and death.

As usual, Shaffer explores a moral subject, in this case vengeance in conflict with an all-encompassing forgiveness. He skillfully merges the classical and the contemporary. The choice of Helen's name is, of course, suggestive of classical restraint. Edward's surname (which he has consciously chosen, changing it from Damsinski) is evocative of his fate. The same is true for Philip, who has taken his father's name, as Edward complains, without permission. The play is almost fiendishly clever and ambiguous, so that at the final curtain the audience may ask: Just *what* is the gift of the Gorgon, and just *who* is the Gorgon?

OTHER MAJOR WORKS

LONG FICTION: *The Woman in the Wardrobe*, 1951 (as Peter Antony; with Anthony Shaffer); *How Doth the Little Crocodile?*, 1952 (as Peter Antony; with Anthony Shaffer); *Withered Murder*, 1955 (with Anthony Shaffer).

SCREENPLAYS: *The Public Eye*, 1972; *Equus*, 1977; *Amadeus*, 1984.

TELEPLAYS: *The Salt Land*, 1955; *Balance of Terror*, 1957.

RADIO PLAY: *The Prodigal Father*, 1955; *Whom Do I Have the Honour of Addressing?*, pr. 1989.

BIBLIOGRAPHY

Beckerman, Bernard. "The Dynamics of Peter Shaffer's Drama." In *The Play and Its Critic: Essays for Eric Bentley*, edited by Michael Bertin. Lanham, Md.: University Press of America, 1986. A structural study, especially of *Equus*, by one of the best dramatic critics of the twentieth century. Examines Shaffer's "binary form . . . the tendency of plays to be a sequence of scenes between two characters" in his work. This essay was originally given in 1983, in Shaffer's presence, at the Modern Language Association (MLA) convention in New York.

Cooke, Virginia, and Malcolm Page, comps. *File on Shaffer*. London: Methuen, 1987. An indispensable source of information in the Methuen series format. Contains brief comments, play by play (not including, however, *Lettice and Lovage*), and Shaffer's own comments on his methods of work, sedulous rewrites, film adaptations, and more. The production dates and publication information are more accessible here than in Eberle Thomas's work (below).

Gianakaris, Constantine J., ed. *Peter Shaffer: A Casebook*. New York: Garland Press, 1991. Volume 10 in the Casebooks on Modern Dramatists Series. Consists of a collection of essays on the playwright's work.

Klein, Dennis A. *Peter Shaffer*. Rev. ed. New York: Twayne, 1993. A combination of biographical and critical information.

Plunka, Gene A. *Peter Shaffer: Roles, Rites, and Rituals in the Theatre*. Rutherford, N.J.: Fairleigh Dickinson University Press, 1988. Disappointing in the absence of coverage of later plays but strong on *The Royal Hunt of the Sun*, *Equus*, and *Amadeus*. This work is part sociology and part mythology, and it is fed by an interview with the playwright in 1986. It contains occasional insights but is generally too scholarly to get at the essence of Shaffer's examination of the ways of God to humankind.

Taylor, John Russell. *Peter Shaffer*. London: Longman, 1974. A brief but provocative essay on Shaffer's contributions through *Equus*. Taylor sees detachment in this work and "a tendency to analyze emotions without too far engaging himself in them as a dramatist." He concludes, however, that "there is no guessing what he can do next, but it seems inevitable that it will be grand and glorious," a foresight of *Amadeus* and *Lettice and Lovage*. Select bibliography.

Thomas, Eberle. *Peter Shaffer: An Annotated Bibliography*. New York: Garland, 1991. A thorough checklist of work on Shaffer, from full-length studies (four) to dissertations and theses (six), to individual studies of plays through *Lettice and Lovage*. The introduction outlines the scope of the book and notes the paucity of biographical information on this private playwright, "the most widely produced and most popular of England's playwrights during the post-World War II era." A general chronology follows, but exact production information is found at each play's entry. Page-number index.

Trussler, Simon, et al., eds. *File on Shaffer*. Methuen Writer-Files series. Westport, Conn.: Methuen, 1988. A concise (eighty-eight-page) treatment of the plays through *Lettice and Lovage*.

Ralph S. Carlson, updated by Thomas J. Taylor and Patrick Adcock

WILLIAM SHAKESPEARE: THE DRAMATIST

PRINCIPAL DRAMA

Henry VI, Part I, wr. 1589-1590, pr. 1592, pb. 1623
Edward III, pr. c. 1589-1595, pb. 1596
Henry VI, Part II, pr. c. 1590-1591, pb. 1594
Henry VI, Part III, pr. c. 1590-1591, pb. 1595
Richard III, pr. c. 1592-1593, pb. 1597
The Comedy of Errors, pr. c. 1592-1594, pb. 1623
The Taming of the Shrew, pr. c. 1593-1594, pb. 1623
Titus Andronicus, pr., pb. 1594
The Two Gentlemen of Verona, pr. c. 1594-1595, pb. 1623
Love's Labour's Lost, pr. c. 1594-1595 (revised 1597 for court performance), pb. 1598
Romeo and Juliet, pr. c. 1595-1596, pb. 1597
Richard II, pr. c. 1595-1596, pb. 1600
A Midsummer Night's Dream, pr. c. 1595-1596, pb. 1600
King John, pr. c. 1596-1597, pb. 1623
The Merchant of Venice, pr. c. 1596-1597, pb. 1600
Henry IV, Part I, pr. c. 1597-1598, pb. 1598
The Merry Wives of Windsor, pr. 1597 (revised c. 1600-1601), pb. 1602
Henry IV, Part II, pr. 1598, pb. 1600
Much Ado About Nothing, pr. c. 1598-1599, pb. 1600
Henry V, pr. c. 1598-1599, pb. 1600
Julius Caesar, pr. c. 1599-1600, pb. 1623
As You Like It, pr. c. 1599-1600, pb. 1623
Hamlet, Prince of Denmark, pr. c. 1600-1601, pb. 1603
Twelfth Night: Or, What You Will, pr. c. 1600-1602, pb. 1623
Troilus and Cressida, pr. c. 1601-1602, pb. 1609
All's Well That Ends Well, pr. c. 1602-1603, pb. 1623
Othello, the Moor of Venice, pr. 1604, pb. 1622 (revised 1623)
Measure for Measure, pr. 1604, pb. 1623
King Lear, pr. c. 1605-1606, pb. 1608
Macbeth, pr. 1606, pb. 1623
Antony and Cleopatra, pr. c. 1606-1607, pb. 1623

Coriolanus, pr. c. 1607-1608, pb. 1623
Timon of Athens, pr. c. 1607-1608, pb. 1623
Pericles, Prince of Tyre, pr. c. 1607-1608, pb. 1609
Cymbeline, pr. c. 1609-1610, pb. 1623
The Winter's Tale, pr. c. 1610-1611, pb. 1623
The Tempest, pr. 1611, pb. 1623
The Two Noble Kinsmen, pr. c. 1612-1613, pb. 1634 (with John Fletcher)
Henry VIII, pr. 1613, pb. 1623 (with Fletcher)

Few dramatists can lay claim to the universal reputation achieved by William Shakespeare. His plays have been translated into many languages and performed on amateur and professional stages throughout the world. Radio, television, and film versions of the plays in English, German, Russian, French, and Japanese have been heard and seen by millions of people. The plays have been revived and reworked by many prominent producers and playwrights, and they have directly influenced the work of others. Novelists and dramatists such as Charles Dickens, Bertolt Brecht, William Faulkner, and Tom Stoppard, inspired by Shakespeare's plots, characters, and poetry, have composed works that attempt to re-create the spirit and style of the originals and to interpret the plays in the light of their own ages. A large and flourishing Shakespeare industry exists in England, America, Japan, and Germany, giving evidence of the playwright's popularity among scholars and the general public alike.

A PLAYWRIGHT FOR ALL TIME

Evidence of the widespread and deep effect of Shakespeare's plays on English and American culture can be found in the number of words and phrases from them that have become embedded in everyday usage: Expressions such as "star-crossed lovers" are used by speakers of English with no consciousness of their Shakespearean source. It is difficult to imagine what the landscape of the English language would be like without the mountain of neologisms and aphorisms contributed by the playwright. Writing at a time when English was quite pliable, Shakespeare's lin-

William Shakespeare (Library of Congress)

guistic facility and poetic sense transformed English into a richly metaphoric tongue.

Working as a popular playwright, Shakespeare was also instrumental in fusing the materials of native and classical drama in his work. *Hamlet, Prince of Denmark*, with its revenge theme, its ghost, and its bombastic set speeches, appears to be a tragedy based on the style of the Roman playwright Seneca, who lived in the first century C.E. Yet the hero's struggle with his conscience and his deep concern over the disposition of his soul reveal the play's roots in the native soil of English miracle and mystery dramas, which grew out of Christian rituals and depicted Christian legends. The product of this fusion is a tragedy that compels spectators and readers to examine their own deepest emotions as they ponder the effects of treacherous murder on individuals and the state. Except for Christopher Marlowe, the predecessor to whom Shakespeare owes a considerable debt, no other Elizabethan playwright was so successful in combining native and classical strains.

Shakespearean characters, many of whom are hybrids, are so vividly realized that they seem to have achieved a life independent of the worlds they inhabit. Hamlet stands as the symbol of a man who, in the words of the famous actor Sir Laurence Olivier, "could not make up his mind." Hamlet's name has become synonymous with excessive rationalizing and idealism. Othello's jealousy, Lear's madness, Macbeth's ambition, Romeo and Juliet's star-crossed love, Shylock's flinty heart—all of these psychic states and the characters who represent them have become familiar landmarks in Western culture. Their lifelikeness can be attributed to Shakespeare's talent for creating the illusion of reality in mannerisms and styles of speech. His use of the soliloquy is especially important in fashioning this illusion; the characters are made to seem fully rounded human beings in the representation of their inner as well as outer nature. Shakespeare's keen ear for conversational rhythms and his ability to reproduce believable speech between figures of high and low social rank also contribute to the liveliness of action and characters.

In addition, Shakespeare excels in the art of grasping the essence of relationships between husbands and wives, lovers, parents and children, and friends. Innocence and youthful exuberance are aptly represented in the fatal love of Romeo and Juliet; the destructive spirit of mature and intensely emotional love is caught in the affair between Antony and Cleopatra. Other relationships reveal the psychic control of one person by another (of Macbeth by Lady Macbeth), the corrupt soul of a seducer (Angelo in *Measure for Measure*), the twisted mind of a vengeful officer (Iago in *Othello*), and the warm fellowship of simple men (Bottom and his followers in *A Midsummer Night's Dream*). The range of emotional states manifested in Shakespeare's characters has never been equaled by succeeding dramatists.

These memorable characters have also been given memorable poetry to speak. In fact, one of the main strengths of Shakespearean drama is its synthesis of action and poetry. Although Shakespeare's poetic style is marked by the bombast and hyperbole that characterize much of Elizabethan drama, it also has a richness and concreteness that make it memorable and quotable. One need think only of Hamlet's "sea of troubles" or Macbeth's daggers "unmannerly breech'd with gore" to substantiate the imagistic power of Shakespearean verse. Such images are also worked into compelling patterns in the major plays, giving them greater structural unity than the plots alone provide. Disease imagery in *Hamlet, Prince of Denmark*, repeated references to blood in *Macbeth*, and allusions to myths of children devouring parents in *King Lear* represent only a few of the many instances of what has been called "reiterated imagery" in Shakespearean drama. Wordplay, puns, songs, and a variety of verse forms, from blank verse to tetrameter couplets—these features, too, contribute to the "movable feast" of Shakespeare's style.

In a more general sense, Shakespeare's achievement can be traced to the skill with which he used his medium—the stage. He created certain characters to fit the abilities of certain actors, as the role of Falstaff in the *Henry IV* and *Henry V* plays so vividly demonstrates. He made use of every facet of the physical stage—the trapdoor, the second level, the inner stage, the "heavens"—to create special effects or illusions. He kept always before him the purpose of entertaining his audience, staying one step ahead of changes in taste among theatergoers. That both kings and tinkers were able to find in a Shakespearean play something to delight and instruct them is testimony to the wide appeal of the playwright. No doubt the universality of his themes and his deep understanding of human nature combined to make his plays so popular. These same strengths generate the magnetic power that brings large audiences into theaters to see the plays today.

GROWTH OF THE DRAMATIST

William Shakespeare was born in Stratford-upon-Avon, England, probably on or near April 23, 1564. His father was John Shakespeare, a glovemaker and later bailiff (or mayor) of the town; his mother was Mary Arden, the daughter of a well-to-do landowner in nearby Wilmcote. His parents had eight children. Although no records exist to prove the fact, Shakespeare probably began attending a Stratford grammar school at six or seven years of age. There, he studied Latin grammar, literature, rhetoric and logic for be-

tween eight and ten hours a day, six days a week. William Lily's largely Latin text, *A Short Introduction of Grammar* (1527), was the staple of the course, but Shakespeare also read Cicero, Plautus, Terence, Vergil, and Ovid. Many of these authors influenced the playwright's later work; Ovid in particular was a favorite source of material, used in such plays as *A Midsummer Night's Dream* and *Romeo and Juliet*. Shakespeare probably knew very little of other languages, although he does exhibit an understanding of French in such plays as *Henry V* and *All's Well That Ends Well*. (The sources for most, if not all, of the plays existed in English translations published during Shakespeare's lifetime.)

Shakespeare may have left school around 1577, the year in which his father fell on hard times. Legend says the young man worked as a butcher's apprentice, but there is no proof to support this notion. His marriage to Anne Hathaway of Shottery took place in 1582; she was eight years his senior and pregnant at the time of the wedding. Whether Shakespeare felt obliged to marry her or simply took pity on her unfortunate predicament is yet another matter for speculation. Their first child, Susanna, was born in May, 1583, and in 1585, twins named Hamnet and Judith were born to the young couple. (It is interesting to note that by 1670, the last of Susanna's descendants died, thereby ending the Shakespeare family line.)

There is no evidence concerning Shakespeare's activities between 1585 and 1592. Legend asserts that he was forced to leave Stratford in order to escape punishment for poaching deer on the estate of Sir Thomas Lucy, one of Stratford's leading citizens. Another popular story has Shakespeare taking a position as schoolmaster at the grammar school, where he supposedly improved his Latin. None of these accounts can be substantiated by fact, yet they continue to seduce modern readers and playgoers. One intriguing suggestion is that Shakespeare joined a troupe of professional actors that was passing through Stratford in 1587. This company, called the Queen's Men, may have been in need of a new performer, since one of their members, William Knell, had been murdered in a brawl with a fellow actor.

SHAKESPEARE AND THE LONDON STAGE

In 1592, Robert Greene, a playwright and pamphleteer, attested Shakespeare's presence in London in a sneering remark about the young upstart whose "tiger's heart [is] wrapt in a player's hide." This reference is a parody of a line from one of Shakespeare's earliest plays, *Henry VI, Part III*. Greene's "Shakescene in a country" is clearly Shakespeare, who by this date was identifiable as both an actor and a playwright. Greene's remark also implies that the uneducated upstart had probably served an apprenticeship of a few years revising old plays, a practice that was common in this period. By 1594, Shakespeare had become a member of the Lord Chamberlain's Men, who were then performing at the Theatre in Shoreditch, to the north of the city. He continued as a member of this essentially stable company, which constructed the Globe Theatre in 1599 and, in 1603, became the King's Men, until he retired from the stage in 1611 or 1612. In part because of the popularity of Shakespeare's plays and in part because of the strong support of Elizabeth and James I, the company achieved considerable financial success. Shakespeare shared in that success by acquiring a one-tenth interest in the corporation. By 1596, he was able to purchase a coat of arms for his father, and in the next year, he acquired the second-best house in Stratford. This degree of prominence and success was unusual for someone in a profession that was not highly regarded in Renaissance England. Greene, Shakespeare's harsh critic, died a pauper, a condition that was typical of many Elizabethan playwrights.

Actors and playwrights were in fact regarded as entertainers whose companions were bearbaiters, clowns, and jugglers. Confirmation of this fact comes from evidence that some public theaters were used both for plays and for bearbaiting and bullbaiting. After 1590, moreover, the playhouses had to be constructed in the Bankside district, across the Thames from London proper. City fathers afraid of plague and opposed to public entertainments felt that the Bankside, notorious for its boisterous inns and houses of prostitution, was the fitting locale for "playing" of all kinds. Indeed, theatrical productions were not regarded as high art; when plays were published, by the company or by individual actors, apparently no effort was made to correct or improve them. As has already been pointed out, Shakespeare himself never corrected or took to the printer any of the plays attributed to him. Poetry was valued as true literature, and there is considerable evidence that Shakespeare hoped to become a recognized and respected poet like Sir Philip Sidney or Edmund Spenser. His poems of the early 1590's (*Venus and Adonis*, 1593, and *The Rape of Lucrece*, 1594) were immensely popular. Still, Shakespeare chose to become a public entertainer, a role that he played with convincing brilliance.

The company to which this best of the entertainers belonged was relatively small—fifteen or twenty players at most. The actors were generally well known to the audience, and their particular talents were exploited by the playwrights. Richard Burbage, the manager of Shakespeare's company for many years, was renowned for his skill in acting tragic parts, while William Kemp and Robert Armin were praised for their talents as comic actors. Shakespeare composed his plays with these actors in mind, a fact borne out by the many comedies featuring fat, drunken men such as Sir John Falstaff (of the *Henry IV* and *Henry V* plays) and Sir Toby Belch (of *Twelfth Night*). Shakespeare could not compose his works for an ideal company; he suited his style to the available talent.

Because his company was underwritten to some degree by the government, Shakespeare and his fellows were often called on to perform at court: 32 times during Elizabeth's reign and 177 times under James I. The king and queen did not venture to the Theatre or the Globe to mingle with the lower classes, depending instead on the actors to bring their wares to them. *Macbeth* was written as a direct compliment to James I: Banquo, the brave general treacherously murdered by the villainous hero, was one of James's ancestors. Shakespeare had to change the facts of history to pay the compliment, but the aim of pleasing his and the company's benefactor justified the change.

There were no women actors on Shakespeare's stage; they made their appearance when Charles II returned to the throne in 1660. Young boys (eleven to fourteen years old) played the female parts, and Shakespeare manipulated this convention with considerable success in his comedies, where disguises created delightful complications and aided him in overcoming the problem of costuming. The lady-disguised-as-page device is worked with particular effect in such plays as *As You Like It*, *Twelfth Night*, and *Cymbeline*.

Because there were few actors and sometimes many parts, members of the company were required to double (and sometimes triple) their roles. The effect of this requirement becomes evident when one notes that certain principal characters do not appear in consecutive scenes. One should likewise remember that performance on the Elizabethan stage was continuous; there was no falling curtain or set change to interrupt the action. No scenery to speak of was employed, although signs may have been used to designate cities or countries and branches may have been tied around pillars to signify trees. The absence of scenery allowed for a peculiar imaginative effect. A place on the stage that had been a throne room could within a few seconds become a hovel hiding its inhabitants from a fierce storm. Shakespeare and his contemporaries could thereby demonstrate the slippery course of Fortune, whose wheel, onstage and in real life, might turn at any moment to transform kings into beggars.

The apronlike stage jutted out into an area called "the pit," where the "groundlings," or those who paid the lowest admission fee (a penny), could stand to watch heroes perform great deeds. The octagon-shaped building had benches on the two levels above the pit for customers willing to pay for the privilege of sitting. Although estimates vary, it is now generally believed that the Globe could accommodate approximately twenty-five hundred people. The design of the stage probably evolved from the model of innyards, where the traveling companies of actors performed before they took up residence in London in the 1570's. On either side of the stage were two doors for entrances and exits and, at the back, some kind of inner stage behind which actors could hide and be discovered at the right moment. A trapdoor was located in the middle of the apron stage, while above it was a cupola-like structure that housed a pulley and chair. This chair could be lowered to the stage level when a *deus ex machina* (literally, a "god from a machine") was required to resolve the action. This small house also contained devices for making sound effects and may have been the place from which the musicians, so much a part of Elizabethan drama, sent forth their special harmonies. The little house was called "the heavens" (stars may have been painted on its underside), while the trapdoor was often referred to as "hell." For Shakespeare's Globe audience, then, the stage was a world in which the great figures of history and imagination were represented doing and speaking momentous things.

In 1608, the King's Men purchased an indoor theater, the Blackfriars, which meant that the company could perform year-round. This theater was located within the city proper, which meant that a somewhat more sophisticated audience attended the plays. Seating capacity was approximately seven hundred; there was no pit to stand in, and there is some evidence that the stage machinery was more elaborate than the equipment at the Globe. Some historians therefore argue that the plays written after 1608— *Cymbeline*, *Pericles, Prince of Tyre*, *The Winter's Tale*, *The Tempest*—were composed especially for performance at the Blackfriars. These tragicomedies or romances teem with special effects and supernatural characters, and this emphasis on spectacle differentiates them from Shakespeare's earlier comedies. Although such a theory is attractive, at least a few of these plays were also performed at the supposedly "primitive" Globe.

By 1608, Shakespeare had achieved the fame and recognition for which he had no doubt hoped. He was in a position to reduce his output to one or two plays per year, a schedule that probably allowed him to spend more time in Stratford with his family. In 1611, he left London for Stratford, returning from time to time to see plays performed at both theaters and possibly to engage in collaborative efforts with new playwrights such as John Fletcher. His last play, *Henry VIII*, was a collaboration with Fletcher; it was produced on June 29, 1613, a fateful day for the Globe. A spark from one of the cannon shot off during the performance set the thatched roof on fire and burned the building to the ground.

From 1613 until his death in 1616, Shakespeare led the life of a prosperous citizen in his native town. No doubt the happiest moment of this period came with the marriage of his daughter Judith in 1616. One of the persistent legends about the cause of the playwright's death is that he celebrated too vigorously at the reception with his friends Ben Jonson and Michael Drayton and contracted a fatal fever. Whatever the cause, Shakespeare died on April 23, 1616, and was buried in Holy Trinity Church. His epitaph gives no hint of the poetic strength that marked his plays, but it does express a concern common among men of his age:

> Good friend for Jesus sake forbear
> To dig the dust enclosed here.
> Blessed be the man that spares these stones
> And cursed be he that moves my bones.

THE HISTORY PLAYS

William Shakespeare began his career as a playwright by experimenting with plays in the three genres—comedy, history, and tragedy—that he would perfect as his career matured. The genre that dominated his attention throughout his early career, however, was history. Interest in the subject as proper stuff for drama was no doubt aroused by England's startling victory over Spain's vaunted navy, the Armada, in 1588. This victory fed the growing popular desire to see depictions of the critical intrigues and battles that had shaped England's destiny as the foremost Protestant power in Europe.

This position of power had been buttressed by the shrewd and ambitious Elizabeth I, England's "Virgin Queen," who, in the popular view, was the flower of the Tudor line. Many critics believe that Shakespeare composed the histories to trace the course of destiny that had led to the emergence of the Tudors as England's greatest kings and queens. The strength of character and patriotic spirit exhibited by Elizabeth seem to be foreshadowed by the personality of Henry V, the Lancastrian monarch who was instrumental in

building an English empire in France. Because the Tudors traced their line back to the Lancastrians, it was an easy step for Shakespeare to flatter his monarch and please his audiences with nationalistic spectacles that reinforced the belief that England was a promised land.

Whatever his reasons for composing the history plays, Shakespeare certainly must be seen as an innovator of the form, for which there was no model in classical or medieval drama. Undoubtedly, he learned much from his immediate predecessors, however—most notably from Christopher Marlowe, whose *Edward II* (pr. c. 1592) treated the subject of a weak king nearly destroying the kingdom through his selfish and indulgent behavior. From Marlowe, Shakespeare also inherited the idea that the purpose of the history play was to vivify the moral dilemmas of power politics and to apply those lessons to contemporary government. Such lessons were heeded by contemporaries, as is amply illustrated by Elizabeth's remark on reading about the life of one of her predecessors: "I am Richard II."

Shakespeare's contribution to the history-play genre is represented by two tetralogies (that is, two series of four plays), each covering a period of English history. He wrote two other plays dealing with English kings, *King John* and *Henry VIII*, but they are not specifically connected to the tetralogies in theme or structure. *Edward III*, written sometime between 1589 and 1595, is, on the other hand, closely related to the second tetralogy in theme, structure, and history. Edward III is the grandfather of Richard II, and his victories in France are repeated by Henry V. Muriel Bradbrook has pointed out the structural similarities between *Edward III* and *Henry V*. Like the second tetralogy as a whole, *Edward III* deals with the education of the prince. King Edward, like Prince Hal, at first neglects his duties and endangers the realm by placing personal pleasure above his country's needs. The Countess of Salisbury begins his education in responsibility, and Queen Philippa completes the process by teaching him compassion. By the end of the play, Edward has become what Shakespeare calls Henry V, "the mirror of all Christian kings."

HENRY VI, PART I

The first tetralogy concerns the period from the death of Henry V in 1422 to the death of Richard III at the Battle of Bosworth Field in 1485. Although he probably began this ambitious project in 1588, Shakespeare apparently did not compose the plays according to a strict chronological schedule. *Henry VI, Part I* is generally considered to have been written after the second and third parts of the Henry story; it may also have been a revision of another play. Using details from Raphael Holinshed's *Chronicles of England, Scotland, and Ireland* (1577) and Edward Hall's *The Union of the Two Noble and Illustre Families of Lancaster and York* (1548)—his chief chronicle sources for the plays in both tetralogies—Shakespeare created in *Henry VI, Part I* an episodic story of the adventures of Lord Talbot, the patriotic soldier who fought bravely to retain England's empire in France. Talbot fails and is defeated primarily because of a combination of intrigues by men such as the Bishop of Winchester and the indecisiveness of young King Henry VI. Here, as in the other history plays, England appears as the central victim of these human actions, betrayed and abandoned by men attempting to satisfy personal desires at the expense of the kingdom. The characters are generally two-dimensional, and their speeches reveal the excesses of Senecan bombast and hyperbole. Although a few of the scenes involving Talbot and Joan of Arc—as well as Talbot's death scene, in which his demise is made more painful by his having to witness a procession bearing his son's corpse—aspire to the level of high drama, the play's characters lack psychological depth, and the plot fails to demonstrate the unity of design that would mark Shakespeare's later history plays. Joan's nature as a strumpet-witch signals the role of other women characters in this tetralogy; Margaret, who will become England's queen, helps to solidify the victory that Joan cleverly achieves at the close of *Henry VI, Part I*. Henry V's French empire is in ruins and England's very soul seems threatened.

HENRY VI, PART II

Henry VI, Part II represents that threat in the form of what might be called "civil-war clouds." The play focuses on the further degeneration of rule under Henry, whose ill-considered marriage to the French Margaret precipitates a power struggle involving the two houses of York and Lancaster. By eliminating wise Duke Humphrey as the chief protector of the king, Margaret in effect seizes control of the throne. In the meantime, however, a rebellion is broached by Jack Cade, the leader of a group of anarchist commoners. This rebellion lends occasion for action and spectacle of the kind that is lacking in *Henry VI, Part I*. It also teaches a favorite Shakespearean lesson: The kingdom's "children" cannot be expected to behave when their "parents" do not. Scenes involving witchcraft, a false miracle, and single combat seem to prove that the country is reverting to a primitive, chaotic state. Though the uprising is finally put down, it provides the excuse for Richard, duke of York, and his ambitious sons to seize power. York precipitates a vengeful struggle with young Clifford by killing his father; in response, Clifford murders York's youngest son, the earl of Rutland. These murders introduce the theme of familial destruction, of fathers killing sons and sons killing fathers, which culminates in the brutal assassination of Prince Edward.

HENRY VI, PART III

As *Henry VI, Part III* begins, England's hopes for a strong successor to weak King Henry are dashed on the rocks of ambition and civil war. When Henry himself is murdered, one witnesses the birth of one of Shakespeare's most fascinating villain-heroes, Richard, duke of Gloucester. Although Richard's brother Edward becomes king and restores an uneasy peace, Shakespeare makes it clear that Richard will emerge as the political force of the future. Richard's driving ambition also appears to characterize the Yorkist cause, which, by contrast with the Lancastrian, can be described as self-destructive on the biblical model of the Cain and Abel story. While one is made to see Richard's wolfish disposition, however, Shakespeare also gives him a superior intellect and wit, which help to attract one's attention and interest. Displaying touches of the irony and cruelty that will mark his behavior in *Richard III*, Richard declares at the close of *Henry VI, Part III*: "See how my sword weeps for the poor king's death."

RICHARD III

In order to present Richard as an arch-villain, Shakespeare was obliged to follow a description of him that was based on a strongly prejudiced biographical portrait written by Sir Thomas More. More painted Richard as a hunchback with fangs, a beast so cruel that he did not flinch at the prospect of murdering the young princes. To More—and to Shakespeare—Richard must be viewed as another Herod; the imagery of the play also regularly compares him to a boar or hedgehog, beasts that know no restraint. Despite these repulsive features, Richard proves to be a consummate actor, outwitting and outperforming those whom he regards as victims. The most theatrical scene in the play is his wooing of the Lady Anne, who is drawn to him despite the knowledge that he has killed her husband (Prince Edward) and father-in-law, whose corpse she is in the process of accompanying to its grave. Many of the audacious wooing tricks used in this scene suggest that one of the sources for Richard's character is the Vice figure from medieval drama.

Richard III documents the breakneck pace and mounting viciousness of Richard's course to the throne. (Steeplechase imagery recurs throughout, culminating in the picture of Richard as an unseated rider trying desperately to find a mount.) He arranges for the murder of his brother Clarence, turns on former supporters such as Hastings and Buckingham, whom he seemed to be grooming for office, and eventually destroys the innocent princes standing in his path. This latter act of barbarism qualifies as a turning point, since Richard's victories, which have been numerous and easily won, now begin to evaporate at almost the same rate of speed. While Richard moves with freedom and abandon from one bloody deed to another, he is hounded by the former Queen Margaret, who delivers curses and prophecies against him in the hope of satisfying her vengeful desires. She plays the role of a Senecan fury, even though her words prove feeble against her Machiavellian foe. Retribution finally comes, however, in the character of the Lancastrian Earl of Richmond, who defeats Richard at Bosworth Field. On the eve of the battle, Richard's victims visit his sleep to announce his fall,

and for the first time in the play, he experiences a twinge of conscience. Unable to respond by confessing and asking forgiveness, Richard fights fiercely, dying like a wounded animal that is finally cornered. With Richmond's marriage to Elizabeth York, the Wars of the Roses end, and England looks forward to a prosperous and peaceful future under Henry Richmond, founder of the Tudor line.

KING JOHN

Whether Shakespeare wrote *King John* in the period between the first and second tetralogies is not known, but there is considerable support for the theory that he did. In the play, he depicts the career of a monarch who reigned into the thirteenth century and who defied papal authority, behavior that made him into something of a Protestant hero for Elizabethans. Shakespeare's John, however, lacks both the dynamism and the charisma of Henry V; he is also guilty of usurping the throne and arranging for the death of the true heir, Arthur. This clouded picture complicates the action and transforms John into a man plagued by guilt. Despite his desire to strengthen England and challenge the supremacy of Rome, John does not achieve either the dimensions of a tragic hero or the sinister quality of a consummate villain; indeed, his death seems anticlimactic. The strongest personality in the play belongs to Faulconbridge the Bastard, whose satiric commentary on the king's maneuvering gives way to patriotic speeches at the close. Faulconbridge speaks out for Anglo-Saxon pride in the face of foreign challenge, but he has also played the part of satirist-onstage throughout much of the action. Something of the same complexity of character will be seen in Prince Hal, the model fighter and king of the second tetralogy. In *King John*, Shakespeare managed only this one touch of brilliant characterization in an otherwise uninteresting and poorly constructed play. He may have been attempting an adaptation of an earlier chronicle drama.

RICHARD II

Shakespeare began writing the second tetralogy, which covers the historical period from 1398 to 1422, in 1595. The first play in this group was *Richard II*, a drama which, like the *Henry VI* series, recounts the follies of a weak king and the consequences of these actions for England. Unlike Henry, however, Richard is a personage with tragic potential; he speaks the language of a poet and possesses a self-dramatizing talent. Richard invites his fall—the fall of princes, or *de casibus virorum illustrium*, being a favorite Elizabethan topic that was well represented in the popular *A Mirror for Magistrates* (first published under Elizabeth I in 1559, although printed earlier under Queen Mary)—by seizing the land of the deceased John of Gaunt to pay for his war preparations against Ireland. This dubious act brings Henry Bolingbroke, Gaunt's son, rushing back from France, where he had been exiled by Richard, for a confrontation with the king. The result of their meeting is Richard's sudden deposition—he gives up the crown almost before he is asked for it—and eventual death, which is so movingly rendered that many critics have been led to describe this as a tragedy rather than a political play. Such a reading must overlook the self-pitying quality in Richard; his actions rarely correspond to the quality of his speech. Yet there has been little disagreement about Shakespeare's achievement in advancing the history-play form by forging a world in which two personalities, one vacillating, the other resourceful, oppose each other in open conflict. *Richard II* likewise qualifies as the first play in which Shakespeare realizes the theme of the fall by means of repeated images comparing England to a garden. Richard, the gardener-king, has failed to attend to pruning; rebels, like choking weeds, grow tall and threaten to blot out the sun. Because Bolingbroke usurps the crown and later arranges for Richard's death, however, he is guilty of watering the garden with the blood of England's rightful—if foolish—ruler. The result must inevitably be civil war, which is stirringly prophesied by the Bishop of Carlisle as the play draws to a close: "The blood of English shall manure the ground,/ And future ages groan for this foul act."

HENRY IV, PART I

The civil strife that Carlisle predicted escalates in *Henry IV, Part I*. Bolingbroke, now King Henry IV, is planning a crusade in the midst of a serious battle involving rebels in the north and west of Britain. This obliviousness to responsibility is clearly motivated by Henry's guilt over the seizing of the crown and Richard's murder. It will take the courage and ingenuity of his son, Prince Hal, the future Henry V, to save England and to restore the order of succession that Shakespeare and his contemporaries saw as the only guarantee of peaceful rule. Thus, *Henry IV, Part I* is really a study of the rise of Hal, who in the opening of the play appears to be a carefree time waster, content with drinking, gambling, and carousing with a motley group of thieves and braggarts led by the infamous coward Sir John Falstaff. Using a kind of Aristotelian mode of characterization, Shakespeare reveals Hal as a balanced hero who possesses the wit and humanity of Falstaff, without the debilitating drunkenness and ego, and the physical courage and ambition of Henry Hotspur, the son of the earl of Northumberland and chief rebel, without his destructive choler and impatience.

The plot of *Henry IV, Part I* advances by means of comparison and contrast of the court, tavern, and rebel worlds, all of which are shown to be in states of disorder. Hal leaves the tavern world at the end of the second act with an explicit rejection of Falstaff's fleshly indulgence; he rejoins his true father and leads the army in battle against the rebels, who are unable to organize the English, Welsh, and Scottish factions of which they are formed. They seem to be leaderless—and "fatherless." Above all, Hal proves capable of surprising both his own family and the rebels, using his reputation as a madcap to fullest advantage until he is ready to throw off his disguise and defeat the bold but foolish Hotspur at Shrewsbury. This emergence is nicely depicted in imagery associated by Hal himself with the sun (punning on "son") breaking through the clouds when least suspected. Falstaff demonstrates consistency of character in the battle by feigning death; even though Hal allows his old friend to claim the prize of Hotspur's body, one can see the utter bankruptcy of the Falstaffian philosophy of self-preservation.

HENRY IV, PART II

In *Henry IV, Part II*, the struggle against the rebels continues. Northumberland, who failed to appear for the Battle of Shrewsbury because of illness, proves unable to call up the spirit of courage demonstrated by his dead son. Glendower, too, seems to fade quickly from the picture, like a dying patient. The main portion of the drama concerns what appears to be a replay of Prince Hal's reformation. Apparently Shakespeare meant to depict Hal's acquisition of honor and valor at the close of *Henry IV, Part I*, while *Part II* traces his education in the virtues of justice and rule. Falstaff is again the humorous but negative example, although he lacks the robustness in sin that marked his character in *Part I*. The positive example or model is the Lord Chief Justice, whose sobriety and sense of responsibility eventually attract Hal to his side. As in *Part I*, Shakespeare adopts the structure of a medieval morality play to depict the rejection of the "bad" angel (or false father) and the embracing of the "good" one (or spiritual father) by the hero. The banishment of Falstaff and his corrupt code takes place during the coronation procession. It is a particularly poignant moment—to which many critics object, since Hal's harshness seems so uncharacteristic and overdone—but this scene is well prepared for by Hal's promise, at the end of act 2 in *Part I*, that he would renounce the world and the flesh at the proper time. The example of Hal's father, whose crown Hal rashly takes from his pillow before his death, demonstrates that for the king there can be no escape from care, no freedom to enjoy the fruits of life. With the Lord Chief Justice at his side, Hal prepares to enter the almost monklike role that the kingship requires him to play.

Henry V

It is this strong and isolated figure that dominates *Henry V*, the play that may have been written for the opening of the Globe Theatre. Appropriately enough, the Chorus speaker who opens the play asks if "this wooden O" can "hold the vasty fields of France," the scene of much of the epic and episodic action. Hal shows himself to be an astute politician—he outwits and traps the rebels Scroop, Cambridge, and Grey— and a heroic leader of men in the battle scenes. His rejection of Falstaff, whose death is recounted here in tragicomic fashion by Mistress Quickly, has transformed Hal's character into something cold and unattractive. There is little or no humor in the play. Yet when Hal moves among his troops on the eve of the

Battle of Agincourt, he reveals a depth of understanding and compassion that helps to humanize his character. His speeches are masterpieces of political rhetoric, even though Pistol, the braggart soldier, tries to parody them. "Once more into the breach, dear friends, once more . . ." introduces one of the best-known prebattle scenes in the language.

With the defeat of the French at Agincourt, Hal wins an empire for England, strengthening the kingdom that had been so sorely threatened by the weakness of Richard II. Both tetralogies depict in sharp outline the pattern of suffering and destruction that results from ineffective leadership. In Henry VII and Henry V, one sees the promise of peace and empire realized through the force of their strong, patriotic identities. At the close of *Henry V*, the hero's wooing of Katherine of France, with its comic touches resulting from her inability to speak English, promises a wedding that will take place in a new garden from which it is hoped humankind will not again fall. The lesson for the audience seems to be that under Elizabeth, the last Tudor monarch, England has achieved stability and glory, and that this role of European power was foreshadowed by the victories of these earlier heroes. Another clear lesson is that England cannot afford another civil war; some capable and clearly designated successor to Elizabeth must be chosen.

Henry VIII

Shakespeare's last drama dealing with English history, a probable collaboration with Henry Fletcher, is *Henry VIII*, which is normally classed with romances such as *The Tempest* and *Cymbeline*. It features none of the military battles typical of earlier history plays, turning instead for its material to the intrigues of Henry's court. The play traces the falls of three famous personages, the duke of Buckingham, Katherine of Aragon, and Cardinal Wolsey. Both Buckingham and Queen Katherine are innocent victims of fortune, while Wolsey proves to be an ambitious man whose scheming is justly punished. Henry seems blind and self-satisfied through much of the play, which is dominated by pageantry and spectacle, but in his judgment against Wolsey and his salvation of Cranmer, he emerges as something of a force for divine justice. The plot ends with the christening of Elizabeth and a prophecy about England's glorious future under her reign. Shakespeare's audience knew, however, that those atop Fortune's wheel at the close—Cranmer and Anne Bullen, in particular—would soon be brought down like the others. This last of Shakespeare's English history plays, then, sounds a patriotic but also an ironic note.

THE COMEDIES

Of the plays that are wholly or partly attributed to Shakespeare, nearly half have been classified as comedies. In addition, many scenes in plays such as *Henry IV, Part I* and *Romeo and Juliet* feature comic characters and situations. Even in the major tragedies, one finds scenes of comic relief: the Porter scene in *Macbeth*, the encounters between the Fool and Lear in *King Lear*, Hamlet's inventive punning and lugubrious satire. There can be little doubt that Shakespeare enjoyed creating comic situations and characters and that audiences came to expect such fare on a regular basis from the playwright.

THE COMEDY OF ERRORS

In his first attempt in the form, *The Comedy of Errors*, Shakespeare turned to a source—Plautus, the Roman playwright—with which he would have become familiar at Stratford's grammar school. Based on Plautus's *Menaechmi* (*The Twin Menaechmi*, 1595), the comedy depicts the misadventures of twins who, after several incidents involving mistaken identity, finally meet and are reunited. The twin brothers are attended by twin servants, compounding the possibilities for humor growing out of mistaken identity. Considerable buffoonery and slapstick characterize the main action involving the twins—both named Antipholus—and their servants. In one hilarious scene, Antipholus of Ephesus is turned away from his own house by a wife who believes he is an impostor. This somewhat frivolous mood is tempered by the presence of the twins' father in the opening and closing scenes. At the play's opening, Egeon is sentenced to death by the Duke of Ephesus; the sentence will be carried out unless someone can pay a ransom set at one thousand marks. Egeon believes that his wife and sons are dead, which casts him deep into the pit of despair. By the play's close, Egeon has been saved from the duke's sentence and has been reunited with his wife, who has spent the many years of their separation as an abbess. This happy scene of reunion and regeneration strikes a note that will come to typify the resolutions of later Shakespearean comedy. Providence appears to smile on those who suffer yet remain true to the principle of family.

Shakespeare also unites the act of unmasking with the concept of winning a new life in the fifth act of *The Comedy of Errors*. Both Antipholus of Syracuse, who in marrying Luciana is transformed into a "new man," and Dromio of Ephesus, who is freed to find a new life, acquire new identities at the conclusion. The characters are, however, largely interchangeable and lacking in individualizing traits. Types rather than full-blown human beings people the world of the play, thus underscoring the theme of supposing or masking. Shakespeare offers a gallery of familiar figures—young lovers, a pedantic doctor, a kitchen maid, merchants, and a courtesan—all of whom are identified by external traits. They are comic because they behave in predictably mechanical ways. Dr. Pinch, the mountebank based on Plautus's *medicus* type, is a good example of this puppetlike caricaturing. The verse is designed to suit the speaker and occasion, but it also reveals Shakespeare's range of styles; blank verse, prose, rhymed stanzas, and alternating rhymed lines can be found throughout the play. This first effort in dramatic comedy was an experiment using numerous Plautine elements, but it also reveals, in the characters Egeon and Emilia, the playwright's talent for humanizing even the most typical of characters and for creating life and vigor in stock situations.

THE TAMING OF THE SHREW

In *The Taming of the Shrew*, Shakespeare turned to another favorite source for the theme of transformation: Ovid's *Metamorphoses* (c. 8 C.E.; English translation, 1567). He had already used this collection for his erotic poems *Venus and Adonis* and *The Rape of Lucrece*; now he plundered it for stories about pairs of lovers and the changes effected in their natures by the power of love. In *The Taming of the Shrew*, he was also improving on an earlier play that dealt with the theme of taming as a means of modifying human behavior. Petruchio changes Kate's conduct by regularly praising her "pleasant, gamesome" nature. By the end of the play, she has been tamed into behaving like a dutiful wife. (Her sister Bianca, on the other hand, has many suitors, but her father will not allow Bianca to marry until Kate has found a husband.) The process of taming sometimes involves rough and boisterous treatment—Petruchio withholds food from his pupil, for example—as well as feigned madness: Petruchio whisks his bride away from the wedding site as if she were a damsel in distress and he were playing the role of her rescuer. In the end, Kate turns out to be more pliant than her sister, suggesting that an ideal wife, like a bird trained for the hunt, must be instructed in the rules of the game.

Shakespeare reinforces the theme of transformation by fashioning a subplot featuring a drunken tinker named Christopher Sly, who believes he has been made into a lord during a ruse performed by a fun-loving noble and his fellows. The Sly episode is not resolved because this interlude ends with the play's first scene, yet by employing this framing device, Shakespeare invites a comparison between Kate and Sly, both of whom are urged to be "better" than they thought they were.

THE TWO GENTLEMEN OF VERONA

The Two Gentlemen of Verona takes a comic tack that depends less on supposing than on actual disguise. Employing a device he would later perfect in *As You Like It* and *Twelfth Night*, Shakespeare put his heroine Julia in a page's outfit in order to woo her beloved Proteus. The main theme of the comedy is the rocky nature of love as revealed in male friendship and romantic contest. Valentine, Proteus's friend, finds him to be fickle and untrue to the courtly code when Proteus tries to force his affections on Silvia, Valentine's love. Although Proteus deserves worse punishment than he receives, he is allowed to find in Julia the true source of the romantic love that he has been seeking throughout the play. These pairs of lovers and their clownish servants, who engage in frequent bouts of punning and of horseplay, perform their rituals—anatomizing lovers, trusting false companions—in a forest world that seems to work its

magic on them by bringing about a happy ending. As in the other festive comedies, *The Two Gentlemen of Verona* concludes with multiple marriages and a mood of inclusiveness that gives even the clowns their proper place in the celebration. The passion of love has led Proteus (whose name, signifying "changeable," symbolizes fickleness) to break oaths and threaten friendships, but in the end, it has also forged a constant love.

LOVE'S LABOUR'S LOST

After this experiment in romantic or festive (as opposed to bourgeois) comedy, Shakespeare next turned his hand to themes and characters that reflect the madness and magic of love. *Love's Labour's Lost* pokes fun at florid poetry, the "taffeta phrases [and] silken terms precise" that typified Elizabethan love verses. There is also a satiric strain in this play, which depicts the foiled attempt of male characters to create a Platonic utopia free of women. The King of Navarre and his court appear ludicrous as, one by one, they violate their vows of abstinence in conceits that gush with sentiment. Even Berowne, the skeptic-onstage, proves unable to resist the temptations of Cupid. As if to underscore the foolishness of their betters, the clowns and fops of this comic world produce an interlude featuring the Nine Worthies, all of whom overdo or distort their roles in the same way as the lover-courtiers have distorted theirs. (This interlude was also the playwright's first attempt at a play-within-a-play.) When every Jack presumes to claim his Jill at the close, however, Shakespeare deputizes the princess to postpone the weddings for one year while the men do penance for breaking their vows. The women here are victorious over the men, but only for the purpose of forcing them to recognize the seriousness of their contracts. Presumably the marriages to come will prove constant and fulfilling, but at the end of this otherwise lighthearted piece, Shakespeare interjects a surprising note of qualification. Perhaps this note represents his commentary on the weight of words, which the courtiers have so carelessly—and sometimes badly—handled.

A MIDSUMMER NIGHT'S DREAM

In *A Midsummer Night's Dream*, Shakespeare demonstrates consummate skill in the use of words to create illusion and dreams. Although he again presents pairs of young lovers whose fickleness causes them to fall out of, and then back into, love, these characters display human dimensions that are missing in the character types found in the earlier comedies. The multiple plots concern not only the lovers' misadventures but also the marriage of Duke Theseus and Hippolyta, the quarrel between Oberon and Titania, king and queen of the fairy band, and the bumbling rehearsal and performance of the play-within-a-play *Pyramus and Thisbe* by Bottom and his companions. All of these actions illustrate the themes of love's errant course and of the power of illusion to deceive the senses. The main action, as in *The Two Gentlemen of Verona*, takes place in a wood, this time outside Athens and at night. The fairy powers are given free rein to deceive the mortals who chase one another there. Puck, Oberon's servant, effects deception of the lovers by mistakenly pouring a potion in the wrong Athenian's eyes. By the end of the play, however, the young lovers have found their proper partners, Oberon and Titania have patched up their quarrel, and Bottom, whose head was changed into that of an ass and who was wooed by the enchanted Titania while he was under this spell, rejoins his fellows to perform their tragic and comic interlude at the wedding reception. This afterpiece is a burlesque rendition of the story of Pyramus and Thisbe, whose tale of misfortune bears a striking resemblance to that of Romeo and Juliet. Through the device of the badly acted play-within-the-play, Shakespeare instructs his audience in the absurdity of lovers' Petrarchan vows and in the power of imagination to transform the bestial or the godlike into human form. In design and execution, *A Midsummer Night's Dream*, with its variety of plots and range of rhyme and blank verse, stands out as Shakespeare's most sophisticated early comedy.

THE MERCHANT OF VENICE

The Merchant of Venice shares bourgeois features with *The Taming of the Shrew* and *The Two Gentlemen of Verona*, but it has a much darker, near-tragic side, too. Shylock's attempt to carve a pound of flesh from the merchant Antonio's heart has all the ingredients of tragedy: deception, hate, ingenuity, and re-

venge. His scheme is frustrated only by the superior wit of the heroine Portia during a trial scene in which she is disguised as a young boy judge. Requiring Shylock to take nothing more than is specified in his bond, while at the same time lecturing him on the quality of mercy, Portia's speeches create the elements of tension and confrontation that will come to epitomize the playwright's mature tragedies. With the defeat and conversion of Shylock, the pairs of lovers can escape the threatening world of Venice and hope for uninterrupted happiness in Belmont, Portia's home. Venice, the scene of business, materialism, and religious hatred, is contrasted with Belmont (or "beautiful world"), the fairy-tale kingdom to which Bassanio, Antonio's friend, has come to win a fair bride and fortune by entering into a game of choice involving golden, silver, and leaden caskets. Though the settings are contrasted and the action of the play alternates between the two societies, Shakespeare makes his audience realize that Portia, like Antonio, is bound to a contract (set by her dead father) which threatens to destroy her happiness. When Bassanio chooses the leaden casket, she is freed to marry the man whom she would have chosen for her own. Thus "converted" (a metaphor that refers one back to Shylock's conversion), Portia then elects to help Antonio, placing herself in jeopardy once again. Portia emerges as Shakespeare's first major heroine-in-disguise, a character-type central to his most stageworthy and mature comedies, *Twelfth Night* and *As You Like It*.

MUCH ADO ABOUT NOTHING

Much Ado About Nothing likewise has a dark side. The main plot represents the love of Claudio and Hero. Hero's reputation is sullied by the melodramatic villain Don Juan. Claudio confronts his supposedly unfaithful partner in the middle of their wedding ceremony, his tirade causing her to faint and apparently expire. The lovers are later reunited, however, after Claudio recognizes his error. This plot is paralleled by one involving Beatrice and Benedick, two witty characters who in the play's beginning are set against each other in verbal combat. Like Claudio and Hero, they are converted into lovers who overcome selfishness and pride to gain a degree of freedom in their new relationships. The comedy ends with the marriage of Claudio and Hero and the promise of union between Beatrice and Benedick.

A central comic figure in the play is Dogberry, the watchman whose blundering contributes to Don Juan's plot but is also the instrument by which his villainy is revealed. His behavior, especially his hilariously inept handling of legal language, is funny in itself, but it also illustrates a favorite Shakespearean theme: Clownish errors often lead to happy consequences. Like Bottom in *A Midsummer Night's Dream*, Dogberry and his men are made an important part of the newly transformed society at the end of the play.

As You Like It

As You Like It and *Twelfth Night* are widely recognized as Shakespeare's wittiest and most stageworthy comedies; they also qualify as masterpieces of design and construction. In *As You Like It*, the action shifts from the court of Duke Frederick, a usurper, to the forest world of Arden, the new "court" of ousted Duke Senior. His daughter Rosalind enters the forest world in disguise, along with her friend Celia, to woo and win the young hero Orlando, forced to wander by his brother Oliver, another usurping figure. Although his florid verses expressing undying love for Rosalind are the object of considerable ridicule, Orlando earns the title of true lover worthy of Rosalind's hand. She proves successful in winning the support of the audience by means of her clever manipulation of Orlando from behind her mask. His inept poetry and her witty commentary can be taken "as we like it," as can the improbable conversions of Oliver and Duke Frederick that allow for a happy ending. Two characters— Touchstone, the clown, and Jacques (pronounced JAYK weez), the cynical courtier—represent extreme attitudes on the subjects of love and human nature. Touchstone serves as Rosalind's protector and as a sentimental observer, commenting wistfully and sometimes wittily on his own early days as a lover of milkmaids. Jacques, the trenchant commentator on the "Seven Ages of Man," sees all this foolery as further evidence, along with political corruption and ambition, of humankind's fallen state. He remains outside the circle of happy couples at the end of the play, a poignant, melancholy figure. His state of self-centeredness, it might be argued, is also "as we like it" when our moods do not identify so strongly with youthful exuberance.

Twelfth Night

Twelfth Night also deals with the themes of love and self-knowledge. Like *As You Like It*, it features a disguised woman, Viola, as its central figure. Motifs from other earlier Shakespearean comedies are also evident in *Twelfth Night*. Viola and Sebastian are twins (a motif found in *The Comedy of Errors*) who have been separated in a shipwreck but, unknown to each other, have landed in the same country, Illyria. From *The Two Gentlemen of Verona*, Shakespeare took the motif of the disguised figure serving as page to the man she loves (Duke Orsino) and even playing the wooer's role with the woman (Olivia) whom the duke wishes to marry. Complications arise when Olivia falls in love with Viola, and the dilemma is brought to a head when Orsino threatens to kill his page in a fit of revenge. Sebastian provides the ready solution to this dilemma, but Shakespeare holds off introducing the twins to each other until the last possible moment, creating effective comic tension. The play's subplot involves an ambitious and vain steward, Malvolio, who, by means of a counterfeited letter (the work of a clever servant named Maria), is made to believe that Olivia loves him. The scene in which Malvolio finds the letter and responds to its hints, while being observed not only by the theater audience but also by an audience onstage, is one of the funniest stretches of comic pantomime in drama. When Malvolio attempts to woo his mistress, he is thought mad and is cast in prison. Although he is finally released (not before being tormented by Feste the clown in disguise), Malvolio does not join the circle of lovers in the close, vowing instead to be revenged on all those who deceived him. In fact, both Feste and Malvolio stand apart from the happy company, representing the dark, somewhat melancholy clouds that cannot be dispelled in actual human experience. By this stage in his career, Shakespeare had acquired a vision of comedy crowded by elements and characters that would be fully developed in the tragedies.

THE MERRY WIVES OF WINDSOR

The Merry Wives of Windsor was probably composed before Shakespeare reached the level of maturity reflected in *As You Like It* and *Twelfth Night*. Legend suggests that he interrupted his work on the second history cycle to compose the play in two weeks for Queen Elizabeth, who wished to see Falstaff (by then familiar from the history plays) portrayed as a lover. What Shakespeare ended up writing was not a romantic but instead a bourgeois comedy that depicts Falstaff attempting to seduce Mistress Ford and Mistress Page, both wives of Windsor citizens. He fails, but in failing he manages to entertain the audience with his bragging and his boldness. Shakespeare may have been reworking an old play based on a Plautine model; in one of Plautus's plays, there is a subplot in which a clever young man (Fenton) and his beloved manage to deceive her parents in order to get married. This is the only strain of romance in the comedy, whose major event is the punishment of Falstaff: He is tossed into the river, then singed with candles and pinched by citizens disguised as fairies. Critics who see Falstaff as the embodiment of Vice argue that this punishment has symbolic weight; his attempted seduction of honest citizens' wives makes him a threat to orderly society. Regardless of whether this act has a ritual purpose, the character of Falstaff, and the characters of Bardolph, Pistol, and Justice Shallow, bear little resemblance to the comic band of *Henry IV, Part I*. In fact, *The Merry Wives of Windsor* might be legitimately seen as an interlude rather than a fully developed comedy, and it is a long distance from the more serious, probing dramas Shakespeare would soon create.

ALL'S WELL THAT ENDS WELL

All's Well That Ends Well and *Measure for Measure* were composed during a period when Shakespeare was also writing his major tragedies. Because they pose questions about sin and guilt that are not satisfactorily resolved, many critics have used the terms "dark comedies" or "problem plays" to describe them. *All's Well That Ends Well* features the familiar disguised heroine (Helena) who pursues the man she loves (Bertram) with skill and determina-

tion. The play differs from the earlier romantic comedies, however, because the hero rejects the heroine, preferring instead to win honor and fame in battle. Even though Helena is "awarded" the prize of Bertram by the King of France, whom she has cured of a near-fatal disease, she must don her disguise and pursue him while undergoing considerable suffering and hardship. In order to trap him, moreover, she must resort to a "bed trick," substituting her body for that of another woman whom Bertram plans to seduce. When Bertram finally assents to the union he bears little resemblance to comic heroes such as Orlando or Sebastian; he could be seen in fact as more a villain (or perhaps a cad) than a deserving lover. The forced resolution makes the play a "problem" for many critics, but for Shakespeare and his audience, the ingenuity of Helena and the multiple marriages at the close probably satisfied the demands of romantic comedy.

MEASURE FOR MEASURE

Measure for Measure has at the center of its plot another bed trick, by which a patient and determined woman (Mariana) manages to capture the man she desires. That man, Angelo, is put in the position of deputy by Duke Vincentio at the opening of the action. He determines to punish a sinful Vienna by strictly enforcing its laws against fornication; his first act is to arrest Claudio for impregnating his betrothed Juliet. When Isabella, Claudio's sister, who is about to take vows as a nun, comes to plead for his life, Angelo attempts to seduce her. He asks for a measure of her body in return for a measure of mercy for her brother. Isabella strongly resists Angelo's advances, although her principled behavior most certainly means her brother will die. Aided by Vincentio, disguised as a holy father, Isabella arranges for Mariana to take her place, since this woman is in fact Angelo's promised partner. Thus, Angelo commits the deed that he would punish Claudio for performing. (Instead of freeing Claudio, moreover, he sends word to have him killed even after seducing his "sister.") Through another substitution, however, Claudio is saved. In an elaborate judgment scene, in which Vincentio plays both duke and holy father, Angelo is forgiven—Isabella being required by the duke to beg for Angelo's life—and marries Mariana. Here, as in *All's Well That Ends Well*, the hero proves to be an unpunished scoundrel who seems to be in fact rewarded for his sin, but the biblical "Judge not lest ye be judged" motivates much of the action, with characters finding themselves in the place of those who would judge them and being forced to display mercy. Some critics have argued that this interpretation transforms Duke Vincentio into a Christ figure, curing the sins of the people while disguised as one of them. Whether or not this interpretation is valid, *Measure for Measure* compels its audience to explore serious questions concerning moral conduct; practically no touches of humor in the play are untainted by satire and irony.

THE ROMANCES

For about four years following the writing of *Measure for Measure*, Shakespeare was busy producing his major tragedies. It is probably accurate to say that the problem comedies were, to a degree, testing grounds for the situations and characters he would perfect in the tragedies, but in the later years of his career, Shakespeare returned to writing comedy of a special kind: tragicomedy or romance. The four plays usually referred to as "the romances" are *Pericles*, *Cymbeline*, *The Winter's Tale*, and *The Tempest*. Three of these portray situations in which fathers are separated from daughters, then are rejoined through some miraculous turn of fortune. Except for *The Tempest*, the events cover many years and involve travel to exotic locales by the heroes and heroines. Sharp contrasts between the court and pastoral settings vivify the theme of nature as the ideal teacher of moral values. In *Pericles*, *Cymbeline*, and *The Winter's Tale*, the plots move inexorably toward tragedy, but through some form of intervention by Providence—or in some cases, by the gods themselves—happiness is restored and characters are reunited. All the plays witness the power of faith as instrumental in the process of regeneration; the loyal counselor or servant is a regular character type in the plays. The general outlook of the romances is optimistic, suggesting that humankind is indeed capable of recovering from the Fall and of creating a new Paradise.

PERICLES

Pericles recounts the adventures of a good king who seems hounded by fortune and forced to wander through the Mediterranean. The plot is faintly reminiscent of that of *The Comedy of Errors*, suggesting that Shakespeare was returning to tested materials from his earliest comedies. During a storm at sea, Pericles' wife, Thaisa, apparently dies in childbirth and is set ashore in a coffin. He then leaves his daughter Marina in the care of a scheming queen, who tries to have her murdered. Instead, Marina is captured by pirates and eventually is sold to a brothel owner. After many years of lonely sojourning, Pericles is finally reunited with his daughter; later, through the offices of a doctor figure named Cerimon, they find Thaisa in the temple of Diana at Ephesus, where she has been resting for years. Throughout, the sea represents both a threatening and a peaceful force; Marina's name points to the theme of the sea as a great restorative power. She "cures" her father aboard a ship.

CYMBELINE

Cymbeline, set in ancient Britain, recounts the misfortunes of its characters against the background of the Roman invasion of England. The tragicomedy has strong patriotic overtones, but it does not qualify as a history play such as those in the two tetralogies. The play depicts the moral education of Posthumus, the hero, whose desire to marry Imogen, Cymbeline's daughter, is frustrated by his low birth. While in exile in Italy, Posthumus brags to an Italian acquaintance, Iachimo, that his beloved would never consider deceiving him. Thus challenged, Iachimo visits Imogen's room while she sleeps and, through a clever ruse involving a ring and a birthmark, convinces Posthumus that he has slept with her. As a result of numerous plot turns, one of which calls for Imogen to disguise herself as a page, the two lovers are finally reunited when Iachimo confesses his sin. Comingled with this strain of plot is another involving two sons of Cymbeline who have been reared in the rugged world of caves and mountains by an old counselor banished by the king. (He originally kidnapped the boys to seek revenge against Cymbeline.) In a climactic scene brought about by the Roman invasion, the mountain-men heroes are reunited with their father and sister, whom all believed was dead. So complex is the plot that many readers and audiences have found the play confusing and sometimes unintentionally humorous. The characters are not fully developed, and it is difficult to determine just what is the central story. Here, too, spectacle overpowers dialogue and characterization, with little or no attention paid to plausibility. Shakespeare seems preoccupied with demonstrating the healthfulness of pastoral life, the patriotic spirit of Englishmen, and the melodramatic quality of evil. Clearly, this agenda of themes and values places one in a comic world that is distinct from the one that typifies the mature comedies.

THE WINTER'S TALE

In *The Winter's Tale*, Shakespeare again explores the motif of the daughter separated from her father, but in this play, the father, King Leontes, must be seen as a potentially tragic figure. His jealousy leads him to accuse his wife, Hermione, of unfaithfulness with his friend and fellow king Polixenes. When Leontes confronts her, even after consultation of the oracle indicates her honesty, she faints and apparently expires. Leontes banishes the child Perdita, who is his daughter but whom he refuses to acknowledge because of his suspicions, and the third act ends with a loyal servant depositing the baby on the shore of Bohemia to be favored or destroyed by Fortune. (A bear pursues and kills the servant, thus destroying any link between Leontes' court and the baby.) Perdita, "the lost one," is found and reared by a shepherd. As sixteen years pass, she grows into a kind of pastoral queen, revealing those traits of goodness and innocence that Shakespeare associates with the Golden Age. When Polixenes repeats Leontes' sin by banishing his son Florizel for falling in love with a lowly shepherdess, the couple, with the help of a rejected servant still loyal to Leontes, returns to Sicilia to seek the aid of the now repentant king. Through a series of revelations and with the help of the old shepherd, Perdita's identity is discovered. She and Florizel are married, and the two kings are reunited in friendship. As a final tour de force, Hermione, who has been hidden away for the whole time by another loyal servant, comes to life as a statue supposedly sculpted by a famous artist. As in the other romances, some divine force has obviously been operating in the affairs of humans to bring about this happy reunion of families, friends, and countries.

The Winter's Tale comes closer than the romances to a realistic treatment of emotion, with all of its destructive possibilities, and to a more nearly honest vision of the pastoral world. Autolycus the clown, for example, pretends to be nothing other than a successful thief, "a snapper-up of unconsidered trifles."

THE TEMPEST

The Tempest is the only romance in which father and daughter are together from the beginning. It also possesses the only plot that observes the classical unities of time and place. Many commentators believe that the play represents Shakespeare's greatest dramatic achievement, blending together beautiful verse, richly realized characters, and the moving wonders of the imagination. There can be no question that *The Tempest* is a refined and elevating statement of the themes of Providence and of order and degree. Prospero, the duke of Milan, exiled by his usurping brother Antonio, vows to punish both Antonio and his chief supporter, King Alonso. The two are aboard a ship sailing near the island on which Prospero and his daughter Miranda reside. Using magical power and the aid of a spirit named Ariel, Prospero apparently wrecks the ship, saving all the voyagers but supposedly drowning Ferdinand, Alonso's son. Once on the island, the party is tormented by disorienting music and distracting sights, especially when Prospero's brother Antonio attempts to convince Alonso's brother Sebastian to kill him and seize the crown. Another rebellion is attempted by Caliban (his name an anagram for "cannibal"), the half-human, half-bestial servant of Prospero. Both rebellions fail, but instead of punishing his victims further, Prospero, moved by the compassion displayed by Ariel, decides to give up his magic and return to civilization. The decision proves crucial, since Prospero was on the verge of becoming a kind of Faust, forgetting his identity as a man. When he acknowledges Caliban, "this thing of darkness," as his own, one realizes that this gesture betokens an internal acceptance of the passions as a legitimate part of his nature. Instead of revenging himself on Alonso, Prospero allows Ferdinand to woo Miranda in a mood and manner that recall Eden before the Fall. It should also be noted that Prospero creates a marriage masque featuring Iris, Ceres, and Juno, at the close of which he delivers the famous "Our revels now are ended" speech. Some critics claim that Prospero's words constitute Shakespeare's farewell to the stage, but there is considerable evidence that he continued to write plays for at least another year.

THE TWO NOBLE KINSMEN

The Two Noble Kinsmen was probably one of the plays composed during that period. It is not included in the First Folio (published 1623). It appeared in print in 1634 and bearing a title page ascribing the comedy to John Fletcher and William Shakespeare. Although collaboration was common among Elizabethan and Jacobean playwrights, it was not a form of composition in which Shakespeare regularly engaged. Because *Henry VIII* was also most likely a collaborative effort, there seems to be compelling evidence that Shakespeare was enjoying a state of semiretirement during this period. Based on Geoffrey Chaucer's "The Knight's Tale" (from his *Canterbury Tales*), *The Two Noble Kinsmen* depicts the love of Palamon and Arcite for Emilia in a polite and mannered style that can easily be identified with Fletcher's other work. The play is similar to the other romances in its emphasis on spectacle. It opens with a magnificent wedding ceremony before the Temple of Hymen, and there are excursions to the shrines of Mars and Diana as well. However, there are no scenes of regeneration involving fathers and daughters, no emphasis on the forgiveness of sin. If this was Shakespeare's last play, it shows him returning to old sources for oft-told tales; his interest in developing new comic forms had obviously waned. On the whole, the romances represent a more sophisticated but less playful and inventive style than that of the character-oriented comedies, such as *Twelfth Night* and *Much Ado About Nothing*.

THE TRAGEDIES

Shakespeare wrote a number of tragedies, among them the famous *Romeo and Juliet*, *Julius Caesar*, *Hamlet, Prince of Denmark*, *Othello, the Moor of Venice*, *King Lear*, and *Anthony and Cleopatra*. His earliest—and clumsiest—attempt at tragedy was *Titus Andronicus*.

TITUS ANDRONICUS

The plot of *Titus Andronicus* no doubt came from the Roman poet Ovid, a school subject and one of the playwright's favorite Roman authors. From Seneca, the Roman playwright whose ten plays had been translated into English in 1559, Shakespeare took the theme of revenge: The inflexible, honor-bound hero seeks satisfaction against a queen who has murdered or maimed his children. She was acting in retaliation, however, because Titus had killed her son. Titus's rage, which is exacerbated by the rape and mutilation of his daughter Lavinia, helps to classify him as a typical Senecan tragic hero. He and the wicked queen Tamora are oversimplified characters who declaim set speeches rather than engaging in realistic dialogue. Tamora's lover and accomplice, the Moor Aaron, is the prototype of the Machiavellian practitioner that Shakespeare would perfect in such villains as Iago and Edmund. While this caricature proves intriguing, and while the play's structure is more balanced and coherent than those of the early history plays, Titus's character lacks the kind of agonizing introspection shown by the heroes of the major tragedies. He never comes to terms with the destructive code of honor that convulses his personal life and that of Rome.

ROMEO AND JULIET

With *Romeo and Juliet*, Shakespeare reached a level of success in characterization and design far above the bombastic and chaotic world of *Titus Andronicus*. Based on a long narrative and heavily moralized poem by Arthur Brooke, this tragedy of "star-crossed lovers" excites the imagination by depicting the fatal consequences of a feud between the Veronese families of Montague and Capulet. Distinguished by some of Shakespeare's most beautiful poetry, the style bears a strong resemblance to that of the sonnets: elaborate conceits, classical allusions, witty paradoxes, and observations on the sad consequences of sudden changes of fortune. Some critics have in fact faulted the tragedy because its plot lacks the integrity of its poetry; Romeo and Juliet come to their fates by a series of accidents and coincidences that strain credulity. The play also features abundant comic touches provided by the remarks of Romeo's bawdy, quick-witted friend Mercutio and the sage but humorous observations of Juliet's nurse. Both of these "humor" characters (character types whose personalities are determined by one trait, or "humor") remark frequently, and often bawdily, on the innocent lovers' dreamy pronouncements about their passion for each other. With the accidental murder of Mercutio, whose last words are "A plague on both your houses!" (referring to the feuding families), the plot accelerates rapidly toward the catastrophe, showing no further touches of humor or satire. The tireless Friar Lawrence attempts, through the use of a potion, to save Juliet from marrying Paris, the nobleman to whom she is betrothed, but the friar proves powerless against the force of fate that seems to be working against the lovers. Although it lacks the compelling power of the mature tragedies, whose heroes are clearly responsible for their fate, *Romeo and Juliet* remains a popular play on the subject of youthful love. The success of various film versions, including Franco Zeffirelli's 1968 feature film, with its teenage hero and heroine and its romantically moving score, proved that the play has a timeless appeal.

JULIUS CAESAR

At least three years passed before Shakespeare again turned his attention to the tragic form. Instead of treating the subject of fatal love, however, he explored Roman history for a political story centering on the tragic dilemma of one man. In *Julius Caesar*, he could have dealt with the tale of the assassination of Caesar, taken from Plutarch's *Bioi paralleloi* (c. 105-115 C.E.; *Parallel Lives*, 1579), as he did with material from English history in the chronicle dramas he had been writing in the 1590's. That is, he might have presented the issue of the republic versus the monarchy as a purely political question, portraying Caesar, Brutus, Cassius, and Antony as pawns in a predestined game. Instead, Shakespeare chose to explore the character of Brutus in detail, revealing the workings of his conscience through moving and incisive soliloquies. By depicting his hero as a man who believes his terrible act is in the best interest of the

country, Shakespeare establishes the precedent for later tragic heroes who likewise justify their destructive deeds as having righteous purposes.

The tragic plot is developed by means of irony and contrast. Cassius, jealous of Caesar's achievements, seduces Brutus into taking part in the conspiracy by appealing to his idealism. This political naiveté stands in sharp contrast to Antony's Machiavellianism, which is so brilliantly demonstrated in his crowd-swaying funeral oration ("Friends, Romans, countrymen, lend me your ears . . ."). Antony's transformation from playboy to power broker displays Shakespeare's belief that the historical moment shapes the natures of great men. Caesar appears to be a superstitious, somewhat petty figure, but in typical fashion, Shakespeare makes his audience see that, just as the conspirators are not free of personal motives such as jealousy, so Caesar is not the cold and uncompromising tyrant they claim he is. With the visit by Caesar's ghost to Brutus's tent on the eve of the final battle at Philippi, Shakespeare foreshadows the ultimate revenge of Caesar in the character of his grandson, Octavius, who emerges as a strong personality at the close of the play. Brutus and Cassius quarrel before the end, but they nevertheless achieve a kind of nobility by committing suicide in the Roman tradition. For Brutus, the events following the assassination demonstrate the flaw in his idealism; he could not destroy the spirit of Caesar, nor could he build a republic on the shifting sand of the populace. In *Julius Caesar*, one witnesses a tragedy that is both politically compelling and morally complex.

HAMLET, PRINCE OF DENMARK

Although the revenge theme is an important part of *Julius Caesar*, it dominates the action of *Hamlet, Prince of Denmark*. Learning from his father's ghost that Claudius, the new king, is a brother-murderer and a usurper, the hero sets out passionately to fulfill his personal duty by destroying the villain-king. Like Brutus, however, Hamlet is a reflective man, given to "saucy doubts" about the veracity of the ghost, about the effect on his soul of committing regicide, and about the final disposition of Claudius's soul. As a result, Hamlet delays his revenge—a delay that has preoccupied audiences, readers, and critics for centuries.

Numerous reasons have been proposed for the delay: Hamlet is melancholic; his morality does not condone murder; he is a coward; he is secretly envious of Claudius for murdering his "rival" for his mother's affections. These explanations, while appealing, tend to shift attention away from other, equally significant elements in the play. Hamlet's soliloquies illustrate the range of Shakespearean blank verse and provide the means for exploring character in detail. The play's trap motif can be seen to represent effectively the doomed, claustrophobic atmosphere of the play. Indeed, those who deliberatively set traps in the play—Polonius, Claudius, Laertes, and Hamlet—find that those traps snap back to catch the "inventor." Hamlet's relationships with Ophelia and with Gertrude amply reveal his self-destructive belief that his mother's marriage to Claudius has tainted his own flesh and transformed all women into strumpets. Throughout the action as well, one becomes aware that Shakespeare is using the theatrical metaphor "All the world's a stage" to illustrate the way in which deceit and corruption can be masked. In another sense, Hamlet's behavior is that of a bad actor, one who either misses his cues (as in the accidental murder of Polonius) or fails to perform when the audience expects action (as in his behavior following the play-within-the-play). There is a good deal of reflection on death and disease in *Hamlet, Prince of Denmark* as well; the hero's preoccupation with these images seems to mirror the sickness of the state and of his own enterprise. When Hamlet finally acts, however, he does so in the role of an avenger and scourge. He murders Claudius after the king has arranged for Laertes to slay him in a duel and after the queen has fallen dead from a poisoned drink intended for Hamlet. With Hamlet's death, the kingdom reverts to the control of young Fortinbras, whose father Hamlet's father had killed in another duel. Though Fortinbras stands as a heroic figure, one cannot help but observe the irony of a situation in which the son, without a struggle, inherits what his father was denied.

TROILUS AND CRESSIDA

In *Troilus and Cressida*, one encounters another kind of irony: satire. This strange play, which may have been composed for a select audience, possibly of lawyers, was placed between the histories and tragedies in the First Folio. The dual plot concerns the political machinations among the Greeks during their siege of Troy and the tortured love affair between Troilus and the unfaithful Cressida. There are no epic battles in the play; indeed, the murder of Hector by a band of Achilles' followers might easily be viewed as cowardly or ignominious at best. Much of the political action consists of debates: Hector argues eloquently that Helen should be sent back to Menelaus; Ulysses produces many pithy arguments urging the reluctant Achilles to fight. Many of these scenes, moreover, end in anticlimax, and action is often frustrated. Throughout, Thersites, the satirist-onstage, bitterly attacks the warring and lecherous instincts of men; even the love affair between Troilus and Cressida seems tainted by the general atmosphere of disillusion. Although the two lovers share genuine affection for each other, one cannot ignore the truth that they are brought together by Pandarus and that their passion has a distinctly physical quality. When Cressida proves unable to resist the advances of Diomedes, Troilus becomes a cuckold like Menelaus; his bitterness and misogyny push one toward Thersites' assessment that the "argument" of the war "is a whore and a cuckold." Still it is possible to see tragic dimensions in the characters of both Hector and Troilus—one the victim of treachery in war, the other the victim of treachery in love.

TIMON OF ATHENS

Although probably written after the other major tragedies, *Timon of Athens* shares a number of similarities with *Troilus and Cressida*. Here again is an ironic vision of humanity, this time in a social rather than martial setting. That vision is expanded by the trenchant comments, usually in the form of references to sexual disease, of Apemantus, another cynical choric commentator. In addition, Timon appears to be a tragic rather than misanthropic figure only if one sees him as the victim of his idealistic reading of humankind. When those on whom he has lavishly bestowed gifts and money consistently refuse to return the favor, Timon then becomes a bitter cynic and outspoken satirist. This exploding of a naïve philosophy or political idea, with its attendant destructive effect on the believer, would seem to be the basis for tragedy in a character such as Brutus or Hamlet, but even Hamlet fails to achieve the degree of misanthropy that typifies Timon's outlook. Although he is loyally followed to the end by his servant Flavius, he dies alone and not as a result of someone else's direct attack. One cannot say that the hero acquires a larger view of humanity or of himself as the result of his experience; he simply seems to swing from one extreme view to its opposite. A comparison of Timon with more sympathetic "railers" such as Hamlet and Lear shows how narrow and shallow are his character and the dimensions of the play. The fragmented nature of the text has led some critics to question Shakespeare's authorship, but it is probably closer to the truth to say that this was an experiment that failed.

OTHELLO, THE MOOR OF VENICE

An experiment that clearly succeeded is *Othello, the Moor of Venice*, an intense and powerful domestic tragedy. Based on an Italian tale by Giambattista Giraldi Cinthio, the story concerns a Moor, a black man who is made to believe by a treacherous, vengeful ensign that his new Venetian bride has cuckolded him with one of his lieutenants, Cassio. In a rage, the Moor suffocates his bride, only to discover too late that his jealousy was unfounded. Rather than face the torture of a trial and his own conscience, he commits suicide as he bitterly accuses himself of blindness. In its simple outline, this story has the appearance of a crude melodrama, but Shakespeare brilliantly complicates the play's texture through skillful manipulation of scenes, characters, and language. He also creates a world with two distinct symbolic settings: Venice and Cyprus. In Venice, Othello shows himself to be a cool, rational captain, deserving of the respect he receives from the senators who send him to Cyprus to defend it from the Turks. Once Othello is on the island, however, Iago begins to chip away at the hero's veneer of self-control until he transforms him into a terrifyingly destructive force. Iago's success depends not only on his close contact with Othello on the island but also on the generally held opinion that he, Iago, is an "honest man." He is thus able to manipulate all the central characters as if he were a puppeteer. These characters share information with Iago

that he later uses to ensnare them in his web, as when Desdemona begs him to find some way to reinstate Cassio in Othello's favor. Iago is especially adept at using the handkerchief Othello gave to Desdemona but which she dropped while trying to ease her husband's headache. When Iago's wife Emilia dutifully hands her husband this handkerchief, he easily makes Othello believe that Desdemona gave it to Cassio as a love token. Although some critics have ridiculed Shakespeare for depending so heavily on one prop to resolve the plot, they fail to note the degree of psychological insight Shakespeare has displayed in using it. The handkerchief represents Othello's wife's honor and his own. She has given both away, in Othello's mind, as if they were trifles.

This play features a hero whose reason is overwhelmed by the passion of jealousy—"the green-eyed monster," in Iago's words. This theme is realized through numerous sea images, by which Shakespeare likens Othello's violent reaction to a storm or tidal wave that drowns everything in its path. Like Shakespeare's other great villains, Iago is a supreme individualist, acknowledging no authority or power beyond himself. That this attitude was a copy of the fallen angel Satan's would not have escaped the attention of Shakespeare's audience, which no doubt interpreted the plot as a replay of the Fall of Man. It may be especially important to perceive Iago as another Satan, since commentators have suspected the sufficiency of his motive (he says he wants revenge because Othello passed over him in appointing Cassio as his lieutenant). The extreme evilness of Iago's nature and the extreme purity of Desdemona's have led others to claim that Shakespeare was simply intent on fashioning a contemporary morality play for his audience. Such a reading tends to simplify what is in fact a thoroughgoing study of the emotions that both elevate and destroy humankind. As Othello discovers before his suicide, he was one "who loved not wisely but too well"; one might observe ironically that it was Iago, and not Desdemona, whom he loved "too well."

KING LEAR

If Othello's tragedy results from the corrosive disease of jealousy, the hero of *King Lear* suffers from the debilitating effects of pride and self-pity. When the play opens, he is in the process of retiring from the kingship by dividing his kingdom into three parts, basing his assignment of land on the degree of affection mouthed by each of the three daughters to whom he plans to assign a part. Cordelia, his youngest and favorite, refuses to enter into this hollow ceremony, and Lear responds by suddenly and violently banishing her. Left in the hands of his evil and ambitious daughters Goneril and Regan, Lear quickly discovers that they plan to pare away any remaining symbols of his power and bring him entirely under their rule. This theme of children controlling, even destroying, their parents is echoed in a fully developed subplot involving old Gloucester and his two sons, Edmund and Edgar. With Cordelia and Edgar cast out—the former to live in France, the latter in disguise as Poor Tom—Lear and Gloucester suffer the punishing consequences of their sins. Lear runs mad into a terrible storm, accompanied by the Fool, a witty and poignant commentator on the unnaturalness of his master's decision. There, Lear goes through a "dark night of the soul" in which he sees for the first time the suffering of others whom he has never regarded. Gloucester, who is also lacking insight into the true natures of his sons, is cruelly blinded by Regan and her husband and cast out from his own house to journey to Dover. On the way, he is joined by his disguised son, who helps Gloucester undergo a regeneration of faith before he expires. Cordelia performs a similar task for Lear, whose recovery can be only partial, because of his madness. After Cordelia is captured and killed by the forces of Edmund, whose brother conquers him in single combat, Lear, too, expires while holding the dead Cordelia in his arms.

This wrenching ending, with its nihilistic overtones, is only one of the elements that places this play among the richest and most complex tragedies in English. Lear's blindness, which is expertly represented in image clusters dealing with sight and insight, leads to cataclysmic suffering for his family and the state. More than any other Shakespearean tragedy, *King Lear* also succeeds in dramatizing the relationship between the microcosm, or little world of humankind, and the macrocosm, or larger world. One sees how the breakdown of the king's reason and control leads to the breakdown of control in the state and in nature. At the moment when Lear bursts into tears, a frightening storm breaks out, and civil war soon follows. Images of human suffering and torture likewise crowd the action, the most compelling of which is the representation of the hero tied to a "wheel of fire" and scalded by his own tears as the wheel turns. The Wheel of Fortune emblem is clearly evoked by this image, revealing Shakespeare's purpose of depicting the king as another fallen prince brought low by his own mistakes and by the caprice of the goddess. That Lear has created the circumstances of his own fall is underscored by the antic remarks of his companion the Fool, the choric speaker who early in the play tries to keep Lear's mind from cracking as he comes to realize how wrong was the banishment of Cordelia. The Fool speaks in riddles and uses barnyard analogies to make the point that Lear has placed the whip in the child's hand and lowered his own breeches. Gloucester must learn a similar lesson, although his dilemma involves a crisis of faith. Lear must strip away the coverings of civilization to discover "unaccommodated man," a discovery he begins to make too late. Just as he realizes that Cordelia represents those qualities of truth and compassion that he has been lacking, she is suddenly and violently taken from him.

MACBETH

Macbeth treats the *de casibus* theme of the fall of princes, but from a different perspective. Unlike Lear, Macbeth is a usurper who is driven to kill King Duncan by the witches' prophecy, by his own ambition, and by his wife's prompting. Once that deed is done, Macbeth finds himself unable to sleep, a victim of conscience and guilt. Although Lady Macbeth tries to control his fears, she proves unsuccessful, and her influence wanes rapidly. Evidence of this loss of power is Macbeth's plot to kill Banquo, his fellow general, to whom the witches announced that he would be the father of kings. During the climactic banquet scene, Duncan's ghost enters, invisible to the other guests, to take Macbeth's place at the table; when the host reacts by raging and throwing his cup at the specter, the celebration is broken up and the guests scatter. Immediately, Macbeth rushes to the witches to seek proof that he is invincible. They tell him that he will not be conquered until Birnam Wood comes to Dunsinane and that no man born of woman can kill him. They also show him a procession of eight child-kings, all of whom represent Banquo's descendants, including the last king, who is meant to be James I. (This procession has helped many critics to conclude that *Macbeth* was written as an occasional play to honor James, who became the company's protector in 1603.)

Seeking to tighten his control of Scotland and to quiet his conscience, Macbeth launches a reign of terror during which his henchmen kill Lady Macduff and her children. Macduff, exiled in England with Duncan's son Malcolm, learns of this vicious deed and spearheads an army that returns to Scotland to destroy the tyrant. In the final battle, which commences with the attacking army tearing down branches from trees in Birnam Wood to camouflage its advance, Macbeth discovers that his nemesis, Macduff, "was from his mother's womb/ Untimely ripped." Thus standing alone (Lady Macbeth commits suicide) and defeated, Macbeth represents himself as a "poor player" who has had his moment onstage and is quickly gone. This use of the theatrical metaphor looks back to the world of *Hamlet, Prince of Denmark* at the same time that it underscores the villain-hero's role as an impostor king. Macbeth is also depicted as a Herod figure (recalling Richard III) when he murders the innocent children of Macduff in an obsessive fit brought on by the realization that he is childless and heirless. Two strains of imagery reinforce this perception, featuring recurring references to blood and to children. When Macbeth kills Duncan, he describes his blood as "gilding" his flesh, suggesting that the king is God's anointed representative on earth. Shakespeare also depicts Macbeth's nemesis as a bloody child; this image hints at the strength-in-innocence theme that dominates the latter part of the play. That is, as Macbeth grows into the "man" that Lady Macbeth claimed he should be, he becomes more destructive and less humane, the caricature of a man. Macduff, on the other hand, in tears over the brutal murder of his wife and children,

emerges as a stronger and more compassionate man because he has shown himself capable of deep feeling. The bloody-babe image might also be defined as a Christ emblem, with the attendant suggestion that Macduff comes to free the land from a tyrant's grasp by spreading a philosophy of goodness and mercy. If the play was written to honor James I, it might also be argued that the comparison between his reign and that of Christ was intended. Whatever the intention of these image patterns, they help one to trace the transformation in Macbeth's character from battlefield hero to usurping tyrant, a transformation brought about by the powerful motive of ambition.

ANTHONY AND CLEOPATRA

Written soon after *Macbeth*, *Antony and Cleopatra* again traces the complex psychological patterns of a male-female relationship. Like Lady Macbeth, Cleopatra appears to control and direct the behavior of her man, Antony, but as the play progresses, she, too, begins to lose power. Unlike Lady Macbeth, Cleopatra outlasts her love, gaining from Antony's death the spirit and stature of rule that was not evident throughout much of the play. Indeed, most of the action involves quarrels between these two mature but jealous and petulant lovers as they struggle to escape the harsh political world created by Octavius Caesar, Antony's rival. Angered by Antony's reveling in Egypt and later by his desertion of Caesar's sister Octavia, whom Antony married only to buy time and an unsteady truce, Octavius begins to move against Antony with a powerful army and navy. During a first encounter between the two forces, in which Antony foolishly decides to fight at sea and also depends on Cleopatra's untested ships, Antony leaves the field in pursuit of the retiring Cleopatra. Angered by her withdrawal and his own alacrity in following her, Antony rages against his "serpent of old Nile" and vows to have nothing further to do with her, but Cleopatra's pull is magnetic, and Antony joins forces with her for a second battle with Caesar. When a similar retreat occurs and Antony finds Cleopatra apparently arranging a separate peace with one of Caesar's representatives, he has the messenger beaten and sent back to Octavius with a challenge to single combat. These wild and desperate moves are commented on by Enobarbus, associate of Antony and choric voice. After the threat of single combat, Enobarbus leaves his master to join forces with Octavius. (Overcome by remorse, however, Enobarbus dies on the eve of battle.)

Believing that Cleopatra has killed herself, Antony decides to commit suicide and calls on his servant Eros to hold his sword so that he can run himself on it. Instead, Eros kills himself, and Antony must strike the blow himself. Still alive, he is carried to the monument where Cleopatra has decided to take up residence. There, Antony expires, "a Roman, by a Roman/ Valiantly vanquished." Almost immediately, Cleopatra's character seems to change into that of a noble partner; her elegant speeches on Antony's heroic proportions are some of the most powerful blank verse in the play. It is also clear that she intends to escape Octavius's grasp, knowing that he intends to parade her and her children before a jeering Roman crowd. Putting on her royal robes and applying the poison asps to her breast, Cleopatra hurries off to join her lover in eternity.

This complicated story is brilliantly organized by means of placing in balance the two worlds of Rome and Egypt. While Rome is presented as a cold, calculating place, reflective of the character of Octavius, Egypt stands out as a lush paradise in which the pursuit of pleasure is the main business of the inhabitants. This contrast is particularly telling because Antony's status as a tragic hero depends on one's seeing him as caught between the two worlds, at home in neither, master of neither. Water and serpent imagery dominate the play, creating a picture of Cleopatra as a Circe figure or a spontaneously generated creature that has seduced the once heroic Antony. Although this is the Roman view of the "gypsy" queen, Shakespeare requires his audience to appreciate her infinite variety. She is beautiful and playful, demanding and witty, cool and explosive. On the other hand, the assessment of Octavius as a puritanical, unfeeling man of destiny is also oversimplified; his reaction to Antony's death reveals genuine emotion. At the close of the play, one realizes that Antony and Cleopatra's vast empire has been reduced to the size of her monument—Caesar must attend a while longer to make this discovery himself. Antony and Cleopatra, how-

ever, have found a world of love that Octavius could never enter, and the tragedy is as much concerned with tracing the boundaries of that empire as it is with marking the triumphs of Octavius.

CORIOLANUS

While reading the story of Antony and Cleopatra in Plutarch's *Parallel Lives*, to which the play reveals a number of similarities, Shakespeare found another Roman figure whose career he saw as appropriate matter for tragedy: Coriolanus. Composed in the period between 1607 and 1608, *Coriolanus* dramatizes the career of a general in Republican Rome. He proves to be a superhuman figure in battle, earning his name by single-handedly subduing the town of Corioles and emerging from its gates covered in blood. (This birth image has a mixed meaning, since the blood is that of his victims.) Unfortunately, Coriolanus refuses to humble himself before the Roman plebeians, whom he despises, as a requirement for holding the office of consul. Indeed, many of his bitter comments about the fickleness and cowardice of the populace remind one of characters such as Thersites and Apemantus. Such contempt and condescension make it hard to identify with Coriolanus, even though one is made aware that the Roman crowd is set against him by the jealous and ambitious tribunes, Brutus and Sicinius. Driven by his pride and anger, Coriolanus challenges the citizens' rights and is subsequently banished. He then joins forces with his former enemy Aufidius, and the two of them lead an army to the very gates of Rome. Coriolanus's mother comes out to plead with her son to spare Rome—and his family—in the most emotional scene of the play. Deeply moved by his mother's arguments, Coriolanus relents and urges his companion to make peace with their enemy. Aufidius agrees but awaits his opportunity to ambush his partner, whom he regards as a lifelong enemy. In a masterstroke of irony, Coriolanus is brought down by the citizens of the very town—Corioles—that he conquered in acquiring his name. Because the play is so heavily laden with swatches of Coriolanus's vitriol and instances of irony such as the final one, it is difficult to classify this tragedy with those in which the heroes present richly complex characters. If Hamlet, Othello,

Macbeth, and Lear possess tragic flaws, those flaws are only a part of their complicated makeup. Coriolanus, on the other hand, can be understood only in terms of his flaw, and the character and play are therefore one-dimensional.

There is little argument, however, that Shakespeare's tragedies constitute the major achievement of his career. These dramas continue to appeal to audiences because their stories are intriguing; because their characters are fully realized human beings, if somewhat larger than life; and because their poetic language is metaphorically rich. Shakespeare possessed a profound insight into human nature and an ability to reveal what he found there in language unequaled in its power and beauty.

OTHER MAJOR WORKS

POETRY: *Venus and Adonis*, 1593; *The Rape of Lucrece*, 1594; *The Passionate Pilgrim*, 1599 (miscellany with poems by Shakespeare and others); *The Phoenix and the Turtle*, 1601; *A Lover's Complaint*, 1609; *Sonnets*, 1609.

BIBLIOGRAPHY

Bloom, Harold. *Shakespeare: The Invention of the Human*. New York: Riverhead, 1998. A drama-by-drama analysis of William Shakespeare's plays, focusing on character development and the playwright's contribution to the modern understanding of the human experience.

Brown, John Russell. *Shakespeare: The Tragedies*. New York: Palgrave, 2001. A study of the tragedies in chronological order.

Danson, Lawrence. *Shakespeare's Dramatic Genres*. New York: Oxford University Press, 2000. Danson's scholarly study examines Shakespeare's philosophy and how it was demonstrated in his dramas. Bibliography and index.

Draper, Ronald P. *Shakespeare, the Comedies*. New York: St. Martin's Press, 2000. Draper provides an analysis of the playwright's comedies. Bibliography and index.

Holderness, Graham. *Shakespeare: The Histories*. New York: St. Martin's Press, 2000. Holderness examines the historical plays of Shakespeare and the historical events on which they were based. Bibliography and index.

McLeish, Kenneth, and Stephen Unwin. *A Pocket Guide to Shakespeare's Plays*. London: Faber and Faber, 1998. This concise guide summarizes the plots and characters of Shakespeare's plays, providing an easy reference.

Marsh, Nicholas. *Shakespeare, the Tragedies*. New York: St. Martin's Press, 2000. Marsh analyzes the tragedies of Shakespeare, providing study guides. Bibliography and index.

Proudfoot, Richard. *Shakespeare: Text, Stage, and Canon*. London: Arden Shakespeare, 2001. A study of Shakespeare's plays, with emphasis on their stage history and how they were produced. Bibliography and index.

Richards, Jennifer, and James Knowles, eds. *Shakespeare's Late Plays: New Readings*. Edinburgh: Edinburgh University Press, 1999. A collection of essays focusing on the playwright's later plays, including *The Winter's Tale*, *The Tempest*, and *The Two Noble Kinsmen*. Bibliography and index.

Robert F. Willson, Jr., updated by John R. Holmes and Joseph Rosenblum

WILLIAM SHAKESPEARE: THE MAN

Born: Stratford-upon-Avon, England; April 23, 1564

Died: Stratford-upon-Avon, England; April 23, 1616

William Shakespeare was born in Stratford-upon-Avon, Warwickshire, England, descended from tenant farmers and landed gentry. His traditional birth date, April 23, 1564, is conjectural. Baptism was on April 26, so April 23 is a good guess—and a tidy one, since that date is also St. George's Day as well as the date of Shakespeare's own death.

One of Shakespeare's grandfathers, Richard Shakespeare of Snitterfield, rented land from the other, Robert Arden of Wilmcote. Shakespeare's father, John, moved to nearby Stratford-upon-Avon, became a prosperous shop owner (dealing in leather goods) and municipal officeholder, and married his former landlord's youngest daughter, Mary Arden. Thus Shakespeare—the third of eight children but the first to survive infancy—was born into a solidly middle-class family in a provincial market town.

During Shakespeare's infancy, his father was one of the town's leading citizens. In 1557, John Shakespeare had become a member of the town council and subsequently held such offices as constable, affeeror (a kind of assessor), and chamberlain (treasurer). In 1568, he became bailiff (mayor) and justice of the peace. As the son of a municipal officer, the young Shakespeare was entitled to a free education in the town's grammar school, which he probably entered around the age of seven. The school's main subject was Latin studies—grammar and readings drilled into the schoolboys year after year. The Avon River, the surrounding farmlands, and the nearby Forest of Arden offered plenty of opportunities for childhood adventures.

When Shakespeare was a teenager, his family fell on hard times. His father stopped attending town council meetings in 1577, and the family's fortunes began to decline. Matters were not improved in 1582 when Shakespeare, at the age of eighteen, hastily married Anne Hathaway, the twenty-six-year-old daughter of a farmer from the nearby village of Shottery. She presented him with a daughter, named Susanna, approximately five months later. In 1585, the couple also became the parents of twins, Hamnet and Judith. As was then customary, the young couple probably lived in his parents' home, which must have seemed increasingly crowded.

The next mention of Shakespeare is in 1592, when he was an actor and playwright in London. His actions during the seven-year interim have been a mat-

ter of much curious speculation, including unproved stories of deer poaching, soldiering, and teaching. It may have taken him those seven years simply to break into and advance in the London theater. His early connections with the theater are unknown, although he was an actor before he became a playwright. He might have joined one of the touring companies that occasionally performed in Stratford-upon-Avon, or he might have gone directly to London to make his fortune, in either the theater or some other trade. Shakespeare was a venturesome and able young man who had good reasons to travel—his confining family circumstances, tinged with just enough disgrace to qualify him to join the disreputable players. The theater was his escape to freedom; he therefore had strong motivation to succeed.

LIFE'S WORK

The London theater, in Shakespeare's day, was made up of companies of men and boys (women were not allowed on the Renaissance English stage but were played by young men or boys). These actors performed in public playhouses roughly modeled on old innyards. The theaters were open to the air, had balconies surrounding the pit and stage, and held from two to three thousand people. A group known as the University Wits—John Lyly, George Peele, Thomas Lodge, Robert Greene, Thomas Nashe, and Christopher Marlowe—dominated the drama. Shakespeare learned his art by imitating these Oxford and Cambridge men, but for him they were a difficult group to join. They looked down on most actors and on those playwrights, such as Thomas Kyd, who had not attended a university. Shakespeare offended on both counts, and Robert Greene expressed his resentment in the posthumously published book *Greene's Groatsworth of Wit Bought with a Million of Repentance* (1592), which included a famous warning to three fellow "gentlemen" playwrights:

Yes, trust them [the players] not: for there is an upstart crow, beautified with our feathers, that with his *Tiger's heart wrapt in a player's hide*, supposes he is as well able to bombast out a blank verse as the best of you: and being an absolute *Johannes Factotum*, is in his own conceit the only Shake-scene in a country.

Greene's literary executor, Henry Chettle, later published an apology for this slur on Shakespeare, with its pun on his name and its parody of a line from *Henry VI, Part III*. On meeting him, Chettle found Shakespeare's "demeanor no less civil than he, excellent in the quality he professes. Besides, divers of worship have reported his uprightness of dealing, which argues his honesty, and his facetious grace in writing, that approves his art."

Actually, Greene's judgment of Shakespeare's early work is more accurate. The early plays are far from excellent; they include some of the most slavish imitations in Renaissance English drama, as Shakespeare tried his hand at the various popular modes. The interminable three-part history play *Henry VI* (Part I, wr. 1589-1590, pr. 1592, pb. 1623; Part II, pr. c. 1590-1591, pb. 1594; Part III, pr. c. 1590-1591, pb. 1595), as Greene notes, makes bombastic attempts at Marlowe's powerful blank verse. In *The Comedy of Errors* (pr. c. 1592-1594), based on Plautus's *Menaechmi* (*The Twin Menaechmi*, 1595), and in the Senecan tragedy *Titus Andronicus* (pr., pb. 1594), Shakespeare showed his ability to copy Roman models down to the smallest detail, even if he did lack a university degree. Apparently, he also lacked confidence in his own imagination and learned slowly. *Richard III* (pr. c. 1592-1593, pb. 1597, revised 1623), however, showed promise in the malignant character of Richard, while *The Taming of the Shrew* (pr. c. 1593-1594, pb. 1623) offered its rambunctious love-fight.

Despite their imitative nature and many other faults, Shakespeare's early plays—notably the *Henry VI* plays—were popular onstage, but his greatest early popularity came from two long narrative poems, *Venus and Adonis* (1593) and *The Rape of Lucrece* (1594). Shakespeare wrote these two poems during the two years that the plague closed down the London theaters. He dedicated the poems to a patron, the young Henry Wriothesley, third earl of Southampton, who may have granted him a substantial monetary reward in return. In any event, when the theaters reopened in 1594, the acting companies were almost decimated financially, but Shakespeare was in a position to buy or otherwise acquire a partnership in one of the newly reorganized companies, the Lord Chamberlain's Men. Henceforth, Shakespeare earned money not only from the plays he had written or in which he acted but also from a share of the profits of every company performance. The financial arrangement seemed to inspire his creative efforts, for he set about writing the plays that made him famous, beginning with *Romeo and Juliet* (pr. c. 1595-1596, pb. 1597) and going on to the great history plays and comedies, including *Richard II* (pr. c. 1595-1596, pb. 1600), *Henry IV* (Part I, pr. c. 1597-1598, pb. 1598; Part II, pr. 1598, pb. 1600), *Henry V* (pr. c. 1598-1599, pb. 1600), *A Midsummer Night's Dream* (pr. c. 1595-1596, pb. 1600), *The Merchant of Venice* (pr. c. 1596-1597, pb. 1600), *Much Ado About Nothing* (pr. c. 1598-1599, pb. 1600), *As You Like It* (pr. c. 1599-1600, pb. 1623), and *Twelfth Night: Or, What You Will* (pr. c. 1600-1602, pb. 1623).

At about the time Shakespeare wrote *Romeo and Juliet* and *Richard II*, he probably also began his great sonnet sequence, not published until 1609. The 154 sonnets, tracing a friendship with a young man, sometimes called the "Fair Youth," and a romance with a "Dark Lady," raise the question of how Shakespeare lived when he was away from Stratford, where his wife and children presumably remained. The young man might be a patron—perhaps Southampton, though other names have also been proposed—and the Dark Lady strictly imaginary, created to overturn the sonnets' trite Petrarchan conventions. Other speculations favor a more personal interpretation, seeing an actual *ménage à trois* of the poet, the Fair Youth, and the Dark Lady. All the questions raised by the sonnets remain open, and the only evidence about how Shakespeare spent his spare time in London indicates that he sometimes frequented taverns (notably the Mermaid) with his fellow playwrights and players.

Evidence also indicates that he remained in close contact with Stratford-upon-Avon, to which he probably returned as frequently as possible. He used his earnings from the theater to install himself as the town's leading citizen, buying New Place as a family residence in 1597 and thereafter steadily amassing other land and property. In 1596, his father John was granted a hereditary coat of arms (or his son may have purchased it for him) and thus became a gentleman, a status he had never achieved on his own. Unfortunately, also in 1596, Shakespeare suffered a setback when his son, Hamnet, died at the age of eleven. Shakespeare's affection for his two remaining children, Susanna and Judith, may be reflected in the witty, saucy, but lovable heroines of his great comedies.

Shakespeare's company in London prospered. In 1599, it stopped renting theaters and built its own, the Globe, which increased company profits. The company was a favorite of the reigning monarchs, who paid well for special performances at court—first Elizabeth I and then, after 1603, James I, who loved the theater even more and renamed Shakespeare's company the King's Men. The company also began performing most of the plays of Ben Jonson, who ranked second only to Shakespeare and who excelled at satiric comedy. Shakespeare turned to tragedy, first writing *Julius Caesar* (pr. c. 1599-1600, pb. 1623) and *Hamlet, Prince of Denmark* (pr. c. 1600-1601, pb. 1603) and then—one after another—*Othello, the Moor of Venice* (pr. 1604, pb. 1622, revised 1623), *King Lear* (pr. c. 1605-1606, pb. 1608), *Macbeth* (pr. 1606, pb. 1623), and *Antony and Cleopatra* (pr. c. 1606-1607, pb. 1623).

Yet even during this period—perhaps the high point in the history of Western drama—Shakespeare's company had its problems. One was the competition of the boys' companies, which performed in the private theaters—small indoor theaters that charged higher admission and appealed to a more exclusive audience than the public theaters. In 1608, the King's Men acquired one of the private theaters, the Blackfriars, plus the services of two playwrights who wrote for it, the collaborators Francis Beaumont and John Fletcher. With their light, witty comedy and melodramatic tragicomedy, represented by such plays as *The Knight of the Burning Pestle* (pr. 1607), *Philaster: Or, Love Lies A-Bleeding* (pr. c. 1609), and *A King and No King* (pr. 1611), Beaumont and Fletcher introduced a new "cavalier" style into Renaissance English drama that ultimately eclipsed even Shakespeare's popularity and perhaps hurried his retirement. It is uncertain whether they or Shakespeare introduced tragicomedy, but Shakespeare's final complete plays are in this fashionable new mode: *Pericles, Prince of Tyre* (pr. c. 1607-1608, pb. 1609), *Cymbeline* (pr. c. 1609-1610, pb. 1623), *The Winter's Tale* (pr. c. 1610-1611, pb. 1623), and *The Tempest* (pr. 1611, pb. 1623). After Beaumont married an heiress and stopped writing plays in 1612 or 1613, Shakespeare collaborated with Fletcher, and possibly others, on *Henry VIII* (pr. 1613, pb. 1623), *The Two Noble Kinsmen* (pr. c. 1612-1613, pb. 1634), and *Cardenio* (now lost).

By 1608, when his productivity dropped to one or two plays per year, Shakespeare may have spent part of each year in Stratford-upon-Avon. In 1607, his elder daughter had married Dr. John Hall, the local physician, and in 1608, with the birth of their daughter, Elizabeth, Shakespeare became a grandfather. Around 1613, he retired completely to Stratford-upon-Avon, though he also joined John Heminge, a partner in the King's Men, and William Johnson, the host of the Mermaid Tavern, in purchasing the gatehouse of the Blackfriars priory, probably for London visits. On February 10, 1616, his younger daughter, Judith, at the age of thirty-one, married Thomas Quiney, a member of another prominent Stratford family. On March 25, 1616, Shakespeare made out his last will and testament, leaving most of his estate to Susanna, a substantial amount of money to Judith, and his "second best bed" to Anne. He died on April 23, 1616, and was buried in Holy Trinity Church, Stratford-upon-Avon.

In 1623, Shakespeare's surviving partners in the King's Men, John Heminge and Henry Condell, published a collection of his plays now known as the First Folio. The portrait included in the First Folio depicts Shakespeare with a short mustache, large, staring eyes, and an oval face accentuated by his high, balding forehead and the remaining hair that almost covers his ears. The bust erected above his grave is similar, except that he has a goatee and the balding has progressed further. The First Folio portrait resembles a soulful intellectual, while the Stratford bust suggests a prominent burgher.

ACHIEVEMENT AND INFLUENCE

The two portraits of Shakespeare portray the two parts of his nature. On one hand, he possessed immense intellectual curiosity about the motives and actions of people. This curiosity, plus his facility with language, enabled him to write his masterpieces and to create characters who are better known than some important figures in world history. On the other hand, reflecting his middle-class background, Shakespeare was himself motivated by strictly bourgeois instincts; he was more concerned with acquiring property and cementing his social position in Stratford than he was with preserving his plays for posterity. If his partners had not published the First Folio, there would be no Shakespeare as he is known today: still acted and enjoyed, the most widely studied and translated writer, the greatest poet and dramatist in the English and perhaps any language.

Besides his ability to create a variety of unforgettable characters, there are at least two other qualities that account for Shakespeare's achievement. One of these is his love of play with language, ranging from the lowest pun to some of the world's best poetry. His love of language sometimes makes him difficult to read, particularly for young students, but frequently the meaning becomes clear in a well-acted version. The second quality is his openness, his lack of any restrictive point of view, ideology, or morality. Shakespeare was able to embrace, identify with, and depict an enormous range of human behavior, from the good to the bad to the indifferent. The capaciousness of his language and vision thus help account for the universality of his appeal.

Shakespeare's lack of commitment to any didactic point of view has often been deplored. Yet he is not entirely uncommitted; rather, he is committed to what is human. Underlying his broad outlook is Renaissance Humanism, a synthesis of Christianity and classicism that is perhaps the best development of the Western mind and finds its best expression in his work. This same generous outlook was apparently expressed in Shakespeare's personality, which, like his bourgeois instincts, defies the Romantic myth of the artist. He was often praised by his fellows, but friendly rival and ferocious satirist Ben Jonson said it best: "He was, indeed, honest, and of an open and free nature," and "He was not of an age, but for all time."

BIBLIOGRAPHY

De Grazia, Margreta, and Stanley Wells, eds. *The Cambridge Companion to Shakespeare.* New York: Cambridge University Press, 2001. This work provides an extensive guide to Shakespeare's life and works.

Dobson, Michael, and Stanley Wells, eds. *The Oxford Companion to Shakespeare.* Oxford, England: Oxford University Press, 2001. An encyclopedic treatment of the life and works of Shakespeare.

Duncan-Jones, Katherine. *Ungentle Shakespeare: Scenes from His Life.* London: Arden Shakespeare, 2001. Duncan-Jones portrays Shakespeare as a man influenced by the political, social, and literary climate in which he found himself. She also examines speculative stories such as his love for a Dark Lady. Bibliography and index.

Honan, Park. *Shakespeare: A Life.* 1999. Reprint. New York: Oxford University Press, 1999. Honan's life of Shakespeare shuns the mythology that has grown up around the playwright and places him in the context of his age.

Kermode, Frank. *Shakespeare's Language.* New York: Farrar Straus & Giroux, 2000. Between 1594 and 1608, Kermode argues, the language of Shakespeare's plays was transformed, acquiring a new complexity that arose out of the playwright's increasingly successful attempts to represent dramatically the excitement and confusion of thought under stress.

McConnell, Louise. *Dictionary of Shakespeare.* Chicago: Fitzroy Dearborn, 2000. A basic reference.

Southworth, John. *Shakespeare, the Player: A Life in the Theatre.* Stroud, England: Sutton, 2000. A biography that focuses on the dramatist as a member of the theater, writing for the theater in collaboration with the theater company.

Thomson, Peter. *Shakespeare's Professional Career.* New York: Cambridge University Press, 1992. Thomson examines the theatrical world of Elizabethan England to illuminate William Shakespeare's life and writings.

Wells, Stanley. *Shakespeare: A Life in Drama.* New York: W. W. Norton, 1995. A critical introduction to William Shakespeare's life and work.

Wilson, Ian. *Shakespeare: The Evidence: Unlocking the Mysteries of the Man and His Work*. London: Headline, 1993. Wilson draws on documents discovered during the excavation of the site of the Globe Theatre to delve into the mysteries surrounding Shakespeare's life, including authorship of his plays, his sexuality, his religion, and the curse he set on his own grave.

Harold Branam

NTOZAKE SHANGE
Paulette Williams

Born: Trenton, New Jersey; October 18, 1948

PRINCIPAL DRAMA

for colored girls who have considered suicide/ when the rainbow is enuf, pr., pb. 1975

A Photograph: Still Life with Shadows; A Photograph: A Study in Cruelty, pr. 1977 (revised as *A Photograph: Lovers in Motion*, pr. 1979, pb. 1981)

Where the Mississippi Meets the Amazon, pr. 1977 (with Thulani Nkabinde and Jessica Hagedorn)

From Okra to Greens: A Different Kinda Love Story, pr. 1978, pb. 1985

Black and White Two Dimensional Planes, pr., 1979

Spell #7: Geechee Jibara Quik Magic Trance Manual for Technologically Stressed Third World People, pr. 1979, pb. 1981

Boogie Woogie Landscapes, pr. 1979, pb. 1981

Mother Courage and Her Children, pr. 1980 (adaptation of Bertolt Brecht's play)

Three Pieces, pb. 1981

Betsey Brown, pr. 1991 (based on her novel)

The Love Space Demands: A Continuing Saga, pb. 1991, pr. 1992

Plays: One, pb. 1992

Three Pieces, pb. 1992

OTHER LITERARY FORMS

Ntozake Shange's three genres—plays, poems, and novels—so overlap that one might say she has invented a new genre, which she has named the "choreopoem." She has published several volumes of poetry, including *Nappy Edges* (1978), parts of which were included in her 1975 play *for colored girls who have considered suicide/ when the rainbow is enuf*; *Natural Disasters and Other Festive Occasions* (1979); *A Daughter's Geography* (1983); *Ridin' the Moon in Texas: Word Paintings* (1987); and *I Live in Music* (1994). Among her novels are *Sassafrass, Cypress, and Indigo* (1982) and *Betsey Brown* (1985). She has gathered writings about her work from 1976 to 1984 into *See No Evil: Prefaces, Essays, and Accounts, 1976-1983* (1984), the study of which is essential to an understanding of her art.

Shange has also distinguished herself as a director, of both her own work and that of others, notably Richard Wesley's *The Mighty Gents* in 1979. In 1980, Shange adapted Bertolt Brecht's *Mutter Courage und ihre Kinder* (1941; *Mother Courage and Her Children*, 1941), changing the scene from mid-seventeenth century Europe to post-Civil War America, making the protagonist an emancipated slave doing business with the army oppressing the Western Indians, and changing the language to black English.

ACHIEVEMENTS

Ntozake Shange's work embodies a rich confusion of genres and all the contradictions inherent in a world in which violence and oppression polarize life and art. These polarizations in Shange's work both contribute to her artistry and complicate it. She has been criticized and praised for her unconventional language and structure, for her almost religious feminism, and for her stand on black/white and male/

female issues. Her first play, *for colored girls who have considered suicide/ when the rainbow is enuf*, produced in 1976 by Joseph Papp's New York Shakespeare Festival, was honored in that year by the Outer Critics Circle, which consists of those who write about the New York theater for out-of-town newspapers. That play also received Obie and Audelco Awards as well as Tony and Grammy Award nominations in 1977. Shange's 1980 adaptation of Bertolt Brecht's *Mother Courage and Her Children* won one of the *The Village Voice*'s Obie awards. Among her many other awards are a *Los Angeles Times* Book Prize for Poetry and a Pushcart Prize.

BIOGRAPHY

Ntozake Shange (pronounced "En-to-zaki Shonggay") was born Paulette Williams in Trenton, New Jersey, on October 18, 1948, daughter of a surgeon and a psychiatric social worker and educator. She grew up surrounded by music, literature, art, and her parents' prominent friends, among them Dizzy Gillespie, Chuck Berry, and W. E. B. Du Bois, as well as Third World writers and musicians. Her ties with her family were strong; she also was close to her family's live-in black maids. She was graduated from Barnard College with honors in 1970, then received a

Ntozake Shange (Jules Allen)

graduate degree at the University of Southern California in Los Angeles. While in California, she began studying dance, writing poetry, and participating in improvisational works (consisting of poems, music, dance, and mime) at bars, cabarets, and schools. These gradually grew into *for colored girls who have considered suicide/ when the rainbow is enuf*, which she carried across the country to perform in workshops in New York, then at the Public Theatre, and eventually on Broadway. The contrasts between her privileged home and education and the realities of the lives of black women led her, in 1971, to change her name legally from what she called the "slave name" of Paulette Williams to Ntozake Shange, meaning "she who comes with her own things" and "she who walks like a lion" in Xhosa (Zulu). Her two failed marriages, her suicide attempts, and her contact with city violence resulted in an anger that found its outlet in her poems. During the late 1970's, she lived in New York City, but she later moved to Houston, Texas, with her daughter, Savannah. She has taught and lectured at many colleges and universities, including Mills College in Oakland California; The State University in Rutgers, New Jersey; the University of California, Berkeley; the University of Houston; Rice University; Yale University; Howard University; and New York University.

Her work with Emily Mann on the script version of *Betsey Brown* brought her into prominence among feminists and experimental theaters. Working under the auspices of the New York Shakespeare Festival, the two women brought the play into its production form through a series of staged readings, workshops, and tryouts, and their collaboration techniques were the subject of forums among dramaturges in 1990.

Shange's poetic "reading/performance" piece *The Love Space Demands*, in which she reads her own work (accompanied by guitarist Billie Patterson), was performed in New Jersey at the Crossroads Theatre and in San Francisco at the Hansberry Theatre in 1992.

ANALYSIS

In Ntozake Shange's introduction to the volume *Three Pieces*, she makes this statement about drama:

"as a poet in american theater/ i find most activity that takes place on our stages overwhelmingly shallow/ stilted & imitative. that is probably one of the reasons i insist on calling myself a poet or writer/ rather than a playwright/ i am interested solely in the poetry of a moment/ the emotional & aesthetic impact of a character or a line."

Her plays have evoked a range of critical responses commensurate with their unconventional nature. Should her work be characterized as poetry or drama, prose or poetry, essay or autobiography? Her choreopoems, made up of poetry, drama, prose, and autobiography, are unified by a militant feminism in which some critics have seen a one-sided attack on black men. Others, however, point out the youthful spirit, flair with language, and lyricism that carry her plays to startling and radical conclusions. Her style and its seeming contradictions, such as the use of both black English and the erudite vocabulary of the educated, are at the heart of her drama. Influenced by their method of development—public poetry reading in bars, cafés, schools, Off-Off-Broadway theaters— the plays are generally somewhere between a poetry reading and a staged play.

First among the contradictions or contrasts is her blending of genres: Her poems shade into drama, her dramas are essentially verse monologues, and her novels incorporate poetic passages. Second, her language varies radically—on a single page and even in a single phrase—from black dialect ("cuz," "wanna," "awready," "chirren") to the language of her middle-class upbringing and education ("i cant count the number of times i have viscerally wanted to attack deform n maim the language that i waz taught to hate myself in/"). In the published texts of her poetry, plays, and essays, in addition to simplified phonetic spellings, she employs the slash instead of the period and omits capitalization. Many recordings of her work are available, and these provide the listener with a much fuller sense of the dynamic quality of her language in performance.

Shange's bold and daring use of language, her respect for people formerly given little value, and her exploration of the roles of black men and women have opened a new dimension in theater. Her blendings of poetry, music, and dance bring theater back to its origins and simultaneously blaze a trail toward the drama of the future.

FOR COLORED GIRLS WHO HAVE CONSIDERED SUICIDE/ WHEN THE RAINBOW IS ENUF

Shange's first dramatic success, *for colored girls who have considered suicide/ when the rainbow is enuf*, is the recital, individually and in chorus, of the lives and growth of seven different black women, named according to their dress colors: "lady in red," "lady in blue," "lady in orange," "lady in brown," "lady in yellow," "lady in purple," and "lady in green." The term "colored girls" in the title evokes a stereotype of black women yet also contains a germ of hope for the future (the "rainbow," both of color and of eventual salvation).

These seven stylized figures are representative voices of black women, and they express their fury at their oppression both as women and as blacks. The first segment shows high school graduation and the social and sexual rite of passage for "colored girls" in the working-class suburbs. Some of the women who have been cruelly disappointed in relationships with men discuss their spiritual quests. A black woman pretends to be Puerto Rican so that she can dance the merengue in Spanish Harlem. A woman breaks up with her lover by returning to him his plant to water. The scenes become more somber, portraying rape, abuse, city dangers, and abortion. Ties with a more heroic black past appear in "Toussaint," while the glamorized prostitute evicts her lover from her bed. The women begin to analyze their predicaments and to assert their independence in segments entitled "somebody almost walked off wid alla my stuff" and "pyramid," in which three women console one another for the actions of the faithless lover whom they share. In the brutal culminating scene, a crazed Vietnam veteran, Beau Willie Brown, abuses his woman Crystal and kills their infant children, dropping them from a window.

The recurrent motif of the recitation is the thwarting of dreams and aspirations for a decent life by forces beyond one's control: war, poverty, and ignorance. There is, however, a saving grace. Toward the end of the play, the seven women fall into a tighter circle of mutual support, much like a religious "laying on of hands" ceremony, in which they say, "i found god in myself/ & i loved her/ i loved her fiercely." Their bitter pain, shown throughout the dramatic episodes, turns into a possibility of regeneration. Thus, the play is a drama of salvation for women who do not receive their full value in society.

Though it was a landmark in the emergence of new black women playwrights, *for colored girls who have considered suicide/ when the rainbow is enuf* has been criticized for its lack of discussion of black traditions in religion, family, and ordinary work, and for its omissions of both black literary and political history and the influence of whites. Its style, considered as an attack on language, part of blacks' "enslavement," has also been criticized. Later plays, however, include these elements in a constantly enriching network of allusions.

A PHOTOGRAPH

In *A Photograph*, a set of meditations and sketches involving an ideal black woman named Michael and her lover Sean, a failed photographer, Shange explores her idea of art—"the poetry of a moment"—as well as representative stages of the African American experience. Photography, dance, and drama are shown to be art forms that capture meaningful moments and present them to viewers and readers so that they might behold and understand the essence and the value of art and life. The young professionals that reside in or pass through Sean's San Francisco apartment-studio are shown to examine the psychological factors that impede and that motivate them and other African Americans.

The five figures of this piece are representative of other aspects of black life than those put forward in her first play. Nevada, a lawyer and lover-supporter of Sean, the struggling artist, sets herself above other "common" African Americans: Her family, she boasts, "was manumitted in 1843/ [when] yall were still slaves/ carrying things for white folks . . . /" The upwardly mobile Earl, also a lawyer, former lover of Claire and long-time friend of Sean, pleads Nevada's case to Sean when the latter rejects her. Claire is a dancer who dances seductively for Sean as he photographs and then ravishes her. Michael is a dancer and the woman Sean comes truly to love as she shares herself and her ideas of art and of the African experience with him.

Early in the drama Sean tells Michael, "i'm a genius for unravelling the mysteries of the darker races/. . . i know who we are." After he rejects Nevada and is rejected by her, Sean reveals his insecurities as a son, a man, an African American, and an artist. The self- and race-assured artist Michael challenges her temporarily broken lover. Sean soon responds to this and to a poetic story danced and told by Michael with his own story and assurances.

> yes. that's right. me. i'ma be it. the photographer of all time. look out ansel/ . . . i can bring you the world shining grainy focused or shaking/ a godlike phenomenon/ sean david . . . i realize you're not accustomed to the visions of a man of color who has a gift/ but fear not/ I'll give it to ya a lil at a time. i am only beginning to startle/ to mesmerize and reverse the reality of all who can see. I gotta thing bout niggahs/ my folks/ that just wont stop/ & we are so correct for the photograph/ we profile all the time/ styling/ giving angle & pattern/ shadows & still life. if somebody sides me cd see the line in niggahs/ the texture of our lives/ they wda done it/ but since nobody has stepped forward/ here I am . . .

Sean seems obviously representative of Shange the artist in his coming-into-his-own response to Michael, who is yet another representative of Shange the artist. This choreopoem seems a particularly significant statement made by Shange, poet and writer: She, like Sean, presents "the contours of life unnoticed" and she, like Michael, speaks "for everybody burdened."

BOOGIE WOOGIE LANDSCAPES

After examining the identity of isolated young black women in *for colored girls who have considered suicide/ when the rainbow is enuf* and of couples in *A Photograph*, Shange concentrates on one woman's visions, dreams, and memories in *Boogie Woogie Landscapes*, which was first produced as a one-woman poetry piece in 1978 and then cast as a play in 1979, with music and dance. Layla, a young black woman, entertains in her dreams a series of nightlife companions who exemplify her perceptions of herself and her memories. "Layla" in Arabic means "born at night," and the entire drama exists in Layla's nighttime subconscious. Layla's dreams of Fidel Castro's Cuba, of primitive cruelties to African women, and of rock and roll and blues interweave with her feelings about growing up, family, brothers and sisters, parents, maids (some of which appear later in Shange's semiautobiographical novel *Betsey Brown*).

SPELL #7

Shange's 1979 play *Spell #7*, like her first play, is structured like a highly electric poetry reading, but this time the cast is mixed male and female. A huge blackface mask forms the backdrop for actors and actresses of an imitation old-time minstrel show, where actors did skits, recited, and joked, all under the direction of a Mr. Interlocutor. The actors come offstage, relax at an actors' bar, and gradually remove their masks, revealing their true selves. Lou, the "practicing magician," reveals that his father gave up his role as magician when a colored child asked for a spell to make her white. The actors tell each other and the audience tall stories. One of these involves a child who thought blacks were immune to dread diseases and disease-ridden passions such as polio and pedophilia. She is disillusioned when, as an adult, she finds that blacks not only can but also do hurt one another, so she buys South African gold "to remind the black people that it cost a lot for us to be here/ our value/ can be known instinctively/ but since so many black people are having a hard time not being like white folks/ i wear these gold pieces to protest their ignorance/ their disconnect from history." Another woman loves her baby, which she names "myself," while it is in the womb but kills it after it is born. Still another girl vows to brush her "nappy" hair constantly so that she can toss it like white girls. By these contrasts and by wry lists and surprising parallels, Shange shows the pain and difficulty, as well as the hopefulness, of being black. Lou refers to the spell that caused his father to give up magic as he (Lou) casts the final spell of Spell #7:

> aint no colored magician in his right mind
> gonna make you white
> cuz this is blk magic you lookin at
> & i'm fixin you up good/ fixin you up good & colored
> & you gonna be colored all yr life
> & you gonna love it/ bein colored

The others join him in celebration of "bein colored"; but the minstrel mask drops down and Lou's final words contain anger as well as celebration:

> crackers are born with the right to be
> alive/ i'm making ours up right here
> in yr face/ & we gonna be
> colored & love it

FROM OKRA TO GREENS

Shange's *From Okra to Greens* draws together and expands on the themes of her earlier theater pieces. The discovery by the lovers Okra and Greens of the beauty and strength—the god—within the individual is like that of the women who populate *for colored girls who have considered suicide/ when the rainbow is enuf*. Similarly, the lovers' discovery of what is sacred—of the fullness and color of life versus the "skinny life" of black and white—is the goal of Layla in *Boogie Woogie Landscapes*, of the actors in *Spell #7*, and of the artists of *A Photograph*. The love between two fully realized human beings, like that experienced by Sean and Michael in *A Photograph*, is fully expanded on in this two-character drama of Okra and Greens. The theme of the responsibility of the artist touched on by Sean and by Michael is also fully developed by the poets Okra and Greens.

In the opening scenes of *From Okra to Greens*, Greens speaks of Okra's plight as single black woman as Okra acts/dances the role. This scene is reminiscent of Sean and Michael speaking in unison about Sean's and then Michael's art in the final scene of *A Photograph* and Ross's talking while Maxine acts out the role that the two are creating together, on the spot, in *Spell #7*. In *From Okra to Greens*, as in her other choreopoems, Shange turns her dramatic poetry into staged drama. She presents verbatim much of the poetry of her collection *A Daughter's Geography*. Although her feminist protests are dramatized in this play as in *for colored girls who have considered suicide/ when the rainbow is enuf* and in *Boogie Woogie Landscapes*, here her feminist protest is given voice by the male character Greens. That both Okra and Greens are poets allows them to have an understanding of one another and of the roles forced on too many African American women and men as well as an understanding of the role that human beings *should* play in the world.

Okra first dances as "the crooked woman" as Greens speaks, showing his and society's distorted view of black women. Okra's dance reflects both her pain and her potential strength and beauty. As the two come together, Greens admits his own crookedness in telling Okra that before their encounter he had not known "what a stood/up straight man felt like." Together the two characters create and present portraits of "some men" who degrade women (as they are encouraged to do by the patriarchy). Once married, the two continue their dialogue, which includes their consideration of one another and of the sociopolitical climate in which they and, later, their daughter, must reside.

Shange's *Okra and Greens* celebrates, as do Sean and Michael in *A Photograph*, the richness of African American life. Her love story extends to the poor of not only her own country but also the world. Okra pleads for the return of Haitian liberators Dessalines, Petion, and L'Ouverture with their visions of "*la liberte, l'egalite, la fraternite.*" As in her other theater pieces, Shange calls here, too, for the return of American visionaries, among them W. E. B. Du Bois.

As the hope of the world's visionaries is shown to have dimmed, so the relationship between the lovers Okra and Greens dims momentarily. Abandoned by Greens, Okra says that "the moon cracked in a ugly rupture." Joined once more, the two encourage each other and others to "rise up" and to "dance with the universe." This story of the love between two poets is a love song to a universe in sad need of hope.

The refrain of *Boogie Woogie Landscapes*, that "we dont recognize what's sacred anymore," is revealed in *From Okra to Greens* in the portrait of the "pretty man" whose pretty floors are covered with the kind of rug that "little girls spend whole/ lives tying." Lack of recognition of the sacred is a theme repeated throughout the work. However, the love between Okra and Greens and their hope for their daughter and for the oppressed peoples of the world shows recognition of the sacred is possible for aware, thinking, and caring individuals. The memory of other visionaries also shows the poets' and others' recognition of

the sacred. It is clear here and throughout her writing that Shange would have her audience recognize the sacred in themselves and in others and do their part in telling the story—in spreading the word—and in fighting for liberty, equality, and fraternity for all.

BETSEY BROWN AND
THE LOVE SPACE DEMANDS

In 1991, Shange adapted her novel *Betsey Brown* into a play. The semiautobiographical work tells the story of a thirteen-year-old African American girl growing up in a middle-class household in 1950's St. Louis. *The Love Space Demands*, a loosely connected series of poems and monologues Shange herself performs with musical accompaniment, revolves around sexual relations in the age of AIDS (acquired immune deficiency syndrome).

OTHER MAJOR WORKS

LONG FICTION: *Sassafras: A Novella*, 1976; *Sassafras, Cypress, and Indigo*, 1982; *Betsey Brown*, 1985; *Liliane: Resurrection of the Daughter*, 1994.

POETRY: *Nappy Edges*, 1978; *Natural Disasters and Other Festive Occasions*, 1979; *A Daughter's Geography*, 1983, 1991; *From Okra to Greens: Poems*, 1984; *Ridin' the Moon in Texas: Word Paintings*, 1987; *I Live in Music*, 1994.

NONFICTION: *See No Evil: Prefaces, Essays, and Accounts, 1976-1983*, 1984; *If I Can Cook, You Know God Can*, 1998.

EDITED TEXT: *The Beacon Best of 1999: Creative Writing by Women and Men of All Colors*, 2000.

BIBLIOGRAPHY

Brown-Guillory, Elizabeth. *Their Place on the Stage: Black Women Playwrights in America*. New York: Greenwood Press, 1988. A good study of Shange, along with Alice Childress and Lorraine Hansberry. Analyzes *for colored girls who have considered suicide/ when the rainbow is enuf* at considerable length, as well as the 1979 trilogy, *Spell #7, Boogie Woogie Landscapes*, and *A Photograph*.

Effiong, Philip Uko. *In Search of a Model for African American Drama: A Study of Selected Plays by Lorraine Hansberry, Amiri Baraka, and Ntozake*

Shange. New York: University Press of America, 2000. Analyzes the historical and sociopolitical considerations that determine the choices made by each dramatist. Considers the ritualization of black theater by each dramatist.

Lester, Neal A. *Ntozake Shange: A Critical Study of the Plays*. New York: Garland, 1995. Lester examines critically Shange's contributions to the American stage, suggests aspects of her work for further study, and contextualizes Shange's drama within appropriate literary traditions. A thorough and insightful study of Shange's *for colored girls who have considered suicide/ when the rainbow is enuf, Spell #7, A Photograph, Boogie Woogie Landscapes*, and *From Okra to Greens*.

Russell, Sandi. *Render Me My Song: African American Women Writers from Slavery to the Present*. New York: St. Martin's Press, 1990. Supplies a list of Shange's work up to *Betsey Brown*. Good biography and comments on the "choreopoem" format. Discusses the trilogy of plays ending with *A Photograph* and examines Shange's version of Bertolt Brecht's *Mother Courage and Her Children*. Puts Shange in context with Alexis DeVeaux, Rita Dove, and Toni Cade Bambara, writers using blues styles fed by oral traditions, of which *for colored girls who have considered suicide/ when the rainbow is enuf* is exemplary.

Shange, Ntozake, and Emily Mann. "The Birth of an R&B Musical." Interview by Douglas J. Keating. *Inquirer* (Philadelphia), March 26, 1989. Follows the story of how Emily Mann and Shange took Shange's *Betsey Brown* from book to stage, in a long interview with both playwrights to mark the opening of the play at the Forum Theater in Philadelphia, as part of the American Music Theater Festival.

Sommers, Michael. "Rays of Hope in a Sky of Blues." Review of *The Love Space Demands* by Ntozake Shange. *Star-Ledger* (Newark, N.J.), March 12, 1992. This appreciative review of *The Love Space Demands* provides an insightful overview of how Shange takes her poetry to the stage. Sommers finds the work "[a] very accessible, dramatically gripping and altogether handsomely-done theater piece."

"*Spell #7* Takes Us on Magical Trip." Review of *Spell #7* by Ntozake Shange. *Times* (Washington, D.C.), May 9, 1991. This descriptive review of *Spell #7* places the piece in the context of a continuing struggle of black women for a dignified place in society: "After all the tribulations and outpourings of feeling, the lingering message is one of racial pride."

Anne Mills King, updated by Thomas J. Taylor
and Judith K. Taylor

JOHN PATRICK SHANLEY

Born: New York, New York; October 13, 1950

PRINCIPAL DRAMA

Saturday Night at the War, pr. 1978

George and the Dragon, pr. 1979

Welcome to the Moon, pr. 1982, pb. 1985

Danny and the Deep Blue Sea: An Apache Dance, pr. 1983, pb. 1984

Welcome to the Moon and Other Plays, pb. 1985

Savage in Limbo, pr. 1985, pb. 1986

the dreamer examines his pillow: A Heterosexual Homily, pr. 1985, pb. 1987

Women of Manhattan, pr., pb. 1986

Italian American Reconciliation, pr. 1986, pb. 1989

All for Charity, pr. 1987

The Big Funk, pr. 1990, pb. 1991

Beggars in the House of Plenty, pr. 1991, pb. 1992

Collected Plays, pb. 1992

What Is This Everything?, pr. 1992

Thirteen by Shanley, pb. 1992

Four Dogs and a Bone, pr. 1993, pb. 1996

Missing/Kissing: Missing Marissa and Kissing Christine, pr. 1996, pb. 1997

Psychopathia Sexualis, pr. 1997, pb. 1998

Cellini, pr. 1998

Where's My Money?, pr. 2001

OTHER LITERARY FORMS

In addition to his dramatic works, John Patrick Shanley wrote screenplays, achieving considerable success with his first effort, *Moonstruck*, in 1987. He followed up with *Five Corners* (1988), *The January Man* (1989), *Joe Versus the Volcano* (1990), *We're Back! A Dinosaur's Story* (1993), *Alive* (1993), and *Congo* (1995). Several of Shanley's plays have been developed into storybooks and novels.

ACHIEVEMENTS

For four consecutive seasons (1983-1986), John Patrick Shanley was selected for participation in the National Playwrights Conference at the Eugene O'Neill Memorial Theater Center. His autobiographical cycle of plays achieved initial success and built his reputation for off-beat, unconventional plays. Several of his plays have enjoyed commercial runs at theaters Off-Off-Broadway and at various theaters across the United States. Since 1988, he has also directed his own plays.

In film, Shanley has achieved even greater success. His screenplay for *Five Corners* was awarded the Special Jury Prize at the Barcelona Film Festival. His screenplay for *Moonstruck* won the Writer's Guild Award, 1981, an Academy Award for Best Original Screenplay, 1987, and the Los Angeles Film Critics Award, 1987. He made his debut as a film director in *Joe Versus the Volcano*.

BIOGRAPHY

John Patrick Shanley was born in New York City on October 13, 1950. The fifth and youngest child of an Irish-born meatpacker and a telephone operator, Shanley grew up on Archer Street in the Bronx, a violent, brutal, racist neighborhood. During his childhood there, he was choked with an iron rod, beaten with a baseball bat, targeted by rock throwers, and at

the age of ten, was hung upside down from the roof of a five-story building by two boys seeking vengeance for a snowball fight. Shanley insists that the development of his off-center, eccentric dialogue began during this time period, issuing from a desperate effort to survive. He perfected an elliptical manner of self-expression that would deflect his true intent and would not appear to offend or challenge his tormentors.

Shanley grew up in a household in which college was perceived as a waste of time. He has acknowledged that, as a child, he had no dreams for his future. He had been expelled three times from high schools in the Bronx when, in 1965, a Roman Catholic priest befriended him and helped him enroll in a boarding school in New Hampshire. At the age of nineteen, he dropped out of New York University, spending two years in the Marine Corps and three years at odd jobs. He returned to college and unexpectedly stumbled on playwriting, an occurrence that allowed him a much-needed means of self-expression. Graduating as class valedictorian, he received a B.S. degree from New York University in 1977. While working toward a master's degree in theater, he was offered two fellowships—one in New York and the other in England. He declined both of them, electing instead to drop out of school and work as a bartender and house painter.

At this time, Shanley found himself in the midst of a prolific imaginative period. In a burst of creativity, he wrote plays and poetry, mainly exploring the memories of his earlier life in the Bronx. Unwilling to continue eking out a living writing plays and perhaps being forced to paint houses again, Shanley turned his out-of-the-ordinary talent toward screenwriting. His success in film granted him the time to continue writing plays.

His marriage of ten years came to an end in 1983, and, in 1988, he married actress Jayne Haynes. They later divorced.

ANALYSIS

John Patrick Shanley has maintained that his motivation for beginning to write at the age of eleven was to provide an outlet for his own difficulties. He has credited playwriting with saving his life by compelling him to remember basic truths he had learned as a child and using them as a means of coping with his own life.

Like other modern playwrights, Shanley seems to be concerned with escalating violence in the world, returning again and again in his plays to violent situations similar to the ones he encountered while growing up and to his unresolved feelings about them. However, Shanley suggests that the greatest violence to individuals seems to manifest itself psychologically through the bitter, binding family ties. As a result, he has mined every step in his relationships with family members in his writing. His characters confront alienation, guilt, betrayal, and love as they attempt to relieve the destructive influences of parent-child kinship. Shanley insists that coming to terms with one's family and resolving the bitterness is a crucial event, and although it may not achieve a state of grace for all concerned, it is necessary to continue living.

Shanley's fatalistic view of life is reflected in his depiction of how love affects his characters. These individuals are doomed to suffer, if not from past family traumas, then from love or its effects. Love brings no happiness to his characters, only pain and loss. It robs individuals of options, of self-respect and peace; it consumes everything, leaving only the pain it generates.

Although Shanley's strength is comedy, the world he depicts is a cynical, gritty one in which individuals confront those who caused them pain, hoping to return it. It is inhabited by eccentric characters, usually blue-collar, working-class people whose explosive dialogue attacks others and themselves with sarcasm, rage, and despair. Frequently, his bombast merges with passionate, poetic lyricism that, to a remarkable degree, compensates for frequent plot deficiencies in his plays. Shanley discovered early in his career a gift for reproducing unpleasant, naturalistic details that depict a neurotic, violent, self-perpetuating, self-defeating world.

DANNY AND THE DEEP BLUE SEA

Shanley's reputation soared with the production of this play. The first of a series of four autobiographical plays, it examines the violence that festers and intermittently explodes. The play centers on a couple who meet at a rough Bronx bar, one violent and eager to maim or kill, and the other guilt-ridden, suicidal, and generally self-destructive. The difficulties that these characters experience with human contact is linked to the horrors in their familial past.

The acrimony and aggression between the two snarling, verbose outcasts, who appear to be engaged in a kind of defensive and combative prize fight with the audience at ringside, create a sense of apprehension as the woman appears to goad Danny into killing her. As the play manages to draw viewers into the strange, impending disaster, suddenly a jolting transformation occurs as the scene shifts to her bedroom, and the characters are talking of love and marriage. Somewhat undeveloped, the startling play seems little more than a vignette, though somewhat too long, that leads to a sentimental and mawkish tribute to the transforming power of love.

Viewers found the shift unsettling and some critics wondered if, indeed, Shanley had lost his nerve and merely retreated from his initial perspective on violence. Still, part of the play's success resulted from the frighteningly real acting of the two main characters and their barrage of seething, graphic dialogue.

ITALIAN AMERICAN RECONCILIATION

Fresh from the success of his screenplay for *Moonstruck*, Shanley returned to the stage with the last play in his four-play cycle, at whose focal point, according to Shanley, is the enormous difficulty of becoming a man in today's society. In this play, Shanley explored his Oscar-winning sentimental vision of ethnic urban romance in New York's Little Italy, specifically suffering characters who are caught in the web of love. The play concerns the farcical scheme of friends to reconcile Huey, the main character, with his former wife, if only for one night. Divorced for three years, Huey is still unable to get on with his life. He yearns desperately for his former wife, who detests him and has shot his dog and threatened him with the same weapon. His sweet, gentle new girlfriend has no power to assuage his obsession with his sharp-tongued, vaguely psychotic former wife.

Despite the ridiculous nature of this comedic plot, Shanley seems to use Huey as a mouthpiece for his own belief in the castrating, consuming powers of love. Those who are blinded by such power see only themselves and their loss and, much like Huey, who cannot continue without his lost manhood, become strangely unable to cope with the world and therefore need the controlling force of love.

BEGGARS IN THE HOUSE OF PLENTY

In this domestic comedy of three acts, Shanley once again turns to autobiographical material as he examines the bitterness that binds family members. Whereas in previous plays, Shanley sought connections between broken romances or marriages and family traumas, in this play, he omits romantic issues to skewer a Roman Catholic family in the Bronx. Shanley's play recalls those of American playwright John Guare, whose plays of Roman Catholic blue-collar families flourished in the 1970's and 1980's.

Unfolding on a set so double-edged that it functions both as a shrine to memories and as a horror house, the action of forty years of family history rushes across the stage in a breathless ninety minutes. Johnny, the narrator growing slowly to manhood, alternates between playing himself as he is now and playing himself as a five-year-old and is the primary victim of the family mayhem.

Shanley's excursion into absurdism or at least a suggestion that his created universe is meaningless replaces his former raw, naturalistic details and borders on outlandish. Parents, who bear the brunt of his indictment, are turned into a demon from hell and a remote creature who regresses into self-absorbed little-girlhood. As is the case with other Shanley plays, the sharp, satiric, surrealistic comedy trails off toward the end into bombast or cracks under the weight of too much bitterness. Johnny's reminiscences end with the questions: Why do parents withhold love and approval? Why does anyone have to beg for love in a family in the land of plenty?

FOUR DOGS AND A BONE

In this two-act sketch, Shanley sets his sights and aims all the verbal weapons in his satiric arsenal at Hollywood. This somewhat structureless play is a series of encounters and confrontations without real resolutions; the four main characters merely battle each other mercilessly in a world Shanley seems to find basically absurd.

The bone in the play's title is fame, which the veteran actress, the scheming ingenue, an unscrupulous producer, and a novice screenwriter attempt to secure through malicious, underhanded intrigues. In a way, Shanley bites the hand that feeds him, in view of his success in films. Shanley begins the play with a quotation from the Roman poet Vergil, lamenting the craving of human beings for gold, but soon turns the focus toward manipulative natures going beyond the realm of point or significance. Juggling absurdism and realism, Shanley shrewdly directs the play that is loaded with details that point to no larger picture. Substituting sharp wit for structure, Shanley shows off barbs, digs and repartee—all illustrating his comic ingenuity for finding new ways to lampoon Hollywood.

PSYCHOPATHIA SEXUALIS

The title of this play is borrowed by Shanley from German author Richard von Krafft-Ebbing, whose 1886 book *Psychopathia Sexualis* was one of many studies read by Shanley during his mid-life crisis. He began a program of self-examination in an effort to understand his own psyche and, at one point, began to find significance in everything. Various characters that began to take shape in his mind inhabit the world of this play.

Shanley's comedy, on the surface, concerns a character whose eccentric behavior reflects his preoccupation with the springs of his own behavior and the outward expressions of inner crises. Typically, Shanley raises more questions than he answers as he focuses on the preposterous, the perverse, and the irrational. Shanley's questions about truth, self-knowledge, and the nature of love or delusions, remain essentially unanswerable, or else the answers appear to change throughout the play.

OTHER MAJOR WORKS

SCREENPLAYS: *Moonstruck*, 1987; *Five Corners*, 1988; *The January Man*, 1989; *Joe Versus the Volcano*, 1990; *We're Back! A Dinosaur's Story*, 1993; *Alive*, 1993; *Congo*, 1995.

BIBLIOGRAPHY

Johnson, Brian D. "Writing His Own Ticket." *Macleans* 101 (1988): 40. Focuses on Shanley's success in plays and films, his tough-guy stance acquired in the Bronx and his modest lifestyle. Shanley discusses his insistence on retaining control of his written material.

Kaplan, Eliot. "A Couple of White Guys Sitting Around Talking." *Gentleman's Quarterly* 60 (1990): 137-139. Kaplan referees a conversation between Shanley's friend, comedian Eric Bogo-sian, and Shanley. Each discusses humor and where, for him, it comes from, what each person's family made of him, and the folly of trying to please everyone.

Roberts, Polly. "Bard of the Bronx." *Harper's Bazaar* 121 (1988): 110-112. Details Shanley's early life in the Bronx, his difficulty with education and family, and his road to success. Argues that Shanley's plays about family dynamics are essentially his confrontations of his own parents.

Mary Hurd

GEORGE BERNARD SHAW

Born: Dublin, Ireland; July 26, 1856
Died: Ayot St. Lawrence, Hertfordshire, England; November 2, 1950

PRINCIPAL DRAMA

Widowers' Houses, wr. 1885-1892, pr. 1892, pb. 1893

Mrs. Warren's Profession, wr. 1893, pb. 1898, pr. 1902

The Philanderer, wr. 1893, pb. 1898, pr. 1905

Arms and the Man, pr. 1894, pb. 1898

Candida: A Mystery, pr. 1897, pb. 1898

The Devil's Disciple, pr. 1897, pb. 1901

The Man of Destiny, pr. 1897, pb. 1898

You Never Can Tell, pb. 1898, pr. 1899

Captain Brassbound's Conversion, pr. 1900, pb. 1901

Caesar and Cleopatra, pb. 1901, pr. 1906

The Admirable Bashville, pr. 1903, pb. 1909 (based on Shaw's novel *Cashel Byron's Profession*)

Man and Superman, pb. 1903, pr. 1905

How He Lied to Her Husband, pr. 1904, pb. 1907

John Bull's Other Island, pr. 1904, pb. 1907

Major Barbara, pr. 1905, pb. 1907

Passion, Poison, and Petrifaction, pr., pb. 1905

The Doctor's Dilemma, pr. 1906, pb. 1911

The Interlude at the Playhouse, pr., pb. 1907 (playlet)

Getting Married, pr. 1908, pb. 1911

Press Cuttings, pr., pb. 1909

The Shewing up of Blanco Posnet, pr. 1909, pb. 1911

The Fascinating Foundling, wr. 1909, pb. 1926, pr. 1928

The Glimpse of Reality, wr. 1909, pb. 1926, pr. 1927

The Dark Lady of the Sonnets, pr. 1910, pb. 1914

Misalliance, pr. 1910, pb. 1914

Fanny's First Play, pr. 1911, pb. 1914

Androcles and the Lion, pr. 1912 (in German), pr. 1913 (in English), pb. 1916

Overruled, pr. 1912, pb. 1916

Pygmalion, pb. 1912, pr. 1914 (in English), pr. 1913 (in German)

Beauty's Duty, wr. 1913, pb. 1932 (playlet)

Great Catherine, pr. 1913, pb. 1919

Heartbreak House, wr. 1913-1919, pb. 1919, pr. 1920

The Music Cure, pr. 1914, pb. 1926

The Inca of Perusalem, pr. 1916, pb. 1919

O'Flaherty, V.C., pr. 1917, pb. 1919

Augustus Does His Bit, pr. 1917, pb. 1919

Annajanska, the Bolshevik Empress, pr. 1918, pb. 1919

Back to Methuselah, pb. 1921, pr. 1922

Jitta's Atonement, pr. 1923, pb. 1926

Saint Joan, pr. 1923, pb. 1924

The Apple Cart, pr. 1929, pb. 1930

Too True to Be Good, pr. 1932, pb. 1934

How These Doctors Love One Another!, pb. 1932
    (playlet)

On the Rocks, pr. 1933, pb. 1934

Village Wooing, pr., pb. 1934

The Six Men of Calais, pr. 1934, pb. 1936

The Simpleton of the Unexpected Isles, pr., pb.
    1935

Arthur and Acetone, pb. 1936

The Millionairess, pr., pb. 1936

Cymbeline Refinished, pr. 1937, pb. 1938
    (adaptation of William Shakespeare's
    Cymbeline, act 5)

Geneva, pr. 1938, pb. 1939

In Good King Charles's Golden Days, pr., pb.
    1939

"The British Party System," wr. 1944 (playlet)

Buoyant Billions, pb. 1947, pr. 1948 (in German),
    pr. 1949 (in English)

Shakes Versus Shaw, pr. 1949, pb. 1950

Far-Fetched Fables, pr., pb. 1950

*The Bodley Head Bernard Shaw: Collected Plays
    with Their Prefaces*, pb. 1970-1974 (7 volumes)

OTHER LITERARY FORMS

Although George Bernard Shaw is generally thought of as a dramatist, he wrote a considerable amount of nondramatic prose. He completed, for example, several novels before turning to the stage, and even though none of them is likely to be remembered for its own sake, all show Shaw's gift for witty dialogue. His *The Intelligent Woman's Guide to Socialism and Capitalism* (1928), written for his sister-in-law, is one of the clearest expositions of socialism or communism ever written. *The Quintessence of Ibsenism* (1891), *The Perfect Wagnerite* (1898), and *The Sanity of Art* (1908) are representative of his criticism in drama, music, and art, respectively. The prefaces to his plays—some of which are longer than the plays they preface and which often explain little about the plays themselves—are brilliantly written

criticisms of everything from the four Gospels to the contemporary prison system.

Other notable Shaw works include *Fabian Essays in Socialism* (1889), *The Common Sense of Municipal Trading* (1904), *Dramatic Opinions and Essays* (1907), *The Adventures of the Black Girl in Her Search for God* (1932), and several collections of letters: *Letters to Miss Alma Murray* (1927), *Ellen Terry and Shaw* (1931), *Correspondence Between George Bernard Shaw and Mrs. Patrick Campbell* (1952), *Collected Letters* (1965-1988, 4 volumes; Dan H. Laurence, editor), and *The Nondramatic Literary Criticism of Bernard Shaw* (1972; Stanley Weintraub, editor).

ACHIEVEMENTS

George Bernard Shaw came to an English theater settled into the well-made play, a theater that had not known a first-rate dramatist for more than a century. The pap on which its audiences had been fed, not very different from television fare today, provided a soothing escape from the realities of the working world. Instead of fitting himself to this unreal mold, Shaw offered reality in all its forms: social, political, economic, and religious. He was a didact, a preacher who readily acknowledged that the stage was his pulpit. In startling contrast to his contemporary Oscar Wilde and Wilde's fellow aesthetes, Shaw asserted that he would not commit a single sentence to paper for art's sake alone; yet he beat the aesthetes at their own artistic game. Though he preached socialism, creative evolution, the abolition of prisons, and real equality for women, and railed against the insincerity of motives for war, he did so as a jester in some of the finest comedy ever written. He had no desire to be a martyr and insisted that, though his contemporaries might merely laugh at his plays, "a joke is an earnest in the womb of time." The next generation would get his point, even if the current generation was only entertained.

Many of the next generations have gotten his point, and Shaw's argument—that he who writes for all time will discover that he writes for no time—seems to have been borne out. Only by saying something to the age can one say something to posterity.

Today, evolution and creationism and Shaw's ideas on creative evolution and the Life Force remain timely issues. In Shaw's own day, as Dan Laurence points out, Henri Bergson changed the dramatist's Life Force into the *élan vital* four years after Shaw wrote of it in *Man and Superman*, and Pierre Teilhard de Chardin's evolutionary ideas, so appealing to moderns, about the movement of the "noosphere" toward an omega man, show the timeliness of Shaw's evolutionary theory that humankind is in the process of creating a God. Shaw's condemnation of the prison system as a vindictive, not a rehabilitative force, matches the widespread concern with the ineffectiveness of that system today. His struggle for the genuine equality of women with men before the law also gives his work a surprisingly contemporary thrust. Shaw brought serious themes back to the trivialized English stage, creating a body of drama that left him second to none among twentieth century dramatists.

BIOGRAPHY

George Bernard Shaw was born in Dublin, Ireland, at No. 3 Upper Synge Street on July 26, 1856. The house still stands, though the address became 33 Synge Street, and the residence is marked by the surprisingly understated plaque, "Bernard Shaw, author of many plays, was born in this house." Shaw's father was a cheerful drunk, and the son's loss of faith in the father might have affected his faith in general. In any event, though he was baptized into the Church of Ireland, he became a lifelong scoffer at organized religion while always remaining a profoundly religious thinker.

Shaw's mother and sister were fine singers and eventually left Shaw's father to move in with the eccentric music teacher, George Vandeleur Lee. From Lee, Shaw himself learned the voice control that would later stand him in good stead as a public debater. He also learned a great deal from respected uncles: From one, a curate at St. Bride's in Dublin, he learned Latin; another, a ship's surgeon, taught him that the Bible was the greatest pack of lies ever invented.

Shaw left secondary school because of boredom. The Latin he had learned early put him too far ahead of his classmates to make the instruction profitable, and by the time the others caught up, he had lost interest and formed poor study habits. He worked for a firm of land agents before finally leaving Ireland when he was nineteen years old, joining his mother and Vandeleur Lee in London.

For a time after arriving in London, Shaw wrote music criticism that Lee had been commissioned to write but turned over to Shaw. Shaw was later to write music criticism (under the pen name "Corno di Bassetto") that qualified him, in the judgment of W. H. Auden and other observers, as the finest music critic ever. By the time he was twenty-three years old, Shaw was convinced that he could not return to office work, and he began a career as a novelist. He wrote five novels, none of which was immediately published, although later, all but the first novel would find publishers.

Around 1884, Shaw made the acquaintance of William Archer at the British Museum. The meeting launched Shaw on his career as a critic, first as an art critic, then as a music critic (as mentioned above), and finally as a drama critic for more than three years for the *Saturday Review*.

While Shaw was a struggling novelist and critic, he became a vegetarian and a socialist; both of these causes were to color his writing for the rest of his life. The conversion to vegetarianism came when he was twenty-five years old and under the influence of Percy Bysshe Shelley's Idealism. His conversion to socialism came somewhat later, probably through the influence of a lecture by Henry George and subsequent reading of Karl Marx. In 1884, Shaw helped Beatrice and Sidney Webb found the Fabian Society, a socialist organization later joined by H. G. Wells. When Shaw's nervousness made him stumble badly during a lecture on John Stuart Mill for the society, he determined to make a public speaker of himself by promptly planting his soapbox for socialism in Hyde Park. Considering the extraordinary public speaker and debater Shaw became, it is hard to believe that he began as a young man who was so shy he could not visit a friend without pacing up and down the street trying to gain courage to ring the door bell.

George Bernard Shaw (© The Nobel Foundation)

In 1892, the Independent Theatre was about to open and needed plays. Shaw quickly finished *Widowers' Houses*, which he had begun seven years earlier with William Archer. The noted drama critic, however, decided Shaw was no playwright and was never to change his mind. Although Shaw had accepted Archer's opinion at first, he gave the play a second try and began a career that was to continue until 1950.

When Shaw was awarded the Nobel Prize in Literature in 1925, he refused it at first, but, on learning he could donate the money to a fund for popularizing Scandinavian literature, he accepted the award and gave the money away. This award marked the high point of his career, though he was still to write seventeen plays. In September, 1950, Shaw, who seemed on the way to becoming the ageless superman he proclaimed, fell from an apple tree he was pruning. He

died in November of that year, of complications stemming from that injury. His ashes were mingled with his wife's and spread on his garden.

ANALYSIS

A religious thinker, George Bernard Shaw saw the stage as his pulpit. His major interest was to advance the Life Force, a kind of immanent Holy Spirit that would help to improve and eventually perfect the world. Shaw believed that to help in this conscious purpose, human beings must live longer in order to use their intellectual maturity. They must be healthier, without the debilitating force of poverty, and—most important—they must be interested in purpose, not simply pleasure. As the giraffe could develop its long neck over aeons because of a need to eat from the tops of trees, so can human beings, with a sense of purpose, work toward the creation of healthier, longer-lived, more intelligent individuals.

According to Shaw, evolution is not merely haphazard but is tied to will. Human beings can know what they want and will what they know. Certainly, individuals cannot simply will that they live longer and expect to do so. Such desire might help, but it is the race, not the individual, that will eventually profit from such a common purpose. Ultimately, Shaw believed, this drive toward a more intelligent and spiritual species would result after aeons in human beings' shucking off matter, which had been taken on by spirit in the world's beginning so that evolution could work toward intelligence. When that intelligence achieves its full potential, matter will no longer be necessary. Humankind is working toward the creation of an infinite God.

Shaw's plays are not restricted to such metaphysics. They treat political, social, and economic concerns: the false notion that people help criminals by putting them in jail or help themselves by atonement (*Major Barbara, Captain Brassbound's Conversion, The Simpleton of the Unexpected Isles*), the need for tolerance (*On the Rocks, Androcles and the Lion*), the superstitious worship of medicine and science (*The Philanderer, The Doctor's Dilemma*), the superiority of socialism to capitalism (*Widowers' Houses, The Apple Cart, The Inca of Perusalem*), the evils of patriotism (*O'Flaherty, V.C., Arms and the Man*), the need for a supranational state (*Geneva*), the necessity for recognizing women's equality with men (*In Good King Charles's Golden Days, Press Cuttings*), and so on. Nevertheless, all of Shaw's efforts to question social and political mores were subsumed by his religious purpose. All were meant to help free the human spirit in its striving toward the creation of a better and more intelligent person, the creation of a superman, the creation, finally, of a God.

ARMS AND THE MAN

In 1894, two years after completing his first play, Shaw wrote *Arms and the Man*. Although lighter and less complex than later plays, it is typical of the later plays in that Shaw uses comedy as a corrective—a corrective, as Louis Crompton effectively puts it, that is intended to shame the audience *out* of conformity, in contrast to Molière's, which is intended to shame the audience *into* conformity.

The year is 1885. Bulgaria and Serbia are at war, the Serbs have just been routed, and the play opens with one of the Serbs' officers, Captain Bluntschli, climbing through the window of a Bulgarian house. The house belongs to Major Petkoff, and Raina Petkoff lies dreaming of her lover, a dashing Byronic hero, Sergius Saranoff, who has led the cavalry charge that routed the Serbs. Bluntschli comes into her room, gun in hand, but convinces her not to give him away, more because a fight will ensue while she is not properly dressed than for any fear she has of being shot.

Bluntschli turns out to be Saranoff's opposite. He is a practical Swiss who joined the Serbs merely because they were the first to enlist his services, not because he believed either side to be in the right. When the Bulgarian soldiers enter the house and demand to search Raina's room, she hides Bluntschli on impulse. After the soldiers' departure, he describes for Raina the recent battle in which some quixotic fool led a cavalry charge of frightened men against a battery of machine guns. All were trying to rein in their horses lest they get there first and be killed. The Serbs, however, happened not to have the right ammunition, and what should have been a slaughter of the Bulgarians turned out to be a rout of the Serbs.

Yet for his irresponsible foolishness, this "Don Quixote" is sure to be rewarded by the Bulgarians. When Raina shows Bluntschli the picture of her lover, and Saranoff turns out to be "Quixote," Bluntschli is duly embarrassed, tries to cover by suggesting that Saranoff might have known in advance of the Serbs' ammunition problem, but only makes it worse by suggesting to this romantic girl that her lover would have been such a crass pretender and coward as to attack under such conditions.

This is Shaw's first ridicule of chivalric notions of war. The viewpoint is corroborated in the next act by Saranoff when he returns disillusioned because he has not been promoted. He did not follow the scientific rules of war and was thus undeserving. Saranoff has discovered that soldiering is the cowardly art of attacking mercilessly when one is strong and keeping out of harm's way when weak.

In this second act, which takes place at the war's end only four months later, the audience is treated to some satire of Victorian "higher love," which Saranoff carries on with Raina before more realistically flirting with her maid, Louka. Later, in a momentary slip from his chivalric treatment of Raina, Saranoff jokes about a practical Swiss who helped them with arrangements for prisoner exchange and who bragged about having been saved by infatuating a Bulgarian woman and her mother after visiting the young woman in her bedroom. Recognizing herself, Raina chides Saranoff for telling such a crass story in front of her, and he immediately apologizes and reverts to his gallant pose.

Finally in act 3, after Bluntschli has returned for an overcoat and Saranoff discovers that Raina and her mother were the women who saved the Swiss, Saranoff challenges Bluntschli to a duel. Bluntschli, however, will not return the romantic pose and calls Saranoff a blockhead for not realizing that Raina had no other choice at gunpoint. When Saranoff realizes that there is no romance in fighting this prosaic shopkeeper, he backs off. Bluntschli wins Raina's hand, Saranoff wins Louka's, and all ends happily. Yet at the very point at which the audience might expect the play to use its romantic, well-made plot to criticize romanticism, Shaw again changes direction by showing his antihero Bluntschli to be a romantic. To everyone's consternation, Saranoff's in particular, Bluntschli points out that most of his problems have been the result of an incurably romantic disposition: He ran away from home twice as a boy, joined the army rather than his father's business, climbed the balcony of the Petkoff house instead of sensibly diving into the nearest cellar, and came back to this young girl, Raina, to get his coat when any man his age would have sent for it. Thus, Shaw uses *Arms and the Man* not only to attack romanticism about war or love but also to assert the importance of knowing and being true to oneself, to one's life force. It matters little whether Bluntschli is a romantic. He knows and is true to himself. He does not pose and does not deceive himself, as do Saranoff and Raina.

Only one who is true to himself and does not deny himself can attune himself to the Life Force and help advance the evolutionary process. Although Saranoff changes his career when he renounces soldiering, he does so because he was not justly rewarded for his dashing cavalry charge. He does not abandon his habitual self-deception. Even his marriage to the servant girl, Louka, has something of the romantic pose about it; it is rebellious. Raina's marriage to Bluntschli has more potential; at least she has come to see her own posing.

Although the play seems light when set beside the later, more complex triumphs, Shaw's "religious" purpose can be seen here at the beginning of his career. It will be better argued in *Man and Superman* and more fully argued in *Back to Methuselah*, but the failure of the latter, more Utopian work shows that Shaw's religious ideas most engaged his audience when they were rooted in the social, political, or economic criticism of his times, as they were in *Arms and the Man*.

CANDIDA

A year after *Arms and the Man*, Shaw wrote *Candida*, his version of Henrik Ibsen's 1879 play, *Et dukkehjem* (*A Doll's House*, 1880). *Candida* showed that, while Shaw was as much a proponent of equality as was his early mentor, he saw women's usual familial role from an opposite perspective. As Ibsen saw it, women suffer in marriage from being treated like children; a wife is denied the larger responsibilities that are the province of her husband. As a consequence, the wife's personal maturity is arrested. She becomes, in a word, a doll. Shaw did not think this the usual marital paradigm; his view of marriage included a husband who does tend to see himself as the dominant force in the family, but the wife is seldom the petted child that Ibsen's Nora is. Much more frequently, she is like Candida, the real strength of the family, who, like her husband's mother before her, allows her husband to live in a "castle of comfort and indulgence" over which she stands sentinel. She makes him master, though he does not know it. Men, in other words, are more often the petted, indulged children, and women more often the sustaining force in the family.

Candida is set entirely in St. Dominic's Parsonage, and the action is ostensibly a very unoriginal love triangle involving the parson, James Morell, his wife, Candida, and a young poet, Eugene Marchbanks. The originality comes from the unique twist given this stock situation. Morell is a liberal, aggressive preacher, worshiped by women and by his curate. Marchbanks is a shy, effeminate eighteen-year-old, in manner somewhat reminiscent of a young Percy Bysshe Shelley, and he is possessed too of Shelley's inner strength, though this is not immediately apparent. The young poet declares to Morell his love for Candida, Morell's beautiful thirty-three-year-old wife. The self-assured Morell indulges the young man and assures him that the whole world loves Candida; his is another version of puppy love that he will outgrow. The ethereal Marchbanks cannot believe that Morell thinks Candida capable of inspiring such trivial love in him. He is able, as no one else is, to see that Morell's brilliant sermons and his equally brilliant conversation are nothing but the gift of gab; Morell is an inflated windbag. Marchbanks forces Morell to see himself in this way, and Morell shows that the poet has hit home when he almost throttles him.

Morell broaches the subject of Marchbanks's love to Candida, at the young man's insistence, and Candida assures her husband that she already knows Eugene is in love with her. She is surprised, however, to find Morell upset by it. Nevertheless, the two foolish men force a crisis by making Candida choose between them. When she plays their game and asks what each has to offer, Morell offers his strength for her defense, his honesty for her surety, his industry for her livelihood, and his authority and position for her dignity. Eugene offers his weakness and desolation.

Candida, bemused that neither offers love and that each wishes to own her, acknowledges that the poet has made a good offer. She informs them that she will give herself, because of his need, to the weaker of the two. Morell is desolate, but Eugene is, too, since he realizes that Candida means Morell. Eugene leaves with the now famous "secret in his heart." The secret the poet knows is that he can live without happiness, that there is another love than that of woman—the love of purpose.

The twist Shaw gives the standard triangle, then, is not merely that the effeminate young poet is stronger than the commanding figure of Morell, but also that Candida is stronger than both. Morell is clearly the doll in this house. Even so, to identify Shaw with Marchbanks, as his fine biographer Archibald Henderson does, makes little sense. Marchbanks is an aesthete like Wilde or the young William Butler Yeats, and the poetic sentiments he expresses to Candida sound very like Shelley's *Epipsychidion*. Shaw, who did not share Shelley's rapture about romantic love and who liked aestheticism so little that he swore he would not face the toil of writing a single sentence for art's sake alone, clearly cannot be confused with Marchbanks. He has more in common with Morell, who is socialistic and industrious. It is Morell who voices Shaw's sentiments when he tells Marchbanks that people have no more right to consume happiness without producing it than they have to consume wealth without producing it. The character in this play who comes closest to Shaw, however, is Candida herself. Much stronger than Ibsen's Nora, she is the only character who does not deceive herself. Morell does not realize that he needs to be coddled in order to play his role as a dynamic, liberal clergyman. Only at the play's end and with Candida's help, does Marchbanks discover the truth she has known all along.

Candida is subtitled *A Mystery*, and, though Shaw is treating a dramatic convention with humor, there is perhaps a more serious sense in which he uses the subtitle: There is some mystery involved in the ties that bind people together in marriage. In the climactic scene, in which Candida is made to choose between the two men, a traditional dramatist might have demonstrated the lover to be a cad and have thrown him out. A more romantic dramatist would have shown the husband to be a tyrant and had the wife and lover elope. Shaw chooses neither solution. He has the wife remain with the husband, but not because the lover is a cad or because she owes it to her husband contractually or for any of the standard reasons Morell offers, but because he needs her and she loves him. In this mystery about what binds partners in marriage, Shaw seems to suggest that it is not the contract, still less any ideal of purity, but simply mutual love and need.

What connects *Candida* with *Arms and the Man*, as well as with the later plays, is the demand that persons be true to themselves. Morell taught Candida to think for herself, she tells him, but it upsets him when that intellectual independence leads to conclusions different from his own. Candida will not submit to Christian moralism any more than she will to poetic romanticism. If there is any salvation for Marchbanks, it is that he has learned from Candida the secret that lies hidden in his heart: He is not dependent on happiness or on the love of a woman. In becoming aware of this, he has the potential to be a true artist, one attuned to purpose and not to self-indulgence. Thus, the play leads to the more lengthy dramatization of the struggle between the philosopher-artist and the woman-mother that is evident in *Man and Superman*.

Man and Superman

Man and Superman promotes Shaw's philosophy of the Life Force more explicitly than do any of his previous plays. Indeed, much of the play is given to discussion, particularly during the long dream sequence in act 3; Shaw never thought that a play's action need be physical. The dynamics of argument, of intellectual and verbal exchange, were for Shaw much more exciting than conventional action.

The drama originated in a suggestion by Arthur Bingham Walkley that Shaw write a Don Juan play. After all, did not Shaw suffer as a playwright from an excess of cerebration and a lack of physicality? Surely, Walkley reasoned, the subject of the amours of Don Juan would force him off his soapbox and into the boudoir. In response to this challenge, Shaw wrote a much more cerebral play than he had ever written before. In his lengthy "Epistle Dedicatory" to Walkley, Shaw explains why. The essence of the Don Juan legend is not, like Casanova's, that its hero is an "oversexed tomcat." Rather, its essence lies in Juan's following his own instincts rather than law or convention.

The play is as diffuse and difficult to stage as *Candida* is concise and delightful to produce. Most of the difficulty has to do with the lengthy Don Juan in Hell dream sequence during act 3, which causes the play to run more than four hours. More often than not, the sequence has been separated from the play. Not until 1964, in fact, when the Association of Producing Artists staged the play at New York City's Phoenix Theatre was the entire play produced in the United States.

As the delightful first act opens, Ann Whitefield has lost her father, and everyone is waiting to learn from the will who her guardian will be. Roebuck Ramsden, close friend of her father and self-styled liberal, is the leading candidate and is at the moment lecturing Ann's young suitor, Octavius, on his friend, Jack Tanner, who is not fit to be seen with Octavius, much less with Ann. Tanner has scandalized this Victorian liberal by his newly published "The Revolutionist's Handbook," whose entire text Shaw appends to the play. "The Revolutionist's Handbook" is a didact's device for getting across some of the ideas that would have been unpalatable in the play, as when Tanner argues (here without opposition) that the Life Force would be served better if people were given more freedom in mating. That is to say, people who might not be compatible as marriage partners might nevertheless produce the finest offspring.

When Tanner appears, the audience is delighted by his wit. He good-humoredly but repeatedly scandalizes Ramsden, particularly when he announces

that he and Ramsden have been named joint guardians of Ann. Tanner is not eager to undertake his role; he knows how manipulative Ann can be, but he does not yet recognize what even his chauffeur could have told him: Ann has designs on him and not on his friend, Octavius. Ann is in the grip of the Life Force, which drives all women in their capacity as mothers to want to reproduce, and she implicitly knows that Tanner would be the proper father for her offspring, not the romantic but spiritually flabby young Octavius. Tanner, however, is Shaw's philosopher-artist and, as such, Tanner knows that he must flee the stifling bliss of marriage and domesticity to pursue his own purpose—something that Marchbanks learned at the end of *Candida*.

When Tanner learns of Ann's designs, he flees to Spain. Here, he and his chauffeur are captured by a group of brigands led by an Englishman named Mendoza. While captive, Tanner dreams the lengthy dream that constitutes the Don Juan in Hell scene. The scene is a brilliant debate involving Don Juan (looking like John Tanner), the Devil (looking like Mendoza), Doña Ana (looking remarkably like Ann Whitefield), and Ana's father, Don Gonzalo (looking like Roebuck Ramsden). The debate centers on the relative merits of Heaven and Hell. Doña Ana, "a good Catholic," is astonished to find herself a newcomer to Hell and has to have it explained to her that some of the best company are here. One can go to Heaven if he or she wishes, but one must remember that the gulf between the two is really a matter of natural inclination or temperament. Hell is a place for those in whom enjoyment predominates over purpose, desires over reason, the heart over the head, the aesthetic over the ideological, and romance over realism. Don Juan is about to depart for Heaven because he is sick of the Devil's cant about the aesthetic values, the enjoyment of music, the pleasures of the heart. An eternity of enjoyment is an intolerable bore. He wishes not to enjoy life but to help it in its struggle upward. The reason Juan went to Hell to begin with was that he thought he was a pleasure-seeker, but he has discovered, as Shaw indicates in the dedicatory epistle, that his amours were more a form of rebellion than of pleasure-seeking. Realizing that he is temperamentally a philosophical man, who seeks to learn in contemplation the inner will of the world, to discover in invention the means of achieving that will, and to follow in action those means, he prefers Heaven.

The dream sequence is also concerned with woman's maternal role in advancing the Life Force. If it seems, at first glance, that the ardent feminist who authored *Candida* has here turned his coat and relegated women to a merely sexual role, it must be remembered that for the moment Shaw is speaking only of one side of woman. When Ana corrects Don Juan's view of woman's mind, he points out to her that he speaks not of woman's whole mind but only of her view of man as a separate sex. Only sexually is woman's nature a contrivance for perpetuating its highest achievement. She too can be the philosopher-artist attuned to the work of advancing the Life Force. Thus, two ways of achieving the inner will of the world are open to her.

In the fourth and final act, having awakened from his dreams, Tanner shows that he is not yet as forceful as his ancestor, Don Juan, when he gives in to Ann's superior force and agrees to marry her. Ironically, the romantic Octavius is the one who resigns himself to bachelorhood.

The play, then, is a philosophical comedy whose theme is that the Life Force is dependent on man and woman if it is to move creation upward. A man or woman possessed of a sense of purpose must attune himself or herself to the Life Force, since the only true joy lies in being used for its purposes, in being willing to burn oneself out and heap oneself on the scrap pile at the end without any promise of a personal reward. Although a number of critics see Tanner as the epitome of Shavian man, Tanner does capitulate to Ann. He lacks the fiber of Don Juan, who realizes the boredom of a life of pleasure. Indeed, Marchbanks of *Candida* is more truly Shavian than Tanner.

Notwithstanding Shaw's overt didacticism in this play, he is true to his belief that, like the Ancient Mariner, he must tell his tale entertainingly if he is to hold the attention of the wedding guest. Consequently, he claims full responsibility for the opinions

of Don Juan but claims equal responsibility for those of the other characters. For the dramatic moment, each character's viewpoint is also Shaw's. Those who believe there is an absolutely right point of view, he says in the "Epistle Dedicatory," usually believe it is their own and cannot, in consequence, be true dramatists.

MAJOR BARBARA

In *Major Barbara*, published not long after *Man and Superman*, Shaw's dramatic means of advancing his theory of the Life Force was to assert that poverty was the world's greatest evil. What critics, even astute ones such as G. K. Chesterton, thought materialistic in Shaw, the author would insist was spiritual. Only with money could one save one's soul.

Major Barbara opens in the home of Lady Britomart Undershaft, whose estranged millionaire husband has been invited to the house for the first time since the children, now adults, were toddlers. Her purpose in inviting this scandalous old atheist to her house is to get more money for her daughters, Barbara and Sarah, who are about to marry. Moreover, she would like Andrew Undershaft to break the ridiculous custom of having the Undershaft munitions business go to an orphan and instead give it to his own son, Stephen. When Undershaft meets his family, he is favorably impressed by Barbara, who is a major in the Salvation Army, and by Adolphus Cusins, her suitor, who is a professor of Greek. He recognizes that Stephen is hopelessly inept and that Charles Lomax, Sarah's young man, is less pompous than Stephen but no less foolish. Barbara invites her father to West Ham so that he might see the constructive work of the Salvation Army, and he agrees, provided that she come to see his munitions plant at Perivale St. Andrews. Thus, the play's structure is neatly determined, with a second act at West Ham and a third at Perivale St. Andrews.

In act 2, Barbara shows her father the Salvation Army's good work, only to learn from her father and the Army's Commissioner, Mrs. Baines, the painful fact that the Army—like all religious organizations—depends on contributions from whiskey distillers and munitions owners such as her father. When Barbara is told that the Army could not subsist without this "tainted" money, she realizes that she is not changing the essential condition of the poor but simply keeping them alive with a bowl of soup; she is helping the capitalists justify themselves with conscience money. She thus serves capital rather than God.

When in act 3 the family visits the munitions factory, Undershaft surprisingly reveals the existence of a model socialist community at Perivale St. Andrews. Though Undershaft lives off the need of people to conduct war, he accepts that need and uses it to destroy society's greatest evil, poverty. In his community, all men work, earn a decent wage, and can thus turn to matters of the soul, such as religion, without being bribed to do so. Since Barbara has come to realize that religious organizations exist by selling themselves to the rich, she decides to get Peter Shirley a job rather than feed him and ask him to pray in thanksgiving at West Ham. She herself joins her father's model village, especially since Cusins is conveniently discovered to be an orphan and the ideal person to inherit the munitions factory.

Shaw's lengthy preface to the play sets out a good deal of his ethical philosophy: Poverty is the worst evil against which man struggles; religious people should work for the betterment of the one world they have and not turn from it for a vision of private bliss in the hereafter. The world will never be bettered by people who believe that they can atone for their sins and who do not understand that their misdeeds are irrevocable. While society should divide wealth equally, no adult should receive his allowance unless he or she produces by personal exertion more than he or she consumes. Society should not punish those guilty of crime, especially by putting them in prisons that render them worse, but neither should it hesitate to put to death anyone whose misconduct is incorrigible, just as people would not hesitate to destroy a mad dog.

Though these ideas are familiar to Shavians, and though most of them are fleshed out in the play itself, *Major Barbara* may first take a reader by surprise. Can the pacifist and socialist Shaw be making a hero of a capitalist who makes his living on the profits of warfare? It is not enough to answer that the capitalist uses his capital to create an ideal socialist community; for this, Shaw could have chosen a banker. On the contrary, he deliberately chooses a munitions manufacturer because the irony helps make his point. However horrid warfare is, it is not so horrid as poverty. Undershaft tells Barbara and Cusins in the final act that poverty is the worst of crimes, for it blights whole cities, spreads pestilence, and strikes dead any souls within its compass. Barbara cannot save souls in West Ham by words and dreams, but if she gives a West Ham ruffian thirty-eight shillings a week, with a sound house in a handsome street and a permanent job, she will save his soul.

When Barbara turns from the Salvation Army to Undershaft's community at Perivale St. Andrews, she is not giving up religion. She is turning, Shaw would have it, from a phony religion dependent on a bribe to the poor and on the maintenance of inequitable present conditions, to a genuine religion that will bring significant social change. Her conversion is completely consistent with her character. When her father asks her to tell Cusins what power is, she answers that before joining the Salvation Army, she was in her own power and, as a consequence, did not know what to do with herself. Once she joined the Army, she thought herself in the power of God and did not have enough time for all that needed to be done. Undershaft helps her to transfer this commitment to a more realistic cause, which will genuinely improve the lot of the poor, but a cause that is still essentially spiritual.

Because Undershaft sees his work in the same light as Barbara sees hers, he can insist that he is not a secularist but a confirmed mystic. Perivale St. Andrews is driven by a will of which he is a part. Thus, once again, Shaw's hero is chosen because he is attuned to the Life Force. It matters little that he is a munitions maker. In *Saint Joan*, the heroine is a saint, yet she is chosen not as a representative of Christian orthodoxy but because she was mystic enough to see that she served a will greater than her own.

In *Major Barbara*, Shaw also makes use of a host of lesser characters to dramatize his political, moral, and ethical theories. When Stephen Undershaft is asked by his father what he is able to do in life, so that Undershaft can give him a fair start, he makes it evident that he is capable of nothing, except—he asserts defensively—of knowing the difference between good and evil, something he implies his father does not know. With this, Undershaft has great fun. Stephen knows nothing of law, of business, of art, or of philosophy, yet he claims to know the secret that has baffled philosophers for ages. Because Stephen knows nothing but claims to know everything, Undershaft declares him fit for politics. To this remark, Stephen takes exception; he will not hear his father insult his country's government. Undershaft once again, however, reflects Shaw's conviction that big business rules government when he sputters, "The government of your country! I am the government of your country."

Peter Shirley, rather than Barbara, provides the real contrast with Undershaft. Barbara shares her father's "heavenly" temper, his sense of purpose. The Army shares with him the recognition that it needs money. Peter Shirley, the unemployed visitor at West Ham, plays Lazarus to Undershaft's Dives, as Shaw puts it. Because the majority of the world believes that an "honest" poor man such as Shirley is morally superior to a "wicked" rich one such as Undershaft, the misery of the world continues. It is significant that when Undershaft gives Shirley a job, the man is unhappy.

Bill Walker, who beats up an old woman visiting the West Ham shelter and then a young woman member of the Army itself, tries to atone by having himself beaten up in turn by a professional boxer, Todger Fermile. Such a grotesque instance of atonement is no more grotesque than any other attempt at atonement, Shaw believes, and both Barbara and Cusins agree with Undershaft that one cannot atone for evil; one does good only by changing evil ways. It can be argued, as in the case of many other Shavian criticisms of Christianity, that Shaw did not understand the Christian doctrine. Perhaps, however, he understood *de facto* Christianity all too well.

Adolphus Cusins also plays a significant role in the drama, certainly the most significant after those of Undershaft and Barbara, and he eventually takes over the munitions factory. A man of greater intelligence and more humane sympathies than Undershaft,

he may be the hope for the Life Force taking a significant step forward. Undershaft repeatedly refers to this professor of Greek as "Dionysius," which suggests in Cusins a capacity to stand outside himself to achieve union with the Life Force. Clearly, Undershaft invites him to make war on war when he turns over the munitions works to him.

Major Barbara is perhaps freighted with too much paradox to do its job convincingly. Certainly, act 1 is sparkling comedy as Undershaft meets his family without knowing who is who. Moreover, the contrast between Undershaft's "gospel" and Barbara's is convincingly set forth. Act 2 is occasionally excellent comedy, and comedy fused with meaning, as when Barbara deals with the bully Bill Walker, but Walker's part becomes a bit too obtrusive a vehicle for attacking atonement, and Undershaft's demonstration of how all religious organizations exist by selling themselves to the rich is somewhat more asserted than dramatized. Perhaps the concluding act is the least successful, since Barbara's and Cusins's conversion is necessarily hurried to preserve the unities, and Shaw has difficulty making his Utopia convincing, a difficulty he later experienced more keenly in *Back to Methuselah*. To do Shaw justice, he acknowledged that, while one can know that the Life Force is driving upward, one cannot know precisely how. Thus, attempts to dramatize future points of progress in creative evolution present insuperable obstacles.

SAINT JOAN

More than in *Major Barbara* and perhaps more than in *Man and Superman*, Shaw found in *Saint Joan* a fit medium to dramatize his major religious ideas. He had intended to write a play about Christ, but he was not permitted to portray divinity on the English stage. Yet no play by Shaw succeeds more unobtrusively in carrying his ideas about the Life Force. As captivating a play as *Major Barbara* is, Undershaft has straw men with whom to do battle, and, though such was not the case in *Man and Superman*, Shaw needed for his purposes the lengthy dream sequence that has made the play so difficult to stage. *Candida* might be a more perfectly structured play, but it does not carry so much of Shaw's mature philosophy. Among Shaw's major dramas, then, *Saint Joan* is perhaps the finest blend of matter and form.

Saint Joan is divided into six scenes and an epilogue. In the first scene, Joan appeals to Robert de Baudricourt for horse and armor to aid in the siege of Orleans and to see to the coronation of the Dauphin. Although he at first scoffs at this request, made through his servant, when faced with Joan, he is persuaded by the strength of her person, as everyone else is. In scene 2, the courtiers try to dupe her and pretend that Gilles de Rais is the Dauphin. Not taken in, she carries the Dauphin, too, by her force of persuasion and convinces this weakling that he, too, has a divine mission that he must be strong enough to accept. In scene 3, Joan joins Dunois, the leader of the French forces, and under their combined leadership, France enjoys a series of victories. In scene 4, the Earl of Warwick and the Bishop of Beauvais plan Joan's eventual execution. The Englishman wants her dead for obvious military reasons; the Frenchman, because she is a dangerous heretic. In scene 5, she is told to give up fighting, that there is no need for more victories. She is told to let the English have Paris. Her sense of destiny, however, convinces her that the English must be driven from French soil. In scene 6, Joan has been arrested. She is given by the Inquisition what Shaw considers a fairer trial than is available to defendants today. She finally recants what the clergymen consider her heresy, but when told that she must remain forever in prison as punishment for her spiritual offenses, she tears up her recantation and goes to the stake under Warwick's authority. The epilogue gets the play back into the comic frame and allows Joan and the rest of the cast of characters to appear twenty-five years later before Charles, now King, and discuss the Church's recent reversal in favor of Joan. There is even a time-shift of several centuries, to the year 1920, so that Joan's canonization can be mentioned. Yet the epilogue ultimately suggests that, were she to return to France in the twentieth century, Joan would again be put to death by the very people who now praise her.

The greatness of *Saint Joan* lies in its scrupulous dramatization of a universal problem. The problem of how one reconciles the dictates of the individual con-

science with the demands of authority is one without easy solutions, whether the individual stands against ecclesiastical, civil, military, or familial authority. The sympathy Shaw extends to Joan in declaring her one of the first "Protestant" saints he extends also to the Inquisitors, who, he asserts, tried Joan more fairly than they themselves were later tried when the judgment on Joan was reversed.

Shaw's fairness is evident in scene 4, for example, when Peter Cauchon makes clear to the Earl of Warwick that, even though both men want Joan captured, they differ in every other respect. Cauchon, Bishop of Beauvais, does not believe that Joan is a witch and will not allow Warwick to get rid of her on this trumped-up charge. Joan is a heretic, much more dangerous than a witch, but he would prefer to save her soul. She is a pious and honest girl who, through pride, is caught up in the Devil's mighty purpose: to wrack the Church with discord and dissension—the same purpose for which the Devil used John Huss and John Wycliffe. If a reformer will not finally effect reform within the pale of Church authority, every crackpot who sees visions will be followed by the naïve populace, and the Church will be wrecked beyond repair.

These arguments are completely familiar to the present age, in which soldiers are told they must obey commanding officers who order the extinction of noncombatants. Can one obey such orders? Yet there surely must be obedience to authority, despite doubts about its wisdom, or there will be anarchy. Humankind has come no closer to finding a solution to the tensions between individual conscience and authority than it had in Joan's day, and it is that insoluble problem that forces audiences to move beyond easy condemnation of the Inquisition and equally easy sanctification of Joan.

Critics have often objected to Shaw's epilogue on the ground that Joan's tragedy is trivialized by it, yet the epilogue is necessary for Shaw's theme: that from the same elements, the same tragedy would come again. The trial at which Joan's judges were judged and she was exonerated was a much more unscrupulous affair than was Joan's trial. Ladvenu, who had been the most sympathetic of those who tried Joan, tells King Charles that the old trial was faultless in every respect except in its unjust verdict, while the new trial is filled with perjury and corruption yet results in a just verdict. Charles, who is concerned only about his having been crowned by a woman who was considered a witch and a heretic, and who is relieved now by having his reign validated, asserts that no matter what the verdict, were Joan brought back to life, her present admirers would burn her within six months.

In his preface, Shaw argues that there was no inconsistency in the Church's reversal on Joan. Although the Catholic Church does not defer to private judgment, it recognizes that the highest wisdom may come to an individual through private revelation and that, on sufficient evidence, the Church will eventually declare such an individual a saint. Thus, many saints have been at odds with the Church before their canonization. In fact, Shaw contends, had Francis of Assisi lived longer, he might have gone to the stake, while Galileo might yet be declared a saint. Thus, the epilogue helps dramatize the complexity inherent in Joan's struggle with the Church.

In none of the plays discussed—perhaps nowhere else in his canon, with the possible exception of *Caesar and Cleopatra*—does Shaw present an example of a character in the grip of the Life Force so convincingly as he does in the character of Joan. Bluntschli is an amusing soldier-adventurer; Marchbanks, a callow poet; Tanner, a failed revolutionary; and Undershaft, a munitions maker who has built a socialist community. Joan is both a Christian and a Shavian saint. She is caught up in a sense of purpose to a degree none of Shaw's other characters is. *Saint Joan*, then, is the culmination of Shaw's art. Although other plays might embrace more of his standard literary and philosophical obsessions, none takes his most central obsessions, those relating to the Life Force and creative evolution, and fleshes them out with such dramatic integrity.

OTHER MAJOR WORKS

LONG FICTION: *Cashel Byron's Profession*, 1886; *An Unsocial Socialist*, 1887; *Love Among the Artists*, 1900; *The Irrational Knot*, 1905; *Immaturity*, 1930.

SHORT FICTION: *The Adventures of the Black Girl in Her Search for God*, 1932.

NONFICTION: *The Quintessence of Ibsenism*, 1891; *The Perfect Wagnerite*, 1898; *The Common Sense of Municipal Trading*, 1904; *Dramatic Opinions and Essays*, 1907; *The Sanity of Art*, 1908 (revised from 1895 serial publication); *Letters to Miss Alma Murray*, 1927; *The Intelligent Woman's Guide to Socialism and Capitalism*, 1928; *Ellen Terry and Shaw*, 1931; *Everybody's Political What's What*, 1944; *Sixteen Self Sketches*, 1949; *Correspondence Between George Bernard Shaw and Mrs. Patrick Campbell*, 1952; *The Matter with Ireland*, 1961; *Platform and Pulpit*, 1961 (Dan H. Laurence, editor); *Collected Letters*, 1965-1988 (4 volumes; Dan H. Laurence, editor); *An Autobiography, 1856-1898*, 1969; *An Autobiography, 1898-1950*, 1970; *The Nondramatic Literary Criticism of Bernard Shaw*, 1972 (Stanley Weintraub, editor); *Shaw: Interviews and Recollections*, 1990 (A. M. Gibbs, editor); *Bernard Shaw's Book Reviews*, 1991 (Brian Tyson, editor).

EDITED TEXT: *Fabian Essays in Socialism*, 1889.

MISCELLANEOUS: *Works*, 1930-1938 (33 volumes); *Short Stories, Scraps, and Shavings*, 1932; *Works*, 1947-1952 (36 volumes).

BIBLIOGRAPHY

Davis, Tracy C. *George Bernard Shaw and the Socialist Theatre*. Westport, Conn.: Greenwood Press, 1994. Davis examines Shaw's belief in socialism and how it affected and was demonstrated in his dramatic works. Bibliography and index.

Dukore, Bernard Frank. *Shaw's Theater*. Gainesville: University Press of Florida, 2000. Part of the Florida Bernard Shaw series, this volume explores the production of Shaw's dramatic works. Bibliography and index.

Holroyd, Michael. *The Search for Love, 1856-1898*. Vol. 1 in *Bernard Shaw*. New York: Random House, 1988. In this superb beginning to his authoritative biography, Holroyd describes Shaw's Irish origins and trials of following his mother to London. His journalistic and musical career is interwoven with various love affairs, culminating in marriage in 1898. Sensitive analyses of political and aesthetic ideas are balanced with insights into early drama. Includes illustrations, a bibliographic note, and an index.

_____. *The Pursuit of Power, 1898-1918.* Vol. 2 in *Bernard Shaw.* New York: Random House, 1989. Describes the complicated interrelationships of Shaw's middle plays (from *Caesar and Cleopatra* to *Heartbreak House*) with ethics, politics, economics, medicine, religion, and war. The popularity of his drama is explained and analyzed, while the sophistication of his personality is narrated through his friendships with such persons as G. K. Chesterton, H. G. Wells, and Mrs. Patrick Campbell. Illustrations, index.

_____. *The Lure of Fantasy, 1918-1950.* Vol. 3 in *Bernard Shaw.* New York: Random House, 1991. The final volume covers Shaw's drama from *Saint Joan,* with late plays such as *Geneva* and *In Good King Charles's Golden Days* receiving balanced attention. Also surveys Shaw's films from his plays, including *Pygmalion* and *Major Barbara.* Shaw's interest in Communism and the Soviet Union receives attention, as does his criticism of American culture. Illustrations, bibliographic note, and index.

Innes, Christopher, ed. *The Cambridge Companion to George Bernard Shaw.* New York: Cambridge University Press, 1998. This reference work in the Cambridge series provides an in-depth look at Bernard Shaw's life, works, and philosophy. Bibliography and index.

Larson, Gale K., ed. *Shaw: Volume 21 in the Annual Bernard Shaw Series.* University Park: Pennsylvania State University Press, 2001. This collection of essays is part of an annual series that examines various aspects of Shaw. This volume contains essays on Shaw's stagecraft, Shaw's and Mark Twain's revisions of Genesis, and Shaw in Sinclair Lewis's writings. Bibliography.

Lenker, Lagretta Tallent. *Fathers and Daughters in Shakespeare and Shaw.* Westport, Conn.: Greenwood Press, 2001. Lenker examines the fathers and daughters portrayed in the plays of William Shakespeare and Shaw. Bibliography and index.

Henry J. Donaghy,
updated by Richard D. McGhee

IRWIN SHAW

Born: New York, New York; February 27, 1913
Died: Davos, Switzerland; May 16, 1984

PRINCIPAL DRAMA
Bury the Dead, pr., pb. 1936
Siege, pr. 1937
The Gentle People: A Brooklyn Fable, pr., pb. 1939
Quiet City, pr. 1939
Retreat to Pleasure, pr. 1940
Sons and Soldiers, pr. 1943, pb. 1944
The Assassin, pr. 1945, pb. 1946
The Survivors, pr., pb. 1948 (with Peter Viertel)
Patate, pr. 1958 (adaptation of a play by Marcel Achard)
Children from Their Games, pb. 1962, pr. 1963

A Choice of Wars, pr. 1967
I, Shaw, pr. 1986 (two one-act plays; *The Shy and the Lonely* and *Sailor off the Bremen*)

OTHER LITERARY FORMS
Irwin Shaw is better known for his short stories and novels than for his plays. His contributions to *The New Yorker* and other magazines in the 1930's earned him a reputation as one of the outstanding short-story writers of his generation, favorably compared to Ernest Hemingway and John Cheever. Many commentators consider the stories Shaw continued to write throughout his career as his main claim to literary immortality. When his *The Young Lions* appeared in 1948, critics called it one of the best novels dealing

with World War II. His later novels were commercial rather than literary successes.

Achievements

Irwin Shaw's failure to win major literary awards disappointed and angered him. Among his few honors were an O. Henry Memorial Award First Prize for his short story "Walking Wounded" in 1944 and an O. Henry Memorial Award Second Prize for "Gunner's Passage" in 1945. In 1946 he received a thousand-dollar grant from the National Institute of Arts and Letters. His only honorary degree came from his alma mater, Brooklyn College, in 1978. Shaw had hoped to have his work recognized by the American Academy of Arts and Letters; their failure to include him among the members embittered him.

Shaw believed that the magnitude of his monetary success prejudiced critics and other writers against him. He was delighted, however, when paperback editions of his late novels sold millions of copies. Dependent solely on his earnings as a writer, Shaw proudly supported his parents, provided a lavish lifestyle for himself, his wife, and his son, and left an estate of several million dollars at his death

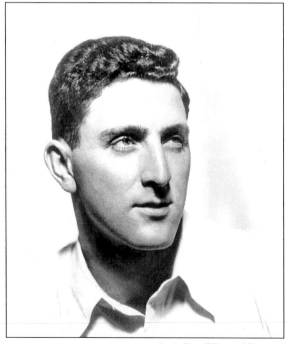

Irwin Shaw (Library of Congress)

Biography

Irwin Gilbert Shaw was the son of William Shamoroff, a Russian Jewish immigrant, and Rose Tompkins Shamoroff, an American-born daughter of Lithuanian Jewish immigrants. In 1923 his father, having begun an initially successful career as a real estate developer, changed the family name to Shaw. The Great Depression destroyed William Shaw's business; after 1932 he was unable to support his family.

Irwin Shaw attended tuition-free Brooklyn College, graduating with a B.A. in 1934, while holding various temporary positions. The most profitable of these was writing dialogue for the *Dick Tracy* and *The Gumps* radio serials, an activity permitting him to provide for his parents and younger brother while learning techniques he would put to effective use in his plays and short stories. In 1935 Shaw heard of a playwrighting contest sponsored by the New Theater League; although he did not win the prize, the group staged his play. The one-act *Bury the Dead* opened for two performances, March 14-15, 1936, before moving to another theater for an extended run. The experimental antiwar drama won almost universal praise, and the twenty-three-year-old author became an overnight celebrity, hailed as a major new American playwright.

Success brought Shaw a contract to write film scripts for Hollywood, the first of many occasions when he would use lucrative earnings from film work to support his serious writing and to maintain a luxurious lifestyle. In Hollywood, during the summer of 1936, Shaw met and fell in love with a young starlet, Marian Edwards. After living together for several years, they married on October 13, 1939. Their son Adam was born on March 27, 1950.

While working on his radio serials, Shaw began writing short stories. Appearing in *The New Yorker*, *Esquire*, and other magazines in the late 1930's and 1940's, they established his reputation as a master of short fiction. In 1939 he published the first of a dozen collections of short stories, winning praise from critics.

On January 6, 1939, the left-wing Group Theatre presented his *The Gentle People: A Brooklyn Fable*. It proved to be Shaw's most profitable drama. Shaw was disappointed by the reception of three other plays he offered the Group Theatre. *Quiet City* was cancelled after two preview performances in April, 1939. *Retreat to Pleasure*, a satirical treatment of the United States' complaisant attitudes as war approached, opened on December 17, 1940, and lasted only twenty-three performances. *Sons and Soldiers*, a multigenerational family story set in 1915, opened May 4, 1943, and closed after twenty-two performances.

When the United States entered World War II, Shaw refused to use his Hollywood connections to get an officer's commission. He waited to be drafted on July 10, 1942, hoping that experiencing the conflict from a private's perspective would provide him with the raw material for a major war novel. The U.S. Army assigned Shaw to a Signal Corps documentary unit as a writer. Shaw helped record the North African campaign, the Normandy invasion, and the liberation of France. He counted entering Paris with the Free French forces on August 25, 1944, as the greatest day of his life.

While in Europe, Shaw worked on a play dramatizing the assassination of a pro-German French admiral by the French Resistance in Algiers. Opening in London in March, 1945, *The Assassins* proved a success there but was a dismal failure in New York in October. Shaw tried one more time to conquer Broadway with *Children from Their Games*, but the play closed after four performances in April, 1963.

His war fiction received a more favorable reception. Two short stories took O. Henry prizes. His first novel, *The Young Lions*, received respectful reviews when it was published in October, 1948, and soon went to the top of best-seller lists, with more than 125,000 copies in print before the end of the year.

In 1951, shortly after publishing *The Troubled Air*, a novel attacking the effect of anticommunist blacklisting on the entertainment industry, Shaw took his family to Europe. Originally intending to stay a year, they remained there twenty-five years.

His steadily increasing income from novels and screenwriting permitted an opulent lifestyle. Shaw maintained an apartment in Paris, moving to winter quarters in a chalet in Klosters, Switzerland, and to various summer homes in the south of France. Despite problems with alcoholism, Shaw kept his mornings free for writing, and produced ten novels while in Europe. His greatest success came after a 1976 television miniseries based on his 1970 novel *Rich Man, Poor Man*, introduced him to a new audience; paperback sales of his novels mounted into the millions. In 1977, asked what he would have done differently if he could live his life over, Shaw answered that he would not have written plays; much as he liked the theater, he believed his work there was a failure.

Shaw's marriage, which had been troubled almost from the start because of his frequent public affairs with other women, ended in divorce in 1970. However, the Shaws reconciled eight years later, and he credited his wife with saving his life during a series of medical crises as his health deteriorated. He eventually died of prostate cancer at the age of seventy-one.

ANALYSIS

Irwin Shaw came of age during the Great Depression of the 1930's, and his plays reflect the world in which he grew up. He identified with President Franklin Roosevelt's New Deal attempt to create a more equitable American society. As a Jew, Shaw was acutely aware of the rise of Adolf Hitler in Germany. He realized Nazism and fascism posed a major threat, not only to Jews but also to all democratic societies.

Shaw's plays fit the social protest style prominent in the 1930's and led to his being classified as a radical. He was often associated with Clifford Odets, whose plays were also sponsored by the left-leaning Group Theatre. Shaw was briefly blacklisted in the 1940's, although he was never a communist. Shaw's first play, *Bury the Dead*, was critical of the military and warfare, and many people thought he was a pacifist, but he firmly believed resistance to fascism was necessary, even if it meant going to war. Violence, and how freedom-loving people should respond to it, provided a recurrent theme for his plays and early stories. His dramas appear realistic on the surface, but Shaw often added fantastic elements to strengthen the impact of his plots.

BURY THE DEAD

This one-act play opens with six dead and decomposing soldiers standing up and refusing to be buried. They reject the pleas of the burial squad, their captain, and three generals, to be good soldiers and go into their graves. Even appeals from their wives, who are brought to the battle scene, fail to dissuade the dead men. Each man describes how he died and what he hoped to experience in life before being put away. The play closes with the dead soldiers marching off stage as a hysterical general attempts to stop them by firing a machine gun.

After its successful two-day production by the New Theater League, *Bury the Dead* moved to Broadway for sixty-five performances. The play was popular in regional theaters across the country as well as in Europe, often presented on a twin bill with Odets's *Waiting for Lefty* (pr., pb. 1935).

THE GENTLE PEOPLE

Two Brooklyn fishermen dream of buying a seaworthy fishing boat and sailing from Brooklyn to Cuba, where they envision becoming commercial successes. They are furious when a young racketeer forces them to pay five dollars a week "protection" money but feel compelled to comply. The gangster courts the daughter of one of the fishermen. When he learns from her that the two men have saved $190 toward their dream, he demands their money. The fishermen decide to resist and succeed in killing the racketeer, thus protecting the young girl from her predator, while preserving their own dream.

Some reviewers disliked Shaw's mixture of fantasy and realism, but perceptive observers recognized that Shaw had written an allegory of resistance to fascism, with the "gentle people" resorting to violence to protect the innocent and to preserve their hope for a better future.

Director Harold Clurman assembled an illustrious cast for the Group Theatre's production. Movie fans flocked to the stage entrance when Sylvia Sidney and Franchot Tone (who played the gangster) returned from Hollywood, joining Sam Jaffe, Karl Malden, Elia Kazan, and Lee J. Cobb in an all-star company.

Although *The Gentle People* did not receive the rave reviews of its predecessor, it proved the greatest commercial success of Shaw's plays, lasting six months on the stage for 141 performances.

THE ASSASSIN

Shaw based this play on the historic assassination of pro-Nazi French admiral Jean-Francois Darlan in Algiers on December 28, 1942. The protagonist, Robert de Mauny, a young Monarchist, despises the admiral commanding the French forces in North Africa, whom he sees as an unprincipled opportunist. After saving several members of the French Resistance from the police, de Mauny joins forces with the Resistance, believing them patriots deserving his aid. When a corrupt general threatens to execute de Mauny's comrades if he does not assassinate the admiral, while also promising to protect him from punishment if he does, de Mauny kills the admiral. His friends are freed as promised, but he is arrested and executed.

Again Shaw explores his favorite theme, the need of good people to meet the violence of fascism with countering violence, whatever the cost. Shaw worked on the play while in Europe from 1943 to 1945. He carefully steered the text through U.S. Army and British censorship and was gratified by an enthusiastic audience and critical response to its March, 1945, London premiere. When the play reached the New York stage in October, however, newspaper critics uniformly and viciously condemned it; the production closed after thirteen performances. Infuriated by his failure, Shaw wrote a lengthy preface to the published version, excoriating the New York Theater for its treatment of playwrights.

OTHER MAJOR WORKS

LONG FICTION: *The Young Lions*, 1948; *The Troubled Air*, 1951; *Lucy Crown*, 1956; *Two Weeks in Another Town*, 1960; *Voices of a Summer Day*, 1965; *Rich Man, Poor Man*, 1970; *Evening in Byzantium*, 1973; *Nightwork*, 1975; *Beggarman, Thief*, 1977; *The Top of the Hill*, 1971; *Bread Upon the Waters*, 1981; *Acceptable Losses*, 1982.

SHORT FICTION: *Sailor off the Bremen and Other Stories*, 1939; *Welcome to the City and Other Stories*, 1942; *Act of Faith and Other Stories*, 1946; *Mixed

Company: Collected Short Stories, 1950; *Tip on a Dead Jockey and Other Stories*, 1957; *Love on a Dark Street and Other Stories*, 1965; *Retreat and Other Stories*, 1970; *God Was Here, but He Left Early*, 1973; *Short Stories: Five Decades*, 1978.

SCREENPLAYS: *The Big Game*, 1936; *Commandos Strike at Dawn*, 1942; *The Hard Way*, 1942 (with Daniel Fuchs and Jerry Wald); *Talk of the Town*, 1942 (with Sidney Buchman); *Take One False Step*, 1949 (with Chester Erskine and David Shaw); *I Want You*, 1951; *Act of Love*, 1954; *Fire Down Below*, 1957; *Desire Under the Elms*, 1958; *This Angry Age*, 1958 (with Rene Clement); *The Big Gamble*, 1961; *In the French Style*, 1963; *Survival*, 1968.

TELEPLAY: *The Top of the Hill*, 1980.

NONFICTION: *Report on Israel*, 1950 (with Robert Capa); *In the Company of Dolphins*, 1964; *Paris! Paris!*, 1977; *Paris/Magnum: Photographs, 1935-1981*, 1981.

BIBLIOGRAPHY

Clurman, Harold. *The Fervent Years: The Story of the Group Theatre and the Thirties*. New York: Da Capo, 1983. The reminiscences of the founder and managing director of the Group Theatre. Clurman depicts the artistic and political ideas that dominated the New York theatrical scene during the years Shaw enjoyed his early success.

Giles, James R. *Irwin Shaw*. Boston: Twayne, 1983. The only full-length critical survey of Shaw's literary work. Chapter three, "The Plays: Fantasy and Protest," analyzes his major dramatic output. Contains a chronology and annotated bibliography.

Placzek, Walter H. "Irwin Shaw (1913-1984)." In *American Playwrights, 1880-1945: A Research and Production Sourcebook*, edited by William W. DeMastes. Greenwood Press, 1995. Provides useful production data on Shaw's plays.

Shaw, Irwin. *The Assassins: A Play in Three Acts*. New York: Random House, 1946. In his twenty-three-page preface, Shaw denounced the treatment of plays dealing with political themes, vigorously attacked New York's drama critics, and suggested ways to improve the New York theatrical world.

Shnayerson, Michael. *Irwin Shaw: A Biography*. New York: G. P. Putnam's Sons, 1989. In his carefully researched biography, Shnayerson describes in detail Shaw's active and increasingly lavish social life. Although he provides little analysis of Shaw's work, the author records the critical reception of Shaw's plays, short stories, and novels.

Milton Berman

WALLACE SHAWN

Born: New York, New York; November 12, 1943

PRINCIPAL DRAMA
The Hotel Play, wr. 1970, pr. 1981, pb. 1982
Play in Seven Scenes, pr. 1974
Our Late Night, pr. 1974, pb. 1984
In the Dark, pr. 1976 (libretto)
Three Short Plays: Summer Evening, The Youth Hostel, Mr. Frivolous, pr. 1976, pr. 1977 (as *A Thought in Three Parts*)
The Mandrake, pr. 1977 (adaptation of Niccolò Machiavelli's play *La mandragola*)
The Famiy Play, pr. 1978

Marie and Bruce, pr. 1979, pb. 1980
My Dinner with André, pr. 1980, pb. 1983 (with André Gregory)
The Music Teacher, pr. 1982 (libretto)
Aunt Dan and Lemon, pr., pb. 1985
The Fever, pr. 1990, pb. 1991
The Designated Mourner, pr., pb. 1996
Four Plays, pb. 1998

OTHER LITERARY FORMS

In addition to his stage plays, Wallace Shawn has written two opera librettos, *In the Dark* and *The Music Teacher*, and two screenplays, *My Dinner with*

André (1981) and *The Designated Mourner* (1997), both adaptations of his stage plays.

ACHIEVEMENTS

After a slow start, Wallace Shawn established himself as a leading writer in the Off-Broadway theater. His first play to receive a major production, *Our Late Night*, as staged by André Gregory's Manhattan Project at the Public Theatre, received an Obie Award in 1975. His play *Aunt Dan and Lemon* shared that same award with several other plays in 1985. *The Fever* won the Obie Award for Best Play of 1991; in accepting the award, he expressed surprise, because he did not consider the lengthy monologue to be a play. Shawn's work, though often taking as its subject extremely violent thoughts or antisocial behavior, has been praised for its accuracy in representing the emotional qualities of contemporary American life. His plays make unusual demands on audiences, who must respond to his characters with comic insight and intellectual energy. Shawn's distinctive voice is one of insidiously timid argumentation, an impression that is reinforced by his frequent appearances as a humorously innocuous character in contemporary films, yet he is also capable of writing shrill, viscerally affecting drama. Shawn's major works are distinctively unconventional, and he is among the most provocative writers in the U.S. theater.

BIOGRAPHY

Wallace Shawn's upbringing was without question a privileged one. His father, William Shawn, was the editor of *The New Yorker* for several decades, and Shawn grew up in the atmosphere of the Manhattan literary society. His education was extensive, including the best schools in the English-speaking world. From the Dalton School (1948-1957) and Putney School (1958-1961), Shawn went on to take a B.A. in history from Harvard (1965). He then took additional degrees at Magdalen College, Oxford: a B.A. in philosophy, politics, and economics (1968) and an M.A. in Latin under G. J. Warnock (1968). The time between universities was spent teaching English on a Fulbright scholarship at Indore Christian College, India.

Shawn's dramatic talents were encouraged by his parents, who provided him with creative tools such as a toy theater and a motion-picture camera. His childhood theatrics included the composition and performance of lurid murder mysteries with his younger brother Allen. Shawn recalls that an important turning point in his perception of drama came when his father took part in a different kind of play, about a botanist in Japan. From this point, Shawn developed the conviction that a play could be almost anything, and other performances included a four-hour version of John Milton's *Paradise Lost* (1667), a play featuring Ludwig Wittgenstein, and a Chinese dynastic drama. Many of these performances featured music by Allen Shawn, with whom Wallace continued to collaborate.

The young Shawn attended frequent professional productions in New York, including acclaimed productions of work as varied as Eugene O'Neill's *The Iceman Cometh* (pr., pb. 1946) and the early classics

Wallace Shawn (Hulton Archive by Getty Images)

of the absurdist drama. This exposure reinforced Shawn's conviction that the potential topics for dramatization are infinite.

Shawn's career after Oxford started with two years of teaching Latin at the Church of the Heavenly Rest Day School in Manhattan. During that time, Shawn began to write regularly, drafting plays such as *Four Meals in May* and *The Old Man*. Shawn then took a succession of odd jobs, including work as a shipping clerk in the garment district and as a copy-machine operator, while drafting a number of short plays and one full-length script, *The Hotel Play*. During this time, Shawn also studied acting with Katherine Sergava at the H.B. studio.

Shawn maintained a long-term relationship with writer Deborah Eisenberg. His play *Marie and Bruce* is dedicated to her, and she is mentioned several times in *My Dinner with André*. She also appeared in the New York production of *The Designated Mourner* in 2000. Her book of short stories, *Transactions in a Foreign Currency* (1986), carries a dedication to Shawn, and her long story "A Cautionary Tale" (published in *The New Yorker*) features characters resembling them both. Eisenberg has also authored one play, *Pastorale* (1982), which features the same sorts of casually cryptic dialogue and frustrated young characters that appear in Shawn's dramatic output.

Shawn's first break came through André Gregory's Manhattan Project. The hourlong production of *Our Late Night*, Shawn's first professional production, was awarded an Obie for Best Play Off-Broadway. Shawn was then engaged by the Public Theatre to prepare the adaptation of Niccolò Machiavelli's *La mandragola* (pr. c. 1519; *The Mandrake*, 1911). The production was staged by Wilford Leach, and Shawn was featured as an actor in the prologue. Leach later directed *Marie and Bruce*, with Louise Lasser and Bob Balaban, in a widely reviewed Public Theatre production in 1980 that led Shawn to a publishing contract with Grove Press.

Shawn's plays have also received several productions in London, including an early stage version of *My Dinner with André* in 1980. The first British production of his work was a *succès de scandale*, a staging of the trilogy *Three Short Plays* by Max Stafford-Clark for the Joint Stock Company in 1977. One part of the trilogy, an orgiastically sexual play called *The Youth Hostel*, aroused a public outcry over alleged obscenity. The author fortunately escaped prosecution, but concern over the representation of sex precluded any impression that might have been created by the play's artistic qualities. Later productions of *Marie and Bruce* and *Aunt Dan and Lemon* were received more responsibly.

The development of Shawn's acting career since 1977 has allowed him the comfort of a regular income and the time to pursue his writing projects. Shawn has had large character roles in a number of films, such as an obsessed psychiatrist in Marshall Brickman's *Lovesick* (1983), a depraved priest in the schoolboy drama *Heaven Help Us* (1985), the diminutive innkeeper Freud in *The Hotel New Hampshire* (1984), and a comic villain in director Rob Reiner's film *The Princess Bride* (1987). He is still perhaps best known for a brief appearance as Diane Keaton's former lover in Woody Allen's *Manhattan* (1979), as well as for his role as himself in the film version of *My Dinner with André*. Shawn has also appeared frequently in his own plays, including the 1981 La Mama E.T.C. production of *The Hotel Play*, the stage and screen versions of *My Dinner with André*, and the London and New York productions of *Aunt Dan and Lemon*. He has also appeared as the sole performer in *The Fever*.

By his own admission, writing does not come particularly easy to Shawn. Nevertheless, he has consistently pursued the images and themes that capture his imagination, always with the assumption that a personal concern with the material will arouse some similar response in the audience. Shawn has not developed any formulaic approach, though his work has distinctive stylistic traits and persistent themes. His plays have shown a steady improvement, and his following has continued to grow as his works enter the repertoire of major regional playhouses such as the Magic Theater and the Mark Taper Forum.

ANALYSIS

Wallace Shawn's major plays exhibit a concern with vivid images of violence, whether political or sexual, as they are manifested in the imaginations and behavior of his contemporary characters. These images connect Shawn's work with the traditional themes of Surrealism, yet the apparently harmless characters and situations in the plays' narrative structures cause a kind of contradictory tension between the force of obsessive imagination and the ordinary experience of daily life. Shawn has consistently improved his ability to express this juxtaposition of qualities, while emphasizing the immediate importance of his major themes.

Shawn's most important works, such as *My Dinner with André* and *Marie and Bruce*, tend to proceed from a narrative framework into a carefully constructed series of dialogues and monologues, arriving finally at a kind of stillness in resolution. Shawn's strengths as a playwright include an unusual flair for formal innovation, in plays as different as *The Hotel Play*, with its innumerable sets and characters, and *The Fever*, almost minimalist in its simple theatricality. He also writes dialogue of enormous sophistication, allowing him to represent the language of intellectuals by credibly imitating rather than satirizing their discourse. His most remarkable quality as a writer, however, comes in his persistent posing of difficult, even painful, questions about contemporary life. Given the temptations of the commercial marketplace, Shawn could easily use his comic skills to write successful teleplays or screenplays. Nevertheless, he has sustained his commitment to the theatrical exploration of obsessive, subconscious desire and the way it shapes human experience, not only in daily life but also in the broader perspectives of the appreciation of history and the value of human culture.

OUR LATE NIGHT

Shawn's first play to receive a major production, *Our Late Night*, raised the eyebrows of critics with its simultaneously scatological and intelligent style. The situation involves a young couple and their party guests and proceeds anecdotally from the final preparations of the couple through the recitations of their guests' unusual feelings and experiences to the empty moments after the party ends. The play's action—or what there is of action in the play—concerns the lust of the partygoers for one another in combination with their visceral reactions to what gets said (and eaten). The longest, most memorable monologue is an impassioned shaggy-dog story about one single-minded male guest's sexual exploits in the tropics.

The language of the play reveals one of Shawn's characteristic devices: the polite utterance of unconscionably rude sentiments. Obscenity begins to flow so freely that it becomes the normal discourse of the play, along with the frequent use of proper names, salutations, and other conventionally respectful phrases. The language becomes the stylistic equivalent of the characters themselves: well-dressed and pleasant-seeming, but sexually obsessed at the core. The final effect of the play, in the right sort of sophisticated performance situation, is not obscene but satirical, exposing the thin veneer of manners that strains to hold back the force of human desire.

THREE SHORT PLAYS

Shawn's second professional production raised more than eyebrows. The London production of *Three Short Plays* provoked antiobscenity complaints that resulted in a government investigation of the theater and an initiative to rewrite British obscenity laws. Of the three plays that constituted the production, the objectionable material was contained in *The Youth Hostel*. The play is unique for Shawn because the actors do not merely talk about their fantasies, they enact the fulfillment of their sexual desires onstage. Yet stylistically, the play has passages very similar to the successful satire of *Our Late Night*. Characters copulate, masturbate, and have violent fistfights, but they continue to express themselves in the polite, matter-of-fact idiom of contemporary young Americans.

The other two plays in the trilogy are less likely to offend audiences than *The Youth Hostel*, but they address the same themes. In *Summer Evening*, a young couple in a foreign hotel pass the time between meals by trying on clothes, discussing the mundane details of their vacation, and snacking. Yet lurking under the surface of the action, which Shawn suggests should have an extremely quick, unrealistic pace, are the desires of the man to possess the woman to the point of death, and the woman's fears of the injury that could come with her submission. The language, dotted with interruptions to encourage the tempo, remains oddly formal and polite, even while the intimacy of the characters' revelations gradually leads them to make love at the play's end. The last play of the set, a monologue titled *Mr. Frivolous*, features the eponymous character at breakfast, fantasizing about companionship and sexual pleasure. The title suggests the principal theme: Despite the intimacy and even the quaintness of his recitation, the young man is vacuous to the point of complete superfluity.

MARIE AND BRUCE

In *Marie and Bruce*, Shawn combines his stylistic habits with his psychological thematic concerns to create an elegantly crafted, if sometimes painful, portrait of a woman's life. Marie narrates the action, a typical day that includes abusing her husband at breakfast, going about her housework, taking a walk, going to a party with her husband, and then abusing him again over dinner. The shrillness of Marie's scatalogical vilifications of Bruce is countered by a patient, quizzical humility on his part, which carries the relationship through a final, horrible denunciation by Marie and back into a pattern of everyday life. The language of the play contains descriptive passages of unusual beauty indicating deep feelings of the characters that are strangely moving. Both of the main characters also have extended narrative solos, in which they describe their adventures when they leave the familiar surroundings of home and office. The images in these monologues are almost lush—erotically charged with the power of each character's frustrated sexuality.

As in *Our Late Night*, Shawn uses the device of a party scene. The supporting characters' scenes are short, with quick crosscutting between snatches of dialogue and actors doubling the many characters in such a way that the overall impression is like an overheard pastiche of party conversation. Some of the scenes, as they are juxtaposed to Marie's narration and short scenes with Bruce, are very funny. Later, at a restaurant, the couple is forced to overhear another conversation, this time a disgusting description of an intestinal ailment. This encounter triggers a blast from Marie that causes the amusing frustration and sexual flirtation of the earlier scenes to be seen from the tragic perspective of human mortality. Her enormous anger and disappointment expressed, Marie settles down at home with Bruce for the quiet end of her Sisyphean day. The dehumanizing experiences of the party scene, of urban confinement, and of powerlessness are reinforced in even the smallest details of the play, such as Bruce's search for the typewriter that Marie has destroyed, a machine made to express human feelings.

THE HOTEL PLAY

The Hotel Play is much less accomplished than *Marie and Bruce* and much more diffuse and vague. Its tropical setting suggests that the play has some connection to the sexual narration of the guest in *Our Late Night*. In fact, the central character of this episodic nightmare play is a diminutive but mysterious hotel clerk. The action shifts between various settings in the hotel, with a human menagerie passing through the more public scenes, while sex and gunfire punctuate the play's more private encounters. Shawn notes in a foreword that the play's atmosphere is intentionally dreamlike, and the most prominent themes are, like those of dreams, full of sexual fascination, eating, laughter, and the fear of death. The random ordering of the work creates the impression of a dream logic as well, which finally culminates in the death of one of the clerk's several paramours. Like the young people in *The Youth Hostel*, the impulsive characters of *The Hotel Play* have a detached, casually polite attitude toward the extreme situations that confront them.

MY DINNER WITH ANDRÉ

My Dinner with André shows a considerable shift away from this relaxed attitude, mostly because André Gregory's part of the extended conversation that constitutes the play is so fraught with concern over the state of humanity and the nature and potential of the human condition. The play's tight form, even as it pretends to be a rambling dialogue in a restaurant, has an important antecedent in the balance and meticulousness of composition in *Marie and Bruce*. Shawn provides a narrative frame for the action, which consists almost entirely of Gregory's extended description of his search for an absolute human meaning in places such as Jerzy Grotowski's retreat in the Polish forest, in Findhorn, in Tibet, and in the Sahara. Once Gregory has almost concluded his fascinating litany of hope and despair, Shawn begins to answer from his domestic perspective, which he views as potentially infinite in its extension. *My Dinner with André*, while not a play in the conventional sense, is a carefully edited, scripted, and objectified conversation with a range of dynamic effects and a wealth of themes that recapitulate those of Shawn's other work: the emptiness of sex, the automatizing influence of routine, the frustrations of desire, and even the horror of the Nazi cruelties. This last point is much more clearly amplified, however, in Shawn's most ambitious play, *Aunt Dan and Lemon*.

AUNT DAN AND LEMON

The narrative frame for *Aunt Dan and Lemon* is provided by Leonora, nicknamed Lemon, as she shares her thoughts and memories with an audience that she welcomes into the theater. The play's progress begins along autobiographical lines, as the audience becomes familiar with Lemon's parents and their friends. Then the action begins to focus on one of the friends, an articulate and conservative Oxford intellectual called Aunt Dan, who forms a peculiar, destructive attachment to Lemon. Once Aunt Dan is introduced, much of the play consists of her storytelling, as she describes sordid acquaintances and political situations to Lemon from her confused, eccentric perspective. The squalid events from Aunt Dan's stories, her conservative background and political instruction, and the impression made on Lemon by her friend's eventual illness and death gradually coalesce into a fascination on the girl's part with the Nazi war crimes. The primary theme of the play, then, seems to be Shawn's demonstration of how an intelligent, sensitive, privileged individual can be persuaded, through the influence of a few frustrated teachers and poor examples, to take a political position sympathetic to radical fascism.

Interestingly, Shawn includes very little material in the play's dialogue that confronts or questions the despicable beliefs of the main characters. Their voices and attitudes, through conventional habits of expression such as those used in the earlier plays, disarm the audience, leading spectators to suppose that the characters are normal, pleasant people. However,

once the stage material begins to include political content, Shawn depends on the audience to carry on a perceptive dialogue of its own, a kind of internal running commentary in the mind of each viewer that confronts and ridicules the beliefs of the characters. Shawn's only manipulation of the audience comes in his choices for the humorous juxtaposition of images and the improbable choice of characters: Aunt Dan's explanation of the Vietnam bombing uses stuffed animals to demonstrate her points, and her story about a seedy group of London friends involves the seduction and murder of an exaggerated Latin Lothario. In the right kind of performance situation, where an educated audience is likely to have strong views that they can oppose to those of the characters, the play is instructive, terrifying, and often quite amusing. Yet the ideological aspect of this play is much like its affective side, almost completely dependent on the competence and the insight of the audience response. For this reason, Shawn was accused of irresponsible playwriting in some of the New York reviews, an accusation that prompted him to write a special afterword on the context of the play.

THE FEVER

In *The Fever*, Shawn brings to the forefront many of the themes and devices of his earlier work in a theatrically severe but verbally complex conversation between an unnamed, Shawn-like narrator and an audience of intimates—a group of ten or twelve people in a private home. Shawn himself considers the work to be a "fable or fairy tale," yet the personal role he took in its performance and the close relation of the material to earlier monologues in his work (such as Lemon's, or the party guest's in *Our Late Night*) caused some critical confusion over Shawn's distance from the character and the fictional experiences narrated in the play. The text concerns the struggle of liberal conscience faced by a genteel American character who must confront and then try to come to terms with the everyday poverty and political torture suffered by ordinary people in a Central American country. The play has no clear narrative, mixing travel episodes about the discovery of another way of life with political ideas, personal moral reflections, descriptions of real or imagined illness, imprisonment, and domestic life. The crucial consideration of the play is one of social justice; why, Shawn's narrator asks, does he lead a life of moneyed privilege, while poor people lead lives of humiliation and terror? The search for answers runs the gamut from commodity fetishism to capitalist defense, but the asking of the play's questions never really implies coherent answers, and no such pat conclusions are forthcoming. Consequently *The Fever* continues, in even more concentrated form, Shawn's call for the audience to consider ambiguous political problems for themselves. Listeners are provoked to ponder, as the feverish character does, the "thin book of life" that comprises their birth, social position, accomplishments, values, and reasons for being in the world. The tale ends not in righteous condemnation but with a plea for forgiveness.

OTHER MAJOR WORKS

SCREENPLAYS: *My Dinner with André*, 1981 (with André Gregory); *The Designated Mourner*, 1997 (adaptation of his play).

BIBLIOGRAPHY

Billington, Michael. "A Play of Ideas Stirs Political Passions." *The New York Times*, October 27, 1985, p. B1. Billington discusses with Shawn the controversy over the political implications of *Aunt Dan and Lemon*. Shawn explains his dialogic theory of audience communication.

King, W. D., John Lahr, and Wallace Shawn. *Writing Wrongs: The Work of Wallace Shawn*. Temple University Press, 1997. The first comprehensive study of Shawn's life and literary output, analyzing each play and placing it in the context of drama from the Greeks to the present.

Posnock, Ross. "New York Phantasmagoria." *Raritan* 11 (Fall, 1991): 142-159. Shawn's concerns in *The Fever* are cleverly juxtaposed with those of New York intellectual Richard Sennett. Both writers are concerned with the contemporary crisis of human values in urban culture.

Rees, Jasper. "A Life in Two Halves." *The Daily Telegraph*, May 3, 1999, p. 18. Discusses the disparity between Shawn's challenging plays and his roles in films he describes as "silly," such as *Toy Story* and *Toy Story 2*. Shawn says that his fifty or so film and television roles pay for his writing.

Savran, David. "Wally Shawn." In *In Their Own Words: Contemporary American Playwrights*. New York: Theatre Communications Group, 1988. This long interview covers Shawn's career up to 1986. Shawn talks specifically about his processes of composition and revision for production.

Shawn, Wallace. "Why Write for the Theater? A Roundtable Report." *The New York Times*, February 9, 1986, p. B1. Shawn discusses his creative process and commitment to theater with Arthur Miller, Athol Fugard, and David Mamet. The most concise statement of his philosophy of composition.

Shawn, Wallace, and William Shawn. "Interview with William and Wally Shawn." Interview by Lucinda Franks. *The New York Times*, August 3, 1980, p. B1. Shawn and his father discuss their memories of Wallace's childhood and their common interests. Shawn recalls his earliest dramatic efforts, which sometimes included his brother and father.

Shewey, Don. "The Secret Life of Wally Shawn." *Esquire* 100 (October, 1983): 90-94. This personal portrait, undertaken in conjunction with the release of *My Dinner with André*, outlines several of the playwright's basic beliefs.

Wetzsteon, Ross. "The Holy Fool of the American Theater." *The Village Voice*, April 2, 1991, p. 35-37. Wetzsteon explains the critical reception of *The Fever*, and Shawn responds to criticisms of his politics and his use of alternative dramatic forms, with some explanations of his intentions.

_____. "Wallace Shawn, Subversive Moralist." *American Theatre* 14, no. 7 (September, 1999): 12(6). Argues that Shawn's later plays not only challenge the audience's sense of morality but also question assumptions about the meaning of theater itself. Includes comments from Shawn, such as his assertion that the audience is the main character in his plays.

Michael L. Quinn,
updated by Irene Struthers Rush

PERCY BYSSHE SHELLEY

Born: Field Place, Sussex, England; August 4, 1792
Died: Off Viareggio, Italy; July 8, 1822

PRINCIPAL DRAMA

The Cenci, pb. 1819, pr. 1886
Prometheus Unbound: A Lyrical Drama in Four Acts, pb. 1820
Oedipus Tyrannus: Or, Swellfoot the Tyrant, pb. 1820
Hellas: A Lyrical Drama, pb. 1822
Charles the First, pb. 1824 (fragment)

OTHER LITERARY FORMS

In addition to his dramas, Percy Bysshe Shelley wrote essays of considerable power and has long been recognized as one of England's greatest poets. His first published work, however, was the thoroughly undistinguished gothic novel *Zastrozzi: A Romance* (1810), which was followed later in the same year by the equally unimpressive *St. Irvyne: Or, The Rosicrucian* (mistakenly dated 1811 on the title page). Also appearing in 1810 were *Original Poetry by Victor and Cazire*, a collaboration with his sister Elizabeth which, despite its title, included plagiarized material, and *Posthumous Fragments of Margaret Nicholson*, a collection of six poems purportedly by the madwoman who had attempted, in 1786, to assassinate George III.

Of considerably greater significance was the appearance in 1811 of *The Necessity of Atheism*, a pamphlet written by Shelley and his Oxford friend, Thomas Jefferson Hogg, and which caused both to be expelled from the university. Having painfully established his credentials as a freethinker, Shelley then published two pamphlets, *An Address to the Irish People* (1812) and *Proposals for an Association of . . . Philanthropists* (1812), and an anonymous broadside, *Declaration of Rights* (1812), which further manifested his extreme liberalism. Another production of 1812, *A Letter to Lord Ellenborough*, expressed Shelley's support for freedom of the press with such passionate eloquence that it was quickly suppressed.

Queen Mab: A Philosophical Poem, whose 2,305 lines were accompanied by 118 pages of notes, was printed in 1813 but was too radical in content for the printer to risk public sale. Instead, copies were circulated privately, and this private dissemination was eventually supplemented by the appearance of pirated editions. In addition, a revision of a part of the poem appeared as *The Daemon of the World* in the 1816 volume *Alastor: Or, The Spirit of Solitude and Other Poems*. At about this time, Shelley also planned to publish a number of his shorter poems, but his plans misfired, and the collection, referred to as *The Esdaile Notebook*, remained unpublished until 1964.

The previously mentioned *Alastor* appeared in February of 1816 and was Shelley's first significant attempt to gain public recognition as a poet. The volume's title poem concerns the destruction of an artistic young man who succumbs to the lure of an unattainable ideal, a temptation to which Shelley himself was highly susceptible. Intricately symbolic in content and abstract in theme, *Alastor* is stylistically consistent with much of the poetry of Shelley's great maturity. The year 1816 also witnessed the writing of the "Hymn to Intellectual Beauty" and "Mont Blanc," two of his finest lyrics.

In 1817, with *A Proposal for Putting Reform to the Vote Throughout the Kingdom* and *An Address to the People on the Death of the Princess Charlotte* (only the former of which is known with certainty to have been published during his lifetime), Shelley brought to a close his career as a political pamphleteer. Political themes continued to be of great importance in his poetry, however, as the title of his next major poem, *The Revolt of Islam* (1818), suggests. A narrative of the struggles of Laon and Cythna, *The Revolt of Islam* is a vision of selfless revolution, revolution·shorn of the vengefulness that produced the Reign of Terror, but revolution ultimately, if gloriously, defeated.

Rosalind and Helen: A Modern Eclogue, with Other Poems was published in 1819, and though *Rosalind and Helen* itself is not among Shelley's more notable works, the volume also included the considerably more successful "Ozymandias" and "Lines Written Among the Euganean Hills." Two other poems of approximately this same period, *Prince Athanase*, a reworking of the *Alastor* theme, and the slightly later *Julian and Maddalo: A Conversation*, an attempt by Shelley to distill the philosophical differences between himself and his famous friend, George Gordon, Lord Byron, appeared first in *Posthumous Poems of Percy Bysshe Shelley* (1824).

Two poems of 1819 that were also published posthumously are *The Mask of Anarchy* (1832), inspired by the Peterloo Massacre, and *Peter Bell the Third* (1839), a parody of William Wordsworth's *Peter Bell* (1819). In addition, the years 1819-1820 produced "Ode to the West Wind," "To a Skylark," "The Sensitive Plant," and "The Cloud," all of which were included in *Prometheus Unbound: A Lyrical Drama in Four Acts, with Other Poems* (1820). "The Indian Serenade," of 1819; the *Letter to Maria Gisborne* and *The Witch of Atlas*, both of 1820; and "When the

Lamp Is Shattered" and *The Triumph of Life*, both of 1822, were contained in the posthumous 1824 volume, only the 1819 poem having appeared during Shelley's lifetime. *The Witch of Atlas* and *The Triumph of Life*, the latter of which Shelley was working on during the days preceding his death, are presented in the intricate symbolic mode characteristic of Shelley's most distinctive poetry.

Two of Shelley's poetic masterworks, *Epipsychidion* (1821) and *Adonais: An Elegy on the Death of John Keats* (1821), remain to be mentioned. The former, inspired by Shelley's acquaintance with Teresa Viviani, whose father had confined her to a convent school during the months preceding her marriage, is an attempt to define humanity's spiritual essence, its *epipsyche*. The latter, written after the death of John Keats, is one of the most beautiful elegies in the English language.

Finally, a great many of Shelley's letters and a number of his more important essays have been published since his death. Among the latter are "A Defence of Poetry," included in *Essays, Letters from Abroad, Translations, and Fragments* (1840), "An Essay on Christianity," contained in *Shelley Memorials* (1859), and the separately printed *A Philosophical View of Reform* (1920).

ACHIEVEMENTS

Percy Bysshe Shelley was long a lover of drama but not always a lover of the theater. Under the influence of Thomas Love Peacock and Leigh Hunt, however, he appears to have overcome much of his natural distaste for theatrical extravagance, and after a number of enjoyable experiences in London, he continued his attendance at plays and operas during his years in Italy. Still, unlike Lord Byron, who acted on more than one occasion in amateur stage productions and served for a time on the Drury Lane Committee of Management, Shelley knew drama from the point of view of the avid reader and occasional spectator, not from the perspective of the practical man of the theater. The strengths and weaknesses of most of his dramatic works, effective—even magnificent—in the study but inappropriate for the stage, are consistent with this indirect knowledge of stagecraft, but the un-

Percy Bysshe Shelley (Library of Congress)

deniable dramatic power of one particular play, *The Cenci*, suggests that, if he had lived longer, Shelley might have become the dramatic genius that England during the Romantic era so sadly lacked.

Very early in his literary career, Shelley is said to have attempted dramatic collaborations with his sister Elizabeth and with a friend, Andrew Amos, but what appear to be the first surviving dramatic fragments are a handful of lines written in Italy in 1818 for a play to have been entitled "Tasso." According to Mary Shelley, her husband, at about this same time, was also thinking of composing a biblical drama based on the Book of Job, no farfetched project when one considers that Byron was about to undertake *Cain: A Mystery* (pb. 1821). If Thomas Medwin, Shelley's cousin and biographer, is to be believed, the plan for *Charles the First* was a product of 1818 as well, though the writing of this promising fragment was deferred to 1819 and thereafter. The only dramatic project of 1818 which Shelley ultimately completed, however, was *Prometheus Unbound*.

As Mary Shelley relates in her notes to the play, *Prometheus Unbound* was begun during a period in which Shelley was thoroughly imbued with the spirit of the Greek tragedies, especially with "the sublime majesty of Aeschylus," which "filled him with wonder and delight." He was also aware, as later critics have pointed out, of the uses of the Promethean myth by his poetic contemporaries, such as Johann Wolfgang von Goethe and Byron. He was familiar, too, with recent experiments, including Goethe's *Faust* (pb. 1808, 1833) and Byron's *Manfred* (pb. 1817), in a highly symbolic mental drama with which his own great talents were wonderfully compatible. The result of this amalgam of influences was Shelley's composition, during 1818 and 1819, of one of literature's great lyric dramas, an exultant statement of Shelley's faith in the ultimate triumph of justice and love over hatred and oppression.

Despite its poetic beauty, however, *Prometheus Unbound* is not a practical stage play. Shelley had long considered himself unsuited for composing such a play, but while he was at work on *Prometheus Unbound*, he was introduced to a subject on which he based one of the few nineteenth century tragedies in

English worthy of continued theatrical attention, *The Cenci*. He had been shown a rare manuscript in which the brutal history of the Cenci family was recorded, and he had been drawn to this tale of incest and murder because it so perfectly illustrated themes that had long obsessed him. As they occur in the play, the savagery of Count Francesco Cenci exemplifying the corrupting influence of absolute, oppressive power, and the vengefulness of his victimized daughter, Beatrice, with its terrible spiritual consequences, illustrate the destructive results of surrendering to hatred. In a sense, the joyous conclusion of *Prometheus Unbound* and the tragic conclusion of *The Cenci* are obverse images of the same truth, that fortitude and forgiveness, rather than violent retaliation, are the proper responses to injustice.

Oedipus Tyrannus was begun on August 24, 1820, a year after Shelley had finished *The Cenci* and soon after he had completed *Prometheus Unbound*. The year before, he had translated Euripides' *Kyklōps* (c. 421 B.C.E.; *Cyclops*, 1782) and had begun the fragment *Charles the First*. Both appeared in *Posthumous Poems of Percy Bysshe Shelley*, as did his translations of scenes from Pedro Calderón de la Barca's *El mágico prodigioso* (1637) and Goethe's *Faust*. An additional fragment, an untitled work centering on an Indian enchantress, was also included in the 1824 volume. Among the above, Shelley had the highest hopes for *Charles the First*, a tragedy which was to trace the complexities of the Cromwell uprising. Unfortunately, the subject presented so many problems that he gave it up by June, 1822.

The Cenci is the only play by Shelley with a substantial stage history, the others having received no more than rare experimental treatment. Even *The Cenci*, in fact, was long neglected, having been performed for the first time in London on May 7, 1886, under the sponsorship of the Shelley Society. During the next forty years, productions occurred in Paris (1891), Coburg (1919), Moscow (1919-1920), Prague (1922), London (1922 and 1926), Leeds (1923), Frankfurt am Main (1924), and New York (1926). The London production of 1922, with Dame Sybil Thorndike as Beatrice, was the most instrumental in establishing *The Cenci*'s fitness for the stage.

BIOGRAPHY

Percy Bysshe Shelley, born on August 4, 1792, at Field Place in Sussex, England, near the town of Horsham, was the eldest of seven children. His father was Timothy Shelley, a longtime member of Parliament and eventual baronet, and his mother, the former Elizabeth Pilfold. The young Shelley lived in privileged comfort, a circumstance that later offended his reformist sensibilities, and was the object of considerable family affection. His education was begun near Field Place by the Reverend Evan Edwards and was continued at Syon House Academy (from 1802 to 1804) and Eton (from 1804 to 1810). His experiences at Syon House and Eton, where he underwent considerable bullying, helped inspire his passionate hatred of oppressive power. These were also the years in which he developed his fascinations with science and literature. The former brought about his successful attempt to burn down a willow tree with a magnifying glass and his unsuccessful attempt to summon the devil; the latter led to the publication of his first book, a gothic novel, before his eighteenth birthday.

Shelley entered University College, Oxford, in October of 1810, and was expelled on March 25, 1811, for his distribution of *The Necessity of Atheism*, a collaboration with Hogg. His expulsion aggravated the difficulties that already existed between him and his father, and finding himself unwelcome at home, Shelley took up residence in London, where he became reacquainted with Harriet Westbrook, a classmate of his sister. Westbrook soon replaced Harriet Grove in Shelley's affections, Grove having rejected the young poet earlier in the year. After the sixteen-year-old Westbrook had made herself irresistible by claiming to be a sufferer of persecution, the two ran off to Edinburgh, where they were married on August 29, 1811. Although the marriage appears to have been reasonably happy at first, it eventually became one of the great disasters of Shelley's life.

Hogg lived with the Shelleys in Edinburgh and later in York, but Hogg's unsuccessful attempt to seduce Harriet during a short trip by Shelley to Sussex resulted in the couple's quick departure for Keswick,

this time accompanied by Harriet's meddlesome sister, Eliza. At Keswick, Shelley became acquainted with Robert Southey, who saw in Shelley's radical ways a reflection of what he had once been, and began corresponding with his future father-in-law, William Godwin, celebrated among liberals as the writer of *An Inquiry Concerning the Principles of Political Justice, and Its Influence on General Virtue and Happiness* (1793). Godwin's ideas were among the most powerful influences on Shelley's own early political ethos.

In February of 1812, Shelley traveled to Dublin, Ireland, where he issued pamphlets and delivered speeches in favor of increased Irish autonomy. He then took himself and his household to Wales and later to Lynmouth, Devon, where *A Letter to Lord Ellenborough* was refused publication, most of the copies being burned by the printer, and where his servant was arrested for handing out sheets of his *Declaration of Rights*. Having come under government surveillance, he then retired to Tremadoc, Wales, after which he departed for London, arriving on October 4, 1812.

During the six weeks he spent in London, Shelley met Godwin, Thomas Hookham, and Peacock, all of whom were to figure prominently in his later career. Shelley's explicit purposes in going to London, however, were to raise money for an engineering project near Tremadoc that was being supported by one of his liberal friends and to deal with some of his own financial difficulties. Having done what he could, he returned to Tremadoc for the winter but left for Ireland after someone purportedly tried to shoot him on February 26, 1813.

Shelley was back in London by April, where *Queen Mab* was published in May (by Hookham) and where Shelley's daughter, Eliza Ianthe, was born in June. During the next several months, the Shelleys' wanderings continued, but most of their time was spent in or near London, thus giving them continuing access to the Godwin household and allowing the growth of their friendship with the amiable Peacock. This seems to be the period, too, when Harriet and Shelley began drifting apart. Their differences in temperament were becoming less easy to ignore, and the annoying presence of the irascible Westbrook was driving her brother-in-law to distraction. The inevitable crisis occurred after Shelley, to Godwin's horror, expressed his love for Godwin's teenage daughter Mary on June 27, 1814. Harriet was not amenable to Shelley's suggestion that Mary become part of the family, and after a period of melodramatic chaos, Shelley and Mary, with Mary's half sister Claire Clairmont, fled to France on July 27, 1814. After an impromptu Continental tour, the errant lovers returned to England on September 13. During the next six months, both Harriet and Mary gave birth to children by Shelley, but only Charles Bysshe Shelley, Harriet's son, survived infancy.

Shelley and Mary found that they were not welcome among most of their old friends, though Peacock remained loyal, and Shelley spent a great deal of his time dodging creditors. His financial troubles were somewhat eased when his father, in June, 1815, began providing him with a generous annual allowance, but his social problems continued. In August of that year, he and Mary rented a cottage outside Bishopsgate, where they lived for a time in somber seclusion. Following a journey up the Thames, however, Shelley recovered his equanimity and began work on the poetry of the *Alastor* volume. *Alastor* was published in February, 1816, shortly after the birth of William Shelley, the poet's second son.

Shelley, with Mary, their son, and Claire Clairmont, embarked on a second Continental tour in May. Claire, who had secretly carried on an affair with Lord Byron and was carrying his child, urged the group on to Lake Geneva, where they soon encountered the celebrated author of *Childe Harold's Pilgrimage* (1812-1818, 1819). Byron and Shelley, though vastly different in personality, quickly became friends, and their many conversations proved fruitful to the poetry of both. The friendship was also beneficial to Mary, who began work on *Frankenstein* (1818) during an evening at Byron's quarters in the Villa Diodati. The encounter was less fortunate for Claire, who discovered that Byron felt no love for her, though he expressed a willingness to rear their child so long as its mother kept discreetly at a distance.

Shelley was generous in his attempts to assist Claire, who accompanied the Shelley household to Bath after their return from the Continent in late summer. Even without the complication of Claire's pregnancy, the next few months were among the most tumultuous of Shelley's life. The first shock occurred in October, when Mary's half sister Fanny Imlay took her own life. This was soon followed by the disappearance of Harriet Shelley, whose body was found on December 10, 1816, floating in the Serpentine, where she, too, had become a suicide. Shelley and Mary were married three weeks later, after which a custody fight for Ianthe and Charles ended in failure on March 27, 1817. Shelley was judged an unfit father because of his "immoral and vicious" principles.

In the midst of these troubles, Shelley found himself winning recognition as a poet, most notably through Leigh Hunt's "Young Poets" article in *The Examiner* in December, 1816. Shelley quickly took advantage of the opportunity offered by the article, which grouped him with John Hamilton Reynolds and Keats, to introduce himself to Hunt, through whom he met Keats, Horace Smith, and other members of the London literary scene. With the birth of Clara Allegra Byron at Bath on January 12, 1817, and with his own involvement in the child custody case, Shelley found it not only possible but also necessary to spend considerable time in the capital, a circumstance that augmented his chances for literary friendships.

A few weeks before the handing down of the Chancery decision, Shelley moved his entourage to Albion House in Great Marlow, where he had easy access to London and where he could accommodate his many literary visitors. The Marlow period, despite its occasional traumas, was a time of comparative stability, during which Shelley did the last of his political pamphleteering and published the longest of his poems, *The Revolt of Islam*. He also began *Rosalind and Helen* and became a father for the fifth time. His daughter Clara was born on September 2, 1817. Unfortunately, because of new financial worries brought on largely by loans to his improvident father-in-law and because of concern that the courts might take custody of William and Clara, Shelley and Mary left Marlow in February, 1818. On March 11, they sailed from England, intending to reach Italy. After that date, Shelley never saw England again.

The Shelley party crossed France and passed through the Alps to Turin and Milan. While in Milan, Shelley exchanged letters with Byron concerning Allegra, and it was finally decided that Byron's daughter would be sent to his apartments in Venice under the protection of a nurse. The Shelleys then traveled to Pisa and Leghorn, where they lingered for several weeks. They next occupied the Casa Bertini at the Baths of Lucca, where Shelley completed *Rosalind and Helen*, which was published during the spring of 1819.

Because of disturbing letters from Allegra's nurse, Shelley and Claire departed for Venice on August 17, 1818, arriving five days later. Byron and Shelley resumed their friendship, a circumstance that inspired Shelley's *Julian and Maddalo*, and Claire was pleased to find Allegra in good health, though the chaos of Byron's bizarre household had necessitated her being placed, for a time, with another family. More significant, as a result of Shelley's misleading statements to Byron concerning the whereabouts of Mary and the annoying Claire, Shelley was forced to ask Mary to make a quick journey from Lucca to Este, where Byron had offered him the use of a house. During the trip, Clara became infected with dysentery; she died in Venice on September 24, 1818.

Clara's death brought Shelley and Mary grief and a cooling of their love, but the months at Este were, nevertheless, productive. In addition to his work on *Julian and Maddalo*, Shelley composed "Lines Written Among the Euganean Hills" and began *Prometheus Unbound*. Their journey to Rome during November showed less production, but their three-month stay in Naples saw the completion of *Prometheus Unbound*, act 1. Following their return to Rome in March, 1819, Shelley wrote the play's second and third acts and became interested in the history of the Cenci family. During June, however, in the midst of the poet's fruitful literary activities, William became ill. The crisis came quickly, and after a sixty-hour struggle, the child died on June 7, 1819.

Soon thereafter, the grieving parents moved to Leghorn, where Shelley immersed himself in further literary endeavors, primarily the writing of *The Cenci*, though *The Mask of Anarchy* was also written there. In October, the Shelleys were again on the move, this time to Florence, where Shelley's last child, Percy Florence, was born on November 12, and where the literary deluge continued. While living at the Palazzo Marino, Shelley wrote *Peter Bell the Third*, "Ode to the West Wind," portions of *A Philosophical View of Reform*, and act 4 of *Prometheus Unbound*. Shelley himself considered *Prometheus Unbound*, published in August of 1820, to be his greatest work, a view which many, if not most, critics have since shared.

In late January, 1820, the Shelleys took inexpensive lodgings in Pisa, in and around which they were to reside during most of the remainder of Shelley's life. With the birth of Percy Florence, Mary's spirits had improved considerably, and much of what had made life bitter for the couple during the previous months appears to have faded from prominence. There were disasters still to come, but there were moments, too, of idyllic tranquillity, as well as further periods of creative accomplishment. Shelley divided 1820 among Pisa itself and nearby Leghorn and San Giuliano. In addition, he traveled with Claire to Florence, where she was to live in the household of a prominent physician. During the year, he seems to have done further work on *A Philosophical View of Reform* and also wrote "The Sensitive Plant," "To a Skylark," the "Letter to Maria Gisborne," *The Witch of Atlas*, and *Oedipus Tyrannus*.

During the first months of 1821, after making the acquaintance of the charming Teresa Viviani, Shelley wrote *Epipsychidion*, a poem inspired by Teresa's virtual imprisonment in the St. Anna convent school. In February and March, after reading a somewhat cynical essay by Peacock, he composed his brilliantly idealistic response, *A Defence of Poetry*, published in 1840. *Adonais* was written on April 11, after he received the shocking news of the death of Keats, whom he had tried to persuade to join him in Pisa for the sake of Keats's health, and the stirring *Hellas* was completed in October.

This was the period, too, when the celebrated Pisan Circle began to form. Thomas Medwin had arrived in late 1819, and Shelley met Edward and Jane Williams in January of 1820. In August of 1820, Shelley traveled to Ravenna to lure Byron to Pisa. Experiencing considerable difficulties because of his own political activities and those of his mistress' family, Byron joined the group late in 1820, along with Teresa Gamba Guiccioli and members of her family. With the addition on January 14, 1822, of Edward Trelawny, a friend of Edward Williams, the Pisan Circle was complete.

With the arrival of Trelawny, 1822 began well, but subsequent months would bring a double catastrophe to Shelley and his friends. The first tragedy occurred in April, when Allegra Byron died in a convent at Ravenna. Claire had been terribly concerned about Allegra from the moment she was told that Byron had left the child behind during his retreat from governmental authorities. He had left Allegra in good hands, but the convent, as Claire had feared, was vulnerable to epidemics, and on April 20, Allegra had succumbed to typhus.

The second tragedy involved Shelley himself. Shelley had continued his literary endeavors in 1822, working primarily on his poems *Charles the First* and *The Triumph of Life*, but with every encouragement from Williams and Trelawny, he also developed an interest in sailing, despite not knowing how to swim. So interested was he, in fact, that he ordered a small boat to be built, delivery of which he accepted on May 12. On July 1, he and Williams sailed the boat, the *Don Juan*, to Leghorn to meet Hunt, whom Shelley had invited to Italy to found a literary journal. On July 8, Williams and Shelley began the return voyage in threatening weather. Their bodies were washed ashore several days later, and under Trelawny's supervision, they were cremated on the beach. In a typically Romantic gesture, Trelawny snatched Shelley's heart from the ashes, and it was eventually given to Mary.

ANALYSIS

For all practical purposes, the narrative of Percy Bysshe Shelley's importance to theatrical history is the tale of *The Cenci*. However, *Prometheus Unbound* was the first of his substantial literary undertakings to be cast in dramatic form and is thematically related to *The Cenci*.

PROMETHEUS UNBOUND

Prometheus Unbound considers on the ideal level what *The Cenci* examines on the level of gritty reality, the relationship between good and evil, between benevolent innocence and that which would corrupt it. Shelley's Prometheus is the traditional fire-giver redefined, as his preface tells us. The primary change that Shelley makes in his subject is a reworking of the events leading to Prometheus's release. In the lost Aeschylean play from which Shelley borrowed his title, there occurred a "reconciliation of Jupiter with his victim" at "the price of the disclosure of the danger threatened to his empire by the consummation of his marriage with Thetis." In Shelley's version, Prometheus earns his freedom more nobly, by overcoming himself, by forswearing hatred and the desire for revenge, embracing love, and achieving, through extraordinary fortitude, a merciful selflessness.

In a sense, Prometheus combines a Christ-like forbearance with the traits the Romantics often admired in Satan. Shelley says Prometheus is like Satan in that "In addition to courage, and majesty, and firm and patient opposition to omnipotent force, he is susceptible of being described as exempt from the taints of ambition, envy, revenge, and a desire for personal aggrandisement." By contrast with Satan, Shelley described Prometheus as "the type of the highest perfection of moral and intellectual nature, impelled by the purest and the truest motives to the best and noblest ends."

This perfection is absent as the play begins, but when, in act 1, Prometheus relents in his hatred and says, "I wish no living thing to suffer pain," his ultimate triumph and Jupiter's defeat are inevitable. Evil can succeed only if it is allowed access to one's innermost being, only if one allows it to re-create oneself in its own vile image. With "Gentleness, Virtue, Wisdom, and Endurance," a person can win out, though the success of goodness requires a great deal of him as is shown in the play's final lines:

To suffer woe which Hope thinks infinite;
To forgive wrongs darker than death or night;
To defy Power, which seems omnipotent;
To love, and bear; to hope till Hope creates
From its own wreck the thing it contemplates;
Neither to change, nor falter, nor repent;
This, like thy glory, Titan, is to be
Good, great and joyous, beautiful and free;
This is alone Life, Joy, Empire, and Victory.

THE CENCI

In *The Cenci*, Beatrice exhibits the necessary defiance of evil, but she lacks the fortitude to resist hatred. She confuses physical violation, which any person with sufficient opportunity can inflict on any other, with spiritual violation, which requires willful complicity. By hating, she comes partially to resemble the thing she hates.

The object of Beatrice's hatred is her father, Count Francesco Cenci, the embodiment of everything the Romantics distrusted in those possessed of power. In characterizing the count, Shelley had a rich gallery of gothic and melodramatic villains on which to draw, and among them all, few can match the count for wickedness. The count is a plunderer, a murderer, and an incestuous rapist. He takes delight in destroying the lives of those around him, and he especially enjoys inflicting spiritual torture. He will only "rarely kill the body," because it "preserves, like a strong prison, the soul within my power,/ Wherein I feed it with the breath of fear/ For hourly pain."

Like many a villain of the period, the count commits his vilest crimes against the holy ties of sentiment. His egomania destroys his capacity for fellow-feeling, and out of the horror of his isolating selfhood, he performs deeds of unnatural viciousness against those who most deserve his love. He abuses Lucretia, his wife, and Bernardo, his innocent young son. He prays for the deaths of two other sons, Rocco and Cristofano, and invites guests to a banquet of thanksgiving when their deaths occur. He refuses to repay the loan of his daughter-in-law's dowry, which he had borrowed from the desperately poor Giacomo, his fourth son. After taking Giacomo's job away and giving it to another man, he alienates this son from his wife and children by claiming that Giacomo used the lost dowry for licentious carousing. He reserves his greatest cruelty, however, for Beatrice. Beatrice possesses the courage to denounce him and to seek redress for the injustices inflicted on herself and her family. She goes so far as to petition the pope for aid in her struggle. In order to break her rebellious spirit, to crush her will to resist him, the count rapes his daughter and threatens to do so again.

The count's unnatural cruelty inspires unnatural hatred in Lucretia, Giacomo, and Beatrice. As Giacomo tells us, "He has cast Nature off, which was his shield,/ And Nature casts him off, who is her shame;/ And I spurn both." The son, "reversing Nature's law," wishes to take the life of the man who "gave life to me." He wishes to kill the man who denied him "happy years" and "memories/ Of tranquil childhood," who deprived him of "home-sheltered love." Beatrice and Lucretia share this wish to destroy the perverter of love. When Count Cenci proves impervious to their pleas that he relent, and when every external authority refuses to intervene, the family members take action against this most unnatural of men.

Because Beatrice is strongest and most sinned against, she becomes the prime mover of her father's murder. Giacomo refers to her victimization as "a higher reason for the act/ Than mine" and speaks of her, in lines ironically recalling the biblical injunction *against* vengeance, as "a holier judge than me,/ A more unblamed avenger." In becoming the avenger, though, Beatrice must steel herself against those qualities of innocence and compassion that have rendered her superior to her persecutor. She thinks, in fact, that exactly those qualities that militate against the murder can be twisted around to give the strength needed to commit it. She advises Giacomo to

. . . Let piety to God,
Brotherly love, justice and clemency,
And all things that make tender hardest hearts
Make thine hard, brother.

When assassins have been recruited to do the deed, Giacomo utters a momentary hope that the assassins may fail. When the first attempt does fail, Lucretia takes the opportunity to urge Francesco to confess his sins so that, if a second attempt succeeds, at least she will have done nothing to condemn his soul to eternal torment. Beatrice, by contrast, is as relentless in pursuing revenge as her father had been in pursuing evil pleasures. At a key moment, when even the assassins quail at taking the life of "an old and sleeping man," Beatrice takes up the knife and shames them into performing the murder by threatening to do it herself.

Beatrice is like her father, too, in claiming that God is on her side. Francesco had seen the hand of God in the deaths of his disobedient sons; the ultimate Father had upheld parental authority by killing the rebellious Rocco and Cristofano. Similarly, as Beatrice plots her father's death, she feels confident of having God's approval for her actions; as his instrument, she is permitted, even obligated, to wreak vengeance on this most terrible of sinners. Neither character is right. Both are appealing to the silent symbol of all external authority to justify the unjustifiable, to second the internal voice that has turned them toward evil.

The dangers of religion are further embodied in the machinations of Orsino and the unconscionable actions of the pope and his representatives. Orsino is God's priest, but his priestly garb merely wraps his lustfulness in the hypocritical guise of sanctity. In order to eliminate Count Cenci, the greatest obstacle to his possession of Beatrice, Orsino urges the conspirators on at every turn. When the conspiracy is discovered, he is the only participant in the count's murder to slink safely away. The pope's role in the play's events is even more reprehensible. For years, he has allowed the count's depredations at the price of an occasional rich bribe. He refuses to intervene to end the count's crimes because it is in his self-interest to allow them to continue. When he finally does take action, apparently because he can now achieve more by eliminating the count than by keeping him alive, the pope is too late; the count is already dead. He then turns on those who have accomplished, outside the law, what he would have done with the full authority of the papal office. As the earthly representative of ultimate power, he orders the deaths of those who have become a threat to all power; the conspirators are to be executed. The irony of this situation is that the force behind the papal authority is the same false notion that lured his victims to act as they did, the assumption that everything, even the shedding of human blood, is allowed to those who have God on their side.

In a world as corrupt as the one in which Beatrice Cenci finds herself, her fall is all the more terrible because it is so easy to sympathize with. The most perceptive comments concerning the nature of Beatrice as a tragic heroine and the appropriateness of her life as a tragic subject are Shelley's own:

> Undoubtedly, no person can be truly dishonoured by the act of another; and the fit return to make to the most enormous injuries is kindness and forbearance, and a resolution to convert the injurer from his dark passions by peace and love. Revenge, retaliation, atonement, are pernicious mistakes. If Beatrice had thought in this manner, she would have been wiser and better; but she would never have been a tragic character. . . . It is in the restless and anatomizing casuistry with which men seek the justification of Beatrice, yet feel that she has done what needs justification; it is in the superstitious horror with which they contemplate alike her wrongs and their revenge, that the dramatic character of what she did and suffered, consists.

In her capacity to endure evil and to forgive the evildoer, Beatrice is no Prometheus, but in her very understandable human frailty, she is a far superior subject for dramatic representation.

OEDIPUS TYRANNUS

Inspired at least in part by the squealing of pigs near Shelley's rooms in the vicinity of Pisa, Italy, *Oedipus Tyrannus* is a raucous burlesque of events surrounding George IV's attempt to divorce his estranged wife, Caroline. Its virulent mockery of commoners, cabinet ministers, and members of the royal family alike brought about its quick suppression.

HELLAS

The last of Shelley's dramatic works to be published during his lifetime, *Hellas*, was written in support of the Greek revolutionaries under the leadership of Prince Alexander Mavrocordato, to whom the play is dedicated. Like *Prometheus Unbound*, *Hellas* has affinities to Aeschylean tragedy. Aeschylus's *Prometheus desmōtēs* (date unknown; *Prometheus Bound*,

1777) provided much of the inspiration for the earlier work, while his *Persai* (472 B.C.E.; *The Persians*, 1777) gave impetus to the writing of *Hellas*. The play's most familiar lines, from the concluding choral song, are an eloquent cry of hope for the regeneration of the world:

> The world's great age begins anew,
> The golden years return,
> The earth doth like a snake renew
> Her winter weeds outworn:
> Heaven smiles, and faiths and empires gleam,
> Like wrecks of a dissolving dream.

OTHER MAJOR WORKS

LONG FICTION: *Zastrozzi: A Romance*, 1810; *St. Irvyne: Or, The Rosicrucian*, 1810.

POETRY: *Original Poetry by Victor and Cazire*, 1810 (with Elizabeth Shelley); *Posthumous Fragments of Margaret Nicholson*, 1810; *Queen Mab: A Philosophical Poem*, 1813 (revised as *The Daemon of the World*, 1816); *Alastor: Or, The Spirit of Solitude and Other Poems*, 1816; *Mont Blanc*, 1817; *The Revolt of Islam*, 1818; *Rosalind and Helen: A Modern Eclogue, with Other Poems*, 1819; *Letter to Maria Gisborne*, 1820; *Epipsychidion*, 1821; *Adonais: An Elegy on the Death of John Keats*, 1821; *Posthumous Poems of Percy Bysshe Shelley*, 1824 (includes *Prince Athanase*, *Julian and Maddalo: A Conversation*, *The Witch of Atlas*, *The Triumph of Life*, *The Cyclops*, and *Charles the First*); *The Mask of Anarchy*, 1832; *Peter Bell the Third*, 1839; *The Poetical Works of Percy Bysshe Shelley*, 1839; *The Wandering Jew*, 1887; *The Complete Poetical Works of Shelley*, 1904 (Thomas Hutchinson, editor); *The Esdaile Notebook: A Volume of Early Poems*, 1964 (K. N. Cameron, editor).

NONFICTION: *The Necessity of Atheism*, 1811 (with Thomas Jefferson Hogg); *An Address to the Irish People*, 1812; *Declaration of Rights*, 1812; *A Letter to Lord Ellenborough*, 1812; *Proposals for an Association of . . . Philanthropists*, 1812; *A Refutation of Deism, in a Dialogue*, 1814; *History of a Six Weeks' Tour Through a Part of France, Switzerland, Germany, and Holland*, 1817 (with Mary Shelley); *A Proposal for Putting Reform to the Vote Throughout the Kingdom*, 1817; *An Address to the People on the Death of the Princess Charlotte*, 1817?; *Essays, Letters from Abroad, Translations, and Fragments*, 1840; *A Defence of Poetry*, 1840; *Shelley Memorials*, 1859; *Shelley's Prose in the Bodleian Manuscripts*, 1910; *Note Books of Shelley*, 1911; *A Philosophical View of Reform*, 1920; *The Letters of Percy Bysshe Shelley*, 1964 (2 volumes; Frederick L. Jones, editor).

TRANSLATIONS: *The Cyclops*, 1824 (of Euripides' play); *Ion*, 1840 (of Plato's dialogue); "The Banquet Translated from Plato," 1931 (of Plato's dialogue *Symposium*).

MISCELLANEOUS: *The Complete Works of Percy Bysshe Shelley*, 1926-1930 (10 volumes; Roger Ingpen and Walter E. Peck, editors); *Shelley's Poetry and Prose: Authoritative Texts and Criticism*, 1977 (Donald H. Reiman and Sharon B. Powers, editors).

BIBLIOGRAPHY

Blumberg, Jane. *Byron and the Shelleys: The Story of a Friendship*. London: Collins & Brown, 1992. Blumberg describes the friendship among George Gordon, Lord Byron, and the Shelleys. Bibliography and index.

Duff, David. *Romance and Revolution: Shelley and the Politics of a Genre*. New York: Cambridge University Press, 1994. Duff examines Romanticism and politics in the work of Shelley. Bibliography and index.

Hamilton, Paul. *Percy Bysshe Shelley*. Tavistock: Northcote House in association with the British Council, 2000. Hamilton's biography provides the story of Shelley's life and criticism and interpretation of his works.

Höhne, Horst. *In Pursuit of Love: The Short and Troublesome Life and Work of Percy Bysshe Shelley*. New York: Peter Lang, 2000. A biography of Shelley that looks at his life and works. Bibliography and index.

Lewis, Linda M. *The Promethean Politics of Milton, Blake, and Shelley*. Columbia: University of Missouri Press, 1992. Lewis examines the Greek myth of Prometheus in Shelley's *Prometheus Unbound*, John Milton's *Paradise Lost*, and the works of William Blake. Bibliography and index.

Simpson, Michael. *Closet Performances: Political Exhibition and Prohibition in the Dramas of Byron and Shelley.* Stanford, Calif.: Stanford University Press, 1998. Simpson examines the role of politics and censorship in the plays of Lord Byron and Shelley. Bibliography and index.

Robert H. O'Connor,
updated by Richard D. McGhee

SAM SHEPARD
Samuel Shepard Rogers VII

Born: Fort Sheridan, Illinois; November 5, 1943

PRINCIPAL DRAMA

Cowboys, pr. 1964 (one act)
The Rock Garden, pr. 1964, pb. 1972 (one act)
Up to Thursday, pr. 1964
Chicago, pr. 1965, pb. 1967
Dog, pr. 1965
Icarus's Mother, pr. 1965, pb. 1967
Rocking Chair, pr. 1965
4-H Club, pr. 1965, pb. 1971
Fourteen Hundred Thousand, pr. 1966, pb. 1967
Melodrama Play, pr. 1966, pb. 1967
Red Cross, pr. 1966, pb. 1967
La Turista, pr. 1966, pb. 1968
Cowboys #2, pr. 1967, pb. 1971
Forensic and the Navigators, pr. 1967, pb. 1969
The Unseen Hand, pr., pb. 1969
Operation Sidewinder, pb. 1969, pr. 1970
Shaved Splits, pr. 1969, pb. 1971
The Holy Ghostly, pr. 1970, pb. 1971
Back Bog Beast Bait, pr., pb. 1971
Cowboy Mouth, pr., pb. 1971 (with Patti Smith)
The Mad Dog Blues, pr. 1971, pb. 1972
Nightwalk, pr., pb. 1972 (with Megan Terry and Jean-Claude van Itallie)
The Tooth of Crime, pr. 1972, pb. 1974
Action, pr. 1974, pb. 1975
Geography of a Horse Dreamer, pr., pb. 1974
Little Ocean, pr. 1974
Killer's Head, pr. 1975, pb. 1976
The Sad Lament of Pecos Bill on the Eve of Killing His Wife, pr. 1975, pb. 1983
Angel City, pr., pb. 1976

Curse of the Starving Class, pb. 1976, pr. 1977
Suicide in B Flat, pr. 1976, pb. 1979
Buried Child, pr. 1978, pb. 1979
Seduced, pr. 1978, pb. 1979
Tongues, pr. 1978, pb. 1981
Savage/Love, pr. 1979, pb. 1981
True West, pr. 1980, pb. 1981
Fool for Love, pr., pb. 1983
A Lie of the Mind, pr. 1985, pb. 1986
States of Shock, pr. 1991, pb. 1992
Simpatico, pr. 1994, pb. 1995
Plays, pb. 1996-1997 (3 volumes)
When the World Was Green, pr. 1996, pb. 2002 (with Joseph Chaikin)
Eyes for Consuela, pr. 1998, pb. 1999
The Late Henry Moss, pr. 2000, pb. 2002

OTHER LITERARY FORMS

Sam Shepard has written a number of screenplays, including the ill-fated *Zabriskie Point* (1969) for Michelangelo Antonioni and the award-winning *Paris, Texas* (1984). He also wrote and directed *Far North* (1988) and *Silent Tongue* (1993). Shepard has also written poetry and short fiction, in *Hawk Moon: A Book of Short Stories, Poems, and Monologues* (1973) and *Motel Chronicles* (1982), and recorded the major events of Bob Dylan's Rolling Thunder Revue tour in a collection of essays titled *Rolling Thunder Logbook* (1977).

ACHIEVEMENTS

Sam Shepard is one of the United States' most prolific, most celebrated, and most honored playwrights. Writing exclusively for the Off-Broadway and Off-

Off-Broadway theater, Shepard has nevertheless won eleven Obie Awards (for *Red Cross, Chicago, Icarus's Mother, Forensic and the Navigators, La Turista, Melodrama Play, Cowboys #2, The Tooth of Crime, Curse of the Starving Class, Buried Child,* and *Fool for Love*). In 1979, he received a Pulitzer Prize for *Buried Child*. His screenplay for Wim Wenders's film *Paris, Texas* won the Palme d'Or at the Cannes Film Festival, and Shepard himself received an Oscar nomination for his portrayal of Colonel Chuck Yeager in *The Right Stuff* (1983). *A Lie of the Mind* was named the outstanding new play of the 1985-1986 season by the Drama Desk. In 1998 Public Broadcasting Service's (PBS) *Great Performances* devoted an hour-long TV program to Shepard's life and plays.

Sam Shepard (Martha Holmes)

BIOGRAPHY

Born Samuel Shepard Rogers VII, on an army base in Fort Sheridan, Illinois, on November 5, 1943, Sam Shepard's early years were marked by repeated moves from one place to another: South Dakota, Utah, Florida, Guam, and eventually Southern California. Shepard's father was severely wounded during World War II, became an alcoholic, and progressively withdrew from the family until he became a desert-dwelling, storytelling recluse; Samuel Rogers VI, the playwright's father, died after being struck by a car in 1983. Shepard recalls that his mother, Jane Schook Rogers, would fire her army-issued Luger pistol at the Japanese soldiers sneaking out of the jungle on Guam in the years following World War II. After Shepard's father retired from the army, the family moved to an avocado ranch in the San Bernardino valley in Southern California, where Shepard spent his adolescent years. In 1962, Shepard joined a barnstorming acting company with a religiously based repertory, the Bishop's Repertory Company. When the company reached New York, Shepard, nineteen years old, dropped out of the company and into the Lower East Side bohemian lifestyle, busing tables at the Village Gate, dabbling with acting, doing drugs, and running the streets with Charles Mingus, Jr., an old California friend.

In 1964, the twin bill of Shepard's first two plays, the original *Cowboys* and *The Rock Garden*, pre-

miered at one of Off-Off-Broadway's most important theaters, Theater Genesis, and Shepard's career was launched. Shepard wrote prolifically for the Off-Off-Broadway theater during the last half of the 1960's, gaining recognition and critical acclaim with each play, many of which contained made-to-order parts for his girlfriend, Joyce Aaron. By 1967, Shepard had gathered three Obie Awards, produced his first full-length play, and could boast of plays being produced on the West Coast, in New York, and in London. In 1969, Shepard married O-Lan Johnson (they had one son, Jesse Mojo), the actress who played the eponymous Oolan in *Forensic and the Navigators*. The following year, however, brought many difficulties for Shepard: *Operation Sidewinder* was produced at the Vivian Beaumont Theater at New York's Lincoln Center, but the frustrations posed by an expensive Broadway production and the generally unfavorable reaction to the play prompted Shepard to return to

Off-Off-Broadway. Further, Shepard's romance with the emerging rock star Patti Smith severely taxed his nascent domestic life. Finally, losing patience with the New York theater scene, Shepard and his family moved to London in 1972. On his return to the United States in 1976, Shepard joined Bob Dylan on his Rolling Thunder Revue Tour and then moved to San Francisco, where he began working with Joseph Chaikin and the Magic Theatre. The move to California also marked the beginning of Shepard's career as a film star; his portrayal of Colonel Chuck Yeager in *The Right Stuff* earned for him an Oscar nomination. While on the set of the film *Frances* (1982), Shepard met Jessica Lange; they later bought a ranch together in New Mexico and subsequently moved to Virginia.

ANALYSIS

Nearly all Sam Shepard's plays examine the functions (and dysfunctions) of the relationships between individuals that constitute either family structures or social structures that approximate family structures—close friendships or tight-knit business alliances. The conflict between the two halves of what can be considered a single unit (brother and brother, father and son, husband and wife, boyfriend and girlfriend) as they struggle either for supremacy or for survival amid surrounding pressures can be found at the core of most of Shepard's plays. Further, his principal characters tend not only to be alienated from their immediate circumstances but also to be victimized by their drive toward a destructive self-isolation. The wake of devastation left by figures who are incapable of bridging the abysses they have created shapes the central conflict in many of Shepard's plays.

The pulsating rhythms of those conflicts can be tracked through Shepard's unique use of dramatic language. Instead of the series of natural exchanges between characters found in plays constructed on the principle of mimetic realism, the language in Shepard's plays reflects his extensive musical background. His dialogue ranges from realistic banter to highly metaphoric and figurative speech, to the beat and patter of rock and roll, to free-form, yet highly complex, jazz-like improvisational riffs. Characters frequently disrupt the flow of the dialogue with abrupt shifts in voice (such as Hoss's switch from the street talk of a rock and roll star to the argot of an old Delta blues singer in *The Tooth of Crime*), sudden shifts in character (such as Chet's and Stu's metamorphosis from modern urban cowboys to old-time prospectors in *Cowboys #2*), or unexpected irruptions into convoluted soliloquies that arrest the flow of the action (such as Wesley's recollection of his drunken father's return in *Curse of the Starving Class*). Even when it is primarily realistic, the plays' language is highly figurative, establishing a layer of metaphoric significance that points toward each play's thematic center.

The settings of Shepard's plays also contribute figurative significance to their dominant themes. The action often unfolds against a backdrop composed of commonplace materials such as bathtubs, old wrecked cars, kitchen tables, refrigerators, living-room sofas, hotel beds, children's bedrooms, or hospital rooms, but these articles suggest an environment that is primarily metaphoric, not realistic. Shepard uses the icons of American pop culture to represent the mythic landscape of the American psyche, thereby demonstrating how personal identity is so often assembled out of the bits and pieces of the social iconography that dominates American culture. His figurative settings also underscore the predominant tensions dramatized, as in *Curse of the Starving Class*, where the lack of food in the refrigerator represents the lack of love and nurture in the family. Because Shepard is primarily interested in depicting figurative conflicts and actions, he is free to draw on a wide variety of materials in the physical setting, as well as the dialogue, in order to create his mythic landscapes. Hence, Shepard's plays are filled with borrowings from, and allusions to, what he sees as the core of the United States' mythology: rock and roll and country-western music, Hollywood and films of all kinds (Westerns in particular), the trappings of middle-class suburbia, the physical geography of the West (the desert in particular), science fiction, and the conflict between generations that shredded American society and culture during the Vietnam era.

Although Shepard has spoken of his personal aversion for the 1960's and early 1970's, the pulsing beat of his scintillating dramatic language, the resonant depth of the mythic images that permeate his plays, and the unwavering intensity of the conflicts that give his plays an unmatched toughness all have their ultimate source in the turmoil both caused and embraced by the sex, drugs, and rock-and-roll generation. The center of Shepard's work moves steadily and inexorably toward a distinctly American version of the domestic drama defined by his predecessors Henrik Ibsen, Anton Chekhov, and Eugene O'Neill, but the conflicts between siblings, husbands and wives, or parents and children are consistently played out against the backdrop of the icons that created the American national identity during the Vietnam era: cowboys, rock and roll music, Hollywood films, middle-class suburbia, science fiction, and the West. It is Shepard's consistent ability, however, to use the particular to suggest the universal that indicates his greatness. In a play written by Shepard, the foreground and shading of a conflict between father and son will inevitably be couched in terms of rock music, cars, gunfights, and liquor, but the outline of that conflict is as old and as evocative as Sophocles' *Oidipous Tyrannos* (c. 429 B.C.E.; *Oedipus Tyrannus*, 1715).

ONE-ACT PLAYS

Shepard's earliest extant play, *The Rock Garden*, sketches many of the themes that resonate throughout his work. In the first of the play's three scenes, Shepard defines the estrangement between generations: A Boy and a Girl sit in silence, sipping milk, while a Man, absorbed in his magazine, ignores them. In the second scene, the Boy signals his alienation from the mother figure (the Woman) by donning more and more clothing, which metaphorically suggests the barriers erected between the family members. The third scene repeats this figurative action, with the mother replaced by the father figure, the Man, who bores his son almost to death. Finally, the Boy shatters the superficial complacency of the relationships with a graphic and intensely personal recounting of his sexual preferences and prowess. Thus, the rock garden metaphorically defines this typical Shepardian family: sterile, arid, and empty.

Most of the one-act plays that Shepard wrote for the Off-Off-Broadway theater during the 1960's explore themes that emerged in *The Rock Garden*. *Chicago* examines the dynamics of isolation. The alienation of Stu—who reposes in a bathtub naked from the waist up but wearing jeans and tennis shoes—from the other cast members cannot be overcome by the figurative barriers that Stu creates through his active imagination. In *4-H Club*, three men, Joe, John, and Bob, take turns imposing improvised antics on the other two; in *Red Cross*, Jim, a tourist infested with crab lice, imposes imaginative scenarios on two women: Carol (Jim's girlfriend) and a hotel maid. All three plays present characters who are markedly alienated from their selves and their surroundings; moreover, Shepard suggests that the imposition of personal desires on others leads typically to irreversible alienation. *Cowboys #2* is perhaps Shepard's best depiction of the ability of the imagination to assert a separate reality, as Chet and Stu, two urban cowboys, take turns imposing imaginative vistas on each other. For example, Chet assumes the voice and posture of an Old West prospector and addresses Stu as Mel, who plays along. The two urban cowboys and old-time prospectors rollick through a number of fanciful incidents: calisthenics, a rainstorm, an Indian attack, a descant on the decay of the modern West, and a trek across the desert. The play suggests that the imaginative world is just as "real" as the actual world.

In a series of plays from the late 1960's to the early 1970's, Shepard explores isolation and alienation by employing metaphoric sets, characterizations, and actions. *Icarus's Mother* depicts a conflict between five metaphorically "grounded" characters and a jet pilot—a transcendent Icarus figure. When the two females (Jill and Pat) respond to the pilot sexually, the pilot reacts sexually, looping, rolling, climbing, and finally plunging to an explosive climax in the ocean. The play suggests that sexual desire is both irresistible and destructive, that permanent transcendence is not possible, and that males and females cannot communicate successfully. *Forensic and the Navigators* examines the American antiwar movement of the 1960's. Two would-be revolutionaries,

Forensic (whose name suggests talk but no action) and Emmet, ineptly attempt to chart out a revolutionary action. When the radicals' hideout is suddenly invaded by California Highway Patrol-like exterminators, the fundamental distinctions between the revolutionaries and the forces of oppression progressively disintegrate, since neither side is capable of significant action.

LA TURISTA

Shepard's first full-length play, *La Turista*, examines the inexorable decay of American society. Set in a Mexican hotel room for the first act, *La Turista* depicts the inability of two middle-class Americans, Kent and Salem, to overcome their cultural and spiritual sickness, symbolized by the dysentery they have contracted. Kent and Salem's internal malaise contrasts sharply with the vitality of the Mexican Boy, who symbolizes both the underdeveloped nations' peoples exploited by American materialism and the son caught in an Oedipal conflict with his father. Moreover, Kent's symbolic role as the epitome of American cultural dominance is undercut by Kent's ironic attack on the obsessions that have made the United States irrecoverably weak. After Kent faints on seeing the Boy in bed with Salem, the remainder of the first act consists of an attempt to revive Kent (who is described as dead), which involves a Witch Doctor, his son, and sacrificial chickens. The second act of *La Turista* duplicates the first in action, although it employs a separate metaphorical structure. Set in a drab American hotel room, Kent's revival continues. The Witch Doctor and the Boy from the first act enter, dressed now like country doctors from the Civil War era. Kent's disease is the result of a psychological and emotional starvation endemically linked to the structure of the typical American family. Kent and the Doctor become enmeshed in a mutually imposed *Frankenstein* scenario that recalls the father/son conflicts of the first act with Kent in the role of monster/son and the Doctor as the creator/father. As the imaginative play reaches its peak, Kent transforms into the monster and escapes his repressive society by crashing through the upstage wall, leaving a cutout of his body. *La Turista* compellingly suggests that the barren American fam-

ily and its disposable society are incurably diseased structures that produce generation after generation of monsters.

THE UNSEEN HAND AND OPERATION SIDEWINDER

The Unseen Hand and *Operation Sidewinder* also explore unresolvable conflicts. *The Unseen Hand*, a cross between a science-fiction adventure and a television Western, pits Willie the Space Freak and the Morphan brothers (a trio of Old West outlaws) against the High Commission of Nogoland with its powerful Unseen Hand, a force that squeezes the mind. The conflict unfolds on a stage cluttered with the detritus of the American consumer society (symbolized by the play's setting: Azusa, everything from A to Z in the United States). Nogoland and Azusa are but two different names for the tyrannizing force of established culture that opposes those who seek true freedom. Willie's ability to escape the Unseen Hand's power seems to be a qualified endorsement of revolutionary action. *Operation Sidewinder*, Shepard's big-budget Broadway production, develops the structure sketched in *The Unseen Hand*.

The plot brings together a group of revolutionaries consisting of Mickey Free (an Indian), a hippie known as the Young Man (who symbolizes all the impatience, violence, and frustrations of American youths during the 1960's and 1970's), and Blood (a Black Panther type), all of whom struggle against the forces of political oppression led by a Central Intelligence Agency goon (Captain Bovine), a mad scientist (Dr. Vector), and Dr. Vector's gigantic and deadly missile/computer shaped like a sidewinder rattlesnake. When Mickey Free liberates Honey, the play's only significant female, by cutting off the Sidewinder's head, the action suggests that violent political confrontation can lead to true liberation, but the remainder of the play does not fulfill that promise. Shepard uses satiric language and irony to undercut the pretentiousness of both the anti-establishment and the establishment. Only Mickey Free's desire to use the Sidewinder's head as a source of spiritual renewal provides a viable alternative to the sterile and debilitating social mythologies embraced by both the revolutionaries and the establishment. The play ends with a pyrotechnic encounter between a group of Desert Tactical troops who futilely discharge their machine guns into Mickey Free, the Young Man, Honey, and a group of Hopi Indians who are caught up in the spirituality of the snake dance and have thereby achieved a higher level of existence. Although the play preaches too much, *Operation Sidewinder* is perhaps Shepard's most hopeful offering, suggesting that the futility of political and generational conflict can at last be transcended.

GEOGRAPHY OF A HORSE DREAMER

Although *Geography of a Horse Dreamer* is on the surface a play about a group of gamblers who are trying to squeeze information from Cody, an artistically minded young man with the ability to dream the winners of horse or dog races, it is really an extended metaphor that reproaches the tendency of a culture to treat its most gifted artists like disposable goods, demanding that they produce more and more until the artists themselves are consumed. Cody's abilities steadily wither, since he cannot meet the demands of the Mafia-like gangsters, until he is liberated from them by his shotgun-wielding brothers from the West in a violent scene at the play's end.

ANGEL CITY

Angel City also examines the role of the artist in society. Rabbit, a film-script fixer, is hired by a motion-picture studio to repair the script of the company's latest big-budget disaster film. The line between films and the "real," however, is a tenuous distinction in *Angel City*. Miss Scoons, the type of the vacuous American female, desires beyond all else to become the people she sees on the silver screen since she believes their lives to be more "real" than hers. Further, the great disaster that Rabbit is supposed to script becomes the cataclysm that destroys both the world without and the world within the play; *Angel City*'s apocalyptic ending suggests that the American film industry, and the mythology it creates, are primary sources of the United States' cultural and spiritual corruption.

THE TOOTH OF CRIME

The Tooth of Crime is best described as a rock-and-roll gunfight between a top-of-the-charts but aging rocker, Hoss, and his up-and-coming rival, Crow.

Set in a stylized future where rockers mark out territory through acts of violence much like members of rival gangs stake out their turf, *The Tooth of Crime* examines the dynamics by which males relate to one another when establishing their fundamental identities. As Hoss and Crow square off in the musical battle that dominates the play's second act, it becomes clear that Hoss and Crow, like so many of Shepard's other male characters, are locked into the battle of identity that pits father against son. Hoss quickly recognizes that "father" and "son" are locked into a generational cycle in which the younger will inevitably usurp the place of the elder, and the play's conclusion, in which Crow takes possession of Hoss's entourage, goods, and status, suggests that father and son are locked in an endless cycle in which the younger generation is doomed to repeat patterns of its forebears.

CURSE OF THE STARVING CLASS

The cyclical pattern etched into the relationship between the generations provides the dominant structure for what have been called Shepard's "family" plays: *Curse of the Starving Class*, *Buried Child*, *True West*, *Fool for Love*, and *A Lie of the Mind*. The "curse" in *Curse of the Starving Class* is quite clearly the curse of generational repetition: Children inevitably duplicate the actions of their parents. The natures of the parents are planted within the psyches of the children and emerge in actions that emphasize the familial curse passed down from generation to generation. Weston, the father, recalls the poison of his father's alcoholism; Wesley, the son, provides a chilling account of Weston's drunken attack on the home's locked front door; and in the third act, Wesley dons Weston's discarded clothes and admits that his father's essence is beginning to control him. Ella, the mother, passes on to her daughter Emma the curse of menstruation as well as the mother's desire to escape her family.

The curse of starvation is overtly symbolized by the perpetually empty refrigerator, which underscores the family's physical, emotional, psychological, and spiritual starvation. Further, the curse of denial pervades all the play's relationships and colors almost every action. Clearly beset from within, this typical

Shepardian family is also beset from without by those forces that Shepard believes threaten the mythic (and therefore true) West: the march of progress that wants to destroy the natural world and replace it with shopping malls, freeways, and tract housing developments. There is, obviously, no salvation for this family. Weston runs off to Mexico with the money he has received from the sale of the farm; Emma is blown up in Weston's car by thugs who are looking to extort money from Weston; Ella refuses to acknowledge what happens right in front of her and repeatedly addresses Wesley as Weston; Wesley completes the transformation into his father by adopting his father's attitudes and behaviors. The anecdote that Ella and Wesley jointly tell to close the play becomes the play's second great symbol: An eagle and a tomcat, tearing at each other in a midair struggle, crash to earth. Like that pair of animals, there is no salvation or escape that awaits the family in *Curse of the Starving Class*, only inevitable destruction.

BURIED CHILD

Shepard's vision of the family in *Buried Child* is even darker; long and deeply buried familial secrets constitute the hereditary curse in Shepard's Pulitzer Prize winner. The family patriarch, Dodge, spends all of his time wrapped in an old blanket on the sofa, staring at the television. His wife, Halie, speaks at her husband (not to him) of trivial matters when she is not busy soliciting the local clergyman, Father Dewis. Their eldest son, Tilden, is a burned out and mentally defective semimute who brings armload after armload of corn onto the stage. The second son, Bradley, had one leg cut off by a chain saw and now spends most of his time wrestling with Dodge for control of the blanket and television set or threatening to cut Dodge's hair. In a series of statements that recalls the pattern of denial that occurs in *Curse of the Starving Class*, Dodge refuses to acknowledge that Bradley is his own son, claiming that his flesh and blood are buried in the backyard. To complicate matters, Halie frequently mentions yet another son, Ansel, who (according to Halie and Halie alone) was a hero and basketball star. Into the midst of this dysfunctional home comes Vince, Tilden's son, who wants to reestablish his family ties, and Shelly,

Vince's girlfriend. Tilden, however, refuses to recognize Vince, claiming that the son he once had is now dead and buried.

The denial of family connections suggests both the physical and the emotional rejection that pervades the home in *Buried Child*. On a physical level, the dead child refers to Halie and Tilden's incestuously conceived child who was killed by Dodge and buried in the field behind the house. Metaphorically, the dead child represents all the children in the family, all of whom are dead to their father and mother and to one another. Unable to gain recognition from any of his progenitors, Vince stomps out one evening and goes on an alcoholic binge, leaving Shelly at the mercy of Bradley, who menaces her sexually. When Vince returns the next morning, thoroughly drunk, his open violence provides Halie and Dodge with the clue to Vince's identity, once again suggesting that behavior is mechanically passed from generation to generation. When Dodge dies, Vince proclaims himself the family's new patriarch just as Tilden enters carrying the exhumed body of the buried child. The play's highly equivocal ending juxtaposes the hope symbolized by the rebirth of a new generation against despairing images of denial, disease, and death.

TRUE WEST

True West explores the conflict between two brothers: Lee, a reclusive and violent thief who has been living in the Mojave desert, and Austin, a suburban Yuppie and screenwriter. Austin is trying to close a motion-picture deal with a Hollywood movie mogul, Saul Kimmer, but when Kimmer hears Lee's impromptu outline for a motion picture about two cowboys chasing each other across the plains of Texas, Kimmer decides to drop Austin's project and develop Lee's. *True West*, in addition to analyzing the fate of the artist in a manner that recalls *Angel City* and *Geography of a Horse Dreamer*, questions which version of the West is indeed true. Lee claims that the desert, with its brutally harsh environment that forces its denizens to live by their wits and strength, is the true West, while Austin claims that suburban California, with its shopping malls, highways, and tract housing, constitutes the real West. Further, the numerous references to famous Western films suggest that the only true West is Hollywood's West.

The pressure of Kimmer's decision to pursue Lee's screenplay causes the brothers to switch roles: Austin, responding to Lee's taunts, steals a variety of toasters from the neighbors; Lee slaves over the typewriter roughing out the dialogue. The reversal of roles indicates the fundamental similarities that bind the brothers. On the abrupt return of their Mother from Alaska, (who, showing rare good sense for a Shepardian mother, claims to recognize nothing and immediately leaves), Lee and Austin square off in a physically violent but unresolved confrontation. *True West* not only questions the mythology that defines the American West but also probes the violence spawned by the fundamental psychological and behavioral equivalence of family members.

Shepard also examines the equivalency of siblings in *Fool for Love*, replacing the brother-brother conflict of *True West* with a love/hate relationship between half-brother and half-sister, Eddie and May. Reared in different towns by different mothers, Eddie and May meet, fall in love, and begin their incestuous relationship before discovering that they share the same father, the Old Man. Although the friction dramatized in Eddie and May's emotional and sexual relationship points toward Shepard's signature characterization of men and women as two opposite animals who cannot coexist, *Fool for Love* also examines how the same event is often shaped and reshaped by different individuals to create widely divergent memories and understandings of what happened. Eddie and May do not share the same recollection of their meeting and cannot come to terms with the implications of their relationship; moreover, none of their stories agrees with versions of the same incidents told by the Old Man, who at times seems to be Eddie's and May's mental projection but who at other times seems to be an independent character. Despite her attempt to establish a different lifestyle with Martin, the new man in her life, May is as inextricably bound to Eddie as he is to her. Even though Eddie leaves at the end of the play and May believes that he is not coming back, the play suggests that the audience has witnessed but one episode in a continually repeating cycle in which Eddie and May are victimized by their repetitive actions just as surely as Wesley and Weston were by theirs in *Curse of the Starving Class*.

A LIE OF THE MIND

A Lie of the Mind explores the dysfunctional structure of the American family as well as the delusions that individuals impose on others and themselves. Beaten nearly to death by her husband Jake, Beth creates lies of the mind—fictions that permit her to survive. The play suggests that each character assembles a personal reality in his or her mind. For example, Jake's mother, Lorraine, blocks out the pain of being abandoned by her husband by pretending indifference; Beth's father, Baylor, hides from his family by erecting a facade of the crusty frontier hunter; Jake represses all of his memories of the race in Mexico that led to his father's death. Further, *A Lie of the Mind* suggests that the "two opposite animals," the male and the female, even when yoked together by an irresistible and consuming love, are torn apart by the violence of their fundamental incompatibility. Both Beth and Jake are trapped by their love—neither can be complete without the other—and their obsessive need to be reunited thrusts Beth into delusions of marriage and propels Jake to Montana to find Beth. Their drive for reunification, however, at last proves futile. After kissing Beth, Jake exits into the darkness, and Beth compulsively turns to Jake's wounded brother, Frankie. *A Lie of the Mind* suggests that the American family, like Beth, is fundamentally crippled.

STATES OF SHOCK

States of Shock is a heavily symbolic exercise in antiwar sentiment that pits a demented, saber-waving colonel against Stubbs, a wheelchair-bound armed-services veteran (who still has a conspicuously large and bloody hole in his chest) in a battle over the symbols and myths that permeate and define large-scale war. Set in a thoroughly American family restaurant, *States of Shock* exposes all the glorious contradictions that surround the concept of war in post-Vietnam America without offering any more than the violence of the inevitable collisions.

SIMPATICO

Simpatico concerns two Californian friends, Carter and Vinnie, who fifteen years earlier had used Vinnie's wife Rosie to blackmail Ames, a horse racing official, into overlooking a race track scam involving look-alike horses. Carter and Rosie then ran off to Kentucky together where they became wealthy. Vinnie uses photographs of Rosie with Ames to extort money from Carter, who returns to California to retrieve the photographs. As in *True West*, the main characters undergo role reversals during the play's progress. Carter becomes an alcoholic ne'er-do-well while Vinnie shaves, puts on a suit, and flies to Kentucky to seek his fortune.

EYES FOR CONSUELA

Eyes for Consuela is based on the short story, "The Blue Bouquet," by Octavio Paz. Henry, a middle-class American whose marriage has disintegrated, flees to a decrepit hotel in a Mexican jungle. There he meets a philosophical Mexican bandit Amado, who threatens to cut out Henry's blue eyes as a gift to his wife Consuela. Henry insists that his eyes are brown, not blue, but this does not impress Amado. Throughout two acts the men argue, drink tequila, and trade life histories, as Amado contends that Henry's despair is an example of anxiety caused by the complexity of American civilization.

THE LATE HENRY MOSS

The Late Henry Moss begins with two brothers, Ray and Earl, sharing a whiskey bottle and memories of their father, who lies dead in the bed behind them. Ray sets out to discover how his father died by interrogating everyone who knows anything about his last day. The story is told in flashbacks as Ray interviews the taxi driver who took Henry Moss on a fatal fishing trip; Esteban, a kindly next-door neighbor; and Conchalla, a sensuous Mexican woman who shared a drinking binge with Henry.

OTHER MAJOR WORKS

SHORT FICTION: *Cruising Paradise*, 1996; *Great Dream of Heaven: Stories*, 2002.

SCREENPLAYS: *Me and My Brother*, 1967 (with Robert Frank); *Zabriskie Point*, 1969; *Ringaleevio*, 1971; *Paris, Texas*, 1984 (with L. M. Kit Carson); *Far North*, 1988; *Silent Tongue*, 1993.

NONFICTION: *Rolling Thunder Logbook*, 1977.

MISCELLANEOUS: *Hawk Moon: A Book of Short Stories, Poems, and Monologues*, 1973; *Motel Chronicles*, 1982 (poetry and short fiction); *Joseph Chaikin and Sam Shepard: Letters and Texts, 1972-1984*, 1989.

BIBLIOGRAPHY

Auerbach, Doris. *Shepard, Kopit, and the Off-Broadway Theater*. Boston: Twayne, 1982. One of the first important academic analyses of Shepard's plays, Auerbach's book provides a valuable analysis of Shepard's work as Off-Broadway drama. Auerbach also provides extensive information on the directors, actors, and theatrical spaces that made up the Off-Broadway theater during the 1960's and 1970's.

Bottoms, Stephen J. *The Theatre of Sam Shepard: States of Crisis*. Cambridge, England: Cambridge University Press, 1998. Along with a thorough examination of Shepard's plays, Bottoms presents an impartial comparison of Shepard's work with that of other leading contemporary dramatists. Contains detailed chronology and bibliography.

DeRose, David J. *Sam Shepard*. New York: Twayne, 1992. DeRose provides a brief overview of Shepard's life and work, analyzing his theatrical and thematic goals. Includes an annotated bibliography of secondary sources and a detailed list of important play reviews.

Hart, Lynda. *Sam Shepard's Metaphorical Stages*. Westport, Conn.: Greenwood Press, 1987. Hart argues that Shepard's plays from *Cowboys #2* to *A Lie of the Mind* are influenced by techniques developed by the Theater of the Absurd, particularly by the work of Samuel Beckett, Antonin Artaud, and Eugène Ionesco. The book contains a brief chapter on Shepard's work for the television and film industries as well as a pithy biography and an extensive bibliography.

King, Kimball, ed. *Sam Shepard: A Casebook*. New York: Garland, 1988. This collection of essays written mostly by academics approaches Shepard's work from many angles and demonstrates the range of response the plays evoke. The casebook includes a solid annotated bibliography and a piece by Patrick Fennel that identifies and discusses Shepard's unperformed and unpublished works.

Marranca, Bonnie, ed. *American Dreams: The Imagination of Sam Shepard*. New York: Performing Arts Journal Publications, 1981. A compendium of essays written by academics, directors, and actors, this volume is a good introduction to Shepard's early work for the Off-Broadway theater. A number of short pieces by Shepard himself round out the volume, including Shepard's influential short essay, "Language, Visualization, and the Inner Library."

Mottram, Ron. *Inner Landscapes: The Theater of Sam Shepard*. Columbia: University of Missouri Press, 1984. Perhaps the best sustained examination of Shepard's plays, Mottram's biographical analysis offers many insightful readings of Shepard's work by comparing incidents in the plays to parallel episodes from Shepard's life or to stories from *Hawk Moon* or *Motel Chronicles* with similar characters or incidents. Mottram also includes a brief chronology of Shepard's work to 1985.

Gregory W. Lanier,
updated by Milton Berman

RICHARD BRINSLEY SHERIDAN

Born: Dublin, Ireland; October 30, 1751
Died: London, England; July 7, 1816

PRINCIPAL DRAMA

The Rivals, pr., pb. 1775
St. Patrick's Day: Or, The Scheming Lieutenant, pr. 1775, pb. 1788
The Duenna: Or, The Double Elopement, pr. 1775, pb. 1776 (libretto; music by Thomas Linley the elder and Thomas Linley the younger, and others)
A Trip to Scarborough, pr. 1777, pb. 1781 (adaptation of Sir John Vanbrugh's *The Relapse*)
The School for Scandal, pr. 1777, pb. 1780
The Critic: Or, A Tragedy Rehearsed, pr. 1779, pb. 1781
Pizarro: A Tragedy in Five Acts, pr., pb. 1799 (adaptation of August von Kotzebue's *Die Spanier in Peru*)
Complete Plays, pb. 1930
Plays, pb. 1956 (L. Gibbs, editor)
The School for Scandal and Other Plays, pb. 1998 (Michael Cordner, editor)

OTHER LITERARY FORMS

Richard Brinsley Sheridan's other literary efforts, all minor, include the early poems "Clio's Protest" and "The Ridotto of Bath," published in *The Bath Chronicle* (1771); a youthful translation, *Love Epistles of Aristaenetus* (1771), in collaboration with Nathaniel Brassey Halhed; and later occasional verses in connection with the theater—such as prologues and epilogues to other writers' plays—the most important being "Verses to the Memory of Garrick, Spoken as a Monody" (1779). Of far greater significance, especially to biographers and historians, are Sheridan's speeches in Parliament, collected in five volumes (1816), and his letters, collected in three volumes, entitled *The Letters of Richard Brinsley Sheridan* (1966). Unfortunately, his speeches are preserved only in summary or imperfect transcript.

ACHIEVEMENTS

Richard Brinsley Sheridan was the best playwright of eighteenth century England, a time of great actors rather than great playwrights. Judged on theatrical rather than strictly literary merit, Sheridan also ranks with the best English writers of comedy: William Shakespeare, Ben Jonson, William Congreve,

Oscar Wilde, George Bernard Shaw. Until the era of Wilde and Shaw, only Shakespeare's plays had held the stage better than Sheridan's.

Of Sheridan's plays, *The School for Scandal*, a comedy of manners, is universally acclaimed as his masterpiece. Also applauded are *The Rivals*, another comedy of manners; *The Duenna*, a comic opera; and *The Critic*, a burlesque. The two comedies of manners have fared better over time than have the two more specialized works, perhaps because their attractions are apparent even in printed form and perhaps because changes of taste have gone against the specialized works. The topical allusions in *The Critic* are mostly lost on modern audiences, and *The Duenna* affronts modern sensibilities with episodes of anti-Catholicism and anti-Semitism. In Sheridan's own opinion, his best piece of work was act 1 of *The Critic*.

In recent times, Sheridan's reputation has waned: His "artificial" comedies lack the high seriousness that the modern age demands. Yet the basis of his appeal remains: effective theater embodied in smooth traditional plots, stock characters fleshed out by Sheridan's observations of his time, and some of the wittiest dialogue ever written. Sheridan has never been known for the originality of his plots and characters, some of which can be traced through Shakespeare and Jonson all the way back to Roman comedy, but—like Shakespeare and Jonson—he had the assimilative genius to transform the old into something lively and new. Revolving around a trickery motif, chronicling the age-old battles of the sexes or the generations, culminating in a marriage or marriages, his plots still entertain with their well-paced intrigues and discoveries. Onto the old stocks he grafted such memorable characters as Mrs. Malaprop, Joseph Surface, Lady Teazle, and Sir Fretful Plagiary. One reason why Sheridan does not seem dated is his language, a distinctly modern prose idiom, supple, utilitarian, informal, expressing the hopeful coherence of the early modern era.

Sheridan's achievement is even more impressive when one considers that he wrote all of his plays (except for the adaptation of *Pizarro*) during a period of five years when he was in his mid-twenties and dur-

Richard Brinsley Sheridan (Hulton Archive by Getty Images)

ing a period of severe restrictions on the theater. The upper- and upper-middle-class establishment controlled the theater with an iron grip through limitations on the number of theaters, official censorship, and the unofficial censorship of its tastes. No play could be presented that did not satisfy the political and social assumptions of the ruling classes. It is remarkable that, under these restrictions, Sheridan could get away with saying as much as he did.

BIOGRAPHY

In eighteenth century Great Britain, Richard Brinsley Sheridan's lot was pretty much cast when he was born into a genteelly poor Irish theatrical family. All of these social disadvantages, however, worked to his advantage in the theater. Being Irish has given numerous British writers of comedy special insight into the vices and follies of their fellow Britons, as well as the rhetorical skills to air their observations. Being in a theatrical family was obviously an advantage for the aspiring playwright. Finally, being genteelly poor sparked his ambitions with both positive and negative charges. Combined, these factors made Sheridan acutely aware of the disparity between his personal worth and his actual place in society—always a great aid to developing a sense of comic incongruity.

Although lacking wealth and social position, Sheridan's family was both well educated and talented. Both his father and mother were children of scholarly clergymen. On being graduated from Trinity College, Dublin, Sheridan's father, Thomas, already a playwright, entered the theater as an actor and soon advanced to manager. Sheridan's mother, the former Frances Chamberlaine, wrote novels and plays. After initial prosperity, the family of six (Richard was the third son) ran into hard times when a minor political indiscretion—reminiscent of an indiscreet sermon that ruined his own father—forced Thomas out of his position. He suppressed some antigovernment lines in a play, thus antagonizing the Irish public. After two years of acting in London, Thomas tried to reestablish himself in Dublin, but without success. Taking his family with him, he returned to England, where, moving from place to place, he pursued an impecunious existence as actor, author, editor, lecturer on elocution, and projector of ambitious undertakings.

After attending Sam Whyte's Seminary for the Instruction of Youth in Dublin, Richard was entered into Harrow School, despite the family's precarious financial situation. How precarious that situation was became evident when, to escape creditors, the rest of the family fled to France, where they lived for several years and where Frances Sheridan died. Left behind at Harrow, Sheridan, lonely and destitute, suffered the abuse heaped on him by his well-bred schoolmates and masters. The unhappy scholar later maintained that he learned little at Harrow.

When his family returned to London, Sheridan, by then a young man, rejoined them. There his education continued informally, and it was completed when, in the fall of 1770, the family moved to Bath, where the father presented entertainments and tried to establish an academy of oratory. The favorite spa of eighteenth century England, Bath gave young Sheridan a closeup study of *le beau monde*, the fashionable world later depicted in his comedies of manners. He managed to join this scene on the basis of few credentials except a ready wit and charm. In Bath, he also met young

Elizabeth Ann Linley, a great beauty and singing member of the musical Linley family, which sometimes collaborated with the Sheridans on entertainments. Elizabeth's public performances brought her the unwanted attentions of numerous suitors, most notably one Thomas Mathews. The boorish Mathews importuned her so closely that, to escape him, Elizabeth (already the subject of a racy play, Samuel Foote's *The Maid of Bath*, 1771) ran away to France—accompanied by Richard Brinsley Sheridan as her protector. After a few weeks, the couple returned, Sheridan fought two duels with Mathews, and, on April 13, 1773, Sheridan and Elizabeth were married.

With this background, Sheridan wrote his plays. He and Elizabeth settled in London, where the need to make a living turned him, like his father, toward the theater. In 1775, he took London by storm, presenting three plays, the first (*The Rivals*) reflecting his recent romantic past. By 1780, however, his playwriting career was over. Although he owned a managing interest in Drury Lane Theatre, he was beginning a distinguished career in Parliament, which consumed much of his efforts.

Sheridan's long service in Parliament has no bearing on his playwriting (aside from the fact that it stopped) but much on his reputation. A liberal Whig, Sheridan sympathized with the American and French revolutions and supported such programs as Catholic emancipation. A principled politician, he could not be bribed despite his constant need for money to pay for elections and entertaining. An independent thinker, he sometimes bucked his own party. Such a man was obviously dangerous, especially when he was also such a powerful speaker. Therefore, the leaders of his party used his powers but never allowed him to become a leader. Sheridan even became an adviser and a friend to the prince of Wales, later George IV, but it was the snobbish prince who led the establishment's strategy against the upstart Sheridan. That strategy was to depict Sheridan as an unreliable lightweight—a strategy dictated at first by Sheridan's background and later by his drinking and debts.

When Drury Lane Theatre burned in 1809, Sheridan's debts drained his resources so that he lacked sufficient funds to win an election in 1812, and his political and princely associates swiftly fell away. Although he died in poverty, he was honored with a lavish funeral in Westminster Abbey, attended by scores of solemn dignitaries and peers of the realm. He is buried in the Poets' Corner of Westminster Abbey.

ANALYSIS

"Poor Sherry," said the prince of Wales, a line echoed by other noble contemporaries of Richard Brinsley Sheridan and even by Sheridan's admirer Lord Byron. Unhappily, the verdict of the prince of Wales and his crowd still represents the official response to Sheridan, coloring understanding of his plays with an *argumentum ad hominem*. This official line runs something as follows: "Poor Sherry was motivated by overwhelming vanity and self-interest. That is why he entered the theater and why he left the theater to enter politics. A poor Irish actor's son, he always wanted to hobnob with the rich and powerful, to be part of *le beau monde*, whose attitudes he reflects in his plays. There was something calculating, something insincere and insubstantial, about the fellow. Same thing about his plays." This is the establishment Sheridan safely tucked away in the Poets' Corner.

There is also, however, an antiestablishment Sheridan—the penniless child suffering at Harrow, the spirited young man dueling for his girl, the member of Parliament sympathizing with the American and French revolutions, whose servants in his plays are smarter than their masters. True, Sheridan's leading characters are usually gentry or better, and Sheridan usually exhibits the doings of *le beau monde*. In addition, he does not issue a clarion call for revolution and the institution of a republic. He was working within the restrictions of accepted traditions, theatrical tastes, and official censorship. Within those restrictions, however, he exhibited *le beau monde* as vain, money-grabbing, and scandalmongering. As a playwright, Sheridan enjoyed the satisfaction of seeing the fashionable world pay and applaud to see itself pilloried.

Sheridan lived in the midst of what one of his characters calls "a luxurious and dissipated age," but

the people enjoying the luxuries and dissipations were standing on the heads of a mass of poor people. He could not attack the upper classes directly, even though they offered big targets for satire. In particular, their illusions about themselves, their pretensions of nobility and gentility, made them vulnerable. Sheridan knew a whoring society when he saw one, and he satirized its illusions and pretensions relentlessly.

Sheridan's satire is milder in tone, however, than that of cynical Restoration comedy or the savage attacks Alexander Pope and Jonathan Swift could deliver. The tone of Restoration comedy harks back to the dark, stinging satire of Ben Jonson, who presented the world as little better than a zoo. Such satire incorporates the conservative vision of the Great Chain of Being, wherein human nature is permanently flawed, half angel, half animal. The animal side must be cynically accepted or flogged into good behavior by Church, State, and satirists. Sheridan's satire is more optimistic, softened by the influence of the sentimental mode that grew up in the eighteenth century as the main competitor of the satiric mode, especially in the novel and drama.

Originating in Nonconformist religious thought and maturing in Romanticism, sentimentalism rested on the revolutionary doctrine that human nature is essentially good. Stressing empathy and the humane emotions, sentimentalism was susceptible to hypocrisy. It also had a devastating effect on drama: Tragedy turned into melodrama, and comedy turned to provoking sympathetic tears. The two most notorious examples of sentimental literature, Henry Mackenzie's novel *The Man of Feeling* and Richard Cumberland's play *The West Indian* both came out in 1771, just before Sheridan began writing. Like his fellow countryman Oliver Goldsmith, Sheridan accepted the underlying doctrine of sentimentalism but reacted against its excesses. Not unnaturally, Goldsmith and Sheridan thought comedy ought to provoke laughter.

To produce "laughing comedy," Sheridan returned to the witty, satiric comedy of manners of the Restoration, but without the Restoration cynicism and sexual license. Whereas the Restoration offered refinement and style as a substitute for goodness, Sheridan still believed in its possibilities. The result is a warmly human balance similar to that in Henry Fielding's novels. As William Hazlitt said of *The School for Scandal*, "it professes a faith in the natural goodness, as well as habitual depravity, of human nature." Human frailties are laughed at and, if acknowledged, usually forgiven. Among prominent failings is hypocrisy, and anyone too good is suspect. Most of all, empathy has become a sense of participation—the author's and the audience's—in the vices and follies of humankind. This laugh of recognition is perhaps Richard Brinsley Sheridan's greatest gift to "high seriousness."

THE RIVALS

Sheridan's first play, *The Rivals*, reflects his own experiences—his life in Bath, his elopement with Elizabeth Linley, his duels—but it is not strictly autobiographical. Nor was it only a *succès de scandale*, although being the talk of the town probably helped Sheridan at the time. Rather than seeing parallels to Sheridan's life in *The Rivals*, modern audiences are more likely to notice parallels to Shakespeare's plays, for Sheridan drew unashamedly not only on his own experiences but also on his predecessors' work. These two seams in the play reveal Sheridan's apprentice patchings, but what is amazing is that he sewed them all up so well. When the play failed in its first performance, Sheridan revised it within a few days and turned *The Rivals* into one of the great English comedies of manners.

Set in the fashionable resort town of Bath, *The Rivals* concerns the efforts of Captain Jack Absolute, "son and heir to Sir Anthony Absolute, a baronet of three thousand a year," to win the hand of Miss Lydia Languish, an heiress who "could pay the national debt." Miss Languish, however, entertains romantic notions of marrying only for love: She is determined to wed a penniless suitor who will elope and live with her in blissful poverty. To humor her fantasies, Captain Absolute pretends to be Beverley, "a half-pay ensign." His wooing is further complicated by the opposition of Mrs. Malaprop, Lydia's battle-ax guardian aunt; and by two rivals, bumbling country squire Bob Acres and duelist Sir Lucius O'Trigger (whose love letters are actually being delivered to Mrs. Malaprop

by the maid, Lucy). The final complication is the appearance of Sir Anthony with news of an arranged marriage for Jack. After a heated confrontation between father and son, this complication proves to be the resolution of the plot: The young lady intended for Jack Absolute is Miss Lydia Languish. The discovery of Beverley's true identity alienates Lydia, but she is brought around when Jack's life is threatened by a duel with the rivals. Averted at the last moment, the threatening duel also convinces Julia Melville to forgive Mr. Faulkland, Jack's friend, for doubting her love.

Drawn out too long, Mr. Faulkland's almost psychotic behavior mars the tone of the play, but his fantasies of doubt correspond to Lydia's fantasies of romance, perhaps pointing up the theme that a good marriage must be rooted in reality: true love and a solid bank account. The other characters provide a display of diverse human nature. Reminiscent of Shakespeare's Sir Andrew Aguecheek, the cowardly suitor Acres contrasts with the equally ridiculous O'Trigger, whose name describes his ready disposition. Lydia's whims and Sir Anthony's commands typify the ludicrous demands that sweethearts and fathers can make, and Mrs. Malaprop's comical misuse of words ("a nice derangement of epitaphs") epitomizes the cavalier misunderstanding of reality that the characters exhibit.

The play is full of notable examples of human illusion—O'Trigger's "honor," Sir Anthony's parental authority, Bob Acres's "polishing" (that is, new clothes, hairdo, dancing lessons, and swearing), Mrs. Malaprop's vanity, Faulkland's doubts, and Lydia's romance. Their illusions make them easy marks for one another and for the streetwise servants. To manipulate them, one simply plays up to their fantasies. For example, Jack is "Beverley" to Lydia, a dutiful son to Sir Anthony, and a flatterer to Mrs. Malaprop. All the characters with illusions are worthy of study, but perhaps the most important are Mrs. Malaprop, Faulkland, and Lydia.

On the periphery of the action, Mrs. Malaprop is symbolically at the play's center. She provides a simplified example of how illusion works. Her funny misuse of words, symbols of reality, epitomizes the break with reality. She thinks her big words make her, as O'Trigger says, "a great mistress of the language," "the queen of the dictionary," or, as Jack says, a leader in "intellectual accomplishments, elegant manners, and unaffected learning." The reality is summed up in Jack's intercepted letter: "I am told that the same ridiculous vanity, which makes her dress up her coarse features, and deck her dull chat with hard words which she don't understand, does also lay her open to the grossest deceptions from flattery and pretended admiration." To Sir Lucius O'Trigger, she is "Delia," a female counterpart of romantic Beverley. When Sir Lucius sees the real thing, however, he turns her down—as do Jack and Acres. Clinging to her illusions, Mrs. Malaprop stomps off the stage, huffing that "men are all barbarians."

The illusions of Faulkland and Lydia are essentially overreactions of the young to the sterile social order represented by Mrs. Malaprop and the older generation: Their illusions are examples of sentimentalism, the gross exaggeration of feeling that Goldsmith and Sheridan deplored. Faulkland is a man of sensibility, but unfortunately, as he notes, love "urges sensibility to madness." His "too exquisite nicety" leads him constantly to question and torture Julia, a "mild and affectionate spirit" any man would be lucky to find. The least suggestion can send him into paroxysms of doubt: Jack and even the "looby" Acres are able to play on his sensibility at will. He is, as he finally admits, a "fool." Lydia's overreaction contrasts with that of Faulkland, but she would agree with him that "when *Love* receives such countenance from *Prudence*, nice minds will be suspicious of its birth." Fed by sentimental novels, her overheated mind throws prudence to the wind. Jack easily deceives her by playing her romantic games and speaking the language of the novels she has read. Thinking to outwit and shock her relatives, she is shocked to discover herself "the only dupe at last." The young lady who had hoped for a "sentimental" elopement with all the trimmings must settle for being "a mere Smithfield bargain." Actually, she gets more than she bargained for: When confronted by the reality of a truly romantic situation—men dueling to the death over her—she comes to her senses.

The illusions of all these characters in *The Rivals* say something about the society in which they live. First, being born in the upper strata apparently encourages illusions about oneself: Only wealth and privilege could create a Mrs. Malaprop. Second, to sustain those illusions apparently requires a lot of lying and deceiving. Third, with all the lying and deceiving, it becomes difficult to find anything genuine—hence the hard search of Faulkland and Lydia for true love. That Sheridan himself sought the genuine is suggested by his repeated use throughout the play of the word "sincerity," apparently a quality he found in short supply in eighteenth century England.

THE DUENNA

Musically untalented, Sheridan wrote the comic opera *The Duenna* in collaboration with his father-in-law and brother-in-law (both named Thomas Linley) and probably with the help of his wife. Despite this piecemeal method of composition, the completed opera was an immense success. In particular, the opera is a testimony to Sheridan's patchwork skill and to the talented Linleys, whose tunes were hummed about London streets. Typically, however, the words of the songs are bland, and so are the opera's stock characters, some of whom are almost indistinguishable from one another. Of all Sheridan's works, *The Duenna* most requires performance, since it depends so much on acting, spectacle, and music (twenty-seven songs in all).

Set in Seville, *The Duenna* features not one but two pairs of lovers thwarted by tyrannical parents. Donna Louisa's father has arranged an unsuitable match for her, notwithstanding her love for Don Antonio, and Donna Clara's father and stepmother are forcing her into a convent, even though she is loved by Don Ferdinand. Both young ladies run off and, assisted by bribed nuns and priests (the latter also drunk), marry their lovers in a convent. Louisa tricks her father, Don Jerome, with the help of her governess, old Margaret the Duenna. When Don Jerome vows "never to see or speak to" Louisa until she marries his choice, Louisa and the Duenna trade places, and the penniless old Duenna marries Louisa's intended, Isaac Mendoza, a rich Jew who has never seen Louisa and who thinks he is adding to his coffers.

Like most of Sheridan's works, *The Duenna* offers sparkling intrigue and dialogue. Here again, a female servant masterminds the plotting, but to a great extent the fathers and the villain outsmart themselves. The scheming Mendoza, recently converted to Christianity and hence standing "like the blank leaves between the Old and New Testament," is well known for being "the dupe of his own art." Of the characters, only the ugly Duenna, the obnoxious Mendoza, and the drunken priest Father Paul stand forth with any distinction, and they are stereotypes.

The broad strokes of the stock characters and action do provide simplified versions of some of Sheridan's themes. For example, the hypocritical nuns and priests show, as Louisa notes, that "in religion, as in friendship, they who profess most are ever the least sincere"—a forewarning of Joseph Surface in *The School for Scandal*. Louisa herself seems of two minds on the relationship of love and wealth. Early in the opera, she sings that she loves Don Antonio "for himself alone," since he has no wealth. Later in the play, faced with the prospect of being disinherited, she changes her tune: "There is a chilling air around poverty that often kills affection that was not nursed in it. If we would make love our household god we had best secure him a comfortable roof." At least her aims are different from her father's, who sets forth his marriage as a proper example: "I married her for her fortune, and she took me in obedience to her father, and a very happy couple we were. We never expected any love from one another, and so we were never disappointed." Such cold-blooded reasoning is a reminder of how often, in Sheridan's plays, the older and younger generations are at odds on the subject of marriage. The two views presuppose radically different ideas not only of marriage but also of personality and society: The vital difference is between valuing someone "for her fortune" and "for himself alone." Thus, in Sheridan's plays, the struggle within the family is a microcosm of the larger struggle between the old and new order in society. There is no doubt about which side Sheridan took, as his own father opposed his marriage to Elizabeth Ann

Linley (old Thomas had the absurd notion that the Sheridans were too good for "musicians").

Another theme in *The Duenna* revolves around the idea of "seeing." There are a number of observations on how subjective states, especially love, affect one's seeing, especially of the beloved. The merging of subject and object here, encouraged perhaps by eighteenth century empathy, foreshadows Romantic "seeing," wherein what is observed takes its coloring from the imagination. *The Duenna* also contains a number of warnings about such "seeing": Don Jerome gets so angry that he does not recognize his daughter posing as the veiled Duenna, and Don Ferdinand gets so jealous he does not recognize his beloved dressed as a nun. In the opera's most philosophical song, however, Don Jerome gets the final word on "seeing":

> Truth, they say, lies in a well,
> Why, I vow I ne'er could see;
> Let the water-drinkers tell,
> There it always lay for me;
> For when sparkling wine went round,
> Never saw I falsehood's mask;
> But still honest truth I found
> In the bottom of each flask.

He seems to say that people need their illusions, or at least their opiates.

Possibly Don Jerome was speaking for Sheridan, since the opium of entertainment is precisely what Sheridan provided in *The Duenna*. The first English comic opera to use specially composed music, *The Duenna* was a forerunner of the operettas by W. S. Gilbert and Sir Arthur Sullivan and the Broadway musical, which by now have institutionalized sentimental "seeing."

THE SCHOOL FOR SCANDAL

If *The Rivals* shows the fashionable world on vacation, *The School for Scandal* shows it back home in London, working hard to "murder characters" and "kill time." If the duelist O'Trigger is deadly, he is nothing to this school of piranhas, which renders "a character dead at every word." The difference between vacation and work is precisely the difference in tone, theme, and achievement between *The Rivals* and *The School for Scandal*. No seams or weaknesses obtrude in *The School for Scandal*, the title of which sums up the play's prevailing imagery and unity.

The play begins with a marvelous expository device: The "scandalous college" is in session, headed by its "president," Lady Sneerwell. As the pupils gather—Snake, Joseph Surface, Mrs. Candour, Crabtree, Sir Benjamin Backbite—the audience hears juicy bits of scandal about the president and each pupil. The key information is that Sir Peter Teazle has a pack of trouble. The Surface brothers, to whom Sir Peter is "a kind of guardian," are competing for Maria, Sir Peter's rich ward. Joseph, the older brother, is a scheming knave who, with "the assistance of his sentiment and hypocrisy," passes for a paragon of virtue, while Charles is "the most dissipated and extravagant young fellow in the kingdom." Joseph enjoys the favor of Sir Peter, and Charles, that of Maria. During a recess, Sir Peter is also shown having fits with his young wife. Country-bred Lady Teazle has blossomed into a London woman of fashion, even joining Lady Sneerwell's group and carrying on a flirtation with Joseph. The scandalmongers, however, have linked her to Charles.

The Surfaces are unmasked when Sir Oliver Surface, a rich uncle, returns from many years in the East Indies and puts the brothers to the test. Posing as a moneylender, Sir Oliver observes Charles's dissipation, even purchases the family portraits from him—but forgives the young man when Charles will not part with the portrait of dear Uncle Oliver. Charles also sends some of the money to old Stanley, a poor relation in distress, but when Sir Oliver, posing as Stanley, applies to Joseph, he is given the brush-off. In a famous scene, Joseph is also discovered hiding Lady Teazle behind a screen and Sir Peter Teazle in a closet, where each has heard an earful. The screen symbolizes Joseph's character and the nature of the society in which he flourishes, and the closet suggests where Sir Peter has been hiding. The truth comes out, however—confirmed by the confessions of Snake—and the people have to live with it. Now the centerpiece of a raging scandal, stodgy Sir Peter mellows; Lady Teazle and Charles will reform; Joseph's punishment is being "known to the world";

and Snake hopes his good deeds will not spoil his professional reputation. Meanwhile, the audience, schooled by a master, has been treated to a delightful exposition of illusion and reality in society.

Sheridan exposes a shallow society in which appearances rule: It is not what you are but what you appear to be that counts; reputation is all. The main proponent of this philosophy—still not entirely discredited even in modern society—is the well-spoken Joseph Surface, whose hypocrisy illustrates another danger inherent in sentimentalism. Actually, the talented Joseph represents both types prominent in his society: the hypocrite, who manipulates appearances to enhance his own reputation, and the scandalmonger, who manipulates appearances to tear down the reputations of others (as Joseph shows, the two callings go together). Behind facades of gentility, both types feel free to indulge their basest instincts. For example, the motives acknowledged by scandalmongers include bitterness over being slandered oneself, personal spite, impersonal malice, fun, and following the fashion, though the dullness of their lives is also a factor. They have nothing better to do than sit around and gossip about other people's lives, with perhaps a touch of envy. As Lady Teazle makes clear, these "are all people of rank and fortune." They represent a society rotten at the core.

Luckily, this decadent society includes a saving remnant that is not fooled by appearances. There is the faithful old servant Rowley, who believes in the goodness of a reprobate's heart. There is crusty Sir Oliver, who is sickened by scraps of morality and who believes that a man is not sincere if he has not made any enemies. There is Lady Teazle, whose personal development through the play marks the course of the plot. At first she is drawn to the world of appearances, of high fashion and rich furnishings, of the circle of scandalmongers and Joseph. Her turning point comes when Joseph suggests that she go to bed with him, literally and figuratively. She returns to her country wisdom and rejects him. When the screen is pulled down and she is caught in Joseph's quarters, she refuses to second his story and dubs him "Good Mr. Hypocrite." Thereafter, she withdraws from the "scandalous college" and turns over a new leaf.

Finally, there is Charles, the reprobate himself. His regeneration is harder to believe than Lady Teazle's, but Sheridan shrewdly keeps him offstage until halfway through the play, by which time he contrasts favorably with Joseph and the scandalmongers. Although dissolute and bankrupt, Charles has two important qualities that Joseph lacks: benevolence and honesty. Unlike the hypocritical Joseph Surface, Charles Surface is exactly what he appears to be. His loss of reputation has, in fact, freed him to be himself, and his experience has prepared him to see himself and others clearly. He is given the two main symbolic gestures in the play: pulling down the screen and selling off the family portraits. Symbolically, he attacks both the pretensions of his society and their hereditary basis. Charles's auction of the family portraits now seems merely funny, but the mockery involved in "knocking down" one's ancestors "with their own pedigree" was probably a shock to the eighteenth century system, even though Sheridan softened the revolutionary gesture by keeping it in the family.

THE CRITIC

In the tradition of *The Rehearsal* (pr. 1671) by George Villiers, duke of Buckingham, and Henry Fielding's *Tom Thumb: A Tragedy* (pr. 1730), Sheridan's *The Critic* is a burlesque, a type of comedy especially popular in eighteenth century England. *The Critic* provides an engaging and informative survey of the theatrical world in Sheridan's time. Despite its many topical references, the play also has potential for revival in the contemporary age of self-conscious art, in which burlesque is a staple of television comedy. The topical references, in fact, would reverberate with a certain irony, since it appears from *The Critic* that things have not changed all that much in the theater.

Act 1 opens on a breakfast scene, where the critic Mr. Dangle holds court, entertaining all sorts of solicitations. This day there appear Mr. Sneer, another critic; Sir Fretful Plagiary, a vain playwright (based on Richard Cumberland); Mr. Puff, an advertising writer who has authored a play; and Signor Pasticcio Ritornello and a chorus of Italian girls come for audition (the scene probably gives some insight into the

Sheridan household). Repartee, malice, and dissimulation fly around the table, in the manner of theatrical shoptalk, with Mrs. Dangle occasionally clearing the air in straightforward language.

In the other two acts, Dangle and Sneer attend a rehearsal of Puff's play, a wretched tragedy entitled *The Spanish Armada*. Again there is much opportunity for satire. Puff has given the actors permission "to cut out or omit whatever they found heavy or unnecessary to the plot"; thus, the play is very brief. Brief as it is, it is a smashing parody of the kind of tragedy written in Sheridan's time, full of clumsy exposition, bombastic verse, stilted characters, and improbable, sensational events, ending with a triumphant sea battle and a procession of all the English rivers accompanied by George Frederick Handel's water music and a chorus.

The faked feelings of the actors in the play-within-the-play are reminders that theater is the essence of illusion, and the framing action of *The Critic* is a reminder of how theater people are often caught up in the illusion. To Mr. Dangle, the theater is more important than the real world: When he reads "the news," it is the theatrical news rather than the news of the impending French invasion. He is such a stargazer because he considers himself a moving force in the theatrical world, as he tells Mrs. Dangle: "You will not easily persuade me that there is no credit or importance in being at the head of a band of critics, who take on them to decide for the whole town, whose opinion and patronage all writers solicit, and whose recommendation no manager dares refuse!" Representing a commonsense point of view, Mrs. Dangle is a counterweight to the vanity that is such an occupational hazard for theatrical (and literary) people. At regular intervals, she tells Mr. Dangle that he is ridiculous: "Why should you affect the character of a critic?" and "Both managers and authors of the least merit laugh at your pretensions. The Public is their Critic."

The real critic in the play is the play itself, as the double meaning in the title indicates. Taking a hard look at the eighteenth century theater, *The Critic* first notes the ideal: "the stage is 'the mirror of Nature.'" The statement is a reminder of how theatrical illusion, and art in general, can paradoxically arrive at the truth. The theater (and art), however, can also go astray, as it did in Sheridan's time. First there is comedy, which strayed into two sorts: "sentimental" comedy, which contains "nothing ridiculous in it from the beginning to the end," and "moral" comedy, which treats "the greater vices and blacker crimes of humanity." To her discredit, Mrs. Dangle prefers the former sort, and Mr. Sneer defends the latter: "The theatre, in proper hands, might certainly be made the school of morality; but now, I am sorry to say it, people seem to go there principally for their entertainment." As for what was happening to tragedy, Mr. Puff's *The Spanish Armada* is sufficient example. Choosing Mr. Puff to be the featured author was an inspired symbolic stroke: as a master of "puffing" (advertising) who commands the language of "panegyrical superlatives," the ability to exaggerate or even invent reality ("to insinuate obsequious rivulets into visionary groves"), he truly represents the spirit of the age in the theater.

Sheridan's remaining plays little enhance his literary reputation, but they do reveal a great deal about his political and social attitudes. The plays are *St. Patrick's Day*, a two-act comedy; *A Trip to Scarborough*, an adaptation of Sir John Vanbrugh's comedy *The Relapse* (pr., pb. 1696); and *Pizarro*, an adaptation of August von Kotzebue's tragedy *Die Spanier in Peru* (1794).

PIZARRO

Pizarro is an embarrassing reminder of the kind of tragedy which Sheridan parodied in *The Critic*. Treating the depredations of European invaders against the noble Incas, the play gives evidence of Sheridan's antipathy to colonial oppression (it echoes his speeches in Parliament against British rule in India) and his ability to satisfy the growing popular taste for romantic melodrama. In its day, *Pizarro* was a tremendous box-office success.

ST. PATRICK'S DAY

Like *Pizarro*, *St. Patrick's Day* was probably a vehicle for specific actors. The short farce also satisfied the requirements of an afterpiece, a slighter work presented after the main play. Full of scheming and disguising, it dramatizes Lieutenant O'Connor's win-

ning of Miss Lauretta Credulous over the opposition of her father, Justice Credulous, who hates Irishmen and soldiers. Aside from its lighthearted action, *St. Patrick's Day* is notable for its Irish sentiments and its sympathy for the lot of poor soldiers (in Sheridan's time, often Irishmen).

A TRIP TO SCARBOROUGH

A Trip to Scarborough, a much more substantial work, was adapted from *The Relapse*, a favorite Restoration comedy. In his adaptation, Sheridan trimmed the plot and cleaned up the sexual innuendo of the original. The adaptation has many features similar to those of Sheridan's other comedies of manners—in particular, an intrigue centering on assumed identity and rivalry between two brothers for a rich heiress. In the course of the intrigue, the penniless Tom Fashion triumphs over his older brother, Lord Foppington, "an ungrateful narrow-minded coxcomb." Furthermore, Lord Foppington is roughly handled by the father-in-law, Sir Tunbelly Clumsy, a jovial Yorkshireman whose personality and household (Muddymoat Hall) are in a tradition stretching to Emily Brontë's *Wuthering Heights* (1847) and Charles Dickens' *Nicholas Nickleby* (1838-1839).

The humbling of a lord in *A Trip to Scarborough* is another example of the antiestablishment Sheridan, a side that the official pronouncements have preferred not to mention. Yet it is as much a part of Sheridan as his inspired ability to write entertaining comedy. A subversive element in eighteenth century Britain, Sheridan was constantly chipping away at the illusions and pretensions of the old order and interjecting stirrings of the egalitarianism that was sweeping away the old order elsewhere. His attack on primogeniture, at the heart of the old system, is typical:

> LORD FOPPINGTON: . . . Nature has made some difference 'twixt me and you.
> TOM FASHION: Yes—she made you older.

Something of a transitional figure in British drama, Sheridan looked back to Restoration comedy for his inspiration, but his social attitudes looked forward to George Bernard Shaw. During the long barren stretch of two hundred years between Restoration comedy and Shaw, Sheridan preserved the comic spirit in British drama largely through the force of his talent.

OTHER MAJOR WORKS

POETRY: "Clio's Protest," 1771; "The Ridotto of Bath," 1771; *A Familiar Epistle to the Author of the Heroic Epistle to Sir William Chambers*, 1774; "Epilogue to *The Rivals*," 1775; "Epilogue to *Semiramis*," 1776; "Verses to the Memory of Garrick, Spoken as a Monody," 1779; "Epilogue to *The Fatal Falsehood*," 1779; "Prologue to *Pizarro*," 1799; "Lines by a Lady of Fashion," 1825.

NONFICTION: *Speeches of the Late Right Honourable Richard Brinsley Sheridan (Several Corrected by Himself)*, 1816 (5 volumes); *The Letters of Richard Brinsley Sheridan*, 1966 (3 volumes; C. J. L. Price, editor).

MISCELLANEOUS: *The Plays and Poems of Richard Brinsley Sheridan*, 1928, 1962 (3 volumes; R. Compton Rhodes, editor).

BIBLIOGRAPHY

Ayling, Stanley. *A Portrait of Sheridan*. London: Constable, 1985. More than two hundred pages on Sheridan's life and work. Ayling offers glimpses of Sheridan's true nature, including the unflattering views on the theater expressed in his letters. The treatment of the early plays is rather brief. Includes some comments on the management of the Drury Lane in later chapters.

Davision, Peter, ed. *Sheridan: Comedies*. Basingstoke, England: Macmillan, 1986. A casebook for the two best-known plays, plus discussions of *The Critic* and *A Trip to Scarborough*. Contains an introductory section on Sheridan's family, his orations, his life and letters; general commentary on Restoration comedy and Sheridan's plays; and final sections on each of the four plays with commentaries by William Hazlitt, Max Beerbohm, George Bernard Shaw, Sir Laurence Olivier, and numerous others. Bibliography and index.

Hare, Arnold. *Richard Brinsley Sheridan*. Windsor, England: Profile Books, 1981. Sketches the major details about Sheridan's life and family. Pays brief attention to the theatrical milieu but analyzes the plays, including some relatively minor ones. Complemented by a select bibliography and a portrait from a pastel by John Russell.

Kelly, Linda. *Richard Brinsley Sheridan: A Life*. London: Sinclair-Stevenson, 1997. The biography looks at Sheridan as both dramatist and legislator. Bibliography and index.

Morwood, James. *The Life and Works of Richard Brinsley Sheridan*. Edinburgh: Scottish Academic Press, 1985. Morwood believes that Sheridan's career as a writer and theatrical manager is inseparable from his private and political life. Makes a fresh effort to evaluate Sheridan's political career and to create a balanced assessment of his thirty-two years as manager of the Drury Lane. Several illustrations, bibliography, index.

Morwood, James, and David Crane, eds. *Sheridan Studies*. New York: Cambridge University Press, 1995. A collection of essays on Sheridan as a dramatist and member of Parliament. Includes a bibliography and index.

O'Toole, Fintan. *A Traitor's Kiss: The Life of Richard Brinsley Sheridan, 1751-1816*. New York: Farrar, Straus and Giroux, 1998. This biography covers Sheridan's earlier years and his plays as well as his later life in Parliament. Also describes his romantic life. Bibliography and index.

Worth, Katharine. *Sheridan and Goldsmith*. New York: St. Martin's Press, 1992. Worth compares and contrasts the writings of Oliver Goldsmith and Sheridan. Bibliography and index.

Harold Branam,
updated by Howard L. Ford

R. C. SHERRIFF

Born: Kingston-on-Thames, England; June 6, 1896
Died: London, England; November 13, 1975

PRINCIPAL DRAMA

Journey's End, pr. 1928, pb. 1929
Badger's Green, pr., pb. 1930
St. Helena, pb. 1934, pr. 1936 (with Jeanne de Casalis)
Miss Mabel, pr. 1948, pb. 1949
Home at Seven, pr., pb. 1950
The White Carnation, pr., pb. 1953
The Long Sunset, pr., pb. 1955
The Telescope, pr., pb. 1957
A Shred of Evidence, pr. 1960, pb. 1961

OTHER LITERARY FORMS

In addition to his nine professionally produced stage plays, R. C. Sherriff wrote five novels. He is, however, remembered chiefly for his first stage play, *Journey's End*, as well as for a number of screenplays that have come to be regarded as classics.

ACHIEVEMENTS

Journey's End, a drama about World War I, is a legend and landmark in the modern British theater. It is notable as the first grimly realistic war play. In it, there is none of the romanticism about war that led the naïve young poet Rupert Brooke to write in his poem "1914," "Now God be thanked who has matched us with His hour" and to sentimentalize the dead soldiers as dreaming happy dreams of "laughter, learnt of friends; and gentleness,/ In hearts at peace, under an English heaven." Both Brooke and the young Thomas Mann saw war as a cleansing, liberating, and purifying process, and Mann called peace "an element of civil corruption." Such views were soon annihilated by the horrors of trench warfare. R. C. Sherriff, a wounded veteran of that war, knew better, and his play shows the stress, boredom, suffering, and slaughter that war produces. When the play was first staged, critic Hannen Swaffer called it "the greatest of all war plays," and in 1962, G. Wilson

Knight still judged it "the greatest war play of the century."

Sherriff's other plays—an ecological drama, a play about Napoleon in exile, several comedy-mysteries, a ghost story, and a drama about Romans in Britain—are literate, civilized, thoughtful, and forgettable, as are his novels. The success of *Journey's End*, however, led its director to hire Sherriff to write screenplays, and as a screenwriter, Sherriff did some of his most notable work, including the production of such classics as *The Invisible Man* (1933), *Goodbye, Mr. Chips* (1939), *The Four Feathers* (1939), *That Hamilton Woman* (1941), *Odd Man Out* (1947), *Quartet* (1949), and *Trio* (1950).

BIOGRAPHY

Robert Cedric Sherriff was born on June 6, 1896, at Kingston-on-Thames, near London. His father, Herbert Hankin Sherriff, worked for the Sun Insurance Company; his mother was Constance Winder Sherriff. Robert grew up in Kingston-on-Thames, where he attended the local grammar school. He was graduated at seventeen, after which he followed his father into the insurance business, but his career was interrupted after nine months by the outbreak of World War I. Sherriff volunteered, became a second lieutenant in the Ninth East Surrey Regiment, was wounded so severely at Ypres (where four-fifths of the original British Expeditionary Force died) that he was hospitalized for six months, returned to active duty, and was mustered out at the war's end as a captain.

Back in civilian life, Sherriff returned to the Sun Insurance Company, where he worked for the next ten years as a claims adjuster. For recreation, he joined the Kingston rowing club, and to raise funds for the organization, he and some fellow members wrote and produced plays. Sherriff took to playwriting with zeal and studied William Archer's *Play-Making* (1912) so thoroughly that he claimed to have memorized it. In addition, he began to read modern plays systematically and commuted to London to see the latest productions. Returning home on the train, he sometimes developed dialogue for a play he had in mind for the rowing club.

After writing plays for six years for amateur productions, Sherriff turned to a more serious project—a drama based on his firsthand knowledge of trench warfare. His parents had saved the letters he had written to them from the trenches, and these helped him revive the immediacy of the experience, its realistic details, and his friendships and feelings at the time. Throughout 1928, he worked alone on the play. Gradually, the play, at first called "Suspense" and then "Waiting," took final shape as *Journey's End*.

Realizing that this drama was not the stuff of amateur theatricals, Sherriff sent it to the Curtis Brown theatrical agency. Impressed but unable to see the play's commercial possibilities, Brown sent it on to Geoffrey Dearmer at the Incorporated Stage Society. Dearmer advised Sherriff to send a copy to George Bernard Shaw, who sent it back with the comment that it was "a document, not a drama," and that as a slice of "horribly abnormal life" it should be "performed by all means, even at the disadvantage of being the newspaper of the day before yesterday." Even so, all the London theatrical managements rejected *Journey's End*; they were strongly opposed to war plays, and this one lacked all the standard ingredients for a popular success. It had no leading lady, no romance, and no conventional heroics, and all the action took place offstage. Though this was the author's seventh play, the first six were all amateur productions, and the insurance agent earning six pounds a week was utterly obscure.

Nevertheless, Dearmer arranged for a production by the noncommercial Incorporated Stage Society. To direct, he picked a minor actor named James Whale. Whale, in turn, looked for a leading actor to play Captain Stanhope. All the eminent London actors had declined the role, but twenty-one-year-old Laurence Olivier, who was hoping to win the lead in a stage version of *Beau Geste* (pr. 1929?) that director Basil Dean was then casting, saw the role of Stanhope as a chance to prove that he could play a soldier and thus handle the lead in the Foreign Legion drama. Ronald Colman had had a smash hit in the film version of *Beau Geste* (1926), and Olivier, an admirer of Col-

man, hoped to repeat the success. As for *Journey's End*, Olivier recalled in his *Confessions of an Actor* (1982) that "Although I could recognize the possibilities of the part of Stanhope, I told James Whale, the director, I didn't think all that highly of the play. 'There's nothing but meals in it,' I complained. He replied: 'That's about all there was to think about in Flanders during the War.'" Though he was performing in a romantic comedy each evening at the Royalty Theatre, with two weekly matinees, and though *Journey's End* was to have only two performances at the Apollo Theatre, Olivier undertook the role as an audition for *Beau Geste*. There were only two weeks for rehearsal, but Olivier dug into the character of the burned-out Stanhope and later called the part his "favorite stage role," though later the actor reserved this designation for Archie Rice in *The Entertainer*.

Cast as young Raleigh was Maurice Evans, then an unknown, who was also hoping to get the lead in *Beau Geste*. George Zucco, later a memorable villain in Hollywood films, was cast as "Uncle" Osborne, the gentle, middle-aged schoolmaster who quotes from Lewis Carroll's *Alice in Wonderland* before going on a virtual suicide mission. Cast as Trotter, the fat officer concerned chiefly about provisions, was Melville Cooper, who later played Mr. Collins in the film version of Jane Austen's *Pride and Prejudice* (1940), in which he again appeared with Olivier. In 1928, no member of the cast was well known.

The first performance, on the evening of Sunday, December 9, 1928, went off flawlessly but received only moderate applause, though Barry Jackson commended the play's honest realism. The critics did not appear *en masse* until the second and final performance at the Monday matinee. The play and production so overwhelmed them that Hannen Swaffer, London's most scathing critic, hailed *Journey's End* as "the greatest of all war plays." James Agate devoted his entire weekly radio talk show to praising it, concluding, "But you will never see this play. I have spoken with several managers, urging them to give you the opportunity of judging it for yourselves, but they are adamant in their belief that war plays have no audience in the theatre."

When six weeks passed with no sign that the play might be revived by a commercial producer, Olivier accepted the lead in *Beau Geste*. Now that the leading man was gone, chances for a revival of *Journey's End* seemed even more unlikely. Sherriff noted that "all the rest of the cast stood by the play. They refused other parts in the hope of remaining in it, and they believed in it so much that they tried in vain to form a combine and raise the cash among themselves. But it seemed hopeless."

Then a fan named Maurice Browne persuaded a millionaire friend to put up the money. There was a search for a new leading man, and a relatively unknown actor named Colin Clive got the part and joined the rest of the cast from the Apollo Theatre. The new production opened on January 21, 1929, at the Savoy Theatre. The first performance received nineteen curtain calls, and the success of *Journey's End* became a theatrical legend. It went on to play 594 performances in London. A second production, also directed by James Whale, with Colin Keith-Johnston in the lead, opened at the Henry Miller Theatre in New York on March 22, 1929, and ran for 485 performances. Translated into twenty-seven languages, *Journey's End* played around the world. *Beau Geste*, a flop, closed after a month, and Olivier went on to act in seven more flops during the nearly two years in which Colin Clive starred as Stanhope.

Journey's End made the reputation and fortune of three men. It raised Sherriff from obscurity to fame and fortune; it established James Whale as an important director; and it made Colin Clive a star. D. W. Griffith wanted to direct the film version, but James Whale was retained as director. Colin Clive again played Stanhope, but the rest of the cast was new, with David Manners replacing Maurice Evans as Raleigh.

As for Sherriff, his friends urged him to write another play. At the moment, he had no ideas for one and instead, collaborating with Vernon Bartlett, turned *Journey's End* into a novel (1930). It did not have the overwhelming success of the play and film versions, and Sherriff turned back to playwriting with his next venture, a problem comedy called *Badger's Green*, about the conflict between developers trying to exploit the imaginary village of the title and the conservationists opposing them. Perhaps the problem, now a vital one, was ahead of its time, for the 1930 production fared poorly.

Discouraged, Sherriff feared that he might not be able to continue supporting himself by his pen, and being unwilling to return to the insurance business, he entered New College at Oxford University to earn a degree in history and become a schoolmaster. While a student, he wrote another novel, *The Fortnight in September* (1931), about a middle-class family's annual vacation at a seaside resort. Favorably reviewed, it sold well in England and abroad. Still at Oxford, Sherriff joined an undergraduate rowing crew, though he was then thirty-five years old, but before he could participate in the annual races or earn his degree, he received an invitation from James Whale to collaborate with Philip Wylie on a screenplay of H. G. Wells's *The Invisible Man* (1897). The scenarios for Whale's *Frankenstein* films had departed drastically from the novel, but the script for *The Invisible Man* followed Wells with reasonable fidelity. To play the lead, who is heard throughout but whose features are seen only in the final shot, Whale wanted an actor with a distinctive voice, and Claude Rains made an impressive film debut in the role. Released in 1933, *The Invisible Man* was one of the year's most memorable films, and its literate script, which constituted the best of all horror and science fiction screenplays until the 1950's, helped make it one of the most successful film adaptations of a Wells novel.

The Invisible Man was important in Sherriff's career, introducing him to screenwriting, a genre in which he was to do some of his most memorable work. Immediately after it, however, he first returned to the stage, collaborating with actress Jeanne de Casalis (the wife of Colin Clive) on *St. Helena*, a play about the exiled and imprisoned Napoleon. Written and published in 1934, it was not produced until 1936, when it had a faltering start until Winston Churchill wrote to *The Times* (London) in its defense, calling it "a work of art of a very high order." Churchill added, "I was among the very first to acclaim the quality of *Journey's End*. Here is the end of the most astonishing journey ever made by mortal man."

The letter boosted ticket sales from fewer than one hundred for a performance to overflow houses; when the demand held for almost two months, the management moved the production to a larger theater in the West End. Possibly the house was wrong for the show, but for whatever reasons, the move was a disaster, and attendance plunged precipitously.

Fortunately for Sherriff, Whale once more invited him to write a screenplay for him, this time an adaptation of Erich Maria Remarque's novel *The Road Back* (1931). Though the 1937 film was only moderately successful, it was important in Sherriff's career in that it returned him to screenwriting; during the next eighteen years, he wrote the scripts for an impressive number of outstanding films, among them *Goodbye, Mr. Chips*, *The Four Feathers*, *That Hamilton Woman*, *This Above All* (1942), *Odd Man Out*, *Quartet*, and *Trio*.

Sherriff did not return to playwriting until 1948, with *Miss Mabel*, a popular comedy-mystery. From 1950 to 1960, he wrote five more plays: *Home at Seven*, *The White Carnation*, *The Long Sunset*, *The Telescope*, and *A Shred of Evidence*. The last two were not successful, and after 1960, Sherriff went into semiretirement. In 1968, he published an autobiography, *No Leading Lady*, the title of which refers to complaints about *Journey's End* before its unexpected triumph. It is valuable as a lively account not only of Sherriff's life and career but also of forty years in the history of British theater and cinema. In those forty years, Sherriff played a prominent part.

ANALYSIS

R. C. Sherriff's major achievement as a playwright, and his only enduring play, is *Journey's End*, the first grimly realistic drama about modern war. Of Sherriff's novels and plays, only *Journey's End* is a masterpiece; the rest are well-crafted, entertaining, but justly forgotten works. Aside from *Journey's End*, it may well be that Sherriff's best work was in films; his screenwriting was always craftsmanlike, and *Journey's End*, *The Invisible Man*, *Goodbye, Mr. Chips*, *The Four Feathers*, *That Hamilton Woman*, *Odd Man Out*, *Quartet*, and *Trio* are film classics. Trench warfare was quite different from anything in

previous wars; instead of dashing cavalry charges and "the pomp and circumstance of glorious war," the men were holed up interminably, suffering from boredom, trench foot, vermin, perpetual bombardment, and shell shock.

JOURNEY'S END

The entire action of *Journey's End* takes place in a dugout in the British trenches before St. Quentin between Monday evening, March 18, 1918, and the following Thursday, toward dawn. As the play opens, Captain Hardy is handing over the command to Captain Stanhope; before Stanhope arrives, Hardy explains the setup to Stanhope's second-in-command, Lieutenant Osborne (and thus to the audience as well). The audience learns that, after a tremendous bombardment, the Germans are planning a major attack. The audience also learns about conditions in the dugout—the rats, vermin, cockroach races, and supplies. Finally, the audience learns that Stanhope, the best company commander in the area, has been drinking so heavily that he is considered a freak. Defending him, Osborne explains that Stanhope, who is only twenty-one years old, has been at the front for three years and has not had a furlough for twelve months. He drinks because his nerves are shattered.

A replacement officer arrives, Second Lieutenant Raleigh, eighteen years old and just out of school. For years, Raleigh has worshiped Stanhope (who was ahead of him in school and who is engaged to his sister) as a hero. Unaware of the change in Stanhope, Raleigh has used the influence of his uncle, General Raleigh, to get a posting under his idol. He tells Osborne about Stanhope in their school days together, and Osborne instructs him about the trenches. The Germans are only a hundred yards away, the length of a football field, and between them is no-man's-land. In the English dugout. the remaining staff include only Second Lieutenant Trotter, short and fat, whose chief concern seems to be food, and Second Lieutenant Hibbert. The minimal plot develops tensions among these men and between the men and the stresses of trench warfare and the impending attack. Hibbert is a coward, and in one dramatic moment, Stanhope threatens to shoot him and then rallies the man's courage temporarily. Raleigh tries to conceal his dismay at Stanhope's nervous drinking. When Raleigh writes a letter to his sister, Stanhope shocks them all by demanding to censor it; he fears that Raleigh will have revealed his deterioration but finds that the younger man has written only praise of him. The colonel assigns Raleigh and Osborne to make a raid to capture a German prisoner; though the Germans are ready and waiting, Raleigh succeeds, but Osborne is killed. Before going over the top, Osborne lays his pipe down with the line, "I do hate leaving a pipe when it's got a nice glow on the top like that"—a finely understated exit. When the attack comes, Raleigh is shot through the spine and dies with only Stanhope present. Stanhope then goes up to join in the fighting as shelling hits the dugout and caves it in. The play ends in darkness with the rattle of machine-gun fire.

In this war, there is no magnificence—only mud, monotony, and mortality. Unlike Ernest Hemingway's *A Farewell to Arms* (1929), an adaptation of which was staged the same year, *Journey's End* offers no romance, except for references to the never-seen sister of Raleigh. The cast is exclusively masculine; women are available only on furlough, which the men seem never to get. Interestingly, the stage version of *A Farewell to Arms*, like *Beau Geste*, died a quick death; apparently it was impossible to mount a believable staging of an Arab attack on Fort Zinderneuf or the retreat from Caporetto, the escape into a raging torrent, the escape across an Alpine lake, or the rest of Hemingway's broad panorama. By confining *Journey's End* to the dugout, Sherriff not only avoided the necessity of trying to stage battle scenes but also conveyed beautifully the claustrophobia of trench warfare, which imprisons the soldiers within their own defenses.

Journey's End is sometimes thought of as an antiwar play, but this is not necessarily the case. Certainly it portrays war as horrible, but it never investigates the causes of war or questions the war's justification. The closest it comes to doing so is a brief scene in which Raleigh says, "The Germans are really quite decent, aren't they? I mean, outside the newspapers?" and Osborne tells how the Germans refrained from shooting a patrol that came out to drag a wounded soldier to safety, and how, instead, a German officer shouted "Carry him!" and fired some flares to help the rescue mission. "The next day," Osborne comments dryly, "we blew each other's trenches to blazes." He and Raleigh agree that "it all seems rather—*silly.* . . ." Otherwise, the play takes warfare for granted. Like Stephen Crane's *The Red Badge of Courage* (1895), which never even mentions the Civil War or the battle at hand, *Journey's End* is concerned with the conduct of men under the stress of warfare. Certainly, it is not an antimilitary play in the way that such films as *All Quiet on the Western Front* (1930), *Paths of Glory* (1957), *Catch-22* (1961), *Gallipoli* (1981), or the novel *Slaughterhouse-Five* (1969) attack the corruption, cruelty, or absurdity of the military mind. Instead, its protagonists do their best to adhere to the British "stiff upper lip" tradition. When they crack momentarily, they show exactly how much they have been holding themselves in under intense pressure.

St. Helena

St. Helena, the play about Napoleon that Sherriff wrote with Jeanne de Casalis, tries to humanize the exiled emperor but never asks about the justice or injustice of his role in keeping all Europe at war for twenty years. In this respect, it resembles *Journey's End*; both plays show the immediate human factor but decline to challenge the morality or necessity of war.

For theatergoers who did not share Churchill's admiration of Napoleon, *St. Helena* lacked impact. A drama of the deposed emperor's frustration and stagnation, it does not build up dramatic intensity but rather winds down in a series of anticlimaxes. The play's structure indicates this, for instead of the traditional three acts, it has twelve scenes spanning six years. Napoleon spends his time dictating his memoirs, frustrating the British authorities, arbitrating petty disputes among members of his staff, complaining about living conditions on the island, reliving his past moments of glory, and wondering whether he should not have died at one of them. The individual roles in *St. Helena* are well written; a good cast could have fun with them, but the overall drama is as tedious as life on the island must have been.

MISS MABEL

After World War II, Sherriff took time out from screenwriting to write several plays. *Miss Mabel* is a comedy-mystery about elderly twin sisters, one a miserly, rich widow, the other, Miss Mabel, a poor, humanitarian spinster. The play begins with the widow dead; to everyone's surprise, her will leaves her sizable fortune to a physician to use in building a hospital, to a vicar to establish a home for children, to the widow's gardener to have his own nursery, and to a nephew to marry and to study architecture. Miss Mabel receives nothing but wants nothing. It turns out that she has poisoned her sister and forged the will. When the heirs discover this crime, they are torn between staying silent and fulfilling their dreams or clearing their consciences by disclosing the crime. They choose to inform the police, but the play implies that the law will be lenient to the murdering philanthropist. The play was quite popular and played to full houses for more than six months.

HOME AT SEVEN

Sherriff's next play appeared in 1950. *Home at Seven* concerns David Preston, a mild-mannered bank teller who comes home one night at seven o'clock to find his wife distraught because he has been missing for more than a day. Preston has no recollection of the lost time, but during his amnesia, five hundred pounds have been stolen from the club of which he is treasurer, and the club steward, whom Preston disliked, has been murdered. Circumstantial evidence seems to point to Preston's guilt, but he is finally proved innocent. Sir Ralph Richardson starred in a successful London run of nearly a year and proceeded to direct as well as star in a film version, retitled *Murder on Monday* (1952).

THE WHITE CARNATION

Sherriff's next play, *The White Carnation*, is a comedy about a ghost. It opens outside the house of John Greenwood, a wealthy stockbroker, who is entertaining his guests at an annual Christmas Eve party. It is close to midnight, supposedly in 1951, in a small town outside London. As the guests depart, "a strange, eerie gust of wind" slams the front door shut, leaving Greenwood locked out in the cold. Unable to rouse anyone, he breaks a window and lets himself

in, only to discover a deserted, unfurnished, partly bombed-out interior. A policeman, attracted by Greenwood's shouting, tries to evict him as a trespasser, but Greenwood refuses to leave his own house. When a sergeant who knows him arrives to establish his identity, the man cries out in horror. A doctor finds Greenwood "healthy" but with no pulse, heartbeat, circulation, or temperature; the doctor informs Greenwood that he has been dead for seven years. According to the sergeant, Greenwood and all of his guests were killed in 1944 when a German fly-bomb fell on the house. The sergeant even attended Greenwood's funeral and saw the corpse dressed, as Greenwood is now, in his dinner clothes, with a white carnation in his buttonhole.

Instead of staying in the twilight zone, the play develops into a droll comedy. As portrayed by Sir Ralph Richardson, Greenwood is not at all an ectoplasmic spook; instead, he is a sturdy, phlegmatic, seemingly flesh-and-blood Englishman. Playing against the expectations of the supernatural, Sherriff derives considerable comedy from satirizing bureaucracy as it comes into conflict with the not-so-spectral Greenwood. The house has been sold and is to be torn down to make room for a housing development, but Greenwood refuses to leave. He does not know how to dematerialize, is utterly ignorant of spectral ways, and wants his furniture and radio back. The question of whether ghosts can own property is debated. What are the legal rights of ghosts? What government bureau has jurisdiction over them? Greenwood's case is passed from the Ministry of Health, which decides that its responsibility ends with death and burial, to the Ministry of Works, which maintains Ancient Monuments but decides that Greenwood's house does not qualify and will not accept him without the house, to the chancellor of the Duchy of Lancaster, who passes the matter on to the Home Office, which deals with passports and which determines that, on his death, Greenwood ceased to be a citizen and that therefore his ghost entered the country illegally and can be deported. No one knows how to deport him, however, and he still refuses to leave.

Meanwhile, Greenwood intends to enjoy himself, reading the greatest literature and listening to the greatest music—pursuits for which he never found time when he was alive. Despite his lofty plans, however, he discovers that he cannot enjoy reading anything but the *Financial Times*; he also learns that he had been insensitive to his wife, thoughtlessly neglecting her and wounding her feelings.

Unable to prevail against Greenwood in any other way, the authorities undermine the house and plan to collapse it at midnight on Christmas Eve, 1952. As they make the final preparations, Greenwood disappears, and we are back at the Christmas Eve party in 1944. In the "interval," however, Greenwood has learned to be more humane, and he is loving and considerate to his wife as once again the bomb falls, together with the final curtain. *The White Carnation* is a *jeu d'esprit*, worlds away from the grim dugout of *Journey's End*, but it shows Sherriff's skill at civilized comedy.

THE LONG SUNSET

Though Sherriff never took his degree in history, he remained an enthusiast of the subject; besides writing *St. Helena* and screenplays for two historical films—*The Four Feathers* and *That Hamilton Woman*—he became an amateur archaeologist and dug among the Roman ruins in southern England. In his play *The Long Sunset*, he tried to reconstruct the life of the Romans in Britain as the empire was dying and the legions were being withdrawn. Sherriff noted in his preface to the play that little is known about the way in which the Romans faced the end. The play deals with Julian, a Roman farmer, and his family. To save their land when the legions leave, they recruit the aid of Arthur and Gawain, who, in Sherriff's play, are much more primitive figures than the romanticized heroes of Camelot. Sherriff's Arthur is closer to the misty figures recorded in the early chronicles by Gildas and Nennius than to the chivalric monarch of Sir Thomas Malory. The play was not a success, but it is noteworthy in that it foreshadowed a whole genre of neo-Arthurian novels that sometimes tried to recapture a sense of the primitive background of the Matter of Britain.

A SHRED OF EVIDENCE

In 1960, Sherriff's last play appeared, a comedy-mystery entitled *A Shred of Evidence*. In it, Richard

Medway learns that while he was out drunk the night before, a cyclist had been killed by a hit-and-run driver on the road Medway had taken. Medway can recall nothing, and the evidence seems to point to him, but his innocence is established. Though the details differ, the play is, in some ways, merely a reprise of *Home at Seven*, and though its plot twists are entertaining, it is Sherriff's weakest work.

OTHER MAJOR WORKS

LONG FICTION: *Journey's End*, 1930 (with Vernon Bartlett; adaptation of Sherriff's play); *The Fortnight in September*, 1931; *Greengates*, 1936; *The Hopkins Manuscript*, 1939; *King John's Treasure*, 1954.

SCREENPLAYS: *The Invisible Man*, 1933 (with Philip Wylie; adaptation of H. G. Wells's novel); *The Road Back*, 1937 (with Charles Kenyon; adaptation of Erich Maria Remarque's novel); *Goodbye, Mr. Chips*, 1939 (with Claudine West and Erich Maschwitz; adaptation of James Hilton's novel); *The Four Feathers*, 1939 (adaptation of A. E. W. Mason's novel); *That Hamilton Woman*, 1941 (with Walter Reisch); *This Above All*, 1942 (adaptation of Eric Knight's novel); *Forever and a Day*, 1943 (with others); *Odd Man Out*, 1947 (with F. L. Green; adaptation of Green's novel); *Quartet*, 1949 (adaptation of W. Somerset Maugham's stories); *Trio*, 1950 (adaptation of Maugham's stories); *No Highway in the Sky*, 1951 (with Oscar Millard and Alec Coppel; adaptation of Nevil Shute's novel); *The Dam Busters*, 1954; *The Night My Number Came Up*, 1955 (based on an article by Air Marshal Sir Victor Goddard).

NONFICTION: *No Leading Lady: An Autobiography*, 1968; *The Siege of Swayne Castle*, 1973.

BIBLIOGRAPHY

Bracco, Rosa Maria. *Merchants of Hope: British Middlebrow Writers and the First World War, 1919-1939*. Legacy of the Great War series. Providence, R.I.: Berg, 1993. Bracco examines British literature written about World War I, focusing on Sherriff's *Journey's End*. Bibliography and index.

Cottrell, John. *Laurence Olivier*. Englewood Cliffs, N.J.: Prentice-Hall, 1975. Olivier, in 1928, was the star of the first production of *Journey's End*, which was staged by the Incorporated Stage Society before it reopened in London. Cottrell gives an elaborately detailed account of the play's first two stagings.

Darlington, William A. "'Keying Down': The Secret of *Journey's End*." Review of *Journey's End*, by R. C. Sherriff. *Theatre Arts Monthly* 13 (July, 1929): 493-497. A critic who had seen all the performances of *Journey's End* compares the play's first two productions and the New York production.

Robert E. Morsberger

ROBERT E. SHERWOOD

Born: New Rochelle, New York; April 4, 1896
Died: New York, New York; November 14, 1955

PRINCIPAL DRAMA

The Road to Rome, pr., pb. 1927
The Love Nest, pr. 1927 (adaptation of Ring Lardner's story)
The Queen's Husband, pr., pb. 1928
Waterloo Bridge, pr., pb. 1930
This Is New York, pr. 1930, pb. 1931
Reunion in Vienna, pr. 1931, pb. 1932
Acropolis, pr. 1933
The Petrified Forest, pr., pb. 1935
Idiot's Delight, pr., pb. 1936
Tovarich, pr., pb. 1936 (adaptation of Jacques Deval's comedy)
Abe Lincoln in Illinois, pr. 1938, pb. 1939
There Shall Be No Night, pr., pb. 1940
The Rugged Path, pr. 1945
Miss Liberty, pr. 1949 (libretto; music by Irving Berlin)
Small War on Murray Hill, pr., pb. 1957

OTHER LITERARY FORMS

Robert E. Sherwood made his reputation as a dramatist, although he received considerable recognition and a Pulitzer Prize for *Roosevelt and Hopkins* (1948), a detailed historical study of the relationship between Franklin D. Roosevelt and Harry Hopkins during the war years; the British edition, entitled *The White House Papers of Harry Hopkins*, followed in 1949. Sherwood also wrote *The Virtuous Knight* (1931), a badly received novel. Both of these works demonstrate Sherwood's interest in history. *The Virtuous Knight* is set in the time of the Crusades and was a product of the period during which some of Sherwood's plays, most notably *The Road to Rome* and *Acropolis*, were based on historical events.

ACHIEVEMENTS

Robert E. Sherwood was not a dramatic innovator. He produced fifteen full-length plays, two of which—*The Love Nest* and *Tovarich*—were adaptations, the former based on a Ring Lardner short story, the latter based on a comedy by Jacques Deval. *Miss Liberty* was a musical for which Irving Berlin wrote the music. Sherwood also wrote the ending for Philip Barry's *Second Threshold* (pr. 1951) after Barry's death. Nine of his plays ran for more than one hundred performances on Broadway, making them commercial successes. *Abe Lincoln in Illinois* had the longest run, 472 performances.

Sherwood received Pulitzer Prizes in drama for *Idiot's Delight, Abe Lincoln in Illinois*, and *There Shall Be No Night*. *Roosevelt and Hopkins* won for Sherwood a fourth Pulitzer Prize. His film script *The Best Years of Our Lives* took an Academy Award for Best Screenplay of 1946, one of nine Academy Awards garnered by the film. Sherwood also received the Gold Medal for Drama of the National Institute of Arts and Letters in 1941, the Gutenberg Award in 1949, and the Bancroft Prize for Distinguished Writing in American History in 1949. He was awarded honorary doctorates by Dartmouth College (1940),

Yale University (1941), Harvard University (1949), and Bishop's University (1950).

Sherwood was also an activist in his profession and in national affairs. In 1935, he became secretary of the Dramatists' Guild and rose to the presidency of that organization in 1937, the year in which he combined forces with Maxwell Anderson, S. N. Behrman, Sidney Howard, and Elmer Rice to form the Playwrights' Producing Company, which was incorporated in 1938 for the purpose of permitting playwrights to stage their own plays, either directing the plays themselves or appointing directors of their own choosing. Sherwood was elected president of the American National Theatre and Academy in 1939.

Although Sherwood had been a strident pacifist, Adolf Hitler's ascendancy in Germany forced him to rethink his stand. A political idealist, Sherwood was finally forced to recognize the impossibility of allowing a dictator to run roughshod over Europe. *There Shall Be No Night* calls for action against aggressors of Hitler's ilk and represents an important turning point in Sherwood's thinking. In his presidential address to the Dramatists' Guild in 1939, Sherwood called on writers to turn their talents to writing in support of freedom. *There Shall Be No Night* is in line with this imperative.

Long a friend and political supporter of Franklin D. Roosevelt, Sherwood was asked by the Roosevelt administration to write war propaganda. He did so willingly and in time became not only a confidant of the president, visiting him often at the White House, but also one of his chief speech writers. In 1940, Sherwood was appointed as a special assistant to the secretary of war, and in 1942, he was appointed director of the overseas branch of the office of war information. In 1945, he served as a special assistant to the secretary of the navy.

Sherwood was also active as a screenwriter. As early as 1932, he had collaborated with Charles Lederer on *Cock of the Air* for United Artists, followed in 1935 by *The Scarlet Pimpernel*, a collaboration with Arthur Wimperis. In 1936, he was involved in writing the screenplay for *Rembrandt*, although he was not the sole author. His screenplay for *The Ghost Goes West* was produced in 1936 by Alexander

Korda. The following year, with Aben Kandel, he wrote the screenplay for *Thunder in the City* and also did considerable rewriting on a Metro-Goldwyn-Mayer script, *Conquest*. In 1938, he was coauthor with Lajos Biro of the screenplay for *The Divorce of Lady X* and also wrote *The Adventures of Marco Polo*, the latter of which was cited by Francis Marion in *How to Write and Sell Fiction Stories* as a splendid example of scenario writing. Sherwood adapted *Idiot's Delight* for the screen in 1939, the year in which *Abe Lincoln in Illinois* was also filmed. *Rebecca* followed in 1940. His finest Hollywood effort was *The Best Years of Our Lives*, in 1946. It was followed in 1947 by *The Bishop's Wife*, on which he collaborated with Leonardo Bercovici, and in 1953 by his last screenplay, *Man on a Tightrope*.

Biography

Robert Emmet Sherwood was the product of an affluent and artistic family. His mother, the former Rosina Emmet, was sufficiently well known as an artist to be listed in *Who's Who*. His father, Arthur Murray Sherwood, was a prominent investment broker and held a seat on the New York Stock Exchange. Arthur Sherwood was a frustrated actor and had been an active member of the Hasty Pudding Club during his student days at Harvard, where he was also the first president of the Harvard *Lampoon*. Robert Sherwood followed in his father's footsteps at Harvard, both as a member of the Hasty Pudding Club and as editor of the *Lampoon*.

Sherwood was named for the Irish patriot Robert Emmet, brother of his mother's great-grandfather, who led an attack on Dublin Castle and was hanged in 1803. Sherwood was proud of his renegade namesake. Mary Elizabeth Wilson Sherwood, mother of Sherwood's father, had been honored both by the French government and by Queen Victoria of Britain. She was active in literary and artistic circles and in her lifetime wrote more than twenty books and hundreds of articles.

Thus, Robert Sherwood, the next to the youngest of five Sherwood children, was born into an artistically active family of considerable means. Shortly after his birth, the family moved to a house on Lexington

Avenue in New York City. The family also maintained a forty-room Georgian mansion, Skene Wood, set on three hundred acres bordering Lake Champlain. It was there that Sherwood spent most of his childhood summers.

During the summers at Skene Wood, Sherwood and his siblings put on amateur dramatic productions, and Sherwood produced a handwritten newspaper, *Children's Life*. At eight, he wrote an ending for Charles Dickens's unfinished novel *The Mystery of Edwin Drood* (1870), and two years later he wrote his first play, *Tom Ruggles' Surprise*, soon to be followed by *How the King Was Saved* and *The Curse of Bacchus*.

When he was nine years old, Sherwood was sent to the Fay School in Southborough, Massachusetts, and at thirteen, he was sent to the Milton Academy near Boston to begin his preparatory studies for Harvard. Both in preparatory school and later at Harvard, Sherwood's energies were to be directed more toward literary matters than toward academic ones. He was managing editor of Milton's monthly magazine, *Orange and Blue*, for much of his final year at Milton; he was deeply in trouble with his studies, however, and in April, the school forced his withdrawal from this post. Ultimately, his grades were so low that Milton Academy refused him a diploma, giving him instead a certificate of attendance. Despite this, Sherwood was elected valedictorian by his classmates, and he gave the valedictory address.

Sherwood's academic career at Harvard was no more distinguished than his career at Milton Academy had been, although his contributions to Harvard's dramatic and literary clubs were substantial. On the brink of expulsion three times during his freshman year alone, Sherwood did not make it through to graduation. In July of 1917, having been rejected on account of his great height by the various branches of the United States armed forces in which he attempted to enlist, Sherwood became a member of the Canadian Expeditionary Force, serving in the Forty-second Battalion of the Fifth Royal Highlanders and achieving the distinction of being very probably the tallest serviceman in World War I to wear kilts. At six feet, seven inches, he towered over

his fellow combatants. He served six months in France, where he was gassed on Vimy Ridge. In 1918, Harvard awarded him a bachelor's degree in absentia although he had not met the academic standards for this degree.

On his return from the war, Sherwood was offered a position at *Vanity Fair*, a magazine that the *Lampoon* under Sherwood's editorship had burlesqued so effectively that its editor wanted Sherwood on his staff. At *Vanity Fair*, Sherwood shared an office with Robert Benchley and Dorothy Parker. The three were fired in 1920 for rebelling against *Vanity Fair*'s editorial staff, but soon they were all hired by *Life* magazine, to whose editorship Sherwood rose in 1924. During this period, Sherwood was a regular participant in the Round Table that met at the Algonquin Hotel.

Sherwood married Mary Brandon in 1922. Their turbulent marriage lasted until 1934, when they were divorced. The following year, Sherwood married Marc Connelly's former wife, actress Madeline Hurlock Connelly. Sherwood's extravagant lifestyle during the early years of his marriage to Mary Brandon caused him to sink deeply into debt, from which he extricated himself in 1926 by writing *The Road to Rome* in three weeks' time. When the play opened on Broadway the following year, it was an immediate success and ran for 392 performances. Throughout his career, Sherwood frequently relied on his gift for rapid composition to free himself from debts.

The activism that had led Sherwood to serve in the armed forces during the war and to speak his mind at *Vanity Fair* shifted its focus to the problems of actors and writers. It led Sherwood to assume prominent roles in the Dramatists' Guild and in the American National Theatre Association and to be instrumental in forming the Playwrights' Producing Company.

It was natural that, with the spread of fascism in Europe, Sherwood's basically activist personality should lead him to encourage his fellow writers to strike out against aggression of the sort that Hitler was practicing and should lead him to write a play, *There Shall Be No Night*, which departed drastically from his romantic liberalism and pacifism of the 1920's and 1930's. It is also significant that Sherwood at this time tried to rewrite his pacifist play *Acropolis*, for which he could never arrange a production in New York and which ran for only twelve performances when it played in London in 1933. Sherwood was unable to rewrite it satisfactorily, probably because he no longer believed in the kind of pacifism that the play promulgated.

Always a man of the world, Sherwood's insights were deepened by his direct contact with high levels of government during the war. His work with the Hopkins papers was meticulously researched, although some scholars think that Sidney Hyman deserves more credit than he was given for the high level of research apparent in *Roosevelt and Hopkins*.

Sherwood became a propagandist in the years following Hitler's invasion of Poland in 1939. The quality and effectiveness of his dramatic writing declined after the war. He died in 1955 at age fifty-nine.

ANALYSIS

Although Robert E. Sherwood's writing was seldom profound, it was often effective and moving. He had an excellent sense of timing and was able to balance his characters and play them off against one another in such a way as to achieve and maintain dramatic tension. His major characters are largely romantics, dreamers of one sort or another, who envision a more perfect world, a more felicitous state of affairs. Sherwood's plays are urbane, idealistic, and often quite witty. They may seem somewhat dated to modern readers. Both the situations on which they are focused and Sherwood's suggested solutions to the problems posed are out of keeping with the pragmatic temper of the modern world.

The most consistent element found in the plays is pacifism. Sherwood was convinced of the futility of war. *There Shall Be No Night*, although it is a war play, wrestles with the question of pacifism quite substantially. In this play, Sherwood was led to abandon his idealism to the extent of calling for action against the sort of aggression that leads to genocide. In nearly all of his other plays, Sherwood examines the options available to humankind to avoid war.

THE ROAD TO ROME

Even Sherwood's earliest play dealt with the question of pacifism and of human conflict in the face of war. *The Road to Rome* would be flippant if it were less urbane. In this historical comedy, Sherwood risks using modern slang and contemporary situations in an ancient Roman setting and gets away with it. The subject of the play had always interested Sherwood: Why had Hannibal and his army come to the very gates of Rome, only to turn away and retreat from a sure victory?

Taking a number of liberties with historical fact, Sherwood suggests an answer: Amytis, the wife of Rome's dictator, Fabius Maximus, allows herself to be captured by the enemy and is about to be stabbed to death by Hannibal when she seduces him. Amytis returns to Rome and to her unexciting husband. Hannibal retreats.

Essentially, *The Road to Rome* is a satire that compares the Rome of Fabius with American society after World War I. Fabius and his mother, Fabia, represent conventional social values. They are much concerned with appearance and with what people think, and they take themselves quite seriously. Amytis, on the other hand, has an Athenian mother; she is an iconoclast in this dreary, somewhat backward Roman society. When she hears that Hannibal is about to invade Rome, Amytis flees to Ostia, admonishing Fabius not to eat too much starch while she is away. She leaves in the company of two slaves, Meta and Varius, around whom a useful subplot is constructed.

Before the end of act 1, it is obvious that Amytis, bored with her life and unsympathetic to her husband and her monotonous mother-in-law, is thrilled by the thought of the aggressor outside the city gates. She claims that Hannibal "sounds like a thoroughly commendable person" and goes on to ask, "Is it wrong for me to admire good, old-fashioned virility in men?"

Thus, the stage is set: When Amytis and her slaves are captured, it is clear that she will entrap Hannibal. More important, through Amytis, Sherwood suggests that Hannibal comes to realize that there is no glory in sacking Rome. Rationality prevails in the tradition of true liberal romanticism found in much of Sherwood's writing before *There Shall Be No Night*.

If Sherwood was attempting to convey the message that reason can prevail over might, he fell somewhat short of his mark. Hannibal can be brought to the point of uttering that "there is a thing called the human equation," but he arrives at this point not through reason so much as because he has yielded to his lust for Amytis. Nevertheless, if the decision not to sack Rome is Hannibal's, it is clear that the focus of the play is on Amytis, whose reason prevails.

The Meta-Varius subplot portrays the true and lasting love the two slaves have for each other. Because they are slaves, they are unable to marry. Their love stands in sharp contrast to the barren relationship that exists between Amytis and Fabius. Amytis persuades Hannibal to free these two lovers so that they can return to their native Sicily and marry.

The last two acts of *The Road to Rome* are weakened by heavy-handed pacifist diatribes, but the play's general wittiness and the excellence of Sherwood's characterizations are sufficient to overcome such shortcomings. It is ironic that Amytis's relationship with her husband is based on her frivolousness, while her relationship with Hannibal succeeds because of her wit and intellect. The play attacks conformity and examines closely the difference between public and private morality. In Amytis, one can see shadows of the bright young Sherwood whose nonconformity led him to disaster on more than one occasion. Amytis is drawn delightfully and convincingly and is ever the recipient of the audience's warm compassion.

As the play ends, Rome has been spared, Hannibal is in retreat, and Amytis returns to Fabius, who will undoubtedly receive the credit for saving Rome. The audience is also left with the strong impression that Amytis has been made pregnant by Hannibal, and it can savor the delicious irony that Hannibal's child will be reared as Fabius's and may himself eventually come to rule Rome. In the final scene of the play, Hannibal says to Fabius, "I wish happiness and prosperity to you, your wife, and your sons." When Fabius responds that he has no sons, Hannibal replies, "You may."

THE LOVE NEST

Sherwood's next play, *The Love Nest*, was based on a splendid Ring Lardner short story, but the adaptation failed utterly, both artistically and commercially, playing only twenty-three performances. Perhaps Sherwood was drawn to the story by his own domestic complications at the time. A secondary theme of the play is censorship, a subject in which Sherwood was becoming quite interested and on which he debated in 1927 with John Sumner, president of the Society for the Prevention of Vice.

The play revolves around Celia Gregg, the actress wife of a much disliked motion-picture director, Lou Gregg. Celia has risen to her present position not through her own talent but because she married a director whose reputation is shady, partly because of nudity in his film, *Hell's Paradise*, and partly because of rumors about his own private life. Celia and the butler, Forbes, an unemployed actor, love each other, and before the play is over, they decide to leave and have a life together, though there is little to suggest that they have any real future. *The Love Nest* has some witty lines, and Celia's dramatic drunk scene in act 2 is splendid, but the play fails because its psychological motivation is unconvincing and underdeveloped, and the dramatic tension is uneven.

THE QUEEN'S HUSBAND

Newspaper accounts of the official visit of Queen Marie of Romania to the United States in 1926 gave Sherwood the substance for his next play, *The Queen's Husband*, a thin yet diverting comedy that ran for 125 performances on Broadway, making it moderately successful commercially. During Queen Marie's visit, her consort was very much in the background. Sherwood's play focuses on the consort, Ferdinand, who in the play becomes Eric VIII, consort of Queen Martha. The principality over which Eric and Martha rule is much in the hands of the military, led by General Northrup, who seeks to annihilate the opposition by executing them. Queen Martha goes along with this. The king, however, must sign the orders for the executions, and he subverts the plan simply by losing the orders. When his private secretary, Freddy Granton, finds the death warrants, Eric tells him to "take them out and lose them again."

Eric is first presented as a doddering nonentity, but it soon becomes apparent that he knows what he is doing and that he ultimately gets his way. In a romantic subplot, Princess Anne is in love with Freddy Granton, but there are impediments to her marrying a commoner; indeed, a royal marriage is being arranged for her. On the day of the wedding, however, the king finally asserts himself, sees to it that Princess Anne marries the man she loves, sends them off on a trip to Panama, and clears the way for free elections by dissolving the Parliament. The play is filled with fairy-tale elements, and its resolution is improbable at best. It was received with some public enthusiasm as a diverting, witty entertainment, well-staged and competently acted, but it is not a play that contributes to Sherwood's artistic stature in any way.

WATERLOO BRIDGE

Waterloo Bridge has little more to recommend it than does *The Queen's Husband*, and its run of only sixty-four performances clearly indicated a lack of public acceptance. The play succeeded better as a film, for which S. N. Behrman wrote the major portion of a screenplay that fleshed out the plot and essentially discarded Sherwood's original script. Universal Studios produced the film in 1931, and Metro-Goldwyn-Mayer released other film versions of the play in 1940 and 1956.

Sherwood wrote the play from the memory of an experience in London in 1918 when he was recovering from war injuries. During the festivities celebrating the Armistice, Sherwood had met an American chorus girl who had been stranded in London, where she was in the cast of *The Pink Lady*. She invited Sherwood to come to her flat, but he lost the address so was unable to accept her invitation.

In the play, a remarkably innocent American soldier, Roy Cronin, meets Myra Deauville on Waterloo Bridge and is too inexperienced to realize that she is a prostitute out plying her trade. He goes to her apartment and, mistaking her for a symbol of purity, proposes marriage to her. She accepts, but then she has a change of heart, leaves Roy a note, and fades from the scene. They meet again by accident on Waterloo Bridge, where she confesses to being a whore, but Roy urges her to forget her past. He loves her and

shows that he does by signing over his life insurance to her and arranging for her to receive part of his pay each month. As the second act of this two-act play ends, enemy bombers are flying overhead and Roy must return to his unit. Myra lights a match and holds it up for the German bombardiers to see. The play ends with a pacifist diatribe that Sherwood puts rather unconvincingly into Roy's mouth. *Waterloo Bridge* was less successful than *The Queen's Husband* because it lacked the wit of its predecessor and because it often wallowed in sentimentality.

THIS IS NEW YORK

Not to be daunted by the failure of *Waterloo Bridge*, Sherwood wrote *This Is New York*, which also failed, running for only fifty-nine performances on Broadway. He produced the play quickly after he had put aside a play about the Crusades entitled "Marching as to War." This historical play was never completed, but much of the material Sherwood used in it found its way into his only novel, *The Virtuous Knight*.

This Is New York shows Sherwood as a loyal and patriotic New Yorker but not as a consummate playwright. Irked by the provincial attitudes that had helped to defeat Al Smith in the 1928 presidential election, Sherwood set out to write a play about the hypocrisy of the provinces. He partially succeeded by lining up Senator Harvey L. Krull of Iowa and his self-righteous wife against a group of New Yorkers, including racketeers, bootleggers, blackmailers, and other such marginal figures. In the end, the Krulls are shown up as the hypocrites Sherwood set out to create, while the socially marginal characters show a warmth and humanity that ingratiate them to audiences. The key figure in the play is the Krulls' daughter Emma, who wants to marry a New Yorker, Joe Gresham. Emma is an appealing character, believably depicted and necessary to the development of the play's theme. After a somewhat tedious and talky first act, the play moves to a dramatically tight second act with a strong climax. The play is significant only as a step in Sherwood's development toward being able to create and control a believable microcosm, an ability that was to serve him well in plays such as *The Petrified Forest* and *Idiot's Delight*.

REUNION IN VIENNA

Sherwood visited Vienna in 1929 to attend a performance of *The Road to Rome*, called *Hannibal ante portes* in the Austrian production. While in Vienna, he met Frau Sacher of the Hotel Sacher, who became the model for Frau Lucher in *Reunion in Vienna*, a sophisticated comedy that came to Broadway in 1931 for a highly successful run. Alfred Lunt and Lynn Fontanne played in the starring roles, with Helen Westley as Frau Lucher. Sherwood called the play an escape from reality. This witty play contained in its printed version a preface as pessimistic as anything Sherwood was ever to write. He warned, "Man may not have time to complete the process of his own doing before the unknown forces have combined to burst the bubble of his universe."

Set in the Vienna of 1930, *Reunion in Vienna* shows a city from which the Habsburgs have been exiled and in which the bourgeoisie has taken command. Frau Lucher—like her prototype, Frau Sacher—works to keep the concept of the nobility alive. She has given clandestine parties for exiled leaders who have returned for visits, and she is now planning a party to celebrate the one hundredth birthday of Franz Josef. Much to everyone's surprise, Archduke Rudolf Maximilian von Habsburg, now a taxicab driver in Nice, returns for the occasion. Rudolf's former mistress, Elena, is married to one of the bourgeoisie who has risen in power, Anton Krug. Anton was a surgeon until the Habsburgs, whom he had opposed, had him sent from his medical post in their army to do hard labor in a rock quarry, where he destroyed his hands. When he finally gained his release, Anton no longer had the manual sensitivity to perform surgery, so he entered the practice of psychiatry.

Anton, who has every reason to hate the Habsburgs, is a rational man. Not only is he able to put past bitterness behind him, but also he is sure enough of his relationship with Elena to encourage her, when they learn that Rudolf is back in Vienna, to see her former lover and to attend Frau Lucher's reunion. She does so and finds that Rudolf is still dashing and romantic. Anton leaves the two of them alone, and the inevitable occurs, much as it did between Amytis and

Hannibal, to whom Elena and Rudolf can legitimately be compared.

Rudolf's entry in act 2 is one of the best-prepared entries in any contemporary play. The deposed archduke is still every inch a Habsburg. The audience has been tantalized through act 1, wondering how Rudolf will appear after a decade away. Two minor characters give hints, but his entry is a breathtaking moment of pure theater. In act 3, the civilized interchange between Rudolf and Anton is well handled. Anton is the voice of reason and control, Rudolf that of emotion and soul. The night that Elena and Rudolf have together does not destroy the Krugs's union but rather strengthens it. If their marriage is dull, it is at least secure; it provides each party with the dependable reference point that husbands and wives need.

Reunion in Vienna helped to reestablish Sherwood's reputation after three plays that had been either outright failures or very limited successes. The play represented a turning point for Sherwood, who, after its production, was a much surer writer, even though he was to produce one more failure, *Acropolis*. *Reunion in Vienna*, dashed off in three weeks, was produced at a time when Sherwood's marriage was foundering and when there was little reason for cheer on the world scene. Hitler and Benito Mussolini were on the rise in Europe, and the world was in the grips of the Depression. Broadway needed a drawing-room drama such as *Reunion in Vienna* to divert its attention from the social and political realitites that caused Sherwood to write such a gloomy preface to the play.

ACROPOLIS

Acropolis was an important play for Sherwood. It deals with ideas concerning human freedom and dignity that Sherwood considered fundamental—ideas present in many of his works but frequently diminished in impact by his witty manner. Sherwood wrote *Acropolis* in 1932 while he was traveling in France with his wife and the Connellys. He had long been mulling over the ideas that were the substance of the play. He gave the script to the Theatre Guild, which turned it down because it was not sufficiently theatrical and because it had too much talk in it. The play was finally produced in London in the fall of 1933, financed largely by Paul Hyde Bonner, Sherwood's neighbor at Grand Enton, Surrey. The play ran for only twelve performances, making it Sherwood's worst commercial disaster.

Unlike Sherwood's other plays, *Acropolis* went through many revisions. Indeed, the author was revising it up to the time he wrote *There Shall Be No Night* in 1940. The play, however, never seemed to coalesce into a dramatic whole, and with Sherwood's shift away from his romantic liberalism of the early 1930's, *Acropolis* in its various forms came to represent his thinking less and less each year. The play remained unpublished, although a number of manuscript versions of it exist.

THE PETRIFIED FOREST

When he went to Reno for six weeks in 1935 to obtain his divorce from Mary Brandon, Sherwood rented an office and began to write. His attention turned to an Arizona tourist attraction, the Petrified Forest, which in his play by that name provides an almost eternal backdrop before which ephemeral men and women play out their small roles. The microcosm of *The Petrified Forest* is the Black Mesa Filling Station. The cast of characters includes Gramp Maple, an old pioneer, now senescent; his son Jason, a bit of a dolt; and his granddaughter, Jason's daughter Gabrielle, nicknamed Gabby.

Gabby's French mother married Jason when he was an American soldier fighting in World War I, and she returned to Arizona with him but could not tolerate the isolation. She returned to France, abandoning both husband and daughter. Boze Hertlinger is a former college football player who pursues Gabby. Into this scene enters Alan Squier, the ideological center of the play in many respects, who has recently come from France and is hitchhiking across the country. Although he is sophisticated, cultivated, and intelligent, Alan is almost bankrupt, and his future is bleak. The cast is rounded out by the Chisholms, a banker and his wife, and their chauffeur, who are all in the filling station when Duke Mantee, a desperado recently escaped from an Oklahoma prison, arrives and holds all of them hostage.

Gabby's dream in life is to visit France, from which her mother came. Gabby, who has the vocabu-

lary of a stevedore, quotes lines from François Villon and paints watercolors, which she will show only to Alan, who predictably begins to be attracted to her. He decides to help her realize her dream by signing over to her his five-thousand-dollar life insurance policy and then getting Duke Mantee to shoot him.

The focus of the play is badly distorted. Alan represents what is good in the world, yet he enters into a suicide pact to help Gabby. One can only conclude that Sherwood is implying that the dark forces will prevail over the bright forces in society, for with Alan's death, which ultimately occurs onstage, the world—or at least Sherwood's microcosm—is left to the Boze Hertlingers and the Jason Maples, people who have ceased to have a discernible purpose in society.

One important theme in *The Petrified Forest* is that the pioneer, who led to the development of the United States, is fading from the scene. Gramp was a pioneer, but now he is too old to qualify as one. If Alan has the potential to be a sort of ideological pioneer, his death precludes that possibility. Duke Mantee comes across as the man of action, suggestive of Harry Glassman, the racketeer in *This Is New York*; Mantee is, despite his criminal record, infinitely more decent and promising than the senator and his wife.

Although *The Petrified Forest* is flawed structurally and thematically, as John Howard Lawson has demonstrated quite brilliantly in his *Theory and Technique of Playwriting* (1936), it was theatrical in the highest sense, and Broadway received it well. It played for nearly two hundred performances. Adapted for the screen in 1936, *The Petrified Forest* featured Leslie Howard as Alan Squier, Bette Davis as Gabby, and Humphrey Bogart as Duke Mantee. It is in its film version that the work is best remembered.

IDIOT'S DELIGHT

In *Idiot's Delight*, Sherwood again employed the device of placing a diverse group of people in a confined microcosm and putting them under considerable tension. *Idiot's Delight* could not have been more appropriate for its time: Its New York opening followed Mussolini's invasion of Ethiopia by two days; its London opening came a week after Hitler had invaded Austria. The world was tense, and Sherwood's play captured and exploited this tension.

As the play opens, the audience is presented with a cast that includes a weapons manufacturer and his mistress; a French Marxist labor leader who is executed before the play is over; two British honeymooners; a German scientist who is about to develop a cure for cancer but must now rush home to the *Vaterland* to work on developing poison gases; and Harry Van, a "hoofer" who is the guardian of a group of traveling showgirls. This mismatched group is stranded at the Hotel Monte Gabriele, just over the Italian border from Austria and Switzerland. All of them are being held by the Italian government because of the international tensions that have developed. They are essentially unable to control their own destinies, much as the people being held by Duke Mantee in *The Petrified Forest* were unable to control their own destinies, save for Alan Squier, who willed his own execution.

Lynn Fontanne, who played the role of Irene, the munitions manufacturer's mistress, urged on Sherwood the revision from which the title is drawn. Sherwood expanded Fontanne's part and wrote into it the speech about God as a "poor, lonely old soul. Sitting up there in heaven, with nothing to do but play solitaire. Poor, dear God. Playing Idiot's Delight."

The play, although it is a delightful comedy, reflects the same sort of futility that was evidenced in *The Petrified Forest*. In it, Sherwood clearly expresses the conviction that intelligent people do not run things but rather are pawns in a system controlled by those of evil intent. In Sherwood's own eyes, the play missed its mark as a seriously intended comedy. Although it ran for more than three hundred performances and won for its author his first Pulitzer Prize in drama, Sherwood was forced to admit that "the trouble with me is that I start off with a big message and end with nothing but good entertainment." The play is best understood if it is viewed essentially as a moral rather than a political statement. Sherwood also wrote the film scenario for *Idiot's Delight*, for which he was paid $135,000 by Metro-Goldwyn-Mayer. The play represented an important step in Sherwood's development and in his public recognition.

ABE LINCOLN IN ILLINOIS

It was two years before Sherwood was to have another opening on Broadway. During this time, he was much occupied with setting up the Playwrights' Producing Company, whose first production was to be *Abe Lincoln in Illinois*. Six feet, seven inches tall himself, Sherwood knew something of the isolation of being very tall, and in significant ways, he identified personally with Lincoln. The play, in three acts, is divided into twelve scenes and covers a thirty-year time span. It begins in New Salem, where the young Lincoln was postmaster, moving in the second act to Springfield, where Lincoln practices law and meets Mary Todd, whom he marries after once refusing to marry her on their appointed wedding day. In the last act, Lincoln is seen debating Stephen Douglas, becoming a presidential candidate, and winning the election. The play ends just as Lincoln is to leave for Washington to assume the presidency.

The character of Lincoln is psychologically well drawn, particularly in regard to his early association with and ultimate marriage to Mary Todd. She represents what the young Lincoln most fears—duty. Had he not married her, one must wonder whether he would ever have become president. Certainly, he is brought to the brink of leaving Illinois and going out to Nebraska with Seth Gale, in which case he could never have become president. Mary is persistent, however, and Lincoln marries her, thus beginning on the course that she has carefully plotted.

The themes of *Abe Lincoln in Illinois* were timely for the late 1930's. The problems that Lincoln faced and the moral dilemmas with which he wrestled were not unlike those that perplexed the pacifist Sherwood, who was being forced to question his moral stand as Hitler threatened the whole of Europe.

Parts of the play are sketchy. The first-act curtain falls on a young Lincoln, immature and uncertain, only to rise years later on a Lincoln who has matured between the acts. Sherwood does not demonstrate the maturing process but rather presents it for the audience to accept, which it can easily do because the Lincoln story is so well known. Similarly, the play ends before the crucial events of Lincoln's term of office, but this is quite immaterial to audiences who are fully aware of the tragic story of the Lincoln presidency. The play, an initial Broadway success that ran longer than any other Sherwood production, has probably been performed more often and been seen by more people that any other Sherwood play, and it is the play with which he is most readily identified today.

THERE SHALL BE NO NIGHT

Sherwood's pacifism had been severely put to the test as the 1930's drew to a close. On the last Christmas Day of the decade, Sherwood heard William Lindsay White's broadcast from Finland called "Christmas in the Mannerheim Line," and it convinced him more than had anything else previously that the United States could not isolate itself from the rest of the world but must intervene to stop the spread of totalitarianism. His patriotism reached new heights, but this was no narrow patriotism. Rather, it had to do with the survival of the highest ideals that Sherwood held. Within six months, he was to make his stand clear, first by writing *There Shall Be No Night*, which he began on January 15, 1940, and which he delivered to the Lunts three weeks later, and then, in May, 1940, by spending $24,000 of his own money to run a full-page advertisement in more than one hundred American newspapers, calling on his compatriots, and particularly on writers, to stop Hitler. It was this advertisement that attracted President Roosevelt's attention and drew Sherwood into government service.

There Shall Be No Night was based on the Russian invasion of Finland in 1939; before the play ran in London, however, by which time Finland had fallen, Sherwood rewrote it, changing the locale from Finland to Greece and making the aggressors German rather than Russian. The play revolves around the Valkonen family and their trials as their country moves into a state of war. Valkonen is an eminent neurologist, a winner of the Nobel Prize. He, his wife Miranda, and his son Erik are gentle people who live lives of great civility in Helsinki, until the war comes and their lives crumble. Before the play is over, they are all dead or about to die except for Erik's fiancé, Kaatri. Pregnant with Erik's child; she escapes to the safety of America, where her delivery will give the

Valkonens "one little link with the future." "It gives us the illusion of survival," says Miranda as the play ends, "and perhaps it isn't just an illusion." The play is filled with ironies, the chief one being that the most worthwhile people are defeated and destroyed. Dr. Ziemssen, the German consul in Helsinki, is by training an anthropologist, yet he is supporting a plan of genocide, clearly stating that the plan outlined in Hitler's *Mein Kampf* is now operative.

An immensely moving play, *There Shall Be No Night* probably did more to mold the consciences of American audiences of its day than any play on the New York stage. It offers no strong ray of hope; rather, Sherwood brings audiences right into the vortex of a cosmic problem and leaves them there to struggle against the forces into which he has plunged them. *There Shall Be No Night*, Sherwood's first full-fledged tragedy, was unrelenting in its pessimistic realism and in its call to action.

LATER PLAYS

Sherwood was never again to write a notably successful play, although he continued to score successes in his screenplays, and his *Roosevelt and Hopkins* was one of the great books to come out of the war period. Of his final plays, *Miss Liberty* was a popular light musical that ran for 308 performances, while *The Rugged Path* and *Small War on Murray Hill* were both artistic and commercial failures. Morey Vinion, the protagonist in *The Rugged Path*, speaks toward the end of the play for Sherwood and helps to explain his inability to write with the verve and wit that he achieved so easily in the 1930's: "I am no longer impressed by the power of the pen. For years I wrote about what was coming. I tried to tell what I had seen and heard and felt. I wrote my heart out. But it did no good." By the time the United States had entered and fought in a world conflict, Sherwood was too dispirited to be able to write with the conviction that earlier drove him.

OTHER MAJOR WORKS

LONG FICTION: *The Virtuous Knight*, 1931.

SCREENPLAYS: *Cock of the Air*, 1932 (with Charles Lederer); *The Scarlet Pimpernel*, 1935 (with Arthur Wimperis; adaptation of Baroness Orczy's novel);

The Ghost Goes West, 1936; *Thunder in the City*, 1937 (with Aben Kandel); *The Adventures of Marco Polo*, 1938; *The Divorce of Lady X*, 1938 (with Lajos Biro; adaptation of Biro's play *Counsel's Opinion*); *Abe Lincoln in Illinois*, 1939 (adaptation of his play); *Idiot's Delight*, 1939 (adaptation of his play); *Rebecca*, 1940 (with Joan Harrison; adaptation of Daphne du Maurier's novel); *The Best Years of Our Lives*, 1946; *The Bishop's Wife*, 1947 (with Leonardo Bercovici); *Man on a Tightrope*, 1953.

NONFICTION: *Roosevelt and Hopkins*, 1948 (also as *The White House Papers of Harry Hopkins*, 1949).

EDITED TEXT: *The Best Moving Pictures of 1922-1923*, 1923.

BIBLIOGRAPHY

Brown, John Mason. *The Ordeal of a Playwright: Robert E. Sherwood and the Challenge of War.* Edited by Norman Cousins. New York: Harper and Row, 1970. Brown's uncompleted second biography furnishes a fragmentary but telling portrait of Sherwood as being wrenched away from devout pacifism to become aroused by world affairs. As a presidential speech writer, he wrote, on the eve of World War II, a pro-interventionist play, *There Shall Be No Night*, portraying a brave Finnish family resisting Finland's invasion. Complemented by an index and a complete text of *There Shall Be No Night*.

_____. *The Worlds of Robert E. Sherwood: Mirror to His Times, 1897-1939.* 1965. Reprint. Westport, Conn.: Greenwood Press, 1979. This thoroughly documented and admiring biography extends from Sherwood's early childhood and up through his career as a critic and playwright to include the writing of *Abe Lincoln in Illinois*. The volume contains a list of Sherwood's work and an index, in addition to twenty-eight illustrations of Sherwood, his family and friends, and several productions.

Meserve, Walter J. *Robert E. Sherwood: Reluctant Moralist.* New York: Pegasus, 1970. In addition to examining Sherwood as a dramatist, Meserve considers the playwright's role as an adviser and speech writer for Franklin D. Roosevelt, as a prominent member of the Author's League, and as a founding partner in the Playwright's Company. The book offers a valuable, objective, detailed analysis of all Sherwood's plays, determining him to be more of a superior maker of plays than a dramatist of searching ideas. Supplemented by an informative, select bibliography and an index.

Mishra, Kshamanidhi. *American Leftist Playwrights of the 1930's: A Study of Ideology and Technique in the Plays of Odets, Lawson, and Sherwood.* New Delhi, India: Classical Publishing, 1991. The author looks at the political and social views of Sherwood, Clifford Odets, and John Lawson. Bibliography.

Shuman, R. Baird. *Robert E. Sherwood.* New York: Twayne, 1964. An accessible and comprehensive biographical and critical treatment of the playwright and his work. It contains a chronology, a detailed examination of Sherwood's plays within the context of his life and career, and an annotated listing of secondary sources.

R. Baird Shuman,
updated by Christian H. Moe

JAMES SHIRLEY

Born: London, England; September 7, 1596 (baptized)

Died: London, England; October 29, 1666

PRINCIPAL DRAMA

The School of Compliment, pr. 1625, pb. 1631 (also known as *Love Tricks: Or, The School of Compliments*)

The Brothers, pr. 1626, pb. 1652

The Maid's Revenge, pr. 1626, pb. 1639

The Wedding, pr. 1626(?), pb. 1629

The Witty Fair One, pr. 1628, pb. 1633

The Grateful Servant, pr. 1629, pb. 1630 (also known as *The Faithful Servant*)

The Traitor, pr. 1631, pb. 1635

Love's Cruelty, pr. 1631, pb. 1640

The Duke, pr. 1631

The Changes: Or, Love in a Maze, pr. 1631, pb. 1632

Hyde Park, pr. 1632, pb. 1637

The Ball, pr. 1632, pb. 1639 (with George Chapman)

The Bird in a Cage, pr. 1632, pb. 1633 (also known as *The Beauties*)

The Young Admiral, pr. 1633, pb. 1637

The Gamester, pr. 1633, pb. 1637

The Triumph of Peace, pr., pb. 1634 (masque)

The Coronation, pr. 1635, pb. 1640

The Lady of Pleasure, pr. 1635, pb. 1637

Chabot, Admiral of France, pr. 1635, pb. 1639 (with George Chapman)

The Duke's Mistress, pr. 1636, pb. 1638

The Constant Maid, pr. 1636-1640(?), pb. 1640

The Royal Master, pr. 1637, pb. 1638

The Doubtful Heir, pr. c. 1638, pb. 1652 (also known as *Rosania: Or, Love's Victory*)

The Politician, pr. 1639(?), pb. 1655

The Gentleman of Venice, pr. 1639, pb. 1655

Patrick for Ireland, pr. 1639(?), pb. 1640

The Humorous Courtier, pr., pb. 1640 (revision of *The Duke*)

The Imposture, pr. 1640, pb. 1652

The Cardinal, pr. 1641, pb. 1652

The Sisters, pr. 1642, pb. 1652

The Court Secret, wr. 1642, pb. 1653, pr. after 1660

The Contention of Ajax and Ulysses for the Armour of Achilles, pr. c. 1645, pb. 1658 (masque)

Dramatic Works and Poems, pb. 1833 (6 volumes)

OTHER LITERARY FORMS

Both before and after his career as a dramatist, James Shirley was a schoolmaster; among the fruits of that vocation are several grammar texts. Of greater significance are his accomplishments as a Cavalier poet, one of the Sons of Ben who sometimes wrote witty verse—"a sort of [Thomas] Carew without Carew's genius," according to Douglas Bush—and whose 1646 collection of poems is in the tradition of the Ovidian poetry of the Elizabethans. In that volume is *Narcissus: Or, The Self-Lover*, which is patterned after William Shakespeare's *Venus and Adonis* (1593). Shirley's best-known poetic work and a frequent anthology piece is a later product: the "noble dirge" from the masque *The Contention of Ajax and Ulysses for the Armour of Achilles*. "The glories of our blood and state/ Are shadows not substantial things. . . ." Though the source of the masque probably is Ovid's *Metamorphoses* (c. 8 C.E.; English translation, 1567), the dirge that Calchas speaks over the body of Ajax strikes an Augustan note. The poetry in Shirley's plays has been praised for its "lightness," "spontaneity of movement," and "richness of decoration," and its similarity to that of John Fletcher has been noted, but because Shirley is a transitional figure between the Elizabethan poetic playwrights and the more prosaic Restoration dramatists, there is little noteworthy verse in his plays, except for the tragicomedies.

ACHIEVEMENTS

For the seventeen years between 1625 and 1642, James Shirley, a prolific playwright in a variety of modes, dominated the Caroline stage. His more than thirty extant plays (several more are lost or of uncertain attribution) demonstrate his facility at creating comedies, tragedies, tragicomedies, and masques for the aristocratic and upper-class audiences of the private theaters. Flourishing as he did in the last years of the golden age of Renaissance drama, he wrote in the traditions of his predecessors: the revenge tragedy of Thomas Kyd and John Webster, the city comedy of Thomas Dekker and Philip Massinger, the humors comedy of Ben Jonson, and the tragicomedy of Francis Beaumont and John Fletcher. Whereas Shirley's tragedies are largely derivative and suggest the decadence common to the serious drama of the decade preceding Oliver Cromwell, the comedies not only recall the past but also look forward to the Restoration comedies of manners written by such men as Sir George Etherege, William Wycherley, and William Congreve, though Shirley is more moral. Among his tragedies, *The Cardinal* does not pale in comparison with Webster's *The Duchess of Malfi* (pr. 1613-1614) or *The White Devil* (pr. 1609-1612), and the comedies *Hyde Park* and *The Lady of Pleasure* still sparkle.

Shirley cannot be credited with any landmark innovations or lasting influence on the stage, but he produced a steady stream of popular plays in which he exploited the themes, devices, and character-types of others while creating dramas uniquely his own, and he was in large measure responsible for the continued vitality of the Renaissance drama into the 1640's. When Massinger died in 1640, Shirley became the principal playwright for the King's Men; only the closing of the theaters two years later ended his career as a dramatist. He had the satisfaction of seeing many of his works (tragedies as well as comedies) revived successfully in the 1660's (though sometimes adapted and presented as if by new playwrights), a distinction

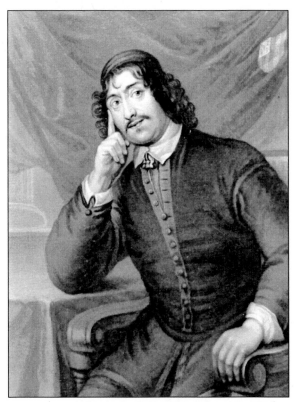

James Shirley (Hulton Archive by Getty Images)

that few of his Renaissance predecessors or contemporaries shared. John Dryden's mocking scorn in *Mac Flecknoe: Or, A Satyre upon the True-Blew-Protestant Poet, T. S.* (1682) is undeserved.

BIOGRAPHY

James Shirley was born in London, probably on September 3, 1596, and baptized on September 7 in St. Mary Woolchurch. On October 4, 1608, he entered the Merchant Taylors' School, which offered the standard classical curriculum, and studied there until 1612. His activities in the next three years are uncertain, though he may have gone to St. John's College, Oxford, while also being apprenticed to a scrivener, Thomas Frith, in London. He was matriculated at St. Catherine's College, Cambridge, in 1615, received the bachelor of arts degree in 1617, and was ordained. Between 1617 and 1625, he worked for his master of arts at Cambridge; married Elizabeth Gilmet; accepted a curacy in Lincolnshire; published his first work, a narrative poem, *Eccho: Or, The Infortunate Lovers* (1618), which is believed to be the same poem as *Narcissus: Or, The Self-Lover*; had two daughters and a son; vacated his living to become headmaster of a St. Albans grammar school; and may have converted to Catholicism.

In 1624, Shirley went to London to become a playwright, and his play *The School of Compliment* was "The first fruits of a muse that before this/ Never saluted audience. . . ." A satiric comedy with a pastoral element that recalls Shakespeare's *As You Like It* (pr. c. 1599-1600), it was revived in the Restoration to Samuel Pepys's delight. During the next decade, Shirley averaged two plays per year, mainly produced for the Phoenix, and became a favorite of Queen Henrietta Maria. When the theaters were closed in 1636 because of the plague, Shirley went to Dublin, where he stayed until 1640, writing plays for John Ogilby's company at the Warburgh Street Theatre. This sojourn in Ireland may have cost him the post of poet laureate, which fell vacant on Jonson's death in 1637 and was awarded the next year to Sir William Davenant. Shirley returned to London in April, 1640, to succeed Philip Massinger as chief dramatist for the King's Men at Blackfriars, but when the Puritans closed the theaters in September, 1642, only three of his plays for the company had been produced; a fourth, *The Court Secret*, was not performed until the Restoration.

Shirley's career as a playwright ended with the Puritan rebellion, at the start of which he reportedly fled London with his patron William Cavendish, later duke of Newcastle, "to join him in the wars." He came back to the city about 1645 and returned to teaching, mainly in the Whitefriars section of London, where he lived. Over the next twenty years he published poetry, masques, a collection of plays, and grammar texts. During the Great Fire of London in October, 1666, Shirley and his second wife, Frances, fled to St. Giles in the Fields, Middlesex, where they died on the same day, October 29, 1666.

ANALYSIS

The pervasive antilicentiousness present in his plays is a trait that links James Shirley to his Elizabethan predecessors more closely than to his Restoration successors. Whatever the genre—tragicomedy, comedy, or tragedy—virtue is either rewarded or, at least, honored. While sexual wrongdoing is not condoned, reformation is accepted. The plays are not, however, homiletic; they are entertainments in the mainstream of earlier Elizabethan practice. As such, careful development of plots and rapid pacing are primary, sometimes to the detriment of characterization. Compare, for example, the Duchess in *The Cardinal* with her counterpart in *The Duchess of Malfi*; the former is shallow, the latter more fully realized. Perhaps because character development is not a central concern in his plays, there are more stereotypes than individuals. This does not detract from the realism of the comedies, however, because the characters are recognizable types, and the action takes place in a realistically portrayed world, a London that Shirley's aristocratic audience would recognize. Not the London of Dekker or Jonson (city merchants and their apprentices are rarely seen in Shirley's comedies), it is closer to the Restoration London of Etherege, Wycherley, and Congreve.

In most of Shirley's plays, there are echoes of earlier dramas. Like his contemporaries and predeces-

sors, he borrowed situations and devices with impunity. Nevertheless, Shirley was more original than most of his fellow playwrights, for though there are frequent similarities or parallels between his and earlier plays, one rarely can point to a direct source. Thus, while *The Cardinal* is in the same revenge tragedy tradition of *The Duchess of Malfi* and certainly must have been written with Webster's play in mind, the earlier work is not its source; there is not even close borrowing. Similarly, although the Enoch Arden motif in *Hyde Park* has an analogue in Dekker's *The Shoemaker's Holiday: Or, The Gentle Craft* (pr. 1600), Dekker's play is not at all a source and, according to Norman Rabkin, "There are no known sources" for *Hyde Park*.

In almost all of his many and varied plays, Shirley uses the old conventions, but he infuses them with a new life. *The Cardinal* may reflect the decadence common to tragedies of the previous decades, but it offers interesting variations on a hackneyed theme. That Shirley's comedies have a distinctive artfulness is confirmed by the critical consensus that they herald the next age as much as they recall the past.

THE WEDDING

Shirley's most noteworthy plays are the comedies *Hyde Park* and *The Lady of Pleasure* and the tragedy *The Cardinal*; a fourth, *The Wedding*, is an early work that is of interest as a Fletcherian tragicomedy. *The Wedding* was a popular play, both on the Caroline stage and in the Restoration. Probably first done at the Phoenix on May 31, 1626, it was printed several times (the first in 1629 with a commendatory poem by John Ford) and was considered a valuable enough property to be included in a 1639 repertory list as a "protected" play. Though Shirley calls it a comedy, it fits Fletcher's description of tragicomedy: "In respect it wants deaths, which is enough to make it no tragedy, yet brings some near it, which is enough to make it no comedy." There are two plots, one serious and one comic, and as in so many early seventeenth century plays, the comic underplot functions fairly independently of the serious business.

The main plot involves the planned marriage of Gratiana, daughter of Sir John Belfare, to Beauford, her "passionate lover." Marwood, Beauford's friend, claims to have seduced Gratiana, which leads to a duel in which Marwood apparently is fatally injured. Beauford then confronts Gratiana, and though she proclaims her chastity and labels Marwood's charge false, Beauford renounces her, and they decide to end their lives. Meanwhile, Marwood, believing he is dying, affirms the truth of his charge, claiming that Cardona, a gentlewoman, had served as bawd. Beauford, having arrayed his quarters as for a funeral, receives news of Marwood's death ("His last breath did forgive you") and a warning that he "must expect/ No safety from the law." Cardona then is brought to Beauford and confesses that while Marwood did "viciously affect" Gratiana, "I knew her virtue was not/ To be corrupted in a thought." Therefore, she reveals, "I did, in hope to make myself a fortune/ And get a husband for my child . . . woo my daughter to/ Supply Gratiana's bed. . . ." Gratiana is brought to Beauford in a coffin, still very much alive, though she has "solicited" her death with prayers, and they renew their vows to each other. Belfare recovers from his temporary madness (brought on by his daughter's disappearance on the eve of her wedding), and Marwood reappears, alive after all and fully recovered. When Cardona tells him of the switch she engineered, he asks forgiveness ("I never had a conscience/ till now.") and agrees to marry Milliscent, the girl he unwittingly had seduced.

The subplot deals with the pursuit of Jane, Justice Lanby's daughter, by three suitors: Rawbone, "a thin citizen," and Lodam, "a fat gentlemen," both Jonsonian humor characters; and Haver, a poor young gentleman who disguises himself as Rawbone's servant in order to have freer access to Jane. The first of the men is a penurious usurer, but Lanby tests his daughter by pretending that he wants her to marry Rawbone. To Lodam—who brings no wealth to a bride, only his own ample self and an imperfect knowledge of foreign languages—Lanby says: "I must refer you, sir, unto my daughter. If you can win her fair opinion, my consent may happily follow." Jane, however, is in love with Haver, who provokes a duel between Lodam and Rawbone and then takes Rawbone's place (in disguise) in the combat. When the men meet at Finsbury to duel, the result is a broadly comic scene.

In its aftermath, the benevolent Lanby pretends to force an immediate marriage between Jane and Rawbone, knowing full well that the apparent Rawbone is Haver in disguise. Jane goes along with the gambit, though believing that her father is cozening her. Lodam's consolation for his lost quest is a dinner; Rawbone gets to deliver the epilogue of the play.

In that epilogue, Rawbone asks the audience "to wake a fool dormant amongst ye. I ha' been kicked, and kicked to that purpose. Maybe they knocked at the wrong door—my brains are asleep in the garret . . . you must clap me . . . I shall hardly come to myself else." Shirley thus draws the attention of the audience to a prevailing theme of the play: people coming to their senses, realizing the truth about themselves, and perhaps even reforming. Hence, the moral ambivalence that is present through most of the play (a trait common to tragicomedy) is confronted in the resolution, when Shirley has his characters face the consequences of their actions. Exclaims Marwood: "Into how many sins hath lust engag'd me!/ Is there a hope you can forgive, and you,/ And she whom I have most dishonour'd?/ I never had a conscience till now."

The Wedding concludes with a typical assembly and reconciliation scene. The plots are linked not only by this scene but also by their common focus on marriage and the subplot's function as a comic contrast to the serious (and potentially tragic) love story of the main plot; the presence of duels in both plots highlights this difference. The device of rival suitors recalls earlier plays, such as Shakespeare's *The Taming of the Shrew* (pr. c. 1593-1594), which also features disguise, while the slapstick duel recalls Shakespeare's *Twelfth Night* (pr. c. 1600-1602) and anticipates Richard Brinsley Sheridan's *The Rivals* (pr. 1775). Belfare's madness harks back to the revenge tragedy of Thomas Kyd, and the bed trick was used earlier in Shakespeare's *Measure for Measure* (pr. 1604), Thomas Middleton and William Rowley's *The Changeling* (pr. 1622), and other Elizabethan plays. In sum, the play is highly derivative, with Shirley utilizing familiar devices, situations, and character types. The combination, however, does work, and the play apparently evoked from audiences the contradictory mix of responses typical of tragicomedy. Because of its genre, it lacks the realistic sophistication of Shirley's later comedies of manners, but considered for what it is—an early work in the Fletcher mode—*The Wedding* certainly succeeds.

HYDE PARK

A better play, *Hyde Park* was licensed on April 20, 1632, and probably was first performed at the Phoenix Theatre on or about that date, to coincide with the seasonal opening of Hyde Park, which King James I had made into a public facility under Sir Henry Rich, earl of Holland. It is an urbane comedy of manners that develops a realistic portrait of Cavalier London at the height of the Caroline period. Popular when it premiered, *Hyde Park* was revived in the Restoration, on which occasion actual horses were brought onstage for the racing scenes.

The action of the play, which occurs on a single day, consists of three plots, each of which, a critic has noted, is "constructed about a love triangle involving a woman and two male rivals." Further, "each plot turns on a surprising change in the woman's position within the triangle," and each is developed as a different kind of comedy: "high comedy appealing to the intellect, sentimental comedy appealing to ethical sensibilities, and simple situation comedy."

On the seventh anniversary of the disappearance at sea of Bonavent, a merchant, his widow finally is ready to remarry, and Lacy is an anxious suitor. Advising against the marriage is the widow's kinswoman, Mistress Carol ("We maids are thought the worse on, for your easiness"), "a malicious piece," according to Lacy, who also says, "'tis pity any place/ But a cold nunnery should be troubled with her." Carol is herself involved in a battle of the sexes with Fairfield, whom she persuades not to make any amorous overtures ("I had rather hear the tedious tales/ Of Holinshed than any thing that trenches/ On love"), and he goes home to "think a satire." She does, however, trifle with two of her servants, she says, "when I have nothing else to do for sport." The supposedly dead Bonavent returns in disguise at the start of the second act, learns of his wife's remarriage that day, and meets Lacy, who invites him to join the wedding celebrations. The third story line concerns Fairfield's

sister Julietta; Trier, who is her suitor; and Lord Bonvile, who intrudes on Trier's turf.

The third and fourth acts are set in Hyde Park and afford an opportunity for Shirley to depict the leisure class at play. Lord Bonvile advances his pursuit of Julietta as Trier hovers, Fairfield bids what he thinks is his final farewell to Carol, and the impending races (among men and horses) become a metaphor for all the competing lovers in the play. As the action progresses, Carol loses a second round to Fairfield, tricked by him and her servant into revealing her true feelings ("O love, I am thy captive . . ."), though still attempting to maintain some distance while Fairfield has the upper hand. The fourth act ends with Bonavent making his first move toward discarding his disguise and revealing himself to his wife.

At the start of the last act, Carol tells Julietta of her fears for Fairfield's well-being as a result of a letter from him. When the presumably distraught suitor is found, Carol proposes to him—not for love, she avers, but because she is merciful and desires to save his life. He denies authorship of the plaintive piece (which was written by one of Carol's servants) and tells her: "To save thy life, I'll not be troubled with thee." She pleads, "I know you love me still; do not refuse me," and he relents: "Each other's now by conquest, come let's to 'em." In the concluding assembly scene, Julietta rejects Trier and accepts Lord Bonvile, and Bonavent removes his disguise and reclaims his wife. In each of the pairings, therefore, a dark horse eventually triumphs, and the losers good-naturedly accept their unexpected misfortune.

Hyde Park is a successful play whose portrait of London life reminds one commentator of the portrayal of London in Dekker's *The Shoemaker's Holiday*. The play is also Elizabethan in other respects, too: clever servants, letters that advance the plots, disguise, and multiple plots. The romance between Carol and Fairfield recalls Beatrice and Benedick of Shakespeare's *Much Ado About Nothing* (pr. c. 1598-1599), and Carol is a descendant of Beaumont and Fletcher's scornful lady character. Shirley also anticipates his Restoration successors, for *Hyde Park* is a comedy of manners—though one in which pre-Restoration standards of sexual propriety are observed. Carol and Fairfield also look ahead to Millamant and Mirabell of Congreve's *The Way of the World* (pr. 1700); their verbal sparring parallels the proviso scene and marital conditions agreement that are central to that play and other Restoration comedies.

Hyde Park, then, is a typical Shirley city comedy, as lively and as realistic as those of Middleton or Dekker, but concerned with a very different London, that of the upper classes and their pastimes. What problems they have revolve about romantic entanglements and intrigues of the love chase and little else, but all of this Shirley handles with dexterity and in conformity with his moral precepts. The thematic core of the play is Lord Bonvile's attempted seduction of Julietta, to which she reacts with a lengthy and eloquent paean to chastity: "unless you prove/ A friend to virtue, were your honor centupled,/ Could you pile titles till you reach the clouds,/ Were every petty manor you possess/ A kingdom, and the blood of many princes/ United in your veins . . . / Yet I . . . am/ As much above you in my innocence." He is moved to immediate repentance: "If this be true, what a wretched thing should I/ Appear now, if I were anything but a lord?/ I do not like myself." He asks for her hand: "since there's no remedy,/ Be honest!" Lord Bonvile's conversion from libertinism not only distinguishes him from the ubiquitous rake of the Restoration but also highlights the primary difference between this play and its successors in the next age.

THE LADY OF PLEASURE

The Lady of Pleasure also is a comedy of manners, and in it Shirley develops variations on the theme of honor. It may even be a commentary on a Platonic love cult in the Caroline court. Licensed in 1635 and performed at the Phoenix Theatre, the satiric play was not as popular in the seventeenth century as other Shirley works, but later playwrights did adapt characters, plot elements, and bits of dialogue from it for their use. Most notable, perhaps, is Sheridan's indebtedness in *The School for Scandal* (pr. 1777); Sheridan's Sir Peter and Lady Teazle are obvious descendants of Shirley's Sir Thomas Bornwell and his wife Aretina, and the conceit of the scandal school also owes something to Shirley.

The play begins with Sir Thomas, a country gentleman, and his wife newly arrived in London so that she can enjoy the city's pleasures, including gambling and partying and wasting their wealth on paintings, furniture, and clothing. The profligate Aretina quickly develops a salon, which includes a bawd named Madam Decoy, and a pair of gallants, Alexander Kickshaw and John Littleworth. The men are interested in Celestina, Lady Bellamour, a young widow whose year of mourning has passed. Aretina sees Celestina as a potential rival, and Bornwell comments: "Now my Lady/ Is troubled, as she feared to be eclipsed/ This news will cost me somewhat." He decides, therefore, to pretend to renounce thrift and embrace her lifestyle, hoping that when she sees an image of herself, she will be frightened into reformation. Meanwhile, Celestina's steward cautions her about living beyond her means, but she resolves "to pay some delight; my estate will bear it." The parallel patterns of the two plots are obvious from the start of the play: Celestina, too, has a gentleman caller and looks forward to lady visitors, whom she will instruct in the social graces.

When Aretine's nephew Frederick arrives from the university in his scholar's black satin uniform, she is appalled: "What luck [misfortune] I did not send him into France!" She commends him to Kickshaw's breeding, Littleworth offers to teach Frederick "postures and rudiments," and Aretina's steward opens the wine cellar to him. The second act ends with Bornwell visiting the young widow Celestina to become acquainted and to invite her to his home; the third act begins at the home of a nobleman who is distantly related to Aretina. Mourning for fair Bella Maria, he rejects Madam Decoy's services as bawd to effect a liaison with Aretina; rather, he warns Aretina of the designs that Decoy has on her honor. When she receives his warning, Aretina decides to use the bawd's services to enter instead into a secret liaison with Kickshaw. She also employs Kickshaw and Littleworth to embarrass Celestina, but the younger woman holds her own against the onslaught, and Bornwell comes to her aid when he realizes that she is being victimized. The act ends with Kickshaw receiving a summons to a tryst with a secret admirer.

In the farcical first scene of the fourth act, Decoy—disguised as a hag—entices Kickshaw to her bedroom, where Aretina awaits him under cover of darkness. The largely satiric second scene focuses initially on young Frederick's transformation into a fop. Then, when Aretina and Bornwell are alone, Bornwell attempts to make his wife jealous by confessing his love for Celestina: "I must/ Acknowledge twas thy cure to disenchant me/ From a dull husband to an active lover." Instead of being offended, Aretina replies: "I must acknowledge Celestina/ Most excellently fair, fair above all/ The beauties I ha' seen. . . ." Further, "she is a piece so angelically moving, I should think/ Frailty excused to dote upon her form,/ And almost virtue to be wicked with her." Bornwell is confused. In the final scene of the act, a seriocomic one, Aretina's distant kinsman visits Celestina, who tests him ("I am man enough, but knew not where,/ Until this meeting, beauty dwelt"), but when he is tempted to make advances, she reminds the nobleman of his honorable reputation and his devotion to the late Bella Maria. Virtue will be rewarded.

The fifth act, though a single scene, also falls into three sections, the first of which has Aretina becoming aware of her husband's large gaming losses and learning that he has "summed up" his estate "and find we may have/ A month good yet." As for their prospects beyond the month, he proposes to become a soldier and suggests that she could "find a trade to live by." As Aretina starts to assess her uncertain future, Decoy, Kickshaw, and Frederick arrive. The boastful talkativeness of Kickshaw and her drunken nephew's romantic overtures ("My blood is rampant too, I must court some body,/ As good my Aunt as any other body") shock her, and she is ready for conversion. Momentarily left alone, she looks in a mirror: "'Tis a false glass; sure I am more deformed./ What have I done? My soul is miserable." The lord who earlier warned his kinswoman Aretina about Decoy comes in, followed by Bornwell and Celestina. While Bornwell consoles his repentant wife, the lord and young widow form "an honorable alliance." The Bornwells will return to the country with "wealth enough,/ If yet we use it nobly," Frederick will return

to college, and Kickshaw is implored to "purge . . . foul blood by repentance."

Although *The Lady of Pleasure* foreshadows Restoration comedies of manners in subject matter, plot, character types, and witty dialogue, its focus on honor and the movement from folly and libertinism to repentance and reformation distinguish it from the later plays, for ultimately it celebrates moderation, honor, and innocence. In addition, Shirley makes it clear, as a critic has noted, that both the highest and the lowest classes share the responsibility for conducting themselves in a manner suiting their station in life.

Notable, too, as a pre-Restoration quality is the unemotional tone of the play, for superficial flirtation rather than romantic involvement is what Shirley largely portrays, and Celestina, wise beyond her sixteen years, delivers the keynote, assuring Mariana and Isabella that "men shall never/ Make my heart lean with sighing, nor with tears/ Draw on my eyes the infamy of spectacles," and then advising them: "'Tis the chief principle to keep your heart/ Under your own obedience; jest, but love not." Finally, there is a shallowness to the upper-class lifestyle depicted in *The Lady of Pleasure*, still another trait that it shares with the post-1660 comedies of manners.

THE CARDINAL

Licensed in 1641, *The Cardinal* is one of four extant tragedies by Shirley and his first tragedy for the King's Men at Blackfriars. Both in his dedication (in which he calls it "the best of my flock") and in his prologue ("this play/ Might rival with his best"), Shirley indicates his own high regard for the play. Many critics agree with him, rating it among the best tragedies of the period, but some point to Shirley's indebtedness to Kyd, Webster, and other predecessors in the revenge tragedy tradition, and one labels the play a "shallow imitation." Derivative though it may be, *The Cardinal* is powerful theater and was a popular stage vehicle both before the closing of the theaters and during the Restoration period. Coming as it does at the end of a half century of revenge tragedy that began with Kyd's *The Spanish Tragedy* (pr. c. 1585-1589), one is surprised at how much originality and vitality it possesses.

The Duchess Rosaura of Navarre, widowed before her youthful marriage was consummated, is betrothed to Don Columbo, a grim-faced and rough-hewn soldier who is nephew to the cardinal, the power behind the throne; her true love is Count d'Alvarez, a young man who is said to be perfectly suited to her (says a lord: "Hymen cannot tie/ A knot of two more equal hearts and blood"), but she has wisely deferred to the king's wishes and "given this treasure up." When war with Aragon begins, the arranged marriage is postponed because Columbo is chosen to lead Navarre's forces. Learning of the unexpected turn of events, the duchess is joyous ("I have not skill to contain myself"), but in the presence of the king, the cardinal, and Columbo himself, she dissembles and maintains the proper facade. When Alvarez comes in, however, she prods him to respect their "mutual vows," but he is unwilling to risk the others' displeasure unless Columbo is killed in battle or renounces his claim.

The action of the second act begins on the battlefield; Columbo is impatient to storm the enemy, but Hernando advises restraint. The disagreement leads Hernando to resign his commission, and he returns to Navarre with a letter giving Columbo's decision to attack. Complementing this action is the arrival of a letter for Columbo from the duchess in which she asks him to resign his "interest to her person, promise, or love." He decides that she is testing him ("'Tis a device to hasten my return;/ Love has a thousand arts") and sends the desired release. The duchess gives Columbo's reply to the king and obtains his permission to wed Alvarez. The cardinal is angry at the unexpected turn of events. He calls Alvarez effeminate and counsels the duchess to leave him, but she is defiant, and the act closes with the cardinal vowing that "action and revenge/ Must calm her fury."

Preparations for the marriage are under way when news arrives of Columbo's triumph and imminent return. The cardinal's passion rises: "He has not won so much upon the Aragon/ As he has lost at home; and his neglect/ Of what my studies had contrived to add/ More lustre to our family by the access/ Of the great duchess' fortune, cools his triumph,/ And makes me wild." Masquers who have prepared a wedding entertainment are asked to delay their presentation so "a company of cavaliers in gallant equipage, newly alighted" can present their revels. At the start, they beckon to the bridegroom, and Alvarez accompanies them. A moment later they return with his body, and Columbo removes his disguise and admits to having committed the murder. The duchess calls for justice, but the king wavers and seeks a way out, for Columbo is a military hero and the cardinal's nephew. Ultimately, though, he decides that not the murder but a breach of decorum deserves punishment: "This contempt/ Of majesty transcends my power to pardon,/ And you shall feel my anger, sir."

Columbo soon is freed, and while not formally pardoned, he is "graced now more than ever" and "courted as preserver of his country." His rehabilitation is attributed to the cardinal's influence, and there is speculation that a match between him and the duchess again may be in prospect. When Columbo visits her, he warns her not to remarry: "I'll kill the next at th' altar and quench all/ The smiling tapers with his blood. . . ." Hernando then comes to her, expresses his devotion to her and Alvarez, and promises to exact vengeance on Columbo and the cardinal. The cardinal then approaches the duchess in a conciliatory manner, but she sees through the deceitful ploys of "this cozening statesman" and remains determined that "this Cardinal must not be long-lived." Toward this end, she will feign madness. The act concludes with a duel between Hernando and Columbo in which the latter is killed.

The death grieves the king and cardinal, and Hernando's disappearance causes suspicion to fall on him. Hernando returns in disguise, renews his pledge to the duchess, and hides in her room when the cardinal (who has been made guardian of the apparently mad duchess) comes for dinner. Though the cleric is troubled that "her loss of brain" means she "is now beneath [his] great revenge" and "is not capable to feel [his] anger," he nevertheless intends to rape and poison her and make it seem as if she committed suicide. Once he embraces and kisses her, however, he feels "a strong enchantment from her lips" and he fears that he "shall forgive Columbo's death" if she yields to him. In the event, she denies his overtures, he forces her, and Hernando rushes from behind the arras, stabs the cardinal, and kills himself. To the king and others, the cardinal (who believes his wounds are fatal) says he has poisoned the duchess, but as proof of his repentance he offers an antidote "to preserve her innocent life." Both drink it, after which he reveals that it really was a deadly poison, and both he and the duchess die. The cardinal, however, has been caught in his "own engine," for the surgeon tells him before his death, "Your wounds, sir, were not desperate."

The Spanish Tragedy, Shakespeare's *Hamlet, Prince of Denmark* (pr. c. 1600-1601), *The Duchess of Malfi*, John Ford's *The Broken Heart* (pr. c. 1627-1631), and Cyril Tourneur's *The Atheist's Tragedy* (pr. c. 1607) are the most obvious antecedents of *The Cardinal*, and the links between it and its predecessors are immediately apparent: murder of a rival by a jealous lover, support for the murderer by a Machiavellian villain anxious for advancement or wealth, madness (real or feigned) as a result of grief, a play-within-a-play, and revenge as an obsessive motive.

Though Fredson Bowers's judgment that *The Cardinal* is "clear-cut, coherent Kydian revenge tragedy" is valid, Shirley departs significantly from past practice in his mystifying prologue. In these lighthearted, even flippant, twenty-six lines of heroic couplets, the playwright teases his audience, refusing to reveal whether *The Cardinal* is a comedy or a tragedy and even suggesting by his style and tone that it is the former: "Whether the comic Muse, or ladies' love,/ Romance, or direful tragedy it prove,/ The bill determines not; and would you be/ Persuaded, I would have 't a Comedy." Self-mockery and a satiric reference to classical dramatic theory increase the mysteriousness of the prologue, and their presence may reflect Shirley's sensitivity at offering an old-fashioned revenge tragedy to his new Blackfriars constituency.

Variations on the color red and frequent allusions to blood pervade *The Cardinal* and create an imagistic texture that complements the horror of the events. The nobility of the duchess, Alvarez, and Hernando contrasts sharply with the depravity of the cardinal and Columbo, and the equivocal morality of the king and Celinda (a court lady) completes the social picture. Shirley falters a bit, however, in his de-lineation of the character of his heroine, for the duchess makes a fundamental error when she misjudges the true nature of Columbo, and her unnecessary avowal to Hernando further diminishes her. Finally, she mistakenly considers the cardinal responsible for the murder of Alvarez. In other words, Duchess Rosaura, memorable though she is, is no Duchess of Malfi, nor has Shirley given her dramatics moments that match Webster's mad scenes.

It is ironic that at the close of his career as a playwright, James Shirley's most memorable work should be one that recalls past stage practice because so many of his earlier plays anticipate those of the next age. The success of *The Cardinal* notwithstanding, Shirley was at his best as a comic playwright, and within the parameters that he set for himself, he wrote creditable comedies of manners that struck a responsive chord not only among his Caroline audience but also on the Restoration stage in the 1660's.

OTHER MAJOR WORKS

POETRY: *Eccho: Or, The Infortunate Lovers*, 1618; *Poems &c. by James Shirley*, 1646 (includes *Narcissus: Or, The Self-Lover*).

NONFICTION: *Via ad Latinam Linguam Complanata: The Way Made Plain to the Latin Tongues*, 1649 (also as *Grammatica anglo-latina*, 1651); *The Rudiments of Grammar*, 1656 (enlarged as *Manductio*, 1660); *An Essay Towards an Universal and Rational Grammar*, 1726 (Jenkin Thomas Philipps, compiler and editor; from Shirley's writings on grammar).

BIBLIOGRAPHY

Burner, Sandra A. *James Shirley: A Study of Literary Coteries and Patronage in Seventeenth Century England*. Lanham, Md.: University Press of America, 1988. This biography of Shirley focuses on the literary circles and patrons of the theater in seventeenth century England. Bibliography and index.

Clark, Ira. *Professional Playwrights: Massinger, Ford, Shirley, and Brome*. Lexington: University Press of Kentucky, 1992. Clark looks at English drama in the seventeenth century, focusing on Shirley, Philip Massinger, John Ford, and Richard Brome. Bibliography and index.

Lucow, Ben. *James Shirley*. New York: Twayne, 1981. Opening chapters on the dramatist's biography, masques, and nondramatic verse are followed by a chronological discussion of the plays. An excellent introduction to Shirley's drama combines plot summaries with pertinent background material and critical analyses. Contains a chronology of the author's life and a select bibliography of primary and secondary sources.

Sanders, Julie. *Caroline Drama: The Plays of Massinger, Ford, Shirley, and Brom.* Plymouth, England: Northcote House, in association with the British Council, 1999. Sanders examines the plays of Shirley as well as those of Philip Massinger,

John Ford, and Richard Brome. Bibliography and index.

Zimmer, Ruth K. *James Shirley: A Reference Guide.* Boston: G. K. Hall, 1980. Zimmer annotates works by and about Shirley published through 1978. The secondary sources include bibliographies, books and articles, commentaries on Shirley within larger works, theses and dissertations, and poems in praise of the dramatist. Also includes a brief sketch of Shirley's life, a chronology of his extant works, and an overview of his dramatic career.

Gerald H. Strauss,
updated by Ayne Cantrell

YEVGENY SHVARTS

Born: Kazan, Russia; October 21, 1896
Died: Komarovo, U.S.S.R.; January 15, 1958

PRINCIPAL DRAMA

Undervud, pr. 1929, pb. 1930
Pustyaki, pr., pb. 1932
Klad, pr. 1933, pb. 1960
Priklyucheniya Gogenshtaufena, pb. 1934
Goly korol, wr. 1934, pr., pb. 1960 (*The Naked King*, 1968)
Krasnaya Shapochka, pr. 1937, pb. 1960
Nashe go stepriimstvo, pb. 1939
Snezhnaya Koroleva, pr. 1939, pb. 1960
Ten, pr. 1940, pb. 1960 (*The Shadow*, 1963)
Dalyokiy Kray, wr. 1942, pb. 1950
Drakon, pr. 1944, pb. 1960 (*The Dragon*, 1961)
Povest o molodykh suprugakh, wr. 1949-1956, pr. 1957, pb. 1960
Dva Klena, pr. 1954, pb. 1960 (*The Two Maples*, 1977)
Pesy, pb. 1962

OTHER LITERARY FORMS

Yevgeny Shvarts began his literary career in the 1920's as a writer of poetry and stories for children.

In the 1930's, he wrote some prose adaptations of Hans Christian Andersen's fairy tales; in the 1940's, he wrote a number of original, realistic stories for children about contemporary life. The best-known of these, *Pervoklassnits* (1947; the first grader), was made into a film in 1948. Other film scenarios by Shvarts include *Razbudite Lenochku* (1933; wake up, Lenochka), *Zolushka* (1947; Cinderella), and *Don Quixote* (1957).

ACHIEVEMENTS

Yevgeny Shvarts succeeded, perhaps better than any other Soviet playwright, in popularizing the formally sophisticated avant-garde theatrical styles that reached their maturity under Vsevolod Meyerhold in the 1920's but then, in the Stalinist years from 1930 to 1956, either were repressed for political reasons or lost out in competition with the old, established realist tradition of the Moscow Art Theatre and the new tradition of socialist realism. Shvarts is an anomaly because he made his major contributions to the Soviet avant-garde tradition in the period from 1934 to 1944, after that tradition was dead or dying or had gone underground elsewhere in Soviet theater.

Shvarts drew the materials for his plays from stories that had become familiar in Soviet mass culture through published translations of fairy tales by Andersen and Charles Perrault and of popular versions of medieval romances. He also drew on nonliterary sources—his audience's collective memory of Russian folktales. He elegantly reworked these materials drawn from popular and folk sources, transforming them in his stylized adaptations. He succeeded in returning them to popular theater and film, where they enriched Soviet popular culture both as individual classics and as continuations of the 1920's avant-garde tradition.

Shvarts is officially recognized in the Soviet Union primarily for his adaptations of fairy tales for children's theater. His versions of "Little Red Riding Hood," "The Snow Queen," and "Cinderella" are part of the standard repertoire of Soviet children's theaters and children's film series. He is also officially recognized for some of the works that he wrote for adult audiences, such as his screenplay for the Soviet version of *Don Quixote*. Yet he receives only unofficial recognition for his three major political plays: *The Naked King*, *The Shadow*, and *The Dragon*.

The political question yet to be resolved in official Russian scholarship is whether, as political satire, these three plays are aimed exclusively at Fascist Germany or whether their target is Stalinist Russia as well. Shvarts's Soviet biographer Sergei Tsimbal asserted that these plays are anti-Fascist satires. In the brief period between 1960 and 1962, however, when Nikita Khrushchev's regime gave official support to anti-Stalinist literature and criticism, there was some official recognition that Shvarts's political plays might have been directed against both Adolf Hitler and Joseph Stalin. For one brief theatrical season in 1960, the political plays were performed in official, professional theaters and were finally published in a 1960 edition of Shvarts's major plays. Yet, 1960 turned out to be the only year when *The Dragon* and *The Shadow* passed official censorship either for publication or for performance in a professional theater. As a result, Shvarts's Soviet reputation as a political satirist is based almost entirely on his place in the repertoire of unofficial, amateur theaters, which frequently perform *The Dragon* and *The Shadow*.

BIOGRAPHY

Yevgeny Lvovich Shvarts was born on October 21, 1896, in the city of Kazan on the Volga River. His father, Lev Borisovich Shvarts, was from a Jewish family and worked as a provincial doctor. He was one of the many liberals of Anton Chekhov's generation who dedicated themselves to the gradual reform of Russian society through their work as educated professionals (doctors, teachers, and so on) within the provincial government. Shvarts's mother, Maria Fyodorovna, came from a Russian Orthodox family, was well educated generally, and was particularly interested in theater. The family moved several times in Shvarts's youth—from Kazan to Dmitrov near Moscow, then back to Kazan, and, at the outbreak of World War I, to Maikop in the northern Caucasus and to Rostov-on-the-Don. Shvarts began the study of law at Moscow University during the first year of the war but then left the university in 1915 and returned to Rostov. In 1917, he joined an amateur avant-garde theater in Rostov called the Theater Workshop, where he became a character actor, specializing in comic roles. His first marriage was to one of the actresses from the Theater Workshop, Gaiane Khaladzieva.

When the Russian Revolution and Civil War were over in 1921, Shvarts moved to Petrograd (rechristened Leningrad in 1924) with other members of Rostov's Theater Workshop. The attempt to establish their experimental workshop as a professional theater failed after its second season, but the move to Petrograd had put Shvarts in touch with the leading members of the literary intelligentsia there. He soon became personal secretary to Kornei Chukovsky; he was an active member of the writers' club known as The Crazy Ship; and in 1925, he became an editor and writer for two children's magazines, *Hedgehog* and *Siskin*. Together with his chief editor, Samuil Marshak, Shvarts encouraged the collaboration of leading experimental prose writers and poets (such as Danil Kharms and Nikolai Zabolotsky) in the writing of children's literature.

Shvarts wrote his first play, *Undervud*, in 1929 for the Leningrad children's theater TIUZ; in 1932, he wrote *Pustyaki* (trifles) for the Leningrad Puppet Theater; and in 1933 and 1934, he wrote three plays: *Klad* (the treasure), *Priklyucheniya Gogenshtaufena* (the adventures of Hohenstauffen), and *The Naked King*. Except for *The Naked King*, all these early plays are clearly written for children and combine a realistic portrayal of contemporary life with fantastic elements (for example, *Undervud* is about the theft of a typewriter from an office by a woman who turns out to be a witch). *The Naked King* is different from the earlier plays in that its erotic and political themes make it more appropriate for adults than for children; it also marks the beginning of Shvarts's works as a dramatic adapter of popular tales.

In 1934, Shvarts also began his friendship and collaboration with Nikolai Akimov, director of the Comedy Theater in Leningrad. With Akimov's encouragement to continue adapting popular stories according to ironic, fantastic, avant-garde styles, Shvarts wrote his *Krasnaya Shapochka* (Little Red Riding Hood) and *Snezhnaya Koroleva* (the Snow Queen), both of which immediately became perennial favorites in the repertoires of Soviet children's theaters. Three of the plays he wrote in the period from 1939 to 1942 were straightforward realistic representations of the Soviet Union's struggle against Germany: *Nashe go stepriimstvo* (our hospitality), *Dalyokiy Kray* (distant region), and "Odna Noch" (one night), the last of which is a modest, unheroic autobiographical account of his own experience of the blockade of Leningrad in 1941 to 1942. In spite of the hardships of the war, Shvarts also wrote his two most innovative and most political plays in this period: *The Shadow* and *The Dragon*.

Shvarts was subjected to criticism and censorship during the "anti-cosmopolitain" campaign that began in Soviet letters in 1946 and continued until after Stalin's death in 1953. He was vulnerable to criticism because both *The Shadow* and *The Dragon* could be interpreted as anti-Stalinist political satire, because so much of his writing was based on Western European models, and because he was Jewish. In this period, he began writing realist plays and stories about problems of family life in contemporary Soviet life. In the 1950's, he returned to writing fairy-tale plays, but he now drew on Russian folk sources (as in *The Two Maples*) rather than on Western European models.

In the late 1950's, Shvarts's health began to fail, but he completed the scenario for Grigori Kozintsev's film version of *Don Quixote* in 1957, shortly before his death.

ANALYSIS

The distinctive feature of Yevgeny Shvarts's style is his use of "old stories" to provide the plots, characters, and even the settings and costumes for his plays. This creates a reflexive sense of dramatic fiction as a playful, ironic variation on narrative fiction. His characters refer to themselves as the roles that they have been designated to play in old stories, and much of their dialogue refers explicitly to how the play's action is progressing in relation to the fairy-tale plot or plots of which it is an adaptation. The dramatic conflict in a Shvarts play is typically a struggle between one group of characters, who want their old stories to be reenacted in accordance with their old plots, and another group of characters, who attempt to change the old story. For example, in *The Shadow*, the hero knows that his life follows the plot of Andersen's tale "The Shadow," in which the hero's romantic idealism is destroyed by the cynicism of his worldly shadow or double. He attempts to change the outcome of the Andersen tale and maintain his idealism, while his shadow attempts to reenact the Andersen plot.

Sometimes the self-conscious ironic emphasis on plot in a Shvarts play serves a comic, lyrical function. For example, in *The Naked King*, the character Christian uses plot devices from Andersen fairy tales to promote the exuberant, comic love between the hero, Henryk, and the heroine, Henrietta. Christian's artful invention of Andersen-inspired twists in the love plot is designed to prevent the impatient heroine from proceeding directly to the kissing and lovemaking that are the desired end of romance, but which, if reached too soon, would silence the aesthetic expression of romantic desire.

Sometimes, however, the plots of Shvarts's plays express his tragic moral philosophy. In *The Shadow*, the shadow's cynical reenactment of the old Andersen plot asserts the powerlessness of moral faith and free will in the real world, while the scholar-hero's attempts to change the Andersen plot assert his faith in his own moral values. In a number of plays, such as *Krasnaya Shapochka*, *The Shadow*, and *The Dragon*, Shvarts uses the plots of old fairy tales to assert the pessimistic view that good is usually defeated by evil, given the endemic strength of evil in human nature and in the "dragons" of political institutions. He then presents his moral heroes and heroines (such as Little Red Riding Hood or Lancelot of *The Dragon*) as possessors of an absurd existentialist faith in the power of their own actions to thwart the seemingly inevitable triumph of evil.

Drawing on the Gogolian models and popular carnivalesque traditions that Meyerhold had introduced to Russian avant-garde theater, Shvarts complemented his main plot lines with a zany, carnivalesque profusion of subplots and verbal banter. This aspect of Shvarts's writing is aptly described by Mikhail Leonidovich Slonimsky's term for Gogolian comedy— "comedy whose name is muddle." *The Naked King* creates a "muddle" by confusing or inverting a number of opposed categories: high and low classes are confused as the heroine-princess falls in love with the hero-swineherd, humans and pigs are confused as the swineherd gives his pigs the names of the king's ladies-in-waiting, and so on. Muddles such as these are at the center of many of Shvarts's most hilarious comic scenes, yet they may also appear in a dark, satiric light in his political plays when they are the creations of rogue-bureaucrats (such as the Mayor and his son in *The Dragon*) who create political muddles to obfuscate and confuse simple moral responses to their corrupt reigns. From Henryk of *The Naked King* to Lancelot of *The Dragon*, Shvarts's heroic characters possess the roguish ability to best their antagonists in duels of obfuscation. Perhaps Shvarts's greatest accomplishment as a playwright is to have created a number of brilliantly witty verbal duels between villains who are geniuses at obfuscation and heroes who can match the villains in this respect while also being able to penetrate muddles of amorality or immorality with their simple, clear moral vision.

The Naked King and *The Dragon* are Shvarts's two best dramatic works. Together, they provide a good example of how the main plots of his plays are adaptations of popular fairy tales and legends, while the subplots are generated according to the zany, comic principles of Gogolian "muddle." Together, they also represent the full spectrum of his moral vision, ranging from the optimistic comedy of *The Naked King* to the pessimistic satire of *The Dragon*.

THE NAKED KING

As the curtain opens in act 1 of *The Naked King*, Henryk, the swineherd, is tending his pigs in a meadow and telling his friend Christian, the weaver, how much he loves the Princess, who lives in the castle nearby. Unlike the swineherd of Andersen's "The Princess and the Swineherd," Henryk is not a prince in disguise; he is a swineherd, but he borrows the plot from Andersen's tale to lure the Princess out of the castle to visit him: He offers to let her see the magic kettle that Christian has made and then offers to exchange the kettle for kisses from the Princess. The premise of the plot in Andersen's tale is the swineherd-prince's need to overcome the Princess's resistance to his love. The Princess covets material things such as the kettle but does not value the prince's spiritual love. Andersen's prince catches his Princess with the material kettle but does not gain her spiritual love. In Shvarts's play, on the other hand, the Princess offers no resistance to Henryk's love. She is quick to offer eighty, then one hundred kisses in exchange for the kettle.

While Henryk and the Princess are in the middle of their first, seemingly endless kiss, they are interrupted by the Princess's father, who tells his daughter: "Tomorrow I'll marry you off to our neighboring king." The scene changes then to an inn along the road that leads to the neighboring king, where that king's Minister of Tender Feelings is arranging a reception for the Princess. He hopes to find out whether the Princess is of royal blood by subjecting her to the test that is at the base of the plot of Andersen's "The Princess and the Pea." He hides a pea under the featherbeds on which the Princess sleeps at the inn: If she notices the pea, she will be proven of royal blood. If this test fails, he has a backup—twelve bottles of strong wine with which he hopes to loosen the tongues of the Chamberlain and Governess accompanying the Princess. The scene in which the Minister interrogates the drunken Chamberlain is a prime example of Gogolian muddle in Shvarts: The Chamberlain imagines in his drunken delirium that he is at a fox hunt; he refers to his princess as "a vixen with a tail"; the Minister taunts him with, "so you've got a king with a tail" and when the drunken chamberlain replies, "Why no, our King's tail-less, but *her* father has a tail," the Minister deduces that the Princess is not of royal blood.

Zany nonsense such as this derails Christian's attempts to bring about the marriage between Henryk and the Princess, but Christian remains undaunted. In act 2, he schemes to prevent the king's marriage to the Princess by borrowing from the plot of Andersen's famous story "The Emperor's New Clothes." He offers to sew the king a wedding suit that only stupid and incompetent people will be unable to see; all the king's ministers therefore pretend to see his new clothes. When the king appears naked at the royal wedding, a child exclaims "He's naked and he's fat!" prompting all the king's subjects to jeer and whistle him offstage and thereby clearing the way for the Princess to marry Henryk. This light, comic ending is delayed and postponed throughout act 2 by more zany Gogolian satire, the object of which is the absurd extremes of pretentiousness and hypocrisy in the king's court. In *The Naked King*, this satire of political hypocrisy simply functions to set up the comic resolution of the romantic plot. In *The Dragon*, however, hypocrisy and pretense are seen as ludicrous but terrifying elements of political despotism.

THE DRAGON

As act 1 of *The Dragon* begins, the hero, Lancelot, stops to rest from his journey at the house of Charlemagne, Chief Archivist of the local Dragon's kingdom. Lancelot is told by a cat that Charlemagne's daughter, Elza, is threatened by a great misfortune: She has been selected as this year's sacrifice to the Dragon that has been ruling the city for nearly four

hundred years. When Charlemagne and Elza return home, they tell Lancelot that he will be able to rest well in their "very quiet city" where "nothing ever happens." Having recently heard that Elza is about to be sacrificed to the Dragon, Lancelot is surprised to hear the city described as quiet, but Charlemagne explains to him that it is quiet because the Dragon is such "an amazing strategist and great tactician" that "as long as he is here, no other dragon will dare touch us."

Asked to tell where he is from, Lancelot says that he is a reader of a book that "records all the crimes of all the criminals, all the misfortunes of those suffering in vain." Dedicated to interceding on behalf of these sufferers, Lancelot admits wearily that he has been "mortally wounded three times by the people [he] was saving by force." Following his script as faithful defender of innocent victims, Lancelot announces that he "will call the dragon out to do battle," even though Elza beseeches him not to fight, fearing that he will be killed.

At this point, the Dragon makes his appearance in a number of guises, some human, some superhuman, but all signifying a combination of invincible power and mystification. Undaunted by the Dragon's displays of power and by blatant evidence that the people of the town would rather be left alone to suffer their Dragon in peace, Lancelot prepares for battle.

In act 2, Lancelot fights the Dragon while the Dragon's top government bureaucrats, the Mayor and his son Henryk, prepare to take credit for Lancelot's brave exploits and set themselves up as the city's new dragons. Seeming to have been mortally wounded in battle, Lancelot withdraws from the city after killing the Dragon, while the mayor's son takes over as the new dragon and prepares to marry Elza.

Meanwhile, in the ironic, unsentimental romantic plot that relates Elza to Lancelot as damsel in distress to faithful knight-savior, Elza's feelings have changed. Early in the first act, she is as cynical as Henryk in accepting the evil reign of the Dragon. By the end of act 1, she is still uncertain about whether she would obey Henryk's order to kill Lancelot. In act 2, however, Elza and Lancelot begin to feel some love for each other in spite of their mutual ironic sense that they are merely going through the motions, playing tired and trite romantic roles. By the end of the play, Elza wants to be saved from the cynicism she shared with Henryk at the beginning of the play; she desires Lancelot's return.

In the final scenes, Lancelot returns to the city, easily deposes Henryk as false pretender to the throne, and berates the citizens of the city for pretending to believe in Henryk's impersonation of the Dragon. Lancelot himself is burdened with Ivan Karamazov's skepticism about the ability of ordinary people to maintain faith in the power of love and virtue, given their fearful, morally lazy desire to surrender their moral freedom to powerful political authorities. *The Dragon* is a pessimistic, satiric play insofar as it is ultimately centered on Lancelot's doubts about his ability to rule the citizens of the city through the moral authority of his own example, rather than through the combination of coercive power and pretense represented in the alliance between the Dragon and Henryk.

The two opposite poles of Shvarts's moral vision are represented in *The Naked King* and *The Dragon*— on one hand, his optimistic faith that adults can regain a simple, childlike sense of right and wrong in their political lives and *see* that the king has no clothes, thereby deposing him, and, on the other hand, his pessimistic sense that people are too likely to surrender to hypocrisy and cowardice and accept despotic rule.

OTHER MAJOR WORKS

SHORT FICTION: *Rasskaz Staroi Balakaiki*, 1925; *Karta S Prikliucheniiami*, 1930; *Prikliucheniia Mukhi*, 1932; *Prikliuchenii V. I. Medvedia*, 1932; *Prikliucheniia Shury i Marusi*, 1937; *Chuzhaia devochka*, 1937; *Pervoklassnits*, 1947.

POETRY: *Voronenok*, 1925; *Rynok*, 1926; *Shariki*, 1926; *Na moroze*, 1927; *Kto bystrei?*, 1930.

SCREENPLAYS: *Razbudite Lenochku*, 1933; *Zolushka*, 1947; *Pervoklassnits*, 1948; *Don Quixote*, 1957 (based on Miguel de Cervantes' novel).

MISCELLANEOUS: *Skazki, povesti, pesy*, 1960 (includes fairy tales, stories, and plays)

BIBLIOGRAPHY

Corten, Irina H. "Evgeny Lvoich Shvarts: A Biographical Sketch and Bibliography." *Russian Literature Triquarterly* 16 (1979). This article presents a brief overview of the life of Shvarts and his works.

_____. "Evgeny Shvarts as an Adapter of Hans Christian Andersen and Charles Perrault." *Russian Review* 37 (1978): 516-567. This essay focuses on Shvarts's adaptations of fairy tales in his plays.

Leach, Robert, and Victor Borovsky, eds. *A History of Russian Theater.* Cambridge, England: Cambridge University Press, 1999. This overview of Russian drama presents background information on the theater during the time in which Shvarts wrote. Bibliography and index.

Metcalf, Amanda T. *Evgenii Shvartz and His Fairy-Tales for Adults.* Birmingham, England: University of Birmingham Press, 1979. A critical analysis of the works of Shvarts, which include fairy tales. Bibliography.

Neill, Heather. "Sinister Fairy Tale." Review of *The Dragon*, by Yevgeny Shvarts. *The Times Educational Supplement*, November 20, 1992, p. 11. A review of a performance of Shvarts's *The Dragon* by the Royal National Theatre in England.

Segel, Harold B. *Twentieth Century Russian Drama: From Gorky to the Present.* Rev. ed. Baltimore, Md.: Johns Hopkins University Press, 1993. This examination of Russian theater in the twentieth century includes coverage of Shvarts's role. Bibliography and index.

Smeliansky, Anatoly. *The Russian Theater After Stalin.* Cambridge, England: Cambridge University Press, 2000. Although this work begins in 1953, toward the end of Shvarts's career, it sheds light on the forces that affected his work. Bibliography and index.

Duffield White

NEIL SIMON

Born: Bronx, New York; July 4, 1927

PRINCIPAL DRAMA

Come Blow Your Horn, pr. 1960, pb. 1961

Little Me, pr. 1962, revised pr. 1982 (music by Cy Coleman, lyrics by Carol Leigh; adaptation of Patrick Dennis's novel)

Barefoot in the Park, pr. 1963, pb. 1964

The Odd Couple, pr. 1965, pb. 1966

Sweet Charity, pr., pb. 1966 (music and lyrics by Coleman and Dorothy Fields; adaptation of Federico Fellini's film *Nights of Cabiria*)

The Star-Spangled Girl, pr. 1966, pb. 1967

Plaza Suite, pr. 1968, pb. 1969

Promises, Promises, pr. 1968, pb. 1969 (music and lyrics by Hal David and Burt Bacharach; adaptation of Billy Wilder and I. A. L. Diamond's film *The Apartment)*

Last of the Red Hot Lovers, pr. 1969, pb. 1970

The Gingerbread Lady, pr. 1970, pb. 1971

The Comedy of Neil Simon, pb. 1971 (volume 1 in *The Collected Plays of Neil Simon*)

The Prisoner of Second Avenue, pr., pb. 1971

The Sunshine Boys, pr. 1972, pb. 1973

The Good Doctor, pr. 1973, pb. 1974 (adaptation of Anton Chekhov's short stories)

God's Favorite, pr. 1974, pb. 1975 (adaptation of the biblical story of Job)

California Suite, pr. 1976, pb. 1977

Chapter Two, pr. 1977, pb. 1979

They're Playing Our Song, pr. 1978, pb. 1980 (music by Marvin Hamlisch, lyrics by Carole Bayer Sager; adaptation of Patrick Dennis's novel)

The Collected Plays of Neil Simon, pb. 1979 (volume 2)

I Ought to Be in Pictures, pr. 1980, pb. 1981

Fools, pr., pb. 1981

Brighton Beach Memoirs, pr. 1982, pb. 1984

Biloxi Blues, pr. 1984, pb. 1986

Broadway Bound, pr. 1986, pb. 1987

The Odd Couple, pr. 1985, pb. 1986 (female version)

Rumors, pr. 1988, pb. 1990

Jake's Women, pr. 1990, pb. 1991

Lost in Yonkers, pr., pb. 1991

The Collected Plays of Neil Simon, pb. 1991 (volume 3)

Laughter on the 23rd Floor, pr. 1993, pb. 1995

London Suite, pr. 1994, pb. 1996

Three from the Stage, pb. 1995

Proposals, pr. 1997, pb. 1998

The Dinner Party, pr. 2000

45 Seconds from Broadway, pr. 2001

OTHER LITERARY FORMS

In addition to his plays, Neil Simon has written numerous scripts for motion pictures. Among these are *After the Fox* (1966, with Cesare Zavattini), *The Out-of-Towners* (1970), *The Heartbreak Kid* (1972), *Murder by Death* (1976), *The Goodbye Girl* (1977), *The Cheap Detective* (1978), *Seems Like Old Times* (1980), *Max Dugan Returns* (1983), *The Lonely Guy* (1984), and *The Slugger's Wife* (1985). He has also adapted dozens of his plays to the screen, from *Barefoot in the Park* (1967) to *I Ought to Be in Pictures* (1982) and *Biloxi Blues* (1988). Along with his brother, Simon wrote during the 1940's and 1950's for a variety of television shows, including *The Phil Silvers Show* (1948), *The Tallulah Bankhead Show* (1951), *The Sid Caesar Show* (1956-1957), and *The Garry Moore Show* (1959-1960). His teleplays include *Broadway Bound* (1992), *Jake's Women* (1996), and *The Sunshine Boys* (1997). Simon published *Rewrites: A Memoir* in 1996, adding a second autobiographical volume, *The Play Goes On: A Memoir*, in 1999.

ACHIEVEMENTS

Neil Simon has established himself as a leading American playwright of the late twentieth century. As a master of domestic comedy and one-line humor, his popular appeal was established early in his career. Though considered by some to be lighter or less serious because of his comedic talents, as his career pro-

Neil Simon (Library of Congress)

BIOGRAPHY

Marvin Neil Simon was born in the Bronx, New York, on July 4, 1927. His father, Irving, was a salesman in Manhattan's garment district; his mother, Mamie, worked at Gimbel's department store. The family moved to Washington Heights in northern Manhattan when Simon was young. The family's life was not always tranquil. Irving was an errant husband who occasionally abandoned the family altogether, leaving Mamie, a frustrated and bitter woman, alone to deal with Neil and his older brother, Danny. Eventually, the parents were divorced, and Neil went to live with relatives in Queens. From an early age, he exhibited a quick wit and an active imagination. He earned the nickname "Doc"—which stayed with him into adult life—because of his penchant for imitating the family doctor. He loved films and sometimes was asked to leave the theater for laughing too loud. In high school, Simon was sometimes ostracized as a Jew, an experience that would later inform his work. That changed, however, when he joined the baseball team and became a star center fielder. Meanwhile, he and his brother began collaborating on comedy material that they sold to stand-up comics and radio announcers. Simon was graduated from DeWitt Clinton High School in 1944 at the age of sixteen.

He entered New York University under the U.S. Army Air Force Reserve program and was sent to basic training in Biloxi, Mississippi, and then to Lowry Field, Colorado. Throughout his military career, he continued to hone his writing skills, reading favorite authors such as Mark Twain and Robert Benchley and writing for military newspapers. Discharged in 1946, Simon took a job in the mail room at Warner Bros. in New York, where Danny worked in the publicity department. The brothers were soon hired to write for Goodman Ace of the Columbia Broadcasting System (CBS), and over the next decade they provided material for such television comedians as Tallulah Bankhead, Jackie Gleason, Carl Reiner, and Red Skelton. During the summers of 1952 and 1953,

gressed, Simon infused his comedy with greater amounts of social relevance, autobiographical inspiration, and dramatic depth. Many of his plays explore the thin line that separates comedy from pathos, provoking audiences to laugh through their tears. His plays focus on character and personal relationships in primarily middle-class, urban settings in the United States. Nevertheless, the stories he dramatizes are about basic human problems and aspirations, and his plays have proven to have universal appeal.

Simon has been the recipient of numerous awards and honors. They include two Emmy Awards for his work in television in 1957 and 1959; a Tony Award for Best Author for *The Odd Couple* in 1965, and another for *Biloxi Blues* in 1985; a New York Drama Critics Circle Award in 1983 for *Brighton Beach Memoirs*; a New York State Governor's Award in 1986; and a Pulitzer Prize in Drama and a Tony Award for Best Play for *Lost in Yonkers*, both in 1991. In 1993 President Bill Clinton hosted Simon at the White House when Simon received Kennedy Center Honors.

they wrote sketches for the professional acting company at Camp Tamiment in Pennsylvania, some of which were featured on Broadway several years later. At Camp Tamiment, Simon fell in love with a young actress named Joan Baim, and the couple was married on September 30, 1953. Five years later, Joan gave birth to a daughter, Ellen; a second daughter, Nancy, was born in 1963.

In 1956, Danny Simon moved to California to be a television director. Neil stayed in New York and wrote for Phil Silvers's *Sergeant Bilko*, Sid Caesar's *Your Show of Shows*, and *The Garry Moore Show*. He also adapted Broadway plays for television, including Lorenz Hart and Richard Rodgers's musical *Dearest Enemy* (pr. 1925). By the later 1950's, however, he wanted more independence than television writing could offer. He began writing a play of his own. For three years, he wrote and revised, as many as fifty times, his first full play. *Come Blow Your Horn* was optioned by twenty-five producers before it was finally staged in 1960 at the Bucks County Playhouse in New Hope, Pennsylvania. A greatly improved version opened on Broadway the following February. The play received positive notice, and, in 1962, Simon's book for the musical *Little Me* reinforced his growing reputation. It was his third full script, however, *Barefoot in the Park*, that firmly established him on the American stage. It ran for four years, with a total of 1,532 performances. In 1965, Simon had a second smash hit with *The Odd Couple*, which ran for two years and earned for him his first Tony Award.

Over the next decade, Simon's work was characteristically prodigious, with a new play appearing every year or two. While the plays were not all unqualified successes, Simon's popularity continued to rise. At the same time, he accrued a list of screenplay credits. Many were adaptations of his own plays; others were original screenplays or adaptations of other people's works. These films helped spread his notoriety beyond primarily urban, middle-class theater audiences to a wider range of viewers. Despite his popular success, however, Simon was still regarded by serious critics as a lightweight scenarist writing for laughs.

In 1972, Simon faced a harrowing personal tragedy. His wife, Joan, was diagnosed with cancer. Simon nursed her through fifteen agonizing months until she succumbed to the disease in 1973. After twenty years of happy marriage, the loss affected him deeply. Later that year, Simon met an actress named Marsha Mason. The two had a whirlwind romance and within weeks were husband and wife. While never rediscovering the deep passion he had known with Joan, Simon enjoyed a good marriage with Mason that lasted nine years.

In 1974, Simon received a special Tony Award for his contributions to the American theater. His plays continued to appear regularly, and on the screen he scored with such films as *The Goodbye Girl* and *The Cheap Detective*. In 1983, he received a singular honor: The Nederlander Organization renamed a Broadway theater after him.

In the mid-1980's, the trilogy composed of *Brighton Beach Memoirs*, *Biloxi Blues*, and *Broadway Bound* showed a more serious, mature, and openly autobiographical Simon. The three plays garnered many awards, including a Tony Award for *Biloxi Blues* as best play of 1985. *Lost in Yonkers* received even more praise, winning the 1991 Pulitzer Prize in Drama and the Tony Award for best play. Most important, critics began to take Simon seriously as a respectable dramatist.

His third marriage came in 1987, to Diane Lander, a former actress and model. Though divorced in 1988, the couple remarried in 1990, and Simon adopted Lander's daughter Bryn. In 1998 Simon divorced Lander a second time. Marrying for a fifth time, he wedded actress Elaine Joyce shortly after divorcing Lander.

By the 1990's, through four decades of diligent writing, Simon had developed great skill and technique. He divided his time between homes in Manhattan and Bel Air, California, and wrote methodically for seven hours every day. Behind each play that reached fruition, Simon had another ten beginnings that had been put aside, and many more ideas not yet even committed to paper. Nevertheless, with the prodigious output already behind him, he has claimed his position in the history of American theater.

ANALYSIS

Neil Simon's plays have so set the standard for American domestic comedy that they almost form a subgenre in themselves. His work is certainly marked by a distinct style and mastery of certain principles of comic writing. Though the mood, subject matter, and focus of his writing have developed over the years, the Neil Simon signature can still be read throughout.

His plays tend to be domestic comedies focusing on family life and relationships. Almost all are set in New York City and, explicitly or not, depict the concerns and values of middle-class, Jewish family life, writers and show business people, and Americans in touch with the liberal movements of the 1960's and 1970's. As a keen observer of contemporary life, Simon fills his plays with recognizable topical references and details. Dealing with such themes as marriage, divorce, sexual liberation, and intergenerational conflict, his work effectively chronicles late twentieth century American lifestyles and values.

Coming as Simon did from a training ground in stand-up comedy and television writing, he is technically expert at coining and structuring one-line jokes. One-liners are not restricted to token "comic" characters; rather, they are distributed among all the characters in his plays. Furthermore, Simon is skilled at connecting the jokes and embedding them in the texture of the conflict in a way that reinforces the integrity of a scene. The jokes serve rather than divert the flow of action; they inform characterization rather than reduce characters to mere mouthpieces for the author's wit. Simon supports his quick humor with characters who are clearly delineated, defined not only by their backgrounds, tastes, idiosyncrasies, and language but also by their larger objectives and outlooks on life. They are drawn with eccentricity and excess, but with sympathy and warmth as well. The tendency toward stereotypes and caricatures that Simon sometimes indulged early in his career gradually disappeared as he honed his craft.

Creating rich characters, Simon serves them well by carefully structuring his plays to maximize the potential for both conflict and humor. Knowing that the line between tragedy and comedy is a thin one, he heightens the stakes of his characters' desires. In-deed, many a Simon play, drained of its wit, could easily be transformed into serious high drama, with situations worthy of Henrik Ibsen or August Strindberg. The people of Simon's plays are frustrated, sometimes nearly neurotic; they take their problems head-on and search earnestly for solutions. Like William Shakespeare, Simon lets the meaning of his plays inhabit the surface, so there is rarely a deep subtext to unearth. As his characters are generally intelligent and perceptive, they police one another against emotional subterfuge. Unlike Shakespeare, however, Simon does not utilize subplots but rather provides a single, clear conflict to propel the action.

Through more than two dozen plays and nearly as many film scripts, Simon has become the wealthiest dramatist in history and the most produced playwright on the contemporary American stage behind Shakespeare. More important, in addition to his supremacy over the popular American theater, his devotion to craft, hard work, simplicity, honesty, and diligence as a playwright have secured him a primary position in its literary annals.

Simon's techniques are clearly evident in his first two major successes, *Barefoot in the Park* and *The Odd Couple*. Both plays are simply constructed, consisting of four scenes in three acts, taking place in a single locale within a span of several weeks, and built on the conflict between two distinctly defined characters.

BAREFOOT IN THE PARK

Barefoot in the Park is about newlyweds Paul and Corie Bratter. The young lawyer and his wife are moving into their first New York apartment, a living space too small, cold, dilapidated, expensive, and high up to induce peaceful living. In the first scene, they take inventory of their new home, amid visits from Corie's well-intentioned mother from New Jersey and a flamboyant older gentleman from the upstairs apartment. Corie hatches a plan to make a match between Mother and the exotic Mr. Velasco.

The second scene is the dinner gathering, pitting Mother's tender stomach against Velasco's gourmet hors d'oeuvres, Corie's enthusiasm against Paul's reluctance, and the foursome against a cold apartment and a catastrophic kitchen. In the third scene, the group returns from a dinner out, Mother leaves with Velasco, and Corie and Paul become embroiled in a fight that ends in a decision to divorce. In facing the challenges of the apartment and the evening, the newlyweds have come to believe that they have nothing in common. Paul considers his wife irrational and irresponsible; she thinks that he is a stuffed shirt incapable of enjoying life.

In the final scene, Mother is unaccounted for, divorce plans proceed apace, and Corie and Paul are miserable. Ultimately, Mother appears, no worse for wear from a night at Velasco's, and Paul and Corie discover the importance of surrender and compromise. She recognizes her need for order, he relaxes enough to take a walk "barefoot in the park," and they both realize the depth of their love.

From the start, Simon creates a situation rife with possibilities. The setting offers opportunities for visual jokes and offstage action: For example, there are ongoing references to the six-flight ascent to the apartment. As newlyweds adapting to a new home, job, and lifestyle, Corie and Paul are portrayed in the midst of major upheaval. The stolid Mother and the splendiferous Velasco are great foils for each other and for the younger couple as well. Furthermore, in Corie and Paul, Simon creates protagonists whose personalities, often in harmony, easily become diametrically opposed through their responses to difficult circumstances.

THE ODD COUPLE

Even more than in *Barefoot in the Park*, the conflict in Simon's next play, *The Odd Couple*, is built squarely on the collision of opposites. Oscar Madison is a divorced sportswriter living alone, who hosts five friends for a weekly poker game, including his good friend Felix Ungar. (During his childhood, Simon's mother used to run poker games in the family home for extra income.) In the first scene, Felix, usually quite punctual, arrives hours late in emotional distress, with the horrific news that his wife kicked him out. Oscar invites Felix to become his roommate, and the "odd couple" is formed.

Simon established Felix's sensitive and fastidious nature in the opening scene, so it is no surprise when, in the second scene, two weeks later, Felix is driving

the slovenly Oscar crazy with his devotion to detail and cleanliness. Their relationship is implicitly a send-up of marriage in an age of rising divorce rates and precarious gender roles. The bachelor life is clearly threatened by Felix's uxoriousness. To break the tension and salve their solitude, Oscar suggests a double date with their upstairs neighbors, the Pigeon sisters. Felix reluctantly agrees.

In the third scene, Cecily and Gwendolyn Pigeon come downstairs for dinner, straight out of an Oscar Wilde drawing room. As in *Barefoot in the Park*, however, the menu is sabotaged by circumstance, and, instead of succumbing to the double seduction that Oscar envisions, the Pigeons both take sisterly pity on the heartbroken Felix. The failed date precipitates a climactic conflagration between the two men, and, as in *Barefoot in the Park*, the only solution seems to be separation.

In the final scene, amid a cold war of silence and anger, Oscar and Felix vent their rage and passion, coming to understand that their conflict reflects an unhappy combination of personality types and the larger tragedies of failed marriages and solitary middle age. These themes reappear time and again in Simon's work—the distance between people, the effects of time on relationships, and the different ways that men and women deal with emotion. In the end, Oscar and Felix reach a mutually respectful peace, forged of patience, humility, and a willingness to laugh.

OTHER EARLY PLAYS

The formula established by these early comedies provides the basis for many of the plays that followed. In 1966, Simon wrote the book for *Sweet Charity*, a Bob Fosse musical based on the Federico Fellini film *Nights of Cabiria* (1957). In *The Star-Spangled Girl*, he pitted liberal journalists against an old-fashioned Southern belle. Both of these pieces met mixed response. Years later, Simon called *The Star-Spangled Girl* "simply a failure," a play "where I did not have a clear visual image of the characters in my mind as I sat down at the typewriter." Nevertheless, with the opening of *The Star-Spangled Girl*, Simon could claim the singular distinction of having four plays running simultaneously on Broadway.

In 1968, Simon tried something new: a series of three one-act plays set in the same hotel room. The result, *Plaza Suite*, is vintage Simon with an added bittersweetness. The first piece focuses on a stale marriage and a revelation of infidelity; the second, on high school flames reuniting in midlife; and the third, on a bride's wedding day jitters and what they bring out in her parents' marriage. That same year, Simon wrote the book for *Promises, Promises*, a Burt Bacharach-Hal David musical version of the 1960 film *The Apartment*.

MID-CAREER PLAYS

A mid-career Simon focused on the romantic woes of a middle-aged man in his next play, *Last of the Red Hot Lovers*. Then came *The Gingerbread Lady*, dealing with the subject of alcoholism; *The Prisoner of Second Avenue*, about the nervous breakdown of a man caught in the vertigo of urban life; and *The Sunshine Boys*, depicting the deteriorating relationship of a pair of old comedians. These plays signaled an attempt by Simon to move into issue-oriented material with a more serious tone. While still striking with characteristic wit and receiving popular acclaim, he sometimes overindulged in sentiment and high seriousness. Some critics lambasted the attempt and urged him to stay on familiar, lighter terrain.

In 1972 and 1973, during the period of his wife's illness and death, Simon's writing reflected his personal tragedy. *The Good Doctor* was his adaptation of the tragicomic stories of Russian dramatist Anton Chekhov. More penetrating was *God's Favorite*, a modern reworking of the biblical story of Job, in which a man challenges God and the universe to help him understand the extremity of his sufferings. It was Simon's attempt to find solace and peace through his writing.

CALIFORNIA SUITE

California Suite, a Pacific Coast retake of the *Plaza Suite* concept, appeared in 1976. Like its predecessor, and much of the intervening work, it takes a more sophisticated approach to relationships and social situations. It consists of four short plays set in a two-room suite at the Beverly Hills Hotel. The first and third have definite pathos beneath their comic gloss; the second and fourth are lighter and broader.

The second of the four pieces is about Marvin and Millie, a husband and wife from Philadelphia who have come to Los Angeles for a nephew's Bar Mitzvah. Marvin arrived a night early and returned to the suite to find a gift from his brother waiting for him: a prostitute. It is the next morning, and Millie arrives; the other woman, however, is still drunk and asleep in the bed, and for most of the play, Marvin scrambles to conceal her inert form. Eventually, he confesses his sin to Millie, and they face the crisis with equal guilt and stoicism. The play runs on frantic energy, physical comedy, and the audience's discrepant awareness of the other woman's presence.

The fourth play is also built on physical comedy emerging from a situation that is out of control. Mort and Beth and Stu and Gert are two couples from Chicago who have taken a three-week vacation together. Best friends at the start, their rapport has steadily eroded. At last, an accidental injury on the tennis court unleashes torrents of accumulated hostility; the feuding then triggers a series of freak accidents, a veritable comedy of mishaps. The barroom brawl-like mayhem ends in unresolved pandemonium. Simon here displays his ability to bring together one-liners, character conflict, and physical comedy into an orchestrated whole.

Set against these two lighter plays are the first and third pieces. In the first, a divorced couple negotiate where their daughter will live for her last year of high school. Billy and Hannah are both brashly intelligent and piercingly sarcastic. What begins as a brittle, venomous battle of words and wits subtly evolves into a deep struggle for pride and control. Knowing each other all too well, they ultimately bring their hopes, fears, and even some of their long-abandoned love into the open. While the characters use humor as a weapon throughout, their true feelings are always evident, and Simon allows and validates their enduring anger. Ultimately, a deal is struck, but the tone and outcome make it clear that there are no winners in this struggle.

The same is true of the third piece, in which a British actress and her husband have come to Hollywood for the Academy Awards. Dividing the action into two scenes, Simon contrasts their hopeful harmony before the ceremony with their bitter and drunken divisiveness after it. Diana has not won the coveted Oscar but instead has made a fool of herself at the ensuing parties. At the heart of her recklessness is a deep dissatisfaction with her marriage. Her husband, Sidney, an unassuming antiques dealer, is a "bisexual homosexual," and his flirtation with a young actor over dinner has brought dangerous issues to the surface. In the end, Sidney will hold, soothe, and probably make love to Diana, but it is evident that the connection is only temporary. That they can come together at all is a sign of hope, but Simon allows no illusions about the sacrifices they are making and the evanescence of their union.

This mix of pieces and tones, all still focused on relationships, marriages, sex, and love, bespeaks an unapologetic honesty that cannot be found in Simon's earlier work. Indeed, in 1979, Simon said that he believed the third play of *California Suite* was his best and most honest writing.

AUTOBIOGRAPHICAL WORKS

While parts of his earlier plays are drawn loosely from personal experience, by the late 1970's Simon was ready to take on autobiographical material more directly. *Chapter Two* was the first play in this direction. It tells the story of a recently widowed man who meets and falls in love with a woman, a story the playwright had known firsthand several years before. During this period, he also wrote a second version of *The Odd Couple*, this time with two women in the leading roles (produced and published a decade later); the book for a Marvin Hamlisch-Carole Bayer Sager musical called *They're Playing Our Song*; a play called *I Ought to Be in Pictures*, about a screenwriter and his daughter; and *Fools*, a comic fable based on a Ukrainian folktale. This last was Simon's only unequivocal flop.

BRIGHTON BEACH MEMOIRS

The real breakthrough came with *Brighton Beach Memoirs*, which, with *Biloxi Blues* and *Broadway Bound*, forms Simon's acclaimed autobiographical trilogy. In these plays, the playwright's own past is clear and unmistakable. The plays center on Eugene Morris Jerome, a teenage writer and baseball enthusiast growing up in Brighton Beach, New York, in the

1940's. Eugene has an older brother, unhappily married parents, and great aspirations. These aspirations lead him to chronicle his family's trials and tribulations, and his writings become a vehicle for narrating and commenting on the action directly to the audience. As Eugene is representative of the young Simon, his direct address offers an intimacy between playwright and audience that Simon had never before attempted or allowed.

In the trilogy, Simon also effectively explores dramatic structure. "I really made a quantum leap in *Brighton Beach* as a playwright," Simon said in 1985, "because it was the first full-bodied play I had ever written, in terms of dealing with a group of people as individuals and telling all their stories." Before, he would focus on a central character or conflict; now, though Eugene was the connecting thread, Simon was portraying a more integrated and balanced world. In *Brighton Beach Memoirs*, Eugene's adolescent fascination with his cousin Nora, his aunt Blanche's quandary over reestablishing her independence, his older brother Stanley's moral crisis at work, Nora's dreams of a show business career, her sister Laurie's fragile health, and Jack and Kate Jerome's precarious marriage and difficult economic straits are all woven together into a delicate tapestry of events and emotions. The play, suffused with characteristic wit but a deeper sense of poignancy, won the New York Drama Critics Circle Award, the first truly critical recognition of Simon's work.

The New York Times critic Frank Rich wrote that he would love to see a "chapter two" to *Brighton Beach Memoirs*, so Simon decided to continue Eugene's story. *Biloxi Blues* takes place at an army training camp in Biloxi, Mississippi, no doubt the camp that Simon had attended four decades earlier. It is one of his few plays set outside New York City and one of the few that feature a group of strangers. Like its predecessor, it balances the stories of several characters. Simon introduces Arnold Epstein, a tender Jewish youth with a will of steel; Sergeant Toomey, a career military man facing his mortality and determined to make soldiers of the last group assigned to him; Wykowski and Selridge, the company bullies; and Carney and Hennesey, who bring other colors of adolescence to the complete picture. Outside the barracks, there are Rowena, the weekend prostitute who takes Eugene's virginity, and Daisy, the lovely schoolgirl who wins his heart.

The play gains steady momentum through a variety of means: the rigors of training, the competitive banter of the barracks, the young men's unrelenting fears and hormones, the often blatant bigotry and anti-Semitism, the lurking suspicions of homosexuality, and the implicit challenges to pride and manhood. In the climactic scene, Simon distills all the play's themes into a tense confrontation between the old soldier Toomey and the unwilling hero Epstein, in a way that seals the play's uncanny, but human, logic.

BILOXI BLUES

In *Biloxi Blues*, Eugene again takes the audience into his confidence, sharing his process of maturing as both man and writer. The one-liners are ever-present, but the world of the play is darkened by the shadow of World War II, establishing a type of meaningful historical context that is unseen in Simon's work before the trilogy. The fourteen scenes, spanning months and moving through a variety of settings, are also unusual for Simon. *Biloxi Blues* is a rite-of-passage play, and Simon treats the inherent issues—adolescence, manhood, fear, sexuality, separation—with deep warmth, sensitivity, and subtlety.

BROADWAY BOUND

Broadway Bound completed the trilogy in 1986. Eugene is back in Brighton Beach, and the tapestry interweaves his fledgling career, writing comedy with his brother Stanley, with the quickly unraveling threads of his parents' marriage. Past and family are inescapable even as the future looks bright, and, when their homegrown skit actually comes across the radio waves, Eugene and Stanley learn an important lesson about the dangers of mixing humor and autobiography. It is no doubt an issue that had crossed the playwright's mind as well.

In *Broadway Bound*, Eugene still narrates and comments, and audiences who followed him through the first two plays can appreciate his ripening maturity. The most powerful scene of the play is remarkably simple: Eugene dances with his mother, Kate, amid the disarray of the kitchen and her crumbling

marriage, to her lyrical reminiscences of a girlhood infatuation with a dashing celebrity and a magical night when she danced with him. The intimacy of the story embarrasses even Eugene, a fact that he candidly confesses to the audience. The Oedipal implications of the scene magnify both the young man's coming-of-age and his mother's life of pain and frustration. By using details taken directly from his own youth, Simon frankly investigates his filial memories and feelings, and the result is powerful. The writing shows a level of dramatic achievement of which the author of *Come Blow Your Horn* could only have dreamed.

The trilogy was followed by *Rumors*, Simon's first attempt at all-out farce, and *Jake's Women*, a whimsical play about a writer and the women who populate his mind. *Jake's Women* endured many rewrites and an aborted out-of-town trial before finally coming to Broadway, a process that testified to Simon's power and diligence as a playwright.

LOST IN YONKERS

In 1991, continuing in the spirit of the trilogy, *Lost in Yonkers* appeared on Broadway. Portraying the sojourn of two boys with their brusque grandmother and eccentric aunt and uncle, it earned Simon critical praise, his second Tony Award for best play, and a prestigious Pulitzer Prize in Drama. The play continues in the spirit of the Brighton Beach trilogy, but with less sense of nostalgia as Simon wrings comedy from the anguish of five deeply disturbed people. Critic David Richards noted that "Were it not for his [Simon's] ready wit and appreciation of life's incongruities, *Lost in Yonkers* could pass for a nightmare."

As in the trilogy, there are two young boys, clearly based on Simon and his older brother, but the other characters and the action are inventions. The place is the apartment over Kurnitz's Kandy Store in Yonkers, where Grandma Kurnitz lives with her thirty-five-year-old, brain-damaged daughter Bella. Grandma Kurnitz's experiences with anti-Semitism as a child in Germany convinced her that to succeed in this world you must be hard as steel. Ignoring her four surviving children's emotional life, she rigidly disciplined them.

The time is 1942, and son Eddie has come to beg his mother to take in his two boys while he travels as a salesman. Having borrowed from loan sharks to pay the medical bills of his recently deceased wife, he desperately needs to earn money. Grandma reluctantly agrees. Following his mother's advice to be hard, a second son, Louie, became a small-time gangster and now comes home to hide from the associates he has cheated. An older daughter Gert also stops by; she suffers from a breathing problem whenever she visits her mother and cannot finish a sentence without gasping for breath.

The emotional center of the play is the struggle of Bella to fashion a life of her own, against the opposition of her mother. Bella falls in love with a mentally retarded movie theater usher and is determined to marry him, despite the grim disapproval of her mother and the skepticism of her siblings, but the usher is too timid to leave the protection of his parents and the romance fails. At the play's end Eddie returns to claim his sons, and Bella asserts herself. She tells her mother she is going to the movies with a new girlfriend who likes her. Further, the girlfriend has a brother, and Bella plans to invite them both for dinner later that week.

LATER PLAYS

Simon continued to send new plays to Broadway, though none repeated the critical or monetary success of *Lost in Yonkers*. *Laughter on the 23rd Floor*, based on Simon's years as a writer for Sid Caesar's television shows, portrays activities in the writers' room as eight conflicting personalities and egos struggle to put together a new comic script every week. *London Suite* echoes *Plaza Suite* and *California Suite* with four one-act dramas, this time taking place in an elegant London hotel. *Proposals*, set in the 1950's at a summer cottage in a resort area of eastern Pennsylvania, revolves around the disagreements between a retired businessman, his former wife, his daughter, and his daughter's various boyfriends, one of whom is the son of a Mafia baron. *The Dinner Party* occurs in a private room at an expensive Parisian restaurant as six diners explore the various reasons their marriages have failed. *45 Seconds from Broadway* takes its title from the time needed to walk from theaters to a coffee shop, familiarly known as the Polish Tea Room, that is a favorite hangout of theater folk. Ten actors exchange banter and good-natured insults with each other and the restaurant's owners.

OTHER MAJOR WORKS

SCREENPLAYS: *After the Fox*, 1966 (with Cesare Zavattini); *Barefoot in the Park*, 1967; *The Odd Couple*, 1968; *The Out-of-Towners*, 1970; *Plaza Suite*, 1971; *The Last of the Red Hot Lovers*, 1972; *The Heartbreak Kid*, 1972; *The Prisoner of Second Avenue*, 1975; *The Sunshine Boys*, 1975; *Murder by Death*, 1976; *The Goodbye Girl*, 1977; *California Suite*, 1978; *The Cheap Detective*, 1978; *Chapter Two*, 1979; *Seems Like Old Times*, 1980; *Only When I Laugh*, 1981; *I Ought to Be in Pictures*, 1982; *Max Dugan Returns*, 1983; *The Lonely Guy*, 1984; *The Slugger's Wife*, 1985; *Brighton Beach Memoirs*, 1987; *Biloxi Blues*, 1988; *The Marrying Man*, 1991; *Lost in Yonkers*, 1993; *The Odd Couple II*, 1998.

TELEPLAYS: *Broadway Bound*, 1992; *Jake's Women*, 1996; *London Suite*, 1996; *The Sunshine Boys*, 1997.

NONFICTION: *Rewrites: A Memoir*, 1996; *The Play Goes On: A Memoir*, 1999.

BIBLIOGRAPHY

Henry, William A., III. "Reliving a Poignant Past." *Time*, December 15, 1986, 72-78. Henry describes the success of the play *Broadway Bound* and its biographical sources, and includes in-depth material about Simon's marriages, lifestyle, writing habits, and older brother Danny. Compares Simon's life with its fictional parallels, especially in *Broadway Bound*.

Johnson, Robert K. *Neil Simon*. Boston: G. K. Hall, 1983. In this thoughtful and penetrating study, Johnson examines Simon's career and output through 1982, providing thorough synopses, analysis, and criticism of both plays and screenplays. Includes a chronology, a select bibliography, notes, and an index.

Konas, Gary, ed. *Neil Simon: A Casebook*. New York: Garland, 1997. Seven scholarly articles examine the influence of Simon's Jewish heritage and compare his work with that of other dramatists. Four essays discuss recurrent patterns in Simon's plays. The volume closes with two Simon interviews.

Koprince, Susan. *Understanding Neil Simon*. Columbia: University of South Carolina Press, 2002. Offering a guide to Simon's work, Koprince provides an overview of Simon's career and an indepth analysis of his major plays. Includes bibliography and index.

McGovern, Edythe. *Not-So-Simple Neil Simon: A Critical Study*. Van Nuys, Calif.: Perivale Press, 1978. McGovern examines twelve of Simon's earliest plays with an even, theoretical, scholarly tone, occasionally tending toward unqualified praise. The slim volume includes a preface by the playwright, a list of characters from the plays, twenty-two production photographs, and seven illustrations by renowned Broadway caricaturist Al Hirschfeld.

Richards, David. "The Last of the Red Hot Playwrights." Review of *Lost in Yonkers*, by Neil Simon. *The New York Times Magazine*, February 17, 1991, 30. Celebrating Simon's success with *Lost in Yonkers*, this reviewer describes the play and production and profiles the playwright. The article brings together personal and professional material, using quotes from Simon, his family members, and actors associated with his plays. Personal and in-depth, with nine photographs.

Simon, Neil. "The Art of Theater X." Interview by James Lipton. *The Paris Review* 34 (Winter, 1992): 166-213. A chatty, revealing interview. The first half of the interview is largely given to discussion of how Simon became a playwright and the strong autobiographical elements in his work: "I think my greatest weakness is that I can't write outside my own experience." Other topics include the "almost invisible line" between comedy and tragedy and the gradually darkening vision of Simon's plays, which he sees as a movement toward greater truthfulness. Simon's ongoing enthusiasm for theater is clear; he concludes, "Every time I write a play it's the beginning of a new life for me."

Barry Mann,
updated by Milton Berman

BERNARD SLADE
Bernard Slade Newbound

Born: St. Catharines, Ontario, Canada; May 2, 1930

PRINCIPAL DRAMA
Simon Says Get Married, pr. 1960
A Very Close Family, pr. 1962
Fling!, wr. 1970, pr. 1977, pb. 1979
Same Time, Next Year, pr., pb. 1975
Tribute, pr., pb. 1978
Romantic Comedy, pr., pb. 1979
Special Occasions, pr., pb. 1982
Fatal Attraction, pr. 1984, pb. 1986
Return Engagements, pr. 1986, pb. 1989
Sweet William, pr. 1986
An Act of the Imagination, pr. 1987
Every Time I See You, pr. 1991
I Remember You, pb. 1994
You Say Tomatoes, pr., pb. 1994
Same Time, Another Year, pb. 1995, pr. 1996

OTHER LITERARY FORMS
Before his first (and highly successful) efforts on Broadway with *Same Time, Next Year*, Bernard Slade spent seventeen years as a writer for television, first as a playwright and later as a series creator and writer. Slade's work in television drama goes back to the days of live broadcasts in the 1950's and 1960's, including a number of hourlong plays first produced by the Canadian Broadcasting Corporation between

1957 and 1963. Several of these plays were also produced on American television for the *U.S. Steel Hour* series. Between 1964 and 1974, Slade wrote a number of pilot films for American television that eventually became successful television series. His major achievements in this genre include *Love on a Rooftop*, *The Flying Nun*, *The Partridge Family*, *Bridget Loves Bernie*, *The Girl with Something Extra*, *The Bobby Sherman Show*, and *Mr. Deeds Goes to Town*, all comedies. Slade's television credits also include authorship of approximately one hundred episodes for these and other series, including *Bewitched* and *My Living Doll*. Slade has said of his experiences as a writer for television that "the controls built into network television, which is basically an advertising medium, don't exactly encourage creativity. Still, TV was my choice. It gave me the financial freedom to sit down and write a play." In 1974, Slade left television to devote full time to writing plays for the theater.

The successful Broadway run of *Same Time, Next Year* made possible Slade's continued work in still another entertainment medium: major motion pictures. Slade has written screenplays for *Stand Up and Be Counted* (1971), *Same Time, Next Year* (1978), *Tribute* (1980), and *Romantic Comedy* (1983). The film versions of Slade's plays will no doubt continue to entertain audiences for years to come.

ACHIEVEMENTS

Throughout Bernard Slade's career, his major works have attracted the prompt and generally enthusiastic attention of the major New York newspapers, including *The New York Times*, the *New York Post*, and the *New York Daily News*. Magazines such as *Time* and *Newsweek* have also carried half-page articles on Slade's works, and scenes from his plays have appeared alongside reviews of all three major television networks. In 1975, *Same Time, Next Year*, long on the list of the top ten longest-running shows, received nominations from all the major awards institutions. The stage version received a Tony nomination, the American Academy of Humor Award, and the prestigious Drama Desk Award, and the screen version received the Academy Award and Writers Guild nominations for Best Screenplay.

Slade's works have also resulted in awards and nominations for actress Ellen Burstyn and actor Jack Lemmon. Burstyn received the Tony Award for Best Actress in 1975 for her portrayal of Doris in *Same Time, Next Year*, and Lemmon earned Tony and Academy Award nominations for his stage and film work as Scottie Templeton in *Tribute*.

Slade is recognized as a major talent both on Broadway and in Hollywood, and his international following continues to increase with each new production. All his major plays have done well in foreign countries, especially England and France, and *Same Time, Next Year* has been produced in some thirty-five countries around the world. Foreign productions of Slade's plays have traditionally retained the plays' American settings. Slade himself was the first to break with tradition when he Anglicized *Special Occasions* for his directorial debut in London in 1983.

BIOGRAPHY

Bernard Slade Newbound was born in St. Catharines, Ontario, Canada, on May 2, 1930. His parents, Fred and Bessie (née Walbourne) Newbound, were originally from England. When he was four, Slade moved to England with his family and settled in London near the Croydon airport, where his father worked as a mechanic. With the threat of war, Slade, like many children, was evacuated from London, spending the year 1939 in a foster home. Shortly after his return to London at the age of ten, the Battle of Britain broke out in full force: The first daylight bombing of London destroyed the Croydon airport, four blocks from Slade's home, and Slade's father was one of the few workers there to survive the attack.

Life in England took on a restless quality during the war years. The family moved often, and Slade attended some thirteen schools around the country between the late 1930's and 1948. Despite the war, Slade found time to attend the theater and to act in several amateur productions, among them Noël Coward's *I'll Leave It to You* (pr. 1919). In 1948, the family left England to return to Canada, Slade taking with him his love for the theater and a few pages of notes for plays of his own.

In Canada, Slade worked briefly at a customs office but soon quit his job to resume acting, first in summer stock and later for year-round theaters, where he often did a different play each week. He acted in more than three hundred plays in all, including virtually every romantic comedy written in the 1930's and 1940's. Although Slade disliked the indignity of looking for work as an actor, the experience of being in front of an audience every night eventually paid off as he absorbed a sense of how and when a play works.

In 1957, after nine years of acting in winter and summer stock theater, Slade sat down during a break in the play in which he was performing and wrote a television play designed to provide himself with a good part. Both the Canadian Broadcasting Corporation and, in the United States, the National Broadcasting Company bought the play but found different actors to take Slade's part. *The Prizewinner*, Slade's first television play, was very much in the tradition of live broadcast drama popularized by the *U.S. Steel Hour* and the *Goodyear TV Playhouse* in New York, particularly the work of such writers as Paddy Chayefsky and Tad Mosel. Slade went on to write many more teleplays, a number of which were produced in the United States as well as in Canada in the late 1950's and early 1960's.

In 1963, having realized that Hollywood was quickly establishing itself as the center for North American television production, Slade moved to California with his wife, Jill Foster Hancock, and their two children and began writing scripts for a new television series entitled *Bewitched*. Soon afterward, he signed a contract (later to become a succession of three-year contracts) with Screen Gems to write pilot films, rarely staying with a show once it became a series. In all, Slade wrote seven pilots, each of which became a successful series, and more than one hundred episode scripts. In 1974, Slade, financially secure, left television and turned his sights on the theater.

Begun on an airplane en route to Hawaii, *Same Time, Next Year* surpassed all Slade's expectations at its opening at Boston's Colonial Theatre in February, 1975. The play quickly moved to New York's Brooks Atkinson Theatre, where it opened on March 13 to standing room only and the unanimous acclamation of New York's best-known theater critics. Soon afterward, Slade wrote the screenplay, and in 1978, Universal Studios released *Same Time, Next Year*, starring Alan Alda and Ellen Burstyn. Earlier, in 1977, Slade had returned to the stage with his wife to star in a Canadian production of *Same Time, Next Year*.

Same Time, Next Year was followed by *Tribute* and, one year later, *Romantic Comedy*, the former originally designed for and offered to Jack Lemmon, who opened the play at Boston's Colonial Theatre on April 6, and in New York on June 1, 1978. Reviews focused primarily on Lemmon's outstanding performance as Scottie Templeton, and criticism of the play was for the most part favorable. Slade then wrote the screenplay for *Tribute*, and, in December, 1980, Twentieth Century-Fox released the film version, starring, once again, Lemmon. Like its predecessors, *Romantic Comedy* opened in Boston and moved to New York, where it played for a year and earned high praise from the critics (Clive Barnes called it Slade's best play) before being adapted for the screen. More than any of Slade's other plays, *Romantic Comedy* reflects the enormous influence of the romantic comedies of the 1930's and 1940's on its author.

By all critical accounts, *Special Occasions* was Slade's first failure: The play closed after only one night at the Music Box in New York. Critics pointed their collective finger at the staging primarily and at the story secondarily and found little to like about either. In 1983, Slade took a slightly different version of *Special Occasions* to England, where the play was received with more sympathy by critics and public alike. Slade thus continues to be a major figure in world theater, although the economic rigors of Broadway have prevented his later works from enjoying the same box-office success as his early plays. The 1987 broadcast of his television play *Moving Day* marked his return to the genre in which he enjoyed his first success.

When asked by *Who's Who in America* to describe his work and career, Slade responded, "I am a prisoner of a childhood dream: to write for the theatre. The fulfillment of that dream has lived up to all my

expectations. I believe the theatre should be a celebration of the human condition and that the artist's
job is to remind us of all that is good about ourselves.
I feel privileged to be given a platform for my particular vision of life, and, whether my plays succeed or
fail, I am always grateful for the use of the hall."

ANALYSIS

One might best approach Bernard Slade's major
works—*Same Time, Next Year*, *Tribute*, *Romantic
Comedy*, and *Special Occasions*—by first surveying
their common ground. All Slade's plays are comedies
for the most part, although *Tribute* and *Special Occasions* contain more frequent departures into the pathetic than do *Same Time, Next Year* and *Romantic
Comedy*. (*Tribute* is, at its simplest level, a story
about a man who knows when and how he is going to
die, while the "special occasions" in the play of that
title include divorce, disfiguring automobile accidents, and alcoholic blackouts.) The time frame of a
typical Slade play is usually quite broad: *Special Occasions* covers one night of Amy and Michael
Ruskin's marriage and ten years of their divorce; *Romantic Comedy* spans thirteen years of an on-again,
off-again professional writing relationship; and *Same
Time, Next Year* begins in 1951 and ends in 1975,
with every indication that its adulterous affair will
continue into a fourth decade.

Time is always significant in Slade's works. All
four major productions plot the maturation of one or
two principal characters over a period of years or
months. Quite often the chief protagonist is a male,
between thirty and fifty years of age, who makes his
living as a writer of one sort or another (Michael
Ruskin in *Special Occasions* and Jason Carmichael in
Romantic Comedy are playwrights). The liberal time
frame allows for a wide variety of situations that cul-
minate in self-recognition on the part of the protagonists and a happy ending for the audience. Slade's
characters typically experience an illicit affair (not always at center stage), a divorce, a career crisis, and
problems with their children and their own maturation. The crowd onstage is always sparse. Two plays—
Special Occasions and *Same Time, Next Year*—have
only two characters each; *Romantic Comedy* and

Tribute have six and seven characters, respectively.
Children rarely appear onstage (*Tribute* is again the
exception), yet despite their absence they are often
crucial to the plot. Amy and Michael Ruskin's children in *Special Occasions* never appear in the spot-
light, but all three younger Ruskins have highly individual personalities, and all are so carefully drawn
that the audience is convinced of their existence even
in their absence. Stephen is at a stage that everyone is
hoping he will grow out of, Jennifer is a musical genius (her piano playing is audible), and Kelly is dull.
One might assess other characters' personalities with
similar ease, even though they are never seen. Indeed,
whole scenes in *Same Time, Next Year* are devoted to
the unsuspecting husband and the more astute wife
(both absent) of the lovers, and most of *Special Occasions* concerns people who are not formally in the
play. Thus, just as the extended time frame convinces
the audience members that they are not simply spectators at a play but observers of continuous human
history, so do Slade's offstage personalities convince
them that the principal characters are real people with
lives beyond the spotlights.

If there is an all-encompassing thesis that one
might extract from Slade's major productions, it is
this: Life does not distill itself into isolated instances
of time but is instead an evolving process that touches
other people who may or may not be present in the
flesh but whose influence is felt from moment to moment. The isolated moment can say much (as is the
case in *Special Occasions*), but every moment has its
context in things outside. While Slade's focus is always on center stage, one senses from the very beginning the presence of a background—historical and
densely populated—that gradually comes to life and
establishes itself as the source of what one sees and
hears onstage. Like his earlier plays for television,
Slade's Broadway productions offer little slices of
life, complete with triumphs and tragedies, while the
whole from which the slice is taken remains conspicuously and deliberately close at hand. Finally, though
they sometimes place a strain on credulity, the triumphs win out over the tragedies with remarkable
consistency. When Slade's world becomes dark—and
it does so almost rhythmically—the darkness lasts

only for its appointed duration. There is always a character ready with a joke, however nervously he may tell it, or a stagehand ready with a curtain, to bring one back to the realization that everything will be all right—in time.

SAME TIME, NEXT YEAR

In no other play does Slade use time more conspicuously than in *Same Time, Next Year*, his most successful Broadway production. The plot is simple enough: George and Doris leave their spouses at home with the children and meet at the same country inn near San Francisco for one weekend every year from 1951 to 1975. They make love 113 times (George, an accountant, uses his calculator to arrive at the figure), taking a brief but unexpected respite in 1961 because of Doris's pregnancy (and early labor) and George's impotence. (The timing is not always so perfect: In 1965, Doris refuses to have sex with him because he voted for Barry Goldwater.) Yet despite the play's dependence on the affair for its plot, *Same Time, Next Year* is only superficially about adultery. Its real focus is on growing up and on the 364 or so days a year that make George and Doris appear different each time the audience sees them.

The play opens on the morning following the pair's initial encounter. There are awkward moments at first, and George has grave misgivings about the whole situation. He tells lies, he calls Doris by a wrong name, and he is sure that his wife knows all about his infidelity. Doris, despite her Roman Catholic upbringing, is much more relaxed. She even eats George's breakfast for him. George's appetite, when it returns, is for sex: "The Russians have the bomb!" he exclaims, using world events and the threat of annihilation to justify sexual license. Having become familiar with each other sexually, the two decide to tell stories about the good and the bad sides of their spouses as a means of getting to know each other better. George already has his stories prepared, so he begins what later will become part of the ritual celebrated every February in the small country inn that never changes.

Despite the static quality of the setting and the fact that each of the five-year intervals follows closely the formula established in the first encounter, *Same Time,*

Next Year is a story about the profound change in the lives of the principal characters and in the larger world outside. The year 1961, for example, matches George's impotence against Doris's pregnancy (both conditions say a good deal about what 1960 must have been like for them). In 1965, Doris is liberated both in her dress and in her philosophical and sociological outlook, while George is on Librium, and by 1970, Doris has bought into the new "chic" establishment and opened an exclusive and highly successful French catering business, while George has exchanged his conservative lifestyle for denim and sandals. His conversation summarizes up the age of analysis with accuracy and charm: "When you first walked into the room I picked up your high tension level. Then after we made love I sensed a certain anxiety reduction but now I'm getting a definite negative feedback."

The source of the high tension level lies in the people and events in the world and outside the inn. George's impotence is only aggravated by his mother calling long distance to discuss possible cures, and his flirtation with Librium dependency is a direct result of his son's death in Vietnam. Although his psychoananalytic jargon is amusing, there are, nevertheless, serious reasons behind his decision to seek psychiatric help. The decision comes not a moment too soon, for, in 1975, George, now a widower, tells his last story about his wife with a degree of equanimity that comes only after years of dealing with life-altering experiences. The years have been kinder to Doris, whose only crisis comes in 1970 when her husband, Harry, leaves her. Significantly, it is George, in the guise of a Father Michael O'Herlihy, who brings about the couple's reconciliation. Once again, analysis has its real-life rewards.

In spite of its occasional crossovers into the realm of domestic tragedy, *Same Time, Next Year* is first and foremost a comedy in the tradition of the 1970's vintage Broadway. With a few notable exceptions, every situation has its comic moments, and the humor always has something to say about character growth. Doris's discussion of what it is like to have grown from a high school dropout to a wealthy businesswoman is a typical example. Fulfillment, she tells

George, is going into Gucci's and buying five suede suits at seven hundred dollars each for her bowling team—simply to spite the unpleasant salesgirl. George, too, has come a long way in twenty years. The same man whose guilt sends him into paroxysms of despair in the 1950's and 1960's is able to confront Doris's husband with amazing composure in 1970. Confessing that honesty is everything, George shamelessly tells Harry about the very intimate relationship he has had with Doris for twenty years. That his first and only conversation with Harry takes place over the telephone makes things a little easier for George and provides one of the play's most humorous moments: "My name? My name is Father Michael O'Herlihy. No, she's out saying a novena right now—Yes, my son, I'll tell her to call you."

One might easily point out any number of similar instances in the play, but the two above will serve to illustrate one final point about the humor in *Same Time, Next Year*. Doris is, from 1956 on, a woman motivated by one outstanding quality—spontaneity. She welcomes every moment as it comes, and she perfectly fits George's definition of life (saying "yes"). So accustomed is the audience to her love of the moment that the episode in the Gucci store comes as no surprise; her reaction represents in every way the classic Doris. George's long-distance triumph is equally revealing. His composure represents an achievement of great proportions, and he revels in it. He knows he is being clever, and so he stretches the moment for as long as he can make it last. Rarely is his self-perception at such a high point; his comic lines come at his own expense for three-quarters of the play. By 1970, a little of Doris has rubbed off on him, and the change is welcome. "I grew up with you," he tells her in 1975, and his words have an unmistakable ring of truth to them. There is only one kind of ending for a play that has so much to celebrate, and that is the kind Doris loves best. "I love—happy—endings!" she says at the end. One feels that she and George have earned one all their own.

TRIBUTE

Same Time, Next Year is one of Slade's most celebrated works. His next play, *Tribute*, is a celebration, for the audience as well as for the characters. The oc-

casion is Scottie Templeton's fifty-first birthday and his first appearance in public since his near-fatal bout with leukemia. His twenty-year-old son, Jud, and his boss, Lou Daniels, have rented a theater in New York and gathered Scottie's friends to pay tribute to the man who has left a legacy of love and laughter to all who know him. Lou opens the evening with a welcome (he knows many of us, he says) and an anecdote about Scottie and a crowded elevator. Dr. Gladys Petrelli, Scottie's physician, appears next and relates a little story about how Scottie's insomnia is contagious.

So much for the play's first beginning. *Tribute* begins a second time in Scottie's New York townhouse as Scottie entertains Sally Haines, a young model he met during an earlier stay in the hospital. The time is three months before the tribute to Scottie. As Sally leaves, Scottie's ex-wife, Maggie Stratton, enters with Jud, whom Scottie has not seen for two years. Still hurting from his parents' divorce and still feeling neglected, Jud is rather cold toward his father and informs him that he will be staying for only a week—he knows it will make little difference one way or the other to Scottie. Jud thus releases his first arrow, but he has brought a full quiver along with the rest of his baggage.

Scottie's stubborn refusal to receive any medical treatment and Jud's aloofness provide the raw materials for a series of confrontations over the next three months. Dr. Petrelli tells Scottie, who remains an incurable jester from start to finish, that using jokes to shut out reality is no longer going to work. She tries to enlist Jud's help, but Jud's "why me?" attitude has only hardened with age. He tells Sally, with whom he is now romantically involved, that his father is little more than a "court jester and a glorified pimp" (in fact, Scottie is a successful public relations man with a few false career starts in his past). Jud's assessment of his father's character only worsens when he accidentally walks in on his parents' lovemaking. The situation looks hopeless until Lou talks to Jud. Scottie's real talent, he tells Jud, is in making friends and in convincing them that life is better than it really is. He is worth saving, says Lou, and there are hundreds of people who feel the same way. Something clicks.

Scottie and Jud have one more confrontation—this one about going to the hospital. Lou interrupts things in mid-crisis only long enough for Jud to pack Scottie's suitcase. They are going to the hospital.

Thus, with a little help, Scottie creates one more friendship where before there was only indifference, and his new friend saves his life and then arranges its celebration. Back onstage for the tribute with which the play began, a handful of Scottie's many friends have been telling stories in between the scenes from Scottie's life, as Jud's slides of his father illuminate the stage. Dr. Petrelli tells of the late hours she has kept because of Scottie's simultaneous attacks of hypochondria and insomnia. Hilary, a retired prostitute, recounts the testimonial dinner that Scottie arranged for her ($250 a plate and a gold watch). Maggie tells a story about a special birthday dinner with Scottie, and Sally sums up what Scottie's new friends in the audience must be saying to themselves by now: "Hi! Whenever I think of Scottie—I smile."

Tribute thus celebrates the little man and dares to call him a hero in spite of his littleness. Life is Scottie Templeton's battleground, and humor, love, and forgiveness are his weapons. He uses them wherever he finds tragedy and indifference—in elevators, on city buses, or in his own townhouse. Hundreds of people have applauded the funny man in the corduroy cap, and it is Slade's intention that hundreds more will follow suit. *Tribute* offers no real clear-cut alternative once Jud's conversion is complete, and Maggie's enduring love for her ex-husband only confirms the rhetorical message of the play. *Tribute* has the effect of transforming the spectator (or reader) into a friend. By the end, the fact that *Tribute* is a play occurs to one only as an afterthought. Slade intends that one's first thoughts should be about one's new friends, and they are.

ROMANTIC COMEDY

Clive Barnes, in a 1978 *New York Post* article, has called *Tribute* an "honest truism" in a "serious funny" vein. A less serious play with less serious truths is *Romantic Comedy*. Slade has called the play a Valentine to the romantic playwrights of the 1930's and 1940's, and the phrase is especially apt. *Romantic Comedy* has all the seriousness of the genre it imi-

tates (which is to say, very little) and all the day-to-day reality of a Valentine card. It achieves, therefore, precisely what it sets out to do: to close the doors on reality and engage in two hours of old-fashioned fun.

Jason Carmichael, a self-centered and highly successful playwright, is about to marry Allison St. James, a young society woman whose father is the ambassador to New Zealand. Anxiously awaiting his prenuptial rubdown at the hands of Boris, Jason walks naked into his study only to find that Phoebe Craddock, a young Vermont schoolteacher and an aspiring playwright, has arrived for a brief interview. She stays for the next ten years and coauthors one Broadway hit after another with the now clothed Jason.

Marriage and partnership go smoothly until Jason decides to use his body where his mind has failed to remedy a bad working relationship with one of his leading ladies. Wife and partner both exit, leaving Jason on his own for the first time in years. He writes nothing of any worth for two years, while Phoebe, now living in Europe with her journalist husband, Leo, writes a best-selling novel called *Romantic Comedy*. She returns to New York to write a stage play based on her novel and to enlist Jason's help. The story is the one that the audience has been viewing onstage, with one supposed difference: Phoebe has "fantasized the relationship to make it interesting."

Romantic Comedy—the play—is already a fantasy, however, and all the crises are resolved: Jason realizes that he loves Phoebe only after a mild heart attack brought on by her return causes him to reevaluate his life; Allison, with qualifications known only to herself, runs for Congress; Leo literally gives Phoebe to Jason and then runs off to Spain to write a novel; and Phoebe outdoes them all by staying with Jason to consummate their unspoken love and to finish the play. There is certainly ample room in *Romantic Comedy* for a little sadness to creep in, but the treatment always says otherwise. *Romantic Comedy* has something of the comedy of manners about it, and, like its eighteenth century forebears, it never opts for realism when a humorous approach presents itself. Still, as Jason remarks in defense of his own plays, it takes a considerable amount of thought to write a play about entertaining an audience for an evening and to make the whole thing look easy.

SPECIAL OCCASIONS

Romantic Comedy has a whole tradition behind its less than serious view of life. *Special Occasions* is an altogether more innovative work that portrays life in all its bittersweet reality. Like *Same Time, Next Year*, *Special Occasions* follows the lives of two characters over a period of years (in this case, ten), charting their ups and downs and their gradual metamorphosis from strangers into friends. The structure is once again episodic, if less neatly so than before. Circumstances and other occasions bring Amy and Michael Ruskin together for brief moments every now and then, often when they least expect an encounter.

The play opens as Amy and Michael celebrate their fifteenth wedding anniversary and discuss their upcoming divorce. Amy's drinking problem quickly suggests itself as one of the reasons behind their separation, and subsequent occasions soon confirm the suggestion as fact. The rest of the play studies the personal growth not only of Amy and Michael but also of their children—Stephen, Kelly, and Jennifer. Michael's decision to undergo analysis marks his first step toward self-understanding, even if he does rehearse what he is going to say to his analyst. The audience next sees him at his mother's funeral, where he plays the flute in compliance with the last request of the deceased. Amy turns up for the viewing but misses the service, attending instead the eulogy for an eighty-five-year-old Japanese woman. Alcohol is responsible for her mistake.

The funeral home incident leads Amy to her next special occasion: her first Alcoholics Anonymous meeting, the rough equivalent of Michael's analysis. The occasion represents her first step toward personal well-being. Unlike Michael, she never deviates from the course she establishes for herself, although the years that follow unfold incident after incident to threaten her serenity. More often than not, it is Michael who suffers from what life offers over the years and Amy who pulls him through. The remaining special occasions follow in quick succession and include the unsuccessful production of Michael's first play,

Stephen's high school graduation, Christmas Eve (an especially *un*festive one), Amy's marriage to Michael's lawyer, the christening of Kelly's son, Stephen's car accident, and Michael's fiftieth birthday. *Special Occasions* has more than enough material for a lifetime—indeed, for several lifetimes—but throughout, the emphasis is on how Amy and Michael come to terms with each occasion and, finally, with each other.

Two questions surface time and time again as Amy and Michael discuss their relationship and the circumstances that bring them together. The first, "Why didn't you tell me?," eventually gives way to the second, "Why did you tell me?" Amy's answer to the second question sums up the theme of the play: Friends, she tells Michael, can tell friends anything. By the end of the play, Amy and Michael, still divorced, have established a firm friendship based on individual growth and shared experience. Like father and son in *Tribute*, they have reframed their relationship out of materials close at hand and can now look forward to filling in the details together. Michael proposes remarriage, but Amy, ever the more sensible of the two, suggests that they pause and enjoy the friendship that has taken ten years and some very special occasions to create.

The critical response to *Special Occasions* was generally unfavorable, but at least part of the negative reaction can be traced to the critics' confusion over what to call the play. *Special Occasions* has been called a comedy, a situation comedy, a soap opera, a television drama, and a failure at each for allowing the others to enter unannounced, yet none of the labels captures the complexity of the play's attitude toward life or the uniqueness of its design. Perhaps it would be more accurate to say that *Special Occasions* is a record of life, complete with its high and its low moments, that seeks to be objective and cumulative. Clearly the play mixes comedy with pathos, but so does life, according to the playwright. The structure is equally mimetic: When one looks back, Slade seems to be saying, one remembers the special occasions. In *Special Occasions*, as in all Slade's plays, looking back turns out to be a pleasurable experience.

Slade has said that no one has yet convinced him that life is not a comedy, and his plays clearly exist to give dramatic expression to his conviction that it is. Slade writes the way he does because he enjoys the sound of laughter and because life regularly affords laughable moments. All Slade's plays are, in the final analysis, profiles in friendship. Doris and George, Scottie and Jud, Jason and Phoebe, Michael and Amy—all affirm Slade's belief that time and a sense of humor can shape experience and bond friend to friend.

FATAL ATTRACTION

Since *Special Occasions*, Slade has experimented with (for him) new dramatic forms as well as returned to the tried and true. *Fatal Attraction* and *An Act of the Imagination* are his attempts at writing mysteries. This murder mystery (not related to the popular film of the same title), centers on Blair, an attractive actress whose husband, Blair, has been fatally stabbed by a paparazzo, whom Blair slays during a rape attempt. Detective Gus does not initially suspect Blair, but her agent shows up and hints of a lesbian relationship with the actress. This play, like many of Slade's other works, contains humorous moments. A *Los Angeles Times* critic, reviewing a 1990 Costa Mesa, California, production, criticized this mix of mystery and comedy.

AN ACT OF THE IMAGINATION

In *An Act of the Imagination*, judged by some critics to be the more successful of the two mysteries, Slade again uses a writer as one of his main characters and revisits the theme of infidelity. British writer Arthur Putnam has written a novel about an adulterous man who is afraid that someone is trying to kill him. Arthur insists that the work is not based on his own life, but his editor and wife have some doubts. The slow-moving first act sets up the dullness of the life Arthur shares with his wife, Julia, then shakes it up with the arrival of a woman, Brenda, who claims to be Arthur's lover and threatens blackmail. This mysterious women ends up dead. The much faster paced second act, in which police officer Fred Burchitt tries to unravel who killed Brenda, is filled with twists and turns that cause the audience to question what is real.

RETURN ENGAGEMENTS

In *Return Engagements*, Slade returned to his time theme. The play consists of six short vignettes, focusing on a room at an inn over a period of twenty-three years. The action revolves around three couples. Bellhop Raymond and ambitious actress Daisy end up, respectively, owning the inn and achieving a modicum of success, as well as marrying. Arrogant writer Keith and his wife, Fern, are having affairs with, respectively, Dawn and Henry. In the end, it is Dawn and Henry who end up married.

SAME TIME, ANOTHER YEAR

According to an article in the *Los Angeles Times*, Slade used the sequel to *Same Time, Next Year* to explore his concerns about aging. In *Same Time, Another Year*, Slade picks up the story of George and Doris in 1976, at the same country inn. In the sequel, filled with jokes about old age, George has a new, young girlfriend named Amber, and Doris has written a book about their affair, which she has sold to Random House. This return to the tried and true in the form of a sequel invited critics to contrast the play with the original, and many critics, including one writing for the *Los Angeles Times*, found the play wanting and its themes less appropriate for the 1990's.

OTHER MAJOR WORKS

SCREENPLAYS: *Stand Up and Be Counted*, 1971; *Same Time, Next Year*, 1978; *Tribute*, 1980; *Romantic Comedy*, 1983.

TELEPLAYS: *The Prizewinner*, 1957; *Moving Day*, 1987.

NONFICTION: *Shared Laughter*, 2000.

BIBLIOGRAPHY

Beaufort, John. "A Twenty-four-Year Love Story." Review of *Same Time, Next Year*, by Bernard Slade. *The Christian Science Monitor*, March 21, 1975. Takes a mildly remonstrative tone, with such phrases as "non-married couple" involved in "illicit, once-a-year trysts" representing "changing mores." Good description of voice-over and set transitions, which "give the new comedy an underlying tone of reminiscent recognition." The play is "slight and facile" but is "graced with humanity."

Breslauer, Jan. "Same Writer, Same Characters, but Next Up, New Adventures." *Los Angeles Times*, January 11, 1996, p. 1. In an interview, Slade discusses what motivated him to write the sequel to *Same Time, Next Year* and what message he hoped to convey.

Kerr, Walter. "Stage: Slade's *Romantic Comedy*." Review of *Romantic Comedy*, by Bernard Slade. *The New Times*, November 9, 1979, p. 63. Anthony Perkins and Mia Farrow star in this Broadway hit, which Kerr faults for some of the comic business and improbable laughs. He cites Perkins for his "smartness, high style, the lofty and chilly bon mot" and finds Farrow's character, "eternally childlike, eternally composed," to be well acted.

Watt, Douglas. "Even in Skilled Hands, Being Glib Isn't Easy." Review of *Romantic Comedy*, by Bernard Slade. *New York Daily News*, November 9, 1979. This review is slightly different in viewpoint and tone from those in other New York newspapers. Watt credits Slade's artistry, mentions the earlier success with *Same Time, Next Year*, and cites Anthony Perkins's and Mia Farrow's personalities, which bring the characters to light in a way that the genre needs.

Wilson, Edwin. "Laughter on Broadway." *The Wall Street Journal*, November 9, 1979. Wilson examines Slade's handling of the writing craft and discusses how the play intentionally works against the form: "Mr. Slade . . . capitulates" to the form in the end, in a noble effort, but "has not solved his [dramatic] problem" entirely.

Winer, Laurie. "Same Jokes, Another Play: It's Deja Vu in Pasadena." Review of *Same Time, Another Year*, by Bernard Slade. *Los Angeles Times*, January 16, 1996, p. 1. In this review of *Same Time, Another Year*, after the opening of its world premiere at the Pasadena Playhouse, Winer criticizes the sequel for lacking the interaction between the two characters that enlivened the initial play and for containing too many old-age jokes.

William A. Davis,
updated by Thomas J. Taylor

JULIUSZ SŁOWACKI

Born: Krzemieniec, Poland; September 4, 1809
Died: Paris, France; April 3, 1849

PRINCIPAL DRAMA

Mindowe Król Litewski, wr. 1829, pb. 1832, pr. 1869

Maria Stuart, pb. 1832, pr. 1862 (*Mary Stuart*, 1937)

Kordian, pb. 1834, pr. 1899

Balladyna, wr. 1834, pb. 1839, pr. 1862 (English translation, 1960)

Horsztyński, wr. 1835, pb. 1866, pr. 1879

Beatrix Cenci, wr. 1839, pb. 1866

Lilla Weneda, pb. 1840, pr. 1863

Mazepa, pb. 1840, pr. 1847 (*Mazeppa*, 1930)

Fantazy, wr. 1841, pb. 1866, pr. 1867 (English translation, 1977)

Złota czaszka, wr. 1842, pb. 1866, pr. 1899

Ksiądz Marek, pb. 1843, pr. 1901

Książę niezłomny, pb. 1844, pr. 1874

Sen srebrny Salomei, pb. 1844, pr. 1900

Agezylausz, wr. 1844, pb. 1844, pr. 1927

Zawisza Czarny, wr. 1844, pb. 1889, pr. 1910

Samuel Zborowski, wr. 1845, pr. 1911, pb. 1928

OTHER LITERARY FORMS

In addition to many masterworks of drama, the literary legacy of Juliusz Słowacki includes much epic and lyric poetry of the highest order. Although the greater part of Słowacki's narrative poetry was published during his own lifetime, very few of his lyric poems were known to his contemporaries. He wrote approximately 130 lyric poems, of which only thirteen appeared in print before his death in 1849. It was only from 1866 onward, when Antoni Malecki began to bring out an edition of Słowacki's collected works incorporating many of the unpublished manuscripts, that Słowacki's countrymen gradually became aware of his genius as a lyric poet. In some of the later poems, it should be noted, Słowacki may be deemed to have transcended the stylistic conventions of Romanticism and to have developed poetic techniques that anticipated those employed by the French Symbolists and the English Pre-Raphaelites.

Słowacki's earliest epic poetry is permeated by a Romantic melancholy and exoticism that is clearly derivative of George Gordon, Lord Byron's writings. Most likely, his first true masterpiece of narrative verse is the elegiac autobiographical sketch entitled *Godzinna myśli* (1833; hour of thought). This work depicts the emotional travail of an adolescent poet growing up in the city of Wilno and its environs, and its sketchy plot focuses on his relationship with two people, a brilliant schoolmate who inexplicably commits suicide and an attractive girl who fails to return his love for her. Before long, however, Słowacki found a political focus for his deep-rooted personal pessimism. Among the noteworthy works of an explicitly political nature is *Anhelli* (1838; English translation, 1930). Written in poetic prose with biblical affinities, it relates the tragic plight of a contentious group of Polish exiles in the frozen wasteland of Siberia during the years following the ill-fated November Insurrection of 1830. His next major narrative poem is the love idyll *W Szwajcarii* (1839; *In Switzerland*, 1953). Set amid the scenic splendor of the Alps, the idyll consists of a series of episodes in the life of a pair of lovers. The reader is told of their meeting, their marriage, the premature death of the bride, and the young man's subsequent departure from Switzerland. The fundamental romantic appeal of this simple tale is, moreover, greatly enhanced by the delicate musicality of its verse.

Some of Słowacki's most successful works of narrative verse are, furthermore, quite unorthodox in

form. One such instance is the posthumously published travel diary *Podróż na wschód* (1836; journey to the east). This poetic journal describes Słowacki's voyage from Naples to Greece as well as his subsequent wanderings in that country. It is, however, frequently interrupted by digressions in which the poet expatiates on various topics of personal concern. The eighth canto of this work was printed separately in 1840 under the title *Grób Agamemnona* (*Agamemnon's Grave*, 1944). At a grotto then believed to be the burial chamber of Agamemnon, the poet recalls the legendary heroism of the ancient Greeks and bemoans the defects in both his own character and that of his countrymen. Similarly topical in nature is the epic entitled *Beniowski* (1841). While most of *Beniowski* is devoted to the adventures of the eponymous hero in the course of an anti-Russian conspiracy that took place in the Polish Ukraine during the 1760's, Słowacki manages, in the plot of this loosely structured narrative poem, to insert numerous satiric attacks directed against the current follies of his compatriots. It was this work, in fact, that first established Słowacki's literary reputation among the Polish émigrés in Paris.

The definitive expression of Słowacki's religious and philosophical convictions is to be found in *Genezis z ducha* (1844; genesis from the spirit) and *Król-Duch* (1847; king-spirit). Both of these works stress the supremacy of the spirit over matter. In the prose poem *Genezis z ducha*, Słowacki presents his readers with a vision of cosmic evolution that has strong affinities with the theories advanced in the twentieth century by the French Jesuit Pierre Teilhard de Chardin. A major role in the evolutionary process that is moving humankind toward spiritual perfection is played by leaders whom Słowacki designates as "king-spirits." The manifestation of the spirit on the historical level is examined in *Król-Duch*, an epic poem written in ottava rima and divided into segments called "rhapsodies." Here, Słowacki employs a concept of metempsychosis that is derived from the tenth book of Plato's *Politeia* (388-368 B.C.E.; *Republic*, 1701), in which the Orphic doctrine of reincarnation is related in the section entitled "The Myth of Er." In Słowacki's adaptation of this episode, a Greek warrior named Er embraces the idea of Poland while awaiting his next reincarnation, and on rebirth, he assumes the identity of Popiel, the legendary Polish king of prehistory. Other reincarnations follow that carry on the historical mission of Poland. Despite the fact that Słowacki was able to give final form to only the first of the five rhapsodies that make up its text, many regard *Król-Duch* as his finest work.

ACHIEVEMENTS

The high point in Polish literature was attained in the Romantic period during the first half of the nineteenth century. The most distinguished poets of this epoch were Adam Mickiewicz, Juliusz Słowacki, and Zygmunt Krasiński. Each of them, to varying degrees, wrote dramatic literature. Mickiewicz, except for two unimportant plays written in French, restricted himself to the composition of three independent dramatic works that he rather arbitrarily chose to link together under the title *Dziady* (1822-1832; *Forefathers' Eve*, 1925, 1944-1946). The third part of *Dziady* is now generally regarded as the single most important play in the history of the Polish theater. Krasiński's contribution to the stage is limited to a pair of plays, both of which soon attained the status of classics: *Nie-Boska komedia* (pb. 1835, pr. 1902; *The Undivine Comedy*, 1846) and *Irydion* (pb. 1836, pr. 1908; *Iridion*, 1875). Słowacki, in contrast, completed nearly twenty full-length plays of great variety, and by virtue of these works, he has been singled out as the founder of modern Polish drama.

Although Słowacki's dramatic works are now part of the standard repertory of the Polish theater, public recognition of their merit came to pass only many decades after the poet's death. The Polish exiles in Paris or elsewhere had no theater of their own, and political conditions in their homeland precluded the staging of works by those engaged in promoting revolutionary activities. The sole dramatic work by Słowacki to be performed during his own lifetime was *Mazeppa*, a translated version of which was staged in Budapest in 1847. It was not until the 1860's that his plays began to be produced in various cities within the Austrian section of partitioned Poland. For the most part, however, they remained proscribed in other parts of the country until the restoration of national independence in the aftermath of World War I. Over the years, six of these works have proved to be especially popular with Polish audiences: *Mary Stuart, Kordian, Balladyna, Lilla Weneda, Mazeppa,* and *Fantazy.* Also noteworthy is Słowacki's free-verse adaptation of Pedro Calderón de la Barca's *El príncipe constante* (1629; *The Constant Prince*, 1893), which he published under the title *Książę niezłomny* (the inflexible prince) in 1844. This work has become one of the most highly regarded presentations of the Laboratory Theater, situated in the city of Wrocław, as produced and directed by the group's founder, Jerzy Grotowski.

BIOGRAPHY

Juliusz Słowacki was born in the year 1809 on September 4 (August 23, Old Style), and hence his life unfolded amid the political turmoil that arose as a result of the partitioning of Poland by Russia, Prussia, and Austria during the closing decades of the eighteenth century. The annexation of Polish territory by its more powerful neighbors occurred in three stages. The first partition took place in 1772; the second, in 1792; and the third, in 1795. The town of Krzemieniec, Słowacki's birthplace, was situated in the province of Volhynia in eastern Poland and came under Russian occupation in 1795. It was here in 1805 that the eminent Polish historian Tadeusz Czacki established a lyceum that was to bring great renown to Krzemieniec. The town was, in fact, called the "Volhynian Athens" and achieved a rank second only to Wilno in terms of importance as a cultural center in the eastern regions of the old Polish Republic. At the time of the poet's birth, his father, Euzebiusz Słowacki, was a professor of literature and rhetoric at the famed lyceum. His mother, Salomea (née Januszewska), was a well-educated woman with a strong penchant for reading literature of a sentimental nature. The bond between mother and son was exceptionally strong, and a number of literary critics have gone so far as to ascribe a mother fixation to Słowacki because of his lifelong need for her emotional support.

A few years after Słowacki's birth, his parents moved to Wilno because of his father's appointment to a chair in literature at the University of Wilno. His tenure in this position proved to be a brief one, owing to his sudden death in 1814, when his son was only five years old. After three years of widowhood, Słowacki's mother decided to enter into a second marriage with Dr. August Bécu, a medical professor at the University of Wilno. Dr. Bécu was himself a widower, with two daughters from his previous marriage. The members of the new household nevertheless lived together quite harmoniously, and Słowacki seems to have developed a genuine attachment to all the members of his adopted family. The future poet was somewhat frail as a child and prone to ill health. As the only boy in the family, he was pampered by his mother and his two stepsisters. Because Dr. Bécu's home was a meeting place for the intellectual elite of Wilno, Słowacki received an early exposure to literary and political controversy. The fact that literature was a matter of importance within the family induced Słowacki to read voraciously in several languages. This idyllic existence came to an abrupt end in 1824, when Dr. Bécu was struck by lightning and died as a result.

After the death of her second husband, Słowacki's mother returned to Krzemieniec, where she was able to live quite comfortably on the pensions that she received as the widow of two university professors. Since Słowacki had already completed his secondary education, it was deemed best that he remain in Wilno and enroll at the university there. Although his mother always encouraged his literary interests, viewing them as social graces, she insisted on his training for a career in law. Shortly before Słowacki's matriculation at the university, the Russians had discovered the existence of clandestine political organizations among the city's youth and took stern measures to suppress them. Many students were among those arrested, and some were forced into Russian exile. As a result of this repression, the intellectual climate at the university became one of cautious conservatism in all fields. Being somewhat aloof by nature, at least outside his family circle, Słowacki formed few intimate relationships among his peers. His only close friend was Ludwik Szpicnagel, and his only love interest was Ludwika Śniadecka. Both were his

seniors by a few years and had fathers who were professors at the university. Szpicnagel was to commit suicide, and Śniadecka proved unresponsive to Słowacki's courtship. Despite these tribulations, Słowacki completed the prescribed course of studies within three years and even managed occasionally to visit his mother in Krzemieniec. After receiving his law degree, he returned to Krzemieniec for a six-month stay before embarking on a career as a civil servant.

In 1829, at the age of nineteen, Słowacki became an employee of the ministry of finance in Warsaw. There he felt free to pursue his literary interests more seriously. Except for a short poetic narrative published anonymously, none of his poetry had ever appeared in print. He had, however, written a number of poetic works while he was a student at the University of Wilno, and he now planned to publish them collectively in a single volume. Inspired by the lively theatrical life in Warsaw, he also decided to try his hand at writing for the stage and swiftly completed two dramas. The first was called *Mindowe Król Litewski*, a play based on events drawn from the history of medieval Lithuania. The second bore the title *Mary Stuart* and dealt with the early life of the Scottish queen. These two plays were to make up the contents of the second volume of his collected works to date. Before Słowacki could complete arrangements for the printing of either volume, however, an anti-Russian insurrection broke out in Warsaw and quickly spread to other parts of the country. Although Słowacki had been largely apolitical up to that time, the upheaval in Warsaw was to alter his life irrevocably.

During that period, Warsaw was the capital of an entity that later came to be called Congress Poland, because it had been created at the Congress of Vienna in 1815 in the aftermath of the Napoleonic wars. Although its official name was the Kingdom of Poland, the Russian czar, Nicholas I, was its mandated ruler, and the czar's brother, Grand Duke Constantine, was commander of its armed forces. Such Russian dominance of their country was deeply resented by most Poles. Another source of dissatisfaction lay in the fact that the reconstituted kingdom embraced but a small portion of the territory that Poland had controlled before the partitions. Thus, Krzemieniec and Wilno were not even a part of the kingdom and lay deep within the Russian-occupied eastern provinces. The insurrection began in November, 1830, when Nicholas I announced that he intended to use Polish troops, along with Russian forces, to suppress revolutions that had recently broken out in France and Belgium. The foremost Polish historian of the day, Joachim Lelewel, formulated the motto "For Our Freedom and Yours" as an appeal for international support, and the insurrectionists duly urged the Russian people to join them in their revolt against czarist tyranny.

The conflict between Russia and Poland was to last ten months before reaching its inevitable end. Słowacki initially greeted the outbreak by writing an ode to freedom in its honor, but despite his personal enthusiasm for the goals of the revolution, he engaged in no further political activity on its behalf for the next few months. Then, for reasons that are not entirely clear, Słowacki left Warsaw early in March and went to Dresden. He remained in Dresden until July, at which time he received orders from the Polish revolutionary government to undertake a diplomatic mission on its behalf. His instructions called for him to go to London via Paris. He traveled posthaste and reached Paris in six days. After five hours in the French capital, he rushed off for Boulogne. Having just missed the daily boat for England, he chartered a vessel of his own to take him to Dover and ordered the Polish flag to be flown from its mast. After spending several weeks in London, he decided to return to Paris. By this time it was clear that the insurrection was doomed to defeat, and Słowacki therefore made no attempt to return to Warsaw. The Polish capital did, in fact, capitulate to the Russians on September 8, 1831. Facing certain arrest if he returned to Poland, Słowacki thought it best to remain in France for the time being. Some ten thousand Poles were to leave their homeland for sanctuary in the West in a move that has come to be called the Great Migration. Unlike most of the other émigrés who left Poland to escape Russian retribution, Słowacki always had sufficient funds to meet his own living expenses. The money, sent to him periodically by his mother throughout his entire life in exile, came from a be-

quest left to him by his father. By investing these modest sums wisely in stocks, Słowacki acquired the wherewithal to pursue his literary ambitions free from financial restrictions.

Although émigrés from Poland also gathered in London, Geneva, and Rome, it was Paris that became the chief center of Polish cultural life for the exiles. Undoubtedly, the two most prominent émigrés in the French capital were Frédéric Chopin and Adam Mickiewicz. Mickiewicz, who had undergone four years of Russian exile for his political activities in the city of Wilno, was slightly more than ten years older than Słowacki and had already earned his reputation as the foremost Polish poet of his generation. Słowacki, on this account, strongly desired Mickiewicz's critical approval of his own poetic endeavors. Being financially independent, he arranged for the publication of a two-volume edition of his works under the title *Poezye* (poems) in 1832 and then anxiously awaited Mickiewicz's reaction. Because the content of these volumes was completely devoid of any political or religious ideology, Mickiewicz dismissed them as "a church without a God inside." Perhaps even more offensive to Słowacki than this harsh verdict on his poetry was the fact that Mickiewicz had used his stepfather, Dr. Bécu, as a model for an extremely unsympathetic character in the newly published part 3 of his dramatic composition *Forefathers' Eve*. Readers could readily identify the doctor in the play with his real-life counterpart because this character is also killed by a lightning bolt, as Słowacki's stepfather had been. Mickiewicz, in this fashion, implied that Dr. Bécu had been punished by Providence because of his refusal to support revolutionary activity aimed at restoring Poland's freedom. Słowacki was so incensed that he wanted to challenge Mickiewicz to a duel, but he was eventually dissuaded from doing so. Since the émigré community proved to be totally indifferent toward his writings, Słowacki saw no compelling reason to remain in Paris, and he left for Switzerland near the end of 1832. The person most sorry to see Słowacki leave Paris was Cora Pinard, the fifteen-year-old daughter of his printer. Her fondness for the young poet was so enduring that she continued to place fresh flowers on his grave for years after his death in 1849, although she was at that time the wife of a rich manufacturer.

Słowacki took up residence in a quiet pension in the suburbs of Geneva. His landlady was extremely well disposed toward him and hoped that he would marry her daughter and remain in Switzerland permanently. Słowacki, however, preferred to court a young Polish aristocrat named Maria Wodzińska. Wodzińska herself was something of a celebrity, since it was common knowledge that Frédéric Chopin was passionately in love with her. On one occasion, Słowacki went on an excursion into the Swiss Alps with her and other members of her family, and this experience inspired him to write the love idyll *In Switzerland*. His chief literary activities during these years, however, were focused on the writing of five dramas, two of which, *Kordian* and *Balladyna*, are considered to be among his most important works for the theater. Despite his contentment with life in Switzerland—first at Geneva and later at Lausanne—Słowacki jumped at the opportunity to go to Rome for the sake of a family reunion with his maternal uncle and one of his foster sisters, who were now husband and wife, and he thereupon terminated his three-year Swiss sojourn, in February, 1836. His relatives were on a grand tour of Italy, and he joined them in seeing the sights in Rome and even went with them on a trip to Naples. Although only six years had elapsed since he had last seen them in Poland, it soon became apparent that he now had little in common with them. Słowacki did, however, meet someone in Rome with whom he shared strong mutual interests: Count Zygmunt Krasiński, a poet who was his junior by a few years. Krasiński, despite his youth, was already the author of two widely acclaimed plays. He quickly recognized Słowacki's genius and did much to inspire him with confidence in his own literary talent and poetic mission.

Słowacki abruptly cut short his stay in Italy when he learned of a possibility of taking a trip to the Near East in the company of two compatriots whom he had met by chance. The trip proved to be beneficial to him in terms of literary productivity, for under the stimulus of travel he wrote constantly and turned out several major works—one of which was the posthu-

mously published travel diary entitled *Podróż na wschód*. Departing from Naples in August, 1836, Słowacki and his companions went first to Greece, next to Egypt, and then to Palestine. While in Jerusalem, Słowacki prayed all night in a church containing Christ's tomb and ordered a mass to be said for Poland. From Palestine, the party went on to Lebanon, at which point Słowacki took leave of his companions in order to spend a few weeks in contemplation at a local monastery. There he wrote the first draft of the long prose poem *Anhelli*.

After a voyage from Beirut to Leghorn, Słowacki arrived back in Italy during the summer of 1837. He then hastened on to Florence and settled down for a protracted stay in that city. Słowacki, as always, worked zealously on his own literary compositions. In addition, he still found time to learn both Italian and Spanish. The small Polish colony in the Tuscan city was prepared to lionize the young poet and gladly opened its homes to him. An accomplished amateur pianist, Słowacki played the music of Chopin in some of the finest salons in Florence, including that of Joseph Bonaparte's daughter, and doting admirers frequently told him that he resembled his distinguished musical compatriot. Despite such pleasures, Słowacki began to grow a bit restless and felt a need to rejoin the Polish émigré colony in Paris so as to be at the center of literary and political activity involving his homeland. The immediate impetus to leave Florence was Krasiński's arrival in the city, bearing ill tidings from Poland. Krasiński, whose family had never supported the November Insurrection, was permitted freedom of movement by the czarist officials, and on a recent trip to Poland he had heard reports that a number of Słowacki's relatives, including the poet's own mother, had been arrested on charges of anti-Russian political activity. Because it was much easier to get news from Poland in Paris, Słowacki soon set out for the French capital and thus ended his eighteen-month stay in Florence.

Although Słowacki arrived in Paris in the later part of December, 1838, he had to wait until May, 1839, before receiving concrete information about his mother's release. Once he knew that his mother was safe, Słowacki felt free to resume writing. Before long, moreover, he was deeply in love again. This time the woman was Joanna Bobrowa, a statuesque beauty from Volhynia who had recently been romantically involved with his friend Krasiński. Even though Krasiński had definitely broken off with her, she remained loyal to him and could not return Słowacki's love. Słowacki eventually decided to settle for her friendship, and the two remained lifelong companions. By the middle of 1842, he also managed to complete four new dramatic works, among which were *Lilla Weneda* and *Mazeppa*. Then, on July 12, 1842, Andrzej Towiański, a religious mystic from Wilno, had a long talk with Słowacki and succeeded in turning him into a disciple. Towiański had been in Paris since September, 1841, and had already converted Mickiewicz to his inner circle. His teachings emphasized the central importance of the Hebrew, French, and Polish peoples in God's scheme for establishing the kingdom of Heaven on Earth as well as the crucial role to be played by great individuals in furthering the historical manifestation of the divine will.

From then on, Słowacki assumed the role of national bard, a position that Mickiewicz had recently vacated by virtue of a decision to abandon poetry in favor of direct political action. As national bard, Słowacki saw himself as both a teacher of spiritual truths and a prophet. He soon expressed his philosophical credo in a remarkable prose poem entitled *Genezis z ducha* and then began work on the grandiose historical epic *Król-Duch*. Notwithstanding his preoccupation with the task of developing a new metaphysical system, Słowacki found time to produce several important dramatic works with strong spiritual overtones. In view of Towiański's partiality toward the dramas of Pedro Calderón de la Barca, moreover, Słowacki persuaded himself to compose a free-verse adaptation of the Spanish playwright's *The Constant Prince*. As befits a national bard, Słowacki also began to take part in the intense political debates of the émigré community in Paris and eventually became estranged from both his erstwhile mentor Towiański and his close friend Krasiński, as a result of ideological differences. In 1846, amid all this activity, Słowacki discovered that he had contracted tuberculosis; in 1847, he made out his will.

The spring of 1848 was a time of political upheaval throughout much of Europe. Although things remained under tight control in Russian-occupied Poland, insurrections broke out in the Polish territories under Prussian and Austrian rule. In order to assist his compatriots in the Prussian area, Słowacki left Paris on short notice and arrived in Poznań on April 10. The revolt there was short-lived, and Słowacki had to flee Poznań to avoid arrest by the Prussian police. For a time he lived under an assumed name in the Silesian city of Breslau, where he was able to arrange for his mother to come from Krzemieniec to visit him. The reunion with his mother, whom he had not seen in more than eighteen years, was a sad one. Both knew that this would be their last meeting, for the effects of tuberculosis had taken a terrible toll on Słowacki's health. He returned to Paris in June, 1848, and spent the last months of his life working feverishly on the epic poem *Król-Duch*. When he was too weak to write, he resorted to dictation. Finally, on an afternoon in April, 1849, Słowacki died with great composure, even though he was so lacking in physical strength that he was unable to open a letter from his mother that had arrived that day. Oddly enough, Chopin himself was to die of the same malady later that year; both he and Słowacki were interred in cemeteries in Paris. At his own request, however, Chopin's heart was removed from his body after his death and taken back to Poland by his sister Ludwika. Today the urn containing his heart rests in the baroque Church of the Holy Cross in Warsaw.

Słowacki's turn to rejoin his homeland physically did not occur until 1927, when the newly independent Polish state arranged for his remains to be transported from Paris and placed in the royal crypt of the Wawel Castle in Kraków amid the tombs of Poland's kings and national heroes. Słowacki's sarcophagus is to be found alongside that of Mickiewicz. Although both Krzemieniec and Wilno were part of the Polish republic in the period between the two world wars, these cities now lie outside the frontiers of present-day Poland as a result of their annexation by the Soviet Union during the course of World War II. Krzemieniec, now called Kremenets, lies within the

Ukraine, while Wilno today bears the name Vilnius and is the capital of Lithuania.

ANALYSIS

It was Juliusz Słowacki's desire to write a variety of plays that could form basis for a repertory of a national theater. Intimately familiar with the masterworks of Western literature, he freely borrowed themes, plots, and techniques from a host of different writers. Because of Słowacki's overt attempts to simulate the aesthetic effects achieved by Shakespeare, Calderón, and other writers, in combination with elements derived from old Polish poetry and Slavic folklore, the eminent Belgian literary scholar Claude Backvis has referred to plays such as *Balladyna* and *Lilla Weneda* as "amazing literary cocktails." In the view of many other critics, Backvis's remark underscores the main weakness in Słowacki's dramatic œuvre: namely, his penchant for mixing the styles of different authors and different periods within one and the same play. Despite this excessive reliance on purely literary inspiration, however, Słowacki's plays possess a genuine spiritual passion that will ensure their continued status as masterworks in the repertory of the classical Polish theater. Along with Mickiewicz and Krasiński, furthermore, Słowacki possessed the creative genius to write works which assured that the cause of Polish independence would never be abandoned.

MARY STUART

Słowacki wrote *Mary Stuart* when he was little more than twenty years of age. Despite its obvious weaknesses, the work still has a large number of admirers. Much of the reason for its continued popularity must be attributed to the subject matter itself. The tragic fate of Mary Stuart has fascinated playwrights throughout the world from the very outset. The first drama about the Queen of Scots appeared in 1589—a play written in Latin by a French Jesuit only two years after her death. Of all the plays written on the topic since then, Friedrich Schiller's *Maria Stuart* (pr. 1800, pb. 1801; *Mary Stuart*, 1801) is undoubtedly the most important. Słowacki had seen a Polish translation of a French version of Schiller's drama in 1830 and completed his own play about the Scottish queen

shortly before the outbreak of the November Insurrection in the same year. Although Schiller limits himself to covering the three days immediately preceding Mary's execution in 1587, the events depicted by Słowacki extend from the autumn of 1565 to February, 1567.

The action of Słowacki's play commences with the Queen of Scots demoting her husband, Lord Darnley, from his status as co-regent. In an apparent act of retribution, Darnley arranges for the murder of Mary's Italian secretary and confidant, Rizzio. The killing takes place under the queen's own eyes. Darnley also witnesses the murder by concealing himself behind her throne. Shortly thereafter, Mary succumbs to the advances of the earl of Bothwell. The ambitious nobleman, by offering her both physical protection and romantic consolation, hopes to advance his personal fortunes. He senses Mary's inner desire for revenge and skillfully maneuvers her into expressing a wish that her husband suffer the same fate as Rizzio. When it is learned that Darnley has become ill and has taken up residence in a house on the outskirts of Edinburgh, Bothwell suggests that Mary visit her husband and induce him to take a sleeping potion that will make him more vulnerable to an assassin's stiletto, which he himself promises to wield. The queen readily agrees to the plan.

Although somewhat distrustful of Bothwell's motives, Mary visits her husband and feigns reconciliation. Afraid that her nervousness might betray her, she leaves before her husband drinks from the goblet. The king's jester, however, suspects that the goblet contains poison and attempts to dissuade his master from drinking the liquid. Darnley, believing in his wife's good faith, takes great offense at the jester's insinuation and orders his execution. The jester quickly imbibes the contents of the goblet and dies within minutes. Unknown to Mary, Bothwell has planned to make her the agent of the king's death. By turning her into a murderess, he seeks to attain the means of dominating Mary psychologically in their personal relationship.

Darnley's reprieve is short-lived, however, for Bothwell has planted explosives under the king's house in order to blow it up and thereby dispose of all evidence pertaining to Mary's direct participation in the death of her husband. The deed accomplished, Bothwell returns to inform Mary that, as partners in crime, they are bound to each other for life. Mary, for her part, protests her innocence and refuses to accept any responsibility for the turn of events. She and her lover are, nevertheless, immediately suspected of being involved in Darnley's death. Mary's Scottish subjects, largely Protestant, deeply disapprove of the queen's Catholic faith. Quick to become indignant at Darnley's murder, the people advance toward the palace, and the play ends with Mary and Bothwell fleeing Edinburgh to escape from the mob's wrath.

It is likely that Słowacki based his characterization of the young Mary on the disclosures contained in the final act of Schiller's play about the Queen of Scots. Here, quite daringly, Schiller depicts an authentic Roman Catholic confession on the stage. Mary bares her soul to her confessor and fully admits to the acts of illicit sex and premeditated vengeance perpetrated in Scotland. Although about to be executed for her complicity in plots recently directed against her cousin Elizabeth I, she resolutely denies her guilt with respect to these charges. Mary transcends her tragic fate by regarding her impending execution as a means of atoning for the transgressions of her youth and thus attains spiritual freedom. Elizabeth, in contrast, refuses to acknowledge that she herself must bear ultimate responsibility for Mary's execution and contrives to make it appear that a minor palace official implemented the execution order prematurely. Elizabeth's vacillations and evasions, as depicted by Schiller, are strikingly similar to those ascribed to Mary in Słowacki's play. Thus, Słowacki owes a twofold debt to the German dramatist. Unlike Schiller, however, Słowacki was content to use poetic prose rather than verse for his own drama about the Queen of Scots.

KORDIAN

Even though several historical personages appear among the *dramatis personae* of his next play, its plot is wholly invented by the author. As originally conceived by Słowacki, *Kordian* was to be the first part of a dramatic trilogy that would cover the history of the November Insurrection. The other two parts were never written, however, and it is uncertain how the problems raised in the first play would subsequently have been resolved. Written in Switzerland in 1833, the play is subtitled "A Coronation Conspiracy" and consists of three acts together with a prologue. Because Słowacki's previously published books had not been received favorably, he thought it best to publish this verse drama anonymously so that it could be judged on its own merits.

In the first act, the fifteen-year-old Count Kordian agonizes over an unhappy love affair as well as over Poland's tragic loss of independence. Believing himself to be incapable of heroic action, he decides to end his existence and duly makes an unsuccessful attempt at suicide. The second act depicts Kordian's journey through Europe in search of self-knowledge. He visits both England and Italy. While in Rome he has an audience with Pope Gregory, whose negative attitude toward Polish independence is excoriated. Then, atop Mont Blanc, the young count resolves to consecrate his life to patriotic activity on behalf of Poland. The third act is set in Warsaw at the time of the coronation of Czar Nicholas I as king of Poland. Kordian now wears the uniform of a Polish military cadet and attempts, with limited success, to persuade other cadets to join him in a conspiracy to kill the czar. By chance he is assigned the duty of standing guard outside the bedroom of the Russian monarch on the eve of the coronation and resolves to carry out the assassination single-handedly. As Kordian enters the czar's bedroom with drawn bayonet, his strength mysteriously deserts him and he falls to the floor unconscious. The authorities place him in an insane asylum in order to determine his mental competence as well as the true intent of his action. While incarcerated in the asylum, Kordian goes through much romantic soul-searching. Meanwhile, he is judged to be responsible for his behavior and is sentenced to death. The czar's viceroy in Poland, Grand Duke Constantine, who was known to be sympathetic toward the Poles, wants Kordian to be pardoned and finally convinces his brother to rescind the death sentence. The final scene of the play takes place at the site of execution, but it is unclear whether the czar's reprieve will arrive in time to spare Kordian's life.

In the view of some critics, the protagonist's name is derived from the Latin word for heart (*cor*) and thus symbolizes the romantic malady of a young man who is unable to translate feelings into action. Other critics view the name as being an anagram of Konrad, the central character in part 3 of Mickiewicz's *Forefathers' Eve*; in this reading, Słowacki's play constitutes a repudiation of the notion that the fate of Poland would be determined by the acts of a "providential man." Since Mickiewicz strongly implied that he himself was this exalted savior, Słowacki was bound to be doubly opposed to this romantic solution to the problem of Poland's plight. In a larger sense, he was also criticizing the revolutionary ardor of his generation for its readiness to sacrifice itself in heroic, but ill-starred, ventures.

BALLADYNA

From the historical concerns of *Kordian*, Słowacki entered the realm of folklore with the dramatic work entitled *Balladyna*. Reduced to its basic plot, the play is a dramatized ballad about a poor woman who has two beautiful daughters: Balladyna and Alina. A rich and powerful nobleman named Kirkor falls in love with both of the sisters to an equal degree. Because he is unable to decide between them, Kirkor accepts the mother's suggestion that the choice be left to fate and that he marry the one who first succeeds in filling a pitcher with raspberries from an adjacent wood. When Alina appears to be on the verge of winning the contest, Balladyna kills her in the wood and appropriates her sister's berries for herself. In this way she becomes Kirkor's wife. Before long, however, Kirkor leaves on a military expedition aimed at overthrowing a usurper of the Polish throne. The usurper is promptly slain, but Kirkor is unable to locate the royal crown and refuses to return home without it. Thus the quest continues.

In Kirkor's absence, Balladyna ejects her own mother from the palace and takes the head of the palace guard as her lover. The two of them succeed in coming into possession of the crown and lead an army against Kirkor and his forces. Kirkor is killed and Balladyna becomes queen of Poland. At her coronation, she proceeds to poison her lover. Shortly thereafter, Balladyna, presiding over a court of jus-

tice, hears a complaint about the actions of a cruel daughter that is lodged by her own mother. Because the mother had become blind after her ejection from the palace, she is unaware of the identity of the new queen. Asked by the court to reveal the name of the offender, the mother declines to do so and is put on a rack. During the interrogation, the mother dies. The royal chancellor nevertheless insists that the queen still pass judgment on the wayward daughter. When Balladyna obliges and decrees a sentence of death, the heavens open up and she is instantly struck dead by lightning.

The setting for this five-act verse drama is in the area near Lake Gopło in western Poland, and the action takes place at a time before recorded Polish history. Hence, Słowacki is able to create a make-believe world in which folkloric and fairy-tale motifs abound. A nymph personifying Lake Gopło plays a prominent role in determining the course of the plot in the same way that supernatural beings interact with humans in William Shakespeare's *A Midsummer Night's Dream* (pr. c. 1595-1596, pb. 1600). Balladyna, moreover, is frequently referred to as the Polish Lady Macbeth. By combining elements from Shakespearean plays with Polish balladry and Slavic folklore, as well as with freely invented materials, Słowacki created a dramatic fantasy of perennial appeal. Ever since *Balladyna* was first produced at the Teatr Skarbka in the city of Lwów on March 7, 1862, this play has been one of the most popular works in the repertory of the Polish theater.

LILLA WENEDA

As in *Balladyna*, the era of prehistory is the setting for the play called *Lilla Weneda*. Here Słowacki wrestles with the question of the origin of the Polish nobility, a historical problem that remains unresolved to this day. Up to the time of the partitions of Poland in the eighteenth century, all political power was vested in the nobility and the masses were totally disenfranchised. The Polish nobility, otherwise known as the *szlachta*, was a relatively large class and constituted approximately 10 percent of the population. They regarded themselves as the nation (*naród*) and believed that they had the moral right to exploit the people (*lud*). Many theories have been set forth over the years to account for the genesis of this strange form of national bifurcation. The view to which Słowacki subscribed held that the nobility in Poland are the descendants of foreign knights who invaded the region at some immemorial period of time. Słowacki had a highly critical attitude toward the nobility and regarded their self-indulgent behavior in the past as the principal cause of Poland's loss of independence. Although he himself was technically a member of this social class, Słowacki did not come from a manor house, like Mickiewicz, nor did he bear a title, like Krasiński. Although both Mickiewicz and Krasiński wanted the nobility to dominate the political and cultural life of reconstituted Polish state, Słowacki advocated a social revolution that would give the people a greater stake in the cause of national restoration.

Słowacki, on the basis of his partiality for the people, imagines a war between a pure-hearted, peaceful Slavic population called the Wenedi and a group of ruthless foreign invaders called the Lechites. The Wenedi are ruled by the elderly King Derwid, and the Lechites are commanded by King Lech. The Wenedi believe that their chances of victory are good, since Derwid is known to be able to inspire his warriors, by playing on a magic harp, to perform feats of great valor. Just before the decisive battle is to take place, however, Derwid and his sons are captured by the forces of King Lech. Gwinona, Lech's sadistic wife, orders Derwid to be tortured and blinded. Meanwhile, Derwid's youngest daughter, Lilla Weneda, resolves to go to the Lechite encampment to make an attempt to obtain the release of her father and brothers. By virtue of her sweetness of character and her ability to overcome all the trials set for her by Gwinona and the Lechites, Lilla succeeds in winning freedom for her brothers but not for her father.

An opportunity to free Derwid arises when the Wenedi capture Lechon, the son of King Lech. The Lechites soon agree to Lilla's proposal that Lechon be exchanged for Derwid. Noticing how anxious the Wenedian king is to hold on to his harp, Gwinona insists that it be left behind, and thus the father and daughter set out for home without the instrument. While the two are still on the way home, Lilla's elder sister, Roza, receives a false report that her father and

sister have been slain by the Lechites, and she responds impulsively by killing Lechon. Although happy over the release of their king, the Wenedi realize that they are doomed to defeat without the magic harp. Lilla thereupon returns to the camp of the Lechites, hoping to persuade them to return the harp. When it becomes known that Lechon is dead, Gwinona kills Lilla. The crucial battle between the opposing nations is then joined in earnest. The Wenedi are on the verge of losing the battle when a chest arrives that they believe contains the magic harp. Once it is opened, they discover that it contains Lilla's corpse. On being told of the chest's contents, Derwid is so overcome by grief that he kills himself immediately. Without king or harp, the Wenedi are quickly vanquished. All of Derwid's sons die, and the sole survivor in his family is Roza. Derwid and Lilla, however, obtain a posthumous victory. Gwinona, by chance, comes on the site where the bodies of Derwid and Lilla are being cremated. On becoming aware of her presence, the black-robed Wenedians seize a number of adjacent burial urns and smother the hapless queen with the ashes of their ancestors. In the epic poem entitled *Król-Duch*, furthermore, Słowacki describes how Roza Weneda is subsequently impregnated with the ashes of her slain brothers and thereupon gives birth to the legendary Polish king of prehistory called Popiel (a name that means "ashes").

The idea of a young woman trying to save her father from imprisonment was apparently inspired by Słowacki's reading of Lord Byron's *Childe Harold* (cantos 1 and 2, 1812; canto 3, 1816; canto 4, 1818). There are also Shakespearean overtones in the play because of the similarities between Derwid and King Lear. In addition, the influence of classical Greek drama is especially strong, since Słowacki introduces a chorus of harpers who express dire forebodings regarding the Polish nation and its future. His message is, however, not entirely pessimistic. It is true that the Lechites embody the vices of the nobility, including, in Słowacki's own words, "a liking for shouting, dill pickles, and coats of arms." The Wenedi, in contrast, represent Poland's "angelic soul," and it is from this source that, in the poet's view, national redemption would eventually manifest itself.

MAZEPPA

Unlike any of the characters in *Lilla Weneda*, Słowacki's protagonist in *Mazeppa* is an authentic historical figure. Mazeppa was born in western Ukraine around 1644 to parents belonging to the native nobility. From about age fourteen to twenty, he served as a page at the court of the Polish king in Warsaw. This royal service was, however, terminated rather abruptly when Mazeppa made advances to a Polish nobleman's wife. The irate nobleman is said to have ordered the youth to be strapped naked to the back of a wild horse and driven off in the direction of the steppes to die. Once having reached the steppes, Mazeppa was befriended by the Cossacks and eventually became their hetman. As hetman, he sought to promote the political objective of making Ukraine independent from either Polish or Russian control. This mission led him to enter into an ill-fated alliance with Charles XII of Sweden directed against his longtime friend Peter the Great. When the forces of the Russian czar inflicted a crushing defeat on the Swedes and their Cossack confederates at the Battle of Poltava (1709), Mazeppa was obliged to seek refuge in the province of Moldavia, controlled by Turkey, and died shortly thereafter. As the history of Ukraine is little known outside the area of Eastern Europe, whatever posthumous fame that Mazeppa has achieved elsewhere stems largely from a number of poems, paintings, and musical compositions created during the Romantic period. There is, for example, Byron's narrative poem entitled *Mazeppa* (1819). What fascinated the English poet about Mazeppa was the legendary incident in which he was strapped naked on a wild horse and set off on a ride into the steppes as punishment for an illicit love affair. Byron's poem, moreover, subsequently inspired the artists Théodore Géricault and Eugène Delacroix, as well as the composer Franz Liszt, to produce versions of the theme in their own respective media. Similarly inspired by Byron is Victor Hugo's lyric poem "Mazeppa," a work that is part of the collection of verse called *Les Orientales* (1829; English translation, 1879).

Słowacki's verse drama on the Mazeppa theme, for its part, is radically different from any previous treatment of the subject. At the outset of the play, Mazeppa is depicted as a libertine courtier of the Polish king Jan Kazimierz, who ruled from 1648 to 1668. While on a visit to a nobleman's castle, both Mazeppa and the king are strongly attracted by their host's young wife, Amalia. She is the nobleman's second wife, and her stepson, Zbigniew, is likewise infatuated with her. Although Amalia is not truly in love with her elderly husband, she is resolved to remain faithful to him. The nobleman, however, soon comes to suspect Mazeppa as his chief rival for Amalia's affections. Because of a quarrel with the king, Mazeppa finds it necessary to hide in an alcove in Amalia's private chambers. The nobleman, suspecting a romantic tryst between the couple, orders the alcove to be walled up even though his wife has assured him in good faith that no one is within it. Sometime later, the nobleman agrees to unseal the alcove after the king promises to turn over anyone within it to his host for further punishment. When Mazeppa emerges, Zbigniew impulsively challenges him to a duel in order to defend the family honor. Despondent over the notion that Amalia may have compromised herself with Mazeppa, however, Zbigniew decides to commit suicide rather than go through with the duel.

On learning of the death of her stepson, Amalia comes to a sudden realization that she herself has been repressing a deep love for Zbigniew ever since the time of her marriage to his father. Completely distraught, she too commits suicide. Once the nobleman becomes aware of the true state of affairs, he orders Mazeppa from his castle and then takes his own life in the throes of utter madness. Notwithstanding the tragic end that befalls the nobleman and his family, Słowacki's play keeps its primary focus on the transformation of the protagonist's character that occurs during the course of the action. Owing to the harrowing entombment that nearly cost him his life, Mazeppa has come to be purified of his former vices and has truly emerged as a new man who is now morally fit to lead his people's struggle against the tyranny of Russian oppression as represented in the person of Czar Peter the Great. The parallel between Mazeppa's entombment and Poland's loss of independence is readily apparent to anyone attuned to the workings of the Polish national psyche.

FANTAZY

The redemptive value of suffering that is underscored in *Mazeppa* is elevated to the level of Christian self-sacrifice and atonement in Słowacki's tragicomedy *Fantazy*. This verse drama depicts the fortunes of the Polish nobility in the aftermath of the failure of the November Insurrection, and its action takes place in two manor houses located in Polish Ukraine around the year 1841. Count and Countess Respekt are the parents of two lovely daughters named Stella and Diana. The family is so much in need of money that the father and mother decide to sell Diana for a large sum of money to a wealthy neighbor, Count Fantazy Dafnicki. Fantazy is somewhat older than Diana and seems to look on the forthcoming marriage as a means of relieving his boredom. Diana, for her part, is highly vocal in her opposition to the union, but this only makes Fantazy all the more eager. To complicate matters, Fantazy's former sweetheart, Countess Idalia, arrives on the scene in order to prevent his marriage to Diana. Many critics believe that Słowacki modeled Fantazy after Zygmunt Krasiński and Idalia after Joanna Bobrowa, both friends of his at the time that the play was being written.

At this juncture, the Count and Countess Respekt receive an unexpected visit from an elderly Russian major and his orderly. The major had befriended the Respekt family when they were sent into Siberian exile as a precautionary measure during the November Insurrection. His orderly, Jan, turns out to be a former lover of Diana who is now impressed into military service as a punishment for past revolutionary activities. The major wishes to help the orderly and Diana to marry, and he therefore challenges Fantazy to a game of cards for very high stakes: The loser must commit suicide. Fantazy loses, and when he prepares to poison himself in a cemetery, Idalia insists on dying with him in true Romantic fashion. The major, however, is too kindhearted to permit Fantazy and Idalia to kill themselves and obligingly shoots himself. This act resolves the situation for all concerned, since the major leaves his considerable estate to be divided between his orderly and the Respekt family. Thus Diana and Jan are free to marry. Through the noble act of the major, Fantazy has come to see the folly of his ways and plans to make a religious pilgrimage to Rome. Idalia hints that she may join him there.

The major's self-sacrifice is not simply the deed of a person who has grown tired of life, but an act of atonement for his immoral involvement in the suppression of the Decembrist revolt back in 1825. He now sees an opportunity to give meaning to his purposeless existence by helping Jan and Diana out of their predicament. The uprighteousness of the major's character is further reflected in the simplicity of his speech—a peculiar mixture of Russian, Ukrainian, and Polish phrases. All other major characters, except for Jan, speak in a florid, convoluted manner replete with gratuitous references to classical mythology, and there is great humor in Słowacki's linguistic parody of pseudo-Romanticism. Beneath his satire on the Polish nobility, however, lies the genuine tragedy of Poland's loss of national independence. In terms of the play's religious dimensions, many critics detect the influence of Calderón and contend that the major acts in the same spirit of Christian self-sacrifice as does the protagonist in the Spanish playwright's *The Constant Prince*. Calderón's influence is even more apparent in two subsequently written plays. Both *Ksiądz Marek* (Father Mark) and *Sen srebrny Salomei* (the silver dream of Salomea) contain a strong element of Spanish mysticism despite the fact that each of these dramas is set in Polish Ukraine. Słowacki's interest in Calderón's plays was, it should be noted, fostered by Andrzej Towiański at the time when the poet was a member of the religious prophet's inner circle.

OTHER MAJOR WORKS

POETRY: *Poezye*, 1932 (2 volumes), 1833 (3 volumes; includes *Żmija*, *Arab*, *Lambro*, *powstańca grecki*, and *Godzinna myśli*); *Anhelli*, 1838 (English translation, 1930); *Trzy poemata*, 1839 (includes *Wacław*, *W Szwajcarii* [*In Switzerland*, 1953], and *Ojciec zadżumionych* [*The Father of the Plague-Stricken*, 1915]); *Poema Piasta Dantyszka o piekle*, 1839; *Grób Agamemnona*, 1840 (*Agamemnon's Grave*, 1944); *Beniowski*, 1841; *Genezis z ducha*, 1844; *Król-Duch*, 1847.

NONFICTION: *Podróż na wschód*, 1836.

MISCELLANEOUS: *Dziela wszystkie*, 1952-1960 (complete works, including *Podróz na Wschód*, wr. 1836; Juliusz Kleiner, editor).

BIBLIOGRAPHY

Babinski, Hubert F. *The Mazeppa Legend in European Romanticism*. New York: Columbia University Press, 1974. The Mazeppa legend as it appeared in the works of Słowacki and others is analyzed.

Dernalowicz, Maria. *Juliusz Słowacki*. Warsaw: Interpress, 1987. This biography of the Polish writer covers both his life and his works. Index.

Krzyżanowski, Julian. *A History of Polish Literature*. Warszawa: PWN-Polish Scientific Publishers, 1978. A study of Polish literature that includes coverage of Słowacki. Bibliography and index.

Miłosz, Czesław. *The History of Polish Literature*. 2d ed. Berkeley: University of California Press, 1983. A scholarly study of Polish literature that includes a discussion of the role of Słowacki. Bibliography and index.

Victor Anthony Rudowski

STEPHEN SONDHEIM

Born: New York, New York; March 22, 1930

PRINCIPAL DRAMA

West Side Story, pr. 1957, pb. 1958 (lyrics; music by Leonard Bernstein; book by Arthur Laurents)

Gypsy, pr. 1959, pb. 1960 (lyrics; music by Jule Styne; book by Laurents)

A Funny Thing Happened on the Way to the Forum, pr., pb. 1962 (lyrics and music; book by Larry Gelbart and Burt Shevelove)

Anyone Can Whistle, pr. 1964, pb. 1965 (lyrics and music; book by Laurents)

Do I Hear a Waltz?, pr. 1965, pb. 1966 (lyrics; music by Richard Rodgers; book by Laurents)

Candide, pr. 1974, pb. 1976 (lyrics with Richard Wilbur and John Latouche; music by Bernstein; book by Hugh Wheeler)

Company, pr., pb. 1970 (lyrics and music; book by George Furth)

Follies, pr., pb. 1971 (lyrics and music; book by James Goldman)

The Frogs, pr. 1974, pb. 1975 (lyrics and music; book by Shevelove)

A Little Night Music, pr., pb. 1973 (lyrics and music; book by Wheeler)

Pacific Overtures, pr. 1976, pb. 1977 (lyrics and music; book by John Weidman)

Sweeney Todd: The Demon Barber of Fleet Street, pr., pb. 1979 (lyrics and music; book by Wheeler)

Marry Me a Little, pr. 1980 (lyrics and music; book by Craig Lucas and Norman René)

Merrily We Roll Along, pr. 1981, pb. 1982 (lyrics and music; book by Furth)

Sunday in the Park with George, pr. 1983, pb. 1986 (lyrics and music; book by James Lapine)

Into the Woods, pr. 1987, pb. 1988 (lyrics and music; book by Lapine)

Assassins, pr. 1990, pb. 1991 (lyrics and music; book by Weidman)

Passion, pr., pb. 1994 (lyrics and music; book by Lapine)

Getting Away with Murder, pr. 1995, pb. 1997 (with George Furth)

Gold!, pr. 2002 (lyrics and music; book by Weidman; originally pr. 1999 as *Wise Guys*)

OTHER LITERARY FORMS

Stephen Sondheim wrote a film script, *The Last of Sheila* (1973), with Anthony Perkins. He has composed music for films as well. He wrote the scores for

Stavisky (1974) and *Reds* (1981) and songs for *Dick Tracy* (1990) and *The Birdcage* (1996). However, Sondheim's reputation is based primarily on his music and lyrics for Broadway-style musicals.

ACHIEVEMENTS

Stephen Sondheim was the most critically acclaimed figure in American musical theater during the last three decades of the twentieth century. Sondheim has won the Tony Award for Best Original Score five times, more than any other individual. These awards were for *Follies* (1972), *A Little Night Music* (1973), *Sweeney Todd* (1979), *Into the Woods* (1988), and *Passion* (1994). In 1971 only, separate Tonys were awarded for score and lyrics, and Sondheim won both for *Company*. Numerous plays on which Sondheim has collaborated have won Tony Awards and New York Drama Critics Circle Awards for Best Musical; these awards were not presented specifically to Sondheim. *Sunday in the Park with George* won the 1985 Pulitzer Prize in Drama.

Sondheim turned down the National Medal of Arts in 1992 in protest because the National Endowment for the Arts, the granting agency, had canceled some of its more controversial grants. He accepted that award in 1997.

BIOGRAPHY

Stephen Joshua Sondheim was born on March 22, 1930, in New York City, the only child of Herbert and Janet Fox Sondheim. His parents owned a clothing company and were both very involved in the business. The Sondheims separated when Stephen was ten, and he attended military school for two years and then attended the George School, a prep school. He was an exceptional student who had skipped two grades and who showed an early talent for music.

In the early 1940's, Sondheim and his mother became close friends with the family of Oscar Hammerstein II, one of the leading figures in musical theater at the time. Sondheim and the Hammersteins' son were close in age, and Sondheim even spent a summer with the family at their home in Bucks County, Pennsylvania. Janet Sondheim bought a house near the Hammersteins' home where her son lived

during his adolescence. Stephen Sondheim asked Hammerstein to read a musical he wrote as a teenager at the George School; Hammerstein critiqued the piece, giving Sondheim valuable training in writing for musical theater. He also hired Sondheim to work on the set of one of his plays.

Sondheim attended Williams College; initially, he majored in English but changed to music. During his college years, he pursued a training program devised by Hammerstein to learn musical theater; the plan involved writing four plays. The first step was to set a play he liked to music, the second was to fix the flaws in a play and set it to music, the third was to write a musical based upon a nondramatic source, and the fourth was to write an original work. After graduation, Sondheim studied music in New York City with Milton Babbitt, an avant-garde composer. As part of his studies, he performed in-depth analyses of classical works; his seriousness about music would be apparent in the complexity of his later compositions.

Sondheim's first big break was as a lyricist for *West Side Story*; he followed by writing lyrics for *Gypsy*. He finally got to write both music and lyrics for *A Funny Thing Happened on the Way to the Forum*, which opened in 1962. Sondheim's reputation and success continued to grow such that he became a central figure in musical theater.

Sondheim's most serious romantic involvement has been with Peter Jones, with whom he exchanged wedding rings in 1994.

ANALYSIS

The most critically acclaimed writer of music and lyrics for Broadway-style musicals in the late twentieth century, Stephen Sondheim has advanced the sophistication of the musical form through his experimentation with content and musical style. One of American musical theater's contributions to drama is the integration of spoken words and music within a production. The majority of Sondheim's lyrics make sense only when sung by the character for whom they are written. Much popular American music earlier in the century came from musical theater. With the exception of "Send in the Clowns" from *A Little Night Music*, Sondheim's songs have not enjoyed popular-

Stephen Sondheim, center, with two young playwrights at the Dramatists Guild in New York City in 1982. (AP/Wide World Photos)

ity, in large part because their meaning is so specific to the dramatic context for which they were written.

The sophistication of Sondheim's compositions has also been an important element in elevating critical assessment of the musical theater genre, which has often been dismissed as pure entertainment rather than serious drama. Sondheim's musical influences range from classical, as seen in the Gregorian chant motif in the score of *Sweeney Todd*, to Asian motifs in *Pacific Overtures*, to contemporary popular music from musical theater and film.

Sondheim's drama, as well, is notable for the range of its sources and themes. For example, *A Funny Thing Happened on the Way to the Forum* is a farce based on the works of the Roman playwright Plautus, *Pacific Overtures* is styled after Japanese Kabuki theater, and *Sunday in the Park with George* draws on the life and work of French Impressionist painter

Georges Seurat. Although collaborative work and drawing on preexisting sources for materials is within the tradition of musical theater, Sondheim's multiple references are also consistent with the practice of postmodernist writers of self-consciously borrowing from existing works. Musical theater, and Sondheim's works in particular, epitomize the postmodernist tendency to reinterpret earlier forms for contemporary uses.

A Funny Thing Happened on the Way to the Forum

Based on plays written by the Roman playwright Plautus, *A Funny Thing Happened on the Way to the Forum* is a farce, with the plot centering on men lusting for beautiful prostitutes and plot twists deriving from coincidences and mistaken identities.

The show's bawdy content and farcical nature pushed the limits of musical theater. The drama is framed as a play-within-a-play, a theatrical device that allows a play to be self-conscious about itself and its intentions. Beginning with the chorus of Greek drama, a tradition has long existed in the theater of voices external to the drama offering commentary on the events. However, most twentieth century drama presents characters going about their business as if unaware of the audience. The framing of Sondheim's drama both ties the play to its classical sources and invites the audience to adopt, despite the lighthearted subject matter, a critical attitude toward the work, as the play offers an explanation of itself as comedy with details about what that means.

A LITTLE NIGHT MUSIC

A Little Night Music is a romantic comedy that draws on the conventional comedic topic of mismatched lovers trying to find their true loves. The idea originally began with a desire by Sondheim and others to make a musical from Jean Anouilh's play *L'Invitation au château* (pr. 1947; *Ring Round the Moon*, 1950). When Anouilh declined an adaptation of his play, Sondheim viewed films with similar plots including Jean Renoir's 1939 *Rules of the Game* and Ingmar Bergman's 1956 *Smiles of a Summer Night*.

The themes and mood of the play draw from a long theatrical tradition, evoking, for example, William Shakespeare's *A Midsummer Night's Dream* (pr. c. 1595-1596), which also portrays mismatched lovers seeking their true loves on a magical evening. In proper comedic form, *A Little Night Music* ends with the lovers properly matched.

Beyond the follies and maneuvering of the lovers, the theme of youth and age is important to both the play's meaning and its structure. Most of the action takes place at the country house of an old woman who, with her young granddaughter, watches the action. The grandmother teaches her young charge that a summer night smiles three times: at the young who know nothing, the fools who know too little, and the old who know too much. The primary plot could occur without the older and younger characters, but they deepen the drama's scope by showing the lovers' plots as part of a stage of life between youth and age.

The musical opens with a quintet of characters who are not part of the main story but who perform lyrics both at the beginning and later in the show that comment on the play's main action. This use of choruslike characters serves to distance the audience from identification with the main characters because of the obvious artifice involved. This distancing evokes an intellectual or critical response from the audience.

SWEENEY TODD

Sweeney Todd blurs the boundaries between musical theater and opera and has, in fact, been performed by various opera companies. The play retells a story about a mass murderer originally written for the stage in the nineteenth century, rewritten by contemporary British playwright Christopher Bond, and finally set to music by Sondheim. The play presents the challenges of portraying murders onstage without disgusting the audience or resorting to slapstick. Further, although the nineteenth century sources were not notable for their psychological subtlety, Sondheim's version seeks to offer insight into the mind of the deranged killer. Beyond the psychological intrigue, the musical explores the themes of revenge and justice. Despite these serious themes, the drama contains significant, albeit black, humor. Todd's accomplice, Mrs. Lovett, bakes the meat from the corpses into pies that she sells in her shop.

The play's significant accomplishment is its ability to interweave tragedy and comedy as well as sophistication and base humor within a musical score that draws on sources ranging from Gregorian chant to contemporary, popular music.

SUNDAY IN THE PARK WITH GEORGE

Inspired by the life and work of Georges Seurat, especially the painting *Un Dimanche, Aprés-Midi à l'Ile de la Grande Jatte* (*A Sunday Afternoon on the Island of La Grande Jatte*), *Sunday in the Park with George* explores what it means to be an artist and the relationship between life and art. In the musical's first act, the people in the painting go about their lives as George sketches them. For example, his pregnant girlfriend Dot decides to marry the baker Louis, and two young women pursue an attractive soldier. At the end of the act, as the characters argue among themselves, the painter stops them and arranges them into the poses and positions for his picture. The dual statement is that the piece of art hides the tensions of life, and at the same time, the artwork turns ordinary life into something beautiful.

The second act continues to explore the meanings of art as Seurat's daughter and her grandson George attend an opening for the grandson's artwork. In contrast to his grandfather, who was focused solely on his artistic vision and never sold a painting, the younger George works the crowd of art patrons and critics, seeking funding for his work. As the play ends, he has decided to move on to new projects rather than repeating variations of his current work. His great-grandmother practiced writing in a book that has been passed down, and George reads from it some of his grandfather's favorite words about art, including order, design, and tension. The grandfather is able, through this medium, to instruct his grandson on the importance of following his own artistic vision.

OTHER MAJOR WORKS

SCREENPLAY: *The Last of Sheila*, 1973 (with Anthony Perkins)

TELEPLAY: *Evening Primrose*, 1966 (lyrics and music)

BIBLIOGRAPHY

Banfield, Stephen. *Sondheim's Broadway Musicals.* Ann Arbor: University of Michigan Press, 1993. A very thorough study of Sondheim's work, this book is particularly useful in its discussions of his music. Although perhaps at times too technical for the typical reader, this book provides much valuable information on Sondheim's life and his musicals. Sondheim himself reviewed the manuscript before publication.

Block, Geoffrey. "Happily Ever After: *West Side Story* with Sondheim." In *Enchanted Evenings: The Broadway Musical from "Show Boat" to Sondheim.* New York: Oxford University Press, 1997. This chapter places Sondheim in the context of the musical theater, arguing that his work is the culmination of the form's development since the late 1920's. The earlier chapters provide a useful history of musical theater.

Goodhart, Sandor, ed. *Reading Stephen Sondheim: A Collection of Critical Essays.* New York: Garland, 2000. The essays in this volume, written by literary critics, treat Sondheim with the seriousness afforded other twentieth century playwrights. The essays range from general treatments to explorations of specific features of the plays.

Gordon, Joanne. *Art Ain't Easy: The Achievement of Stephen Sondheim.* Carbondale: Southern Illinois University Press, 1990. Gordon argues for the recognition of Sondheim and musical theater as art rather than merely as escapist entertainment. This study notes many connections between Sondheim's works and works considered high art. Gordon's analysis of the musical qualities of Sondheim's numbers is thorough.

Secrest, Meryle. *Stephen Sondheim: A Life.* New York: Delta, 1998. This full-length biography is based primarily on interviews with Sondheim's friends and associates. It describes not only the events of Sondheim's life but also the history of each of the musicals on which Sondheim worked, including the inspiration for the story, the process the collaborators went through to see the project to production, and the critical and audience response to the play.

Zadan, Craig. *Sondheim and Company.* 2d ed. New York: Da Capo, 1994. This book provides analysis and history of each of Sondheim's musicals. Its many photographs offer a good sense of the style of the productions as well as the process of their preparation. A useful appendix lists who worked on the various productions, provides Broadway performance histories, and lists nonmusical projects in which Sondheim participated.

Joan Hope

SOPHOCLES

Born: Colonus, Greece; c. 496 B.C.E.
Died: Athens, Greece; 406 B.C.E.

PRINCIPAL DRAMA

Aias, early 440's B.C.E. (*Ajax*, 1729)
Antigonē, 441 B.C.E. (*Antigone*, 1729)
Trachinai, 435-429 B.C.E. (*The Women of Trachis*, 1729)
Oidipous Tyrannos, c. 429 B.C.E. (*Oedipus Tyrannus*, 1715)
Ēlektra, 418-410 B.C.E. (*Electra*, 1649)
Philoktētēs, 409 B.C.E. (*Philoctetes*, 1729)
Oidipous epi Kolōnōi, 401 B.C.E. (*Oedipus at Colonus*, 1729)
Sophocles: The Plays and Fragments with Critical Notes, Commentary, and Translation in English Prose, pb. 1897 (7 volumes)

OTHER LITERARY FORMS

In addition to his plays, Sophocles also wrote paeans and elegies. Fragments exist of a paean to the god Asclepius, of an ode to the historian Herodotus, and of an elegy to the philosopher Archelaus. An apparently complete epigram addressed to the poet Euripides also survives. According to ancient tradition, Sophocles wrote a literary treatise in prose, *On the Chorus*. Unfortunately, this work, which may have discussed the tragedian's increase in the size of the chorus, is lost.

ACHIEVEMENTS

Sophocles' dramatic career, which intersects both Aeschylus's and Euripides' periods of production, was noted in antiquity for several important theatrical innovations, and his plays have experienced a remarkably constant popularity beginning in his own lifetime and continuing into the present. Perhaps no other playwright has had as great an influence on both ancient and modern concepts of the dramatic art.

Like Aeschylus, Sophocles acted in his own plays. His performances as a ball-playing Nausicaa and as a lyre-playing Thamyras in lost plays were well known

in the fifth century. Sophocles is said by ancient sources, however, to have been the first playwright to have abandoned the practice of acting in his own works. It is now impossible to determine whether this change, which became the norm among later Greek tragedians, was a true Sophoclean innovation, the result of, as the sources state, Sophocles' own weakening voice, or was rather the result of a general trend toward increasing specialization in later fifth century B.C.E. tragedies.

Sophocles is also said to have increased the size of the tragic chorus from twelve to fifteen members and to have added a third actor. If Aeschylus's *Oresteia*, produced in 458 B.C.E., can be used as chronological evidence, the former innovation had not yet become the rule by 458, but the latter change had most certainly been introduced by that date. All the surviving plays of Sophocles make use of three actors, but the size of the chorus in a given play is rarely easy to document. The introduction of the third actor was the final evolutionary stage in the development of Greek tragedy, which probably had its origins in a choral song to which one, two, and, finally, three actors were added. With the use of three actors, Sophocles was able to concentrate dramatic attention on the actors and the spoken dialogues and agons or "debates" for which his plays are noted. Sophocles' mastery of dialogue is especially evident in his prologues, which almost always begin not with the static, expository monologues of Euripides, but with dramatic, plot-advancing dialogues, such as the bitter exchange between Antigone and Ismene at the beginning of *Antigone*.

In general, Sophocles accomplishes this development of the actor's role in tragedy without neglecting the choral portions of the play. Sophocles' interest in the chorus is suggested not only by the tradition that he wrote a prose treatise on the chorus and increased its size, but also by the extant plays themselves. While the choruses of Sophocles' tragedies do not have the central importance of such Aeschylean choruses as those in *Hiketides* (463 B.C.E.?; *The Suppli-*

ants, 1777) and *Eumenides* (English translation, 1777; one of three parts of *Oresteia*, 458 B.C.E.), nevertheless, several Sophoclean odes, such as the "Ode to Man" in *Antigone* and the Colonus ode in *Oedipus at Colonus*, are among the most beautiful in Greek tragedy. Sophocles also shows himself able to manipulate dramatic mood through the tone of his odes, as in *Ajax*, when he places a joyful song just before disaster. Only in *Philoctetes*, which has only one true choral ode, does a work of Sophocles exhibit the diminished choral role common in Greek tragedy of the last decades of the fifth century B.C.E.

Two other innovations attributed in antiquity to Sophocles suggest that the playwright was interested in the visual as well as the verbal effects of drama. The ancient biography on the life of Sophocles states that he designed boots and staffs for both actors and the chorus, and in *De poetica* (c. 334-323 B.C.E.; *Poetics*, 1705), Aristotle says that Sophocles invented scene painting. In general, however, the extant plays show little of the spectacular stagecraft found in both Aeschylus and Euripides. The closest Sophocles comes to Aeschylus's use of ghosts is the supernatural disappearance of Oedipus in *Oedipus at Colonus*, and he employs the favorite Euripidean technique of the *deus ex machina* only once, in *Philoctetes*.

Modern scholars often state that Sophocles was responsible for the abandonment of connected tragic trilogies in favor of thematically independent plays, a conclusion based on the tenuous assumption that all mid-fifth century B.C.E. productions of three tragedies and one satyr play were connected in theme. Another possible interpretation of the scanty ancient evidence on trilogies is that connected trilogies were an Aeschylean experiment that few, if any, later tragedians repeated. Sophocles' composition *Telepheia*, usually considered to be his only connected trilogy, may not have been a connected group at all. Not even the names of the plays that made up *Telepheia* are known, and there is no evidence that the *-eia* ending signifies a connected trilogy in fifth century B.C.E. terminology, despite the *-eia* ending in *Oresteia*.

Although it is unlikely, then, that Sophocles was an innovator in the production of unconnected trilogies, several of his individual plays do possess another distinctive structural feature, diptych composition. Composed of two nearly independent parts or with two separate main characters, *Ajax*, *Antigone*, and *The Women of Trachis* all divide neatly into two parts, with the departures or deaths of Ajax, Antigone, and Deianira, respectively. Only Euripides' *Alkēstis* (438 B.C.E.; *Alcestis*, 1781) approaches the two-part structure of these Sophoclean plays, the "disunity" of which has been noted by both ancient and modern critics. Yet dipytch form appears to have been an intentional feature of these tragedies, perhaps even a Sophoclean experiment made in response to the Aeschylean connected trilogy. This Sophoclean form is based not on structural disunity but rather on structural flexibility and demonstrates a general deemphasis on the need for single central characters that is notable not only in Sophocles but also in extant Greek tragedy in general. Sophocles' *Oedipus Tyrannus*, with its nearly exclusive attention to the fate of a single character, is rather the exception than the rule in this respect.

Sophocles (Library of Congress)

The esteem in which Sophocles' work was held in the fifth century B.C.E. is evident from such contemporary evidence as Aristophanes' *Batrachoi* (405 B.C.E.; *The Frogs*, 1780), in which praise of the late Sophocles as "good-natured while alive and good-natured in Hades," is clearly comic understatement, and Phrynichus's *Muses*, produced in the same year, in which Sophocles is described as "a prosperous and clever man who wrote many good tragedies." This fifth century B.C.E. respect for Sophocles was intensified in the fourth century B.C.E., under the influence of Aristotle, whose high praise of Sophoclean tragedy in *The Poetics* has shaped all subsequent critical approaches, not only to Sophocles but also to tragedy in general. Aristotle, for whom Sophoclean tragedy, and specifically *Oedipus Tyrannus*, was an ideal tragedy, particularly admired Sophocles' dramatic development of character and quoted the playwright as saying that "he [Sophocles] made men as they ought to be; Euripides as they are."

Along with the works of Aeschylus and Euripides, Sophocles' plays were widely adapted by Roman tragedians in the second and first centuries B.C.E., but Seneca's *Oedipus* (c. 40-55 C.E.; English translation, 1581) is the only extant Roman imitation of Sophocles. Seneca follows closely the plot of Sophocles' *Oedipus Tyrannus*, but with a typically Roman overemphasis on Teiresias's rites of prophecy and with a compressed version of Oedipus's discovery of his true identity that pales beside its Sophoclean source. Seneca's play also lacks the great mood of irony for which Sophocles is justly famous.

The role of Sophoclean tragedy in the history of ideas would be incomplete without mention of Sophocles' influence on the philosophy of Georg Wilhelm Friedrich Hegel in the nineteenth century and on the psychological theories of Sigmund Freud in the twentieth century. In his *Ästhetik* (1835; *The Philosophy of Fine Art*, 1920), Hegel praised *Antigone* for its ideal tragic form—that is, its dramatic reconciliation of conflicting positions, which conformed well with the Hegelian concept of dialectics, of thesis-antithesis-synthesis. In *The Interpretation of Dreams* (1900), Freud cited *Oedipus Tyrannus* as an expression of a child's love of one parent and hatred of the other, the psychic impulse that Freud came to call the "Oedipus complex."

Despite such influence outside the theater, it is on Sophocles' tragic art, and in particular on his skilled use of character development, dialogue, and dramatic irony, that his reputation has justly rested for more than two thousand years.

BIOGRAPHY

The main events of Sophocles' life are known from several ancient sources, including inscriptions and especially an Alexandrian biography that survives in the manuscript tradition. Although it is difficult at times to distinguish fact from anecdote in these sources, even the fiction is a useful gauge of Sophocles' image and reputation in antiquity.

Sophocles' lifetime coincides with the glorious rise of Athenian democracy and Athens's naval empire and with the horrors of the Peloponnesian War. Born a generation later than Aeschylus and a generation earlier than Euripides, Sophocles won dramatic victories over both of these playwrights. He was born c. 496 B.C.E. to Sophilus, a wealthy industrialist and slave owner from the Athenian *deme* of Colonus. Although Sophocles generally avoids personal references in his plays, his love for his native Colonus is evident in his last work, *Oedipus at Colonus*, and especially in the famous Colonus ode of that play.

Sophocles received a good education. According to ancient sources, as a youth he won competitions in wrestling and in music. His music teacher, Lamprus, was known for his epic and conservative compositions, for which he was ranked in his day with the great lyric poet Pindar. Sophocles himself is said to have been chosen to lead the victory song with lyre after the Athenian sea victory at Salamis in 480 B.C.E.

The patriotism of Sophocles was well known in antiquity. In the ancient biography, he is called *philathenaiotatos*, "a very great lover of Athens," and, unlike both Aeschylus and Euripides, he is said never to have left his native city for the court of a foreign king. Sophocles was also unlike his fellow dramatists in that he held public office several times: In 443/442 B.C.E., he was *Hellenotamias*, a financial overseer of the Delian League in Athens; in 441/440, he was general along with Pericles in the Samian Revolt. Sophocles may have been general again, around 427, this time with Nicias; and in 413, he was elected *proboulos*, a member of a special executive committee formed after the Sicilian disaster.

No clear conclusions concerning the dramatist's political sentiments can be derived from Sophocles' political career, especially since fifth century Athenian democracy often survived on noncareer appointments from among its citizens. There are several hints in Sophocles' biography, however, of links with the pro-Spartan and aristocratic circle of the Athenian statesman Cimon: Plutarch says that Sophocles won his first dramatic victory in 468 B.C.E., when, as requested, Cimon and his nine fellow generals took the place of judges chosen by lot for the tragic competition. Sophocles, as general in 441/440, is said to have visited the poet Ion of Chios, a close friend of Cimon. Sophocles wrote an elegy, of which fragments survive, to another member of Cimon's circle, the philosopher Archelaus of Miletus. Finally, Sophocles is also connected with Polygnotus, the famous painter and friend of Cimon who is said to have made a well-known portrait of Sophocles holding a lyre. On the other hand, Sophocles may have also been a friend of Pericles, the great Athenian statesman and Cimon's political rival, with whom Sophocles was general in 441/440. So, it may be that Sophocles attempted to separate his probable friendship with Cimon from his civic duty and patriotic sentiments. At the least, this evidence shows that Sophocles was not politically detached, but rather, very much involved in the political and intellectual life of his day. The ancient biography mentions that Sophocles established a *thiasos*, or religious guild, in honor of the Muses. Other members of this intellectual group are unknown, but it may have included Sophocles' good friend, the historian Herodotus, whom the dramatist occasionally used as a source and to whom he wrote an ode.

Sophocles won his first dramatic victory in 468 B.C.E. by defeating Aeschylus, probably with a group that included a *Triptolemus*, now lost. Whether this was Sophocles' first dramatic competition is not known, but it is recorded that the playwright went on to win twenty-three more victories, to earn second

place many times, and third place never. With four plays in each production, this means that ninety-two out of Sophocles' approximately 124 dramas won for him first prizes. This great contemporary success contrasts strikingly with the career of Euripides, who won first place only five times. Sophocles did not compete in 467 B.C.E. but probably won second place against Aeschylus's Danaid trilogy in 463 (?).

Unfortunately, no plays from Sophocles' earliest years survive. The earliest extant play is probably *Ajax*, from the early 440's B.C.E. In his *Ethika* (after c. 100; *Moralia*, 1603), Plutarch distinguishes three periods of Sophoclean style: a "weighty" period with Aeschylean similarities; a "harsh and artificial stage"; and a final group "most suited to express character and best." No extant plays, except perhaps *Ajax*, belong to the first two periods. Because the categories themselves, with their progression toward increasing worth, are obviously peripatetic in origin, it is doubtful that these periods can be accepted as reliable statements about Sophoclean drama.

In 441 B.C.E., Sophocles probably produced *Antigone*, for which he may have won first prize, since the *hypothesis*, or ancient introduction, to this play states that the dramatist was elected general in 441/440, based on the merit of *Antigone*. The Athenian democracy of that period was perfectly capable of making political appointments on such an apolitical basis. Other ancient sources imply that Sophocles saw no military action as general in the Samian Revolt that year but that he did travel to Ionia with the Athenian fleet.

Sophocles was certainly back in Athens in 438 B.C.E., when he won first prize with unknown plays against an Euripidean group which included *Alcestis*. The dating of *The Women of Trachis* is perhaps the most fiercely debated of all extant Sophoclean tragedies, but the stylistic and thematic similarities of this play to the firmly dated *Alcestis* make possible at least an approximate dating of *The Women of Trachis* to the period between 435 and 429.

In 431, Sophocles, competing with an unknown group of plays, came in second to the dramatist Euphorion, Aeschylus's son. Euripides came in third in that year with *Mēdeia* (431 B.C.E.; *Medea*, 1781).

Sophocles made no production at the Greater Dionysia of 428. *Electra* is another play that is difficult to date accurately, but based on its links with Euripides' *Ēlektra* (413 B.C.E.; *Electra*, 1782), Sophocles' play can at least be dated to the decade beginning 420 B.C.E., except for the year 415, when it is known that Sophocles made no production. Only the last two extant plays are firmly dated: *Philoctetes*, which won for him first prize in 409 B.C.E., and *Oedipus at Colonus*, produced posthumously in 401 B.C.E. by Sophocles' grandson of the same name, which also won for him first prize.

In addition to his patriotism, Sophocles was also noted for his piety. Specifically, he is linked with the cult of the healing god Asclepius, whose cult the dramatist helped establish in Athens in 420 B.C.E. Sophocles' paean to Asclepius was quite famous in antiquity and still survives in fragments. Sophocles was a priest of the hero Halon, who was ritually connected with Asclepius and under whose epithet, Dexion or "Receiver," Sophocles was honored posthumously. Such associations with public cults, however, were distinct in fifth century B.C.E. Athens from intellectual belief, and the classical view of Sophocles as calm, pious, and moderate has come to be questioned by such modern scholars as C. H. Whitman, who notes that the extant tragedies exhibit little of that blind piety that tradition links with the dramatist. Sophocles' true religious sentiments are lost behind the poetic veil of his tragedies.

There are indications in ancient sources that Sophocles had a troubled family life in his old age. The playwright had two sons: Iophon by Nicostrata and Ariston by the Sicyonian woman Theoris. Iophon was a dramatist in his own right and even competed against his father at least once. Less is known about Ariston, except that his son, Sophocles, was so favored by the grandfather that Iophon brought a lawsuit to have the old man made a legal ward of his son on the grounds of senility. Sophocles, speaking in his own defense at the trial, is said to have stated: "If I am Sophocles, I am not insane; if I am insane, I am not Sophocles." When Sophocles concluded by reciting lines from *Oedipus at Colonus*, his work in progress, the case was dismissed.

In March of 406 B.C.E., at the *proagon*, or preview to the Greater Dionysia, Sophocles dressed a chorus in mourning for the recent death of Euripides. This appearance at the *proagon* is evidence for a Sophoclean production in that year, but Sophocles must have died shortly after the dramatic festival, because in Aristophanes' *The Frogs*, produced in early 405, Sophocles is mentioned as already dead. Despite Sophocles' advanced age, the ancient sources still sought to embellish his death with several spurious causes: that he choked on a grape (like Anacreon), that he became overexerted while reciting *Antigone*, or that he died for joy after a dramatic victory. More reliable is the report that Sophocles' family was granted special permission from the Spartan general Lysander to bury the dramatist in his family plot on the road to Decelea, where the Spartans maintained a garrison. Death thus spared Sophocles from witnessing the complete collapse of the Athenian empire and the submission of Athens to Sparta in 405 to 404 B.C.E.

ANALYSIS

The textual transmission of Sophocles is remarkably similar to that of Aeschylus, with a first complete ancient edition by the Athenian orator Lycurgus in the late fourth century B.C.E. and a definitive Alexandrian edition by Aristophanes of Byzantium in the second century B.C.E. A school selection of the seven extant tragedies was made sometime after the second century C.E. and was reedited by the late fourth century rhetorician Salustius. The plays may have survived the medieval period in only one manuscript, although this has been debated. The present text was extensively revised in the fourteenth century by several Byzantine scholars, including Planudes, Thomas Magister, and Triclinius. The plays reached the West in the fifteenth century, and the first printed edition of Sophocles was the Aldine edition of Venice (1502).

The *Life of Sophocles* devotes a lengthy paragraph to describing the playwright's links with the epic poetry of Homer, and scholars of all periods have continued to note Sophoclean imitation of Homeric subject matter and language. Sophocles achieved his greatest success in the art of character development and especially in the depiction of the hero, for which he owes a major debt to Homer. Many Sophoclean characters, including nearly all the *dramatis personae* of *Ajax* and the Odysseus of *Philoctetes*, are derived from Homeric sources at least in part, but even where Sophocles treats a subject not directly handled by Homer, such as the stories of Oedipus and Antigone, the poetic techniques of Homer and Sophocles intersect in their methods of character development, in the types of characters depicted, and especially in their focus on the heroic qualities of particular individuals.

Even Aristotle recognized the importance of character development to Sophoclean studies. In his *Poetics*, he frequently cited Sophocles' Oedipus as the ideal tragic character and stated that "Sophocles is the same kind of imitator as Homer, for both imitate characters of a higher type." Much modern scholarship, too, has been devoted to a study of Sophocles' technique of character development and of the "Sophoclean hero." In particular, the works of C. H. Whitman and of B. M. W. Knox have both helped to clarify the characteristics of the Sophoclean hero and to show his affinities with the Homeric hero. It is impossible to analyze a Sophoclean play without studying Sophocles' character development and without taking into account the Aristotelian and later interpretations of the Sophoclean hero that have molded a modern understanding of this dramatist and his work. At the same time, such an analysis must not lose sight of Sophocles' other dramatic skills, such as his mastery of dialogue and his use of the chorus, both of which complement the development of Sophocles' main characters.

THE THEBAN PLAYS

Sophocles' so-called Theban plays have always been considered the center of his corpus. Although *Antigone*, *Oedipus Tyrannus*, and *Oedipus at Colonus* do not form a connected trilogy and, indeed, represent productions spanning a period of forty years, these plays project many consistencies of style and character development that suggest some continuity in Sophoclean dramatic art. The story of the unfortunate house of Laius was a popular theme of fifth century B.C.E. Greek tragedy, but except for Aeschylus's *Hepta epi Thēbas* (467 B.C.E.; *Seven Against Thebes*, 1777) and Euripides' *Phoinissai* (c. 410 B.C.E.; *The Phoenician Women*, 1781), which are extant, far too little is known about any of these lost plays to judge their relationship to the Sophoclean versions. The misfortunes of the house of Laius, including Oedipus's destiny to kill his father and marry his mother as well as the mutual fratricide of his sons, were mentioned by Homer, and several epics on this Theban cycle are known to have survived past the fifth century B.C.E. Knowledge of these epics is scanty, but Sophoclean innovations in this mythic cycle may include the blinding of Oedipus, the dramatic use of a local Athenian legend concerning the death of Oedipus in Sophocles' native *deme* of Colonus, and the development of the story of Antigone.

ANTIGONE

Antigone concerns the events after the deaths of her brothers Eteocles and Polyneices and her decision to bury Polyneices despite the decree of Creon, the new ruler of Thebes, that the body remain unburied as a lesson to traitors. Sophocles begins the play with a dramatic prologue in which Antigone announces her decision to her sister Ismene, asks for her help and is refused, and finally determines in anger to act alone. This scene between the sisters, which Sophocles later skillfully imitated in *Electra*, demonstrates Sophocles' ability to employ action to develop his characters. Absent are the long, choral, narrative beginnings of Aeschylus's *Persai* (472 B.C.E.; *The Persians*, 1777) and *Agamemnōn* (*Agamemnon*, 1777; one of three parts of *Oresteia*, 458 B.C.E.), and the expository prologues of Euripides. Within one hundred lines of dialogue, Sophocles not only has significantly advanced the action but also has vividly depicted Antigone's character. Antigone's stubbornness, isolation, and strong sense of self-righteous nobility are well developed in this scene and help to define not only her character but also that of the Sophoclean hero in general. Much like the Homeric hero, especially Achilles, the Sophoclean hero projects *arete*, an untranslatable Greek word implying a "pattern of virtue." *Arete* sets the hero apart from other people and is inevitably self-destructive through its greatness. Thus, from the outset, Antigone is determined to face death for what she believes to be the noble course of action.

By contrast to the gloom of the prologue, the parodos, or choral entrance song, is a jubilant victory song celebrating the end of the siege of Thebes by Polyneices and is a striking example of Sophoclean manipulation of mood through choral passages. The chorus in Sophocles is usually considered to be a mouthpiece for the playwright's own views, but the interest in dramatic effect that Sophocles demonstrates in this chorus and others should be sufficient warning against reading such direct authorial intrusion into the dramatic text. Therefore, the chorus's Aeschylean sentiments in the parodos, that an insolent—that is, hubristic—Polyneices has been justly punished by Zeus, cannot necessarily be applied to Antigone's situation or to Sophocles' belief. Rather, the Sophoclean chorus tends to speak in character and with little extradramatic insight. *Antigone*'s chorus of elders express their own views in the parodos, views that serve as an excellent dramatic transition from Antigone in the prologue to Creon in the next scene.

In the first episode, Sophocles once again moves events along swiftly while developing character, this time that of Creon. Hardly has Creon finished his long and self-revealing inaugural address as ruler of Thebes and announced his decree concerning Polyneices, than a messenger arrives to report that this decree has already been disobeyed. Hegel used Creon's insistence in this scene on the primacy of the state and positive law over the individual to argue that the meaning of *Antigone* lay in the inevitable resolution or synthesis of Creon's conflict with Antigone, who stands for the right of the individual and the family and for the superiority of divine law. This interpretation of *Antigone*, however, is Hegelian, not Sophoclean, for there is no real synthesis in *Antigone*. Rather, there is a constant affirmation of the righteousness of the heroine that is evident even in this first episode, in which the messenger's suggestion that certain bizarre circumstances surrounding Polyneices' burial may hint at divine complicity is roundly rejected by Creon. Divine sanction for Antigone's action is inherent in the ancient Greek belief that all human corpses must be buried, a law to be challenged only under pain of punishment by the gods.

The choral ode that follows, often called the "Ode to Man," is probably the most famous ode of Sophocles, if not of all Greek tragedy. With its thematic links with Homer's *Odyssey* (c. 725 B.C.E.; English translation, 1614) and Aeschylus's *Choēphoroi* (*Libation Bearers*, 1777; one of three parts of *Oresteia*, 458 B.C.E.), as well as its philosophical connections with Protagoras and other thinkers of that time, this ode is a poetic statement of the wonder of humankind, of the ability of the human intellect to surmount the limitations of nature, and of the dangers inherent in such a powerful intelligence. Application of this ode to the dramatic events of *Antigone* is ambiguous. Clearly, the chorus is thinking of the unknown lawbreaker who buried Polyneices and whose deeds are a good example of humankind's dangerous intellect. As early as Homer, a hero's greatness had led to self-destruction, and this is no less true of Antigone. On the other hand, later events in the play will prove the relevance of the chorus's words as well to Creon, whose decree has dishonored the "sworn right of the gods." The multiplicity of interpretations that can be applied to this ode enhances its dramatic value and emphasizes once again Sophocles' skilled use of the chorus.

The "Ode to Man" also illustrates the power of Sophocles' so-called diptych structure and shows the futility of searching for a single main character in this or several other Sophoclean plays. Antigone and Creon complement each other. Antigone could not be Antigone without Creon, who, like Antigone, possesses some of the qualities of a Sophoclean hero, including stubbornness, isolation, and a self-righteous nobility. Creon's encounter with his son Haemon in the third episode is particularly revealing of the king's character. The scene is a brilliant combination of set speeches by both Creon and Haemon followed by rapid and emotional stichomythia, or line-by-line interchange, between father and son. This dialogue reveals Creon's stubborn inability to yield to reason and a lack of understanding of and isolation from his son Haemon that lead inevitably to disaster.

Haemon's appearance in the play may have been another Sophoclean innovation in the myth. As Creon's son and Antigone's fiancé, Haemon serves an an excellent illuminator not only of Creon's but also of Antigone's character. Sophocles does not present Haemon's relationship to Antigone in a romantic manner; the two are certainly not "lovers" in the modern sense because they never meet onstage. If the manuscript attribution of line 572 to Ismene is correct, Antigone never even speaks of her betrothed. Rather, Haemon's loyalty for Antigone, even unto death, serves as another, and perhaps the most vivid, proof of the heroine's isolation from all human contact in pursuit of her noble goal.

Antigone ends as quickly as it began, with a decision to free Antigone forced on Creon by the seer Teiresias, but not before it is too late. In rapid succession, the suicides of Antigone, Haemon, and his mother, Eurydice, are announced, and Creon returns in the exodos, or last scene, as a broken man. It is Creon, not Antigone, who comes closest to fitting the requirements of an Aristotelian tragic hero, with a peripeteia, or "fall," caused by hamartia, a "tragic flaw." Like both Xerxes in *The Persians* and Agamemnon in the first play of *Oresteia*, Creon's hamartia may be a form of faulty thinking that is punished by the gods. (Creon himself realizes this and uses the word "hamartemata.") By contrast, Antigone has no true peripeteia; while she does die, she dies as a Sophoclean hero in the glory and isolation of her self-conscious nobility. An Aristotelian tragic hero can thus be found in this play, but only at Antigone's expense.

OEDIPUS TYRANNUS

Oedipus Tyrannus concerns an earlier stage in the same myth, with the discovery by Oedipus, Antigone's father, that he has fulfilled a Delphic oracle by unwittingly killing his father, Laius, and marrying his mother, Jocasta. The play is perhaps better known by its Latin title, *Oedipus Rex* or *Oedipus the King*, but the Greek title, while probably not Sophoclean (fifth century B.C.E. playwrights apparently did not title their plays, which were usually identified by their first lines), is more dramatically accurate. Technically, the Greek word *tyrannos*, means not a "harsh ruler"

but an "unconstitutional" one. At the beginning of the play, Oedipus, having gained power by solving the Sphinx's riddle, rules Thebes as a true *tyrannos*; yet, dramatic events prove that Oedipus is also Thebes's true *basileus* or "king" because he is really the son of the late King Laius. This irony in Oedipus's situation is the focus of the drama, which was so admired by Aristotle for its depiction of peripeteia caused directly by anagnorisis or "recognition." Sophocles further developed this irony, if not by actually inventing the blinding of Oedipus (who does not blind himself in Homer), then by using the theme of sight and blindness to great dramatic effect in the famous scene with Teiresias, in which the blind prophet is forced by Oedipus to contrast his own true knowledge with the ruler's ignorance; Teiresias tells Oedipus: "You have eyes but cannot see in what evil you are." In an ironic sense, then, the action of the play is directed toward an Oedipus, who sees with his eyes but not with his mind, becoming like Teiresias, who sees with his mind but not with his eyes. *Oedipus Tyrannus* is a true tragedy of discovery.

Many of the same dramatic skills found in *Antigone* can also be seen in *Oedipus Tyrannus*. In this play, too, Sophocles combines rapid action and dialogue with careful character development. One striking difference between *Antigone* and *Oedipus Tyrannus*, however, is structural: *Oedipus Tyrannus* lacks the diptych form and vacillation between two main characters that are found in *Antigone*. Rather, *Oedipus Tyrannus* is focused entirely on Oedipus and the development of his personality. This development is accomplished through a series of dialogues between Oedipus and most of the other *dramatis personae*, beginning in the prologue and not ending until Oedipus learns the fatal truth of his identity in the fourth episode. In these scenes, the qualities of a Sophoclean hero are again and again revealed in Oedipus: in his heroic intransigence, his determination to discover the murderer of Laius and his own identity, in his sense of nobility and self-worth, in his angry alienation from all who try to help. Oedipus's own heroic nature—like that of Antigone—leads him on to self-destruction.

Aristotle's admiration of *Oedipus Tyrannus* as the

ideal tragedy has, in a sense, been a Trojan horse for this play, because it has directed too much scholarly attention to Aristotle's interpretation of the play, an interpretation that is more Aristotle's reaction to Plato's prohibition of tragedy in *Politeia* (388-368 B.C.E.; *Republic*, 1701) than it is a close reading of *Oedipus Tyrannus*. Aristotle sought to counter Plato's objections to tragedy by making Oedipus into a morally satisfying character, by seeing in Oedipus a man, neither outstandingly virtuous nor evil, who falls into misfortune through hamartia. By doing this, Aristotle has created several thorny questions for the play: Does Oedipus really have a tragic flaw? Could he have acted any differently and still have been himself? Finally, is Oedipus of only average virtue? The Sophoclean answer to all these questions could only have been negative. Oedipus is not an ordinary person. He is the solver of the Sphinx's riddle and a man of superior intelligence. He is a man of outstanding virtue. In short, he is a Sophoclean hero. To have acted other than he did would have meant a denial of his heroic identity, a denial of himself. This heroic firmness is a remarkably constant theme in the Sophoclean corpus. It can be found in the suicide of Ajax, in the desperate love of Deianeira, in the civil disobedience of Antigone, in the inquest of Oedipus the *tyrannus*, in the hatred of Electra, in the suffering of Philoctetes, and in the mysterious death of Oedipus at Colonus. Sophocles' primary contribution to the history of drama, then, is his masterful focus on character development, and, in particular, his portrayal of the unyielding hero.

BIBLIOGRAPHY

Budelmann, Felix. *The Language of Sophocles: Communality, Communication, and Involvement.* New York: Cambridge University Press, 2000. A scholarly study of the language used in Sophocles' works. Bibliography and indexes.

Daniels, Charles B. *What Really Goes on in Sophocles' Theban Plays.* Lanham, Md.: University Press of America, 1996. Daniels examines Sophocles' Theban plays with reference to Greek mythology. Bibliography and index.

Kirkwood, Gordon MacDonald. *A Study of Sophoclean Drama: With a New Preface and Enlarged Bibliographical Note.* Ithaca, N.Y.: Cornell University Press, 1994. A scholarly look at the tragedies of Sophocles. Bibliography and indexes.

Pucci, Pietro. *Oedipus and the Fabrication of the Father: "Oedipus Tyrannus" in Modern Criticism and Philosophy.* Baltimore, Md.: Johns Hopkins University Press, 1992. A study of Sophocles' works that focuses on the Oedipus character. Bibliography and index.

Segal, Charles. *Oedipus Tyrannus: Tragic Heroism and the Limits of Knowledge.* 2d ed. New York: Oxford University Press, 2001. A close examination of the role of heroes in Sophocles' tragedies, particularly Oedipus in *Oedipus Tyrannus*. Bibliography and index.

_____. *Sophocles' Tragic World: Divinity, Nature, Society.* Cambridge, Mass.: Harvard University Press, 1995. The tragedies of Sophocles are analyzed in respect to religion, nature, and society. Bibliography and indexes.

_____. *Tragedy and Civilization: An Interpretation of Sophocles.* Norman: University of Oklahoma Press, 1999. In this work, Segal examines Sophocles' major plays as well as the role of Greek mythology and civilization in his works. Bibliography and indexes.

Van Nortwick, Thomas. *Oedipus: The Meaning of a Masculine Life.* Norman: University of Oklahoma Press, 1998. A scholarly study of the Oedipus character, particularly in *Oedipus Tyrannus* and *Oedipus at Colonus*. Bibliography and index.

Thomas J. Sienkewicz

WOLE SOYINKA

Born: Ijebu Isara, near Abeokuta, Nigeria; July 13,
1934

PRINCIPAL DRAMA

The Swamp Dwellers, pr. 1958, pb. 1963
The Invention, pr. 1959 (one act)
The Lion and the Jewel, pr. 1959, pb. 1963
Camwood on the Leaves, pr. 1960, pb. 1973 (radio
   play)
A Dance of the Forests, pr. 1960, pb. 1963
The Trials of Brother Jero, pr. 1960, pb. 1963
The Strong Breed, pb. 1963, pr. 1964
Three Plays, pb. 1963
Five Plays, pb. 1964
Kongi's Harvest, pr. 1964, pb. 1967
The Road, pr., pb. 1965
Madmen and Specialists, pr. 1970, revised pr., pb.
   1971
The Bacchae, pr., pb. 1973 (adaptation of
   Euripides' play)
Jero's Metamorphosis, pb. 1973, pr. 1975
Collected Plays, pb. 1973-1974 (2 volumes)
Death and the King's Horseman, pb. 1975, pr.
   1976
Opera Wonyosi, pr. 1977, pb. 1980 (adaptation of
   Bertolt Brecht's play *The Three-Penny Opera*)
Requiem for a Futurologist, pr. 1983, pb. 1985
A Play of Giants, pr., pb. 1984
Six Plays, pb. 1984
A Scourge of Hyacinths, pr. 1990, pb. 1992 (radio
   play)
From Zia, with Love, pr., pb. 1992
*The Beatification of Area Boy: A Lagosian
   Kaleidoscope*, pb. 1995, pr. 1996
Plays: Two, pb. 1999

OTHER LITERARY FORMS

Wole Soyinka is not only a dramatist but also a
poet, novelist, and critic. His poetry has appeared in
several collections, including *Idanre and Other
Poems* (1967), *Poems from Prison* (1969), *A Shuttle
in the Crypt* (1972), and *Mandela's Earth and Other*
Poems (1988). The long poem *Ogun Abibiman*, connecting Yoruba mythology with African liberation,
was first published in 1976. Soyinka has also written
a few short stories as well as *The Interpreters* (1965)
and *Season of Anomy* (1973), two novels. He has also
translated the Yoruba novel of D. O. Fagunwa, *Forest
of a Thousand Daemons: A Hunter's Saga* (1968).
His most famous piece of criticism is *Myth, Literature, and the African World* (1976). In addition,
Soyinka has produced two autobiographical works—
"The Man Died": Prison Notes of Wole Soyinka
(1972), a memoir of his prison experiences, and *Aké:
The Years of Childhood* (1981), a dramatic and imaginative re-creation of his early life—and a memoir to
his father, *Ìsarà: A Voyage Around "Essay"* (1989).

ACHIEVEMENTS

In spite of frequent criticism of his obscure and
difficult style, Wole Soyinka is generally regarded as
a major literary figure in the contemporary world;
by some he is considered to be the most sophisticated writer to emerge in Anglophone Africa. He has
achieved success in the three major forms—poetry,
fiction, and drama—and in the drama, for which he is
best known, his range extends from broad farce and
satire to tragedy. If he seems obscure, it is usually because of the density of the text: the constant reliance
on imagistic and rhythmic expression and on the ever-
present mythic and metaphysical dimension. An ambitious and experimental writer, he invites close textual
analysis. His success as a dramatist extends to the
practical arts of acting and directing. He has been the
prime mover in the establishment of theater companies
and the encouragement of the theatrical arts in Nigeria.

Behind all this literary activity lies Soyinka's loyalty to traditional Yoruba culture. He has had the intellectual capacity to understand and adapt it to his
own needs and to the needs of his country. This has,
perhaps inevitably, led him into the political arena,
since his primary concern for human freedom is
based largely on the identity of Ogun, the dynamic
god of Yoruba mythology. Ogun is not necessarily the

god of all Nigerian society. Soyinka is one of those rare writers of genius whose productions appeal both to the professional critic and to the general public. Soyinka's social consciousness has given his works a moral force that has made him a leader among political activists in Africa. His plays are translated into French and have been produced in Africa's Franco-phone countries. His influence on African theater has been tremendous, and the fear of Soyinka's revolutionary themes has led at least one African country to ban his plays.

Soyinka was awarded the Nobel Prize in Literature in 1986. Other prizes include the Jock Campbell Award for Fiction in 1968, the John Whiting Drama Prize in 1966, and his first prize at the Dakar Negro Arts Festival in 1960.

BIOGRAPHY

Akinwande Oluwole Soyinka was born July 13, 1934, at Abeokuta in Western Nigeria. His mother was a strong-willed businesswoman; his father, a

Wole Soyinka (© The Nobel Foundation)

school supervisor. Soyinka is a member of the Yoruba tribe whose culture is dominant in Western Nigeria. He has studied Yoruban mythology and theology as a scholar, and he has developed a theory of tragedy from Yoruban culture and has used it as the basis and inspiration of his fiction, poetry, and drama. His works are filled with its gods and spirits and its rituals and festivals. The traditional leader, the Oba, retains his spiritual and moral authority. The Yoruba language influences Soyinka's rhythmic and imagistic English style. Soyinka's formal education, however, has been basically Christian and European. Biblical and literary echoes pervade his work. Still, he considers himself African, writing for an African audience. He defends his eclecticism as the right of any artist and insists that even his representation of Yoruba culture is necessarily and justifiably personal.

Soyinka's primary and secondary education was in Nigeria. He attended St. Peter's School in Aké, Abeokuta (1938-1943), Abeokuta Grammar School (1944-1945), and Government College in Ibadan (1946-1950). His undergraduate preparation began at University College, Ibadan (later the University of Ibadan), where he studied from 1952 to 1954 with such future notables as Chinua Achebe and Christopher Okigbo. He then went to the University of Leeds in England, where he received his bachelor of arts degree with honors in English in 1957. He was later to receive an honorary degree from Leeds in 1973. His academic career began four years after graduation. He received a Rockefeller Research Fellowship to the University of Ibadan (1961-1962) and became lecturer at the University of Ife (1962-1964). In 1969, he became drama director, and he soon established a drama department and an acting company at the University of Ibadan. He has held various university academic posts, including a visiting professorship at Yale University in 1981, and has also delivered papers at academic meetings and published critical reviews and articles.

As early as his high school days, Soyinka was writing sketches for presentation and, soon after, clever comedies for the radio. At Leeds, he concentrated on the dramatic component in his course work. His career as a dramatist actually began when he became a play reader at the Royal Court Theatre in London, where some of his own early work was performed. Believing that special skills were necessary for the performance of his Nigerian plays, after his return to Lagos in 1960, he organized two theater companies: the Masks Company (1960) in Lagos and the Orison Theatre Group (1964) in Ibadan. Since then, he has argued that the best place for such companies, to ensure that they remain nonpolitical, is the university campus. This insistence on political nonalignment points to a final aspect of Soyinka's life—his social commitment. He has continually spoken out on public issues and, as a result, has risked the constant displeasure of existing authorities and institutions; he was detained in prison during the Biafran War, from August, 1967, to October, 1969. Even his early work contains political themes, but the Biafran War and his prison experiences have made his subsequent work more explicitly committed to social justice. He lived in exile from Nigeria for five years (1970-1975). His plays of those years and afterward, produced both abroad and at home, exhibit a political pessimism and employ varying degrees of political rhetoric, from subtle, intricate, metaphysical exploration to overt, satirical attack in public forums and over the radio. The dominant theme in his drama, as well as in his poetry and fiction, is individual human freedom, with its capacity for creation and destruction. Soyinka's own life is an example of that exertion of will, the responsibility of the individual to understand, reinterpret, and act on his or her cultural surroundings.

Given the political climate of Nigeria since 1993, Soyinka frequently led the exile's life, shuttling back and forth between the United States and Europe. Some reforms after 1998 have allowed him to return intermittently to his country. He continues his outspoken criticism of repressive regimes.

ANALYSIS

For Wole Soyinka, art and morality are inseparable. This does not mean simply that sensitivity to beauty is a good indicator of moral awareness, though that is strongly suggested in *A Dance of the Forests*. What is more to the point is that the primary obligation of art is to tell the truth: That obligation implies exposure and denunciation of falsehood. Even in Soyinka's broad farces—for example, the two plays that feature the prophet Jero—the object is not entertainment for its own sake but satire against any religious, social, or political leader who makes a mockery of human freedom. Soyinka also insists—with an eye on the romantic notion of negritude—that human beings have a dual nature whether they be African or Western; that is, they have destructive as well as creative urges. Part of his purpose as an artist is to expose the self-serving idealization of primitive African virtue; the problems in contemporary Africa may exist in a context of Western colonial oppression, but moral responsibility lies within the individual person as much as in the cultural milieu.

What is special about the moral content of Soyinka's drama is its metaphysical dimension, based on his own personal rendering of Yoruba myth. It assumes a continuum between the worlds of the dead, the living, and the unborn. That continuum is made possible by a fourth realm, which, in *Myth, Literature, and the African World*, Soyinka calls "the fourth stage," a realm that links the living with their ancestors and with the future. The myth of Ogun, the god who risked the dangers of the abyss and created a road from the spiritual to the human world, is the key to an understanding of all Soyinka's work, including his drama. The worship of Ogun is a ritual repetition of the god's feat. Yoruba drama, in a comparison that Soyinka himself makes, thus resembles Greek drama in its ritual essence and its origin. Ogun is the Yoruba counterpart of Dionysus. To emphasize its ritual nature, Soyinka incorporates in his drama elements of dance, music, mime, and masquerade. Characters are not merely actors playing a role—which in itself has ritual suggestions—but, in moments of high tension, are symbolically possessed by a god. The central actions are variations of rites of passage, with transformation or death-rebirth being the central archetypal pattern. Soyinka's most frequently used term for the terrifying experience of the numinous fourth stage is "transition." In some plays, the transition experience is artificial or incomplete, or it is parodied (the Jero plays); in others, it is the most pervasive theme.

Soyinka has a remarkable ability to combine the dramatic and theatrical device of peripeteia with the metaphysical experience of transition. The peripeteia, or climactic event of the play, is at the same time as the moment of divine possession. Generally, the plays move from ordinary realism to ritual enactment, with the nonverbal elements of dance, song, and masquerade receiving increasing prominence as the climax approaches. Thus, for Soyinka, drama is a serious matter. He may say in a facetious moment that it must be primarily entertainment, but in fact he treats it not only as a social and moral force but also as an act of human freedom and a ritual reenactment of human beings' relationship to divinity.

EARLY PLAYS

Among Soyinka's early plays, *A Dance of the Forests* is the most ambitious; it is also the most complex treatment of the chthonic, or underworld, realm of gods and spirits of transition. Even in Soyinka's earliest major play, *The Swamp Dwellers*, the sensitive protagonist, Igwezu, appears as an outcast from ordinary society, as one who has returned from a confrontation with the gods and is not yet able to deal with the compromising and capricious worlds of society and nature. His climactic decisions are those of a man dazed by his revolutionary experiences. The wise old Beggar (an incarnation of the god?) cannot persuade him to turn his knowledge to account. *The Lion and the Jewel*, a comic rendition of society, presents the archetype of transition in at least two ways: through a parody of transformation as the ridiculous country schoolteacher, Lakunle, imagines his passage from bachelor to husband, and through the real rite of passage experienced by the heroine, Sidi, from maiden to wife.

A DANCE OF THE FORESTS

A Dance of the Forests, as the title itself suggests, is in another world entirely. All the action is set in the forest, a universal symbol of the unknown, of the mysterious secrets of nature. It relies heavily on ritual, with its accompanying music, mime, dance, and masquerade. In the forest are representatives of the three other realms—the ancestors from the past, the living, and spiritual projections of posterity—as well as the gods and spirits who participate in and organize an extraordinary ritual to bridge the abyss between them.

A Dance of the Forests was written for the Nigerian independence celebrations in 1960, represented in the play as the Gathering of the Tribes. The principal human figures, Adenebi, Rola, and Demoke, have left the public festivities and sought the solitude of the forest. They are all guilty of some crime, hence uneasy in public, though the degree of their awareness varies considerably. Adenebi remains a lost soul because he cannot admit his guilt, even to himself. Rola, a prostitute, and Demoke, an artist who has just murdered his rival, at first, like Adenebi, try to hide their shame, but eventually they face the truth about themselves as human beings and achieve redemption. This is the essential plot of the play; it requires that these three characters—especially Demoke, as the central figure on whom the climax turns—pass from the ordinary world of the living to the world of the dead and the gods—that is, that they enter the "fourth stage." The first people they meet are Dead Man and Dead Woman, who have come in answer to the summons of the tribes. These ancestors turn out to be not the glorious heroes of Africa's imaginary past but fallen human beings who led unsatisfactory lives. They are accusers rather than celebrators of humankind.

Part 1 ends with some of the townspeople trying, through divination, ritual proverbs, dance and song, and a smoking, air-polluting lorry, to chase them away. Early in part 1, the three human protagonists also meet the Supreme Deity, called in the play Forest Head and temporarily disguised as an ordinary man named Obaneji. He guides them to the appointed place for the ritual Welcome of the Dead, which he has decided to hold in the forest because human society has refused to acknowledge the two dead guests as true ancestors out of their past.

Part 2 depicts a conflict between the forces of chance, retribution, and destruction, represented by the god Eshuoro, and the creative forces, represented by the god Ogun and his human agent, Demoke. It is a spiritual conflict that takes place in the realm of transition, symbolically rendered by the swamplike setting deep in the forest. The actual conflict between

Eshuoro and Demoke is preceded by an elaborate Welcome of the Dead. Forest Head, in Prospero-like fashion, stages a drama that re-creates the crucial event in the lives of Dead Man and Dead Woman. Dead Man, a warrior in the court of Mata Kharibu three centuries earlier, had defied the order of his ruler and refused to fight a senseless war. His punishment was emasculation and slavery, which he had to endure in two subsequent incarnations. What he wants now is rest. Forest Head is sympathetic, but Eshuoro is not. Dead Woman was Dead Man's pregnant wife, who, overcome by grief, committed suicide and hence doomed her unborn child to the fate of an *abiku*, an infant that dies repeatedly in childbirth. This scene, designed to arouse fear and pity for the suffering in human life, especially of those whose motives are pure, becomes in the hands of Eshuoro, an uninvited guest who appears in disguise as the Questioner of the Dead, further evidence of the weakness and sinfulness of human nature. The scene also includes two other figures, previous incarnations of Rola and Demoke as Madame Tortoise, the archetypal prostitute, and the Court Poet, who along with the Warrior resists her charms. What the scene also suggests, therefore, is the ever-recurring cycle of human history, and what follows is a dramatic and symbolic investigation of the question: Do human beings have the freedom and the will to change the pattern? Again it is Eshuoro who attempts to control the inquisition.

Up to this point, the three human protagonists have remained in the background (partly through dramatic necessity, since Rola and Demoke are actors in the flashback), but now the magic of Forest Head concentrates on their redemption. He insists that he cannot change anything himself; he can only provoke self-awareness. Thus, he designs a spiritual projection of the future but remains a passive observer. Significantly, the three humans are masked and become possessed by the spirits who speak through them. Having lost their identities, they enter totally the abyss of transition. The spirit voices from the intangible void are purposely obscure in their dire warnings. Scattered among them are the cries of Half-Child, whom Forest Head has meanwhile taken from the womb of Dead Woman. Its voice, too, is a voice of the future; it wants a full existence with a living mother.

With Eshuoro directing the action, the future of humankind appears desolate, but Eshuoro's power is not absolute. The play's climactic events, couched as they are in symbolic mime and dance, have elicited numerous interpretations. Eshuoro appears bent on separating Half-Child from its mother, as though a reunion would mean salvation. Demoke becomes a principal actor (once Forest Head has restored his consciousness), as he attempts to protect the child. With Ogun's help, he succeeds in returning the child to the mother, but Eshuoro emits a shout of victory even at this, suggesting perhaps that Demoke's act may save the child but place his own life in jeopardy, for he is taking on the responsibility of changing the pattern of history. A ritual scene follows in which Eshuoro forces Demoke, a "sacrificial basket" on his head, to climb the totem that Demoke had carved for the tribal festivities. Eshuoro then sets fire to the totem in order to kill both the artist and his creation, but his vengeance is foiled by Ogun, who catches the falling Demoke.

These scenes, depicting the saving of the child and of Demoke himself, are symbolically taking place within the unconscious and are a resolution to Demoke's particular problem and to the central issue raised by the play. As the tribe's carver, Demoke occupies a vital position. Without his art, ritual contact with the gods is impossible, yet in the act of carving the totem he had through jealousy flung his assistant and rival to his death. The incident reflects Soyinka's insistence on the creative and destructive tendencies in humankind. How can Demoke atone for his crime? The play dramatizes his inner acceptance of his human nature, his admission of guilt, and his redemption through the saving of Half-Child. Soyinka seems to suggest that all salvation is essentially personal and must follow the path of self-awareness, confession, and risk—a rite of passage across the abyss that separates human beings and the gods. The public celebration at the Gathering of the Tribes is pointless and meaningless, even hypocritical, because it denies the realities of the past and the destructive, darker side of human nature. The play thus offers both a tragic vision of life and hope for the future through the courageous acts of individual people. It also identifies the artist as the key provoker of self-awareness. Like Demoke, he is closest to the abyss; he possesses "fingers of the dead."

THE STRONG BREED AND KONGI'S HARVEST

Between *A Dance of the Forests* in 1960 and *The Road* in 1965, Soyinka devoted his energies to the writing of his first novel, *The Interpreters*, but he did complete two plays, *The Strong Breed* and *Kongi's Harvest*, both of which present a young man taking the responsibilities of the community on his own shoulders. In *The Strong Breed*, Eman first tries to deny the very fact of ritual atonement, especially his own inherited role as the "carrier" of tribal guilt; eventually, however, he plays out this role in another tribe with such obsession that he pays for his rebellion with his life. Daodu, in *Kongi's Harvest*, assumes the Hamlet-like role of avenger as he challenges the authority of the usurping President Kongi, forcing him in the climactic scene to face the horrors of death, of the abyss, which in his egotism he had ignored. In both plays, the myth of transition clearly remains the key to self-awareness.

THE ROAD

These two plays were followed by *The Road*, Soyinka's first drama centered on the danger to human sanity posed by contact with the chthonic realm. The setting of *The Road* differs significantly from that of *A Dance of the Forests*. The latter takes place entirely within the realm of passage—symbolically the forest—and hence is essentially an inner experience; in contrast, *The Road* takes place in society—although a very specialized and symbolic segment of it—and is mainly concerned with the effects of death on social behavior. The vision of *A Dance of the Forests* is, broadly speaking, tragic, but with a comic ending: Demoke receives both atonement and a sobering projection of the future. *The Road*, on the other hand, maintains a comic atmosphere through most of its scenes but ends on a tragic note; it actually contains every conceivable dramatic mode, from satire and realism to Symbolism and the absurd. Like *A Dance of the Forests*, it is a complex, multifaceted, and ambiguous play.

Structurally, *The Road* proceeds in a manner similar to *A Dance of the Forests*, from the ordinary to the ritualistic. Throughout, Soyinka maintains a tension between the practical world of survival and the spiritual world of essences, between the self and the other. Samson is a realist. He always retains contact with the ordinary world and fulfills the role of mirror or "narrator" even though he never steps out of his role as character. He is the reference point by which one measures the psychological states and obsessions of the other characters. In part 1, he remains onstage and controls the action until the final scene, when Professor, the epitome of obsession with death and the other major figure in the play, takes over the action. The same pattern emerges in part 2, in which Samson and Professor are usually onstage together and in which the balance gradually shifts in the direction of ritual. The setting for the play is a kind of rundown truck stop. Samson is a "tout" for the truck driver Kotonu, who has recently given up his job for psychological reasons that the play gradually makes clear. Professor, a former lay reader in the adjacent church, now runs the truckers' rest stop, which doubles as a spare-parts shop and headquarters of his Quest for the meaning of Death. He holds his own communion every evening for his followers and hangers-on. Murano, his assistant and palm-wine tapster, symbol of the transition stage and Professor's best hope for enlightenment, leaves every morning and returns in the evening with wine for the ritual service.

The play deals with one day in the lives of these characters, a day made decisive by two recent occurrences that bring Professor's Quest to its crisis. In part 1, the occurrences are merely suggested; part 2 contains their reenactment as past merges with present. Kotonu and Samson narrowly missed being killed in an accident on the road; a truck passed them and then fell through a rotted portion of a bridge. Though Samson viewed the near miss stoically, Kotonu was so disturbed by the thought of death that he has given up driving, much to the displeasure of Samson, whose main preoccupation throughout the play is to restore Kotonu to his common sense. To this end, Samson solicits the aid of Professor, who has hired Kotonu to manage the spare-parts store.

Samson insists that Kotonu's genius is in driving, not in scavenging parts off wrecked vehicles and selling them. Professor, however, is sympathetic with Kotonu's sudden concern with death. The second incident is even more significant. Kotonu and Samson were involved in a hit-and-run accident in which they "killed" a man masquerading as Ogun (the "guardian of the road") in a ritual ceremony; he was in the *agemo* phase, in transition from the human to the divine essence. They hid the body in the back of the truck and carried it to the truck stop, where Professor found it. This victim is the Murano of the play, in dumb suspension between life and death and, hence, supposedly in possession of secrets that Professor is after. The incident intensified Kotonu's withdrawal, especially since he was required to don Murano's bloody mask to escape capture by the other celebrants. Thus, Kotonu himself symbolically became the god Ogun in the rite of passage. The reenactment of these scenes, together with several others in which Samson mimics Professor or recalls past incidents, dramatizes the impact of death on the living and structurally prepares for the final ritual act.

One other significant event has also recently occurred. Usually Professor leaves every morning for his tour of the road and, like Murano, does not return until evening. On this particular day, he has broken that pattern after coming upon a wreck and finding a road sign with the word "Bend" on it, which he takes to be symbolic. He returns to his headquarters more absentminded than usual and then departs in a daze. Part 1 ends at noon with a funeral service for the victims of the accident at the bridge, and with the return of Murano, confused by the organ music that usually calls him back in the evening. The day is clearly ominous. Murano is almost "killed" as a thief by one of the hangers-on.

The communion service at the end of part 2 is the culmination of the various "performances" during the play that have become progressively more intense. The policeman, Particulars Joe, is at the truck stop in search of the hit-and-run victim, whom no one has as yet identified as Murano. The identification soon becomes clear as Murano discovers the Mask he had worn, puts it on, and begins the dance that is to continue until Professor's closing speech. Everyone at the communion, already intoxicated by the wine, senses the power of the moment, the traditional reenactment of the rite of passage from human to divine. Murano is becoming possessed by the god Ogun. Professor hopes to use the moment to gain secret knowledge of death without dying himself. Salubi, to retain his sanity, wants to leave. Say Tokyo Kid, apparently the Eshuoro figure, symbolic of retribution and destruction, skeptical of such ritual behavior, challenges Murano and, during the struggle, stabs Professor with a knife passed to him by Salubi. Murano, completely possessed by the god, hurls Say Tokyo Kid to his death. Professor ends the play with a sermon to his followers, enjoining them to imitate the Road by lying in wait and treacherously destroying the unsuspecting traveler.

The key figure in this play is Professor, but he is such a strange composite that the play remains an ambiguous statement. He is an archetypal character, or rather a composite of archetypes. He is Faust, Falstaff, Jesus, and Don Quixote mixed up in a bundle of conflicting motives. Like Falstaff, he insists on the survival instincts in human nature. Like Faust, he challenges the gods to achieve knowledge denied to the descendants of Adam. He has messianic fantasies, but he is maddened by his preoccupation with death as surely as Don Quixote's romance with literature blinds him to ordinary reality. It is as though the mind of Professor has become a chaotic image of the chthonic realm that he so desperately searches out but that he as a human being cannot understand. He never learns that the road of his daily wanderings on which his drivers make their living is not a real substitute for the Road that Ogun traveled to make contact with the human. Whereas Demoke in *A Dance of the Forests* undergoes the transition experience but retains his human perspective, Professor becomes obsessed with the realm itself and intellectualizes himself out of human society. To a large extent, of course, he is a comic figure—the proverbial absentminded professor—but the ambivalent messianic-Machiavellian Quest gives him a certain magnificent dimension and elevates his flaw to the hubris of classical tragedy.

THE TRIALS OF BROTHER JERO AND JERO'S METAMORPHOSIS

The chaotic misdirection of *The Road*—and, indeed, of much of Soyinka's work in the 1960's, with its motifs of political chicanery, moral inertia, and death in modern Nigeria—anticipated the horrors of the Biafran War at the end of the decade. The war and Soyinka's two-year detention in prison did not, in fact, drastically change his philosophical approach to his craft, but they did intensify his concerns. *The Trials of Brother Jero*, for example, written before the war, is political and social satire, but Jero as the trickster is essentially a comic figure mixing farce and wit. The political caricature who undergoes a mock transformation in the final scene is more ridiculous than dangerous. In a companion piece, however, *Jero's Metamorphosis*, written after the war, the ritual transformation of the beach prophets into an Apostolic Salvation Army is a thinly veiled attack on a military regime that has, as the play reiterates, made public execution a national spectacle. Jero, dressed in his general's uniform, sitting underneath his own portrait as the curtain falls, is a sinister threat to moral sanity.

MADMEN AND SPECIALISTS

The very subject of *Madmen and Specialists*, written soon after Soyinka's release from prison, is the war's devastating effect on every phase of human life. Its central character, Bero, is hubris itself in his absolute denial of the essence of Yoruba culture: the continuity of life, the gods, the ancestors, and humankind's responsibility toward the future. He renders meaningless the realm that links human beings with the gods, and he violates the primary law of existence—return to nature as much as or more than is taken from it—and reduces people to organisms.

THE BACCHAE

Soyinka's willingness to undertake an adaptation of Euripides' *Bakchai* (405 B.C.E.; *The Bacchae*, 1781) thus comes as no surprise: It, too, deals with a madman in defiance of the gods and of the basic rhythms of human society and human nature. Dionysian possession and retribution are the closest thing in Western culture to the worship of Ogun among the Yoruba: *The Bacchae*, like *Madmen and Specialists*, constitutes a warning to militaristic oppression. In all

three of these postwar plays, the motif of death, the numinous realm of passage, has retained its central place within the philosophical and dramatic structure; it has simply taken on added significance and urgency because of the realities through which Soyinka has had to live. Death has become part of a greater political commitment and a deeper pessimism.

DEATH AND THE KING'S HORSEMAN

The new commitment and tone are nowhere more evident than in *Death and the King's Horseman*, a play that addresses the failure of the older generation to preserve intact the traditional Yoruba culture and that pessimistically depicts the attempt of their children to undertake the responsibility. According to Yoruba custom, when a king dies, his horseman must, at the end of the thirty days of mourning, commit suicide and join him in the passage to the underworld; otherwise, the king remains in the passage, subject to evil forces. Soyinka builds his play around the king's horseman, Elesin Oba, whose weakness of will breaks the age-old formula and places the entire society in danger of extinction. As with the other plays, much of the action is ritual, and, as is common in Soyinka, the climactic scenes combine dramatic peripeteia with divine possession and entrance into the transition phase. The structure also reflects the clash of African and Western cultures, a theme common in African literature but rather rare in Soyinka; the scenes alternate between Nigerian and British settings. Soyinka insists in a prefatory note that the British presence is only accidental: Elesin's failure is not imposed from without but is self-inflicted.

Soyinka organizes the play with his usual economy. All the action takes place within the span of a few hours. Act 1 presents Elesin's procession through the market just at closing time, on the way to his own death: He and his Praise Singer chant his fate. His love of the market as a symbol of earthly activity and life, however, suggests his ambivalence toward his role, and when he sees a beautiful young girl and arranges with Iyaloja, her future mother-in-law and leader of the market women, to marry and enjoy this maiden as his last earthly act, his eventual failure to carry out his appointed role is almost certain. Both Iyaloja and the audience, however, yield temporarily to Elesin's sophistic arguments. He insists that this is not mere sexual indulgence but a mingling of the "seeds of passage" with the life of the unborn; he deceives himself and his audience with poetic fancies and beautiful language. Iyaloja grants him the gift of the girl but warns him of his responsibility. His poetic fancy will not become a reality unless he dies.

In act 2, the scene changes to the home of the British District Officer, Simon Pilkings, and his wife, Jane; the accompanying music changes from sacred chant and rhythm to the tango. The *egungun* mask, used in Ogun worship to represent divine possession, has been turned into a costume for the masquerade later that evening. Here, Soyinka presents ritual suicide through the eyes of the supercilious Pilkings, who rejects Yoruba culture as barbaric; Jane is more sympathetic but still uncomprehending. Simon arranges for Amusa, a Nigerian sergeant in his employ, to arrest Elesin and prevent the completion of the ritual.

Act 3 begins with a comic scene in which the market women and their daughters turn Sergeant Amusa's duty into a mockery and send him packing back to his white superior. This moment of hilarious triumph gives way to what appears to be the climactic scene of the play, Elesin's emergence from his wedding chamber and his hypnotic dance of possession as he symbolically enters the abyss of transition.

This sacred event is replaced again by the artificiality of British custom, as act 4 begins with a mime at the masquerade ball, with the prince of Wales (having come to Nigeria as a gesture of courage and solidarity during World War II) and his entourage dressed in seventeenth century costume, dancing to a Viennese waltz and admiring Pilkings's demonstration of the *egungun* dance movements and vocal accompaniments. When he learns that Amusa has failed in his mission, Pilkings departs for the market to halt the suicide. Meanwhile, Jane has a long discussion with Elesin's son, Olunde, who has just returned from studying medicine in England to oversee his father's ritual burial. Jane is shocked that Olunde still clings to barbaric customs in spite of his Western education; in turn, Olunde suggests the greater barbarism of world wars, and there is no meeting of minds. The act

closes with the unexpected return of Pilkings with Elesin. Olunde, who had assumed with absolute confidence that his father had completed the ritual obligation, senses immediately the cosmic reversal of roles, represented onstage by the father on his knees begging forgiveness from his son and the son judging the father.

Act 5 sees Elesin in chains imprisoned at the Residency. Iyaloja and the other market women bear the body of Olunde to his cell. She condemns Elesin for forcing his son to die in his place, thus reversing the cycle of nature. At the sight of his son, Elesin strangles himself with his chain and enters the abyss, though perhaps too late to satisfy the demands of the gods. What is especially significant about this scene is Elesin's second attempt to conceal the truth from himself. In act 2, he had refused to face his excessive love of life, his inability to leave the world of pleasure to the young. Now, in his conversation with Iyaloja before his recognition of his son, he is denying responsibility for his failure of will. He blames the tempting touch of young flesh and mentions Iyaloja's own complicity in the temptation; he blames especially Pilkings for his abrupt intervention. His most significant statement, however, is his self-serving appeal to the cultural situation. The power and influence of British culture, he says, caused him to question the loyalty of his own gods, and he came to doubt the validity of the ritual itself. The play ends with a dirge over the deaths of Olunde and Elesin, but also, perhaps, over the death of a culture. Iyaloja and Olunde have completed the ritual as best they could, but she is not sure whether the son's death will satisfy the gods. The question remains, whether the younger generation of Nigerians will be able to save the civilization that their parents, in self-indulgence, doubt, and cowardice, have abandoned.

A PLAY OF GIANTS AND REQUIEM FOR A FUTUROLOGIST

Two satirical plays of the 1980's, *A Play of Giants* and *Requiem for a Futurologist*, insist that neither the political leaders nor the people have emerged from the chaos. In the first, set in New York City, Field-Marshal Kamini (a thinly disguised Idi Amin of Uganda) is a con artist who leads three other heads of state in a hostage-taking, blackmailing, terrorist challenge against the United Nations. It is an all-out, farcical attack on the worship of power by those who wield it and those who submit to it. In the second play, the con artist is an opportunistic servant, Alaba, who uses various disguises to "overthrow" his master, Dr. Godspeak, a well-known prophet or "futurologist," by convincing the public and the doctor himself that he is dead. At Godspeak's "death," Alaba becomes the futurologist, a reincarnation of the famous French astrologer Nostradamus, who can use his supposed powers to exploit a gullible population. In Kamini and Alaba, Soyinka thus metamorphoses once again the Jero of the 1960 play. Nigeria—and the world—still plays the grotesque, exhausting, and futile game of the quack and the dupe.

PLAYS OF THE 1990'S

Three plays written in the 1990's, *From Zia, with Love*, *A Scourge of Hyacinths*, and *The Beatification of Area Boy: A Lagosian Kaleidoscope*, are Soyinka's direct responses to the military dictators and irresponsible government of Nigeria. For his critical portrayals, Soyinka paid an additional four years (1993 to 1998) of self-imposed exile. During that period, he taught and traveled in the United States and England.

Both *From Zia, with Love* and *A Scourge of Hyacinths* were originally written as radio plays. Each grew out of real situations. Whether parodying the dictatorship of General Sani Abachu by comparing life under him to living in a prison in *From Zia, with Love* or likening the destruction of civil liberties to an invasion of water hyacinths in *A Scourge of Hyacinths*, Soyinka used his position as a world-respected writer to protest and was charged with treason for his efforts.

THE BEATIFICATION OF AREA BOY

The Beatification of Area Boy shows the suffering of the average Nigerian at the hands of both the military and corrupt politicians. Soyinka's protagonist is Sanda, a university dropout, who is the leader of a group of small-time vendors on Broad Street in Lagos, the capital. This one-act play, written in 1995, combines many of Soyinka's writing strengths with his political determination. He uses the setting of the streets of modern Lagos to illustrate the huge dispari-

ties in the lives of Nigerians and to show that while at one time the country's problems may have been imposed on it by outsiders, usually Western powers, current difficulties are primarily indigenous, rooted in the corruption and greed of the Nigerian military and political parties.

The title is taken from the name given to the Area Boys, or young men who operate more or less like gang leaders in specific, assigned turf in Lagos, basically conning and blackmailing wealthy businesspeople and tourists. Their quasi-director and the play's protagonist is Sanda. What becomes quickly apparent is that Sanda and all the other characters hustling on the street really have no other choice. The corruption and brutality in the country have made it all but impossible for them to have legitimate jobs and the chance at a better life.

Soyinka's sympathy for the ordinary Nigerian is obvious because the characters exude charm and warmth and care for each other in addition to exhibiting a realistic assessment of their situation and the powers that persecute them. On this busy street, working from their humble stalls, exists a community of people like Mama Put, who sells food; Judge, a vagrant; Barber; Cyclist; Boyko; Sanda; and Sanda's former girlfriend Miseyi, although she is actually from a well-connected family. The police, military officers, and a military governor use their considerable positions and thugs against these people, who are merely trying to survive. A public wedding and the bride's last-minute rejection of the groom force a showdown between the street people and the military and political powers. Despite a serious skirmish complete with gunshots and beatings, the street people escape to try another day, showing that Soyinka still harbors hope for his country.

Soyinka's considerable skill at presenting song and dance in his plays is evident in *The Beatification of Area Boy*. For example, upset because the Area Boys have overcome some of his soldiers, a screeching military officer belts out a tune entitled, "DON'T TOUCH MY UNIFORM!!!" Another song example is "Maroko," which describes a "wretched shanty town." Both are funny despite the pathetic and miserable situations being described.

Other major works

LONG FICTION: *The Interpreters*, 1965; *Season of Anomy*, 1973.

POETRY: *Idanre and Other Poems*, 1967; *Poems from Prison*, 1969; *A Shuttle in the Crypt*, 1972; *Ogun Abibiman*, 1976; *Mandela's Earth and Other Poems*, 1988; *Early Poems*, 1997.

NONFICTION: *"The Man Died": Prison Notes of Wole Soyinka*, 1972 (autobiography); *Myth, Literature, and the African World*, 1976; *Aké: The Years of Childhood*, 1981 (autobiography); *Art, Dialogue, and Outrage*, 1988; *Ìsarà: A Voyage Around "Essay,"* 1989; *The Credo of Being and Nothingness*, 1991; *Wole Soyinka on "Identity,"* 1992; *Orisha Liberated the Mind: Wole Soyinka in Conversation with Ulli Beier on Yoruba Religion*, 1992; *"Death and the Kings' Horseman": A Conversation Between Wole Soyinka and Ulli Beier*, 1993; *Ibadan: The Penkelemes Years: A Memoir, 1946-1965*, 1994; *The Open Sore of a Continent: A Personal Narrative of the Nigerian Crisis*, 1996; *The Burden of Memory, the Muse of Forgiveness*, 1999; *Seven Signposts of Existence: Knowledge, Humour, Justice, and Other Virtues*, 1999; *Conversations with Wole Soyinka*, 2001 (Biodun Jeyifo, editor).

TRANSLATION: *Forest of a Thousand Daemons: A Hunter's Saga*, 1968 (of D. O. Fagunwa's novel *Ogboju Ode Ninu Igbo Irunmale*).

BIBLIOGRAPHY

Gates, Henry Louis, Jr., ed. *In the House of Oshugbo: Critical Essays on Wole Soyinka*. London: Oxford University Press, 2002. This large collection of essays includes analyses of specific plays, biographical information, comparative studies involving contemporary writers such as Bertolt Brecht and James Joyce, and discussions of literary theory, the art of writing, and Yoruba culture.

Jeyifo, Biodun, ed. *Conversations with Wole Soyinka*. Jackson: University Press of Mississippi, 2001. The first book to feature recorded interviews of Soyinka. Interviewers include Henry Louis Gates, Jr., Anthony Appiah, and Biodun Jeyifo. These interviews help clarify what are called the obscurities in Soyinka's most difficult plays.

_____. *Perspectives on Wole Soyinka*. Jackson: University Press of Mississippi, 2001. This collection of critical essays covers three decades. Its major contribution is analyzing Soyinka's work using many kinds of contemporary schools of critical theory from feminism to recuperated phenomenology. Also discussed are his postcolonial politics and aestheticism.

Jones, Eldred Durosimi. *The Writing of Wole Soyinka*. 3d ed. Portsmouth, N.H.: Heinemann, 1988. This introductory survey of Soyinka's works opens with a background essay on the author. Subsequent essays deal with individual texts under the general chapter headings "Autobiography," "Plays," "Poetry," and "Fiction." Essays on thirteen plays follow a summary-commentary format, approaching them as individual, literary texts, but with some cross-referencing, a few production and theatrical notes, and occasional attention to stylistic development. Includes a biographical outline and a brief bibliography.

Lindfors, Bernth, and James Gibbs, eds. *Research on Wole Soyinka*. Lawrenceville, N.J.: Africa World Press, 1992. These essays represent a wide variety of critical methodologies applied to Soyinka's works, including linguistics and structural, textual, and cultural interpretations.

Maja-Pearce, Adewale, ed. *Wole Soyinka: An Appraisal*. Portsmouth, N.H.: Heinemann, 1994. This book is a collection of essays primarily by African writers. Topics include Soyinka's fiction, poetry, and drama, as well as the African culture from which he writes. His Noble lecture is the lead entry. An interview with Soyinka is also presented.

Okome, Onookome. *Ogun's Children: The Literature and Politics of Wole Soyinka Since the Nobel Prize*. Lawrenceville, N.J.: Africa World Press, 2002. An analysis of Soyinka that focuses on his work since receiving the Nobel Prize.

Wright, Derek. *Wole Soyinka Revisited*. New York: Twayne, 1992. This introductory study of Soyinka includes critical studies of his works, biographical information, and a chronology of his life and works.

Thomas Banks,
updated by Judith Steininger

SIR RICHARD STEELE

Born: Dublin, Ireland; March, 1672
Died: Carmarthen, Wales; September 1, 1729

PRINCIPAL DRAMA

The Funeral: Or, Grief à-la-mode, pr. 1701, pb.
1702
The Lying Lover: Or, The Ladies' Friendship, pr.
1703, pb. 1704 (adaptation of Pierre Corneille's
play *Le Menteur*)
The Tender Husband: Or, The Accomplished Fools,
pr., pb. 1705 (adaptation of Molière's play *Le
Sicilien*)
The Conscious Lovers, pr. 1722, pb. 1723
(adaptation of Terence's play *Andria*)
The Plays of Richard Steele, pb. 1971 (Shirley
Strum Kenny, editor)

OTHER LITERARY FORMS

Sir Richard Steele's periodical essays, even more
than his four plays, had a major impact on early
eighteenth century sensibility. Beginning his journalistic career as the anonymous author of the Whig
government's *The London Gazette*, Steele later joined
with Joseph Addison to produce *The Tatler* (1709-
1711; 188 periodicals by Steele) and *The Spectator* (1711-1712, 1714; 236 periodicals by Steele), the
most influential vehicles of opinion and taste of
their day, which consisted of short, fictional essays
illustrating an idea, theme, or moral. Steele later
wrote, also with Addison, *The Guardian* (1713), also
a vehicle for periodical essays. *The Englishman*
(1713-1714, first series; 1715, second series; periodical essays), *The Theatre* (1720, later edited by
John Loftis and published as *Richard Steele's "The
Theatre,"* 1920, 1962), and lesser periodicals also
came from Steele's pen. Taken together, these more
than seven hundred essays constitute Steele's major literary achievement. Steele was also an occasional poet, a writer of political tracts such as *The
Importance of Dunkirk Considered* (1713), and a
moral philosopher, author of *The Christian Hero*
(1701).

ACHIEVEMENTS

Although not a dramatist of the first rank, Sir
Richard Steele had some notable successes and is important in theater history. He came to write for the
theater when, in his words, successful comedies were
"built upon the ruin of virtue and innocence." An advocate of reform, Steele hoped to demonstrate that a
play could provide effective entertainment without
pandering to the worst tastes of the town. He believed
that high spirits and a healthy didacticism could coexist. In practice, his demonstrations were mixed successes. Steele stressed domestic virtues and worked
hard to make them seem attractive. He appealed to
emotion in ways not customary in comedy, helping to
usher in a hybrid form known as sentimental comedy,
a forerunner of melodrama. These features, as well as
Steele's characters and themes, caused him to be
among the first to reflect the consciousness of the
new middle class.

Steele was a competent manager of dramatic
structure, a fashioner of believable characters who
speak intelligibly and who, when they are not whining excessively, can gain one's sympathy. Often robust in movement, Steele's comedies sometimes suffer from being too studied, too obviously written as
prescriptions and thus lacking in natural ease.
Steele's plays, along with his drama criticism, had
considerable influence in England and in France. Unfortunately, it was an influence in a direction that has
not found much esteem—though the enormous audience for the modern-day soap opera may owe him a
debt of gratitude.

BIOGRAPHY

Sir Richard Steele was born into a family of the
English governing class in Ireland. His paternal
grandfather was a successful merchant adventurer
and courtier who enjoyed the favor of both James I
and Charles I. Steele's father (both forebears were
also named Richard) led a less colorful life, but he
had begun a promising career as a lawyer when
young Richard was born in 1672. Steele's mother,

born Elinor Sheyles (a Celtic name), was the widow of Thomas Symes of Dublin. She became Mrs. Steele in 1670. Because Steele's father died at a young age without establishing a sure footing for his children, it fell to Richard's aunt, Katherine Steele Mildmay, to provide for the family. Her second marriage, to Henry Gascoigne in 1675, placed her in a position to help her nephew, and it was through Gascoigne's influence (he was private secretary to the duke of Ormonde) that Steele entered Charterhouse, a prestigious public school, in the fall of 1684. At Charterhouse, Steele met his famous friend and collaborator, Joseph Addison, though the two men attended different colleges at Oxford. In 1695, Steele became an ensign in Lord Cutt's regiment, and, partly as a result of his earliest literary efforts, he soon gained a commission and later a captaincy.

Steele made his mark in literary circles with his essay *The Christian Hero* and then with a series of comedies—*The Funeral*, *The Lying Lover*, and *The Tender Husband*—all produced between 1701 and 1705. His success made him an early member of the Kit-Kat Club, founded by leading Whigs, where he enjoyed the company of London's literary intelligentsia and made important Whig connections. By 1707, Steele was "the Gazetteer," the writer of the official government newspaper. After this political hackwork, he joined forces with Addison to create two successful and influential papers, *The Tatler* and *The Spectator*. These periodicals, of which Steele wrote more than four hundred between 1709 and 1712, established for him a second and more permanent reputation. First befriended and then attacked by Jonathan Swift, Steele found himself increasingly a political creature and gave less attention to his other periodical ventures during the last years of the Tory ministry under Queen Anne. An active Whig scribe, Steele found himself in and out of the House of Commons and ready to share the spoils of the coming Whig triumph of 1714.

Early in 1715, Steele was made governor of Drury Lane Theatre, regained a seat in Parliament, and (in April) was knighted by George I. He held the Drury Lane post, at least nominally, until his death. Reform of the stage was Steele's mission, as it had been in his

Sir Richard Steele (Library of Congress)

early plays and in his many essays about the theater, but only during the first five years was he active in his duties, and even then he had only limited success in administering the reforms he advocated. His last play, *The Conscious Lovers*, is the best testimony to the sincerity of his goals. Ill health plagued Steele's later years, which he divided between Hereford and Carmarthen, Wales, where he died in 1729.

Steele's domestic life was a study in contrasts. He had an illegitimate daughter by Elizabeth Tonson, the sister of his then future publisher. His first marriage, in the spring of 1705 to Margaret Ford Stretch, a widow of considerable property, ended with her death late the following year. Steele managed to encumber her estate with debts. In 1707, he married Mary Scurlock of Carmarthen. Their marriage of eleven years was marked by Steele's utmost tenderness and devotion, as his constant letters to her attest. She died in childbirth. Neither of Steele's two legitimate daughters lived to have children, though his illegitimate daughter did. His two sons did not survive childhood.

ANALYSIS

Of Sir Richard Steele's four plays, *The Funeral* and *The Tender Husband* are at once the most humorous and the least sentimental. *The Funeral*, Steele's most original play, was written in part to relieve him of the reputation he had made as a pious drone through his essay *The Christian Hero*. Even these sprightly pieces, however, reveal Steele's concern with curing the corruption of the London stage. He shunned the licentiousness that had been rampant but gave each piece enough wit, zest, and characterization to make it popular for many years to come. It is as the author of *The Lying Lover* and *The Conscious Lovers* that Steele's reputation as a founder of the sentimental comedy rests. The earlier play was not a stage success, and it is clearly the weakest of Steele's dramatic efforts. *The Conscious Lovers* was both a success and a major influence. An analysis of *The Tender Husband* and *The Conscious Lovers* allows representation of what M. E. Hare called Steele's "purely amusing and his didactic veins."

THE TENDER HUSBAND

The Tender Husband presents Biddy Tipkin, a young girl whose guardian uncle has arranged her marriage to a country cousin, one Humphry Gubbin. Biddy, whose head is filled with the excesses of the airy romances she reads so voraciously, has let herself imagine something far more exotic and impassioned than this dry arrangement. For his part, Humphry does not want to be forced into anything. When the two meet, they pledge to be friendly enemies; they will not have each other, but they will cooperate toward each other's freedom.

Before the audience is introduced to this pair, it learns that Captain Jack Clerimont is seeking his financial ease through a careful marriage. His older brother, Clerimont Senior, has heard of Biddy and helps set a plot in motion that will give Jack a chance at that prize. Everything Jack hears about Biddy's wealth is translated into a positive personal attribute in his playful formulations. Apprised of her fortune of ten thousand pounds, Jack responds: "Such a statute, such a blooming countenance, so easy a shape!" The play's humor, and part of its meaning, derives from interchanges of this sort. By making Jack a good-natured rogue, Steele softens the cynicism in this conventional equation of love and money.

With the wily lawyer Samuel Pounce as helpful (and bribed) intermediary, Jack is given the opportunity to meet and to woo Biddy. He imitates the manner and language of romance literature, quickly winning her heart. He has already convinced himself that he is rescuing her from the hard fate her uncle has in mind. Biddy, because she wants to be, is an easy conquest. Pounce, by distracting Biddy's stern Aunt Barsheba with talk of the stock market (her true passion), makes Jack's path as smooth as can be.

In a later scene, Jack, disguised as the artist hired by Barsheba to paint her niece's portrait, completes his courtship of Biddy while warning her of how her romantic notions will have to be adjusted to reality. By this time, Steele has modulated Jack's intentions so that his cynical first motive has changed into something far more acceptable; he has discovered a genuine affection for the girl. No longer simply deceiving her for her money, he has been transformed from Restoration rake into earnest suitor.

Wrapped around the Humphry-Biddy-Jack plot is another, more sinister one. Clerimont Senior has been using his soon-to-be-cast-off mistress, Lucy Fainlove, in a most despicable manner. He has had her disguise herself as a man, not only to pass unsuspected before Mrs. Clerimont but also to put that lady in a compromising position so that her husband can "discover" the infidelity that he assumes to be the consequence of the fashionable liberty she desires and he seems to grant. Although his scheme works, he gains little by it. Because he is softened by his wife's tears and somewhat sorry for his deceit, Clerimont Senior becomes Steele's way of suggesting that even a man of generous heart can be temporarily led astray by social fashions that magnify vice by encouraging human frailties. His wife, too, has allowed herself to be victimized. Her love of appearances and affectations provided her, for a while at least, with more pain than pleasure.

Everyone ends up reconciled and happy with the final state of affairs. Jack gets Biddy, the older Clerimonts passionately patch things up, and Lucy Fainlove captures Humphry, who is quite pleased with himself. Lucy turns out to be the sister of lawyer Pounce, a neat twist that allows Steele to link the two plots together.

If *The Tender Husband* (an ironic title) says anything, it says that people will behave as these people do. It also suggests that those most concerned with forms and appearances are most easily deceived. Steele, like William Congreve in *The Way of the World* (pr. 1700), advocates marriages based on love rather than on parental arrangements, but he (again like Congreve) recognizes the importance of financial security. Jack begins by seeking a fortune; Biddy begins by longing for a romantic dream. Each ends up at a humane, caring, yet practical middle ground.

In many ways, *The Tender Husband* is like much of the Restoration comedy that predates it. Clerimont Senior is the familiar libertine type, though his reformation precludes either a significant victory or any kind of punishment. The far more appealing Jack is still not a paragon of virtue, as the true sentimental hero must be. The tone of the play, however, is far less cynical and the satire is far more gentle than that to which audiences had been accustomed. It is easy to feel sympathy for Jack, for Biddy, and even for Humphry, who is a very special version of the stock country bumpkin and a clear model for Oliver Goldsmith's famous Tony Lumpkin in *She Stoops to Conquer* (pr. 1773). Biddy's aunt, her Uncle Hezekiah, and Humphry's father are all recognizable types, but Steele gives them life. The many songs in the play add their own charm. Colloquially convincing, witty, unburdened by preachiness, *The Tender Husband* is to many critics Steele's best play. It "reforms" the excesses of Restoration comedy without losing touch with what made them work. It remains, first and last, an entertainment.

THE CONSCIOUS LOVERS

The same cannot be said for *The Conscious Lovers*. In his preface to the first edition, Steele asserted that "the chief design of this was to be an innocent performance." The prologue asked the audience to value "wit that scorns the aids of vice" and to help "moralize the stage" by giving the work a kind reception. Clearly, then, *The Conscious Lovers* was designed as a model for a new type of drama. As governor of Drury Lane, Steele had made but the slightest

advances in his campaign for reform. With his own play he hoped to make his intentions clear while pleasing a discriminating audience.

The play's plot concerns Bevil Junior's desire to please his heart without displeasing his father. Bevil is a model son: loving, respectful, and particularly unwilling to bring his father any pain. Sir John, though a bit formal, is a caring father who has his son's interests at heart. In standard comic tradition, he has arranged a marriage between his son and Lucinda Sealand. It would be a sensible match, except that the two are not in love. Because Bevil does not wish to go against his father, he has not given any hint of his dismay. He acts exactly as his father wishes as the marriage day approaches. The audience learns that he is counting on being rebuffed, as he knows that Lucinda has her heart set elsewhere. This is a very risky charade, however, especially since Mr. Sealand has favored the match with Bevil.

Recently, though, Mr. Sealand has begun to have doubts about Bevil, and he is about to break off the engagement. Bevil was seen paying suspicious attentions to a mysterious young lady at a masked ball. Questioned by Sir John, Bevil insists that everything is honorable, that he is still worthy of his father's trust, and that the planned marriage should take place.

The mysterious beauty is Indiana, an unfortunate girl who has lost first her parents and then her guardians in a series of calamities. She had been threatened by pirates and sent to prison; then fortune sent Bevil into her life. Her rescuer has set her up in respectable London lodgings with her Aunt Isabella and is "keeping" the young lady without making any demands. Believing himself tied to Lucinda, Bevil has not spoken to Indiana of his love for her, but she hopes that she has read signs of love in his deeds and in his eyes. Isabella expects base motives and keeps her niece worried. Poor Indiana is desperately in love with her benefactor and is tortured by doubt.

There are two genuine suitors for Lucinda's hand. One is Bevil's friend Mr. Myrtle, whose sincere love is returned by Lucinda. The other is Cimberton, a formal, distant, wealthy oaf who is Mrs. Sealand's choice. These complications introduce a battle of wills between Lucinda's parents concerning who will control the girl's future. A conflict, thus, springs up between Bevil, whose behavior is confusing to those around him, and Myrtle, whose jealousy leads him to suspect Bevil of treachery.

The play is a framework for Bevil's moral dilemmas. Should he disobey his father? Can he do so without hurting him? When Myrtle challenges him to a duel, should he partake of this honorable custom—or should he prove to Myrtle that his jealousy is groundless by revealing an exchange of letters between Lucinda and himself against Lucinda's wishes? The audience is intended to feel the struggle within the sensitive and scrupulous young man, and, to some extent, Steele's strategy does succeed. Because Steele detested the dueling custom, he has Bevil argue his way out of the challenge, though Bevil finally must break the confidence that Lucinda has placed in him. Myrtle, once enlightened, is properly thankful, almost tearful, as he recognizes the difficulty of Bevil's stance and the purity of his motives. In true sentimental-comedy form, the two can now work together toward the end of matching Myrtle with Lucinda.

While Mr. Sealand is planning to seek out the mysterious Indiana to discover the truth about Bevil's behavior, Mrs. Sealand is busy concluding arrangements for Lucinda's marriage to Cimberton. She calls in lawyers to determine if Cimberton can bestow an estate on Lucinda without his uncle's consent. Seeing an opportunity for information and delay, Myrtle and Bevil's man Tom disguise themselves as the lawyers. Their expert exchange of opinion naturally ends in confusion. Sir Geoffry Cimberton is then expected. Now Myrtle disguises himself as the uncle, buying time for himself, slightly discouraging the match, then revealing himself and his bold, passionate nature to Lucinda. Mrs. Sealand, not sure what to do next, decides to take everyone and follow her husband as he inquires into the Indiana matter.

A tearful discovery scene ensues as Indiana first reveals the delicacy of her situation and then, by reviewing her history, leads Mr. Sealand to understand that he is face-to-face with his daughter (by a first wife) who was lost in infancy. Through this happy accident, a Bevil-Sealand match is made possible after all. Sir John, when he learns all, is properly proud of

his son's behavior and is happy to welcome Indiana in Lucinda's place. He has learned his lesson about arranged marriages. Cimberton, on hearing that Lucinda's fortune has now diminished by one half (that becomes her sister's), leaves the field, and Myrtle is quick to take advantage of the opening. The play concludes with assurances that "Whate'er the generous mind itself denies/The secret care of Providence supplies."

Though Steele has made virtue attractive in terms of the plot, the stock discovery scene cheapens the resolution somewhat. One cannot depend on providence being this fantastic. The question is whether Steele has made virtue attractive in terms of the virtuous characters themselves. The moral scruples of Bevil Senior and Junior create a strained situation in which they cannot deal frankly with each other, and Bevil's constant rationalizing of his behavior is not especially attractive. One is made to believe that, in the end, Bevil would not have gone through with the marriage to Lucinda. Thus, saving a miracle, a rupture between father and son would be inevitable. Would it not be better for Bevil to make an early declaration of his feelings for Indiana? Certainly Indiana would have been spared much anguish. Although it is clear that the hero never acts out of malice, his caution and sensibility lead him into behavior that is deceitful and hurtful.

Isabella's constant questioning of Bevil's motives creates the trial of Indiana's fortitude that is an emotional center of the play; more important, this persistent doubt reveals the pervasive cynicism of the play's social world. To others, if not to the audience, Bevil's behavior is unbelievable if understood as altruistic. Isabella is sure there is a trap somewhere: Bevil must expect something for paying Indiana's bills. Thus, Steele creates a sort of Platonic mistress while keeping vice off stage. Because Bevil, however, perceives Indiana's warm feelings for him, is it fair—is it manly—for him to withhold his own?

The Bevils, father and son, remain compromised and tedious figures, whatever Steele's intentions. Real wisdom lies in Sir John's servant, Humphrey, and to a lesser extent in the truly comic characters, Tom and Phillis. The romance between Tom and

Lucinda's maid is high-spirited and reasonably straightforward. Their bantering and jests at the upper classes are a source of genuine humor, as are the disguise scenes of Tom and Myrtle and the stuffy indifference of Cimberton. It is as if Steele has two plays going on at once: a solemn, didactic tearjerker and an old-fashioned farce. The sentimental part is not comic, and the comic part is not sentimental.

If he had continued to write for the theater, Steele might have improved on the formula—he had the tools and the inspiration. In itself, *The Conscious Lovers* only points in a direction it cannot reach.

OTHER MAJOR WORKS

POETRY: *The Procession*, 1695; *Prologue to the University of Oxford*, 1706; *Epilogue to the Town*, 1721; *The Occasional Verse of Richard Steele*, 1952 (Rae Blanchard, editor).

NONFICTION: *The Christian Hero*, 1701; *The Tatler*, 1709-1711 (with Joseph Addison; periodical essays); *The Spectator*, 1711-1712, 1714 (with Addison; periodical essays); *The Importance of Dunkirk Considered*, 1713; *The Englishman*, 1713-1714, 1715 (periodical essays); *The Guardian*, 1713 (with Addison; periodical essays); *The Lover*, 1714 (with Addison; periodical essays); *The Reader*, 1714 (with Joseph Addison); *The Plebiean*, 1718; *The Theatre*, 1720 (later published as *Richard Steele's "The Theatre,"* 1920, 1962; John Loftis, editor); *Tracts and Pamphlets by Richard Steele*, 1944 (Rae Blanchard, editor); *The Correspondence of Richard Steele*, 1968 (Blanchard, editor).

BIBLIOGRAPHY

Bloom, Edward A., and Lillian D. Bloom, eds. *Addison and Steele: The Critical Heritage*. Boston: Routledge & K. Paul, 1980. A collection of critical analyses of the works of Steele and Joseph Addison. Bibliography and index.

_____. *Educating the Audience: Addison, Steele, and Eighteenth Century Culture: Papers Presented at a Clark Library Seminar, 15 November 1980*. Los Angeles: William Andrews Clark Memorial Library, University of California, Los Angeles, 1984. A collection of essays presenting critical analysis of the works of Steele and Addison as well as essays on the theater of their time.

Dammers, Richard H. *Richard Steele*. Boston: Twayne, 1982. A basic biography of Steele that also provides critical analysis of his works. Bibliography and index.

Kenny, Shirley S. *The Plays of Richard Steele*. Oxford, England: Clarendon Press, 1971. Contains a substantial introduction to each Steele play, providing information on the sources, the manner of composition, the stage history, and the fame and influence of the play, with notes on the text.

Knight, Charles A. *Joseph Addison and Richard Steele: A Reference Guide, 1730-1991*. A Reference Guide to Literature. New York: G. K. Hall, 1993. Annotated bibliographies of works about and by Steele and Joseph Addison. Indexes.

Schneider, Ben Ross, Jr. *The Ethos of Restoration Comedy*. Urbana: University of Illinois Press, 1971. Schneider discusses Steele passim but provides a commentary related to major elements in late seventeenth century comedy: satire, the plaindealing versus the double-dealing characters, criticism of characters who show self-love, and others.

Philip K. Jason,
updated by Howard L. Ford

CARL STERNHEIM

Born: Leipzig, Germany; April 1, 1878
Died: Brussels, Belgium; November 3, 1942

PRINCIPAL DRAMA
Die Hose, pr., pb. 1911 (*The Bloomers*, 1927)

Die Kassette, pr. 1911, pb. 1912 (*The Strongbox*, 1963)

Bürger Schippel, pr., pb. 1913 (*Paul Schippel Esq.*, 1970)

Der Snob, pr., pb. 1914 (*The Snob*, 1927)

1913, pb. 1915, pr. 1919 (English translation, 1939)

Tabula rasa, pb. 1916, pr. 1919

Der entfesselte Zeitgenosse, pr. 1921

Der Nebbich, pr. 1922

Das Fossil, pb. 1922, pr. 1923 (*The Fossil*, 1970)

Aus dem bürgerlichen Heldenleben, pb. 1922

Scenes from the Heroic Life of the Middle Classes: Five Plays, pb. 1970

OTHER LITERARY FORMS

In addition to plays, Carl Sternheim wrote a novel, several novellas, and a number of essays. A typical example of his fiction is the novella *Busekow* (1913), the prose style of which marks a transition from naturalism to a condensed expressionistic narrative technique. Sternheim deliberately omits insignificant details, highlighting in a woodcutlike fashion only the essential facts and events. This style shows a strong tendency toward abstraction, overstatement, and satiric exaggeration. The novella *Meta* (1916) is written in similar fashion. In it, Sternheim traces the psychological development of a maid who loses her sweetheart in the war and spends the rest of her life trying to compensate in various ways for the loss. The essay *Gauguin und van Gogh* (1924) and the novella *Heidenstam* (1918) are of particular significance, because Sternheim uses them to discuss the central issue of expressionist aesthetics: the attempt to penetrate beneath the surface of the "appearance" of reality toward its true "essence." The expressionist artist attempts to tear off the "mask" of reality as it appears to sensory perception to reach the true being of things (*das Wesen*).

ACHIEVEMENTS

During the two decades between 1910 and 1930, Carl Sternheim was one of the most prominent playwrights in Germany. His plays were staged at most of the prestigious German theaters, with occasional per-formances in Rome, Paris, and London. His influence is evident in the work of modern German and Swiss dramatists who are critical of the middle class and of capitalist industrial society—in particular, Bertolt Brecht and Friedrich Dürrenmatt. After World War II, some of his plays were successfully revived in West Germany. Several of his works have been translated into English, French, and Italian.

BIOGRAPHY

Wilhelm Adolf Carl Sternheim was born on April 1, 1878, in Leipzig, Germany. He spent his early childhood in Hannover. In 1884, his family moved to Berlin, where Sternheim attended high school (he was graduated in 1897). In 1897, he attended Munich University, where he took courses in literary history, history, and the theory of knowledge. He continued his studies at the University of Leipzig, and the University of Göttingen, where he studied law and literary history. In 1900, he married Eugenie Hauth and moved first to Weimar, then to Berlin. In order to strengthen his physical health, he voluntarily served for a year in a cavalry regiment in 1902. In 1903, he moved to Munich, and four years later, he married for the second time. The wealth of his second wife, Thea Bauer, enabled him to live the life of the upper-middle class. He collected paintings (among them, ten van Goghs) and had a castlelike mansion built for himself and his family on the outskirts of Munich (and later in the suburbs of Brussels). With the success of his play *The Bloomers* in 1911, he began to establish himself as one of the most prominent German playwrights of his time. His plays written after 1918, however, did not achieve the success of his plays written between 1911 and the end of World War I.

Repeatedly, Sternheim ran into trouble with the censors. His plays *The Bloomers*, *The Snob*, and *1913* were allowed to be staged only after certain lines were stricken and other textual revisions were made. The reasons given by the authorities were either moral (Sternheim's plays were labeled obscene) or sociopolitical (the censors claimed that the plays would antagonize certain classes of German society and thereby jeopardize the peace.) Some of Sternheim's plays indeed caused scandals when first performed (notably *The Strongbox*). The middle-class audience felt attacked and offended, much to the delight of the author.

After 1914, Sternheim temporarily took up the cause of the workers in Germany. He published articles in the leftist expressionist journal *Die Aktion* and became a member of an anarchistic splinter party called "The General Unity Organization of the Workers," which called for a society free of any form of domination and for the destruction of all workers' unions and all political parties. This "political" period in Sternheim's life, though, was short-lived and was followed by a withdrawal into privacy. After living in various other European cities, Sternheim moved back to Brussels in 1930. In the same year, he was married for the third time, to the daughter of German playwright Frank Wedekind. Under National Socialism (1933-1945), Sternheim's plays were banned from German and Austrian stages. On November 3, 1942, he died in Brussels of pneumonia.

ANALYSIS

Carl Sternheim's major plays describe German society during the period from the late nineteenth century to the end of World War I. This was the so-called "Wilhelminian era" (after Emperor William II), a time of rapid industrialization in Germany. This period also saw the founding of the Social Democratic Party, which, under Chancellor Bismarck, was soon repressed and whose loyalty to the Reich was questioned because of its ties with international communism. The German government, authoritarian and dominated by the aristocracy, attempted to contain the growing pressure from the rising middle class and from the militant workers' movement by means of an increasingly aggressive foreign policy (which ultimately led to World War I).

During the 1890's and during the first years of the new century, social legislation (no work on Sundays, protection of children against abuses in child labor, accident and health insurance) was designed to appease the workers, whose political strength was partially paralyzed by the growing conflict between the revolutionary communists and the reformist Social Democrats. Germany was ruled by a coalition of the old aristocracy and the new bourgeois plutocracy (the former still being the dominant factor). Among this elite there developed a strong sense of nationalistic expansionism fostered by a number of well-funded and organized interest groups and sometimes coupled with outbreaks of anti-Semitism. Thus, a precarious balance between inner social unrest and an aggressive expansionist foreign policy constituted the political and social climate in which Sternheim's plays were conceived.

Although Sternheim did not consider himself an expressionist (in fact, he uses the terms "expressionism" and "expressionist" in some of his plays to characterize an overly agitated, conspicuous, and spectacular mode of behavior on the part of particular characters), he shares some common ground with expressionism in terms of both style and content. Most of Sternheim's characters are types representing their respective social classes. Because they are not psychologically differentiated individuals, the German spoken by them is an extremely artificial and abstract idiom. Although Sternheim's aristocrats speak in somewhat more stilted fashion and use a different vocabulary from that of the other characters, language does not function as an instrument of social or psychological differentiation in his plays. The elimination of the definite article, the frequent use of past participles, the end position of the subject, and other stylistic devices run counter to "normal" German usage. Their function is not to help describe life in a realistic true-to-life fashion. Sternheim, like his expressionist contemporaries, does not attempt to copy or reproduce reality. Rather, he proceeds from essential truths underlying social interaction, which are then "expressed" in the way his characters speak and act, regardless of any mimetic norms.

Sternheim's comedies often present a protagonist who is powerful, successful, and victorious from the outset and who, withstanding all challenges, inevitably triumphs in the happy ending typical of traditional comedy. Whereas traditional comedies often expose the discrepancy between a character's actions and the norms, values, and ideals that society represents, Sternheim's comedies seem to celebrate the triumph of the material norms of the German middle and upper classes from the first to the last scene. The glory of bourgeois and aristocratic existence, however, always contains an element of caricature. Sternheim's satiric mode of presentation (although it is never totally critical or skeptical in terms of social change and leaves room for positive evaluation) confronts the flaws of social reality (in all classes) with an ideal that is never quite explicit in his texts. The author does not openly call for a "new man" or a utopian social order, as many of the expressionists did at that time. The implicit ideal must be deduced by the reader or audience from the negativity of the world presented in Sternheim's plays. Glimpses of this ideal can be seen in the theoretical statements made by Sternheim's "revolutionary" characters, such as *The Bloomers'* Mandelstam, *1913*'s Krey, and *The Fossil*'s von Bohna. Yet these characters remain helpless theorists. Their ideas have no impact on social reality, and some of them—such as Krey and von Bohna—even adapt to the status quo by betraying their cause.

THE BLOOMERS

Sternheim's biting criticism of the German bourgeois pervades his first successful play, *The Bloomers*. Its plot is simple: Luise, the wife of a civil servant, Theobald Maske, loses her bloomers during a Sunday afternoon walk on a crowded street. The embarrassing incident is noticed by a few bystanders. Maske acts as though a major disaster has happened, which might threaten his position. The only consequence of the event, though, is the appearance of two men at Maske's home. They both witnessed the incident and have come to rent a room. Both Scarron, whose social status remains mysterious (he appears to be wealthy; he is a writer, an educated intellectual, a follower of Friedrich Nietzsche, and a passionate Don Juan all in one) and Mandelstam, a sickly barber's apprentice, have come to Maske's place because they have been attracted by Maske's beautiful but naïve wife. Their only function in the play, though, is to serve as contrasting characters vis-à-vis the boisterous and smug protagonist Maske. After some amorous overtures to Luise, which meet with little resistance on her part, Scarron abandons her and his room for a whore, whereas the unlucky lover Mandelstam stays on.

This is the framework within which Theobald Maske makes his buoyant appearance. Sternheim's

satiric portrait of the German bourgeois around the turn of the century reveals the following features: He is a loyal subject of his superiors, especially the king; hating daydreaming and disorder, his mind is focused entirely and exclusively on the daily practical matters at hand; and nothing matters more to him than his secure position. He would never dream of striving toward a higher office. If everything stays the same until the day of his retirement, he will be totally satisfied. Maske exhibits anti-Semitic leanings (although he does not admit it). He talks like a staunch nationalist, but he has no interest in politics. To him, happiness is a good meal, good health, and physical strength. He regards women as inferior to men, beats his wife, and indulges in an occasional adulterous adventure. Although he is not a religious man, he feels it is "all right" to go to church because it is the proper thing to do for people of his kind. He likes to think of himself as one of the "little people" and makes every effort to live as inconspicuously as possible. By the same token, he turns out to be a greedy profiteer when it comes to squeezing money out of Scarron and Mandelstam. Whereas he knows nothing about literature, music, or art, he does have a vague sense of "culture" as something that is supposed to give his drab existence some luster and status. Yet his attitude toward cultural activities is truly philistine.

THE SNOB

The Bloomers was the first play of a tetralogy published in both *Aus dem bürgerlichen Heldenleben* and *Scenes from the Heroic Life of the Middle Classes*. The second play of this tetralogy, *The Snob*, focuses on the tendency among members of the German middle and upper-middle classes to emulate the lifestyle of the aristocracy. In the late nineteenth and early twentieth centuries, the German aristocracy witnessed the decline of its wealth while it was still able to hold on to political power. A new financial elite had arisen. Wealthy capitalists from the upper-middle class had acquired high social status, yet they continued to look up to the members of the aristocracy as their role models for social behavior.

Christian Maske, Theobald Maske's son, is a case in point. Through hard work and shrewd business deals, he has acquired a fortune and is about to be appointed president of a mining company. Count Palen is a member of the board of directors of that company. Christian wishes to marry the count's daughter Marianne. To him, that marriage means the ultimate authentication of the fact that he has arrived at the top of his society. Count Palen views this marriage with mixed feelings. On one hand, he welcomes the influx of the money of the nouveau riche into his impoverished family. On the other hand, Christian is a parvenu, an upstart who does not really "belong" in aristocratic circles.

The character of Christian is—as is so often the case with Sternheim's protagonists—portrayed satirically, but not without a certain degree of sympathy and even admiration on the part of the author. The adjective "heroic" in the title of the English translation that includes the entire tetralogy must be understood exactly in this twofold (and only seemingly self-contradictory) sense: The Maskes are not truly heroes, yet their vitality, energy, and success are admirable. The satire exposes Christian's lack of compassion, love, and gratitude. Once he has amassed his wealth, he literally pays back those who helped him achieve his goal, especially his parents, whom he then shoves off to Zurich because he does not want to be reminded of his petty bourgeois background, which might prove to be an embarrassment to him in an aristocratic environment. His cold and calculating behavior as well as his efforts to emulate aristocratic style (exemplified by such details as how to tie a necktie properly, how to phrase a letter, or how to use art as a status symbol) are attempts at playing a prescribed role. Behind Christian's aristocratic persona (in the Jungian sense) there remains, however, the original individual who is still capable of showing grief when his father brings him the news of his mother's death. Yet he tries to impress Marianne by boasting of his ancestors, by emphasizing that his financial genius is something that is "in his blood," and finally by claiming that he is really the illegitimate son of a French viscount because the one thing that money cannot buy is a genuine aristocratic lineage (as documented in the famous register of the aristocracy, the *Gotha Almanac*).

Christian Maske is indeed a "snob," both in the accepted sense of the word and in its original sense—*sine nobilitate*—yet the sheer energy and self-discipline that enable him to advance in society not only are duly admired and envied by the aristocracy but also positively impress the reader or spectator. Christian is an ambivalent character. His success is both baffling and questionable, especially because it is based on the exploitation of millions of workers (as Christian himself cynically admits).

1913

The third play in the tetralogy, *1913*, shows Christian Maske at the end of a successful life. Having risen to the ranks of the aristocracy, he is now Baron Christian Maske von Buchow, the wealthy owner of many factories, a still-powerful and energetic patriarch. His cold and ambitious oldest daughter, Sophie, tries to wrest the power from her father's hands by striking on her own a deal with the government of the Netherlands involving the sale of weapons. The fact that the members of the Maske family are Lutherans (conveniently publicized by Sophie) facilitates the negotiations with the Dutch. When Maske hears about the deal, he has all the major newspapers print the news that the Maskes have converted to Catholicism. This is his way of striking back at his daughter. Maske is able to reestablish his authority but at a deadly cost. The excitement is too much for him, and he dies of a heart attack.

More significant than the plot (the triumph and fall of the patriarch) are Maske's views about the state of his society. He is able to anticipate the dangers of mass production, and he foresees the stifling impact of a materialistic consumer mentality. Furthermore, he forecasts World War I and fully recognizes the revolutionary potential of the masses once they are stirred up by Socialist ideas. He even goes so far as to say that he would welcome social change along Socialist lines, if only a great leader of the underprivileged masses would appear. Maske's secretary, Wilhelm Krey, is an articulate theorist who combines radical socialism with a strong sense of nationalism. As so often in Sternheim's plays, the herald of social change is not a leader but merely an apolitical intellectual, an ideologist. Not only does he fail to make the slightest practical impact on social life, but also he compromises his position at the end by attaching himself to the social class he is supposed to crush: the aristocracy. His liaison with Ottilie (Maske's daughter) and the symbolic act of trying on (or rather, masquerading in) certain garments worn only by aristocrats attest the discrepancy between theory and practice that characterizes this Socialist who turns out to be a would-be aristocrat.

As in *The Snob*, Christian Maske is portrayed in *1913* as a complex character. On one hand, he represents bourgeois capitalism and ruthless materialism at their zenith. The accumulation of wealth appears to be the only goal in his otherwise aimless and directionless life. On the other hand, he also represents Sternheim's ideal of the strong-willed individual who realizes his potential regardless of any social or financial obstacles. This individualism is based on a combination of Darwinism and a Nietzschean philosophy of the will to power, though Sternheim's attitude toward both thinkers was ambivalent. He deplored in Darwinism the lack of a spiritual goal and feared that Nietzsche's thought would unleash the animal instincts in humankind.

Although Krey, the socialist thinker, fails, there is another character in the play, Stadler, who vows that he will carry forward the torch of socialism. This shows that Sternheim, in spite of his admiration for the successful industrialist Maske, is fully aware of the "social question" and sees the necessity of social change.

THE FOSSIL

The last play of the tetralogy, *The Fossil*, has two protagonists: a retired general of the cavalry, Traugott von Beeskow, and an aristocrat, Ago von Bohna. Von Beeskow, who is completely out of touch with his time, still doggedly clings to the ideals and to the lifestyle of his class. Before World War I, his daughter Ursula was engaged to Ago von Bohna, who subsequently spent many years in Moscow. The dreadful experience of the war and his stay in Russia have converted von Bohna to communism. Like most of Sternheim's communist characters, he is a pure theoretician who shows little interest in practical politics. Von Bohna has summed up his ideas and insights in a

manuscript. He returns to Prussia in order to see Ursula and to confront her father. When he meets Ursula again, he realizes that he still loves her. Ursula, reared in the aristocratic tradition, finds herself unable to accept von Bohna's views. She even goes one step further and promises her father (who detests the renegade) to get hold of von Bohna's manuscript and destroy it. The lover in von Bohna is stronger than the communist theoretician. He sacrifices his manuscript (which Ursula throws into the fire) in return for Ursula's love. When the old von Beeskow surprises the two lovers, he kills them both in a fit of rage before surrendering to the police.

Two different worlds clash here, and both sides discredit themselves. Von Beeskow is indeed a "fossil," a survivor from an extinct social class. His position becomes strikingly and graphically clear when—in one scene of the play—he mounts his rocking horse and acts out (in full uniform) a fantasy about commanding a cavalry attack. Two types of aristocrats challenge each other in this play: the "fossil" who knows no other way than to adhere stubbornly to his ancient values and ideals and the radical social reformer von Bohna. Like Krey in *1913*, von Bohna does not know how to translate theory into action. In his case, personal matters have priority over his "mission." He preaches that the individual must subordinate himself to the needs of the collective. His own actions, however, belie his social theories. Thus, the play shows the last gasp of an aristocracy that has become its own caricature while necessary social reforms have not yet progressed beyond the stage of theory and have not yet found—as far as Germany is concerned—a qualified champion.

THE STRONGBOX

In 1912, Sternheim published the play *The Strongbox*, which focuses on the idolization of material wealth on the part of the typical bourgeois. Krull, a teacher, finds himself torn between two women: Fanny, his second wife, and Elsbeth Treu, a middle-aged woman who possesses stocks and bonds of considerable worth. She keeps those papers in a heavy iron coffer. Krull, his wife, and his daughter Lydia (from a previous marriage) are the only relatives to whom Elsbeth could bequeath the money. Elsbeth hates Fanny and is jealous of her, while Krull tries very hard to please both women. The coffer becomes more and more the focal point of his entire existence. He is allowed to draw up a list of its contents and to drag it from place to place. Elsbeth lets him have the strongbox while hesitating to write the will that will make him its rightful owner. Krull even takes the coffer to bed, where it literally replaces his wife. He is portrayed as an egotist whose sole purpose in life has become the quest for pleasure and enjoyment. The prospect of inheriting Elsbeth's money keeps alive his hope of escape from the drudgery of a poorly paid teacher's life. Egotism, nationalism, and mammonism are the striking features of this typical specimen of the German middle class. He is intelligent enough to realize that the international nature of high finance (not all the stocks one may own represent German assets) conflicts with his nationalistic instincts. What is good for one's wallet might not be so good for one's nation. Krull also understands quite well (and accepts) the fact that those stocks that he hopes to inherit are the fruit of the exploitation of millions of workers.

Elsbeth, whose hopes and expectations with regard to Krull remain unfulfilled, finally bequeaths all her wealth to the Catholic Church. The play does not proceed to the point where Krull finds out about Elsbeth's move. The shattering of his grand illusion and the dashing of his hopes can only be imagined by the audience or the reader.

PAUL SCHIPPEL ESQ.

Although Sternheim's comedy *Paul Schippel Esq.* confronts a member of the German proletariat with a number of representatives of the middle class, this confrontation does not lead to conflict but to the rise of the proletarian Schippel to the status of the bourgeois. Schippel, an illegitimate child, is a poor musician who plays in beer halls. His only asset is his beautiful voice, which earns for him a place in a quartet that has recently lost its tenor. The three other members of the quartet are all men of the middle class: Hicketier, a goldsmith; Krey, a civil servant; and Wolke, the owner of a printing shop. The proletarian is reluctantly accepted simply because he is needed. Hicketier, Krey, and Wolke hope to win first prize at a competition, and they cannot compete without a good tenor. At first, Schippel is overly conscious of his low social position. At the same time, he hates the middle class for their wealth and their secure and carefree life. His only desire is to move up in society. Yet the other members of the quartet keep their distance and, whenever the occasion arises, impress on Schippel the fact that he does not "belong" in their circle (just as Count Palen in *The Snob* felt that Christian Maske did not "belong" in aristocratic circles). Schippel, unsure of himself, vacillates between a humble expression of his déclassé social status and bold attempts to usurp the role of the bourgeois now that "they" cannot do without him. He has set his eyes on Thekla, Hicketier's beautiful sister. When he asks Hicketier for her hand, he learns that someone else, namely the prince himself, has just spent the night with Thekla. Now that the girl has lost her "finest luster," as her brother tactfully puts it, Hicketier is willing to give her to Schippel. Schippel, however, in a moment of glory, refuses the girl under the changed circumstances. His moral principles and his honor, so he claims, do not allow him to marry a girl who is no longer a virgin. Krey, who does not know about Thekla's escapade with the prince and wants to marry her, is told about the incident by Schippel. Because Schippel gloats over Krey's dilemma and because Krey cannot but take Schippel's condescending attitude as an insult, he is obliged to challenge Schippel to a duel. The duel, originally a social ritual of the aristocracy, in particular of the high-ranking aristocratic officers of the military, had become an integral part of the bourgeois emulation of aristocratic behavior.

Ironically, both Schippel and Krey are deadly afraid of the duel. Schippel makes an unsuccessful attempt to flee (at this point, he is ready to sacrifice his social ambitions), while Krey almost faints on his arrival at the spot where the duel is supposed to take place. The duel begins, and Schippel happens to inflict a slight injury to Krey's arm. This "victory" prompts Wolke and Hicketier to elevate Schippel to the social rank of the middle class, as though he had thereby passed the ultimate test. Therefore, it is not Schippel's artistic talents that determine his fate but rather the totally accidental outcome of a social ritual in which none of the combatants really believes.

Paul Schippel Esq. illustrates once more Sternheim's conviction that the German proletariat of the early twentieth century did not strive for social revolution, but either had dreams of moving "up" (as in Schippel's case) or simply accepted the status quo. Everybody knows his "place" in this society. There are boundaries that one should not transgress. The only transgression allowed in certain situations is a downward one. The prince has the privilege to ruin the reputation of a middle-class girl (whether or not she consents). The girl then can—against her will—be shoved "down" to the proletariat (as Hicketier intends to do with his sister). Both "transgressions" involve an appalling lack of moral decency in a society that gives only the appearance of moral propriety. Oddly enough, the proletarian (Schippel) finds himself in the position to violate the bourgeois code of honor and thereby to place himself on the same level as the members of the bourgeoisie (the duel). Once he is allowed to play the "game" of the duel, his "victory" legitimizes his new position as a respected bourgeois. The play satirically exposes the artificiality of the social structure and the arrogance and the banality of the lifestyle of the German middle class, in particular its cultural pretentiousness and its hollow claims to dignity, importance, and moral integrity. It both describes and ridicules, but it lacks any intention to offer a blueprint for social change.

OTHER MAJOR WORKS

LONG FICTION: *Busekow*, 1913; *Napoleon*, 1915; *Meta*, 1916; *Mädchen*, 1917; *Heidenstam*, 1918; *Europa*, 1919-1920 (2 volumes); *Mädchen: Novellen*, 1926; *Napoleon: Novellen*, 1927; *Busekow: Novellen*, 1928.

NONFICTION: *Berlin: Oder, Juste Milieu*, 1920; *Tasso: Oder, Kunst des Juste Milieu*, 1921; *Gauguin und van Gogh*, 1924; *Lutetia, Berichte über europäische Politik, Kunst und Volksleben*, 1926; *Kleiner Katechismus für das Jahr 1930/31*, 1930; *Vorkriegseuropa im Gleichnis meines Lebens*, 1936.

BIBLIOGRAPHY

Chick, Edson M. *Dances of Death: Wedekind, Brecht, Dürrenmatt, and the Satiric Tradition*. Columbia, S.C.: Camden House, 1984. Chick examines the use of satire in the works of Sternheim, Frank Wedekind, Bertolt Brecht, and Friedrich Dürrenmatt. Bibliography and index.

Dedner, Burghard. *Carl Sternheim*. Boston: Twayne, 1982. A basic biography of Sternheim and critical analyses of his works. Bibliography and index.

Sturges, Dugald S. *The German Molière Revival and the Comedies of Hugo von Hofmannsthal and Carl Sternheim*. New York: Peter Lang, 1993. Sturges examines the influence of Molière on the plays of Sternheim and von Hofmannsthal. Bibliography and index.

William, Rhys W. *Carl Sternheim: A Critical Study*. Bern, Switzerland: Peter Lang, 1982. William provides an analysis of Sternheim's life and his works. Bibliography.

Christoph Eykman

TOM STOPPARD
Tomas Straussler

Born: Zlin, Czechoslovakia; July 3, 1937

PRINCIPAL DRAMA

A Walk on the Water, pr. 1963 (televised; revised and televised as *The Preservation of George Riley*, 1964; revised and staged as *Enter a Free Man*, pr., pb. 1968)

The Gamblers, pr. 1965

Rosencrantz and Guildenstern Are Dead, pr. 1966, pb. 1967

Tango, pr. 1966, pb. 1968 (adapted from the play by Sławomir Mrożek)

Albert's Bridge, pr. 1967 (radio play), pr. 1969 (staged), pb. 1969

The Real Inspector Hound, pr., pb. 1968 (one act)

After Magritte, pr. 1970, pb. 1971 (one act)

Dogg's Our Pet, pr. 1971, pb. 1976 (one act)

Jumpers, pr., pb. 1972

Travesties, pr. 1974, pb. 1975

Dirty Linen and New-Found-Land, pr., pb. 1976

The Fifteen-Minute Hamlet, pr. 1976, pb. 1978

Every Good Boy Deserves Favour, pr. 1977, pb. 1978 (music by André Previn)

Night and Day, pr., pb. 1978

Dogg's Hamlet, Cahoot's Macbeth, pr. 1979, pb. 1980

Undiscovered Country, pr. 1979, pb. 1980 (adapted from Arthur Schnitzler's play *Das weite Land*)

On the Razzle, pr., pb. 1981 (adaptation of Johann Nestroy's play *Einen Jux will er sich machen*)

The Real Thing, pr., pb. 1982

The Dog It Was That Died, and Other Plays, pb. 1983

The Love for Three Oranges, pr. 1983 (adaptation of Sergei Prokofiev's opera)

Rough Crossing, pr. 1984, pb. 1985 (adaptation of Ferenc Molnár's play *Play at the Castle*)

Dalliance, pr., pb. 1986 (adapted from Arthur Schnitzler's play *Liebelei*)

Hapgood, pr., pb. 1988

The Boundary, pb. 1991 (with Clive Exton)

Arcadia, pr., pb. 1993

The Real Inspector Hound and Other Entertainments, pb. 1993

Indian Ink, pr., pb. 1995

The Invention of Love, pr., pb. 1997

The Seagull, pr., pb. 1997 (adaptation of Anton Chekhov's play)

Plays: Four, pb. 1999

Plays: Five, pb. 1999

OTHER LITERARY FORMS

In addition to composing plays and occasionally adapting the dramas of others, Tom Stoppard has written several short stories, radio plays, teleplays, screenplays, and the novel *Lord Malquist and Mr. Moon* (1966). He prides himself on his versatility, eschewing the notion of the dedicated author plowing a lonely furrow and sacrificing almost all other concerns on the altar of high art. Instead, as he told an interviewer in 1976:

> I've got a weakness . . . for rather shallow people who knock off a telly play and write a rather good novel and . . . interview Castro and write a good poem and a bad poem and . . . every five years do a really good piece of work as well. That sort of eclectic, trivial person who's very gifted.

Stoppard's novel *Lord Malquist and Mr. Moon* is "rather good." It is an exuberant farce that uses a collage of literary styles and allusions ranging from those of Joseph Conrad to Oscar Wilde, and from James Joyce to T. S. Eliot. Lord Malquist is a modern-day earl who seeks to sustain the dandyish refinements of his eighteenth century ancestors. His hired diarist, Mr. Moon, is a pathetically ineffectual man obsessively nursing a homemade bomb. Where the imperious and selfish Malquist anticipates such later dramatic characters as Sir Archibald Jumper of *Jumpers*, the confused, Prufrockian Moon models for the rebuffs experienced by the same text's George Moore. Malquist sums up what seems to be the novel's thesis when he declares, "since we cannot hope for order, let us withdraw with style from the chaos."

ACHIEVEMENTS

Tom Stoppard's dramaturgy has a uniquely wide appeal in the contemporary theater because he often manages to combine comedy with social concern, farce with moral philosophy, and sometimes absurdism with naturalism. He and Harold Pinter, beginning in the 1960's, came to be considered the English-speaking world's leading playwrights. Both owe a large debt to Samuel Beckett and exhibit a willingness to experiment with theatrical forms. Pinter's sparse language, pauses, and silences, however, con-

Tom Stoppard in 1996. (AP/Wide World Photos)

Eliot, and many more to combine them with "whodunit" thrillers, journalistic techniques, music-hall comedies, and popular love songs.

The leading debate among Stoppard's critics is whether his works are too frivolous and waggish to be taken seriously and whether, despite his eye for striking situations and ear for witty talk, he is no more than an ingenious but juvenile sprinter, too short-winded to complete the potential of his promising situations. His supporters insist that Stoppard is able to fuse his fertile comic sense with intellectual substance. They find his vision of life mature and profound as he dramatizes such concerns as free will versus fate (*Rosencrantz and Guildenstern Are Dead*), moral philosophy (*Jumpers*), art versus politics (*Travesties*), totalitarianism (*Every Good Boy Deserves Favour*), the press's freedoms and responsibilities (*Night and Day*), and married love (*The Real Thing*). They assert that Stoppard's career has shown an increasing commitment to ethical humanism and freedom of conscience while his dramatic craft has forged a rare compact between high comedy and the drama of ideas.

BIOGRAPHY

Tomas Straussler was born on July 3, 1937, in the town of Zlin, Czechoslovakia, since renamed Gottwaldov. He was the youngest of two sons of a physician, Eugene Straussler, and his wife, Martha. Stoppard's parents were Jewish, although Stoppard did not know this until much later in life. Their religious background caused the family to move to Singapore in early 1939, on the eve of the German invasion of their homeland. In 1942, all but the father moved again, to India, just before the Japanese invasion, in which Dr. Straussler was killed. In 1946, Martha Straussler married Kenneth Stoppard, a major in the British army who was stationed in India. Both children took their stepfather's name when the family moved to England later that year. Demobilized, Kenneth Stoppard prospered as a machine-tool salesperson.

Despite this globe-trotting background—in one interview he called himself "a bounced Czech"—Stoppard has spoken and written in English since the

trast sharply with Stoppard's free-flowing fountains of verbal play and display. Moreover, Pinter's carefully guarded characters and often baffling, static plots could not differ more from Stoppard's accessible people and vividly detailed, fast-paced action sequences. His plays have won Tony and Olivier awards. The film of *Rosencrantz and Guildenstern Are Dead* won the Golden Lion at the Venice film festival in 1990. In 1999 *Shakespeare in Love*, for which he wrote the screenplay, won seven Academy awards and three Golden Globes. In 1997 Stoppard became the first British playwright to be knighted since Terence Rattigan.

Stoppard's work is postmodernist in its self-conscious artfulness and intricate game playing. He loves to confound his audience with abrupt shifts of time and convention, unreliable narrations, and surprising twists of plot. His eclectic borrowings fuse high and low culture, invading the texts of William Shakespeare, George Bernard Shaw, Wilde, Joyce, age of five. His first school in Darjeeling, India, was an English-language, American-run institution. He attended preparatory schools in Nottingham and Yorkshire, leaving at the age of seventeen after having completed his "A" levels. In 1954, he began working as a local journalist in Bristol, rejoicing in the life of a newspaper reporter for the next six years. He did not consider becoming a playwright until the late 1950's, when a new breed of English dramatists, led by John Osborne and Arnold Wesker, asserted themselves on the London stage. Simultaneously, a new breed of actors emerged, prominent among them Peter O'Toole, whose blazing performances for the Bristol Old Vic repertory company definitively turned Stoppard to the theater.

In July, 1960, Stoppard wrote *The Gamblers*—a one-act clumsily derived from Beckett's *En attendant Godot* (pb. 1952, pr. 1953; *Waiting for Godot*, 1954)—which was unsuccessfully staged in Bristol in 1965. Later in 1960, he composed his first full-length play, *A Walk on the Water*. Considerably rewritten and retitled *Enter a Free Man*, it was staged in London in 1968 after *Rosencrantz and Guildenstern Are Dead* had established Stoppard as a major playwright. In 1962, Stoppard moved to a London suburb and became the drama critic of a new magazine, *Scene*, which folded after eight months. Fortunately, he had begun by then a steady career as a writer of radio plays for the British Broadcasting Corporation (BBC).

With the aid of a Ford Foundation grant, he wrote, in 1964, a one-act version of *Rosencrantz and Guildenstern Are Dead*, which he rewrote and expanded for the Royal Shakespeare Company in 1965, then for the Oxford Theatre Group in 1966, which performed it at that year's Edinburgh Festival. An enthusiastic review in *The Observer* caused Laurence Olivier to buy the play for his National Theatre, which staged it in 1967. Critical acclaim showered on this production, which continued in the National Theatre's repertoire for an unprecedented three and a half years.

In 1965, Stoppard married Jose Ingle; they became the parents of two sons, Oliver and Barnaby. They were divorced in 1972, and the same year,

Stoppard married Dr. Miriam Moore-Robinson, a physician and television personality, with whom he had two sons, William and Edmond.

After the worldwide success of *Rosencrantz and Guildenstern Are Dead*, Stoppard not only has produced a number of one-act and full-length dramas but also has adapted the plays of several European writers. He has written film scripts as well as radio and television plays. He has directed several stage plays, usually but not always his own, and has supervised the filming of *Rosencrantz and Guildenstern Are Dead*. In 1983, he adapted Sergei Prokofiev's *The Love for Three Oranges* for the Glyndebourne Opera.

Although he had known that one or two of his grandparents were Jewish, Stoppard learned in 1994 that, in fact, all of his grandparents were Jewish and all were killed by the Nazis. His adopted father's anti-Semitism became public when he asked Stoppard in 1996 to stop using the name Stoppard because the playwright had been working for the cause of Russian Jews. In 1999 he wrote an article entitled "On Turning Out to Be Jewish" in which he discusses how these discoveries fundamentally altered his sense of self.

ANALYSIS

Tom Stoppard's dramaturgy reveals a cyclical pattern of activity. He tends to explore certain subjects or techniques in several minor works, then creates a major play that integrates the fruits of his earlier trial runs. Thus *Rosencrantz and Guildenstern Are Dead* explores the dialectic of individual freedom opposed to entrapment, which such earlier plays as *A Walk on the Water* had rehearsed.

ROSENCRANTZ AND GUILDENSTERN ARE DEAD

In *Rosencrantz and Guildenstern Are Dead*, Stoppard assumes the audience's close knowledge of Shakespeare's *Hamlet, Prince of Denmark* (pr. c. 1600-1601, pb. 1603). In the Elizabethan tragedy, Rosencrantz and Guildenstern are two former schoolmates of Hamlet who have been summoned to Elsinore by King Claudius to probe the puzzling behavior of the prince. Hamlet soon intuits that they have become Claudius's spies. When Claudius has them accompany Hamlet on the ship to England,

Hamlet discovers the King's letter ordering his execution. He coolly substitutes his escorts' names for his in the letter and shrugs off their consequent deaths as resulting from their dangerous trade of espionage.

From a total of nine scenes in *Hamlet, Prince of Denmark* involving Rosencrantz and Guildenstern, Stoppard incorporates six, omits two, and distributes the other in scenes wholly devised by him. Stoppard's Ros and Guil know that they have been summoned to Elsinore but can remember nothing more of their past. They are two bewildered young men playing pointless games (such as coin flipping) in a theatrical void, while the real action unfolds off stage. They are adrift in a predetermined plot, bumbling Shakespeare's lines on the occasions when the palace intrigue sweeps their way. Just as Beckett's Vladimir and Estragon engage in mock-philosophizing disputations and vain recollections as they await Godot, so Ros and Guil pursue frequent speculations about their past, their identity, and the baffling world around them.

Stoppard has here constructed an absurdist drama that owes its largest debts to Franz Kafka and Beckett. His Ros and Guil are unaccountably summoned to a mysterious castle where, between long periods of waiting, they receive cryptic instructions that eventually lead to their deaths. They remain uncertain whether they are the victims of chance or fate, mystified by events that are within the boundaries of their awareness but outside the circumference of their understanding.

Like Beckett's Vladimir, Ros is the one who worries and protects; like Beckett's Estragon, Guil is the one who feels and follows. Beckett's world is, however, considerably bleaker than Stoppard's. He offers no comforting irony behind his characters' somber metaphysical flights, while Stoppard's buffoonery is humane. He presents his coprotagonists as likable though confused and frightened strangers in a world somebody else seems to have organized.

Stoppard's literary borrowings include a generous slice of Eliot's poetry, as Ros and Guil imitate Prufock in their roles as attendants and easy tools, playing insignificant parts in a ferociously patterned plot featuring mightier powers. This sympathy for the ineffectual underdog is a constant in Stoppard's dramatic world, as he demonstrates, over and over, his compassionate concern for decent people shouldered aside and manipulated by more brutal peers. Is *Rosencrantz and Guildenstern Are Dead* an immensely entertaining but ultimately shallow exercise, or is it a brilliant transposition of Shakespeare's universe to Beckett's absurdist world? Most critics and large audiences have cast their votes in favor of this erudite, witty, crackling clever drama.

JUMPERS

A second group of Stoppard's plays dramatizes the conflict between a protagonist's wish to know and the many difficulties that frustrate this desire, such as the limitations of human perceptions, the frequent deceptiveness of one's senses, and the complexity of ethical choices in a world in which guidance is either uncertain or unavailable. Plays belonging to this category include such one-acts as *After Magritte* and the radio play *Artist Descending a Staircase* (1972), as well as Stoppard's two most ambitious, full-length dramas, *Jumpers* and *Travesties*.

Jumpers is a kaleidoscopic work, part bedroom farce, part murder mystery, part political satire, part metaphysical inquiry, and part cosmic tragedy, creating new configurations of ideas and themes from each angle of vision. Stoppard's hero is George Moore, a work-obsessed, seedy, middle-aged professor of moral philosophy, whose name is identical with that of the great English thinker who wrote *Principia Ethica* (1903). George's career has ground to a halt because his adherence to absolute values—beauty, goodness, God—makes him odd man out in a university dominated by logical positivists who hold that value judgments cannot be empirically verified and are therefore relative and meaningless.

George's main adversary is Sir Archibald Jumper, vice chancellor of the university, who is authoritative in a staggering number of roles: He holds degrees in medicine, philosophy, literature, and law, and diplomas in psychiatry and gymnastics. He is organizer of the Jumpers—a combination of philosophical gymnasts and gymnastic philosophers—all members of the Radical Liberal Party that Archie also heads. The Radical Liberals embody Stoppard's satiric vision of socialism in action. Having just won an election—which they may have rigged—they have taken over the broadcasting services, arrested all newspaper owners, and appointed a veterinary surgeon Archbishop of Canterbury.

The female principal in the George-Archie struggle is represented by George's beautiful but aptly named wife, Dotty. She is a neurotic musical-comedy star, many years younger than her husband, who retired from the stage after having suffered a nervous breakdown because she believed that the landing of a human being on the Moon had eliminated that planet as a source of romance and thousands of songs. In an ironic reversal of the selflessly heroic British Antarctic Expedition of 1912, Dotty sees, on her bedroom television set, a fight for survival between the damaged space capsule's commander, Captain Scott, and his subordinate officer, Oates. To reduce the weight load, Scott kicks Oates off the capsule's ladder, thereby condemning him to death. Pragmatism has sacrificed moral values—an indictment of logical positivism's slippery ethics. George and Archie are not only philosophic but also erotic rivals. While Dotty has barred her husband from her body—and he makes little effort to overcome her resistance—she is available at all hours to Archie, who visits her in the mornings in her bedroom and is her doctor and psychiatrist and presumably her lover, leaving her room "looking more than a little complacent."

In the first scene, as the Jumpers tumble in the Moores' apartment to celebrate the Rad-Lib victory, a bullet suddenly kills one of them. He turns out to be Duncan McFee, a logical positivist who was scheduled to debate with George at a symposium the next day. Dotty is left whimpering with the corpse, while George, concentrating on composing his lecture, knows nothing of the killing, so that he and his wife talk at cross-purposes while the body hangs behind her bedroom door, always unseen by him. Stoppard parodies the whodunit formula by having Inspector Bones bumble the murder investigation. The resourceful Archie persuades Bones to drop the case by having Dotty trap him in an apparently compromising position. At the close of act 2, McFee is revealed as probably the victim of George's vengeful secre-

tary, who had been McFee's mistress and had learned that he was married and planned to enter a monastery.

Holding together the frequently delirious action is the shabby but lovable person of George, shuffling distractedly between his study and Dotty's bedroom, preparing his case against Archie's cynical materialism, which insists that observability has to be a predicate of all genuine knowledge. He does his best—and clearly advocates Stoppard's position—to defend a God in whom he cannot wholly bring himself to believe, so as to support his adherence to moral and aesthetic standards, which he considers a necessary basis for civilization.

The condescending Archie dismisses George as no more than the local eccentric: "[He] is our tame believer, pointed out to visitors in much the same spirit as we point out the magnificent stained glass in what is now the gymnasium." George is less mocked by Stoppard as bumbler and clown than he is admired as a fragmented culture's last humanist, clinging with mad gallantry to lasting values.

In *Jumpers*, Stoppard has written his best play. It is not only a swiftly paced farce and mystery but also a brilliantly humane comedy about the only animal in the cosmos trapped in the toils of an overdeveloped consciousness: the human being. The ultimate mystery, *Jumpers* suggests, is the meaning of life. The work constitutes Stoppard's richest and most brilliant exploration of ethical concerns.

ARTIST DESCENDING A STAIRCASE

In *Artist Descending a Staircase*, a radio play, Stoppard undertook what he has called "a dry run" of *Travesties*. *Artist Descending a Staircase* uses a continuous loop of recording tape to involve the audience with three artists engaged in an inquiry into the meaning of art. A more striking bond, between *Jumpers* and *Travesties*, has been summarized by Stoppard in an interview:

Jumpers and *Travesties* are very similar plays. . . . You start with a prologue which is slightly strange. Then you have an interminable monologue which is rather funny. Then you have scenes. Then you end up with another monologue. And you have unexpected bits of music and dance, and at the same time people are playing ping-pong with various intellectual arguments.

TRAVESTIES

Travesties is aptly named. In one of those travesties of probability, the writer James Joyce, the Romanian poet Tristan Tzara, and the Russian revolutionary Vladimir Ilich Ulyanov (who assumed the name of Lenin) were all living in Zurich in 1917: the Irishman working on *Ulysses*, the Romanian helping to set off the Dadaist explosion, and the Russian planning the Armageddon of the Bolshevik Revolution. Stoppard uses his literary license to have the trio interact, and adds, as his protagonist, a British consular official, Henry Carr, historically a minor clerk but promoted by the author to head the British consulate, while the name of the real consul in Zurich—Bennett—is assigned to Carr's butler. Old Carr, like Beckett's Krapp, replays the spool that contains his past.

The play's plot is both a pastiche and a travesty of Oscar Wilde's great comedy *The Importance of Being Earnest* (pr. 1895, pb. 1899). Stoppard discovered that Joyce had been the business manager of an amateur theatrical company that had staged Wilde's work in Zurich in 1918 and had cast Carr in one of the leading roles as Algernon Moncrieff. This prompted Stoppard not only to have his Carr also echo Algernon but also to double Tzara as Wilde's Jack Worthing, Bennett as Wilde's manservant Lane, and to name his romantic interests Gwendolen and Cecily to mirror Wilde's Gwendolen and Cecily. Rather surprisingly, Joyce intermittently becomes Lady Bracknell; after all, his middle name, Augusta, corresponds to Bracknell's first.

Travesties is a tour de force of spirited language and convoluted situations that fuses Wilde's high comedy of manners with Shavian dialectic, Joycean fiction, Epic theater, Dadaist spontaneity, music-hall sketches, and limerick word-games. Underneath the bouncy mattress of witty farce is a hard board: Stoppard's lust for ideas. He takes a piercingly cross-eyed look at those movers and shakers of everything that is not nailed down: artists and revolutionaries. The drama revolves four views on art through its ironic prism: Tzara represents Dadaist antiart; Joyce advocates the formalist tradition of art that emphasizes its long-meditated artifice; Lenin subordinates art to an instrument of state policy; and Carr holds a Philistine suspicion of the artist as an ungrateful drone.

In an interview, Stoppard declared himself particularly pleased with a scene, late in act 1, in which Tzara and Joyce confront each other on several levels: Joyce quizzes Tzara along the lines of the catechism chapter involving Bloom and Dedalus in *Ulysses*; Lady Bracknell quizzes Jack about his eligibility for her niece's hand; Tzara informs the audience about the nature of Dadaism; and Joyce affirms the mission of art to shape the ephemeral fragmentation of life into quasi-eternal objects.

Tzara may be the play's most attractive personality. He is not only a Romanian eccentric but also a sardonic social critic and an irreverent deconstructionist of platitudinous slogans. Stoppard has Tzara demand the right both to create a poem out of words jumbled in his hat and to urinate in different colors. Stoppard's Joyce is eloquent in his devout allegiance to the religion of art but less convincing as a shamrock-jacketed spouter of limericks and scrounger of money.

The characterization of Lenin, encountered in the public library but never in Carr's drawing room, proves most problematic. While the artists and bourgeoisie play, he acts, preparing to depart for Russia. His admirer, the librarian Cecily, opens the second act with an earnest lecture on Marxism, interrupted only by Carr's wooing of her. Lenin does not participate in any parallel pairing with Wilde's play—his political weight negates travesty except, perhaps, that his role as Cecily's instructor faintly resembles Miss Prism's. Theatrically, Stoppard's shift from the high-spirited merriment of act 1 to the solemn opening of act 2 is audacious and controversial; some critics have demurred at the drastic undercutting of comic momentum, since it upsets the audience's assumption that the play is made up of the blurred and unreliable recollections of a senile Henry Carr.

Carr is shocked by Tzara's and Lenin's demands that society should be transformed. He tells Tzara, who has expressed sympathy for Lenin's ideas, "You're an amiable bourgeois . . . and if the revolution came you wouldn't know what hit you. . . .

Multicoloured micturition is no trick to these boys, they'll have you pissing blood." Yet Carr, while inveighing against artists as self-centered and hostile, also insists that an individual artist's freedom is the most reliable test of a society's freedom.

In the play's coda, old Carr concludes that he learned these lessons from his Zurich experiences: One should be a revolutionary; if not, one should be an artist; and then there is a third lesson—which he cannot recall. Carr may well be a travesty of the sentiments of the public at large, trying to make sense of the meaning of history and the nature of art—and usually failing to do so.

In *Travesties*, Stoppard has composed a witty test whose laughs may outweigh the moral force of its ideas. "In the future," he told Ronald Hayman in June, 1974, "I must stop compromising my plays with this whiff of social application. . . . I should have the courage of my lack of convictions." Yet most of Stoppard's plays after *Travesties* show a marked increase in his political concerns and the deepening of his social conscience.

Dirty Linen and New-Found-Land

In *Dirty Linen and New-Found-Land*, Stoppard for the first time takes an unequivocal political stance, opposing any absolute right of the press to wash any and all linen in the glare of trash journalism's exposures. Even politicians, the play contends, are entitled to their confidential lives, as long as their private conduct does not handicap their public performance.

Starting in 1975 with his participation in a protest march against the mistreatment of Soviet dissidents, Stoppard has consistently voiced, both on and off the stage, his outrage at totalitarian violations of human rights. He has particularly befriended and championed the Czech playwright and later statesman Václav Havel, who is in significant ways his mirror image: Havel was born nine months before Stoppard, shares Stoppard's perspectives of absurdism and penchant for wordplay as well as Czech nativity, but he has consistently committed his work as well as his person to social causes, while Stoppard's recognition of social responsibilities has been intermittent. Both playwrights value as their highest goods freedom of expression and individualism.

Every Good Boy Deserves Favour

In *Every Good Boy Deserves Favour*, Stoppard created what he termed "a piece for actors and orchestra." With music by André Previn and a setting in a psychiatric prison in the Soviet Union, the work uses for its title a mnemonic phrase familiar to students of music because the initial letters, EGBDF, represent in ascending order the notes signified by the black lines of the treble clef. This play-oratorio is a sharply ironic, point-blank attack on the ways in which Soviet law is perverted to stifle dissent. The work is unfortunately flawed by Stoppard's and Previn's self-contradictory uses of the orchestra: On one hand, it evokes a totalitarian society based on a rigid notion of harmonious order in which improvisation and nonconformity are forbidden; on the other hand, the orchestra seeks to offer a lyrical and humane commentary on the action. The text fails to resolve these opposing purposes.

A far more accomplished attack on the suppression of individual freedom is Stoppard's teleplay *Professional Foul* (1977), dedicated to Havel. The text explores the same ethical problems posed in *Jumpers* and is one of Stoppard's most impressive works.

Night and Day

Although *Every Good Boy Deserves Favour* and *Professional Foul* represent ambitious advances in Stoppard's dramaturgy, *Night and Day* is a disappointing sidestep into a naturalism that none of Stoppard's previous plays has embraced. He does continue his new role as a didact, opposing any force that might inhibit the untrammeled passage of information, whether it be a union-closed shop or venal media tycoons or a totalitarian state. The drama takes place in a convulsed African country, possibly Uganda, which is agitated by a rebellion against a despotic government led by equally despotic officers. The play's serious concerns, however, are often obscured by stylish posturing and excessive verbal sparks that subvert the serious circumstances of the action. As a result, the text toys with difficult subjects, trivializing them in a manner reminiscent of Noël Coward's flip cleverness.

The Real Thing

In *The Real Thing*, Stoppard again harks back to Coward (as well as Wilde) for an exercise in love among the leisured classes, in which aristocrats of style spend their time polishing epigrams and tiptoeing into one another's penthouse souls. This play, however, also has a heart, throbbing with the domestic passion to which even an intellectual playwright, the protagonist Henry, can succumb. Henry has an affair with his good friend's wife, Annie; they fall in love, divorce their spouses, and marry. They are happy for two years, but Annie takes Henry's complaisance for complacence and has trysts with other men. Henry discovers howling-wolf pain in his cuckoldry before he and Annie realize that their marriage is, for better and worse, the real thing.

As so often in his dramatic practice, Stoppard mines his play with parallel phrases and repeated allusions. Yet this time his characters do more than skate on brittle surfaces. They suffer recognizable pain in the throes of romance, sharp darts of regret and ardor, frustration and anguish as they find themselves betrayed and rejected by those they love. This time, Stoppard has created recognizable people as well as flashed the laser beams of his intellect.

LATER PLAYS

Stoppard's major theatrical work in the late twentieth century, *Hapgood*, *Arcadia*, *Indian Ink*, and *The Invention of Love* show a depth to his characters and ideas that did not exist in his earlier work. Unlike his early plays, which were often described by critics as being too academic, his later work demonstrates Stoppard's discovery of lyricism. Although just as complex intellectually, these later plays are equally about ideas and emotions and present fully realized characters, rather than the witty, though ultimately shallow ones that populate his work before *The Real Thing*. Despite greater emphasis on developed characters, these late plays still manage to tackle concepts as diverse and complex as Heisenberg's uncertainty principle (in *Hapgood*), chaos theory (in *Arcadia*), colonialism (in *Indian Ink*), and classicism (in *The Invention of Love*). Stoppard has already earned an honored place in the ranks of England's playwrights. Like Wilde, his ferocious wit and intellectual acuity dazzle audiences; like Shaw, he stylishly explores intellectual and emotional dilemmas; and like Beckett, his comedy is sometimes bathed in pain and sadness.

Altogether, Stoppard is an immensely talented, uniquely unclassifiable writer who invites his public to discover the humaneness of plays and the glory of the English language's density and richness.

HAPGOOD

More than five years after *The Real Thing*, and after a series of adaptations, Stoppard wrote *Hapgood*, first performed in London in 1988 and subsequently revised for its American tour. Stoppard was inspired by quantum mechanics and the discovery that light consists of particles and waves. He took his fascination with physics' duality and applied it to *Hapgood*, in the form of dual human nature, that is, double agents and double dealings—or, more specifically, espionage. The principal character, Hapgood (also code-named Mother), is a female spy who has been ordered by the Central Intelligence Agency to get rid of a double agent who has been serving the Soviet government. The kind but at the same time merciless Hapgood carries out her mission amid thrilling scenes of kidnappings that are not exactly what they seem to be, double agents who may actually be triple or even quadruple agents, and sexual delusions, in a cerebral drama unequivocally demonstrating its author's love of paradox.

INDIAN INK

Between screenplays, adaptations, and original dramas, Stoppard wrote perhaps one of his best works, the 1991 radio play *In the Native State*, which he later adapted for the stage as *Indian Ink*. Like other writers fascinated with British imperialism and India, such as E. M. Forster, Stoppard deals here with the ambiguous theme of India's gaining of independence or, as it can also be seen, India's losing its status as a territory of the British Empire. *In the Native State* is also about the Anglo-Indian taboo of sexual relations between British women and Indian men.

While on a visit to India, the young poet Flora Crewe has her portrait painted by Nirad Das, an Indian artist. Das, however, has painted two portraits of Crewe: a "proper" one and a nude, the latter remaining in the possession of his son. The nude represents the "more Indian" side of Nirad Das, which is exactly how Crewe wants him to be, for if he anglicized himself she would despise him, since he would be attempting to bring the bloodlines closer together and eventually erase the distinction between ruler and ruled.

ARCADIA

Although after *The Real Thing* Stoppard began devoting most of his time to screenplays and to adapting other writers' dramas, his 1993 play *Arcadia*, which was produced after a break of five years, was greeted with enthusiasm among theater critics, who saw the play returning Stoppard to the stage world.

In *Arcadia*, Stoppard again manages to throw his audience into confusion with sudden shifts from one time period to another; he also continues his experiment of borrowing authentic literary figures, such as Lord Byron, whom spectators find here involved in a murder mystery, one requiring a certain level of intellectual gymnastics on their part.

Arcadia is set in 1809 in the garden room of a beautiful country house in Derbyshire, England. The play's two principal characters, Thomasina Coverly, a thirteen-year-old pupil of Lord Byron's contemporary Septimus Hodge, and Bernard Nightingale, a detective/academic, are separated in time by 180 years. Nightingale, who visits the Coverly house in the 1990's, has as a motive a desire to expose a scandal that occurred in the country house and that involved Lord Byron. According to Nightingale, the fictional poet Ezra Chater, whom Byron criticized in *English Bards and Scotch Reviewers*, is shot following an erotic meeting in the country house. The supposed shooting of Chater, his fictitiousness (as viewers discover that he is Nightingale's invention), and the insinuated quarrel between him and Lord Byron are only some of the mysteries that engage spectators into becoming detectives.

THE INVENTION OF LOVE

Stoppard's last play written in the twentieth century, *The Invention of Love*, is also one of his most ambitious. The play is a memory play again based on a real-life writer: A. E. Housman, poet and classics scholar of the late nineteenth and early twentieth centuries. It begins with Housman's arrival in Hades upon his death in 1936. As he travels down the river Styx with Charon, the ferryman, he remembers/encounters/relives important moments in his life, particularly those that involve Moses Jackson, the man Housman loved unrequitedly throughout his entire life. Here again Stoppard plays with the audiences' perception of time, showing both the young Housman and the old, even allowing them to interact at the ends of both acts.

Stoppard parallels the life of Housman with the life of Oscar Wilde, his contemporary. Where Wilde acted on his homosexual tendencies, ultimately leading to his imprisonment, Housman repressed his own leanings. Rather than simply being a play about denial of love, Stoppard uses Housman to question the nature of many types of love, including brotherly, scholarly and physical. When Housman encounters Wilde in Hades the two discuss the differences between artist and scholar, as well as the two types of love that can be created by these two types of men. *The Invention of Love* is Stoppard's most complex musings on the nature of love, time, life, and death. It is arguably his densest, and most rewarding, work at the time of its first performances.

OTHER MAJOR WORKS

LONG FICTION: *Lord Malquist and Mr. Moon*, 1966.

SCREENPLAYS: *The Engagement*, 1970; *The Romantic Englishwoman*, 1975 (with Thomas Wiseman); *Despair*, 1978 (adaptation of Vladimir Nabokov's novel); *The Human Factor*, 1979 (adaptation of Graham Greene's novel); *Brazil*, 1986; *Empire of the Sun*, 1987 (adaptation of J. G. Ballard's novel); *The Russia House*, 1990 (adaptation of John Le Carré's novel); *Rosencrantz and Guildenstern Are Dead*, 1990; *Billy Bathgate*, 1991 (adaptation of E. L. Doctorow's novel); *Medicine Man*, 1992; *Vatel*, 1997 (translation and adaptation of Jeanne LaBrune's screenplay); *Shakespeare in Love*, 1998; *Enigma*, 1999.

TELEPLAYS: *A Separate Peace*, 1966; *Teeth*, 1967; *Another Moon Called Earth*, 1967; *Neutral Ground*, 1968; *The Engagement*, 1970; *One Pair of Eyes*, 1972 (documentary); *Boundaries*, 1975 (with Clive Exton); *Three Men in a Boat*, 1975 (adaptation of Jerome K. Jerome's novel); *Professional Foul*, 1977; *Squaring the Circle*, 1984; *The Television Plays, 1965-1984*, 1993; *Poodle Springs*, 1998.

RADIO PLAYS: *The Dissolution of Dominic Boot*, 1964; *M Is for Moon Among Other Things*, 1964; *If You're Glad I'll Be Frank*, 1965; *Where Are They Now?*, 1970; *Artist Descending a Staircase*, 1972; *In the Native State*, 1991; *Stoppard: The Plays for Radio, 1964-1991*, 1994.

NONFICTION: *Conversations with Stoppard*, 1995.

TRANSLATION: *Largo Desolato*, 1986 (of Václav Havel's play).

BIBLIOGRAPHY

Billington, Michael. *Stoppard the Playwright*. London: Methuen, 1987. Long the drama critic of *The Guardian*, Billington, who writes from a leftist perspective, admires Stoppard's eloquence but mistrusts his conservative ideas. Still, Billington praises *The Real Thing* and expresses his hopes that Stoppard will increase his passion for both people and causes.

Brassell, Tim. *Tom Stoppard: An Assessment*. New York: St. Martin's Press, 1985. Brassell's study is detailed, elegantly written, and learned. He applies a considerable knowledge of modern drama as well as philosophy.

Gusso, Mel. *Conversations with Stoppard*. New York: Limelight Editions, 1995. A collection of interviews between *New York Times* drama critic Gusso and the playwright that covers the time from 1972 to 1995 when the playwright's *Indian Ink* was about to open in London. Presents Stoppard's own erudite thoughts on his work.

Hayman, Ronald. *Tom Stoppard*. London: Heinemann, 1977. Hayman's compact text is chiefly valuable for two highly revealing interviews conducted in 1974 and 1976.

Kelly, Katherine E., ed. *The Cambridge Companion to Tom Stoppard*. Cambridge, England: Cambridge University Press, 2001. Provides essays on all things Stoppard, including an in-depth biography, as well as scholarly criticism on his plays, radio plays, and screenplays. Also contains a very extensive bibliography.

Rusinko, Susan. *Tom Stoppard*. Boston: Twayne, 1986. Mainly summarizes the views of other critics and reviewers. Its chief service is an extended bibliography of secondary as well as primary sources.

Whitaker, Thomas. *Tom Stoppard*. New York: Grove Press, 1983. Whitaker's text is succinct, perceptive, and smoothly worded. He stresses the performance aspects of Stoppard's plays, often commenting on particular productions that he has seen.

Gerhard Brand,
updated by Matthew J. Kopans

DAVID STOREY

Born: Wakefield, England; July 13, 1933

PRINCIPAL DRAMA

The Restoration of Arnold Middleton, wr. 1959, pr. 1966, pb. 1967
In Celebration, pr., pb. 1969
The Contractor, pr. 1969, pb. 1970
Home, pr., pb. 1970
The Changing Room, pr. 1971, pb. 1972
Cromwell, pr., pb. 1973
The Farm, pr., pb. 1973

Life Class, pr. 1974, pb. 1975
Mother's Day, pr. 1976, pb. 1977
Sisters, pr. 1978, pb. 1980
Early Days, pr., pb. 1980
Phoenix, pr. 1984, pb. 1993
The March on Russia, pr., pb. 1989
Stages, pr., pb. 1992
Caring, pb. 1992
Plays: One, pb. 1992
Plays: Two, pb. 1994
Plays: Three, pb. 1998

OTHER LITERARY FORMS

This Sporting Life, David Storey's first—and still most widely read—novel, appeared in 1960; it won the Macmillan Fiction Award and was later made into a successful film with a screenplay by Storey (1963). Storey also adapted his *In Celebration* to film in 1975. *Flight into Camden*, which received both the John Llewelyn Rhys Memorial Prize and the Somerset Maugham Award, also reached print in 1960. Among Storey's many other novels are *Pasmore*, published in 1972 and winner of the Faber Memorial Prize; the autobiographical *Saville* (1976), awarded the prestigious Booker Prize; and *Present Times* (1984). Storey has also written *Edward* (1973), a book for children, and *Storey's Lives: Poems, 1951-1991* (1992).

ACHIEVEMENTS

David Storey's writing has won several awards. His first play, *The Restoration of Arnold Middleton*, won the *Evening Standard* Award for Most Promising Playwright (1967), and *The Contractor* received both the London Theatre Critics Award for Best Play (1970) and the Writer of the Year Award from the Variety Club of Great Britain (1971). *Home* was a critical success on both sides of the Atlantic, garnering the *Evening Standard* Drama Award, a Tony Award nomination, and an award from the New York Drama Critics (1971). Two years later he again received an award from the New York Drama Critics and another Tony nomination, this time for *The Changing Room*.

BIOGRAPHY

Although a character in one of David Malcolm Storey's plays remarks that "sport and art don't mix," those two apparent opposites did indeed mix at a crucial period in Storey's own development. The son of a coal miner, Storey was born on July 13, 1933, in Wakefield, Yorkshire—located in northeastern England. In 1953, after attending local schools, Storey began his studies at the Slade School of Fine Art in London, receiving his diploma in 1956. During that time, he commuted on weekends back up to the north, where he played professional football for the Leeds Rugby League Club from 1952 to 1956. After his marriage in 1956, he worked at a number of odd jobs—among them teacher, farm worker, and erector of circus tents, all of which would be reflected in his plays—before he turned to writing. In 1959, when his earliest attempts at fiction proved to be unmarketable, he tried drama, but his first work in the medium, *The Restoration of Arnold Middleton*, did not finally reach the stage until it was produced in Edinburgh, Scotland, in 1966. Following the phenomenal success of *This Sporting Life* in 1960 and the publication of two more novels within three years, Storey turned his energies once again to the theater and, in a tremendous burst of creative inspiration, wrote four of his most important plays: *In Celebration* and *The Contractor*, both written in 1969; *Home*, written in 1970; and *The Changing Room*, written in 1971. With the production of *In Celebration*, Storey began his long and fruitful association with George Devine's English Stage Company at the Royal Court Theatre in London's Sloane Square (where John Osborne's *Look Back in Anger* had premiered in 1956) and director Lindsay Anderson; Anderson would later direct the movie version of *In Celebration* for the American Film Theater's second season. In 1971 Storey's *The Changing*

David Storey in 1972. (AP/Wide World Photos)

Room and *The Contractor* were presented by The Long Wharf group of New Haven, which provided the kind of ensemble acting that, in America, a regional theater seems best able to provide. Storey's theatrical activity continued unabated during the 1970's with more plays, including *The Farm* and *Cromwell*, *Life Class*, *Mother's Day*, *Sisters*, and *Early Days*. Of these, only *Life Class* and *Early Days* appear likely to have much continued life in the theater.

By the early 1980's, Storey hinted that his career as a dramatist was winding down, declaring that "the plays are a dead duck now." In fact, only one play, *Phoenix*—about the artistic director of a theater that loses its government subsidy and is finally demolished—would be produced mid-decade and only in the provinces rather than in London. Another play, *Stages*, was produced in 1992, followed by the publication of *Caring* in the same year.

ANALYSIS

Although David Storey considers himself primarily a novelist whose plays are offshoots of his fiction, it now appears certain, at least on the American side of the Atlantic, that he will be known and remembered more as a dramatist. If his novels are in the vein of D. H. Lawrence—with their attention to human beings' physical and spiritual disharmony and their criticism of modern humankind's separation from the elemental processes of nature—his plays qualify him as the principal disciple of Anton Chekhov in postwar British theater. Like the Russian master before him, Storey writes dramas in the mode of symbolic naturalism that, while they are firmly rooted in a specific social milieu, touch on the most universal of themes at the same time that they become swan songs for a dying civilization. Storey admits to finishing his plays very quickly, sometimes within a few days during periods when he is blocked in his novel writing, claiming that they "compose themselves" after a first sentence flashes into his mind. Several of the plays, in fact, reveal a close connection to one or another of the novels; *The Changing Room*, for example, takes a situation from *This Sporting Life* and expands on it, as *The Contractor* does from *Radcliffe* (1963) and *Life Class* from *A Temporary Life* (1973).

Storey finds the writing of drama therapeutic, since work in the theater removes him from the solitary, inner process of creating a novel and transplants him into the outer, communal world of theatrical production.

Not that such a split is at all an unusual experience for this man of letters who was simultaneously both rugby player and art student. Such dichotomies are the wellspring of his creativity, and if they converge fortuitously with the central disharmonies of twentieth century life, so much the better. If the twentieth century is the century of the disintegration of society, of the dissociation of sensibility, and of schizophrenic humankind, fragmented and alienated, then Storey perfectly captures this widespread sense of vulnerability and mortality within both his fiction and his drama. Several of his works (especially *This Sporting Life* and *The Changing Room*) focus on the split between flesh and spirit, body and soul, the physical and the mental; others (such as *Life Class*), on the pull between life and art, reality and illusion, form and feeling; still others (including *This Sporting Life*, *Radcliffe*, and *The Farm*), on the conflict between the masculine and feminine sensibilities, discipline and intuition, activity and passivity. Further polarities that Storey explores include those between past fact and present memory (*Home* and *Early Days*), between nature and progress (*The Contractor*), between the word and the sword as well as between existence and essence (*Cromwell*), and between commitment and betrayal and dreams and practicality (*Sisters*). Furthermore, throughout Storey's plays there is a wealth of imagery of the sterile wasteland, of what one of his characters terms the "computerized, mechanized, de-humanized, antiseptic society" that is modern industrial culture. As his characters search for meaning and order and some means to achieve integration, they look to the values of work, of communal spirit and support, and of an art whose essence is faithfully to record life so that human beings can see not only the literary reality but also the way in which moments in that reality, especially daily rituals, can achieve a transcendent, sacramental effect that allow people to reclaim some purpose and value—at least temporarily.

In nearly all of his plays, Storey practices an almost documentary realism, an absolute fidelity to the facts, even to the minutiae, of daily existence; yet in his best dramas he transcends this level of realism so that the events become, as they do for Chekhov, symbolic of much larger concerns, even allegories of human beings in the modern age. In 1973, Storey himself distinguished between the three types of plays that he writes: the decidedly literary plays, those written in the mode of poetic naturalism, and the overtly stylized works. Among the first group, he included *The Restoration of Arnold Middleton*, which focuses on one man's use of elaborate pretense to escape confronting reality; *In Celebration*, which is set, like Storey's own early life, in a coal-mining town in the North Country; and *The Farm*, which, while revolving like Arnold Wesker's *Roots* (pr., pb. 1959) around an engagement that does not come to pass, explores a mother's attachment to the poet-son and a father's anger over his daughters' failures to regenerate life. To these must be added *Mother's Day*, an unsuccessful farce in the manner of Joe Orton, and *Sisters*, which, like Tennessee Williams's *A Streetcar Named Desire* (pr., pb. 1947), sees a woman's arrival threaten the arrangement between her sister and brother-in-law, until the woman's retreat into insanity saves them all. These works, all of which are family problem plays, are literary in that their dialogue and handling of character are novelistic, their plots are linear and generally well made, and their settings are basically representational and not overtly symbolic.

The second group, those works that Storey designates as poetic naturalism, are closest to Chekhov in that their plots are minimal, with the external action that does exist unfolding on a highly symbolic plane. In the two plays that Storey included in this category, *The Contractor* and *The Changing Room*, the event that would appear to be central actually happens off stage (as is also true of *In Celebration*). One can add to this group *Life Class*, in which Storey hints at his philosophy of the artist as a singer of life, recording life in order that others may see it; if human beings partake of existence simply by "being" in the fullest sense of that word, then for Storey the work of art primarily "should not mean but be." Storey's opening direction for *Life Class*, as for *Cromwell*, specifies simply "A Stage," providing an aesthetic comment about the empty space that needs to be filled, in the same way that the dramatist's mind (like a blank page) is peopled through the imaginative act.

Among his third group of overtly stylized works for the stage, Storey had completed only *Home* and *Cromwell*—a history play for an unlocalized Shakespearean stage filled with imagery of light and dark—by 1973, but also belonging to this group is *Early Days*, as Pinteresque in its language of lyric threnody as is *Home*. Most characteristic of the plays in this category is the manner in which stage activity is stripped down to a minimum, in which the rhythmic dialogue becomes sparser and more poetic, sometimes elegiac, and almost at times a liturgical sequence of antiphons with responses. No matter, however, which of the three groups they fall into, almost all Storey's plays are characterized by a use of the visual and verbal rituals of everyday life, the communal celebrations through which his men and women attempt to redeem the fallen world and to discover a validation for their own existence and some shared values in a diminished and precarious world akin to a modern wasteland.

IN CELEBRATION

In its surface details, *In Celebration* is Storey's most Lawrentian and openly autobiographical play. Set in a coal-mining town in the North Country, it focuses on the conflict between the mother and the son-artist. In its structure, *In Celebration* is a traditional family problem play: Three sons return home to honor their parents' fortieth wedding anniversary, and, while there, they dredge up a hurt from the past that continues to influence the present. The play's observance of the unities of time and place, the emphasis on the parents' guilt and its effects on the children, and the complex mix of love and hate that binds the family together, all make the work reminiscent of Eugene O'Neill's *Long Day's Journey into Night* (pr., pb. 1956). Furthermore, the strategy of a slow disclosure of a secret from the past puts the audience in mind of the realistic, well-made plays of Henrik Ibsen's middle period, such as *Gengangere* (pb. 1881, pr. 1882; *Ghosts*, 1885). Mr. Shaw, proud head of the family, refuses to retire even after forty-nine years in the mines, despite seemingly tenuous health, since hard work serves as a means of making retribution for his "sins." Shaw idolizes his wife, whom he got pregnant before they married. The daughter of a pig breeder, better educated than her husband (ironically, she holds a diploma in domestic hygiene), and significantly more religious, she must have felt it a "letdown" to marry him. Their first child, Jamey, who could "draw like an angel," was only seven when he died; Shaw had prayed, to no avail, that the son be spared and his own life taken instead, and Mrs. Shaw, six months pregnant at the time with their youngest child, Steven, had attempted to commit suicide. Shaw refused to have his three surviving sons follow him into the mines, seeing instead that they all went to college. Consequently, they have been forced from the working class into the lower middle class, with all the problems in social dislocation that this change traditionally causes for a Britisher.

The youngest son, Steven, a father of four, teacher, and sometime writer, is a brooding, sensitive, mostly silent man disturbed by what he terms a "feeling of disfigurement." Although he would have died in the womb had his mother's attempted suicide succeeded, he now appears to be her favorite. As a young man, he was disdainful of the establishment and for several years worked on a novel highly critical of the moral flabbiness of modern industrial society. Recently, however, he has reached an accommodation with life and given up his writing; he views this not as a compromise, but rather as an acceptance of things as they are. What deeply disturbs him now is more personal: nightmares and crying spells about the dead brother.

The middle son, Colin, a card-carrying communist during his school days, is now an industrial arbitrator of disputes between workers and management. Colin insists that the family not measure one another by their failures and, solely to raise his mother's spirits at a troubled time and ease her mind about the future, fabricates the news that he will finally marry.

The eldest living son, Andrew, has left a career in law to become an artist, a painter of—as he describes them—abstracts with "no sign of life." As a thirteen-

year-old boy, he announced to his family that he had no belief in anything, and he continues to be an angry young man, reviling the factory automation that turns workers into robots and continually goading Steven into reasserting his lost venom. Most of all, Andrew's present intention is revenge against his parents, particularly against his mother, who, after Jamey's death, had sent him off for six weeks to stay at a neighbor's and repeatedly had been deaf to his desperate cries to be let back into the house.

Andrew resents the way in which his father has always enshrined his mother as a goddess out of some mishandled sense of guilt for having violated her, and he accuses the parents of needing to fashion Jamey into some impossible ideal of perfection to atone for their sins and of having too strictly controlled his life and that of his brothers as well. The home, to him, was a fetid atmosphere, and the parents' guilt was responsible for their sons' problems. Now, as his anniversary memento, he wants to bring all this out into the open, which to some extent he does—although Mrs. Shaw seems oblivious to much of it, perhaps deliberately refusing to face these truths. Steven, however, forbids Andrew to harm or damage their mother and father, and so a full confrontation is narrowly averted. Andrew dances with his mother—tellingly, with no music playing—and, like Arnold in Storey's first play, somewhat unaccountably senses redemption, "salvation in his bones." What undercuts the resolution, however, and marks the ending with uneasiness, is the way that the family's final meal together—a breakfast of cold tea and dry toast—is left uneaten. No real communion has been established as the sons go off, leaving Mrs. Shaw with only Mr. Shaw to support her, a stage image much like that which concludes Storey's next and finest play.

THE CONTRACTOR

The Contractor retains elements of the conventional family problem play that Storey mined in *In Celebration*, but overlaying this probing of a family's deterioration through three generations are new directions in Storey's dramatic artistry that might even warrant the adjective "Storeyean": the minimization of plot, the fascination with exact reproduction of minute details of daily activity (here the onstage erecting of a huge canvas marquee for a wedding reception), and the investing of concrete image and event with a multilayered network of symbolic meaning.

To describe the external action of *The Contractor* is to discover, from one perspective, how much meaning Storey can evoke from so little. Five workmen erect a tent on the lawn of the company owner's house in the first two acts, then dismantle the tent in act 3, so that the stage image of three tent poles at the end of the play exactly replicates that at the beginning. The tent, like everything else that exists—family relationships, social institutions and structures, value systems—is transitory and ephemeral: All things under the sun pass away, and Storey examines the bedrock, if any, that remains. The workmen are carefully individuated (especially Kay, the foreman, who has been in prison for embezzlement and is sensitive to the emotional distress of others, and Glendenning, the sweets-loving, stuttering half-wit), but it is the group activity, the common goal of erecting the tent, that matters. Ewbank, the tent company owner and father of the bride, is set apart from his workmen by his economic and social status, and yet he insists on pitching in and helping. Not jaded by his station in life, he feels more comfortable with the laborers; he disparages money as more trouble than it is worth, and responds with compassion to Glenny, whom the others torment, and with heartbreak at the senseless damage done to the tent during the party. If Ewbank as overseer of the sewing of the beautifully stitched tent is a craftsman, Old Ewbank, his father, who is a rope maker, is an artisan. Throughout the play, Old Ewbank walks on and off, carrying a piece of rope that he is weaving (but that he eventually misplaces), contrasting it with today's machine-made rope that lacks resilience, and commenting that the laborers, too, have lost their stamina, dependent on pills and drink. His handmade rope is a precious bit of the past, which loses out to the machine-made product of the present.

In contemporary life, there exists a dissociation between art and work, a devaluing of the artifact as impractical. Nevertheless, the possibility that work and art might once again merge, at least fleetingly, is hinted at in the setting up of the marquee. The third generation of the family is represented by Ewbank's indolent son Paul, university-educated yet lacking any marketable skill. He admits to having no incentive to work purposefully and is content to loaf around the world (unsure of his destination) after the wedding. Alienated, rootless, not knowing his place in modern society, Paul does, however, have a flair for arranging the pots of flowers that decorate the tent. His grandmother recognizes this talent as the lingering touch of the artist in him, as the remnant of his grandfather's artistry, yet his father can only disparage such a nonutilitarian skill.

The tent as symbol is amenable to richly various interpretations. Storey himself has spoken of it, first, in terms of "a metaphor for artistic creation": the imaginative act of beginning with very little (three tent poles) and spinning around it a marvelous and ingenious structure, but then wondering, or having others wonder, what it is all worth. Second, Storey has connected the tent with "the decline of capitalistic society." It is being erected on the grounds below the Ewbank home, itself beautiful yet tainted because it was built from the sweat of the laborers, and on a rise above the town. Once the valley boasted only farms and mills, yet now it is covered by a cloud of smoke from the industrialized city, where a television aerial adorns every roof. If human beings have become separated from nature and lost the connection between themselves and the earth, they have also lost any fixed point of reference for themselves as social beings. The long-overdue breakdown of the oppressive class system has arrived, and yet people, particularly those of the middle class, find it difficult to know where they belong in the new society, while many in the lower class still look back wistfully on the old stratification.

If the tent symbolizes art and empire, it also suggests the transitoriness of relationships between parent and child, and husband and wife, and the brevity of life itself. The action of *The Contractor*, which occurs in very late summer, exudes an autumnal air: Ewbank remarks that he wishes he had time to do everything over again but that he is too old to start anew. "Come today. Gone tomorrow" might well serve as the play's epigraph. The only things that might endure in the face of constant change and diminishment are close personal relationships—though even those may no longer be lasting—and the value of work. The picture at play's end of Ewbank and his wife, alone now that their children have left, standing arm-in-arm and mouthing stoically "We'll manage" in the face of loss, is somewhat consoling, even if a shadow is cast over the new marriage of daughter Claire to a doctor when she must plead with him to stay sober at their reception. With everything else breaking down and dying out, what provides cohesion and meaning is work, in which individuals lose their egotism and exert their energies to create something together outside themselves. If the ritual dance of the family members, which in traditional romantic drama would signify generativity, is here undercut since it is performed without music, the shared meal retains all its religious force as a secular sacrament. After the tent is dismantled, Ewbank comes out from the house carrying a tray with a bottle of whiskey and the leftover wedding cake. The men partake in a ritual of eating and drinking that symbolizes the communion, however temporary, between them—with Ewbank even hiding away a little extra cake for Glenny.

The Contractor remains Storey's most Chekhovian play—and perhaps the most Chekhovian in all of modern British drama—as well as his most impressive work for the theater. It even verbally echoes *Dyadya Vanya* (pb. 1897, pr. 1899; *Uncle Vanya*, 1914) when Mrs. Ewbank announces near the end, "They've gone, then." The departure is yet another among the many symbols in the play of things passing away with nothing new to take their place.

HOME

Storey received his inspiration for *Home* from an image at the end of *The Contractor* of an ornamental metal table and two chairs, which become virtually the only elements in the setting of the later play. If plot in drama is understood as a causally connected series of events that rises to some resolution of a conflict, then *Home* is nearly plotless. Storey here eschews action in favor of a more lyric structure, related to musical composition in its reverberation of

motifs: It is a tone poem for voices. The play opens with two early-middle-aged men in a garden: Harry, who in his youth played amateur football, acted bit parts in the theater, and dreamed of becoming either a dancer or a flutist, and Jack, more dandyish in his dress, formerly in the Royal Air Force, who in his youth thought of becoming a priest. They talk and, in scene 2, walk on and off the stage as they are joined by two women of a lower social class. It is here, when Kathleen reveals that her shoelaces have been taken away and that she has painted on the walls, that the audience first realizes that the characters live in an asylum. The gentlemen, each of whom breaks into tears at three points in the play, escort the ladies to lunch. When they return for act 2, the furniture has been disarranged by Alfred, the play's only other— and totally silent—character, whose ritualized movements of lifting and carrying off the metalwork chairs and table suggest that this apparently purposeless activity is all that remains of their lives.

On its literal level, the simple action creates the impression of lost souls, each locked into the home of his or her own psyche, only able to break out sporadically by means of communication with another person. Marjorie is Kathleen's helpmeet, someone the other woman can physically lean on; the basis of their camaraderie is gossiping and tattling on others and sharing slightly bawdy ripostes. Harry and Jack, less well adjusted because clearly more sensitive, have developed a private language of their own, answering each other's incomplete sentences almost intuitively. They are aware of time passing, very slowly, and of eventual mortality. Although they must wait—a favorite image in the contemporary theater—for their next meal to interrupt the monotony of the day and have devised other private means for filling up time, they do not, unlike the tramps in Samuel Beckett's *En attendant Godot* (pb. 1952, pr. 1953; *Waiting for Godot*, 1954), wait in hopeless expectation for anything astounding and meaningful to happen to them. Rather, the mood is again elegiac: Everything notable and noble has already happened in the past, and is not likely to occur again.

If, in this play, with its multivalent symbolism, the home of the title is the psychic retreat of these four souls, it is also England itself, just as Chekhov's orchard was Russia. At one time, a lord and lady occupied the house now turned into the asylum; at one time, England's unique geography as an island led to the creation of a civilized culture and democracy. In a reverent litany of the poets and discoverers and inventions that once made England great, Harry and Jack name Charles Darwin, Sir Isaac Newton, John Milton, and Sir Walter Raleigh; radar, the steam engine, and penicillin.

Perhaps Storey even wishes his audience to recall John of Gaunt's famous set piece from William Shakespeare's *Richard II* (pr. c. 1595-1596) apostrophizing England as "this sceptred isle" and "other Eden, demiparadise," for one of the characters inhabiting what little garden remains at the asylum recalls the local tale that Adam and Eve actually lived in the Vale of Evesham. As the characters remark, however, the "sun has set" on the Empire, and its like will not be seen again. Where once great minds and great ideas flourished, now there is only uniformity and boredom; where once there was camaraderie in battle, responsibility for family members in need, and respect for the "gentler sex," now there is aimlessness, appalling manners, and lack of moral fiber; where once there was sun, now there is little beauty in an industrialized, soot-covered wasteland. Everything, now, has become little, and just as the patients have no hope of release from their home, there is little hope of a future for the larger home that is England. Kathleen yearns for death, lest she go mad—not realizing that she already has; Harry recognizes that there no longer exist any great roles for the actors on the great stage of the world, but only tiny parts on a little platform. Jack muses over metaphysical concerns, the why for God's actions, the mystery at the center of existence, finding no answers. To make life bearable, one can only hold out a hand to another person once in a while and be tolerant of the lapses of others, of the little falls from grace in the midst of the larger fall that has overtaken Western civilization. This swan song for a dying world that apparently is not waiting for anything to be born ends with an image of Harry and Jack desolate and in tears over their awareness of loss.

THE CHANGING ROOM

Just as the central action of the wedding reception that the audience expects to see in *The Contractor* happens between the acts, so, too, the action of the rugby match occurs off stage in *The Changing Room*. What the audience does see is the preparation for the football game (the stripping, bandaging, greasing of bodies, and suiting up), the treatment of the wounded gladiator during the match, and the aftermath of victory (the ritual of bathing, locker-room badinage, singing, and dressing in street clothes before returning to the world). Much of this activity, observed with Storey's usual eye for concrete detail, is choreographed almost like a ballet in performance. Storey manages, despite the large ensemble cast of twenty-two, to give some individuality to members of the team, among them the narcissistic Patsy, who lovingly stands in front of mirrors combing and recombing his hair; the studious-looking schoolmaster Trevor, who wears a club blazer and has an economist for a wife; the fastidious team captain Owens, evidently in his next to last season in the rugged sport, who takes full advantage of the special privileges due him; Walsh, quick with bawdy jokes and gestures as a cover for his sexual insecurity; and most of all the childlike Kendal, who treasures the electric tool kit he has bought to build bookshelves for his wife and who is brought in bloodied from a broken nose.

If the location of Storey's play is literally a changing room where men discard their everyday clothes and don their rugby shirts and shorts, it is also a setting employed symbolically, for these men undergo not only a change in clothing; they change from individuals into a group, as the lining up and passing of the ball from one to another before the match indicates, imbued with a sense of team spirit and commitment. The team breaks down social distinctions, equalizing workers and professionals, who can use the game as a means of improving, on one level, their economic condition; even the team's owner, Sir Frederick Thornton, though he sees the players as robots, likes to feel himself one of the men, as Ewbank does in *The Contractor*.

More important, playing rugby is a way of escaping the dulling routine of a machine-dominated existence through a physical ritual that takes on religious overtones of purification and renewal, since it enables these men to get in touch with the energies of their bodies (playing football is "life at the extreme," claims Storey, who knows from his own experience); the bodily exertion becomes a means of enlivening the spirit and, even though the fusion is only temporary, an organic harmony replaces fragmentation and dissociation. Like man alone, however, even men together are still subject to vulnerability and mortality. Storey even turns the nudity, occurring naturally here and with greater aesthetic justification than in almost any other contemporary drama, into a visual symbol of man's shared humanity: Bodies may be fine-tuned, yet they can become broken, and they do age; even pain, however, can be a measure of a man. If it is fashionable for contemporary writers to use sport as a metaphor for war or for the struggle for existence, or to portray it as a sublimation for sex or a substitution for power, Storey eschews such negative connotations to focus instead on the way in which sport, like art, can be a transcendence of the moment in time and of the purely self-centered tendency in man.

If there is a central character in *The Changing Room*, it is, ironically, the only one on stage who neither participates in nor watches the game—the menial workman Harry, who hoses out the bath, stokes the fire, lays out the clothes and towels, and sweeps up after the men. The broken-down, hymn-singing Harry, mentally deficient as the result of an accident years ago, is, for the players, a nearly anonymous presence, taken for granted and noticed only when he fails to supply their needs. Harry is obsessively paranoid over the threat of Russia and what he sees as its vast plot to destroy the West. Russia is even responsible for the cold weather that has turned the playing field into a frozen waste; the communists, he claims, have planted listening devices in the changing room and are using a poison gas to slow the thinking processes and thus brainwash humankind. What Harry says about England is more pointed and closer to the truth: Convinced that his own job has value, that he knows precisely who he works for, he decries—as Old Ewbank had—the detrimental effects of machinery on man's energy and the blurring of class distinc-

tions that mean that men no longer know their place. Like old Fiers in Chekhov's *Vishnyovy sad* (pr., pb. 1904; *The Cherry Orchard*, 1908), who longed to maintain the days of serfdom when he felt secure in a lowly station in life, Harry questions progress, feeling that the present cannot measure up to the past, that it is "too late" for any redemption. The final image of Harry sweeping the empty room symbolizes the way that the present continually displaces the past and all that it stands for. The certainty of old values has broken down, and man appears unable to discover ways to reinvigorate and renew his existence. Even the game can serve only as a temporary ritual that gives the pain of existence during the rest of the week a meaning. Storey's final attitude, then, is deliberately ambiguous and as double-edged as Chekhov's: There is mostly loss, but there is also some possibility for gain. The only certainty for man, however, is the fact of change, which is always unsettling.

The Changing Room, like other plays by Storey, such as *The Contractor* and *Home*, might seem, on the surface, to be apolitical, to be an exercise in documentary realism raised to the level of art. The surface reality is so precisely observed and re-created that the symbolic levels and allegorical equivalencies never seem to be imposed from without but always appear to be discovered by Storey as emanating from within that very reality and then subtly articulated. It could, however, be argued that Storey is the quintessential nonproselytizer among the contemporary British social and political dramatists. His plays are about England. He differs from most other—and usually younger—British social dramatists of the present day in the breadth of his vision. Working by symbol and indirection, he reveals the ills of the time but espouses no narrow platform for curing them. His political attitude, as he suggested in a remark in *Cromwell*, might sound like a self-serving excuse, but perhaps it is simply the realistic if somewhat cynical conclusion of a sensitive man thrown up against an insensitive system: No matter what side a person takes politically, and no matter what political decision that person makes, the decision ends by defeating the very values that the person originally tried to uphold. Storey proposes no answer, for probably none exists. He recurrently dramatizes diminution, decay, and mortality, with every once in a while a moment of compassion and shared humanity, through a daily ritual such as a bath or a meal, to help his oftentimes desolate people along the way.

CARING

In *Caring*, an experimental one-act play published in 1992, Storey avoids politics but continues to focus on diminished and decaying people who simultaneously "care" for and castigate each other. The play, which resembles the drama of Samuel Beckett, has no set, no props, no plot, no stage directions, and characters whose identities are never really defined. The play centers on a couple, presumably aging theatrical or vaudeville performers, who seem to be at the end of their careers. As the play progresses, Zena and Clarke correct each other, argue, insult, and perhaps even rehearse lines from a play or plays that have been staged or are in rehearsal. As they reproach each other for the affairs both have had with other performers, they also defend their lovers, whom they tend to romanticize. In fact, it is difficult to tell what is theatrical and what is real. At first the two characters seem to be a married couple, but later they appear to be married to other people. When Clarke asks, "Same time, next week?" he seems to suggest that this is a regular assignation with well-established dialogue and clearly both characters derive some pleasure from the acerbic repartee. Near the end of the play, Storey's use of rhymed dialogue implies that their conversation is a routine or performance for their own entertainment. As such, it can be altered to suit their needs.

OTHER MAJOR WORKS

LONG FICTION: *This Sporting Life*, 1960; *Flight into Camden*, 1960; *Radcliffe*, 1963; *Pasmore*, 1972; *A Temporary Life*, 1973; *Saville*, 1976; *A Prodigal Child*, 1982; *Present Times*, 1984; *A Serious Man*, 1998; *As It Happened*, 2002.

POETRY: *Storey's Lives: Poems, 1951-1991*, 1992.

SCREENPLAYS: *This Sporting Life*, 1963 (adaptation of his novel); *In Celebration*, 1975 (adaptation of his play).

CHILDREN'S LITERATURE: *Edward*, 1973.

BIBLIOGRAPHY

Hutchings, William. *The Plays of David Storey: A Thematic Study*. Carbondale: Southern Illinois University Press, 1988. The first full-length study devoted solely to Storey's work for the theater, Hutchings's valuable book provides detailed critical analyses of each drama. Hutchings sees Storey as stressing the importance of physical work and daily rituals to help the individual achieve a sense of community in a modern society that has been radically desacralized by industrialism and technology. Contains an extensive bibliography.

_____, ed. *David Storey: A Casebook*. New York: Garland, 1992. The essays on Storey's plays concern the role of the artist, the depiction of women, the relationship between family and madness, and the use of comedy. Hutchings provides an introduction, a chronology, and an extensive bibliography dealing with Storey's dramas. One of the only collections devoted exclusively to Storey's dramatic output.

Kerensky, Oleg. *The New British Drama: Fourteen Playwrights Since Osborne and Pinter*. New York: Taplinger, 1977. Kerensky focuses on the conflict between working-class parents and well-educated middle-class sons in Storey's plays, wherein fidelity to naturalistic detail often takes precedence over plot. He devotes his lengthiest comments to *Mother's Day*, Storey's negatively reviewed farce about English domestic life.

Liebman, Herbert. *The Dramatic Art of David Storey: The Journey of a Playwright*. Westport, Conn.: Greenwood Press, 1996. Liebman provides some biographical information, comments on the ties between Storey's novels and his films, and groups the plays into three categories for purposes of analysis: plays of madness, plays of work, and family plays. He also provides a selected bibliography.

Quigley, Austin E. "The Emblematic Structure and Setting of David Storey's Plays." *Modern Drama* 22, no. 3 (1979): 276-279. In response to conflicting assessments over whether Storey should be regarded as a traditional or an experimental playwright, Quigley probes the basis for Storey's originality as a dramatist. He proposes that it rests in his uncanny ability to reconceive conventional theatrical devices as "structuring images" that contain the plays' themes.

Randall, Phyllis R. "Division and Unity in David Storye." In *Essays on Contemporary British Drama*, edited by Hedwig Bock and Albert Wertheim. Munich: Max Hueber Verlag, 1981. Randall sees as major themes in Storey's writing the disintegration of both the individual and the family or social unit, and "the struggle to make life work on both the external and internal levels." The dramas, she argues, accept the impossibility of full integration, often ironically undercutting the spiritual values. Concludes with a useful chart indicating the interrelationships between Storey's novels and plays.

Taylor, John Russell. *David Storey*. London: Longman, 1974. This pamphlet, written by one of the principal authorities on contemporary British drama as part of the British council's Writers and Their Work series, charts the connections between Storey's novels and plays up through 1973. Taylor emphasizes the tension between the physical and the spiritual in the fiction and the blending of realistic with symbolic or allegorical levels in the dramas. Includes a photograph of Storey as a frontispiece.

Worth, Katharine J. *Revolutions in Modern English Drama*. London: G. Bell and Sons, 1972. In brief yet sensitive remarks, Worth explores Storey's use of physical objects as a focal point and his expert handling of space (stage space in *The Contractor* and screen space in the television adaptation of *Home*). Worth believes that audiences relish the process through which space is transformed, and the characters too, as they participate in fleeting moments of communion.

Thomas P. Adler,
updated by Thomas L. Erskine

BOTHO STRAUSS

Born: Naumburg an der Saale, Germany; December 2, 1944

PRINCIPAL DRAMA

Peer Gynt: Nach Henrik Ibsen, pb. 1971
Die Hypochonder, pr., pb. 1972 (*The Hypochondriacs*, 1977)
Prinz Friedrich von Homburg: Nach Heinrich von Kleist, pb. 1972
Bekannte Gesichter, gemischte Gefühle, pb. 1974, pr. 1975 (*Familiar Faces, Confused Feelings*, 1976)
Sommergäste: Nach Maxim Gorky, pb. 1974
Trilogie des Wiedersehens, pb. 1976, pr. 1977 (*Three Acts of Recognition*, 1981)
Gross und Klein, pr., pb. 1978 (*Big and Little*, 1979)
Kalldewey: Farce, pb. 1981, pr. 1982

Der Park, pb. 1983, pr. 1984 (*The Park*, 1988)
Die Fremdenführerin, pr., pb. 1986 (*The Tour Guide*, 1995)
Besucher, pr., pb. 1988
Sieben Türen, Bagatellen, pr., pb. 1988
Die Zeit und das Zimmer, pb. 1988, pr. 1989 (*Time and the Room*, 1995)
Angelas Kleider, pr., pb. 1991
Schlusschor, pr., pb. 1991
Das Gleichgewicht: Stück in drei Akten, pr., pb. 1993
Ithaka, pr., pb. 1996
Jeffers: Akt I & II, pr., pb. 1998
Der Kuss des Vergessens, pr., pb. 1998
Die Ähnlichen, pr., pb. 1998
Der Narr und seine Frau heute abend in Pancomedia, pr., pb. 2001
Unerwartet Rückkehr, pr., pb. 2002

OTHER LITERARY FORMS

Botho Strauss is a major German writer whose contributions to drama and fiction are equally important. Indeed, Strauss seems to alternate between writing both genres. His prose texts have a reflective quality; and some of them, especially *Der junge Mann* (1984; *The Young Man*, 1989), belong to the core of German postmodern writing.

Strauss has also written essays, ranging from his early theater reviews to political statements. Even the latter show Strauss's aesthetic and elitist approach to dealing with issues. Most controversial was "Anschwellender Bocksgesang," published in the German news magazine *Der Spiegel* (February 8, 1993), in which he analyzed contemporary democracy as self-satisfied and unable to make the changes necessary for its survival. To many people, this seemed close in word and spirit to the dangerous German conservatism of the 1920's. However, in the post-Cold War 1990's, the dichotomies of political left and right were somewhat elusive, and Strauss's analysis still could be understood in keeping with his earlier, more progressive views.

ACHIEVEMENTS

The talent of Botho Strauss was recognized early on when he was awarded a prestigious scholarship to live in Rome at the Villa Massimo (1976). Among his many other awards, the Georg Büchner Prize (1989) carries the most recognition. Strauss is a very private person who shies away from public appearances and did not attend the award ceremony for this prize but instead had somebody else read his acceptance speech.

BIOGRAPHY

Botho Strauss was born in Naumburg an der Saale. He studied German literature, theater, and sociology for five semesters at the universities of Cologne and Munich. He found his way to the theater first as an actor in amateur performances. From 1967 to 1970 he wrote theater reviews for *Theater heute*, the most important German journal for contemporary drama.

Then he turned to practical theater work as dramaturge in Berlin from 1970 to 1975, where he collaborated with Peter Stein, one of Germany's most influential theatrical directors. Their work was groundbreaking, and Strauss contributed extensively to the 1974 production of Maxim Gorky's *Dachniki* (pr., pb. 1904; *Summer Folk*, 1905), which shows affinities with Strauss's own work.

In the mid-1970's, at about the time that Gorky's *Summer Folk* premiered and toured internationally, Strauss's plays met with increasing success. His breakthrough as a dramatist came in 1978 with *Big and Little*. A popular playwright by the end of the 1970's, he became one of the preeminent German-language playwrights of the 1980's and has remained a prolific and influential writer.

ANALYSIS

Botho Strauss's career shows movement from his groundbreaking theater work with Peter Stein and the German New Subjectivity in the 1970's to a new conservatism in the 1990's. However, this movement does not completely describe Strauss's work because he has always done things his way. For example, while New Subjectivity usually is limited to exploring the individual response, Strauss has always had a larger picture in mind. This picture sees the individual human being dominated by an abstract system of meaningless repetition, a typically postmodern assumption that is called the "end of history."

In fact, basic assumptions and linguistic brilliance are strong postmodern elements in Strauss's dramas and prose texts. This is even more important because postmodernism is a literary movement that did not dominate German literature of the twentieth century to the same extent that it dominated the literature of the United States. In keeping with postmodern thinking, Strauss approaches an increasingly complex world in terms of a game that encompasses the way he uses language and in the way he manipulates characters and plot. This game quality reveals a pessimistic worldview: Strauss's plays are about the failure of the human search for belonging and certainty in a world that has nothing to offer but uncertainty.

This general approach determines the specifics of Strauss's themes, characters, and plot. The themes elaborate on the failed search for belonging and suggest elusive answers: shifting and uncertain identities and realities, alienation, failure to communicate, isolation versus relationships, frustrated yearning for happiness, a fine line between sanity and madness, and myth. The characters embody these themes; they are isolated and neurotic, but also well-spoken and often painfully self-conscious as well as uncertain as to their identity. As a result of these uncertainties, the plot in a play by Strauss is often no longer linear and usually merges realistic and nonrealistic elements (especially myth).

Strauss's specific way of using characters and plot in his plays is best understood as a response to broad literary developments. Beginning in the late nineteenth century, playwrights began to question how it was possible to tell complete stories (plot) and have meaningful communication (dialogue) in a world in which events no longer seemed to make sense. As a result, neither a play's plot or the function of its dialogue could be taken for granted.

Strauss's plays do not pretend to solve the problem; rather, they use action and dialogue as a means to evoke the issues that have made plot and dialogue problematic. First, as a basic principle of his plays, action is focused (on a character) yet often arbitrary (as to the identity of that character and as to the classical unities of time, place, and plot): Some characters seem to be passing by as if coming from or going to another play. The plot of *Time and the Room* is held together by the central character Marie, but she seems to be different persons depending on the specific scene: For example, in the first scene of the play's second part, she has met the right person at the airport, although during the first part she had missed that person on the very same occasion. This is also an example of how Strauss dissolves the traditionally linear plot.

Second, the questioning of dialogue as an expression of meaningful communication is evident in the so-called well-made plays of the late nineteenth and early twentieth centuries, whose sophisticated conversations among eloquent members of high society represent language without true meaning. The tradition of the well-made play is in part revived by Strauss in the use of superficial small talk, especially

at parties. In his plays, such conversation has even less meaning because dialogue often degenerates into monologue. Portraying the ineffectuality of language can produce interesting theatrical effects. For example, in *Three Acts of Recognition*, Susanne expresses her innermost feelings to Moritz about their stale love affair; however, she has turned her back toward her lover and has not noticed that he has left. She keeps talking while virtually all other characters pass by, overhearing what she says. Just before she is done and turns around, Moritz returns so that she never realizes that he has no idea what she tried to tell him.

This use of theme, character, plot, and dialogue/monologue is typical even in Strauss's early plays. In his first major play, *The Hypochondriacs*, a clear plot line gives way to a farcical murder mystery with characters whose identities are unclear and include possible doppelgängers. Early on, Strauss uses myth or magical elements to at least temporarily suspend the confusion of human relationships, for example, with the magician Karl in *Familiar Faces, Confused Feelings*. Other plays are grounded more in the realities of disillusioned modern society; however, from *Three Acts of Recognition* to *Der Narr und seine Frau heute abend in Pancomedia* (the fool and his wife in tonight's pancomedia), there seems to be a residual element of irrationality that exists both in the sense of impending doom and in an underlying mythical level. For example, in *The Tour Guide*, the myth of Pan is not treated explicitly but rather alluded to by the complicated affair between an older tourist and a young female tour guide in the summer in the Greek countryside.

THREE ACTS OF RECOGNITION

The plot is as clear as the comings and goings of a party with its small talk can be. The play shows the members of a local Arts Foundation gathered for a preopening event at the gallery. In its eerie presentation of miscommunication and noncommunication, this play seems unreal, but it is also realistic as a parody of such public cultural events. Yet it can be argued that this plot of busy small talk masks the true action behind the scenes: the power struggle between a member of the board who objects to the choice of paintings and the gallery director Moritz. In the end, censorship is victorious.

BIG AND LITTLE

This play—Strauss's breakthrough as a playwright—presents a series of ten scenes that chronicle the decline of Lotte, an unemployed graphic artist who is separated from her husband, into the margins of society. The uncertainty of some elements—for example, the passing of time can be only estimated by the increasing deterioration of Lotte's dress—heighten the sense of threat and inevitability of becoming homeless in a society that just does not care. The setting is urban and contemporary but the location of the scenes is as arbitrary as Lotte's search for belonging. In her failure, she becomes a tragicomic character because she remains ever hopeful although she is utterly isolated. In the final scene, she "calls" her husband from a telephone booth, which has become her home; however, their "conversation" is a monologue because she does not even dial his number.

KALLDEWEY: FARCE

Although Strauss's other plays seem unreal, this play is more directly surreal. The battle of the sexes is literally choreographed as the stage directions call for hands, arms, and legs to protrude from door frames at the beginning and, at the end, for the actors to "seemingly" shed their roles. In between, the play's three acts and one interlude present a woman who can find freedom only in having her husband murdered by two lesbians, a therapeutic housing cooperative that includes the formerly murdered husband, and reminiscences by the couple that has now grown old. Full of mythical and literary allusions, the play is aptly focused on the mysterious stranger Kalldewey, whose name can be seen as connected to carnival, a topsy-turvy world in which the normal rules of behavior have been temporarily suspended, thus emphasizing the gamelike character of Strauss's plays in general.

THE PARK

This five-act play presents itself as a thought experiment: Many theories and myths have been applied to make this world a better one—now what if people applied the genius of a great work of art to make the world better? This is the premise with which Strauss brings William Shakespeare's *A Midsummer Night's Dream* (pr. c. 1595-1596) to the reality of a contemporary German city. The experiment fails. The fairies' forest itself symbolizes how much things have changed: As a city park it is a place of ambiguities between civilization and nature, order and chaos, and reason and instinct. Now people no longer have a sense of the magic of love. Not only have the old myths become ineffectual but also the old mythical characters Oberon and Titania are transformed into normal contemporary middle-class people with worries about their jobs.

TIME AND THE ROOM

This is Strauss's most advanced play concerning the abandonment of the classical unities of time, place, and plot in favor of parallel realities. The play is held together by a central character Marie, but she seems to be different people in different scenes. Also, time itself seems warped: Just as Marie finishes telling a story about how a man rescued a woman, the door opens and a man carries in a woman whom he has just rescued.

DER NARR UND SEINE FRAU HEUTE ABEND IN PANCOMEDIA

In his first play of the new millennium, Strauss pursues the ambitious—and lengthy—endeavor of presenting a kind of balance sheet of contemporary society and a sum of his work. He picks a setting that is symbolic of people in transition and transit: a hotel with the ironically conforting name "Confidence." The plot operates on several levels: There are about one hundred characters coming and going between exchanges of superficial small talk; there is the ill-fated love story of a wheeling-and-dealing fledgling publisher Zacharius Werner and a young rising-star writer Sylvia Kessel; and there is an attempt to understand the essence of the contemporary "new economy," which lies somewhere between love and money. Toward the end of the play, Sylvia has written a novel about Zacharius and herself, which seems the only way for them to be together. The disillusionment and sense of flux at the end of the play emphasize the themes that Strauss has employed throughout his writing career.

OTHER MAJOR WORKS

LONG FICTION: *Schützenehre*, 1974; *Marlenes Schwester*, 1975; *Die Widmung*, 1977 (*Devotion*, 1979); *Rumor*, 1980 (*Tumult*, 1984); *Paare, Passanten*, 1981 (*Couples, Passersby*, 1996); *Der junge Mann*, 1984 (*The Young Man*, 1989); *Niemand anderes*, 1987; *Kongress: Die Kette der Demütigungen*, 1989; *Beginnlosigkeit*, 1992; *Wohnen, Dämmern, Lügen*, 1994 (*Living, Glimmering, Lying*, 1999); *Die Fehler des Kopisten*, 1997; *Das Partikular*, 2000.

POETRY: *Unüberwindliche Nähe*, 1976; *Diese Erinnerung an einen, der nur einen Tag zu Gast war*, 1985.

NONFICTION: *Versuch, ästhetische und politische Ereignisse zusammenzudenken: Texte über Theater 1967-1986*, 1987; *Der Gebärdensammler: Texte zum Theater*, 1999.

BIBLIOGRAPHY

Calandra, Dennis. *New German Dramatists: A Study of Peter Handke, Franz Xaver Kroetz, Rainer Werner Fassbinder, Heiner Müller, Thomas Brasch, Thomas Bernhard, and Botho Strauss.* New York: Grove Press, 1983. Includes a section on Strauss's plays of the 1970's with emphasis on characters and themes (isolation, relationships, shifting identities). Also discusses specific stage productions, especially premieres.

McGowan, Moray. "Past, Present, and Future: Myth in Three West German Dramas of the 1980's." *German Life and Letters* 43, no. 3 (April, 1990): 267-279. Looks at the growing interest in myth during the 1980's and places Strauss's use of Shakespeare's *Midsummer Night's Dream* in the context of other playwrights adapting Arthurian and Germanic myths. None of the authors uses myth as an escape from reality.

Stoehr, Ingo R. *German Literature of the Twentieth Century: From Aestheticism to Postmodernism.* Rochester, N.Y.: Camden House, 2001. Provides a broad survey of twentieth century German literature with brief sections on plays and novels by Strauss that allow the reader to see Strauss's contribution to literature.

Ingo R. Stoehr

AUGUST STRINDBERG

Born: Stockholm, Sweden; January 22, 1849
Died: Stockholm, Sweden; May 14, 1912

PRINCIPAL DRAMA
Fritänkaren, pb. 1870
I Rom, pr., pb. 1870
Den fredlöse, pr. 1871, pb. 1876 (*The Outlaw*, 1912)
Hermione, pb. 1871
Anno fyrtioåtta, wr. 1876, pb. 1881
Mäster Olof, pb. 1878, pr. 1890 (*Master Olof*, 1915)
Gillets hemlighet, pr., pb. 1880
Herr Bengts hustru, pr., pb. 1882
Lycko-Pers resa, pr., pb. 1883 (*Lucky Peter's Travels*, 1912)
Fadren, pr., pb. 1887 (*The Father*, 1899)
Marodörer, pr. 1887
Fröken Julie, pb. 1888, pr. 1889 (*Miss Julie*, 1912)
Kamraterna, pb. 1888, pr. 1905 (with Axel Lundegård; *Comrades*, 1912)
Fordringsägare, pb. in Danish 1888, pr. 1889, pb. 1890 (*Creditors*, 1910)
Hemsöborna, pr. 1889, pb. 1905 (adaptation of his novel)
Paria, pr. 1889, pb. 1890 (*Pariah*, 1913)
Den starkare, pr. 1889, pb. 1890 (*The Stronger*, 1912)
Samum, pr., pb. 1890 (*Simoom*, 1906)
Himmelrikets nycklar, eller Sankte Per vandrar på jorden, pb. 1892, pr. 1929 (*The Keys of Heaven*, 1965)

Moderskärlek, pb. 1893, pr. 1894 (*Mother Love*, 1910)

Bandet, pb. in German 1893, pb. 1897, pr. 1902 (*The Bond*, 1960)

Debet och kredit, pb. 1893, pr. 1900 (*Debit and Credit*, 1906)

Första varningen, pr., pb. 1893 (*The First Warning*, 1915)

Inför döden, pr., pb. 1893 (*In the Face of Death*, 1916)

Leka med elden, pb. 1893, pr. in German 1893, pr. 1897 (*Playing with Fire*, 1930)

Till Damaskus, forsta delen, pb. 1898, pr. 1900 (*To Damascus I*, 1913)

Till Damaskus, andra delen, pb. 1898, pr. 1916 (*To Damascus II*, 1913)

Advent, ett mysterium, pb. 1899, pr. 1915 (*Advent*, 1912)

Brott och Brott, pb. 1899, pr. 1900 (*Crime and Crime*, 1913; also known as *There Are Crimes and Crimes*)

Erik XIV, pr., pb. 1899 (English translation, 1931)

Folkungasagan, pb. 1899, pr. 1901 (*The Saga of the Folkungs*, 1931)

Gustav Vasa, pr., pb. 1899 (English translation, 1916)

Gustav Adolf, pb. 1900, pr. 1903 (English translation, 1957)

Carl XII, pb. 1901, pr. 1902 (*Charles XII*, 1955)

Dödsdansen, första delen, pb. 1901, pr. 1905 (*The Dance of Death I*, 1912)

Dödsdansen, andra delen, pb. 1901, pr. 1905 (*The Dance of Death II*, 1912)

Engelbrekt, pr., pb. 1901 (English translation, 1949)

Kaspers fet-tisdag, pr. 1901, pb. 1915

Kristina, pb. 1901, pr. 1908 (*Queen Christina*, 1955)

Midsommar, pr., pb. 1901 (*Midsummertide*, 1912)

Påsk, pr., pb. 1901 (*Easter*, 1912)

Ett drömspel, pb. 1902, pr. 1907 (*A Dream Play*, 1912)

Halländarn, wr. 1902, pb. 1918, pr. 1923

Kronbruden, pb. 1902, pr. 1906 (*The Bridal Crown*, 1916)

Svanevit, pb. 1902, pr. 1908 (*Swanwhite*, 1914)

Genom öknar till arvland, eller Moses, wr. 1903, pb. 1918, pr. 1922 (*Through Deserts to Ancestral Lands*, 1970)

Gustav III, pb. 1903, pr. 1916 (English translation, 1955)

Lammet och vilddjuret: Eller, Kristus, wr. 1903, pb. 1918, pr. 1922 (*The Lamb and the Beast*, 1970)

Näktergalen i Wittenberg, pb. 1904, pr. 1914 (*The Nightingale of Whittenberg*, 1970)

Till Damaskus, tredje delen, pb. 1904, pr. 1916 (*To Damascus III*, 1913)

Brända tomten, pr., pb. 1907 (*After the Fire*, 1913)

Oväder, pr., pb. 1907 (*Storm*, 1913)

Pelikanen, pr., pb. 1907 (*The Pelican*, 1962)

Spöksonaten, pb. 1907, pr. 1908 (*The Ghost Sonata*, 1916)

Abu Casems tofflor, pr., pb. 1908

Bjälbo-Jarlen, pr., pb. 1909 (*Earl Birger of Bjälbo*, 1956)

Riksföreståndaren, pb. 1909, pr. 1911 (*The Regent*, 1956)

Siste riddaren, pr., pb. 1909 (*The Last of the Knights*, 1956)

Stora landsvägen, pb. 1909, pr. 1910 (*The Great Highway*, 1954)

Svarta handsken, pb. 1909, pr. 1911 (*The Black Glove*, 1916)

Hellas: Eller, Sokrates, pb. 1918, pr. 1922 (*Hellas*, 1970)

Toten-Insel: Eller, Hades, pb. 1918 (*Isle of the Dead*, 1962)

Six Plays, pb. 1955

Eight Expressionist Plays, pb. 1965

OTHER LITERARY FORMS

August Strindberg wrote nearly two dozen novels, many of which are autobiographical; several volumes of short stories and poems; and more than twenty book-length essays, including writings about the history of Sweden, philosophy, religion, language, and dramatic theory. In addition to the individual Swedish- and English-language editions of Strindberg's work, translated selections appear in *The Strindberg*

Reader (1968), edited by Arvid Paulson, and *Inferno, Alone and Other Writings* (1968), edited by Evert Sprinchorn.

ACHIEVEMENTS

Tremendously influential in both Europe and the United States, August Strindberg was begrudgingly praised by Henrik Ibsen as one who would be greater than he, and more generously lauded half a century later by Eugene O'Neill as the writer to whom the American playwright owed his greatest debt. Although Strindberg wrote some seventy dramatic pieces, he is best known outside his native Sweden for a small number of plays that represent the range of his achievement. Of these, *The Father, Miss Julie, A Dream Play*, and *The Ghost Sonata* have earned for Strindberg his stature alongside Ibsen, Anton Chekhov, and George Bernard Shaw as a seminal figure in the first stage (1880-1920) of modern drama.

Strindberg's intensity and versatility are generally considered as much a product of his own neuroses as of his literary genius. The turbulent male-female relationships that his plays portray are commonly accepted as the playwright's expression of his own ambivalent feelings toward women, just as his treatment of the class conflict would seem to have its impulse in his domestic position as "the son of a servant." His late, expressionistic plays, written after a period of intense despair and nonproductivity, reflect the emphasis on atonement that characterizes Strindberg's later writing.

Aside from the provocative autobiographical content of his work, however, Strindberg's achievement rests on his perfection of the naturalistic form, his extension of that form into an imaginative forum for modern psychology, and his movement from dramatic realism to expressionism.

Most of Strindberg's plays that were translated into English and published early in the century are no longer in print. There are, however, a number of more recent translations that have appeared in collections, including, among others, Elizabeth Sprigge's *Six Plays* (1955), Arvid Paulson's *Eight Expressionist Plays* (1965), and the translations of Strindberg's drama by Walter Johnson.

BIOGRAPHY

Born in Stockholm on January 22, 1849, Johan August Strindberg was the fourth child of twelve born to Ulrika Eleonora Norling, formerly a waitress, and Carl Oscar Strindberg, a shipping agent. Strindberg's early life was spent in poverty, in the aftermath of his father's bankruptcy. When he was thirteen, his mother died, and his father married a housemaid. In 1867, Strindberg entered the University of Uppsala, where he studied, intermittently, until 1872, only to leave the university without a degree. In 1869, during one of his respites from university life, he tried acting at the Royal Theater and completed an acting course at the Dramatic Academy, though with little promise of success on the stage. By the following year, Strindberg had turned to playwriting, returned to the university, and had a modest theatrical success with the production of *I Rom* by Runa, a local literary club. The play had been preceded by several other dramatic efforts, and its production encouraged Strindberg to begin work on *Master Olof*, a play about the Swedish

August Strindberg (Courtesy of the D.C. Public Library)

religious reformer Olaus Petri, on which Strindberg was to work for nearly a decade. When he left the university, Strindberg worked as a journalist in Stockholm. In 1874, following a second unsuccessful attempt at acting, he took a position at the Royal Library in Stockholm, which he retained for eight years as he continued writing plays.

In 1875, Strindberg met the first of his three wives, Siri von Essen, who was married at the time to Baron Carl Gustaf Wrangel. The actress divorced her husband following an attempted suicide by Strindberg and, late in 1877, married the man who had been a frequent guest in their home. The marriage lasted until 1891, producing three children (a fourth, born two months after the wedding, did not live). During this period, Strindberg wrote a number of naturalistic plays that reflected the class and gender struggles that were to characterize his best-known work.

Though reasonably secure in his reputation among Swedish writers, Strindberg became disillusioned with the theater when *Herr Bengts hustru* (Sir Bengt's wife), a play he wrote in response to Ibsen's *Et dukkehjem* (pr., pb. 1879; *A Doll's House*, 1880), with his wife in the lead role, failed in production, and he and Siri entered the period of their lives that critics have called "the wander years." From 1883 through 1891, the pair traveled extensively, settling at various times in France, Switzerland, Bavaria, and, in 1889, again in Sweden. Following their divorce, Strindberg continued his nomadic life, moving to Berlin, Paris, London, Lund, and, finally, back to Stockholm. Strindberg was particularly creative during the wander years, publishing a short story collection in two volumes, entitled *Giftas I* and *Giftas II* (1884, 1886; *Married*, 1913), a historical novel, two autobiographical works, and three naturalistic dramas, two of which, *The Father* and *Miss Julie*, are among the most successful of his plays.

Immediately after the divorce, Strindberg entered a six-year period during which his literary achievements were nearly nonexistent. Distraught over a blasphemy trial centering on statements made in his short-story collection and deeply disturbed by his suspicions concerning Siri's infidelity, Strindberg married Frida Uhl, an Austrian journalist whom he met in Berlin. A year and a half later, in 1894, the couple were divorced, with Frida taking custody of their infant daughter.

For the next three years, Strindberg endured poverty and humiliation and suffered fantastic visions and unfounded fears. Displaying the classic symptoms of paranoia, he entered the torment about which he was to write in *Inferno* (1897; English translation, 1912). It was a time during which he experimented with alchemy, hypnotism, and black magic. He surfaced from his Inferno a self-styled religious man, practicing a hybrid of Catholicism and Swedenborgianism and working on the first play in the allegorical Damascus trilogy.

In Stockholm, Strindberg met a young actress, Harriet Bosse, and, despite nearly thirty years difference in their ages, married her. During a separation from Harriet, Strindberg began writing his expressionistic *A Dream Play*, with intentions of having his wife play the Daughter of Indra. In 1903, however, after only two years of marriage, Harriet left with their infant daughter, apparently unable to accommodate Strindberg's excessive jealousy.

In 1907, Strindberg became codirector, with August Falck, of the Intimate Theater, founded especially for the production of Strindberg's "chamber plays." The theater closed three years later, and in 1912 Strindberg died of stomach cancer. Though the Swedish writer did not have the honor of receiving the prestigious Nobel Prize, he was awarded the Anti-Nobel Prize—fifty thousand crowns through public subscription—two months before his death.

ANALYSIS

Because August Strindberg's drama falls into two distinct periods, separated by the years of his personal Inferno, it is easy to generalize about his work. The pre-Inferno plays are naturalistic in form and are insistently concerned with sexual and class struggles bringing to the philosophy of naturalism a psychological realism that validates his characters as among the most excitingly credible in modern drama. The post-Inferno plays reflect Strindberg's experience with mysticism and a variety of religions, along with his preoccupation in later life with guilt, expiation, and reconciliation. These plays are important especially for the ways in which they extend the boundaries of dramatic form, introducing expressionism and Symbolism into the mainstream of world drama.

Strindberg's early plays reflect the literary preoccupation of the time with the philosophy of naturalism, which holds forces beyond the control of the individual will responsible for human behavior yet also poses the question of individual choice. The resulting complexity of character allowed Strindberg to approach with renewed intensity the two conflicts that for him both personally and artistically were never resolved.

Though Strindberg's work was published as early as 1869, *The Father*, produced and published in 1887, is considered the first of his great naturalistic plays. In that play, as in a number of others that followed, Strindberg dramatizes a major concern of his life and work: the eternal power struggle between men and women. Laura stands as a prototypical Strindbergian woman: immensely powerful and in control yet perhaps not so by design. The play does not clarify whether Laura's triumph over her husband is the consequence of malevolent cunning or of an innocent but nevertheless destructive wielding of a natural female power. That same power is evident in the relationship between Miss Julie and Jean in *Miss Julie*, in which the sexual encounter between mistress and servant is initiated through Julie's aggression, though here the male ultimately achieves superiority as Julie endures postcoital humiliation and finally commits suicide. A concurrent struggle in *Miss Julie*, which is a second preoccupation of Strindberg, is that between the classes. Julie may be seduced to her death by Jean, but she reestablishes class honor, whereas the intimidated servant reverts to subservience.

Strindberg's personal conflicts were to expand during the Inferno period and were reflected in the religious and historical plays produced between 1897 and 1901. In those years, the playwright turned to mysticism and allegory, as in the Damascus trilogy. During this period, he also devoted considerable attention to Swedish history, dramatizing the lives of its people and several of its kings in such plays as *The*

Saga of the Folkungs, *Gustav Vasa*, *Gustav Adolf*, and *Carl XII*. In *The Dance of Death I* and *The Dance of Death II*, he confirmed that his obsession with the battle of the sexes was still alive.

Strindberg's most interesting work, however, comes with his later plays, which attempt to capture the dream form in drama. In both *A Dream Play* and *The Ghost Sonata*, his two most successful efforts, the playwright violates the laws of causality and logic, creating a fluid and subjective sequence of events that is dominated by the vision of an implied dreamer. In *A Dream Play*, the Daughter of Indra visits Earth and both observes and participates in the activities of those she encounters. In *The Ghost Sonata*, a young student passes through several rooms in a symbolic house en route to an encounter with a symbolic hyacinth girl. In the earlier play, the recurrent lament of the Daughter of Indra is, "Humankind is to be pitied," reflecting the deep sadness of the playwright, who had been through several religious conversions and had himself seen the condition of humankind. In *The Ghost Sonata*, a similar pessimism prevails but is redeemed in that play by a final tone of reconciliation. A statue of Buddha in the inner room suggests the religious preoccupation and the need to reconcile good and evil that characterizes Strindberg's post-Inferno plays.

THE FATHER

Strindberg once remarked that he did not know whether *The Father* was an invention or a reflection of his own life. The play, in which a man is driven mad by doubts concerning his parenthood, was written at a time when Strindberg's marriage to Siri von Essen was near collapse. Like the Captain in *The Father*, Strindberg was haunted by the knowledge that a man can never know with certainty that he is his child's father, as his suspicions of Siri developed into an obsession with whether he had fathered their first child, born two months after the wedding.

The sexual power struggle that takes place between husband and wife when the two disagree on the future of their daughter, Bertha, forms the dramatic center of the play. Determined to have her way, Laura, the Captain's wife, devises ways of undermining her husband's credibility and confidence. Her goal is to have the Captain certified insane so that he loses his legal claim to their daughter. Her method is psychological torment: Only she, not he, can know whether Bertha is his natural child. Made suspicious by her suggestion, the Captain becomes obsessed with the need to know, devising biological, experiential, and literary tests to affirm his paternity, only to be driven to madness by the impossibility of knowing. In the final tableau, the straitjacketed Captain, surrounded by the women in the household, lies helpless at the nurse's breast, repudiating his child, then falling in a fatal stroke; his wife, embracing Bertha, cries, "My child! My own child!"

Laura's manipulations are not less effective than those of an Iago, and she emerges as uncontested champion in this domestic duel of wills. Yet the play—and she herself—question how conscious her manipulations have been. Moments before the Captain's defeat, Laura claims that she never meant for any of this to happen, that she never thought through her behavior to its consequence. Allusions throughout the play to Omphale and to other women in classical literature suggest that for Strindberg, Laura represents a prototypical evil, a curiously innocent power that is uniquely and naturally feminine. Laura achieves control less by design than by instinct.

In a letter to Friedrich Nietzsche, Strindberg reported the reaction to the production of his play: One woman died, another miscarried, and most of the audience ran from the theater, bellowing. Strindberg's hyperbole, though obviously intended to be frivolous, nevertheless reflects the excitement generated by this highly personal but powerful portrayal of women and of marriage.

MISS JULIE

The best known of Strindberg's plays, *Miss Julie* takes place on a midsummer eve in Sweden. In the absence of her father, a nobleman, the twenty-five-year-old Julie, a member of Strindberg's degenerate, emancipated "third sex," initiates a psychological battle with Jean, the valet, that culminates in his sexual triumph. The battle, however, is a social conflict as well, and, in a dramatic suicide-seduction scene, Julie regains her social honor, leaving Jean to tremble at the return of her father, the count. Throughout their

encounter, the sexual and social lines separating the two shift, as each lives out the respective dreams of rising and falling that unify the work's images and give dramatic design to the play.

Jean's dream is one of aspiration: He is lying under a tree in a thick and darkened wood; he wants to climb to the top of the tree to look out over the brightly lit landscape and rob a bird's nest of its golden eggs. Despite persistent climbing, however, he never arrives at the first branch, much less the top. When Jean was younger, he once found himself in a compromising position. A servant who had no business being in the gentry's outhouse (the Turkish pavilion), Jean avoided discovery by leaving through the sewer, only to surface to spy Julie, in pink dress and white stockings, standing in the fields. Since that time, he has been symbolically cleansing himself of the dirt and excrement that characterize his servile status, hoping to become proprietor of a Swiss hotel and, eventually, a Rumanian count.

Julie's dream is one of degradation and fall. She is on top of a pillar, longing to descend to the ground, but she does not have the courage to jump. The daughter of an aristocratic father and a common but feminist mother, Julie has developed a hostility toward men (she forces her fiancé to jump over her slashing whip) and an attraction to the servant class. At the Midsummer Eve's festivity, both she and Jean find occasion to act out their perversities and temporarily realize their dreams.

Jean's aspiration and Julie's desire to fall meet in an offstage sexual consummation, signaled onstage by the crescendo of the sounds of the reveling peasants. When the couple emerge from Jean's bedroom, it is clear that Jean is in control. Just as Julie had flaunted her superiority before the sexual act, Jean flaunts his now, ruthlessly abusing the younger woman by refusing to be tender and by calling her a whore. Yet any sense of triumph or defeat is neutralized by the couple's awareness of the consequences of their act; the two plan their departure for Switzerland, Jean to start his hotel, Julie to escape her shame.

Julie reappears in traveling clothes, a smudge of dirt on her face, her pet bird in hand. Asserting his masculine strength, Jean refuses to let Julie take the bird along, decapitating it as Julie expresses a brutal death wish for the entire male sex. Recovering from the fantasy that allowed her hope, she urges Jean to seduce her into killing herself. Jean's dream of self-advancement dissipates as Julie, in her willingness to die to atone for the sacrifice of her honor, endorses an aristocratic principle of reputation and personal integrity that the servant cannot understand. Julie's social victory is affirmed when Jean flinches at the sound of the bell announcing the count's return.

In his preface to the play, Strindberg identifies the factors that were responsible for Julie's tragic fate, including her parents' and her fiancé's characters, the mood of the Midsummer Eve, the urgency of the sexually aroused Jean, Julie's "monthly indisposition," chance, and other biological and environmental conditions. Strindberg's analysis of Julie's behavior reflects the extent to which the playwright incorporated into the play the naturalistic philosophy first given literary expression by novelist Émile Zola. As Strindberg himself notes in the preface, however, *Miss Julie* also includes a psychological dimension that implies Julie's complicity in her fate.

Because it articulates the philosophy of naturalistic drama and suggests both the psychological and the expressionistic, Strindberg's preface has become one of the most widely reprinted statements of modern dramatic theory. Similarly, *Miss Julie*, as the dramatic representation of that theory, and as an emotionally and intellectually engaging play as well, has become an acknowledged masterpiece of world drama.

A DREAM PLAY

An example of Strindberg's post-Inferno work, *A Dream Play* replaces the causal structure of the early naturalistic plays with a loosely constructed series of events that approximate the form of a dream. Though seemingly random, spontaneous, and formless, the action of the play is carefully contrived to re-create the unconscious and reveal inner truth. *A Dream Play* is an astonishing foray into expressionistic drama that testifies to Strindberg's quest for a form to accommodate the polyphonic thinking that characterizes his later work.

A Dream Play has a cast of thirty-nine, as well as a sizable number of walk-on performers. Its central character is the supernatural Daughter of Indra, who visits Earth both as an observer and as a participant. As emissary of her father, she is to report back to him on whether human complaint is justified; as a result of her sojourn, she concludes that humankind is to be pitied.

The Daughter of Indra's earthly enterprise first brings her in contact with an imprisoned officer, whom she frees from punishing labor, and then with the officer's family, whom she observes as the mother, preparing for death, saddens her husband by offering a servant the shawl that he once gave her. The Daughter of Indra's preliminary judgment is that humankind is to be pitied, but that love conquers all.

In an alley leading to the opera house, the Daughter of Indra witnesses the disappointments of auditioning opera singers, who tell their troubles to the doorkeeper, who wears the mother's shawl. Roses in hand, the officer awaits Miss Victoria, who never appears. In the alley, there is a locked door with a cloverleaf cutout that presumably shields the mysteries of life, but a court order is needed to open it.

In a lawyer's office, a white-faced divorce attorney, sitting in the stench of crime, prompts the Daughter of Indra's judgment. The office is transformed into a church, where a commencement ceremony, presided over by four deans of the faculties, is in progress. When the lawyer steps forward to receive his laurels, he receives only a crown of thorns. Unable to understand the cries for mercy that surround the lawyer or the tears dropping to the pavement, the Daughter of Indra offers to marry the lawyer to test the redemptive power of love, marriage, and home.

Yet in the next scene, she is a poor, tired housewife, cooking over a hot stove while the baby screams. Announcing that he now has his degree, the lawyer offers to take his wife to Fairhaven, where the world is more pleasant. By mistake, however, they wind up in Foulstrand, a contemporary inferno, to be greeted by the Quarantine Master and an assortment of miserable people. A dragon boat arrives with newlyweds at the helm, but the blissful couple kill themselves. At Fairhaven, strains of a Johann Sebastian Bach toccata and a waltz conflict to ruin the dance, while at a Mediterranean resort, two men shovel coal in the heat, complaining of their misfortune.

Finally, at Fingal's Cave, or Indra's Ear, the Daughter of Indra again encounters the poet whom she first met at Foulstrand, and here she invokes the Kingdom of Heaven and speaks of what she has learned, asking, with the poet, why humankind must be so miserable. Though much time has passed since her descent to Earth, a telescoping now takes place that transports the Daughter of Indra back to the opera house and the cloverleaf stage door. She listens as the deans of the faculties quarrel over whether it should be opened, then watches as it swings ajar to reveal nothing.

The Daughter of Indra returns to the Growing Castle that had appeared on her descent and prepares to return to the ethereal world. As she offers her assessment of the divided nature of humankind, promising to carry the world's lamentations to her father's throne, the Castle bursts into flame, revealing a wall of human faces in despair, and, finally, a chrysanthemum. The Daughter of Indra departs, leaving behind the poet, the one visionary capable of articulating the coexistence of misery and joy that is the story of humankind.

Influenced by Indian religion and Oriental philosophy, Strindberg envisions the world in this play as a mirage, caught in the eternal conflict between spirit and form. In a diary entry made two days before he completed the play, Strindberg equated love with sin, remarking on the paradox that the world (if it exists at all) exists through sin, making life an endless vacillation between "the pleasures of love and the agony of penance." *A Dream Play* remained unproduced for five years after it was published in 1902, finally seeing production during the same year in which *The Ghost Sonata* was published.

THE GHOST SONATA

The Ghost Sonata is one of Strindberg's chamber plays, so named for their intimacy, their lyricism, and their simplicity of theme. Like chamber music, the chamber plays were designed for small audiences, particularly those at Strindberg's Intimate Theater. Like *A Dream Play*, *The Ghost Sonata* is abstract in form, presenting a series of images suggestive of a dream.

The dominant consciousness in the play is a student named Arkenholz, who progresses through the symbolic episodes of the dream until he acquires understanding, at which point the dream ends through his awakening. While he is in the dream, Arkenholz is poet-seeker, possessing exceptional acuity of perception. He is limited, however, by an equally powerful, ambivalently evil old man named Hummel, who guides Arkenholz into a house in which strange and symbolic characters reside. In the deepest room of the house is the Hyacinth Girl, the vision of beauty and love that the student cannot resist.

Arkenholz's mythic quest begins at the facade of the building, where he encounters a milkmaid and Hummel, an old man in a wheelchair who tells him that by sitting through a Richard Wagner opera he will gain entrance to the house. Excited by Arkenholz's fondness for the house, Hummel identifies its inhabitants: the colonel who beats his wife; the marble statue of the colonel's wife, who is now a mummy; the Lady in Black; the dead consul; the decrepit fiancé, who is mad; the caretaker's wife; and, in the Hyacinth Room, the Girl.

Once inside, the student observes the unnatural coterie in the Round Room, where he witnesses Hummel's inhumane treatment of the colonel and hears of a network of sexual relationships as the residents of the house gather for their ritual supper. The student pauses for introductions to the mummy, who comes out of her closet squawking like a parrot, and to the marble statue of her youthful form, while Hummel, who has fathered the woman's child, hangs himself in the closet. Without his guide, Arkenholz continues his journey into the timeless world of the Hyacinth Room, in which the clock that stood prominently on the mantle in the Round Room and strikes to signal the last minutes of the old man's life is replaced by a statue of the Buddha.

The Hyacinth Girl turns out to be an emaciated woman, drained of her strength by a vampire cook who boils the nourishment out of the meat, but the student is awed by her beauty. When she hears that Arkenholz wants to marry her, the Hyacinth Girl reveals the secrets of the house, transforming his vision of innocence and beauty into a lamentation, then a plea for redemption. As the student begins to awaken from his dream, he speaks of what he has learned, reconciling the woe that he has discovered and the innocence in which he had believed.

A "world of intimations," suggestively inviting its readers into its seemingly strange but curiously familiar landscape, *The Ghost Sonata* is a richly evocative vision of guilt and expiation, of innocence and evil, that extends to all humankind. Strindberg claimed that writing the play was a painful experience, that he hardly knew himself what he had written, but that he felt in it the sublime.

OTHER MAJOR WORKS

LONG FICTION: *Från Fjärdingen och Svartbäcken*, 1877; *Röda rummet*, 1879 (*The Red Room*, 1913); *Jäsningstiden*, 1886 (*The Growth of the Soul*, 1914); *Hemsöborna*, 1887 (*The Natives of Hemsö*, 1959); *Tschandala*, in Danish 1889, in Swedish 1897; *I havsbandet*, 1890 (*By the Open Sea*, 1913); *Le Plaidoyer d'un fou*, 1893 in German, 1895 in Swedish (*A Madman's Defense*, 1912, also known as *The Confession of a Fool*); *Inferno*, 1897 (English translation, 1912); *Ensam*, 1903 (*Alone*, 1968); *Götiska rummen*, 1904; *Svarta fanor*, 1907; *Taklagsöl*, 1907; *Syndabocken*, 1907 (*The Scapegoat*, 1967); *Författaren*, 1909.

SHORT FICTION: *Giftas I*, 1884; *Svenska öden och äventyr*, 1882-1892; *Giftas II*, 1886 (*Married*, 1913; also known as *Getting Married*, 1973; includes *Giftas I* and *Giftas II*); *Utopier i verkligheten*, 1885; *Skärkarlsliv*, 1888; *Legender*, 1898 (*Legends*, 1912); *Fagervik och Skamsund*, 1902 (*Fair Haven and Foul Strand*, 1913); *Sagor*, 1903 (*Tales*, 1930); *Historiska miniatyrer*, 1905 (*Historical Miniatures*, 1913).

POETRY: *Dikter och verkligheter*, 1881; *Dikter på vers och prosa*, 1883; *Sömngångarnätter på vakna dagar*, 1884.

NONFICTION: *Gamla Stockholm*, 1880; *Det nya riket*, 1882; *Svenska folket i helg och söcken, krig och fred, hemma och ute eller Ett tusen år av svenska bildningens och sedernas historia*, 1882; *Tjänstekvinnans son: En s äls utvecklingshistoria*, 1886

(4 volumes; *The Son of a Servant: The Story of the Evolution of a Human Being*, 1966, volume 1 only); *Vivisektioner*, 1887; *Blomstermalningar och djurstycken*, 1888; *Bland franska bönder*, 1889; *Antibarbarus*, 1896; *Jardin des plantes*, 1896; *Svensk natur*, 1897; *Världshistoriens mystik*, 1903; *Modersmålets anor*, 1910; *Religiös renässans*, 1910; *Folkstaten*, 1910-1911; *Tal till svenska nationen*, 1910-1911; *Världsspråkens rötter*, 1910; *Oppna brev till Intima Teatern*, 1911-1912 (*Open Letters to the Intimate Theater*, 1959); *Zones of the Spirit: A Book of Thoughts*, 1913.

BIBLIOGRAPHY

Carlson, Harry Gilbert. *Out of "Inferno": Strindberg's Reawakening as an Artist*. Seattle: University of Washington Press, 1996. A study of the change in Strindberg's literary works after his publication of *Inferno*. Bibliography and index.

Ekman, Hans-Göran. *Strindberg and the Five Senses: Studies in Strindberg's Chamber Plays*. Somerset, N.J.: Transaction, 2000. A critical analysis of Strindberg's chamber plays, with particular emphasis on the five senses. Bibliography and index.

Marker, Frederick J., and Christopher Innes, eds. *Modernism in European Drama: Ibsen, Strindberg, Pirandello, Beckett: Essays from Modern Drama*. Buffalo, N.Y.: University of Toronto Press, 1998. A collection of essays from *Modern Drama* published between 1963 and 1994 on modernism in the dramatic works of Strindberg, Henrik Ibsen, Luigi Pirandello, and Samuel Beckett. Bibliography and index.

Martinus, Eivor. *Strindberg and Love*. Charlbury, Oxford, England: Amber Lane Press, 2001. A study of Strindberg's relations with women, including how it manifested in his literary works. Bibliography and index.

Robinson, Michael. *Studies in Strindberg*. Norwich: Norvik Press, 1998. A critical analysis and interpretation of the literary works of Strindberg. Bibliography and index.

Robinson, Michael, and Sven Hakon Rossel, eds. *Expressionism and Modernism: New Approaches to August Strindberg*. Vienna: Edition Praesens,

1999. A collection of papers from the Thirteenth International Strindberg Conference, Linz Austria, October, 1997, and one essay from the Internationale Strindberg-Tage, Vienna, October, 1997, that examine the literary works of Strindberg. Bibliography and index.

Törnqvist, Egil. *Strindberg's "The Ghost Sonata" from Text to Performance*. Amsterdam: Amsterdam University Press, 2000. An in-depth analysis of Strindberg's *The Ghost Sonata*. Bibliography and index.

June Schlueter

HERMANN SUDERMANN

Born: Matziken, East Prussia (now Macikai, Lithuania); September 30, 1857
Died: Berlin, Germany; November 21, 1928

PRINCIPAL DRAMA

Die Ehre, pr., pb. 1889 (*Honor*, 1915)
Sodoms Ende, pr. 1890, pb. 1891 (*A Man and His Picture*, 1903)
Heimat, pr., pb. 1893 (*Magda*, 1895)
Die Schmetterlingsschlacht, pr. 1894, pb. 1895
Das Glück im Winkel, pr. 1895, pb. 1896 (*The Vale of Content*, 1915)
Teja, pr., pb. 1896 (English translation, 1897)
Fritzchen, pr., pb. 1896 (English translation, 1910)
Das ewig Männliche, pr., pb. 1896 (*The Eternal Masculine*, 1910)
Morituri, pr., pb. 1896 (includes *Teja, Fritzchen,* and *Das ewig Männliche*; English translation, 1910)
Johannes, pr., pb. 1898 (*John the Baptist*, 1899)
Die drei Reiherfedern, pr., pb. 1899 (*The Three Heron's Feathers*, 1900)
Johannisfeuer, pr., pb. 1900 (*Fires of St. John*, 1904)
Es lebe das Leben!, pr., pb. 1902 (*The Joy of Living*, 1902)
Der Sturmgeselle Sokrates, pr., pb. 1903
Stein unter Steinen, pr., pb. 1905
Das Blumenboot, pr., pb. 1906
Die Lichtbänder, pr., pb. 1907 (*Streaks of Light*, 1909)
Margot, pr., pb. 1907 (English translation, 1909)

Der letzte Besuch, pr., pb. 1907 (*The Last Visit*, 1909)
Die ferne Prinzessin, pr., pb. 1907 (*The Far-away Princess*, 1909)
Rosen, pr., pb. 1907 (includes *Streaks of Light, Margot, The Last Visit,* and *The Far-away Princess; Roses*, 1909)
Strandkinder, pr. 1909, pb. 1910
Der Bettler von Syrakus, pr., pb. 1911
Der gute Ruf, pr., pb. 1913
Die Lobgesänge des Claudian, pr., pb. 1914
Die Freundin, pr., pb. 1916
Die gutgeschnittene Ecke, pr., pb. 1916
Das höhere Leben, pr., pb. 1916
Die entgötterte Welt: Bilder aus kranker Zeit, pr., pb. 1916 (includes *Die Freundin, Die gutgeschnittene Ecke,* and *Das höhere Leben*)
Regine, pr. 1916
Die Raschoffs, pr., pb. 1919
Heilige Zeit, pb. 1921
Opfer, pb. 1921
Das deutsche Schicksal, pb. 1921 (includes *Heilige Zeit, Opfer,* and *Notruf*)
Wie die Träumenden, pb. 1922
Die Denkmalsweihe, pb. 1923
Dramatische Werke, pb. 1923 (6 volumes)
Der Hasenfellhändler, pb. 1927

OTHER LITERARY FORMS

Hermann Sudermann was known as a novelist and short-story writer as well as a dramatist. Best known among his novels are *Frau Sorge* (1887; *Dame Care,*

1891), *Der Katzensteg* (1889; *Regina*, 1894), *Es war* (1894; *The Undying Past*, 1906), *Das hohe Lied* (1908; *The Song of Songs*, 1909), *Der tolle Professor* (1926; *The Mad Professor*, 1928), and *Die Frau des Steffen Tromholt* (1927; *The Wife of Steffen Tromholt*, 1929). Best known among his stories and collections are *Iolanthes Hochzeit* (1892; *Iolantha's Wedding*, 1918), *Die indische Lilie* (1911; *The Indian Lily*, 1911), and *Litauische Geschichten* (1917; *The Excursion to Tilsit*, 1930). Sudermann also wrote a literary autobiography, *Das Bilderbuch meiner Jugend* (1922; *The Book of My Youth*, 1923).

ACHIEVEMENTS

For many years, the East Prussian Hermann Sudermann successfully competed for the favor of the German theatergoing public with the poet laureate of the age of naturalism, the Silesian Gerhart Hauptmann. Both writers had come to Berlin from the eastern provinces of Germany and had triumphed within a few months of each other in the artistic and political capital of the empire. The innovative and revolutionary Freie Bühne (free stage) performed Hauptmann's first drama, *Vor Sonnenaufgang* (pr., pb. 1889; *Before Dawn*, 1909), in 1889, and followed it with Sudermann's first play, in 1890, after it had premiered at Berlin's Lessing Theater on November 27, 1889. Sudermann's next two plays, *A Man and His Picture* and *Magda*, were enthusiastically received as well. They established him as a favorite Berlin playwright for the decade up to 1902. By then, the Berlin critics, under the leadership of the renowned and despotic Alfred Kerr, had begun to consider Sudermann inferior to the towering genius of Hauptmann.

With his move to Berlin, Sudermann more or less abandoned the form of the novel, which he had previously employed to describe the land and the people of his native East Prussia, and turned his attention primarily to drama, perhaps because it better captured the fast pace of the big city. From the outset, the critics perceived a certain shallowness in his characters and in the world that he depicted in his plays. Entrances and exits occurred altogether too conveniently, characters seemed to lack motivation at times and flip-flopped incomprehensibly. In spite of these

Hermann Sudermann (Hulton Archive by Getty Images)

shortcomings, Sudermann's plays were considered well-made everyday theatrical fare. They seized on the themes and problems of the day, boiled them down into a dramatically effective piece, created admirable roles for stars such as the part of Magda for Eleonora Duse but left most questions unresolved in the end. Such superficiality, some argued, might have been a result of the newness of the environment for Sudermann, since he had entered Berlin as an outsider. Thus, only when he returned to the subject of his East Prussian homeland in the drama *Fires of St. John*, did these critics again perceive the honesty and intensity that distinguished his early prose.

Relatively few of Sudermann's plays are actually situated in Berlin. Nevertheless, the restlessness of that city, the decay of its moral fiber, its replacement of old values by questionable new ones, and the uncertainties of existence for the various classes are themes explored in many of them. Yet Sudermann's affinity with the best-known Berlin naturalists, Arno Holz and Johannes Schlaf, remains only slight because he describes the working-class setting only once, in *Stein unter Steinen* (stone among stones), and never deals with the utter hopelessness and degeneration encountered in Holz and Schlaf's most famous work, *Die Familie Selicke* (1890; the Selicke family). Sudermann's plays are considerably more bourgeois and conservative than the typical naturalist drama, usually ending on an optimistic or, at least, conciliatory note, and permitting the hero or heroine to escape at the last minute from the almost insurmountable obstacles of life. It has been observed that Suderman did not grow with, but rather in opposition to, the metropolis of Berlin and its problems. Parallels are easily drawn between his characters and classes and those that Henrik Ibsen depicted. Sudermann also stands close to the French conversational boulevard theater of such authors as Alexandre Dumas, *fils*, and Victorien Sardou.

BIOGRAPHY

Hermann Sudermann came from a peasant family of Dutch Mennonites who had immigrated to East Prussia because of religious persecution. By the time Sudermann was born, his father had given up farming and was leasing a small brewery on the estate of Matziken. Although his father soon succeeded in buying a somewhat larger brewery in the Lithuanian town of Heydekrug, Sudermann's youth was spent in petit bourgeois circumstances. His parents sent him to the middle school in the town of Elbing, but he did not remain there for long. On his return to Heydekrug, he became a drugstore apprentice for a brief time, until a knee ailment forced him to quit his apprenticeship. He was then allowed to attend the gymnasium (high school) in Tilsit. After graduation, he gained his father's permission to study at the University of Königsberg. A stipend provided by distant relatives living in Russia contributed to his support. In 1877, he transferred to the University of Berlin, carrying some drama scripts tucked away in his luggage. Left by this time without any support from home, he tried to improve his financial state by submitting his poetry to some literary journals in that city. One of the editors took pity on him and engaged him as a tutor for his children. Soon, Sudermann accepted a second tu-

toring post at the home of an influential Berlin banker. The wealth of the Berlin upper classes, which so starkly contrasted with his own poverty, soon disgusted him, and he quit his job. Later, he drew on this experience for the rather biting portrayals of the leisure class in *A Man and His Picture* and *Das Blumenboot* (the flowerboat). In 1882, Sudermann finally landed a job as editor at the liberal magazine *Der Reichsfreund*, where he also published his first short stories. In 1887, he gained wider recognition with his novel *Dame Care*, which was hailed by the critics as one of the first naturalistic works in the genre known as *Heimatkunst* (native art).

With the premiere of *Honor*, Sudermann became famous virtually overnight. He had escaped poverty and, in 1891, was able to marry the widow Clara Lauckner, a writer in her own right. They had a daughter and also reared two children from Mrs. Lauckner's first marriage. Sudermann wrote a considerable number of plays during the next decade, initially clinging to the Berlin setting, but soon widening his scope to include subjects as far-reaching as folk myths in *The Three Heron's Feathers*, biblical themes in *John the Baptist*, historical lore in *Teja*, and his native East Prussia in *Fires of St. John* as well as in his third drama, *Magda*.

In 1902, Sudermann published a small critique of his own about Berlin's rampant theater criticism, entitled *Die Verrohung in der Theaterkritik* (brutalization in theater criticism). In it, he documented recent excesses among the local theater critics and their writings. The critics reacted predictably: Sudermann experienced an ever-growing harshness in their treatment of him, which led to his eventual decline in popularity on the stages of the capital as well as elsewhere; even the relatively uncontroversial play *Stein unter Steinen* provoked a theater scandal in 1905. Yet Sudermann's withdrawal from the stage did not signal an end to his writing of drama. World War I brought him into the limelight once again with the trilogy *Die entgötterte Welt*, which bore the subtitle *Bilder aus kranker Zeit* (pictures from a sick time), and with *Die Raschoffs* (the Raschoff family).

In 1924, Sudermann's wife died and he withdrew to his small castle outside Berlin, where he continued to write, having returned to the genre of the novel in his last years. The two novels of note from this period are *The Mad Professor* and *The Wife of Steffen Tromholt*. Sudermann's nobility of mind, his integrity, and his ability to cultivate friendships became manifest in his last will and testament, which bequeathed his estate to a foundation for needy actors.

ANALYSIS

"His worth lies in his character. He is an achievement in himself, clear and uniform in his merits as well as in his deficiencies, not everywhere of equal value, but always honest." This admission comes from Kurt Busse, Hermann Sudermann's most ardent admirer, in his often defensive analysis of the author and his work. It appeared in 1927, about a year before Sudermann's death. Busse's attempt at vindication of an author who had been undervalued and mistreated by the critics ever since his *Die Verrohung in der Theaterkritik* did not succeed, and the novelist and playwright remained virtually forgotten in Germany after World War II. Such oblivion is not entirely deserved. Circumstances made Sudermann a political liability after the end of the Nazi era. His perennial themes were *Heimat* (homeland), *Ehre* (honor), *Treue* (faithfulness), *Blut und Familien-bande* (blood and family ties), and *Sittlichkeit* (morality), all of which had become suspect through their exploitation by the Nazis.

There have been some signs of at least a partial rediscovery of Sudermann as a playwright. After he had been absent from the German theater for many years, his *Der Sturmgeselle Sokrates* (storm companion Socrates) was staged in 1981, and a collection of modern essays on the artist and his work appeared in 1980. Perhaps his views were more acceptable in the prosperous West Germany of the 1980's. His early obsolescence was hastened because he never fully incorporated the new currents of naturalism into his works. Such naturalistic catchwords as "environment" and "heredity" played important parts in his early plays, yet Sudermann's characters usually eluded the dire consequences of these two factors, overcoming the misery for which they seemed initially destined. Thus, his plays essentially remained

attached to the optimism of the middle classes, to the ideas of political liberalism, and to the philosophy of the eighteenth century Königsberg philosopher Immanuel Kant. Although he absorbed the intellectual currents of his time only superficially, it is probably exaggerated to call him simply a *Routinier* (slick writer), as some critics have done.

Busse calls Sudermann the late heir of the French sociocritical salon drama, whose principal representatives were the older and the younger Dumas and Sardou. Their dramas had inspired German playwrights after the middle of the nineteenth century and had thus rejuvenated German bourgeois drama without, however, instilling in it the same sociocritical fervor of its French models. The German copies remained somewhat unaggressive and complacent, reflecting the restoration mood after the failure of the Revolution of 1848. After Germany's victory in the Franco-Prussian War in 1871, historical plays and tragedies of major proportions experienced great popularity in the newly founded nation, relegating the bourgeois drama almost entirely to the realm of comedy and farce. During this era of national euphoria, the plays of Henrik Ibsen, and, later, August Strindberg, made only little impact in Germany and were not fully comprehended even by the two German theater revolutionaries of 1889, Hauptmann and Sudermann. Busse concedes that Sudermann "learned from Ibsen, he received an impetus from the characters and problems in Ibsen's works, but he remained untouched by Ibsen's technique and therefore by the new intellectual sphere, into which Ibsen had placed his characters." He observes further that the rift in Ibsen's drama, which fatefully divides the old and the new time, is not present in that of Sudermann. The German playwright certainly juxtaposed old and new times, old and new generations, old and new morality, but he lacked the scope and depth displayed in Ibsen's *Peer Gynt* (1867; English translation, 1892), for example. Sudermann depicted, accused, and educated; his work was reform rather than confession.

Reform, especially political reform, or rather the lack of it, was very much a current topic in Germany when Sudermann began his career. The *Sozialisten-gesetze* (laws dissolving the Socialist Party) which had been passed in 1878, are reflected in his work and significantly influenced his attitudes. Indeed, Sudermann's alert social conscience and his biting social criticism are as characteristic of his drama as his ability to create vivid and genuine dialogue and a naturalistic milieu. If one examines the psychological presuppositions in Sudermann's plays, on the other hand, one will find them as cheap as the conflicts are banal.

HONOR

Sudermann's plays were written with the average theater audience in mind, focusing on an engaging story rather than on characterization; his stories were often superior to those of Hauptmann, who remained the master of characterization. Many of Sudermann's plots depend on a contrast between different milieus, and such a contrast is central to his first work, *Honor.* The manufacturer Mühlingk lives with his wife and their two children, Kurt and Lenore, in the mansion on Mühlingk's factory grounds, while the family of the old and crippled Heineke dwells in a shabby cottage on the other end of the large estate. Years ago, Heineke was seriously injured in an accident caused by a coach leaving a ball at the mansion. In order to placate his own conscience and avoid any further litigation, Mühlingk has provided Heineke and his family with free lodging at the cottage and has also seen to the education of Heineke's son Robert.

Robert has just returned home from India, where he has been Mühlingk's factory representative for the past ten years. While abroad, he had longed for his *Heimat* (homeland) and his family. Now that he is back, however, it becomes obvious that he no longer fits. A different environment abroad and a new circle of friends have allowed him to grow beyond the narrow confines at home. He has developed a new code of honor that his destitute parents and younger sisters could never afford themselves. He can be proud of his achievements, but he must also remember his place in this class-conscious society. Now, however, he has the disconcerting suspicion that his beloved younger sister Alma, in whom he has put all of his hope, has apparently been compromised by Mühlingk's son Kurt, whom she has repeatedly met at a secret hideaway. The couple has also been observed at a dance

by Robert's wealthy friend Count Trast-Saarburg, who has traveled home from India with Robert. As Robert's suspicion becomes a certainty, he demands satisfaction from Kurt. Kurt's father, who wants to avoid a scandal, has a different sort of satisfaction in mind. He demands that the Heinekes vacate their cottage and thereby remove the temptation for his son. In turn, he will pay them forty thousand marks for their silence.

When Robert finds out that his family's honor has been sold in this manner, he plans to take his family with him to India, in order to start a new life there, but not before he has gained satisfaction. His friend Trast-Saarburg dissuades him from his plans. He also convinces Robert that honor is part of the inner man and cannot be stolen from him by a scoundrel. Trast-Saarburg admonishes Robert not to despise his family for their perceived lack of honor. The Mühlingks have after all given them back the only honor useful in their circumstances—namely, sufficient capital to make them respectable. At this moment Lenore, Mühlingk's daughter, appears. She has not been corrupted by her family's wealth, and she has always loved Robert, with whom she had grown up. Trast-Saarburg has noticed their fondness for each other, while Robert does not even dare to admit his love for Lenore to himself. Trast-Saarburg will help the relationship to blossom by lending Robert enough money to repay the Mühlingks the amount they paid to bribe his parents. Lenore, who loathes her family's practice of righting every wrong with money, openly declares her admiration and love for Robert. She will become his wife, and Robert, in turn, will become the new partner in Trast-Saarburg's vast business and, eventually, his heir.

After the premiere of *Honor,* Sudermann was hailed as the "rightful heir to young Schiller," presumably the Friedrich Schiller of *Kabale und Liebe* (pr., pb. 1784; *Cabal and Love,* 1795). He had put his finger on the pulse of the times and had accentuated the social problems welling up in industrial Berlin, particularly those problems arising from the juxtaposition of extreme leisure and wealth with abject poverty. He had also added exactly the right amount of naturalism through his infusion of inescapable family bonds and constricting milieu; but not so much naturalism as to spoil the experience for the middle- and upper-class playgoers who constituted the theater audience.

Honor already displayed all the strengths and weaknesses of Sudermann. The story is well conceived and engaging but ultimately rather banal. The conflicts of his characters often seem concocted. Robert's concern about his sister's honor, for example, remains simply unbelievable for a man who has seen so much of the world and carried so many responsibilities. This is especially true in that nothing dishonorable seems to have happened between her and Kurt. Even audiences of Sudermann's time must have questioned Robert's concern. Moreover, character development remains sketchy. The best example is Count Trast-Saarburg, who is Sudermann's mouthpiece and a character of some scope. He remains noble but hollow in his platitudes; his statement that honor should be replaced by duty for decent men exemplifies Sudermann's middle-class morality. The many asides of the characters throughout the work do not match the otherwise naturalistic setting. This device, which betrays a certain ineptness on the part of the budding playwright, is not so prominent in his later works. Sudermann's reliance on convenient but implausible entrances and exits, on the other hand, was a flaw that would persist throughout most of his works. In *Honor*, it is the timely but unmotivated appearance of Lenore toward the end of the last act that is especially disturbing. Busse remarks that *Honor* became fateful for the author in two respects: It was the work that had made him famous, and it remained the one by which critics continued to judge him, even after he had written better plays.

A MAN AND HIS PICTURE

A Man and His Picture, Sudermann's second drama, again employs the contrast between classes. The first and the fourth acts are situated in the mansion of the wealthy stockbroker Barczinowski, and the second and third acts, at the petit bourgeois home of the dairy inspector Janikow. The play is again set in Berlin. Honor has been replaced by morality as a theme. Barczinowski's wife, Adah, a forerunner of Frank Wedekind's Lulu in her consumption of able-bodied men, has a love affair with Janikow's son, the

painter Willy. Willy's claim to fame is the painting *The End of Sodom*, which hangs in Barczinowski's house. Decadence and *fin de siècle* attitudes permeate the characters in Frau Adah's salon. She recognizes that she must grant Willy more freedom in order to bind him ever closer to herself. She thus intends to have him marry her young niece Kitty, but Willy remains reluctant. He wants to remove himself from Adah's sphere of decadence, which has robbed him of his strength and artistic talent.

He has another reason for this change: He has discovered the purity of Klärchen Fröhlich (the name Klärchen is derived from Clara, which indicates purity). Klärchen is the illegitimate child of Willy's professor at the academy, entrusted to Willy by the professor shortly before his death. Klärchen has now blossomed into womanhood, and Willy is attracted by her beauty and her innocence, but his eventual seduction of her drives her to suicide. Her fiancé, Kramer, wants to avenge her, but he is thwarted. Willy dies, even though Kramer's attack never takes place.

A Man and His Picture is Sudermann's first homage to the perennial turn-of-the-century German theme of the artist versus society. In this case, the artist shows willing complicity in letting himself be corrupted by a society that is all too tempting. Sudermann's condemnation of the upper class has intensified, compared to his first play. The wealthy have now become parasites of society, as exemplified by Barczinowski's profession: He is a manipulator of wealth, while Mühlingk had been the manufacturer of a still tangible good. Sudermann characterizes Barczinowski as "the typical stockbroker, but without the Jewish mask." Adah is described as a cold and vain woman who has surrounded herself with decadent art that "revels in the flesh." Willy has perfectly sensed the atmosphere of her salon when he quotes Johann Wolfgang von Goethe's *Faust* (1808, 1833) in describing it: "*Und im Genuss verschmacht' ich nach Begierde*" (And in pleasure I long for desire).

As the protagonist, Willy has lost the moral fiber that Robert Heineke still possessed, because he has allowed himself to be absorbed into this decadence. Thus, the society with which he is in conflict is clearly represented by the household of his father and mother, while Robert Heineke had at least found himself in a double conflict: with the house of his parents but also, and much more important, with that of the Mühlingks. Willy again revealed Sudermann's weakness in drawing convincing characters. One contemporary German critic referred to him as a "washrag," vaguely reminiscent of Osvald Alving from Ibsen's *Gengangere* (1881; *Ghosts*, 1885) in his inability to work. Others were incredulous that three women (Adah, Kitty, and Klärchen) desire this milksop, who does not even possess enough courage to kill himself in the end, thus forcing the playwright "to invoke a most improbable, but fortunately fatal, hemorrhage," according to scholar Otto Heller.

The portrayals of Adah and her niece Kitty Tattenberg are somewhat more successful, while that of Klärchen must be termed infelicitous. Kurt Busse argued that Sudermann's ability to draw lifelike characters had improved when compared with *Honor*. He noted that the figures this time are neither altogether good nor altogether evil, that they are, however, "shallow people without a solid core." He also observed that Sudermann had paid a greater homage to naturalism this time, since the milieu is the driving influence on all the characters. Asides, as well as contrived exits and entrances, still mar the otherwise naturalistic setting of *A Man and His Picture*. The exaggerations in characterization, on the other hand, may indicate that Sudermann had a satire in mind, but that he did not always succeed in distancing himself sufficiently from his subject.

DAS BLUMENBOOT

In *Das Blumenboot*, immorality has been replaced by amorality, suggesting that an idle brain is the devil's workshop. The play lacks the engaging plot of many of Sudermann's other dramas; it is instead cumbersome and confusing. The theme, that love does not exist within marriage and that longing kills without marriage, is expounded in a rather trivial manner. The idle rich are no longer held up to scorn, but rather to ridicule.

THE JOY OF LIVING

The circle of plays about the Berlin upper classes includes one of Sudermann's masterpieces, *The Joy of Living*. It depicts a rather stereotypical love trian-

gle, but it does so with a mature understanding and compassion for its characters, who are drawn more believably than most of the playwright's others. The play's topic is morality, and beyond that, renunciation, sacrifice, and human decency. Baron Richard Völkerlingk, a young nobleman, rich and talented but without any goals in life, has married a beautiful but hollow and gossipy woman. Their relationship is dead from the beginning. He finds the ideal woman, who can restore his faith in himself and give him goals and tasks for his empty existence. Beate, however, is the wife of his best friend, Count von Kellinghausen. Incapable of living with their lie and convinced that great accomplishments, if they are to be achieved, need total honesty, they renounce their love. In friendship, they work together to support her husband's political career. For fifteen years they live next to each other, up to the point when she urges Völkerlingk to continue the political work of her husband (who has retired) as the conservative candidate in his district. To prevent his victory, the opposition candidate has unearthed some long forgotten love letters. "I live because I am dead": These words, repeated twice in the play, are also Beate's last words as she feigns a heart attack while actually having poisoned herself. Her death opens the door for Völkerlingk's unencumbered political career. The children from the two marriages will marry, fulfilling what was not granted to their parents.

MAGDA

In his third play, *Magda*, Sudermann shifted the setting from Berlin to a provincial capital, presumably somewhere in East Prussia. Magda is a younger version of Claire Zachanassian from Friedrich Dürrenmatt's *Der Besuch der alten Dame* (1956; *The Visit*, 1958). Disgraced by bearing an illegitimate child, conceived by a friend of the family, she was driven out. Now she has returned home after having risen far above her domestic and small-town environment. Like Robert Heineke in *Honor*, she wants to find her way back into the family, and like Robert, she fails because she has liberated herself from its strictures. The German title *Heimat* (homeland) must be interpreted ironically, since this *Heimat* does not provide comfort and shelter any longer.

In some ways, *Magda* seems to represent a settling of accounts for the author: Sudermann's own provincial past, the narrow-mindedness of his father and his frustrating struggle to attain fame as an artist, loom behind the play. The theme of the woman who breaks out of the mold into which marriage, family, or even society have wanted to press her, occurs in a number of Sudermann's works. Contemporary critics noted, however, that *Magda* was not simply a play about the emancipation of women; rather, in *Magda*, Sudermann again took up the topic of Honor, this time the honor of the artist and the brilliant prodigal daughter, who makes an impassioned plea for wanting "to live her own life." *Magda*'s antagonist, the pastor Heffterdingk, who had wanted to marry Magda when she was a young girl, seems to betray the author's chief effort within the play. Thus *Magda* revealed to its time the contrast between provincial life and the larger world, the conflict between the quiet virtues of home and the brilliant temptations of art, the difference between fulfilling one's own personality and following the narrow path of middle-class morality and duty. In *Magda*, the heroine survives. Her father, the incarnation of petit bougeois virtue, perishes, and the pastor is thrown back into his narrow existence. Thus, Sudermann reversed the fate that the artist Willy had suffered in *A Man and His Picture*. Finally, it is notable that, as Dürrenmatt's *The Visit* would do fifty years later, *Magda* provided one of the most impressive leading roles for the great actresses of its age. Eleanora Duse, for example, had her own English translation fashioned for her American performance.

DER STURMGESELLE SOKRATES

The mendacity of the age and its pretense at democracy under Emperor Wilhelm II are the themes of Sudermann's only political satire, *Der Sturmgeselle Sokrates*. The dentist Albert Hartmeyer is known as "Socrates" in the secret society of "Storm Companions." In the middle of the 1870's, somewhere in East Prussia, this group of leftover fighters from the Revolution of 1848 tries to preserve its democratic ideals, which have become as dusty as the flags in their meeting room. "What would we be today, if we were not uncompromising?" Hartmeyer proudly announces to his companions. In his private life, however, this dyed-in-the-wool fighter for democracy does not tolerate any democratic notions. While he composes poems to the glory of German womanhood, his wife, whom he treats like a scullery maid, must ask him for the key to the wine cellar, safely tucked away in his vest pocket. Her former life as a waitress leads Hartmeyer to scorn and despise her. In his profession, Hartmeyer is also hopelessly outdated. His older son, Fritz, a dentist as well, has taken over almost all of Hartmeyer's former patients with his modern and painless treatments. The younger son, Reinhold, has just returned from the university, where he did not, as his father had expected, join the venerated national-democratic fraternity of his father, but rather an exclusive student corps espousing the good life without the fight for democracy. It is Hartmeyer's most ardent wish that both sons should now join the Storm Companions. At their planned initiation, the old Baron von Laucken-Neuhof, the past leader of the Storm Companions and Sudermann's mouthpiece, unmasks the rhetoric of the society as empty talk and its ideals as dead and buried. In the end, even the "uncompromising" Hartmeyer sells out his ideals, as he accepts a medal given him in recognition for dental treatment that Fritz has administered to a nobleman's favorite hound.

Almost prophetic are the statements by Siegfried, the son of the fellow Storm Companion and Rabbi Dr. Markuse, who warns his father,

> With one foot you are still in the old ghetto and you feel that you must be thankful because they let you out. I can already smell the air of a new ghetto, into which they want to lock us, because they fear us. . . . This ghetto will have no walls and fences, it will be nothing more than a cold smile, a polite refusal, an unanswered visit.

Der Sturmgeselle Sokrates is relevant even today in its satiric reflection on an age that mirrors the all-too-human traits of modern German society. Overtly, it is a satire about misguided nationalism, the follies of democracy, and the lip service rendered to hollow ideals. The drama was singularly unsuccessful at its first performance, since it ridiculed the venerated

German revolutionaries of 1848 by depicting them as idiots and hypocrites. Critics and audiences alike seemed to have overlooked, however, the fact that Sudermann's satire was aimed more bitingly at the German character of his time—the Bismarck era and those saber-rattling days before World War I—than at revolutionaries of an age long passed. Moreover, there are some striking parallels between the Storm Companions and the disappointed reformers of the late twentieth century, as was evident when the play was revived on the German stage in 1981. The Storm Companions are petty, humorless, stodgy, malicious, and arrogant men who have lost sight of the times and events around them. It is only fitting, therefore, that Sudermann's mouthpiece, the old Baron von Laucken-Neuhof, should warn Hartmeyer about his isolation from the rest of the world; he plans to send him Miguel de Cervantes's *El ingenioso hidalgo don Quixote de la Mancha* (1605, 1615; *The History of the Valorous and White Knight-Errant, Don Quixote of the Mancha*, 1612-1620; better known as *Don Quixote de la Mancha*) to console him in his loneliness. Sudermann's satire about generational conflict drawn along political lines, in which old liberals have turned conservative and the children cling to the establishment, is a fitting counterpiece to Carl Zuckmayer's *Der Hauptmann von Köpenick* (1931; *The Captain of Köpenick*, 1932).

FIRES OF ST. JOHN

In *Magda*, *The Vale of Content*, and *Der Sturmgeselle Sokrates*, Sudermann had returned for his settings to the provinces away from Berlin. All three describe life in provincial towns, two in East Prussia, one in Northern Germany. In *Fires of St. John*, the author chose a setting even more similar to the place of his birth. It is the estate of the Vogelreuters in Prussian Lithuania. The time is the end of the 1880's. Vogelreuter, a man of middle-class origin, lacks the trappings of the Prussian Junkers but has adopted their way of thinking. He and he alone will give the orders on the estate, and he has decided that his daughter Trude shall marry his nephew Georg von Hartwig. Many years earlier, the family had adopted a foundling Marikke, who is called *Heimchen* (the homebody) by everyone, and who is the daughter of

Weszkalnene, a sluttish figure who still roams the countryside and tries to confront her child from time to time, mainly in order to obtain money from the family. Heimchen is a *Notstandskind* (a child brought to them during a famine), and she is treated by them as both servant and daughter. She knows that she must be grateful, and she works hard to repay the Vogelreuters. At present, she spends every free hour in Königsberg in order to furnish a new house for Trude and Georg, who are to be married soon. During her last stay in town, she has found among Georg's belongings a blue notebook with love poems that are addressed to her; Georg had secretly written them about four years earlier. She confronts him with her knowledge, and both confess their love for each other, as the fires of St. John are burning everywhere in the land (this is the night when forbidden desires can well up in the heart), but just for one brief moment, because Marikke must accept the marriage proposal from the village's assistant pastor so that no disgrace will befall the house of Vogelreuter.

Fires of St. John has been lauded as Sudermann's best drama by some, perhaps because of its moving portrayal of the author's Lithuanian homeland and the excellent development of its major characters, Vogelreuter, Marikke, and Georg. Sudermann finally perfected his art of portraiture in the East Prussian "Krautjunker" or country squire Vogelreuter, described by critic Otto Heller as "a puzzling mixture of thick-headedness and jovial humor, generosity and crude bigotry, caste conceit and patriotic devotion, materialism and staunch belief in ideals." With Marikke, the author drew his most naturalistic portrait. Heredity and environment are the two major factors that determine her character. The environment of Vogelreuter's house has "domesticated" her, but her mother's wild and untamed nature, her desire to roam, always seem to seethe in Marikke just below the surface. While the old Lithuanian Weszkalnene steals from the barns of the peasants, Marikke, her daughter, steals from Trude's happiness because she also cannot control her desire. "Can it be against nature that a child longs for its mother?" she asks Georg. Everyone in Vogelreuter's house has acted as if Weszkalnene were not Marikke's mother, as if Marikke were one of them. Yet the truth will out, and Sudermann uses the example of a Lithuanian folk song, which Marikke has heard only once and yet which she remembers word for word, to illustrate the point of heritage. Uncontrollable forces from within drive Marikke toward ruin, and the counterforces of her adoptive family are barely strong enough to prevent the worst. No blood flows in *Fires of St. John*, yet two lives are consumed in sacrifice to the ruling power of law and morality. Georg von Hartwig stands between Vogelreuter and Marikke. He, too, is a *Notstandskind*, having been taken in by the Vogelreuters as well. In contrast to Marikke, however, he will inherit the estate through his family relationship and through his marriage to Trude. Reared to become master of the house, he secretly longs for freedom from entrapment—a freedom that only Marikke can give him. The relationship between Marikke, Georg, and Trude is somewhat similar to that of Adah, Willy, and Klärchen in *A Man and His Picture*. Trude, however, is a distinct improvement over Klärchen. Despite her youth and innocence, she possesses enough strength to remain an equal in the love triangle.

With *Fires of St. John*, Sudermann had rendered character portrayals on a par with those of Hauptmann. Curiously enough, this improvement was bought at the expense of the tidy plot for which Sudermann was otherwise known. In particular, Georg's long monologue about the fires of St. John, in which he lectures on the spark of heathenism in all people and on that burning desire that must be fulfilled to make existence bearable again, is ill conceived; it is doubtful that the drama gains in probability from the simultaneous kindling of the fires of St. John and the love of Georg and Marikke. In this instance, Sudermann may have succumbed to his love for symbolism, but this excess is balanced in *Fires of St. John* by a strict adherence to the unities of classical drama: The action is confined to one location and takes place within twenty-four hours. Classical restraint also dominates its message; Sudermann's usual praise of individualism and self-fulfillment has been replaced by the approbation of social authority, and the insubordination of the individual is rebuked.

OTHER MAJOR WORKS

LONG FICTION: *Frau Sorge*, 1887 (*Dame Care*, 1891); *Der Katzensteg*, 1889 (*Regina*, 1894); *Es war*, 1894 (*The Undying Past*, 1906); *Das hohe Lied*, 1908 (*The Song of Songs*, 1909); *Der tolle Professor*, 1926 (*The Mad Professor*, 1928); *Die Frau des Steffen Tromholt*, 1927 (*The Wife of Steffen Tromholt*, 1929); *Purzelchen*, 1928 (*The Dance of Youth*, 1930).

SHORT FICTION: *Im Zwielicht: Zwanglose Geschichten*, 1887; *Iolanthes Hochzeit*, 1892 (*Iolantha's Wedding*, 1918); *Die indische Lilie*, 1911 (*The Indian Lily*, 1911); *Litauische Geschichten*, 1917 (*The Excursion to Tilsit*, 1930).

NONFICTION: *Die Verrohung in der Theaterkritik*, 1902; *Das Bilderbuch meiner Jugend*, 1922 (*The Book of My Youth*, 1923).

MISCELLANEOUS: *Romane und Novellen*, 1919 (6 volumes).

BIBLIOGRAPHY

Friesen, Lauren. "Dramatic Arts and Mennonite Culture." *Melus* 21, no. 3 (Fall, 1996): 107-124. In her essay about Mennonite plays, Friesen examines the role played by Sudermann, a Mennonite.

Leydecker, Karl. *Marriage and Divorce in the Plays of Hermann Sudermann*. New York: Peter Lang, 1996. Leydecker analyzes the concepts of marriage and divorce as they appear in the plays of Sudermann. Bibliography.

Matulis, Anatole C. *Lithuanian Culture in Modern German Prose Literature: Hermann Sudermann, Ernest Wiechert, Agnes Miegel*. Lafayette, Ind.: Purdue University, 1966. This study of the Lithuanian culture's presence in German literature focuses on prose, but it sheds light on Sudermann's plays as well. Bibliography.

Stroinigg, Cordelia E. *Sudermann's "Frau Sorge": Jugendstil, Archetype, Fairy Tale*. New York: Peter Lang, 1995. Although this work deals primarily with *Dame Care*, one of Sudermann's novels, it discusses the naturalism to be found in his plays. Bibliography and index.

Klaus D. Hanson

ALEXANDER SUKHOVO-KOBYLIN

Born: Moscow, Russia; September 17, 1817
Died: Beaulieu, France; March 11, 1903

PRINCIPAL DRAMA

Svadba Krechinskogo, pr. 1855, pb. 1856
    (*Krechinsky's Wedding*, 1961)
Delo, pb. 1861, censored version pr. 1882 as
    Otzhitoye vremya (*The Case*, 1969)
Smert Tarelkina, pb. 1869, censored version pr.
    1900 (*The Death of Tarelkin*, 1969)
Trilogiya, pb. 1869, censored version pr. 1901
    (includes *Krechinsky's Wedding*, *The Case*, and
    The Death of Tarelkin; *The Trilogy of Alexander
    Sukhovo-Kobylin*, 1969)

OTHER LITERARY FORMS

Alexander Sukhovo-Kobylin is best known for his
drama.

ACHIEVEMENTS

Alexander Sukhovo-Kobylin can be considered
one of the greatest Russian dramatists of the nineteenth century and is generally ranked with such lu-
minaries of the theater as Nikolai Gogol, Alexander
Griboyedov, and Alexander Ostrovsky. His three
plays, which treat related events, constitute the sum
of his literary output. They are distinguished for their
sharp delineation of character, their dynamic plots,
and their witty, racy style. As with his predecessor
Griboyedov, many lines from Sukhovo-Kobylin's
plays have become aphorisms in modern Russian.

Sukhovo-Kobylin was strongly influenced by
Gogol, with whom he was in fact acquainted, and his
buffoonery and the names of his characters, particularly in *The Death of Tarelkin*, are reminiscent of
Gogol's writing. The other great influence on his
work was that of the French theater. He visited
France frequently and was friends with a number of
French actors and actresses, as well as with Alexandre Dumas, *fils*. Sukhovo-Kobylin was particularly
drawn to the *pièce bien faite* (the "well-made play"),
a style of comedy characterized by an intricate plot

based on an intrigue, which was brought to perfection
by such writers as the popular Eugène Scribe, the
younger Dumas, Émile Augier, and Victorien Sardou.
He also frequented the small boulevard theaters of
Paris and was exposed to the rapid onstage character
transformations of the great comics Marie Bouffe and
Pierre Levassor. The impact of the boulevard theater
is especially marked in *The Death of Tarelkin*.

In his introduction to the English translation of
Sukhovo-Kobylin's plays, *The Trilogy of Alexander
Sukhovo-Kobylin*, Harold B. Segel notes that the standard subjects for French comedies of manners during the period when Sukhovo-Kobylin was writing
the first part of the trilogy were related to money.
Gambling, swindling, speculation, and the impecunious nobleman who wanted to make a match with
an heiress were the most common themes. Scribe's
literary heirs combined the structure of the well-
made play with social comedy in plays that aptly described the situation prevailing in France at the time
of the Second Empire. Like his French counterparts,
Sukhovo-Kobylin united the well-made play with social comedy, satirizing the socially ambitious nou-
veaux riche from the provinces. His adroitness at
blending the traditions of the French with the Absurd
elements of Gogol and applying the result to contemporary social conditions is a mark of his mastery as a
playwright.

BIOGRAPHY

Alexander Vasilievich Sukhovo-Kobylin was born
in Moscow, Russia, on an estate belonging to his family, on September 17, 1817. His father, Vasily, was a
colonel who had fought in the War of 1812 and was a
well-read and a religious man. His mother, Marya,
from the aristocratic Shepelev family, turned her
Moscow home into a salon to which scholars, artists,
and writers were drawn. She was a cultivated woman
who was particularly interested in French philosophical literature, some of which she translated into Russian. All of her children achieved at least a modest
degree of success; Alexander's older sister Elizaveta

was a well-known author in the later 1800's (writing under the pen name of Evgeniya Tur), and his younger sister was a landscape painter of note.

Sukhovo-Kobylin excelled in philosophical studies at Moscow University, obtaining a gold medal for excellence in 1838. He was especially interested in the study of Georg Wilhelm Friedrich Hegel, but he dropped his preoccupation with philosophy when he plunged into society life during the late 1830's and early 1840's. While on a visit to Paris, Sukhovo-Kobylin met Louise Simon-Dimanche and brought her back to Russia as his mistress. His subsequent passion for Countess Naryshkina altered his relationship with Louise, but before she was able to return to France, she was found brutally murdered on November 9, 1850. It was this murder and Sukhovo-Kobylin's resultant involvement in the legal machinations of the case that provided him with the impetus to write his three great plays.

Although there were no signs of violence at Simon-Dimanche's apartment, blood was found on the staircase of the private quarters of the house that Sukhovo-Kobylin shared with his parents, and he was arrested. Four of his house serfs, who had originally claimed to know nothing about the crime, confessed that it was they who had murdered her and cited her difficult personality as the reason for their action, but they retracted this statement after their conviction. According to Nina Brodiansky in a 1946 essay on Sukhovo-Kobylin, Efim Egorov, who was Simon-Dimanche's coachman and the principal culprit in the affair, claimed that his confession had been obtained by police torture and by a bribe tendered by Sukhovo-Kobylin himself. Sukhovo-Kobylin was arrested for a second time in 1854 and was imprisoned for four months. As a result of family appeals and petitions to the grand duchess and to the new empress, the latter herself intervened. Sukhovo-Kobylin was acquitted of the crime, although many considered him guilty. Because his private papers were almost entirely destroyed in a fire on his estate in 1899, the details will always remain a mystery, and controversy has continued to surround the case.

Sukhovo-Kobylin's life drastically changed as a result of the murder and the subsequent interminable

investigation and harassment, and he withdrew from society to devote himself again to the study of philosophy. His experiences became the material from which he wrote his three plays. In them, he expressed his bitter vision of an evil and corrupt bureaucracy and his belief that an accident of fate can condemn the good while the evil triumph, a dark view of life reminiscent of Gogol.

Sukhovo-Kobylin was married twice, both times to foreigners. His later life was marked by financial difficulties resulting from his having given enormous sums as bribes to secure his freedom. He died in Beaulieu on the French Riviera in 1903 at the age of eighty-five, having finally tasted international recognition when *The Death of Tarelkin* was performed in French in Paris in 1902.

ANALYSIS

The importance of Alexander Sukhovo-Kobylin is twofold. His genius for blending disparate components of the well-made play with Gogolian characters and stylistic elements, puppet theater, and techniques of the French boulevard theaters enabled him to write plays unique not only for their time and place but also in European theater generally. They are modern even today. Second, Sukhovo-Kobylin, by coupling absurd plot and stylistic elements with the depiction of evil, causes the audience to see life as a nightmare in which chance plays a major role, a vision not so far, as Segel observes, from the haunting realm of Franz Kafka. In his depiction of the virtuous man victimized by the machinery of a corrupt state, and in his conception of corruption as essentially meaningless and absurd (as in *The Death of Tarelkin*), Sukhovo-Kobylin anticipates the banality and evil of twentieth century totalitarian systems. Thus, he was a philosophical forerunner as well as a theatrical one.

KRECHINSKY'S WEDDING

Krechinsky's Wedding, written in 1854 and first performed in 1855, is the first play of the trilogy that constitutes Sukhovo-Kobylin's entire œuvre. In this play, the author draws on the French *comédies-vaudevilles* (vaudeville comedies), with which he had become familiar in Paris, as well as on native Russian traditions. The impact of Gogol's *Revizor* (pr., pb.

1836; *The Inspector General*, 1836), with its satire and buffoonery, is particularly marked. There is also a resemblance to Griboyedov's *Gore ot uma* (wr. 1824, uncensored pr. 1831, censored pb. 1833, uncensored pb. 1861; *The Mischief of Being Clever*, 1857) in the plot structure and characters, with the major difference from this latter work being that the action centers on a negative rather than a positive character.

The plot, according to Brodiansky's short study, was based on an anecdote the author had heard in Moscow, but the play acquired an intricate symbolism that went far beyond the original tale. Set in Moscow, *Krechinsky's Wedding* has six major characters. The Muromsky family consists of Muromsky himself, a wealthy landowner who is unaffected and honest; his eligible daughter Lidochka, who has fallen in love with the society dandy Krechinsky; and Muromsky's sister-in-law Atuyeva, who adores the mannerisms of the seemingly sophisticated Muscovites. The other characters are Vladimir Nelkin, the Muromskys' unaffected country neighbor; Mikhail Krechinsky, a man-about-town; and Krechinsky's cohort, the cardsharp Ivan Raspluev.

The plot revolves around the attempt of Krechinsky, a gambler constantly in debt, to obtain Lidochka's hand in marriage and gain access to her estate. Atuyeva and Lidochka are taken in by Krechinsky's cosmopolitan veneer and his ability to speak some French. Muromsky, on the other hand, is suspicious of Krechinsky, preferring the simple honesty of Nelkin. He is eventually won over by Lidochka's choice, partly because Krechinsky presents him with a prize bullock, waxes eloquent about life in the country, and speaks of his fictitious estates.

Krechinsky suddenly discovers that he must pay his gambling debts at his club or be publicly disgraced. In an attempt to raise a large sum overnight, he sends Raspluev to ask Lidochka for the loan of her diamond pin, supposedly the object of a wager with a Prince Belsky. Krechinsky takes the pin to the pawnbroker Bek, but at the last minute, he substitutes a virtually identical pin with an imitation stone. He returns the authentic jewel to Lidochka that evening while she is visiting him with her family.

Nelkin, in love with Lidochka, is dubious about Krechinsky's sincerity and financial worth, and he is amazed when the real pin is produced. The pawnbroker Bek, who has discovered Krechinsky's substitution, comes in with the police after Nelkin has been thrown out and while the Muromskys are leaving. Just as Krechinsky is about to be arrested, Lidochka, in a effort to save him, runs to Bek with the real pin and says that the substitution was a mistake. The Muromskys now leave, but not before Lidochka herself has been implicated in the swindle. It is this last section that connects *Krechinsky's Wedding* with the second play in the trilogy, *The Case*.

In her essay about Sukhovo-Kobylin, Brodiansky asserts that he maintains the unities of time and action, although not that of place. Such devices as the use of the bell, the presence of a bullock on the stage, Raspluev's addressing the audience, and Krechinsky's deft substitution of the pin with the paste jewel for the genuine article are all in the tradition of the boulevard theaters of Paris. The two principal characters, Krechinsky and Raspluev, are braggarts and scoundrels who bear a marked resemblance to Gogol's characters in *The Inspector General*. Raspluev in particular seems to be the adherent of no special moral code, and he enjoys swindling other people simply to amuse himself. The fact that the Muromskys are accidentally ensnared in the trap of these two scoundrels underlines Sukhovo-Kobylin's thesis that the innocent are the victims of the guilty.

The Case

The Case, originally entitled "Lidochka," was published in a very limited edition in 1861; because of the disapproval of the censor, however, it was not staged until 1882, and then only in a cut, censored version, and only after Sukhovo-Kobylin had renamed it *Otzhitoye vremya* (bygone times) to remove all references to contemporary Russia. *The Case* attained great success when staged by Vsevolod Meyerhold in 1917, the original version being used in this uncensored production.

The Case is set in St. Petersburg, where the Muromskys are living in order to fight the case that has developed out of Lidochka's unfortunate remark, "It's a mistake," uttered when giving the authentic diamond pin to Bek. This statement, occasioned by her fear that Krechinsky would be arrested, has caused suspicion to focus on her as well, for she and her former fiancé are now viewed in official circles as having perpetrated a fraud against her father and as having had a love affair. Krechinsky has sent Muromsky a letter advising him to pay whatever bribes are necessary to bring the case to a speedy and satisfactory conclusion. Krechinsky seems genuinely sorry for the trouble that he has brought on the family, but Muromsky, inexperienced in such matters, has refused up to this point to pay bribes in order to exonerate Lidochka.

The action of *The Case* has now become centered on the amount of the bribe that Muromsky must pay, how he can raise this sum of money, and what the state of the case will be after the funds have been extracted from him. In order to determine Muromsky's financial worth, Kandid Tarelkin has been sent into their home. While ostensibly a friend who purports to use his influence on their behalf, Tarelkin is actually anticipating the gain of a tidy sum once the bribe has been given. Muromsky's estate steward, who is aware of Tarelkin's true motives, has suggested that the latter be bribed to arrange a meeting between the departmental director of affairs, Varravin, and Muromsky. When Varravin asks for an enormous amount to settle the case, the shocked Muromsky then asks Tarelkin to set up another interview, this time with the head of the department himself, referred to in the cast of characters as "An Important Person."

In order to procure as much money as possible from Muromsky, Tarelkin arranges for the meeting to take place in the morning, when the "Important Person" is at his worst and is bound to demand the largest possible sum. Having failed with the higher official, Muromsky tries to buy a settlement by paying off Varravin. Varravin has hit on a scheme to avoid sharing money with Tarelkin: He accuses Muromsky of attempting to bribe him and ostentatiously gives his money back, having first extracted all but a few thousand rubles. Unable to withstand this final blow, Muromsky succumbs to a stroke. The "Very Important Person" arrives and is advised that Muromsky is actually drunk, whereupon the poor man is placed in

a carriage and dies on the way home. When Tarelkin attempts to get his "share" of the bribe money, he is told falsely that Varravin has refused it. Tarelkin himself ends up with nothing.

In contrast to the French orientation of *Krechinsky's Wedding*, that of *The Case* is almost exclusively Russian. It is part of the St. Petersburg tradition in Russian literature, a tradition that is traceable to *Medniy vsadnik* (1841; *The Bronze Horseman*, 1936) by Alexander Pushkin. Like Pushkin's poem, *The Case* also addresses the issue of the little man versus the state, and, in both works, the state wins. There is an air of unreality in *The Case* reminiscent of the mood in such classic "Petersburg" works as Gogol's tales "Shinel" ("The Overcoat") and "Nos" ("The Nose") and Fyodor Dostoevski's "White Nights." Muromsky cannot believe that his beloved daughter has been caught in such an unrelenting trap, nor that the machinery of the government bureaucracy is so corrupt. It is not simply stress that causes his death; it is primarily the horror of the evil and degradation to which he has been subjected. Muromsky in fact attains a higher stature in this play than in the preceding one, for here both he and Lidochka symbolize the good of the ordinary person against the evil of the system.

Varravin and the Muromskys' estate steward, Razuvaev, emerge as central characters. Varravin stands for the wicked government that has the blood of the common citizen—Muromsky—on its hands. Razuvaev is an "Old Believer," close to the Russian rural traditions so beloved by such writers as Leo Tolstoy and untainted by the Western European patina that defiled a potentially good man, Krechinsky. That Varravin wins in the end is inevitable, given Sukhovo-Kobylin's own negative experiences with the system and considering the abyss into which he believed he had fallen.

The resemblance to Gogol does not end with the choice of the setting. Like his predecessor, Sukhovo-Kobylin gave his characters symbolic rather than real names ("A Very Important Person," "An Important Person," "Varravin"). Several minor figures (Chibisov-Ibisov, Gerts-Sherts-Shmerts) have rhyming names similar to Bobchinsky-Dobchinsky in *The Inspector General*. As with Gogol, the use of rhyming names for some characters and of titles rather than names for others creates an air of absurd unreality that is linked with the insubstantiality of the Petersburg setting and that forces the reader to see the triumph of evil as the only actuality.

THE DEATH OF TARELKIN

The Death of Tarelkin unites the absurd elements of Gogol's stories and plays with aspects of the French boulevard theaters and with Russian puppet theater to produce a work unique in Russian drama. Begun in 1857 but not completed until 1869, the play ran into problems with the censors and was performed for the first time in 1900. According to Segel, the entire trilogy was staged on three successive evenings in 1901. *The Death of Tarelkin* was then banned from performance until 1917, when Meyerhold presented it in its original version. Meyerhold produced it again in 1922, with constructivist sets and costumes designed by the brilliant avant-garde artist Varvara Stepanova.

The Death of Tarelkin centers on the rivalry among three villains introduced in the earlier plays, Raspluev from *Krechinsky's Wedding*, and Varravin and Tarelkin from *The Case*. Tarelkin, who was unable to procure any of Muromsky's bribe money in *The Case*, has been haunted by creditors. He decides to steal incriminating documents from Varravin in order to blackmail him later, and he attempts to escape punishment and evade his creditors by assuming the identity of the recently deceased bureaucrat Sila Kopylov. Sukhovo-Kobylin's genius for creating a dynamic plot is evident at the very beginning of the first act, when the action gets off to a fast start as Tarelkin orders his cook Mavrusha to arrange rotten fish around a wax dummy representing a corpse. He removes and hides his false teeth and toupee and passes himself off as Kopylov when his fellow clerks, accompanied by Varravin, arrive for the funeral. Although Varravin is suspicious, Tarelkin's trick succeeds. All the clerks are forced to pay for the funeral of their destitute colleague, and in a hilarious scene, each takes money for this purpose from the pockets of the others.

Raspluev, who has become a police officer and has been left to stand guard over the bureaucrat's cof-

fin, has developed from the cardsharp and coward of *Krechinsky's Wedding* into a bully. Tarelkin carelessly believes that danger is behind him and invites Raspluev for a drink. This celebration is interrupted by a visit from the corpulent laundress Lyudmilla Brandakhlystova, who claims that Kopylov (impersonated by Tarelkin) is the father of her horde of children. Her visit is followed by one from Varravin, who, now disguised as Captain Polutatarinov ("Half-Tatar"), still hopes to discover the whereabouts of his stolen documents. He delivers an insulting description of Tarelkin to Raspluev, who immediately recognizes the missing man in the so-called Kopylov. The disclosure of Tarelkin's toupee and dentures, coupled with the unearthing of Kopylov's passport containing evidence of his recent demise, provides incontrovertible evidence that the supposed Kopylov is in fact Tarelkin.

Tarelkin is tied up and garroted to force him to confess to his true identity and reveal the location of Varravin's papers. Polutatarinov now invents the tale that Tarelkin is actually a vampire. Varravin then reappears in his true guise and tells Inspector Okh that Tarelkin must not have any water, for water gives vampires inordinate strength. Tarelkin confesses readily to being a vampire and, in a reference to *The Case*, Tarelkin admits to having killed Muromsky by "sucking him dry." This is the only somber note in *The Death of Tarelkin*, and it serves as a reminder of the author's own persecution at the hands of the government.

The Death of Tarelkin not only combines Gogol's employment of absurd names ("Half-Tatar") with incredible situations (the wax dummy surrounded by rotten fish) but also is a precursor of the grotesque satire characterizing the Surrealist theater that flourished at the turn of the twentieth century. Sukhovo-Kobylin's wordplay and use of noncommunicative language (as in Raspluev's questioning of Lyudmilla) also foreshadow the Theater of the Absurd.

BIBLIOGRAPHY

Adrianow, Gennadij Y. *Anthroponyms: Their Symbolism as a Literary Devise in the Trilogy of A. V. Sukhovo-Kobylin, "The Pictures of the Past."*

Northfield, Vt.: Norwich University Press, 1979. The author examines the types of names given to characters in Sukhovo-Kobylin's trilogy.

Borowitz, Albert. *Eternal Suspect: The Tragedy of Alexander Sukhovo-Kobylin.* Kent, Ohio: Kent State University Press, 1990. This work, part of a true crime series, looks at Sukhovo-Kobylin's role as murder suspect.

Fortune, Richard. *Alexander Sukhovo-Kobylin.* Bos-

ton: Twayne, 1982. A basic treatment of the writer, examining his life and plays.

Segel, Harold B. Introduction to *"The Death of Tarelkin" and Other Plays: The Trilogy of Alexander Sukhovo-Kobylin.* 2d ed. New York: Harwood Academic Publishers, 1995. The introduction provides a biography of Sukhovo-Kobylin as well as critical analysis of his works.

Janet G. Tucker

ALEKSANDR PETROVICH SUMAROKOV

Born: St. Petersburg, Russia; November 25, 1717
Died: Moscow, Russia; October 12, 1777

PRINCIPAL DRAMA

Khorev, pb. 1747, pr. 1750 (English translation, 1970)

Gamlet, pb. 1748, pr. 1750

Sinav i Truvor, pr., pb. 1750

Tresotinius, pb. 1750

Aristona, pb. 1751

Semira, pr., pb. 1751 (English translation, 1970)

Opekun, pb. 1765

Yaropolk i Dimiza, pb. 1768 (revision of an earlier play)

Vysheslav, pb. 1770

Dimitri Samozvanets, pr., pb. 1771 (*Dimitri the Imposter,* 1806)

Mstislav, pb. 1774

Selected Tragedies of A. P. Sumarokov, pb. 1970

OTHER LITERARY FORMS

Aleksandr Petrovich Sumarokov is by common consent the first full-fledged representative of Russian classicism. Consciously assuming the role of Russia's Jean Racine, Molière, Jean de La Fontaine, and Nicolas Boileau all in one, Sumarokov wrote prolifically in all the literary genres fashionable for French neoclassicism: tragedies, comedies, pastorals, lyrics, odes, satires, fables, epistles, elegies, heroides, sonnets, songs, ballads, rondos, madrigals, epigrams, and inscriptions. A complete ten-volume collection of his works was first published in Moscow, *Polnoe sobranie vsekh sochineniy v stikhakh i proze* (1781-1787). A more recent collection of his works in verse, *Izbrannye proizvedeniya,* was published in Leningrad by the Library of the Poet in 1953. A second edition was published by the Library of the Poet in 1957.

Most of Sumarokov's literary work is in verse, with the exception of his comedies, which in themselves represent a break from the true classical tradition inasmuch as tragedy was the genre most highly valued by the classicists. The higher, more solemn verse forms Sumarokov wrote in the "lofty style," using Alexandrine meter adapted to Russian in a close imitation of French neoclassical poetry. In contrast, Sumarokov's numerous fables have a more open Russian form without a fixed stanza or rhyme scheme, in the manner of the free verse of La Fontaine's fables. Sumarokov's songs show still greater variety of form, reflecting in part his admiration for seventeenth century German verse, which he himself translated into Russian.

In competing with his rival, Mikhail Vasilievich Lomonosov, Sumarokov composed more than eighty religious and solemn odes along with numerous fervent dithyrambs, many of which were addressed to Empress Elizabeth, the daughter of Sumarokov's idol, Peter the Great. In these odes, as well as those addressed to Catherine the Great, Sumarokov portrays not realistic images of the imperial figures, but ideals of the benevolent, enlightened despot in true classical fashion. For example, in "An Ode to the Sovereign Empress Catherine II on the Day of Her Birth, April 21, 1768," Sumarokov extols her virtue as "Mother to all Russia's children," while in an earlier ode in honor of her name day, he praises her wisdom and beauty, likening her to a "lily of Paradise." This ideal image was later mocked by the younger generation of writers because of its incongruity with Catherine's real personality, which gradually revealed itself to the public eye. Nevertheless, the didactic tone and humble adulation of Sumarokov's odes represent the dominant spirit of Russian classical poetry.

Sumarokov's satires, which belong to the "low style" of verse, often ridiculed, in typical Horatian fashion, human weaknesses and vices such as false pride, idleness, ignorance, and rascality, and were devoted to the portrayal of numerous swindlers, dandies, misers, gluttons, and ignoramuses. Other satires rebuked the dandified young aristocrats of the day, who flaunted their Parisian manners and language but who could not speak proper Russian—a theme that was to become prominent in many nineteenth century works.

ACHIEVEMENTS

Aleksandr Petrovich Sumarokov was not only a prolific and innovative writer but also one of Russia's first theoreticians of literature. His "Epistle on the Art of Poetry," which espoused a "doctrine of genres," secured a permanent place for Sumarokov among the pages of Russian literary criticism. In 1759, Sumarokov founded a literary periodical *Trudolyubivoya pchela* (industrious bee), in which he published articles on the history of Russia, philosophy, political economy, and the Russian language. Although Sumarokov's works are somewhat imitative in nature, lacking great innovative genius, his contribution to eighteenth century Russian letters was enormous, and he is remembered for the distinctness of his pictures of local life, his pride in Russian history,

his humanitarian ideas, and his intensity of feeling, which permeates most of his works.

BIOGRAPHY

Aleksandr Petrovich Sumarokov was born in St. Petersburg on November 25, 1717. Of noble descent, Sumarokov was the son of a St. Petersburg military man who was reared in the tradition of the Petrine epoch, with an acute consciousness of the family's high social standing and a strong desire to maintain it. Being a sufficiently wealthy nobleman of the old order, Sumarokov's father owned six estates with approximately 1,670 serfs; he eventually transferred from active military duty to St. Petersburg, where he held a prominent place in civilian life.

At the age of fourteen, young Sumarokov, along with other children of high-ranking nobility, entered the then recently opened school for the Gentlemen's Cadet Corps of the Land Forces in St. Petersburg. At this academy, he received a diverse education that included the French classics. Of great significance for Sumarokov's future literary career as a dramatist was his participation in and enthusiastic support of the amateur theatrical interludes, performed by pupils of the Cadet Corps for audiences from the royal court. For these occasions, Sumarokov, along with other talented poets and budding actors, composed poetry and dramatic pieces, imitating the models of contemporary French poetry to which they had been introduced. As novices, they all (including Sumarokov) followed the working rules of the newly emerging Russian classicism, first developed by Vasily Kirillovich Trediakovsky, who was at that time a leading writer and theoretician, enjoying great popularity, and with whom Sumarokov was later to quarrel.

Although Sumarokov wrote verses and tragedies while at the Cadet School, he did not immediately embark on a full-fledged career as a writer and dramatist on completion of his education. At that time, there was in Russia's capital no theater specifically for Russian playwrights and Russian actors; while theatrical performances were the chief source of entertainment for the court during the reign of Anna Ivanovna (1730-1740), these performances usually consisted of Italian, French, and German plays, and ballets and operas performed by dramatic companies from abroad in a room equipped for the theater in the newly built Winter Palace. Given such limitations, it is not surprising that Sumarokov first chose to pursue a military career. In 1740, when Sumarokov finished the Corps, he was graduated as an adjutant to the vice counselor, Count M. G. Golovkin, who had become one of the most eminent magnates by the end of the reign of Anne I. Following Golovkin's death, coinciding with the ascension to the throne of Elizabeth Petrovna (1741), Sumarokov's fate hardly changed, as he soon became an adjutant to Elizabeth's favorite, A. G. Razumovskiy, and served in that capacity for more than a decade.

Carrying on her father's keen interest in the theater, Empress Elizabeth (Peter the Great's daughter) forced the members of her court to attend theatrical events. A successful performance of Sumarokov's first tragedy, *Khorev*, proved to be a turning point in his life, drawing the favorable attention and admiration of the empress herself and firmly establishing his reputation as a dramatist. In 1756, this notable patroness of the theater sent an official decree to the senate, announcing the establishment of a Russian theater for the performance of tragedies and comedies in the Golovinskiy stone house on Vasilevskiy Island near the Cadet House. Sumarokov, who by then had already produced three more tragedies (including *Gamlet*), was appointed the director of this new theater's first company, consisting exclusively of Russian actors, brought to St. Petersburg by Elizabeth I from Jaroslav and headed by the famous Russian merchant actor, Fyodor Grigorievich Volkov.

From the onset, Sumarokov's career as theater director was tenuous. The initial assistance allocated for the management of the theater was far from sufficient, threatening the company with financial disaster. Sumarokov was continually forced to lodge complaints about the lack of funds. Only after great difficulties did he finally succeed in having the theater come under the financial protectorate of the court. As a result, the Russian theater found itself in a position of submission to court control. Indeed, the management of the theater fell into the hands of the imperial procurator, a German by the name of K. Sivers,

who was indifferent to its fate. A writer and dramatist of high integrity, Sumarokov could not help but be greatly incensed at this bureaucratic interference, and as a sign of protest, he offered his resignation, which, in 1761, was unceremoniously accepted. From this date, Sumarokov had no direct relation to the theater's management but was allowed to continue his association with the company in the capacity of playwright. In spite of his quarrelsome, somewhat overbearing personality, his service to the struggling theater was enormous: It was largely because of his efforts in the face of court opposition that the first Russian theater survived.

Soon after his retirement as theater director, Sumarokov migrated to Moscow, where he occupied himself almost solely with literary activity, writing his last two tragedies, *Dimitri the Imposter* and *Mstislav*. This activity also included a zealous correspondence directed at Catherine II (1762-1796), whose ear he allegedly deafened with complaints about excessive censorship and the lack of official support for the theater. Because of his annoying behavior and sometimes excessive idealism, he soon lost favor with the Empress. Catherine II eventually commanded him to cease writing to her.

As noted above, Sumarokov was generally considered to be an irascible and disagreeable man whose excessive egotism caused him to quarrel constantly with many of his rivals, Trediakovskiy and Lomonosov in particular. He even quarreled with the governor of Moscow, P. S. Saltykov, and ultimately died in abject poverty, a neglected and rejected man.

ANALYSIS

Aleksandr Petrovich Sumarokov's prominence in the literary world of his time was a product not only of his dramatic successes but also of two well-known "Epistles," in which he established certain rules for Russian literature and for Russian as a literary language. Any in-depth analysis of Sumarokov's dramaturgy must consider the rules that he first set down as the basis for his subsequent plays. Sumarokov's "Epistle on Art" proposes a doctrine of genres, classifying each kind of poetry (or prose) and its appropriate style according to the subject matter treated. Accordingly, all elements that contradict the nature of any specific genre must be eliminated. The poet must be selective: A tragedy cannot be marred by elements contradictory to the simple tragic ideal; the pastoral must employ the most natural kind of poetry to depict the plight of a shepherdess, while the elegy ought to treat the torturous moments of love or the sorrow of the heart.

Sumarokov's doctrine of genres is based on the notion that art must "mirror the universe" and depict the "simplicity of essential nature." He strictly adheres to the classical conception of the poet's duty to convey a certain order in the apparent chaos of the universe. This view of art typifies the belief of classical aestheticians, that at the core of the universe there exist certain essential principles that emanate from divine life. It is these principles that govern the hearts of human beings and must be conveyed by the poet.

Both Sumarokov's theory of literature and his works in verse grew out of his love for the great French writers of the seventeenth and eighteenth centuries—Voltaire, Pierre Corneille, Racine, Boileau—and for the principles derived from classical drama. Following the rules already established by French classicism, Sumarokov recognized tragedy as the most favored genre, for it had been handed down to the contemporary world by the great ancient Greek writers such as Aeschylus, Sophocles, and Euripides. In a tragedy, simplicity and unity must be maintained so that the tragic tone is not broken by the intrusion of comic effects. Above all, Sumarokov proposes the Corneillian conflict between reason and the passions as the pivotal point of the tragedy, with the obvious outcome of the triumph of reason and duty over feelings and personal gain. Hence, the play's happy ending for most of the characters presumably serves as a moral lesson to the audience. While two of his tragedies, *Khorev* and *Dimitri the Imposter*, do result in the deaths of the principal characters, such a fate is the inevitable destiny for all those who give full reign to self-centered instincts, subjugating others to their every tyrannical whim. Sumarokov also adopted Aristotle's "pity" and "fear" as the springs of tragic emotion.

Perhaps most important, Sumarokov took from his French models the notion of the three unities: of time, place, and action. According to this formula, time in any tragedy must be limited so that the critical moment being represented on the stage more nearly corresponds to the short span of time of the actual performance. In order not to confuse or deceive the audience, only one fairly limited place (usually a palace) should be chosen so that the viewer need not make unreasonable mental and visual leaps—for example, from Moscow to Rome or from court to countryside. Last, irrelevant episodes or secondary plot lines must not actually take place on stage inasmuch as they would obscure the principal inner conflict of the main character. Any external or secondary events, such as riots, military battles, and so forth, must be reported by a secondary character such as a confidant or messenger in a conversation with the hero of the play.

All Sumarokov's tragedies testify to the classic concept of character: Certain fixed personal qualities lead to an inevitable fate. As in the Greek tragedies, these specific qualities are consistently and uniformly revealed in both the speech and the action of Sumarokov's tragic hero. In regard to subject matter, however, Sumarokov broke with the classic canons by not selecting subjects from the legends of ancient Greek or Roman history. With the exception of *Gamlet*, set in Denmark, and *Aristona*, set in Persia, his tragedies are based on legends from Russian history. While the names of several characters, such as Kij from *Khorev* and Mstislav from the play of that title, actually stem from the Russian chronicles, many names are merely invented to create a sense of the Slavic world. In fact, Sumarokov strives to present not the particular in history but the universal: the enlightened, patriotic nobleman or woman who voluntarily subordinates personal private passions to reason and duty, putting the good of all the people as a whole ahead of individual gain. In order not to obscure this ideal, Sumarokov seldom includes any significant degree of local or national color in his tragedies.

Sumarokov's tragedies enjoyed great success during his lifetime. As William Brown points out in *A History of Eighteenth Century Russian Literature* (1980), Sumarokov was revered by lesser, classical Russian dramatists such as Mikhail Matveyevich and

Vasily Ivanovich Maikov, whose attempts to invade their "master's theatrical realm" fell short of the mark. Although imitative in nature, Sumarokov's tragedies still remain, as Brown writes, "the best examples of this classical genre." Moreover, but for the success of these tragedies, the Russian theater would have been far slower in coming to the cultural forefront of eighteenth century Russian society.

In stark contrast to his tragedies in verse, the far less classical nature of Sumarokov's comedies often became the object of criticism from both his contemporaries and subsequent literary critics. In spite of the fact that he set down fundamental laws for writing comedy as well as tragedy, his own productions in this area do not strictly adhere to these laws. In the "Second Epistle," Sumarokov states that above all, one must avoid amusement for its own sake, yet the majority of his comedies appear to many critics to be no more than popular farces, the sole intent of which is entertainment. Sumarokov himself declared that his own efforts in the realm of comedy were only mediocre. Still, the ground rules that he put forth for this genre played an important role in establishing the basis of Russian comedy. His statement, based on the classical concept of comedy, that "the function of comedy is by mockery to correct morals," reflects the very essence of the comic spirit of such playwrights as Nikolai Gogol in the nineteenth century and Mikhail Bulgakov in the twentieth.

In prose, these comedies present as objects of derision the vices and vicious types already well known in the world of satire: pompous, French-speaking dandies; inhumane, corrupt judges; insipid country bumpkins; greedy usurers; jealous husbands; puffed-up pedants; and vulgar ignoramuses. Although these satiric types were not his invention, Sumarokov was the first Russian dramatist to introduce genuine Russian types who speak colloquial Russian, laced with choice proverbs and folk sayings. Many of his comic characters seem to be genuine products of the Russian countryside. In particular, Sumarokov's obtuse, vegetating country squire became familiar to future Russian audiences in the works of Denis Ivanovich Fonvizin, Alexander Griboyedov, and Nikolai Gogol. In regard to the promotion of natural spoken Russian

and Russian types, Sumarokov's comedies made a substantial contribution to the development of Russian drama.

Only since the twentieth century has Sumarokov begun to be recognized as the founder of the modern Russian stage. It is now the consensus that Sumarokov's plays, particularly his comedies, brought Russian literary language nearer to modern spoken Russian, avoiding the archaisms and biblical constructions for which his rival Lomonosov was famous. His introduction of classical tragedy to the Russian stage constitutes a significant contribution to the realm of Russian literature.

KHOREV

Sumarokov's first tragedy, *Khorev*, thoroughly attests his classical disposition. Based on a story from the legendary Russian past, the play centers on a feud between Zavolox, onetime Prince of Kiev, and a rival, Prince Kij. The feud evolves into a major conflict for the two principal characters: Khorev, Prince Kij's son, falls in love with Osnelda, the daughter of his father's enemy, who has been taken into captivity by Prince Kij during a raid on the ancient capital city. This irresolvable struggle between love and loyalty ultimately culminates in the death of the unfortunate couple, whose private feelings are cruelly subordinated to the greater concerns of state. Even though this tragedy concerns the remote past, the contemporary political environment of the 1740's through the 1760's may in part be represented in the dramatist's plea to allow a foreigner to occupy the throne to ensure that peace and harmony exist without needless bloodshed. (Like Prince Zavolox from the play, Empress Elizabeth and Empress Catherine were of distant non-Slavic ancestry, causing some dissension among those of ancient Russian blood.)

GAMLET

No tragedy of Sumarokov has been more criticized than *Gamlet*, his second tragedy and his version of *Hamlet, Prince of Denmark* (pr. c. 1600-1601), which reflects both his interest in William Shakespeare and his belief that a poet may alter any particularity of a given time or event to conform to the overriding rules of classicism. He therefore changed or eliminated many of the events and *dramatis personae* of Shakespeare's play, which he knew chiefly through La Place's French version as it appeared in 1746 and was first performed by the St. Petersburg Cadet Corps in 1750. In the opening scene of Sumarokov's *Gamlet*, the Danish Prince Hamlet reveals his suspicions of his usurper uncle, Claudius, who, with the encouragement of the wicked Polonius, has murdered Hamlet's father, the former Danish king, and now schemes to poison his wife Gertrude in order to marry Polonius's daughter, Ophelia (Hamlet's fiancé). The plot develops in a traditional classical manner with a confrontation between love and duty. Hamlet struggles to overcome his passion for Ophelia in order to do battle with Polonius and Claudius, in the hope of fully revealing their villainy. Similarly, putting duty before love, Ophelia threatens to renounce her love for Hamlet if he does not spare her father's life.

The conflict happily resolves itself on stage with two pronouncements: Hamlet announces mutiny by the people, and a soldier arrives to announce Polonius's suicide. The play ends not with the tragic deaths of Ophelia and then Hamlet (as in Shakespeare's *Hamlet*), but with the preparations for their wedding and ascension to the Danish throne. The tragic ideal is underscored by the demise of those who would tyrannize others, putting private interests ahead of universal harmony and the welfare of their subjects. Sumarokov clearly takes significant liberties with Shakespeare's plot to achieve this end.

In *Gamlet*, Sumarokov fully realizes the neoclassical treatment of character. As Brown points out, the principals engage in conversations with "secondary persons whose sole function is to listen to the utmost thoughts and intentions of the principals." Sumarokov departs slightly from this tradition by having his principals further reveal their own character in brief soliloquies in which they recognize their own impotence or loathsomeness. For example, the tyrant and murderer Claudius, in a plea to God for grace and mercy, confesses that repentance is not compatible with his wicked and shameless nature: "I cannot find this longing within myself, filled as I am with all ungodly passions. No spark of goodness is in my con-

science. How can I conceive a way to bring about my repentance?"

Through the character of Ophelia, Sumarokov expresses his most cherished ideal of a person in conflict with mortal weaknesses. Ophelia protests Claudius's villainous ways proclaiming that a king should be a divinely inspired ruler who is benevolent toward his people; otherwise, he will act as a mere mortal with barbaric instincts and a criminal nature. Sumarokov's *Gamlet*, for the most part, cannot be judged as a mere imitation of Shakespeare's play, for this eighteenth century classicist carefully reworked the principal characters in concert with the rules for a tragedy that he established in his "Epistle on Art." In spite of the fact that Sumarokov has been severely criticized for his alteration of Shakespeare's work, his *Gamlet* enjoyed great popularity on the Russian stage in the eighteenth century.

DIMITRI THE IMPOSTER

The distinct antidespotic trend that is evident throughout all Sumarokov's tragedies is the dominant theme in his next to last and perhaps best-known play, *Dimitri the Imposter*. Alexander Pushkin, in his later play on the same historical period, *Boris Godunov* (1824-1825; English translation, 1918), presented the full range of dramatic events of the Time of Troubles, but Sumarokov's tragedy, in keeping with the canons of classicism, concentrates on the tragic nature of the central character, Dimitri, who, in Brown's words, "represents the ultimate claim to autocracy, that the monarch possesses his subjects soul and body." As is true for most of Sumarokov's *dramatis personae*, Dimitri embodies a single character trait that governs all of his actions. Some "evil fury" inhabits his soul and is an unchangeable aspect of his personality. This is revealed in several soliloquies in the form of a vain drive to place himself on an equal level with God in order to control completely the lives of others: "Before me you are but a shadow and a cobweb. All that is God's is mine."

The plot line is fabricated to expose fully Dimitri's fated character and revolves around a love triangle between the tyrant himself and two nonhistorical characters: Ksenija, Šuskij's daughter, and her faithful fiancé, Prince Georgij. As in all

Sumarokov's tragedies, passion is stilled and duty obeyed. Georgij and Ksenija must sacrifice their love for the lives of others and their cherished land. In the final act, Dimitri's design on Ksenija is thwarted by the threat of a popular uprising, which occurs off-stage. Dimitri's character remains consistent to the very end; rather than be subdued by the approaching mob, heard in the wings, Dimitri dramatically takes his own life with a dagger as he utters one last defiant curse on all those left behind: "Ah, if only the whole universe might perish with me."

In conjunction with the classical concept of unity and simplicity, all the playwright's secondary *dramatis personae* are simply drawn, conforming to two distinct categories: The virtuous and the villainous. In this way, the didactic strain of the play is not in the least obstructed or confused. No attempt is made to present a realistic portrayal of these characters or the actual historical epoch. In the image of Ksenija, the exalted traits of womanhood are extolled: virtue, beauty, and fidelity. The character of Georgij serves as a mere abstraction of Sumarokov's own liberalism: "Am I not then my own? My heart, blood, soul and mind—are these not my possessions?" Similarly, Prince Šuskij, an actual historical personage, becomes the mouthpiece for Sumarokov's progressive conception of the monarchy as the servant of the people—a view he shared with members of the popular political Panin group, whose ideals are echoed in Šuskij's naïve proclamation: "He is a greater man who will lay down his life and perish for his people."

OTHER MAJOR WORKS

MISCELLANEOUS: *Polnoe sobranie vsekh sochineniy v stikhakh i proze*, 1781-1787 (10 volumes); *Izbrannye proizvedeniya*, 1953, 1957.

BIBLIOGRAPHY

Brown, William Edward. *A History of Eighteenth Century Russian Literature*. Ann Arbor, Mich.: Ardis, 1980. Brown examines Sumarokov within his broader discussion of eighteenth century Russian literature.

Levitt, Marcus C. "The Illegal Staging of Sumarokov's *Sinav i Truvor* in 1770 and the Problem of Authorial Status in Eighteenth Century Russia." *Slavic and East European Journal* 43, no. 2 (Summer, 1999): 299-323. The author examines the illegal staging of one of Sumarokov's plays, focusing on the author's defense strategies.

_____. "Russianized *Hamlet*: Text and Contexts." *Slavic and East European Journal* 38, no. 2 (Summer, 1994): 319. Levitt examines the meaning and context of Sumarokov's *Gamlet*, which was considerably changed, as well as the source materials that Sumarokov probably used in developing his play.

Nebel, Henry M., Jr. *Selected Aesthetic Works of Sumarokov and Karamazin*. Washington, D.C.: University Press of America, 1982. Nebel critiques and presents translations of some of Sumarokov's works as well as some of those of Nikolay Mikhaylovich Karamzin, historian and novelist who reformed the literary language.

Sheidley, William E. "Hamlets and Hierarchy." *Peace Review* 11, no. 2 (June, 1999): 243-249. Sheidley examines the portrayal of official hierarchies as injust, inadequate, or incoherent in literature, especially Sumarokov's version of Hamlet. Sumarokov's portrayal of the fall of a selfish and corrupt ruler shows his belief in a monarchy that concerns itself with the welfare of its subjects.

Jane E. Knox

ALGERNON CHARLES SWINBURNE

Born: London, England; April 5, 1837
Died: Putney, England; April 10, 1909

PRINCIPAL DRAMA
The Queen-Mother, pb. 1860

Rosamond, pb. 1860
Atalanta in Calydon, pb. 1865
Chastelard, pb. 1865
Bothwell, pb. 1874
Erechtheus, pb. 1876
Mary Stuart, pb. 1881
Marino Faliero, pb. 1885
Locrine, pb. 1887
The Sisters, pb. 1892
Rosamund, Queen of the Lombards, pb. 1899
The Duke of Gandia, pb. 1908

OTHER LITERARY FORMS

Algernon Charles Swinburne is best known as a poet, though he also wrote literary criticism and fiction. His drama must be considered a part of his poetic output as it is written exclusively in verse, the bulk of it in blank verse (unrhymed iambic pentameter). His poetic drama is among his least distinguished work and shares many of the shortcomings of his nondramatic poetry: overdecoration, excessive use of alliteration, and an uneasy tension between vulgarity and pomposity. Conversely, the best passages in his plays reveal the brilliancies that ensure him a place among the best of the late Victorian poets: a remarkable verbal facility and an equally remarkable capacity for metric innovation.

Swinburne is generally classified among the Pre-Raphaelite poets and painters of the latter third of the nineteenth century. Along with his friends and associates Dante Gabriel Rossetti, William Morris, and Sir Edward Burne-Jones, Swinburne was committed to a theory of art that rebelled against the smugness and prudishness of Victorian England by insisting that art must be considered on its own terms, quite apart from any moral value it might possess. Swinburne was a latecomer to the so-called Pre-Raphaelite Brotherhood, a group of writers and painters whose founding members included the painters Holman Hunt and Sir John Everett Millais. The Pre-Raphaelites took their name from an aesthetic theory propounded by the essayist John Ruskin. Simply stated, the idea is this: Art must seek to reproduce nature to the smallest detail, using only nature as a model. For Ruskin, his contemporaries erred in studying Raphael, for in doing

so they imitated and reproduced Raphael's mistakes. Artists should instead do what Raphael did: study nature only—hence the term "Pre-Raphaelite."

This original doctrine was eventually abandoned by Rossetti and his disciples—among them Swinburne—who replaced it with a philosophy closely resembling the French critic Théophile Gautier's *l'art pour l'art* (art for art's sake). It is perhaps to this later school, subsequently known as the Aesthetes, that Swinburne properly belongs. Though some of his poems, notably those contained in *A Song of Italy* (1867), do have some sort of moral or political purpose behind them, his best work is truly concerned with art for its own sake and with the role of the artist. He was perhaps one of the last of the Romantic poets, his best work showing many more affinities with George Gordon, Lord Byron, Percy Bysshe Shelley, and John Keats than with his contemporaries, Alfred, Lord Tennyson, Robert Browning, and Matthew Arnold.

Swinburne's novels *Lesbia Brandon* (1952) and *Love's Cross-Currents* (1901) deserve more attention than they have yet received. The latter, a satire on Victorian morality, is one of Swinburne's most consistently interesting works. His literary criticism, much of it published in periodicals, is unhappily short on objectivity. It is too personal, too full of unrestrained praise and harsh invective to be of much value except as Victoriana.

ACHIEVEMENTS

Any discussion of Algernon Charles Swinburne must take into account that his career was divided into two pronounced stages: that up to 1879 and that after 1879. From 1879 until his death in 1909, Swinburne lived a reclusive life under the guardianship of his agent and friend, Walter Theodore Watts-Dunton, removed from the literary mainstream, and although he continued to write prolifically, there was a certain falling off in quality and imagination in the works he produced during this later period. The works of the 1860's and 1870's are the portions of Swinburne's canon that remain of interest today, and similarly it is the drama of the early period that is most noteworthy.

The bulk of Swinburne's plays deal with history or myth, a choice of subject matter that was both a blessing and a curse to his career as a playwright. Although he was widely read in British and continental history, his scholarliness often gets the best of his artistry in his plays: Artistic license is far too seldom exercised. In the Mary, Queen of Scots trilogy, for example—*Chastelard*, *Bothwell*, and *Mary Stuart*—Swinburne is far too steeped in the history of the era to exploit fully the dramatic possibilities of Mary Stuart, the woman and the myth.

This tension between history and art does not exist in his myth plays—to this group belong *Atalanta in Calydon* and *Erechtheus*—and in these works, the modern reader finds an overly heavy dependence on Greek tragedy. Although it could be argued that *Atalanta in Calydon* (Swinburne's only acclaimed play) substantially subverts Greek conventions, adapting the methods of Sophocles to serve Swinburne's nineteenth century intentions, still one finds the speeches too long, the meter too forced, the cho-

rus too vocal. *Erechtheus* is even more derivative than *Atalanta in Calydon*, more often than not a virtuosic imitation of Sophoclean tragedy. Similarly, Swinburne's plays in the Elizabethan mode are much too obviously derivative of Thomas Kyd, Francis Beaumont, John Fletcher, and their contemporaries. Replete with bloodshed, vendettas, and murders, such early pieces as *Rosamond* and *The Queen-Mother* are heavily influenced by the revenge tragedies of the minor Renaissance dramatists, but they, too, often lack the dramaturgical mastery of their precursors.

Swinburne must therefore be considered an imitative rather than an original playwright. His most interesting plays—*Atalanta in Calydon*, *Chastelard*, and (for very different reasons) *The Sisters*—succeed not because of their dramatic merit but because of the poetic ingenuity of many of their parts. Like his early nineteenth century precursors, Swinburne was an innovative poet who felt compelled to try his hand at the drama. Too often the results are such that one wishes he had devoted his time to the lyric poetry of which he was an undisputed master. Nevertheless, like the closet dramas of his great Romantic predecessors, Swinburne's plays retain historical interest.

BIOGRAPHY

Algernon Charles Swinburne was born into two of England's proudest old aristocratic families, the Swinburnes and the Ashburnhams. His father was Captain (later Admiral) Charles Henry Swinburne; his mother, the former Lady Jane Henrietta Hamilton, the daughter of the third earl of Ashburnham. He enjoyed a privileged childhood, dividing his time between the estate of his parents, East Dene on the Isle of Wight, and Capheaton Hall, the Swinburne family seat in Northumberland near the Scottish border. For the rest of his life, he would be fascinated by Scottish history and myth, using it as subject matter for works of such diverse merit as the early poem "The Queen's Tragedy" (1854) and his dramatic trilogy centering on Mary Stuart. He was never close to his father—a conventional man who was away much of the time—but he was pampered by his mother, to whom he remained close until her death in 1896. His paternal grandfather, Sir John Swinburne, was a surrogate fa-

Algernon Charles Swinburne (Library of Congress)

ther to the boy, treating him with an affection and respect that the poet never forgot.

Although he was the eldest of six children, young "Hadji" Swinburne was a lonely child, made, from early childhood, to feel like an outcast. He was at best unusual in appearance, with bright red hair, a too-slight build, and a perpetual nervous twitch. In the midst of a notably red-blooded extended family, Swinburne appeared effeminate, reared as he was in the company of his mother and four sisters. As a hedge against solitude, he turned to books. Taught to read by his mother, Swinburne at a young age mastered the Bible, Sir Walter Scott's novels, and the plays of William Shakespeare.

In 1849, Swinburne was enrolled at Eton, a move that ultimately proved disastrous. The sensitive boy did not fare well in the restrictive and patriarchal public-school atmosphere, where conformity and team spirit reigned. Always a rebel, young Swinburne was at once terrified and enraged by the oppressive discipline that characterized the place. Though a brilliant student—he was able to profit at least from Eton's heavily classical curriculum, which emphasized Latin and Greek—he was a social failure and a constant source of embarrassment to the school's administration. In the summer of 1853, Swinburne left Eton for good, at least two years earlier than expected.

Swinburne had begun writing even while at Eton, turning out heavily Elizabethan tragedies and even a mock eighteenth century poetic tribute to Queen Victoria entitled "The Triumph of Gloriana." On entering Oxford in 1856, he continued his literary career, falling naturally and almost instantly into membership in Old Mortality, a literary group that later published the short-lived literary magazine *Undergraduate Papers*. A more important and farther-reaching influence came in 1857, when Swinburne met Dante Gabriel Rossetti, who, along with his disciples Sir Edward Burne-Jones and William Morris, was down from London decorating the Oxford Union Society building with murals. Swinburne, already seriously questioning religious and political orthodoxy and the hypocrisies of official Victorian morality, was immediately drawn to Rossetti's Svengali-like personality

and to the doctrine of art for art's sake. In Swinburne, Rossetti had found his newest disciple.

Rossetti's influence on Swinburne cannot be overstated, and it is generally considered an unhealthy one. Rossetti seems to have cultivated an apostlelike devotion from the young men who constantly surrounded him, often then publicly ridiculing them or dropping them altogether. In addition, Swinburne found Rossetti's bohemian lifestyle much too enticing. Rossetti practiced to a remarkable degree the decadent doctrine that he preached. His life was riddled with alcoholic bouts and heterosexual affairs, and under this master's influence, Swinburne learned to give free rein to the sadomasochistic sexual urges that had been festering in him since his Eton days. Swinburne's love of bondage and flagellation figures prominently in some of his best poetry; indeed, such poems as "Dolores" and "Laus Veneris" are anomalies of English literature: They are poetic works of the highest order that until recently could not be candidly or openly discussed by the literary establishment.

Whatever else Rossetti's aesthetic doctrines accomplished, they at least succeeded in prompting Swinburne to take up writing more seriously than ever before. While at Oxford, Swinburne produced a number of poems, plays, and essays, among them the "Ode to Mazzini," a tribute to the leader of the fight for Italian democracy (later to become a friend and admirer of Swinburne); the long poem "Queen Iseult," a treatment of the Tristram and Isolde legend; and the two tragedies mentioned earlier, *The Queen-Mother* and *Rosamond*. As a result of Swinburne's intense literary activity, his academic standing suffered. In 1860, he left Oxford as he had left Eton—for reasons never made public.

The story of Swinburne's subsequent life in London is one of personal dissipation, literary acclaim (and notoriety), and sexual liberation to the point of excess and beyond. Through the offices of Rossetti and his friends—the politician and biographer Richard Monckton Milnes, the explorer Richard Burton, the painter Simeon Solomon—Swinburne led a life of unrestrained bohemianism, as if to make up for years of repression and conformity at Eton and Oxford. He discovered the poetry of Charles Baudelaire and the sexually explicit writing of the Marquis de Sade. Both of these writers he championed through editorials and reviews in the British popular press in a deliberate attempt to shock the staid literary establishment. The publication of *Atalanta in Calydon* in 1865 met with official approval, but in the same year *Chastelard*, the first of the Mary Stuart plays, brought condemnation, scandalizing, among countless others, the poet laureate Tennyson. *Poems and Ballads* (1866), which includes such "abnormal" poems as "Anactoria" and "Sapphics," gave Swinburne the reputation that he had long craved. He would forever be known as the British Baudelaire, the deviant rebel of English letters.

Swinburne's physical frailty was never quite able to withstand his excesses, and from time to time, his father would quietly come to London and fetch Swinburne home to recuperate. One such rescue occurred in 1871 during a long and bitter public battle in which the minor poet Robert Buchanan attacked Rossetti and Swinburne as members of the amoral "Fleshly School of Poetry." Naturally, Swinburne mounted a counterattack. The peevish and juvenile mudslinging continued for five years, culminating in a libel suit in 1876—a suit that Buchanan won. In 1877, Swinburne's father died, and the poet returned to London, hell-bent on spending his inheritance on liquor and sexual pleasure. In June, 1879, his friend Walter Theodore Watts (later Watts-Dunton) did what Admiral Swinburne had so often done: He rescued the poet from a collision course with death and installed him at The Pines, Watts's home in suburban Putney.

Swinburne never left The Pines, and little is known of the last thirty years of his life. He continued to write and to publish, with Watts-Dunton acting as a shrewd literary agent. The poet who everyone thought would die young died at the age of seventy-two on April 10, 1909.

ANALYSIS

Like such varied Romantic poets as Byron, Shelley, Keats, and William Wordsworth, Algernon Charles Swinburne wrote "closet dramas," plays never intended to be performed, but rather to be read as works of literature. His plays have seldom if ever been produced on the stage, and for good reason: Swinburne knew next to nothing about stagecraft, and his poetic dramas betray his ignorance of the practical demands of the theater. They are, almost without exception, too long; the dialogue is often unnaturally poetic, even for verse drama; and the character motivation is too often obscure, with too much background being assumed of the audience.

ATALANTA IN CALYDON

Swinburne very likely got the idea for his most renowned drama, *Atalanta in Calydon*, from Ovid's *Metamorphoses* (c. 8 C.E.; English translation, 1567). The myth concerns Meleager, son of King Oeneus and Queen Althaea of Calydon, at whose birth the three Fates decree a glorious life and an early death: Meleager will die, say the Fates, when the brand then in the fire is consumed. To circumvent their prophecy, Althaea takes the brand from the fire and conceals it. Years later, Artemis, goddess of chastity and of the hunt, demonstrates her anger at Oeneus, who has neglected to pay her sufficient homage, by sending a wild boar to Calydon to devastate the fields and vineyards. The world's greatest hunters are convened to try to slay the boar, among them Meleager, recently returned from Jason's voyage in quest of the Golden Fleece, and Atalanta, skilled huntress and priestess of Artemis, a native of Arcadia.

Meleager falls in love with Atalanta almost immediately, despite his parents' misgivings. When he succeeds in killing the boar, he presents the head and skin to Atalanta. His mother's brothers Plexippus and Toxeus, however, who are angry that a woman should be allowed to join the hunt in the first place, take exception to Meleager's action and threaten to take the trophies for themselves. Meleager, provoked by their challenge to his manhood and by their treatment of Atalanta, kills both of his uncles in a fit of rage. When Althaea hears the news of her brothers' murders, she resurrects and destroys the forgotten brand, in effect killing her son. Meleager dies, but not before forgiving his mother and restating his love for Atalanta.

Too much has been made of the play's classicism. Although it is in many ways a skillful imitation of the plays of the Greek masters Sophocles and Euripides—a Greek chorus, for example, intermittently intones the tragic themes, and the Aristotelian unities of time, place, and action are for the most part observed—the most compelling aspects of *Atalanta in Calydon* are decidedly nineteenth century. The theme of the play is the unavoidable control of fate over human life. More specifically, the play questions the benevolence of gods (and, by implication, the Christian God) who allow human tragedies to occur. Some of the most beautiful passages are those in which the chorus takes the gods to task, and the modern reader cannot but detect in these passages a direct affront by Swinburne to Victorian religious piety.

The play is also fundamentally modern in its treatment of love. Althaea repeatedly warns her son against the snares of love, and the chorus frequently takes up Althaea's sentiment, solemnly chanting about the dangers of romantic involvement and the attractions of celibacy. Oeneus is concerned specifically with Meleager's attraction to Atalanta, who is throughout the play presented as a somewhat masculine girl, a worshiper of the goddess of chastity. To Oeneus, Meleager's devotion to Atalanta is somehow unnatural, and no good can come of it. Toxeus and Plexippus also question Meleager's sexuality, though in a much more derisively confrontational manner. To them, Meleager's feelings for Atalanta are unmanly, as is his awarding of the hunting trophies to the chaste huntress. Meleager kills his uncles as much in overzealous defense of his manhood as in defense of Atalanta.

The drama received almost universal acclaim on its publication, giving Swinburne a popular acceptance that he would never again enjoy. Despite its reputation as a masterpiece, however, *Atalanta in Calydon* is a rather dull poem and a very inadequate piece of drama. The plot is difficult to follow, and the dramatic business of the play is handled ineptly. Except for Althaea, no character is fully enough realized to be convincing; Atalanta in particular is a remarkably shallow creation. The metric adeptness that characterizes Swinburne's best poems is present in *Atalanta in Calydon*, but it does not always lend itself to dialogue. One wonders if the play has not received so much attention because it is for the most part

"clean," capable of being discussed without indelicacy. At any rate, it is unhappily short on the Swinburnian genius that the Victorians considered perverse.

CHASTELARD, BOTHWELL, AND MARY STUART

Swinburne's Mary Stuart trilogy is, as has been noted, more the work of a scholarly poet than of a playwright. Swinburne's obsession with the queen got the better of him in these plays. He seems to have been intent on providing the artistic final word on her life and legend, an intention that becomes most grotesquely obvious in *Bothwell*, the second installment of the trilogy, an interminable play of surpassing dullness. By far the most interesting of the three is the first, *Chastelard*, which treats the love triangle between Mary, her future husband Lord Darnley, and the courtier Chastelard. Quite possibly Swinburne wrote the play as an attack on conventional Victorian morality, and as such it succeeds. The love between Mary and Chastelard is as unconventional as the love described in the most daring of Swinburne's lyric poems. Passionate, highly sexual, and reckless in the extreme, the relationship between the courtier and his queen is a prime example of *amour fou*, a mad love whose element of danger is irresistibly attractive to the lovers. Mary is treated as a beautiful, dangerous woman, a direct descendant of Keats's "La Belle Dame Sans Merci." Chastelard, one of the most compelling characters in Swinburne's dramatic canon, is a reckless swain, willing to sacrifice all for the sake of passion. It is Swinburne's most decadently Romantic play, brimming with suggestions of sadomasochism and sexual cruelty: Parts of it, in other words, are pure Swinburne. Predictably, however, the drama was misunderstood. A reading public that had approved of the neoclassical pomp of *Atalanta in Calydon* was scandalized by *Chastelard*, and Swinburne's reputation as an amoral deviant—a reputation finally and incontrovertibly established by the *Poems and Ballads* of 1866—was well under way.

MARINO FALIERO, LOCRINE, AND ERECHTHEUS

Swinburne's remaining poetic dramas deserve only passing mention, flawed as they are in various ways. *Marino Faliero*, a deliberate answer to Byron's play of the same name, is a revenge tragedy set in Renaissance Italy. It is of interest solely as a testimonial to Swinburne's sustained championship of Italian Republicanism. *Locrine* is another reworking of a myth, this one concerning a love triangle between a king, a queen, and the king's mistress. It is fascinating as an exercise in prosody, employing nearly every English stanza form, from the heroic couplet to the Shakespearean sonnet. As a dramatic work, it is embarrassingly bad. *Erechtheus*, like *Atalanta in Calydon* an imitation of the Greeks, is too stately and solemn for its own good.

THE SISTERS

The Sisters is Swinburne's only attempt at dramatic realism. Set in 1816, it explores yet another love triangle, this one involving two sisters, both of whom are in love with the same man. When the hero, Reginald Clavering, becomes promised to one, the other poisons them both. Swinburne admitted that the play was autobiographical, with Reginald Clavering a direct attempt to portray himself as a dramatic character. *The Sisters* is at its best a provocative study of love, rejection, and jealousy, but it is more often an awkward tale of courtship among the upper classes.

THE DUKE OF GANDIA

The last dramatic work that Swinburne published was *The Duke of Gandia*, a perverse playlet about murder, incest, and intrigue in the court of the Borgia pope, Alexander VI. In it, one sees flashes of the old Swinburne, for the play is deliberately and violently irreligious. It is perhaps telling that so late in life Swinburne chose to write and to publish a play that is monstrous in its view of religion, authority, and familial love. *The Duke of Gandia* serves as a reminder that Swinburne never lost the decadent rebelliousness that had made him famous during the reign of Queen Victoria.

OTHER MAJOR WORKS

LONG FICTION: *Love's Cross-Currents*, 1901 (serialized as *A Year's Letters* in 1877); *Lesbia Brandon*, 1952.

POETRY: *Poems and Ballads*, 1866; *A Song of Italy*, 1867; *Ode on the Proclamation of the French Republic*, 1870; *Songs Before Sunrise*, 1871; *Songs of Two Nations*, 1875; *Poems and Ballads: Second Series*, 1878; *Songs of the Springtides*, 1880; *The Heptalogia*, 1880; *Tristram of Lyonesse and Other Poems*, 1882; *A Century of Roundels*, 1883; *A Midsummer Holiday and Other Poems*, 1884; *Gathered Songs*, 1887; *Poems and Ballads: Third Series*, 1889; *Astrophel and Other Poems*, 1894; *The Tale of Balen*, 1896; *A Channel Passage and Other Poems*, 1904; *Posthumous Poems*, 1917; *Rondeaux Parisiens*, 1917; *Ballads of the English Border*, 1925.

NONFICTION: *Byron*, 1866; *Notes on Poems and Reviews*, 1866; *William Blake: A Critical Essay*, 1868; *Under the Microscope*, 1872; *George Chapman*, 1875; *Essays and Studies*, 1875; *A Note on Charlotte Brontë*, 1877; *A Study of Shakespeare*, 1880; *Miscellanies*, 1886; *A Study of Victor Hugo*, 1886; *A Study of Ben Jonson*, 1889; *Studies in Prose and Poetry*, 1894; *The Age of Shakespeare*, 1908; *Three Plays of Shakespeare*, 1909; *Shakespeare*, 1909; *Contemporaries of Shakespeare*, 1919.

MISCELLANEOUS: *The Complete Works of Algernon Charles Swinburne*, 1925-1927 (20 volumes; reprinted 1968).

BIBLIOGRAPHY

Louis, Margot Kathleen. *Swinburne and His Gods: The Roots and Growth of an Agnostic Poetry*. Buffalo, N.Y.: McGill-Queen's University Press, 1990. Louis examines Swinburne's views on religion as they were demonstrated in his writings.

Pease, Allison. *Modernism, Mass Culture, and the Aesthetics of Obscenity*. New York: Cambridge University Press, 2000. Pease's scholarly study of erotic literature and views of obscenity looks at the works of Swinburne as well as those of D. H. Lawrence, Aubrey Beardsley, and James Joyce. Bibliography and index.

Reide, David G. *Swinburne: A Study of Romantic Mythmaking*. Charlottesville: University Press of Virginia, 1978. Reide argues that Swinburne is the link between the first English Romantics and the modern Romantics. Traces Swinburne's development from unthinking acceptance of earlier modes to creative affirmation, reflecting the development of a literary tradition insisting on the creative continuation of tradition itself as the one certainty against meaninglessness.

Rooksby, Rikky. *A. C. Swinburne: A Poet's Life.* Brookfield, Vt.: Ashgate, 1997. This biography of Swinburne looks at his life and works, focusing on his poetry and his critical writings. Bibliography and index.

Rooksby, Rikky, and Nicholas Shrimpton, eds. *The Whole Music of Passion: New Essays on Swinburne.* Brookfield, Vt.: Ashgate, 1993. A collection of essays providing literary criticism of Swinburne's works. Bibliography and index.

Thomas, Donald Serrell. *Swinburne: The Poet in His World.* New York: Oxford University Press, 1979. This volume depicts Swinburne in relation to the society in which he lived. An insightful biography of what the author deems to be one of the most eccentric and original writers of the Victorian period. Contains illustrations and a select bibliography.

J. D. Daubs,
updated by Genevieve Slomski

JOHN MILLINGTON SYNGE

Born: Rathfarnham, Ireland; April 16, 1871
Died: Dublin, Ireland; March 24, 1909

PRINCIPAL DRAMA

When the Moon Has Set, wr. 1900-1901, pb. 1968
Luasnad, Capa, and Laine, wr. 1902, pb. 1968
A Vernal Play, wr. 1902, pb. 1968
The Tinker's Wedding, wr. 1903, pb. 1908, pr. 1909
In the Shadow of the Glen, pr. 1903, pb. 1904 (one act)
Riders to the Sea, pb. 1903, pr. 1904 (one act)
The Well of the Saints, pr., pb. 1905
The Playboy of the Western World, pr., pb. 1907
Deirdre of the Sorrows, pr., pb. 1910
The Complete Plays, pb. 1981

OTHER LITERARY FORMS

John Millington Synge's nondramatic works— autobiographical sketches, essays, reviews, and diaries—document the proposition that his dramatic career began with his response to William Butler Yeats's advice to abandon Paris for Ireland's remote regions. Synge's observations of the lives of the country people of Aran, Connemara, Kerry, and Wicklow indicate that until he lived in these repositories of folk tradition, he had not found either theme or style. The diaries and essays from these visits report Synge's compilation of dramatic incidents, details of local color, images, and turns of speech, and show an understanding of that way of life that encompassed its dialect, character, and fatalism. Although these accounts show an acute eye for the dramatic, they have less-than-scientific reliability, permeated as they are with Synge's nature mysticism, his brooding remove from social engagement, and his lack of sympathy with the religious traditions of the people. Synge's direct, precise prose is chiefly valuable as a record of the sources for his plays and of his developing creative consciousness.

With a few exceptions—"In Kerry," "Queens," and "Danny"—Synge's poetry merits the same judgment. Ironic, romantic, and morbid, it is rich with Celtic and folk reference. It also shows, however, the influence of various European poets—François Villon, Giacomo Leopardi, Petrarch—whose works Synge translated. There is some evidence that Synge's direct idiom contributed to Yeats's abandonment of romantic idealism after 1902.

Synge's photographs (*My Wallet of Photographs,* 1971) are valuable documents of turn-of-the-century life on the Irish seaboard. His *Letters to Molly* (1971) and *Some Letters of John M. Synge to Lady Gregory and W. B. Yeats* (1971) are equally valuable in coming to an appreciation of Synge's personal and business struggles in his final and more creative years.

ACHIEVEMENTS

The Irish Literary Renaissance was the result of the collective efforts of diverse talents in the fields of translation, folklore, fiction, poetry, and drama. Under the leadership of the Olympian William Butler Yeats, the movement counted the folklorist Douglas Hyde, the novelists James Joyce and George Moore, the translator and dramatist Lady Augusta Gregory, and the poet and editor George Russell (whose pseudonym was Æ) among its contributors. These writers shared the desire for the establishment of a national literature that would express what they considered distinctive about the Irish imagination. Each contributed to the dramatic literature presented on the stage of the Abbey Theatre, but John Millington Synge is the only one of this group whose contribution lies mainly in the drama. Indeed, Synge is generally regarded as the most distinguished dramatist of the Irish Literary Renaissance.

This reputation rests on the output of his final seven years: six plays, two of which, *Riders to the Sea* and *The Playboy of the Western World*, are masterpieces. These plays in particular exhibit the characteristic qualities of intense lyric speech drawn from the native language and dialects of Ireland, romantic characterization in primitive settings, and dramatic construction after the classics of European drama. Three central theses dominate Synge's work: the enmity between romantic dreams and life's hard necessities, the relationship between human beings and the natural world, and the mutability of all things. These plays are the expressions of a complex personality, formed by Synge's early musical training, his alienation from his own Anglo-Irish roots, his love for the landscapes and country people of Ireland, the tension between romantic impulse and realistic imperatives, and his persistent morbidity and personal loneliness.

Synge has had considerable influence in shaping the style and themes of subsequent Irish dramatists, such as George Fitzmaurice and M. J. Malloy, and some influence outside Ireland, most notably in the work of Federico García Lorca and Eugene O'Neill.

John Millington Synge (Library of Congress)

BIOGRAPHY

Edmund John Millington Synge was born April 16, 1871, in Rathfarnham, County Dublin, the youngest of the five children of a comfortable Anglo-Irish Protestant family. His schooling was mostly private until, at the age of seventeen, he entered Trinity College, Dublin, where he won prizes in Irish and Hebrew even though he put most of his energy into the study of the piano, violin, and flute. During his youth, he developed a strong reaction to his mother's religiosity and an enthusiasm for the antiquities and natural beauty of the Irish countryside. He went to Germany in 1893 to study music but the following year abandoned his plans to move to Paris and attend lectures in European language and literature at the Sorbonne. Instead, he traveled through Germany, Italy, and France between 1894 and 1896. He wrote some poetry and dramatic fragments, gave lessons in English, and studied French and Italian, returning during the summers to Dublin, where he furthered his interests in the Irish language and Irish antiquities.

In December, 1896, Yeats encountered Synge in Paris and discerned a literary talent in search of a subject. He advised Synge to go to the Aran Islands off the Atlantic coast of Ireland, where the people spoke Irish and still led lives free of modern convention. Synge complied, and for a portion of each summer from 1898 to 1902, he lived among the fisherfolk and recorded his observations with notebook and camera. He continued to write dramatic sketches and literary reviews and edited his notes under the title *The Aran Islands* (1907). His first plays, *When the Moon Has Set*, written in prose, and *A Vernal Play* and *Luasnad, Capa, and Laine*, written in verse—although apprenticeship works—exhibit fragmentary characteristics of his mature work. This maturity came rapidly, for during the summer of 1902, he wrote *Riders to the Sea* and *In the Shadow of the Glen* and began *The Tinker's Wedding*. *Riders to the Sea* was the first of Synge's plays to be published (October, 1903), but *In the Shadow of the Glen* was the first to be produced on the stage—by the Irish National Theatre Society (October, 1903). An acrimonious public debate over the play's depiction of Irish life followed this production, a debate to which its author contributed little. When *Riders to the Sea* was produced, Synge's reputation improved, especially following the London presentation of the two plays in March, 1904.

When the Abbey Theatre opened in December of 1904, Synge was appointed literary adviser and later director, along with Lady Augusta Gregory and W. B. Yeats. The following February, *The Well of the Saints* was produced there, though it was poorly received. Meanwhile, Synge was visiting Counties Kerry, Galway, and Mayo and was working on his masterpiece, *The Playboy of the Western World*. As he drafted and revised this play throughout 1906, a romantic relationship was growing with Molly Allgood (known on stage as Máire O'Neill), the Abbey actress who played the role of Pegeen Mike in the first production, on January 26, 1907. The play offended Irish sensibilities, provoking a week of riots and a bitter public debate over the play and freedom of expression on the stage. Again, Synge took little part in the argument, leaving the burden of defending his work to Yeats.

Synge commenced his last play, *Deirdre of the Sorrows*, which is based on a story of the Sons of Usnach from the Ulster cycle of Celtic tales, during 1907. During this same year, the symptoms of Hodgkin's disease, which had first manifested themselves in 1897, reappeared. The resultant operations interfered with Synge's revisions of the play, caused the postponement of his wedding, and failed to arrest the disease. He died on March 24, 1909. In January, 1910, *Deirdre of the Sorrows* was first performed, with Molly Allgood in the title role.

ANALYSIS

When, in 1893, John Millington Synge was choosing between musical and literary careers, two seminal documents were published that would profoundly affect his decision and form the character of his subsequent work. These were Stopford Brooke's lecture "The Need of Use of Getting Irish Literature into the English Tongue," and Douglas Hyde's *Love Songs of Connaught* (1893). Brooke's lecture identified four tasks essential to the development of an Irish national literature: the translation of ancient Irish texts, the molding of the various mythological and historical cycles into an imaginative unity, the treatment in verse of selected episodes from these materials, and the collection of folk stories surviving in the Irish countryside. Some of these tasks had already been undertaken, but none had an impact on the developing revival to equal that of Hyde's slim volume of the same year. He showed that the living song tradition in the Irish Gaelic-speaking areas was rich, complex, and sensitive; that a strong link with an ancient cultural tradition still persisted; and that a translation of these songs into Hiberno-English opened new avenues of expression to the literary artist.

By the early 1890's, Yeats was already committed to some of the tasks outlined by Brooke, and he also greeted Hyde's work enthusiastically. Yeats wrote in an 1893 issue of *The Bookman*: "These poor peasants lived in a beautiful if somewhat inhospitable world, where little has changed since Adam delved and Eve span. Everything was so old that it was steeped in the heart, and every powerful emotion found at once noble types and symbols for its expression." When

Yeats encountered Synge in Paris three years later, it was with these principles and sentiments that he persuaded him to abandon the French capital for the Aran Islands. The plays that resulted do indeed constitute a distinguished translation of folk and heroic materials to the modern stage.

Synge set himself not only against the mystical excesses of the Irish writers of his time but also against the intellectual drama of Henrik Ibsen and George Bernard Shaw and produced works of narrow but intense passion. Synge's plays realize, more successfully than those of any of his contemporaries, Yeats's dictum that Irish writers should seek their form among the classical writers, but their language at home.

RIDERS TO THE SEA

Riders to the Sea was the first play Synge wrote, and it draws most heavily and directly on his experience of life on the Aran Islands; many of the details, along with the main incident on which the play is based, can be found in the journals Synge kept during his visits there. It was Synge's first successful use of Hiberno-English to serve his own dramatic and poetic purposes, and it is regarded by most commentators as one of the finest short plays in that literature.

The action of the play is simple and highly compressed. An old woman of the Aran Islands, Maurya, has lost her husband, father-in-law, and four sons to the sea. She now awaits news of the fate of Michael, another son, as her last and youngest son, Bartley, prepares to make the crossing to Galway with two horses. Maurya's two daughters have just received a bundle of clothes which they identify as those of Michael. As the young women attempt to keep the news from her, she attempts to dissuade Bartley from the hazardous journey—in vain, for just as Bartley must play the provider's part, Maurya's timeworn experience has taught her to anticipate the truth. While her daughters find confirmation of Michael's death in the bundle of clothes, Maurya sees a vision of what is about to happen: Bartley's drowning. As the daughters tell Maurya of Michael's death, the neighbors carry in Bartley's body. The play climaxes with Maurya's lament for these and all her menfolk, ending with a prayer for all the living and the dead.

Although it requires less than thirty minutes to perform, the play encompasses a succession of moods and a universe of action. By contrasting the young women's particular, objective attitudes (their preoccupation with the physical evidence of Michael's death) with Maurya's subjective, universal, even mystical, consciousness (her forgetting the blessing and the nails, and her visionary experience), Synge establishes a pattern of dramatic ironies. Maurya's feelings in regard to the external action of the play, moreover, are seen to evolve from a subdued disquiet, to a higher anxiety, to a visionary sympathy with her last two sons, and finally to a threnody of disinterested compassion for the mothers and sons of all humankind. Maurya is, therefore, not only a credible individual character but also an archetypal figure: She is cast among domestic details yet is inattentive to them because her awareness of commonality and community eventually obscures particular concerns. Only her indomitable attitude in those eloquent, passionate speeches offers a nearly adequate human response to the implacable antagonist, the sea.

The sea that surrounds the bare islands is both the islanders' source of sustenance and their principal natural enemy; in the play, it insistently reminds the characters that, contend with it or not, they are doomed. Synge has carefully selected the domestic details to develop his themes—the bread, the nets, boards, knife, rope, and knot—details which establish a practical and symbolic relationship between the smaller and larger worlds of action, onstage and offstage, practical and moral. Other elements in the play act as religious or mystical allusions: the apocalyptic horses, the fateful dropped stitches, the ineffectual young priest, the omens in the sky and in the holy well. Many aspects of the setting—the door, the colors, the blessing—repeat and reverse themselves as images of the life-and-death ritual that sets Maurya and the sea against each other again and again. Maurya's maternal mysticism is solemnly expressed by her prayers, blessings, gestures, litanies, and pitiful elegy for the cavalcade of death.

Although Maurya's speeches are interlaced with Christian invocation, her response to the catastrophe does not, at its most profound depths, derive from conventional Christian feelings. Maurya confronts a system of natural elements that confounds all human aspirations, and her response is in the tradition of characters from grand tragedy. Thus Synge has written a play that combines elements from Greek tragedy (it reminded Yeats of the plays of Aeschylus), the attitudes of primitive Gaelic society (its fatalism and impersonality), and the modern world, with its nihilism and cultivation of a sense of the absurd. There has been considerable argument over the compatibility of these ethics with one another, but there is no disagreement over the intensity and complexity of the emotions engendered by the play, whether read or staged.

In the Shadow of the Glen

Synge's second produced play, *In the Shadow of the Glen* (written under the title *The Shadow of the Glen*) is set in the Wicklow Mountains south of Dublin, a remote area familiar to Synge, in which he had a cottage and about which he had written several essays gathered under the title *In Wicklow* (1910). The play shows the influence of Ibsen's *Et dukkehjem* (pr., pb. 1879; *A Doll's House*, 1880), but its direct source is "An Old Man's Story," which Synge had heard from the Aran Island storyteller Pat Dirane; it is found in Synge's prose work *The Aran Islands*. The question of the play's origin is significant because it was immediately attacked for its depiction of an unfaithful wife and its unfair portrayal of Irishwomen. Synge unquestionably took considerable liberty with his raw materials—drawing, for example, on an episode from Petronius's *Satyricon* (c. 60 C.E.; *The Satyricon*, 1694), "The Widow of Ephesus"—and the result was an original, concise, complex comedy.

A "Tramp" is admitted to a lonely cottage by one Nora Burke, whose husband is laid out as if for a wake. Conversation between the two reveals that Nora has been living unhappily with her relatively well-off but aged husband, a situation that has led to a number of dalliances with other men, including the now deceased Patch Darcy. Nora then exits to rendezvous with another young man, Michael Dara, leaving the Tramp to maintain the wake. The Tramp, however, is soon shocked to find that Nora's husband, Dan Burke, is feigning death in order to trap his wife

and either bring her to heel or eject her from his house. No sooner has the Tramp agreed to cooperate with Dan's scheme than Nora returns with Michael Dara. The pair discuss their prospects of marriage now that Nora is apparently free. Suddenly Dan springs from the bed to confront the pair. Michael Dara backs off immediately, and Nora is left to face her husband alone; at this point, the Tramp reintroduces himself with renewed eloquence, offering Nora a romantic life with him outside material security. This appeal finally releases Nora's imaginative energies, and she departs with him, leaving Dan Burke and Michael Dara to share a bottle of whiskey.

In the Shadow of the Glen offered the first explicit treatment of sexual frustration on the modern Irish stage; at the same time, the play's symbolic setting and the rich imagery of its language enlarge its reference to register a protest against the constraints of time and space (represented by the mists moving up and down the Wicklow glen). Synge sympathizes with Nora and identifies with the Tramp, the two developing characters in the play, in opposition to their static counterparts, Dan Burke and Michael Dara. The Tramp's sympathetic nature and colorful talk awaken hitherto untapped imaginative reserves in Nora, so that the surroundings of mountain mist and road become reinvested with their primary magic. The play thus dramatizes Synge's central preoccupations: the conflict between actuality and human aspirations, the awareness of human mutability, and human beings' intimate relation with the natural world.

In the Shadow of the Glen dramatizes life-and-death issues in many ways, both literally and metaphorically, and on different levels of seriousness and comedy: Daniel Burke appears dead but rises twice. His ploy is to test the convention of life (his wife's fidelity) with the perspective of death, and he succeeds in exposing it as illusory. The audience begins with a conventional view of death; proceeds, after Dan's first resurrection (through the sharing of his vantage point, but not his point of view), to a seriocomic view of life; and ends, after his second resurrection, with a romantic sharing of the Tramp's vantage point and point of view on both life and death. As its sympathies shift, the audience proceeds from an ironic view of Nora's infidelity to an ironic view of Dan's righteousness. The first revelation is that the conventional phenomena of death are deceptive; the final revelation is that the conventional phenomena of life are equally deceptive. The playgoer begins by believing Dan to be dead in body and ends by believing him dead in soul. These ambiguities and shifts in the plot are reflected in the language and imagery of the play, which propose states of animality, madness, and age as relative conditions between life and death.

It is clear, for example, that Nora's memories of Patch Darcy condition her response to the Tramp, and as the play progresses, the connections between these two male figures multiply, as do the associations of the Tramp with death. Thus, as the image of Patch Darcy (his life-in-death counterpart), the Tramp is at once the antagonist of Dan and Michael, death-in-life counterparts. The Tramp is, in an important sense, the ghost of Patch Darcy, for he is the counterpart, in Nora's consciousness, of her dead lover. She seems to recognize the affinity, at first dimly but with sufficient clarity at the end to follow her Patch into the mists on the mountainside to romance, and probably to madness and death. Thus, the Tramp, as Patch Darcy revenant, is Nora's shadow of the Wicklow glen. By a combination of poetic language, naturalistic action, and farce, the play transforms its source into a small triumph, preparing the way for Synge's greatest achievement, *The Playboy of the Western World.*

THE PLAYBOY OF THE WESTERN WORLD

The Playboy of the Western World originated in a story, recorded in 1898, about a man named Lynchenaun "who killed his father with the blow of a spade when he was in a passion" and, with the aid of the people of Inishmaan, evaded the police to escape eventually to the United States. When later (1903-1905) Synge visited Counties Kerry and Mayo, he gathered further materials for this work: observations of the lonely landscapes of the western seaboard, the moodiness and rebellious temperament of the people, and their religiosity, alcoholism, and fanciful language. For the next two years, he worked steadily on the play under five successive titles, almost twenty

scenarios, and a dozen complete drafts, before it was finally produced on January 26, 1907.

The play develops the Lynchenaun story into that of Christy Mahon, a timorous Kerry farmboy who has fled north from the scene of his parricide to a lonely stretch of the coastline of Mayo. There he happens on a remote public house where he tells his story. The villagers give him refuge, and as he is called on to retell his story to a succession of curious neighbors, his embellishments become more colorful, and his self-confidence grows in proportion to the hyperbole. The villagers respond to these accounts with increasing admiration, so that Christy is soon regarded as a hero for his passionate deed. He strikes fear in the men and desire in the women, especially in the daughter of the house, Pegeen Mike. She rejects her fiancé, the pious Shawn Keogh, for Christy's attentions, which she seeks to retain against the competition of the village women, especially the Widow Quin. All this attention drives Christy to further heights of eloquence—especially in the love scene with Pegeen—and to feats of athletic skill at the village sports.

These triumphs, however, are rudely deflated by the appearance of another, older Kerryman, with a bandaged head: Christy's father, very much alive. He exposes Christy as a coward and a liar, and the crowd, Pegeen included, immediately rejects their erstwhile champion. Christy has been changed, however, and to prove his father wrong and regain his reputation and Pegeen's affections, he attacks his father again, this time laying him low "in the sight of all." Christy, however, has misjudged the effect of such an action on the villagers, who distinguish between the admirable "gallous story" and the shocking "dirty deed," and they capture Christy to bring him to justice. He is disillusioned with all of them and threatens indiscriminate vengeance, whereupon his father again revives, recognizes Christy's newfound character, and invites him back to Kerry as master of the house. Christy agrees, and they depart, casting aspersions on the "villainy of Mayo and the fools in here." Too late, Pegeen realizes that she has lost a true champion.

The play provoked immediate outrage among the Dublin audiences: They considered it an insult to national pride, to Catholicism, and to common decency.

Among a people hoping for a fair, if not positive, treatment in support of their long-standing grievance against British rule, the play was a cruel disappointment. For his part, Synge refused to tone down the play's oaths and irreverent allusions, even when appealed to privately by the actors and by his fellow Protestants Yeats and Lady Gregory. The protests, in fact, turned into a full-scale riot with Christy's reference to "a drift of chosen females standing in their shifts," which was considered an intolerable obscenity. In the week that followed, the police protected the stage and players from nightly attack, Yeats defended the freedom of the stage in public debate, Synge himself granted an unfortunate interview to the press, and the newspapers were full of acrimonious argument. In retrospect, it is not difficult to understand why a Dublin audience, sensitive to signs of religious and ethnic derogation, should react so vehemently to the work of a son of the landed class produced at the "national" theater and composed of such an original blend of Rabelaisian humor, lyricism, romance, and exaggeration.

In his preface to the play, Synge anticipates a hostile reaction by praising the "popular imagination that is fiery and magnificent, and tender" that he found among the people of the remote regions. He proposes that the language and images are authentic, "that the wildest sayings and ideas in this play are tame indeed compared with the fancies one may hear in any little hillside cabin." Although it is true that Synge's sources—in plot, language, and characterization—are sound, the combination here, more than in his other works, is uniquely his own. Just as the action and characterization lack normal constraints, so, too, is the language compressed and heightened.

The distinctive language of *The Playboy of the Western World* derives from several sources: the Hiberno-English dialects of the West of Ireland, vestiges of Tudor English still found in Ireland, popular sermons, and Synge's own penchant for musical, rhythmic prose. Chief among these is the influence of Irish Gaelic syntax, vocabulary, and idiom, with its rich lode of religious and natural imagery. This convention is particularly effective at the romantic climax in act 3, although it can sound parodic in scenes of less excitement. Even so, Synge's particular artistic use of local dialect is considerably more flexible and expressive than the comparable experiments of Lady Gregory or Yeats.

In this dialect, Synge found an ideal vehicle for his own passionate vision of the lonely outsider. Christy is the poet whose creative gifts are only superficially appreciated by a convention-bound society; Christy not only invests the language with new zest and daring but also unknowingly transforms himself, by the same process of imaginative energy, from a cowering lout into a master of his destiny. His transformation begins as the people of Mayo trust his story and continues as he realizes his own narrative skills; it is completed when, with full moral awareness, he strikes his father down a second time. His father is the first to recognize the new Christy; Pegeen Mike does so, too, but for her it is too late; for the rest, the episode is no more than a subject for gossip.

Christy's path to his apotheosis comes only after an erratic journey of surges and reversals; *The Playboy of the Western World* is exuberant comedy in its action as well as in its language and characterization. It contains moments of farce, satire, tragicomedy, and the mock heroic. As Ann Saddlemyer's standard edition shows, Synge's revisions were vigorous and meticulous, act 3 giving him the most difficulties; some of these difficulties—Pegeen's motivations and the resolution of the Widow Quin's role—arguably remain unresolved. For all of its difficulties, however, this act achieves brilliant closure and includes perhaps the finest dramatic writing to come from the Irish theater.

The power of *The Playboy of the Western World* rests on more than its verbal pyrotechnics and comic structure; as many critics have argued, it exhibits features of the scapegoat archetype, the Oedipus myth, and the Messiah theme. It has relationships with Irish folk legend, with the early Irish Ulster cycle of heroic tales, and with Ibsen's *Peer Gynt* (1867). Whatever the relevance of these sources or analogues to an appreciation of this great play, the play's qualities derive from the happy collaboration of Synge's instinctive sense of the dramatic and the quality of his material. He describes it thus to an admirer: "The wildness and, if you will, the vices of the Irish peasantry are due, like their extraordinary good points of all kinds, to the *richness* of their nature—a thing that is priceless beyond words."

DEIRDRE OF THE SORROWS

In his unfinished last play, *Deirdre of the Sorrows*, Synge was in the process of making a new departure. He found that the challenge of writing on a heroic theme from the Ulster cycle presented fresh difficulties, which he took satisfaction in solving. It is generally conceded that his version humanizes the legend: It is more realistic than the versions by Æ and Yeats, with which it is often compared.

OTHER MAJOR WORKS

NONFICTION: *The Aran Islands*, 1907; *In Wicklow*, 1910; *The Autobiography of J. M. Synge*, 1965; *Letters to Molly: John Millington Synge to Máire O'Neill, 1906-1909*, 1971 (Ann Saddlemyer, editor); *My Wallet of Photographs*, 1971 (Lilo Stephens, introducer and arranger); *Some Letters of John M. Synge to Lady Gregory and W. B. Yeats*, 1971 (Saddlemyer, editor); *The Collected Letters of John Millington Synge*, 1983-1984 (2 volumes; Saddlemyer, editor).

MISCELLANEOUS: *Plays, Poems, and Prose*, 1941; *Collected Works*, 1962-1968 (Ann Saddlemyer and Robin Skelton, editors).

BIBLIOGRAPHY

Casey, Daniel J. *Critical Essays on John Millington Synge*. New York: G. K. Hall, 1994. These essays by Synge scholars cover topics such as Synge's use of language, his poems, and most of his plays, including *The Well of the Saints* and *The Tinker's Wedding* as well as the more famous *The Playboy of the Western World*. Bibliography and index.

Gerstenberger, Donna Lorine. *John Millington Synge*. Rev. ed. Boston: Twayne, 1990. A basic biography and critical evaluation of Synge's works. Bibliography.

Kiely, David M. *John Millington Synge: A Biography*. New York: St. Martin's Press, 1995. Kiely covers the life of this complex and difficult dramatist. Bibliography and index.

Krause, Joseph. *The Regeneration of Ireland: Essays*. Bethesda, Md.: Academica Press, 2001. This scholarly work focuses on the intellectual life of Ireland in the late nineteenth and early twentieth centuries, focusing on Synge's life and works. Bibliography and index.

McCormack, W. J. *Fool of the Family: A Life of J. M. Synge*. New York: New York University Press, 2000. McCormack draws on previously unpublished material in his depiction of Synge, which places the dramatist in the context of the cultural changes taking place around him.

McDonald, Ronan. *Tragedy and Irish Writing: Synge, O'Casey, Beckett*. New York: Palgrave, 2001. McDonald examines the treatment of tragedy in Irish literature, focusing on the works of Synge, Sean O'Casey, and Samuel Beckett. Bibliography and index.

Watson, George J. *Irish Identity and the Literary Revival: Synge, Yeats, Joyce, and O'Casey*. 2d ed. Washington D.C.: Catholic University of America Press, 1994. Watson looks at the historical and sociological developments taking place in Ireland while Synge, W. B. Yeats, James Joyce, and Sean O'Casey were writing and the influence these events had on their works. Bibliography and index.

Cóilín D. Owens,
updated by Peter C. Holloran

T

GEORGE TABORI

Born: Budapest, Hungary; May 24, 1914

PRINCIPAL DRAMA

Flight into Egypt, pr. 1952, pb. 1953
The Emperor's Clothes, pr. 1953
Miss Julie, pr. 1956 (adaptation of August
    Strindberg's play)
Brouhaha, pr. 1958
Brecht on Brecht: An Improvisation, pr. 1962, pb.
    1967 (adaptation of selections of Bertolt
    Brecht's work)
*The Resistable Rise of Arturo Ui: A Gangster
    Spectacle*, pr. 1962, pb. 1968 (adaptation of
    Brecht's play *Der aufhaltsame Aufstieg des
    Arturo Ui*)
Andorra, pr. 1963 (adaptation of Max Frisch's play)
The Nigger-lovers, pr. 1967
The Cannibals, pr. 1968, pb. 1973
The Guns of Carrar, pr. 1968, pb. 1970 (adaptation
    of Brecht's play *Die Gesehre der Frau Carras*)
Pinkville, pr. 1970
Mother Courage, pr. 1970 (adaptation of Brecht's
    Mutter Courage und ihre Kinder)
Clowns, pr. 1972
The 25th Hour, pr. 1974
Talk Show, pr. 1976
Changes, pr. 1976
Weisman und Rotgesicht, pr. 1978 (radio play), pr.
    1990 (staged; *Weisman and Copperface*, 1991)
My Mother's Courage, pr. 1979
Der Voyeur, pr. 1982
Jubiläum, pr. 1983
Mein Kampf, pr. 1987 (*Mein Kampf: A Farce*, pr.
    1989)
Die Goldberg-Variationen, pr. 1991
Nathans Tod, pr. 1991
Requiem for a Spy, pr. 1993
A Mass Murderer and Her Friends, pr. 1995
Die Ballade vom Wiener Schnitzel, pr. 1996

OTHER LITERARY FORMS

Although George Tabori gained the greater part of his fame in the United States as the writer of award-winning dramatic screenplays, he originally was lauded (particularly in European literary circles) as the writer of such critically acclaimed novels as *Original Sin* (1947). Tabori's novels *Beneath the Stone* (1945) and *The Caravan Passes* (1951), for example, preceded his earliest drama, *Flight into Egypt* (1952), and deal almost exclusively with the philosophical contemplation of evil. On the other hand, later novels such as *The Journey: A Confession* (1958) and the memoir *My Mother's Courage* (1979) tend to focus on personal issues such as love and family in the face of inhumanity. Tabori's plays remain the primary focus of his career, although such works as *Frohes Fest* (1981), in which he both wrote the screenplay and directed the film, show his extensive range beyond the theatrical drama.

ACHIEVEMENTS

Resembling in many ways his mentor, Bertolt Brecht, George Tabori spent decades developing his skills as a playwright, screenwriter, novelist, and essayist. Given his literary zeal, then, it is not surprising that he was honored for his contributions to the areas of theater, screen, and text by a number of wide-ranging awards. In 1969, Tabori won the Best Foreign Film award. In 1981, *Frohes Fest*, a film that he directed and for which he wrote the screenplay, received the International Filmfest Mannheim-Heidelberg Grand Prize. In 1992, he was awarded the George Büchner Prize for Literature, and, perhaps most remarkably, given his background as one of the last surviving witnesses to the Holocaust, was extended honorary Austrian citizenship. These awards, however, do not fully demonstrate the esteem in which Tabori is held by European audiences. Despite the tragedies of his own life, Tabori's writings unflinchingly take on the most difficult of topics—death, hatred, and personal moral responsibility—with great integrity and honesty.

BIOGRAPHY

The son of journalist Kornel (Cornelius) Tabori and Elsa Ziffer, George Tabori was born May 24, 1914, in Budapest, Hungary, and raised in a Jewish, though secular, family. Coming of age during the nascence of the Nazi Party in Europe, Tabori completed high school in 1932 and then traveled to Berlin, where he worked in a hotel for two years. He returned afterward to Budapest but decided that his interest in writing and journalism would be more easily pursued in London.

Tabori spent the war years serving as a journalist and war correspondent for the British Broadcasting Corporation and the British army, not realizing that his own life would be irrevocably altered by the rise of German leader Adolf Hitler. As Tabori would later describe in his moving memoir, *My Mother's Courage*, his father, Kornel Tabori, was deported to Auschwitz, and his mother, Elsa Ziffer, only barely escaped the same fate. Although George Tabori was safe in London, he would be haunted ever after by his father's 1944 murder—a scenario that would be played out endlessly in his tragedy *The Cannibals*.

After the war, Tabori emigrated to the United States, where he began writing novels and adapting plays for the Hollywood film industry. Although he was married twice in the United States (first to Hanna Freund, whom he divorced in 1954, and then to the actress Viveca Lindfors, whom he divorced in 1970) and had two children (John and Lena, both by his second marriage), he never truly felt at home in America. Therefore, it was no coincidence that when a German theater agent offered to stage *The Cannibals*, a play set in a concentration camp, in Europe, Tabori found the idea to be too compelling to ignore. Moving in 1968 to Germany, he pursued an extensive career in the theatre, finally culminating in the acquisition of his own drama company in Vienna.

ANALYSIS

As one of last survivors of a terrible, but distant era, George Tabori imbues all of his dramatic works with the underlying fear that the horrors of the past, however many years distant, simply lie sleeping beneath the surface of "civilized" society and may, once again, rise up to destroy humanity. Tabori implicitly asks: Who and what are determining how Jews should lead their lives? *The Cannibals*, *Mein Kampf: A Farce*, and *My Mother's Courage*, all provide examples of how individuals can be reduced to mere symbols or stereotypes by the circumstances of their lives while still managing, through adherence to inner principles and agapic love, to retain their dignity. The true evil of the Holocaust seems to be that the choice between life and death can be reduced to a mere matter of expediency should one's humanity cease to play a role in one's perceptions of others. On the other hand, it is also the refusal of an individual to allow his or her dignity to be stripped from him or her that, paradoxically, allows that individual to remain human.

THE CANNIBALS

In *The Cannibals*, a play Tabori dedicated to his father, the playwright examines the extent to which individuals can be forced to abandon even the most basic elements of morality. When Puffi, an inmate of a concentration camp, is accidentally killed, his fellow prisoners are ordered by the sadistic Capo to eat his body or be similarly killed. Stripped of their individuality by their shaved heads and identical clothing, the concentration camp inmates are denied any identity beyond that of their individual stereotypes; one is a gypsy, one is a homosexual, one is a Jew, and so forth—a condition that is intended to encourage distance and vicious competition between the inmates. However, even under such horrific conditions as starvation and sadistic coercion, most of the prisoners still refuse to yield their humanity—only two prisoners choose to eat their former companion. Even though this choice allows the two prisoners to survive the death camp and, eventually, become prosperous

American citizens, the loss of their dignity haunts them far more intensely than the pain of loss suffered by the children and grandchildren of those inmates who refused to defile themselves.

The central character, "Uncle Tabori" (clearly a reference to Tabori's father Kornel), is a voice for morality whose vivid recollection of a dream stirs most of the other prisoners to retain the dignity refused them by their German captors. Even when Uncle Tabori is stripped of his clothing (the last, tattered vestiges of "society" clinging to his wasted body) and led, naked, to his execution, the old man refuses to yield. Only the outer trapping of his humanity can be taken from him—not his inner soul. Following Jewish ritual, he tries to gather together a "minyan" of prisoners to jointly resist defilement. Even in death, he remains the noble leader of his group.

Mein Kampf: A Farce

In *Mein Kampf*, another of Tabori's Holocaust plays, Herzl, a poor Austrian Jew, encounters a very young, impoverished Hitler in a flophouse in Vienna. Herzl, too compassionate to accept his new "friend's" impending death without feeling guilt too intense to bear, finds himself confronted with a choice of saving Hitler, fully aware that if he does he will thus be responsible for the Holocaust. Herzl feels that, to remain human, he must have a respect for life that encompasses even the life of a madman like Hitler. He also hopes, in vain, that his act of kindness may motivate the young Hitler to pursue different avenues of greatness beyond those of the political sphere. The irony, that a single act of love can be the cause of great evil, is a quandary that never fully resolves in Tabori's work. Kindness, love, and respect, although frequently demonstrated in Tabori's plays, do not have reliably positive consequences for those who practice them—in fact, the practice of virtue seems to condemn the practitioner to certain death as often as it saves him or her. The sole purpose, Tabori seems to suggest, in practicing virtue, is to reinforce the nobler aspects of one's character—not to expect any kind of external-world benefit.

My Mother's Courage

In most of his plays, Tabori seems to suggest that it is comic resistance in the face of death that makes

Jews "Jewish." If Tabori has an answer to the Jewish question, then it is in his insistence on keeping Jewish humor alive and transcending the absurd with dignity. This transcendence is perhaps what makes *My Mother's Courage* so unique. Of all Tabori's plays, *My Mother's Courage* is undoubtedly the most poetic and most optimistic, perhaps because it embodies all the elements that Tabori remembered existing in his real-life relationship with his mother. The play tells a personal, as well as universal, story about how it is the quirks and accidents of life that affect people far more than any real intent on their part.

My Mother's Courage is Tabori's eloquent depiction of how an ordinary Jewish housewife—his own mother, in fact—accidentally survives a deportation to Auschwitz by appealing to the quirky nature of an ordinarily vicious Nazi officer. She does not expect to be called heroic, although her solemn protection of a young, raped girl also caught up in the violence of a forced deportation might make her seem so, and she does not attribute her escape from death to anything but blind luck (the true account of Elsa Ziffer's survival, in fact). Her son, Tabori the playwright and Tabori the character, wants the world to remember her story about her chance encounter with a German officer because of the sheer absurdity of it—it is not kindness but perverse luck that causes the Nazi officer to let Tabori's mother live. Understanding that it is this very absurdity that rules life is what allows Jews to carry on in the midst of madness—that it is the humor inherent in the absurd that encourages survival.

With its obvious reference to Brecht's *Mutter Courage und ihre Kinder* (pr. 1941, pb. 1949; *Mother Courage and Her Children*, 1941), Tabori portrays a mother who is honest and naïve—the exact opposite of Brecht's tragic camp-follower. The mother and son in this play gain a measure of pleasure and dignity by maintaining their honesty and integrity in the face of certain death. As in *Mein Kampf*, the pursuit of virtue is a worthy goal unto itself. In this play, fortunately, such gentle idealism does not also end up costing lives. Perhaps it is this gentleness, in fact, that makes *My Mother's Courage* the most popular of Tabori's plays.

OTHER MAJOR WORKS

LONG FICTION: *Beneath the Stone*, 1945; *Companions of the Left Hand*, 1946; *Original Sin*, 1947; *The Caravan Passes*, 1951; *The Journey: A Confession*, 1958; *The Good One*, 1960.

SCREENPLAYS: *I Confess*, 1953; *The Journey*, 1959; *No Exit*, 1962 (adaptation of Jean-Paul Sartre's play); *Secret Ceremony*, 1968; *Parades*, 1972; *Insomnia*, 1975; *Frohes Fest*, 1981; *My Mother's Courage*, 1996 (adaptation of his play).

NONFICTION: *Ich wollte meine Tochter läge tot zu meinen Füssen und hätte die Juwelen in den Ohren: Improvisationen über Shakespeares Shylock: Dokumentation einer Theaterarbeit*, 1979; *My Mother's Courage*, 1979 (memoir).

BIBLIOGRAPHY

Feinberg, Anat. *Embodied Memory: The Theatre of George Tabori*. Iowa City: University of Iowa Press, 1999. Feinberg provides readers the first English-language study of the dramatic works of Tabori. Feinberg states that Tabori, like his predecessor, Brecht, tries to embody "the ideal union" of playwright, director, theater manager, and actor. He also suggests that Tabori rejects sentimentality and philosemitism in his plays, preferring stark realism in both the depictions of scenes and the frailties of the characters. Feinberg does not address the autobiographical elements of Tabori's works because he sees them as the most commonly addressed issues in his plays.

Garforth, Julian A. "George Tabori's Bare Essentials: A Perspective on Beckett Staging in Germany." *Forum Modernes Theater* (Tubingen) 9, no. 1 (1994): 59-75. A great deal has been written about Tabori's admiration for the works of Brecht. Garforth focuses instead on another of Tabori's inspirations, Samuel Beckett, and how the playwright has chosen to adapt absurdist motifs in general and Beckett's themes in particular within his own works. Tabori's *The 25th Hour* is presented as having classic absurdist traits—death counterbalanced with zany humor, farce, wit, and slapstick.

Gottfried, Martin. "Theatre: *Merchant of Venice* in Munich." *Saturday Review* 6:3 (1979): 36. Gottfried describes Tabori's "improvisations" on William Shakespeare's *The Merchant of Venice*. The rereading of this classic play for the modern stage, including references to Hitler, Joseph Goebbels, and brownshirts, particularly emphasizes the absurdly overdrawn hatred that Shakespeare has for his Jewish villain. Shylock's character, according to Tabori's vision, becomes a symbolic thread connecting ancient anti-Semitism with its modern counterpart.

Zipes, Jack. "George Tabori and the Jewish Question," *Theater* 29, no. 2 (1999): 98-107. Zipes analyzes several of George Tabori's dramas in the light not of their autobiographical or historical significance but of their universal depiction of the nature of identity. Zipes asserts that Tabori's primary purpose in writing such works as *The Cannibals* is not to horrify or disgust audiences but to determine what it means to be Jewish today or what are the politics of identity, especially when one is not entirely sure of the implications of not knowing one's own identity.

Julia M. Meyers

RABINDRANATH TAGORE

Born: Calcutta, India; May 7, 1861
Died: Calcutta, India; August 7, 1941

PRINCIPAL DRAMA
Prakritir Pratishodh, pb. 1884 (verse play; *Sanyasi: Or, The Ascetic*, 1917)

Rājā o Rāni, pb. 1889 (verse play; *The King and the Queen*, 1918)

Visarjan, pb. 1890 (verse play; based on his novel *Rajarshi; Sacrifice*, 1917)

Chitrāngadā, pb. 1892 (verse play; *Chitra*, 1913)

Prayaschitta, pr. 1909 (based on his novel *Bau-Thakuranir Hat*)

Rājā, pb. 1910 (*The King of the Dark Chamber*, 1914)

Dākghar, pb. 1912 (*The Post Office*, 1914)

Phālguni, pb. 1916 (*The Cycle of Spring*, 1917)

Arupratan, pb. 1920 (revision of his play *Rājā*)

Muktadhārā, pb. 1922 (English translation, 1950)

Raktakarabi, pb. 1924 (*Red Oleanders*, 1925)

Chirakumār Sabhā, pb. 1926

Natir Pujā, pb. 1926 (*Worship of the Dancing Girl*, 1950)

Sesh Rakshā, pb. 1928

Paritrān, pb. 1929 (revision of *Prayaschitta*)

Tapati, pb. 1929 (revision of *Rājā o Rāni*)

Chandālikā, pr., pb. 1933 (English translation, 1938)

Bānsari, pb. 1933

Nritya-natya Chitrāngadā, pb. 1936 (revision of his play *Chitrāngadā*)

Nritya-natya Chandālikā, pb. 1938 (revision of his play *Chandālikā*)

Three Plays, pb. 1950

OTHER LITERARY FORMS

A multifaceted genius, Rabindranath Tagore did not leave any literary genre unexplored. His worldwide fame rests chiefly on his achievements as a poet; the quality and quantity of his poetry have tended to overshadow his contributions in the areas of drama, fiction, and nonfiction. He published nearly sixty collections of poetry, consisting of short lyrics generally characterized by a unique metaphysical strain, a yearning spiritual quest set against the beauty of the natural landscape of Bengal, his home state. This elemental force also manifested itself in the production of about three thousand *Rabindrasangit*, poignantly evocative songs for which Tagore both wrote the lyrics and composed the music.

Tagore produced ten novels and close to one hundred short stories in a comparatively "realistic" mode, unflinchingly examining social problems of the day and depicting their impact on representative characters. He translated many of his Bengali works into English, albeit with varying degrees of artistic success; some are justifiably regarded as original compositions in English. Tagore also wrote essays and letters, travelogues and memoirs, and delivered lectures and sermons on a wide variety of subjects; these considerable prose writings illuminate his personality and provide important insights into Tagore's intellectual life as well as into the lives and times of the many people with whom he came into contact. He was both a pragmatist and philosopher, writing simple and eminently practical manuals (for example, on methods of village reconstruction in Bengal) and significant treatises on social, political, and educational, as well as religious and literary, matters. Toward the end of his life, he began to take up painting seriously, creating several striking works that are included in two portfolio collections.

ACHIEVEMENTS

Poet, dramatist, novelist, composer, critic, translator, philosopher, educator, nationalist, reformer, painter, director, choreographer, actor—Rabindranath Tagore's talents were manifold. Any account of his accomplishments runs the risk of being inadvertently incomplete. The range and variety of his work prompted one respected Bengali scholar to comment that "Rabindranath is the world's most complete writer." He straddles the world of Bengali literature like a colossus; his writing is the yardstick against which other writers are compared. In all modern Indian literatures—let alone Bengali—Tagore's influence was pervasive, inspiring a contemporary cultural renaissance. He is perhaps the one person readily identifiable as *the* modern Indian writer. At the popular level, Indians to a large degree venerate him as a seer: Mahatma Gandhi is known as the *Mahātmā* ("Great Soul"), Tagore as the *Gurudeva* ("Revered Guru").

In Tagore's hands, the Bengali language underwent a rapid progression toward flexibility and modernization. The advance of Bengali literature telescoped into Tagore's career what normally might have taken three or four generations of writers to achieve. Tagore revolutionized Bengali poetry by pioneering the use of colloquial diction in place of the stiff, formal Bengali rhetoric based on Sanskrit, by experimenting with and inventing many new verse forms and meters, and by choosing his subjects from every aspect of life. As an author of fiction, Tagore introduced and perfected the art of the short story in Bengali, and he refined the existing trend of dealing with realistic material. In the area of music, he rebelled against orthodoxy by combining in his songs the conventions of classical *rāga* with the popular modes of folk music. His work in the theater featured an insistence on nonrepresentational stagecraft and the importance of the imagination, and an antipathy toward spectacle and illusionistic devices.

A firm believer in education as a natural, pleasurable, and creative experience, Tagore set a precedent by establishing his own open-classroom school away from the city of Calcutta, which grew into an interna-

Rabindranath Tagore (© The Nobel Foundation)

tional university founded on his idealistic concept of universal humanity. Actively concerned with social and economic reform, he later conceived of a rural reconstruction center near the university, where he implemented his ideas on community development, the earliest such experiment in India. Even in matters of politics, he was a visionary: Years before Gandhi arrived in India, Tagore had laid down the theoretical tenets of the doctrine of nonviolent noncooperation. One of the earliest prophets of internationalism, in his travels, Tagore interpreted India to the rest of the world, and the East to the West, in an appeal for universal understanding and cooperation.

Tagore received the Nobel Prize in Literature in 1913, becoming the first non-European to win this award. Knighthood was conferred on him in 1915, which he resigned four years later to protest the Jalianwalla Bagh massacre at Amritsar, where British troops fired into a crowd of unarmed Indians, causing two thousand casualties. Tagore's songs "Jana-gana-mana adhināyaka jaya he" (hail, the leader of the minds of our people) and "Āmār sonār bānglā" (my golden Bengal) were chosen respectively as the national anthems of India in 1947 and Bangladesh in 1971.

BIOGRAPHY

The youngest of fourteen children, Rabindranath Tagore was born into the gifted and aristocratic Tagore family, one of the most important households in the history of nineteenth century Calcutta, capital of British India. He received an enlightened upbringing at home, in an atmosphere in which the spirit of knowledge reigned supreme, in which intellectual discussions on international subjects were encouraged, and in which all members of the large joint family regularly participated in a variety of cultural activities. His career in school was undistinguished— he disliked its institutionalized discipline and often played truant. In any case the education imparted at home in tutorial sessions conducted by his elder brothers was probably more substantial, as was the influence of the personality, erudition, and spiritualism of Debendranath Tagore, his father. He wrote his first poem when he was eight years old and had his first poem published at the age of fourteen. At sixteen he made his acting debut, in his brother Jyotirindranath's adaptation of Molière's *Le Bourgeois Gentilhomme* (1670; *The Would-Be Gentleman*, 1675). At the age of eighteen, he began writing his first play, in verse, and at twenty, he had composed and acted the lead role in his first musical.

In 1878, Tagore was sent to England to complete his studies, but with characteristic indifference he left University College, London (where he was to study law), and returned home. He married Mrinalini Devi, of Jessore (now in Bangladesh), in 1883. His father dispatched him in 1890 to Shelaidaha in East Bengal, to oversee the family estates there. This sojourn placed him in intimate contact with rural Bengal and her people. The exposure at home to the world of learning, humanities, and the arts had been one permanent influence on Tagore. The deep religious convictions and philosophical nature of his father had also affected him. His experience with formal academics had made a significant impact on his attitude toward human-made institutions. In Shelaidaha, he absorbed the physical details that he would use in his writings: The empathic observation of nature in all its moods and the keen awareness of the simple life of the Bengali peasant led him to perceive the strong bond between nature and humans immanent in the physical world. His most romantic and lyrical plays (notably *Chitra*) date from this period. They were all written in verse.

The Shelaidaha period came to an end in 1901, when Tagore moved to Shantiniketan, a starkly beautiful spot in West Bengal that his father used as a retreat for meditation. Here he decided to establish his own school, but finances were short, and a series of private tragedies beset him. Mrinalini Devi died prematurely in 1902, his thirteen-year-old daughter, Renuka, died in 1903, Debendranath Tagore, in 1905, and his youngest son, Somendranath, in 1907. The pain of these deaths expresses itself to some extent explicitly in *The Post Office* and implicitly in *The King of the Dark Chamber* and *The Cycle of Spring*. At this point, prose became the dominant medium of his plays; he would never revert to writing verse drama again. Tagore took part during this time in na-

tionalist protests against the British but soon withdrew from active politics. In 1912, he accompanied his son Rathindranath—who had been graduated from and wished to complete a doctorate at the University of Illinois—to the United States. On their way, in London, he showed his acquaintance the painter William Rothenstein a few English translations he had made of his own poems from the collection *Gitānjali* (1910). Through Rothenstein's good offices, these exercises were published in 1912 as *Gitanjali* (*Song Offerings*), which eventually won for Tagore the Nobel Prize.

Tagore spent the winter of 1912-1913 in the United States, lecturing in several cities. The announcement of his Nobel Prize later in 1913 made him an instant celebrity all over the world. For the remainder of his life, his presence was in such great demand everywhere that he had to undertake about a dozen foreign tours of North and South America, England, Europe, Russia, the Middle East, Southeast Asia, and the Far East. In 1918, he laid the foundation stone for the Visvabharati University at Shantiniketan and, in 1922, inaugurated Shriniketan, its sister township and rural development center. The amazing thing is that in spite of all these commitments, the prodigious flow of his writing continued unabated. In fact, he wrote as many as twelve of his major plays in this last period, the 1920's and 1930's being particularly productive in the field of drama.

ANALYSIS

To say that Rabindranath Tagore was a prolific dramatist would be an understatement. In his sixty-year career as a playwright, he wrote more than fifty works in the dramatic mode. He tried his hand at so many different styles that a classification of his dramatic output is essential. Tagore himself applied the following terms to his plays: *nātak* or *nātya* (drama), *nātyakāvya* (dramatic poem), *nātikā* (playlet), *prahasan* (farce), *gitinātya* (musical drama), and *nritya-nātya* (dance drama). His conventional *nātya* can be further subdivided into two categories—the early blank-verse dramas *The King and the Queen* and *Sacrifice*, and the others, numbering twenty, all written in prose and, with one exception, published after 1907. Although Tagore separately classified seven of his works as "dramatic poems," they are technically similar to the two verse *nātya*, the only substantial difference being that the latter are in five acts. Because all seven "dramatic poems" were printed by 1900, it would be appropriate to categorize them chronologically, together with the two poetic plays, as his early dramatic work in verse. To them should be added two of Tagore's "playlets," both written in verse, published during this same period. The author also labeled as "playlets" four other dramatic works in prose, published after 1907, of which the most important is *Chandālikā*. While *Chandālikā* is a short play, two of the other "playlets" are about as long as some of the full-length plays. Once again, therefore, it may be more helpful in an analysis to place these four pieces with Tagore's later plays, which are exclusively in prose.

Tagore wrote four "farces," three of them during the 1890's. Of all of his plays, these lively and relevant social comedies were the only popular successes he had for a long time on the professional stage. Tagore also attempted several artistically successful adventures in fusing music with drama. Songs are incorporated into the scripts of virtually every Tagore play, but in some of his works, the music and songs command precedence over spoken dialogue. He initiated his dramatic career with three such "musical dramas" published in the 1880's. Six more exercises in this genre appeared between 1923 and 1934, but they were more in the vein of collected songs linked by a loose plot on a common theme, for example, the advent of a particular season. Finally, in the last five years of his life, Tagore introduced his "dance dramas," in which Indian dance and musical forms merge with stories borrowed from earlier writings. Two of the three dance dramas published before his death, for example, were based on *Chitrāngadā* and *Chandālikā*, respectively. In addition, he wrote many minor dramatic miscellanea: sketches, dialogues, satiric and comic skits, and short riddles "in imitation of European charades."

Tagore constantly revised, reworked, or abridged his existing work and made dramatizations of his own fiction. Apart from the two pieces that became dance

dramas, three plays (including *Sacrifice*) had their origins in novels and five others in various short stories; *Worship of the Dancing Girl* had its genesis in a poem. Tagore's last dance drama began in the form of a poem written in 1899, metamorphosed into a dance drama in 1936, and was transformed a second time in 1939 to its present fully developed shape. Similarly, the play *Paritrān* started off as a novel published in 1883, was dramatized with a different title in 1909, and ultimately rewritten under another title. In the cases of five other plays, including *The King of the Dark Chamber*, Tagore constructed concise acting editions with altogether different titles, the stageworthy versions succeeding the originals sometimes by as many as forty years, sometimes by as few as six. In recasting *The King and the Queen* as *Tapati* forty years later, Tagore indicated his dissatisfaction with the verse original, observing that he had virtually to write a new play in prose in order to make it suitable as theater. Indeed, the very existence of his acting editions indicates his concern for the staging of his plays and should serve as compelling evidence against those critics who dismiss them as mere closet drama.

The literary influences of Tagore offer important insights into his plays. Above all writers, Tagore perhaps revered the classical Sanskrit master Kālidāsa the most; his early drama contains much proof of the impact of Kālidāsa's heroic themes, nature imagery, and lyric language. The mysticism of the fifteenth century poet Kabir attracted Tagore, too, as did the devotional fervor of Vaishnava religious poetry, presenting human love as simultaneously sacred and profane, and the folk songs of his native Bengal, particularly those with a spiritual flavor, as of the wandering minstrel *bāul*. Among Western dramatists, he respected William Shakespeare. It is significant that he liked *Antony and Cleopatra* (pr. c. 1606-1607, pb. 1623) "very much" and found *Othello, the Moor of Venice* (pr. 1604, pb. 1622, revised 1623) fascinating, a "harrowing" experience. His early verse drama was to a great extent modeled after Shakespeare. Tagore admired as well the Romantic idealism of Percy Bysshe Shelley and John Keats. In later years, he acknowledged the debt to Maurice Maeterlinck in his mature "symbolic" plays. Although the initial spark may have come from a reading of Maeterlinck, there is considerable difference between the uses of symbolism as practiced by the Belgian poet and by Tagore.

The Western concepts of illusionism and naturalism in the theater, much in fashion among Tagore's contemporaries in late nineteenth century India, did not find a place in Tagore's theory of drama. Many critics, ignorant of the principal consideration that realistic drama and the representational stage (a "childish intrusion") did not in the least appeal to Tagore, are quick to point out flaws in Tagore's dramaturgy. This well-entrenched vogue of Tagore criticism has rarely been opposed, fostering the article of faith among scholarly and theatrical circles that his plays are weak on stage. That this attitude is patently false has been proved on several occasions in the theater, especially in the capable hands of the Bengali director Sombhu Mitra. Tagore is no Henrik Ibsen, and his plays consequently should not be judged by realist standards. If a comparison must be made to a Western author, the proper analogy might be William Butler Yeats, perhaps the Yeats who composed *Four Plays for Dancers* (pb. 1921) and other such later works. Tagore derived his mature drama mainly from Indian traditions, from sources as apparently divergent as Bharata's ancient theoretical discourse, the *Nātyashāstra*, and the indigenous folk theater of Bengal, the *jātrā*. From Bharata, Tagore enlisted support to vindicate his practice of discouraging painted sets in productions of his plays; as for the *jātrā*, he pointed out that "there is no forbidding separation of the actors from the spectators." Referring to the *jātrā*, he noted that "The poetry, which after all is the main thing, flows like a spreading fountain through the medium of acting." Tagore insisted, "The art of acting has to be subservient to the poetry of the written word. But that should not mean that acting must be a slave to all the other arts." He thought that actors had a special responsibility to "draw apart the curtain of naturalism and reveal the inner reality of things. If there is too much emphasis on imitative naturalism the inner view becomes clouded." For this reason, he said, "I never humour the adolescent habit of frequently changing scenes and moving the curtain up and down."

One can glean from these comments the four major characteristics of Tagore's drama. First, it is meant ideally for a completely flexible, totally open (perhaps even open-air) stage. Second, it is fluid and imaginative in the widest sense, requiring an appropriately nonillusionistic production style. Third, whether written in verse or prose, its essence is poetry, demanding heightened participatory and auditory awareness. Fourth, it purports to "reveal the inner reality of things." As in his other writings, Tagore explores in his plays the nature of humankind and its relation to divinity or the spiritual world. Some themes are immediately indicative of Tagore's spiritual preoccupations—renunciation of the world (*Sanyasi*), the realization of religious duty (*Sacrifice*), the true attributes of divinity (*The King of the Dark Chamber*), the death of a bed-ridden child (*The Post Office*), the death of winter followed by the rebirth of spring (*The Cycle of Spring*), the worship performed by a dancing girl (*Worship of the Dancing Girl*). In many plays, Tagore's choice of key characters reveals his predilection for the spiritual side of life. Besides the ascetic in *Sanyasi*, the priest in *Sacrifice*, and the Buddhist dancing girl in *Worship of the Dancing Girl*, there is Dhananjaya, the ascetic who appears in *Muktadhārā* and *Paritrān*, the Buddhist monk Ananda in *Chandālikā*, and the spiritual preceptor Purandar in *Bānsari*. In other plays, Tagore deals with people's relations with other people. Human conceptions of love and feminine beauty are the themes of *Chitra* and *Chandālikā*. The attachment between adults and children figures strongly in *Sanyasi* and *The Post Office*. *Muktadhārā* treats the invention of the machine and its adverse effects on common people. In *Red Oleanders*, the subject is the dehumanizing impact of organization and of greed for wealth. Political repression is examined in *Paritrān*, and the duties of a ruler in *The King and the Queen*. He also examines the caste structure of Hinduism in *Chandālikā*, and the conflict between love and duty in *Bānsari*. Despite the ostensibly spiritual import of many of Tagore's plays, he was actually involved with the ramifications of these issues in everyday life.

Thus the undesirable aspects of organized religion are specifically attacked in several works: namely, ritual sacrifice in *Sacrifice*, religious intolerance in *Worship of the Dancing Girl*, and untouchability in *Chandālikā*.

THE POST OFFICE

The adjectives commonly applied to Tagore's mature prose drama are "symbolic" and "allegorical," but the playwright frequently disclaimed these notions, stating instead that his plays were indeed "just like other plays . . . very concrete." *The Post Office*, perhaps Tagore's most famous play outside Bengal, presents a fine example of how commentators trip over themselves attempting to lace his plays with significant meaning. A generally accepted theory suggests that this short play symbolizes and fulfills in its action the human desire for union with God. Such an interpretation, if correct, would cruelly contradict the actual situation depicted. A terminally ill boy, the center of attention, dies in the course of this play. Amal (the name signifies "pure") is too young even to understand the concept of God, much less wish to be united with Him. On the contrary, he is full of genuine *joie de vivre*, constantly imagining what he would do once able to walk again. The ordinary person would feel only sadness, not joy, for Amal's passing. The meaning of the play, as Yeats observed, is "less intellectual, more emotional and simple." Tagore's sensitive portrayal, however, evokes a double response at the conclusion. Yeats also recognized that *The Post Office* "conveys to the right audience an emotion of gentleness and peace." Although the audience grieves for Amal, perhaps distressed that so young a boy could not have the chance to enjoy life fully, it simultaneously rejoices that he has been liberated—according to Hindu beliefs—from the shackles of the material world. The pathos in the play is like that of an epiphany, but thoroughly real and only remotely symbolic. There remains a final consciousness that life is tragic yet beautiful, in equal, counterbalanced proportions, and must be lived fully.

THE KING OF THE DARK CHAMBER

The idea of duality in life expresses itself with relation to divinity in *The King of the Dark Chamber*. This play is undoubtedly allegorical in intent, tracing the spiritual enlightenment of humankind from a one-dimensional vision of God to an all-inclusive vision. The figure of the nameless King whom no one has seen, which recurs in so many of Tagore's plays, represents the Supreme Godhead. His queen, Sudarshanā ("the beautiful one"), stands for humanity, and they meet each other always in complete darkness. She is puzzled by the King's assertion that she will not be able to bear the sight of his face. Eventually she does get to see him and is horrified by the vision. Her spontaneous rejection of him leads her deeper into an already existing infatuation with a king manqué named Suvarna (which means "golden"). In the end, having learned through suffering, she returns to her King and accepts his appearance in total submission. Sudarshanā's development in the play is analogous to the spiritual maturation of people during their lifetime. People's originally innocent conception of life and divinity as happy and benign is usually shattered at some point by a confrontation with the harsh, pitiless cruelty of reality, which leads people immediately to question God and to negate life, sometimes as a result embracing false ideals—as signified here by the impostor Suvarna. Experience makes people mature, bringing them to a full understanding of the fact that life and divinity are simultaneously terrible and beautiful, ultimately reconciling them with God. The spiritual allegory of growth from the state of innocence through experience to the state of acceptance is by no means original, but Tagore's treatment of it shows a simple and unfettered purity. There is also, as the characters' names imply, the secondary motif that people should look not at externals but at inner truths for spiritual inspiration and purification.

RED OLEANDERS

Tagore's preoccupation with life, death, and God in the first decade of the twentieth century gave way to a more overt analysis of political and social subjects during the 1920's. *Red Oleanders* epitomizes the best work of this phase. Set in an imaginary town called Yakshapuri (in Hindu mythology, the god of wealth rules over the city of this name), the play presents a society in which the hoarding of gold demands strict discipline and a stratified class structure based on the suppression of human rights. Tagore himself explained its several layers of meaning later to his English readers: He had condemned the principle of organization for utilitarian purposes, which subjugates the individuality of people and turns "a multitude of men . . . into a gigantic system"; the passion of greed among colonial powers, "stalking abroad in the name of European civilization," and humiliating subject races; and the impersonal attitude in modern humanity that transforms the spirit of science into the tyranny of the machine, preferring mechanization over humanitarianism. The playwright had become increasingly troubled by the evils of twentieth century civilization and seemed to offer an alternative solution in the person of Nandini, the heroine of this play. Nandini symbolizes spontaneity, love, altruism, and the spirit of humanity in communion with nature. The rebellion she instigates against the dehumanizing and exploitative order succeeds; the invisible King of Yakshapuri comes out and joins forces with her to destroy his own Frankenstein after he sees the havoc it has wrought. *Red Oleanders* has been variously interpreted as a call to Indians to take up arms against the British government and as a socialistic revolt against the agencies of capitalism. Such flag-waving restrictions of its theme only constrict its essential beauty, which exists in its universal qualities, applicable to all societies.

TAPATI

In his last prose plays, published around the early 1930's, Tagore appears to have withdrawn into a less strident, more contemplative mood, exploring the struggle between love and duty in his protagonists. The mode of these late plays is comparatively realistic, the dialogue bare and incisive, devoid of the poetic overtones of Tagore's earlier prose. *Tapati*, the rewritten version of *The King and the Queen*, serves as a typical example from this period. The story deals with the obsessive passion of a king, Vikram—significantly, the king is no longer anonymous—for his queen, Sumitrā, at the expense of his royal duties. Sumitrā feels he should not neglect his kingly responsibilities because of love for her and leaves the palace. The conclusion is tragic, precipitated by an almost malevolent transformation in Vikram's char-

acter, but the chief interest in the play lies in the characterization of Sumitrā, who exemplifies the strong heroines of Tagore's later work. Although she has reminded critics of the liberated Nora in Ibsen's *Et dukkehjem* (pr., pb. 1879; *A Doll's House*, 1880), she fulfills a far more important role in Tagore's world, integral to an understanding of his canon. Tagore wrote,

> I have a stronger faith in the simple personality of man than in the prolific brood of machinery that wants to crowd it out. This personality—the divine essence of the infinite in the vessel of the finite—has its last treasure-house in woman's heart. Her pervading influence will some day restore the human to the desolated world of man. As in the animal world the physically meek has to-day inherited the earth, woman will one day prove that the meek in soul, through the sure power of love, will rescue this world from the dominance of the unholy spirit of rapacity.

Nandini and Sumitrā, among others, are creations in this mold. In the final analysis, Tagore's drama reveals a powerful underlying current of optimism and a deep faith in the feminine principle. His affirmative feeling for life, the beauty of the natural world, and the inviolable relationship between humanity and the divine, contribute to the pervasive sense of harmony and the invincible spirit of hope in his plays.

OTHER MAJOR WORKS

LONG FICTION: *Bau-Thakuranir Hat*, 1883; *Rajarshi*, 1887; *Chokher bāli*, 1902 (*Binodini*, 1959); *Naukadubi*, 1906 (*The Wreck*, 1921); *Gora*, 1910 (English translation, 1924); *Chaturanga*, 1916 (English translation, 1963); *Ghare bāire*, 1916 (*Home and the World*, 1919); *Jogajog*, 1929; *Shesher kabita*, 1929 (*Farewell, My Friend*, 1946); *Dui bon*, 1933 (*Two Sisters*, 1945).

SHORT FICTION: *The Hungry Stones and Other Stories*, 1916; *Mashi and Other Stories*, 1918; *Stories from Tagore*, 1918; *Broken Ties and Other Stories*, 1925; *The Runaway and Other Stories*, 1959.

POETRY: *Saisab sangit*, 1881; *Sandhya sangit*, 1882; *Prabhat sangit*, 1883; *Chabi o gan*, 1884; *Kari o komal*, 1887; *Mānashi*, 1890; *Sonār tari*, 1893 (*The*

Golden Boat, 1932); *Chitra*, 1895; *Chaitāli*, 1896; *Kanika*, 1899; *Kalpana*, 1900; *Katha o kahini*, 1900; *Kshanikā*, 1900; *Naivedya*, 1901; *Sisu*, 1903 (*The Crescent Moon*, 1913); *Smaran*, 1903; *Utsarga*, 1904; *Kheya*, 1905; *Gitānjali*, 1910 (*Gitanjali* [*Song Offerings*], 1912); *The Gardener*, 1913; *Gitali*, 1914; *Balāka*, 1916 (*A Flight of Swans*, 1955, 1962); *Fruit-Gathering*, 1916; *Gan*, 1916; *Stray Birds*, 1917; *Love's Gift, and Crossing*, 1918; *Palataka*, 1918 (*The Fugitive*, 1921); *Lipika*, 1922; *Poems*, 1922; *Sisu bholanath*, 1922; *The Curse at Farewell*, 1924; *Prabahini*, 1925; *Purabi*, 1925; *Fifteen Poems*, 1928; *Fireflies*, 1928; *Mahuya*, 1929; *Sheaves: Poems and Songs*, 1929; *Banabani*, 1931; *The Child*, 1931; *Parisesh*, 1932; *Punascha*, 1932; *Vicitrita*, 1933; *Bithika*, 1935; *Ses saptak*, 1935; *Patraput*, 1936, 1938 (English translation, 1969); *Syamali*, 1936 (English translation, 1955); *Khapchada*, 1937; *Prantik*, 1938; *Senjuti*, 1938; *Navajatak*, 1940; *Rogsajya*, 1940; *Sanai*, 1940; *Arogya*, 1941; *Janmadine*, 1941; *Poems*, 1942; *Sesh lekha*, 1942; *The Herald of Spring*, 1957; *Wings of Death: The Last Poems*, 1960; *Devouring Love*, 1961; *A Bunch of Poems*, 1966; *One Hundred and One*, 1967; *Last Poems*, 1973; *Later Poems*, 1974.

NONFICTION: *Jivansmriti*, 1912 (*My Reminiscences*, 1917); *Sadhana*, 1913; *Personality*, 1917; *Nationalism*, 1919; *Greater India*, 1921; *Glimpses of Bengal*, 1921; *Creative Unity*, 1922; *Talks in China*, 1925; *Lectures and Addresses*, 1928; *Letters to a Friend*, 1928; *The Religion of Man*, 1931; *Mahatmaji and the Depressed Humanity*, 1932; *Man*, 1937; *Chhelebela*, 1940 (*My Boyhood Days*, 1940); *Sabhyatar Samkat*, 1941 (*Crisis in Civilization*, 1941); *Towards Universal Man*, 1961.

MISCELLANEOUS: *Collected Poems and Plays*, 1936; *A Tagore Reader*, 1961.

BIBLIOGRAPHY

Chakraverty, Bishweshwar. *Tagore, the Dramatist: A Critical Study*. 4 vols. Delhi: B. R. Publishing, 2000. A scholarly study of Tagore's drama, organized by genre type. Bibliography and index.

Dutta, Krishna, and Andrew Robinson. *Rabindranath Tagore: The Myriad-Minded Man*. New York: St. Martin's Press, 1996. This biography of Tagore looks at the man, his philosophy, and his works. Bibliography and index.

Ivbulis, Viktors. *Tagore: East and West Cultural Unity*. Calcutta: Rabindra Bharati University, 1999. The author looks at the influence of both the West and the East in Tagore's work. Bibliography.

Nandi, Sudhirakumara. *Art and Aesthetics of Rabindra Nath Tagore*. Calcutta, India: Asiatic Society, 1999. Nandi analyzes the Tagore's aesthetics as expressed in his writings. Bibliography and index.

Nandy, Ashis. *The Illegitimacy of Nationalism: Rabindranath Tagore and the Politics of Self*. New York: Oxford University Press, 1994. This study focuses on the political and social views of Tagore as demonstrated by his life and writings. Bibliography and index.

Roy, R. N. *Rabindranath Tagore, the Dramatist*. Calcutta, India: A. Mukherjee, 1992. A study of Tagore that focuses on his dramatic works.

Ananda Lal

MANUEL TAMAYO Y BAUS

Born: Madrid, Spain; September 15, 1829
Died: Madrid, Spain; June 20, 1898

PRINCIPAL DRAMA

Juana de Arco, pr., pb. 1847 (based on Friedrich Schiller's play *Die Jungfrau von Orleans*)

Un juramento, pr., pb. 1848 (with Luis Fernández-Guerra y Orbe and Manuel Cañete)

El cinco de agosto, pr. 1848, pb. 1849

Un marido duplicado, pr. 1849, pb. 1850 (with Miguel Ruiz y Torrent)

Tran-Tran, pr., pb. 1850 (with Victorino Tamayo y

Baus; based on Jean François Alfred Bayard
and Edmond Desnoyers de Biéville's play *Les
Enfants de troupe*)

Centellas y Moncada, pr., pb. 1850 (with Benito de
Llanza y Esquibel)

Una apuesta, pr., pb. 1851 (based on the French *La
Gageure imprévue*)

Una aventura de Richelieu, pr., pb. 1851

El don del cielo, pr., pb. 1852 (with Cañete)

La esperanza de la patria, pr., pb. 1852 (with
Cañete)

Angela, pr., pb. 1852 (based on Schiller's play
Kabale und Liebe)

El peluquero de su alteza, pr. 1852, pb. 1853 (with
Cañete and Luis Fernández-Guerra y Orbe)

Huyendo del perejil, pr. 1853, pb. 1857

Virginia, pr., pb. 1853

La Ricahembra, pr., pb. 1854 (with Aureliano
Fernández-Guerra y Orbe)

El castillo de Balsaín, pr. 1854, pb. 1855 (with
Luis Fernández-Guerra y Orbe)

La locura de amor, pr., pb. 1855

Hija y madre, pr., pb. 1855

A escape, pr., pb. 1855

La bola de nieve, pr., pb. 1856

Lo positivo, pr., pb. 1862 (based on Léon Laya's
play *Le Duc Job*)

Del dicho al hecho, pr. 1862, pb. 1864 (based on
Jules Sandeau's novel *Un Héritage*)

Lances de honor, pr., pb. 1863

Más vale maña que fuerza, pr. 1866, pb. 1870

Un drama nuevo, pr., pb. 1867 (*A New Drama*,
1915)

No hay mal que por bien no venga, pr., pb. 1868

Los hombres de bien, pr., pb. 1870

Oᴛʜᴇʀ ʟɪᴛᴇʀᴀʀʏ ꜰᴏʀᴍs

The reputation of Manuel Tamayo y Baus rests almost exclusively on some twenty years of creative
work for the theater. Historical dramas and thesis
plays concerned with contemporary mores were the
centerpieces of this literary activity. Abundant, too,
were the contributions that he made to subdivisions
of the primary genre for which he wrote, inasmuch as
he authored many humorous one-act plays, cultivated

the short dramatic allegory called the *loa*, and composed librettos for the Spanish version of the musical
comedy, the *zarzuela*. In addition to plays, he wrote
three disquisitions on theatrical matters: his prologue
to *Angela*; a formal letter meant for publication addressed to his closest friend, Manuel Cañete, concerning the tragedy *Virginia*; and his maiden speech
before the Royal Spanish Academy on his public reception into that body in June of 1859. These essays
on poetics provide valuable insights into his own art
and into the dramatic theory and aesthetics of the day.

Aᴄʜɪᴇᴠᴇᴍᴇɴᴛs

Some critics consider Manuel Tamayo y Baus to
have been Spain's foremost playwright of the nineteenth century. Agreement seems fairly general that
his masterpiece is *A New Drama* and that his was a
leading role during a period of transition, uncertainty,
and tentativeness for the national theater, then somewhat in decline. His best writing came to the fore
when the Romantic school was in the process of being supplanted and when there was a reorientation in
the direction of greater realism on stage, more penetrating psychological study, and a new insistence on
moralizing satire aimed at unwholesome aspects of
the acquisitiveness of an emerging middle class. All
these tendencies were grist for his own dramatic mill.

For Tamayo y Baus, realism involved a certain degree of poetizing; however, he called for an idealized
imitation of nature rather than advocate the painting
of harsh realities exactly as they are. In his treatises,
he propounded the depiction of a purified reality, in
which conformity to fact still implied a kind of truthfulness never devoid of beauty. He himself succeeded
in incorporating this unifying technical process into
his own work. Clarín (Leopoldo Alas), one of the
most prestigious and demanding critics of the day,
found human truth in Tamayo y Baus's greatest masterpiece, *A New Drama*, but truth in combination with
what Clarín defined as the two ultimate elements of
beauty: the rudimentary integrals of forcefulness and
harmony.

These descriptive norms of Tamayo y Baus were
somewhat classical in spirit, and he endorsed them
both as critic and as dramatist. His admiration for an-

tiquity led him to believe that the ancient genre of tragedy symbolized dramatic expression in its highest form. Unsurprisingly, Tamayo y Baus would choose to bring before the public his own effort in this area of composition. The immediate fruit of his labors, *Virginia*, dated 1853, constituted the first of his two versions of that play, for he revised and perfected it over a considerable period of time. Always the author's favorite from among the many and diverse works that he had written, *Virginia* would come to be known as Spain's finest modern tragedy.

Several other plays by Tamayo y Baus either triumphed on the stage or were well received. A list of the best known and most respected would doubtless include such titles as *La Ricahembra*, *La locura de amor*, *La bola de nieve*, *Lo positivo*, and *Lances de honor*. From the points of view of critical acclaim and international attention, however, none of these plays surpassed *A New Drama*. Hispanists from outside Spain have attested the range of its influence. For example, Boris Tannenberg, writing in Paris in 1902, suggested that *A New Drama* provided a likely prototype for one of the most famous of selections from the operatic repertoire, Ruggiero Leoncavallo's *I pagliacci* (1892).

Another critic, Gerard Flynn, in an important biographical study, *Manuel Tamayo y Baus* (1973), remarks that the greatly differing degrees of imitation and originality shown by Tamayo y Baus in his many rather free arrangements of foreign plays has served to render more difficult an accurate accounting of what truly constitutes the playwright's own works; for this reason they have been estimated to number, variously, between thirty-five and fifty. Tamayo y Baus seems to have been the Spanish dramatist of the nineteenth century most oriented to German theater, and he imitated in particular Friedrich Schiller.

BIOGRAPHY

Manuel Tamayo y Baus began his life practically on stage because his family both managed and formed part of a company of itinerant players. After the birth of Manuel, which occurred in Madrid in 1829, the traveling troupe was to center its activities in the south of Spain, touring cities of Andalusia.

His parents, José Tamayo and Joaquina Baus, were able and distinguished artists. His father, an actor, directed the company, while the beautiful and talented Joaquina was a major leading lady of the day. Two of Manuel's brothers, Andrés and Victorino, were also associated with the family's enterprise in various professional undertakings. Indeed, Victorino and Manuel would eventually collaborate as writers, specifically on *Tran-Tran*, a minor play of the year 1850; of much greater import would be, however, another, later instance of their work together: Performing admirably as an actor in Manuel's *A New Drama*, Victorino would introduce to the Spanish public for the first time the powerful and moving role of the tragic figure Yorick.

That triumph, however, would not come soon; it would have to wait until 1867, when Manuel's activities as a playwright would be drawing very near their close. Being a principal role, and a masculine one, Yorick is a reminder, by way of stark contrast, of a fundamental characteristic of Tamayo y Baus's professional inclinations. In the years that represent the very beginnings of his career, the young Tamayo y Baus had shown a marked preference for plays in which the leading character was female.

The partiality shown in his theater for feminine characters, clearly reflected in the titles of several of his earliest works—*Juana de Arco*, *Angela*, *Virginia*, and *La Ricahembra*—initially arose from his exceedingly close relationship with his mother. He adored her, and he yearned to compose dramatic parts that would provide her with vehicles to display her unusual acting skill. From Joaquina Baus, Manuel had received much of his initial training, his first lessons in the arts of stagecraft. He was intellectually prepared to reap the benefits of this guidance at a remarkably early age. What quite likely constitutes the most frequently repeated story regarding incidents in Tamayo y Baus's life deals precisely with that particular. His biographers, beginning with Aureliano Fernández-Guerra y Orbe, invariably relate that when the youngster was still only eleven, his first successful effort was presented on the stage. Entitled *Genoveva de Brabante*, it appeared in Granada in 1841 and was an arrangement of a foreign work from France.

Not unexpectedly, his mother performed in that drama, portraying the principal role. When the final curtain fell, a highly emotional scene transpired: Embracing and accompanying each other to the proscenium, the proud mother and son joyfully received together the audience's warm ovation.

The script for *Genoveva de Brabante* has not survived, but in another, later play that has been published, Joaquina Baus's name is to be found listed among the members of the cast. Thus, in 1847, she was Saint Joan in *Juana de Arco*, a work first presented in Madrid in October of that year. José Tamayo was to appear in that same production also. With filial devotion, Manuel had dedicated this version of Schiller's *Die Jungfrau von Orleans* (1801; *The Maid of Orleans*, 1835) to both of his parents— the objects of all of his affections, according to a statement contained within its prologue.

This sentiment and others expressed in the dedication suggest that *Juana de Arco* may have been written quite some time before the date of its first performance. Less than two years later, in September of 1849, Tamayo y Baus would marry María Amalia Máiquez, a young lady whom he had first met in Granada before his return to Madrid in 1843. These dates and the sequence of events leading to the marriage make highly questionable the thought that his parents in 1847 would still be the sole object of his affections. The marriage, a very happy one, served to strengthen the ties of Tamayo y Baus to the theatrical life of his country. The Máiquez family was very prominent in Spanish acting circles, and Amalia's father, also called José, was himself an impresario. Apart from making possible Amalia's loving presence at his side, the betrothal and the union must have had other immediate consequences for Tamayo y Baus's life—emotional results of a consolatory nature—for soon he would suffer the grievous loss of his mother and, indeed, sorrowful and bereft, would find himself dedicating *Angela* to her memory in 1852.

With these antecedents, Tamayo y Baus, for nearly two decades of his life, would grind out play after play with only an occasional interruption. From the total perspective of his professional life and fame,

his career in the theater would provide him with many distinctive moments of singular success, especially when he triumphed with *Virginia* in 1853, with *La locura de amor* in 1855, and with *A New Drama* in 1867. Yet only three years after the gratifying reception of *A New Drama*, Tamayo y Baus would leave behind the theater and cease to be a playwright. Several explanations for this peremptory action might be properly adduced. *Los hombres de bien*, his last play, had been coolly received in 1870, and Tamayo y Baus was sensitive to this. Furthermore, a great change had taken place in Spain in 1868 with the downfall of the monarchy; Tamayo y Baus's conservative ideology, reflected in his plays, now seemed out of date.

Divorced from his former career, Tamayo y Baus would devote the last twenty-eight years of his life to other duties and activities. Elected to the Spanish Royal Academy in 1858, this body would now occupy a great part of his time. Indeed, only shortly after his retirement from the theater, he would be elected the Academy's secretary in 1874. Also, having had prior service as the administrator in charge of the Library of San Isidro, he would assume the prestigious post of director of the Spanish National Library. Beginning in 1884, he would discharge this duty until his death in 1898.

ANALYSIS

Another hard experience for Manuel Tamayo y Baus, one that followed more immediately on his marriage than the death of his mother, was the failure of *El cinco de agosto* in December of 1849. Composed by Tamayo y Baus in an exaggerated Romantic style, gloomy and lugubrious, it was in fact his first attempt at an original drama worked out entirely on his own. Its reception was sufficiently negative to compel the writer to retreat, to fall back once again to the protective aura of Schiller. Thus, his *Angela*, based on the German playwright's *Kabale und Liebe* (pr., pb. 1784; *Cabal and Love*, 1795), was another adaptation. Nevertheless, a considerable portion of the creative invention demonstrated in the play came directly from Tamayo y Baus.

During the period 1848 to 1852, Tamayo y Baus readily accepted several collaborations. He produced, writing in this manner, a number of minor works, some original in their themes and some in the form of arrangements. A brief listing of these collaborations with other playwrights could be presented as follows: With Luis Fernández-Guerra y Orbe and Manuel Cañete, he wrote *Un juramento*, 1848; with Miguel Ruiz y Torrent, *Un marido duplicado*, 1849; with Victorino Tamay y Baus, *Tran-Tran*, 1850; with Benito de Llanza y Esquibel, *Centellas y Moncada*, 1850; with Cañete, once more, two *loas* in 1852, *El don del cielo* and *La esperanza de la patria*; and again with Fernández-Guerra y Orbe and Cañete, *El peluquero de su alteza*, 1852. The itemizing of these minor works is worthwhile, for it throws light on just how much, even in this early stage of his career, Tamayo y Baus's name was kept before the public. This occurred not only in Madrid, where almost all these plays were produced and published, but elsewhere, too, for *Centellas y Moncada* was a work first performed in Barcelona. Moreover, some of the entries in the list reflect indirectly the intimate personal relationships that existed not only between the two Manuels, Tamayo y Baus and Cañete, but also between them and Aureliano and Luis, the brothers Fernández-Guerra y Orbe. Theirs were enduring bonds of friendship, going back to a former part of Tamayo y Baus's lifetime, his years of residence in Granada.

UNA APUESTA AND HUYENDO DEL PEREJIL

Two pieces by the dramatic poet also belonging to the initial period of his production were delightful, entertaining one-act plays: *Una apuesta*, of 1851, and *Huyendo del perejil*, dated 1853. *Una apuesta* was another arrangement, derived from a French work that dates back to 1768, *La Gageure imprévue*. Both of the one-act plays were popular with the public because by this time Tamayo y Baus had thoroughly mastered uncomplicated plot lines and clever dialogue. He himself discounted these shorter works as mere trifles, yet these short plays have a certain sprightliness that maintains the freshness of their appeal. Thus, in 1930, Cony Sturgis and Juanita Robinson published in New York a classroom edition of precisely these two plays. The reader is indebted to them for an explanation of the odd title *Huyendo del perejil*, which means literally in English "fleeing from the parsley." This puzzling phraseology, the coeditors make clear, is the first half of the Spanish saying "huyendo del perejil, le nació en la frente," which can be translated to English as, "fleeing from the parsley, it sprouted on his brow." This curious and seemingly unintelligible proverb is the Spanish equivalent of "out of the frying pan into the fire." In the play, a nobleman, fearful that his son is being pursued by a seductress interested only in his money, blindly sets out to prevent their projected marriage. Without realizing who she is, the Marquis meets the young lady in question and falls deeply in love with her himself. When her true identity is finally revealed to him, the outwitted father, now well aware of her beauty, intelligence, and other admirable qualities, abashedly relents.

It is somewhat astonishing that in the very same year, 1853, that Tamayo y Baus authored such a lighthearted and amusing work, he would also compose and present to his public so deeply pondered and erudite a play as his tragedy *Virginia*. The contrast between the two compositions is a measure of his extraordinary aesthetic breadth.

LA RICAHEMBRA

The following year, 1854, Tamayo y Baus and Aureliano Fernández-Guerra y Orbe collaborated on *La Ricahembra*. Written in verse, this was a historical drama stylistically reminiscent of the theater of the Golden Age. Tamayo y Baus, still interested in probing the hearts of determined women, paints in *La Ricahembra* the proud figure of Doña de Mendoza, who, finding herself a rich and powerful widow, rejects a multitude of suitors. She believes her noble lineage is superior to theirs. Finally, a gentleman who seeks to enter into courtship is so incensed by her hauteur that he slaps her face in pure frustration. Her pride now dictates that she must marry him, lest it be bandied about that any man other than her husband has ever dared to strike her.

LA BOLA DE NIEVE

Both in *La locura de amor*, of 1855, and in *La bola de nieve*, of 1856, jealousy is once again the central theme. In the latter play, the fierce and self-destructive fault is completely groundless, affecting two principal characters instead of one, a brother and a sister. Their overactive minds suspect that the respective objects of their love have been dallying with others. Their imagination on this score grows ever wilder—indeed, it snowballs, as is suggested by the title of the play. Estranged at last from Luis and Clara, the guiltless pair to whom the siblings were previously betrothed, María and Fernando now become attracted to each other.

After the composition of *La bola de nieve*, Tamayo turned away from verse, probably sensing that prose was preferable for the realistic dramas on contemporary themes to which he now wished to dedicate his art. It was only with some reluctance that Spanish dramatists of the century were forsaking the use of versification; Adelardo López de Ayala y Herrera, for example, who ably shared the limelight with Tamayo y Baus in the production of modern thesis plays, used metrics in *Consuelo* as late as 1878. Tamayo y Baus, however, who had had great success using prose in *La locura de amor*, must have felt quite comfortable employing it.

HIJA Y MADRE

At this time, he began to write a series of dramas with contemporary settings. These were his thesis plays, works that normally contained a strong moral and religious message, one that reflected the firm Catholic piety of the author and his equally staunch conservative ideology. *Hija y madre*, of 1855, was one such play, and its fundamental lesson in morality dealt with filial obligations and respect.

LO POSITIVO

Lo positivo of 1862, *Lances de honor* of 1863, and *Los hombres de bien* of 1870 are three more of the social dramas typical of his later work. The first was inspired by a French piece, Léon Laya's *Le Duc Job*. Tamayo y Baus greatly simplified the original, reducing what had been its eleven characters to merely four. Like Ayala y Herrera's *Consuelo*, *Lo positivo* was an attack on loveless marriage; it condemned the idea of entering into wedlock for the sake of mere convenience and for materialistic gain. This play, like many of Tamayo y Baus's later works oriented toward morality, ends on a happy note. The protagonist, Cecilia, torn between opposing senti-

ments of love and interest, finally decides in favor of the poor but good man and rejects the unscrupulous millionaire. Cleverly adapted, *Lo positivo* was favorably received.

LANCES DE HONOR

The institution of dueling would be denounced in *Lances de honor*. Tamayo y Baus privately considered such mortal combat an act too savage to be allowed in any civilized society. The principal character of the play, Don Fabián García, is a memorable one, ranking among the most powerful of the masculine roles created by Tamayo y Baus. A noble-minded figure, he has been challenged to a duel. Though constantly provoked and publicly shamed by his implacable adversary, who is completely in the wrong, Don Fabián's deep religious convictions will not let him participate in acts of bloodshed. His son Miguel becomes dismayed by the ignominious treatment his father now receives from those who judge him to be a coward. The relentless challenger, a politician named Don Pedro, even slaps Don Fabián. At this point, the sons of the two rivals decide to carry out the duel themselves. Miguel is wounded unto death. Don Pedro, now cognizant of his egotism and of the enormity of his guilt, kneels in repentance before God.

LES HOMBRES DE BIEN

Yet another religious message is to be found in *Los hombres de bien*. Here Tamayo y Baus showed his displeasure with Ernest Renan's *Vie de Jésus* (1863; *The Life of Jesus*, 1864), which denied the divinity of Christ. *Los hombres de bien* was coldly received and, indeed, nothing more would be written by Tamayo y Baus for the theater after its production.

Already, long before 1870, he had begun what could be called a nominal withdrawal or disassociation from the stage through the use of pseudonyms in place of his real name. Instead of signing works with "Manuel Tamayo," he employed pen names such as "José María García," "Don Fulano de Tal," or "Joaquín Estébanez." It was with the last of these fictitious designations, a favorite, that he acknowledged authorship of *Lo positivo*, *Lances de honor*, *Más vale maña que fuerza*, *A New Drama*, *No hay mal que por bien no venga*, and *Los hombres de bien*. Estébanez was a family name, inherited from the maternal side.

A New Drama has always been seen as a prodigious proof of Tamayo y Baus's eminent gifts. In view of the universal praise that it has received for its uniqueness, *A New Drama* merits in this analysis separate and more extended exposition. *Virginia*, his tragedy, and *La locura de amor*, the finest production of the dramatist within the historical genre, are similarly deserving of additional attention and regard.

VIRGINIA

It was the second of these plays that came first in time. In a period when neoclassical tragedy no longer was in vogue, Tamayo y Baus attempted to rehabilitate this form of literature with *Virginia*, modernizing it through greater realism, stronger sentiments, more dramatic vigor, and an increased emphasis on the psychological study of individual characters. He made these changes with the intention of still respecting and blending into his tragedy what he considered to be sublime characteristics of this class of literature, its loftiness and distinctive air of dignity. Yet he must have felt a certain dubiousness about this type of experimentation. While *Virginia* proved successful and although he kept reworking it, Tamayo y Baus would write no further tragic works along these same lines.

Virginia was a beautiful Roman girl besieged by the cruel and tyrannical decemvir Appius Claudius. In a final, desperate effort to escape the powerful magistrate's ruthless attempts to possess her physically, she heroically freed herself and her family from disgrace by not resisting when her father came to kill her. Virginia's story, an ancient one recorded in the works of Livy, has many points of contact with the legend of Lucretia. The nature of the death of the latter heroine supposedly excited the Romans to expulse the monarchy, for—as the tale goes—having been raped by Sextus Tarquinius, the son of the despotic king of Rome, the chaste victim informed her husband and her father of what had happened and then dutifully proceeded to commit suicide. Virginia's sacrifice, like that of the virtuous Lucretia, would be the signal for an oppressed people's popular revolt.

Tamayo y Baus's play had been preceded by many theatrical versions of this theme. In his prologue addressed to Cañete, he discounted the value of those that had been written earlier in Spain and seemed particularly drawn to more modern, foreign arrangements of the tragedy, such as the Italian Vittorio Alfieri's *Virginia* of 1784 and that of the Frenchman Isidore La Tour de Saint-Ybars, dated 1845. The plot line of Tamayo y Baus's first version of 1853 can be sketched as follows: Invading the home of Virginia while her husband and father are gone to war, the perfidious decemvir Appius Claudius professes his love to her. The new young bride angrily spurns these unwanted attentions. The intruder, intoxicated with his own political power and determined to satisfy his whim, orders his client Marcus to have Virginia seized on a pretext. The two conspire to distort the law by falsely claiming that Virginia was not the daughter of the brave soldier Virginius, but was instead the offspring of a slave of Marcus. Adamant, oblivious to every entreaty, Appius Claudius presides over the trial and cynically awards Virginia to his client Marcus. The judicial travesty is so patently extreme that it horrifies the Romans who are present. At this point Virginius, who has hastened back from the wars, humbly steps forward. The magistrate unconcernedly grants him permission to do what he beseeches, to speak for one last time to the daughter that he has lost. Both he and Virginia now realize that only death can free her from a miserable bondage that will place her at the beck and call of their lascivious adversary. Acquiescent, she dies at the hands of her father, stabbed by the knife that she herself was able to slip secretly to Virginius at the moment of their last embrace. This final touch, the provision of the weapon by the victim, was an innovation, a highly effective dramatic device added by Tamayo y Baus to the total legend of Virginia.

Both of Tamayo y Baus's versions of Virginia can be read in his complete works, published between 1898 and 1900 and reissued as a single volume in 1947. Alejandro Pidal y Mon provided the prologue to this handy and useful work, which constitutes, if not in truth a collection of all Tamayo y Baus's writings, the most comprehensive and readily available anthology on the subject. Pidal contended that *La locura de amor*, the play devoted to the deranged queen "Juana la loca," was Tamayo y Baus's best. Indeed, if quantity of translations can be at all accepted as a reliable indicator, then surely *La locura de amor* must rank at least a healthy second in popularity to *A New Drama*, taking into account the international reception afforded to each individual piece within the total corpus of Tamayo y Baus's works.

LA LOCURA DE AMOR

Normally, historical dramas were written in verse, but *La locura de amor*, of 1855, is an intensely emotional work expressed in a very beautiful if somewhat archaic prose. The title itself is highly suggestive, since it seems to indicate that Juana's insanity was caused by love, by an uncontrollable jealousy aroused by the faithlessness of her husband. Tamayo y Baus seems sympathetic to Juana in his liberal interpretation of the theme. He depicts her, the heretrix to the throne of the great Isabel of Castile, as ennobled by her afflictions, raging with passion while beset by conspirators hovering near the throne. Yet she is driven to madness as much by the fears and the agitations that excite her thoughts as by the licentiousness of her royal consort. Even he, in the denouement of *La locura de amor*, is treated in rehabilitative fashion. When the young king, Felipe, lies dying, he confesses with fervor his contrition; too late, he realizes to his sorrow how deep his love for Juana really was.

In the final scene of *La locura de amor*, the queen's mental illness can no longer be doubted. As she tenderly contemplates the body of her now dead spouse, Juana addresses all who are assembled, imposing general silence. In her mind, and to the dismay of all who stand about her, Felipe is not deceased; he has merely gone to sleep.

The true Juana la Loca was one of the most pathetic figures of the royal chronicles of Spain. Historical facts reveal that while Juana became queen of Castile in 1504, it was only two years later, in 1506, that she lost her husband. After the continued deterioration of her mental health, Juana would begin a period of some forty-seven years of seclusion, or of imprisonment, in the palace of Tordesillas. This would last until her own death in 1555. Interestingly, two playwrights who came after Tamayo y Baus, Benito Pérez Galdós and José Martín Recuerda, focused their attention on those years of her widowhood, the

former with his play *Santa Juana de Castilla*, first presented in 1918, and the latter with *El engañao*, of 1981.

A NEW DRAMA

A New Drama was first performed in March of 1867. It is undeniably exceptional and, even within the bounds of Tamayo y Baus's own production, stands apart as something of an anomaly. Set in Elizabethan England, in 1605, it bears precious little relation to the thesis plays dealing with contemporary middle-class society that Tamayo y Baus was so actively composing at the time.

Envy and infidelity are central to its argument. Its characters are eight in number, and all the parts are male roles except for that of Alicia. All are in some way involved with William Shakespeare's company of actors and with the rehearsal and presentation of a brand-new play. Alicia is married to Yorick, a popular comic actor who is old enough to be her father. He loves her intensely, but her feelings for him are nearer to gratitude than love. Alicia has married Yorick for two reasons: to satisfy the wishes of her now dead mother and because Yorick was the selfless benefactor of the older woman in a time of tribulation. Yorick also took in an orphan, Edmundo, and had reared him like a son and protégé. Both Alicia and Edmundo must struggle to suppress their true sentiments, the fact that even before the marriage they fell in love. These feelings emerged when they performed *Romeo and Juliet* together.

The play begins peacefully. Yorick is overjoyed. Ambitious to try more than comic roles and having learned of the new play, he has finally persuaded Shakespeare to give him the tragic lead. A first work by a fledgling author, the new drama tells the story of Count Octavio; this nobleman, having generously favored an indigent young man, now learns that the treacherous ingrate coveted his wife.

Shakespeare was hesitant in casting Yorick as Octavio. Normally another talented member of his company, Walton, would be awarded such a tragic role. Walton pretends to accept his replacement, but he is envious and swears in his heart to have vengeance. Well aware that Edmundo and Alicia are in love, he recalls bitterly that he, too, suffered a wife's infidelity. He undertakes a campaign to awaken the suspicions of Yorick through constant insinuation.

Shakespeare, almost omniscient, fully understands the true emotions of all four: Yorick, Alicia, Walton, and Edmundo. He directs their real lives with the same air of authority with which he directs fantasy on the stage. He warns Walton to cease his meddling, and his ascendancy at first works its effect.

Edmundo and Alicia have never expressed their love physically; indeed, theirs is a totally joyless love, heavily riddled with guilt. When Edmundo sees how Yorick's suspicions of Alicia grow, he writes her a letter proposing that they flee. The night of the performance, Walton, who has intercepted the letter, substitutes it on stage for the one that Count Octavio is to read.

The final scene of *A New Drama* is a play-within-a-play. Landolfo (Walton) hands over to Count Octavio (Yorick) an incriminating letter dealing with his wife Beatriz' infidelity (she is played by Alicia). Immediately thereafter, in the new drama, Count Octavio is to kill Manfredo, the young lover (Edmundo), an act that becomes a terrible reality when Yorick, at the very height of a triumphant performance, does, indeed, slay Edmundo on the stage. Fiction is now truth. What the audience wildly applauded as artistic make-believe is no longer dramatic imitation.

A New Drama ends when Shakespeare emerges to deliver his last lines. He announces to the public that Yorick, irrationally caught up in his characterization, has killed the actor who played Manfredo. There is a second disaster as well: Another performer in the play is also dead. Walton's body, pierced by a sword, has been found lying on the street. There is every reason to believe that Shakespeare himself knows the answer to that mystery.

Mixing reality with fiction, *A New Drama* presents both the historical figure of Shakespeare and characters that are based on that poet's own creations. Reminiscent of Othello and Iago are Yorick, the jealous husband, and Walton, his evil confidant. In Alicia and Edmundo, Romeo and Juliet vaguely are repeated. The play-within-a-play structure, masterfully handled by Tamayo, also has antecedents. One's thoughts immediately turn to Shakespeare again and to *Hamlet,*

Prince of Denmark (pr. c. 1600-1601). Lope de Vega Carpio also made use of the same kind of formal arrangement, as did Alexandre Dumas, *père*, in his play called *Kean: Ou, Désordre et génie* (pr., pb. 1836, with Théaulon de Lambert and Frédéric de Courcy; *Edmund Kean: Or, The Genius and the Libertine,* 1847). Moreover, *Edmund Kean* has numerous points of contact with the plot of *A New Drama.*

Once again, as in *La locura de amor*, Tamayo y Baus stands supreme in the psychological analysis of character. Yorick, Alicia, and Edmundo are not merely symbols of good or bad behavior. They are depicted at all times as extremely human, overwhelmed by indecisiveness and by personal insecurity. Even the villain Walton is provided logical motivation. Finally, Clarín, whose political orientation was much more liberal than that of Tamayo y Baus, did not allow his politics to obscure his judgment regarding the playwright's great worth. It was his prediction that the play *A New Drama* would be considered for centuries a priceless jewel in the treasury of Spanish drama.

OTHER MAJOR WORKS

NONFICTION: *Discursos leidos ante la Real Academia española*, 1859.

MISCELLANEOUS: *Obras*, 1898-1900 (4 volumes); *Obras completas*, 1947.

BIBLIOGRAPHY

Flynn, Gerard. *Manuel Tamayo y Baus.* New York: Twayne, 1973. A basic biography of Tamayo y Baus that also provides literary criticism of his works.

Mazzeo, Guido E. "Yorick's Covert Motives in *Un Drama Nuevo.*" *MLN* 83 (1968): 275-278. Mazzeo maintains that the character of Yorick already suspected that his wife was not faithful and therefore wanted to play the part of Octavio.

Podol, Peter L. "The Evolution of the Honor Theme in Modern Spanish Drama." *Hispanic Review* 40, no. 1 (Winter, 1972): 53-72. Podol looks at the concept of honor in *Lances de honor* and *A New Drama.*

Donald A. Randolph

TORQUATO TASSO

Born: Sorrento, Kingdom of Naples (now in Italy);
   March 11, 1544
Died: Rome; April 25, 1595

PRINCIPAL DRAMA

Aminta, pr. 1573, pb. 1580 (verse play; English
   translation, 1591)
Il re Torrismondo, pb. 1587, pr. 1618 (verse play)

OTHER LITERARY FORMS

Torquato Tasso's significant literary output reflects the eclectic interests of the Renaissance intellectual and includes poetry, drama, theoretical works,
dialogues, and religious compositions. His lifelong
love and greatest involvement was with the epic, and
he sought to given modern expression to the ancient
form, from *Rinaldo* (1562; English translation, 1792)
to *Gerusalemme conquistata* (1593; *Jerusalem Conquered*, 1907). Tasso appeared destined for this artistic preference. His lengthy stay at the court of
Ferrara, the Italian home of chivalric romances, and
his paternal legacy naturally drew him to the epic
form. Also influenced by the current debates on literary theory and the religious concerns of the Counter-
Reformation, Tasso sought to create a work that
would integrate the pleasures of chivalric romance
and the gravity of the classical epic, while adhering
to the Aristotelian canons expressed in *De poetica*
(c. 334-323 B.C.E.; *Poetics*, 1705). To clarify his
stand, the author also produced a series of theoretical
works on poetics and the epic and an apologia of his
own poem. Occasionally self-serving, these writings
do clarify Tasso's views, his adherence to traditions
and standards, and his position as a literary critic.
They also explain Tasso's intentions and aspirations
in composing *Gerusalemme liberata* (1581; *Jerusalem Delivered*, 1600), his major work. While imitating both the classics and the chivalric romances of his
time, Tasso wanted to renew the epic by placing it in
a historical Christian context. From Aristotle, he took
the concepts of verisimilitude, unity of action, and
religious/supernatural associations, as well as an insistence on "sublime" exploits, "heroic" protagonists,
"illustrious" deeds, and a high tone. From the romances, he borrowed the atmosphere of enchantment,
sensual love, and the desire to amuse his public.

ACHIEVEMENTS

Torquato Tasso became a literary celebrity at an
early age with the positive reception given his first
published work, *Rinaldo*, a chivalric romance. It was,
as his father noted, an excellent endeavor for a boy of
eighteen. His sustained renown as an intellectual and
literary figure caused the writer both joy and grief.
Plagued by criticism as well as praise, victimized by
unscrupulous publishers who pirated his writings, and
tortured by his own artistic doubts and perfectionism,
Tasso depended on his pen for his livelihood not only
as a courtier whose patrons exacted services in ink
but also for his personal sense of self-worth. The toll
on his mental stability was high, and, by 1580, he was
equally famous as a poet and infamous as a madman.
As a result, Tasso became a protagonist as well as a
propagator of literature. Viewed as the prototype of
the mad, inspired artist, he lives in the pages of such
Romantic works as Johann Wolfgang von Goethe's
Torquato Tasso (1790; English translation, 1827) and
Lord Byron's *The Lament of Tasso* (1817).

BIOGRAPHY

A man of letters, cultured but without means,
Torquato Tasso's father, Bernardo, entered the most
logical profession for a man of his condition: courtier
to princes. His longest service was with Ferrante
Sanseverino, prince of Salerno, who paid him well
and respected his need to write. During the good
years of this association, Bernardo, then more than
forty years old, decided to marry a noblewoman of
Tuscan descent, Porzia de' Rossi. The union was
happy, and, in 1544, a son, Torquato, was born. Educated in the classics, the boy was happy until international political intrigue shattered the family's existence. Sanseverino was branded a rebel and forced
into exile, a fate Bernardo chose to share. At the age

Torquato Tasso (Library of Congress)

of ten, Torquato was allowed to join his now impoverished father in a life of exile, wandering from court to court across Northern Italy, separated from his only sister, Cornelia, and soon orphaned by the sudden death of his beloved mother. His education continued, culminating in legal and philosophical studies at the University of Padua. Torquato proved a less than exemplary student in conduct but a promising poet and intellectual. At eighteen, he published his first important work, *Rinaldo*, and began writing the first of his love *canzonieri*, conventional compositions but works that reflected his lifelong commitment to epic literature and lyric poetry. On completion of his studies, he chose to follow his father's example and his own inclinations, and he became a courtier-poet.

From 1565 to 1577, Tasso was attached to the court of Cardinal Luigi d'Este, in Ferrara, first under Cardinal Luigi and later as "gentleman" of Alfonso Il d'Este, duke of Ferrara. Ferrara was then a major cultural center and an intellectual mecca; there, the chi-

valric epic romance had flourished under Matteo Maria Boiardo and Ludovico Ariosto, music and theater were patronized, and a solid library had been assembled. Court life was spirited, somewhat amoral, and highly competitive. The young writer found two allies in the duke's unmarried sisters and a relatively tranquil atmosphere in which to write. His major labor was *Gerusalemme liberata*, with which he hoped to achieve greatness as an epic poet. As he toiled on the long work, he found time to compose poetry, philosophical and literary treatises, and *Aminta*. This serene state, however, was temporary.

Of delicate constitution, suffering from periods of ague, and hypersensitive, Tasso began to show signs of severe mental strain after the age of thirty. He experienced lapses of mental lucidity, periods of irrational behavior, and religious crises that led him to seek absolution and confirmation of his Catholic orthodoxy from the Inquisition. Restlessness, paranoia, and dissatisfaction with his position at court soon followed. His sensitivity and egotism made him feel slighted and unappreciated. The victim of unscrupulous editors and envious rivals, Tasso created imaginary enemies as well, adding to his fears. Prone to fits of violence and loss of control, at one point he attacked a servant with a knife and, as a result, was put under house arrest. Within a few months, he had escaped to his sister's home in Sorrento but later begged forgiveness of the duke. Reconciled with the Este family, the poet returned to Ferrara but soon departed again for the first of his courtly peregrinations.

Moving from city to city, palace to palace, the wandering courtier sought the perfect haven, only to return once again to Ferrara. His timing was poor, as the family was celebrating a new ducal marriage. Feeling slighted, an angry Tasso burst into a violent diatribe against the Este family, could not be restrained, and was sent to an asylum. This imprisonment lasted seven years. At first he was chained and kept in confinement; then gradually, he acquired more autonomy and was allowed some measure of freedom to come and go, write, and receive visitors. His symptoms included psychopathic behavior, hallucinations, visions, periods of extreme irritability, and profound depressions. During his incarceration, he continued to write and declare his sanity. It was during this period that his major works were first printed, without his consent.

Released in 1586, Tasso left Ferrara and resumed his wanderings, crisscrossing the Italian peninsula. Always uncertain about the quality of his work, he constantly polished it, even rewriting his epic so that it would more fully conform to the Aristotelian standard. At the request of a patron, he completed a tragedy, *Il re Torrismondo*, left unfinished since 1573. Famous and about to be crowned poet laureate, Tasso had earned little from his publications. He requested, or rather, demanded, money and gifts from friends and benefactors. Alone, having never married, the poet died in the solitude of a Roman convent. What had been a tragic, agitated, and self-centered existence came to a quiet close, leaving behind the works and the myth.

ANALYSIS

As a historical figure, Torquato Tasso appears to embody two cultural eras: the High Renaissance and the Counter-Reformation. Some critics divide his literary production evenly and narrowly along such lines, assigning *Aminta* to the Renaissance, the *Gerusalemme liberata* to a transitional mode, and the last works to the triumph of the poet's conservative Catholicism. This division is too facile: Like all great artists, Tasso was a complex figure. Immersed in the humanistic culture of his time, Tasso had an extraordinary facility in assimilating the works of others and integrating them in his own works. Echoes of Vergil, Horace, Homer, Sophocles, Dante, and Petrarch resound through his works, recognizable but transfused. At best, Tasso's borrowings are poetic references and cultural commentary, enriching his text, infusing it with the familiar reverberations of tradition. His emulation is as much art as erudition. At worst, the writer can be pedantic, weighed down by his learning: Art gives way to artifice, and knowledge substitutes for inspiration. In all situations, Tasso has control of his language and mastery of his style; his verse is fine-tuned, polished, and elegant.

The taste of the Renaissance elite formed Tasso's style. It manifests itself in his predilection for pomp,

ornamentation, and decorum, and in his esteem of honor, heroism, and power. The sheer musicality of his poetry is legendary; the sound obliterates the everyday meaning of the words, freeing them to create new meanings through rhythm. His mastery of the Italian literary tradition led Tasso to experiment, to circumvent intentionally the prevailing Petrarchism of his age and play with the poetic devices available to him. His use of metaphor, conceit, hyperbole, and musical phrasing predates the Baroque, when poets sought to astonish the public with their manipulation of language. Tasso was both the heir of an ancient literary tradition and the prophet of a new style and a new approach to the written word.

As a teller of stories, whether in epic poetry or in drama, Tasso was again a harbinger of new attitudes and an inspiration to future artists. His characterizations are often unique. Drawn from traditional models, Tasso's protagonists possess an interior life, rich in contradictions and marked by introspection. The tone of their lives is neither epic nor Arcadian, but melancholy, suffused with a voluptuous sense of death and loss. The heroic nature of the Crusaders is modified by a lingering atmospheric evanescence. They are warriors fraught with inner demons, beset by illusions, destined to disappointments. An existential angst surrounds the men and women of his poetic world. Joy, love, pleasure, and success are all fleeting or tainted. Even the bucolic world of *Aminta* is elegiac, tinged with melancholy and nostalgia; its happy ending cannot erase totally the various protagonists' considerations on the loss of love, the fear of rejection, the onset of old age, and the ambiguous attractions of death.

One of Tasso's greatest talents lies in his ability to infuse nature with a mood akin to the emotional state of the characters. The bees, the plants, the birds mate in a paean to the same instinctive love that draws Aminta to Silvia, just as the raging storm of *Il re Torrismondo*, in act 1, denotes the furious and confused state of mind of the protagonist, caught in the whirlwind of his guilt-ridden passion. As often, the protagonists find no outlet or communion, becoming trapped in themselves, victims of their own subjectivity. The warrior Clorinda's femininity is hidden beneath her armor, her "external" self; Rinaldo's suppressed sexuality develops into effeminate passivity in Armida's garden; Aminta's frustrated love is transformed into a death wish. Tasso's world is peopled with individuals hungering for recognition, reaching for the unattainable, frustrated and frustrating. His ability to capture psychological nuance is matched by his mastery of the poetic form. At his best, as in *Aminta*, form and content merge in perfect symbiosis, achieving the harmony of great art. Whether in the epic, the pastoral, or the lyric, Tasso emerges as the voice of humankind's inner, emotional self speaking in the language of renewed tradition.

AMINTA

Although Tasso did not consider himself a playwright and gave relatively minor attention to his dramatic production, *Aminta* is universally considered a masterpiece in its genre. The piece was the fruit of a particularly happy, peaceful period in the writer's disturbed life. The work flowed easily and naturally from Tasso's pen during a two-month period in the spring of 1573, whereas his second play, *Il re Torrismondo*, took fourteen years from inception to completion. This short compositional time, highly unusual for the perfectionist Tasso, reflects a conceptual ease that makes *Aminta* the most unified of the writer's longer works. Probably meant as a divertissement for the court, the play responds to the taste and expectations of its intended public. It is a stylistically refined drama in which Tasso effortlessly incorporates numerous literary references that blend easily with his own poetry. The entire pastoral tradition, both classical and Renaissance, runs through the play. Traces of Giovanni Boccaccio's *Il ninfale fiesolano* (1344-1346; *The Nymph of Fiesole*, 1597) and *Il ninfale d'Ameto* (1341-1342; also known as *Commedia delle ninfe*), Poliziano's *Orfeo* (pr. c. 1480; English translation, 1879; also known as *Orpheus*), Jacopo Sannazaro's *Arcadia* (1489; English translation, 1966), and the poetry of Dante, Petrarch, and Lorenzo de' Medici combine with traces of Vergil's *Eclogues* (43-37 B.C.E.; also known as *Bucolics*; English translation, 1575), Theocritus's *Idylls* (1566; English translation, 1684), and the poetry of Ovid and Catullus and Greek romances. Sixteenth century

Ferrara had also seen a revival of modern interest in the dramatic pastoral. Despite these debts, *Aminta* is also an original work, difficult to categorize and unrestricted by its sources.

Tasso's contemporaries variously defined the work as a pastoral comedy or fable, an eclogue, or simply a pastoral. The playwright termed it a *favola boschereccia*, or woodland fable. The play contains elements of comedy, tragedy, bucolic poetry, and the dramatic eclogue. Written in an extraordinarily effective mix of seven- and eleven-syllable lines, known as polymetric verse, the work follows the classical unities rigidly. Its Italian blank verse is often quite musical and occasionally rhymed, constituting the foundation and inspiration for the recitative of eighteenth century melodrama and opera. This hybrid play is lyric, descriptive, and narrative, rather than dramatic. It is theater without action.

The plot, divided into the standard five acts, is extremely simple. Set in a metahistorical world of shepherds, Satyrs, nymphs, and gods, it is timeless. The general tone is serene, although tragic, comic, and satiric elements are present. Aminta, a young shepherd, is desperately in love with Silvia, his childhood friend. She has forsworn all men, rebuffed the boy, and chosen service to Diana and the hunt. Dafne, an aging nymph, seeks to convince the girl of her error, urging her to give up the state of useless virginity in exchange for the joys of love. Tirsi attempts to console Aminta but neither he nor Dafne are able to sway their young friends. The third act initiates a series of crises. Aminta, incited by Tirsi, has decided to act with more boldness in his courtship, only to discover that the Satyr has abducted his love, tied her to a tree, and is about to assault her. Silvia is saved and liberated by her devoted lover but does not stop to thank him. A second blow to the youth soon follows: Silvia's bloody veil has been found, and it is presumed that the girl has fallen victim to wolves. In act 4, Silvia is safe and sound but Aminta has gone off to die. It is only at this moment that the huntress, overcome by pity for the dead shepherd, acknowledges her love for him. All ends well, however; some vegetation, an appropriately bucolic *deus ex machina*, had broken the youth's fall from a cliff. As the play ends, he is contentedly lying in the arms of his love. It is important to note that all the action is narrated, not seen, in a series of conversations, monologues, and commentaries from the chorus, the protagonists, and a few minor characters. As is common in Renaissance theater, there is a prologue, recited by Cupid masquerading as a shepherd. Some editions also include choral and individual intermezzos and an epilogue by Venus, although these were probably not included in the first productions and in some early printings of the text.

The partition of the drama into five acts, the series of tragic misunderstandings and vicissitudes, the suicidal desperation of the hero, and the continuing references to violence would place the work in the realm of tragedy were it not for its idyllic atmosphere. The natural setting tempers all negativity. Indeed, nature itself is one of the text's presences, if not an actual protagonist. *Aminta*'s world borders on anthropomorphism: The tree helps the Satyr bind the nymph with its pliable branches while the grasses and branches weave a net to break the shepherd's fall. It was only appropriate that the first performance took place on a small island in the middle of the Po River—an actual woodland setting for this Arcadian fable. The major theme of the work—love—is also presented in natural and naturalistic terms. As Dafne points out to Silvia, love is instinctive, while its rejection is abnormal: Does not the dove kiss its companion? Does not the nightingale sing of love? Does not the serpent abandon its poison to mate? Silvia's enforced virginity is defined as aberration, not virtue. Even the Satyr's unbridled lust is not actually condemned because lust is appropriate to his essence. In contrast to the girl's rejection of her sexual nature, Aminta's gradual shift from playmate to enamored youth is both understandable and acceptable, an inevitable transition from childhood to adolescence. Love is valued not as a means of spiritual enlightenment but as a sensual pleasure; possession is gratification; chastity is frustration. This message both Tirsi and Dafne seek to communicate to their young friends, but Aminta is too timid to seek satisfaction and Silvia, too obdurate. Eros is the god of this world, presented in the guise of Cupid in the prologue. The only law is that of natural instinct, introduced by the chorus at the close of act 1. The Golden Age, the chorus declares, was not so called because of flowing milk and honey, fruit-laden trees, eternal spring, or tranquillity, but because nature's single law was still observed before the existence of suffocating honor: "What pleases, is permitted." In Tasso's presentation, the Golden Age is an era of freedom, unfettered by societal impositions, where people could live according to their instincts rather than by synthetic rules of conduct. *Aminta*'s underlying philosophy is fundamentally amoral, but it does not shock because it operates in a timeless dreamworld of primitive innocence.

Love is the major concern of all the characters of this Renaissance pastoral. Taken together, these characters represent different attitudes toward love and variations on the act of loving. On the most primitive level, there is the Satyr, with his animalistic needs. Aminta's love is rarefied, his passion sublimated by his devotion. He is the despair of love, its proximity to death. Silvia is the rejection of love, the reluctant virgin destined finally to capitulate. In the older protagonists, experience has created skepticism but the expert and aging Dafne still hopes to love again, whereas Tirsi has known only love's pain and desires sensual fulfillment, not emotional involvement. The two couples formed are quite different. The adolescents symbolize youthful idealism, whereas the mature confidants are worldly-wise, even cynical, representatives of sophistication and experience. All celebrate the right to love and to make love by the conclusion of the work. Only one character, however, undergoes any change: Silvia. Psychologically, *Aminta* is a static play with few emotional chords. Its enchantment lies in its representation of a simple, serene, and sensual idyll, an interlude from reality.

Tasso's mastery of language makes this world come to life. His musical, smooth, and persuasive poetry is the perfect linguistic accompaniment to this sensual and airy tale. His lyric expertise and mastery of prosody is put to excellent use in creating a sensual environment. The vocabulary, phrasing, and sentence structures are kept simple, agile, and graceful, in keeping with his protagonists' world. The language is refined and elegant but not affected or pompous.

Nothing appears forced or artificial, although Tasso's art is always at work. The very musicality of the verse merely emphasizes the dreamlike quality of the play. The shepherds may speak like courtiers, but they exist in a mythic, not a realistic setting. As Cupid points out in the prologue, love enobles, inspiring primitive hearts and sweetening rough speech. Art also inspires, and *Aminta* proved tremendously successful as a literary stimulus to future generations. The French, English, and Spanish national literatures were all affected by the publication of the play in the original, in numerous translations, and in paraphrased reworkings. In Italy alone, E. Carrara estimates, eighty-five pastoral plays existed by 1615, while there were more than two hundred by 1700. The popularity of *Aminta* was partially responsible for this significant growth. It is not excessive to state that the pastoral genre—lyric or dramatic—was renewed and strengthened by Tasso's contribution.

IL RE TORRISMONDO

Il re Torrismondo was neither as successful nor as influential, although it, too, enjoyed popularity in the sixteenth century. Begun in 1573, the play was left incomplete in the middle of its second act, probably because of the playwright's obsession with his epic poem. More than a dozen years later, after his mental collapse and incarceration, Tasso returned to his tragedy. The work, however, proved to be tired and uninspired. Influenced by *Poetics*, Tasso hoped to create a modern classical tragedy, as similar as possible to Sophocles' *Oidipous Tyrannos* (c. 429 B.C.E.; *Oedipus Tyrannus*, 1715) in theme and structure. The Aristotelian canons are strictly observed: five acts, the three unities, a chorus, elevated theme and style, no death on stage, sudden changes of fortune, vicissitudes accompanied by unexpected recognitions, religious significance, and a final catharsis. In this respect, the play is similar to other Renaissance attempts at tragedy. It also reflects the era's predilection for horrible actions and gloom, as well as the tendency to moralize on stage. Tasso's insistence on the use of ancient standards added to the lack of spontaneity and energy in his second dramatic effort. Although the playwright praised the Greeks' simplicity of language, he himself opted for a rhetorical

work devoid of their tragic severity. From first to second draft, the play had also changed title, if not basic plot. Two classic motifs run through *Il re Torrismondo*: incest with resulting misfortune and the enduring bond of male friendship. Because of two coexisting moral themes, the story line is contrived and complex.

Germondo is hopelessly in love with Alvida, princess of Norway. They cannot marry, however, because of political animosities. Torrismondo has agreed to ask for Alvida's hand, bring the princess back to his kingdom, and there present her to Germondo, who is his great friend. Unfortunately, during the sea voyage, Torrismondo and Alvida fall passionately in love. She, presuming that they are betrothed, allows their mutual passion to be consummated. The tragedy begins on the eve of the wedding. The "false" groom is distraught with love for Alvida and with guilt at having betrayed his friend. Thus, he is quick to accept his *consigliere*'s suggestion that Germondo be married to Torrismondo's sister Rosmunda as compensation for his loss. This second marriage would strengthen their political and personal ties and permit him to wed Alvida. Germondo agrees to the *consigliere*'s offer, sacrificing his fruitless love to his friendship for Torrismondo. Just as all appears resolved, Rosmunda rejects the alliance. Forced to explain her action, she informs the family that she is not Torrismondo's sister but a substitute. Nymphs had predicted that the baby sister would cause her brother's untimely death. The father had secretly taken the newborn away and put a false Rosmunda in her place.

In Aristotelian fashion, a series of sudden recognitions and revelations follow. It is learned that Alvida is the true Rosmunda: The young couple have unwittingly committed incest. Torrismondo rejects his biological sister, offering her hand once again to his good friend. The young woman, feeling rejected by the man she loves, chooses to die. It is only on her deathbed that Alvida learns the truth, discovering that her passion is still shared by her brother-lover, who joins her in death. For both, life had become unbearable and unacceptable without the presence of the beloved. Indeed, all Tasso's characters are doomed to an unhappy fate. Germondo loses both the woman and the friend. The queen, his mother, learns the identity of her real daughter at the moment that the newly discovered child dies, followed by the sorrowful mother's only son. Rosmunda is destined to a celibate life, when she actually would prefer the love of her false brother. Indeed, the dead lovers appear to have chosen the better fate.

As a tragedy, *Il re Torrismondo* possesses all the trappings and none of the soul of classical drama. According to the Aristotelian definition, tragedy is meant to elicit pity intermixed with terror from the spectators, who experience their own catharsis through their passive participation. Tasso's lovers do evoke a sympathetic response: Unknowing victims of circumstance, they are doomed without true guilt. The elements for a successful tragedy are present, but the playwright does not succeed. He himself lacks the moral outrage necessary to produce a shocked reaction from the audience. The motive of fraternal incest does not serve this function, because it is not felt. There is no catharsis in either Alvida or Torrismondo's deaths because their motivations are not suitable. Alvida's suicide is not the result of spiritual guilt, as was Jocasta's, but of unrequited love. She feels scorned by the man who had possessed her body and her affections. Having given all, she believes herself bankrupt. Death is her escape from unhappiness. Torrismondo is closer in spirit to Juliet than he is to the guilt-ridden Oedipus. While suspicion, doubt, and anguish torment these protagonists, the moral issue is subservient to the development of the love motif.

The tragedy resembles *Aminta* in its atmosphere of gloom and fatalism, possibly because both works were conceived at the same time. Both plays emphasize the pain of unrequited love and the joys of satisfied passions, the frustrations of amorous doubts and the fear of betrayal. Both are sensual in their description of physical closeness—in fact, the first draft of *Il re Torrismondo* stressed the erotic implications, an emphasis that Tasso suppressed in the final work—and posit the enduring nature of sexual passion. The lovers are the truly interesting characters, especially Alvida. The other protagonists are wooden abstractions of the types they personify: perfect friend, grave

virgin, motherly wet-nurse, maternal queen. The only novelty is the *consigliere*, or correspondent figure, who will regularly reappear in seventeenth century French tragedy; he is the amoral voice of convenience in opposition to the chorus, the collective spokesman for virtue and moral conventions. Unfortunately, even the positive characterizations are often uneven. While in the throes of guilt, Torrismondo is given to long digressions on proper etiquette for his banquet or lengthy unsuitable descriptions, as in act 1, when he spends considerable time recounting the force of the storm that shipwrecked him while explaining his passion for Alvida. These undramatic moments recur, slowing the text and destroying the symmetry of the action. Such tangential dialogue is destructive of the simplicity that Tasso admired in the Greeks and sought to imitate.

Like all Tasso's major works, *Il re Torrismondo* was written under the sign of love and death. Unlike *Aminta, Gerusalemme liberata*, and many of the poems, it lacks the artist's inimitable lyricism. Yet the last few lines of the tragedy's close, intoned by the chorus, serve as a fitting epitaph for Tasso, the man and the writer, a commentary on a spent existence and a tired poetic vein: "Of what use is friendship, of what use love? oh tears, oh sorrow."

OTHER MAJOR WORKS

POETRY: *Rinaldo*, 1562 (English translation, 1792); *Gerusalemme liberata*, 1581 (*Jerusalem Delivered*, 1600); *Rime*, 1581, 1591, 1593 (*From the Italian of Tasso's Sonnets*, 1867); *Gerusalemme conquistata*, 1593 (*Jerusalem Conquered*, 1907); *Le sette giornate del mondo creato*, 1607.

NONFICTION: *Allegoria del poema*, 1581; *Dialoghi*, 1581; *Apologia*, 1586; *Discorsi dell'arte poetica*, 1587; *Lettere*, 1587, 1588, 1616-1617; *Discorsi del poema eroico*, 1594 (*Discourses on the Heroic Poem*, 1973).

BIBLIOGRAPHY

Boulting, William. *Tasso and His Times*. New York: Haskell House, 1968. A biography of Tasso that places him temporarily, identifying the influences on his work.

Looney, Dennis. *Compromising the Classics: Romance Epic Narrative in the Italian Renaissance.* Detroit, Mich.: Wayne State University Press, 1996. Looney examines Italian Romance epic narratives, including those of Tasso, Matteo Maria Boiardo, and Lodovico Ariosto. Bibliography and index.

Niccoli, Gabriel Adriano. *Cupid, Satyr, and the Golden Age: Pastoral Dramatic Scenes of the Late Renaissance.* New York: Peter Lang, 1989. Nic-

coli examines the works of a number of pastoral dramatists from the late Renaissance, including Tasso's *Aminta.* Bibliography and index included.

Reynolds, Henry. *Tasso's "Aminta" and Other Poems.* Salzburg: Instit für Anglistik und Amerikanistik, Universität Salzburg, 1991. A modern publication of seventeenth century writer Reynolds's analysis of Tasso's famous work. Bibliography and index.

Fiora A. Bassanese

ALFRED, LORD TENNYSON

Born: Somersby, England; August 6, 1809
Died: Near Haslemere, England; October 6, 1892

PRINCIPAL DRAMA

Queen Mary, pb. 1875, pr. 1876
Harold, pb. 1876, pr. 1928
Becket, wr. 1879, pb. 1884, pr. 1893
The Falcon, pr. 1879, pb. 1884 (one act)
The Cup, pr. 1881, pb. 1884
The Foresters, wr. 1881, pr., pb. 1892
The Promise of May, pr. 1882, pb. 1886
The Devil and the Lady, pb. 1930 (unfinished)

OTHER LITERARY FORMS

Alfred, Lord Tennyson's plays were an interlude in his long and distinguished career as a poet. During his lifetime, he published more than fifteen volumes of poetry, which have been collected into the nine-volume *The Works of Tennyson* (1907-1908), edited by his son, Hallam, Lord Tennyson. At the insistence of Sir Arthur Sullivan, Tennyson wrote a song cycle, *The Window* (1870), which Sullivan set to music. Several songs from *The Princess* (1847) were also set to music, one by Benjamin Britten in *Serenade for Tenor, Horn, and Strings*, Opus 31. Tennyson's letters from 1821 to 1892 have been edited by Cecil Y. Lang and Edgar F. Shannon and have been published in three volumes.

ACHIEVEMENTS

Alfred, Lord Tennyson's achievements as a dramatist are of interest primarily for the light they shed on his poetry. Tennyson was the best known and most loved poet of the Victorian period, but his fame and popularity were purchased at a high price. Honors were plentiful: his appointment as poet laureate after William Wordsworth's death, his audiences with the Queen, his peerage, his burial in Westminster Abbey. During his last twenty years, his birthdays were solemnized almost as national holidays. Lakes in New Zealand, agricultural colonies in South Africa, and roses in England were named for him. His views on all subjects were eagerly sought and accepted. With such great expectations, it would take a most exceptional man to resist, and Tennyson, unfortunately, was not exceptional enough. He tried to be the spokesperson of his country, and he published more than he should have. Earlier in his career, he showed that he could profit from sound criticism and became a better poet, but once the criticism stopped, he lost his own critical sense.

After his death, the inevitable reaction occurred, and it became so radical a shift that "Tennysonian" became a term of mockery and contempt. Tennyson had been the symbol of his age, and the twentieth century could see nothing worthy of preserving from the Victorian era. Tennyson's ability to inspire and

Alfred, Lord Tennyson (Library of Congress)

console his age led later readers to denounce him for his moralizing. This "debunking period" was perhaps necessary to achieve a more balanced view of his accomplishments. Modern assessments have emphasized the division within Tennyson, who was caught between the mysticism of the Romantics and the dogmatism of the Victorians. He was a poet who wrote about the eternal tensions of withdrawal and involvement, of doubt and faith, of the fanciful and the real. His technical virtuosity, his impressionistic rendering of scenes, his dedication to the poet's calling, and his place in a tradition all contribute to his reputation as a major poet and assure him a lasting place in the history of English literature.

BIOGRAPHY

Alfred, Lord Tennyson was born in 1809 at Somersby Rectory in Lincolnshire, but his father, the Reverend Dr. George Tennyson, was not the typical Anglican clergyman. As the dispossessed eldest son

of a wealthy landowner, he was forced to accept a profession he disliked, but it afforded him time to educate his children. A man of culture and intelligence himself, he noticed early that Alfred, the fourth of his twelve children, had a gift for poetry, which he readily encouraged. Alfred began writing verses during his earliest years, and at twelve he began an epic poem in imitation of Sir Walter Scott. This caused his father to remark: "If that boy dies, one of our greatest poets will have gone." Tennyson was spurred on by this encouragement and by collaboration with his brother Charles; *Poems by Two Brothers* was published when Alfred was still in his teens.

When Tennyson went to Cambridge in 1827, he became associated with a group of brilliant young men who called themselves the Apostles. One of the most gifted of them, Arthur Hallam, became his best friend and chief advocate. This group of friends helped him to overcome his initial shyness; they gave him confidence and broadened his experience so that in the next few years he published two volumes of poetry: *Poems, Chiefly Lyrical* (1830) and *Poems* (1832, imprinted 1833).

All seemed to be going well in a promising literary career but then came a series of shocks. The most traumatic was certainly the sudden death of Hallam in 1833; their friendship had become so close and deep that Tennyson went into a long period of depression following his friend's death. He published very little over the next nine years, but rather than attribute these years of silence completely to Hallam's death, one has to recognize several other serious blows that fell at about the same time. In 1831, two years before Hallam's death, Tennyson's family suffered a series of grievous troubles: Alfred's father died, his brother Edward had to be confined because of insanity, and his favorite brother, Charles, became addicted to opium. Added to these troubles were the hostile reviews of his poetry. For one who had received only encouragement and praise from family and friends, the reviews, which called his poetry "obscure" and "affected" and branded him "the pet of a cockney coterie," were sufficient to cause Tennyson to question his poetic gifts. Though stung by these losses and criticism, he became a much better poet. When he did publish again, in 1842, he showed a remarkable advance over his earlier work, and the critical reception that followed assured him a place in English literature. Even Wordsworth acknowledged, "He is decidedly the first of our living poets." Tennyson followed this triumph with the publication of his long elegy on Hallam, *In Memoriam* (1850), and that same year, he was named poet laureate to succeed Wordsworth.

The remaining years of Tennyson's long life were productive. Financially secure, he was able to marry Emily Sellwood, whom he had loved for fourteen years. They purchased a country estate, which freed him somewhat from the public demands that accompanied his growing popularity. After publishing the experimental monologue *Maud* in 1855, he devoted nearly twenty-five years to the twelve books of the epic *Idylls of the King* (1859-1885). During the last third of his life, he published six other volumes of poetry, which contained some good poems and a great number of popular poems. Works such as *Enoch Arden* (1864), full of domestic sentimentality, added to his popularity but detracted from his lasting reputation. It was also during this period that he began writing his verse dramas. Reassured by his almost universal fame and his belief that someone needed to restore the lagging stature of English drama, he disregarded his own lack of knowledge of the theater and wrote seven plays in the hope that someone else would make them acceptable for public performance.

Tennyson remained for fifty years the most popular poet of his age. After he accepted the peerage in 1883, he lived out the last years of his life as beloved poet and respected sage, mostly at his country estate of Aldworth. When he died in October, 1892, he was buried in Westminster Abbey, and a whole nation mourned the loss.

ANALYSIS

The fact that Alfred, Lord Tennyson began writing plays at the age of sixty-five is unusual and perhaps accounts in part for the relative failure of his poetic dramas. His friend Robert Browning had begun his career writing plays, but Browning realized that his gifts were not suited to playwriting, and he shifted with great success to the dramatic monologue and narrative poetry. Tennyson must have felt that he would succeed where Browning and others had failed. English drama during the nineteenth century had reached a low point with facile plots, melodramatic endings, stock characters, bombastic language, and pseudo-Elizabethan techniques. Every major poet of the century recognized the problem and wrote dramas, hoping to resurrect the proud past of the English stage. They, like Tennyson, failed. Tennyson might have had a better chance of success since, writing after others had failed, he could profit from their mistakes.

Drama was not for him a completely new turn. One of his earliest works was a blank-verse drama, *The Devil and the Lady*, which he wrote when he was fourteen or fifteen and which remained unfinished and unpublished until long after his death. His poetry had included dramatic elements, such as his dramatic monologues and the monodrama *Maud*. Moreover, he had an interest in the stage throughout his life—an interest that led to friendships with a number of actors and directors. He believed that he possessed the dramatic instinct and that he was a competent judge of acting and play production. Because of this background, limited though it was, he believed that he could overcome his lack of any real knowledge of stagecraft or the practical necessities of the theater. He expected his plays to be edited for stage production by those who had the special training. Such editing did occur, but his primary difficulty was his inability to portray the subjective action of the characters within the constraints of the dramatic form.

When Tennyson as a boy began writing blank-verse plays, his model was William Shakespeare. It is not surprising that when he later turned to drama, he would again look to Shakespeare, particularly Shakespeare's historical plays. Tennyson, however, was careful to select subjects that had not been used by Shakespeare. He envisioned a trilogy of plays— *Harold*, *Becket*, and *Queen Mary*—that would portray the making of England. *Harold* centers on the great conflict among Danes, Saxons, and Normans for predominance, the awakening of the English people and the Church from their long sleep, and the forecast of greatness for England's composite race.

Becket concentrates on the struggle between the Crown and the Church for supremacy, a struggle that continued for hundreds of years. *Queen Mary* portrays the final defeat of Roman Catholicism in England and the beginning of a new age in which freedom of the individual replaced the priestly domination of the past.

QUEEN MARY

Queen Mary, the last in the trilogy, was the first play that Tennyson completed. He became interested in the subject because of the resurgence of Roman Catholicism brought on by the Tractarian movement. Several of his friends had converted, and the pronouncements of the Vatican were alarming to staunch Protestants. Tennyson, as spokesperson and sage, believed that he should write a poetic play on the life of Queen Mary and show the fiercest crisis of his country's religious struggle. He was firmly on the side of the Protestants, but he was sympathetic to the tragic life of Mary, who was cast off by her father and treated with shameless contempt before her accession to the throne. Hallam, Lord Tennyson wrote that his father believed that "there was nothing more mournful than the final tragedy of this woman, who, with her deep longing for love, found herself hated by her people, abandoned by her husband, and harassed in the hour of her death by the restlessness of despair."

Although Tennyson set out to relate the tragic story of this misunderstood queen, his desire to be faithful to the historical record caused him to include far more than a play could hold. A summary of the five acts suggests a harmonious pattern. Act 1 opens with Mary's coronation and her decision to reinstate Catholicism, which she will cement through her marriage to Philip. Act 2 introduces the major military challenge to her authority with the unsuccessful rebellion by Thomas Wyatt. Act 3 deals with the marriage of Philip and Mary and the absolution of the members of the English Parliament by Cardinal Pole, the pope's legate. Act 4 is used to present Thomas Cranmer's death, which is the major spiritual challenge to Mary's authority. Act 5 depicts the nation beginning to fall apart because of the military threats from abroad and the religious dissension within—a dissension that Mary, trapped in her marriage to the loveless Philip, is unable to combat. At her death, Elizabeth succeeds her to the throne, and a Protestant England is assured.

What distracts from this harmonious pattern is the loose structure, with capricious changes of scene to include a number of background events and characters that intrude on the main story. The political ploys and stratagems of France and Spain, the rise and fall of minor characters such as Edward Courtenay and Stephen Gardiner, even the major episodes of Wyatt's rebellion and Cranmer's death—all distract from the central character of the play. Tennyson's published version of *Queen Mary* has twenty-three scenes and forty-five speaking characters. Although many of the scenes and characters were omitted in Henry Irving's production of the play, the separate treatment of so many parts causes the reader or the spectator to become confused and lose sight of the central figure in the drama.

Tennyson set out to be fair to the queen, but he almost lost sight of her in the panorama of her struggles. One question that is left unanswered by the play is what caused her to change from the merciful, forgiving queen who could pitifully speak of "good Lady Jane as a poor innocent child who had but obeyed her father" to the vengeful queen who at her wedding wore red shoes, "as if her feet were washed in blood." Not only does she have Lady Jane beheaded, but also she renounces the nobles' plea for Cranmer's exile by saying, "It is God's will, the Holy Father's will,/ And Philip's will, and mine, that he should burn." Her only motive throughout the play is to win the love of Philip, but such a motive is weak because Philip is almost a caricature of the ruthless, self-serving, loveless husband. Moreover, Mary knew this before she ever met Philip; she was told that he is a man "Stonehard, ice-cold—no dash of daring in him," who lives a "very wanton life." As Tennyson provides no insight into another, more favorable, side of Philip's character, Mary's devotion to him, which causes her to sacrifice the lives of so many "heretics" and almost causes her to lose her country, seems more pitiable than tragic.

Queen Mary, as Tennyson's first play, is seriously flawed, but it also has some strengths. The multiple scenes and subjects suggest the confused temper of the age. There is also some good characterization, such as that of Thomas Cranmer, who is torn between his fear and his faith, his desire to live and his call to martyrdom, his pride and his humility. The play was not an unmitigated failure; indeed, after major editing, it enjoyed a fairly successful run.

HAROLD

Tennyson, more fully aware of his inexperience in the theater after seeing *Queen Mary* on the stage, read several contemporary plays before he began to write his second play, *Harold*, which would be the first in the completed trilogy. The structural improvement is apparent: He halved the number of scenes to eleven and the number of characters to twenty-three. Nevertheless, this was the only one of Tennyson's plays not to be produced during his lifetime; there was no public performance until 1928.

The action of the play follows roughly the order of events represented on the Bayeux tapestry, which Tennyson had seen in Brittany some years earlier. The tapestry, two hundred twelve feet long and one and a half feet wide, shows Harold's hunting expedition in Flanders, his capture and enforced stay with William of Normandy, his oath to assist William in becoming king of England, the return to England, the death of Edward, the coronation of Harold, and William's invasion and victory at Hastings. Tennyson adds to his play Harold's love for Edith and his political marriage to Aldwyth.

The story has the ingredients to make a fine tragedy. Harold is a strong character who is destined to be king because he had driven out the Normans and brought peace. He is presented in contrast to the other two kings—Edward the Confessor, pious and incompetent, and William of Normandy, strong but deceitful. Harold has both strength and honor, as he shows when he initially refuses to take an oath that he knows he cannot honor: "Better die than lie." He cannot maintain this resolve, however, and he is doomed by fate to lose both the woman he loves and the country he tries to defend. On his deathbed, Edward commands Edith to be a virgin saint, to spend her life in prayer against the curse that Harold brought on himself and on England when he broke his oath.

Despite these potentially dramatic conflicts, the play is a failure, largely because all the major characters are weakly conceived and developed. Edward's piety and saintliness are overemphasized, as are William's cruelty and deceitfulness. There is nothing in the play to suggest the qualities of one who would unify the country and, in Tennyson's own words, "mold the greatness of our composite race." Edith is a stereotype of the lovely, faithful woman who will sacrifice her own happiness for Harold's safety. Aldwyth, conversely, is the scheming, ambitious female who will destroy her country if it will make her its queen. Even Harold is a confusing portrait. He is presented as a strong leader and man of honor, but his actions too often belie his words. He naïvely believes that he can go to Normandy for a hunting holiday because the Normans certainly have forgotten and forgiven him and his father, who drove them out of England. He pledges his undying love to Edith but then quickly makes a political marriage with Aldwyth. His final defeat is expected and accepted because the inconsistencies in his character have confused the reader and muted the desired sympathy.

BECKET

Tennyson did not have much better success with the final drama of his historical trilogy, *Becket*. Failing in his initial effort to have the play accepted for production, he published it with the apologetic statement that it "was not intended in its present form to meet the exigencies of our modern theatre." In the last year of his life, it was accepted, and four months after his death it began a successful run of 112 nights.

Tennyson's failure in this play, as in the two earlier plays, was twofold: his inability to control the historical material and his inability to develop character. He had chosen a fitting subject in the confrontation of temporal power with spiritual power, but he was not able to reveal the subjective crises that motivated Henry and Becket. The play opens with a chess game that obviously foreshadows the play's theme. After Becket moves, he says, "Why—there then, for you see my bishop/ Hath brought your king to a standstill. You are beaten." The struggle between Archbishop Becket and King Henry should now begin, but it fails to materialize because of the introduction of a subplot. Rather than allowing the two chess players to discuss the conflict of Church and State that will surely come, Henry urges Becket to help him protect his paramour, Rosamund de Clifford, from his jealous Queen Eleanor. The two plots war against each other throughout the play.

Tennyson must have felt that he could not sustain the interest of the audience solely by the spiritual conflict within Becket, and thus he brought in the love triangle with Becket as an unwilling accomplice. The unsatisfactory union of history and romantic legend confuses and distorts the conflict between the two men. Because of the Rosamund story, Becket appears only briefly in the third and fourth acts. The principal distortion is that Rosamund becomes the cause of Becket's death. In Tennyson's version of the story, it is after Eleanor tells Harold a lie, saying "Your cleric has your lady," that Henry utters the famous words, "Will no man free me from this pestilent priest?" The great conflict between Church and State is incidental to the king's love for his paramour.

The subplot also prevents Tennyson from exploring Becket's inner conflict. Becket often mentions his doubts, but whenever he begins to engage in serious introspection, the demands of the plot intrude and the reader cannot experience his spiritual crisis. After Becket is told that he will become archbishop, he begins to doubt his calling, asking, "Am I the man?" Twenty-five lines later, however, he concludes, "I do believe thee, then. I am the man." When he is asked to sign the "customs," which will restrict the power of the Church, he does so impulsively, without introspection, and then, just as quickly, he recants and refuses to seal them. Too often in the play the act of deciding is omitted, and only the decision itself is presented. Even before his martyrdom, his friends try to persuade him to save himself, but Becket ignores them. Again, the decision is already made.

Tennyson's real success in the play lies in his portrayal of Becket as a man who becomes consumed by his spiritual pride. Once he assumes the robes of the Church, he begins to confuse his will with the will of God. He even uses Christ's words to refer to himself: "Why, John, my kingdom is not of this world," but John answers him: "We are self-uncertain creatures,

and we may,/ Yea, even when we know not, mix our spites/ And private hates with our defense of Heaven." It is clear that Tennyson admires Becket, but he sees the fundamental flaw of those who will themselves to martyrdom.

THE FALCON

Tennyson was not discouraged by his failure readily to find a producer for his last two plays. He wrote four more plays, but he did not again try to write a history play. His next play, *The Falcon*, was a sentimental comedy in one act based on a tale from Giovanni Boccaccio's *Decameron: O, Prencipe Galetto* (1349-1351; *The Decameron*, 1620). Count Federigo, who has squandered all of his wealth in the vain pursuit of the widowed Lady Giovanni, is forced to live in a cottage with only his falcon to delight him. When Lady Giovanni unexpectedly comes to visit him, he realizes that he has no food to offer her, but he does not hesitate to order the killing of the falcon to provide a suitable meal for her. He then discovers the reason for her visit. Her desperately ill son had begged for the falcon to help him recover. It is a rather touching and mournful story, but the lady is won over by the gentleman's sacrifice, and the play ends as they embrace. Though there is not much substance to the work, it enjoyed a limited success on the stage.

THE CUP

The Cup is a two-act play based on a story in Plutarch, a tale of revenge in which the beautiful Galatian priestess Camma avenges the death of her husband, the victim of the lecherous and devious Synorix. When Synorix pursues her into the temple, she feigns a willingness to yield, but she says they must drink together from one cup. After she has poisoned the cup, she drinks half and gives the other half to her guilty lover, rejoicing that she has been permitted to avenge and then rejoin her dead husband.

The Cup had a long run, but its success was largely the result of spectacular staging. In this lavish production, more than two thousand pounds was spent on costumes and sets, and one hundred beautiful actresses were selected as vestal virgins, Camma's attendants in the temple. A review in *The Times* of London praised the magnificence of the production and the excellence of the acting, but it found "something shadowy and unreal" in the play.

THE FORESTERS

Tennyson returned to a full-length play with *The Foresters*, an old man's nostalgic dream of Robin Hood and Sherwood Forest. Robin Hood, the ideal outlaw, appears as a dubious shadow of King Arthur, the ideal king; his merry men's efforts to revolt against tyranny are marred by sentimentality and boyish antics. Interestingly, although the play was a failure in England, it was very successful in the United States.

THE PROMISE OF MAY

The Promise of May is noteworthy for several reasons: It was Tennyson's only play on a contemporary subject, it is predominantly prose, and it was his last play. It was also a dismal failure on the stage. Tennyson intended to present "a surface man of many theories," but his central character, Philip Edgar, is really an insincere hedonist with no ideology at all. The contrived plot involves an intellectual from the city corrupting and then abandoning a simple country girl, only to be forgiven by her at the end. Tennyson himself realized that it was a failure, and he did not try again to write plays.

OTHER MAJOR WORKS

POETRY: *Poems, Chiefly Lyrical*, 1830; *Poems*, 1832 (imprinted 1833); *Poems*, 1842; *The Princess*, 1847; *In Memoriam*, 1850; *Maud and Other Poems*, 1855; *Idylls of the King*, 1859-1885; *Enoch Arden and Other Poems*, 1864; *The Holy Grail and Other Poems*, 1869 (imprinted 1870); *Gareth and Lynette*, 1872; *The Lover's Tale*, 1879; *Ballads and Other Poems*, 1880; *Tiresias and Other Poems*, 1885; *Locksley Hall Sixty Years After, Etc.*, 1886; *Demeter and Other Poems*, 1889; *The Death of Œnone and Other Poems*, 1892.

NONFICTION: *The Letters of Alfred Lord Tennyson: Volume 1, 1821-1850*, 1981 (Cecil Y. Lang and Edgar F. Shannon, editors); *The Letters of Alfred Lord Tennyson: Volume 2, 1851-1870*, 1987 (Lang and Shannon, editors); *The Letters of Alfred Lord Tennyson: Volume 3, 1871-1892*, 1990 (Lang and Shannon, editors).

MISCELLANEOUS: *The Works of Tennyson*, 1907-1908 (9 volumes; Hallam, Lord Tennyson, editor).

BIBLIOGRAPHY

Hood, James W. *Divining Desire: Tennyson and the Poetics of Transcendence*. Aldershot, Vt.: Ashgate, 2000. Hood examines religious transcendence in the works of Tennyson. Bibliography and index.

Howe, Elisabeth A. *The Dramatic Monologue*. New York: Twayne, 1996. This study of dramatic monologues looks at the works of Tennyson, Robert Browning, T. S. Eliot, and Ezra Pound. Bibliography and index.

Levi, Peter. *Tennyson*. London: Macmillan, 1994. This biography examines the life and work of the poet Tennyson.

Ormond, Leonée. *Alfred Tennyson: A Literary Life*. New York: St. Martin's Press, 1993. A biographical study that examines Tennyson's life as a poet and writer. Bibliography and index.

Potter, Lois, ed. *Playing Robin Hood: The Legend as Performance in Five Centuries*. Newark: University of Delaware Press, 1998. This study of the legend of Robin Hood examines how the story has been presented in literature, including in Tennyson's *The Foresters*. Bibliography and index.

Smith, Elton Edward. *Tennyson's "Epic Drama."* Lanham, Md.: University Press of America, 1997. Smith examines the dramatic works of Tennyson. Bibliography and index.

Thorn, Michael. *Tennyson*. New York: St. Martin's Press, 1993. A biography of Tennyson that covers his life and works. Bibliography and index.

Tucker, Herbert F., ed. *Critical Essays on Alfred, Lord Tennyson*. New York: Maxwell Macmillan International, 1993. A collection of essays on the poet Tennyson. Bibliography and index.

Edwin W. Williams,
updated by Richard D. McGhee

TERENCE
Publius Terentius Afer

Born: Carthage; c. 190 B.C.E.
Died: En route from Greece; 159 B.C.E.

PRINCIPAL DRAMA

Andria, 166 B.C.E. (English translation, 1598)
Hecyra, 165 B.C.E. (*The Mother-in-Law*, 1598)
Heautontimorumenos, 163 B.C.E. (*The Self-Tormentor*, 1598)
Eunuchus, 161 B.C.E. (*The Eunuch*, 1598)
Phormio, 161 B.C.E. (English translation, 1598)
Adelphoe, 160 B.C.E. (*The Brothers*, 1598)

OTHER LITERARY FORMS

Terence is remembered only for his plays.

ACHIEVEMENTS

Latin literature took an important step in its development when Terence arrived on the scene. Although Plautus had done much to improve the Latin tongue and to refine the stage, he was hindered in his efforts by an audience lacking in culture. It was otherwise with Terence. In the interval that separated Plautus and Terence, a society of literary men had grown up at Rome, and their tastes were dominated by admiration of Greek literature and culture. It was in this circle that Terence moved and formed his literary aspirations and ideals. As a result, his main purpose differed from that of Plautus, who aimed at securing the applause of the people. Instead, Terence directed his efforts especially toward the attainment of elegance and correctness of expression and toward symmetry in the elaboration of his plots. Terence believed that the best way to obtain these results and the surest method for building up a national literature was a faithful reproduction of Greek works. Accordingly, he set himself the task of Hellenizing Roman comedy more completely, and by a close imitation of his Greek models, he succeeded in combining with the refined Latin of the cultivated class much of the flexibility, delicacy, and smoothness of the Attic idiom.

BIOGRAPHY

Publius Terentius Afer (Terence) is said to have been a native of Carthage and to have been brought in his childhood to Rome as a slave. There he was educated as a free man, by Terentius Lucanus, the senator, by whom he was afterward set free. Although originally a slave, Terence cannot have been a prisoner of war because there was no war between Rome and Carthage during his lifetime. He may, however, have fallen into the hands of a slave-dealer at Carthage because many of the native African tribes were subject to the Carthaginians. In Carthage, there must have been enslaved *Afri* whose children were in bondage with their parents. The children of such parents were often sold into foreign lands, and it is easy to conceive how Terence, if born at Carthage under these or similar circumstances, may have been sold by a slave-dealer to Lucanus at Rome. Such an explanation of his origin and deportation to Rome is justified in part by his cognomen Afer, which points to his being of other than Phoenician blood. Had Terence been of Phoenician origin, the last of his three names would more naturally have been Poenulus, since the Carthaginians were commonly distinguished from the Africans and it was customary to give names to slaves to indicate the nation to which they belonged. On receiving his freedom, Terence would have added to his praenomen, Publius, the Gentile name of his master (Terentius), which then would become his nomen, while as cognomen he might retain the title of "the African" (Afer) as a mark of particular distinction.

Terence's personal attractions and intellectual gifts, which had helped him to obtain his freedom, were the cause also of his permanent reception within the aristocratic circle of younger literary men at Rome. Terence probably became known to these men while he was still a member of his master's household. This circle included many of the nobility who were mainly responsible for introducing into Roman life Greek culture and refinement.

Among the noble young men who were friends of Terence and members of the same literary circle was Scipio Africanus the Younger; it was he who gave his name to what has since been known as the Scipionic circle of literati, a small group of people who made Greek literature their special study and Greek refinement and education their standard. It was the men of this class and character whom Terence especially endeavored to please with his comedies. He seems to have been indifferent to the general public.

Reportedly, when Terence submitted his first play to the aediles for production, he was told to obtain the opinion of Caecilius, who was then an established author. Going to Caecilius's house, where a dinner was in progress, Terence sat at the side of the room and began reading his play aloud. Soon he was invited to join the guests on the couches, where he finished reading it to great applause.

Having gained the support of Caecilius and Scipio and other members of the literary and aristocratic class at Rome, he was able to repel the attacks of his enemies, who, moved by jealousy, brought against

Terence (Library of Congress)

Terence the unfounded charge of plagiarism—or more exactly, hypocrisy—in representing as his own compositions dramas that were written at least in part by his noble friends. The truth appears to be that Terence read his compositions aloud to his literary friends and employed, independently and according to his choice, their criticisms and suggestions.

After producing six comedies between 166 and 160 B.C.E., Terence went to Greece, probably for the purpose of studying Greek life and institutions, which, according to his habit, he portrayed in his comedies. In 159 B.C.E., he died, just as he was about to return to Rome with translations, which he had made in Greece, of a number of Menander's plays. Accounts vary as to the place and manner of his death. One story relates that he was lost at sea off the island of Leucas while on his way to Italy and that his translations perished with him. Another account reports that he died at Stymphalus in Arcadia, after having lost his baggage and manuscripts in a shipwreck.

ANALYSIS

Terence's literary activity displayed itself wholly in the production of *palliatae*, plays that are fundamentally Greek and are representations of Greek habits, morals, and customs. The name *palliatae* comes from the *pallium*, a Greek cloak worn by the actor. It is clear that Terence deliberately tried not to break the Greek illusion. The characters must have seemed distinctly foreign to the Roman audience to such an extent that sometimes it appears that the only truly Latin element in his plays is the language. He based all of his plays on the Greek New Comedy; his favorite model was Menander, on whose plays four of Terence's are based (*Andria*, *The Self-Tormentor*, *The Eunuch*, and *The Brothers*). The remaining two (*Phormio* and *The Mother-in-Law*) are based on originals by the later writer Apollodorus.

Terence's use of the Greek plays led to an accusation of *contamnatio* (contamination). Normally, the use of a Greek original meant the closest possible adherence to it. Terence, contrary to the artistic usage of the time, used parts and materials drawn from more than one Greek model in the construction of a play.

Terence countered the charge in the prologues of several plays, most notably in *Andria*. It is now generally accepted that the charge was malicious and inspired by the jealousy of his enemies.

All six of Terence's plays tend to be conservative and more staid than those of Plautus. The scene is always "a street in Athens"; the characters are the standard old man, young man, courtesan, and slave; the chief variation is the more frequent introduction of the elderly married lady, and of the young couple already married when the play begins. The parasite, when he appears in *Phormio* and *The Eunuch*, has been elevated from the status of buffoon to that of an intelligent man-about-town; similarly the pimp, when he appears in *Phormio* and *The Brothers*, is much more the businessman than the scoundrel. The plays show almost no clowning and no slapstick whatever. Nearest to rowdy foolishness are the scenes in *The Eunuch* in which a braggart soldier, in the company of his parasite and an "army" consisting of two or three ragged numbskulls, lays siege to the house of a prostitute. The plays are nearly perfect in form; every scene is functional and serves to forward the action of the plot or to provide necessary elaboration on some character trait. There are no wasted scenes, introduced merely for comic diversion; indeed, there is hardly a wasted word. There are no immoral scenes, no drunken revels, few remarks that even smack of impropriety, let alone of obscenity, and no violence at all. Action on stage is quiet and rarely undignified. That the plays move smoothly, gracefully, and rapidly is a tribute to the skill with which they were put together; for all their quietness, they never lose the fast action that is the essence of Terence's comedy.

Terence's plays move on a higher moral level than Plautus's. In every one of the six, there is a "recognition" of one sort or another; in every one, except for *The Mother-in-Law* in which the characters are already married when the story begins, the hero and heroine properly end by becoming husband and wife. In *Andria*, *The Self-Tormentor*, and *Phormio*, a long-lost daughter is found and recognized. In *The Eunuch*, the girl turns out to be the sister of a proper Athenian citizen. In *The Mother-in-Law* and *The Brothers*, the girls had been foolish enough to go out on the streets at night in the course of a wildly sexual festival and had been raped by unknown young men. In *The Mother-in-Law*, the young man in question has subsequently married the girl he raped, without realizing who she was. His self-righteous anxiety on discovering that she was already pregnant, presumably by some man other than himself, causes the complications that Terence sets out to solve. In *The Brothers*, the young man has acknowledged his act and has promised to marry the girl, even though she is poor and of a lower class. The suspicion on the part of the girl's mother that the young man is about to renege on his promise forms one of the problems that this intricate play tries to solve.

In all of his plays, Terence is a thoroughly gentle and tactful poet, never overly forceful or blatant. Still, through all of his plays runs a persistent note of social criticism, directed particularly at the position of slaves and of women in Greek and Roman society. There is not a single slave or female character who is not decent, honorable, resourceful, and intelligent. This is certainly not the result of inadvertence, nor can it be brushed aside as simple sentimentality. It is rather Terence's way of arraigning ancient society for the heartless indifference that it commonly demonstrated toward its slave population and for the hypocritical and specious reasoning with which it handled prostitutes. Terence, perhaps because he himself had been a slave, shows sympathy toward them, and this gains for him respect for his understanding and courage. Terence's plays, as documents of human nature, are not much better than Plautus's, but where Plautus saw in other people chiefly an opportunity for creating an amusing situation, Terence viewed humanity with affection and regard.

THE BROTHERS

The critical consensus has been that *The Brothers* is Terence's masterpiece. First, it is a serious comedy because it deals with the theme of education and works out the consequences of opposing theories in ways that are simultaneously logical and amusing. Second, it is a tour de force of double plotting hardly equaled in drama: There are two systems of upbringing; two young products thereof, with their two love affairs, as well as the two brothers of the older generation who are the cause of it all. Last, in spite of the play's clever plot, its characters remain complex.

Although the plot elements of all the plays are conventional and repetitive, they form no more than a base on which Terence erects a remarkably varied set of stories, which hold the attention of the audience not only by unfolding a tale but even more by the sympathetic presentation of an interesting set of human problems and by a remarkable, gentle, unobtrusive, yet persistent note of social criticism.

THE EUNUCH

A good example of a conventional play of New Comedy is *The Eunuch*. The play presents two stories. In the primary plot, the young man has lost his position as lover of a courtesan to a braggart soldier. The courtesan hopes to regain possession of a young Athenian girl who had been like a sister to her and who has been lost to her for many years. By coincidence, the young girl has turned up in the soldier's possession. Once the problem of getting the young girl back has been solved, the courtesan is presumably ready to take the young man back as her lover.

The chief interest of the play centers on its subplot, in which the Athenian girl herself is the central figure, even though she appears on the stage briefly and speaks no lines. The young man's brother falls in love with her and substitutes himself for a eunuch who was given to the courtesan by the young man. The "eunuch" and the Athenian girl make love, and the other slaves wonder wide-eyed how a eunuch managed it. In the meantime, the Athenian girl is recognized as the sister of an Athenian citizen, and after disentangling the identity of the brother from that of the eunuch, he (the brother) is engaged to the girl. The play comes very near to being foolish; it is certainly the least interesting of all of them, yet it is said to have been the most popular and Terence's greatest success in his lifetime. One reason may be that it is the most lively and vivid of Terence's plays; although it is noted for its bawdy scenes, its vulgarity is greatly minimized by Terence's tasteful treatment.

PHORMIO

Phormio has a double plot somewhat better balanced than that of *The Eunuch*. There are two love affairs, one concerned with the love of the young man

Antipho for an orphan girl, Phanium, who never appears on the stage, and the other with the passion of Phaedria, the second young man, for the usual courtesan. By a series of clever tricks, the parasite Phormio succeeds in getting Antipho married to Phanium and obtaining the money that Phaedria needs to purchase his ladylove. At the end of the play, Phanium turns out to be an Athenian citizen, in fact, the daughter of Phaedria's father Chremes, who is cajoled into letting Phaedria keep his courtesan.

Aside from *The Brothers*, *Phormio* has earned more praise than any other Terentian comedy. It is more comical than the others; the handling of the improbable plot is masterly; the characters, as is usual with Terence, are complex and sympathetic; and in a variation on a theme, it is interesting to see the parasite rather than the slave carry the burden of intrigue.

ANDRIA

Andria is the closest of all Terence's plays to a tender love story and probably the best known of all of his plays. The play centers on the usual love-of-young-man-for-long-lost-daughter theme. The conflict is occasioned by the young man, Pamphilus, and his determination to keep the girl whom he has married without his father's consent and without adequate proof of her citizenship. Pamphilus has to withstand the equally strong determination of his father, Simo, to separate the couple, not so much because he disapproves of the girl, Glycerium, as because of Simo's hurt that a son of his flouted both Athenian law and custom by, apparently, marrying a noncitizen.

In the end, Glycerium turns out to be a citizen, in fact, the daughter of Simo's old friend, Chremes. The story might be quite commonplace except for the curious way in which the character of a dead woman, Chrysis, pervades it. She is the true "woman from Andros." She came to Athens a penniless orphan, tried with courage and persistence to earn an honest living, but, finding this too difficult, dropped into the less happy but more prosperous trade of the prostitute, and died just before the story of the play opens. Her courage, kindness, generosity, and devotion to Glycerium makes the whole play shine and gives it a human warmth and sympathy that would not be possible otherwise.

Interest inevitably centers on the slave Davus, who considerably outdoes his master in matters of intelligence and sheer manliness. Davus is clever, quick, and resourceful. He has a buoyant spirit that even the abuse of slavery cannot break. More than that, he never loses his human dignity; he may be a slave, but he is nevertheless a man.

THE SELF-TORMENTOR

Terence apparently believed that there is no one right way to rear sons, and this is confirmed in *The Self-Tormentor*. The bewildered and self-pitying father in this play, with his foolish attempts to punish himself for what he perceives as a mistake in bringing up his son, represents Terence's opinion of fathers. The play once again involves two fathers. One is Menedemus, whose son Cinia has joined the Persian army because his love for a poor woman, Antiphila, has shamed his father. The other is Chremes whose son Clitipho has as a mistress a prostitute, Bacchis. The plot centers on the attempts of the young men to obtain their respective ladyloves. *The Self-Tormentor* is usually considered a less successful *The Brothers*. Its theme is similar and its characterization almost as good. Terence is thought to have started weaving more threads here than he could effectively manage; the general pattern, even when completed, is hard to follow. There is one unique feature in the plot: In this play, the recognition scene adds to the complication rather than leading to the denouement.

THE MOTHER-IN-LAW

The remaining play, *The Mother-in-Law*, had a curious history. On the first two occasions when it was presented, the audience walked out before the play was over to go and see, on one occasion, a tightrope walker, and on the other, a gladiatorial exhibition. Only on the third attempt did the play succeed in holding the audience until the final curtain. This original bad luck has been at least in part responsible for the generally low rating that the play still enjoys. Actually, it tells an unusual story and tells it remarkably well. The plot concerns a young man who has raped a girl during a religious festival and later has married her without knowing that she was this same person, only to be greatly distressed on discovering that she was pregnant, apparently by some other man. The resolution of this tangle comes about through a variation of the recognition device: A ring, pulled from the girl's finger by the young man in the act of raping her and later presented by him to his mistress, a prostitute, is produced by the prostitute at the critical moment and establishes the identity of the young man's wife.

The role of the prostitute immediately attracts the attention of the audience; generous and sympathetic courtesans are not unknown in the comedy of Terence, but this one is the only one who deliberately, and out of sheer kindness and generosity, engages in an act that must inevitably and permanently sever her from her former lover. The young man, too, presents an interesting variant, for unlike other young men in Roman comedy who seem to have had mothers only through biological necessity, this one is devoted to his mother—so much so, in fact, that he considers her happiness more important than his wife's.

BIBLIOGRAPHY

Forehand, Walter. *Terence.* Boston: Twayne, 1985. A basic biography of Terence with literary criticism of his works. Includes some general discussion of Latin drama. Bibliography and index.

Goldberg, Sander M. *Understanding Terence.* Princeton, N.J.: Princeton University Press, 1986. Goldberg provides a brief biography of Terence along with analysis of his works and of Latin drama in general.

Snowden, Frank M., Jr. *Blacks in Antiquity: Ethiopians in the Greco-Roman Experience.* Cambridge, Mass.: Belknap Press of Harvard University Press, 1970. The author examines the role of blacks in the Greek and Roman worlds.

Sutton, Dana Ferrin. *Ancient Comedy: The War of the Generations.* New York: Maxwell Macmillan International, 1993. This study of ancient comedy looks at Terence, Menander, and Plautus. Bibliography and index.

Shelley P. Haley

MEGAN TERRY

Born: Seattle, Washington; July 22, 1932

PRINCIPAL DRAMA

Ex-Miss Copper Queen on a Set of Pills, pr. 1963,
   pb. 1966

Calm Down Mother, pr. 1965, pb. 1966

Keep Tightly Closed in a Cool Dry Place, pr. 1965,
   pb. 1966

Comings and Goings, pr. 1966, pb. 1967

The Gloaming, Oh My Darling, pr. 1966, pb. 1967

Viet Rock: A Folk War Movie, pr., pb. 1966 (music
   by Marianne de Pury)

The Magic Realists, pr. 1966, pb. 1968

The People vs. Ranchman, pr. 1967, pb. 1968

Massachusetts Trust, pr. 1968, pb. 1972

Megan Terry's Home: Or, Future Soap, pr. 1968
   (televised), pb. 1972, pr. 1974 (staged)

The Tommy Allen Show, pr. 1969, pb. 1971

Approaching Simone, pr. 1970, pb. 1973

Three One-Act Plays, pb. 1970

Couplings and Groupings, pb. 1973

Nightwalk, pr. 1973, pb. 1975 (with Sam Shepard
   and Jean-Claude van Itallie)

Babes in the Bighouse, pr., pb. 1974

Hothouse, pr., pb. 1974

The Pioneer, pr. 1974, pb. 1975

Pro Game, pr. 1974, pb. 1975

100,001 Horror Stories of the Plains, pr. 1976,
   pb. 1978 (with Judith Katz, James Larson, and
   others)

Brazil Fado, pr., pb. 1977

Sleazing Toward Athens, pr. 1977, revised pr., pb.
   1986

Willa-Willa-Bill's Dope Garden, pb. 1977

American King's English for Queens, pr., pb. 1978

*Attempted Rescue on Avenue B: A Beat Fifties
   Comic Opera*, pr., pb. 1979

Goona Goona, pr. 1979, pb. 1981

Advances, pb. 1980

*Mollie Bailey's Traveling Family Circus: Featuring
   Scenes from the Life of Mother Jones*, pr. 1981,
   pb. 1983

Kegger, pr. 1982

Family Talk, pr., pb. 1986

Sea of Forms, pr. 1986, pb. 1987 (with Jo Ann
   Schmidman)

Dinner's in the Blender, pr., pb. 1987

Walking Through Walls, pr., pb. 1987 (with
   Schmidman)

Amtrak, pr. 1988, pb. 1990

Headlights, pr., pb. 1988

Retro, pr. 1988

Do You See What I'm Saying?, pr., pb. 1990

Belches on Couches, pr. 1992 (with Schmidman
   and Kimberlain)

India Plays, pr. 1992

Sound Fields: Are We Hear, pr. 1992 (with
   Schmidman and Sora Kimberlain)

Star Path Moon Stop, pr. 1995

Plays, pb. 2000

No Kissing in the Hall, pr. 2002

OTHER LITERARY FORMS

Megan Terry wrote lyrics for *Thoughts* (1973), a
musical by Lamar Alford, and she has contributed
prose pieces to *The New York Times* and *Valhalla: A
Modern Drama Issue*. She has also written teleplays
and radio plays.

ACHIEVEMENTS

One of the most prolific playwrights of the New
Theater in the United States, Megan Terry is linked
with the Open Theatre, which she helped form with
Joseph Chaikin and Michael Smith in 1963. The
work that brought international attention to Terry is
Viet Rock, the first well-publicized play about Vietnam to be produced in the United States. Terry and
the Open Theatre created an improvisational workshop atmosphere, in which actors, directors, and
playwrights could form a living theater experience,
disorienting audience expectations through "transformations" in which actors, settings, times, or moods
may alter without transition or apparent logic. Although some critics find this experience alienating or

confusing, others hail the technique as a significant contribution to the development of a truly living theater experience. Her plays' earthy language, sexual and political content, musical segments, humor, and vaudeville touches all blend to create lively, dynamic experiences for audiences. Her innovative work has received numerous awards, including the Stanley Drama Award (1965), WGBH Award (1968), Latin American Festival Award (1969), Obie Award (1970), Earplay Award (1972), Dramatists Guild Award (1983), and grants from the National Endowment for the Arts, Creative Artists Public Service Grant, Rockefeller Foundation, and the Guggenheim Foundation. In 1971, she became resident playwright at the Omaha Magic Theater.

BIOGRAPHY

Megan Terry was born in Seattle, Washington, on July 22, 1932, as Marguerite Duffy. Throughout grade school, Terry was fascinated with the theater, and she was exposed at an early age to the influence of the Seattle Repertory Playhouse. In 1951, the theater closed under pressure from a state committee investigating so-called un-American activities, an event that both radicalized the young Terry and confirmed her in her view of the theater as a powerful political tool. Terry received a B.Ed. from the University of Washington, and she taught at the Cornish School of Allied Arts. She traveled to New York, where she became involved with the Playwrights' Unit Workshop, which included Edward Albee, Richard Barr, and Clinton Wilder, in the 1963 production of *Ex-Miss Copper Queen on a Set of Pills*, a work based on her fascination with a pill-popping prostitute who had once been a beauty queen. Terry's career includes several attempts at realistic drama, including *Hothouse* and an early version of *Attempted Rescue on Avenue B*, but she found that she wanted to create new techniques for conveying her messages about the destructiveness of the United States' economic and political power structures. In working with the Open Theatre on *Calm Down Mother* and *Keep Tightly Closed in a Cool Dry Place*, Terry created two of her most successful one-act transformation plays. Using three female actors, *Calm Down Mother* explored

what is possible for women and what role limitations women encounter in society. In a similar fashion, *Keep Tightly Closed in a Cool Dry Place* used three male actors, whose characters begin in a prison setting and transform from gangsters to drag queens to soldiers, testing various kinds of enclosures, both imagined and real. Her fascination with sexuality appeared in another transformation play entitled *Comings and Goings*, which stretched actors' technique and delighted its original audiences, many of whom were actors themselves. The first collaboration play to be created in a workshop situation was also Terry's most renowned, *Viet Rock*. Gerome Ragni was among the actors in the workshop, and he later collaborated with James Rado to produce *Hair* in 1967. *Viet Rock* created a number of firsts, including the combination of rock music with the traditional musical-theater genre, treatment of the controversial Vietnam War theme, and the intrusion of actors touching and interacting with audience members.

After receiving an American Broadcasting Company "Writing for the Camera" Fellowship from Yale, Terry wrote *The People vs. Ranchman*, a work dealing with the creation of stars out of people such as Charles Manson and Angela Davis. After receiving negative reviews for this work, Terry went on to produce *Megan Terry's Home*, a futuristic play commissioned by Channel Thirteen's *New York Television Theater*, the first commissioned play ever presented on National Educational Television (NET) Playhouse. With an increasing interest in feminist issues, Terry wrote *Approaching Simone* (winner of the Obie Award for Best New Play of 1969-1970) in 1970, studying the life of Simone Weil, a Jewish-French philosopher who starved herself to death in protest over the World War II soldiers who were starving at the front. Turning again to historical sources, Terry created *100,001 Horror Stories of the Plains* in 1976 from the accounts of family stories, poems, and songs collected while Terry was playwright-in-residence for the Magic Theater in Omaha, Nebraska. Another controversial work combining her concern over violence and women's rights was *Goona Goona*, a burlesque treatment of child abuse and wife abuse in the imaginary Goon family. Terry further explores feminist themes in *Mollie Bailey's Traveling Family Circus*, first produced in 1981 at the Mark Taper Laboratory Theater of Los Angeles, a play dealing with real and imagined events in the lives of Mollie Bailey and Mother Jones.

After Terry became playwright-in-residence at the Omaha Magic Theater, she became increasingly well known as a feminist playwright. Her work continued to deal with such domestic issues as family violence, illiteracy, and alcoholism, but she also expanded it to include musical collaborations, in such works as *Sea of Forms*, *Walking Through Walls*, and *Headlights*, which was produced in 1988. *Belches on Couches*, *Sound Fields: Are We Hear*, and *Star Path Moon Stop* deal respectively with the effects of television on society, critical issues regarding abuse of the natural environment, and the meaning of "home" in a postmodern world.

In 2002, after thirty-three years as an experimental theater, the Omaha Magic Theater closed, ending Terry's tenure as resident playwright there. Terry's first project in the twenty-first century was a play commissioned by the Omaha Theatre for Young People called *No Kissing in the Hall*, about teenagers dealing with their sexuality.

ANALYSIS

Megan Terry's works, although varied in structure, length, technique, and subject matter, are linked by a dynamic emphasis on emotion over reason; a lively use of earthy language, humor, music, metaphors, and symbols; a fearless treatment of timely controversial subjects; and a dedication to collaboration and spontaneity in acting and production. Because of her quickness to address controversial issues, some of her most noted works may not be her best plays, but rather those works that elicited the strongest public reaction at the time of first production.

The Magic Realists drew sharp criticism and publicity for its failure to touch ground with some realistic setting or situation, but it merits analysis in that it marks the beginning of Terry's shift to her own distinctive theatrical style, rooted in the traditions of vaudeville and early film comedy. *Viet Rock*, while

characterized by some critics as naïve and simplistic, clearly captures the spirit of early protest reactions to the war in Vietnam, and as such it is Terry's best-known play. Two of her most representative works, *Keep Tightly Closed in a Cool Dry Place* and *Megan Terry's Home*, explore the theme of enclosure and entrapment, at both personal and cultural levels. *Mollie Bailey's Traveling Family Circus* represents yet another phase in the development of Terry's playwriting, combining her love of music and strong female characters with a deep commitment to exploring ethical and political issues.

Terry's work demonstrates adaptability, variety, and a consistent dedication to political and ethical ideals, qualities that provoke criticism as well as praise. Analysis of the body of her work reveals a prolific and imaginative mind at work, constantly striving and reworking themes as old as drama: family and gender roles, violence and pacifism, individual and social welfare, subordination and freedom. Her plays represent a substantial contribution to American drama, both in their innovative forms and in their political and philosophical substance.

THE MAGIC REALISTS

The Magic Realists premiered in 1966 at La Mama Experimental Theatre Club in New York and drew sharp criticism from *Village Voice* reviewer Michael Smith for its lack of connection to any outside reality. Terry's first break from realistic theater styles, *The Magic Realists* presents a combination of obscure dialogue and stereotyped characterizations. The action of the play centers on T. P. Chester's attempts to find a clone of himself who can carry on his non-stop wheelings and dealings. He chooses Don, a teen-age escaped convict, in whom he recognizes the same total lack of scruples and the same "hunger" that have brought him to his esteemed position in the world of high finance. Occasionally, a "person" enters the stage, representing one of his numerous children, whom Chester views solely as tax exemptions. When a beautiful black woman named Dana arrives on the scene, she manages to seduce Don from Chester's influence. Dana, a Japanese American, and an American Indian, who all turn out to be secret agents, attempt to arrest Chester, but one of Chester's offspring persons appears to rescue him with a submachine gun. At last united, the father and child inadvertently gun down the secret agents as the weapon is held between them in a wild, whirling embrace.

The action demonstrates in vaudeville style how the capitalist economic power structure creates machinelike human beings whose sense of family, justice, and human emotion are entirely subordinated to the drive for money. Although the plot and characterizations are admittedly thin, this early work reveals several of Terry's strong points. She captures natural speech rhythms and the comedy inherent in juxtaposition of radically differing character types. The combined elements of violence and sexuality create lively slapstick comedy and a few thought-provoking insults to the status quo.

VIET ROCK

In a similar vein, *Viet Rock* garnered much attention but little praise for its earnest, naïve attack on the brutality and absurdity of the Vietnam War. The play uses all the familiar clichés about honor, duty, and love of country to demonstrate that the soldiers who deliver these lines are basically automatons. Women in the play share responsibility for creating males who are infantile, obedient, and easily manipulated by brainless sentimentality. *Viet Rock* depicts events as varied as senate hearings and soldiers writing home to mothers and sweethearts in a collection of vignettes linked by few or no transitions. Although the music and satire received negative reviews for failure to achieve depth or complexity, Terry also drew admiration for her canny sense of theater and her ability to create a "happening" that captured the current mood of public outrage. Critics argued, however, that the play did very little to deepen anyone's understanding of issues or to undermine self-satisfaction, two principal aims of satire. The play may not be notable for its depth, but its innovative use of rock lyrics and interaction between actors and audience broke ground for the creation of *Hair*, one of the best-known rock musicals to come out of the Vietnam War era.

KEEP TIGHTLY CLOSED IN A COOL DRY PLACE

Receiving much more critical acclaim but less publicity, *Keep Tightly Closed in a Cool Dry Place*

premiered at the Sheridan Square Playhouse in 1965 under the aegis of the Open Theatre. Dedicated to Joseph Chaikin, one of the founders of the group, the play typifies the concept of "transformation," a theater style in which actors, setting, and mood metamorphose, often without transition. The play has only three characters: Jaspers, an intellectual lawyer; Michaels, a burly type; and Gregory, a bewildered, handsome young man destined to become victim of the other two characters. In jail, Jaspers and Michaels consider how to undermine Gregory's confession, which has revealed that Jaspers hired Michaels to get Gregory to kill Jaspers's wife. The first transformation turns Jaspers into General George Armstrong Custer, with Michaels as one of his soldiers, whom he instructs to kill Gregory, now a "redskin." Just as abruptly, the characters become themselves again, and Gregory dreams of rape, achieving orgasm as Jaspers and Michaels berate him for his lack of control, his ineptitude, and his unprofessionalism.

If the audience members believe that they understand the character types established in the opening, the remainder of the play shatters these assumptions. The three men join to become a machine, apparently a gun, and each actor describes a part of the machine's features. In the next transformation, Jaspers becomes a dying English soldier under Captain John Smith, alias Gregory. Later, Jaspers becomes mother to Michaels, then victim of a murderer, then an evangelist, and finally father to Michaels and Gregory. The play closes with a dancing chant in which the three form a human wheel, with Jaspers offering the closing line, "This side should face you!" Although the unexpected transformations are jarring and disorienting, the play offers the unifying notion that all human beings go through a series of roles, presenting different facets of human behavior, as dictated by society and circumstance. The prison setting suggests that people are locked into these roles, just as unwillingly and randomly as prisoners are incarcerated.

MEGAN TERRY'S HOME

Another play examining confinement, this time in a futuristic setting, is *Megan Terry's Home*, originally created for Channel Thirteen in New York and later commissioned for NET and nationally broadcast in January of 1968. The principal characters, Mother Ruth, Cynthia, and Roy, constitute part of a unit of nine people, forced by overpopulation to live and die together in a room smaller than a jail cell. Central Control, the governing body, ministers to their physical, spiritual, and psychological needs, through the total organization of their sleeping and waking time. They pop pills for nourishment and psychological well-being, watch multiple television screens for news of past and present, and dream, chant, and perform isometrics for social and physical interaction.

The central conflict of the play rests in Cynthia and Roy's desire to marry and have their own real baby for the group, a privilege rarely granted to units, regardless of how obedient, efficient, or patient they are. When the air-venting system temporarily breaks down, allowing another human to enter their cell, Ruth panics, overrides her socialization, and kills the intruder. The group of nine quickly disposes of the body and the marriage ceremony of Roy and Cynthia continues, with all nine hoping that they may one day be allowed by the state to have a baby of their own.

Terry's play cleverly creates an alternative world, complete with values, customs, and mannerisms convincingly appropriate to a highly technological civilization coping with overpopulation and limited resources. It confronts the idea that human instincts for survival may be exactly the impulses that will lead to self-destruction. The overcrowded society places a premium on cooperation, self-sacrifice, obedience, and nonviolence, but it is unable to overcome the women's urges to become mothers to their own children. One of her most sophisticated and intellectually complex works, *Megan Terry's Home* calls on audiences to question human nature, media culture, religious values, and Western notions of progress. The action of the play suggests the possibility that brutality in the name of survival may be unavoidable, and it does so in a way that creates dramatic suspense and empathy for believable characters. Terry effectively exploits the medium of television, but stage directions make the work easily adaptable for live presentation as well.

MOLLIE BAILEY'S TRAVELING FAMILY CIRCUS

Terry's dedication to feminism appears in numerous plays, nowhere more openly than in *Mollie Bailey's Traveling Family Circus*. This piece, dedicated to Mollie Bailey and Mother Jones, alternates between scenes of Mollie and Gus Bailey and children and the life of Mother Jones. As with some of her earlier work, this play is at times heavy-handed in its delineation of good and evil, with heartless capitalists and their flunkies as adversaries to Mother Jones, who bravely seeks justice and protection for victimized children. Women are portrayed as the preservers of civilization, of all that is good and brave and true, and males appear in the play as little more than sperm banks. Music and humor carry the play, however, creating an entertaining spectacle with the timely obsessions of contemporaneous culture at its heart.

FAMILY TALK

Terry continued with her interest in music, humor, and family issues in such works as *Family Talk*, a play that dramatizes the breakdown in communication within the family. Showing how television acts as a substitute for real communication, this play demonstrates what happens when Mother Kraaz unplugs the television. The seven family members literally and figuratively stumble and grope as they attempt to communicate with one another without the escape hatch of the huge, centrally located television set. Dian Ostdiek's stage design includes a monopoly board setup with such location markings as "Danger—Mom at Work" or "Stargazing Strip," where family members retreat when the stress of communication becomes too great. The music and lyrics, by Joe Budenholzer and John J. Sheehan, range from Andrews Sisters style, to country western or folk rock, to sound effects in the tradition of John Cage. While the vision is at times grim, the humor and musical play of *Family Talk* suggest healing and reconciliation.

HEADLIGHTS

In a similar vein, *Headlights* presents an alarming portrait of American society, pointing out that one of every eight Americans cannot read and then focusing on solutions to illiteracy. The play uses music, choral speech, multiple actors for single characters, and standard dialogue to relay the devastating effects of illiteracy. Multimedia presentations of slides and collages combine with props—fluorescent tubes, rings, rubber balls, and lampshade hats that illuminate when a character is "enlightened"—to illustrate how the system fails to educate. At the same time, the play's portrayal of individual characters learning to read serves as an inspiration to nonreaders and teaching volunteers alike. As with *Family Talk*, the subject matter for *Headlights* came from interaction with audiences encountered by the Omaha Magic Theater's touring group.

STAR PATH MOON STOP

Star Path Moon Stop, the Omaha Magic Theater's last piece, is the outgrowth of collaboration with the Dallas Children's Theatre. It was inspired by Terry's realization that the audience and the world in which they live are changing—that even after living for almost thirty years in Omaha, she was no longer assured to be served by the same printer or other merchant from one month to the next. Through hundreds of interviews, she explored the concept of this ever-changing, even nomadic world. *Star Path Moon Stop* utilizes a modular text and includes structural actions, "stops" or "reality frames" that serve as distancing for the audience. The performance text can be constructed to create recurring patterns and to emphasize themes. The play's dramatic form and subject matter confirm Terry as a playwright who is consistently attuned to contemporary issues and unafraid to explore them in her works.

OTHER MAJOR WORKS

TELEPLAYS: *The Dirt Boat*, 1955; *One More Little Drinkie*, 1969.

RADIO PLAYS: *Sanibel and Captiva*, 1968; *American Wedding Ritual Monitored/Transmitted by the Planet Jupiter*, 1972.

EDITED TEXT: *Right Brain Vacation Photos: New Plays and Production Photographs, 1972-1992*, 1992 (with Jo Ann Schmidman and Sora Kimberlain).

BIBLIOGRAPHY

Babnich, Judith. "Family Talk." Review of *Family Talk*. *Theatre Review* 39 (May, 1987): 240-241. Although this article is only a brief review of one play, it reveals important details about how many of Terry's works are produced through collaboration with psychologists, social workers, artists, and community activists. Babnich points out how Terry uses music, multimedia effects, and comedy to achieve serious social criticism and a call for action and social healing.

Betsko, Kathleen, and Rachel Koenig. "Megan Terry." In *Interviews with Contemporary Women Playwrights*. New York: Beech Tree, 1987. An interview with Terry on her writing and life.

Keyssar, Helene. "Megan Terry: Mother of American Feminist Theatre." In *Feminist Theatre*. New York: Grove Press, 1985. This article details the contributions of Terry to the development of a collaborative feminist theater in the United States. In addition to providing thorough bibliographic information and notes, this essay offers a valuable overview and analysis of Terry's vital impact on American drama, from her early work as a founding member of the Women's Theatre Council in 1971 to her community-based collaborative playwriting techniques, developed with the Omaha Magic Theater.

Klein, Kathleen Gregory. "Language and Meaning in Megan Terry's 'Musicals.'" *Modern Drama* 27 (December, 1984): 574-583. Focusing on the plays *American King's English for Queens*, *Babes in the Bighouse*, *Brazil Fado*, and *The Tommy Allen Show*, Klein details how Terry's work elucidates the relationship of language to gender. This insightful article draws connections between Terry's work and the traditions of B-movie musicals, television, and popular culture, with an emphasis on the language of Terry's musicals.

Leavitt, Dinah L. "Megan Terry." In *Women in American Theatre*, edited by Helen Krich Chinoy and Linda Walsh Jenkins. New York: Crown, 1981. A brief overview of Terry's works and life.

Murphy, Brenda, ed. *The Cambridge Companion to American Women Playswrights*. New York: Cambridge University Press, 1999. This broad work contains information on Terry and her place in American theater.

Natalle, Elizabeth. *Feminist Theatre: A Study in Persuasion*. Metuchen, N.J.: Scarecrow Press, 1985. This survey of feminist theater features a ten-page bibliography, an index, and nine pages of analysis of Terry's role in the development of feminist theater. The discussion focuses primarily on *American King's English for Queens* and *Babes in the Bighouse*, placing them in the context of feminist concerns.

Rebecca Bell-Metereau,
updated by Anne Fletcher

STEVE TESICH

Born: Titovo Užice, Yugoslavia; September 29, 1942
Died: Sydney, Nova Scotia, Canada; July 1, 1996

PRINCIPAL DRAMA

The Carpenters, pr. 1970, pb. 1971 (one act)
Lake of the Woods, pr. 1971, pb. 1981 (one act)
Baba Goya, pr. 1973, pb. 1981 (also published as *Nourish the Beast*, 1974)
Gorky, pr. 1975, pb. 1976 (musical)
Passing Game, pr. 1977, pb. 1978
Touching Bottom, pr. 1978, pb. 1980 (includes the one-acts *The Road*, *A Life*, and *Baptismal*)
Division Street, pr. 1980, pb. 1981
The Speed of Darkness, pr., pb. 1989
Square One, pr., pb. 1990
On the Open Road, pr., pb. 1992
Arts and Leisure, pr. 1996, pb. 1997

OTHER LITERARY FORMS

Steve Tesich is best known as a screenwriter because of the critical and popular success of his first screenplay, *Breaking Away* (1979). He had five screenplays produced in the 1980's, the most successful of which was *The World According to Garp* (1982), an adaptation of John Irving's novel. Tesich also published the novel *Summer Crossing* (1982), a coming-of-age story set in East Chicago, Indiana. Both the screenplays and the novel draw heavily on his own experiences and have been praised for their intriguing characters.

ACHIEVEMENTS

Steve Tesich has been called the United States' cheerleader because of the optimism expressed in his early absurdist comedies for the land "where anything is possible." He demonstrated a unique ability to create fully developed, if eccentric, characters, individualized dialogue, and outrageous situations. His early plays are significant as commentaries on the faith of the United States' promise in the 1970's and his later plays on the outrage of that nation's unrealized promise in the late 1980's. He received many awards including the Vernon Rice Award and Drama Desk Award for *Baba Goya*; the Writer's Guild Award, the New York Film Critics Circle Award, the National Society of Film Critics Award, and the Academy of Motion Picture Arts and Sciences Best Original Screenplay Award for *Breaking Away*; and the National Board of Review Exceptional Film Award for *The World According to Garp*.

BIOGRAPHY

Steve (Stoyan) Tesich was born September 29, 1942, in Titovo Užice, Yugoslavia, where he learned the art of storytelling from his mother, Gospava (Bulaich) Tesich. His favorite boyhood theme was going to the United States to find his father, Radisa, who was missing in the war. Eventually, Radisa contacted his family from England, where he turned up after fleeing Yugoslavia to join its government in exile. The Tesich family was finally reunited in 1957, but in the United States, because Stoyan had led a family revolution against going to England: He wanted to go to the land "where anything could happen." Therefore, at age fourteen, Stoyan became Steve, living in East Chicago, Indiana, where his machinist father found work in the steel mills. Although the unrelenting red glow of the smokestacks was not the great American West that he had learned to love in motion pictures, he optimistically believed that he had found the "frontier of possibility." Tesich quickly learned English and was assimilated into the high school culture of the late 1950's. He won a wrestling scholarship to Indiana University, where he made Phi Beta Kappa, won the Little Five Hundred bicycle race, and was graduated in 1965. Tesich has often used his Indiana years as the background for his stories.

After Columbia University awarded Tesich a graduate scholarship, he moved to New York City to study Russian literature, with the notion that he might become an academic. As he began to understand the characters in Russian novels, however, he began to get excited about the idea of becoming a writer, and he augmented his literary studies with writing classes. He also met Rebecca Fletcher, who encouraged him in a writing career. Tesich was graduated from Columbia University with his master of arts degree in Russian in 1967 and married Fletcher on May 24, 1971. He worked briefly as a caseworker for the Brooklyn Department of Welfare while he tried his hand at novels and scripts. The American Place Theatre agreed to produce *The Carpenters* in 1970. Over the next eight years, the American Place Theatre actively supported his playwriting by producing several of his plays. The most successful of these was *Baba Goya* (later retitled *Nourish the Beast*), which won the 1973 Vernon Rice and Drama Desk awards and was produced on public television.

Tesich had also been writing screenplays during this time, with no success. Director Peter Yates suggested that he merge two of his scripts, one about four college-town locals, the other about the Little Five Hundred bicycle race. The result was the award-winning *Breaking Away*, which established Tesich as a major American writer. He immediately returned to the theater in 1980 with the political farce *Division*

Street. The play was first staged in Los Angeles at the Mark Taper Forum, where it was a resounding success. It then became his first Broadway production, where it was savaged by New York critics.

Tesich did not return to the theater for almost ten years, during which time five of his screenplays were filmed and his novel *Summer Crossing* was published. He was not "lured away by Hollywood" or disgruntled by all the criticism. He simply intended to stay away from the theater until he could approach playwriting from a new angle. In 1989, Tesich emerged with a daughter, Amy, and two new plays, *The Speed of Darkness* and *Square One*, which do present a new Tesich vision of his adopted homeland. Instead of his personal perspective, he developed the ability to write from a societal perspective, to write about moral issues in the dramatic form. His last play, *Arts and Leisure*, which completed an Off-Broadway run shortly before his death in July, 1996, of a heart attack, portrays a theater critic. This critic's work, Tesich says, encourages passivity in the face of violence or tragedy in Americans because it teaches people to act like theater critics—sitting on the sidelines, taking notes, and experiencing the crisis, catharsis, and climax of plays.

Analysis

Steve Tesich's plays are divided into two groups by a ten-year, self-imposed exile from the theater. The early plays, beginning with *The Carpenters* and ending with *Division Street*, share the personal viewpoint of "immigrant optimism," an America where anything is possible, where a Yugoslavian teenager who does not speak English can win an Academy Award before his fortieth birthday. The later plays, beginning with *The Speed of Darkness*, are based on a social viewpoint that mourns for an America that has not lived up to its promise. The early plays are noted for their bizarre portraits of family life full of eccentric characters, outrageous comedy, wordplay, and individualized dialogue, as well as for their extensive, often burdensome symbolism. The later plays demonstrate the unique comic perspective and symbolism together with the vivid characterization, dialogue, and extreme situation of the early plays, while charting new dramatic territory dealing with moral issues. As he is an intensely personal writer, the plays are a commentary on Tesich's life.

THE CARPENTERS AND LAKE OF THE WOODS

Tesich always experimented with dramatic forms, most prevalently the absurdist worldview. *The Carpenters* depicts a dysfunctional American family living in a house that is breaking down around them, just as their family relationships are breaking down. The father tries but is unable to understand his existence. *Lake of the Woods* shows another family, on vacation in America's wonderlands. When they reach their scenic destination, however, they find only a desolate wasteland. Their intentions are hobbled, their mobile home and car are vandalized, and it seems as though their hardships will kill them. Instead of giving up, however, the father rallies his family and sets out on an optimistic trek, away from the lapidation of modern urbanism toward a wilderness of happy people. Both plays have moments of brilliance, with clever dialogue and surprise comic twists, but they are often self-conscious and deteriorate into heavy-handed symbolism that becomes preachy and banal.

BABA GOYA

The absurdist comedy *Baba Goya* is Tesich's most successful early play. Often called a 1970's *You Can't Take It with You* (pr. 1936, pb. 1937, by George S. Kaufman and Moss Hart), it depicts another outlandish family, this time headed by a raunchy mother who is intent on making every screwball who darkens her door a member of her family. In the mistaken belief that he is dying, her fourth husband, Mario, takes out a newspaper advertisement to find his replacement. Baba interviews applicants as she tries to help her depressed son and disparaged daughter develop enough strength to leave her nest. Baba can forgive her daughter for divorcing her liberal husband who talked her into getting pregnant just so an abortion law could be tested. She can forgive her daughter's starring in a pornographic film, selling drugs, and becoming a thief, but never her voting for Richard M. Nixon. Detractors of *Baba Goya* condemn it as a silly and pointless contrivance of sight gags and clever

one-liners. They are, however, blind to this play's subtler symbolism. Baba Goya is Tesich's America, taking in all no matter what their idiosyncrasies or problems and helping them to stand on their own two feet, becoming productive members of the family.

GORKY

Tesich's next effort was a musical, *Gorky*, based on the life of the Russian writer Maxim Gorky. In what has become a recurring pattern, the play was resoundingly criticized by some but highly praised by others. Tesich had become an acknowledged voice in the theater but one that struck either a nerve or a chord. *Gorky* is one of his least successful efforts, with not enough facts to be a biography and hardly enough opinion to be a political commentary. What remains is a conversation between three actors depicting Gorky as an innocent youth, a passionate revolutionary, and a disillusioned victim of a Stalin purge.

PASSING GAME AND TOUCHING BOTTOM

Tesich returned to his absurdist viewpoint in *Passing Game* and *Touching Bottom*, the latter containing three one-act plays in the tradition of Samuel Beckett. Both plays return to the skewed lives that have become the hallmark of his plays. He also returned, however, to his heavy-handed symbolism.

DIVISION STREET

Division Street, the last of Tesich's early plays, combines all of his most successful elements into a political farce that emphasizes character and plot over symbolism. A metaphor borrowed from Studs Terkel, *Division Street* is the story of Chris, an aging radical from the 1960's, who has sold out to the establishment and is intent on starting a career. As chance would have it, however, he is served a putrid cabbage in a Yugoslavian restaurant and is photographed regurgitating on the street. The picture makes the newspaper, and his past gallops unwanted to his door. What follows is a brilliant farce complete with slamming doors and windows, mistaken identities, reunited orphans, outrageous characters and situations, and clever dialogue full of Tesich wordplay, one-liners, and repartee. The script is filled with radicals who have no place in the "Me" generation but who long for the good old days of "the movement." The original, published version has a weakly resolved ending, with Chris once again leading the displaced radicals in a new movement and a patriotic rendition of "America the Beautiful." A revised production eliminated the song, along with two characters, but still ended in sentimental patriotism. Tesich did not intend for the characters to be perceived as shallow hippies without a cause, as it is sometimes interpreted, becoming a mindless romp, a shallow farce and nothing more. When it is understood that Tesich intended the play to be a remembrance of his own college activist days ending with a call to continued activism, to find and eliminate injustice, the play becomes a comedy of ideas.

Even when Tesich is criticized, he is praised for his ability to create fascinating characters and intriguing dialogue. This talent is the result of his mastery of American English, his keen ear for the ways people speak, and his unusual approach to creating characters first, and then situation and conflict. When studying Russian literature, he recognized how he felt about the United States as he observed what happened when Russian characters with differing ideologies bumped into each other. In the Russian novels, the ideas and beliefs were heavy burdens; in the United States the divergent ideas were energizers. This notion of interacting and reacting ideas evolved into the methodology of Tesich's writing. He begins by writing character notes: anecdotal biographies, snatches of dialogue, and philosophical questions, often accumulating as much as a hundred pages of background material. Next, he begins to write about his characters, to explore and see what they do. As the divergent characters collide, something happens, and *that* is what he writes about. He discards the preliminary material and writes the story of what happens when his intricately delineated, conflicting, and contradicting characters collide.

The Speed of Darkness

When Tesich returned to the theater after almost ten years of absence, that method was still in evidence. Even though his perspective and motivation for writing changed, his later plays were based squarely on character. While the early plays sprang from his own perspective, emanating from his own experience, in his later plays he wrote from the experience of others. He was the disappointed American, still loving the United States for what it should be, but he was outraged at the moral bankruptcy that he saw around him. *The Speed of Darkness* was written in response to what he perceived as creeping revisionism in the United States' memory of the Vietnam War. Tesich adopted a traditional dramatic structure that goes back to Henrik Ibsen's plays, where the present is jeopardized, if not destroyed, by the secrets of the past. Joe and Lou are emotionally destroyed by the war. Angry and bitter, they return to the United States with no hopes or dreams. They vent their anger by getting drunk and illegally disposing of toxic waste on a bluff outside a South Dakota town. Their lives part, however, when Joe meets Anne, falls in love, and finds some meaning in life. Eighteen years later, Joe is being honored as the state Man of the Year at the same time that Lou shows up, a dirty, homeless Vietnam veteran, aimlessly carrying his life in a bundle as he follows the traveling Vietnam Memorial from city to city. His return opens the floodgates of guilt for past crimes and infidelities, which lead to tragedy and catharsis for this American family. Earlier Tesich themes of the displaced, the foreign, and the guilt of the past are played out against a new moral backdrop of social commentary. The symbolism is somewhat more successfully integrated into character and action, and the theatricality of the crises is not so gratuitous.

Square One

The absurdist comedy *Square One* creates outlandish characters and situations for social comment. It grew out of Tesich's observation that humankind's aspirations have become small and that society satisfies its obligations merely by becoming informed, not by acting on any indignation or moral outrage. He creates a future world in a dysfunctional society where almost no one acknowledges pain. The masses are emotionally massaged by a constant barrage of entertainment presented by "artists, third class." Tesich's two characters, who never call each other by name, meet, marry, reproduce, and separate against a background in which Wagnerian tenors are janitors and in which politicians do not appear in public but hire actors to deliver their hollow election promises. The strength of the play is its delicious wordplay. It is the aesthetic counterpart to Larry Gelbart's political and satirical play *Mastergate* (pr. 1989). As it did in the early plays, however, the symbolism takes over, becoming too literal and heavy-handed, overwhelming the fun of the language and the outrageousness of the situation.

ON THE OPEN ROAD

On the Open Road is a dark comedy about two men trying to find a safe place after the end of a very destructive civil war. In this Beckett-tinged drama, Angel, the "scum of the earth," hopes to be educated by Al as they wander through a ruined city. At one point, they betray Jesus to obtain their freedom and are assured by a Monk that they have not sinned because the Bible does not forbid anyone killing God. The two men's search for and collection of art from ruined museums is meant to represent a misguided notion that becoming cultured can be substituted for developing a sense of morality.

ARTS AND LEISURE

Tesich's last play takes a similarly dark view of humanity. *Arts and Leisure* is the story of a drama critic, Alex Chaney, who attempts to spice up his life by creating dramatic confrontations, with unfortunate effects. At the end, Chaney is left alone, deserted by even his maid, who acts as the play's conscience. The critic's approach to life, particularly his desire to observe drama, is causing a problem in American society. By encouraging people to act as drama critics—searching for and observing crisis, climax, and denouements while they take notes and experience feelings without actually participating—Tesich suggests that the drama critic is responsible for the passivity in American society. When faced with personal or larger tragedy, people act like theater critics. Even when the desire for drama provides action, that action is not necessarily positive. Critic Chaney claims that "racism works," meaning that it is dramatic on stage. Tesich suggests that if racism were absent from the world, some people would miss it because it provided a sense of drama, giving their work a heightened sense of meaning and importance that would vanish in the absence of racism.

OTHER MAJOR WORKS

LONG FICTION: *Summer Crossing*, 1982; *Karoo*, 1998 (posthumously).

SCREENPLAYS: *Breaking Away*, 1979; *Eyewitness*, 1981; *Four Friends*, 1981; *The World According to Garp*, 1982; *American Flyers*, 1985; *Eleni*, 1985.

BIBLIOGRAPHY

Brandes, Philip. "Theater Beat: Tesich's Dark Humor Drives This *Open Road*." Review of *On the Open Road*, by Steve Tesich. *Los Angeles Times*, October 20, 2000, p. F28. This review of a performance of Tesich's *On the Open Road* provides insight into this play as a vehicle for conveying the playwright's views about morality in modern life.

Coen, Stephanie. "Steve Tesich: The Only Kind of Real Rebel Left, He Figures, Is a Moral Person." *American Theatre* 9, no. 4 (July, 1992): 30. This profile of Tesich concentrates on his views of moral issues and how they are reflected in plays such as *On the Open Road*.

Dudar, Helen. "As One Playwright Strikes Out for the Future . . ." *The New York Times*, February 19, 1990, p. B5, 20. Written on the premiere eve of *Square One*, then the first new Tesich play in New York in ten years, this article briefly describes the "new Tesich." Dudar finds that he is no longer the United States' cheerleader, having lost his sense of wonder, and that he has learned to write from others' experiences, not only from his own.

"Playwright Steve Tesich Dies at Age Fifty-Three." *The Washington Post*, July 4, 1996, p. B5. This obituary sums up the life and works of the playwright and screenwriter.

Rothstein, Mervyn. "Morality's the Thing for This Playwright." *The New York Times*, March 12, 1991, p. C11, 13. In response to the relatively successful Broadway opening of *The Speed of Darkness*, Tesich explains how he has changed in the decade since his early plays. He now is concerned with "moral issues," such as this play's decrial of the United States' refusal to deal with the aftermath of the Vietnam War. Photograph.

Shteir, Rachel. "The World According to Tesich." *The Village Voice*, June 18, 1996, 88. Tesich discusses *Arts and Leisure* and explains how the play about a drama critic is critical of what he views as people's excessive desire to dramatize their lives. "Steve Tesich." In *Current Biography Yearbook*. New York: H. W. Wilson, 1991. This profile of Tesich, published five years before his death, examines his plays and screenplays.

Gerald S. Argetsinger

DYLAN THOMAS

Born: Swansea, Wales; October 27, 1914
Died: New York, New York; November 9, 1953

PRINCIPAL DRAMA

Under Milk Wood: A Play for Voices, pr. 1953 (public reading), pr. 1954 (radio play), pb. 1954, pr. 1956 (staged; musical settings by Daniel Jones)

OTHER LITERARY FORMS

Dylan Thomas was above all else a poet. His main collections of poems are *Eighteen Poems* (1934), *Twenty-five Poems* (1936), *The Map of Love* (1939), *New Poems* (1943), *Deaths and Entrances* (1946), *Twenty-six Poems* (1950), *In Country Sleep* (1952), *Collected Poems, 1934-1952* (1952), and *The Poems of Dylan Thomas* (1971), a posthumous collection edited by Daniel Jones.

Thomas was also a writer of prose. With John Davenport, he wrote a novel, *The Death of the King's Canary* (1976), published more than twenty years after Thomas's death. Among his major collections of short stories are *Portrait of the Artist as a Young Dog* (1940) and two collections published posthumously, *A Prospect of the Sea and Other Stories* (1955) and *Adventures in the Skin Trade and Other Stories* (1955). A definitive edition of his short fiction, *The Collected Stories*, was published in 1984.

Particularly germane to a consideration of Thomas the dramatist are his radio scripts. The collection *Quite Early One Morning* (1954) contains twenty-two scripts for broadcast by the British Broadcasting Corporation. Two of these scripts, *Quite Early One Morning* (1944) and *Return Journey* (1947), contrib-

uted to the evolution of *Under Milk Wood*. A third radio script, *The Londoner* (1946), also contributed to the evolution of the play and is included in the volume *"The Doctor and the Devils" and Other Scripts* (1966). This volume also contains two film scripts, *The Doctor and the Devils* (1953) and *Twenty Years A'Growing* (1964). Other film scripts by Thomas include three published posthumously: *The Beach at Falesá*, published in 1963; *Rebecca's Daughters*, published in 1965; and *Me and My Bike*, also published in 1965. Thomas also wrote two potboilers, *Three Weird Sisters* (1948), with Louise Birt and David Evans, and *No Room at the Inn* (1948), with Ivan Foxwell for British National.

Thomas's notebooks and letters have also been published: *Letters to Vernon Watkins* (1957), edited by Watkins; *Selected Letters of Dylan Thomas* (1966), edited by Constantine FitzGibbon; *Poet in the Making: The Notebooks of Dylan Thomas* (1968), edited by Ralph Maud; and *Twelve More Letters by Dylan Thomas* (1969), edited by FitzGibbon.

ACHIEVEMENTS

Dylan Thomas is probably one of the half-dozen most significant poets to have written in English in the twentieth century, although critical opinion about his work has been divided. By the end of his life, Thomas had become a popular poet. The sales of his *Collected Poems, 1934-1952*, published the year before he died, showed that the popularity of his work was unequaled by any other serious modern poet in English. The interest in Thomas was partly a result of the "legend" that developed during his lifetime, fostered by Thomas's eccentric mode of life, his striking originality, and his extraordinary ability to read his poetry aloud. Perhaps in reaction to the Thomas cult, academic critics in Great Britain were slower than were their American counterparts to recognize his status as a major poet.

Although Thomas wrote only one play, its incorporation into the repertory of most theaters was extremely rapid after its initial performance in 1953. More so than the poetic dramas of T. S. Eliot or Christopher Fry, *Under Milk Wood* has become one of the major contemporary challenges to conventional notions of theater. It is likely that *Under Milk Wood* will remain the primary example and measure for future experiments in this important domain of the theater.

BIOGRAPHY

Dylan Thomas was born in Swansea, Wales, in 1914. He had a sister, Nancy, older than he by some eight years. Thomas spoke no Welsh, although both of his parents had spoken Welsh in their childhood homes. Thomas's father had written poetry in his youth; he was a schoolmaster, an atheist, and had deliberately rejected the Welsh language. Thomas attended the Swansea grammar school. When he was seventeen, he became an apprentice reporter and proofreader for the *South Wales Daily Post*, and he did not attend a university. He began to publish his first poems in newspapers in the early 1930's. He was also an amateur actor with the Swansea Little Theatre. (A friend and fellow actor, Malcolm Graham, has written, "The more fantastic the part, the better Dylan was.") It was during these years that Thomas's voice became strong and acquired the resonance that was to make him as famous as his poetry.

In 1934, Thomas moved to London, and in that year, his first collection, *Eighteen Poems*, was published. In 1937, Thomas married Caitlin Macnamara, and their first child, Lewelyn, was born in 1939. After the outbreak of World War II, Thomas tried to enlist for military service but was rejected. His second child, Aeron, was born in 1943. The family spent the years from 1940 to 1945 living in or near London, Thomas working on scenarios for documentary films. His first radio broadcast for the British Broadcasting

Dylan Thomas (Library of Congress)

Corporation had been made in 1937, but after 1945, he made more frequent broadcasts for the corporation on a freelance basis. In 1948, he began the production of feature-length films. During the postwar years, he traveled to Italy and to Prague, Czechoslovakia, and in 1951 he went to Persia with a commission to write a film for the Anglo-Iranian Oil Company. His third child, Colm, was born in 1949.

In 1950, Thomas made his first trip to the United States at the invitation of John Malcolm Brinnin. He read at the Poetry Center at the Young Men's and Women's Hebrew Association in New York, and for three months he visited American colleges, reading his own work as well as that of other nineteenth and twentieth century poets. In 1952, he made his second trip to the United States, and he returned in 1953 for his third visit. In May, 1953, *Under Milk Wood* was given its first performances in Cambridge, Massachusetts, and in New York. In October, 1953, Thomas returned to the United States for a fourth time; on November 9, he died in New York City at the age of thirty-nine. He was buried in St. Martin's Churchyard in Laugharne, Wales.

ANALYSIS

Although Dylan Thomas wrote only a single work for the theater, its originality, importance, and influence are far-reaching. *Under Milk Wood* is distinguished by the density, sonority, and expressiveness of its language. Although it does not achieve the full Shakespearean synthesis of poetry and drama, the play has restored one aspect of that synthesis—the expressive potential of the human voice—to its former prominence.

UNDER MILK WOOD

Under Milk Wood was not the product of a career that developed in the theater; rather, it developed from a poet's experience with radio drama. Indeed, one of the most pertinent questions to be asked about *Under Milk Wood* is whether it is really a play at all. Is it, in fact, a radio script (or exotic poem) that has been railroaded by enthusiasts into the dramatic repertory? One must answer emphatically that *Under Milk Wood* is a play, written with a deliberateness and a consciousness of different genres and alternate modes of expression of which few readers are aware. Like many works at the frontier of a medium of expression, it is a synthesis. It had a long and complicated evolution in the author's mind over the course of a decade, ending as "a play for voices" performed by professional actors.

At the time the play was first performed—only a few months before Thomas's death—he was turning away from the more strictly personal, lyric poetry he had written previously, toward a more public form of expression with large-scale dramatic works that would provide scope for his versatility and for his gifts of humor and characterization, as well as for his ability as poet. He had planned to collaborate with Igor Stravinsky on an opera; according to Thomas's concept and in Stravinsky's words, "The opera was to be about the rediscovery of our planet following an atomic misadventure. There would be a re-creation of language, only the new one would have no abstractions; there would only be people, objects, and words." Far from being the eccentric excursion of a poet into the domain of theater, *Under Milk Wood* was to have been the first of a series of large-scale mixed-media productions for the stage. Death intervened, however, leaving only the first work of this projected cycle.

There is a reasonably good text available for *Under Milk Wood* and considerable commentary on it, yet a simple definition of the play is elusive. Its subtitle, *A Play for Voices*, indicates to many that it is not "normal" theater, yet this begs the question of what normal theater is. A tradition of what might be called dramatic realism is very much alive in British and American theater, and plays that do not fit into this mold are often seen as suspect, or not viable commercially, by theater professionals. To stage Thomas's play successfully, a theater company must have actors capable of using their voices to render a dense, highly articulated text, and many groups do not have actors with the necessary ability or training. An actor—the "First Voice"—must be able to speak the following words in a convincing, effective manner:

> It is Spring, moonless night in the small town, starless and bible-black, the cobble-streets silent and the hunched, courters'-and-rabbits' wood limping invisible down to the sloeblack, slow, black, crowblack, fishing-boat-bobbing sea. The houses are blind as moles (though moles see fine tonight in the snouting, velvet dingles) or blind as Captain Cat there in the muffled middle by the pump and the town clock, the shops in mourning, the Welfare Hall in widows' weeds.

For the actor, not only is there the problem of the use of his voice, but also there remains the all-important matter of interpretation. Words such as "hunched," "limping," "muffled middle," and "mourning" must be interpreted and understood before they can be spoken effectively. Many actors and also directors will not be able to perform this basic act of interpretation and consequently will turn with relief to a different kind of play that is less demanding.

Thomas's language is rooted in place, dialect, and province. It is not literary—at least it is not literary in an English sense. The dialect is Anglo-Welsh. There are a certain number of literary additions, largely rhythmic, and there is consonance, assonance, and alliteration, but Thomas has the advantage that his dialect, or the voices he knows, can make use of these devices without becoming stilted or artificial; hence, they are not literary, strictly speaking.

Perhaps more than any other twentieth century play, *Under Milk Wood* poses the question: What is the function of language in theater? For those who instinctively reply that its function is to be the most economic vehicle for the plot, *Under Milk Wood* will be a disappointment. Yet the theater is always subject to historical evolution, and for long periods in the past, poetry and drama were combined. In the late nineteenth and early twentieth centuries, they were kept separate, but it could be argued that this span was atypical. The British critic Raymond Williams has observed that "many of our deepest and richest experiences are unlikely to be reducible to conversational terms, and it is precisely the faculty we honor in poets that, by means of art, such experiences can find expression." An important function of the older pieces in the theatrical repertory, especially those of William Shakespeare and the Elizabethans, is that their language keeps this broader sense of realism alive. Perhaps it is the deprivation of this older tradition that accounts in part for the revolt against the naturalism of the past fifty years and also for the special sense of discovery that the experience of poetic drama can offer—for example, the poetic drama of Federico García Lorca, or that of Thomas and *Under Milk Wood*.

What is the main dramatic action of *Under Milk Wood*? As in the first act of Thornton Wilder's *Our Town* (pr. 1938), it is a day in the life of a small town, in this case Llareggub, modeled after Laugherne on the coast of Southern Wales. The notion of the single day's span might have derived from James Joyce's *Ulysses* (1922); at any rate, the drama of a town waking in the morning was prefigured in Thomas's radio script *Quite Early One Morning*, and a full day served as the frame of his radio script *The Londoner*. Wilder had felt that one day was not enough for all three acts of his play, and he introduced huge lapses of time between acts to dramatize his characters growing, aging, and dying—this is what "happens" in his play. In *Under Milk Wood*, there is a constant process of what might be called the exposition of

character, but this exposition is in no way abstract, purely informative, or staid; rather, each character is in a state of uniquely dynamic flux. This applies to their dreams at the beginning of the play (the first twenty-five pages are dreams), and to the movement of time itself, with dawn finally lifting: "The principality of the sky lightens now, over our green hill, into spring morning larked and crowed and belling."

Is it enough, as one listens to the various characters of the play (who are quite unusual), to wonder what they will do next, and how they will act? For example, will Mr. Pugh give expression to his desires and poison Mrs. Pugh? Will Polly Garter, once again, be unable to say no. Will the ghosts of Ogmore and Pritchard live on in obedience to Mrs. Ogmore-Pritchard, or will they disappear. Will the clock collection of Lord Cut-Glass continue to tick and multiply. Will the two Mrs. Dai Breads continue living with the same husband? Why cannot Mog Edwards and Myfanwy Price marry and live together; what will happen to Lily Smalls and Rose May Cottage (will they sail into the spring sky?). What will happen to the blind Captain Cat as he sails among the drowned. Will *all* the dead come out in the end? One of the unique features of the play is that all of these characters and many more (sixty-three are included in the cast) are acting simultaneously, and their voices are skillfully interwoven to flow naturally and unexpectedly into one another. For example, the First Voice is describing the afternoon:

FIRST VOICE: Clouds sag and pillow on Llareggub Hill. Pigs grunt in a wet wallow-bath, and smile as they snort and dream. They dream of the acorned swill of the world, the rooting for pig-fruit, the bagpipe dugs of the mother sow, the squeal and snuffle of yesses of the women pigs in rut. They mud-bask and snout in the pig-loving sun; their tails curl; they rollick and slobber and snore to deep, smug, after-swill sleep. Donkeys angelically drowse on Donkey Down.

MRS. PUGH: Persons with manners,

SECOND VOICE: snaps cold Mrs. Pugh

MRS. PUGH: do not nod at table.

FIRST VOICE: Mr. Pugh cringes awake. He puts on a soft-soaping smile: it is sad and gray under his nicotine-eggyellow weeping walrus Victorian moustache worn thick and long in memory of Doctor Crippen.

MRS. PUGH: You should wait until you retire to your sty,

SECOND VOICE: Mrs. Pugh, sweet as a razor. . . .

Throughout the play, transitions between voices are handled with great dexterity, as with the repetition of the pig motif in a totally unexpected place. The voices interweave, break away from one another, and suddenly flow back together again when least anticipated. It has been said that the characters in the play are "eccentrics," but this is not quite correct. They are held in a very dynamic imbalance that becomes, as the play progresses, a strange type of dramatic balance constantly undone and reestablished again. The dynamism is such that one does not perceive a static day at all; rather, one sees the people growing and dying and hears the dreams and voices of both the living and the dead.

Toward the end of the play the First Voice says:

Dusk is drowned forever until tomorrow. It is all at once night now. The windy town is a hill of windows, and from the larruped waves the lights of the lamps in the windows call back the day and the dead that have run away to sea. All over the calling dark, babies and old men are bribed and lullabied to sleep.

The play deals with multiplicity, a carefully worked out multiplicity of diverse characters who are drawn with sharpness and exuberance and who obey a large variety of types of motivation. There is, for example, much ribaldry, reaching its peak with the song near the end, addressed to the "chimbley sweep." The abundant sexual fantasy in the play has been censured by Thomas's dourer critics; two observations may clarify the function of this element. The lines expressing sexual fantasy are filled with humor and verbal life, and regardless of whether they are to the actor's or to the audience's taste, they must be spoken so that they communicate these qualities. They are not all of the same mold (Mae Rose's, Lily's, Captain Cat's, Mr. Waldo's); clearly it is a mistake to attribute them to the author. Perhaps the soundest approach to this aspect of the play is to see it as analytical, similar, for example, to the endeavor of Arthur Schnitzler,

who probed behind the repressive mechanisms of his characters and described their private, outlandish fantasies and illusions.

As the voices weave in and out of one another, a major problem remains: How is the play to be visualized? Thomas provided only a minimum of stage directions, and it is far from clear, especially for actors brought up on domestic naturalism, how they should position themselves. *Under Milk Wood* is not a radio play with disembodied voices invisible behind a microphone. On the contrary, the "voices" must be fully visible and the actors are the focus of attention, lit on the stage. It is a mistake to have the actors sit—they must be choreographed. Many cues will be found in the language, yet there is much room for the creative imaginations of the director and the actors. In a 1968 production by the American Conservatory Theater in San Francisco, the actor playing Lord Cut-Glass moved from clock to clock to clock on stage, performing a hilarious dumb show that lasted several minutes. Not a single word was spoken. The audience left the theater thinking, perhaps, that Lord Cut-Glass was one of the most effectively drawn characters in the play. This, however, was an illusion of creative staging, for there are many characters with longer or more important roles. Thomas himself did not spell out these stage directions; their absence, when combined with an unimaginative director, can lead to a production that is a resounding failure. This represents a potential weakness of the play; the language, however, contains innumerable possibilities for action, movement, and gesture. *Under Milk Wood* provides maximum challenge, and freedom, for a resourceful director.

The question remains: What is the structure or plot of *Under Milk Wood*? The play is not divided into acts or scenes in the traditional manner; the introduction of each new voice—and personage—brings with it a new "scene." As indicated above, this is, in itself, a structural feature of the play, and the fluidity, the simultaneous presence, of all the inhabitants of the town is rendered by the play's language. Some critics have argued that Thomas had no talent for structure. Thomas's biographer Paul Ferris, generally objective and sympathetic, writes: "His gift was for dialogue; when he had to construct a story, he was in difficulties. His idea of a plot was a straight line moving forward in time, as in *Under Milk Wood*." John Davenport has written that Thomas was "incapable of dramatic structure." No doubt Thomas's main talents were for sound, rhythm, and dialogue: the spoken voice. Yet if one reads his film scripts, one sees that he paid meticulous, practical attention to visual detail when required to do so: ample directions for the camera, to "dissolve and track downwards," "pan up" or "pan down," or the carefully imagined "close-ups." He made everything painstakingly visual.

During one stage of the composition of *Under Milk Wood*, Thomas considered introducing an action and plot into the play that was to have been highly dramatic in the traditional or naturalistic sense. According to Thomas's project of 1943, the town was to be literally put on trial, with Captain Cat as Counsel for the Defense. This was to highlight the contrast between the town and the outside world. The trial was to have a surprise ending: The final speech of the Prosecution was to prescribe an ideally sane town, and when the inhabitants of Llareggub heard it, they were to withdraw their defense, begging to be cordoned off from the "sane" world as soon as possible. Thomas's working title for the play at this time was "The Town Was Mad." At least one critic (Raymond Williams) thinks it unfortunate that Thomas abandoned this plan. Later, in 1944-1945, Thomas had new ideas for the play; according to Constantine Fitz-Gibbon,

After the revelations of the German concentration camps, Dylan outlined the idea to me one afternoon in an underground drinking club called the Gateways. The village was declared insane, anti-social, dangerous. Barbed wire was strung about it and patrolled by sentries, lest its dotty inhabitants infect the rest of the world with their feckless and futile view of life. They do not mind at all, though they grumble about the disappearance of the buses. The village is the only place that is left free in the whole world, for the authorities have got it wrong. This is not a concentration camp; the rest of the globe is the camp, is mad, and only this little place is sane and happy.

FitzGibbon adds that he thinks Thomas rightly discarded all of this superstructure when he wrote the play, for he was "far too skilled a writer to underline his plots."

For several years after the war, Thomas continued to be uncertain about the direction his play should take. According to Daniel Jones, Thomas was unable to decide on the form of the work:

There was much discussion with friends about a stage play, a comedy in verse, and a radio play with a blind man as narrator and central character. The blind man, a natural bridge between eye and ear for the radio listener, survives in *Under Milk Wood*, with the difference that Captain Cat is made to share his central position with two anonymous narrators.

By the time the play appeared in *Botteghe Oscure* in 1952, Thomas had partly returned to the plan of *Quite Early One Morning*, limiting the picture to the town itself, with hardly a suggestion of a world beyond the town, and the time sequence was extended to form a complete cycle. Yet Thomas was not writing another radio play, and he was developing the project in a specific direction. As Aneirin Davies, Thomas's employer for the British Broadcasting Corporation, has written, "By leaving the stage himself, the poet has taken the step from dialogue to drama." Another British Broadcasting Corporation producer, Douglas Cleverdon, has written that Thomas found the form of the radio play too confining. He thinks that Thomas developed the structure of "The Town Was Mad" with a full-length radio play in mind, but that he switched to the form of the "radio feature" because of its relative freedom: "It has no rules determining what can or cannot be done. And though it may be in dramatic form, it has no need of dramatic plot. Consequently, when the development of *The Village of the Mad* proved complicated, it was natural that Dylan should turn to the more fluid form of the feature."

Slowly, yet deliberately and consciously, Thomas rejected the plot of "Madtown"; as Cleverdon has noted, he seemed relieved when the decision was finally made. At the same time, he was also moving away from the form of the radio feature. By October, 1951, he had written to Countess Caetani saying he had abandoned one play ("Madtown") because "the comedy was lost in the complicated violence of the words." The new play was described as "a piece, a play, an impression for voices, an entertainment out of the darkness of the town I live in."

Thomas continued to work on the play until the last moment before its reading on May 3, 1953, at the Fogg Museum at Harvard, and he continued to write additional material until the production of the play in New York eleven days later. An hour before the play was to begin, he still had not written the conclusion. As John Malcolm Brinnin has recorded:

> But in these last minutes he devised a tentative conclusion that would serve. Twenty minutes before curtain time, fragments of *Under Milk Wood* were still being handed to the actors as they applied makeup, read their telegrams and tested their new accents on one another. Some lines of dialogue did not actually come into the hands of the readers until they were already taking their places onstage.

Thomas himself took the parts of the First Voice and the Reverend Eli Jenkins. At the end of the performance, when the lights had faded, the thousand spectators sat as if stunned. "But within a few moments," Brinnin goes on, "the lights went up and applause crescendoed and bravos were shouted by half the standing audience while the cast came back for curtain call after curtain call until, at the fifteenth of these, squat and boyish in his happily flustered modesty, Dylan stepped out alone."

More than anything else, the evolution of the play shows that traditional plot was found to be awkward and unsuitable. By a deliberate decision it was rejected, and only after this was Thomas able to write the play that now exists. The rejection was both conscious and subconscious. For years he had worked on the version with the plot, trying to reconcile it with his new ideas and conceptions, but artistically they proved to be irreconcilable. One can assume that if he had lowered his standards and tried to produce a version that would "work," analogous to his film scripts, he would have had no difficulties, but he was aiming much higher. The answer to the question of what "happens" in the play is clear. No traditional, natural-istic plot, with an orderly sequence of delimited actions, "happens." Something much more happens: An entire town, represented by more than sixty characters on stage, acts out all of its innermost desires, intentions, thoughts, and dreams—often highly contradictory—and these take place as close to simultaneously as the medium permits. The characters are interwoven in a seamless web—or, if there are seams, they are interconnected with an astonishingly high degree of art. The characters develop, age, and are engaged in the act of dying as the audience sees and listens to them. The process might be called "dynamic integration"—it constantly threatens to become undone, and it is intensely dramatic. At the same time, the play is one of the most demanding in the repertory: The voices must be skillful and highly trained, and more than in any other play the director is required to find visual counterparts, on stage, for words and their voices.

OTHER MAJOR WORKS

LONG FICTION: *The Death of the King's Canary*, 1976 (with John Davenport).

SHORT FICTION: *Portrait of the Artist as a Young Dog*, 1940; *Selected Writings of Dylan Thomas*, 1946; *A Child's Christmas in Wales*, 1954; *Adventures in the Skin Trade and Other Stories*, 1955; *A Prospect of the Sea and Other Stories*, 1955; *Early Prose Writings*, 1971; *The Followers*, 1976; *The Collected Stories*, 1984.

POETRY: *Eighteen Poems*, 1934; *Twenty-five Poems*, 1936; *The Map of Love*, 1939; *New Poems*, 1943; *Deaths and Entrances*, 1946; *Twenty-six Poems*, 1950; *In Country Sleep*, 1952; *Collected Poems, 1934-1952*, 1952; *The Poems of Dylan Thomas*, 1971 (Daniel Jones, editor).

SCREENPLAYS: *Three Weird Sisters*, 1948 (with Louise Birt and David Evans); *No Room at the Inn*, 1948 (with Ivan Foxwell); *The Doctor and the Devils*, 1953; *The Beach at Falesá*, 1963; *Twenty Years A'Growing*, 1964; *Rebecca's Daughters*, 1965; *Me and My Bike*, 1965.

RADIO PLAYS: *Quite Early One Morning*, 1944; *The Londoner*, 1946; *Return Journey*, 1947; *Quite Early One Morning*, 1954 (twenty-two radio plays).

NONFICTION: *Letters to Vernon Watkins*, 1957 (Vernon Watkins, editor); *Selected Letters of Dylan Thomas*, 1966 (Constantine FitzGibbon, editor); *Poet in the Making: The Notebooks of Dylan Thomas*, 1968 (Ralph Maud, editor); *Twelve More Letters by Dylan Thomas*, 1969 (FitzGibbon, editor).

MISCELLANEOUS: *"The Doctor and the Devils" and Other Scripts*, 1966 (two screenplays and one radio play).

BIBLIOGRAPHY

Ackerman, John. *Dylan Thomas: His Life and Work*. New York: St. Martin's Press, 1996. A biography describing the life and writings of Thomas.

_____. *Welsh Dylan: Dylan Thomas's Life, Writing, and His Wales*. 2d ed. Bridgend, Wales: Seren, 1998. This biography of Dylan looks at his homeland, Wales, and shows how the area influenced his writings.

Davies, James A. *A Reference Companion to Dylan Thomas*. Westport, Conn.: Greenwood Press, 1998. A handbook that provides quick and easy reference to facts about the poet and his life. Bibliography and index.

Ferris, Paul. *Dylan Thomas: The Biography*. Rev. ed. Washington, D.C.: Counterpoint, 2000. This volume presents an account of the playwright's upbringing in Swansea, Wales, his education, his move to London and marriage, his travels during the postwar years, and his drama. Bibliography and index.

Hardy, Barbara Nathan. *Dylan Thomas: An Original Language*. Athens: University of Georgia Press, 2000. Hardy looks at Thomas's use of language in his writings, including his use of Welsh-derived terms. Bibliography and index.

Jones, R. F. G. *Time Passes: Dylan Thomas's Journey to "Under Milk Wood."* Sydney: Woodworm Press, 1994. An account of the literary development of Thomas, including analysis of *Under Milk Wood*. Bibliography and index.

Korg, Jacob. *Dylan Thomas*. Rev. ed. New York: Twayne, 1992. A basic biography of Thomas that covers his life and works. Bibliography and index.

Sinclair, Andrew. *Dylan the Bard: A Life of Dylan Thomas*. New York: Thomas Dunne Books, 2000. Sinclair provides the story of Thomas's life as a poet and writer. Bibliography and index.

John Carpenter,
updated by Peter C. Holloran

LUDWIG TIECK

Born: Berlin, Prussia (now in Germany); May 31, 1773

Died: Berlin, Prussia (now in Germany); April 28, 1853

PRINCIPAL DRAMA

Karl von Berneck, pb. 1795

Ritter Blaubert, pb. 1797, pr. 1835

Der gestiefelte Kater, pb. 1797, pr. 1844 (verse play; *Puss-in-Boots*, 1913-1914)

Die verkehrte Welt, pb. 1797

Prinz Zerbino: Oder, Die Reise nach dem guten Geschmack, pb. 1798

Das Ungeheuer und der verzauberte Wald, pb. 1798

Leben und Tod der heiligen Genoveva, pb. 1800, pr. 1807

Leben und Tod das kleinen Rotkäppchens, pb. 1800 (*The Life and Death of Little Red Riding Hood*, 1851)

Kaiser Octavianus, pb. 1801, revised pb. 1828

Der Anti-Faust: Oder, Die Geschichte des dummen Teufels, pb. 1801

Fortunat, pb. 1816

Ludwig Tiecks Schriften, pb. 1828-1854

Werke, pb. 1963-1965

Other literary forms

Ludwig Tieck is best known for his novels *Geschichte des Herrn William Lovell* (1795-1796) and *Franz Sternbalds Wanderungen* (1798) and for his numerous short stories, fairy tales, and poems. His important critical works are collected in a four-volume set, *Kritische Schriften* (1848-1852), and in a recent selective edition, *Ausgewählte Kritische Schriften* (1975). Another of Tieck's major contributions is his publication of editions of his contemporaries' works, including *Heinrich von Kleists hinterlassene Schriften* (1821), *Lenz Gesammelte Schriften* (1828), and *Novalis Schriften* (1802; *Novalis: His Life, Thoughts, and Works*, 1891).

Tieck published translations of Miguel de Cervantes and William Shakespeare (*Don Quixote*, 1799-1800, four volumes; *Shakespeares dramatische Werke*, 1825-1833, nine volumes), and of other English plays (*Alt englisches Theater: Oder, Supplement zum Shakespeare*, 1811). He edited German medieval works including Ulrich von Lichtenstein's *Frauendienst* (1810) and plays of the Baroque, which appeared in *Deutsches Theater* (1817).

Achievements

Ludwig Tieck's achievements are the more remarkable because they were made at a time when it was difficult for a member of the lower classes to gain access to a university education and to make the social connections necessary for success. Tieck, an indefatigable worker, began to write while still at school and sold his stories to paying journals. In 1797, he published the *Herzensergiessungen eines kunstliebenden Klosterbruders* (*The Outpourings of an Art Loving Friar*, 1974), written with his friend Wilhelm Heinrich Wackenroder, who died the following year. This and similar stories established his literary connection with the early Romantic school. In 1799, he joined the circle of the brothers Schlegel (August Wilhelm and Friedrich) in Jena, where he also became a close friend of Novalis (Friedrich von Hardenberg).

Tieck exemplified the Romantics' interest in medieval literature, in contrast to the classicist tradition, which attempted to emulate the ancients. Like the Brothers Grimm (Jacob and Wilhelm), Schlegel, Sophie Mereau, and Achim von Arnim, Tieck contributed to the immense surge of philological activity at that time, which made long-forgotten medieval works accessible to the public in linguistically modernized, printed versions. Therefore, Tieck published an edition of Ulrich von Lichtenstein's *Frauendienst* in 1810; his interest in the theater is reflected in a collection of older German plays, *Deutsches Theater*, containing works by Hans Sachs, Martin Opitz, Andreas Gryphius, and others. In addition, Tieck shared the Romantics' interest in Shakespeare and Cervantes, whom they considered to be ideological and literary forerunners of their own school of thought. Tieck translated Cervantes' *Don Quixote* into German, but his chief interest remained the theater. Tieck's translations in the two-volume *Alt englisches Theater*, published in 1811, introduced pre-Shakespearean drama to German readers. Also significant was his publication of a Shakespeare translation by August Wilhelm Schlegel, Tieck's daughter Dorothea, and Count Baudissin, which quickly su-

Ludwig Tieck (Hulton Archive by Getty Images)

perseded Johann Heinrich Voss's translation. Among Tieck's other Shakespearean works are his translation of *The Tempest* as *Der Sturm* (1796), prefaced by the important essay "Shakespeares Behandlung des Wunderbaren," his "Briefe über Shakespeare," and *Shakespeares Vorschule* (1823-1829).

No less notable was Tieck's effort to publish editions of his contemporaries' works. Among these were Novalis, Friedrich Müller, Heinrich von Kleist, Jakob Michael Reinhold Lenz, and the collected works of Friedrich August Schulze.

BIOGRAPHY

Johann Ludwig Tieck was born on May 31, 1773, in Berlin as the son of a master rope-maker. Although he wanted to go on the stage, it was decided that he should study theology—the field most readily open to young men who were gifted but not affluent or well-connected. Tieck attended the universities at Halle, Erlangen, and Göttingen from 1792 to 1794, devoting himself more and more to the study of the humanities (literature, philology, history). After returning to Berlin, Tieck wrote in quick succession a horror novel, *Abdallah* (1795), the three volumes of *Geschichte des Herrn William Lovell* (1795-1796), and the novel *Peter Leberecht* (1795). From 1795 to 1798, Tieck contributed substantially to Friedrich Nicolai's magazine *Straussfedern* on a freelance basis. Under the pseudonym Peter Leberecht (taken from his own novel), he published three volumes of *Volksmärchen* (1797), which included the tale of the beautiful Magelone. Johannes Brahms set the poems in it to music as *Romanzen aus der "schönen Magelone,"* opus 33. In the same year appeared *The Outpourings of an Art Loving Friar,* which as noted above, Tieck wrote in collaboration with his friend Wackenroder. These aesthetic reflections on art and music are still read and perceived as the epitome of the early Romantic program. The novel *Franz Sternbalds Wanderungen* also deals with aesthetic concepts; it is a *Künstlerroman* and has as its protagonist a fictitious pupil of Albrecht Dürer.

In 1798, Tieck married a pastor's daughter, Amalia Alberti, from Hamburg. In 1799, he went to Jena, joining the Schlegels' circle (August Wilhelm

and Friedrich Schlegel, Novalis, and Friedrich Wilhelm Joseph Schelling). Increasingly, he turned to the dramatic genre in his writing. Particularly in the *Märchendrama* (*Puss-in-Boots*, *Ritter Blaubert*, *Prinz Zerbino*, *The Life and Death of Little Red Riding Hood*, *Das Ungeheuer und der verzauberte Wald*, and others) he was able to combine innocent humor with biting satire on contemporary political and social topics. Longer plays of a more serious nature include *Karl von Berneck*, *Leben und Tod der heiligen Genoveva*, and *Fortunat*. The latter, although called a fairy tale, is highly didactic.

In 1801, after a brief stay in Berlin, Tieck moved to Dresden, attending to his philological interests (*Minnelieder aus dem Schwäbischen Zeitalter*, 1803), as well as to writing in various genres and topics (*Der Anti-Faust*, a satiric comedy; "Der Runenberg," a short horror story; *Kaiser Octavianus*, a two-part dramatic fantasy). In 1805-1806, Tieck traveled to Italy with a group of friends, attempting to recover from an illness that befell him in 1804 in Munich, where he had accompanied his divorced sister Sophie Bernhardi. One of the most prominent Romantics, Tieck's almost obsessive creativity began to suffer because of his continuing health problems, and he turned more and more to editorial work. After his return from Rome, he went to Ziebingen, traveled to Vienna and Munich in 1808, and to the health spa in Baden-Baden in 1810. After visiting Heidelberg, he returned to Ziebingen. The summer of 1813 Tieck spent in Prague together with his family, and he traveled to London in 1817 with his friend Wilhelm von Burgsdorff in order to have rare manuscripts copied for his Shakespearean studies.

In 1819, Tieck settled in Dresden, where he participated in an advisory capacity at the Dresden theater beginning in 1825. Although his own plays lacked public support for successful performances, Tieck had become well-known as cofounder of the early Romantic school, as a universal talent, as a theoretician and critic of the theater, as a master of Romantic irony, and as a reader of his own plays and poetry. In 1841, King Friedrich Wilhelm IV of Prussia appointed Tieck as his reader, gave him the title of Geheimer Hofrat, and called him as adviser to the

Royal Theater in Berlin. Until his death, Tieck lived alternately in Berlin and in Potsdam, where he had been given the use of a villa near the royal residence. His stage productions of *Antigone*, and especially that of *A Midsummer Night's Dream*, created a great sensation. Although the dramatic works of his youth were not theatrically successful and indeed rarely staged, they have survived as *Lesedramen* because of their exquisite wit, satiric content, and ironic treatment.

ANALYSIS

It is impossible to find a common denominator for Ludwig Tieck's plays because his talents and interests explored every aspect of the stage. Disguised as a farce, the two-part, five-hundred-page play *Fortunat* (published in a volume of his collected works) has a didactic nucleus that explores not only the follies of human nature but also the relationship between the sexes, the generations, and the social classes. The tragedy *Leben und Tod der heiligen Genoveva* represents a dramatic treatment of a legend and has been perceived as an attempt to bridge the gap of religious understanding initiated by historical occurrences. It earned for Tieck the reputation of having spurred numerous conversions to Catholicism within the Romantic movement, as well as within his own family. Yet even in this hallowed setting, the playfully destructive element of Romantic irony is not lacking when at the very beginning, on being told the story behind the artistic depictions of martyr scenes, Benno exclaims: "Who knows whether everything really happened that way," and Grimoald agrees: "I think so, too; it was long ago." Doubt is being cast on the veracity of the legend and the play. The popular genre of the *Schicksalstragödie* (fate tragedy) is mirrored in the nihilism of *Karl von Berneck*, and the dramatization of the popular fairy tale of Little Red Riding Hood (*The Life and Death of Little Red Riding Hood*) is far removed from the innocent entertainment its subject and length might suggest. The plot, adapted from the tale by Charles Perrault, contains so many political allegorizations and references to social inequities that critics have called the little red bonnet a Phrygian (Jacobin's) cap.

Although Ludwig Tieck's dramatic works have seldom been staged, they created an impact on literary developments in Germany because of their exemplification of Romantic postulates and techniques. Much of the satiric innuendo is lost for today's reader because Tieck's references to contemporary literary feuds, quips, and quotes are no longer identifiable. This, in addition to the difficulty involved in translating puns and jokes, has hindered acceptance of his dramatic work outside Germany—a circumstance partly overcome by good modern translations.

Among the plays by Tieck that are still read today are several of the fairy dramas. They also represent the Romantic style—not only because of the atmosphere of illusion and the grotesque that they convey but also because of the manipulative literary techniques they employ. Several of them also show a certain continuity of plot as well as thematic affinities and therefore lend themselves to a coherent discussion in limited terms. These are the dramatizations of *Puss-in-Boots*, *Die verkehrte Welt*, called a historical play, and *Prinz Zerbino*.

PUSS-IN-BOOTS

Puss-in-Boots is based on the familiar story of the cat who wins a kingdom for his poor and lowly master. Tieck wrote the play within one evening, Perrault having furnished the plot and Carlo Gozzi the spirit of the work. Despite its rapid genesis, it is not a simplistic piece but is created on three constantly interacting levels of consciousness. The first is the level of the fairy tale itself and its characters. The reader's expectation of a romantic, charming tale is immediately destroyed by the appearance of the cat. This magic and quasi-supernatural figure astounds the audience with an utterly prosaic, bourgeois, and philistine personality, which mocks with its sobriety not only the reader's, but also the other characters' hopes and fears. This yoking of the magical and the realistic—an ambivalence that characterizes the entire play—is the basis for the Romantic irony with which the author manipulates the reader: Illusions or expectations are created only to be destroyed again and to give rise to new ones. No character in this play is safe from ridicule because of his office or function: The king, who has an insatiable craving for roast rabbit, the princess, who writes poetry but has not mastered grammar, the poet, who needs an official "Pacifier" to escape the wrath of the audience—all are mere puppets in the hands of their author, created to facilitate his display of wit and to foster an atmosphere of contrast and confusion intended to perplex and startle Tieck's contemporaries. This is not a classical comedy but a Romantic negation of it, which scoffs at rules and proprieties and is an end in itself.

The second level of the play is that of a depicted reality that constantly encroaches on the action taking place on the level of the fairy tale. Tieck accomplishes this by making the stage itself the theater and the fairy tale a play-within-the-play. By creating a fictitious audience on stage that reacts with scorn, derision, and even violence to the production of the fairy tale, Tieck can imbue it with all the characteristics that he perceives as ridiculous or inane in contemporary individuals and society. At the same time, he maintains complete control over both sets of characters (those of the play and those of the play-within-the-play) and creates an objective distance between the reader and the depicted reality, subtly manipulating the reader toward a critical view of the real world.

The real world, seen through the playwright's eyes, is grotesque and ridiculous. The audience on stage is composed of enlightened commoners— enlightened (not unlike Tieck himself) in the sense of eighteenth century citizens, educated in the virtues of reason and the classical arts, and armed with a set of philosophical and literary rules governing all aspects thereof. If Tieck exposes the nobility's inadequacies in the play-within-the-play (critics have perceived parallels between the kind and Frederick William II of Prussia, between the princess and Wilhelmine Ritz, countess of Lichtenau, and between Nathanael von Malsinki and Czar Paul I), he derides the pervading rationalism of members of his own class in the characters who compose the fictitious audience. Their names are drawn from the sphere of workers and craftsmen: They include a "Schlosser" (locksmith), "Fischer" (fisherman), "Müller" (miller), "Bötticher" (cooper), and others.

These emancipated citizens criticize the play in a manner that shows their acquired "culture" and pur-

portedly discriminating taste to be merely a confused repetition of professional critics' opinions. Having no real understanding of artistic creativity, they cling to platitudes and mindless imitation in the discussion before the play's beginning. Fischer expects an "imitation in the New Arcadian" (idyllic) manner, and Müller concurs: "That wouldn't be bad, for I have long desired to see such a magic opera without music for once." This is an obvious reference to the popularity which musical offerings such as Wolfgang Amadeus Mozart's *Die Zauberflote* (1791; *The Magic Flute*) enjoyed. Later, when pandemonium erupts among the disappointed audience, the Pacifier sings Mozart's "In diesen heil'gen Hallen kennt man die Rache nieht" ("we know no thoughts of vengeance within these temple walls") and brings decorations from the *The Magic Flute* on stage. Fischer disagrees with Müller's judgment, arguing that only if accompanied by the "heavenly art" (music) is it possible "to swallow all these stupidities. Egad, strictly speaking we are beyond such distortions and superstitions; the Enlightenment has borne its fruits, as indeed it should." This comment, which belies the later reactions of the audience, ridicules not only the rationalists but also Tieck's own concoction. Schlosser expects a "revolutionary drama," and indeed, Tieck occasionally uses political overtones such as the cat's proclamation of a "tiers état." Fischer and Müller agree that the age of phantoms, witches, and ghosts is past, as also is that of a Puss-in-Boots. Bötticher, named by Tieck with a sly reference to Karl August Böttiger and his book of praise for the then popular August Wilhelm Iffland, wishes to see a play in the classical sense: "We shall have a feast fit for gods. How this genius, who so intimately experiences and finely tints all characters, will carve out the individuality of this tomcat! As an ideal, undoubtedly, in the sense of the ancients, not unlike Pygmalion." In this depicted reality of the theater, Tieck ridicules that contemporary, aloof rationalism and "vapidity which, devoid of understanding for depth and mystery, dragged everything it could not and would not understand before the bar of so-called human reason." In 1828, more than thirty years after its publication, Tieck reminisced about the play: "All my recollections—what I had heard at different times in the pit, in the loges or the salons—awoke, and so this arose and was written in a few happy hours."

The third level of the play is the level of literary criticism. Unless the reader consults an annotated edition, many of the witticisms that give the play its satiric edge will be lost. Indeed, even Tieck's contemporaries were unaware of many of his allusions. On December 19, 1797, Nicolai wrote to Tieck: "When you allude to anecdotes of the local stage in *Puss-in-Boots*, it is perhaps not even interesting for local readers, who regard unimportant anecdotes of the theater and the pit as despicable. But what, then, are readers in other places to think, if they do not know what they are reading about?" Nicolai's comment is well-meaning but based on the instinctive dislike of what began to emerge as a distinctive genre of the Romantic play. This type of literary satire is no more opaque than the scenes of Johann Wolfgang von Goethe's Walpurgis Night in *Faust* (1808-1833) nor is it less legitimate than political or social satire; it is also one of Tieck's favorite outlets for his brilliant humor.

The difficulty that the poet within the play encounters with his audience, the negative reception that he and his work are accorded, the misunderstanding of the plot and the literary intent—all of these were factors in the public reception of Tieck's work and in the public reception of Romantic plays in general. The theatergoing public was educated to accept the literary standards of the post-Enlightenment era: A spiritually edifying tragedy was expected to be classical in style; an entertaining comedy was to comply with the standard rules as implemented, for example, by Iffland and August von Kotzebue. The plays of Tieck and other Romantics mixed the genres, destroyed the illusions, and confused the audience. The creative new element was viewed as theatrical incompetence. Fischer's comments in the play particularly mirror this very real public reaction: "It is impossible for me to enter into a sensible illusion," he asserts, when confronted with the talking cat. He fails to realize that a rational illusion is in itself an incongruity. When he is later told by another character that the audience in the play is well depicted,

he reacts with consternation: "The audience? But there isn't an audience in the play." The entire comedy is an attempt to reeducate the public, and it fails. At the beginning, the Poet confronts his audience, which tells him that they want "a tasteful play." He asks, "of what kind? Of what color?" and is told: "Family histories," "Life savings," "Morality and German sentiment." When it becomes apparent that the play which is about to commence is not of this variety, Fischer scolds: "How can you write such pieces? Why didn't you educate yourself?" The Poet's noncompliance with the public's wishes and expectations is perceived as a lack of education in the literary arts, and his "new kind of poetic invention" is utterly rejected. When he pleads, "Show me first that you understand me at least to some extent," he is pelted with rotten apples. All of his explanations fail and he leaves the theater with the words: "O thankless century!"

DIE VERKEHRTE WELT

Like his fictitious poet, Tieck himself met considerable misunderstanding among his contemporaries with this fairy drama and with *Die verkehrte Welt*. The latter was so incomprehensible to Nicolai, who was to publish it in his journal *Straussfedern*, that he mistakenly believed he was receiving a second play when Tieck sent him the fourth and fifth acts after having previously delivered the first three. This time Nicolai admonished Tieck not to continue on his eccentric path but to cultivate the noble, the natural, and the interesting. Tieck considered a world in which the public determined literary taste, a world awry. (*Die verkehrte Welt* may be translated as "perverted world," or "topsy-turvy world"). In *Die verkehrte Welt*, to a much greater extent than in *Puss-in-Boots*, Tieck criticizes contemporary literary production. The idea expressed by Nicolai that public taste should coincide with literary production is vehemently exposed to satiric treatment. This play, too, draws on a Poet and on diverse members of a fictitious audience for its characters. The confusion begins when members of the cast decide that they would prefer to be the audience, and when the audience expresses the wish to act. The distraught Poet, worrying about his play, expresses great concern but is overruled by Grünhelm (one of the spectators) and by the theater's director. Grünhelm admonishes the Poet not to worry about his art, for "almost everything depends on the good-will of the audience. I know that as well as you do; therefore, true art is what uplifts this good humor." When the Poet turns to the director for help, the latter merely asserts: "Look, I think of it this way: The public has already paid, and that takes care of the most important thing." Commercialism, the whims of the public, and the demands of individual actors determine what passes for artistic production on the stage, and that is what is wrong with the literary world. Tieck expresses in these plays the basic tenets of the Romantic revolution: the need to reevaluate and revise literary production and its principles and the need to reeducate the public, its tastes, and its standards.

In this sense, Tieck's *Die verkehrte Welt* is programmatic and didactic. The figuration reveals this intent in its apposition of Scaramuz and Apollo. In the absence of Apollo (the leader of the muses), Scaramuz insists on playing the role of Apollo and taking charge of artistic developments. Over the objections of the Poet but with the aid of the theater's director and the public, he is granted that right. Scaramuz (Scaramouch) is a stock character from the *commedia dell'arte*, a buffoon and ne'er-do-well who is never cast in the role of a tragic hero such as he wishes to portray here. In Tieck's play, Scaramuz represents the contemporary materialistic, enlightened, and self-satisfied citizen to whom art and the theater is surrendered. Under his rule, egotism, materialism, and triteness govern: Actors (as well as members of the audience) play only the roles that suit them; on Mount Parnassus (the seat of the gods, or, figuratively speaking, that of the arts), a bakery and a brewery are erected by means of a mortgage; and when one of the writers complains to His Majesty, Scaramuz, that his readers have no taste and wish him to write trashy books, Scaramuz replies: "And why not, since in the end it is their lot to read your scribblings? Therefore you shall have the taste which is demanded of you." In the figure of Scaramuz and his followers, Tieck portrays the representatives of a false, materialistic kind of art, derived from the age of rationalism

and nurtured by the political, social, and economic changes that have permitted the rise of the masses to positions of power and have given rein to money and credit.

Democracy (reference is again made to the French Revolution) and capitalism have created havoc and terror for the arts, Tieck claims, but this is so only because the true artists have failed to act and to take charge. The personification of this true artist is Apollo, the second major figure in the play. Tieck's placement of this figure, with the inclusion of the myth in which Apollo had to perform the duties of a shepherd for King Admetus, gives the play a strange and anachronistic twist and is the more surprising because Tieck normally excludes classic forms and figures from his plays. Its function is precisely to draw attention to this character and his actions, however, inasmuch as he mirrors that most venerated of poets, Goethe, to whom the Romantics looked for approval and guidance. As Tieck's letters and essays show, he perceived Goethe at the time this play was written as somewhat of a messianic figure who could and would rescue the literary arts from that state of deterioration in which Tieck saw them. The younger Goethe had indeed embarked on a new, intrinsically German form of literature with his *Götz von Berlichingen mit der eisernen Hand* (1773; *Götz von Berlichingen with the Iron Hand*, 1799) and his *Faust*, which appealed to the Romantics as works akin to those of their own school of thought. To their great disappointment, Goethe increasingly devoted his efforts to a revival of classicism in Germany, both in his function as director of the Weimar theater and in his own later production; he even went so far as to condemn Romanticism, calling its influence corruptive and destructive of literature. In his later letter, Tieck bitterly accuses Goethe of having betrayed Germany and German literature by embracing classicism: "No poet without a country [Vaterland]; to separate oneself from it is to deny the muses." Tieck's retrospective critical discussion of Goethe's tenure as director of the Weimar theater is also unflattering: "His influence was more negative rather than that the theater might have progressed through him," and no school of art was founded or furthered by him. "Here, as . . . in history and politics, he has failed to recognize the spirit of his time."

When Tieck wrote *Die verkehrte Welt*, the direction Goethe was to take later was not yet apparent. Goethe had secluded himself in the small-town atmosphere of Weimar, directing plays and shepherding the tastes of the local audience. Tieck uses the myth of Apollo as shepherd for King Admetus in describing Goethe's retreat: Apollo (Goethe) "has fled" and practices "simple shepherd's songs in solitude" instead of taking charge of his role in the theater and preventing the takeover by Scaramuz. The programmatic aspect of Tieck's play (which, incidentally, he calls a "historical" play) is evident in the happy ending that he provides: When Apollo recognizes the havoc created by Scaramuz's reign, he returns from his isolation to take charge once again of his domain and to return true artistry to its rightful place: "Victory is ours, friends," says Apollo at the end. "Take Scaramuz prisoner, and then we will reorganize the kingdom anew." Considering the high hopes Tieck held for Goethe's leadership, one can understand the depth of his disappointment at the realization that Goethe, who was fast approaching fifty years of age, preferred a sedentary life and had no intention of leading a revolution of the theater.

PRINZ ZERBINO

A quest for restoration of true artistry to art is also the main theme of *Prinz Zerbino*. (The German subtitle translates literally as "the journey in quest of good taste.") Tieck prefaces the comedy with a dedication to his brother, the sculptor Friedrich Tieck of Berlin, whose work is not sufficiently appreciated, he believes. Friedrich's works "may be compared to the best of the new and old era, yet many of them . . . have remained crated in Munich for years, awaiting an edifice which will bring them to light. This is a major misfortune for an artist." The comedy, too, revolves around the misunderstanding and misrepresentation of genius. The setting is a courtly environment (unmistakably patterned after Berlin's royal quarters), populated with some of the same characters already encountered in *Puss-in-Boots*. The cat Hinze, now a nobleman of great power, rules with other representatives of enlightened ambition and

misdirected science. The truly philosophical, inquisitive, and fertile minds (Prince Zerbino, heir to the throne and son of the cat's owner, Gottlieb; the court jester; and to some extent the old king) are believed to suffer from an insidious type of insanity that the physicians are unable to cure: "It is the illness which so frequently accompanies greatness." The old king's symptoms include his wish to read what he has to sign, and Zerbino even says to his jester: "Although you are a born fool you are still the most rational man in the entire country." Because his interest in literature and philosophy has stimulated his imagination excessively, his physicians perceive him in a stage of crisis: His illness must necessarily pass "soon into lunacy or common sense—it is impossible for it to remain in this impasse much longer. The noble patient asked me today what form of government I considered best."

In his effort to discover good taste, Zerbino sets out on an allegorical journey that brings him into contact with the catastrophic influence that so-called "good taste" has had on artistic endeavors. Tieck uses this allegory as an opportunity for literary satire and for attacks on Nicolai, Kotzebue, Immanuel Kant, Friedrich Schiller, Iffland, Johann Daniel Falk, and others. Zerbino's traveling companion Nestor, thought to be a caricature of Nicolai, offers the suggestion, "perhaps we have found good taste long ago and just don't know it," but Zerbino laments, "Taste! Where are you hiding to elude me on all paths?" In order to achieve the objective distance necessary for the destructive element of Romantic irony, Tieck employed techniques that anticipated Bertolt Brecht's influential concept of *Verfremdung*, the so-called alienation effect: Personifications of the "blue of heaven" as well as of trees, bushes, flowers, and birds become articulate and thereby destroy the illusion of reality or authenticity into which the reader may have slipped, forcing him to confront the ultimate illusion with the facts—good taste cannot be defined. Not even Tieck's own play is able to illustrate the term, and when Zerbino realizes this, he acts out of character and threatens: "I will enter into all scenes of this comedy, they shall break and burst, so that I either find good taste in this present play, or at least destroy the entire play and myself." In turning the plot back scene by scene, Nestor remarks that it does not seem to matter whether it goes backward or forward, but the playwright, the critic, and the other actors object to Zerbino and Nestor's undertaking. The play itself is a failure, and good taste remains an elusive commodity. The final irony is the restoration of the status quo at court in a scene depicting a "great Circus." Fatalistic overtones are evident in Tieck's conclusion that change is not likely to occur.

OTHER MAJOR WORKS

LONG FICTION: *Abdallah*, 1795; *Peter Leberecht*, 1795; *Geschichte des Herrn William Lovell*, 1795-1796 (3 volumes); *Franz Sternbalds Wanderungen*, 1798 (2 volumes); *Vittoria Accorombona*, 1840 (*The Roman Matron*, 1845).

SHORT FICTION: *Volksmärchen*, 1797; *Novellen*, 1823-1828 (7 volumes).

POETRY: *Gedichte*, 1821-1823 (3 volumes).

NONFICTION: *Minnelieder aus dem Schwäbischen Zeitalter*, 1803; *Shakespeares Vorschule*, 1823-1829 (2 volumes); *Kritische Schriften*, 1848-1852 (4 volumes); *Ausgewählte Kritische Schriften*, 1975.

TRANSLATIONS: *Don Quixote*, 1799-1800 (4 volumes; of Miguel de Cervantes' novel); *Alt englisches Theater: Oder, Supplement zum Shakespeare*, 1811 (2 volumes); *Shakespeares dramatische Werke*, 1825-1833 (9 volumes).

EDITED TEXTS: *Novalis Schriften*, 1802 (2 volumes; *Novalis: His Life, Thoughts, and Works*, 1891); *Frauendienst*, 1810 (works by Ulrich von Lichtenstein); *Schriften*, 1811 (3 volumes; works by Friedrich Müller); *Deutsches Theater*, 1817 (2 volumes; includes medieval and Baroque plays); *Heinrich von Kleists hinterlassene Schriften*, 1821; *Gesammelte Schriften*, 1826 (3 volumes; works by Heinrich von Kleist); *Lenz Gesammelte Schriften*, 1828 (works of Jakob Michael Reinhold Lenz); *Sämtliche Schriften*, 1843 (collected works of Friedrich August Schulze).

MISCELLANEOUS: *Herzensergiessungen eines kunstliebenden Klosterbruders*, 1797 (written with Wilhelm Heinrich Wackenroder; *The Outpourings of an Art Loving Friar*, 1974); *Phantasus*, 1812-1816 (3 volumes; *Tales from the Phantasus*, 1845).

BIBLIOGRAPHY

Birrell, Gordon. *The Boundless Present: Space and Time in the Literary Fairy Tales of Novalis and Tieck*. Chapel Hill: University of North Carolina Press, 1979. This study examines how old fairy tales and folk tales featured in the works of Novalis and Tieck.

Klett, Dwight A. *Ludwig Tieck: An Annotated Guide to Research*. New York: Garland, 1993. This reference guide provides extensive bibliographical material. Index.

Paulin, Roger. *Ludwig Tieck: A Literary Biography*. New York: Oxford University Press, 1986. A critical look at the life and works of Tieck. Bibliography and index.

Sullivan, Heather I. *The Intercontextuality of Self and Nature in Ludwig Tieck's Early Works*. New York: Peter Lang, 1997. Sullivan examines the self and nature in Tieck's earlier writings. Bibliography and index.

Yee, Kevin F. *Aesthetic Homosociality in Wackenroder and Tieck*. New York: Peter Lang, 2000. This study looks at Romanticism and patriarchy in literature in the works of Wilhelm Heinrich Wackenroder and Tieck. Bibliography and index.

Zeydel, Edwin H. *Ludwig Tieck, the German Romanticist: A Critical Study*. 2d ed. Hildesheim, New York: G. Olms, 1971. An update of the classic 1935 study on the German writer. Bibliography.

Helene M. Kastinger Riley

TIRSO DE MOLINA
Gabriel Téllez

Born: Madrid, Spain; 1580(?)
Died: Almazán, Spain; February, 1648

PRINCIPAL DRAMA

El vergonzoso en palacio, wr. 1611?, pb. 1624 (*The Bashful Man at Court*, 1991)

Marta la piadosa, wr. 1615, pb. 1636

Don Gil de las calzas verdes, wr. 1615, pb. 1635 (*Don Gil of the Green Breeches*, 1991)

El condenado por desconfiado, wr. 1615?, pb. 1634 (*The Saint and the Sinner*, 1952; also known as *Damned for Despair*, 1986)

La venganza de Tamar, wr. 1621, pb. 1634 (*Tamar's Revenge*, 1988; also known as *The Rape of Tamar*, 1999)

El burlador de Sevilla, wr. 1625?, pb. 1630 (*The Trickster of Seville*, 1923)

La prudencia en la mujer, wr. 1627-1633, pb. 1634 (*Prudence in Woman*, 1964)

OTHER LITERARY FORMS

Though Tirso de Molina is remembered primarily as a dramatist, he also wrote two prose miscellanies, *Los cigarrales de Toledo* (1624; the country houses of Toledo) and *Deleytar aprovechando* (1635; teaching while entertaining), as well as *Historia general de la orden de Nuestra Señora de las Mercedes* (1639; general history of the Mercedarian order).

ACHIEVEMENTS

Tirso de Molina is recognized—along with Lope de Vega Carpio, Pedro Calderón de la Barca, and Juan Ruiz de Alarcón—as one of the four major dramatists of Spain's great period of literary and artistic excellence known as its Golden Age (c. 1592-1681). The exact nature of his contribution to the drama of this period is, however, somewhat difficult to define. A comparison with Lope de Vega and Calderón shows him to lack both the poetic humanity of the former and the intellectual majesty of the latter; unlike Ruiz de Alarcón, Tirso does not excel in the pro-

duction of a particular type of drama. An examination of the fifty-four plays of which he is the undisputed author reveals a diverse collection of historical dramas, pious saints' lives, and frivolous comedies of seduction and marriage.

Tirso is known internationally as the author of the famous theological play *The Trickster of Seville*, a work that is indirectly the source of the libretto of Wolfgang Amadeus Mozart's *Don Giovanni* (1787), and he probably is in fact the author of this drama, though there is some uncertainty concerning this. The authorship of *The Saint and the Sinner*, the other great theological drama attributed to him, is similarly subject to question.

BIOGRAPHY

Not only does uncertainty exist involving the authorship of two plays considered to be the masterpieces of Gabriel Téllez (known best as Tirso de Molina), but also his life is shrouded in mystery. The identity of his parents is unknown, and even the date of his birth is uncertain. An eighteenth century portrait indicates that he was born in 1572. The same portrait, however, indicates that he died at the age of seventy-six years and five months on March 12, 1648 (for which he would necessarily have been born in 1571). On the other hand, a royal authorization for a party of monks to travel to the West Indies in 1616 lists his age as thirty-three years, suggesting a 1583 birth date, and in a deposition made by Tirso himself in 1638, the dramatist listed his age as fifty-seven, so that most scholars assume he was born in 1580 or early 1581 and died in February, 1648.

A fourth alternative—and a dramatic theory concerning Tirso's parentage—has been suggested by Blanca de los Ríos, the editor of the standard Spanish edition of Tirso's complete works, who bases her conclusions on the 1584 baptismal record of a child named Gabriel. Three lines of this document have been heavily crossed out, but Ríos believes that she has deciphered the obliterated words as reading:

"Téllez Girón, son of the duke of Osuna." Such a reading would indicate that Tirso was the illegitimate son of one of the most important men in sixteenth century Spain, and it might also explain the many puzzling vicissitudes in Tirso's career as well as his fondness for underdogs and his antipathy toward noblemen who abuse their power. The reading suggested by Ríos, however, has not been accepted by a majority of Tirso scholars.

The scant factual material available on Tirso's life must be gleaned from his own writings and from the records of the Mercedarian order, which he entered in 1600. Following his profession, he studied for a time in Salamanca, Toledo, Guadalajara, and (possibly) Alcalá de Henares before residing briefly in Soria, Segovia, and Madrid, where he presumably wrote and saw staged his first plays. From there he moved to Toledo, where he enjoyed the company of the local aristocracy (leading him to comment later in *Los cigarrales de Toledo* that he was more generously received by the citizens of Toledo than he had been in his own native town, Madrid). In 1616, he was sent with five other Mercedarian monks to Hispaniola (present-day Dominican Republic), where he served for almost two years as a member of the order's governing body and as a professor of theology before returning to Spain in 1618. In 1620 or 1621, he was sent again to Madrid and enjoyed several years as a successful dramatist in the capital before a 1625 edict censured him for writing profane plays and ordered his superiors to remove him from Madrid and to forbid him, on pain of excommunication, to write any more dramas. Because other priests of the period (notably Lope de Vega) were also accustomed to writing highly secular plays but were never bothered by the authorities, the edict is a bit puzzling. Ríos has used it—along with the dramatist's complaint that he was unfavorably received by the natives of his own city—as evidence to support her theory of Tirso's illegitimate birth, suggesting that his presence in the Spanish capital was an embarrassment to his father or to his father's family. Other critics, however, believe that Tirso's banishment is attributable to his attack in several of his dramas on the institution of *privado* (royal favorite) and to the resulting wrath of the

count-duke of Olivares, the favorite and chief minister of Philip IV. Whatever the reasons for the edict, Tirso apparently continued to enjoy the esteem of the leaders of the Mercedarian order, who appointed him in 1626 to the position of *comendador* (commander) and in 1632 named him chronicler, charging him with writing the order's history. The order allowed him to continue the publication of his collected dramatic works.

In 1640, however, the order's vicar provincial, Fray Marcos Salmerón, removed Tirso from the office of chronicler and banished him to the remote monastery of Cuenca; at the same time, Salmerón issued an edict forbidding any of the Mercedarians to write satires against the government—leading critics to assume that Tirso had again incurred Olivares's ire by composing a now-lost satire. Olivares died in 1643, and in 1645 Tirso was recalled from his exile in Cuenca and was appointed *comendador* of the monastery of Soria. He died in Almazán, Spain, in February of 1648.

ANALYSIS

Formally, Tirso de Molina's theater follows the dramatic norms established by his older contemporary, "the father of Spanish theater," Lope de Vega Carpio. Like Lope de Vega, Tirso valued variety and thus produced a diverse collection of plays ranging from serious biblical histories to frivolous comedies about courtship. Like Lope de Vega, he violated classical decorum by including in even his most serious dramas some humor—often in the form of a stock character known as a *gracioso* (clown). Tirso also followed Lope de Vega's practice of writing his plays in a mixture of verse forms and organizing the action in three acts; like Lope de Vega, he deliberately disregarded the dramatic unities of time and place, which sought to limit a play's setting to a single place and decreed that its action should occur in a single day.

Without departing from the norms established by Lope de Vega, Tirso endowed his plays with an individual style. One notices in his works, for example, a fondness for incorporating humor based on rustics' mispronunciation of Spanish. One also notices a surprising lack of interest in the theme of honor or reputation—a theme recommended by Lope de Vega as particularly appropriate for drama because of its power to arouse the audience. Thus, Tirso never wrote a "wife-murder play" such as Lope de Vega's *El eastigo sin venganza* (pb. 1635; *Justice Without Revenge*, 1936) or Calderón's *El médico de su honra* (pb. 1637; *The Surgeon of His Honor*, 1853), works that dramatize a husband's need to kill his wife in order to protect his reputation.

Because "wife-murder plays" generally appear to endorse (at least superficially) Spain's bloody honor code, Tirso's neglect of the genre is significant. It is quite likely that he found plays dealing with the honor code distasteful because of his sympathy for society's victims and his concomitant antipathy for its victimizers. Such an attitude is clearly evident in his theater, which is fond of dramatizing a victim's recovery of his lost estate or the visitation of retribution on the proud and mighty who abuse their power. The role of women in Tirso's dramas is particularly interesting. Rather than portray women as passive victims of an unjust social code, Tirso excels in the portrayal of female characters who act with intelligence and decisiveness in order to control their destinies in difficult circumstances.

THE BASHFUL MAN AT COURT

This attitude is already apparent in one of Tirso's earliest works, *The Bashful Man at Court*, which (like many Golden Age plays) strikes a modern reader as a jumbled combination of rather remotely related plots. The central action revolves around the courtship of Magdalena, a duke's daughter, and her secretary Mireno (the bashful man at court), whom both Magdalena and Mireno believe to be of peasant stock but who is actually the son of the Portuguese duke Pedro de Coimbra, who has lived for twenty years in exile after being wrongly accused of treason.

Two obstacles stand in the way of Magdalena and Mireno's romance: his shyness and the supposed difference in their social stations. The first of these is overcome by Magdalena, who, behaving in a manner typical of many of Tirso's female protagonists, uses initiative and ingenuity to encourage Mireno to over-

come his timidity and to declare his interest in her. The second obstacle is resolved by an unexpected public announcement from Lisbon that Mireno's father's name has been cleared, thus allowing his father to reveal his true identity to him—and to Magdalena's father. Although this rather abrupt *deus ex machina* detracts somewhat from the drama's ending, Tirso handles it in a way that emphasizes the play's underlying psychological intention. Thus, Mireno, who has used the more noble sounding name of Dionís while in Magdalena's employ, discovers that his name is indeed Dionís. Through Mireno/Dionís, Tirso implies that an individual can attain his true, more noble identity only when he is able to overcome the limitations that he places on himself.

Except for the noble background of its characters, *The Bashful Man at Court* resembles a Spanish Golden Age genre referred to as the *comedia de capa y espada*, or cape and sword play. These plays, which derive their name from the costume worn by the actors playing the leading male roles, have complicated plots dealing with the courtship of one or more sets of middle-class youths who devise ingenious measures to overcome the obstacles to their love. The young protagonists frequently resort to disguise and other forms of deception, which often backfire with comic results. Though there are frequent duels, they never produce serious results, since cape and sword plays (seventeenth century Spain's equivalent to the modern situation comedy) invariably end happily with at least one wedding.

MARTA LA PIADOSA

Such plays provide a natural framework for Tirso to create female characters endowed with ingenuity and initiative, and the protagonist Marta of *Marta la piadosa* (pious Martha) is a nice illustration of how he uses the opportunity to its fullest advantage. Marta, who is in love with Don Felipe, deftly overcomes almost overwhelming obstacles to their marriage. When her father decrees that she must marry a wealthy old man named Urbina, she circumvents this decision by feigning religious vocation. Moreover, she uses this same feigned vocation as grounds to have Don Felipe, disguised as a Latin teacher, visit her regularly. With Felipe's help, she maneuvers her sister Lucía (who is also in love with Felipe) into a relationship with Urbina's son. The play thus ends, typically for the genre, with multiple weddings.

DON GIL OF THE GREEN BREECHES

Probably Tirso's best cape and sword play, *Don Gil of the Green Breeches* again centers on the clever maneuvers of a quick-witted and active female protagonist, Doña Juana, who, having been courted and abandoned by Don Martín, assumes a series of false identities in order to impede Don Martín's courtship of the wealthy Doña Inés. Doña Juana assumes both male and female identities. Disguised as Doña Elvira, she maligns Don Martín's character; disguised as Don Gil, she wins Inés's affection herself, thus causing Inés to lose interest in Martín. In the course of the play, the fictitious Don Gil assumes increasing importance and attracts various other characters to assume the same disguise. The climactic moment of the play occurs when four "Don Gils," each dressed in green breeches, appear on the stage simultaneously, producing a moment of uproarious confusion, which, when finally cleared up, prepares the way for a denouement involving three weddings.

THE TRICKSTER OF SEVILLE

Tirso's lighthearted cape and sword plays provide a sharp contrast to his serious masterpiece *The Trickster of Seville*. As has been mentioned, the authorship of this play is uncertain. It was not included in the series of collected works published under Tirso's direction but appeared instead, attributed to him, in a collection of works by various dramatists published in 1630. Such collections are notoriously unreliable sources concerning the authorship of the works they publish, but in the case of *The Trickster of Seville*, critics, basing their theories on similarities between this work and other works known to be written by Tirso, generally accept the attribution as accurate.

The play is noteworthy, among other reasons, because it is one of the earliest works based on the legendary character Don Juan. Modern scholars (such as philosopher José Ortega y Gasset) often see Don Juan as the archetypal personification of unrestrained vitality, and there is much in *The Trickster of Seville* to support such an interpretation. Examples include the opening scene in which Don Juan, "a man without a name," materializes in the darkness of the Duchess Isabela's bedroom, and the scene in which he emerges from the ocean in order to seduce the fishing peasant girl, Tisbea. It is clear, however, that Tirso (consciously, at least) views Don Juan as a malign disturber of social order. For Tirso, Don Juan's lack of discipline and his influential relatives' abuse of their position in order to protect him from punishment are destablizing social forces that must ultimately be punished. In *The Trickster of Seville*, the punishment is of divine origin. In the play's conclusion, Don Juan is dragged off to Hell by the statue of a man he has killed in a duel, and the Spanish king, on being informed of this, pronounces it a just punishment from Heaven.

PRUDENCE IN WOMAN

Tirso's most famous historical drama, *Prudence in Woman*, blends the theme of the abuse of power, which is evident in *The Trickster of Seville*, with that of the resourceful woman, which is dramatized in *The Bashful Man at Court*, *Marta la piadosa*, and *Don Gil of the Green Breeches*. Based on incidents occurring during the early years of the reign of Fernando IV (1285-1312), the play is an encomium to his regent mother María de Molina's restrained and sagacious use of power in order to guide the Castilian kingdom through desperately trying times.

The play's treatment of Fernando's advisers, who, in order to improve their own lot, intentionally deceive the young king by giving him false advice, is particularly interesting in the light of the previously mentioned conflict between Tirso and Spain's current royal favorite, the count-duke of Olivares. Indeed, much of the plot of *Prudence in Woman* corresponds in some detail to conditions and incidents in Spain at the time of the play's composition, and there can be little doubt that the work is an expression of Tirso's worries regarding what he saw as an unhealthy political situation. As theater, this play is less successful than the other works discussed. Its plot is highly repetitious, and its tone is overtly didactic. Quite possibly, both defects may be attributed to a lack of artistic distance—to a too intimate involvement of the author in the material.

THE SAINT AND THE SINNER

The authorship of *The Saint and the Sinner*—like that of *The Trickster of Seville*—is uncertain. This play was first published in 1634, under Tirso's direction, in the second volume of his collected works. In the prologue of this volume, Tirso remarks that only four of the twelve dramas that it contains are by him; the remaining eight are by authors whom he fails to identify. Because two of the plays contained in this volume can be identified as Tirso's because of the mention of his name in their closing lines, the chances are only 20 percent that any of the remaining ten are by him. Despite these odds, the authorship of *The Saint and the Sinner* continues to be assigned to Tirso, and many critics see this work as a companion piece to *The Trickster of Seville*.

In many ways, the protagonists of these two works are diametrically opposed. Don Juan is a wanton libertine, while Paulo of *The Saint and the Sinner* is an ascetic hermit. Don Juan is overly confident, while Paulo is lacking in confidence. In spite of these differences, both share the fate of eternal damnation.

Paulo is damned because he fails to trust God. Though he has long lived a virtuous and religious life, he does not feel confident of his salvation and, following a disturbing dream, prays for a sign to show him what his ultimate fate will be. His prayer is answered not by God but by the Devil in the guise of an angel. The Devil tells Paulo that his fate will be the same as that of a man from Naples named Enrico. On going to Naples and learning that Enrico is a thief who is guilty of both rape and murder, Paulo despairs and abandons his religious life to become an outlaw. Ironically, Enrico is eventually converted, and at the end of the play his soul is shown born aloft while Paulo is consumed by flames.

While, from a modern point of view, *The Saint and the Sinner* may seem a bit puzzling, it is an accurate dramatization of the fundamental Christian dogma of salvation by faith. It is probably no accident that the protagonist's name is an ironic reflection of that of the apostle Paul, whose writings emphasize this dogma. The Pauline message is that salvation is a divine gift that cannot be earned through good works; Paulo's tragic flaw is that he does not understand this message.

TAMAR'S REVENGE

Based on a biblical account in 2 Samuel, *Tamar's Revenge* dramatizes the rape of King David's daughter Tamar by her half brother Amnon and his subsequent murder by Tamar's brother Absalom, who wishes to avenge his sister's lost honor. As might be surmised from this outline of its plot, the play is typical of the Senecan tragic style, popular in Spain at the time, which sought to amaze the audience with spectacular violence. This is particularly true of its ending, in which the slain Amnon's bloody body is revealed lying among food spread on a banquet table.

This denouement should not, however, be interpreted as pandering to a bloodthirsty public's desire for titillation. By having Amnon speak of Tamar throughout the play as a morsel of food and by building into the work numerous other uses of food imagery, Tirso makes clear that Amnon's sin is his unrestrained appetite. It is thus appropriate that Absalom and Tamar accomplish their revenge by inviting him to a banquet and converting the banquet table into an executioner's block. The form of Amnon's punishment is thus closely related to his sin; he is the victim of his own appetite. In essence, Tirso implies that sin is its own punishment.

In the light of this implication, the drama's treatment of Absalom is particularly interesting. Throughout the play, Absalom answers his father's pleas for mercy with the demand for justice. Tirso's audience was familiar with the biblical account of Absalom's rebellion against his father and his execution by one of David's soldiers—again in spite of his father's pleas for mercy. Thus, in one sense Absalom can be seen as the victim of his own refusal to show mercy.

For seventeenth century viewers this would have been particularly interesting because they could not have failed to perceive *Tamar's Revenge* as an indictment of Spain's honor code, which held husbands, fathers, and brothers responsible for avenging—through the murder of the offending party—acts dishonoring any female members of their family. Because the avenging party in *Tamar's Revenge* is David's rebellious son Absalom, there can be little doubt that Tirso condemns this code as a hypocritical sham. Moreover, by showing Absalom as the victim of his own refusal to show mercy, he emphasizes the contrast between the honor code's dependence on justice and revenge and the Christian concept of mercy.

OTHER MAJOR WORKS

NONFICTION: *Los cigarrales de Toledo*, 1624; *Deleytar aprovechando*, 1635; *Historia general de la orden de Nuestra Señora de las Mercedes*, 1639.

BIBLIOGRAPHY

Albrecht, Jane. *Irony and Theatricality in Tirso de Molina*. Ottawa Hispanic Studies 16. Ottawa: Dovehouse Editions, 1994. This study of Tirso de Molina also examines the Spanish theater of the time. Bibliography and index.

Halkhoree, P. R. K. *Social and Literary Satire in the Comedies of Tirso de Molina*. Ottawa Hispanic Studies 5. Ottawa: Dovehouse Editions, 1989. This study examines the use of social satire in the comedies of Tirso de Molina. Bibliography.

Hesse, Everett Wesley. *Tirso's Art in "La venganza de Tamar": Tragedy of Sex and Violence*. York, S.C.: Spanish Literature Publishing, 1991. Provides a critical analysis of Tirso de Molina's *Tamar's Revenge*. Bibliography.

Hughes, Ann Nickerson. *Religious Imagery in the Theater of Tirso de Molina*. Macon, Ga.: Mercer, 1984. Hughes presents a study of Tirso de Molina's plays in respect to his handling of religious imagery. Bibliography.

Levin, Leslie. *Metaphors of Conversion in Seventeenth Century Spanish Drama*. Rochester, N.Y.: Tamesis, 1999. This study of seventeenth century Spanish theater focuses on Tirso de Molina and Pedro Calderón de la Barca and the topic of conversion. Bibliography.

Sola-Solé, Josep M., and George E. Gingras, eds. *Tirso's Don Juan: The Metamorphosis of a Theme*. Washington, D.C.: Catholic University of America Press, 1988. This collection of papers from a symposium on Tirso de Molina held in Washington, D.C., in November, 1985, discusses the dramatist's depiction of the Don Juan character in *The Trickster of Seville*. Bibliography.

Sullivan, Henry W. *Tirso de Molina and the Drama of the Counter Reformation*. 2d ed. Amsterdam: Rodopi, 1981. An examination of the dramatic works of Tirso de Molina. Bibliography and index.

Sullivan, Henry W., and Raúl A. Galoppe, eds. *Tirso de Molina: His Originality Then and Now*. Ottawa Hispanic Studies 20. Ottawa: Dovehouse Editions, 1996. A critical analysis and interpretation of Tirso de Molina's works with reference to his originality. Bibliography.

Wilson, Margaret. *Tirso de Molina*. Boston: Twayne, 1977. A basic biography of Tirso de Molina that covers his life and works. Bibliography and index.

Currie K. Thompson

ERNST TOLLER

Born: Samotschin, Germany (now Szamocin, Poland); December 1, 1893
Died: New York, New York; May 22, 1939

PRINCIPAL DRAMA
Die Wandlung, pr., pb. 1919 (*Transfiguration*, 1935)

Masse-Mensch, pr. 1920, pb. 1921 (*Masses and Man*, 1924)
Die Maschinenstürmer, pr., pb. 1922 (*The Machine-wreckers*, 1923)
Hinkemann, pr., pb. 1923 (English translation, 1926)
Der entfesselte Wotan, pb. 1923, pr. 1925

Die Rache des verhöhnten Liebhabers, pr. 1923, pb. 1925 (*The Scorned Lover's Revenge*, 1936)

Hoppla, wir leben!, pr., pb. 1927 (*Hoppla! Such Is Life!*, 1928)

Feuer aus den Kesseln, pr., pb. 1930 (*Draw the Fires!*, 1935)

Wunder in Amerika, pr., pb. 1931 (with Hermann Kesten; *Miracle in America*, 1934)

Die blinde Göttin, pr. 1932, pb. 1933 (*The Blind Goddess*, 1934)

Seven Plays, pb. 1935

Blind Man's Buff, pr. 1936, pb. 1938 (with Denis Johnston, based in part on Toller's play *Die blinde Göttin*)

Nie wieder Friede!, wr. 1936, pb. 1978 (*No More Peace!*, 1936)

Pastor Hall, wr. 1938-1939, pb. 1946, pr. 1947 (English translation, 1939)

OTHER LITERARY FORMS

Apart from his plays, Ernst Toller is best known for his autobiographical writings, especially *Eine Jugend in Deutschland* (1933; *I Was a German*, 1934), as well as a volume of verse entitled *Das Schwalbenbuch* (1924; *The Swallow-book*, 1924).

ACHIEVEMENTS

Ernst Toller was one of the best-known dramatists in the Germany of the Weimar Republic. In his lifetime, his reputation rested largely on five plays written between the years 1917 and 1927, half of which he spent behind bars. These plays, connected with his experiences as a revolutionary and a political prisoner, made Toller one of the most liked as well as one of the most hated artists of his time. His renown or notoriety was the result of the controversial topicality of his plays, of the innovative stagings they received at the hands of a series of first-rate directors, and of the playwright's considerable talents, more lyric than dramatic, perhaps, but abetted by a keen and fantastic imagination.

When the Nazis came to power and suppressed "degenerate" literature, Toller, a socialist and a Jew, became a nonperson. After his death in exile in 1939, he remained relatively obscure until the middle 1960's,

when the thaw in the Cold War climate promoted during the Adenauer "restoration period" took effect. With the growth of the New Left, the politicizing of West German universities, and the rise of a counterculture, scholars and critics began to focus on those periods of German literature predating 1945, which had been neglected because this literature was politically uncomfortable. The result for Toller has been triple rediscovery, first as the representative dramatist of activist or political expressionism; second, as one of the more significant authors of neofactualism, the literary movement associated most closely with the Weimar culture; and finally, as one of the foremost spokespersons of German literature in exile. In addition, thanks in large measure to the liberalizing influence of Bertolt Brecht's aesthetic theories, East German critics have come to regard Toller as a pioneer in the development of a socialist drama. Toller will in all likelihood prove to be the most enduring of the major expressionist playwrights and the only one to enjoy more than a provincial reputation.

BIOGRAPHY

Ernst Toller was born on December 1, 1893, in the little town of Samotschin near Posen in what was then eastern Prussia and is now western Poland. His father was a fairly well-to-do shopkeeper and, as a member of the town council, one of the most prominent Jewish citizens in the area. Toller attended the local Jewish grade school and in 1913 was graduated from the Realgymnasium (academic high school) in Bromberg, the county seat.

Among his more vivid recollections were experiences of national, religious, and class hatred. Toller once wrote a piece in the local press condemning the authorities. Only the intervention of Toller's father saved the high school student from a libel suit by the mayor. The young Toller clearly evinced the symptoms of a vulnerable heart. The sensitive side of his nature succumbed to the fear of alienation as a "dirty Jew." Security lay in becoming more German than the kaiser himself, in drowning himself in the narrow ambience of Wilhelminian nationalism; hence, his choice of university: Grenoble in France. It was the fashionable thing for solid middle-class burghers to send their sons abroad, and one of the foreign centers of higher learning favored by the Germans was Grenoble with its attractive location. Here Toller spent most of his time at the German Students' Union and adopted a supercilious attitude toward France and its civilization. There was an occasional tug of guilt at being able to live it up because of his parents' money while his former childhood "Polack" friends were drowning in poverty.

When World War I broke out, Toller managed to catch the last train to Switzerland before the closing of the frontier. From there he rushed to Munich. His jingoistic enthusiasm knew no bounds. After being rejected by both infantry and cavalry because of poor health, he lied his way into the artillery but not before being almost beaten to death by some irate citizens who took him for a spy because of the French label in the lining of his hat. Toller went out of his way to volunteer for frontline duty and saw thirteen months of almost continuous action in some of the bloodiest fighting on the western front. Then his frail constitution and his hypersensitivity betrayed him. He col-

Ernst Toller (Hulton Archive by Getty Images)

lapsed from psychosomatic exhaustion. He was honorably discharged as a corporal in January, 1917, haunted by the feeling that the soldiers dying at the front were not Frenchmen and Germans but men—in fact, brothers.

Toller sought to bury his memories of the war in an orgy of work at the University of Munich, but to no avail. At a gathering in Castle Lauenstein of some of Germany's most respected intellectuals, including the renowned sociologist, Max Weber, to which Toller was invited as a promising student, the former soldier, Toller, was appalled at the bankruptcy of ideas evinced by the older generation in its discussion of Germany's future. Later, he was shocked to learn through his readings that the German government and the German industrialists bore considerable responsibility for the war and that the former had, in fact, lied to the nation about its aims, that its policy of aggrandizement was needlessly prolonging the war.

In the meantime, determined to take the easiest route to the fashionable but meaningless doctor's degree, Toller had transferred to the University of Heidelberg, which had a notorious reputation as a degree factory. He opted for economics because it was the rage; his topic, "Pig-breeding in East Prussia," would allow him time to cater to his newly acquired pacifist convictions. He set up an antiwar organization called Young Germans' Cultural and Political Union. The group was outlawed by order of the High Command and its members pressed into military service regardless of physical fitness. Toller managed to escape to Berlin, where he met the man who was to have the greatest influence on the course of his life: Kurt Eisner, the leader of the Independent Socialist Party (USPD) in Bavaria, under whose influence Toller became a non-Marxist socialist. This conversion to socialism was at the core of the play on which Toller was working (entitled appropriately enough *Transfiguration*) when he followed Eisner to Munich, where early in 1918 the socialist leader organized a strike of munitions workers to end the war. Toller distributed excerpts from his uncompleted play to the strikers and very quickly assumed a position of leadership. He was arrested, put back into uniform, and jailed. In prison, he read the works of Karl Marx, Friedrich

Engels, and Rosa Luxemburg, grounding himself in the theoretical side of classical Marxism and embracing its central indictment of capitalism, although he rejected much else. In prison, Toller also managed to complete the final scenes of his play. On his release, he was assigned to a reserve unit. Then, at the instigation of his patriotic mother, who was convinced that her son had gone out of his mind, Toller was put into a psychiatric clinic in Munich. He was discharged from both the clinic and the army in time to become fully enmeshed in the so-called November Revolution of 1918, one of the most complicated and tragic events in the history of Germany. On November 7, 1918, the Democratic and Social Republic of Bavaria was proclaimed by Kurt Eisner, the first republic on German soil since the Revolution of 1848. Toller became deputy chairman of the Central Council of Workers', Peasants', and Soldiers' Councils, a type of grassroots governmental organization that, in the opinion of Eisner and Toller, was far more democratic than the parliamentary system represented by the Bavarian Landtag.

In February, 1919, Eisner was assassinated by a young ultrarightist determined to prove that he was more patriotic than the neo-Fascist members of the Thule Society, which had blackballed him because of a Jewish skeleton in his family closet. The Landtag, controlled by the SPD, established a government under Johannes Hoffmann akin in counterrevolutionary sentiment to the Ebert government in Berlin. Inspired by the establishment of a Soviet Republic in Hungary, strongly urged on by the workers' and soldiers' councils in outlying cities, and determined not to let the policies of Eisner go to rack and ruin, the revolutionary workers of Munich proclaimed on April 7, 1919, the existence of the (first) Bavarian Republic of Councils. Within a day, Toller was elected head of state. The rival government of Prime Minister Hoffmann retreated to Bamberg. The politically inexperienced Toller accepted his position reluctantly and only out of a deep sense of responsibility to the workers. He proceeded to do what the SPD should have done in Berlin but had not, overthrow the old order of things responsible for Germany's sorry state. He issued decrees for establishing a proletarian army and a

revolutionary tribunal to replace the military and judicial systems of the old regime.

On April 13, 1919, a coup by soldiers in Munich loyal to Hoffmann was squelched with the help of the Communists, who until this point had refused to participate in the council government for reasons that have always remained a mystery. The next day, the Communists took over, convinced that Toller was not running a tight ship of state. Under the leadership of Eugen Leviné, a second council republic was set up, called by some historians the Soviet Republic of Bavaria to distinguish it from its predecessor, run in the main by Independents, left-wing Social Democrats, and sundry anarchosocialists. Because of his popularity, Toller was appointed field commander of the Red Army; there is a certain irony in the fact that he, an avowed pacifist, gained the distinction of being the only "general" to score a victory for the republic. At Dachau, the Reds defeated the White forces of Hoffmann, composed of Bavarian SPD workers. The outnumbered Hoffmann appealed to Berlin, and a large force of Free Corps, fresh from crushing the revolution in Berlin, Brunswick, and Saxony, swarmed into Bavaria. The military and economic situation for the republic became hopeless. Toller wanted to negotiate with the enemy. The Communists insisted on a fight to the bitter end to secure a moral victory. Toller resigned his commission in protest and took his place in the ranks. The Communist leadership resigned on April 27, after a vote of no confidence by the councils, but it retained control of the army. That was the official end of the Soviet Republic.

Toller was appointed head of a provisional executive committee to enter into negotiations with the White generals, an act that made the first head of state of the Council Republic its last as well. The mercenaries demanded unconditional surrender. The Red Army refused to lay down its arms. The Whites advanced so rapidly that, contrary to their intention, they entered Munich on May 1, the international workingmen's holiday, and proceeded at once to create martyrs. They massacred some six hundred individuals and executed, after a trial of sorts, two hundred more. One of the martyred was Gustav Landauer, whose slaying rivaled in brutality the murders of Liebknecht and Luxemburg. Among the "legally" dispatched was Leviné. If Toller had not been able to go underground for a month he would have shared the fate of Landauer. During the intensive manhunt for him, Hoffmann's mercenaries shot to death a detective that they mistook for Toller.

In the end, the ten-thousand-mark reward for his capture did him in. Despite the fact that he courageously declared his solidarity with the revolution and accepted responsibility even for those actions that were clearly beyond his control, the tribunal sentenced Toller to five years of fortress imprisonment rather than to death. Among the factors that saved his life were the following: He was not a Communist; he seemed to be a decent middle-class young man (witness his fine war record) who had momentarily been led astray (witness his stay in a psychiatric clinic); his impeccable character witnesses, among them Max Weber and Thomas Mann; his moderating influence on the course of the revolution; his humanitarian efforts to reduce the bloodshed. Ironically, he was severely taken to task by the Communists on these last two points.

In the meantime, Toller's first play, *Transfiguration*, opened in Berlin to an enthusiastic reception by critics and spectators alike; in its plea for an end to violence and the reconciliation of all people regardless of class, creed, or nationality, it struck a highly nostalgic chord in a nation worn out by almost five years of war and revolution. Toller became an overnight celebrity. There was a nationwide movement to secure the freedom of the most famous political prisoner in Germany. When the offer of a pardon came from an opportunistic Bavarian government, Toller turned it down in an act of solidarity with his fellow inmates. With *Masses and Man* and the other major plays written during his confinement, Toller cemented his reputation as the leading playwright of political expressionism and acquired another as the most controversial author of the Weimar Republic, for the plays that followed *Transfiguration* succeeded in offending not only nationalist sentiment but also large segments of the Left. Toller obliquely took the shine off the mystique of the proletariat as the saviors of humankind in *The Machine-*

wreckers, and in *Hinkemann*, he proffered the thesis that socialism is by no means the answer to all human ills.

On his release from prison in 1924, Toller resumed his active struggle against injustice. His party, the USPD, had dissolved itself in 1920, one-third of its members having joined the left wing of the SPD, one-third having become progressive Communists who would later oppose Stalinization, and the remaining third having drifted out of politics or having become "members" of what German political historians have dubbed the "homeless Left"—individuals unable to endure the capitulation of the Social Democrats to capitalism or the stern dogmatism of the Communists but retaining their belief in socialism. Toller joined the homeless Left, whose rallying point was the magazine *Die Weltbühne*; between 1925 and 1933, he traveled widely, including trips to Africa, the Near East, Russia, and the United States, to gather material for his documentary exposés.

Despite his reservations about the republic, Toller found it infinitely preferable to a rightist dictatorship. His warnings and those of a few other equally perspicacious left-wing intellectuals went unheeded. Shortly after Hitler came to power, the Reichstag burned down. Hitler seized on the incident as a pretext to do away with his opponents. Fortunately Toller was on a lecture tour in Switzerland when the Schutzstaffel (SS) entered his apartment to arrest him. It is practically certain that his fate would have been similar to that of his friend and fellow anarchosocialist, the pacifist poet, Erich Mühsam, who, like Toller, had endured some five years of fortress imprisonment for his participation in the government of the Bavarian Republic: Mühsam was murdered by the SS in a concentration camp in July, 1934. Toller was among the first to have his books burned by the Nazis and among the first to be deprived of his German citizenship. He became in effect a professional anti-Fascist, devoting much of his time to warning about the dangers of Nazism. At the International PEN Club congress in 1933, he exposed to the world the Nazi persecution of writers. The outraged Nazi-dominated German section seceded and was replaced by an emigrant group led by Toller.

Toller helped his fellow refugees achieve stability and security and raised funds for the victims on both sides in the Spanish Civil War. He did an enormous amount of traveling, including a lecture tour of the United States and Canada from October, 1936, to February, 1937. Naturally, the quality of his creative writings declined—as a playwright he enjoyed a modest success in England and Ireland, none whatsoever in the United States. A stint as a screenwriter for Metro-Goldwyn-Mayer came to an end when Toller's conscience would not permit him to take any more pay for work that Hollywood was obviously not going to find to its taste.

Not long after being invited to the White House by Eleanor Roosevelt in recognition of his humanitarian work, the playwright suddenly decided to give up the good fight that he had been waging in one form or another since 1917. On May 22, 1939, at the age of forty-five, Toller hanged himself with the belt of his dressing gown in the shower stall of his hotel room in New York City. His greatest strength proved in the end to be his tragic flaw: a sensitivity, which took on a manic-depressive form. He had been shaken by Francisco Franco's victory in Spain and by the news that the relief funds collected to alleviate the suffering of homeless children had been confiscated by Franco. He was increasingly concerned over the Allied policy of appeasement and indifference toward a Hitler who seemed unstoppable, and he was penniless (for months he had been unable to pay for a divorce from his young actress wife, who had recently left him). He was almost friendless, meticulously avoided by acquaintances on whom he always seemed to be making excessive demands in the struggle against Fascism, and he was physically and mentally drained by his political activities as well as his efforts to establish himself as an author in the non-German-speaking world.

In his suitcase was the manuscript of his last play, *Pastor Hall*, inspired by Protestant leader Martin Niemöller's public stance against the Hitler regime and the solitary witness of Erich Mühsam, who, having been forced by his concentration camp guards to dig his grave and then told his life would be spared only if he sang a Nazi anthem, defiantly burst into the "International." Not a single producer approached by Toller would touch the play. Spread out all over his desk were photos of emaciated Spanish children. Theirs were probably the last human faces he gazed on in this life.

Analysis

In summarizing the achievement of Ernest Toller as a synthesis of literature and life unmatched in the history of expressionism, literary historian Manfred Durzak wondered what critical categories can apply to a man who paid for the shattering of his ideal of the human community with his life.

Transfiguration

Toller's first play, *Transfiguration*, is the recapitulation of his spiritual journey from the parochialism of organized religion through the exclusiveness of nationalism to an all-embracing pacifism. It also epitomizes the search of the expressionist intellectual for the truly human community and captures the aspirations of millions of war-weary Germans for peace and some sort of radical transformation in the body politic as the natural issue of years of untold suffering and sacrifice for the fatherland.

The work is conceived on the lines of a *Stationendrama*, a structure that harks back to August Strindberg's confessional Damascus trilogy (pb. 1898-1904) and derives its name from the Stations of the Cross. This type of play depicts the internal development of its hero to higher things in a series of loosely connected stations or steps. There is no real antagonist, and the individuals encountered along the protagonist's path serve as his embodied obstacles or signposts or aspirations. In Toller's play, the stations are divided into thirteen "pictures," both "real" and "unreal." The latter, called "dream pictures," serve as projections of the hero's subconscious or as counterparts to or commentaries on his development. The play opens with a surrealistic prologue in which the skeletons of dead soldiers rise up from their graves and line up smartly according to rank, the crosses in their hands taking the place of rifles and swords. The message is clear. The kaiser's pronouncement at the outbreak of the war that he will recognize no distinctions, class or otherwise, among his Germans, is revealed in all its falsity. Even in death, the inhuman community rests on the principle of hierarchy.

Toller's hero, Friedrich, is likened to Ahasuerus, the Jew, who, because he refused to help Christ on his way to Golgotha, was condemned to wander restlessly in his search for redemption until the return of the Savior. Friedrich's quest for roots focuses on the nation-state in the first half of the play. In an effort to overcome his alienation as a Jew and an artist not at home in the middle-class world, he seizes the opportunity to serve in a colonial war and share in the white man's burden to bring the blessings of civilization to the savages. Friedrich volunteers for a dangerous mission and is awarded the iron cross as a sign that he is now one of "them." He has been severely rattled by the brutalities of war. The elation of a Red Cross nurse, a Sister of Mercy, on hearing the news that ten thousand natives have been butchered in a single battle, leaves its mark on Friedrich's psyche. After his medical discharge, he tries hard to salvage what is left of his patriotic zeal by creating a huge sculpture symbolizing the "victory of the fatherland." Friedrich smashes the statue to bits when it dawns on him that he has been creating a cover-up for inexcusable human suffering. The catalyst is a personal encounter with a crippled war veteran and his wife, riddled with venereal disease contracted through her husband. They reveal to the hero the social causes of the war.

In the second half of the play, Friedrich takes on the features of a secular Christ as he reaches out to the wider community of his fellow human beings. Descending to the depths and sharing in the sufferings of the poor in slums, factories, and prisons, he develops the sense of compassion that Ahasuerus lacked. He thwarts the urge to overthrow the old order by a violence commensurate with the violence inflicted on the poor by the forces of capitalism and militarism. Exuding charisma, Friedrich issues a successful summons to a revolution of the heart as a prerequisite for the classless society of human brotherhood. Because both the rich and the poor have been victimized and dehumanized by the "system" and because both are, deep down, equally human and equally good, the summons is all-inclusive. The transfiguration of humankind is accomplished without bloodshed.

The play has been praised for the power of its surrealistic war scenes and the haunting lyricism of some of its lines (a few critics have drawn a favorable comparison between the free verse in *Transfiguration* and that in *The Swallow-book*, Toller's only major contribution to the poetry of expressionism). *Transfiguration* has been criticized for its excessive rhetoric, for padding, for disjointedness, and for sloppy motivation. Some commentators are particularly critical of the ending, which they regard as utterly unbelievable; the emphasis on a voluntaristic socialism based on Socratic rationalism (knowledge equals virtue), they contend, is both naïve and far-fetched. The historical apologia for the emphasis can be found in the opposition of the expressionists to the contention of their literary predecessors, the naturalists, that people are rather helpless and passive victims of their heredity and environment, without free will. Apart from this, the fact remains that, for a few relatively euphoric months, Toller's revolution in *Transfiguration* became a spontaneous and bloodless reality of sorts, in the Democratic and Social Republic of Bavaria, where someone who was at the same time a playwright, a Jew, and an anarchistic socialist, was head of state of one of the most conservative regions of Germany. With its vision of a world "without misery, without war, and without hatred," Toller's play is as timelessly relevant or as foolish as the dream of a Martin Luther King, Jr., in its appeal to the finest instincts in humankind.

MASSES AND MAN

Masses and Man, Toller's second play, was written in a creative outburst of some three days duration in his first year of confinement for high treason. It was an attempt to come to grips with a seemingly insoluble problem that had haunted him ever since he, a socialist who despised force and hated bloodshed, had caused blood to be shed: the ultimate moral and tragic dilemma confronting the revolutionary as an ethical person, an individual striving for his own ideals in the ivory tower, and as a political person, a mass-man swept toward his goal by social impulses at the expense of these ideals. The main figure of

Toller's play, Sonja Irene L., is modeled on a professor's wife who played an important role in the January, 1917, illegal strike for peace by the Munich munitions workers, and who (in actuality) committed suicide in prison. The strike, the real beginning of Toller's revolutionary activities, marks the point in time at which *Transfiguration* ends and *Masses and Man* begins. The latter play is, at least outwardly, also a station drama, depicting as it does in a series of episodes, reinforced by dream projections, the painful spiritual odyssey of the inexperienced and naïve "good" person intent on alleviating human suffering through the excruciatingly real world of revolution in all of its phases, from peaceful demonstrations to revengeful retribution. When the leader of the masses, called the Nameless One (who resembles the Communist leader Eugen Leviné), argues, rather forcefully, that strikes may bring an end to the war but that they will not change a system that enslaves the workers and that only force will do this, Sonja Irene L. acquiesces in this policy. The momentary capitulation to violence is motivated by her total rejection of a status quo beyond redemption and is made absolutely clear in a brilliantly conceived dream picture depicting a group of capitalists doing a fox-trot around the desks of the stock exchange as they celebrate the enormous profits they are making out of war. As the situation of the revolutionaries becomes hopeless and they give vent to their years of pent-up misery by shooting hostages, Sonja protests vigorously, calling for the total repudiation of violence. The Nameless One demands a fight to the end in the conviction that the blood of martyrs is the seedbed for future revolutionaries. He carries the day. Sonja is branded a bourgeois intellectual and condemned to death. Before the sentence can be carried out, however, the revolutionary army is overrun. Sonja is taken prisoner and executed by the state.

The structural backbone of the play is a series of dialectical encounters between Sonja and her ideological antagonists; hence, the formal element that makes the play much more than a station drama also makes it an intensely exciting work. Each clash of ideas results in a crucial decision for the heroine and defines the course of future action. In the first three debates, she is the loser (once with her husband, a government official who tries to convince her to put charity before "justice" and with whom she returns home in a moment of existential weakness; twice with the Nameless One—when she tacitly assents to violence and when he convinces the workers that she is a counterrevolutionary). In the fourth debate, again with the Nameless One as he steals into her prison cell to help her escape, she scores her big victory. Like Toller in the real world, she refuses to escape because it can only be accomplished at the expense of a human life. In her final confrontation, with the priest sent to hear her last confession, she categorically rejects the doctrine of Original Sin and of the innate corruption of humankind, doctrines exploited by the Church to buttress an economic system whose prime mover is fear. Having reaffirmed her belief in human goodness, she goes to her death in witness of that belief. Two female inmates—and it is deliberately left uncertain whether they are political prisoners or common criminals—are inspired by her example and undergo a transfiguration.

Ethos, structure, and language (Toller actually improves on the telegram style popularized by Georg Kaiser) combine to make *Masses and Man* the best-known expressionist play throughout the world. Walter Sokel has astutely suggested that it comes closer than any other play of this literary movement to being a tragedy in the classical sense of the term. Sonja's guilt is caused by a tragic flaw which is the result of her greatest virtue: active compassion for the downtrodden. Rejecting the offer of clemency proffered by the state because of her moderating influence on the revolutionaries, she goes to her death deliberately to atone for her "crime." When Sonja puts the revolutionary state (the dictatorship of the proletariat) on the same level as the capitalist state that it is to replace, *Masses and Man* becomes one of the most prophetic works of the century in its anticipation of both Stalinism and of the rejection of Soviet statism by the neoanarchists of the later twentieth century. The truly human community can only be effected by a quantum leap inspired by the transfiguration of individuals. Toller writes:

What else could I tell you, that I believe that above all else we must combat war, poverty, and the state (which in the final analysis knows nothing but force and not justice) . . . and put in its place community bound together in an economic sense by the peaceful exchange of the products of one's labor for others of equal value, the community of free men which is permeated by creative spirit.

THE MACHINE-WRECKERS

In the second play written during the playwright's fortress imprisonment, *The Machine-wreckers*, Toller wanted to delve more deeply than he had in *Masses and Man* into the reasons for the failure of the German Revolution of 1918-1919 from the vantage point of the proletariat. He was convinced that the dehumanization of the workers over a long period of time made it extremely difficult for them to embrace actively a set of humanitarian, pacifist ideals. One sad result had been the breakdown of international solidarity in 1914 as the Socialist parties of France, England, and Germany reneged on their solemn pledge not to fight in any nationalist war that would pit brother-worker against brother-worker. A second sad result had been the disunity created in the ranks of the workers' movement by the split into majority and minority Socialism in 1917. A third sad result had been the excess of revolutionary violence that led to the needless slaying of Liebknecht and Luxemburg in 1919. The playwright sought to flesh out this thesis, presented abstractly in *Masses and Man*, by writing a more realistic play about the revolt of the English Luddites in 1815. In order to document the nearly unbearable miseries of the proletariat, he would use Engels's *Die Lage der arbeitenden Klasse in England* (1845; *The Condition of the Working Class in England in 1844*, 1887) and Marx's *Das Kapital* (1867-1904; *Capital: A Critique of Political Economy*, 1886-1909) as sources.

The plot concerns the attempt of the weavers of Nottingham to cope with the new machines that are causing massive layoffs. A strike is in progress when the hero, Jimmy Cobbett, a weaver who has traveled extensively and has learned to read and write, returns to his hometown. The strike is obviously ineffectual, thanks to the scabs, a ready supply of whom is available. The striking weavers decide to take direct action by destroying the machines, the apparent cause of all their woes. Jimmy convinces them for the moment that the machines are here to stay and that if the workers of the town will develop a sense of solidarity with their fellow workers in England and on the Continent, they will eventually become the masters of the machines that are now enslaving them. In the end, Jimmy is betrayed by the envious leader of the weavers whom he has replaced, a man whose mind has been warped by suffering and abuse. His murder at the hands of exasperated workers takes on Christlike dimensions; Ned Lud, the most representative weaver in the play, whose relation to Jimmy is akin to that of Peter to Christ, undergoes a transformation after Jimmy's slaying. The weavers go off to jail willingly to atone for his death and the hope is expressed that the legacy of Jimmy Cobbett will not be lost on a "more faithful" generation of workers.

The play was a smashing success in its day, partly because the audience enthusiastically identified the sentiments of the murdered Jimmy on humankind's relation to technology with those of Walther Rathenau, the prestigious Weimar politician who had been cut down by right-wing terrorists less than a week before the premiere. Despite some individual highlights, however, the play can no longer be considered part of the living theater. Toller had much trouble trying to fuse the symbolic and ideological elements with the psychological in what is a transition play from expressionism to neorealism (five acts, a plot, and unity of time and place). There is also much uncertainty about the function of language—one is seldom sure why Toller used verse at one point and prose at another. The realistic details were shocking enough in their day but now, in the present media-happy age, they seem to slow down an already overloaded plot, many of whose characters, including all the females, are not directly germane to the action.

The strengths of the play are, surprisingly, three scenes done in the expressionist manner. The first is the confrontation in the House of Lords between Lords Byron and Castlereagh in a prologue that serves as a neat exposition of the historical background. A corresponding confrontation between Jimmy and Ure, the factory owner, in the fourth act is remarkable for its terse poetization of the mentality both of the communist-anarchist (Peter Kropotkin and Gustav Landauer) and of the social Darwinist (Herbert Spencer). In this scene, the brief moment of Ure's recognition of Jimmy's sincerity, if not sanctity, and of his profound regret that he cannot share the weaver's belief in a brotherly world to come, represents Toller at his dramatic best. The third outstanding scene is the confrontation at the end between the workers and their archnemesis, the steam engine, presented as a supernatural being of demoniac proportions not unlike the mine-monster in Émile Zola's adaptation of *Germinal* (1885).

The reputation of the play has suffered at the hands of commentators who claim that the author borrowed too heavily from Gerhart Hauptmann's *Die Weber* (pb. 1892; *The Weavers*, 1899), generally regarded as the unparalleled showpiece of German naturalist drama, an accusation vehemently denied by Toller. It is true that there are many parallels between the two plays, but perhaps the fairly obvious reason for these similarities is that certain elements are bound to be common to works that treat the same theme, here the effects of the industrial revolution on human relationships. They are, in the words of Michael Ossar, "clichés of the genre." *The Machine-wreckers* can stand (or fall) on Toller's merits alone.

HINKEMANN

The failure of human beings in the mass to heed the anguished admonition to be good and help one another, the last words of *The Machine-wreckers*, is scrutinized on the level of the individual worker in *Hinkemann*, the last major play Toller wrote in prison. The setting is contemporary: a Germany marked by unemployment, hunger, discord, and cynicism in the aftermath of a lost war and an aborted revolution. Hinkemann, the protagonist, is a robust-looking unemployed laborer emasculated in the war and supporting his childless wife, Grete, on a very inadequate disability pension. The psychological consequences of his impotence have made him acutely sympathetic to the sufferings of humans and animals.

On a mission of last resort to his mother-in-law to borrow coal and money, Hinkemann flies into a rage when the woman coolly puts out the eyes of a goldfinch so that it will sing better. He sees in this act a paradigm of humankind's inhumanity, and, more specifically, an indication that his long-suffering wife has the capacity to commit a similarly shameful act. For all he knows, she may be secretly looking down on him. To assert what is left of his manhood and bring home more than the bare essentials to his wife, he hires himself out as a carnival geek. In the meantime, Grete succumbs to the advances of a lascivious hulk of a man, the soon-to-be foreman, Paul Grosshahn, and in a moment of very human weakness betrays Hinkemann's secret. Later and unknown to the hero, the adulterous couple catch Hinkemann's act. His billing as the strong man of Germany and the darling of elegant German womanhood sends Grosshahn into gales of sneering laughter. Grete, on the other hand, is shocked into a realization of the great wrong she has done her husband. To retain her, he has sacrificed his most sacred feelings: The gentle-hearted man who would not set mousetraps in the kitchen because it is wicked to torture animals has reduced himself to the level of his mother-in-law by biting into the throats of rats and mice and sucking their blood. Grete abandons Grosshahn, determined to be good to Hinkemann for the rest of her life.

After his performance, the hero goes to a pub to chat with his proletarian cronies. This scene gives Toller a chance to point up the bitter disharmony in the ranks of the Left and the limitations of a socialism that will not be able to cure the metaphysical ills of humankind, the wounds of the soul. When Grosshahn shows up, half-drunk and in a jealous rage as a result of his rejection by Grete, he reveals to one and all Hinkemann's infirmity, and for good measure throws in the devastating lie that Grete finds her husband ludicrous. Laughed at by his comrades, purportedly ridiculed by his wife, Hinkemann leaves the pub and collapses in the street tormented by a nightmare vision of callousness and cruelty on a worldwide scale in a scene that harks back to the dream picture of the expressionists but also points the way to the political theater of Erwin Piscator with its use of such epic devices as filmstrips, newsreel inserts, and illuminated statistics. The scene cements the link between the lovelessness of society at large, in which the socialists are a major participant, and the personal tragedy that befalls Hinkemann and his wife. He is ultimately crushed by the gradually growing awareness of a universal indifference to suffering. Insight into the nature of contemporary society ("They stabbed my eyes open") turns his ideals of a better world into illusion. It robs him of the strength to continue with his wife, even after he, in the moment of his greatest compassion, recognizes that she is as much a victim of things as he is and believes her when she says that she did not laugh at his infirmity. Unable to face alone a world the nature of which Hinkemann has brought home to her, Grete kills herself.

Contrary to what a number of commentators have asserted, *Hinkemann* is not a totally bleak play. The transformation of Grete and the basic humanity of one of the workers who laughs at Hinkemann in the pub and later apologizes and offers his sympathetic support (not coincidentally, this character espouses the anarchosocialism of the author) are certainly hints of hopefulness. More tellingly, Hinkemann's final denunciation of a world in which people make themselves "poor" when they might be "rich" is really a not so very concealed cry for its opposite, for a mystical union of all humankind, for a world in which all are "one soul in one body," a plea directed mainly at the proletarian audiences of Toller's play. As a human document, *Hinkemann* is the author's greatest achievement, a credible transmutation into literature of what is at the core of his ethos:

> The suffering that man inflicts on man is beyond my comprehension. Are people naturally so cruel? Have they as little imagination that they cannot realize the manifold torments that humanity endures? I do not believe in the essential "weakness" of man. I believe that the worst things are done from lack of imagination, from "laziness of heart."

As a proletarian tragedy, it does not rank too far below the German masterpieces of the genre: Georg Büchner's *Woyzeck* (wr. 1836, pb. 1879; English translation, 1927) and Hauptmann's *Fuhrmann Henschel* (pr., pb. 1898; *Drayman Henschel*, 1913).

HOPPLA! SUCH IS LIFE!

Three years after his release from prison in 1924, Toller completed the last of the plays directly connected with his experiences as a revolutionary. *Hoppla! Such Is Life!*, a grimly sober assessment of the past, present, and future of the Weimar Republic, is one of the most noteworthy of politicoliterary documents of the era. The play can be regarded as the swansong of activist expressionism and, as such, a kind of anti-*Transfiguration*, and its hero, Karl Thomas, an anti-Friedrich. Toller has his hero confront the momentarily prosperous, highly conservative, and firmly capitalistic Germany of 1927 with the ardor and optimistic mentality of the revolutionary of 1917-1919. As the play opens, Thomas, an anarchosocialist of bourgeois origins like Friedrich, has been awaiting his execution for ten days. When his death sentence is unexpectedly commuted to a term in prison, his mind snaps from the shock. He spends the next eight years in a sanatorium in a total blackout. Cured, he is released into the world of the "roaring twenties" with its cynicism and toughness and search for thrills, a world in which the notion of the brotherhood of humanity can only be treated as a stale joke (the title of the play derives from a hit song whose theme suggests "jazzing it up" before the deluge comes). Thomas's downward journey to total despair therefore begins where Friedrich's sojourn to the heights had ended. In fact, the latter's eloquent summons to the receptive populace of the world to erect the cathedral of socialism at the end of *Transfiguration* has its disillusioning counterpart in Thomas's antipathetic recapitulation of the credo of the expressionist who attempts to teach the ideals of the revolution to two unreceptive schoolchildren. To them, the recent past is just a collection of meaningless dates, and like their elders, they are primarily interested in fun and games. In the end, Thomas reaches the conclusion that Germany is one gigantic mental institution (the direct opposite of the world of Socratic rationalism that greeted Friedrich at the conclusion of his odyssey). Powerless to effect a cure and refusing to compromise his revolutionary principles by becoming part of the scene, he commits suicide.

In the course of his journey through 1927, Thomas

has encountered various groups of characters who sum up the political spectrum of the Weimar Republic: reactionaries resorting to terror, to the "propaganda of the deed" because of their intense hatred of the republic; conservative bankers and generals who put up with the republic for the moment because its democratic facade serves as a sop to the masses and a cover for their machinations; socialists who have betrayed the aspirations of the working class in their eagerness to demonstrate their ability to help run a capitalist state and their worthiness to hobnob with the upper classes; former revolutionaries who have lost the spark, if not the will to revolution, and who are reduced to performing the day-to-day chores of the party functionary or union organizer. To keep things as historically objective as possible, Toller lets them all have their day in court, and, in fact, does not identify totally with his hero—certainly a radical break with his own dramatic past.

An alternate ending, in which Thomas converts from "an inconvenient dreamer" to someone willing to promote his ideals through "onerous, routine work" in the face of almost overwhelming discouragement, suggests that, intellectually, Toller sided with the last mentioned group. The fact, however, that only the suicide ending was ever printed points to an almost total despair of the heart. In its ambiguous attitude toward its hero, and in its uncanny insight into the future, its prophecy of the coming of a Fascist dictatorship infinitely worse than the republic that had betrayed the cause of socialism, the play anticipates Toller's end.

OTHER MAJOR WORKS

POETRY: *Gedichte der Gefangenen*, 1921; *Das Schwalbenbuch*, 1924 (*The Swallow-book*, 1924); *Vormorgen*, 1924.

NONFICTION: *Justiz: Erlebnisse*, 1927; *Quer durch: Reisebilder und Reden*, 1930 (*Which World—Which Way? Travel Pictures from America and Russia*, 1931); *Eine Jugend in Deutschland*, 1933 (*I Was a German*, 1934); *Briefe aus dem Gefängnis*, 1935 (*Letters from Prison*, 1936).

BIBLIOGRAPHY

Benson, Renate. *German Expressionist Drama: Ernst Toller and George Kaiser*. New York: Grove Press, 1984. A study of expressionism in German drama, focusing on Toller and Kaiser. Bibliography and index.

Chen, Huimin. *Inversion of Revolutionary Ideals: A Study of the Tragic Essence of Georg Büchner's "Dantons Tod," Ernst Toller's "Masse Mensch," and Bertolt Brecht's "Die Massnahme."* New York: Peter Lang, 1998. Chen compares and contrasts Büchner's *Danton's Death*, Toller's *Masses and Man*, and Brecht's *The Measures Taken*, examining the revolutionary ideals expressed by each writer. Bibliography.

Davies, Cecil. *The Plays of Ernst Toller: A Revaluation*. Amsterdam: Harwood Academic Publishers, 1996. A critical reexamination of the plays of Toller. Bibliography and indexes.

Dove, Richard. *He Was a German: A Biography of Ernst Toller*. London: Libris, 1990. Dove discusses the political efforts of Toller as well as his dramatic works. Bibliography and index.

_____. *Revolutionary Socialism in the Work of Ernst Toller*. New York: Peter Lang, 1986. The author studies how Toller's belief in revolutionary socialism manifested itself in his works. Bibliography.

Ralph Ley

BARTOLOMÉ DE TORRES NAHARRO

Born: Torre de Miguel Sesmero, Spain; c. 1485
Died: Seville?, Spain; c. 1524

PRINCIPAL DRAMA

Diálogo del nascimiento, wr. c. 1505, pb. 1517
Addición del diálogo, wr. c. 1505, pb. 1517
Comedia seraphina, wr. c. 1508, pb. 1517
Comedia jacinta, pr. c. 1509, pb. 1517
Comedia soldadesca, wr. 1510, pb. 1517
Comedia trophea, pr. 1514, pb. 1517
Comedia tinellaria, pr. 1516, pb. 1517 (*The Buttery*, 1964)
Comedia Himenea, pr. 1516, pb. 1517 (*Hymen*, 1903)
Comedia Calamita, pb. 1520

OTHER LITERARY FORMS

On March 26, 1517, Bartolomé de Torres Naharro's collection of previously unedited plays and poetry appeared in published form in his *Propalladia* (the first fruits of Pallas). Several other poetic works, published separately after this date, were incorporated in subsequent editions of this collection. The total number of extant poems is fifty. (One of the difficulties in fixing the date of Torres Naharro's death arises from the circulation of certain of his poems in contents until 1530.)

Most of his poetry seems to date from the period 1513-1516 and is quite closely related to his drama. Comparable themes and modes of expression appear in both literary forms. Themes common throughout his *Cancionero* (songbook), which makes up the first part of *Propalladia*, are love, disenchantment with life, respect for great men and sincere patriotism for Spain, and devotion to Christ, the Virgin, and God.

ACHIEVEMENTS

Bartolomé de Torres Naharro was a quintessential Renaissance man: soldier, writer, thinker, and social critic. His was the age of Spanish maritime and overland expansion, the age of Castilian political unification, and the age of the influence of the Italian Hu-

manists. The critic Joseph E. Gillet, who prepared a scholarly edition of the playwright's works, credits Torres Naharro with bringing "form to the inchoate half-medieval drama of his predecessors." Before this time, Spanish drama consisted largely of ritualistic religious and devotional plays, more static than dramatic, more intent on educating the ignorant masses in liturgical dogma than on entertaining with novel artistic experiments. Torres Naharro, with Juan del Encina (the "father" of Spanish secular drama), Lucas Fernández (author of several quasi-religious plays that incorporate farcical scenes), Gil Vicente (the "father" of the Portuguese theater), and Diego Sánchez de Badajoz, attended the University of Salamanca at the end of the fifteenth century. At this university, humanistic ideas fresh from Italy were debated, imitated, and commented; it was here that the new Spanish drama was to emerge. Encina, several years older than the others, staged plays for the household of the dukes of Alba and enlisted young actor-students from the university population to perform his pastoral eclogues for palace audiences. Undoubtedly, Torres Naharro and his friends were initiated into the theater spirit under Encina's tutelage.

If Encina began the development of Spanish drama from religious to a predominantly secular stage, Torres Naharro was to advance it much further, creating a finely wrought body of drama surpassed only by Lope de Vega Carpio.

Torres Naharro is the first Spanish playwright and critic to express his ideas on drama in a treatise. In his "Prohemio" ("Prologue") to *Propalladia*, Torres Naharro formulated his own dramatic theory, one based in part on acute observation of the Roman comedies of Plautus and Terence in Italian translation. It should be noted that Aristotle's enormously influential precepts on the theater were not readily available in the vernacular until well into the decade of the 1530's, some twenty years after Torres Naharro published his theory of drama.

In the "Prologue," Torres Naharro proposes the following concepts: that a play be divided into five acts (following Horace's advice in the "Epistle to the Pisos"), with intermission periods between acts providing "resting places" for both actors and audiences; that there be a limited number of actors—between six and twelve, he suggests—so as neither to bore with too few nor to overwhelm with too many; that decorum reign in a play—rustics and aristocrats should speak and act according to their various places in society (a theory not consistently practiced in his own plays); that the term *comedia* be used to designate a work encompassing both potentially tragic and obviously comic elements; that drama be performed and not read; that plot predominate over character; that drama-*comedias* be reduced to *comedias a noticia* (realistic vignettes of life) and to equally believable *comedias a fantasía* (invented plots); that the *comedias* have a happy ending; that a play be divided into two basic parts: the introit and fable (plot); and that a play present a variety of notable and enjoyable events in its plot structure. What Torres is postulating in his "Prologue" is, in effect, a formula for the Spanish *comedia*, which was to assume its definitive form with Lope de Vega at the beginning of the seventeenth century.

Another of Torres Naharro's contributions to Hispanic letters is clarity of expression and precision in language. Torres Naharro's writing was instrumental in making Castilian the accepted linguistic vehicle for lucid communication; Castilian's supremacy over Latin was only a recent development.

Although Torres Naharro was not recalled in the later years of the sixteenth century as a precursor and theorizer of the *comedia*, he created the *comedia* or tragicomedy undercurrent that pervades the theater in Spain during that century. He left a group of servile imitators but no school of dramaturgy. In his age, permanent theaters were nonexistent in Spain; Kings Charles V and Phillip II provided little encouragement for writing "frivolous" literature. The Reformation and Counter-Reformation were enemies of fictional fantasies, and advocates, instead, of doctrinal pieces. Thus, Torres Naharro was born too soon and in a sense, forgotten too early. Yet his works have survived; their immense popularity attests their influence on the continued development of Spanish theater.

BIOGRAPHY

Bartolomé de Torres Naharro was born in the second half of the fifteenth century; the precise date of his birth is unknown. On the evidence of certain references in the *Comedia jacinta*, scholars have assumed that Torres Naharro attended the University of Salamanca, either as a full-time student or as a servant to a wealthy boy, at the end of the fifteenth and beginning of the sixteenth centuries.

In several of his poems, Juan del Encina indicates a friendly relationship with one Bartolo, a priest from Extremadura. He is no doubt referring to Bartolomé de Torres Naharro, whom he most assuredly first met in Salamanca at some point in the 1490's in his capacity as a producer-director, with Torres Naharro a student-actor. Both playwrights undertook their real apprenticeship in humanistic studies at Rome during the period 1503-1512.

A mecca for the adventuresome, a haven for religious outcasts, a battleground for the Spanish soldier, and the center for Renaissance thought, Italy proved a powerful magnet for the young Torres Naharro. The route to Rome was, however, indirect; Torres Naharro could very possibly have entered the military in the service of the Catholic monarchs, Ferdinand and Isabella, before arriving there. It has been suggested that military expeditions took him first to Andalusia, Valencia, and Catalonia. In his diverse travels in Spain and Italy, Torres Naharro likely acquired his knowledge of the Valencian dialect of Catalan, and of various dialects of Italian. These languages, in addition to classical and vulgar Latin, a smattering of Portuguese and French, and, naturally, Castilian, found their way into *Comedia seraphina* and *The Buttery*. Torres Naharro's Italian experience began in 1503-1507. As a soldier, he may have served in squadrons in the employ of Cesare Borgia, at Faenza, Forli, and Rimini. In his play *Comedia soldadesca*, the playwright provides one with ample, firsthand information concerning many facets of Spanish military life in Italy.

A few years after arriving in Italy, Torres Naharro probably staged a wedding play, *Comedia jacinta*, as entertainment for the 1509 marriage ceremony of Fernando de Avalos and Vittoria Colonna, held on the Italian isle of Ischia. By 1510, Torres Naharro had firmly established residence in Rome and was producing and acting in his first full-length plays: *Comedia seraphina* and *Comedia soldadesca*. His first known performed play, however, is *Diálogo del nascimiento* (the Christmas dialogue), with its accompanying *Addición del diálogo* (addition to the dialogue), performed for a non-Roman theater audience at a Yuletide marriage festival.

By 1513, Gillet conjectures, Torres Naharro had secured a literary patron in the person of either Giulio de Medici or Giovanni de Medici, the latter of whom became Pope Leo X (1513-1523). To have secured such favors means that Torres Naharro must have already proven his ability as both poet and dramatist.

Torres Naharro's performance places would have been palace meeting halls visited while accompanying his first protector throughout Italy. For many Renaissance playwrights, noble marriages and inaugural ceremonies for public officials provided occasions to display dramatic talents. In addition to reading, attending, and acting in neoclassical, humanistic comedies, Torres Naharro would have had the opportunity to be in the presence of such literary figures as Ludovico Ariosto, Niccolò Machiavelli, Pietro Aretino, and Alessandro Piccolomini. Ultimately, however, he rejected such influences, essentially becoming an anticlassicist.

In 1515-1516, Torres Naharro served in the employ of Cardinal Bernardino de Carvajal, a fellow Spaniard living in Rome. At this time, Torres Naharro and Juan del Encina were competing for "acceptance and favor" with other artists in numerous Roman Spanish colonies. A year later, Torres Naharro left Rome and arrived in Naples, where he had secured the favors of Fabrizio Colonna. He was also in the employ of Fernando de Avalos, marquis of Pescara, husband of Fabrizio Colonna's daughter, Vittoria. It was in Naples, on the twenty-sixth of March, 1517, that the *editio princeps* of *Propalladia* appeared, dedicated to Fabrizio Colonna.

Biographer John Lihani supposes that Torres Naharro's constant dissatisfaction with life, his hypersensitive cynicism, and "an inborn wanderlust" compelled the writer to abandon Naples and return to his homeland. He took up temporary residence in Seville, and in 1520, a new edition of *Propalladia* appeared in that city.

From available documents (later family wills), Gillet surmises that Torres Naharro died in Seville either in 1520 or 1524. Some of Torres Naharro's poems, however, were circulating in poetic contests during the 1520's, a fact that suggests 1530 as a possible date of death. Torres Naharro may have retired to a monastic life for the remaining years of his life.

ANALYSIS

Unconventional in his theater, philosophical if not truly lyrical in his nondramatic verse, universal in spirit and expression, Bartolomé de Torres Naharro is one of those rare individuals who advances art to a new level of awareness and social consciousness.

HYMEN

Hymen is divided according to Torres Naharro's simplistic pre-Aristotelian formula for composition: introit and plot. Following a pattern that Torres Naharro establishes for the majority of his introits—or dramatic prologues—a rustic enters speaking in Sayagués (a dialect of northwestern Spain), greets his public, and—although it is Christmas Eve—proceeds to boast of his erotic exploits with various country wenches.

The rustic in *Hymen* recounts his only marriage; his only child resembled the village priest, who obviously frequented their home with more than purely religious intentions. His most ardent extramarital affair was with Juana the Washerwoman, a soapmaker. The rustic describes their lovemaking in graphic and playful detail, then realizes that perhaps he is straying too far from his proposed intentions; he asks pardon for his rude and gross speech, and announces the play to be performed. The play will be divided into five acts, a *comedia*, though not a hilarious comedy (*comedia de risadas*). It will be subtle, something unexplainable, something completely novel. What *Hymen* is, indeed, is a tragicomedy, in which plot predominates over character, in which ethics and morality predominate over fortune or fate. It is the prototype of what was to be known as the Spanish *comedia* in the seventeenth century.

The introit completed, the plot begins. Act 1 opens on a night scene, possibly the first in Castilian theater. Ymeneo, a young aristocrat, approaches Phebea's window in order to woo her. It is love at first sight for Ymeneo. He pines, laments, and suffers the severe pangs of lovesickness, for his "lady" does not answer his calls. His two manservants, Eliso and Boreas, advise him to return home, while they stand vigil over the home of the beloved. Ymeneo leaves in a crazed state, but his men are more fearful of the Marquis, Phebea's brother, who carefully guards his sister's reputation. The two servants then talk of love; Boreas, the selfish and astute servant, is deeply in love with Doresta, Phebea's handmaiden. Both men depart, as the Marquis and his manservant, Turpedio, enter. Though it is still night, the presumably decent Marquis, on the alert for the suspected Ymeneo, retires to a girlfriend's house for breakfast; obviously, he maintains a double standard for sexual behavior, prohibiting his sister from practicing precisely what he does.

Act 2 evolves later that same night. Ymeneo has returned to serenade Phebea. His love song, well suited for the occasion, tells of the glory in suffering for his *belle dame sans merci*. Phebea now approaches her jalousied window. She shows some compassion for Ymeneo, whose sadness would soften even the hardest of hearts. He entreats her to give him entry to her boudoir. She, in turn, attempts to protect her public reputation, rejecting such advances as scandalous and lascivious, but more swooning by Ymeneo breaks her hold, and she finally capitulates: Ymeneo can come the following evening. Content, Ymeneo offers his belongings to his men. Eliso, however, denies the favor, for he believes in loyalty to master and not in self-interest. His master appreciates the gesture and will offer brotherly love in its place. Ymeneo's departure is immediately followed by the entrance of the Marquis and Turpedio: The Marquis vows that Ymeneo and Phebea must be killed in order to preserve the family's "unblemished" honor.

It is late afternoon when act 3 commences. Eliso and Boreas are arguing about Eliso's refusal to accept gifts from Ymeneo. Boreas's philosophy is to take whatever one can whenever possible. Eliso accedes to Boreas's line of reasoning because he knows that the

worthy are often left unrewarded. Doresta enters and Boreas proceeds to woo her in cavalier fashion. She, a bit ugly in appearance and gross in expression, is convinced, like her mistress, by the courtly hyperbolic metaphors. Doresta will also open her door for new love. The exit of Ymeneo's manservants is followed by the entrance of the Marquis's manservant Turpedio. He too attempts to woo Phebea's servant, who effectively parries his advances. Doresta spurns his attempt by insulting his masculinity; Turpedio hurls rough and sexual insults at her.

Act 4 is set that night, the "appointed night" for the important rendezvous. As Ymeneo makes his way to Phebea's bedroom, the dramatic action itself develops in the street. Boreas and Eliso flee for their lives, as they fear impending death at the hands of the Marquis. The Marquis and Turpedio enter; their trap for the lovers is set, for Ymeneo and Phebea are now together. The front door is locked, however, so it will have to be broken down.

Act 5 opens with a confrontation scene between the Marquis and Phebea. Ymeneo has escaped. She is to confess her sexual sins before her death. Although accepting her brother's authority in family affairs, Phebea makes a tearful, emotional peroration to unfulfilled love desire: Nature will turn unnatural on learning of her unfortunate and unfair death. Ready to strike the mortal blow, the Marquis is stopped by the gallant Ymeneo, sword in hand, ready to save his beloved. Phebea is his wife, he contends. Furthermore, no intermediaries were needed in this honest arrangement, because the two are in love and because Ymeneo decides for himself in such matters. The Marquis has little recourse but to bless the couple, who in turn vow to love their respective servants as family members, not as hired help. Doresta is to choose a husband, but the end is left ambiguous, for the choice is to be made in the future, outside the frame of action of this *comedia a fantasía* (play of invented plots).

Hymen is the quintessence of Torres Naharro's theatrical and lyric art. In this play, elements from his previous *comedias a fantasía*, such as *Comedia seraphina* and *Comedia jacinta*, from his semirealistic commentary plays (*comedias a noticia*), such as *Comedia soldadesca* and *The Buttery*, from his farcical medieval *Diálogo del nascimiento* and from *Comedia trophea* (a type of medieval mummer's representation in which illusion appears as reality), are blended masterfully. Elements that existed separately and in less polished form in Torres Naharro's earlier theater, such as comic relief, repartee, lyric fluidity, foreshadowing, asides, song, the use of a *gracioso* (servant-confidant schemer), courtly love themes, and appropriate language for characters of differing sociointellectual levels, fuse in *Hymen*. His later plays, including the longer and more complex *Comedia Calamita*, are basically imitations of the *Hymen* formula. In *Hymen*, there are none of the static, irregularly long, prolix monologues characteristic of most of Encina's and, to some degree, Torres Naharro's earlier theater. Language moves briskly forward. The hilariously gross introit, with its scatological references, is quite appropriate for a wedding festivity—references to fertility and to sexual practices equally shock and instruct the audience.

Boreas and Eliso are *graciosos*, earlier versions of a character type that was to become second only to the major protagonist in the *comedia* of Spain's seventeenth century. Before Torres Naharro's expert and more complex handling, earlier Spanish dramatists had characters of the *gracioso* type in a simplistic fashion, as mere country bumpkins, dolts, or humorous shepherds.

In terms of theme, *Hymen* reflects many of its author's fundamental values: It mocks the concept of courtly lovesickness; it criticizes the aristocracy's typical ingratitude for the work of menials; it condemns the double standard for the sexes; it advocates a free choice of a marriage partner; and it scorns the absurdity of the archaic and rigid Spanish code of family honor. Torres Naharro's plays should be considered early examples of social theater; they have a didactic as well as entertainment function. Torres Naharro advocates a humanistic egalitarianism in *Hymen*: Aristocrats and plebeians will be brothers before God and among themselves.

COMEDIA SOLDADESCA

Comedia soldadesca (the military comedy) is a plotless, near-realistic *comedia a noticia*, or "documentary play." *Comedia soldadesca* is Torres Na-

harro's exploration into the scheming, corrupt, and "inglorious" transactions of characters employed in the Spanish military stationed in Italy. What Torres Naharro offers his audience in this early play is an attempt at representing realistic vignettes of corrupt soldiering. He employs here some of the techniques tested in his earlier *Comedia seraphina*, particularly the use of several different languages—Castilian, Italian, and Latin—no doubt to satisfy the linguistic appetites of his multilingual audience.

The structure is binary, divided into introit and a five-act body. In the introit an anonymous shepherd, probably the author-playwright himself, addressed the princely audience in Sayagués. He insults the courtiers, most of whom are learned; they are presumptuous, he says. One might be surprised at such license, but Torres Naharro is closely following the medieval court jester tradition, whereby the jester was immune to criticism and punishment for playing the fool. The Naharresque jester thus condemns the courtiers' lack of common sense. In order to prove his point, he begins to test their so-called knowledge by posing absurd, self-answering enigmas, such as: "In what month do we celebrate Saint Mary of August?" The courtiers are the real fools, for they are insulted. He, the poor peasant, sleeps more soundly than they, and enjoys his hardy meals more than does the Pope, a man blessed with a thousand preoccupations. According to this character, simple country life is superior to that of the court, where intrigue and anxiety reign.

The rustic then recounts the dramatic action, a procedure quite helpful to an audience unaccustomed to sitting and paying attention to a dramatic performance for two hours. The synopsis also offers the audience the opportunity to appreciate those technical subtleties that Torres Naharro was beginning consciously to employ in his theater.

Comedia soldadesca presents a realistic picture of a corrupt Spanish army corps in service in Italy in the first decade of the sixteenth century. Torres Naharro attacks both the aristocratic establishment in his introit as well as the military in the play proper. This critical perspective is surely humanistic in scope, and represents one of the many "modern" aspects of his worldview. The employment of different languages in the work offers evidence of Torres Naharro's linguistic awareness and desire for greater realism on stage. Italians must speak in their native tongue; so must Spaniards, men of the Church, and country bumpkins. The impetus of *Comedia soldadesca* is obviously not generated by plot structure in the conventional sense; rather, the play is a vignette of realistic, rather loosely connected scenes. Indeed, in addition to its value as a work of art, *Comedia soldadesca* has significance as a historical document, recording early sixteenth century military customs and practices — the first such document in Castilian literature.

It is ironic that those members of the military class to benefit least from the spoils of glorious war were the foot soldiers, for whom Torres Naharro shows little sympathy. The playwright is cold, starkly realistic; he is telling his audience that "this is the way things are." One must fend for oneself. Torres Naharro exposes the ills of society but does not always provide a cure for them, as his major artistic purpose at this early stage of his career was to delight his audience, rather than to shock them. In Horatian terms, his play is more *dulce* (entertaining) than *utile* (edifying). As the critic Lihani concludes, "He felt the need to make the risible deliberately clear in a time of economic distress and social chaos. . . . The *Comedia soldadesca* is a drama of radical, combined with Christian, inspiration, decrying injustices inherent in human systems."

DIÁLOGO DEL NASCIMIENTO

In the Nativity play and farcical epilogue, *Diálogo del nascimiento* and *Addición del diálogo*, Torres Naharro follows patterns established by the Salamancan school of playwrights: Gil Vicente, Lucas Fernández, Juan del Encina, and Diego Sánchez de Badajoz. It is Torres Naharro's earliest known play.

The introit speaker, not a rustic, pleads for decorum: Those with donkeys must tie them up. This indicates that the play was performed outdoors and in a semirustic environment. He proceeds to recount his sexual exploits with a country girl. She had evaded him once, but they had met again at a wedding ceremony (not unlike that for which this playlet was to be performed). Deeply in love, he had sent this "dog-faced, cat-eyed wench" a love epistle, in which he had expressed his devotion to her, swearing by his guts, skin, flesh, and blood. She had responded in an equally uncouth fashion. They were to meet at an upcoming wedding ceremony where he could tickle her as much as he wished, so long as her father did not catch them. The prologuist was drawn into a marriage with the girl, even though Miguel the sexton was said to have slept with her on occasion.

The mock courtly tradition gives way to more pressing matters: The play to be performed will tell of "news from Spain" and "all of the mysteries surrounding the life of Christ." In the epilogue, two yokels will entertain with their nonsense. The author demands silence; the play is to begin.

Patrispano, a Spanish pilgrim, enters, having returned from Jerusalem. In an extremely long monologue, he asks God when he may rest at Christ's side after having suffered so much on the way of life. It is a lovely December evening, one apt for recalling the beauty involved in the virgin birth. Past then becomes present, and evangelical legend or history becomes participatory reality as Patrispano speaks in present tense of Christ's coming. It will cause special wonder and happiness. At the conclusion of his speech, Patrispano rests beside a font. Betiseo, a fellow Spaniard, now enters. He has been robbed of his most prized possession: a wine jug. Patrispano shares his jug with this new friend, and as they drink, they philosophize on the simple virtues of Christianity and the beneficence of God. Of peace, there is none this Yuletide. Patrispano describes the manger scene, explains the mystery of the Trinity, and discusses with his friend biblical events in the life of Christ. They will continue on to Rome; on their way, they sing the popular ballad, "Sad was Adam the Father," which tells of Christ's triumph over the forces of evil in the world.

ADDICIÓN DEL DIÁLOGO

Here *Diálogo del nascimiento* ends and its continuation, *Addición del diálogo*, commences. Two shepherds enter: Herrando and Garrapata. According to Herrando, Christ has been born wearing a skirt. He then corrects the absurdity by stating that the child has been born in his mother's lap. Furthermore, he has been born holding a shield and a sword, symbolizing "patience and justice," respectively. What follows are a series of questions and answers regarding the birth: Why was Christ crying at birth? Why did Mary give birth unaided? Why does one mourn the death of Christ if one has already mourned the year before? Herrando explains that the enactment of the mysteries is part of a ritualistic ceremony; this play, too, is a ritualistic, participatory exercise. The yokels follow with a series of *pullas* or "debasing witticisms," absurd remarks and questions intended to weaken one's opponent by ridiculing him. After this section, the two agree to attend midnight mass. When asked how he will reply to the village abbot, Hernando answers with more absurdities, from gross mispronunciations of Latin incipits and the liturgy to other silly offenses. For common man he wishes an unfaithful wife and the pox. As for woman, he wishes to have her first and then leave her to his friends. The epilogue finishes with a humorous hymn of praise to the Virgin.

On either side of the devotional scene of this Christmas play are bits of slapstick. At this very early stage in Torres Naharro's theatrical career, the playwright had learned, if in a rather primitive, schematic way, one of the most important of dramaturgical skills: to keep one's audience amused and interested at all times. He had learned well from his predecessors: the use of the introit from Lucas Fernández, from Italian drama, and possibly from Latin plays being performed in Italian translation. Encina's eclogues and Fernández's farces taught the young Torres Naharro how to entertain with rustic humor: One could play with words, speak in a peasant dialect, or talk of sex in animalistic, crude terms. The themes in this *Diálogo del nascimiento* include a satire of the clergy, a call for peace, and the beauty of essential Christianity and sharing with one's fellowman. All of these subjects find expression in more sophisticated ways in Torres Naharro's later theater.

OTHER MAJOR WORK

MISCELLANEOUS: *Propalladia*, 1517 (English translation, in *"Propalladia" and Other Works of Bartolomé de Torres Naharro*, 1943-1961 [4 volumes]).

BIBLIOGRAPHY

Gillet, Joseph E., ed. *"Propalladia" and Other Works of Bartolomé de Torres Naharro*. 4 vols. Bryn Mawr, Pa.: George Banta, 1943-1951. This collection of Torres Naharro's works details his life and provides critical analysis of his works.

Lihani, John. *Bartolomé de Torres Naharro*. Boston: Twayne, 1979. A basic biography of Torres Naharro that addresses both his life and works.

Stern, Charolotte. "The Early Spanish Drama: From Medieval Ritual to Renaissance Art." *Renaissance Drama* no. 6 (1974): 177-201. This essay examines how Spanish drama changed from Medieval times to the Renaissance. Contains some discussion of Torres Naharro.

Kenneth Brown

CYRIL TOURNEUR

Born: Place unknown; c. 1575
Died: Kinsale, Ireland; February 28, 1626

PRINCIPAL DRAMA
The Revenger's Tragedy, pr. 1606-1607, pb. 1607
The Atheist's Tragedy: Or, The Honest Man's Revenge, pr. c. 1607, pb. 1611
The Plays of Cyril Tourneur, pb. 1978

OTHER LITERARY FORMS

Cyril Tourneur's only noteworthy work in addition to his plays is *The Transformed Metamorphosis* (1600), an obscure allegorical verse satire on religion in a metaphysical style. He also wrote three elegiac works on prominent figures. A few short prose works and occasional verses, signed only "C. T.," have been attributed to him without further evidence of his authorship.

Achievements

If Cyril Tourneur was the author of *The Revenger's Tragedy* (its authorship is still a matter of debate), his achievement is considerable: He ranks among the chief Jacobean dramatists for a brilliantly structured drama that rings interesting changes on all the conventions of revenge tragedy and dexterously fuses irony, satire, burlesque, and moral purpose in its characterizations. The language of the play is remarkable for its concentrated imagery and its sense of frenzied intensity and haste. If he wrote only *The Atheist's Tragedy*, he must be recognized as the talented author of a well-structured and interesting variant of the revenge tragedy. In this thesis play, Tourneur creates a memorable villain and several interesting minor characters, shows a deft hand at the farcical twist, and daringly and successfully blends medieval structural devices with more modern ideological concepts.

Biography

There is no documentation relating to Cyril Tourneur's birth or early life. Scholar Allardyce Nicoll plausibly conjectures his connection with the Tourneur family of Great Parndon, Essex, suggesting that he might have been son to Edward Tourneur, a Middle Temple barrister. Nothing is known of Cyril Tourneur's education. He might have accompanied the Cádiz expedition of 1596, perhaps under the command of Sir Christopher Heydon, to whom he dedicated his first published work, *The Transformed Metamorphosis*. He served as secretary of Sir Francis Vere, on whose death in 1609 he wrote a funeral elegy. *The Atheist's Tragedy* depicts in its hero Charlemont a character resembling Vere in some respects. A lost tragicomedy by Tourneur, *The Nobleman*, was entered in the Stationers' Register in 1612. As far as is known, the play was never printed, but it was performed, as was *The Revenger's Tragedy*, by the King's Men. Tourneur's elegiac works on Robert Cecil, earl of Salisbury (wr. 1612), and Prince Henry (1613) complete the recorded corpus of his work, except for a 1613 reference to his being given an act of "The Arraignment of London," a play of which no other record exists, to write for Philip Henslowe's

company. Some critics have tried to credit Tourneur with the composition of, or at least his hand in, other plays, but without significant evidence.

A career in military and public service surrounded Tourneur's short period of literary activity. He served the Cecils and carried official letters to Brussels in 1613 and seems later to have been employed in Holland, where he saw military service in 1614. In 1617, Tourneur was arrested—on grounds that are not known—and released on the bond of Sir Edward Cecil, whom he accompanied as secretary of the Council of War and the Marshal's Court on a voyage to raid Spanish treasure ships at Cádiz in 1625. On the way home from this abortive expedition, he died in Kinsale, Ireland, of an illness that attacked many of the crew. The petitions of his wife, Mary, after his death show that he died destitute.

Analysis

Anyone approaching the study of Cyril Tourneur's work encounters two major debates. The first is the problem of whether he wrote *The Revenger's Tragedy*. No author's name is given in the Stationers' Register entry, and this uncertainty is complicated by the play's being coupled in double entry with *A Trick to Catch the Old One* (pr. c. 1605-1606), known to be by Thomas Middleton. *The Revenger's Tragedy* was not ascribed to Tourneur until 1656, when it appeared in Edward Archer's play lists; ascription to Tourneur was repeated in Francis Kirkman's lists of 1661 and 1671. These lists are not invariably accurate, but their tendency in erroneous ascriptions is to attach inferior plays to well-known authors, not major plays to lesser-known ones.

The Revenger's Tragedy

Because there is so little external evidence of authorship, studies have been made on internal evidence to identify the author, the favored alternative candidate being Middleton, whose chief supporters include E. H. C. Oliphant, Samuel Schoenbaum, and Peter Murray. The arguments include differences in style and phraseology from *The Atheist's Tragedy*, of which Tourneur's authorship is unquestioned, and similarities to Middleton's. The former, however, may be explained by the normal variations and developments in a single author's style, and the latter by influence. That two independent but concurrent studies of imagery, by Marco Mincoff and by Una Ellis-Fermor, conducted on the same principles, produced precisely opposite results—one ascribing the play to Middleton, the other to Tourneur—illustrates the subjectivity of such examinations. Studies of versification are at the mercy of compositors' and editors' mislineation. Although studies based on preferred spelling and word forms are more objective, there is not enough of Tourneur's writing extant to apply them confidently, and they can do little more than suggest that Middleton may have supplied the copy from which the play was printed not that he wrote the play.

Among the chief supporters of Tourneur's authorship are R. A. Foakes, Irving Ribner, and Inga-Stina Ekeblad (later Ewbank). Against Middleton's authorship may be cited the fact that his work before 1607 and for some time after included only city comedies for boy companies; he did not begin writing tragedies until fifteen years later. The title page of *The Revenger's Tragedy* claims it to have been acted by the King's Men, for whom Tourneur is known to have written. In favor of Tourneur's authorship, there are similarities in tone, theme, and imagery between *The Revenger's Tragedy* and *The Transformed Metamorphosis*. Between *The Revenger's Tragedy* and *The Atheist's Tragedy*, there seems to be a thematic development, a common moral view, and a similar use of medieval dramatic concepts and techniques. There are other minor similarities between the two plays, in the characters' type names based on Italian words (something Middleton and other dramatists also did), the central use of a skull, and the debts of both to John Marston and William Shakespeare. Foakes sees a stylistic development, arguing that while *The Revenger's Tragedy* gains atmosphere by swift alternation of dialogue and of verse and prose, *The Atheist's Tragedy* contains more varied verse. Because the slim external evidence points to Tourneur while the internal evidence that might point to Middleton is inconclusive, there seems no choice but to continue ascribing the play to Tourneur—a perfectly plausible ascription. As Allardyce Nicoll points out, the uncer-

tainty of authorship may be an advantage, because it directs critical attention to the play's artistry and to its position in the Jacobean age.

The second debate concerns the worldview of *The Revenger's Tragedy*. The arguments range from that of T. S. Eliot—who sees the play as affirming evil—to that of John Peter, who sees Tourneur's mind as a moral one, which guides the characters' natures and their fates; the action, in its series of peripeteia; the irony and satire; and the references to moral and religious norms throughout the play to a moral conclusion. This dichotomy in critical opinion has arisen largely from an inability to distinguish Vindice's voice from his author's (on the surface, this distinction may not be easy, since the play is seen from Vindice's point of view), from a failure to see the firm authorial control in the irony of language and action, and from lack of attention to the moral elements in both language and action. These failures result in part from a neglect of the theatrical situation. Stage production makes quite clear the variations in Vindice's voice, especially his asides, which, in the scenes with Lussurioso and with Castiza and Gratiana, express an anguish and a bitter sarcasm that contrast with the energetic amorality and insinuation of the pander he is pretending to be. Vindice's close relationship to the audience reveals how the author has judged him by making him the ironic butt of many of his own remarks. Those who see in *The Revenger's Tragedy* an amoral world also fail to give the moral action of Gratiana's fall and conversion the full force and emphasis that they attain in the theater.

The play's sources are to be found in several areas. Some of the main plot elements derive from tales of the houses of Este and Medici told in the Italian *novelle* and especially from the revenge of Lorenzo de' Medici on his cousin Alessandro, duke of Florence, as told in *The Heptameron* (1559) of Marguerite de Navarre, translated into English in William Painter's *Palace of Pleasure* (1566): The cruel and licentious duke asked Lorenzo to supply his own sister as a mistress, whereupon Lorenzo sets up an assignation at which he had Alessandro killed. (The story was later treated by Alfred de Musset in his play *Lorenzaccio*, pb. 1834; English translation, 1905.)

The Italian setting was popular in English Renaissance tragedy, Italy as depicted on the stage being a land of sophisticated perversion, revenge, murder, and intrigue. The Italian setting and satiric vein recall John Marston, who clearly influenced *The Revenger's Tragedy*. Tourneur seems to be answering Marston with a more moral approach to similar problems. In Marston's *Antonio's Revenge* (pr. 1599), the perpetrators of a horrible revenge go unpunished, while in his *The Malcontent* (pr. 1604), Duke Altofronte appears disguised in the court of the man who usurped his dukedom and emerges undisillusioned and untainted by participation in intrigue to win it back. Vindice is a variant of Marston's malcontent, disguised among his enemies, in a position to comment as a satirizing observer.

Distancing the action of their plays to Italy left dramatists free to comment on English life. Here, reference may be intended to the court of James I, famous for its banquets, for its promiscuity, and for its costly attire. Leo Salingar, in his famous article "*The Revenger's Tragedy* and the Morality Tradition," interprets Tourneur as equating the decay of moral order with the manorial system, as capitalism replaced divine providence.

Several critics have noted *The Revenger's Tragedy*'s dependence on the medieval morality tradition. Its opening action follows that of such plays as Henry Medwall's *Nature* (pr. c. 1500), a journey of humankind to the world, where he loses his virtue: Vindice, the Everyman character, leaves the abode of Grace (Gratiana) and Chastity (Castiza) and journeys to the court of the World ("for to be honest is not to be in the world"), where he attires himself as "a man of the time" and mingles with characters whose names and actions recall the morality Vices. In addition to the allegorical formalization of characters and action, the medieval grounding of the play is evident in the *contemptus mundi* and *memento mori* elements. The skull stands as the play's central symbol, stressing—as does the series of peripeteia—the futility of human plans and acquisitions: "O, thou terror to fat folks,/ To have their costly three-pil'd flesh worn off/ As bare as this." The hectic violence of the play-world's pleasures and vices and its verbal rhythms remind

Samuel Schoenbaum of *danse macabre* iconography, with its combination of the horrible and the humorous, its sensuality, and its banquets and revelry, which are indulged in to divert minds from death.

Tourneur adapts and blends these medieval elements with the various motifs of a newer tradition, the revenge tragedy, which had established itself from Thomas Kyd's *The Spanish Tragedy* (pr. c. 1585-1589) through William Shakespeare's *Hamlet, Prince of Denmark* (pr. c. 1600-1601). The court setting, the delayed vengeance, the complicated intrigues, and the spectacular catastrophe, familiar from Kyd and his followers, are all there, as are, in some form, the emissary from beyond the grave and the revenger's insanity. The delay, which normally gains sympathy for the revenger by showing his internal conflict, has already occurred when the play opens. *The Revenger's Tragedy* focuses on the mind's decay from the point of decision to its self-destruction in excessive addiction to violence, and even more on the moral problem of revenge, not—like *The Spanish Tragedy* and *Hamlet*—on the conflict leading up to the point where passion takes control. Thus, the murder has taken place nine years earlier, and Vindice, who has brooded on it all that time, has had the balance of his mind tipped before the play begins: Love has already turned to poison ("My poison'd love," as he addresses the skull, has a double sense), and his anger to vengeful plotting.

Vindice's deterioration is delineated in several ways. The most dramatic is through his disguise, his dangerous toying with his own identity. He begins with a self-hatred evident in his contempt for men ("the uprightest man [if such there be/ That sin but seven times a day]") and in depression ("since my worthy father's funeral,/ My life's unnatural to me, e'en compell'd/ As if I liv'd now when I should be dead"). He resolves to "turn into another," thinking that he can do so temporarily ("for once"). Still somewhat tentative about his disguise as a pander, he asks Hippolito, "Am I far enough from myself?" Like Lady Macbeth, he must conjure a warping of his nature, praying to "Impudence" to mask his real feelings, and like Macbeth, he prays that he may avoid seeing himself: "O suff'ring heaven, with thy invisible finger,/ . . . turn the precious side/ Of both mine eyeballs inward, not to see myself."

In time, his embarrassment and his anguish both vanish as he loses himself in the cleverness of his exquisitely plotted revenge ("I'm lost again, you cannot find me yet"), and in his enjoyment of bloodshed, he begins to see himself as an instrument of God's justice in the purgation of the sinful state. He takes on a new disguise, that of a dangerous, malcontent revenger, which is what, ironically, he has actually become. His task in this role is to kill "himself" in his previous role as pander. The most poignant irony in this progressive loss of self comes when the blessing he feels in Gratiana's conversion leads him momentarily to forget his vengeance: "Joy's a subtle elf;/ I think man's happiest when he forgets himself"—which in a religious sense is true; unfortunately, Vindice has here confused "self" with his (self-congratulatory) revenge pursuit. For a moment, there seems to be a chance for his salvation, but he takes leave of his mother to pursue his role as avenger. The self-destructiveness in these rejections of identity culminates in the compulsive confession that condemns him to death, the ultimate loss of personal identity.

The skull takes the place of Hamlet's ghost in keeping the image of the offense before Vindice's mind. This is a particularly interesting variant of revenge tragedy motifs, showing that the impulse to revenge arises from *inside* the revenger, because, inanimate and without a will of its own, the skull can only reflect the thoughts of its observer. The skull is a unifying symbol, drawing together the imagery of disguise, dissimulation, and transformation, and also serving as a memento mori. It also proves Vindice's abnormality of mind at the beginning of the play and is an index of the deterioration in his worldview. When he first addresses it, he is aware of Gloriana's rare chastity and appreciates her natural beauty. After Gratiana's fall has shaken his faith in chastity altogether, he sees Gloriana's beauty as artificial, too, covering only the unsightliness of the skull: "see, ladies, with false forms/ You deceive men, but cannot deceive worms." In keeping with this jaundiced view, he makes the skull serve as a whore. The revenger's

traditional madness is realized in Vindice's macabre sensibility and his growing obsession with lust. Recognizing this, it can be seen that the jaundiced vision is Vindice's, not Tourneur's; since Vindice is the play's presenter, it is his mind that the play reflects; his is the "intense and unique and horrible vision of life," as T. S. Eliot describes it.

As Charles and Elaine Hallett explain in *The Revenger's Madness* (1981), when the revenger's insanity reaches its height, it takes him out of the real world into a play-within-a-play, and in a closed room, where he assumes complete control, he acts out his own rough and poetic justice. Tourneur rings various changes on the play-within-a-play technique, first having *The Revenger's Tragedy* itself begin as one, with Vindice as presenter introducing a procession of the vicious court characters bodied forth by his imagination. It appears again in the theatrical disguise motif, in the dramatic imagery surrounding the duke's murder, and finally in the concluding masque. In the end, Vindice's pageant fades, leaving him to face both earthly justice—flawed at best—and divine justice, whose law he has transgressed in committing murder.

The play contrasts divine with earthly justice. The revenger's tragedy lies in the conflict between the Christian view, in which murder is strictly forbidden, and an older tradition, still privately recognized, which urged personal vengeance for the death of kin. The revenger's downfall lies in his denial of God's providence, his distrust of heaven's efficacy, shown by his taking vengeance into his own hands. The audience sympathizes with the revenger's wrong, his grief, his indignation against the murderer, his search for justice and order, and the dilemma he faces when human justice provides no remedy and divine and civil law prohibit action. That the audience, carefully guided by the author to view the play's inherent order, can see a world order beyond Vindice's ken and that they can see the failure of his insight to comprehend his own error does not inhibit their sympathy with Vindice. His energy, his intelligence, his direct address to them draw them to him. In the very minute of his sadistic fury, they may experience vicariously their own fantasies of wreaking poetic justice on their own offenders. To say, as many critics have done, that the audience cannot sympathize with Vindice is to deny a major aspect of the play's theatrical technique and moral function. Vindice bridges good and evil, play and real world. The audience, having indulged their passion vicariously, may be recalled from their participation with Vindice by Antonio's voice of sanity, standing back while their scapegoat goes to execution. Vindice's death is necessary on one level because the audience needs to impose control on its own urge to unbridled passion. (This may, of course, be the reason that so many critics protest the impossibility of sympathizing with Vindice at all.) On another level, his death is essential because he has taken God's authority into his own hands, seeing himself as God's instrument (he hubristically interprets the thunder as a sign of God's approval), thus disrupting God's order and questioning God's justice.

As the duke's excess of passion leads to his death and Junior's to his, so Vindice's leads to his. Antonio survives. Many critics see Antonio as a cynical comment on human justice. Indeed, his justice is imperfect, for he condemns to death a masquer whom too many readers mistake for innocent. In fact, this particular masquer, though innocent of Lussurioso's death (Antonio condemns him as "Dipp'd in a prince's blood"), has committed murder: By his own admission, he has killed Spurio. This is simply another illustration of the play's main theme, first illustrated by Junior's trial at the beginning and Junior's death through other means: Though human justice is imperfect and unreliable, God's justice is not. God has used Antonio to punish sin: It is God, not Antonio (as Antonio acknowledges), who is in control. Antonio's own fortune in contrast to Vindice's figures this pattern. Like Vindice, Antonio begins as a discontented nobleman. Discontent is the frame of mind most open to temptation. Like Vindice, Antonio has lost his wife through the ruling family's viciousness, and, having sought human justice, has not found it. He is privy to an oath of vengeance—which he does not initiate—but this vengeance is to wait for the outcome of the next judicial sitting. The sitting never takes place: Justice on Junior comes instead through Supervacuo and Ambitioso's misguided machina-

tions. Antonio's patience is rewarded with state power at the end of the play.

Tourneur carefully shows the audience how each of Vindice's grievances would have righted itself without his intervention. Instead of waiting for God to dispense justice, however, Vindice has taken it into his own hands, and thus, according to poetic, divine, and human justice, he is deprived of all power. In sentencing Vindice and Hippolito to death, Antonio passes the only judgment he can. Murder must be condemned by law. Antonio's words, "You that would murder him would murder me," are not egocentric but politic: In murdering a ruler—it is irrelevant how evil the ruler—Vindice has committed treason and disrupted the social order.

To emphasize the play's moral view, several other characters are given revenge motives: Ambitioso and Supervacuo against Spurio, the duchess and Spurio against the duke, Lussurioso against Piato. Their pettiness and failures, the incredible series of ironic reversals in which their plans rebound on themselves, point to the moral of the play and show that personal vengeance is ineffectual (farcically so in the case of Ambitioso and Supervacuo), evil, and self-defeating. In the end, evil has destroyed itself. The play's pervading moral view is upheld by Vindice, whose asides, more profusely toward the beginning of the play before he usurps God's function, have as their basis conventional moral and religious standards—even his cynical remarks, such as "Save Grace the bawd, I seldom hear grace nam'd!" ("Grace" is the name of a major character in the play.) Though temporarily obscured, tempted through human frailty made frailer by poverty, Gratiana, whose name means Grace, is redeemed. Castiza, except when pretending in a ploy to test her mother's penitence, is true to her allegorical name. It is these two, with the values they represent, whom Vindice recalls in his final words, when he has cast off his roles as Piato, Vindice, murderer, masquer, and returned to an impoverished self—which, cherishing these values, proves not so impoverished after all. Acknowledging the order these values imply, he is able to accept death.

Foakes postulates in his edition that the play and the central character's lack of "the common touch" may account for neglect by theater professionals from 1607 to 1965. Yet in a play that presents a gallery of enviable roles, Vindice is one of the most satisfying roles for an actor, for he himself is so highly theatrical. The range of the part in its various disguises demands immense virtuosity of imagination, voice, and body, and the subtle variety of the language, the range from poetry to prose in countless moods and variations, requires a sensitive and practiced speaker. In constructing the duke's murder, Vindice is inventing a work of dramatic art, aesthetic motives having for him entirely displaced moral ones. Portraying his orgiastic involvement in the execution of this vengeance and his satisfaction with it, the actor is playing his own excitement with his own artistry in a manner rarely offered him by any playwright. The fact that in doing so he is performing a dramatic role absolves him from hubris. The play began to be performed again in the twentieth century, first by universities, finally in 1965 by the Pitlochry Festival Theatre, and then in 1967 by the Royal Shakespeare Company in a brilliant and memorable several-year run. Other productions followed.

THE ATHEIST'S TRAGEDY

The Atheist's Tragedy is an idea play, a moral exemplum demonstrating the failure of faith in nature instead of faith in God. It shows also that human striving is vain and that God's justice prevails effectively. The play uses the medieval *de casibus* structure, substituting Providence for Fortune, paralleling the rise and fall of the atheist d'Amville (the atheist's tragedy) with the fall and rise of the patient Christian Charlemont (the honest man's revenge). The moral premise is the same as that of *The Revenger's Tragedy*: that vengeance belongs to God, who will punish those who disturb his order and reward those who suffer patiently. Some of the methods are the same, particularly the use of symbolic rather than naturalistic characters. The structure, like that of *The Revenger's Tragedy*, shows the influence of the morality tradition: Humankind is shown as it should be in an ordered patriarchal society headed by Montferrers and Belforest, is led away from God during d'Amville's amoral machinations (which destroy the social

order by attacking primogeniture while at the same time questioning the fatherhood of God), and then is restored in Charlemont's self-conquest, which achieves a right relationship of humankind with God. As in the morality play, characters are sharply divided into good and evil, and the vicious characters, more energetic than the virtuous, are more interesting to the audience.

The play was probably composed as an answer to George Chapman's *The Revenge of Bussy d'Ambois* (pr. c. 1610), as *The Revenger's Tragedy* seems to answer Marston. The names Charlemont and d'Amville echo those of Clermont and Bussy d'Ambois, Chapman's passive revenger and supreme individualist. Tourneur refutes Clermont's self-sufficient stoicism by showing the failure of d'Amville's self-sufficiency and the success of Charlemont's positive Christianity.

As a revenge-play variant, *The Atheist's Tragedy* is daringly experimental. It calls attention to this fact by recalling *Hamlet* in the two appearances of the ghost and in the graveyard scene. Its ghost, however, is used to urge a son *not* to revenge. This results in a dramatic problem: how to maintain sympathy for a passive hero. Tourneur attempts to solve this, first by having the ghost—unlike that which appears to Clermont d'Ambois—give reasons for not avenging, and then by arranging for Charlemont almost to give way to passion once and be restrained by the ghost, after which he is under physical restraint throughout most of the rest of the play so that he *cannot* act. In addition, Charlemont is given a clear moral development, learning to balance passion and reason and submit both to God.

As this play has no stage history (all that is known from its title page is that it had been performed in "diuers places"), it has not been possible to see how successful Tourneur was in his experimentation. D'Amville, unquestionably the more active character, dominates the play's interest, manipulating most of its plot. His tragedy, like Vindice's, springs from his lack of trust in God. The intellectual position he represents is that nature is simply a mechanism to be manipulated by people's reason to their own advantage, and that in the absence of moral sanctions, the only rational aims of life are pleasure and wealth.

For spiritual immortality, d'Amville substitutes immortality through posterity, and all of his schemes are directed to making his posterity rich. Thus, he is ironically undermined from the very start, as can be seen in the vanity of his efforts. When he prides himself on the power of his reason to provide against all accidents, he neglects to consider the possibility of his posterity's demise. At the same time, his imagery undermines him, for it traditionally describes not the relationship of earthly father to son so much as that of God to humankind, a relationship he rejects:

> And for my children, they are as near to me
> As branches to the tree whereon they grow,
> And may as numerously be multiply'd
> As they increase, so should my providence,
> For from my substance they receive the sap
> Whereby they live and flourish.

All aspects of the play coherently and economically work to show the folly of denying God. The verse, precise and regular, accords with d'Amville's rationalism. The main image, that of building, suggests the transitory nature of humanity's works, and the presence of the stars symbolizes God's presence, even though d'Amville, like Shakespeare's Edmund, scoffs at their power and tries to substitute the power of gold. Other characters, particularly Levidulcia and Snuffe, underscore particular aspects of d'Amville's nature or serve as extensions of it. Whereas he is a rational atheist, Levidulcia is a sensual atheist, led only by physical lust, which she justifies by nature. She dies when her lust betrays her, as d'Amville does when his reason betrays him. Both experience a revelation of the truth before they die. Snuffe, the Puritan hypocrite, parodies d'Amville, especially in the graveyard scene where his seduction of Soquette, gone ludicrously wrong, sends up d'Amville's attempted murder and rape. The association also stresses d'Amville's Puritan traits. The minor characters' obscenity and wit caricature his materialism and rationalism.

The final ironic reversal shows the man who tried to destroy others destroying himself. Although naturalistically not as far-fetched as critics have claimed (it is remarkably easy to deal oneself such a blow, and

under the influence of wine it would be more so), the final scene is intended symbolically, to show God's justice in all its appropriateness.

The play is carefully patterned, with a major debate between nature philosophy and Christian patience and a subsidiary debate between chastity and lust. The characters' ideas and experiences are increasingly closely paralleled, d'Amville losing his reason as Charlemont gains in certainty of his faith, d'Amville's increasing fear of death contrasted to Charlemont's contempt for it.

Though it lacks the intensity of *The Revenger's Tragedy*, *The Atheist's Tragedy* has considerable stage potential. D'Amville, the stage Machiavel, is a marvelous role: His energy, manipulativeness, variety of action, and power of poetry—particularly at points where his reason is giving way—recommend him to a powerful actor and should have challenged the actor-managers of the nineteenth century. The role contains numerous theatrical effects: a ghost, a murder on stage, a suicide before the eyes of the audience, a formal funeral, seductions, an attempted rape, a duel, farcical concealment of lovers, and a graveyard romp. Several of the subsidiary characters are tempting to an actor, especially Snuffe, and the likable and surprisingly moral sensualist Sebastian, whose lines inject an element of humor similar to that provided by Spurio in *The Revenger's Tragedy*. As in *The Revenger's Tragedy*, Tourneur shows a very sure grasp of humor, which has not dated, and this would virtually ensure stage success. The play is certainly more inviting to production than many of the equally or more obscure plays that were produced in the twentieth century, and not until it has been staged, preferably compared in different productions, will it be possible to judge the extent of its success as drama. It is likely that this would also provide critics further insight into the question of the two plays' common authorship, as well as a more comprehensive view of the art of Tourneur.

OTHER MAJOR WORKS
POETRY: *The Transformed Metamorphosis*, 1600.
MISCELLANEOUS: *The Works of Cyril Tourneur*, 1929, 1963 (Allardyce Nicoll, editor).

BIBLIOGRAPHY

Camoin, François A. *The Revenge Convention in Tourneur, Webster, and Middleton.* Salzburg: Institut für Englische Sprache und Literatur, Universität Salzburg, 1972. Stresses the complexity of moral views among Jacobean playwrights, which led to the questioning nature of their works. Emphasizes the different techniques of Elizabethan and Jacobean playwrights writing revenge plays. Finds that *The Atheist's Tragedy* offers a more frightening view of the conditions of mortals than Tourneur's earlier *The Revenger's Tragedy.*

Jacobson, Daniel J. *The Language of "The Revenger's Tragedy."* Salzburg: Institut für Englische Sprache and Literatur. Universität Salzburg, 1974. Jacobson investigates such aspects of Tourneur's language as antithesis, irony, and paradox. The sections on imagery relate it to function and theme, finding great thematic emphasis on corruption and damnation. Discusses metaphor, metonomy, and metalepsis as elements of the play's figurative language.

Murray, Peter. *A Study of Cyril Tourneur.* Philadelphia: University of Pennsylvania Press, 1964. This full-length study of Tourneur provides a definitive discussion of the authorship question for *The Revenger's Tragedy.* Tourneur's two plays are analyzed in detail for their art and thought. Murray also gives considerable attention to *The Transformed Metamorphosis* but little or no attention to other minor works.

Schuman, Samuel. *Cyril Tourneur.* Boston: Twayne, 1977. A basic biography covering the life and providing critical analysis of the works of Tourneur. Index.

White, Martin. *Middleton and Tourneur.* New York: St. Martin's Press, 1992. White compares and contrasts the works of Thomas Middleton and Tourneur. Bibliography and index.

Arthur Kincaid,
updated by Howard L. Ford

MICHEL TREMBLAY

Born: Montreal, Canada; June 25, 1942

PRINCIPAL DRAMA

Le Train, pr. 1964 (televised), pb. 1990

Cinq, pr. 1966, pb. 1971 (English translation, 1976; includes *Berthe, Johnny Mangano and His Astonishing Dogs*, and *Gloria Star*)

Les Belles-sœurs, pr., pb. 1968 (English translation, 1973; also as *The Guid Sisters*, 1988)

En pièces détachées, pr. 1969, pb. 1970 (revision of *Cinq; Like Death Warmed Over*, 1973; also as *Broken Pieces* and *Montreal Smoked Meat*)

La Duchesse de Langeais, pr. 1969, pb. 1970 (English translation, 1976)

Demain matin, Montréal m'attend, pr. 1970, pb. 1972 (musical)

À toi, pour toujours, ta Marie-Lòu, pr., pb. 1971 (*Forever Yours, Marie-Lou*, 1972)

Les Paons, pr. 1971

Hosanna, pr., pb. 1973 (English translation, 1974)

Bonjour, là, bonjour, pr., pb. 1974 (English translation, 1975)

Surprise! Surprise!, pr. 1975, pb. 1977 (English translation, 1976)

La Duchess de Langeais and Other Plays, pb. 1976 (includes *La Duchesse de Langeais, Berthe, Johnny Mangano and His Astonishing Dogs, Gloria Star*, and *Surprise! Surprise!*)

Les Héros de mon enfance, pr., pb. 1976 (musical; music by Sylvain Lelièvre)

Sainte-Carmen de la Main, pr., pb. 1976 (*Saint Carmen of the Main*, 1978)

Damnée Manon, Sacrée Sandra, pr., pb. 1977 (English translation, 1979)

Les Socles, pb. 1979 (*The Pedestals*, 1979)

L'Impromptu d'Outrement, pr., pb. 1980 (*The Impromptu of Outrement*, 1981)

Les Anciennes Odeurs, pr., pb. 1981 (*Remember Me*, 1984)

Albertine en cinq temps, pr. 1985, pb. 1986 (*Albertine in Five Times*, 1986)

Le Vrai Monde?, pr., pb. 1987 (*The Real World?*, 1988)

La Maison suspendue, pr., pb. 1990

Nelligan, pr., pb. 1990 (libretto; music by Andre Gagnon)

Théâtre: Volume 1, pb. 1991

Marcel poursuivi par les chiens, pr., pb. 1992 (*Marcel Pursued by the Hounds*, 1992)

En circuit fermé, pb. 1994

Messe solenelle pour une pleine lune d'été, pr., pb. 1996 (*Solemn Mass for a Full Moon in Summer*, 2000)

Encore une fois, si vous le permettez, pr., pb. 1998 (*For the Pleasure of Seeing Her Again*, 1998)

L'Etat des lieux, pr., pb. 2002

OTHER LITERARY FORMS

Although Michel Tremblay is best known for his drama, he is also the author of a number of short stories, film scripts, and television plays; in addition, he translated into French Aristophanes' *Lysistratē* (411 B.C.E.; *Lysistratē*, 1837), Paul Zindel's *And Miss Reardon Drinks a Little* (pr. 1967, pb. 1972) and *The Effect of Gamma Rays on Man-in-the-Moon Marigolds* (pr. 1965, pb. 1971), four short plays by Tennessee Williams, and Dario Fo's *Mistero buffo: Giullarata popolare* (pr. 1969, pb. 1970; *Mistero Buffo: Comic Mysteries*, 1983). He has also published a number of novels, including *La Grosse Femme d'à côté est enceinte* (1978; *The Fat Woman Next Door Is Pregnant*, 1981); *Thérèse et Pierrette à l'École des saintes-anges* (1980; *Thérèse and Pierrette and the Little Hanging Angel*, 1984); *Le Cœur découvert* (1986; *The Heart Laid Bare*, 1989; also as *Making Room*, 1990), and *Hotel Bristol: New York, NY* (1999). In 1990, Tremblay wrote and published the libretto for an opera, *Nelligan*, which was produced the same year.

ACHIEVEMENTS

Michel Tremblay is part of a new generation of playwrights that emerged in Quebec during the 1960's and 1970's, a time of profound political and cultural change for this province. Led by Tremblay, these writers saw as their primary task the liberation of Quebec culture from the shackles of foreign domination. With very few exceptions, the theater of Quebec to the mid-twentieth century had never treated issues genuinely French-Canadian; it was a theater enslaved to the thematic, stylistic, and linguistic control of "mother" France. With the opening of Tremblay's *Les Belles-sœurs*, at the Théâtre du Rideau Vert in Montreal on August 28, 1968, a new and autonomous Québécois theater was born. Significant partly for its thematic focus on the realities of the working class of Quebec, *Les Belles-sœurs* is the first play to be written in the distinctive French of Tremblay's people—*joual*. A peculiar mixture of Anglicanisms, Old French, neologisms, and standard French, *joual* (from the Québécois pronunciation of the French word *cheval*) is the popular idiom of Quebec and especially of Montreal's working class. To the French and to Quebec's cultural elite, *joual* was a bastard tongue, emphasizing the pitiful nature of Quebec culture. To Tremblay, however, *joual* was a symbol of identity, a language not to be silenced but to be celebrated for its richness and for its distinctive flavor. To discuss Tremblay's greatest achievements is thus not simply to focus on the fact that he has become Canada's leading playwright, that his enormous creative output in the areas of theater, literature, film, and television has won for him international fame, that he has influenced the development of Canadian drama, and that he has won countless awards for his work. Though all of this is true, it is also important to recognize him as a cultural leader with a commitment to articulate and grapple with the problems of an oppressed community.

Tremblay has accumulated a long list of literary prizes and distinctions. Among the most important are his being named a Chevalier de l'Ordre des Arts et des Lettres de France; his *Albertine in Five Times* brought him the Chalmers Prize in 1986; in 1988, Tremblay received the Prix Athanase-David for his work as a whole; in 1989, he received the Grand Prix du Livre de Montréal for *Le Premier Quartier de la lune* (*The First Quarter of the Moon*, 1994), a prose work. Tremblay was named Chevalier de l'Ordre national du Québec in 1991. In 1994, he was given the Molson Prize for Lifetime Achievement in the Arts. In 1999, Tremblay received a Governor-General's Award. A controversy developed when some Quebec nationalists expected him to refuse the award. However, Tremblay accepted it—announcing for the first time, however, that he had refused the Order of Canada award in 1990. Tremblay won two prizes, the Chalmers Award and a Dora Mavor Moore Award, for *For the Pleasure of Seeing Her Again*.

BIOGRAPHY

Michel Tremblay was born in east-end Montreal on June 25, 1942, the youngest child of a working-class family. His family lived in a small seven-room house with two other families, and Tremblay remembers distinctly the first voices of his life: women who would speak candidly to one another about their lives and who would censor nothing in front of the young child. Indeed, these are the voices sounded in many of his plays, especially *Les Belles-sœurs*. In 1955, he won a scholarship to a school for gifted children; his innate distaste for the cultural elite soon caused him to return to the public schools.

Tremblay speaks of his adolescence as a time of personal anguish, a time when writing became his primary channel of expression. Moreover, as a young man he became obsessed with television: "It was the only theatre I knew." In 1959, he took a job as a linotype operator and during this period wrote his first television play, *Le Train*, for which he eventually won first prize in the 1964 Radio-Canada Contest for Young Authors. It is also in 1964 that he met André Brassard, who became one of his closest friends, his principal collaborator, and the director of many of the premier performances of his plays. His publishing career began in 1966 with a book of short stories, *Contes pour buveurs attardés* (*Stories for Late Night Drinkers*, 1978). In the same year, he submitted his first full-length play, *Les Belles-sœurs* (written in 1965), to the Dominion Drama Festival, but the revolutionary piece was rejected. Two years later, however, it was produced, with great success, at

the Théâtre du Rideau Vert in Montreal and later in Paris.

The years following 1968 marked a creative and prolific period for Tremblay. For English-speaking Canadians, however, Tremblay was not so widely publicized, partly because of the playwright's desire to restrict his work to his French compatriots. It was only after 1976, the year the Separatists' Parti Québécois under René Lévesque took power in the provincial House, that Tremblay opened his work to the English-speaking world. After 1976, translations of his plays appeared, productions abounded, and Tremblay emerged as Canada's leading playwright, recognized as such in both North America and Europe. That he has achieved international acclaim testifies to the fact that his work is as universal in meaning as it is specific to contemporary Quebec life.

In the late 1980's, Tremblay's work became increasingly autobiographical with such plays as *The Real World?* and *For the Pleasure of Seeing Her Again* and the series of autobiographical novels, *Chroniques du Plateau-Mont-Royal*. In 1989 he added *Le Premier Quartier de la lune* to the series, and *Un Objet de beauté* (*A Thing of Beauty*, 1998) was published in 1997. He has also written the memoirs *Les Vues animées* (1995; *Bambi and Me*, 1998) and *Douze coups de théâtre* (1992; *Twelve Opening Acts*, 2002).

In general, Tremblay is so productive in so many artistic genres—musical theater, opera, fiction, painting, and film among them—that an observer may find it difficult to keep track of what Tremblay has done and is doing. His career is certainly one of the richest in literary history.

ANALYSIS

Antecedents in the history of dramatic literature help to characterize the plays of Michel Tremblay. The playwright himself cites as most influential the ancient Greek tragedians on one hand and Samuel Beckett on the other. The influence of the ancient playwrights shows itself most notably in Tremblay's repeated use of choruses and in the rhythmic precision of his work. Indeed, much of his theatrical power stems from a native musical sensibility that informs the structure of his plays. Like the Greeks, Tremblay writes dramatic pieces that operate, at least in part, as rhythmic scores for performance; his plays abound with overlapping voices and interwoven monologues, and possess a rhythm so peculiar to the language and intonations of the Québécois that there is often as much power in how his characters speak as there is in what they say.

Beckett's influence on Tremblay manifests itself in the specific context in which Tremblay places his characters and in the way those characters grapple with the struggles of life. Tremblay celebrates the notion that, despite the seeming despair of Beckett's figures, there is a beauty in their struggle to face and accept their lives: "I never read or see a Beckett play without experiencing a lift." His appreciation of Beckett is significant; although Tremblay's characters seem trapped in the underbelly of culture, in seedy nightclubs, confined apartments, in a world of whores, pimps, and transvestites, or trapped even in their own social roles and family relationships, still there is a sense of uplift in their struggles and in the courage they find in themselves.

LES BELLES-SŒURS

Stylistically, Tremblay's dramas are eclectic, not only when looked at as a body of work, but also within single plays. In *Les Belles-sœurs*, for example, he creates a realistic setting, utilizes realistic dialogue, and then counters that realism with stylized elements reminiscent of the Theater of the Absurd. The premise of the play is simple: Fifteen women of the neighborhood gather to help Germaine Lauzon paste a million Blue Chip stamps in booklets for a contest she has won. The women of the title ("the sisters-in-law" or "the beautiful sisters," an ambiguity in French that accounts for the original title maintained in translation) gossip as they paste. When Germaine is not looking, however, the women secretly steal the stamps. This ostensible, realistic line of the story unfolds in a dynamic relationship with stylized, isolated monologues spoken by the women to express the more honest, individual problems of their miserable, trapped lives: Marriage, family, and sex—the basis of their worlds—have achieved a level of banality that seems to reduce all of life to sheer endurance.

Perhaps the clearest example of the juxtaposition of styles comes at the end of the play. Germaine discovers the thieves, throws them out of her home, and feels a profound sense of loneliness and isolation. She falls to her knees to pick up the stamps that scattered on the floor during the chaos of discovering the theft. At that moment, Tremblay breaks out of the realistic structure once again. From off stage the women begin to sing a chorus of "O Canada," while simultaneously a rain of stamps falls from the ceiling. The stylized "shower" of prosperity is parallel to Germaine's windfall of stamps at the beginning of the play. Yet the playwright creates his final image as a self-consciously artificial construct, an image that contrasts with the conventionally realistic form used at the outset. Like a Euripidean *deus ex machina*, Tremblay's rain of stamps is a theatrical joke; humanity is in turmoil and has reached an impasse within the realistic conventions of the play. The playwright's ending undercuts that impasse, however, and, with a broad satirical gesture, he clarifies the source of the problem itself; the values of the Canadian middle class have their price.

THE FAMILY CYCLE

The body of Tremblay's dramatic work possesses a remarkable consistency both in theme and in focus. His *dramatis personae* are the underprivileged, the people on the fringe of society, people who live in disguise. His plays also have a striking similarity of context; indeed, in the bulk of his work, he examines two specific worlds. On one hand, he looks at the family, at the home, and at the nature of the individual within the family construct. On the other hand, he looks to a horrifying world external to the family: the world of the Main in Montreal, with its host of transvestites, whores, and pimps, all set against a backdrop of "gambling joints, cabarets, lights and noise." In the words of André Brassard, "The Main is the Kingdom of the marginals . . . the underprivileged and forgotten part of the proletariat . . . the underlayer of society." The Tremblay opus can thus be examined to a large degree in two major cycles: the family cycle and the Main cycle. The two worlds do intersect at points, creating a potent juxtaposition. Indeed, when considered as a whole, Tremblay's work is interesting not only because of his investigation into these two separate worlds but also because of his ability to show how those worlds mirror each other. In effect, the two cycles intersect to illuminate the "family" of the Main and the "underbelly" of the home.

LIKE DEATH WARMED OVER

Like Death Warmed Over, the first play of the family cycle, was actually written, in its original version, before *Les Belles-sœurs* but published and performed at a later date. It unfolds in four loosely connected episodes. The play begins in the inner courtyard of an east-end Montreal tenement on a sweltering summer afternoon. For the chorus of neighbors, the single point of interest is the window across the way—the home of Robertine, her daughter Hélène, Hélène's husband, Henri, and their daughter Francine. The neighbors are fascinated with the peculiar and unsavory domestic battles in Robertine's home. They offer a detailed description of the troubled family and its history as they wait for Hélène to come home, for the "show" of the evening to begin.

The middle two episodes tell the story of Hélène, how she spends her time slinging smoked meat in a cheap restaurant on Papineau Street after having lost her job in a bar on the Main. She gets drunk, returns to the bar, only to have the frustrations of her life become that much more glaring as she confronts the figures of her past. The final episode takes place back in Robertine's living room. Hélène comes home, verbally abuses Henri (who spends all of his time watching cartoons on television) and Robertine, and gives the neighbors the "show" for which they have waited. Toward the end, Claude, the retarded brother, returns home for a visit after escaping from his sanatorium. He wears "sunglasses and speaks English" and believes that doing so gives him ultimate power: It makes him invisible. In Tremblay's world, the madman overturns his alienation to make it an illusory source of strength. Claude's presence thus provides a sharp contrast to the feeling of humiliation and powerlessness among the other members of the family. Typically, the play ends in a series of stylized monologues in which the family members express their despair. They repeat a refrain in unison during this final section, a refrain that sums up their despon-

dency and languor: "There's not a goddamn thing I can do."

FOREVER YOURS, MARIE-LOU

Although *Like Death Warmed Over* is a play about failure and ultimate despair in family relationships, Tremblay's next play in the family cycle, *Forever Yours, Marie-Lou*, presents the attempt of two sisters, Carmen and Manon, to find refuge from the traumas of family life. In this play, two conversations transpire simultaneously, one between Marie-Louise and her husband, Leopold, and the other between their daughters Carmen and Manon. The two conversations take place in the family home, but ten years apart. Carmen and Manon (in the 1970's) recall the past, ten years earlier, when their parents and younger brother Roger died in a car accident. Manon, a religious zealot, believes her father Leopold was responsible for the accident, an act of suicide and filial murder. Carmen denies this account, although her rejection is undermined when Leopold (in the action of the 1960's) threatens Marie-Louise with that very scenario.

Structurally, the play is a quartet of interweaving voices as each level of action comments on the other through a powerful theatrical juxtaposition. Each character has complaints about the others, each feels abused, each feels as if life has dealt him or her an unfair blow. In the turbulence of the marriage, Marie-Louise turns to religion and Leopold to his drinking and television. The daughters, too, have their share of trouble, not only as products of their repressive and abusive home but also as individuals who must cope with the tragic past. Carmen has turned to the Main and to singing in cabarets. Manon has, on the other hand, withdrawn entirely into a lonely life of religious fanaticism. The two women have clearly gone in opposite directions, but it is evident that they are both striving to find shelter from the traumas of the family.

While Marie-Louise and Manon hide in an existence of religious repression, and Leopold in an escape into alcohol and boredom that finally erupts in the violence of murder and suicide, Carmen achieves a degree of liberation from her repressive past. This is evident only when one realizes that the core of

Tremblay's play is the collision of real human needs with the religious and social constructs that make the fulfillment of those needs impossible. That Carmen turns to the Main is perhaps only a limited alternative, another subculture with its own restrictions. Yet, within the context of the play, Carmen's choice is the most fruitful; she has at least discovered a part of herself that opens the way toward personal creativity. This notion is the center of the play in which she next appears: *Saint Carmen of the Main*, a play in which issues of the family and the Main intersect in a subtle but provocative way.

SAINT CARMEN OF THE MAIN

In this later play, Carmen is returning from a stay in Nashville, where she has been sent to improve her yodeling technique; the play opens with the chorus (the people of the Main) celebrating her return. Indeed, her education away from the Main was more than simply a time to improve technique: Carmen comes back as a leader of the people, as their voice; it is a voice expressed through her new lyrics and songs that relate directly to the concerns of the community. Carmen's journey from repression to release is a model of realized human potential and gives her strength to speak for others. Despite the ecstasy of the people over their newfound leader, however, Carmen must face her antagonists: the cabaret owner Maurice, who wants her to sing the "old songs," and Carmen's rival, Gloria, who fights for her "rightful place." When he challenges Carmen, Maurice articulates the political question of the play, a question that perhaps haunts the playwright himself: "All right. Let's say they take our advice. Let's say they smarten up, they wake up and they get mad. Then what? It's fine to wake people up, but once they're awake, what do you do with them?"

Shortly after her performance at the cabaret, Carmen is brutally murdered; she is denounced as a lesbian so that the crime may be pinned on her innocent dresser, Harelip. "The lights go out completely on the Choruses"; the sun is down, the fire of awakening quelled. This is a play about the possibility of awakening, of fighting repression, of the change that can come about when human beings are acknowledged for their strengths. Carmen has found that

strength within herself and is a beacon for the people. Yet the figures of the status quo—threatened for reasons both political and financial—end the triumph of humanity that lit the world for an instant.

BONJOUR, LÀ, BONJOUR

If in the story of Carmen, Tremblay suggests that personal strength can come only from a freedom discovered outside the repressive home, then in *Bonjour, là, bonjour*, he explores the act of personal acceptance within the family itself. Again, this play is inspired by musical principles; there are thirty-one sections entitled "solo," "duo," "trio," and so forth, up to "octuor," depending on the number of voices involved in a given episode. The central figure in *Bonjour, là, bonjour*, Serge, is a young man who has just returned from a three-month stay in Paris, where he has tried to deal with his love for his sister Nicole. Though the odds are against him, Serge breaks through the oppressive structures of his family life to assert his integrity and express his love both to Nicole and to his aging and deaf father, Gabriel. Serge must defend himself against the invasion of his relatives (two spinster aunts and three sisters other than Nicole), who try to use his vitality to serve their needs. Once he sees past moral taboo to admit fully his incestuous love, he is able to triumph and communicate with his father. Like Carmen, in her relationship to the people of the Main, Serge becomes a figure who releases his father from a suffocating life. He invites his father to live with him and Nicole and, in the end, finds the strength to shout the words "I love you" into Gabriel's deaf ears.

THE MAIN CYCLE

The plays of the family cycle are clearly parables of the political and cultural repression Tremblay sees within Quebec culture. Like Tremblay's characters, the Québécois must begin a long journey to self-acceptance. Still, there is another "family" Tremblay explores: the family of the Main. In the Main cycle, he focuses on the individual desperately trying to find himself in a chaotic and frightening world, a world in which the search for identity is no less difficult, nor alienation less painful, than it is within the home. Perhaps most indicative of his concern is the recurring transvestite figure, whose multiple personas epitomize the alienation of the individual in the Main.

Tremblay began his investigation of the Main in three short plays written early in his career: *Berthe, Johnny Mangano and His Astonishing Dogs*, and *Gloria Star*. The three plays function as a trilogy and were originally part of the collection entitled *Cinq*, written in 1966. The trilogy examines the individual's alienation from the self by focusing on the collision of one's dreams and fantasies of fame and glory with the stark realities of a boring and desperate life. Tremblay once again works toward a stylized ending to the trilogy in which he communicates how dreams of success and perfection are the offspring of artifice; the playwright makes this abundantly clear in a surrealistic conclusion of theatrical make-believe.

LA DUCHESSE DE LANGEAIS

La Duchesse de Langeais, a piece in which the past of an aging transvestite unravels in monologue, is the next play of the Main cycle and represents Tremblay's first treatment of this sexually complex figure. The Duchesse is a human being who is desperately alone. She speaks of how she became the Duchesse, "the biggest faggot ever," how she envisions herself as a "woman of the world," how she spent her life whoring for hundreds of men, how she was sexually abused as a child by her cousin Leopold (later to appear in *Forever Yours, Marie-Lou*), and how she entered a life of obsessive sexual activity from the age of six.

The theme of alienation operates on many levels in *La Duchesse de Langeais*. She is a transvestite locked in a sexually ambiguous role. She is aware of her age and feels a frightening sense of attenuation in her life. She has a history of being a female impersonator, trapped in a Pirandellian disparity between the roles performed and the actress/actor underneath. Yet the monologue itself attests her alienation in a more immediate way. Is there any possibility of verifying the past she describes? Is she merely creating a fiction for the audience? Is she creating the fiction for herself? Indeed, reality and illusion are so disconnected in this play that it is impossible to verify much. Tremblay (the primary illusion-maker) communicates through this onslaught of unverifiable information the pain and suffering that accompanies

the life of one lost in a labyrinth of insubstantiality and artifice.

HOSANNA

Hosanna, on the other hand, probes deeper into the tensions of the multiple roles of the transvestite and female impersonator. The play takes place in the early hours of the morning in the confined and oppressive apartment of Hosanna, a transvestite whose original name is Claude, and "her" lover Cuirette ("Leatherette" in French, but also suggesting the English "Queerette"), whose original name is Raymond. Hosanna has returned from a night of humiliation and ridicule, a night that will ultimately lead her to a painful acceptance of self.

Hosanna and Cuirette represent two extremes. The former is a highly effeminate drag queen whose excessive perfume, makeup, jewels, and clothing constitute her mask. The latter is a "leather-man," who has grown too fat for the clothes that once expressed his exaggerated machismo image; nevertheless, his leather jacket, motorcycle, and tough persona are all the accoutrements through which he defines himself. The first act deals with the tensions and collisions of the relationship, the inability of the two individuals to recognize each other's needs and, more important, to recognize and accept themselves for who they are. When the second act begins, Hosanna is alone; she tells the story of how the people of the cabaret (including the Duchesse) played a practical joke on her, how they faked plans for a costume party for which they were all to dress as famous women in history. For weeks, Hosanna prepares her role as Elizabeth Taylor playing Cleopatra; when she arrives, however, everyone at the club is dressed in a Cleopatra costume—"Everyone made up better than me!" She tries to keep her composure, even through the taunting repetition of the chant that haunts the audience as much as Hosanna herself: "Hosanna, Hosanna, Hosanna, Ho!"

The event is enough to shock Hosanna into a state of self-reflection and to force her to confront the mask she wears. Cuirette, who is absent for most of the second act in a frustrated sexual escapade, and who had been privy to the joke played on Hosanna, returns home to shed his own mask and to be with the one he loves. It is, thus, Raymond and Claude present at the last moment of the play, not Cuirette and Hosanna. In the end, Tremblay shows two human beings who have begun the difficult journey involved with the abandonment of self-hatred. Raymond and Claude must accept who they are, together and as individuals.

DAMNÉE MANON, SACRÉE SANDRA

The theme of reconciliation with the self dominant in the Main cycle is also at the core of *Damnée Manon, Sacrée Sandra*. (The literal English translation would be "doomed Manon, holy Sandra," but is finally inadequate because of the ambiguous implication of *sacrée* in French, a word with meanings both sacred and profane. Indeed, this ambiguity is precisely what this conceptually complex piece is about.) Manon, the religious sister from *Forever Yours, Marie-Lou*, and Sandra, the transvestite cabaret owner from *Hosanna*, are the characters of the drama. Tremblay again creates a double action by juxtaposing two monologues. The double action eventually moves to a single point that articulates the place in which the sacred and profane meet. Moreover, the play ends with the kind of theatrical self-consciousness that informs much of the playwright's work: Both characters realize that they are the invention of the same author. As Manon comes to recognize the erotic nature of her religious devotion and Sandra the obsessive religiosity of her sexual escapades, the playwright himself seems to imply a reconciliation of seeming opposites within himself. He is the creator of both characters; indeed, as an individual, he, too, embodies both the sacred and profane.

THE IMPROMPTU OF OUTREMENT

Tremblay wrote three major plays after 1979: *The Impromptu of Outrement*, *Remember Me*, and *Albertine in Five Times*. In these plays, he plucks his characters out of the Main and places them back in a domestic context. In *The Impromptu of Outrement*, Tremblay presents four sisters who were brought up in a middle-class Montreal suburb, Outrement, and who are meeting for the occasion of Yvette's birthday. The party has become an annual custom, a time for a little "impromptu." The real purpose of their meeting, however, is to have a chance to lash out against one another, to complain about one another's lives, to scream about one another's failures and life choices. Ultimately, however, it is an occasion when they feel disgust with who they are; the sisters mirror to one another what they deem ugliest in themselves. The play is Tremblay's version of Anton Chekhov's *Tri sestry* (pr., pb. 1901, revised pb. 1904; *The Three Sisters*, 1920), a work that explores the torture of languishing potentiality, of the trap of the middle class, of unrealized dreams and bourgeois isolation.

REMEMBER ME

Remember Me examines two men who are meeting long after the end of their relationship of seven years. Each man has continued with his career and with other relationships; each, however, feels the burden of his own mediocrity and a profound discontent with life. Like *The Impromptu of Outrement*, therefore, *Remember Me* centers on the individual who feels disenfranchised from his own potential; both plays demonstrate how middle-class promise quickly turns to mundane routine. In addition, by focusing on four women in one play, and two homosexual men in the other, Tremblay makes a clear statement about the frustrations minorities feel with the false promises of acceptance in bourgeois society.

ALBERTINE IN FIVE TIMES

Albertine in Five Times is a play about the life of one woman at five different points in her life. Tremblay presents the fragmented individual in many of his dramas, but this time he exploits his art to realize all pieces simultaneously. In this play, Tremblay pursues his preoccupation with self-alienation by grappling with the problem of the ever-changing self in time; as in Beckett's *Krapp's Last Tape* (pr., pb. 1958), *Albertine in Five Times* creates a picture of the individual estranged from the past and from the self that has emerged over time. Nevertheless, the play provides a moving portrait of the stages of one woman's struggle. Like so many of Tremblay's characters, Albertine, though desperate, does struggle; the search for identity is the most challenging task for any individual. Tremblay celebrates the courage of his characters, and of the Québécois themselves; he celebrates their strength to look at themselves and begin the long journey to freedom.

THE REAL WORLD?

Almost all Tremblay's plays since the mid-1980's have to do, in one way or another, with the family—in particular, how troubled characters fit into their families and how members of those families respond to threat from within or without. Another important theme in the plays of this period is artistic creation—its sources and its problems. *The Real World?* focuses on both of these concerns.

This piece deals with a young playwright whose first drama features characters named after his father, mother, and sister—the sources of his inspiration. As the play's characters look more and more like their models, Claude, the writer, is troubled by what he is doing. He wonders if he has the right to plunder his private life and to invade the lives of his family members in order to create. And, as the title suggests, where does a writer draw the line between what is fact and what is imagined? Clearly, this subject is of importance to Tremblay, and he has said that he and Claude have shared the same concerns.

LA MAISON SUSPENDUE

La Maison suspendue presents a couple, Jean-Marc and Mathieu, who come to spend a summer vacation with Mathieu's son, Sébastien, in a log cabin in the Laurentian Mountains. The cabin has been in Jean-Marc's family for three generations, and when he opens the front door, he takes off on a discovery of his roots.

The couple finds that the cabin contains vibrations of fiddler-tale teller Josaphat-le-violon who had a son by his sister, Victoire. In 1950, the home witnesses the trials of Edouard, who fantasizes his ambiguous sexuality while living with his sister, Albertine, who rejects such fantasies. Jean-Marc, who has had to deal with his own sexual identity, reconciles his identity and his new family with the figures from the past.

MARCEL PURSUED BY THE HOUNDS

In *Marcel Pursued by the Hounds*, the protagonist is fifteen-year-old Marcel—who is subject to hallucinations that suspend him between dream and reality. He hopes to makes things better by living with his sister, Thérèse, but it may be too late: He seems hopelessly trapped by imagination, even madness. The play is a form of dialogue between Marcel and Thérèse, in which other characters constitute a kind of Greek-tragedy chorus. The ultimate point is the extent to which people's childhood games and fantasies come back to haunt them in their adult lives—which are full of the dangers and cruel realities that people did not recognize when they were children.

SOLEMN MASS FOR A FULL MOON IN SUMMER

The form of *Solemn Mass for a Full Moon in Summer* resembles that of *Marcel Pursued by the Hounds*. The title of this play is an accurate one: *Solemn Mass for a Full Moon in Summer* is an incantatory rite, in which the voices of the characters—Isabelle, Yannick, Jeannine, Louise, Rose, Mathieu, Gaston, Mireille, Yvon, Gérard, and the Widow—mingle in a liturgical drama. All the characters complain about their lives, yet they try hard to not succumb to bitterness. Instead, they long for some kind of self-liberation—and when the summer moon appears, a solution, hope, and consolation seem possible.

FOR THE PLEASURE OF SEEING HER AGAIN

For the Pleasure of Seeing Her Again is a short play but one of Tremblay's most moving works. It is an extended conversation between the Narrator (a stand-in for Tremblay himself) and Nana (who represents the playwright's late mother). The play contains wonderfully funny reminiscences by both the Narrator and his mother—about growing up in Montreal and Saskatchewan, about oddball family members, about Tremblay's choice of career and his mother's ambivalent attitude toward the latter. However, the tone takes a deeply somber turn near the play's end, when Nana tells about the cancer that she carried for a time, the pain, and her death. The finale features an angel descending to take Nana to Heaven.

L'ETAT DES LIEUX

L'Etat des lieux is, on one hand, a riotous comedy and on the other, an investigation into such subjects as aging, failure, and artistic energy. It all begins when soprano Patricia Pasquetti has a crisis during the final scene of Richard Strauss's *Salome*. Before a packed house, Patricia hits a grotesquely false note. It is not surprising that Patricia's life starts to fall apart. Through the sympathetic eyes of her longtime accompanist, the audience sees Patricia struggle for a while in Paris before returning home to Quebec's L'Ile des Soeurs. Once she gets home, Patricia takes out her disappointment on her daughter, who is an actress. Mother accuses daughter of lacking creative élan. However, Patricia's own mother—another actress—intervenes. She knows firsthand how artists decline with age—but she also knows the immense power of artistic freedom that transcends aging.

OTHER MAJOR WORKS

LONG FICTION: *La Cité dans l'œuf*, 1969 (*The City in the Egg*, 1999); *C't'à ton tour, Laura Cadieux*, 1973; *Le Cœur découvert*, 1986 (*The Heart Laid Bare*, 1989; also as *Making Room*, 1990); *Le Cœur éclaté*, 1993; *La Nuit des princes charmants*, 1995; *Quarante-quatre minutes, quarante-quatre secondes*, 1997; *Hotel Bristol: New York, NY*, 1999; *Chroniques du Plateau-Mont-Royal*, 2000 (series of six novels including: *La Grosse Femme d'à côté est enceinte*, 1978 [*The Fat Woman Next Door Is Pregnant*, 1981]; *Thérèse et Pierrette à l'École des saintes-anges*, 1980 [*Thérèse and Pierrette and the Little Hanging Angel*, 1984]; *La Duchesse et le roturier* 1982 [*The Duchess and the Commoner*, 1999]; *Le Premier Quartier de la lune*, 1989 [*The First Quarter of the Moon*, 1994]; *Des Nouveles d'Édouard*, 1984 [*News from Edouard*, 2000]; and *Un Objet de beauté*, 1997 [*A Thing of Beauty*, 1998]); *L'Homme qui entendait siffler une bouilloire*, 2001.

SHORT FICTION: *Contes pour buveurs attardés*, 1966 (*Stories for Late Night Drinkers*, 1978); *Manoua*, 1966.

SCREENPLAYS: *Françoise Durocher, Waitress*, 1971; *Backyard Theatre*, 1972; *Il était une fois dans l'est*, 1974; *Parlez-nous d'amour*, 1974.

TELEPLAYS: *Trois Petits Tours*, 1969; *En pièces détachées*, 1971; *Le Soleil se lèvue en retard*, 1975; *Bonheur d'occasion*, 1977; *Les Belles-sœurs*, 1978.

NONFICTION: *Douze coups de théâtre*, 1992 (memoir; *Twelve Opening Acts*, 2002); *Un Ange cornu avec des ailes de tôle*, 1994 (memoir; *Les Vues animées*, 1995 (memoir; *Bambi and Me*, 1998);

Pièces à conviction: Entreitiens avec Michel Tremblay, 2001 (interviews).

TRANSLATIONS: *Lysistrata*, 1964 (of Aristophanes' play); *L'Effet des rayons gamma sur les vieux garçons*, 1970 (of Paul Zindel's play *The Effect of Gamma Rays on Man-in-the-Moon Marigolds*); *Et Madame Roberge boit un peu*, 1971 (of Paul Zindel's play *And Miss Reardon Drinks a Little*); *Mistero buffo*, 1973 (of Dario Fo's play); *Mademoiselle Marguerite*, 1975 (of Roberto Athayde's play *Apareceu a Margarida*); *Oncle Vania*, 1983 (with Kim Yaroshevskaya; of Anton Chekhov's play); *Le Gars de Quebec*, 1985 (of Nikolai Gogol's play *Revizor*).

BIBLIOGRAPHY

Anthony, G., ed. *Stage Voices: Twelve Canadian Playwrights Talk About Their Lives and Work.* Garden City, N.Y.: Doubleday, 1978. Canadian playwrights, including Tremblay, discuss their plays and their lives. Index.

David, Gilbert, and Pierre Lavoie, eds. *Le Monde de Michel Tremblay.* Montreal: Cahiers de Théâtre Jeu, 1993. Presents a series of studies relevant to Tremblay's entire body of work from *Les Belles-sœurs* to *Marcel Pursued by the Hounds*. In French.

Godin, Jean-Cléo, and Laurent Mailhot, eds. *Théâtre Québecois II.* Montreal: Bibliothèque Québecoise, 1988. A collection of essays on theater in Quebec. In French.

Massey, Irving. *Identity and Community: Reflections on English, Yiddish, and French Literature in Canada.* Detroit, Mich.: Wayne State University Press, 1994. Provides a section containing criticism and interpretation of Tremblay's works. Bibliography and index.

Usmiani, Renate. *Michel Tremblay.* Vancouver: Douglas & McIntyre, 1982. An analysis of Tremblay's works and discussion of his life. Bibliography.

_____. *The Theatre of Frustration: Super Realism in the Dramatic Work of F. X. Kroetz and Michel Tremblay.* New York: Garland, 1990. A comparative study of the realism in the works of Tremblay and Franz Xaver Kroetz. Bibliography and index.

Lorne M. Buchman,
updated by Gordon Walters

WILLIAM TREVOR

Born: Mitchelstown, County Cork, Ireland; May 24,
1928

PRINCIPAL DRAMA

The Elephant's Foot, pr. 1965
The Girl, pr. 1967 (televised), pr., pb. 1968 (staged)
A Night with Mrs. da Tanka, pr. 1968 (televised),
    pr., pb. 1972 (staged)
Going Home, pr. 1970 (radio play), pr., pb. 1972
    (staged)
The Old Boys, pr., pb. 1971 (adaptation of his novel)
The Fifty-Seventh Saturday, pr. 1973
Marriages, pr., pb. 1973
A Perfect Relationship, pr. 1973
Scenes from an Album, pr. 1975 (radio play), pr.,
    pb. 1981 (staged)

OTHER LITERARY FORMS

William Trevor's reputation rests primarily on his
fiction, especially the short stories that have been
published widely in periodicals in the United States
and Great Britain and in collections. His novels have
received acclaim as well. Approximately thirty-seven
of his stories have been adapted for British television.
At least fifteen of his plays have been adapted for radio, a few specifically written for radio. Some of his
stories and novels have been adapted to the screen.
He also has written some nonfiction, *A Writer's Ireland: Landscape in Literature* (1984) and *Excursions
in the Real World* (1993), a collection of memoirs.

ACHIEVEMENTS

William Trevor has been a prolific writer, capturing scenes of ordinary life and winning many awards.
Although he no longer lives in his native Ireland, he
considers himself an Irish writer. Many of his works
deal with the history of strife and animosity that has
plagued Irish life. His novel *The Old Boys* (1964)
won the Hawthornden Prize for literature in 1965. In
1976 his novel *The Children of Dynmouth* (1976)
won the Whitbread Award for fiction as did his novel
Fools of Fortune (1983) in 1983. He received *The*

Hudson Review Bennett Award in 1991. His novel
Felicia's Journey (1994) won the Sunday Express
Book of the Year Award and the Whitbread Book of
the Year Award in 1994. *The Hill Bachelors* (2000)
received the *Irish Times* Irish Literature Prize for fiction in 2001. He has been awarded the Royal Society
of Literature award and the Allied Irish Banks prize
for literature. His radio play, *Beyond the Pale*, received the Giles Cooper Award for the best radio play
of 1980. Another radio play, *Autumn Sunshine*, was
included in the 1982 collection of the best radio plays
of the year. In recognition for his standing as a world-
class author, he was made honorary Commander of
the British Empire, a distinction awarded few Irish
citizens. He is a member of the Irish Academy of Letters. In 1999, he received the David Cohen British
Literature Prize.

BIOGRAPHY

William Trevor was born William Trevor Cox on
May 24, 1928, in Mitchelstown, County Cork, Ireland. His parents, William Cox and Gertie Davis,
married in Dublin during a period of civil war. By the
time of his birth, the war had abated, and his parents
had moved from the city. His father, a bank official,
was required by his position to relocate frequently.
As a result, Trevor's early education was sporadic. At
one time, he was tutored by a young girl; at another,
he was the only Irish Protestant enrolled in a Catholic
convent school. The daily life and Catholic customs
in small Irish towns that he came to know as a youngster provided many of the images and much of the
content of his later work. As a young boy living in
Tipperary, he developed a love for films and enjoyed
reading detective fiction. Both of these genres influenced his style.

Trevor attended boarding school in Dublin at age
twelve. He studied sculpture under Oisin Kelly at
St. Columba's College. Later he attended Trinity College, Dublin, graduating with a B.A. in history. There
he met Jane Ryan, who he would marry in 1951.
They moved to County Armagh, Northern Ireland,

where both worked as teachers. He continued in sculpture, winning a competition in 1952. He and his wife emigrated to England, where he continued as an artist, holding a one-man show in Bath in 1958 and another in Dublin in 1959. By the end of the decade, his sculpture had become abstract, and he was no longer happy with it. He turned to writing, publishing his first novel, *A Standard of Behaviour*, under the name William Trevor in 1958.

After the couple's first child was born, Trevor sought a more lucrative position in advertising while continuing to write short stories. Encouraged by an editor at Bodley, he wrote another novel. When the novel, *The Old Boys*, won the Hawthornden Prize in 1965, Trevor left his position in advertising and turned to writing full time.

ANALYSIS

William Trevor would be more well known among fiction readers than theatergoers if it were not for the popularity of his stories on radio and television and in popular film in Great Britain. Although he has stated that his favorite medium is the one in which he develops a relationship with the individual reader, he has, from the earliest stages of his writing career, written and adapted works for the stage, radio, television, and screen. This adaptation has come easily because much of his fiction explores themes and character motivation as presented through the character's own words or perceptions and through juxtaposed scenes or episodes. In other words, his fiction, rich with dialogue, is itself dramatic. It is not surprising then that the themes, style, and evolution of Trevor's drama parallel those of his fiction.

Throughout his work, certain themes emerge. The most persistent is the lonely, alienated, fragmented experience of contemporary human beings. Characters are cut off from others for many reasons. Many of them have been scarred by the abuse of another. The nature of that abuse is generally reported or implied rather than depicted. He also explores the abuse inherent in and resulting from one group or nation exploiting another. Loneliness also results from ordinary loss or limited possibilities presented by circumstance and chance.

Related to the theme of lonely, fragmented lives is the prevalence of evil, a force surprisingly mundane. Ordinary people inflict great harm, sometimes intentionally, sometimes through a thoughtless selfishness that motivates them to set off a chain of events or revelations that wreak havoc in other lives. His works demonstrate that past evils continue to infect the present. Evil committed by groups or individuals affect the entire social fabric. Fanatics emerge who cannot forgive what has happened in the past and continually subvert attempts at reconciliation through new violence. Evil, guilt, and violence are inextricably related.

His works also show the ways that difficult lives are endured. Because of his many stories of individuals coping with the inevitability of fate, Trevor is often compared to Anton Chekov, who also describes characters' recognition of their need to accept reality. Trevor still finds the possibility of hope and affirmation. Some characters demonstrate the redeeming effects of compassion and commitment, reflecting a hopeful vision that lives can be different when people connect with one another and the larger community.

Stylistically, Trevor's drama holds more affinity to his short stories than to plays of other dramatists. Conflict and resolution are not what shape his works. They are instead shaped by exploration of character (the effects of loneliness, for example) or theme (the effects of the past). At times, characters, reminiscent of characters of James Joyce, achieve a new realization or epiphany; at other times, they simply struggle to cope with the circumstances in their lives.

Trevor's style lends itself to drama. He has claimed that being an Irish Protestant in a predominantly Catholic society provided him with an outsider/observer perspective. Developing the habit of quietly listening to what people say, he perfected voice and tone, enabling him to delineate a variety of characters who reveal themselves in words, thoughts, and actions. Evidence of Trevor's appreciation of film and detective stories appears in the juxtaposition of significant scenes, the revelation of significant details through innuendo, and incrementally disclosed detail. Parallel structuring and repetition reinforce themes.

Although Trevor emphasizes compassion and connection throughout his work, the earlier plays and stories tend to focus more on England, exploring English characters who are comic and eccentric as well as lonely and alienated. These humorous portrayals have often been compared to the characters of novelist Charles Dickens. Later works focus on Ireland, exploring the small and often tragic lives of ordinary people, the influence of the past, and the disappearance of cultures.

A NIGHT WITH MRS. DA TANKA

This play reflects Trevor's early work in that it presents two lonely, highly comic, eccentric characters. Mrs. da Tanka, having a drink in the bar of a hotel, notices the entrance of Mr. Mileson, whom the bartender identifies as a man coming to this hotel annually in memory of a honeymoon he dreamed of that never took place. Mrs. da Tanka sees in him an opportunity to alleviate her own solitary state and immediately sets out to snare him, at least for the night. The extent of her manipulation and his adamant refusal explain the particular lifestyle of each.

GOING HOME

This play depicts the outrageous behavior of one character, a young boy named Carruthers. The boy's unhappy life, which provokes the aggressive behavior, has its roots in his family. Ignored by his father and made to feel a nuisance by his mother, who is always recalled in a red silk dress accompanied by a new, demanding boyfriend, the boy realizes he is unwanted and unloved.

He has just been expelled from school and is traveling home with the house matron, Beryl Fanshawe, who realizes that having spent her youth and her prime at this school, now both are gone. Because she and the boy travel in the same direction, she has always been called on to accompany him to his station. Like him, she is returning to a home in which she is viewed as an annoyance. Her parents make it evident that she is a bother, yet they still restrict her opportunities for new adventures or even simple diversions.

She understands the source of the boy's suffering and feels compassion for him even though she is, on these trips, the victim of his aggressive misbehavior. Recalling how she comforted him when he felt lonely and abandoned at his first arrival at the school, she longs to provide him with the love and care that he desperately needs and that would fill her with happiness. Though the boy, the woman, and the audience all recognize the benefits of this, all also recognize that class and circumstance make such a connection impossible.

MARRIAGES

This two-act play, which presents the irony of circumstance, the manipulation of others, and the damaging effect a revelation can have, is set in a bedroom of an inn, the site of a husband's affair. Mrs. Landsowne, whose husband of twenty-five years has died suddenly, is meeting with Mrs. Swingland, his mistress. The widow explains how shocked she was after her husband's death to find the rapturous love letters from his mistress in his drawer. Devastated by the sudden turn her life has taken, Mrs. Landsowne describes the history and seeming importance to her and her husband of their love, marriage, and family. Learning of this relationship has disillusioned her, shaking her view of the world, herself, her husband, and their life together.

In the second act, the other woman speaks, explaining her privileged circumstances and her life of boredom. She details how she met her lover, seduced him, and then through tears and pleading begged him to meet her weekly. She asserts that the husband truly loved his wife and family and met her reluctantly and out of compassion. Mrs. Landsowne is left to make sense of this revelation.

SCENES FROM AN ALBUM

Reflecting Trevor's turn to Irish issues and themes, this two-act play develops through four vignettes at different periods. It explores responses to significant events associated with a family home and, in so doing, presents the impact of history on lives centuries later. The first period begins in 1610 just after English captain Eustance Malcolmson surveys the land he has been granted for defeating the Irish. He decides to build a great house there, relocating the Catholic tenants. He naïvely expresses the hope that one day his family will love the subjected people as their own. This violent birth of sectarianism ignites a long series of acts of hatred and violence by fanatics, both Catholics and Orangemen, who can never let the past rest or sins be forgiven.

Opening with the surreal effect of a group of Irish Republican Army members taking aim at the audience, the second act moves the scene to the 1980's. The remaining members of the Malcolmson family view letting their line die out and their house become a relic of Ireland's past like an abbey or a burial mound as the only solution to generations of conflict. Two spinster sisters and their sister-in-law, mother of the inheritor of the estate, have commissioned a scholar to write the history of the family. While the current Eustace Malcolmson, an ineffectual alcoholic, lounges on a chair, they explain what they would like recorded. They want it stated that their family had once helped William of Orange to victory; for this they are guilty. More important, they want it said that they were a noble, gracious, and fair people, more Irish than the Irish. Although they recognize that attitudes have not changed much since 1610, Eustace, the heir, prays to God that they will.

Other major works

LONG FICTION: *A Standard of Behaviour*, 1958; *The Old Boys*, 1964; *The Boarding-House*, 1965; *The Love Department*, 1966; *Mrs. Eckdorf in O'Neills Hotel*, 1969; *Miss Gomez and the Brethren*, 1971; *Elizabeth Alone*, 1973; *The Children of Dynmouth*, 1976; *Other People's Worlds*, 1980; *Fools of Fortune*, 1983; *Nights at the Alexandra*, 1987; *The Silence in the Garden*, 1988; *Two Lives*, 1991; *Juliet's Story*, 1991; *Felicia's Journey*, 1994; *Death in Summer*, 1998; *The Story of Lucy Gault*, 2002.

SHORT FICTION: *The Day We Got Drunk on Cake and Other Stories*, 1967; *The Ballroom of Romance and Other Stories*, 1972; *The Last Lunch of the Season*, 1973; *Angels at the Ritz and Other Stories*, 1975; *Lovers of Their Time and Other Stories*, 1978; *Beyond the Pale and Other Stories*, 1981; *The Stories of William Trevor*, 1983; *The News from Ireland and Other Stories*, 1986; *Family Sins and Other Stories*, 1990; *Collected Stories*, 1992; *Ireland: Selected Stories*, 1995; *Outside Ireland: Selected Stories*, 1995; *Marrying Damian*, 1995 (limited edition); *After Rain*, 1996; *The Hill Bachelors*, 2000.

RADIO PLAYS: *Beyond the Pale*, 1980; *Autumn Sunshine*, 1982.

NONFICTION: *A Writer's Ireland: Landscape in Literature*, 1984; *Excursions in the Real World*, 1993.

EDITED TEXT: *The Oxford Book of Irish Short Stories*, 1989.

Bibliography

MacKenna, Dolores. *William Trevor: The Writer and His Work*. Dublin: New Island Books, 1999. Analyzes influences on his work during forty years of writing. Shows his particular concerns—individual lives of ordinary people—and his strengths. Devotes a chapter to his work for radio, television, and the screen. Contains excellent bibliography.

Morrison, Kristen. *William Trevor*. New York: Twayne, 1993. Analyzes important themes and rhetorical strategies; argues for evidence of what she calls his "system of correspondences" and child murder as a metaphor for colonial exploitation.

Morrow Paulson, Suzanne. *William Trevor: A Study of the Short Fiction*. New York: Twayne, 1993. Provides analysis of Trevor's short fiction in addition to interviews with the author and compilations of reviews of his work.

Shirmer, Gregory A. *William Trevor: A Study of His Fiction*. London: Routledge, 1990. Traces the evolution of Trevor's fiction exploring certain themes, especially the importance of human connections, the influence of history, and the connection between public and private worlds. Provides analysis of consistent stylistic techniques.

Bernadette Flynn Low